CASES AND MATERIALS

ECONOMIC JUSTICE:
RACE, GENDER, IDENTITY AND ECONOMICS

SECOND EDITION

by

EMMA COLEMAN JORDAN
Professor of Law
Georgetown University Law Center

ANGELA P. HARRIS
Professor of Law
Boalt Hall—School of Law, University of California, Berkeley

FOUNDATION PRESS
2011

THOMSON REUTERS™

© 2005 THOMSON REUTERS/FOUNDATION PRESS
© 2011 By THOMSON REUTERS/FOUNDATION PRESS

    1 New York Plaza, 34th Floor

    New York, NY 10004

    Phone Toll Free 1–877–888–1330

    Fax (646) 424–5201

    foundation–press.com

Printed in the United States of America

ISBN 978–1–59941–958–9

Mat #40929476

For the late E. W. Coleman and M. H. Coleman,
my daughters Kristen and Allison and my sisters Betty, Jean and Earlene

INTRODUCTION TO THE
SECOND EDITION

We live in a society organized according to two master principles: capitalism and democracy. Although principles and their associated values, institutions, and norms are integral to American life, they often seem to exist in different worlds. Capitalism is often thought of as belonging to the "private" sphere, whereas democracy belongs in the "public" sphere. Capitalism is the business of business organizations and of economic analysis; democracy is the business of politicians and voters and of political analysis. Within the academy, a similar split seems to have created two cultures, like the "two cultures" of science and the humanities of which C.P. Snow originally spoke. Economic analysis has developed a culture of scientific expertise in which developing testable hypotheses with mathematical rigor, constructing quantitative analyses, and making predictions are principal values. Although social scientists increasingly analyze democratic institutions in this way as well, discussions of democracy have more traditionally been the bailiwick of moral philosophers, and more recently critical theorists, who use the language of morality, justice, and the methodological tools associated with the humanities to pursue the "ought" rather than the "is."

The split obtains in legal scholarship as well. In the last few decades, the law and economics movement has had a tremendous impact on legal studies. Like its parent discipline economics, law and economics focuses on questions of transactional efficiency and tends to ignore questions of distribution or justice; it seeks to accurately describe how legal rules work (or don't work), and to the extent it is normative rather than descriptive, the assumed goal is greater efficiency. Traditional legal scholarship, however, has taken the pursuit of distributional justice, fairness, and democratic process as central to its analyses. In the last few decades critical legal scholarship has developed an even more openly moral discourse of justice, focused on the pursuit of equality. Traditional and critical scholars, however, have seldom ventured into the territory of efficiency or the systematic analysis of transactions, just as law and economics scholars have seldom ventured into the territory of fairness and equality.

Interesting exchanges between the two cultures have begun to occur in the last few years. Economics generally, and law and economics in particular, has begun to alter its once iron-clad assumption that people always act as rational maximizers; with the abandonment of perfect rationality, economic analysis is increasingly equipped to address issues, like cooperative behavior, that involve trust as well as immediate self-interest, and motivations more complicated than direct instrumentality. For their part, philosophers and traditional scholars–and even a few critical scholars—have become increasingly interested in what economic analysis can tell us about institutions and the aggregate behavior of groups in response to incentives. New sub-disciplines like "socio-economics" have emerged to explore the convergence between traditional legal scholarship and law and economics. Yet, a productive conversation between critical legal scholarship and law and economics has only tentatively begun. This casebook is offered as a means of furthering that conversation.

The phrase "economic justice" signals our aim: rather than maintaining the tacit assumption that "justice" has nothing to do with economics and economics nothing to do with social justice, we hope to engage the two cultures with one another. What can economics tell us about democracy and the law? What can theories of justice tell us about economic theory and the law? Why is there no legal language of "class" in the United States, and what might one look like? Rather than asking students to specialize in one or the other discourse, as current legal pedagogy implicitly does, this casebook openly engages students in the project of learning from both discourses, and using each as a means to gain insights on the other.

Moreover, our project here is not only to engage traditional legal scholarship with law and economics, but more specifically critical legal scholarship with law and economics. Critical legal scholarship is not only distinctive in its wholehearted embrace of a moral perspective on politics and law and in its commitment to equality as the master principle; it is also distinctive in its ambition to place issues that have long stymied American society, especially the issue of racial and gender justice, at the center of its normative agenda. Race and gender are so thorny, in part, because they introduce a third principle—community—into the debate between liberty and equality. Neither traditional legal analysis nor economic analysis has paid much attention to the question of who constitutes America, what full citizenship means to those who were originally not included in the American vision, and how a multicultural, multinational society can function within a single economic and political system. Neither traditional legal analysis nor economic analysis has adequately addressed issues like the market value of racialized culture and sexual difference, the borders of national and cultural community, and the problem of remediating long-standing inequalities in both economic and social spheres.

In this casebook, we use the problem of racial and gender injustice as a vehicle for engaging both critical theory and economic theory. Just as race, gender, and class seem inextricably intertwined, economic and critical analysis both seem crucial to unraveling the knot of racial and gender inequality. Moreover, economic analysis and critical analysis may need to influence and be influenced by one another in order for a truly incisive and transformative dialogue about race and gender to emerge in the legal academy and in American society more generally.

This casebook involves students in creating this dialogue. In Chapter 1, we identify a central tension between the culture of traditional legal analysis, with its claims of neutrality and the culture of critical race theory with its emphasis on subjective narrative. We ask whether legal analysis is (or should it be) a science? Or is legal reasoning inherently interpretive, more art than science? Is the law a neutral and objective forum for conflict resolution, or is it a tool of the powerful? As legal scholars concerned with the impact of subordination in law and in markets, we examine the role that traditional legal analysis plays in reinforcing the rational choice, efficiency, and wealth maximization assumptions of traditional economic views of the operation of markets. It is not surprising to find that claims of neutrality play as central a role in traditional legal theory, as they do in traditional economic analysis.

The challenge to the premise of legal neutrality has brought to the surface the conflict between the two cultures of law. In this first chapter we extend the anti-subordination critique to classic market economics and to law and economics. We believe that the question of method—whether there is an objective science of society, or whether knowledge is inherently perspectival—is of such central importance to understanding the structure of economic inequality that it is the indispensable starting point from which we must begin the three-way conversation between the traditionalists in economics, the traditionalists in law, and the anti-subordination-oriented legal theorists.

The central organizing question of this first chapter: what methods and normative assumptions are most useful in evaluating the complex landscape of law, markets, and culture? What tools are best suited to sort truth from ideology and myth? What would "truth" look like if we found it? We begin with these questions because we believe that unless these intensely contested, yet often invisible, first premises of analysis are explored, it will be impossible to make sense of the claims and arguments of the traditionalists in economics and in law or the contradictory positions of critical race feminist scholars concerned with the problem of intertwined structures of subordination. Throughout this book we will use a variety of tools to pursue our interest in fostering a conversation between economics and the critical perspectives. We will use methodologies and insights from sociology, psychology, and behavioral economics, as well as the various schools of modern legal thought.

Chapter 2 is an entirely new chapter in which we explore the economic and financial collapse of 2008. This crisis began with unregulated and often predatory origination of high cost loans. American financial institutions operated free of important regulatory constraints. In the years between 2004 and 2007, banks and mortgage brokers escalated irresponsible origination and underwriting standards. These loans were then packaged and structured into pools of derivatives linked to subprime home mortgages. The securitization process was an essential element in creating an interdependent a global financial market. However, when the basic assumption of rising home prices proved to be wrong, the home price asset bubble burst, launching a worldwide financial panic. The crisis produced an extraordinarily painful natural experiment in which the neoclassical model of macroeconomic theory and the deregulatory legal arguments of law and economics failed spectacularly. The failure of the economic and legal theories that we challenged in the first edition gives us no comfort because the economic dislocation of so many ordinary citizens is still unfolding.

Chapter 2 examines the conflicting narratives of the crisis. Members of the private financial sector portray the crisis as an unpredictable natural disaster, a once-in-a-century "tsunami" that "no one could have predicted." Financial regulators, including the Securities and Exchange Commission and the Federal Reserve, tell a story of a stealthy, unregulated "shadow banking" sector over which they had no statutory. In the political narrative, the collapse was a triumph of private greed over civic responsibility, the "fat cat bankers" of Wall Street gaming the system against Main Street. For homeowners, this is a story of easy subprime home loans that turned the American Dream into a personal finance nightmare of foreclosures, job losses, vanishing home equity, constrained family finances for college, and disappearing retirement portfolios. Finally, for taxpayers, the bailout unleashed a deep seated populist outrage that was directed at both politicians and bankers. The competition among these stories continues, more than two years later.

As the second edition goes to press in the fall of 2010, the official autopsy of the crisis is still in progress. The Financial Crisis Inquiry Commission was established to "examine the causes, domestic and global, of the current financial and economic crisis in the United States.".

In Chapter 2 we extend our evaluation of law and economics and its inattention to pervasive problems of economic and social inequality. We begin with a history the Federal Housing Administration (FHA) policies that laid the foundation for racially discriminatory housing finance. One consequence of this FHA history was the creation of a persistent asset gap based on disparities in housing ownership. We provide a history of the subprime loan market. The financial collapse brought a wave of foreclosures on homes that had been financed with deeply flawed loans. The wave of foreclosures has overwhelmed courts and lawyers representing lenders. The problem of mistaken foreclosures and incomplete or fraudulent legal documentation of foreclosure proceeding prompted two important extralegal reactions that we document here: strategic default and squatters. We conclude with a discussion of sustainable housing for low wealth borrowers.

Chapter 3 introduces students to two ways of thinking about the idea of economic justice: one drawing on the Weberian notion of class stratification, and the other drawing on Marx (who drew on early economists like Adam Smith and John Stuart Mill) and the notion of political economy. It introduces students as well to the concept of the United States as a capitalist democracy in which capitalism and democracy popularly inhabit two different spheres, a "public" and a "private," and it helps students see how law is actively engaged in creating and maintaining both spheres, as well as in drawing the line between them. Chapter 1 also engages students in trying to answer the question why there is no developed discourse of economic inequality within American constitutional law. In pursuing answers to this question, the chapter introduces themes that will reappear throughout the book, including racial injustice and the tangled relationship between racial inequality and economic inequality.

Chapter 4 introduces students to the basic principles of economic theory and the key ideological assumptions that undergird the discipline of economics and thereby law and economics, through an engagement with "classical," free-market economics and some of its critics. We use familiar cases from the first year curriculum in torts and property to provide examples of judicial reasoning that relies upon the law and economics theoretical premises.

Chapters 5 and 6 extend the exploration of the basic tenets of modern economic theory as it has been applied in legal reasoning. Chapter 5 is concerned with the critiques of classic market theory coming from those who share its basic premises. Chapter 6 introduces students to the major challenges to market economics from those who reject the basic premises of that field. In this chapter, we explore the challenges to price theory, rational choice, and wealth maximization premises that have come from those who do not share the faith in markets and private ordering. Within law, these criticisms include doctrinalists who are unconvinced by the positive claim that the common law converges on efficiency, critical legal scholars who reject the normative premise that wealth maximization is a coherent value for evaluating the legal rules that govern the distribution of material goods in a democracy.

In Chapters 7 and 8 we take up the data that confirms the picture of economic inequality. Beyond the numbers, we listen to the voices and narratives of those who are at the bottom rung of wealth and income. We see the role of class and the influence of material culture in degrading the participation of those with the least in the common forums of this society. Finally, these two chapters are concerned with the barriers to economic mobility.

Chapters 9, 10, 11, and 12 take up specific topics that illuminate the interactions among race, gender, and economic inequality, and the sometimes complementary, sometimes conflicting values of liberty, equality, and community. Chapter 9 concerns the family; Chapter 10 concerns culture and identity; Chapter 11 concerns the market value of culture; Chapter 12 concerns underground and informal economies; and Chapter 13 concerns economic borders to community.

Finally, Chapter 14 addresses questions of remediation and transformation. How might familiar legal debates like the one on "affirmative action" be transformed when seen from a perspective that incorporates a sophisticated understanding of the relationship between race and class, and a vision that is enriched by both efficiency and justice concerns?

ACKNOWLEDGEMENTS FOR THE SECOND EDITION

I am deeply grateful for the support of my Georgetown students, especially William Steinwedel, Ugochi C Igbokwe and Jahlionais Gaston for their devotion as research assistants through many long hours.

The faculty support at Georgetown continues to be superb. I thank Anna Selden, Lindsay Pullen, Angie Villarreal, Sylvia Johnson, Toni Stedmon, Monica Stearns, Jennifer Davitt and Jennifer Klein. Working with my co-author has been a casebook author's dream: exceptional imagination, timeliness, and above all an even temperament.

EMMA COLEMAN JORDAN

Washington, D.C.
October 2010

I would like to thank my faculty assistant at the University at Buffalo, Sue Martin, for getting so quickly up to speed on the thankless task of collecting permissions to reprint; the participants in the 2010 ClassCrits workshop at the University at Buffalo, for provocative and insightful discussion and commentary on the global financial crisis and the state of heterodox economics; and, as always, my brilliant co-author Emma Jordan.

ANGELA HARRIS

Berkeley, California
October 2010

ACKNOWLEDGEMENTS FOR THE FIRST EDITION

The idea for creating teaching materials to introduce law students to a systematic examination of the interdisciplinary dimensions of increasing economic inequality and the role of identity in the distribution of wealth first occurred to me more than ten years ago. My decision to create this casebook arose from my mounting frustration with the conceptual limitations of the consumer protection features of commercial law and banking, the two traditional areas in which I had been working over the course of my career. I deeply appreciate the contributions of Nancy Ota who came to Georgetown Law Center in 1992–93 as a graduate Fellow in the Future Law Professor Program to work with me. She invested her unique imagination and commitment to assist me in creating the first set of teaching materials for the first course on Economic Justice.

This casebook owes much to the confidence and support I enjoyed from my publisher, Steven Errick. His enthusiasm and shared vision for the innovations of this effort and his never-failing generosity in responding to and initiating additional publishing opportunities for the Economic Justice topic were important at critical points in the process. Steve's departure in the weeks before this book went to press was a real personal loss. I look forward to working with the new publisher, John Bloomquist in future editions.

I especially want to thank the many Georgetown University Law Center students who enrolled in the early courses in Economic Justice, and who became my most enthusiastic cheering section (offering rap and pop lyrics, African proverbs, Equal Access to Justice/E.A.T. Justice, a socially conscious business venture and strong counterarguments) as this project moved forward to completion. I learned so much from our intense classroom investigations of some of my then forming hypotheses about educational capital, wealth and income inequalities, intergenerational economic effects, linguistic differences, the relationship of the Constitution to economic outcomes, and the limits of conventional market theory. The richness and complexity of this project owe much to my students.

From my Georgetown law students, I chose outstanding research assistants who worked with passion and conviction on the research for this book. They found many truly important additions to the materials. They designed the critical copyright accounting system, chased elusive copyright holders with the zeal of a "repo" man/woman They kept me laughing when I might have otherwise turned grouchy. They discussed this newly emerging field with me with intelligence and energy. My special thanks go to Angela Ahern '05, Rashida Baskerville '06, Katherine Buell '04, Cassandra Charles '05, Kenneth Leichter '06, William Morriss '05, Michael Radolinski '06, and Joshua Soszynski '07.

Shaping the boundaries of this project required many hours of conversation with colleagues. Steven Salop was exceptionally generous with his time and the contents of his library on economics. The time we spent talking about economics and shuttling from my office to his across the hall, undoubtedly accelerated my understanding of the intellectual framework of modern economics. I benefited greatly from the expertise and gentle prodding of several colleagues: Alex Aleinikoff, William Braxton, Jerry Kang (during his visit in 2004–5), Carrie Menkel–Meadow, Michael Seidman, Gerry Spann, Rebecca Tushnet, Kathy Zeiler and the colleagues who participated in the Georgetown Law Center Summer Faculty Workshop in 2004. If there are any errors in what follows, it must be because I didn't listen to their sage advice.

This project could not have been finished without the superb institutional arrangements in place at Georgetown University Law Center to support faculty manuscripts. Georgetown enjoys an organizational structure that would be the envy of most casebook writers. I received several summer research grants to allow me to devote time to developing and completing the project. In their capacities as lead manuscript editor and faculty services librarian for this book, Zinta Saulkans and Jennifer Locke and her staff were truly indispensable to achieving a high technical quality for the final manuscript. Diane McDonald, my faculty assistant, Derreck Brown, Sylvia Johnson, Toni Patterson, Ronnie Reese, and Anna Selden in the Office of Faculty Support were always optimistic in the face of frustrations and the unexpected nightmares of formatting, and other technical melt-downs. They were responsive to my many requests during the development of this book. Finally, the Office of Information Systems and Technology introduced me to new equipment and software for managing the project. My special thanks go to Dianne H. Ferro Mesarch, Dimo Michailov, Pablo Molina and Barry Wileman.

In 2001, Angela Harris visited at Georgetown from Boalt Hall at the Univ. of California at Berkeley. As we discussed her work on class and race, it became clear that I could benefit from working with her on this casebook. When she agreed to join the project, I could not know then what a terrific contributor she would be. Her intelligence and humor made the work flow effortlessly to conclusion. We truly had fun doing this work; my only regret is that I didn't think to ask her to join me sooner.

Finally, I want to thank my two daughters Kristen and Allison for their patience and understanding during the many hours I devoted to completing this project.

EMMA COLEMAN JORDAN

Washington, D.C. August, 2005

I would like to thank my students at Boalt and at Georgetown (Wealth and Class Relations, fall 2000; Wealth and Class Relations, fall 2001; and Law, Markets, and Culture, fall 2004) for their excitement, hard work, and insight as we tried to think through the complicated mutual entanglements of "fairness," "efficiency," "markets," "culture," and "law," and as we struggled toward an institutional theory of human flourishing.

I would like to thank my assistant, Ayn Lowry, for her skill and dedication at tracking down copyright holders across the globe, and for her enthusiasm for this project despite the many last-minute headaches it caused.

I owe a huge debt to my co-author, Emma Coleman Jordan, for talking me into joining and then sticking with the project, and for her wonderful combination of brilliant vision, sisterly solidarity, and can-do spirit.

Last, but not least, I would like to thank my amazing research assistants, Tucker Bolt Culbertson and Naomi Ruth Tsu, for everything: research, pep talks, proofreading, formatting, article suggestions, critical feedback, and, of course, cookies.

ANGELA HARRIS

Berkeley, California
August 2005

SUMMARY OF CONTENTS

TABLE OF CONTENTS

TABLE OF CASES

Principal cases are in bold type. Non-principal cases are in roman type. References are to Pages.

CASES AND MATERIALS

ECONOMIC JUSTICE:
RACE, GENDER, IDENTITY AND ECONOMICS

SECOND EDITION

CHAPTER 1

RACE, MARKETS, AND NEUTRALITY IN TWO DISCIPLINES

Introduction and Overview

Almost fifty years ago, Charles P. Snow, the British novelist and physicist, identified an important communications gap between the literary and scientific cultures. In a now famous lecture, he used the metaphor of "two cultures" to represent the often incompatible world views of science and literature. He worried that the progress of knowledge in the western world would be compromised by the incomprehension then existing between scientists on one hand, and scholars in the humanities on the other. For Snow, science embodied a culture of objectivity, neutrality, and detached factual inquiry. Literary intellectuals, on the other hand were concerned with questions of meaning, identity, and history.

We conclude that an analogous gap exists today between two groups of legal scholars who think seriously about markets. On one hand, traditional law and economics scholars, like economists, are interested in questions of rational choice, efficiency, wealth maximization, and production and transactions costs. On the other hand, legal scholars concerned with questions of identity, including race, gender, and sexual orientation have focused their scholarly investigations on issues of subordination, identity, cultural context, and legal indeterminacy. These two groups of scholars might have much to learn from each other. However, these "two cultures" of law, with few exceptions, remain in separate conversations, with separate world views and separate, even antagonistic, operating assumptions about how to evaluate market phenomena.

In this book, we investigate the problems of the market domain with respect for both cultures. We suspect that the economics perspective, with its reliance on scientific measurement and numerical representation of experience, offers much that can be useful. Our vantage point as scholars who have been active in anti-subordination theory, however, also leads us to be attentive to questions of identity, culture, context, history, and dominance.

Central to the tension between the two cultures of law is the question of method. Is legal analysis (or should it be) a science? Or is legal reasoning inherently interpretive, more art than science? Is the law a neutral and objective forum for conflict resolution, or is it a tool of the powerful? Scholars concerned with the problem of subordination—especially subordination based on race and gender identity—have challenged the claims of

1

neutrality of traditional legal theory. This challenge has brought to the surface the conflict between the two cultures of law. In this book we extend the anti-subordination critique to classic market economics and to law and economics. We believe that the question of method—whether there is an objective science of society, or whether knowledge is inherently perspectival—is of such central importance to understanding the structure of economic inequality that it provides a promising field upon which to begin the three-way conversation between the traditionalists in economics, the traditionalists in law, and the anti-subordination-oriented legal theorists.

As legal scholars concerned with the impact of subordination in law and in markets, we want to examine the role that traditional legal analysis plays in reinforcing the rational choice, efficiency, and wealth maximization assumptions of traditional economic views of the operation of markets. It is not surprising to find that claims of neutrality play as central a role in traditional legal theory as they do in traditional economic analysis.

We turn now to the central organizing question of this first chapter: what methods and normative assumptions are most useful in evaluating the complex landscape of law, markets, and culture? What tools are best suited to sort truth from ideology and myth? What would "truth" look like if we found it? We begin with these questions because we believe that unless these intensely contested, yet often invisible, first premises of analysis are explored, it will be impossible to make sense of the claims and arguments of the traditionalists in economics and in law or the contradictory positions of critical race, feminist, and other scholars concerned with the problem of intertwined structures of subordination. Throughout this book we will use a variety of tools to pursue our interest in fostering a conversation between economics and the critical perspectives. We will use methodologies and insights from sociology, psychology, and behavioral economics, as well as the various schools of modern legal thought.

To begin our discussion we have chosen a now-famous narrative account by Professor Patricia Williams. Williams is a part of the critical race theory movement, described below. Our choice to begin with a narrative reflects our view about neutrality and truth. Stories can provide a potent starting point for identifying and examining buried assumptions. As you work through this material keep in mind the structure and sources of the neutrality claims identified above. See if you can detect them on your own.

A. CRITICAL RACE THEORY: NARRATIVE, NEUTRALITY, AND THE MARKETPLACE

The Death of the Profane
THE ALCHEMY OF RACE AND RIGHTS 44–51 (1991).

■ PATRICIA J. WILLIAMS

Buzzers are big in New York City. Favored particularly by smaller stores and boutiques, merchants throughout the city have installed them as screening devices to reduce the incidence of robbery: if the face at the door looks desirable, the buzzer is pressed and the door is unlocked. If the face is that of an undesirable, the door stays locked. Predictably, the issue of undesirability has revealed itself to be a racial determination. While controversial enough at first, even civil-rights organizations backed down eventually in the face of arguments that the buzzer system is a "necessary evil," that it is a "mere inconvenience" in comparison to the risks of being murdered, that suffering discrimination is not as bad as being assaulted, and that in any event it is not all blacks who are barred, just "17–year–old black males wearing running shoes and hooded sweatshirts."

The installation of these buzzers happened swiftly in New York; stores that had always had their doors wide open suddenly became exclusive or received people by appointment only. I discovered them and their meaning one Saturday in 1986. I was shopping in Soho and saw in a store window a sweater that I wanted to buy for my mother. I pressed my round brown face to the window and my finger to the buzzer, seeking admittance. A narrow-eyed, white teenager wearing running shoes and feasting on bubble gum glared out, evaluating me for signs that would pit me against the limits of his social understanding. After about five seconds, he mouthed "We're closed," and blew pink rubber at me. It was two Saturdays before Christmas, at one o'clock in the afternoon; there were several white people in the store who appeared to be shopping for things for *their* mothers.

I was enraged. At that moment I literally wanted to break all the windows of the store and *take* lots of sweaters for my mother. In the flicker of his judgmental gray eyes, that saleschild had transformed my brightly sentimental, joy-to-the-world, pre-Christmas spree to a shambles. He snuffed my sense of humanitarian catholicity, and there was nothing I could do to snuff his, without making a spectacle of myself.

I am still struck by the structure of power that drove me into such a blizzard of rage. There was almost nothing I could do, short of physically intruding upon him, that would humiliate him the way he humiliated me. No words, no gestures, no prejudices of my own would make a bit of difference to him; his refusal to let me into the store—it was Benetton's, whose colorfully punish ad campaign is premised on wrapping every one of the world's peoples in its cottons and woolens—was an outward manifestation of his never having let someone like me into the realm of his reality. He had no compassion, no remorse, no reference to me; and no desire to acknowledge me even at the estranged level of arm's-length transactor. He saw me only as one who would take his money and therefore could not conceive that I was there to give him money.

In this weird ontological imbalance, I realized that buying something in that store was like bestowing a gift, the gift of my commerce, the lucre of my patronage. In the wake of my outrage, I wanted to take back the gift of appreciation that my peering in the window must have appeared to be. I wanted to take it back in the form of unappreciation, disrespect, defilement. I wanted to work so hard at wishing he could feel what I felt that he would never again mistake my hatred for some sort of plaintive wish to be included. I was quite willing to disenfranchise myself, in the heat of my need to revoke the flattery of my purchasing power. I was willing to boycott Benetton's, random white-owned businesses, and anyone who ever blew bubble gum in my face again.

My rage was admittedly diffuse, even self-destructive, but it was symmetrical. The perhaps loose-ended but utter propriety of that rage is no doubt lost not just to the young man who actually barred me, but to those who would appreciate my being barred only as an abstract precaution, who approve of those who would bar even as they deny that they would bar *me*.

The violence of my desire to burst into Benetton's is probably quite apparent. I often wonder if the violence, the exclusionary hatred, is equally apparent in the repeated public urgings that blacks understand the buzzer system by putting themselves in the shoes of white storeowners—that, in effect, blacks look into the mirror of frightened white faces for the reality of their undesirability; and that then blacks would "just as surely conclude that they would not let themselves in under similar circumstances." (That some blacks might agree merely shows that some of us have learned too well the lessons of privatized intimacies of self-hatred and rationalized away the fullness of our public, participatory selves.)

On the same day I was barred from Benetton's, I went home and wrote the above impassioned account in my journal. On the day after that, I found I was still brooding, so I turned to a form of catharsis I have always found healing. I typed up as much of the story as I have just told, made a big poster of it, put a nice colorful border around it, and, after Benetton's was truly closed, stuck it to their big sweater-filled window. I exercised my first amendment right to place my business with them right out in the street.

So that was the first telling of this story. The second telling came a few months later, for a symposium on Excluded Voices sponsored by a law review. I wrote an essay summing up my feelings about being excluded from Benetton's and analyzing "how the rhetoric of increased privatization, in response to racial issues, functions as the rationalizing agent of public unaccountability and, ultimately, irresponsibility." Weeks later, I received the first edit. From the first page to the last, my fury had been carefully cut out. My rushing, run-on-rage had been reduced to simple declarative sentences. The active personal had been inverted in favor of the passive impersonal. My words were different; they spoke to me upside down. I was afraid to read too much of it at a time—meanings rose up at me oddly, stolen and strange.

A week and a half later, I received the second edit. All reference to Benetton's had been deleted because, according to the editors and the faculty adviser, it was defamatory; they feared harassment and liability; they said printing it would be irresponsible. I called them and offered to supply a footnote attesting to this as my personal experience at one particular location and of a buzzer system not limited to Benetton's; the editors told me that they were not in the habit of publishing things that were unverifiable. I could not but wonder, in this refusal even to let me file an affidavit, what it would take to make my experience verifiable. The testimony of an independent white bystander? (a requirement in fact imposed in U.S. Supreme Court holdings through the first part of the century).

Two days *after* the piece was sent to press, I received copies of the final page proofs. All reference to my race had been eliminated because it was against "editorial policy" to permit descriptions of physiognomy. "I realize," wrote one editor, "that this was a very personal experience, but any reader will know what you must have looked like when standing at that window." In a telephone conversation to them, I ranted wildly about the significance of such an omission. "It's irrelevant," another editor explained in a voice gummy with soothing and patience; "It's nice and poetic" but it doesn't "advance the discussion of any principle.... This is a law review, after all." Frustrated, I accused him of censorship; calmly he assured me it was not. "This is just a matter of style," he said with firmness and finality.

Ultimately I did convince the editors that mention of my race was central to the whole sense of the subsequent text; that my story became one of extreme paranoia without the information that I am black; or that it became one in which the reader had to fill in the gap by assumption, presumption, prejudgment, or prejudice. What was most interesting to me in this experience was how the blind application of principles of neutrality, through the device of omission, acted either to make me look crazy or to make the reader participate in old habits of cultural bias.

That was the second telling of my story. The third telling came last April, when I was invited to participate in a law-school conference on Equality and Difference. I retold my sad tale of exclusion from Soho's most glitzy boutique, focusing in this version on the law-review editing process as a consequence of an ideology of style rooted in a social text of neutrality, I opined:

> Law and legal writing aspire to formalized, color-blind, liberal ideals. Neutrality is the standard for assuring these ideals; yet the adherence to it is often determined by reference to an aesthetic of uniformity, in which difference is simply omitted. For example, when segregation was eradicated from the American lexicon, its omission led many to actually believe that racism therefore no longer existed. Race-neutrality in law has become the presumed antidote for race bias in real life. With the entrenchment of the notion of race-neutrality came attacks on the concept of affirmative action and the rise of reverse discrimination suits. Blacks, for so many generations deprived of jobs based on the color of our skin, are now told that we ought to find it demeaning to be hired, based on the color of our skin. Such is the silliness of simplistic either-or inversions as remedies to complex problems.

What is truly demeaning in this era of double-speak-no-evil is going on interviews and not getting hired because someone doesn't think we'll be comfortable. It is demeaning not to get promoted because we're judged "too weak," then putting in a lot of energy the next time and getting fired because we're "too strong." It is demeaning to be told what we find demeaning. It is very demeaning to stand on street corners unemployed and begging. It is downright demeaning to have to explain why we haven't been employed for months and then watch the job go to someone who is "more experienced." It is outrageously demeaning that none of this can be called racism, even if it happens only to, or to large numbers of, black people; as long is it's done with a smile, a handshake and a shrug; as long as the phantom-word "race" is never used.

The image of race as a phantom-word came to me after I moved into my late godmother's home. In an attempt to make it my own, I cleared the bedroom for painting. The following morning the room asserted itself, came rushing and raging at me through the emptiness, exactly as it had been for twenty-five years. One day filled with profuse and overwhelming complexity, the next day filled with persistently recurring memories. The shape of the past came to haunt me, the shape of the emptiness confronted me each time I was about to enter the room. The force of its spirit still drifts like an odor throughout the house.

The power of that room, I have thought since, is very like the power of racism as status quo: it is deep, angry, eradicated from view, but strong enough to make everyone who enters the room walk around the bed that isn't there, avoiding the phantom as they did the substance, for fear of bodily harm. They do not even know they are avoiding; they defer to the unseen shapes of things with subtle responsiveness, guided by an impulsive awareness of nothingness, and the deep knowledge and denial of witchcraft at work.

The phantom room to me is symbolic of the emptiness of formal equal opportunity, particularly as propounded by President Reagan, the Reagan Civil Rights Commission and the Reagan Supreme Court. Blindly formalized constructions of equal opportunity are the creation of a space that is filled in by a meandering stream of unguided hopes, dreams, fantasies, fears, recollections. They are the presence of the past imaginary, imagistic form—the phantom-roomed exile of our longing.

It is thus that I strongly believe in the efficacy of programs and paradigms like affirmative action. Blacks are the objects of constitutional omission which has been incorporated into a theory of neutrality. It is thus that omission is really a form of expression, as oxymoronic as that sounds: racial omission is a literal part of original intent; it is the fixed, reiterated prophecy of the Founding Fathers. It is thus that affirmative action is an affirmation; the affirmative act of hiring—or hearing—blacks is a recognition of individuality that replaces blacks as a social statistic that is profoundly interconnective to the fate of blacks and whites either as subgroups or as one group. In this sense, affirmative action is as mystical and beyond-the-self as an initiation ceremony. It is an act of verification and of vision. It is an act of social as well as professional responsibility.

The following morning I opened the local newspaper, to find that the event of my speech had commanded two columns on the front page of the Metro section. I quote only the opening lines: "Affirmative action promotes prejudice by denying the status of women and blacks, instead of affirming them as its name suggests. So said New York City attorney Patricia Williams to an audience Wednesday."

I clipped out the article and put it in my journal. In the margin there is a note to myself: eventually, it says, I should try to pull all these threads together into yet another law-review article. The problem, of course, will be that in the hierarchy of law-review citation, the article in the newspaper will have more authoritative weight about me, as a so-called "primary resource," than I will have; it will take precedence over my own citation of the unverifiable testimony of my speech.

I have used the Benetton's story a lot, in speaking engagements at various schools. I tell it whenever I am too tired to whip up an original speech from scratch. Here are some of the questions I have been asked in the wake of its telling:

Am I not privileging a racial perspective, by considering only the black point of view? Don't I have an obligation to include the "salesman's side" of the story?

Am I not putting the salesman on trial and finding him guilty of racism without giving him a chance to respond to or cross-examine me?

Am I not using the store window as a "metaphorical fence" against the potential of his explanation in order to represent my side as "authentic"?

How can I be sure I'm right?

What makes my experience the real black one anyway?

Isn't it possible that another black person would disagree with my experience? If so, doesn't that render my story too unempirical and subjective to pay any attention to?

Always a major objection is to my having put the poster on Benetton's window. As one law professor put it: "It's one thing to publish this in a law review, where no one can take it personally, but it's another thing altogether to put your own interpretation right out there, just like that, uncontested, I mean, with nothing to counter it."

NOTES AND QUESTIONS

1. Shared claims of neutrality: legal neutrality and economic neutrality. In their declarations of "truth," legal opinions are presented as objective, indifferent, and neutral. Similarly, the market is based on the notion that a willing buyer and a willing seller will participate in an arm's-length transaction according to their preferences. The sum total of these discrete transactions is a market expressing cumulative preferences that are neutral, in that they do not reflect central government control. It was

Adam Smith, one of the founding fathers of modern economics, who asserted that the greater good for all could be best achieved through such a market of free exchanges, guided by the invisible hand. But, what happens when only one party is willing to participate in a transaction? How do individual preferences and choices affect the market? What role does legal neutrality play in weakening or reinforcing these preferences?

2. Wechslerian principles of neutrality. Lawyer and legal scholar Herbert Wechsler promoted constitutional interpretation based on neutral principles, not the immediate results of particular cases. He described the "ad hoc evaluation" based on individual outcome as "the deepest problem of our constitutionalism." Herbert Wechsler, *Toward Neutral Principles of Constitutional Law*, 73 HARV. L. REV. 1 (1959).

> A principled decision, in the sense I have in mind, is one that rests on reasons with respect to all the issues in the case, reasons that in their generality and their neutrality transcend any immediate result that is involved. When no sufficient reasons of this kind can be assigned for overturning value choices of the other branches of the Government or of a state, those choices must, of course, survive. Otherwise, as Holmes said in his first opinion for the Court, "a constitution, instead of embodying only relatively fundamental rules of right, as generally understood by all English-speaking communities, would become the partisan of a particular set of ethical or economical opinions...." *Id.* at 19.

Wechsler recognizes the potential for constitutional decisions that do not reflect personal views of justice, and he points to use of the Fourteenth Amendment to remedy racial discrimination as "the hardest test." *Id.* at 26. Though he claimed to be in favor of desegregated schools, he says:

> I find it hard to think the judgment [in *Brown v. Board of Education*] really turned upon the facts. Rather, it seems to me, it must have rested on the view that racial segregation is, in principle, a denial of equality to the minority against whom it is directed; that is, the group that is not dominant politically and, therefore, does not make the choice involved. For many who support the Court's decision this assuredly is the decisive ground. But this position also presents problems. Does it not involve an inquiry into the motive of the legislature, which is generally foreclosed to the courts? Is it alternatively defensible to make the measure of validity of legislation the way it is interpreted by those who are affected by it? In the context of a charge that segregation *with equal facilities* is a denial of equality, is there not a point in *Plessy* in the statement that if "enforced separation stamps the colored race with a badge of inferiority" it is solely because its members choose "to put that construction upon it"? . . .

> For me, assuming equal facilities, the question posed by state-enforced segregation is not one of discrimination at all. Its human and its constitutional dimensions lie entirely elsewhere, in the denial by the

state of freedom to associate, a denial that impinges in the same way on any groups or races that may be involved.

* * *

But if the freedom of association is denied by segregation, integration forces an association upon those for whom it is unpleasant or repugnant.... Given a situation where the state must practically choose between denying the association to those individuals who wish it or imposing it on those who would avoid it, is there a basis in neutral principles for holding that the Constitution demands that the claims for association should prevail? (I should like to think there is, but I confess that I have not yet written the opinion. To write it is for me the challenge of the school-segregation cases.)

Id, at 33–34.

The requirement of neutrality in law, as described by Wechsler, limits the judiciary's ability to make law based on value judgments. Is it more important for the legal system to make decisions based on neutral principles or outcomes? Are "neutral" principles really neutral, or do they promote value judgments as well? Is the refusal of the courts to inquire into the motive of the legislature a neutral principle or one which upholds the power of the political majority? In what ways has this philosophy influenced the development of the common law? We return to the question of motive in *Washington v. Davis* infra at 44.

Williams challenges the "blind application of principles of neutrality," claiming, "[b]lacks are the objects of a constitutional omission which has been incorporated into a theory of neutrality." Williams, *supra,* at 50. How would Williams respond to Wechsler's question whether there is a neutral principle upon which *Brown v. Board of Education* could have, or should have, been decided?

3. Neutrality of facts in appellate opinions. Courts use the law as a screen through which certain facts emerge as relevant while other facts are sifted out as irrelevant. *See* Richard Delgado, *Storytelling for Oppositionists and Others: A Plea for Narrative*, 87 Mich. L. Rev. 2411, 2428 (1989). Sometimes the facts after they pass through this screen are startlingly dissimilar to the experiences of the parties involved.

For example, the Supreme Court's opinion in *United States v. Cruikshank*, 92 U.S. 542 (1875) did not include any significant discussion of the facts, only stating the indictments at issue:

The general charge ... that of "banding," and ... that of "conspiring" together to injure, oppress, threaten, and intimidate Levi Nelson and Alexander Tillman, citizens of the United States, of African descent and persons of color, with the intent thereby to hinder and prevent them in their free exercise and enjoyment of rights and privileges "granted and secured" to them "in common with all other good citizens of the United States by the constitution and law of the United States." United States v. Cruikshank, 92 U.S. 542, 548 (1875).

The Court found that the charges were insufficiently specific under the Civil Rights Enforcement Act of 1870, and the convictions were overturned. *Id.* at 559. The Court failed to mention that the charges stemmed from the "bloodiest violence of the Reconstruction." ENCYCLOPEDIA OF AFRICAN AMERICAN CIVIL RIGHTS: FROM EMANCIPATION TO THE PRESENT 541 (Charles D. Lowery & John F. Marszalek, eds., 1992). On Easter Sunday of 1873 in Colfax, Louisiana, 280 African Americans were massacred. *Id.* at 541. In *Cruikshank*, the Court overturned the only convictions among scores of federal prosecutions for the Colfax Riot, but the significance of the opinion's blow to the post–Civil War civil rights movement is lost without a factual setting.

Rather than failing to include significant facts, Justice Cardozo seems to have invented his own version of what took place in the famous torts case *Palsgraf v. Long Island Railroad*. After reading Cardozo's impossible account of Mrs. Palsgraf being injured from across the station platform after a small package exploded, her attorney requested a rehearing because "there was an apparent error in the understanding of the facts of the case." Manz, *Palsgraf, Cardozo's Urban Legend?*, 107 DICK. L. REV. 785, 818 (Spring 2003). Manz asserts that the importance of this case, despite its questionable fact pattern, does not indicate disregard for the truth so much as academic interest in the opinion itself, not the underlying event. Manz, *supra* at 789. As Wechsler advocated, principled reasoning, not the immediate outcome, is important. *See* Wechsler, *supra* text at note 2. Perhaps the outcome of this case is relevant, however. Mrs. Palsgraf was reportedly upset by the lost case for the rest of her life. Manz, *supra* at 840. Additionally, Cardozo's version of the facts has raised questions about his attitudes toward women and the poor. *Id.* at 786. For more on the Palsgraf case factual history, see JOHN T. NOONAN, JR., PERSONS AND MASKS OF THE LAW (1976).

The law review board attempted to screen references to Williams's race as irrelevant and the role of Benetton's as unverifiable. Is Williams correct in asserting that these facts were relevant to her story?

Questioning the neutrality of law, Richard Delgado observed:

Traditional legal writing purports to be neutral and dispassionately analytical, but too often it is not. In part, this is so because legal writers rarely focus on their own mindsets, the received wisdoms that serve as their starting points, themselves no more than stories, that lie behind their quasi-scientific string of deductions. The supposedly objective point of view often mischaracterizes, minimizes, dismisses, or derides without fully understanding opposing viewpoints. Implying that objective, correct answers can be given to legal questions also obscures the moral and political value judgments that lie at the heart of any legal inquiry. Delgado, *supra* at 2440–41.

Delgado is describing the indeterminacy of the law and challenging the notion of neutral application—central themes in the critical legal studies movement. *See* RICHARD W. BAUMAN, CRITICAL LEGAL STUDIES: A GUIDE TO THE LITERATURE 3 (1996). Although "[n]o single manifesto" can summarize the diversity of critical legal thought, "[t]he critique of law, its theories, and its institutions is meant to break down hierarchies of gender, race, class, or so-called merit." *Id.* at 3–4.

4.   Challenging neutrality in practice. Law students generally learn the language of law through legal writing courses, which teach the tone, culture, factual analysis, and reasoning of the practice of law. Kathryn M. Stanchi, *Resistance is Futile: How Legal Writing Pedagogy Contributes to the Law's Marginalization of the Outsider*, 103 DICK. L. REV. 1, 11 (1998).

In addition to internalizing the labels of "relevant" and "irrelevant" facts, students learn how to write objectively. The dominant perspective is described as neutral and objective, and the subjective is disregarded as personal, as opposed to professional. *Id.* at 40. "[O]bjectivity is a hallmark of legal language, of the professional voice." *Id.* at 35.

To counteract the negative effects of objectivity, instructors must incorporate critical legal theory into teaching lawyering skills, but critical writing has generally been focused on legal scholarship instead of the practice of law. Stanchi, *supra* at 56; Brook K. Baker, *Transcending Legacies of Literacy and Transforming the Traditional Repertoire: Critical Discourse Strategies for Practice*, 23 WM. MITCHELL L. REV. 491, 516 (1997).

> Developing a critical discourse is fraught with contradictions arising from lawyers' competing obligations to act and write zealously on behalf of clients on the one hand, and to resist dogma and write transformatively in furtherance of community interests and social justice on the other. Nonetheless, legal writing specialists might consider the efficacy of increased reliance on: (1) using subversive outsider-narratives; (2) confronting and avoiding appeals to bias; and (3) using a more dialogic, less adversarial, more feminist discourse. *Id.* at 517.

Narratives, when subversive instead of hegemonic, use an individual story to reveal a collective wrong. *Id.* at 528–29, 532. The adversarial nature of legal representation allows lawyers to use almost any relevant tactic and prevents only the most blatant appeals to biases. The backlash of color-blind jurisprudence restricts the means to counteract stereotypes, employing biases as well. *Id.* at 543. Using feminist ideals to counteract the male ideology of legal representation as combat, "a nonadversarial advocacy might tone down excessive rhetoric, decrease competitive posturing, and instead engage in a more serious legal, moral, and political dialogue with opponents and legal decision-makers." *Id.* at 555–56.

How might Williams have used her experience in a discrimination suit against Benetton's? Could she find a role for her narrative in the formality of legal documents, thereby avoiding appeals to biases and creating a dialogue about retailers' use of buzzers? *See* Williams at 48, in which she claims omission of her race would make the reader participate in old habits of cultural bias.

5.   Narratives in legal discourse. Narratives are a powerful means of constructing moral and social realities, which are indeterminate and therefore subject to interpretation. Richard Delgado, *Storytelling for Opposition-*

ists and Others: A Plea for Narrative, 87 Mich. L. Rev. 2411, 2415–16 (1989) (illustrating how the reality of a single event changes with the perspective of five different stories).

The stories of the dominant ingroup are used to construct a "shared reality in which its own superior position is seen as natural," by picking and choosing facts to justify the world as it is. But " 'neutrality' can feel [different] from the perspective of an outsider." *Id.* at 2412, 2421, 2425.

Members of outgroups use counterstories, which directly challenge the stories of the ingroup, as (1) a means of self-preservation and (2) a means of lessening their own subordination. *Id.* at 2436.

> [S]tories about oppression, about victimization, about one's own bru-talization—far from deepening the despair of the oppressed, lead to healing, liberation, mental health. They also promote group solidarity. Storytelling emboldens the hearer, who may have had the same thoughts and experiences the storyteller describes, but hesitated to give them voice. Having heard another express them, he or she realizes, I am not alone.

> Yet, stories help oppressed groups in a second way—through their effect on the oppressor. Most oppression ... does not seem like oppression to those perpetrating it. It is rationalized, causing few pangs of conscience. The dominant group justifies its privileged posi-tion by means of stories, stock explanations that construct reality in ways favorable to it....

> This story is drastically at odds with the way most people of color would describe their condition.... Counterstories can attack that complacency.

> What is more, they can do so in ways that promise at least the possibility of success. Most civil rights strategies confront the obstacle of blacks' otherness. The dominant group, noticing that a particular effort is waged on behalf of blacks, increases its resistance. Stories at times can overcome that otherness, hold that instinctive resistance in abeyance. Stories are the oldest, most primordial meeting ground in human experience. Their allure will often provide the most effective means of overcoming otherness, of forming a new collectivity based on the shared story.

> *Id.* at 2436–38.

Listeners asked Patricia Williams why she did not feel obligated to include the salesman's side of the story and why her individual experience was worth their attention. How could Williams, had she chosen to answer the questions, have defended putting "[her] own interpretation right out there"?

6. Significance of Williams's self description. While describing her face in a manner that reinforces connections with this country's segregated history, is Williams giving short shrift to descriptive accuracy? What relationship should the accuracy of Williams's self description have with her publication of the Benetton's story in a law review? If the law review editors believe Williams's description was wholly inaccurate, should they refuse to publish her work? Would the answer change if Williams's piece were written in the traditional, "objective" law review style? For an especially heated exchange between two critical legal scholars about exactly the point raised in the notes above, and the credibility of Patricia Williams's Benetton story, see Mark Tushnet, *The Degradation of Constitutional Discourse*, 81 GEO. L.J. 251, 265–78 (1992) and Gary Peller, *The Discourse of Constitutional Degradation*, 81 GEO. L.J. 313 (1992). *See generally* Richard Posner, *The Skin Trade*, THE NEW REPUBLIC, Oct. 13, 1997, at 40; DANIEL A. FARBER AND SUZANNA SHERRY, BEYOND ALL REASON (1997).

One possible criticism that can be made of Williams's decision to describe her face as round and brown is that it paints a much more familiar picture of racism. Discrimination against Patricia Williams implies a difficult problem which can not be solved simply by assimilation or affirmative action. Law review readers who believe in marketplace neutrality will not want to believe in discrimination against Patricia Williams because it may raise issues of their own culpability for not finding ways of combating prejudice beyond assimilation.

Does Williams's article lose some of its effectiveness by perpetuating a comforting picture of racism? *See also* Devon W. Carbado & Mitu Gulati, *The Law and Economics of Critical Race Theory: Crossroads, Directions, and a New Critical Race Theory*, 112 YALE. L.J. 1757, 1817 (2003) (book review).

7. Williams and anonymous clerk. In *Death of the Profane*, Williams describes not one, but two transactions. First, there is the actual transaction between her and the clerk: the gift of her commerce in exchange for his permission to enter Benetton's. Second, there is the hypothetical exchange which never took place: Williams's money in exchange for Benetton's sweater. When analyzing the situation in this way, doesn't it seem simply as though Williams didn't meet the clerk's asking price for admittance? Obviously, the clerk undervalued Williams's cultural capital. Since the clerk did not open the door, should Williams have pressed a twenty dollar bill against the window in order to sweeten her offer? Would it indicate that the market was functioning properly, at least in the first exchange, if the clerk who refused Williams entry was fired because of bringing bad publicity to Benetton's?

8. Note on Williams's "marketplace." Williams's poignant personal account details her exclusion from participating in the marketplace, an environment where, theoretically, a willing buyer and a willing seller make a connection based on each of their preferences and enter into agreements to buy and sell products and services. The marketplace is fundamentally associated with freedom, functional objectivity, and deference to personal preference. DEBORAH WAIRE POST ET AL., CONTRACTING LAW 1 (1996). In making exchanges for goods and services, willing buyers and sellers usually engage in single transactions or once-only interactions. CRAIG CALHOUN ET AL.,

STRUCTURES OF POWER AND CONSTRAINT: PAPERS IN HONOR OF PETER M. BLAU 134 (1990). These transactions are not based on personal trust between these buying and selling actors; rather, individuals depend on the independent system of law, official contracts, courts, and enforcement agencies to regulate interaction and exchange in the marketplace. *Id.* In this case, Williams requesting to enter Benetton's was an offer to participate in the marketplace, a manifestation of intent to enter into an exchange of her money for a Benetton's product. POST, *supra* at 196. However, Williams's offer created the power of acceptance in the sales associate—the "narrow-eyed, white teenager"—and in denying her admittance into the store, the young clerk abruptly ended a potential exchange in the retail market. *Id.* Therefore, economists may claim that there was no acceptance on the part of the sales clerk, thereby making no obligation on the part of Benetton's to sell Williams any goods or services. The absence of an acceptance failed to complete the formation of a contract between Benetton's to sell goods and Williams to grant "the gift of her commerce."

Though the marketplace paradigm explicates exchanges between buying and selling actors in a straightforward, ostensibly neutral model, it largely ignores several ideological, cultural, and social implications of everyday human interaction. The simple paradigm assumes that actors voluntarily enter into these transactions and that these buyers and sellers do not consider salient issues, such as the other actor's race, class, gender, or ethnicity. *Id.* at 2. As societal norms, citizens' biases, and the nation's socioeconomic hierarchy play a large role in social life, economic models of exchange in the marketplace fail to consider the varied rule systems that constitute and control social transactions. CALHOUN, *supra* at 142.

Williams challenges the simple economic model by asserting that the market is not an impartial setting, but a partial milieu where market players are significantly influenced by their own prejudices and self-indulgence to exclude certain actors from participating in the process of exchange. Williams claims the white clerk's rejection of her admittance into the store was an overt "manifestation of his never having let someone like me into the realm of his reality"; this clerk was only a willing seller to certain willing buyers, not buyers like Williams. Rather than a simple economic transaction, where two players are interested in generating an efficient exchange with one another, negotiating, and creating bilateral decisions, Williams is not given a chance to enter into the bargain; she is on the receiving end of a unilateral decision. According to Williams, a critical race scholar, the marketplace is not an environment where players are on equal footing and make decisions based on individual preferences, but a place where her "round brown face" banishes her from creating stable economic relationships.

9. ***Death of the Profane*** **as demonstrating market power.** At first glance, Professor Williams's experience seems to imply a market failure. However, market economics does not say that businesses (like Benetton's) always make correct decisions; it says that when businesses make bad decisions, they are punished by lost profits which provide an incentive to make better decisions in the future. According to this model, if a business does not stop making bad decisions, its competitors will eventually drive it out of business. With this in mind, is Williams's story an example of the market in action? Benetton's has certainly suffered for its bad decision. Not only did Professor Williams not patronize Benetton's, she also posted a sign in Benetton's window and immortalized the episode in a law review article. Will the loss of business and bad publicity generated by this incident lead Benetton's to change its ways, demonstrating that there wasn't a market failure after all?

10. *Death of the Profane* as demonstrating market impotence. If Williams's experience was not a market failure, does that mean that the market provides no means of dealing with any particular act of injustice, and that it can only (theoretically) work to minimize possible future injustice? However, if the market can not deal with actual acts of injustice, does that argue strongly for legislative solutions?

11.   Does a famous black face make any difference? In the summer of 2005, Oprah Winfrey, the billionare entertainer and entrepreneur, went shopping in Paris. Just fifteen minutes after closing, Oprah approached the very exclusive Hermes store, accompanied by a small party of friends. She noticed a group of people still milling about in the store, and she tried to enter. She was firmly turned away by a clerk. Oprah's best friend, Gayle King, who witnessed the incident reports that: " 'People were in the store and they were shopping. **Oprah** was at the door and she was not allowed into the store.' '**Oprah** describes it herself as "one of the most humillating moments of her life." ' "

King said it's unlikely that Winfrey will shop there again. *Store Sorry for Closed Door Policy*, CHI. TRIB., June 24, 2005, at p. 23.

Oprah was as enraged as Patricia Williams at this shopping slight. Oprah turned her considerable publicity apparatus to respond to the store's refusal. Although she received an apology, she promised to devote an entire show to the episode when she begins taping for the new season in the fall of 2005.

Does the Oprah incident reinforce, undercut, or complicate the racial explanation of Patricia Williams story? Like Williams, Oprah concluded that this was an example of racism. What weight should we give the store's explanation that it refused entry to Oprah because it was preparing for a special promotional event? Does it matter that the store did not fire or demote the clerk who denied entry to Oprah and friends?

12.   Buzzer's role in market model. Does the buzzer fit into the conventional model of the market discussed above? Rather than a tradition- al negotiation between a willing buyer and a willing seller, the buzzer creates a unilateral decision made by an unwilling seller to exclude a willing buyer from the market. What factors might have influenced the clerk's decision to exclude Williams?

13.   Buzzer and racism in marketplace. Williams notes that some deemed the buzzer system to be a "necessary evil" to mitigate the risk of crime in retail establishments. Another possible interpretation of the cultural and social context of the buzzer is that it symbolizes an elevated economic status or a means to establish economic segregation, utilized to prevent theft by excluding people who do not look as if they could afford the merchandise.

If the buzzer system was created to serve this purpose, why did the sales clerk choose to exclude Williams from the store? What is the basis of his belief that a black woman like Williams cannot afford clothes from Benetton's? Did the clerk exclude Williams based on the pervasive cultural representations of African Americans' socioeconomic background in the media or in the courts? Teun A. Van Dijk's study of racism and prejudice at a micro level observed interpersonal communication in everyday life. Van Dijk asserts that the media and the law are major vehicles that create ethnic prejudices in society. TEUN A. VAN DIJK, COMMUNICATING RACISM: ETHNIC PREJUDICE IN THOUGHT AND TALK 361 (1987). These representations of minorities may have a deleterious effect on interpersonal relations in the marketplace:

> Prejudices about aggression and crime of ethnic groups largely derive from biased media stories that mention the ethnic backgrounds of suspects, which are again based on police reports or court trials, as well as on media articles about crime statistics or crime "waves" that are also partly derived from information supplied by the authorities. This is one of the most socially destructive ethnic prejudices, and there is much empirical evidence that the law and the media together help construct public attitudes about crime, deviance, or similar negative properties attributed to ethnic minority groups. *Id.* at 364.

Do you share Van Dijk's view? Do court trials aid in creating derogatory beliefs about the socioeconomic status of minorities and thus reinforce the legitimacy of the buzzer system?

An article in the *Washington Post Magazine* created heated debate concerning the buzzer system when it ran a column that supported the use of locks and buzzers as a security measure to discriminatorily screen young black male customers entering retail shops.

> As for me, I'm with the store owners, although I was not at first.... Young black males commit an inordinate amount of urban crime.... [R]ace is only one factor in their admissions policy. Age and sex count, too. And while race is clearly the most compelling factor, ask yourself what their policies would be if young white males were responsible for most urban crime.

> A nation with our history is entitled to be sensitive to race and racism—and we are all wary of behavior that would bring a charge of racism. But the mere recognition of race as a factor—especially if those of the same race recognize the same factor—is not in itself racism. This may apply as much to some opponents of busing or public housing in their own neighborhood as it does to who gets admitted to jewelry stores. Let he who would open the door throw the first stone.

Richard Cohen, *Closing the Door on Crime*, WASH. POST, Sept. 7, 1986 (magazine), at W13; *see also* Jane Gross, *When "By Appointment" Means Keep Out*, N.Y. TIMES, Dec. 17, 1986, at B1.

Was race "only one factor" in the exclusion of Williams, a successful female law professor? How does race as a factor in exclusion affect the model of the market described above? Is using race as a factor in excluding a willing buyer from the market racist? If not, what would meet the commentator's definition of racism?

14.   More screening based on race. Discriminatory screening practices are not an isolated occurrence. In New York, small shops on the Upper East Side have used, in addition to locks and buzzers, signs that read, "Men by appointment only." *Fear of Blacks, Fear of Crime*, N.Y. TIMES, Dec. 28, 1986, at § 4, 10. In addition, an African American man in Philadelphia filed a complaint with the Human Rights Commission after he was denied entrance to Mums & Pops Confectionary, which employs a lock and buzzer system. *See* Tamar Charry, *Bitter Sweets Battle*, PHILADELPHIA CITY PAPER, Dec. 7–14, 1995.

The retailers employing such security measures seem to equate blackness with criminality, and the *New York Times* editorial board warned, "discrimination, cumulatively, can be as poisonous as mugging or burglary." *Fear of Blacks, supra.* "Fearful whites need to put themselves in the shoes of innocent blacks. Doing so will not dissipate fear, but it can steadily inspire the understanding and reason that keep fear in its place." *Id.* A letter to the editor disagreed "that a society in which prejudice is rampant is as bad as one in which violent crime is rampant." Michael Levin and Margarita Levin, *Howard Beach Turns a Beam on Racial Tension*, N.Y. TIMES, Jan. 11, 1987, at § 4, 30. The letter concluded that an innocent black person would not let himself into the shop if standing in the owner's shoes. After reading Williams's description of the humiliation and rage she felt, do you think she would agree with the letter's conclusion? For an array of responses to a hypothetical involving decisions to screen customers based on race, see *The Jeweler's Dilemma* in THE NEW REPUBLIC, Nov. 10, 1986, at 18.

15.   Law and economics criticisms of critical race narrative methodology. Judge Richard Posner, a leading law and economics scholar, faults the critical race narrative methodology as non scientific, selective, and unreliable when compared to economic methodology. Posner, Overcoming Law, 368–384, "Nuance, Narrative and Empathy in Critical Race Theory." This argument is discussed in the next section of this chapter.

B.   A LAW AND ECONOMICS CHALLENGE TO THE NEUTRALITY OF THE CRITICAL RACE NARRATIVE METHODOLOGY

Nuance, Narrative, and Empathy in Critical Race Theory

OVERCOMING LAW 368–84 (1995).

■ RICHARD POSNER

The Alchemy of Race and Rights describes its author, Patricia Williams, as a young black female law professor of contracts and commercial law whose abiding interest is the plight of the American black. Or plights, for she is particularly concerned with the lack of fit that her condition of being a black professional woman makes with the attitudes and expectations of the predominantly white community in which, as a professor in an academic field that has relatively few women, very few blacks, and therefore almost no black women, she mainly circulates. The lack of fit induces in her at times a sense of disorientation that is almost vertiginous. So it is a book about both "privileged" blacks like herself and her underprivileged coracialists at the bottom of the social totem pole.

The book offers a black feminist perspective on a variety of practices and institutions: law's pretense to objectivity and impersonality, surrogate motherhood, consumerism, constitutional protection of hate speech and condemnation of governmental efforts at affirmative action, the inept and insensitive behavior of well-meaning white liberal academics, and above all white racism in what she considers its hydra-headed manifestations. There is little that is new in the paraphrasable content of her criticisms. The novelty is the form, which can aptly be described as literary, in which Williams has cast her discussion of these legal and social issues. She is not unique in employing literary methods in legal scholarship; earlier and essentially isolated examples of this genre to one side, it is the methodological signature of critical race theory. But she is one of the most skillful practitioners of the genre.

The subtitle of the book—"Diary of a Law Professor"—is a clue to her technique. The book is not literally a diary, although it contains some excerpts from the author's diary. But it is like a diary in presenting the author's analyses of legal and social issues in the form of reactions to her daily experiences, whether as consumer, law professor, television viewer, or daughter. The reader comes to understand that Williams's way of coping with the many stresses of her life is to write down her reactions to stressful or arresting events as soon after they occur as she can. Writing in a diary-like format is thus a form of therapy. But it also gives scope for her powerful gift for narration. * * *

The rhetorical highlight of the book, however, is the description of an episode at a Benetton clothing store. "Buzzers are big in New York City. Favored particularly by smaller stores and boutiques, merchants throughout the city have installed them as screening devices to reduce the incidence of robbery: if the face at the door looks desirable, the buzzer is pressed and the door is unlocked. If the face is that of an undesirable, the door stays locked. Predictably, the issue of undesirability has revealed itself to be a racial determination," as Williams discovers one Saturday afternoon when she

> was shopping in Soho and saw in a store window a sweater that I wanted to buy for my mother. * * *

The power of this sketch lies in its compression, its vivid contrasting of the round brown face with the sales clerk's narrow eyes and pink bubble gum, its use of physical exclusion as a metaphor for social exclusion, its suggestion that the least significant of whites (this gum-chewing bubble-blowing teenage sales clerk) is utterly comfortable with exercising power over an older and more accomplished black, and its elegant summation of the clerk's reaction to her ("evaluating me for signs that would pit me against the limits of his social understanding"). Yet here at the very pinnacle of Williams's art the careful reader will begin to feel a sense of disquiet. Did Williams really press her face against the window—that is, did her face actually touch the glass? Or is she embroidering the facts for dramatic effect—making the insult to her seem even graver than it was because it shattered a childlike eagerness and innocence? Also, how does she know that the sales clerk refused to let her in the store because she's black? The only evidence she cites is that, since Christmas was approaching, it was unlikely that the store had closed, and that there were other shoppers in the store. The second point has no force. Stores normally stop admitting customers before all the customers already in the store have left—otherwise the store might never be able to close. The first point has greater force. Although many stores close early on Saturday, the likelihood that a Benetton store in New York City during the Christmas shopping season would be one of them is slight. Yet Williams does not suggest that she has tried to find out whether the store was open. She does not suggest that she saw any customers admitted after she was turned away. The absence of a sign indicating that the store was closed would be some evidence that it was not, but she doesn't say anything about the presence or absence of a sign. Many stores list their hours on the front door. She makes no mention of this either. In all likelihood the store was open, but I am surprised that she—a lawyer—did not attempt to verify the point.

But of course the attempt might have been futile. And it is even possible, though I find no clues to this in the text, that her anger at the episode reflects in part a pervasive, debilitating uncertainty that confronts blacks in their encounters with whites. Not every disappointment that a black person encounters is a result of discrimination, and yet it may be impossible to determine which is and which is not. We like to know where we stand with other people, and this may be difficult for blacks in their dealings with whites.

Yet she had told us at the outset, in defense of doing legal scholarship in the form of story telling, "that one of the most important results of reconceptualizing from 'objective truth' to rhetorical event will be a more nuanced sense of legal and social responsibility" (p. 11). Unless "nuanced" is a euphemism for fictive, Williams has promised to get the particulars of an event or situation right, rather than submerging them in a generality, such as that whites hate blacks. That promise implies an effort to find out what *really* was going on in that white teenager's mind when he told her the store was closed. Maybe, as I said, it was closed; or maybe it wasn't but the clerk had his hands full with the customers inside. Maybe he was a disloyal employee who wanted to get his employer in trouble; maybe he was lazy, mischievous, rude, irresponsible, or just plain dumb.

The Alchemy of Race and Rights suppresses every perspective other than that of the suffering, oppressed black. * * *

This is a pattern. In discussing the case of Bernhard Goetz, who shot four black youths in a subway car and was acquitted of all but an illegal weapons charge even though he could not have been acting in *reasonable* self-defense, Williams disparages white fear of black crime by characterizing the criminal records of Goetz's victims as mere "allegations" by asking rhetorically how the community would have reacted to Goetz's action if he had been black and his victims white *and the crime had occurred in a department store rather than in the subway*—an added fictive touch that magnifies the malignant irrationality of Goetz's action—and by reciting irrelevant statistics showing that whites commit more crimes than blacks. What is omitted is that the prison population is almost half black, although blacks are only 12 percent of the population, and that urban street (and subway) crime is committed mostly by blacks. Black criminality is a serious social problem. To pretend otherwise is an evasion. AIDS, drug addiction, homophobia, neglect of children, anti-Semitism, and poor political leadership are other problems of the black community that Williams ignores. * * *

Mention of black anti-Semitism brings me back to the question of Beethoven's color. That Beethoven was black is a typical and recurrent claim of the Afrocentrist movement, members of which have also asserted that melanin is positively correlated with intelligence, that the ancient Greeks stole philosophy from black Egyptians and, specifically, that Alexander the Great pillaged the library at Alexandria to steal Egyptian philosophical ideas for his old tutor, Aristotle (never mind that Alexander *founded* Alexandria and that the library was built long after his death), that Napoleon shot off the sphinx's nose so that no one would know that the sphinx had Negroid features, that not only Beethoven but also Haydn, Cleopatra, and Lincoln were black, that Beethoven's blackness is shown by (among other things) his confidence in his abilities, a confidence similar to that of Mohammed Ali, that Dwight Eisenhower's mother was black, that America was first discovered by Africans, that AIDS was invented by whites to exterminate the black race, that the telephone and carbon steel were invented in Africa along with science, medicine, and mathematics, that "the [African] Blacks' conception of God was on a scale too grand to be acceptable to Western minds"—and that Jews controlled the African slave trade and today are plotting with the Mafia the financial destruction of the black race. *Not all Afrocentrists are anti-Semitic; but irresponsible claims appear to be the hallmark of the movement* [emphasis added], and I should have thought that Williams, as a lawyer and an academic, would have wanted to place as much distance as possible between herself and it rather than to embrace uncritically one of its representative wild claims.

Could it be—despite Martha Nussbaum's argument that imaginative literature in general and the novel in particular renders social reality with a degree of balance, nuance, and concreteness that provides a needed antidote to the partial visions furnished by abstract, generalizing social-scientific approaches, such as that of economics—that one-sidedness is an endemic risk of the literary depiction of reality, rather than a particular characteristic of Patricia Williams? * * *

We accept one-sidedness in literature, moreover, because we make allowance for *autres temps, autres moeurs* and because factual accuracy and scholarly detachment are not rules of the literature game. But they are rules of the scholarly game, and Williams is writing as a scholar. If my criticisms of her in this chapter should turn out to be one-sided, misleading, and tendentious, she would not be impressed by my rejoining that mine is only one voice in an ongoing conversation and I can leave it to others to rectify any omissions or imbalance in my contribution.

If one-sidedness is the other side of literature's empathetic concreteness, empathetic awareness of strangers' pains and pleasures is the unexpected other side of the economist's Gradgrindian detachment. Consider rent control. The beneficiaries are plain to see: they are the tenants when the rent-control law is adopted. The victims are invisible: they are the future would-be tenants, who will face a restricted supply of rental housing because landowners will have a diminished incentive to build rental housing and owners of existing apartment buildings will prefer to sell rather than to rent the apartments in them. Economics brings these victims before the analyst's eye; literature, and the type of legal scholarship that imitates literature, does not.

Maybe economic scholarship is not *really* empathetic. The economist does not enter imaginatively into the distress of the disappointed quester for rental housing; all he does is tote up some additional costs. But that may be a sounder way of doing policy than by cultivating empathy. A jurisprudence of empathy can foster short-sighted substantive justice because the power to enter imaginatively into another person's outlook, emotions, and experiences diminishes with physical, social, and temporal distance.[30] Compare the maxims *tout comprendre c'est tout pardoner* and no man is a villain in his own eyes (an actor's adage). The second maxim should remind us that when we succeed in looking at the world through another's eyes, we lose the perspective necessary for judgment. We find ourselves in a stew of rationalization, warped perception, and overmastering emotion. (Any lawyer knows the risk of overidentification with his client.) The *tout comprendre* maxim expresses a different point: To understand another person completely is to understand the causality of his behavior, to see that behavior as the end of a chain of causes and thus as determined rather than responsible. It is to understand the person as completely as a scientist understands an animal, which is to say as a phenomenon of nature rather than as a free agent. If we understand a criminal's behavior as well as we understand a rattlesnake's behavior, we are unlikely to accord him much dignity and respect.

---

30. A more basic point is that the internal perspective—the putting oneself in the other person's shoes—that is achieved by the exercise of empathetic imagination lacks normative significance *[Emphasis added]*.

The project of empathetic jurisprudence invites us to choose between achieving a warped internal perspective and an inhumanly clinical detachment: between becoming too hot and too cold. The affective dimension of empathy leads to identification with the person whose fate or welfare is at stake; the intellectual dimension leads to embedding the person in a web of causes that transforms him from a free human being into (in Nietzsche's phrase) an irresponsible piece of fate. I take back nothing I said in discussing the German judges about the importance of remembering that other human beings are—human. That does not require us to be able to crawl into their minds. Indeed, a lively awareness that other people are in an important sense closed to us—that they have their own plans and perspectives, into which we can enter imperfectly if at all—is one of the planks of the liberal platform. It is a presupposition of individuality.

Another problem with Williams's method is a lack of clarity. Here is the ending of the chapter in which Williams stands up for rights against the critical legal studies movement: "Give [rights] to trees. Give them to cows. Give them to history. Give them to rivers and rocks. Give to all of society's objects and untouchables the rights of privacy, integrity, and self-assertion; give them distance and respect" (p. 165). "What does it *mean* to give rights to history, or to entitle cows to privacy, integrity, and self-assertion? Is the reference to cows meant to put us in mind of Hindu doctrine regarding the sacredness of animals? Is Williams an animist, a 'Green'? Is she the second coming of Walt Whitman? (likely Carl Sandburg.) How can all this be squared with her being a fashion-conscious shopper. * * *

Narrative has two aspects, Narrative in the sense of the telling of a story is the way we make sense of a sequence of events unfolding in history. Black scholars like it because they believe that the current condition of the American black population cannot be understood without reference to the history of Negro slavery. But despite Williams's references to her great-great-grandmother, a slave, her book does not employ historical narration.

Narration is also a literary technique. To present an issue, such as the clash between critical legal studies and critical race theory, in the form of a story, * * * is to reinforce or replace abstract argument with a portrait. Portraits, including the verbal portraits that we call literature—works that depict rather than overtly argue—can change minds. This role of verbal portraiture, as also of photographs, is especially valuable in situations in which we have difficulty *seeing* important aspects of a problem because it involves people whose experiences are remote from ours. In education and occupation Patricia Williams is like other establishment legal figures, but in race and all that that connotes in this country (at least when the race is black) she is not, and maybe one has to learn to see the world through her eyes as well as one's own before one can fully evaluate the arguments pro and con various racial policies. On this view the very one-sidedness of her presentation, however questionable by the conventional standards of scholarship and even by the professed standards of critical race theory (which promised us, remember, nuance), has value in providing insight into the psychology and rhetoric of many blacks. But if whites must acquire a stereoscopic biracial perspective in order to cope effectively with our society's racial problems, blacks must too.

———

NOTES AND QUESTIONS

1.   Standards of proof and burden of persuasion in narrative. What standards of proof and persuasion does Judge Posner rely upon to assess the Williams narrative? *See* Richard H. Gaskins, Burdens of Proof in Modern Discourse (1993) (New Haven, Yale University Press).

2.   Throwing rhetorical stones from glass houses? Does Posner's essay exhibit any of the problems that he sees in Williams work? Lack of clarity, exaggeration for rhetorical effect, manipulation of empathy, one-sidedness?

3.   Difference between legal and economic standards of proof. Is the Posner essay structured by the standards of economic proof, or legal proof?

4.   Finding "truth" in law or economics. What would persuade Judge Posner that a report of racism or microaggression is "true"?

5.   Valuing collective experience. What place does group experience with subordination have in the Posnerian schema? *But see* Charles R. Lawrence, III, *The Id, the Ego, and Equal Protection: Reckoning with Unconscious Racism*, 39 Stan. L. Rev. 317 (1987) (arguing for "cultural meaning test" based on a community's collective experience as the targets of racism).

6.   Statistics as a scientific form of collective experience. In economics, collective experience is represented in statistical forms of aggregate data, including the mode, mean, average, and regression analysis. *Mode* is the value or item occurring most frequently in a series of observations or statistical data. *Mean* is the sum of all the members of the set divided by the number of items in the set. *Average* is something, as a type, number, quantity, or degree, that represents a midpoint between points on a scale of valuation. In statistics, *regression analysis* is a mathematical method of modeling the relationships among three or more variables. It is used to predict the value of one variable given the values of the others.

C.   The Narrative of Post-Modern Racism: The "Microaggressions"

Popular Legal Culture: Law as Microaggression
98 Yale L.J. 1559 (1989).

■ Peggy C. Davis

   [*The scene is a courthouse in Bronx, New York. A white assistant city attorney "takes the court elevator up to the ninth floor. At the fifth floor, the doors open. A black woman asks: 'Going down?' 'Up,' says [the city attorney]. And then, as the doors close: 'You see? They can't even tell up from down. I'm sorry, but it's true.' "]*

The black woman's words are subject to a variety of interpretations. She may have thought it efficient, appropriate, or congenial to ask the direction of the elevator rather than to search for the indicator. The indicator may have been broken. Or, the woman may have been incapable of competent elevator travel. The city attorney is led, by cognitive habit and by personal and cultural history, to seize upon the pejorative interpretation.

The city attorney lives in a society in which blacks are commonly regarded as incompetent. The traditional stereotype of blacks includes inferior mentality, primitive morality, emotional instability, laziness, boisterousness, closeness to anthropoid ancestors, occupational instability, superstition, care-free attitude, and ignorance. Common culture reinforces the belief in black incompetence in that the black is "less often depicted as a thinking being." If, for example, the city attorney watches television, she has observed that whites, but not blacks, are likely to exert authority or display superior knowledge; that whites, but not blacks, dispense goods and favors; and that blacks are disproportionately likely to be dependent and subservient. Cognitive psychologists tell us that the city attorney shares with all human beings a need to "categorize in order to make sense of experience. Too many events occur daily for us to deal successfully with each one on an individual basis; we must categorize in order to cope." In a world in which sidewalk grates routinely collapsed under the weight of an average person, we would walk around sidewalk grates. We would not stop to inspect them and distinguish secure ones from loose ones: It is more efficient to act on the basis of a stereotyping heuristic. In a world in which blacks are commonly thought to be incompetent (or dangerous, or musical, or highly sexed), it is more efficient for the city attorney to rely on the generalization than to make individuating judgments.

It is likely that the city attorney assimilated negative stereotypes about blacks before she reached the age of judgment. She will, therefore, have accepted them as truth rather than opinion. Having assimilated the stereotypes, the city attorney will have developed a pattern of interpreting and remembering ambiguous events in ways that confirm, rather than unsettle, her stereotyped beliefs. If she sees or hears of two people on a subway, one white, one black, and one holding a knife, she is predisposed to form an impression that the black person held the knife, regardless of the truth of the matter. She will remember examples of black incompetence and may fail to remember examples of black competence.

Psychoanalysts tell us that the stereotype serves the city attorney as a mental repository for traits and impulses that she senses within herself and dislikes or fears. According to this view, people manage normal developmental conflicts involving impulse control by projecting forbidden impulses onto an outgroup. This defense mechanism allows the city attorney to distance herself psychologically from threatening traits and thoughts. In this respect, the pejorative outgroup stereotype serves to reduce her level of stress and anxiety.

Historians tell us of the rootedness of the city attorney's views. During the early seventeenth century, the circumstances of blacks living in what was to become the United States were consistent with principles of open, although not equal, opportunity. African–Americans lived both as indentured servants and as free people. This early potential for egalitarianism was destroyed by the creation of a color-caste system. Colonial legislatures enacted slavery laws that transformed black servitude from a temporary status, under which both blacks and whites labored, to a lifelong status that was hereditary and racially defined. Slavery required a system of beliefs that would rationalize white domination, and laws and customs that would assure control of the slave population.

The beliefs that served to rationalize white domination are documented in an 1858 treatise. In many respects, they echo the beliefs identified one hundred years later as constitutive of the twentieth century black stereotype:

> [T]he negro, . . . whether in a state of bondage or in his native wilds, exhibits such a weakness of intellect that . . . 'when he has the fortune to live in subjection to a wise director, he is, without doubt, fixed in such a state of life as is most agreeable to his genius and capacity.' . . .
>
> . . . So debased is their [moral] condition generally, that their humanity has been even doubted. . . . [T]he negro race is habitually indolent and indisposed to exertion. . . . * * *
>
> The negro is naturally mendacious, and as a concomitant, thievish. . . .
>
> . . . Lust is his strongest passion; and hence, rape is an offence of too frequent occurrence.

The laws and customs that assured control of the slave population reinforced the image of blacks as incompetent and in need of white governance. The master was afforded ownership, the right to command labor, and the virtually absolute right of discipline. Social controls extending beyond the master-slave relationship served to exclude the slave—and in some respects to exclude free blacks—from independent, self-defining activity. * * * Social relationships between whites and blacks were regulated on the basis of caste hierarchy: Breaches of the social order, such as "insolence" of a slave towards a white person, were criminally punishable.

This history is part of the cultural heritage of the city attorney. The system of legal segregation, which maintained caste distinctions after abolition, is part of her life experience. This "new system continued to place all Negroes in inferior positions and all whites in superior positions." The city attorney is among the

> two-thirds of the current population [that] lived during a time when it was legal and customary in some parts of this country to require that

blacks sit in the back of a bus, give up their seats to whites, use different rest rooms and drinking fountains, and eat at different restaurants.

The civil rights movement and post–1954 desegregation efforts are also part of the city attorney's cultural heritage. As an educated woman in the 1980s, she understands racial prejudice to be socially and morally unacceptable. Psychological research that targets her contemporaries reveals an expressed commitment to egalitarian ideals along with lingering negative beliefs and aversive feelings about blacks. "Prejudiced thinking and discrimination still exist, but the contemporary forms are more subtle, more indirect, and less overtly negative than are more traditional forms."

Recent research also suggests that the city attorney can be expected to conceal her anti-black feelings except in private, homoracial settings. Many of her white contemporaries will suppress such feelings from their conscious thoughts. White Americans of the city attorney's generation do not wish to appear prejudiced. "[T]he contemporary form[ ] of prejudice is expressed [at least in testing situations] in ways that protect and perpetuate a nonprejudiced, nondiscriminating self-image." Americans of the city attorney's generation live under the combined influence of egalitarian ideology and "cultural forces and cognitive processes that ... promote prejudice and racism." Anti-black attitudes persist in a climate of denial.

The denial and the persistence are related. It is difficult to change an attitude that is unacknowledged. Thus, "like a virus that mutates into new forms, old-fashioned prejudice seems to have evolved into a new type that is, at least temporarily, resistant to traditional ... remedies."

II.   THE VIEW FROM THE OTHER SIDE OF THE LENS: MICROAGGRESSION

Return to the fifth floor and to the moment at which the elevator door opened. The black woman sees two white passengers. She inquires and perceives the response to her inquiry. She sees and hears, or thinks she sees and hears, condescension. It is in the tone and body language that surround the word, "Up." Perhaps the tone is flat, the head turns slowly in the direction of the second passenger and the eyes roll upward in apparent exasperation. Perhaps the head remains lowered, and the word is uttered as the eyes are raised to a stare that suggests mock disbelief. The woman does not hear the words spoken behind the closed elevator doors. Yet she feels that she has been branded incompetent, even for elevator travel. This feeling produces anger, frustration, and a need to be hypervigilant against subsequent, similar brandings.

The elevator encounter is a microaggression. "These are subtle, stunning, often automatic, and non-verbal exchanges which are 'put downs' of blacks by offenders." Psychiatrists who have studied black populations view them as "incessant and cumulative" assaults on black self-esteem.

Microaggressions simultaneously sustain defensive-deferential

thinking and erode self confidence in Blacks.... [B]y monopolizing ... perception and action through regularly irregular disruptions, they contribute to relative paralysis of action, planning and self-esteem.

They seem to be the principal foundation for the verification of Black inferiority for both whites and Blacks.

The management of these assaults is a preoccupying activity, simultaneously necessary to and disruptive of black adaptation.

> [The black person's] self-esteem suffers ... because he is constantly receiving an unpleasant image of himself from the behavior of others to him. This is the subjective impact of social discrimination.... It seems to be an ever-present and unrelieved irritant. Its influence is not alone due to the fact that it is painful in its intensity, but also because the individual, in order to maintain internal balance and to protect himself from being overwhelmed by it, must initiate restitutive maneuvers ...—all quite automatic and unconscious. In addition to maintaining an internal balance, the individual must continue to maintain a social facade and some kind of adaptation to the offending stimuli so that he can preserve some social effectiveness. All of this requires a constant preoccupation, notwithstanding ... that these adaptational processes ... take place on a low order of awareness.

Vigilance and psychic energy are required not only to marshall adaptational techniques, but also to distinguish microaggressions from differently motivated actions and to determine "which of many daily microaggressions one must undercut."

The microaggressive acts that characterize interracial encounters are carried out in "automatic, preconscious, or unconscious fashion" and "stem from the mental attitude of presumed superiority." They are the product of the factors described in Part I. The elevator incident represents their least insidious form. This is so for three reasons. First, the black woman at the elevator initiated an interaction, thereby providing social cues that would predictably result in an expressed judgment. The microaggression she suffered was avoidable. The black woman can in the future decline to initiate an exchange with a white stranger. To the extent that she minimizes such exchanges, she can protect against further insult. Moreover, the microaggression was arguably content-based. The reaction of the city attorney can be interpreted as a response to the woman's question—to the data gathered in the interaction—rather than a response to the person. Susceptibility to content-based microaggression can be minimized or controlled, not only by avoiding interactions, but also by avoiding ambiguity when interactions occur: The black woman might have said, "The indicator is broken. Is this elevator going up or down?" The more frequent and more insidious microaggressions, however, are unavoidable in that they are neither initiated by blacks nor based in any apparent way on the behavior of blacks. Finally, the elevator incident is benign among microaggressions because the white woman's implicit assertion of superiority did not culminate in an achievement of subordination. A fictitious continuation of the elevator incident illustrates microaggressions that are not only unprovoked in the sense described above but also complete in their achievement of subordination:

[*The city attorney decides to leave the elevator. She is standing at the right side of the car—directly opposite, but several feet away from, the black woman. Although she might easily exit by walking a path angled toward the center of the car, she takes a step directly forward. After a moment's hesitation, the black woman steps aside.*]

This is microaggression in its most potent form. It is the direct descendent of an aspect of color-caste behavior described fifty years ago as "deference":

> The most striking form of . . . "caste behavior" is deference, the respectful yielding exhibited by the Negroes in their contacts with whites. According to the dogma and to a large extent actually, the behavior of both Negroes and white people must be such as to indicate that the two are socially distinct and that the Negro is subordinate. Thus . . . [i]n places of business the Negro should stand back and wait until the white has been served before receiving any attention, and in entering or leaving he should not precede a white but should stand back and hold the door for him. On the streets and sidewalks the Negro should "give way" to the white person.

The wordless interchange was not initiated by the black woman. It was not based upon any action taken by her. It was a natural manifestation of an imbedded interactive pattern in which "skin color determines whether or not one is expected to operate from an inferior or superior vantage point. Both races have come to expect and accept as unremarkable that the blacks' time, energy, space, and mobility will be at the service of the white." The inferiority of the black is more than an implicit assertion; it is a background assumption that supports the seizure of a prerogative.

　　　* * *

———

NOTES AND QUESTIONS

1. Neutrality in law: its sources. In the public law debates over constitutional principle, the once well-accepted idea that legal rules are neutral, formal, and even scientific has been a vigorously contested terrain. In the 1980s, critical legal scholars mounted a broad challenge to the neutrality of legal rules. They argued that legal rules are indeterminate, lacking in objective neutrality, controlled instead by context, politics, and discretionary incorporation of the decision maker's perspective. However, when we turn to the debates about the rules that control outcomes in the market, skepticism about neutrality and rationality has emerged among legal scholars more recently.

In what follows we offer a preliminary map, tracing the role of the neutrality claim in legal theory. We start with the formalism of Christopher C. Langdell, a late nineteenth century dean of Harvard Law School, who introduced the study of appellate cases and the classification of legal subjects into categories that he defined as based upon a scientifically rigorous organization of legal thought, derived from provable "principles" of law. Langdell's formalism thus served to introduce the early framework of the neutrality claim through its assertion that legal reasoning was based upon "scientifically provable premises."

In the practice of law, legal neutrality is featured in several professional norms. First, we have the expectation of professional detachment in which the lawyer serves as a vigorous advocate on behalf of the client, without becoming so identified with the client as to lose perspective on sound professional assessments of what best serves the client's interest. Second, in litigation, neutrality expectations are on display in the rules that govern judicial conduct. Judges are expected to maintain an even temperament. Our chosen garb for judges, black robes, strips them of their ordinary clothing and the signifiers of class status that are a part of ordinary "street" clothing. Thus, the black robe is chosen to signal to participants in the legal process that judges have left behind personal identity in the service of their professional obligation of fair treatment and neutrality for every litigant.

In the dynamics of the courtroom, we can see the contest model of truth-seeking neutrality at work. In the contest model opposing lawyers may introduce palpably false testimony, misleading evidence, and they may use harsh tactics to destroy the credibility of witnesses who speak the objective truth. However, in the contest model, neutrality does not depend upon the truth or unbiased participation of litigants, but depends instead upon the dynamics of contested assertions. Neutrality emerges from the competing vectors of truth introduced by the interested parties. The contest model is also carried over into our expectations for jury deliberation. Juries are expected to rely upon their diverse identities, experience, and preferences to arrive at a verdict in both the criminal and civil cases. The verdict is the product of a contest of competing points of view, ultimately produces a compromise that represents a fair and neutral adjudication of the disputed claims.

In constitutional frameworks, the ideal of neutrality finds its home in the Equal Protection Clause. The equality norm has, at least since Wechsler (see note 2, *supra* at page 8), merged with legal formalism to insist on the application of "neutral principles." The concept of legal neutrality therefore can be traced to many complex and mutually reinforcing structures in legal theory, legal practice, and doctrine.

2. Neutrality in economics: its sources. In the market domain, belief in the insights of the first modern economist, Adam Smith, is still very firmly entrenched. Smith's central argument, in the 1759 classic the *Theory of Moral Sentiments*, was that private markets operate on the self-interested decisions of each individual participant. He argued that society achieved its maximum productivity when individuals were left alone to figure out from whom they wanted to buy and to whom they wanted to sell. Smith's famous metaphor for the social good that would arise from the cumulative impact of these buyer-seller decisions is the "invisible hand." In the centuries since Smith wrote, the argument that individuals are "led by an invisible hand to promote" what was good for society by choosing what was good for themselves has been enormously influential across all social-science disciplines, such as law, sociology, psychology, and economics.

Traditional economic analysis does not incorporate variables for either culture or identity. The language of economic analysis is built upon the implicit assumption that economic activity is natural and pre-political, and that economic actors possess abstract, identity-free preferences, devoid of the influences of culture or the dynamics of social groups. We adopt an opposing view that economic institutions are suffused with cultural power. We know that identity matters, and that economic subordination is not an abstract preference to those excluded from participation in the material comforts of our wealthy economic system.

As in traditional models of legal practice, traditional economic methodologies are framed with the claim of neutrality in seeking truth. Truth seeking in the hard sciences, like mathematics, physics, and chemistry depends upon the use of the scientific method, in which researchers do not have a normative stake in the outcome of the investigations. So, empiricism, and experimental procedures that can be duplicated by any trained scientist, insure that the "truth" is not subject to manipulation. Economics associates itself with the scientific culture. This association plays a role in advancing the neutrality premises, as well. In this culture, professional detachment is a prerequisite. There is a preference for laboratory experiments over *in vivo* (life), in which variables can be controlled, unlike the messy multivariate environments of real human interaction.

Despite the association of economics with the physical sciences and mathematics, we notice that contemporary economics imposes crucial limitations upon its fields of inquiry. For example, questions of distribution—who has how much wealth—have been defined as outside the scope of research for the discipline. The problems of economic inequality and the structures of identity-based subordination have no place in the equations featuring wealth maximization, zero transactions costs, rational choice, and perfect competition.

3. Critical race theory objections to neutrality frameworks: sources and central themes. Critical race theory rejects the neutrality and objectivity of law, elevating a personal, subjective, outsider experience to the center of jurisprudence, and demanding non-neutral laws to eradicate the ramifications of oppression. In addition to its anti-neutrality position, critical race theory explores other themes, including the following characteristic viewpoints:

    a. **Race as a social construction.** Critical race theorists deem the notion of race developed as a function of communal needs, economics, and politics. This belief aids in explaining the simplicity and prevalence of race as a social category (the mere existence of race) and the derogatory and positive connotations related to particular racial identities.

Because race is a social construct, it does not exist a priori; rather, it is created by discourses in politics, law, and science. In addition, the constructs that support race formation are mutable and volatile. The meaning of race, the number of racial groupings, and the cultural definition of particular racial personalities have all changed over time.

b. **Narrative.** Critical race scholars write narratives to liberate themselves from the constraining effects of conformity. With narratives, scholars can choose from a range of techniques—autobiographies, parables, and self-portraits—to communicate race and equality issues. Narrative provides a framework about the character of discrimination from the view of those who experience it and also challenges the "truth" (the objective reasoning) of American jurisprudence. Carbado & Gulati, *supra*, at 1784–86. Though there is some "storytelling" in the legal world—in the courtroom and in legal documents—stories told through a detached lens fail to capture central experiences.

c. **Color-blind society.** Critical race theorists reject the notion of colorblindness and embrace race consciousness. According to these scholars, colorblindness promotes nonwhites to assimilate and to deny their racial background because association with that group would cause these nonwhites to appear to be different. Critical race theory scholars argue that one simply cannot be "blind" to race because it is impossible not to notice an individual's attributes without having first thought about such traits at least once before. Neil Gotanda elaborates on this notion as he discusses the difference between medical colorblindness and liberal theorists' "nonrecognition" of race:

> A medically color-blind person is someone who cannot see what others can. It is a partial nonperception of what is "really" there. To be racially color-blind, on the other hand, is to ignore what one has already noticed. The medically color-blind individual never perceives color in the first place; the racially color-blind individual perceives race and then ignores it.... The characteristics of race that are noticed ... are situated within an already existing understanding of race.... This preexisting race consciousness makes it impossible for an individual to be truly nonconscious of race.

Neil Gotanda, *A Critique of "Our Constitution is Color–Blind,"* 44 Stan. L. Rev. 1, 18–19 (1991).

d. **Race as performative identity.** Legal scholars Devon Carbado and Mitu Gulati argue that the social definition of an individual's racial identity is a function of the way that person "performs" his or her race—for example, how an Asian person presents her "Asianness." In everyday encounters, people create or project specific images of race. This implies that the simplicity of an African American's racial identity partly originates from (1) the image of blackness he presents, and (2) how that racial projection is interpreted. Carbado and Gulati argue that they often have to suppress their racial or ethnic attributes in speech, clothing, and hair in order to dispel derogatory stereotypes about their demographic groups. This implies that racial minorities have some power to configure the parameters upon which they are experienced.

The racial "performance" an individual exhibits can span a wide range, and that individual's susceptibility to racism largely depends on where he falls on the racial spectrum:

> On one side of the spectrum are "conventional" black people. They are black prototypes—that is, people who are perceived to be stereotypically black. Their performance of blackness is consistent with society's understanding of who black people really are. On the other side are "unconventional" black people—people who are not stereotypically black. Their performance of blackness is outside of what society perceives to be conventional black behavior. A black person's vulnerability to discrimination is shaped in part by her racial position on this spectrum. The less stereotypically black she is, the more palatable her identity is. The more palatable her identity is, the less vulnerable she is to discrimination. The relationship among black unconventionality, racial palatability, and vulnerability to discrimination creates an incentive for black people to signal—through identity performances—that they are unconventionally black. These signals convey the idea that the sender is black in a phenotypic but not a social sense. Put another way, the signals function as a marketing device. They brand the black person so as to make clear that she is not a black prototype.

Devon W. Carbado & Mitu Gulati, *The Law and Economics of Critical Race Theory*, 112 YALE L.J. 1757, 1769 (2003) (book review).

e. **Essentialism.** To "essentialize" about race is to assume that a specific racial or gender personality has a singular and particular essence, isolated from other parts of identity. Some critical race scholars choose not to follow this essentialized methodology and are instead committed to intersectionality, a theory that insinuates that people's identities are intersectional—that is raced, gendered, sexually oriented, etc.—and that people's susceptibility to racism is a function of their specific intersectional identities. *Id. See* Kimberlé W. Crenshaw, *Mapping the Margins: Intersectionality, Identity Politics, and Violence Against Women of Color*, 43 STAN. L. REV. 1241 (1991); Angela P. Harris, *Race and Essentialism in Feminist Legal Theory*, 42 STAN. L. REV. 581 (1990).

f. **Identity privilege.** Critical race theorists argue that because racial discrimination is an enduring social predicament, there will be victims and recipients of this discrimination.

g. **Multiracialism.** A primary premise of critical race theory is a multiracial concept. This implies that the effects of racism are larger than any particular racial group. Certain critical race scholars condemn the black/white paradigm, asserting that most legal and political discussions concerning race focus on black and white experiences, failing to consider or marginalizing the experiences of nonblack minorities.

D. Economics and Law: Two Cultures in Tension

Economics and Law: Two Cultures in Tension

54 Tenn. L. Rev. 161 (1986).

■ James Boyd White

* * *

Many people think of economics solely as a scientific, conceptual, and cognitive system, apparently unaware that there are any other dimensions of meaning in economic talk. But all expression is loaded with values, ethical and otherwise; all expression defines a self and another and proposes a relation between them; all expression remakes its language; in these senses all expression proposes the creation of a community and a culture. All expression, in short, is ethical, cultural, and political, and it can be analyzed and judged as such. To claim that economics is a science is perhaps to claim that it cannot be judged in such terms. But "sciences" are cultures too, with their own created worlds and values. One way to describe my aim in this talk, then, is to say that it reverses the usual flow: we are used to economic analyses of this or that aspect of our common life—voting, the family, war, etc. I propose here to begin what I would call a rhetorical or cultural analysis of a certain kind of economics.

* * *

III. Economics as a Language of Theory

Neoclassical microeconomics proceeds upon certain assumptions that can be summarized this way. The universe is populated by a number of discrete human actors, each of whom is competent, rational, and motivated solely by self-interest. External to the human actors is a natural universe that affords what are called "resources," which are acted upon by human actors to create something called "wealth." Partly for reasons of practicality, this kind of economics defines economic activity, and hence wealth, in terms of the process of exchange by which one actor exchanges some item within his dominion for an item within the dominion of another, or, far more commonly, for money which is the medium of exchange. To look at everything from the point of view of exchange is, naturally enough, to regard the universe as a collection of items for potential exchange, and in this sense to itemize it. When an exchange takes place these items enter the economic system and become part of what we mean by productivity. Where no exchange actually takes place—as where wealth is created and consumed by the same person, or where leisure is chosen over work—the economic effect of the actor's decision is not disregarded by professional economics, as it often is in popular economic thought, but it is still measured by the value of an imagined exchange, the one the actor has forgone. The central principle of the system is that everything is at least hypothetically interchangeable and thus of necessity quantifiable in ways that permit meaningful commensuration, at any rate by the actors who are faced with the choices to which economics speaks.

As the natural universe is itemized by these real or imagined exchanges, the social world is atomized, conceived of as a set of actors of equal competence, without race, gender, age, or culture. Each actor is assumed to be motivated by an unlimited desire to acquire or consume. Since each is interested only in its own welfare, each is in structural competition with all the others. This in turn creates a severe scarcity with respect to the resources. Where there is no scarcity, as there once was not with respect to clean air or water, there can be no economics of this kind. The final ingredient is money, a medium in which surplus can be accumulated with convenience and, in principle, without limit. So far as possible, all human interaction is reduced to the single model of exchange. Economics is the study of what life would be like on such assumptions.

Exchange is a method of determining value, which, tautologically, is said to be the price for which items are sold. This is the value that is put upon them by the economic system, and the only kind of value that economics can express. Obviously individuals may put different values on different items—indeed, this is ordinarily necessary for the exchange to occur in the first place—but although these private values drive the economic system, they are not directly expressible in its terms.

In the world of economics individual actors function according to what economists call "rationality." This is a reasoning process that consists of identifying items of potential consumption or dominion in the world, calculating their value in dollar or other common terms, and then estimating various kinds of positive and negative risks. Reason is thus reducible to calculation and risk assessment. * * *

  * * *

IV.   ECONOMICS AS A SYSTEM OF VALUES

We can start with the question of value. In its purest form economics claims to be a value-free social science. But as I suggested earlier I think it in fact enacts a set of values, including political ones, values to which the speaker of the language cannot avoid finding himself at least in part committed.

A.   *In the World*

Think, for example, of the way in which economics defines the economic actor and the processes by which he functions. He is for the most part assumed to be an individual of indeterminate age, sex, race and cultural background, but of adequate competence at manipulating economic relations. He acts as one who is both perfectly aware of his own wishes and wholly rational—in the special sense in which that term is used, to mean "calculating"—in his pursuit of them. He exists as an individual, not as part of a community, except insofar as he establishes contractual or exchange relations with others. He is assumed to be motivated by self-interest, which in turn is defined in terms of competition, acquisition, and dominion, at least in relation to resources and other actors, for in the process of exchange the self is reduced to those desires.

Of course a particular individual may have other values—indeed the economist insists that he must, calling them "tastes" or "preferences"—perhaps including a "taste" for altruism, for peace and quiet, for heavy metal music, for appreciating nature unspoiled, for beautiful or ugly art, and so forth. These values will drive his participation in the exchange process, or his decision to withdraw from it. But in either case they are themselves valued by the method of exchange: either by an actual exchange that takes place or by a hypothetical or imagined exchange that is forgone (or in a more complicated case by a combination of exchanges made and forgone). In both cases these external values are converted by the discourse into the acquisitive or instrumental values—the desire to extend the dominion of the will—that all economic actors are assumed to have, for this is the only kind of value about which economics can directly talk.

With respect to the external values in their original form, the system is purportedly "value neutral." That is, it regards individual values as simply exogenous to the system itself. Economics of course recognizes that these values exist, but it demeans them by calling them "tastes" or "preferences," names that imply that no serious conversation can proceed on such subjects. And economics itself is by definition not about those values, but about the process by which they are reflected in the activity of exchange. This means that economics cannot, in principle, talk about any value other than the acquisitive or instrumental one that it universalizes. (Indeed it does not talk about this value either, but merely assumes and acts upon it.) This is not to be "value free," as its apologists claim, but to make self-interest the central, indeed almost the only, value, for it is the only one that can be talked about in these terms. To come at it the other way, it is to claim that all values can be talked about, at least for some purposes, as if they were selfish, quantifiable, and interchangeable.

      * * *

Yet economics is troubling not only for the self-interested values it directly asserts, but also for the very neutrality, the "value freedom," that it claims. It is in principle neutral on all questions of value that are external to the acquisitive and competitive ones enacted in the exchange game, which it lumps together as "tastes" or "preferences" among which no distinctions can be drawn. But this is to be silent on all the great questions of human life: questions of beauty and ugliness in art and music, sincerity and falsity in human relations, wisdom and folly in conduct and judgment, and the greatest of all questions, which is how we ought to lead our lives. Economic analysis assumes as a given the existence of "tastes" or "preferences" which drive the system, but economics as a language can provide no way of talking about these values, whether in oneself or another, no way of thinking about which to prefer and which not. To the extent that economics does reach out for these questions it may be worse than silent, for silence after all can be a mode of controlling a discourse. When economics tries to speak about these matters it does so in the only way it knows how to speak, in purely quantitative terms and on the assumption that all human transactions can be reduced to the model of exchange.

* * *

For the purposes of economic analysis all human wishes and desires are thus reduced to the same level, as though no principled choices could be made among them, as though it didn't matter what choices one made. This in turn means that it is impossible to talk in these terms about our most important choices as individuals and communities, or about the education of mind or heart, for any impulse that we or others may happen to have is as good, valid, and entitled to respect as any other.

* * * We must and do have preferences, as the economist knows; and these necessarily commit those who have them to the inquiry of better and worse, as well as to that of greater and less. To refuse to engage in this inquiry—to privatize it—as economics in its neutral phase necessarily does, is to deny an essential and necessary aspect of human life. To reduce all value to self-interest, as it does the rest of the time, is intellectually and ethically intolerable. How could one educate one's children or oneself to live in a world that was neutral on all the great questions of life, except that it reduced them to acquisition, competition, and calculation?

B. Among Economists

There is another dimension to economics, as a discourse among economists. Here too, in the discourse, values are of necessity enacted. For example, economics necessarily values the reduction of life to terms such as I describe, for this is what it achieves. It values linear reasoning and competition for dominance. This last is especially so among economists, for it is ostensibly a premise of economic discourse, as a rule of proof appropriate to a science, that we will believe only what we are forced by logic and fact to believe. This means that economic conversations—like certain other academic discussions—are often attempts to compel others to submit to one's views, or to resist such submission. In doing so they necessarily perform a claim that this is the most appropriate and valuable way to converse on these subjects, itself a most dubious position.

* * *

The claim that microeconomics is a value-free science is thus false in at least two ways. First, even as a science it is not value-free, for no science can be. It values the positivist and behaviorist premises from which it functions, the reduction of reason to calculation, the performed conversion of the world into quantifiable units, and so on. Second, economics attributes motives and values to its actors, those of acquisitiveness and self-interest, and invests itself in these attributions, which it assumes to be universal. This assumption is qualified by the recognition that one actor may choose to act for others, but in the end economics always reduces motive to self-interest, the only kind of motive it can conceive of and speak about. The reduction of all human interaction to the model of exchange, actual or imagined, simply erases whole fields of life and thought, from art to morals, for economics recognizes no ground, other than competitive survivability, upon which one can choose one form of life or one work of art over another, or even upon which one can choose to favor the market and its methods of analysis over others.

In saying that "value-free" economics is actually committed to certain values, both in the assumptions it makes about the world and in the conventions by which its own discourse operates, I do not mean to suggest that the field is in this respect peculiar. Quite the contrary. As I say above I think that all systems of discourse commit their users to values and do so in both domains, that is in one's account of the "other world" one talks about and in the here-and-now world one creates by talking. Science does this, and so do law and literary criticism too. Economics is not to be blamed, then, for having values. But no one should be allowed to claim value-neutrality where it does not exist, and economics, like other disciplines, can be praised or blamed for the values it has. All of us, economists and lawyers and lecturers among the rest, should be held responsible for the values we enact in our talking.

All this is not to say that economics is wrong to do what it does, namely, to isolate the practices of exchange for study, especially when its results are applied to spheres of life that are in fact characterized by exchanges that take place on conditions roughly matching the assumptions of the discourse. This is, after all, a good deal of the economic life of the investor or entrepreneur in a capitalist economy. But it is to say that this study would lead to insanity unless it were premised on a recognition that these activities, and the culture they and their study together create, require subordination to other activities and cultures, both at the level of the individual and of the polity.

V. ECONOMICS AS A POLITICAL SYSTEM

An economist might agree with most of this and say that the language and practices in which he engages as an economist must somehow be put together with the languages and practices that make up the rest of his life, both public and private. This would raise the wonderfully interesting and important question, how this might be done, and with what effect on economics itself, a question to which I shall return below.

But another line of justification is possible as well, one that neither denies the political character of this discourse nor seeks to subordinate it to other languages and practices, but affirmatively celebrates the politics and ethics that this kind of economics entails, mainly on the ground that the market is affirmatively desirable both as a model of life and as a political and social institution. The premises of the analytic method, in other words, can be regarded as the proper premises upon which to build our collective life. In talking this way the economist moves off the ground of purportedly pure science. He begins to use his language not as a "filing system" but as a way of expressing overt social and political attitudes, largely in support of the institution of the market. I should stress that not all economists would take this step. But some would. They are of course perfectly entitled to do so, but only to the extent that their politics and ethics, not their economics, persuade us of the rightness of their vision.

A.   *Justifying the Market as a Model of Life*

The institution of the market is celebrated by its proponents because in their view it is democratic—each person brings to the market his own values and can "maximize" them his own way—and because it is creative and open, leaving the widest room for individual choice and action. The market establishes a community based upon a competitive process that allows each person freedom to choose what to do with what is his. These merits mean, for some economists at least, that all social institutions ought to be modified to approximate the market—to conform to the analytic model of life as exchange—or at least to be analyzed and judged on that presumption.

The market is further justified, when such justification is thought necessary, in either of two rather conflicting ways. The first is to say that the market is good because it promotes efficiency, that is to say it maximizes the "welfare" of all participants in the process. It does this by definition, because each person participates in the process only because he thinks he gets more that way than he would any other way, and who are we to tell him differently? In maximizing the welfare of all participants it does the same for society as a whole, which is nothing more or less than the sum of all the participants in the market. The obvious trouble with this is that it takes for granted not only the existing values (or "tastes") of the actors, but also the existing distributions among them of wealth, capacity, and entitlement, which it has no way of criticizing. Yet these may of course be eminently criticizable.

The "welfare" defense of the market would justify all transactions—including the sale of oneself into slavery or prostitution—that are not in an obvious sense "coerced" by another because they are marginal improvements for the actors involved. But an economy might provide a different set of starting points for its actors, so that such degrading activities would no longer be "improvements" for anyone. We would all benefit from living in such a world. But the economist has no way of saying this. On the premises I have described he cannot deny the desirability of redistribution, but he cannot affirm it either. Even to discuss the question requires a shift of discourse, to ways of talking that economics of the sort I have been discussing excludes.

The second ground upon which the market is justified is that not of its gross effects but of its fairness. In one version this justification rests upon the ethical standing of voluntary action and holds that the results of the market process are justified with respect to every actor because the choices by which the market works are voluntary. In another version, it becomes the affirmative celebration of autonomy or liberty: whether or not it is efficient, the market is good because it gives the widest possible range to freedom of choice and action. Here the claim moves beyond justifying market results by the voluntary character of the choices upon which they rest to the point of asserting autonomy as the central social and political value. The obvious trouble with this line of defense, in both of its forms, is that it assumes that all exchanges are for all actors equally voluntary and equally expressive of autonomy, a position that common sense denies.

    * * *

The market purports to rest upon an assumption of the equality of all the actors in the system. In fact, it rests upon a different assumption, namely, the equality of every dollar in the system. Since some players have many more dollars, and through this fact are at a competitive advantage, it is a system that actively supports inequality among its actors.

It is not too much to say, I think, that the modern celebration of the market as the central social institution—the most fair, the most respecting of autonomy, and the most efficient—threatens to destroy the single greatest achievement of Western political culture: the discovery that a community can govern itself through a rule of law that attempts to create a fundamental moral and political equality among human beings. The great phrase in the Declaration of Independence—"all men are created equal"— is partly a theological statement about the conditions under which we are created and partly a political statement about the obligation of the government to acknowledge, indeed to create or recreate, that equality. This value is the heart of what is meant both by equality under law and by our democratic institutions more generally, resting as they do on the premise that each person's vote is worth exactly what everyone else's is. The ideology of the market, if it prevailed in its desire to convert all institutions into markets, would destroy this set of political relations and would create another in its stead, based upon the dollar.

    * * *

The market ideology claims to be radically democratic and egalitarian because it leaves every person free to do with her own what she will. But this freedom of choice is not equally distributed among all people. The market is democratic not on the principle of one person one vote, but on the far different principle of one dollar, one vote. One could hardly make a greater mistake than to equate, as so much modern public talk carelessly does, the "free market" with democracy.

There are two distinct points here. First, the exchange transactions that the market celebrates are not entitled to the special respect claimed for them as free and voluntary, and hence fair, unless each person has roughly the same amount of money and the same competence and freedom in its use, which is demonstrably not the case. The accumulations of wealth it permits thus cannot be justified by the fairness of the transactions by which the accumulation occurs. Second, if the advocates of the market succeeded in converting other institutions into markets, the result would be to transfer to those who have wealth not only the economic power that inescapably follows it but also the political power that in our democratic tradition the people have claimed for themselves and have exercised through the institutions of self-government. This would validate and institutionalize private economic power held by one person over another, of the rich over the poor. If we were to yield entirely to its claims, we would gradually find our traditional government, which operates by collective deliberation on a premise of fundamental equality of citizens, replaced by a private-sector government of the few over the many, wholly unregulated by collective judgment.

VI.   ECONOMICS AS A SYSTEM OF ECONOMIC ANALYSIS

But it is not only as a system of value and politics that this kind of economics, and the ways of thought it encourages, are troubling. I think that it is distorted and unrealistic as a way of imagining, thinking about, and shaping the processes of production and exchange that we think of as the economy itself.

A.   *The Social and Natural Matrix*

The first distortion I wish to consider has to do with the relationship between the exchange system and the cultural and natural world that it necessarily presupposes. What I mean is this. The economic activity of exchange takes place under natural and cultural conditions that are absolutely essential to it, but about which economics has no way of talking except by itemization, quantification, and conversion into the material of actual or hypothetical exchange. All talk about exchanges, that is, necessarily presupposes that the exchangers live in the natural world of sun, air, and water, subject to the powers of growth and health and disease, a world the organization of which is complex far beyond our understanding. Each of the exchangers is part of that world in another sense as well, for each is himself an organism, and one that incompletely understands both himself and his relation to the natural world upon which he absolutely depends for his existence. The language of economics similarly assumes the existence of a society and culture, a set of human understandings and expectations upon which each exchanger can rely: that promises will normally be kept, that one can get one's money home without being robbed, that it is worth thinking about the future, for oneself or for one's children, and so on. What is more, the actor's motives or values (what the economists call his "preferences") are themselves formed by interactions both with his culture and with nature. This is how we are made as individuals, how we cohere as a community, and how we connect ourselves to the past and to the future.

But on all this economics is silent, for it begins to speak only when an actor has, at least in his mind, identified some item in the world and begun to think of exchanging it for something else. It is his judgment of its worth, in exchanging it or in declining to do so, that is for the economist its value. But what confidence can we have in such judgments of worth, by actors necessarily imperfectly aware both of themselves and of the cultural and natural worlds they inhabit? To put it in epistemological terms, the economist assumes that there is nothing to be known about the natural or cultural world that cannot be known through the process of exchange itself. But in order to judge the value of an item now, or to predict one for the future (which is very much the same thing), one must make estimates about possible changes in the social, cultural, and natural matrix in which all exchange takes place, and about the effect of this and similar exchanges upon that matrix. There is no reason to be especially confident in anyone's capacity to make such estimates.

* * *

This is to talk about it in terms of knowledge, the knowledge that the economist assumes we have. But it can be cast in terms of value as well, for the language of economics assumes that the relation between humanity and nature should be one of dominion, that the expanded assertion of control by individual actors over nature—called "natural resources"—is inherently a good thing. But why should one grant such an assumption? As Wendell Berry repeatedly points out in his works on agricultural economics, modern agriculture can be considered a great technological success only if one uses the measure of present-day output per man-hour, disregarding both the destructive effects of modern farming on soil and water and the costs, natural and economic, of the fossil fuels used for both fertilizer and power. If productivity over decades or per acre is the test, as in a world of five billion perhaps it should be, our agriculture falls well below that of many more "primitive" peoples. If one includes the meaning of the work the farmer does, its rhythms and its harmonies or disharmonies with nature, the picture is complicated further; still further if one asks how important it is in a nuclear age for a particular polity, or for humanity, that the capacity for fruitful and stable survival on a small scale be maintained. Economic language assumes, with what a theologian like James Gustafson might call a foolish pride, that man's wants and wishes are the ultimate measure of value; it then claims that these wishes are constrained only in ways that traders can see and account for. These are assumptions of fact and value that one might generously regard as dubious.

The only kind of meaning economics can reflect is one that can be expressed in the medium of exchange, that is, quantifiable and comparative. This is in turn to give the world itself a meaning of a new kind, reflected in the Japanese phrase for the blue sky that can rarely be seen over Tokyo these days: it is called a "recession sky."

* * *

D. Erasing Community

For similar reasons this kind of economics has the greatest difficulty in reflecting the reality of human community and the value of communal institutions. Its necessary tendency seems to be to destroy the idea of public action, indeed the idea of community itself. This is partly because this methodology tends to resolve all communities and organizations into the individual human actors who constitute them, partly because commitment to the market system leads one to think that everything that can be made the subject of the market should be. The idea is that every economic actor should pay for what he wants, and should not have to pay for what he doesn't want. But this tends to destroy our public institutions, all of which extend benefits far beyond those who would pay (if they were reduced to markets) or who do pay (when they are supported by taxes). Such institutions reflect a communal judgment that we need to educate ourselves and each other, that our "tastes" are not all of equal value but need to be formed, and formed well rather than badly. Public universities, libraries, orchestras, museums, parks—all these would fall before the ideology that denies the existence and reality of community and reduces all institutions, all human production, to the language of the market.

Think here of the way economists explain why people who will probably never visit, say, the Everglades or an art museum are happy to have their taxes used to maintain them. The economist says it is because the actor wants to maintain the option of visiting them some day, and calls this an "option demand." But may it not be that the voter simply takes pleasure in what other people have and in what other people can do, in belonging to a community that is good for all its members? Or that he respects their desires and wants a community based on that kind of mutual respect? This possibility is systematically denied by the assumption of economic talk, that individuals and communities are in principle incapable of generosity, or more precisely, that "altruism" can adequately be talked about as a species of selfishness.

The language of self and self-interest not only fails to reflect the reality of community and of shared interests, it draws attention away from those aspects of life and devalues them. To continue to talk on these assumptions, even hypothetically, is to encourage "self-interest" in an ethical sense and to erode the commitments we have to each other that underlie such essential practices of citizenship as the willingness to pay taxes, to work for the local school, or to serve in the army, upon which everything depends. To adopt the economic view would in fact threaten the very existence of community, for on these premises no one would conceivably die or seriously risk his life for his community: at the point of danger one's self-interest in survival would outweigh all other self-interests. And to speak of all "tastes" as if they were equivalent is to invite oneself and others to think that they are, and to confirm the premises of our culture, already drummed into the mind by the consumer economy, that the consumer is king, that whatever you happen to want is a good that you should seek to satisfy, that no distinction can be drawn between the beautiful and ugly, the wise and foolish, and so on. It is to confirm a vulgar view of democracy that makes the preference or will supreme, as if we functioned by instant referendum. It erases the sense that a democracy is a mode of communal self-constitution and self-education that may have higher ends than the satisfaction of wants, namely the creation of a community of a certain sort, at once based upon a set of responsibilities and offering us a set of opportunities for civic and social action.

————

NOTES AND QUESTIONS

1. Effect of terminology on White's critique. White states that "all systems of discourse commit their users to values . . . [and that] economics is [not] wrong to do what it does." James Boyd White, *Economics and Law: Two Cultures in Tension*, 54 TENN. L. REV. 161, 176 (1986). If all White wishes is for economics to acknowledge that it is no different from other systems of discourse, does his critique of law and economics have any value? Would the problems White identifies with law and economics be solved by acknowledging that law and economics has values without making any substantive changes to the discipline? Would White be satisfied with this solution?

2. Pernicious nature of law and economics. At the close of his article, White states that "to continue to talk on . . . [law and economics'] assumptions, even hypothetically, is to encourage 'self interest' in an ethical sense and to erode the commitments we have to each other that underlie such essential practices of citizenship as the willingness to pay taxes, to work for the local school, or to serve in the army, upon which everything depends. To adopt the economic view would in fact threaten the very existence of community. . . ." *Id.* at 192. If White is correct about the dire consequences of even hypothesizing in an economic framework, how can he assert that economics is not wrong to "do what it does"? *Id.* at 176.

E. JUDGING RACE: THE DOCTRINE OF DISCRIMINATORY INTENT

Note About Neutrality in Form, Discriminatory Impact and the Paradox of Statistical Correlation vs. Motivation

The debate about race, neutrality, and markets has not been limited to economic theories of rationality contesting the subjective narratives of critical race scholars. Conflicting perspectives about neutrality also extend to disputes about what evidence can trigger a constitutional violation of the Equal Protection Clause. In this debate, the liberal and conservative positions have been reversed. Civil rights advocates sought to rely upon scientific measures of statistical racial disparity to show that the impact of a facially neutral policy violated the Equal Protection standard. The Court rejected statistical measures of the disparate impact of the employment screening test on black applicants.

For "facially neutral" policies, such as this employment screening test, the Court introduced a motive-focused standard that required evidence of intentional racial discrimination to establish a violation of the Fourteenth Amendment. The demise of disparate impact theory to prove an Equal Protection violation was a major setback for the use of civil rights legal theory seeking to challenge government policies and practices, even though such policies did not contain a race-specific classification.

Consider how this case contributes to our understanding of the uses of the concept of neutrality. Does the fact that scientific tools, such as statistical proof of disproportionate harm to racial minority groups, were rejected in this case turn the conservative (scientific) vs. liberal (empathetic, seeking to enter the subjective experience of another) on its head? As you read the case that follows, recall that it was Judge Posner who said:

> Maybe economic scholarship is not *really* empathetic. The economist does not enter imaginatively into the distress of the disappointed quester for rental housing; all he does is tote up some additional costs. But that may be a sounder way of doing policy than by cultivating empathy. A jurisprudence of empathy can foster short-sighted substantive justice . . . [1]

Posner, OVERCOMING LAW, *supra* at 381.

On the basis of the observations above, had he been a Justice, do you think Judge Posner would have dissented in the following case?

———

Washington v. Davis

426 U.S. 229 (1976).

■ MR. JUSTICE WHITE delivered the opinion of the Court.

This case involves the validity of a qualifying test administered to applicants for positions as police officers in the District of Columbia Metropolitan Police Department. The test was sustained by the District Court, but invalidated by the Court of Appeals. We are in agreement with the District Court and hence reverse the judgment of the Court of Appeals.

[The action was filed by black applicants to become police officers in the District of Columbia. The claimants were unsuccessful in passing a test that was designed to measure verbal skills, vocabulary and reading. They introduced evidence in the District Court showing that a greater percentage of blacks failed, than did whites. In addition, the claimants alleged that the test had not been validated, by accepted test measurement methodology, to provide reliable test results for predicting future job performance.]

The central purpose of the Equal Protection Clause of the Fourteenth Amendment is the prevention of official conduct discriminating on the basis of race. It is also true that the Due Process Clause of the Fifth Amendment

---

1. A more basic point is that the internal perspective—putting oneself in the other person's shoes—that is achieved by the exercise of empathic imagination lacks normative significance.

contains an equal protection component prohibiting the United States from invidiously discriminating between individuals or groups. *Bolling* v. *Sharpe,* 347 U.S. 497 (1954). But our cases have not embraced the proposition that a law or other official act, without regard to whether it reflects a racially discriminatory purpose, is unconstitutional *solely* because it has a racially disproportionate impact.

Almost 100 years ago, *Strauder* v. *West Virginia,* 100 U.S. 303 (1880), established that the exclusion of Negroes from grand and petit juries in criminal proceedings violated the Equal Protection Clause, but the fact that a particular jury or a series of juries does not statistically reflect the racial composition of the community does not in itself make out an invidious discrimination forbidden by the Clause. "A purpose to discriminate must be present which may be proven by systematic exclusion of eligible jurymen of the proscribed race or by unequal application of the law to such an extent as to show intentional discrimination." A defendant in a criminal case is entitled "to require that the State not deliberately and systematically deny to members of his race the right to participate as jurors in the administration of justice."

The rule is the same in other contexts [a 1964 case] upheld a New York congressional apportionment statute against claims that district lines had been racially gerrymandered. The challenged districts were made up predominantly of whites or of minority races and their boundaries were irregularly drawn. The challengers did not prevail because they failed to prove that the New York Legislature "was either motivated by racial considerations or in fact drew the districts on racial lines"; the plaintiffs had not shown that the statute "was the product of a state contrivance to segregate on the basis of race or place of origin." * * *

The school desegregation cases have also adhered to the basic equal protection principle that the invidious quality of a law claimed to be racially discriminatory must ultimately be traced to a racially discriminatory purpose. That there are both predominantly black and predominantly white schools in a community is not alone violative of the Equal Protection Clause. The essential element of *de jure* segregation is "a current condition of segregation resulting from intentional state action." *Keyes* v. *School Dist. No. 1,* 413 U.S. 189, 205 (1973). "The differentiating factor between *de jure* segregation and so-called *de facto* segregation ... is *purpose* or *intent* to *segregate.*" *Id.,* at 208. See also *id.,* at 199, 211, and 213. The Court has also recently rejected allegations of racial discrimination based solely on the statistically disproportionate racial impact of various provisions of the Social Security Act because "[t]he acceptance of appellants' constitutional theory would render suspect each difference in treatment among the grant classes, however lacking in racial motivation and however otherwise rational the treatment might be."

This is not to say that the necessary discriminatory racial purpose must be express or appear on the face of the statute, or that a law's disproportionate impact is irrelevant in cases involving Constitution-based claims of racial discrimination. A statute, otherwise neutral on its face, must not be applied so as invidiously to discriminate on the basis of race. *Yick Wo v. Hopkins,* 118 U.S. 356 (1886). It is also clear from the cases dealing with racial discrimination in the selection of juries that the systematic exclusion of Negroes is itself such an "unequal application of the law ... as to show intentional discrimination." A prima facie case of discriminatory purpose may be proved as well by the absence of Negroes on a particular jury combined with the failure of the jury commissioners to be informed of eligible Negro jurors in a community, or with racially nonneutral selection procedures. With a prima facie case made out, "the burden of proof shifts to the State to rebut the presumption of unconstitutional action by showing that permissible racially neutral selection criteria and procedures have produced the monochromatic result."

Necessarily, an invidious discriminatory purpose may often be inferred from the totality of the relevant facts, including the fact, if it is true, that the law bears more heavily on one race than another. It is also not infrequently true that the discriminatory impact—in the jury cases for example, the total or seriously disproportionate exclusion of Negroes from jury venires—may for all practical purposes demonstrate unconstitutionality because in various circumstances the discrimination is very difficult to explain on nonracial grounds. Nevertheless, we have not held that a law, neutral on its face and serving ends otherwise within the power of government to pursue, is invalid under the Equal Protection Clause simply because it may affect a greater proportion of one race than of another. Disproportionate impact is not irrelevant, but it is not the sole touchstone of an invidious racial discrimination forbidden by the Constitution. Standing alone, it does not trigger the rule, that racial classifications are to be subjected to the strictest scrutiny and are justifiable only by the weightiest of considerations. * * *

As an initial matter, we have difficulty understanding how a law establishing a racially neutral qualification for employment is nevertheless racially discriminatory and denies "any person ... equal protection of the laws" simply because a greater proportion of Negroes fail to qualify than members of other racial or ethnic groups. Had respondents, along with all others who had failed Test 21, whether white or black, brought an action claiming that the test denied each of them equal protection of the laws as compared with those who had passed with high enough scores to qualify them as police recruits, it is most unlikely that their challenge would have been sustained. Test 21, which is administered generally to prospective Government employees, concededly seeks to ascertain whether those who take it have acquired a particular level of verbal skill; and it is untenable that the Constitution prevents the Government from seeking modestly to upgrade the communicative abilities of its employees rather than to be satisfied with some lower level of competence, particularly where the job requires special ability to communicate orally and in writing. Respondents, as Negroes, could no more successfully claim that the test denied them equal protection than could white applicants who also failed. The conclusion would not be different in the face of proof that more Negroes than whites had been disqualified by Test 21. That other Negroes also failed to score well would, alone, not demonstrate that respondents individually were being denied equal protection of the laws by the application of an otherwise valid qualifying test being administered to prospective police recruits.

Nor on the facts of the case before us would the disproportionate impact of Test 21 warrant the conclusion that it is a purposeful device to discriminate against Negroes and hence an infringement of the constitutional rights of respondents as well as other black applicants. As we have said, the test is neutral on its face and rationally may be said to serve a purpose the Government is constitutionally empowered to pursue. Even agreeing with the District Court that the differential racial effect of Test 21 called for further inquiry, we think the District Court correctly held that the affirmative efforts of the Metropolitan Police Department to recruit black officers, the changing racial composition of the recruit classes and of the force in general, and the relationship of the test to the training program negated any inference that the Department discriminated on the basis of race or that "a police officer qualifies on the color of his skin rather than ability."[13] * * *

A rule that a statute designed to serve neutral ends is nevertheless invalid, absent compelling justification, if in practice it benefits or burdens one race more than another would be far reaching and would raise serious questions about, and perhaps invalidate, a whole range of tax, welfare, public service, regulatory, and licensing statutes that may be more burdensome to the poor and to the average black than to the more affluent white....

We also hold that the Court of Appeals should have affirmed the judgment of the District Court granting the motions for summary judgment filed by petitioners and the federal parties. Respondents were entitled to relief on neither constitutional nor statutory grounds. * * *

■ MR. JUSTICE STEVENS concurring....

While I agree with the Court's disposition of this case, I add these comments on the constitutional issue discussed....

The requirement of purposeful discrimination is a common thread running through the cases summarized in Part II. These cases include

---

13. It appears beyond doubt by now that there is no single method for appropriately validating employment tests for their relationship to job performance. Professional standards developed by the American Psychological Association in its Standards for Educational and Psychological Tests and Manuals (1966), accept three basic methods of validation: "empirical" or "criterion" validity (demonstrated by identifying criteria that indicate successful job performance and then correlating test scores and the criteria so identified); "construct" validity (demonstrated by examinations structured to measure the degree to which job applicants have identifiable characteristics that have been determined to be important in successful job performance); and "content" validity (demonstrated by tests whose content closely approximates tasks to be performed on the job by the applicant). These standards have been relied upon by the Equal Employment Opportunity Commission in fashioning its Guidelines on Employee Selection Procedures, 29 CFR pt. 1607 (1975), and have been judicially noted in cases where validation of employment tests has been in issue.

criminal convictions which were set aside because blacks were excluded from the grand jury, a reapportionment case in which political boundaries were obviously influenced to some extent by racial considerations, a school desegregation case, and a case involving the unequal administration of an ordinance purporting to prohibit the operation of laundries in frame buildings. Although it may be proper to use the same language to describe the constitutional claim in each of these contexts, the burden of proving a prima facie case may well involve differing evidentiary considerations. The extent of deference that one pays to the trial court's determination of the factual issue, and indeed, the extent to which one characterizes the intent issue as a question of fact or a question of law, will vary in different contexts.

Frequently the most probative evidence of intent will be objective evidence of what actually happened rather than evidence describing the subjective state of mind of the actor. For normally the actor is presumed to have intended the natural consequences of his deeds. This is particularly true in the case of governmental action which is frequently the product of compromise, of collective decision-making, and of mixed motivation. It is unrealistic, on the one hand, to require the victim of alleged discrimination to uncover the actual subjective intent of the decision-maker or, conversely, to invalidate otherwise legitimate action simply because an improper motive affected the deliberation of a participant in the decisional process. A law conscripting clerics should not be invalidated because an atheist voted for it.

My point in making this observation is to suggest that the line between discriminatory purpose and discriminatory impact is not nearly as bright, and perhaps not quite as critical, as the reader of the Court's opinion might assume. I agree, of course, that a constitutional issue does not arise every time some disproportionate impact is shown. On the other hand, when the disproportion is as dramatic as in *Gomillion* v. *Lightfoot,* 364 U.S. 339, or *Yick Wo* v. *Hopkins,* 118 U.S. 356, it really does not matter whether the standard is phrased in terms of purpose or effect. Therefore, although I accept the statement of the general rule in the Court's opinion, I am not yet prepared to indicate how that standard should be applied in the many cases which have formulated the governing standard in different language.
* * *

My agreement ... rests on a ground narrower than the Court describes. I do not rely at all on the evidence of good-faith efforts to recruit black police officers. In my judgment, neither those efforts nor the subjective good faith of the District administration, would save Test 21 if it were otherwise invalid.

There are two reasons why I am convinced that the challenge to Test 21 is insufficient. First, the test serves the neutral and legitimate purpose of requiring all applicants to meet a uniform minimum standard of literacy. Reading ability is manifestly relevant to the police function, there is no evidence that the required passing grade was set at an arbitrarily high level, and there is sufficient disparity among high schools and high school graduates to justify the use of a separate uniform test. Second, the same test is used throughout the federal service. The applicants for employment in the District Columbia Police Department represent such a small fraction of the total number of persons who have taken the test that their experience is of minimal probative value in assessing the neutrality of the test itself. That evidence, without more, is not sufficient to overcome the presumption that a test which is this widely used by the Federal Government is in fact neutral in its effect as well as its "purpose" as that term is used in constitutional adjudication. * * *

■ MR. JUSTICE BRENNAN and MR. JUSTICE MARSHALL dissent

[I]t should be observed that every federal court, except the District Court in this case, presented with proof identical to that offered to validate Test 21 has reached a conclusion directly opposite to that of the Court today. * * *

Empirical Evidence

PERVASIVE PREJUDICE, UNCONVENTIONAL EVIDENCE OF RACE AND GENDER DISCRIMINATION 3–8 (2001).

■ IAN AYRES

Indeed, there seems to be a widespread, implicit belief (at least among white males) that race and gender discrimination is not a serious problem in retail markets. The civil rights laws of the 1960s focused on only a handful of non-retail markets—chiefly concerning employment, housing, and public accommodation services. Indeed, the most gaping hole in our civil rights law concerns retail gender discrimination. No federal law prohibits gender discrimination in the sale of goods or services. A seller could flatly refuse to deal with a potential buyer of a car or a paperclip because of her gender. And while the civil rights laws of the 1860s prohibited race discrimination in contracting, the civil rights laws a century later only prohibited sex discrimination in a narrow range of "titled" markets. The thousands of other markets that make up our economy are completely unregulated with regard to gender (as well as to religion and national origin) discrimination and only somewhat more regulated with regard to race. And only a handful of cities and states (chief among them California) make up for this failing by prohibiting gender discrimination in contracting generally.

The non-regulation of retail discrimination seems to be premised on a vague coterie of assumptions: (1) retail discrimination does not exist because retailers have no motive to discriminate; (2) retail discrimination does not exist because competition forces retailers not to discriminate; and (3) any retail discrimination that does occur does not have serious consequences because of effective counterstrategies by potential victims. It is also argued that any discrimination in the sale of goods or services is less important than the potential effects of discrimination in the markets for employment and housing. But without denying the primacy of employment, the current regulatory regime leaves approximately 66 percent of the dollars we spend—and 35 percent of the dollars we earn—unregulated (with respect to gender discrimination) or less regulated (with respect to race discrimination).

In this book, I contest the idea that race and gender discrimination in the retail sale of goods is nonexistent or unimportant. My thesis is that race and gender discrimination is neither a thing of the past nor is it limited to the narrow set of "titled" markets regulated by the civil rights legislation of the 1960s (Title VII, Title II, and so on). The book's primary contribution is empirical, but let me begin with a few theoretical reasons why we should take the possibility of retail discrimination seriously.

RETAILERS MAY HAVE A MOTIVE TO DISCRIMINATE

The argument that discrimination in the sale of goods and services does not exist because retailers lack any disparate treatment motive is itself premised on the twin ideas that discriminating against economically marginal groups would not be profitable and that racial animus would not manifest itself in discrete retail transactions.

The latter idea is that while animus might cause race discrimination in the more relational settings employment, apartment rental, and restaurants—which civil rights laws regulate, regulated retail transactions are sufficiently discrete that seller and/or customer prejudice would not induce disparate treatment. There are, however, several problems with this theory. First, as pointed out by Ian MacNeil, contractual arrangements are not as discrete as they initially appear. Barbers may have much more tactile and repeated contact with their customers than one-time sellers of a house, but the law much more vigorously regulates the latter transaction. Second, the thought that prejudice is less likely to be acted upon in discrete transactions is premised on a narrow theory of what might be called "associational" animus—that is, that bigots don't like associating with particular groups. But, * * * there are other types of animus that might persist even in discrete markets. For example, if sellers enjoy extracting an extra dollar of profit from people of color more than from whites, we might expect to see disparate racial treatment in pricing or quality of service. Finally, appreciating the pervasive discretion given to employees as agents open up the possibility that even profit-maximizing principals will by necessity countenance some disparate treatment by their subordinates.

Discriminating retailers may also be actuated by profit. Sellers may have a profit-maximizing incentive to price discriminate against minorities and women—even if sellers believe that members of these groups are on average poorer. It has long been known that "statistical discrimination" might cause rational, profit-maximizing sellers to charge more to groups that on average cause sellers to incur higher costs. Thus, as a theoretical matter, the drivers of taxis might discriminate against African American men if the drivers perceive a higher chance of being robbed by such passengers. But, more provocatively, focusing on the example of new car sales, I argue that profit-maximizing sellers may engage in "revenue-based" race and gender disparate treatment. Dealerships may discriminate not because they expect higher costs but because they expect to be able to extract higher revenues. This is a surprising possibility because, as an empirical matter, people of color have a substantially lower ability to pay for new cars. But profit-maximizing sellers care far more about the variability in willingness to pay than in the mean willingness. The presence of a few minority members who are willing to pay a large markup can make it rational for the dealership to offer higher prices to all members of the group-even if group members are on average poorer.

It is correct and useful to ask whether sellers would plausibly be motivated to engage in a particular type of discrimination. But treating this issue seriously opens up a variety of dimensions where discrimination in the retail sale of goods and services could be a plausible seller strategy for either profit or non-profit-based reasons.

COMPETITION MAY NOT DRIVE OUT RETAIL DISCRIMINATION

Nobel-prize winning economist Gary Becker emphasized how competition could provide a much-needed antidote for the disease of discrimination. Non-discriminating sellers could earn higher profits by picking up the sales of those minorities and/or women excluded from equal access to the discriminating sellers. One problem with this theory is that it focuses on the ability of competition to drive out discriminating sellers, but competition may not be as effective at driving out the preferences of discriminating customers. If fixed costs of production limit the number of firms selling and if a substantial number of, say, white customers prefer dealing with a firm that discriminates against (by excluding or offering inferior service to) people of color, then firms may decide that it is more profitable to exclude minorities than to lose the patronage of whites.

As an empirical matter, however, my guess is that most firms would not find overt race or gender discrimination to be a profit-maximizing strategy. While Lester Maddox may have increased his sales by excluding African Americans, in most markets a "whites only" or "males only" policy or overtly charging higher prices to particular demographic groups would lead to a general negative consumer reaction-by both minorities and progressive white consumers.

A more important limitation on competition is consumer information. In order for discrimination to cause the competitive shift of consumers toward nondiscriminatory sellers, consumers must know which sellers are discriminating and which are not. There is thus an important informational prerequisite for competition to have the predicted Beckerian effect. But as described above, there are many aspects of treatment where consumers may not be able to compare how sellers treat similarly situated counterparts. Retail discrimination is most likely to persist where consumers do not learn the benchmark treatment of fellow consumers. Thus, while there is little opportunity for a single fast food franchise to charge different prices for hamburgers, it is possible for a dealership to charge different prices to potential buyers of cars. Since bargained prices diverge from the list price, it is very difficult for a consumer to know whether she has received a nondiscriminatory price. And it will be more difficult for a nondiscriminatory seller to credibly market itself on the basis that the race or gender of customers do not influence its bargaining strategy.

Markets in which price or other terms of trade are individually bargained for provide much greater opportunities for race or gender discrimination than markets with homogeneous product attributes and posted prices. However, even retailers that sell standardized products at posted prices might discriminate on the basis of race or gender with regard to discretionary aspects of service. Anyone watching the *Prime Time* segment could vividly see that record and department stores could substantially increase the "transaction costs" of minority customers. This is not just an issue of whether the retailer provides "service with a smile" but, as in the *Prime Time Live* testing, whether the retailers make minority customers wait substantially longer before being served (or whether the minority customers are conspicuously shadowed to scrutinize whether they are shoplifting).

Retailers may also discriminate in their willingness to accommodate private and somewhat idiosyncratic consumer requests. For example, Jane Connor is currently testing retailers in Binghamton, New York, to see whether there are racial differences in their willingness to accede to a request to use a restroom or a request to return a sweater without a receipt. Economists (and others) tend to ignore or downplay the harms of such discrimination. But nontrivial injury may be visited on people of color in terms of both higher transactions costs and taking more precaution to comply strictly with retailer policies. One audit study showed that African Americans in Washington, D.C., had to wait 27 percent longer to hail a cab If this seems a minor inconvenience, white readers should try to imagine what their life would be like if *every* (or even just many) transactions took 27 percent longer. Even a single incident can impose real psychological costs. Consider, for example, Patricia Williams's story of being denied entrance to an open Benneton store by a gum-chewing, buzzerwielding store clerk.

NOTES AND QUESTIONS

1. Statistical discrimination. Statistical discrimination exists when a seller or provider of services or property owner treats two equally suitable persons differently, solely on the basis of the average characteristics of members of a race, gender, or other subordinated group.

2. References for statistical discrimination. For more extensive discussion of statistical discrimination, see D.J. Aigner and G.C. Cain, *Statistical Theories of Discrimination in the Labor Market*, 30 INDUS. & LAB. REL. REV. 175 (1977); K.J. Arrow, *The Theory of Discrimination; in* DISCRIMINATION IN LABOR MARKETS (Ashenfelter and Rees eds.) (1973); A. Moro & P. Norman, *A General Equilibrium Model of Statistical Discrimination*, 114 J. OF ECON. THEORY 1 (2004); S. SCHWAB, *Is Statistical Discrimination Efficient?*,

76 Amer. Econ. Rev. 228 (1986); P. Norman, *Statistical Discrimination and Efficiency*, 70 Rev. of Econ. Studies 615 (2003).

3. Does statistical discrimination account for the proliferation of stereotypes and the presence of negative cognitive associations for subordinated groups whose average characteristics are the product of a societal history of exclusion from opportunity?

————

F.   NEUTRALITY CHALLENGES FROM OTHER SOCIAL SCIENCE METHODOLOGIES:

1.   COGNITIVE PSYCHOLOGY—SCIENTIFIC EVIDENCE OF COGNITIVE BIAS?

Racism lost its explicit social endorsement in the aftermath of the civil rights revolution that followed in the more than half-century since the 1954 Supreme Court decision in *Brown v. Board of Education*. Hostile racial attitudes and prejudicial belief systems gradually went underground, flourishing in the subterranean world of personal cognition, family norms, and private conversations in racially homogeneous settings. Until recently, this bias was undetectable by scientifically reliable assessment tools. Moreover, both economic theory and legal theory operated on heuristics that assumed that significant racial bias no longer existed.

As Ian Ayres has shown, with a series of empirical research studies of racial discrimination in retail markets, this assumption is probably false. *See* Ayres, Pervasive Prejudice? Unconventional Evidence of Race and Gender Discrimination, *infra* at 801. However, notwithstanding Ayres path-breaking empirical research, the difficulty for those seeking to challenge the neutrality heuristics of economics and law has been to find ways to identify individual biases, and more importantly to link those biases to racially harmful behavior.

Note on the Implicit Association Test (I.A.T.)

The development of the Implicit Association Test has provided a method to penetrate the web of latent individual bias. The test, in its most widely used version, is administered to individuals who choose to take it on the internet. Test takers are asked to sort a randomly shown series of faces into two categories: black American or white American. The test instructions encourage speedy responses using two keys on the computer keyboard that require the use of either the left or right hand. In the second stage of the test, a sequence of value-laden words, such as "joy" and "failure" appear on the screen. The test taker is asked to associate these words with a random distribution of the same set of faces representing the two racial groups. In the final step, the words and faces are reversed, and the test taker is asked again to associate the words with the, now racialized faces.

The existence of bias is measured by the time difference between the length of time it takes to match the faces to words that are consistent with the racial stereotype, and the length of time required to match the faces with words associated with the other group, so that matching blacks with joy takes longer than matching blacks with "failure." The test is built on the psychological phenomenon of cognitive dissonance, in which there is discrepancy between beliefs, and new facts require more mental effort to process. The test results, from tens of thousands of self-selected test takers who described themselves as liberal, identified 88 percent of white test takers as having an anti-black bias. Perhaps even more interesting than the bias of whites against blacks, were the results of black bias against other blacks, revealing an internalization of the cultural tilt against all blacks. A startling 48 percent of blacks showed an anti-black bias.

The test is not without its critics who charge that even if it accurately measures interior states of mind, it should not be the basis for policymaking, or legal intervention by government, because it only reveals "thoughts." Psychologist Hal Arkes argues that the problem with the test is "where we are going to set our threshold of proof for saying something represents prejudice. My view is the implicit prejudice program sets the threshold at a historical low." Quoted in, Shankar Vedantam, "See No Bias," *The Washington Post Magazine*, 12, at 40, Jan. 23, 2005.

Taking the I.A.T. We encourage you to take a moment to take the test for yourself. The website is https://implicit.harvard.edu. A full explanation of the research design can be found at https://implicit.harvard.edu/implicit/demo/faqs.html.

Pro–Black Bias. Courtland Milloy, a black columnist for the *Washington Post*, took the Implict Association Test. He reports that his results told him that: "your data suggest a strong automatic preference for Black relative to White." Milloy notes:

> For some readers, no doubt, this is confirmation that I am a reverse racist . . . The last thing I wanted [was] to end up in that group of African Americans who showed a pro-white or anti-black bias [48 percent]. . . . A conscious effort is what it has taken for me not to absorb the worst of white society's stereotypes about blacks.

Courtland Milloy, "Out From Under the Thumb of White Bias," *Washington Post*, B1, January 26, 2005.

————

Civil Rights Perestroika: Intergroup Relations After Affirmative Action

86 CAL. L. REV. 1251 (1998).

■ LINDA HAMILTON KRIEGER

Here at the University of California at Berkeley, there was a surreal quality to November 6, 1996, the day after voters, in enacting Proposition

209, elected to end affirmative action in California state hiring, contracting, and education. The few protests that had been organized ended quickly and quietly. At the law school, students seemed uncharacteristically subdued: quietly resigned—or quietly pleased. In the newspapers that morning and on the mornings that followed, articles about Texaco executives referring to their African–American employees as "niggers" and "black jelly beans" were oddly juxtaposed against others in which Proposition 209's triumphant sponsors heralded a glorious new era of truly equal opportunity and the long-awaited dawning of a colorblind society.

Now, many months later and well into the first of Berkeley's "post-affirmative action" years, the atmosphere here is no less strange. On the first day of classes in 1997, the halls and courtyards swarmed with television cameras and reporters, attempting, I noted with a sense of irony, to identify the lone African–American member of Boalt Hall's first "colorblind" class. We were no longer supposed to consider race, but race was everywhere in these halls on that first morning of the new school year.
* * *

If history is any guide, the trend started in California will spread to other states and to the national stage in the months ahead. The 105th Congress witnessed the introduction of three separate bills that would have "nationalized" Proposition 209, and, events in Houston notwithstanding, many States are contemplating similar legislation.

But before proceeding further down this road, it might be wise to pause and ask some hard questions. * * * What can we expect to occur with respect to intergroup relations, and with race relations in particular, in a post-affirmative action environment? If affirmative action is eliminated, will remaining policy tools prove adequate to effectuate racial and gender equity and to prevent the resegregation of American society? Will the idea of "colorblindness" suffice as a theoretical model for understanding what it means not to discriminate? Or will we find instead that affirmative action actually served to mask a "multiplicity of sins"—critical failings in our approach to intergroup relations and serious defects in the tools available to make the equal opportunity society a reality instead of a hazy, unattainable dream?* * *

[This article] inquires whether, absent preferential forms of affirmative action, remaining policy tools would prove adequate to control discrimination and prevent the further segregation of American society. It concludes that these remaining tools, which include a colorblindness model of nondiscrimination, an objective concept of merit, and individualized adjudication as a primary policy enforcement tool, are unequal to the task. In short, we still lack adequate tools for coping successfully with the problems of intergroup competition and cooperation in a pluralistic society.

This failure, which I will argue has been masked to a certain extent by preferential forms of affirmative action, derives from a misunderstanding of the nature and sources of intergroup bias, from a failure to recognize its tendency to persist over time, and from over-reliance on limited adjudicatory and regulatory approaches to address what is fundamentally a complex cultural problem. Accordingly, I argue that unless we develop a broadened understanding of intergroup bias and new approaches to reducing it, the problems of discrimination and inequality of opportunity will worsen in a post-affirmative action environment.

[D]iscrimination does not solely derive from stable, dispositional traits internal to actors we call "discriminators." Rather, intergroup bias increases or decreases in response to contextual, environmental factors which shape how social actors perceive, judge, and make decisions about members of their own and other social reference groups. Accordingly, an anti-discrimination policy grounded in an individualized search for discriminatory intent cannot be expected to succeed either in identifying and preventing intergroup bias or in managing social tendencies toward intergroup conflict. If we are to solve the problem of intergroup discrimination, we must attend more closely to the ecology of intergroup relations. Eliminating affirmative action before we have developed an effective alternative theoretical and doctrinal approach to managing intergroup bias is a strategy more risky than many might assume. * * *

II

AFTER AFFIRMATIVE ACTION: RECOGNIZING DISCRIMINATION IN THE LAND OF THE COLORBLIND

What might we expect if every institution in the nation—every college and university, every corporation, every state and local public agency, and every arm and organ of the federal government—suddenly prohibited its employees from considering the race, sex, or national origin of applicants or employees in hiring, contracting, promotion, or admission to educational programs? What would happen if every employment and admissions decision maker was told simply to "be colorblind," to base his or her decisions only on "considerations of merit"? Would they do it? Could they do it? Could we identify those who did not do it, whose decisions were tainted by intergroup bias?

The answers to these questions are, quite simply, "no," "no," and "no." Perhaps constitutions can be colorblind. Perhaps official government or corporate policies can be colorblind. But human beings living in a society in which history, ideology, law, and patterns of social, economic, and political distribution have made race, sex, and ethnicity salient, cannot be colorblind. The "colorblindness" approach to nondiscrimination will prove ineffective because it provides neither a framework for enabling people to recognize the effects of race, gender, or national origin on their perceptions and judgments, nor the tools required to help them counteract those effects. Indeed, a color blindness-centered interpretation of the nondiscrimination principle, coupled with well-meaning people's awareness that they do categorize along racial and ethnic lines, may exacerbate the very intergroup anxiety and ambivalence that lead to what social psychologists refer to as aversive racism.

Furthermore, decision makers cannot base selection decisions only on colorblind considerations of merit for the simple reason that merit has a color. Conceptions of merit are socially and politically constructed and are shaped by the same ingroup preferences that give rise to other subtle forms of intergroup bias. Affirmative action preferences have, in many ways, diverted our attention from the biases inherent in the construction of merit. But if preferences are eliminated, this problem and the inequities it generates will soon rise into sharp relief.

Finally, there is substantial reason to doubt that remaining law enforcement tools, particularly the adjudication of individual disparate treatment cases, will prove effective in identifying and remedying subtle but pervasive forms of intergroup bias. For a variety of reasons, reliance on individual disparate treatment adjudication can be expected to result in the serious underidentification of discrimination by judicial decision makers, victims, and private fact finders.

A. The Inefficacy of Colorblindness as a Normative Construct

[E]xisting antidiscrimination law constructs intergroup bias as something that occurs when a "discriminatory purpose" motivates a decision. In other words, in order for a decision to be considered "discriminatory" under a statute such as Title VII, the disparate treatment plaintiff must show that the employer chose to take the negative action against him because of his membership in a particular protected class. Thus, to say that discrimination is intentional means that the decision stands in a particular sort of close relation to the target person's group status. Specifically, in the decision maker's mental process, there must be some syllogistic connection between the two.

So, for example, existing antidiscrimination law understands cognitive stereotypes as causing discrimination through the operation of a conscious, syllogistic reasoning process, through which the decision maker uses a person's group status in the following sort of way:

Major Premise: Women with young children are preoccupied with family responsibilities and do not put their jobs first;

Minor Premise: This applicant is a woman with young children;

Conclusion: This applicant cannot be expected to put the job first.

Current antidiscrimination law further conceives gender role expectations, or normative stereotypes, as causing discrimination through the operation of a similar sort of syllogistic reasoning:

Major Premise: Women with young children should be preoccupied with family responsibilities and should not hold jobs that will compete with the responsibilities associated with raising children;

Minor Premise (1) The rigors of this job can be expected to conflict with family responsibilities associated with raising young children;

Minor Premise (2) This applicant is a mother with young children;

Conclusion: This applicant should not hold this job.

According to the existing jurisprudential model of discrimination, personal animosity may also lead to discrimination through the operation of implicit syllogistic reasoning:

Major Premise: Working with black coworkers makes me feel uncomfortable;

Minor Premise: This applicant is black;

Conclusion: Working with him would make me feel uncomfortable.

In each of these contexts, the decision maker's thinking moves directly through the target person's group status. So long as we understand discrimination as operating in this way, we can rely on a color-blindness model of nondiscrimination to function as an effective normative principle. A social decision maker can refrain from discriminating simply by refraining from any syllogistic use of the target person's group status, in other words, by being "colorblind."

But as I have also attempted to demonstrate, not all discrimination is of this sort. Much discrimination has little connection with discriminatory motive or intent. This sort of discrimination occurs when an individual's group status subtly, even unconsciously, affects a decision makers' subjective perception of relevant traits, on which ostensibly non-discriminatory decision are subsequently based. This form of discrimination results from a variety of categorization-related cognitive biases, and can result in disparate treatment based on race, sex, national origin, or other factors, even among the well-intentioned.

I do not wish to rehash the evidence supporting this proposition described at length elsewhere. Rather, using related but more recent research, I wish to demonstrate that only "color-consciousness" can control these cognitive forms of intergroup bias. This research strongly suggests that cognitive biases in social judgment operate automatically, without intention or awareness, and can be controlled only through subsequent, deliberate "mental correction" that takes group status squarely into account.

1.   Automatic Processes in Intergroup Judgment

In his early work on perceptual readiness, Jerome Bruner observed that when a person receives information with the goal of forming an impression, his or her first cognitive task is to fit that information into some existing knowledge structure. As Bruner described, only when behavioral information is encoded in this way does it becomes useful, or even meaningful.

Of course, in many situations incoming information is ambiguous in that it is susceptible to varied interpretations. A student's volunteered but halting response to a question can be interpreted as reflecting dull-wittedness—or courageous engagement with a difficult subject. An employee's hesitancy in the face of an important decision may evince timidity—or prudence. As Bruner suggested, "All perception is generic," meaning that observed actions, like objects, take on meaning only when they are assigned to a particular trait construct—a preexisting knowledge structure residing in the observer's mind.

In their attempts to understand this process more fully, cognitive psychologists originally assumed that assigning an action to a particular trait construct depended primarily on the extent of the "match" between the features of the action and those of the construct. Then in the late 1970s through the early 1980s, encouraged no doubt by Amos Tversky and Daniel Kahneman's seminal work on the availability heuristic, various researchers began investigating the role of trait construct accessibility in social perception. Their work showed that the readiness with which a person will characterize a particular behavior in terms of any given trait construct is a function of that construct's availability in memory at the time the behavior is perceived. Any activity, conscious or unconscious, that "primes" a particular trait construct will tend to increase its accessibility and the corresponding likelihood that ambiguous information will be assimilated or encoded in a manner consistent with that trait.

Social stereotypes bias perception in this general manner. As numerous researchers have demonstrated, one learns at an early age stereotypes of the major social groups in the United States. These stereotypes have a long history of activation, and are likely to be highly accessible, regardless of whether they are believed. They are invoked automatically when people encounter members of a stereotyped outgroup. Once activated, stereotypes serve to "prime" the trait constructs with which they are associated. Incoming behavioral information, especially if capable of various interpretations, is accordingly assimilated into those traits associated with the stereotype.

This tendency to assimilate ambiguous information into stereotypic trait constructs might not be so serious if people were aware that they were doing it. To understand the significance of this process and its implications for the debate over affirmative action, it is useful to understand a phenomenon which attribution theorists refer to as spontaneous trait inference.

People are highly concerned with understanding why things happen in their social environments. Rightly or wrongly, we assume that understanding why something has happened will improve our power to predict or even control what will happen in the future. To the extent that personality traits play an important role in understanding people's actions, one might expect the process of translating observed behaviors into trait-related meanings to occur with great frequency. Given that social perception and judgment processes become increasingly efficient with repeated execution, one might further hypothesize that trait inference processes could become so overlearned as to operate without intention or awareness, much like the processes involved in recognizing a word or a face.

This hypothesis appears to be correct. In a number of studies replicated in a variety of contexts by other researchers, New York University psychologist James S. Uleman and his colleagues demonstrated that European–American subjects spontaneously encode behaviors into stable trait constructs without intention or awareness. Thus, there is a strong tendency, at least among European Americans, to attribute stable dispositional qualities spontaneously, as part of the process of perceiving and encoding information about another person's behavior. To say that trait inference is "spontaneous" however is not quite the same as saying it is "automatic," and the difference is critical to equal opportunity policy.

Through the early–1980s, it was generally believed that a particular mental process was either entirely automatic or entirely deliberate. Over time, however, cognitive processes came to be understood as falling along a continuum. On one side of that continuum lie "controlled processes," which require substantial processing capacity and occur with greater levels of focus and awareness. On the other side lie fully automatic processes, which occur without intention or awareness, are difficult if not impossible to control once triggered, and interfere little with other ongoing mental activity. Eventually, it became apparent that complex mental processes such as causal attribution and other forms of social inference were neither exclusively automatic nor exclusively controlled, but rather combined aspects of both. Specifically, social inference came to be understood as comprising a chain of three sequential subprocesses: "categorization," in which the person perceived is identified and placed within an existing categorical structure; "characterization," in which spontaneous dispositional inferences are drawn from the observed behavior; and "correction," in which those dispositional inferences are adjusted to account for situational factors. While categorization and characterization are automatic, correction is controlled. It requires deliberate, effortful mental processing and will compete for cognitive resources with other information processing demands. * * *

The significance of these processes and their implications for the colorblindness approach to nondiscrimination can hardly be overemphasized. Very little information shapes a social perceiver's impression of a target person. Rather, it is the perceiver's interpretation of the raw information that influences social judgment. If the target's social group membership influences these interpretations, and if one is unaware of the effect of such status on those interpretations, how can we expect a colorblindness approach to nondiscrimination to function successfully as a normative principle? Given the realities of social perception, we can anticipate that similarly situated people will be treated differently based on their group membership, because decision makers, influenced by these subtle forms of intergroup bias, will not perceive them as similarly situated at all. Nothing in the colorblindness approach to nondiscrimination provides social decision makers with the tools required to recognize or to correct for biases of this sort.

According to spontaneous trait inference theory, only the application of deliberate, controlled, corrective processes can prevent stereotypes and subtle ingroup priming valences from biasing interpersonal judgment. As social cognition researchers Patricia Devine and Susan Fiske observe, it is neither that nonprejudiced individuals "do not notice" such traits as gender or ethnicity nor that the presence of a member of another group does not "prime" the stereotypes associated with those groups. Rather, insofar as cognitive sources of bias are concerned, the difference between people who discriminate and those who do not is that members of the latter group notice the influences of stereotypes on their thinking and counteract those influences by consciously adjusting responses in a nonprejudiced direction. This process, however, is effortful: it requires both strong motivation and a great deal of capacity, attention, and practice. In short, controlling the biases stemming from such processes as spontaneous trait inference is substantially more complicated than it might at first seem.

2.   Controlled Processes and Nondiscrimination: Taming the Beast of Automaticity

The major sources of error in human judgment divide into two broad types. Errors of the first type stem from a failure to know or apply normative rules of inference. Errors of the second type result from a phenomenon which Timothy Wilson and Nancy Brekke refer to as "mental contamination." Mental contamination occurs when a person's judgment or behavior is corrupted by unconscious or uncontrollable mental processes which she would rather not have influence her behavior or decisions. Judgment errors deriving from rule ignorance or incorrect rule application are easier to remedy than those resulting from mental contamination. Normative rules of inference, like the rule of regression to the mean, supply specific procedures for solving the problems to which they pertain and can be consciously learned and deliberately applied.

Correcting judgmental errors resulting from mental contamination is more difficult, in large part because simply teaching people a particular decision rule is unlikely to control biases of which they are unaware. This will be particularly true if the biases in question are difficult to recognize, or easily mistaken for valid, decision-relevant considerations. A supervisor evaluating employees for promotion, or a professor considering which student to hire as a research assistant, may know the rule, "don't discriminate against the black guy." But that kind of rule, in this case the colorblindness rule, cannot be applied in the same way as cost-benefit analysis or the rule of regression to the mean. It can be applied to eliminate facial discrimination—that is, a conscious, explicit policy of excluding a certain group of persons from consideration. It might even be applied to eliminate the conscious, deliberate use of group status as a proxy for decision-relevant traits like initiative or writing ability. But it cannot be applied to prevent or correct biases caused by emotional discomfort, the subconscious effects of stereotypes, causal attribution, or spontaneous trait inference, because it fails to provide a specific set of procedures or techniques which can be applied to the evaluation or decision task at hand. A normative decision rule, such as one prohibiting discrimination on the basis of race, cannot be applied to eliminate a source of bias if the decision maker is unaware that her judgment might be biased or is unable to control the effects of such bias for lack of applicable remedial tools.

As Wilson and Brekke explain, four discrete conditions must be satisfied if people are to control the effects of nonconscious biases. First, one must become aware of the nature of the particular mental process which threatens to bias one's judgment. Second, one must be motivated to correct its unwanted influence once it has been recognized. Third, one must be able to discern the direction and magnitude of the bias, lest it be "overcorrected" and judgment skewed in the opposite direction. And finally, one must have sufficient control over his or her mental processes to correct the effect of the unwanted influences. While it is beyond the scope of this Article to review all of the problems encountered at each of these four stages, those with the most serious implications for the colorblindness model of nondiscrimination warrant attention here.

a.   Unawareness of Mental Process

During the fall of 1996, while the campaign on Proposition 209 swirled around the University, I was teaching a class on employment discrimination law. Every day, I called on a different student to respond to questions about the cases prepared for that day's class. Most of my students were Caucasian; only three of sixty-five were African American. Let us assume for purposes of illustration, that one day I had called on one of these three African–American students, and that he experienced a certain amount of difficulty answering various questions. He was not unprepared, but many of his answers were halting and somewhat confused, leaving me with the initial impression that he was not particularly capable.

I flatly reject the belief that African–American law students are less intelligent than others. If asked at the beginning of the semester to predict how any one of my three African–American students would perform relative to their classmates, I would have vigorously objected to making a prediction in the absence of individuating information. Given that I am familiar with certain normative rules of inference such as the principle of regression to the mean, I would probably, if pushed, have predicted that his or her performance would be about average.

But it is also true that, although I reject them as untrue, I am aware of the stereotypes associated with intelligence, academic achievement, and African–American males. I too was exposed to those stereotypes at a very early age, before I developed my own powers of critical and moral intelligence and made a conscious decision to reject these stereotypes as inaccurate and unfair. But my nonprejudiced beliefs did not displace the stereotypes, which exist alongside and function independently of these beliefs. The stereotypes are triggered whether I believe in them or not. And, once triggered, those stereotypes prime the trait constructs associated with them, constructs like "not too bright" or "underachieving," rather than "grappling courageously with a difficult subject."

So, what should one conclude if I had taken from this hypothetical encounter the initial impression that the student in question was "not particularly capable?" His performance had not been very good. Why then, should I even question whether the student's race had anything to do with my judgment?

If such a situation were to arise, I would likely question my initial impression only if: (1) I was aware of the possibility that negative stereotypes of African–American males, or some other aspects of the situation had subtly influenced my judgment; and (2) I was motivated to do something about it.

Of course, other subtle cognitive sources of bias besides racial stereotypes could have "contaminated" my judgment as well. If I approached the issue mindfully, I would probably have noticed that over the course of the semester, a number of students I had called on had performed relatively poorly, some just as poorly as the student in question. But try as I might, if I had not made contemporaneous notes, I probably could not now remember just who those students were. I would remember the African–American student, but I would most likely have forgotten the others.

This scenario illustrates a common unconscious source of bias—the polarized evaluation of distinctive members of an otherwise largely homogeneous group. It is well-established that people pay particularly close attention to distinctive stimulus objects, such as a "token" woman or minority group member. And the more attention we pay to something, the more about it we perceive, encode, and store in memory. Indeed, under conditions of high attention, we are more likely to encode an event visually, which makes it more readily available in memory and more influential in the formation of subsequent judgments. Accordingly, the poor performance of a distinctive minority student is more likely to be remembered, and will tend to be charged with a more powerful negative valence, than the poor performance of a majority white student.

If I were unschooled in these sorts of salience or expectancy-related biases, I would likely remain unaware that the student's race had played any role in the formation of my initial impression that he was "not particularly capable." But could I fairly deny that he had been negatively judged, at least in part, because of his race?

The colorblindness approach to nondiscrimination is dangerous because it leads a decision maker to believe that, so long as she is not consciously thinking about race, she is not discriminating. But social cognition theory teaches that, in a culture pervaded by racial stereotypes, or where persons of one race constitute a small minority in an otherwise homogeneous group, one must think about race in order not to discriminate. In short, the colorblindness principle discourages the first step prerequisite to controlling cognitive sources of intergroup bias.

b.   The Role of Motivation

All "dual process" models of social inference posit that in order to correct errors caused by an automatic mental process, people must not only be aware of the process, but must also be motivated to control its biasing effects. Of course, the development of awareness itself requires motivation.

Despite early controversy on particular issues, it is now relatively well-accepted that people lack awareness of a large proportion of mental processing, including the processes comprising impression formation.

Developing self-awareness of such processes and correcting for the various biases inherent in them is in any context objectively difficult. Even after they are activated, the controlled processes required for mental correction require a great deal of capacity and attention and will compete for cognitive resources with other mental demands. But in the context of intergroup discrimination, the order is taller still. Increasing awareness of and sustained attention to the biasing effects of racial, ethnic, or gender stereotypes on one's social judgments is apt to engender fear of moral opprobrium and substantial psychological discomfort. Thus, especially in the context of reducing intergroup bias, there is little reason to assume that people will expend the effort or bear the psychological discomfort associated with mental correction unless they have strong motivations for so doing. Thus, the colorblindness approach not only fails to provide incentives for developing an awareness of mental contamination, but the model itself and the rhetoric that often accompanies it actually establish disincentives for so doing. * * *

c.   The Limits of Mental Correction

As Timothy Wilson and Nancy Brekke observe, even if a person becomes aware that some unwanted mental process has tainted her judgment, she may not be able to determine the magnitude of the resulting bias. For example, in my hypothetical interaction with my African–American student, I might have become aware that stereotype or salience-related biases had influenced my assessment of his performance. But assuming that I were eventually required to formulate an evaluation, how far, if at all, should I adjust it? There is really no way for me to assess how much of my impression is fairly attributable to bias and how much to the student's flawed performance.

Even more troubling is the question whether "correction" is feasible at all. Once the initial impression that the student was "not particularly capable" had been formed, would I be able to erase it from my mind, or prevent it from influencing my impressions of him in connection with future interactions?

There is ample reason to fear that I would not. In a series of now classic studies, Stanford psychologist Lee Ross and his colleagues demonstrated that, even after a belief is discredited, the causal explanations generated to support it persist, giving the discredited belief a kind of cognitive life after death. More recently, University of Texas psychologists Daniel Gilbert and Randall Osborne extended these observations to the process of spontaneous trait inference. Their work demonstrates that once a trait inference is made, subsequent efforts to adjust it may prove ineffective. As they observed, misperceptions are "metastatic." Controlled processing may correct the original misperception, but it often fails to eliminate subsidiary changes that the original misperception engendered.

These endure and influence subsequent judgments of the person perceived. It is easier to forbear from action based on a biased impression than to eliminate the impression itself.

Assuming I realized that my impression formation process was potentially biased, I might have decided to reject the view that the student was not particularly capable. I might even have decided not to take action based on my initial impression of his in-class performance, for example, deciding not to use it in calculating his grade. But I would probably not be able to erase the impression from my mind. Given its enduring presence, I would likely experience any adjustments in my subsequent behavior toward or expressed beliefs about the student as a form of racial preferencing. "After all," I might tell myself, "if the student weren't African–American, I wouldn't be bending over backwards like this." What the colorblindness perspective would allow me to forget, or never teach me in the first place, is that if the student were not African–American, I probably would not have remembered his performance at all. * * *

[Krieger's discussion of how conceptions of "merit" are "defined and assessed through the same complex, largely unconscious cognitive processes which subtly bias social judgment in other contexts and give rise to more easily recognizable forms of discrimination" is omitted.]

b. Schematic Expectancies and the Problem of Ingroup Favoritism * * *

iii. Ingroup Helping Discrimination and the Leniency Effect

Patterns of modern discrimination turn in large measure on the answer to one simple question: Who gets cut slack, and who does not? What happens when an employee violates a rule? Is she subjected to discipline under established policies, or are her transgressions overlooked, or attributed to factors beyond her control? When an ambiguous aspect of a person's background can be interpreted in various ways, one negative, one neutral, which attribution is made? And when a person simply needs help, does she receive it?

Type II bias in large measure shapes people's tendencies to assist or ignore, to excuse others' transgressions or hold them accountable under objective standards of conduct. The earliest, and perhaps still the most vivid of the studies illustrating this effect, was conducted in the early 1970s, in front of a Kansas supermarket. In this study, one black woman and one white woman, whom researchers matched for age and social class-related appearance, dropped a bag of groceries while leaving a supermarket, right in the path of oncoming shoppers. Researchers investigated whether white shoppers would help a white "bag dropper" more frequently than a black bag dropper.

The results were complex and intriguing. Overall, the experimenters found no significant effect of race on the provision of help per se: approximately the same percentage of incoming white shoppers in either condition stopped to help. Subsequent analysis of the data however, revealed an important, if more subtle, phenomenon. When the bag dropper was white, sixty three percent of those who stopped continued to provide assistance until the job was done. When the bag dropper was black, helpers tended to pick up one or two items and then leave, providing complete assistance only thirty percent of the time.

Additional studies provide further evidence of an ingroup helping bias. In 1977, Samuel Gaertner and John Dovidio conducted an experiment in which white subjects were led to believe that they were participating in an investigation of extrasensory perception (ESP). Researchers assigned subjects to serve as either a "sender" or a "receiver," and paired each with a partner/confederate, who was either white or black. Senders and receivers sat in different rooms. Researchers told some subjects that a second person was sitting with their partner in the other room, and told other subjects that the partner was alone.

During the course of the "ESP" experiment, researchers staged an emergency. Subjects heard the sound of falling chairs and the screams of the partner in the other room, followed by prolonged silence. Researchers investigated whether the partner's race would effect the rates at which subjects would go to the aid of their partner.

When subjects believed that their partner was alone in the other room, the partner's race had no significant effect on responses. However, when subjects believed that there was another person in the room with the partner, race made a dramatic difference. Where the apparently imperiled partner was white, seventy-five percent of subjects offered aid, but where the partner was black, the rate dropped to thirty-seven percent. Perhaps even more significantly, subjects showed greater physiological arousal, measured by change in heart rate, when the partner/confederate was white than when he was black.

Gaertner and Dovidio interpreted these results as indicating that whites do not deliberately avoid providing assistance to blacks. However, when features of the situation are ambiguous, when it is unclear whether help is called for, they tend to resolve uncertainty in favor of helping whites and against helping blacks. * * *

As the tendency to assist is biased, so is the tendency to overlook or excuse transgression. For example, in a 1974 field study of whites' reactions to apparent shoplifting, Max Dertke and his colleagues demonstrated that when the shoplifter/confederate was black, white shoppers spontaneously reported and followed up on an observed shoplifting incident at a much higher rate than when the shoplifter/confederate was white. * * *

One can easily see how over time, these subtle forms of ingroup favoritism would result in markedly different outcomes for ingroup and outgroup members. If decision makers react to members of their own social reference groups with more positive associations, a quicker willingness to help, and a stronger inclination to ignore or excuse shortcomings, it is easy to predict who will be systematically advantaged in hiring and promotion decisions. Disparities will develop even absent hostile animus or negative actions directed towards the outgroup. * * *

[Krieger's discussion of how current anti-discrimination law is poorly equipped to control Type II discrimination is omitted.]

D.   Individualized Adjudication, Hypothesis Testing, and Causal Attribution: The Effects of Intergroup Bias

Consider for a moment the judgment task involved in adjudicating an individual employment discrimination suit. Determining in any given case whether discrimination has occurred is fundamentally an exercise in causal attribution. The employer has taken some negative action, most frequently a termination of employment, against the plaintiff. The jury's role is to determine why that negative action was taken. Was it, as the plaintiff alleges, because the decision maker discriminated against her because of her membership in a protected group? Or was it, as the defendant argues, because of some legitimate, nondiscriminatory reason, usually some malfeasance or deficiency on the plaintiff's part? In a hiring case, did the plaintiff fail to get the job because the decision maker took her group status into account in making the challenged decision? Or did the decision maker believe that some other candidate would do a better job? The trial of such a case will essentially entail a battle between two competing causal theories. Seeking to convince the jury that discrimination is to blame, the plaintiff will portray the decision makers as discriminators. Seeking to convince the jury that the plaintiff is to blame, the defendant will do everything possible to make his or her deficiencies salient.

Why should we expect a jury to approach this social decision task free from the various forms of intergroup bias that distort intergroup perception and judgment in other contexts? As we have seen, unconscious stereotypes about members of different social groups create implicit expectancies in the minds of social perceivers. These expectancies in turn distort the perception, interpretation, and recall of information about members of the targeted groups, pulling subsequent social judgments in a stereotype-consistent direction. Stereotypic expectancies and other forms of intergroup bias also affect causal attribution, causing unconscious distortions in the interpretation and perceived predictiveness of past behavior.

Attributing the causes of employment decisions implicates the very processes of social perception and judgment bound up in the challenged employment decisions themselves. Unless the demographic characteristics of fact finders vary in some dramatic way from those of the decision makers, we cannot reasonably expect that the level of intergroup discrimination reflected in employment decisions will vary in any meaningful way from the level reflected in discrimination verdicts. Indeed, the analytical structure and content of disparate treatment adjudications, focusing as it does on the plausibility of defendant's proffered legitimate nondiscriminatory reasons for a challenged employment decision, can be expected to potentiate those forms of intergroup bias caused by stereotypic expectancies. Discrimination adjudications therefore may be even more vulnerable to cognitive forms of intergroup bias than the decision tasks which give rise to them.

An employer's determination, for example, whether a particular employee should be terminated is not much different from a court's determination whether an employer believed in good faith that a particular employee deserved to be terminated. Similarly, an employer judging whether a particular candidate is best qualified for a position is not particularly different from a court judging whether a particular candidate would reasonably have been viewed by a well-intentioned employer as the best qualified person for a position. Expectancy confirmation effects, such as those illustrated in Darley's and Gross's study discussed above, will distort both types of judgments. Thus, there is no reason to believe that the incidence of stereotype-induced judgment error in discrimination adjudications will differ in any significant way from its incidence in employment or educational decision making. Indeed, if as Darley and Gross suggest, exposure to ambiguous but ostensibly diagnostic collections of information potentiates expectancy confirmation bias, we can expect disparate treatment adjudications, with their "information rich texture," to suffer even more from such biases than hiring or educational admissions decisions, where relatively little diagnostic information is available and decision makers may be more on guard against making stereotypic judgments.

In short, from a cognitive process standpoint we cannot expect disparate treatment adjudications to be any less subject to subtle forms of intergroup bias than the decisions which give rise to them. Correspondingly, we cannot expect individualized adjudication of disparate treatment claims to be particularly effective in identifying or redressing cognitive discrimination. For this reason as for others, disparate treatment adjudication, like the colorblindness model of nondiscrimination and reliance on an objective concept of merit, is an extremely weak tool for combating cognitive forms of intergroup bias. We cannot expect these policies to do the work once accomplished by disparate impact theory, numerical standards, and the systematic, self-critical analysis of selection procedures. Unfortunately, when a person is color-blind, there is simply much he will not see.
* * *

What is the explanation for the stubborn persistence of pervasive discrimination today? In what follows, R.A. Lenhardt draws on sociological research to argue that the focus should be on the racial harm, including citizenship harms arising from exclusion, instead of either disparate impact, or intent.

2.   SOCIOLOGY AND LAW: STIGMA THEORY

Understanding the Mark: Race, Stigma, and Equality in Context

79 N.Y.U. L. REV. 803 (2005).

■ R.A. LENHARDT
     * * *

     * * * In fact, we are approaching a state in which many minority youths arguably stand a greater chance of being incarcerated than of

obtaining a college degree and entering the economic mainstream. According to a recent study, of the approximately two million people in adult correctional facilities in the United States, an astounding 1.2 million, or 63%, are African–American or Latino, even though these groups together comprise only 25% of the total population.

These statistics paint a devastating picture of increasing racial separation and inequality along several fundamental life axes and demonstrate how far away we actually are from remedying the problem of racial disadvantage. The truth is that, in many ways, we are as racially divided a society today as we were before the Supreme Court's landmark decision in *Brown v. Board of Education* and the enactment of the Civil Rights Act of 1964. Where we live, go to school, and work are all still greatly determined by race. The question we must ask is: Why? What accounts for the stubborn persistence of the color line DuBois identified so many years ago? Why do racial disparities still exist?

For some time, the only legal framework available for understanding questions of racial inequity and disadvantage, reflected in cases such as *Washington v. Davis*, was that of intentional discrimination. Then, more than fifteen years ago, Professor Charles Lawrence revolutionized legal scholarship by arguing that the source of racial harm lay principally in unconsciously racist acts. Drawing on psychoanalytic theory and cognitive psychology, Lawrence's article, *The Id, The Ego, and Equal Protection: Reckoning with Unconscious Racism*, challenged the view that only intentionally discriminatory conduct ran the risk of imposing racial harm. Because of the cognitive processes and meanings associated with race in this country, Lawrence argued, racial motive was most often reflected in unconscious conduct bearing a disparate racial impact. He maintained that the messages communicated by facially neutral governmental actions were the best indicator of racist motive, and he therefore advocated greater judicial attention to the cultural or racial meaning of policy choices and initiatives.

This Article seeks to advance the conversation about the nature and contours of racial harm by asserting that we should be concerned, not with the meanings associated with conduct, but rather with the meanings associated with race itself. My argument is that racial stigma, not intentional discrimination or unconscious racism, is the true source of racial injury in the United States. This theory accounts for the persistence of racial disparities that mark the color line, as well as the incidence of intentionally discriminatory or racialized behavior. It conceives of these problems as a function of racial stigma, not vice versa. In this respect, it is perhaps the most comprehensive theory of racial harm advanced thus far.

[Lenhardt defines racial stigma as consisting of the following 4 characteristics:]

I.   WHAT IS RACIAL STIGMA?

* * * Brands were used as a way of identifying African slaves as human property up until the latter part of the eighteenth century and as a method of punishment well into the nineteenth century. When we talk about racial stigma today, however, we are almost never referring directly to the brands and cuts that were used to demarcate slave or outsider status. We plainly mean something different, something less physical and perhaps more cognitive in nature. The question is: What?

Even as the term racial stigma has become part of common parlance, it has escaped clear definition. An informal survey of individuals on the street likely would generate as many definitions as people interviewed. For some, it refers to demeaning racial insults or stereotypes. For others, it is synonymous with the concept of racial inferiority. Still others see it principally as a by-product of discriminatory treatment that excludes or denies a benefit on the basis of race. The connotation given the term seems to vary by individual and even by context.

Significantly, this holds true even among courts and legal scholars, who ordinarily might be expected to have a more uniform understanding of a concept that has been embraced as a key constitutional principle in the race context. The legal approach to racial stigma, for the most part, has mirrored the strategy that former Justice Potter Stewart infamously adopted in obscenity cases: "I know it when I see it." By contrast, with only a few refinements, social scientists seem to have employed the same basic understanding of stigma for some time. In this Section, I thus look principally outside the legal arena to social science for direction in defining what racial stigma is and how it functions.

1.   DEHUMANIZATION AND THE IMPOSITION OF VIRTUAL IDENTITY

Most lawyers are probably familiar with the social research on racial stigma that Dr. Kenneth Clark completed nearly fifty years ago as an expert in the litigation surrounding *Brown v. Board of Education*. In the social science world, however, the work of another social scientist—Erving Goffman—is most often cited in connection with questions surrounding the problem of racial stigma. Nearly forty years after it was first published, Goffman's book, STIGMA: NOTES ON THE MANAGEMENT OF SPOILED IDENTITY, continues to be regarded as one of the definitive texts in this area.

In Stigma, Goffman concerned himself with a single purpose: defining the problem of stigma. Looking to a variety of psychological, sociological, and historical studies and texts, he explored a range of stigma-inducing conditions and situations, including the so-called "tribal" or group-based stigmas such as "race, nation, and religion." Although Goffman also studied the etiology and function of stigmas relating to physical deformities and character "blemishes" attributed to a variety of conditions, the many insights he garnered through his research are extremely relevant to the race-focused inquiry that I take up here. Even today, virtually all social scientists accept the broad definition of stigma developed through his work, namely that "stigmatized persons possess an attribute that is deeply discrediting and that they are viewed as less than fully human because of it." * * *

2. Shared Negative Meanings about the Racially Stigmatized

* * * Racial stigma, at bottom, concerns the relationship between a group of individuals perceived as essentially similar and shared community beliefs about that group and the attributes they possess. While racist attitudes are held at an individual level as well, the group-level responses to racial difference are most important here. Part of the strength of the "societal devaluations" associated with race in this country is that "they cannot be dismissed as the ravings of some idiosyncratic bigot." They are shared and consensual, which means that they cannot easily be ignored. This, perhaps even more than the precise character of the messages conveyed about race, is what makes racial stigma such a powerful social force. The meanings ascribed to an attribute—i.e., that dark skin or an accent provide meaningful evidence of intellectual or moral inferiority—begin to form what constitutes "a socially shared sense of 'reality.' " * * *

3. The Automatic Nature of Responses to the Racially Stigmatized

The next stigma factor that contributes to broad-scale racial inequality relates to the automatic or unconscious nature of the responses the nonstigmatized—and sometimes even minorities themselves—have to the racially stigmatized. The prevailing constitutional paradigm in the race context is, of course, the discrimination model discussed earlier. Under that model, embodied in cases such as *Washington v. Davis*, only conduct and policies that reflect discriminatory intent or motive can be actionable. No remedies exist for racialized, unconsciously committed behavior or policies that have merely a discriminatory impact.* * *

4. The Reinforcing Nature of Racial Stigma and Stereotypes

As previously noted, when asked to define racial stigma, people often confuse it with the problem of racial stereotypes, which have historically been defined as inaccurate or overbroad generalizations, but have more recently come to be understood as "cognitive categories" employed in processing information. Most "profoundly stigmatized social identities" have a myriad of well-accepted stereotypes associated with them: "Blacks are dumb"; "Latinos are lazy"; "Asians are smart, but conniving." The terms racial stigma and racial stereotype are, however, two analytically distinct concepts. Whereas racial stigma provides the negative meanings associated with race and accounts for the initial affective reactions individuals often have toward racial minorities, racial stereotypes help to explain the persistence of certain attitudes about and responses toward race and the racially stigmatized. In this way, they also are directly related not just to discrimination but to the broader problem of racial inequality.

Racial stigma and stereotypes, in some sense, play mutually reinforcing roles in the dehumanization and marginalization—social, as well as economic and political—of minority groups. On the one hand, racial stigma contributes to the development of negative racial stereotypes about stigmatized groups. It is thought that the social meanings conveyed by racial stigma actually influence the cognitive processes that lead to stereotype formation. As Glenn Loury notes, "The 'social meaning of race'—that is, the tacit understanding associated with 'blackness' [or dark skin] in the public's imagination, especially the negative connotations—biases the social cognitions and distorts the specifications of observing agents, inducing them to make causal misattributions [or categorizations] detrimental to" racial minorities.

CHAPTER 2

THE SUBPRIME CRISIS OF 2008: A CASE STUDY IN MARKET FAILURE AND ECONOMIC INJUSTICE

"As in *Rashomon*, perspective took hold. Sometimes what we are left to deal with are not the facts—that is why there is a controversy—but the different stories people tell as a way of making sense of the uncertainties and complexities that matter to them." Marcel Janssens, *Witnesses and "truth" in the multiple-I narrative*, JOURNAL OF LITERARY STUDIES, 1753–5387, Volume 13, Issue 3, 1997, Pages 334–42.

A. CONFLICTING NARRATIVES OF THE FINANCIAL CRISIS

The failure of global credit markets in the fall of 2008 is a complex social and economic story with many subplots and twists. Akiro Kurosawa's film *Rashomon*, Grand Prize winner at the 1951 Venice Film Festival, is synonymous with subjectivity and indeterminacy in personal narrative. Rashomon (RKO Pictures 1951). This film provides a useful framework for understanding what is at stake in sorting out the truth from radically conflicting accounts of the same event.

The collapse of global credit markets in the fall of 2008 is widely agreed to be the most severe economic dislocation since the Great Depression of the 1920s. But what caused the interconnected housing and financial markets to panic? In this chapter, we look at accounts of the meltdown from the perspective of a variety of actors: legislators, financial regulators, economists, bankers and other financial intermediaries, taxpayers, and subprime borrowers in racially subordinated communities. This examination of conflicting narratives allows us to apply the insights that we gained in Chapter 1 about the power of stories and contested ideas about legal and economic neutrality.

We take a brief detour into the film itself to construct a conceptual platform for understanding the inconsistent narratives of the financial crisis. The only uncontested fact in the film is that a man lies dead in the woods. In the murder trial of a bandit, we hear the irreconcilable stories of the bandit himself, the dead man, the dead man's wife, and a woodcutter. The bandit claims that he killed in self-defense during mutual combat with the dead man, who discovered the bandit having passionate sex with the dead man's wife. The wife testifies that she was helpless to resist the

73

bandit's brutal rape. The dead husband, speaking through a medium, tells a very different story of his obligatory honor-bound suicide when confronted with the sexual violation of his wife. The fourth story—told by a woodcutter who came upon the rape—bears no resemblance to the others. In the woodcutter's version, the bandit killed the dead man when the selfish wife goaded the two men into fighting over her honor, after the husband heard the bandit proposing to marry the wife after raping her.

In Kurosawa's master narrative, each character tells truths and lies. The contradictory stories can be understood from the perspective of the storyteller, but never reconciled. One lesson of the film is that humans cling to accounts that affirm their own view of themselves in the world. The irreconcilable narratives and counter-narratives of the causes of the financial panic of 2008 may be similarly self-reinforcing.

Members of the private financial sector have chosen to portray the crisis as an unpredictable natural disaster, a once-in-a-century "tsunami" that "no one could have predicted." Financial regulators, including the Securities and Exchange Commission and the Federal Reserve, tell a story of a stealthy, unregulated "shadow banking" sector over which they had no statutory authority. The Shadow Banking System Financial Crisis Inquiry Commission Hearing, http://www.judicialwatch.org/foiablog (May 7, 2010, 13:55 EST). In Congress and the White House, the political narrative of the crisis is that the collapse was caused by the triumph of private greed over civic responsibility, the "fat cat bankers" of Wall Street gaming the system against Main Street. For homeowners, this is a story of easy subprime home loans that turned the American Dream into a personal finance nightmare of foreclosures, job losses, vanishing home equity, constrained family finances for college, and disappearing retirement portfolios. Finally, for taxpayers, the bailout unleashed a deep seated populist outrage that was directed at both politicians and bankers. The competition among these stories continues, more than two years later.

Narratives have power to challenge hidden perceptions and to shape outcomes. Thus, this chapter will look at the crisis to ask which stories makes sense, and which stories explain the most about a terrifying period of global finance in which millions of homeowners lost their homes. We now take up, in order, a brief overview (in film parlance, the "back story") of the financial crisis; stories from borrowers in zip codes targeted for subprime loan origination and underwriting; and the accounts of bankers and economists.

B. THE SUBPRIME MORTGAGE CRISIS: A BACK STORY

Embedded in the subprime crisis were preexisting economic inequalities and housing credit starvation. Following World War II, families were encouraged to see owning their own home as part of the American Dream. *See* Alyssa Katz, Our Lot: How Real Estate Came to Own Us (2009) (discussing how government interventions to promote homeownership contributed to the subprime mortgage crisis). Government policies and the real estate industry helped make this dream real for many households through favorable terms for home mortgages and a boom in new homebuilding in the suburbs. However, low income Black and Hispanic families were systematically excluded from the market for homeownership and wealth accumulation by a combination of government policies and market factors. An untapped market of potential homebuyers thus emerged.

Risk-based residential mortgage pricing, introduced in the late 1990s, allowed bankers to design new mortgage loan products and origination systems meant to neutralize the credit risk of default by low net worth borrowers, or overextended high-net worth borrowers. The heart of the new lending system was the financial innovation of loan "securitization." Securitization meant that individual home mortgages were assigned to pools based on their likelihood of default. These pools were then divided into separate interests that could be freely bought and sold in financial markets to individual and institutional investors. In theory, securitization reduced the risk associated with lending to shaky borrowers, because the risk would be spread across the financial system.

The result of this perceived reduction of risk was the opening of new "subprime" mortgage loan markets, based upon aggressive origination of loans by independent mortgage brokers operating in formerly credit-starved communities. These communities, of course, included many disproportionately African American and Hispanic neighborhoods. Edward Gramlich, the late Federal Reserve Board member, found that "[b]rokers have become pervasive and operate in virtually all communities, but they are especially plentiful in areas underserved by old-line commercial banks and thrifts, such as minority communities." Edward M. Gramlich, Subprime Mortgages, America's Latest Boom and Bust, 15 (2007).

Subprime loan originators and every component of the residential mortgage investment and funding system collected commissions for each transaction. By 2005, 60 percent of the originators of subprime loans were not regulated by either state or federal governments. Citing Apgar and Fishbein, Gramlich found that "there has been a huge rise in the number of independent [largely unregulated] mortgage brokers, from an estimated 7,000 firms in 1987 to an estimated 53,000 firms in 2004." These brokers were originating "about 60% of all subprime mortgages, compared with 25 percent for the prime market [by 2005]." Gramlich, at 19.

Loan originators did not have any legal liability for loans that failed. In the old system, the bank making the loan would take the loss if a borrower defaulted. In the new system, mortgage loans were quickly bundled together and sold in groups as securities to individual and institutional investors. Thus, there was very little incentive for the originators to be careful about the loans they made. In addition, the commission compensation structure provided an incentive for lenders to encourage repeated refinances, because for each transaction the lender earned a fee.

Another key to the success of the new system was the willingness of credit rating agencies to give AAA credit ratings to subprime mortgage pools. Because the AAA rating is given to U.S. Treasury securities, considered the safest investment possible, investors concluded that there was little risk of default. Moreover, the potential profits were huge. Mortgage-based securities carried high yields for a global pool of investors with surplus savings. The managers of the pools of investment capital that purchased these securities received huge bonuses. The CEOs of investment banks and commercial banks that purchased mortgage-backed securities were also well compensated, and would continue to be so even by 2008, when the entire private securitization investment structure was in free fall.

A final element of the story was the rising housing market in the United States in the years leading up to the crash. It was easy for homeowners, bankers, and investors to conclude that housing prices would continue to rise, even while some onlookers uneasily warned of a housing "bubble." Even if the bubble would someday burst, no one wanted to miss out on the enormous short-term profits to be made in the meantime.

Kevin Phillips, a finance and politics writer, captures the dynamics of this new mortgage lending system: "[T]here were huge institutional pressures to entice as many customers as possible, reflecting the enormous profits to be made from taking mortgages and securitizing and repackaging them en masse . . . Lenders needed to woo high-risk borrowers for the good commercial reason that there weren't enough low risk borrowers to meet the volume demanded by the big commercial banks, investment firms, and other packagers, all pursuing lucrative fees." Kevin Phillips, Bad Money, Reckless Finance, Failed Politics, and the Global Crisis of American Capitalism (2008).

2008 marked the beginning of the end for many Wall Street investment banks. In March, Bear Stearns was sold under government supervision to JPMorgan Chase & Co. Then, government-sponsored enterprises "Fannie Mae" (the Federal National Mortgage Association) and "Freddie Mac" (the Federal Home Loan Mortgage Corporation) became insolvent and were placed under conservatorship. By September, the abrupt and disorderly failure of Lehman Brothers sparked a mortgage-finance global credit panic, which in turn precipitated a massive government rescue.

Housing values in the United States became the focus of uncontrolled speculation. Robert Shiller notes that By the end of 2005, "the share of residential investment in the U.S. gross domestic product (GDP) rose to 6.3% the highest level since the pre-Korean War housing boom of 1950–51." Robert Shiller, The Subprime Solution (2008). Housing speculation found a home on Wall Street in the rapid growth of the volume of individual loans that were transferred, pooled, and used to support securities bought by global pools of investors. The irrationally strong demand by investors to profit from the run up in housing values in the "safe" U.S. market created a classic asset bubble in which the supply of housing soon produced a glut.

By the middle of 2006, housing prices began to fall. Investors income agreements and models were based on the false assumption that prices would never fall. Soon, fraud and rising defaults on loans that were unsuited for subprime borrowers produced accelerating losses. The initial losses on mortgage-backed securities then spooked investors world wide. As investors rushed to withdraw from these investments, the psychology of fear of further losses produced a complete breakdown in confidence among banks.

When a bank loses confidence in the solvency of other banks it hoards cash and refuses to make loans. If the loss of confidence is pervasive, as it was by March of 2008 when the investment bank Bear Stearns became insolvent, then a sudden disruption of normal short-term lending spreads like wildfire. The resulting freeze in bank-to-bank lending is called a credit panic. In the subprime crisis, the credit panic was the product of the bursting of the inflated house price asset bubble. In this financial climate the largest banks could no longer operate because they were either illiquid, or they were insolvent. The prospect that the weakest of the large investment banks and commercial banks might fail all at one time triggered government intervention to either prop them up with massive transfusions of cash through arrangements for sales to healthier institutions or taxpayer financed bailouts.

Congress established the Troubled Assets Relief Fund (TARP) to provide a $700 billion taxpayer-supported fund to buy non-performing subprime loans and mortgage-backed securities based on subprime loans from banks and investment firms that were on the edge of insolvency. Many taxpayers were outraged that public funds would be committed without major conditions on how they were spent.

Taxpayers were also sensitive to the seeming unfairness of being asked to provide support for the very financial institutions that caused the financial crisis. By July of 2009, a national poll found that 80 percent of Americans said that Wall Street benefited more from the bailout of the financial industry than the average U.S. taxpayer. Only 8 percent of adults said the taxpayer benefited more. Rasmussen Reports, July 17, 2009.

Based on this fairness argument, some taxpayers and policymakers pressed elected representatives to vote against the authorization of the TARP fund. Supporters of the bailout argued, however, that the $700 billion TARP fund and the $1 trillion of Federal Reserve lending to failing financial institutions were, although regrettable, necessary to prevent further damage throughout the national and global economy, because every sector depends on healthy financial institutions and the flow of sufficient credit.

Economists are conceptually divided into two camps, one camp, led by Nobel Prize Winner, Paul Krugman claims that economics installed a flawed macroeconomic models that rested on assumptions of self-limiting market dynamics and rational choice. The other is convinced that neoclassical assumptions continue to provide a valuable way of predicting economic behavior in financial markets.

We explore this intellectual division among economists in Chapter 5, Internal Critiques. We include several new debates about the subprime crisis. When we get to Chapter 5, we will encourage you to return to this chapter to see how the divided narratives of the economics profession enhance your understanding of the bankers' and borrowers' stories featured here.

As we move through the remainder of this chapter, consider the following questions. Did the combination of the commission and compensation structure for subprime loans, the pooling of loans into vast, complex pools of securities, create a mechanism that exacerbated income inequality? What role did the legal theories of law and economics play in providing ideological support for the creation of the unregulated "shadow" banking system? Did neo-classical economic theory contribute to disabling regulatory intervention, whether that intervention sought to limit securitization or to prohibit "reverse racial redlining" of subprime mortgages?

C. THE SUBPRIME BORROWERS STORY

1. HISTORY OF HOUSING FINANCE DISCRIMINATION

a. The Origins of Redlining—FHA Sec. 203 Guidelines

The Creation of Homeownership: How New Deal Changes in Banking Regulation Simultaneously Made Homeownership Accessible to Whites and Out of Reach for Blacks

115 YALE L.J. 186, 188–218 (2005) (footnotes omitted).

■ ADAM GORDON

From 1920 to 1960, the rate of owner occupancy in the American housing market rose from 46% to 62%. These numbers, however, explain only a small part of the significance of the federal government's New Deal intervention in the housing market. The creation of the Federal Housing Administration (FHA) to insure lenders against the risk of default on single-family mortgages fundamentally transformed what it meant to own a house in America. Prior to the 1930s, owner-occupied housing was a good held primarily for reasons of consumption—not investment—and usually acquired late in life. Through New Deal reforms, homeownership became the primary mechanism that middle-class Americans use to build assets. Today, 60% of the total assets of middle-class Americans are held in owner-occupied homes.

* * * In order to make homeownership affordable to most Americans over the majority of their working lives, lenders had to accept far lower down payments than they ever had before—saving up for the pre-New Deal standard of one-third or more of the value of the home could take many years. And they had to allow homebuyers to spread out loan payments over far longer terms than they had before—the prior practice of making a mortgage to a homebuyer for only five to seven years made it impossible for

most people to ever fully own their homes. State and federal banking law prohibited lenders from lowering down payment requirements and lengthening terms, and for good reason. Such changes would pose genuine threats to lenders' "safety and soundness" because they would expose lenders to greater risks of default.

Despite the risk involved, the FHA decided that it would insure low-down payment, long-term mortgages in order to promote homeownership. * * * [T]he FHA, as an insurer, would take over payments in case of default. * * *

[T]hese policies, while logical and benign on the surface, in fact produced devastating results for African–Americans. As historian Kenneth Jackson and others have described, the FHA's core insurance program, section 203(b), systematically discriminated against African–Americans. * * * Commentators such as Paul Boudreaux and Robert Ellickson have downplayed the importance of the FHA's racial discrimination, instead arguing that personal preferences have driven racial segregation. Underlying their skepticism of the FHA's importance is the reasonable question: "If substantial numbers of African–Americans would have taken out insured mortgages, why didn't businesses develop to serve that market?" * * *

Congress and state legislatures granted exemptions to bank safety-and-soundness regulations only for FHA-insured mortgages—not for mortgages insured by the private sector. Thus, if the FHA would not insure a particular borrower, that borrower could not get a low-down payment, long-term mortgage from any source. The FHA's discretionary guidelines effectively became binding law, giving whites a generation's head start on accumulating wealth through homeownership, a fact reflected in concrete data from the census and land records. This reality suggests that government policy fostered segregated housing patterns to a greater degree than many commentators have previously thought.

[T]he integration of section 203(b) forty years ago through an Executive Order by President Kennedy did not sufficiently remedy the pervasive system of FHA discrimination against African–Americans. Simply making FHA-insured loans available to blacks did not compensate for the dramatic advantage that whites had enjoyed for decades in the homebuying market, an advantage that may explain why the median white household has ten times as much wealth as the median black household today. In addition, the end of discrimination in the FHA program failed to eliminate the view of neighborhood racial transition and composition that the FHA's insurance guidelines cemented in the American mind: that whites could prosper only by living separately from blacks, and that blacks moving into a neighborhood signified imminent price decline. The past acceptance of these empirically faulty characterizations as official federal policy may help account for why American metropolitan areas remain highly segregated by race. * * *

I.   Creating an Asset Class: How the New Deal Redefined Homeownership
* * *

B.   How Mortgage Market Collapse Produced New Deal Reforms

As a result of the Great Depression, home mortgage foreclosures rose from sixty-eight thousand per year in 1926 to one thousand homes per day in early 1933, when half of all mortgages in the United States were in default. As urban historian Kenneth Jackson has pointed out, these foreclosures affected not just the poor, but also middle-class families. * * *

The federal government first reacted to the situation by buying up defaulted loans from banks under the auspices of the Home Owners' Loan Corporation (HOLC) and refinancing them on more favorable terms. But HOLC did not have a long-term effect on the American housing market. * * *

The Federal Housing Administration (FHA), created by the National Housing Act of 1934, restarted the slow lending market, limiting the risk of future foreclosures for lenders by insuring them against default on mortgages. Borrowers paid a premium of a half-percent on top of the standard interest rates paid to the lender, which went into a reserve fund held by the FHA that indemnified lenders in case of default. In addition, in case the reserve fund ran out of money, the federal government promised to pay lenders from general funds. In effect, the federal government enabled lenders to provide home mortgage credit without any risk of loss—a vital guarantee given how much money those lenders had lost in the foreclosures of the early Depression.

The FHA did far more than simply restart a lending industry that had faltered at the onset of the Depression. Through guidelines that specified which loans would be eligible for insurance, the FHA fundamentally transformed the mortgage market. The FHA standards allowed mortgages with low down payments—initially 20%, then 10%, and by the mid–1960s, 3%. Moreover, these mortgages extended for long terms—initially twenty years, soon twenty-five, and then thirty. At the end of those terms, the homeowner fully owned the home and did not need another mortgage. The FHA thus allowed younger households to buy homes with the assurance that they would not be forced out of those homes at the end of a short-term mortgage, and granted them an opportunity to build significant assets through homeownership.

The FHA pursued these policy objectives even though they made providing insurance more risky. Lowering down payment requirements meant that, all other things being equal, foreclosure was more likely because the buyer had less equity in the house. Thus, if home values declined even a small amount, it would make economic sense for the borrower to walk away from the home instead of continuing payments on her mortgage.

Similarly, longer terms meant that banks received smaller payments each month than they would have with a short-term loan of the same size. A long term also includes more turns of the business cycle, making borrower defaults (and FHA payouts) more likely. Finally, for the entire term, the same amount of money remained unavailable for making other loans, creating the additional risk that the bank would not be able to either take advantage of better business opportunities as they came up or adjust to higher-interest-rate environments. These changes are what fundamentally transformed homeownership from a short-term, consumption-driven experience for a minority of Americans to the main tool that most Americans use for asset building over the long term. Being able to borrow larger sums over longer terms made homeownership radically more affordable. The federal government took on significantly more risk in its insurance program in order to satisfy mounting public pressure to increase affordable homeownership opportunities. This pressure came not just from citizens, but, perhaps even more vehemently, from developers and related businesses hit hard by the Depression. * * *

Effectively, FHA-insured buyers got better homes than conventional borrowers without paying anything close to the full cost of the difference in quality. This disparity reflects the regulatory differences that allowed FHA-insured loans to have longer terms and lower down payments. Furthermore, an FHA-insured home was much more likely to be a new home—59% of FHA-insured mortgages outstanding in 1950 had gone for new homes, compared with 23% of conventional mortgages. Most of those new homes were in the suburbs, the place that would experience the greatest rate of property-value appreciation in the coming decades and thus enable asset development. In sum, America had two housing markets from 1934 until the mid–1960s: a conventional market, with tight regulations on loan terms and down payments, and an effectively unregulated market of loans insured by the FHA, allowing extremely liberal loan terms and miniscule down payments.

III. How the Banking Safety-and-Soundness Changes Hurt African–Americans and Urban Neighborhoods

A. Discrimination in Section 203(b)

This data, and the power of banking regulation in creating separate markets for FHA-insured and conventional mortgages that they demonstrate, raise two critical questions. First, why did the American housing market not comport with the semi-strong form of the efficient capital markets hypothesis, which predicts that interest rate and down payment differences should have been immediately capitalized into higher home prices? Contrary to the theory of efficient markets, monthly payments remained lower for FHA insured homes than for non-FHA-insured homes, even though the FHA insured homes tended to be newer and of better quality. Second, given the lack of such capitalization, why would anyone choose a conventional mortgage over an FHA-insured mortgage?

Both of these questions hint at the serious problem caused by having safety-and-soundness regulations that, in effect, gave a monopoly to the FHA for most of the American first-time homebuyer market. Many would argue that such a government monopoly is bad enough simply because monopolies generally raise prices and discourage innovation. But, even worse, the government monopoly created by the FHA refused to offer its product to wide swaths of the American population, thus creating separate mortgage markets in urban neighborhoods and for African–Americans.

People excluded by the FHA had to find a way to afford the steep down payment and higher monthly payments needed for conventional mortgages, or give up the dream of homeownership.

The discriminatory policies of the FHA in its first three decades of existence are well known. As Kenneth Jackson has described, HOLC rated every urban and suburban neighborhood in America as "A," "B," "C," or "D" quality, color coding maps of every metropolitan area ("D," or lowest quality, was colored red—the origin of the term "redlining"). Quality ratings were based on age and type of housing stock, but also very much on race. "A" neighborhoods had to be "homogenous"—meaning "American business and professional men"—and "American"—meaning white and often, native-born. Predominantly black neighborhoods received a "D" grade. HOLC did not use these categories as major criteria for distribution of its loans; indeed, in many counties HOLC made loans mainly in "C" and "D" areas. This wide distribution of loans proved to be a good business decision for HOLC; often, residents of "C" and "D" areas had lower rates of default than residents of "A" and "B" areas.

The FHA, in contrast, used the HOLC system as a basis for developing criteria to select which loans it would insure. It set up a pseudoscientific rating system for neighborhoods, in which 60% of the available points were awarded based on "relative economic stability" and "protection from adverse influences"—both code words for segregation. "If a neighborhood is to retain stability, it is necessary that properties shall continue to be occupied by the same social and racial classes," the FHA's Underwriting Manual counseled. The FHA strongly suggested racial covenants as a means of protecting against such transitions. Furthermore, FHA underwriting standards frowned upon homes with rental units or stores (historically most of the homeownership stock in urban neighborhoods), favoring instead single family homes in single-use neighborhoods.

The FHA's underwriting standards reflected the model of neighborhood change developed by economist Homer Hoyt. In this model, neighborhoods started out new and white. Over time, housing stock deteriorated, and the neighborhood transitioned from white Protestant to Jewish and finally black. The FHA assigned every neighborhood a place somewhere along this supposedly inevitable continuum. The FHA's standards, however, ignored countervailing realities of neighborhood integration and change. In the early twentieth century, as Richard Sander has described, "[al]though many cities ... had 'Negro districts,' most blacks lived outside these districts; .... [A]s late as 1910, housing segregation was one of the least significant problems facing blacks." And even when neighborhoods did become segregated, their values did not necessarily decline as they transitioned from white to black. A comprehensive study of racial transition in seven cities from 1943 to 1955 that carefully separated race from other factors found that "the entry of nonwhites into previously all-white neighborhoods was much more often associated with price improvement or stability than with price weakening." Even Hoyt himself cautioned that race was so often conflated with other neighborhood characteristics that race could not be seen simply as an independent factor driving changes in neighborhood value.

The FHA ignored these complex realities, making simple racial categorizations both by grading neighborhoods based on racial composition and by encouraging racial covenants. With these brightline rules, the FHA encouraged housing segregation, much as municipal racial-zoning laws mandated segregation before the Supreme Court invalidated these laws in 1917.

B.   The Results of Discrimination in Section 203(b)

The FHA's underwriting criteria resulted in much lower rates of lending in urban neighborhoods than in suburban neighborhoods. For example, Jackson found that 91% of a sample of homes insured by the FHA in metropolitan St. Louis from 1935 to 1939 were located in the suburbs. In addition, these criteria resulted in much lower rates of lending to nonwhites than to whites, even when compared with the market as a whole. Only 2.3% of FHA-insured mortgages outstanding in 1950 were for nonwhites, while 5.0% of conventional mortgages were for nonwhites. Furthermore, the few loans that were made to nonwhites were for properties of below-average value. The median purchase price of nonwhite-purchased properties in the FHA insurance program in 1950 was under $6000 for all properties in the program, the equivalent value was $7900. This disparity reflects differences in income between white and nonwhite buyers in the FHA program; the median family income of all buyers with outstanding FHA-insured loans in 1950 was $4400, while the figure for nonwhites was closer to $3500.

One might speculate that the disparity between the conventional market's rate of lending to nonwhites and the FHA-insured market's rate of lending to nonwhites reflects discrimination based on income, not race. Because nonwhites on average had lower incomes than whites, discrimination based on income alone would result in fewer nonwhites getting FHA-insured loans. However, from the limited data available on this point, it does not appear to be the case that the FHA program provided fewer opportunities for lower income households than the market as a whole. While the median household income of a household receiving a conventional mortgage was lower than the median for a household receiving an FHA-insured mortgage, it appears that this gap may have come mostly or entirely from higher rates of lending through the FHA insurance program inside metropolitan areas (as opposed to rural areas).

Similarly, some might see the FHA's racial policies as solely trying to minimize the risk of default. But faced with the contradictory example of HOLC's program, in which default rates were lower on lower-grade, urban homes, and the empirical evidence that race alone did not determine home value, such a justification appears tenuous at best. Even if there had been some additional risk in insuring urban homes, or those occupied by blacks, the FHA had already decided that it would be willing to take on the massive additional risks associated with making low-down-payment, long-term loans. It is hard to characterize the FHA's view of blacks and urban neighborhoods as anything but outright discrimination. * * *

IV.   Ending FHA Redlining: Why The Remedy Did Not Match The Harm

A.   Opening Up Section 203(b)

The FHA ended its racially discriminatory policies gradually. From 1948 to 1962, the FHA moved from active preference for racially homogenous neighborhoods and developments with racial covenants to a supposedly neutral policy of insuring homes whether or not they were open to purchase by blacks. In 1962, President Kennedy issued an Executive Order that took the next step, actively refusing FHA insurance to anyone who would not sell homes to blacks.

In 1948, the Supreme Court held in *Shelley v. Kraemer* that courts could not enforce racial covenants. If courts could not enforce racial covenants, surely government agencies could not actively use racial covenants as a criterion for deciding where to insure mortgages. But it took the FHA a year to react to *Shelley*. When it did, it announced that its policy would not change until February 15, 1950, giving builders a sufficient amount of time to file covenants and secure FHA insurance for projects already planned.

Even after the FHA stopped using race as a direct criterion, it left developers to choose whether they wanted to impose racial restrictions on their own—a practice generally legal and frequently employed until the passage of the Fair Housing Act of 1968. The head of the FHA stated: "The role of the Federal Government in the housing programs is to assist, to stimulate, to lead, and sometimes to prod, but never to dictate or coerce, and never to stifle the proper exercise of private and local responsibility." In practice, leaving the choice to discriminate to developers produced the same results as explicitly including race as a criterion: Only 2.5% of FHA-insured loans reported in the 1960 census went to nonwhites. And of new homes insured by the FHA 1949 to 1959, less than 2% were available for sale to nonwhites—and even that paltry number came mainly from all-black developments.

One commentator explains the continuation of discriminatory results despite FHA "neutrality" by referring back to the "self-fulfilling prophecy" created by the adoption of Hoyt's model of neighborhood change by the FHA and other market actors. The longstanding belief among developers, realtors, and homebuyers, backed by the FHA, that racial transition was a harbinger of neighborhood decline induced all these actors to try to keep neighborhoods white. In doing so, they made Hoyt's false assumption increasingly true.

Drawing on Robert Ellickson's work on the power of social norms, Carol Rose has argued that "[w]hen nudged along by judicial recognition, norms *become* law, in the formal as well as the informal sense." After the FHA had helped establish a norm of racial segregation in housing in its early era of explicit discrimination, it continued to recognize discriminatory housing practices by developers through "neutrally" insuring homes with discrimination clauses, allowing the norm of segregation to continue as law.

President Kennedy finally truly ended redlining in the FHA's core section 203(b) program by signing Executive Order 11,062 on November 20,

1962. The Executive Order recognized that "discriminatory policies and practices based upon race, color, creed, or national origin now operate to deny many Americans the benefits of housing financed through Federal assistance," and directed "all departments and agencies in the executive branch of the Federal Government, insofar as their functions relate to the provision, rehabilitation, or operation of housing and related facilities, to take all action necessary and appropriate to prevent discrimination because of race, color, creed, or national origin" in a series of areas including "loans hereafter insured, guaranteed, or otherwise secured by the credit of the Federal Government." The action was the only one needed to make the FHA change its underwriting practices, because its discrimination resulted from administrative policy, not legislative requirement.

Indeed, the FHA dramatically changed its practices, going from making 2.5% of its loans to nonwhites in 1960—far below the rate of the market as a whole—to 12.5% in 1970 and 19.8% in 1980, both far above the rate of the market as a whole. One commentator notes that by 1969, "FHA's standard mortgage program had become increasingly . . . an active tool of social policy by directing homeownership and affordable private-market rental opportunities to low-income households in inner-city neighborhoods."

b.   Housing Asset Disparity: The Wealth Gap

1.   The Wealth Gap

One notable effect of FHA's past discriminatory policies was the creation of a persistent asset gap. Consider whether the FHA practice of redlining limited residents of the redlined communities' ability to transfer housing appreciation to the next generation. The next chart shows the size of the wealth gap is between whites and blacks.

The Racial Wealth Gap Increases Fourfold

INSTITUTE ON ASSETS AND SOCIAL POLICY, RESEARCH AND POLICY BRIEF, May, 2010.

■ THOMAS M. SHAPIRO, TATJANA MESCHEDE, and LAURA SULLIVAN

New evidence reveals that the wealth gap between white and African–American families has more than quadrupled over the course of a generation. Using economic data collected from the same set of families over 23 years (1984–2007), we find that the real wealth gains and losses of families over that time period demonstrate the stampede toward an escalating racial wealth gap. * * *

Wealth, what you own minus what you owe, allows people to start a business, buy a home, send children to college, and ensure an economically secure retirement. Without wealth, families and communities cannot become and remain economically secure. Recognizing the importance of building wealth over a lifetime, our nation has created public policies that provide incentives and subsidies for asset building activities. However, reforms are needed to ensure that such opportunities and rewards are distributed equitably.

KEY FINDINGS

Following the financial trajectories of the same cohort of families between 1984 and 2007:

- The wealth gap between whites and African Americans increased more than 4 times, from $20,000 to $95,000.

- Middle-income white households had greater gains in financial assets than high-income African Americans; by 2007, they had accumulated $74,000, whereas the average high-income African American family owned only $18,000.

- In 2007, one in ten African–Americans owed at least $3,600, almost doubling their debt burden since 1984.

- At least 25% of African-American families had no assets at all to turn to in times of economic hardship.

Accelerating Racial Wealth Gap

In 23 years, the racial wealth gap increased by $75,000, from $20,000 to $95,000. Figure 1 underscores the dramatic growth in financial assets (excluding home equity) among white families from a median value of $22,000 to $100,000, while at the same time showing that African–Americans saw very little increase in assets (in real dollars). The growth of the racial wealth gap significantly affects the economic future of American families. For example, the racial wealth gap in 1984 amounted to less than three years tuition payment for one child at a public university. By 2007, the dollar amount of the gap is enough to pay full tuition at a four-year public university for two children, plus tuition at a public medical school. The gap is opportunity denied and assures racial economic inequality for the next generation.

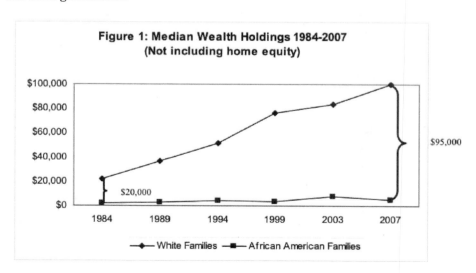

Figure 1: Median Wealth Holdings 1984-2007 (Not including home equity)

What Happened in the Past 25 Years?

The racial wealth gap results from historical and contemporary factors but the disturbing four-fold increase in such a short time reflects public policies, such as tax cuts on investment income and inheritances which benefit the wealthiest, and redistributes wealth and opportunities. Tax deductions for home mortgages, retirement accounts, and college savings all disproportionately benefit higher income families. At the same time, evidence from multiple sources demonstrates the powerful role of persistent discrimination in housing, credit, and labor markets. For example, African-Americans and Hispanics were at least twice as likely to receive high-cost home mortgages as whites with similar incomes. These reckless high-cost loans unnecessarily impeded wealth building in minority communities and triggered the foreclosure crisis that is wiping out the largest source of wealth for minorities.

Broken Chain of Achievement

For African–Americans, the data shows that income equality doesn't lead to racial wealth equality. Figure 2 provides a more nuanced picture of wealth holdings by looking at families by income groups in 1984 (the base year for family wealth data). Households are divided into income thirds: low-income, middle-income group and high-income. This figure shows two important findings.

1. The great wealth produced in this period accrues primarily to highest income whites, and

2. Job achievements cannot adequately predict family wealth holdings given the huge disparities in wealth between whites and blacks in the same income categories. While those who begin the period with roughly similar incomes would be expected to have the same opportunities to build wealth, the differences in accumulation by race remain stark even accounting for income.

Most notable is the large gap in wealth among the highest income whites and blacks. By 2007, the average middle-income white household accumulated $74,000, whereas average high-income African Americans owned only $18,000.

The result is a wealth gap of $56,000 for an African American family earning more than $50,000 in 1984 compared to a white family earning about $30,000 in the same year.

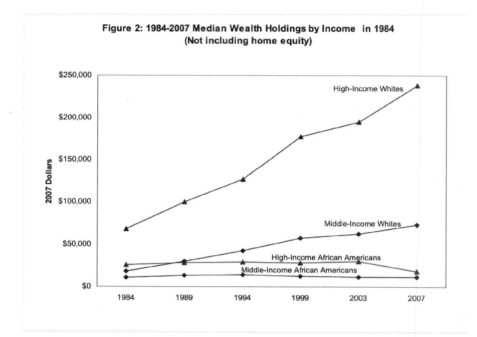

Figure 2: 1984-2007 Median Wealth Holdings by Income in 1984
(Not including home equity)

Debt Increases for the Poorest African American Families

Economic stagnation and decline was experienced by both low-wealth whites and low-wealth African Americans. However, African–Americans were found to be more likely to have very low levels of wealth. In fact, for every year of the study at least one in four African–American families had no assets all.

The increase in negative wealth experienced by many households at the lowest positions on the wealth distribution reveals a new dependence on credit to make ends meet. Among those with no financial assets, credit is often an emergency resource.

Summing all assets and debt, one in ten African–Americans owe at least $3,600 (see Figure 3), while their debt burden in 1984 was at about half of this in real terms in 1984 ($2000). In sum, many African Americans hold more debt than assets.

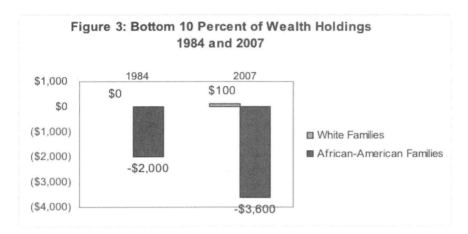

Figure 3: Bottom 10 Percent of Wealth Holdings 1984 and 2007

Why Do People of Color Rely on Debt

The growth of debt comes after years of deregulation of the lending market. The segmentation of the mortgage lending market highlights a general trend in lending in which low-income people and consumers of color pay more for accessing credit. In credit-starved minority communities across the country, the deregulated market brought a proliferation of high-cost lending, including securitized subprime and predatory loans, payday lending and check cashing stores. With greater numbers of families struggling with ever-growing debt, that far outstrips their income and savings, many low-income and minority households must turn to costly lending products because they have no other options. Minorities and low-income consumers resort more frequently to credit card debt and other forms of high cost debt in the absence of assets. A Consumer Financial Protection Agency that ensures fairness for consumers of all financial products would help equalize and regularize the terms on which cash-strapped families are borrowing to make ends meet.

Closing the Racial Wealth Gap

Efforts to increase asset-building opportunities for low and moderate-income households have expanded as the importance of assets for economic stability and mobility becomes more fully recognized. But, as the data show, these efforts are not yet strong enough or at scale to make a significant difference in people's lives. The data presented here reveal that income alone does not tell the story of economic security or future opportunities. African–Americans who have worked hard at well-paying jobs to achieve the American Dream are still not able to achieve the wealth of their peers in the workforce, which translates into very different life chances. We can do much more to support wealth building for vulnerable families. Universal policies alone will not address the race gap; wealth building opportunities must be targeted to families of color whose lives are made even more precarious by not having enough assets to make ends meet when economic challenges arise.

A U–Turn is needed. Public policies have and continue to play a major role in creating and sustaining the racial wealth gap, and they must play a role in closing it.

c.   Home Equity

Home equity accounts for 1/3 of the average net wealth of U.S. households. A recent Pew Hispanic Center study found that the median African American family held 88% of its total wealth in the form of home equity. Pew Hispanic Center, Wealth of Hispanic Households: 1996–2002 (Oct. 18, 2004), Table 10.

Some observers now blame banks for impoverishing African American households. "The Center for Responsible Lending estimates that families lose 2.3 billion each year from their home equity wealth because of prepayment penalties in subprime mortgage loans. By targeting African Americans for the sale of its highest-cost and riskiest loans, Wells Fargo drained wealth from families and neighborhoods and added to the stockpile of boarded-up homes that are an open invitation to criminals." Press Release, Illinois Attorney General Lisa Madigan, Madigan Sues Wells Fargo for Discriminatory and Deceptive Mortgage Lending Practices (July 31, 2009). http://www.illinoisattorneygeneral.gov/pressroom/2009_07/20090731.html.

Chart 2–1

Home Equity by Race

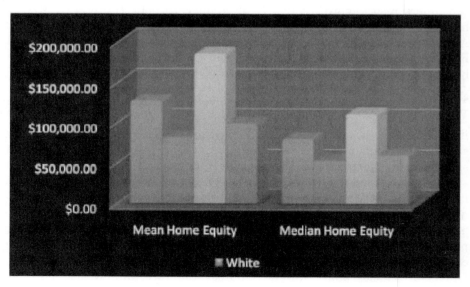

Source: Lauren J. Krivo & Robert L. Kaufman, *Housing and Wealth Inequality: Racial–Ethnic Differences in Home Equity in the United States.* Demography, Vol. 41, No. 3, 585 (Aug. 2004)

Chart 2–2   Homeownership by Race

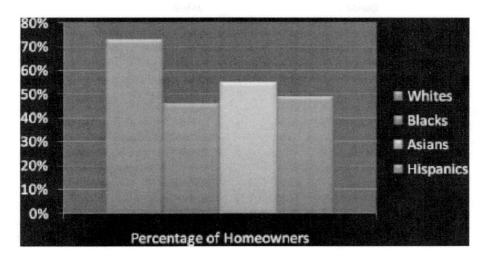

Source: Lauren J. Krivo & Robert L. Kaufman, *Housing and Wealth Inequality: Racial–Ethnic Differences in Home Equity in the United States.* Demography, Vol. 41, No. 3, 585 (Aug. 2004)

White—73%

Black—46%

Asian—55%

Hispanic—49%

NOTES AND QUESTIONS

1. Considering The Wealth Gap. Can Gordon's arguments about FHA's past discriminatory policies fully explain a persistent asset gap? What other factors might have contributed to the wealth disparity described below?

The average African–American owned 8 cents of wealth for every dollar owned by whites—Thomas Shapiro

Wealth Gap between Whites and African Americans:

Year—1998; Gap Amount—$100,700.00

Year—2007; Gap Amount—$142,600.00

Note: The median net-wealth of non-whites has increased $6,600 per person from 1998–2007. However, the racial wealth gap is widening. Source: Thomas Shapiro, Commentary, *Close The Racial Wealth Gap.*, CNN (2009) at http://www.cnn.com/2009/LIVING/06/10/shapiro.wealth/index html.

2. Lack of Regulation or Reverse Redlining? What is the better explanation for the lack of black wealth and the concentrated distribution of subprime mortgages in poor and minority communities—racial discrimination, or poor government regulation that permitted exploitation of the most vulnerable borrowers? For an overview of the origins and effects of government deregulation on the financial markets, see Simon Johnson and James Kwack, 13 Bankers: The Wall Street Takeover and the Next Financial Meltdown (2010).

3. The Weakness of the Minority Middle Class. Even before the subprime crisis of 2008, the stability of the African–American middle class was tenuous. One researcher observed in 2000:

> The population of Black and Hispanic families is growing rapidly, but individual households have significantly fewer opportunities than whites to enter the middle class. Our Index shows that African Americans and Latinos are less likely to enjoy long-term middle class financial security than whites. These groups are also significantly more likely to be in danger of slipping out of the middle class. While 34 percent of white middle-class families enjoy long-term financial security. This figure is even lower for African Americans and Latinos. Only 26 percent of African–American families and 18 percent of Latino families enjoy long-term financial security... Thirty-three percent of African–American families and 41 percent of Latino families are in danger of losing their middle-class status.

See Jennifer Wheary, et. al., *By a Thread: The New Experience of the American Middle Class,* Demos, 2000, 10.

4. Regulation of Home Mortgages: Paternalist or Protective? Should some borrowers never have become homeowners in the first place? Or was the subprime mortgage boom good for minority neighborhoods, at least at the beginning? Chicago School economist Gary Becker, a Nobel Prize winner in economics and one of the foremost proponents of neoclassical economic theory, made the following arguments about reverse redlining in the mortgage markets at the beginning of the crisis:

> Some have proposed that families should not be allowed to get mortgages if they do not meet minimum standards of income and assets, even if lenders would be willing to provide mortgages, and would-be borrowers still want a mortgage after being informed of the risks. This proposal is a dangerous form of paternalism that denies the rights of both borrowers and lenders to make their own decisions. Moreover, it is ironic that only a few years ago, banks were being investigated for "redlining" that is, for avoiding lending to blacks and other residents of poor neighborhoods. The Fair Housing Act of 1968 prohibits discrimination in lending, and the Community Reinvestment Act of 1977 requires banks to use the same lending criteria in all communities, regardless of the living standards of residents. As a result of the present crisis, however, banks and other lenders are being criticized for equal opportunity lenient lending to all, including black residents of depressed neighborhoods.

5. "Reverse Redlining" in Litigation. In addition to the NAACP-initiated structural discrimination lawsuits, individuals have challenged reverse redlining and racial discrimination by banks in the distribution of subprime loans. An example of an individual lawsuit is a case in Massachusetts in which an African–American couple brought a discrimination action against Countrywide Mortgage for discrimination, alleging that Countrywide set up a discretionary pricing policy under which loan officers could set their own rates for each customer. The couple argued that this resulted in disparate impact discrimination, because loan officers used their discretion to charge African–Americans a disproportionately larger amount. See Plaintiff's Opposition to Countrywide's Motion to Dismiss, (D. Mass. 2007), included in Russell J. Brummer and Andrew L. Sandler, Subprime Credit Crisis: Everything You Need To Know Now, Practicing Law Institute, 2008. 404–406. [Can you say more about the elements of the causes of action, in particular whether intent to discriminate is required?] For a review of several cases that discuss reverse redlining in the era of subprime lending, see Raymond H. Brescia, *Subprime Communities: Reverse Redlining, the Fair Housing Act and Emerging Issues in Litigation Regarding the Subprime Mortgage Crisis,* 2 ALBANY GOV'T L. REV. 164 (2009).

6. The End of Redlining Did Not Solve All the Problems. Despite the fact that for the most part, official redlining ended in the 1960s, redlining continued to color some actions by FHA long afterwards, according to a study by Elvin K. Wyly:

> Even after the government officially ended discrimination in the FHA, there were still schemes to defraud black investors. For example, the insurance programs of the early 1970s designed a program to serve first time and low-income homebuyers. Very quickly, however, fraudulent operators learned that FHA guarantees could easily be exploited by making loans designed to default so a lender could collect the FHA insurance.

Elvin K. Wyly, "The Subprime State of Race," University of British Columbia, October 2008. In this essay, the author argues that the subprime mortgage crisis was partly the result of previous discrimination and previous government inaction in the mortgage market.

7. Did the "Prosperity Gospel" Play a Role? Observers have pointed out that the subprime credit crisis and the rise of debt spending in minority communities coincided with the rise of the "Prosperity Gospel" in minority churches. The Prosperity Gospel holds that those who are favored by God will become rich, and it was promulgated by several "mega-church" pastors with predominantly minority congregations, such as Creflo Dollar and Joel Osteen. What impact might the endorsement of debt by these churches have had in stimulating acceptance of predatory loans? See Robert J. Weems, Jr., "Bling–Bling and Other Recent Trends in Black Consumerism," *African–Americans in the U.S. Economy,* (Celia Conrad, et al. ed. 2005), 249; Creola Johnson, *The Magic of Group Identity: How Predatory Lenders Use Minorities to Target Communities of Color,* 17 GEO.J.POV.L. &

POL'Y 165 (2010). Ralph Blumenthal, *Joel Osteen's Credo: Eliminate the Negative, Accentuate Prosperity,* N.Y. TIMES, Mar. 30, 2006, at E1.

8. Post Racialism and the Subprime Crisis. Is the racial analysis of the Gordon article still persuasive? Since the election of Barack Obama, the first African-American president of the United States, there has been a vigorous discussion of post-racialism. The argument supporting this concept is that the emergence of powerful African-American leaders signals the end of the old order of racial discrimination. White voters abandoned old stereotypes and prejudices to support his election. Some have argued that this presages important changes in racial thinking that should soon yield many other social and economic changes. Post-racialist herald the development of a new, post-racial paradigm.

Andre Douglas Pond Cummings challenges the accuracy of the post-racial perspective in Racial Coding and the Financial Market Crisis, 2011 UTAH L. REV. (forthcoming 2011):

> While markets were roiling in September and October 2008, with financial Armageddon at the nation's doorstep and two Presidential candidates debating the possible effects and solutions, a simple message emerged from the right and was peddled to the consuming American public as the primary reason that the global markets were collapsing: Minorities. African American and Latino borrowers were provided as the scapegoat to explain why the global economy was failing. The dirty little myth maintains that because of Governmental intrusion into the home lending industry, through the Community Reinvestment Act of 1977, lenders were forced to provide loans to extremely risky minority borrowers, who themselves were overreaching by trying to purchase homes that they had no business buying. Because lenders had no choice but to provide loans to risky minority borrowers, subprime loans became the avenue of choice for lenders to overreaching minority borrowers and it was the current failure of black and brown homeowners to pay their mortgages that the subprime mortgage industry collapsed. Thus, as the myth purports, the financial market crisis is ultimately traceable to minority Americans and governmental social welfare.
>
> With precious little evidence to support this scapegoating, many U.S. citizens have embraced the dirty little myth hook, line and sinker. And, this percolating resonance continues to survive as myth proponents today include economists, conservative think tank employees, Wall Street insiders, mutual fund presidents, pundits and average citizens. That the dirty little myth would spring up at the onset of this generation's greatest economic ordeal is disappointing. That the dirty little myth would be embraced by so many with so little to support it, with scant questioning or thought is demoralizing. The myth is particularly mystifying in an era where many post-racialist Americans are determined to believe that with the election of an African American President Obama that our nation has crossed over into a colorblind

era. Critical Race Theory, however, provides insight into how a 21st century dirty little myth can still find traction in the United States.

The powerful continuing dynamism of entrenched traditional American racism persists in our newly acclaimed "post-racial" United States. This static feature, relentless U.S. racial discrimination, simply evolves, and as the laws change to outlaw various manifestations of overt racism, it merely mutates into new and sophisticated, complex manifestations of race hatred. This mutation involves racist embrace of any available mechanism or adjacent expression to subordinate the interests of minorities in the United States and oft-times seeks to attach liability in careless ways to any available minority scapegoat.

The dynamism and continuing intensity of American racism is clearly evident in the financial market crisis of 2008. The market collapse was caused by intense and complex economic forces and failures, not by minority borrowers.

d. Subprime America

Subprime Mortgages: America's Latest Boom and Bust

The Urban Institute (2007).

■ EDWARD M. GRAMLICH

Figure 3-1. Homeownership Rates by Race or Ethnicity, 1970-2005

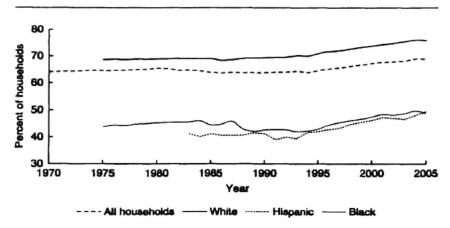

Source: U.S. Census Bureau data.

1.   Subprime Mortgages

Figure 3-2 Homeownership Rates, 1940 – 2005

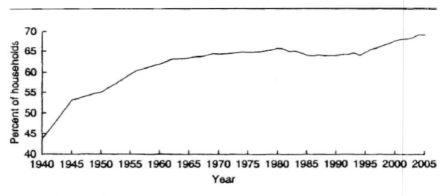

Source: U.S. Census Bureau data.

The earlier homeownership boom focused on the middle classes and the prime mortgage market. These prime borrowers took out long-term mortgages, secured by their homes, generally for 30 years. They paid mortgage rates of around 6 percent, and their mortgages covered 80 or 90 percent of their home price. The new ownership boom has moved one step down the income scale, focusing largely (though not exclusively) on the so-called subprime market. Subprime borrowers generally have lower incomes and often are not able to put as much down—their loan-to-value ratios often go up to 100 percent. Because of their worse credit history, subprime borrowers have to pay much higher interest rates, points, and fees, and they normally must accept prepayment penalties to get their home-secured loans. When the points and fees are amortized, the effective mortgage rate, called the average percentage rate (APR), is often in the double digits.

With rates this high, and with continuing pressures to expand ownership, people have been tempted to stretch the limits. Borrowers have sought ways to get in a house by keeping their down payments and monthly payments as low as possible. Lenders have sought new business. The combination has led to shortcuts that can often cause problems— excessive reliance on adjustable rate mortgages (ARMs), not verifying the repayment ability of the borrower, or not escrowing taxes and insurance payments. * * *

While all income groups have participated in this new opening up of the mortgage market and rise in homeownership, low- and moderate- income households and racial and ethnic minorities have been at the center of the boom. From 1994 to 2005, the overall ownership rate rose from 64 to 69 percent. The rate for blacks rose from 42 to 49 percent, a rise that contributed to the increase of nearly 1.5 million black homeowners over the period. The rate for Hispanics went from 42 to 50 percent, accounting for many of the 2 million additional Hispanic homeowners (figure 1.2). The rate for households indicating more than one race rose from 52 to 60 percent, helping to add another 2 million homeowners. The rate for homeowners in the lowest tenth of the income distribution rose from 39 to 43 percent, in the second tenth from 45 to 49 percent, and so forth. An unusual number of all these groups is first-time homebuyers.

The subprime mortgage market developed for several reasons. One important factor was the Depository Institutions Deregulatory and Monetary Control Act of 1980. This act effectively abolished usury laws on first-lien mortgages. Usury laws, which prevent mortgages above a certain rate from even being made, acted to shut low- and moderate-income borrowers out of credit markets. As these usury laws passed from the scene, instead of denying mortgage credit, mortgage lenders could now make loans, though with higher interest rates to conform to the worse credit prospects of the new borrowers. * * *

There were other factors. The 1990s saw the development and refinement of automated techniques for approving credit applications. Lenders now use credit scoring and similar techniques much more often than earlier, in the mortgage market and in other credit markets, leading to a faster and more inclusive mechanism for generating mortgage approvals. Some lenders now make mortgage approvals in a few minutes. Many old-line lenders such as banks and thrifts have set up subprime mortgage affiliates to make loans in the new part of the mortgage market. The 1990s saw the advent of mortgage brokers, intermediaries between lenders and borrowers, who are open, in the neighborhood, and available to place mortgages for a fee. * * *

On the nonprofit side of the ledger, there was also a substantial increase in community-based organizations (CBOs). These CBOs receive funds to subsidize affordable mortgages and make them to low- and moderate-income groups. Groups including NeighborWorks America (NWA) and the Opportunity Finance Network (OFN) have organized many local CBOs into vigorous and effective national networks.

Government regulations have had an impact as well. One that is particularly important is the Community Reinvestment Act (CRA), which gives banks and thrifts a responsibility to plow back funds to low- and moderate-income borrowers in their business areas, called assessment areas. CRA was first passed back in 1977, over the strong objections of the banks. But now, banks have made many low- and moderate-income mortgages to fulfill their CRA obligations, they have found default rates pleasantly low, and they generally charge low mortgages rates. Thirty years later, CRA lending has become a very good business.

Yet another factor has been the economy itself. Recessions have been less severe and frequent in recent decades; in fact, there were only two between 1982 and 2006, and they were relatively mild. Meanwhile, the continual dampening of inflation in the 1980s and early 1990s eventually translated to lower nominal interest rates (both long-term and short-term). The combination of more stable employment and lower payments to support a mortgage created ideal economic conditions for expansion of the mortgage market.

One factor that does *not* seem to have influenced the growth in the sub-prime market much is a factor common for housing and mortgages in general, the well-known income tax preferences for housing—both the deductions for mortgage interest and property taxes and the generous treatment of capital gains on houses. The deductions for interest and taxes are unlikely to matter much because most low- and moderate-income homeowners do not itemize deductions. The generous capital gains treatment may not matter much either for households that are not paying a large amount in income taxes.

Reflecting all these positive factors, back in 1994 subprime mortgage originations were $35 billion, less than 5 percent of total mortgage origina- tions. By 2005 subprime mortgage originations had risen to $625 billion, 20 percent of total originations (figure 1.4). This works out to a whopping 26 percent annual rate of increase over the whole decade. From being essen- tially nonexistent back in 1994, subprime mortgages are now 7 percent of the total mortgage stock. The subprime market was barely known in 1994, but merely a decade later, it is a huge factor. And the prime mortgage market expanded as well, again to accommodate the new loan demand emanating from all households, again including those low- and moderate- income households and racial minorities who could qualify for prime loans.

While it seems highly desirable to open up mortgage markets to these new borrowers, often for the first time, any major social movement on this scale will likely have drawbacks. And there are drawbacks associated with the subprime mortgage market. A first is simply its novelty. The subprime market opened for the first time, and as described above, an unusual share of the new mortgages were nontraditional products that featured adjustable rates. Short-term interest rates were very low in this period, for good macroeconomic reasons, and the initial cost of these new subprime mort- gages was low. In addition, many lenders treated the two-year rate as a teaser and advertised on this basis. Now that short-term rates have returned to more realistic (higher) levels, many subprime borrowers are suffering large payment shocks.

Figure 3-3 Mortgage Originations by Type of Mortgage, 1994 – 2005 (billions of dollars)

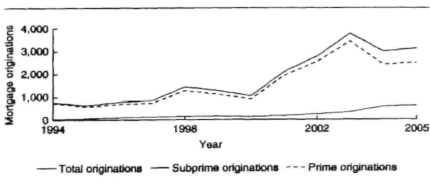

Source: Home Mortgage Disclosure Act data, 2005.

Further, house prices have been rising smartly in many local markets, permitting many borrowers who may have gotten in trouble on their mortgage to sell the house, pay the prepayment penalty, and walk away from the whole deal without much loss. But this period is ending too. House price increases began to slack off in 2006. Because of the rise in short-term rates, combined with reduced house price appreciation, the new subprime mortgage market is now being stress-tested in a major way.

There are added complications. While the prime mortgage market is well regulated and supervised, with the major lenders—banks and thrifts—undergoing arduous examinations every three years, the subprime market is much less so. All mortgage markets operate under general federal statutes preventing discrimination, insuring proper disclosures, and regulating other aspects of mortgage transactions. But in the subprime market, 30 percent of the loans are made by subsidiaries of banks and thrifts, less tightly supervised than their parent company, and 50 percent are made by independent mortgage companies, state-chartered but not subject to much federal supervision at all.' Mortgage brokers are largely unsupervised, with minimal incentives to see that borrowers get their best deal and only indirect incentives to see that borrowers will be able to make their mortgage payments. And many subprime borrowers are from lower-income households, not well-versed in financial matters and vulnerable to losses in income or payment ability.

The consequence of all these factors is that many borrowers could fall behind on their mortgage payments and go into delinquency status, sometimes even getting foreclosed on their loans. In a foreclosure, a borrower's house is taken away and the borrower has to move out, typically losing any equity that has been accumulated in the house in the process. Foreclosures have never been much of a problem in the prime mortgage market, with overall foreclosure rates staying below 1 percent for many years. In the sub-prime market, by contrast, they *have been* about ten times as high, more like 7 percent (Joint Center for Housing Studies 2006, figure 25). And what happens now that short-term interest rates have risen and house price increases have slacked off is anyone's guess. The Center for Responsible Lending (CRL), having studied 6 million recent subprime mortgages, predicts a sharp increase in foreclosure rates, up to 20 percent for newly made subprime loans (Schloemer et al. 2006).

There are problems on the other side of the market too. By February 2007, the *Wall Street Journal* reported that at least 20 subprime lenders had filed for bankruptcy, with more likely to follow. On April 2 they were joined by New Century Financial, the third-largest subprime lender in 2005 and a poster child for the go-go subprime market. A bond index fund that registers investors' expectation that the value of low-rated subprime mortgage bonds will fail lost 30 percent of its value in the first two months of 2007.

A mortgage foreclosure is the dramatic culmination of a process. But for every mortgage that is foreclosed, many others are very near foreclosure. A household may be struggling to make payments and in a situation where if the least little thing goes wrong, the household will fall behind. Things that could go wrong include loss of a job, a health problem (many of these families are among the 45 million Americans now without health insurance), or a problem with the house itself, such as a leaky roof.

There are indications that these pre-foreclosure issues may be serious as well. According to macroeconomic data, personal saving rates are negative and consumer debt burdens and personal bankruptcies are at all-time highs.' Studies of longitudinal income data indicate that about 40 percent of first-time low-income homebuyers go back to renting after their first homeowning experience. It is not clear why, but this share is much higher than for other higher-income new homeowning groups, leading to the suspicion that many low-income homeowners are making distress sales. Further studies from panel data indicate that the volatility of income flows for low- and moderate-income households has increased from earlier decades. And there are other ways in which households are now subject to increased risk. Putting this all together, the CRL estimates that another 5 to 10 percent of recent subprime mortgages are likely to be resolved by distress prepayments.

When something does go wrong, or even if it does not, the family may be at the mercy of predatory lenders, a group that often takes advantage of low-income, less-literate, less financially savvy, and more vulnerable borrowers. Such terms as asset-based lending (lending on the basis of the value of an asset in a foreclosure proceeding, not on the loan payment prospects), loan-flipping (rapid refinance of mortgages often without cause, but with big closing costs), equity-stripping (losing the equity in one's house), and outright fraud and abuse have colored the foreclosure discussions.

So there it is. There is both good news and bad news in the opening up of the mortgage market, particularly the subprime market. The good news is that millions of new homeowners, who formerly would have been denied mortgage credit, can now take out mortgage loans, buy homes, live in better neighborhoods, and send their kids to better schools. A great many of these new homeowners, most likely a majority, are making their mortgage payments on schedule and building wealth in their homes.

The bad news is that a smaller share of these new homeowners is stretched thin, vulnerable to the least shock, saving very little, with high levels of consumer debt, at the mercy of predatory lenders, being forced to sell their houses early, and often ending up in foreclosure.

If the new homeowners had not become that, of course, they would have rented. Hence it is important to examine rental markets along with ownership markets, to make sure that these new homeowners are attracted into homeowning, not pushed in by the absence of available rental properties.

Unfortunately, conditions in the rental market are not very good either. Many renters have low and moderate incomes, and wages in these income levels declined in the 1980s, leading to the so-called hollowing out of the income distribution. Yet the nation has gone through an overall housing boom where prices have risen sharply, much more so than incomes for low- and moderate-income households.

The combination has put the squeeze on low-and moderate-income households, whether they own or rent. According to tabulations by the Joint Center for Housing Studies using data from the American Community Surveys, very large shares of low-income households–45 percent among owners and 57 percent among renters—are spending more than half their disposable income on housing, the normal definition of households with serious affordability issues. Another 21 percent faces moderate cost burdens, spending between 30 and 50 percent of their disposable income on housing.' With spending at this level, households have very little left over for other needs. They are also likely to spend enormous amounts of time commuting to their jobs and away from their families.

On the supply side of the market, many properties have been removed from the available rental stock. There are numerous federal rent subsidy programs, but their effectiveness has been called into question, and expenditures have leveled off.

A number of state and local policies also operate, perhaps unintentionally, to constrict the supply of affordable rental housing. The overall situation is not promising, especially if millions of foreclosed homes are taken out of supply (at least temporarily) and these homeowners are pushed back into an already-inadequate supply of rental housing.

* * * The Department of Housing and Urban Development (HUD) has some experimental approaches for converting rent subsidies into down payment-escrow accounts. While at this point small numbers of potential homeowners have taken advantage of these possibilities, the particular experiences of these homeowners have been very favorable, with very low foreclosure rates. Unlike the open subprime mortgage market described earlier, most graduates of rent subsidy programs have undergone extensive homeowner counseling, and they may be more ready to take the step to ownership.

Of more quantitative importance is a new interest in manufactured housing, factory-built structures that can be located either on land owned by the homeowner or on land owned by an investor. In the former case, manufactured housing comes very close to normal single-family housing; in the latter case, it is a hybrid situation where the homeowner owns the structure and the landlord owns the land. Either way, manufactured housing is clearly cheaper than site-built housing. It is starting to make a real quantitative impact in many rural areas, particularly in the south. On the lending side, however, the results in the manufactured housing sector are essentially the same as in the rest of the subprime market, with low down payments and high foreclosures.

It might be tempting to evaluate the subprime market, weighing the gains of homeowners who seem better off against the losses of those who seem worse off. But this type of assessment is not very meaningful. The opening up of mortgage markets happened, and at this point the changes are so fundamental that realistically they cannot be reversed.

The nation cannot just close up the subprime mortgage market and go back to the ownership rates of a decade ago. Rather, the task is to manage the new situation and see if policy measures can retain the benefits of the new burst in ownership while lessening the costs.

2. MASS FORECLOSURES DURING THE SUBPRIME CRISIS

Foreclosures are both an economic and a psychological phenomenon. The trauma of eviction extends from adults to the youngest child in the household and beyond, engulfing entire neighborhoods. The contagion effect of concentrated foreclosures leads to dramatic losses of city revenues and boarded up buildings have become havens for crime that further drain city services. According to a study by New York University's Center for Real Estate and Public Policy, African–Americans and Latinos have been disproportionately affected by foreclosures. Between January 2007 and the end of 2009, nearly 8 percent of African–American and Latino homeowners lost their homes to foreclosures, compared to 4.5 percent of Whites. http://www.responsiblelending.org/mortgage-lending/research-analysis/foreclosures-by-race-and-ethnicity.pdf.

This is the story of one New York community experience with concentrated foreclosures within miles of the world headquarters of global banking giant Citibank.

a. A Story of Middle Class Foreclosures in Williamsbridge, The Bronx[1]

The Williamsbridge area of the Bronx is a representative ground zero in the subprime devastation that has wracked the nation. This northeast Bronx neighborhood is home to working-class families. Sixty-five percent of its residents are black. Many are first-time homeowners who are immigrants from Nigeria, Ghana, and Jamaica. Today, there is block after block of broken windows and abandoned homes with multiple foreclosure and auction notices plastered on the doors. The empty buildings, the loss of jobs, decreased business and tax revenue and the broken dreams of families who thought they were moving up the ladder of life to grasp their share of future family stability and the prospects for intergenerational wealth embodied in their first home purchase are the scars that remain.

New York University's Furman Center for Real Estate and Public Policy found that Williamsbridge stands out among subprime-affected communities in New York City for two reasons: it had high rates of home-ownership and later high rates of default. At the peak of the housing bubble in 2006, this neighborhood had one of the highest rates of home-ownership in the Bronx. The 31% ownership rate here nearly equals the average for the entire city. These high rates of ownership masked deeper financial defects in the loan products that residents used to become homeowners. Traditional banks once avoided lending in Williamsbridge, engaging in redlining (the practice of refusing to make mortgage loans in geographically defined areas that followed boundaries of racial segregation.) In the years 2000–2007, unregulated mortgage brokers and mortgage subsidiaries of the biggest banks filled the void created by years of redlining this community, with high-cost loans. These flexible loan products had unconscionable features that virtually ensured default. The median annual income in Williamsbridge is a modest $31,000. However, according to one account, half of the mortgages originated there were subprime, and fully 51 percent of all home equity loans were subprime as well.

The distance from Citibank headquarters in Manhattan to Williamsbridge, in the Bronx, is not measured in miles. Citigroup's signature building, a diagonal-roofed, glass and steel skyscraper sits on East 153rd across the street from its world headquarters on Park Avenue, an economic world away from the devastated blocks of Williamsbridge, filled with a mixture of older wooden homes and new, yet vacant, condos.

The trail from Citibank's headquarters on Park Avenue to Williamsbridge is a literal trail of tears for families who took out mortgages, some of which approached one-half million dollars, based on incomes of less than $40,000/year. Many of the loans originated by unregulated mortgage bro-

---

1. Emma Coleman Jordan, Race and the New Economic Connection in the Subprime Crisis: A Paradox of Individualism and Community, Fourteenth Annual Derrick Bell Lecture on Race in American Society, New York University School of Law, Nov. 12, 2009. An earlier version of this story was published as the Derrick Bell Lecture, October 12, 2009. NYU Law School.

kers were based on a clearly unsustainable debt-to-income ratios. Families in the bottom quintile of the income distribution were solicited for loans that promised to deliver the American dream of affordable monthly payments leading to full ownership in thirty years.

For the residents of Williamsbridge, this longshot opportunity to achieve a cherished aspiration led to a maze of misrepresentation, deceptive practices, high pressure tactics for repeated refinancing, deceptively low teaser rates, and undisclosed payment shocks that led to the foreclosure epidemic now visible. The subprime foreclosure crisis has now decimated the sense of community that once thrived in the summertime front porch conversations of the proud working class neighbors of Williamsbridge, no less than crack, violence and infectious disease in other working-class communities in years past.

Citibank has received more than 45 billion in government bailouts from three rounds of direct federal assistance. Citibank has a portfolio of "toxic assets," many of which are derivative securities that are based on the collateral of private residences in communities like Williamsbridge, in the northeast Bronx. The modern financial titans of Citibank, like Sherman McCoy, the central character of Tom Wolfe's The Bonfire of the Vanities, unwound with a series of strategic wrong turns that carried them from the heights of money, power and privilege on Wall Street to the anger and rage of the ordinary folks in the South Bronx, and the klieg lights of Congressional hearing rooms. For better or worse, as the foreclosures mount, and housing prices fall, the value of the complex securities, such as collateralized debt obligations, credit default swaps, and pools of securitized loans originated or purchased for its off balance sheet entities by Citibank's subprime mortgage banking division, CitiFinancial, have bound the fate of these two very different worlds together.

NOTES AND QUESTIONS

1. A Public Nuisance? Similar to Williamsbridge, Cleveland suffered a blight of many foreclosures in the post-subprime period. In response, the City of Cleveland sued mortgage lenders for creating a public nuisance by concentrating unsustainable subprime lending in inner city neighborhoods. This later led to large sections of some neighborhoods with high rates of defaulting homeowners, which in turn led to an overall drop in property values and an increased need for police and fire services. The suit was later dismissed. City of Cleveland v. Deutsche Bank Trust Company, et. al., CV–08–646970, Ct. of Comm. Pleas, Ohio, 2008.

Do you believe that Williamsbridge and other cities have valid causes of action against the subprime originators for causing economic hardship for all in minority neighborhoods? If such a rule were adopted, what might be the impact on the availability of future credit?

2. Gramlich points out that because of lower credit scores, "subprime borrowers have to pay much higher interest rates, points, and fees, and they normally must accept pre-payment penalties to get their home-secured loans." Gramlich, Subprime Mortgages: America's Latest Bloom and Bust, *supra*.

Some scholars argue that the way credit scores are calculated might have a disparate impact on people of color. See Chi Chi Wu, Credit Scoring and Insurance: Costing Consumers Billions and Perpetuating the Economic Racial Divide (2007), available at http://www.consumerlaw.org/reports/content/InsuranceScoring.pdf. Do you think individual borrowers who live in neighborhoods with high concentrations of foreclosures will receive a negative credit score component that is based upon neighborhood foreclosures?

3. Has There Been a Loss of Power for Community Organizations? Alan Fishbein, a noted consumer lawyer, argues that the eventual collapse of non-profit organization-supported mortgages in poor neighborhoods was caused by the weakening strength of community organizations, which had traditionally played an important role as advocates for affordable housing in poor neighborhoods. Fishbein offers these observations about the changing mortgage industry:

> "This dangerous marketing of subprime mortgages to minorities was additionally damaging because of the slowness of community-based organizations, which were once vital to loaning to poor communities, to adjust to the subprime market. Many such organizations struggled to adjust to the increasing automation of the mortgage market. Even bankers themselves conceded this fact: 'Several bankers conceded that as they have grown in scale, there is less of a need to work with community groups.'"

William C. Apagan and Allen J. Fishbein, "The Changing Industrial Organization of Housing Finance and the Changing Role of Community Based Organizations," Cambridge: Harvard University Joint Center for Housing Studies, May 2004.

Community based organizations did not develop the market expertise to sell packages of loans on the secondary market through mortgage brokers, so this became a problem in the new mortgage market. Banks, who were externalizing their risk and enhancing the liquidity of their balance sheets, soon began to ignore community based organizations altogether. Instead, banks referred prospective low wealth customers to unregulated mortgage brokers.

4. To the Point of No Return. The economic crisis of 2009 has caused a massive loss of jobs, and some estimate that if all of the unemployed were included in the numbers, the unemployment rate might exceed 20 percent. That has led some observers to speculate that jobs in some sectors such as manufacturing are never going to come back in the numbers that they once enjoyed. Indeed, some argue that America has entered a decline in which the economy produces very few new jobs.

Economists who take this viewpoint out that there are only three industries that are expected to grow jobs in the U.S. under current models in the next 20 years: restaurants, education, and health care. Do you agree with this theory? What additional information would you need to come to a more confident conclusion? What would you suggest Americans do about this problem? Joshua Cooper Ramo addresses these questions in "Jobless in America: Is Double Digit Unemployment Here to Stay?" *Time*, Sept. 11, 2009.

5. The New Economy. In an essay in the New York Review of Books, Amartya Sen argues that capitalism must be significantly reworked in order for it to respond to twenty-first century concerns. Amartya Sen, Capitalism Beyond the Crisis, THE NEW YORK REVIEW OF BOOKS, Mar. 26, 2009. Do you believe this? Why or why not? What economic changes do you believe are necessary in response to this crisis? Is the Chinese model of state authoritarianism/capitalism a more stable model for the future?

b. Mortgage Delinquency Rates

Figure 3
Mortgage delinquency rates rise with cooling of house prices

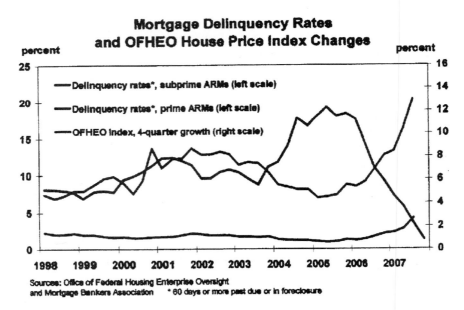

The sharp increase in the number of mortgage delinquencies of subprime mortgages from 2006–2008 increased the number of erroneous foreclosure filings, and even mistaken completed foreclosures. For the homeowners who have been subjected to these process defects, the economic nightmare that ensues brings a cascade of distress. ProPublica, a non-profit investigative news organization, captures the dramatic consequences of the large number of foreclosures that have simply overwhelmed banks ability to keep accurate ownership records.

c.   Disorganization at Banks Causing Mistaken Foreclosure

By Paul Kiel, ProPublica—May 4, 2010 at http://www.propublica.org/feature/disorganization-at-banks-causing-mistaken-foreclosures–050410   on May 4, 2010.

Millions of people face losing their homes in the continuing foreclosure crisis, but homeowners often have more than the struggling economy and slumping house prices to worry about: Disorganization within the big banks that service mortgages has made a bad problem worse.

Sometimes the communication breakdown within the banks is so complete that it leads to premature or mistaken foreclosures. Some homeowners, with the help of an attorney or housing counselor, have eventually been able to reverse a foreclosure. Others have lost their homes.

"We believe in many cases people are losing their homes when they should not have," said Kevin Stein, associate director of the California Reinvestment Coalition, which counts dozens of nonprofits that work with homeowners among its members.

In the worst breakdowns, banks—and other companies that service loans—actually work at cross-purposes, with one arm of the company foreclosing on the home while the other offers help. Servicers say such mistakes are rare and result from the high volume of defaults and foreclosures.

The problems happen even among servicers participating in the administration's $75 billion foreclosure-prevention program. Servicers operating under the year-old program are forbidden from auctioning someone's home while a modification decision is pending. It happens anyway.

Consumer advocates say the lapses continue because they go unpunished. "We've had too much of the carrot, and we need a stick," Stein says. The Treasury Department has yet to penalize a servicer for breaking the program's rules. The program provides federal subsidies to encourage modifications.

Treasury officials overseeing the program say they're aware of the problems and have moved to fix them. But some states are going further to protect homeowners, with recent rules that stop the foreclosure process if the homeowner requests a modification.

Many homeowners, seeing no other option, have gone to court to reclaim their homes. At least 50 homeowners have recently filed lawsuits alleging the servicer foreclosed with a loan mod request pending or even while they were on a payment plan.

Homeowners have long waits for help

In good times, banks and other servicers—Bank of America is the biggest, followed by Chase and Wells Fargo—were known mainly to homeowners simply as where they sent their monthly mortgage payments. But the companies have been deluged over the past couple of years by requests for help from millions of struggling homeowners.

Homeowners commonly wait six months for an answer on a loan mod application. The federal program for encouraging loan mods includes a three-month trial period, after which servicers are supposed to decide whether to make the modifications permanent. But some homeowners have waited as long as 10 months for a final answer.

Communication breakdowns occur because of the way the servicers are structured. One division typically deals with modifications and another with foreclosures. Servicers also hire a local trustee or attorney to actually pursue foreclosure.

"Often they just simply don't communicate with each other," said Laurie Maggiano, the Treasury official in charge of setting policy for the modification program. Such problems were particularly bad last summer, in the first few months of the program, she said. "Basically, you have the right hand at the mortgage company not knowing what the left hand is doing," said Mark Pearce, North Carolina's deputy commissioner of banks. Communication glitches and mistakes are "systemic, more than anecdotal" among mortgage servicers, he said.

"We've had cases where we've informed the mortgage company that they're about to foreclose on someone." The experience for the homeowner, he said, can be "Kafkaesque."

"We're all human, and the servicers are overworked and trying their best," said Vicki Vidal, of the Mortgage Bankers Association. She said foreclosure errors are rare, particularly if struggling homeowners are prompt in contacting their servicer.

Frances Gomez, of Tempe, Ariz., lived in her house for over 30 years. Three years ago, she refinanced it with Countrywide, now part of Bank of America, for nearly $300,000. The home's value has declined dramatically, said Gomez, who put some of the money from the refinancing into her hair salon.

Last year, the recession forced her to close her shop. Gomez fell behind on her mortgage, and after striking out with a company that promised to work with Bank of America to get her a loan mod, she learned in December that her home was scheduled for foreclosure.

So Gomez applied herself. She twice succeeded in getting Bank of America to postpone the sale date and said she was assured it would not happen until her application was reviewed. Gomez had opened a smaller salon and understood there was a good chance she would qualify.

She was still waiting in March when a Realtor, representing the new owner of her home, showed up. Her house had sold at auction—for less than half of what Gomez owed. "They don't give you an opportunity," she said. "They just go and do it with no warning."

It's not supposed to work that way.

Under the federal program, which requires servicers to follow a set of guidelines for modifications, servicers must give borrowers a written denial before foreclosing. When Gomez called Bank of America about the sale, she said she was told there was a mistake but nothing could be done. She did get a denial notice—some three weeks after the house was sold and just days before she was evicted.

"I just want people to know what they're doing," Gomez, now living with family members, said.

After being contacted by ProPublica, Bank of America reviewed Gomez's case. Bank spokesman Rick Simon acknowledged that Gomez might not have been told her house would be sold and that the bank made a mistake in denying Gomez, because it did not take into account the income from her new salon business. Simon said a Bank of America representative would seek to negotiate with the new owner of Gomez's house to see if the sale could be unwound.

Simon said the bank regrets when such mistakes happen due to the "very high volume" of cases and that any errors in Gomez's case were "inadvertent."

Even avoiding a mistaken sale can also be a stressful process.

One day in February, a man approached Ron Bermudez of Emeryville, Calif., in front of his house and told him his home would be sold in a few hours. This came as a shock to Bermudez; Bank of America had told him weeks prior that he'd been approved for a trial modification and the papers would soon arrive. He made a panicked phone call to an attorney, who was able to make sure there was no auction.

Last November, Michael Hill of Lexington, S.C., finally got the call he'd been waiting for. Congratulations, a rep from JPMorgan Chase told him, your trial mortgage modification is approved. Hill's monthly payment, around $900, would be nearly halved.

Except there was a problem. Chase had foreclosed on Hill's home a month earlier, and his family was just days away from eviction.

"I listened to her and then I just said, 'Well, that sounds good,'" recalled Hill, who is married and has two children. "'Tell me how we're going to do this, seeing as how you sold the house.'" That, he found out, was news to Chase.

Hill was able to avoid eviction—for now. Chase reversed the sale by paying the man who'd bought the home an extra $19,500 on top of the $86,000 he'd paid at the auction.

After the mistaken foreclosure, he began the trial modification last December. He made those payments, but two months after his trial period was supposed to end, Hill is still waiting for a final answer from Chase.

The miscommunications have continued. He received a letter in January saying that he'd been approved for a permanent modification, but he was then told he'd received it in error.

His family remains partially packed, ready to move should the modification not go through. "I'm on pins and needles every time someone's knocking on the door or calling," he said.

Christine Holevas, a Chase spokeswoman, said that Chase had "agreed with Hill's request to rescind the foreclosure" and was "now reviewing his loan for permanent modification." She said Chase services "more than 10 million mortgages—the vast majority without a hitch."

To contest a foreclosure under the federal program, [homeowners must call] a Treasury Department-endorsed hotline staffed by housing counselors. Those counselors can escalate the case if the servicer still won't correct the problem.

That escalation process has saved "a number" of homeowners from being wrongfully booted out of their homes, Maggiano said. Hill, the South Carolina homeowner, is an example of someone helped by the HOPE Hotline.

Of course, the homeowner must know about the hotline to call it. Gomez, the Arizona homeowner who lost her home to foreclosure, said she'd never heard of it.

Many homeowner advocates say the government's effort has been largely ineffective at resolving problems with servicers.

"I uniformly hear from attorneys and counseling advocates on the ground that the HOPE Hotline simply parrots back what the servicers have said," said Alys Cohen, an attorney with the National Consumer Law Center. Cohen said she'd voiced her concerns with Treasury officials, who indicated they'd make improvements.

New rules to offer more protection

Under the current rules for the federal program, servicers have been barred from conducting a foreclosure sale if the homeowner requested a modification, but are allowed to push along the process, even set a sale date. That allows them to foreclose more quickly if they determine the homeowner doesn't qualify for a modification.

As a result, a homeowner might get a modification offer one day and a foreclosure notice the next. As of March, servicers were pursuing foreclosure on 1.8 million residences, according to LPS Applied Analytics.

Maggiano, the Treasury official, said that's been confusing for homeowners. Some "just got discouraged and gave up."

New rules issued by the Treasury in March say the servicer must first give the homeowner a shot at a modification before beginning the process that leads to foreclosure.

They also require the servicer to adopt new policies to prevent mishaps. For instance, the servicer will be required to provide a written certification to its attorney or trustee that the homeowner does not qualify for the federal program before the house can be sold.

Maggiano said the changes resulted from visits to the servicers' offices last December that allowed Treasury officials to "much better understand (their) inner workings."

The rules, however, don't take effect until June. Nor do they apply to hundreds of thousands of homeowners seeking a modification for whom the process leading to foreclosure has already started. Maggiano said Treasury's new rule struck a balance to help homeowners who were responsive to servicer communications to stay out of foreclosure while not introducing unnecessary delays for servicers. Some borrowers don't respond at all to offers of help from the servicers until they're faced with foreclosure.

Some states, such as North Carolina, have recently gone further to delay moving toward foreclosure if a homeowner requests a modification. State regulators there passed a law that requires a servicer to halt the process if a homeowner requests a modification.

Pearce, the North Carolina official, said the rule was prompted by the delays homeowners have been facing and puts the burden on the servicers to expeditiously review the request. "They're in total control."

Stopping the process not only removes the possibility of a sudden foreclosure, he said, but also stops the accumulation of fees, which build up and can add thousands to the homeowner's debt as the servicer moves toward foreclosure.

NOTES AND QUESTIONS

1. Liability for Debt Collection Attorneys. Should debt collection attorneys who make foreclosure collection mistakes be civilly liable?

Jerman v. Carlisle, 130 S.Ct. 1605 (2010) addresses this question. In this case, a debtor sued a law firm representing her creditor, Countrywide Mortgage, a prolific originator of subprime mortgages.

The law firm and one of its attorneys (collectively Carlisle), filed a lawsuit in Ohio state court on behalf of a mortgage company to foreclose a mortgage on real property owned by petitioner Jerman. The complaint included a notice that the mortgage debt would be assumed valid unless Jerman disputed it in writing. Jerman's lawyer sent a letter disputing the debt, and, when the mortgage company acknowledged that the debt had in fact been paid, Carlisle withdrew the suit. Jerman then filed an action under the Fair Debt Collection Practices Act (FDCPA), *15 U.S.C. § 1692 et seq.*, contending that by sending the notice requiring her to dispute the debt in writing, Carlisle had violated *§ 1692g(a) of the act*, which governs the contents of notices to debtors.

The FDCPA, imposes civil liability on "debt collector[s]" for certain prohibited debt collection practices. A debt collector who "fails to comply with any [FDCPA] provision . . . with respect to any person is liable to such person" for "actual damage[s]," costs, "a reasonable attorney's fee as determined by the court," and statutory "additional damages." *§ 1692k(a).* In addition, violations of the FDCPA are deemed unfair or deceptive acts or practices under the Federal Trade Commission Act (FTC Act), *§ 41 et seq.*, which is enforced by the Federal Trade Commission (FTC). See *§ 1692l.* A debt collector who acts with "actual knowledge or knowledge fairly implied on the basis of objective circumstances that such act is [prohibited under the FDCPA]" is subject to civil penalties enforced by the FTC. *§§ 45(m)(1)(A), (C).* A debt collector is not liable in any action brought under the FDCPA, however, if it "shows by a preponderance of evidence that the violation was not intentional and resulted from a bona fide error notwithstanding the maintenance of procedures reasonably adapted to avoid any such error." *§ 1692k(c).*

The District Court, acknowledging a division of authority on the question, held that Carlisle had violated *§ 1692g(a)* but ultimately granted Carlisle summary judgment under *§ 1692k(c)*'s "bona fide error" defense. The Sixth Circuit affirmed, holding that the defense in *§ 1692k(c)* is not limited to clerical or factual errors, but extends to mistakes of law. However, Justice Sotomayor, writing for the Supreme Court in a 7–2 decision, held that the bona fide error defense in *§ 1692k(c)* does not apply to a violation resulting from a debt collector's mistaken interpretation of the legal requirements of the FDCPA.

2. Collection Lawyers' Conflicts of Interest Arising From Personal Liability for Legal Errors. Will the imposition of personal liability create a conflict of interest between the financial interests of collection lawyers and their duty to mount an aggressive foreclosure enforcement for their clients?

The lawyers who were sued in *Jerman* raised practical concerns about the impact of a decision that eliminated the legal mistake defense for debt collecting lawyers. The debt collection bar filed amici curiae briefs arguing that the private enforcement provisions awarding attorneys fees to prevailing plaintiffs have created "a cottage industry" of professional plaintiffs who sue debt collectors for insignificant violations. Brief of National Association of Retail Collection Attorneys at 18, Jerman v. Carlisle, 130 S.Ct. 1605 (2010). The potential for a "flood of lawsuits" against collection attorneys could raise direct conflicts between the collection attorney's personal financial interests and the zealous representation of their clients. *Id.* at 5.

How do you expect collection lawyers to modify their contractual relationship with clients in light of *Jerman*? Are there other protections for debt collection lawyers who make mistaken legal interpretations? How should the risk of "abusive" lawsuits by debtors be weighed in a judicial system that is flooded with erroneous foreclosures? The Court concluded that "this decision does not place unmanageable burdens on debt-collecting lawyers."

3. Mediation. Another idea, which has grown in popularity since the foreclosure crisis, is to require banks and mortgage companies to enter mediation before they are allowed to foreclose on a home. Many states have adopted this approach, with varying success.

There have been several problems, however. In some cases, the banks make one take-it-or-leave-it offer. Moreover, some states do not require banks to negotiate in good faith. Geoff Walsh, "State and Local Foreclosure Mediation Programs: Can They Save Homes?" National Consumer Law Center, September 2009.

4. The Justice of Wall Street Bailouts and Bonuses. In the early spring of 2009, there was a great uproar over bonuses given to CEOs at AIG, despite the fact that it was only surviving as a corporation on government assistance. Some, however, insisted that the only way to attract the best people and not lose them to companies overseas was to offer them large bonuses.

Philosopher Michael Sandel frames the issue as follows:

> "At the heart of the bailout outrage was a sense of injustice . . . morally speaking it had felt all along like a kind of extortion. Underlying the bailout outrage was a belief about moral desert. The executives receiving the bonuses (and the companies receiving the bailouts) didn't deserve them. But why didn't they? The reason may be less obvious than it seems. Consider two possible answers—one is about greed, the other about failure."

Sandel argues that "greed is a vice, . . . an excessive single-minded desire for gain . . . that people aren't keen to reward." Greed and failure are linked when, as Sandel contends, "the reason the bonuses [after the collapse] are coming from the taxpayer is that the companies have failed . . . The public's real objection to the bonuses and the bailout-is not that they reward greed but that they reward failure." Sandel, Justice, What's The Right thing To Do? at 14–15 (2009).

5. Why Not Let Banks and Borrowers Fail? Gary Becker argued at the beginning of the crisis that people in default on their mortgages should be allowed to go into foreclosure without government help. Posting of Gary Becker to the Becker–Posner Blog, http://www.becker-posner-blog.com (Mar. 16, 2008, 17:34 EST). He argued that Bear Stearns should have been allowed to collapse as well. Instead, the federal government intervened to subsidize its sale to a healthy investment bank, Morgan Stanley. *Id.*

During the Great Depression, Andrew Mellon, then the Treasury Secretary, suggested that the whole financial system should be allowed to collapse on itself. What evidence would you rely on to evaluate the Becker and Mellon arguments? Would widespread unmediated failures have produced greater economic stability in the long term? Are these questions which require advanced training in economics to answer persuasively? What is the economic difference between allowing individual borrowers to lose their homes and allowing global financial institutions to fail? Is it possible to separate the consequences of these two types of failure?

6. Formality Bites: How Electronic Efficiencies in Property Recordation Ran Afoul of Ancient Reification Rules. Several courts have refused to honor evidence of the lender's title because the Mortgage Electronic Record System (MERS) is not the mortgagee and therefore does not hold title to the property. MERS is an electronic registry designed to track servicing rights and ownership of mortgage loans in the United States. It is the mortgagee of record for lenders, investors, and their loan servicers in the county land records. The system was developed to facilitate the large volume of residential loans that became the basic collateral for a complex securitization system.

In *Landmark Nat. Bank v. Kesler*, 216 P.3d 158, 168 (Kan. 2009), the court held that MERS, as the representative of the second mortgage holder, did not have a sufficient ownership interest in a house that was subject to foreclosure action by the first lienholder to be entitled to notice of the action.

This case relies upon a traditional, largely physical view of property title registration. Real property law links proof of ownership to the registration of a deed in the land title office of the local jurisdiction in which the property is located. Ownership, in this older view, is an artifact of physical possession of a properly registered deed. Thus, by observing ancient concepts of deeds and land title registration, the abstract property represented by mortgage securitizations become unenforceable if they do not comply with local title registration. Of course, the entire purpose for creating the MERS system was to make mortgage securitizations more efficent by introducing a national electronic registry that would avoid the time and expense of meeting local title requirements. The Kansas Supreme Court, in a case of first impression reasoned that:

> MERS and the amicus curiae American Land Title Association argue that MERS provides a cost-efficient method of tracking mortgage transactions without the complications of county by county registration and title searches. The amicus suggests the statutory recording system is grounded in seventeenth-century property law that is entirely unsuited to twentieth-century financial transactions. While this may be true the MERS system introduces its own problems and complications.

> The practices of the various MERS members, including both [the original lender] and [the mortgage purchaser], in obscuring from the public the actual ownership of a mortgage, thereby creating the opportunity for substantial abuses and prejudice to mortgagors . . . should not be permitted to insulate [the mortgage purchaser] from the consequences of its actions in accepting a mortgage from [the original lender] that was already the subject of litigation in which [the original lender] erroneously represented that it had authority to act as mortgagee.

> A protected property right must have some ascertainable monetary value. Indirect monetary benefits do not establish protection under the Fourteenth Amendment. An entitlement to a procedure does not constitute a protected property interest. * * *

> MERS did not demonstrate, in fact did not attempt to demonstrate, that it possessed any tangible interest in the mortgage beyond a nominal designation as the mortgagor. It lent no money and received no payments from the borrower. It suffered no direct, ascertainable monetary loss as a consequence of litigation.

The relationship the MERS has to Sovereign is more akin to that of a straw man than to a party possessing all the rights given a buyer. A mortgagee and a lender have intertwined rights that defy a clear separation of interests, especially when such a purported separation relies on ambiguous contractual language. The law generally understands that a mortgagee is not distinct from a lender: a mortgagee is "[o]ne to whom property is mortgaged: the mortgage creditor or lender."

Landmark Nat. Bank v. Kesler, 216 P.3d 158, 168 (Kan. 2009).

The MERS lawsuit demonstrates how new technologies have had unintended consequences. A system designed to make it easier to divide and package home mortgages for sale as the basis for complex securities, became in at least one jurisdiction, a barrier to enforcement of the right of property owners to exclude borrowers upon default. See also, *Blau v. America's Servicing Co.*, 2009 WL 3174823 (D. Ariz. 2009); *Nicholson v. OneWest Bank*, 2010 WL 2732325 (N.D. Ga. 2010), and *In re Relka*, 2009 WL 5149262 (Bkrtcy. D. Wyo. 2009).

7. The Role of Courts in the Banking and the Mortgage Industry: Will this crisis engender more judicial involvement in the mortgage and banking industries? What doctrines might support a more active role for common law adjudication?

Some scholars have begun to argue that the courts should play a greater role in the formation and interpretation of financial contracts:

[C]ourts * * * have institutional advantages over legislators in dealing with adhesion contracts as the source of financial meltdowns. Courts have greater flexibility than legislators in responding quickly to new deceptive schemes implemented through adhesion contracts. And the judiciary is better suited to apply the law consistently through the booms and the busts of the economy, since judges are not subject to the lobbying efforts and campaign contributions made by the regulated entities.

Shelley Smith, *Reforming The Law of Adhesion Contracts: A Judicial Response To The Subprime Mortgage Crisis*, Marquette University Law School, October 2009 available at http://works.bepress.com/cgi/viewcontent. cgi?article=1002&context=shelley_smith.

Is Smith right that courts have institutional advantages over legislatures in dealing with financial adhesion contracts? What about regulatory agencies?

In *Tainted Loans: The Value of a Mass Torts Approach in Subprime Mortgage Litigation*, 78 U. CIN. L. REV. 1 (2009), Raymond H. Brescia argues that an approach to subprime litigation which adopts the techniques used in mass torts cases (such as "the ready use of class action procedures; consolidation of related cases; global settlements; and aggregation of factual, liability and damages assessments") can help bring about better policy responses to the subprime mortgage crisis, and force banks to be more aggressive with meaningful mortgage modifications.

d. Counter Claims Against Foreclosure?

Associates Equity Homes Services, Inc., below, was decided before the peak of the subprime foreclosure crisis. However, it adopts the common-law doctrine of close-connectedness that was used to defeat the holder-in-due-course doctrine.

The holder in due course doctrine is an eighteenth century concept that protects the assignee of a negotiable instrument from the underlying contract claims of the maker or drawer. These claims include misrepresentation or failure to perform. In the 1960s the holder in due course doctrine became a favored tool of finance companies that worked regularly with often unscrupulous contractors who provided a service, obtained a note from the homeowner, and immediately transferred the note to the finance company who could rely on the holder in due course doctrine to defend against conventional fraud claims.

A series of cases beginning in the 1960s found that the transferee of the negotiable instrument, usually a note, was "too closely connected" to the underlying sales or service transaction for which the note was issued to be protected by the holder in due course doctrine. Courts used a variety of tests to determine close connection. Here are a few of those tests:

1. Did the transferee have any knowledge of the transferor's poor performance of similar contracts?

2. Was the transferee involved in setting the credit criteria for the note, or directly approving the credit report?

3. Did the transferee determine the terms of the original note?

4. Does the transferee take all, or substantially all of the notes generated by the transferor?

Does *Associates Equity Homes Services* actually rely on the close-connectedness doctrine?

Associates Home Equity Services Inc. v. Troup

Superior Court of New Jersey, Appellate Division.
343 N.J.Super. 254, 778 A.2d 529 (2001).

This is a foreclosure action. Defendants Beatrice and Curtis Troup, African–Americans, obtained a mortgage loan from third-party defendant East Coast Mortgage Corp. (ECM) to pay for repairs on their Newark home made by third-party defendants Gary Wishnia, General Builders Supply, Inc. and Property Redevelopment Center, Inc. (collectively Wishnia). The mortgage and note were assigned by ECM to Associates Home Equity Services, Inc. (Associates). When the Troups defaulted, Associates instituted this foreclosure proceeding. The Troups filed a counterclaim against Associates and a third-party complaint against Wishnia and ECM, claiming violations of the Consumer Fraud Act (CFA), N.J.S.A. 56:8–1 to –106, the Law Against Discrimination (LAD), N.J.S.A. 10:5–1 to –49, the Fair Housing Act (FHA), 42 *U.S.C.A.* §§ 3601 to 3631, the Civil Rights Act (CRA), 42

U.S.C.A. § 1981, and the Truth–In–Lending Act (TILA), 15 *U.S.C.A.* § 1635.

The trial court granted summary judgment dismissing all of the Troups' claims against Associates and ECM, and entered a judgment of foreclosure in favor of Associates. * * *

We affirm in part and reverse in part.

Considering the evidentiary material in a light most favorable to the Troups, these are the facts. Beatrice Troup, a seventy-four year old African American, has lived at 62 Vanderpool Street in Newark for approximately forty years. Following a telephone solicitation by Gary Wishnia, an agent for General Builders Supply, Inc., Beatrice and her son Curtis executed a contract for exterior home repairs with General on September 1, 1995. The contract price was $38,500, payable "$479.75 for 240 months." Beatrice claims that Wishnia told her "not to worry, he would get me financing." An amended contract was executed on November 16, 1995, for additional interior home repairs, increasing the contract price to $49,990. The agreement provided that "[payments] are to be made beginning January 1, 1996 payable to Property Redevelopment Center, Inc. until permanent financing is obtained."

Some time before September 14, 1995, Jeffrey Ahrens, ECM's representative, prepared the Troups' loan application. A credit search was conducted. According to Beatrice, the Troups had no personal dealings with ECM. She and her son Curtis dealt directly with Wishnia who arranged a limousine to transport the Troups to ECM's office to close the loan. Also, Wishnia did the "leg work" in processing the loan and obtained all income documentation required by ECM.

The Troups' loan application, dated September 14, 1995, but not signed by them until the closing date of April 27, 1996, provided for a $46,500 loan at an annual interest rate of 11.65 percent, adjustable after six months. The Truth–In–Lending disclosure form signed by the Troups at closing stated that the loan was a "balloon" type, payable in fifteen years, with the last payment being $41,603.58. The Troups were also charged four points, or four percent of the total loan amount. At the closing, Beatrice was required to execute a deed conveying the property to herself and her son.

At some point after April 27, 1996, ECM assigned the mortgage and note to Associates. On May 11, 1998, Associates filed a foreclosure complaint alleging that the Troups had failed to make the required payments under the mortgage and note. The Troups filed an answer, counterclaim and third-party complaint consisting of fifteen counts against the Wishnia defendants, ECM and Associates. Pertinent here are the counts charging Wishnia with "unconscionably poor" workmanship, and that Wishnia had conspired with ECM to place the mortgage financing with ECM and "to reap profits by subjecting the Troups to unconscionable, illegal and fraudulent home repair and financing transactions." The Troups charged Associates and third-party defendants with unconscionable and deceptive conduct in violation of the CFA. They further allege that ECM violated the TILA by failing to provide them with a "clear and conspicuous notice" of the expiration date of their right to rescind, failing to make proper disclosures, and materially understating the finance charges. Finally, the Troups asserted that Associates "participated in, authorized and/or ratified and/or had constructive knowledge of" the deceptive unconscionable acts of ECM and engaged in predatory lending practices in violation of the FHA, the CRA, and the LAD.

In dismissing all of the Troups' claims against ECM and Associates, and entering a judgment of foreclosure in Associates' favor, the trial court found that the terms of the mortgage loan given to the Troups were not "unconscionable when looked at in its entirety," given the fact that, although a 6.6 percent rate was available to "prime borrowers," the Troups "did not appear to be AAA rating." The claims against ECM based on Wishnia's deceptive and unconscionable conduct and workmanship were dismissed because, according to the court, ECM could not be held accountable for Wishnia's conduct. The court also determined that all of the Troups' claims against ECM and Associates were barred by the governing statutes of limitations under the LAD, the FHA and the CFA. Finally, the court dismissed the Troups' demand for rescission under the TILA, concluding that "there was conspicuous notice given" of the right to rescind.

The Troups and *amicus* claim that Associates engaged in a predatory lending practice by actively discriminating against them in consort with ECM by treating the Troups, African–Americans, less favorably than white borrowers in violation of the FHA, the CRA, and the LAD. *Amicus* adds that Associates may also be held accountable for ECM's discriminatory practice on the theory that Associates "controlled" ECM's conduct. The Troups do not seek money damages against Associates for any violation of these statutes. Rather, they argue that Associates' discriminatory conduct supports the affirmative defense of equitable recoupment in these foreclosure proceedings. The trial court did not address this issue.

Specifically, the Troups and *amicus* charge "reverse redlining" in this case. * * * Reverse redlining has been held to violate the FHA and the CRA. We do not hesitate to conclude that the practice violates the LAD as well. See N.J.S.A. 10:5–12i(1). (It is unlawful for a mortgage company to "discriminate against any person . . . because of race, . . . in the granting, . . . or in the fixing of the rates, terms, conditions or provisions" of a mortgage loan).

A plaintiff may establish a colorable claim of reverse redlining by demonstrating that "defendants' lending practices and loan terms were 'unfair' and 'predatory,' and that the defendants either intentionally targeted on the basis of race, or that there is a disparate impact on the basis of race." . . . (the FHA prohibits "not only direct discrimination but practices with racially discouraging effects"); and . . . (FHA violation can be demonstrated by a showing of either direct discrimination or discriminatory effects).

In this case the Troups' predatory lending claim was dismissed without permitting them to conduct meaningful discovery on the issue. The Troups laid the foundation for a reverse redlining case by establishing that they are African Americans living in a predominately African–American neighborhood in Newark. Their expert stated that the 11.65 percent interest rate and other terms of the loan were unjustified from an objective viewpoint, given the Troups' credit history and favorable debt-to-income ratio. Moreover, an Associates' representative testified during deposition that Associates paid a premium of $2,325 to ECM for securing the Troups' loan. He explained that "[w]e [Associates] pay a premium for the loan . . . [which] increase[s] as the interest rate of the loan increased," a practice recognized in the lending community as "yield spread premium."

Also significant is the fact that Associates gave ECM a "pre-approval determination" on February 23, 1996, two months before the Troups executed their loan application with ECM and ECM assigned the loan to Associates nine days after the loan was closed. The Troups argue that a fair inference can be drawn from these facts that Associates participated in inflating the interest rate and imposed the terms of the loan characterized by the Troups' expert as "onerous." These facts at the very least are supportive of the Troups' claim that Associates participated in the targeting of inner-city borrowers who lack access to traditional lending institutions, charged them a discriminatory interest rate, and imposed unreasonable terms.

* * * Further, we agree with the Troups that they are entitled to be informed concerning loans made by ECM and Associates to other New Jersey borrowers during the time period when the loan was made to the Troups. This information may or may not disclose a pattern of discriminatory lending practice in New Jersey's inner cities. If it does, the trial court should consider the Troups' request for further information about the loans, such as the location of the property, and race and income of the borrowers. The discovery order must not, of course, be overly burdensome and should be made subject to any legitimate claim of confidentiality, appropriate protective orders and redaction. * * *

However, the Troups' claims under the pertinent federal and state statutes are cognizable under the theory of equitable recoupment as an affirmative defense to Associates' foreclosure complaint. "[T]he fundamental purpose of recoupment . . . is the examination of a transaction in all its aspects to achieve a just result." A successful recoupment defense acts to reduce the amount the plaintiff can recover on the claim for the debt when the counterclaim arises from the same transaction.

[T]he Troups may assert their recoupment defense under both New Jersey and federal law notwithstanding expiration of the controlling statutes of limitations. The recoupment defense in this case arises out of the same transaction as the claim for the debt. The underlying loan transaction was the common source of both the Troups' liability to pay the debt and their correlative rights under the fair housing and civil rights statutes. The Troups' recoupment defense is not intended to invalidate the debt; it is asserted to reduce the amount that Associates may recover on its claim.

Associates argue that the underlying premise of recoupment is inapplicable here because its complaint is for foreclosure, rather than for collection of a debt. * * * As stated, what the Troups seek is a diminution of the amount due based on Associates' violation of statutory fair housing and civil rights laws. In our view, it would be fundamentally unfair and contrary to the remedial goals expressed by these statutes to preclude the recoupment remedy simply because it is invoked in a foreclosure proceeding. Without the defense, the mortgagee could simply take the mortgaged premises, leaving the borrower without a remedy. We therefore, reverse the summary judgment order dismissing the Troups' claim against Associates, and direct that an appropriate discovery order be entered.

The Troups and *amicus* argue that the trial court erred in dismissing the Troups' claims against ECM and Ahrens based on the so-called "Holder Rule." [Of the Federal Trade Commission that requires any consumer credit contract must contain a bold face, ten point type the following: NOTICE

ANY HOLDER OF THIS CONSUMER CREDIT CONTRACT IS SUBJECT TO ALL CLAIMS AND DEFENSES WHICH THE DEBTOR COULD ASSERT AGAINST THE SELLER OF GOODS OR SERVICES OBTAINED WITH THE PROCEEDS HEREOF. RECOVERY HEREUNDER BY THE DEBTOR SHALL NOT EXCEED AMOUNTS PAID BY THE DEBTOR HEREUNDER.]

* * *

Essentially, the Holder Rule strips the ultimate holder of the paper of its traditional status as a holder-in-due-course and subjects it to any potential defenses which the purchaser might have against the seller. *Federal Trade Comm'n v. Winters Nat'l Bank & Trust Co.*, 601 F.2d 395, 397 (6th Cir.1979). The Federal Trade Commission has included within the reach of the Holder Rule those sellers and creditors who "employ procedures in the course of arranging the financing of a consumer sale which separate the buyer's duty to pay for goods or services rendered from the seller's reciprocal duty to perform as promised." 40 F.Reg. 53,506, 53,522 (1975).

Consequently, the Holder Rule expressly incorporates "purchase money loan[s]" within the scope of the rule. *See* 16 *C.F.R.* § 433.2(b). A "[p]urchase money loan" is defined as "[a] cash advance which is received by a consumer" which is applied "in whole or substantial part, to a purchase of goods or services from a seller who (1) refers consumers to the creditor or (2) is affiliated with the creditor by common control, contract or business arrangement." 16 *C.F.R.* § 431.1(d).

Here, there is at the very least a fact issue concerning whether ECM's note constituted a "purchase money loan." ECM's financing provided the Troups with a "cash advance" totaling $49,990 which was applied in "substantial part" to pay for the improvements made to the home by Wishnia. *Ibid.* There is also evidence that Wishnia "refers consumers" to ECM. *Ibid.* Indeed, in this case Wishnia made all the arrangements for the loan and had the Troups chauffeured to ECM's offices to close. A reasonable jury could also conclude that Wishnia was "affiliated with" ECM by "business arrangement." *Ibid.* The Troups presented evidence that Wishnia and ECM had mutually arranged at least six other home improvement or equity loans to other customers living in the City of Newark or the Newark area. * * *

Nevertheless, ECM argues that the Holder Rule is inapplicable for three reasons. First, it claims that it did not "purchase" a "consumer credit contract" because initially the Troups paid Wishnia's affiliated companies monthly payments on the home repair contracts before the loan was made by ECM. This argument ignores the undisputed evidence that, before the Troups signed the first contract, Wishnia told Beatrice "not to worry, he would get [her] financing." Further, the second contract provides that "[payments] are to be made beginning January 1, 1996 payable to Property Redevelopment Center, Inc. *until permanent financing is obtained.*" Indeed, after the contract was executed, Wishnia promptly arranged the loan with ECM, with whom he had placed other home repair contracts on behalf of other borrowers. In our view, reasonable minds could conclude that Wishnia and ECM contemplated from the outset that the loan to finance Wishnia's contracting work would be placed by ECM. We agree with the Troups that, under these circumstances, Wishnia and ECM should not be permitted to circumvent the consequences of the Holder Rule simply because Wishnia arranged for temporary financing with his affiliated companies.

Second, ECM argues that the Holder Rule is inapplicable because the bold-typed notice required by 16 *C.F.R.* 433.2 was never placed on the relevant documents. We reject that argument. Although it is true that the documents did not contain the requisite notice, it is inconceivable to us that ECM and Ahrens may evade the remedial reach of the Holder Rule simply because of that omission. It was their responsibility to insert the notice. Indeed, as a financing institution, ECM must be charged with notice of the requirement. Moreover, the bold-typed notice is required by New Jersey law. N.J.A.C. 13:45A–16.2(a)(13)ii, states:

No home improvement contract shall require or entail the execution of any note, unless such note shall have conspicuously printed thereon the disclosures required by ... Federal law concerning the preservation of buyers' claims and defenses.

"[T]he law is a silent factor in every contract." *Silverstein v. Keane*, 19 N.J. 1, 13, 115 A.2d 1 (1955) (citation and quotation marks omitted). Moreover, equity looks to substance rather than form. *Kleinberg v. Schwartz*, 87 N.J. Super. 216, 222, 208 A.2d 803 (App.Div.), *aff'd*, 46 N.J. 2, 214 A.2d 313 (1965). These well-settled maxims should apply here to effectuate New Jersey's regulatory goal by "reading into" the pertinent documents the notice required by 16 *C.F.R.* § 433.2 and *N.J.A.C.* 13:45A–16.2(a)(13)ii.

Third, ECM claims that the Holder Rule is inapplicable because it has assigned the note to Associates. We reject that argument as well. The clear and unambiguous language of the Rule "notifies *all potential holders* that, if they accept an assignment of the contract, they will be 'stepping into the seller's shoes.' " *Lozada v. Dale Baker Oldsmobile, Inc.*, 91 F. Supp. 2d 1087, 1094 (W.D.Mich.2000) (quoting *Oxford Fin. Cos., Inc. v. Velez*, 807 S.W.2d 460, 463 (Tex.Ct.App.1991) (emphasis added)). Thus, the creditor-assignee becomes " 'subject to' *any* claims or defenses the debtor can assert against the seller." *Oxford Fin.*, *supra*, 807 S.W.2d at 463; and *see Simpson v. Anthony Auto Sales, Inc.*, 32 F. Supp. 2d 405, 409 n.10 (W.D.La.1998) (holding that the Holder Rule permits consumers to bring claims against assignee without regard to whether damages warranted rescission). Here, ECM, as "a potential holder" had notice that if it procured the purchase money loan arranged by Wishnia, it may be stepping into Wishnia's shoes. We cannot accept the proposition that the FTC contemplated that such result would not attach simply because of a subsequent assignment of the loan, especially when, as here, it is claimed that ECM actively participated with Wishnia, the seller, in placing the loan with the Troups.

We conclude that fact issues exist respecting ECM's liability under the Holder Rule. Summary judgment dismissing the Troups' claims is therefore reversed. Ahrens' argument that there is no basis to hold him personally liable may be revisited after conclusion of all discovery concerning application of the Holder Rule.

The Troups argue that the trial court erred in dismissing their consumer fraud claims against Associates and third-party defendants.

N.J.S.A. 56:8–2 prohibits:

[t]he act, use or employment by any person of *any unconscionable commercial practice,* deception, fraud, false pretense, false promise, misrepresentation, or the knowing, concealment, suppression, or omission of any material fact with intent that others rely upon [it] . . . *in connection with the sale or advertisement of . . . merchandise.* . . .

Loans are included in the definition of "advertisement," . . . and the definition of "merchandise," . . . has been held to include "the offering, sale, or provision of consumer credit. . . ."

The word "unconscionable" must be interpreted liberally so as to effectuate the public purpose of the CFA. . . . It is not intended to "erase the doctrine of freedom of contract, but to make realistic the assumption of the law that the agreement has resulted from real bargaining between parties who had freedom of choice and understanding and ability to negotiate in a meaningful fashion." . . . The standard of conduct contemplated by the unconscionability clause is "good faith, honesty in fact and observance of fair dealing[,]" and the need for application of that standard "is most acute when the professional seller is seeking the trade of those most subject to exploitation-the uneducated, the inexperienced and the people of low incomes." *Ibid.* Whether a particular practice is unconscionable must be determined on a case-by-case basis. *Id.* at 543, 279 A.2d 640. In this case, whether the acts of Associates and third-party defendants were unconscionable was for the jury to decide. * * *

We affirm the trial court's dismissal of the Troups' demand for rescission under the TILA. * * *

The purpose of the three-day waiting period under § 1635(a) is to give the consumer the opportunity to reconsider any transaction which would have the serious consequence of encumbering title to his or her home. If a lender's notice of the right to rescind is deficient, a mortgagor's rescission rights are extended to three years. 15 *U.S.C.A.* § 1635(f). If the creditor fails to comply with the written requirements of the notice to rescind, or if a "material" disclosure is not correctly made, the rescission period is extended for three years. *Ibid.,* 12 *C.F.R.* § 226.23(a)(3).

We agree with the trial court's determination that the notice of right to cancel in this case complied with the mandates of the TILA. * * *

Affirmed in part, reversed and remanded in part.

D. THE BANKERS' STORY

Bankers argue that they were surprised by the panic of 2008 and that no one could have predicted the collapse of the five major investment banks of Wall Street. The failure to predict argument compares the man-made financial crisis to natural calamities, such as unusually severe hurricanes or tornadoes. The natural disaster metaphor provides a formulation that avoids accountability for making mistakes of judgment and for taking irresponsible risks with other people's money. "Nobody has yet admitted that they have made mistakes, would you like to be the first?" Financial Crisis Inquiry Commission (FCIC) member Heather Murren pointedly asked former Treasury Secretary Henry ("Hank") Paulson during a hearing on the "shadow banking system." Only Treasury Secretary Timothy Geithner, former President of the New York Federal Reserve Bank in the period leading up to and including the crisis was willing to confess "absolutely we could have done more . . . I do not agree [that it was inevitable] . . . I do not believe we were powerless." The Shadow Banking System Financial Crisis Inquiry Commission Hearing, http://www.judicialwatch.org/foiblog (May 7, 2010, 13:55 EST). Most [bankers], however, repeatedly defended themselves with statements like the one former Bear Stearns CEO Alan D. Schwartz made: "I can't think of anything I could have done within the context of the model." *Id.*

Warren Buffet, the legendary investor whose company, Berkshire Hathaway, is a big shareholder in Moody's credit rating agency. He is one of the richest men in the world. Buffet echoes the "no mistakes, not predictable" story of the financial sector. For example, in his testimony to the Financial Inquiry Commission, he "defended the actions of the credit rating agencies during the run-up to the subprime mortgage crisis, calling the housing boom a "four-star" bubble that not even he was able to anticipate." New York Times, Legal, Deal Book, June 2, 2010. http://dealbook.blogs.nytimes.com/2010/06/02/buffett-defends-how-rating-agencies-are-paid/?hp. For the stories of three investors who predicted and profited from the subprime mortgage meltdown, see Michael Lewis, The Big Short: Inside the Doomsday Machine (2010).

The argument that the crisis was unforeseeable and that the bankers did not make any errors of judgment contrasts with the narrative deployed by, financial regulators, who soon developed their own self-protective narrative. Regulators were defensive about their failure to control the extreme dependence of investment banks on daily loans, their failure to detect the massive Ponzi scheme of financier Bernard Madoff, and the low levels of capital held by investment and commercial banks to cushion against the very risks that came to fruition in 2007. The regulators' narrative is a story of limited statutory authority and the cleverness and anti-social greed of financial wizards who built a "shadow banking system" in the vacant legal space created by weak statutes and regulations. The Shadow Banking System Financial Crisis Inquiry Commission Hearing, http://www.judicialwatch.org/foiblog (May 7, 2010, 13:55 EST).

E.   GOING FORWARD: REMEDIES AND RAGE

1.   DEMOCRACY AND CONTRACTS: LISTENING TO THE OUTRAGE

During the worst financial crisis since the Great Depression, there are a cluster of developments that demonstrate democratic resistance to the perception that Wall Street has taken unfair advantage of ordinary citizens, by changing the rules of finance to allow them to develop and then exploit information asymmetries among financial firms and between banks and borrowers.

Two legal scholars have argued that intentional law breaking by squatters can affirmatively improve legal regulation. They note that there is inherent tension in property law between dynamic forces of change and the static expectation of societies for economic stability. They argue further that intentional law breaking "is a strategy for change employed by those who cannot afford to file civil suits ... In other words, intentional law breaking is typically,(though not always) a tool of the havenots." Property Outlaws: How Squatters, Pirates, and Protesters Improve the Law of Ownership Eduardo M. Penalver and Sonia Katyal (2010).

This section examines evidence that a dynamic process of change to the property rules of home mortgages is in fact visible in the aftermath of the financial crisis.

2.   SQUATTERS AND STRATEGIC DEFAULTERS

a.   Squatters

One aftermath of the concentration of foreclosures is that evicted residents have exercised unregulated self-help remedies, including illegally occupying homes or refusing to pay the mortgage for homes that have lost value and the mortgage balance exceeds the market value of the property. Owners Stop Paying Mortgages, and Stop Fretting, New York Times, May 31, 2010. Thomas J. Sheeran, "Foreclosed Homes Occupied by Homeless," USA Today (accessed 9/25/2009). Derek K., "Ex Owners Turning Aggressive in Effort," Washington Post (access 9/25/2009).

Some squatters act alone and in secret, other do so openly, with organizational support as an act of civil disobedience. The New York Times reported on the growth of the squatting phenomenon. "Michael Stoops, executive director of the *National Coalition for the Homeless,* said about a dozen advocacy groups around the country were actively moving homeless people into vacant homes—some working in secret, others, like Take Back the Land, operating openly. In addition to squatting, some advocacy groups have organized civil disobedience actions in which borrowers or renters refuse to leave homes after foreclosure. The groups say that they have sometimes received support from neighbors and that beleaguered police departments have not aggressively gone after squatters." "With Advocates' Help, Squatters Call Foreclosures Home," John Leland, New York Times, April 9, 2009, http://www.nytimes.com/2009/04/10/us/10squatter.html.

b.   **Strategic Default**

One legal scholar makes the argument directly that in the context of the current crisis strategic defaults are not morally wrong. "Beyond Guilt in the Housing Crisis: The Morality of Strategic Default," Brent T. White. *Arizona Legal Studies,* Discussion Paper No. 10–15 and "Take This House and Shove It: The Emotional Drivers of Strategic Default," *Arizona Legal Studies Discussion Paper No. 10–17*, May 14, 2010. White summarizes his argument for the role of emotion in the strategy of defaulting on "underwater" loans, in the following:

> "An increasingly influential view is that strategic defaulters make a rational choice to default because they have substantial negative equity. Based upon the personal accounts of over 350 individuals, [White] argues that this depiction of strategic defaulters as rational actors is woefully incomplete. Negative equity alone does not drive many strategic defaulters' decisions to intentionally stop paying their mortgages. Rather, their decisions to default are driven primarily by emotion— typically anxiety and hopelessness about their financial futures and anger at their lenders' and the government's unwillingness to help. If the government and the mortgage industry wish to stem the tide of strategic default, they must address these emotions.

> "Because emotions are primary, however, principal reductions may not be necessary. Rather, many underwater homeowners simply need some reason to feel less apprehensive about the financial consequences of continuing to pay their underwater mortgages. One possible way to provide this comfort would be a "rent-based loan program," allowing underwater homeowners to refinance their entire balances to an interest rate that would bring their mortgage payment in line with the rental cost of a comparable home. Indeed, a rent-based approach would relieve many underwater homeowners' financial anxiety and likely be enough alone to stem the tide of strategic default." Brent White, Abstract of "Take This House and Shove it: The Emotional Drivers of Strategic Default," *Arizona Legal Studies Discussion Paper No. 10–17,* May 14, 2010.

3.   JUDGES AND SHERIFFS NULLIFY FLAWED FORECLOSURES

Judge John Doyle, Florida (Volusia County Ct.)

Doyle ended his previous practice of allowing bank lawyers to appear by telephone in the 3,000 pending foreclosure cases in his court. He found that many lawyers simply did not pick up the phone. Doyle thought that it was "unfair for homeowners who take time off from work, only to find that the bank lawyers are too busy to participate in the hearing." Doyle decried the "[s]hoddy work of what he called 'foreclosure mills,' which he says train young attorneys that it is not a big deal to miss a hearing." Deutsche National Bank Trust Co. v. Vincent Virgilio, No. 200814169CIDL (Fla. Volusia County Ct. filed Nov. 12, 2008). www.jonathanturley.org (accessed 9/25/2009).

4.   ALTERNATIVES TO SUBPRIME LENDING

Research reveals that appropriately structured affordable housing programs have a proven record of successful, sustainable mortgages that have default rates far below those of subprime loans for borrowers with similar characteristics. In "Homeownership Done Right: What Experience and Research Teaches Us," David Abromowitz and Janneke Ratcliffe of the Center For American Progress found that:

> [A] 2009 examination of the foreclosure experiences of five city-based affordable homeownership programs in Boston, Chicago, Los Angeles, New York, and San Francisco found that out of nearly 9,000 low-income families who turned to these programs to purchase their homes, the overall default rate was below 1 percent. All of these lending programs boasted default rates below the average for their cities. Similarly, a recent report on New York City's affordable home-ownership program showed only 13 foreclosures out of more than 20,000 homes sold to low-income buyers since 2004.

NOTES AND QUESTIONS

1.   What Works for Sustainable Housing For Low Wealth Borrowers? The following are features common to all programs that work according to Abromowitz and Ratcliffe:

- Fixed-rate, fully amortizing loan terms over 30 years
- Full documentation of income and demonstrated ability to pay the mortgage
- Escrows of taxes and insurance to ensure regular payment

Prohibitions against refinancing to extract home equity through subprime mortgages.

2.   Lingering Effects of The Great Recession. What will be required to increase government investment in affordable housing programs? Ironically, the financial collapse caused by the effects of lax underwriting standards for subprime mortgage lending has constrained future spending. There is a growing consensus that deficit reduction will be required for many years. Tax increases, benefit cuts, and slower growth in spending in virtually every category will be required in order to reduce the already substantial fiscal deficits which were enlarged by bailouts, and stimulus spending to mitigate the harshest effects of the Great Recession.

In February 2010, while the recovery from the recession was not yet firmly established, President Obama established the **National Commission on Fiscal Responsibility and Reform**. The Commission will make recommendations that put the budget in primary balance so that we are paying for all operations and programs for the federal government (achieving deficits of about 3 percent of GDP) by 2015 and meaningfully improve the long-term fiscal outlook.

3.   Why were the most risky loan products sold to the least sophisticated borrowers? Federal Reserve Board Governor Edward Gramlich noted that high-risk, high-cost loan products were frequently targeted at lower-income and minority borrowers. Abromowitz and Ratcliffe, cited above, conclude that this question "answers itself. The least sophisticated borrowers are probably duped into taking these products. But that does not explain how lenders, policymakers, regulators, and investors lost sight of the difference between making mortgages possible and making as many mortgages as possible."

4.   Did residential segregation cause the foreclosure crisis? Two leading sociologists argue in this important new study that:

> The rise in subprime lending and the ensuing wave of foreclosures was partly a result of market forces that have been well-identified in the literature, but it was also a highly racialized process. We argue that residential segregation created a unique niche of minority clients who were differentially marketed risky subprime loans that were in great demand for use in mortgage-backed securities that could be sold on secondary markets. We test this argument by regressing foreclosure actions in the top 100 U.S. metropolitan areas on measures of black, Hispanic, and Asian segregation while controlling for a variety of housing market conditions, including average creditworthiness, the extent of coverage under the Community Reinvestment Act, the degree of zoning regulation, and the overall rate of subprime lending. We find that black residential dissimilarity and spatial isolation are powerful predictors of foreclosures across U.S. metropolitan areas. To isolate subprime lending as the causal mechanism through which segregation influences foreclosures, we estimate a two-stage least squares model that confirms the causal effect of black segregation on the number and rate of foreclosures across metropolitan areas. We thus conclude that segregation was an important contributing cause of the foreclosure crisis, along with overbuilding, risky lending practices, lax regulation, and the bursting of the housing price bubble.

Jacob S. Rugh and Douglas S. Massey, Racial Segregation and the American Foreclosure Crisis, 75 Amer. Sociological Rev. 629 (2010).

CHAPTER 3

STATES, MARKETS, AND THE PROBLEM OF GOVERNANCE

Introduction

Many decades ago, economist Arthur Okun observed:

American society proclaims the worth of every human being. All citizens are guaranteed equal justice and equal political rights. Everyone has a pledge of speedy response from the fire department and access to national monuments. As American citizens, we are all members of the same club.

Yet at the same time, our institutions say "find a job or go hungry," "succeed or suffer." They prod us to get ahead of our neighbors economically after telling us to stay in line socially. They award prizes that allow the big winners to feed their pets better than the losers can feed their children.[a]

Okun's point was that the United States is a capitalist democracy, with a "split-level institutional structure." Thus, many of the social institutions in which Americans live their daily lives are organized around capitalist "market" principles, according to which inequality of many kinds is a fact of life. At the same time, other social institutions in which Americans live their daily lives—particularly those institutions connected to government— are organized around egalitarian, "democratic" principles. In addition, democracy and equality are touchstones for how Americans talk about their group identities outside the state. When people speak of their racial and gender identities, for example, they often speak of the importance of social, cultural, and legal equality.

Legal rules create, regulate, and maintain both our "capitalist" institutions and our "democratic" ones. This book is designed to introduce readers to descriptive and normative issues concerning the operation of law in a capitalist democracy. Thinking about what might constitute "economic justice" requires us to think about markets, about culture, and about the state, and to think about their interrelationship. It requires us, as well, to think about how law operates in both capitalist and democratic realms, and about the shadow of the law in social worlds not governed directly either by state or market.

---

a. ARTHUR M. OKUN, EQUALITY AND EFFICIENCY: THE BIG TRADEOFF 1 (1975).

This chapter introduces a number of questions. In what ways does the law shape our market culture and our political culture? How does our society negotiate the tensions between the inequalities our market culture produces and exploits and the equality idealized by our political culture? What role does the law play in these negotiations? Which aspects of our social life should be governed by market principles and which by non-market principles? How should our society negotiate the resulting tensions? What role should the law play in negotiating these tensions? In light of all these considerations, what does economic justice mean?

It may be useful to begin with some terminology. The broadest way to think about economic justice is through the idea of political economy. Our capitalist democracy is made up of different kinds of institutions, some labeled political and some economic, and different sorts of institutions are organized according to different rules and norms. What is the relationship between the political and the economic realms? How do the norms of each differ? How does the law constitute and regulate each of these realms, and how does it conceptualize the relationship between them? Finally, how might the conventional distinctions between the political and the economic be criticized?

A.   Law and Political Economy

Before economics existed as a discipline, there was political economy. As we will see in greater detail in chapter 4, the foundational thinkers in economics—including Adam Smith, Thomas Malthus, David Ricardo, and Karl Marx—considered their subject to include not only economic activity in the modern sense, but also the connection between economic activity and human flourishing. Adam Smith's great works, for example, include the *Wealth of Nations* and *The Theory of Moral Sentiments*: books that travel far beyond the contemporary purview of the discipline of economics.

In contemporary times, however—perhaps partly as a consequence of the nineteenth-century ideology of domesticity described in the excerpt from Frances Olsen below—we tend to think about the social world as being divided into separate spheres. The most common division—between the state, the market, and the family—places the political in the sphere of the state and the economic in the sphere of the market. This division, which we can call structural liberalism, suggests that the realms of the state, the market, and the family are inherently very different.

The assumption that the state, the market, and the family are separate and very different spheres of life has led to a number of consequences. One consequence is the way these spheres are described. As the excerpt from Olsen below explains in more detail, the state is usually conceptualized as public, whereas the family is usually described as private. The market is sometimes described as public and sometimes as private. The public/private distinction, moreover, is imagined as a relationship of opposites.

A second consequence of structural liberalism is the emergence of different kinds of methods to describe and analyze different spheres. Thus, in contemporary life, people often use the language of economics and efficiency to talk about market institutions, whereas they use the moral language of fairness or equity to talk about state institutions. Efficiency and equity, like the public and the private, are popularly believed to be opposites, inherently in tension with one another. The language of economics, moreover, employs rhetoric of objectivity and neutrality, eschewing questions of values, meaning, and justice. The language of fairness and equity, in contrast, has recently attracted postmodern and critical thinkers who are skeptical of concepts of objectivity and neutrality.

Structural liberalism affects how students are trained and what experts see as the proper domain of their expertise. A third consequence of structural liberalism, then, is a specialization of expertise between those who study the world of facts and those who study the world of meaning—a dichotomy deplored by C.P. Snow in a famous article on what he called the two cultures of the sciences and the humanities. Students in economics departments learn very little about moral philosophy or other disciplines that take fairness seriously. Conversely, philosophy students and humanities scholars typically know very little about economics. The split continues in professional life. Economic experts and policymakers tend not to use the language of fairness or investigate questions of distribution, while experts and policymakers interested in questions of justice and fairness tend not to have much to say about economic efficiency. The essay by Anthony Taibi excerpted below deplores this consequence of structural liberalism from the perspective of people who care about racial justice.

A fourth consequence of structural liberalism is the tendency to speak of the division between state, family, and market not only as a descriptive truth but as a prescription for action. For instance, it is commonly debated whether and when government should or should not intervene in the market, or whether and when government should or should not interfere with the family. This kind of debate can be very misleading, however, for at some level the state is always involved in creating and maintaining both market and family institutions. Governments, for example, formulate and enforce contract and property rights, without which markets could not function; and markets are regulated by domestic and international trade rules, including antitrust laws and tariff regulation. Similarly, marriage is a recognized legal institution with rights and responsibilities that are formulated by legislatures and enforced by courts, as well as being a private relationship of love and intimacy. It is important, therefore, not to confuse description with prescription, and to understand that arguments for or against government interference in the market or the family are really arguments about the costs and benefits of specific kinds of government action.

As you read the materials below, consider the various ways in which state, market, and family are defined as being separate and distinct. Consider also the ways in which they are interrelated with one another, and the ways in which they are all regulated by law. How is the split between public and private reflected in constitutional law? How is the distinction between political and civil rights, on the one hand, and social and economic rights, on the other, reflected in international and in U.S. law? How might things be different?

1. STRUCTURAL LIBERALISM AND ITS CRITIQUES

The Family and the Market: A Study of Ideology and Legal Reform

96 HARV. L. REV. 1497 (1983).

■ FRANCES OLSEN

* * * In the early nineteenth century, as men's work was largely removed to the factory while women's work remained primarily in the home, there came to be a sharp dichotomy between "the home" and "the [workaday] world." This dichotomy took on many of the moral overtones developed in the theological dichotomy between heaven and earth. Often the home was referred to as "sacred," and home life was the reward for which men should be willing to suffer in the earthly world of work. The family and home were seen as safe repositories for the virtues and emotions that people believed were being banished from the world of commerce and industry. The home was said to provide a haven from the anxieties of modern life—"a shelter for those moral and spiritual values which the commercial spirit and the critical spirit were threatening to destroy."

At the same time that the home was being glorified, it was being devalued. The woman's sphere was for men "the object of yearning, and yet of scorn." Ann Douglas has pointed out that, while men sentimentalized the family and exalted domesticity, they continued to behave in the marketplace as if they believed that "profane," worldly goals represented the greatest good. * * *

Further, while the world of the marketplace was decried for being selfish, debasing, and exploitative, it was also admired and esteemed. Self-reliance, progress, modernization—each had positive connotations that were associated with the world of commerce and industry. Rationality, discipline, and a focus on objective reality were considered desirable aspects of the "male" sphere of the market. Moreover, although the values of domesticity were used to criticize the destructiveness of marketplace values and the pursuit of wealth, they nevertheless served to "undercut opposition to exploitative pecuniary standards in the work world, by upholding a 'separate sphere' of comfort and compensation, instilling a morality that would encourage self control, and fostering the idea that preservation of home and family sentiment was an ultimate goal."

Given this simultaneous glorification and denigration of both the home and the marketplace, it should be no surprise that the sharp split between the two spheres had complex effects upon women. The market/family dichotomy tended to exclude women from the world of the marketplace while promising them a central role in the supposedly equally important domestic sphere. The dichotomy encouraged women to be generous and nurturant but discouraged them from being strong and self reliant; it insulated women from the world's corruption but denied them the world's stimulation. While the dichotomy tended to mask the inferior, degraded position of women, it also provided a degree of autonomy and a base from which women could and did elevate their status. * * *

A.   The Free Market and the Private Family: The Principle of Nonintervention

Although the woman's sphere has been described as "private" and contrasted with the "public sphere of the marketplace and government," such a characterization can be misleading. There are two different dichotomies involved in this contrast: on one hand, a dichotomy between the market, considered public, and the family, considered private; on the other hand, a dichotomy between the state, considered public, and civil society, considered private. Both the market and the family are thought of as part of "private" civil society in opposition to the "public" state. Calling both the marketplace and the state "public" can thus confuse our thinking about the two dichotomies.

It is important to recognize the distinction between the state/civil society dichotomy and the market/family dichotomy, because the former dichotomy plays itself out in an analogous manner on both sides of the latter. In discourse on the market, the state/civil society dichotomy appears as the issue of state regulation of the economy; in discourse on the family, it appears as the issue of state interference in the family. The classic laissez-faire arguments against state regulation of the free market find a striking parallel in the arguments against state interference with the private family. The two sets of arguments, and the ideals that underlie them, share a great deal more than just hostility to government. Both are constructed of similar elements and subject to similar attacks; our understanding of each is enriched by our understanding of the other.

1.   The Free Market.—It is possible briefly to summarize the basic themes of laissez-faire theory without denying the richness or complexity of the theory. Laissez-faire theory depends upon the notion of a free and autonomous market. Although the free market does not have to be considered an object or a thing, "the market" must at least be considered a coherent and sensible way of talking and thinking about economic relations among people. Further, laissez-faire theory posits that the market is "natural" in that it reflects actual supply and demand, and "autonomous" in that it was not created by the state and can function independently of the state. Laissez faire theory both assumes and asserts that it makes sense to advocate state neutrality with respect to the market. Economic and social inequalities that persist after the institution of the liberal state (that is, the institution of "political equality") are deemed to be natural and beyond the proper scope of state activity. Thus, although laissez-faire theorists believe that people should be considered equal in their relations with the state, these theorists characterize the domination and subordination that accompany economic and social inequality in civil society as private matters that do not implicate the political state. A departure from laissez-faire policies is asserted to constitute an effort by the state to alter an inequality that otherwise exists quite independently of the state. Enforcement of contract, tort, and property law is compatible with laissez-faire doctrine only as long as the courts merely facilitate free market transactions without jeopardizing or compromising state neutrality.

Some critics of laissez faire accept the claim that laissez-faire policies would actually represent state neutrality with respect to an autonomous free market, but nevertheless reject these policies and urge that the state should regulate the economy to lessen some of the damaging effects of free market inequality. Thus, proponents of laissez-faire policy have had to assert not only that nonintervention is possible, but also that it is preferable to any form of state intervention.

Two classic arguments have been advanced to support nonintervention. The first is based on the theory that, although the natural market functions effectively, it is fragile. Just as introducing rabbits into Australia disrupted the continent's natural ecology, so, too, the attempt to mitigate human suffering by tinkering with one aspect of the market may cause quite unexpected and severe suffering with regard to other aspects of the market.

The second classic argument emphasizes the extreme strength and durability of the market. The claim here is that the free market is characterized by strong natural forces that will overcome and nullify any but the most radical efforts to impose state control on the economy, and that nothing less than socialism or total state abolition of the free market will have any lasting effect. Such theorists consider a court's refusal to enforce "harsh" or "oppressive" contract terms or a legislature's attempt to abolish cognovit notes to be reforms doomed to failure. The very same "unequal bargaining position" that is appealed to in support of such reforms can be used to demonstrate their futility. One contract term may be forbidden, but it will be replaced by another or by an adjustment in price; thus, assuming that the basic conditions of supply and demand remain unchanged, bargaining power will stay about the same, and parties will continue to form contracts that reflect this bargaining power.

2. The Private Family.—* * *The basic assumptions that underlie arguments in favor of the private family are similar to those underlying the arguments in favor of the free market. The first assumption is that "the family" is a coherent way of talking about certain relations among people. Another assumption is that the family is capable of existing in some sense apart from state activity, as a natural formation rather than only as a creation of the state.

The issue of state neutrality with respect to the family is more complicated than that of neutrality with respect to the market. Neutrality toward the market means treating the participants in economic life as juridical equals. The state is said to take a neutral stance toward the family, however, when it ratifies the preexisting social roles within the family.

In contrast to the market, in which universal selfish behavior is supposed to result in the betterment of society, the family has generally been expected to be based on less individualistic principles. The good of all is to be achieved not by each family member's pursuit of individual goals, but rather by sharing and sacrifice among family members. At one time the social good was thought to require the husband to control his wife; and children were, and to an extent still are, expected to obey their parents for the sake of a better society. Parents have often been expected to sacrifice their immediate individual interests for the sake of their children. The morality of altruism has been supposed to animate the family to the same extent that the morality of individualism has been supposed to pervade the marketplace.

The state has traditionally been expected to facilitate sacrifice and sharing within the family by ratifying the social roles assigned to family members; thus, it would be considered intervention for the state to treat the members of a family as juridical equals. At one time, for example, the father's social role entitled him to control the children. If the mother were to leave him and take the children with her, the courts would ordinarily be expected to force her to return them to him; for courts to refuse to do so would be considered state interference with the family.

Today, courts are still ordinarily expected to ratify the social role of parents as disciplinarians. For example, if a court were to allow a child to recover tort damages from her parents for confining her to her room as punishment, most people would consider this a serious state intrusion into the family, even though the parents' act would have been false imprisonment had it been committed by a third party.

The notion of noninterference in the family depends upon some shared conception of proper family roles, and "neutrality" can be understood only with reference to such roles. For example, one of the bases upon which statutes limiting access to contraceptives have been struck down is that such statutes intrude upon the marital relation. Governmental programs providing minors with access to contraceptives, however, are also condemned as state interference in the family. Thus, "interference" is not a simple description of state action or inaction, but rather a way of condemning particular state policies, usually those aimed at changing the status quo. The status quo itself is treated as something natural and not as the responsibility of the state. Actual inequality and domination in the family— as in the free market—are represented as private matters that the state did not bring about, although it could undertake to change them.

* * *

B.   Standard Critiques of the Free Market and the Private Family

1.   The Market.—The attack upon the accuracy and coherence of the laissez-faire image of the free market had two major components. First, the notion that the market is private and capable of existing separately from the state was challenged. Commentators argued that "systems advocated by professed upholders of laissez faire" were "in reality permeated with coercive restrictions of individual freedom." Furthermore, these coercive restrictions did not conform to "any formula of 'equal opportunity' or of 'preserving the equal rights of others.'" State interference, it was claimed, was unavoidable and would inevitably "affect the distribution of income and the direction of economic activities." Because government neutrality was an impossibility, a laissez-faire economy was a false ideal.

The second component of this attack was a demonstration that the government was not in fact neutral, but instead benefited certain entrepreneurs at the expense of working people. In making this argument, some commentators assumed that it would be theoretically possible to fashion workable laissez-faire policies, but pointed out that in practice these were "never ... carried out consistently." The extreme version of this argument would suggest that laissez faire is a smokescreen used by representatives of large industries to limit popular control of business. The same industries, it could be argued, would not really want an across-the-board laissez-faire policy, because they actually depend upon probusiness regulation.

An argument that draws on both components of the attack on laissez faire treats so called "private law as a state grant of partial sovereignty to one of the economic actors." Thus, contract law does not simply put into effect the agreement of the parties; rather, the mechanisms for enforcing contract put "the sovereign power of the state at the disposal of one party to be exercised over the other party." Similarly, private property is seen to confer on its owner the "sovereign power [of] compelling service and obedience" from those who need access to the property. This vision of property and contract law undermines the notion that the state can be a noncoercive, neutral arbiter in the market.

2. The Family.—Arguments similar to those developed in the attack on laissez faire have been used to undermine the basis for state refusal to "intervene" in the private family. One such argument attempts to demonstrate that the state cannot be neutral because it cannot help imposing coercive restrictions upon the freedom of family members. For example, although noninterventionists argue that the state should not interfere to prevent wife abuse, courts will have to deal somehow with cases in which battered wives kill their husbands. The simple principle of nonintervention in the family gives no clear direction for deciding such cases; it will not dictate whether criminal charges should be brought against these women or whether wife battering should mitigate or provide a defense to homicide. Yet the determination of such questions will inevitably affect the distribution of power within violent marriages and thus the social relations of families.

The second component of the attack on the private nature of the family is the claim that, even if the state could be neutral vis-à-vis the family, it in fact is not. The theory of the private family, it is argued, is not consistently carried out. Instead, the assertion that family affairs should be private has been made by men to prevent women and children from using state power to improve the conditions of their lives. By insisting that the family should not be subject to state regulation, men have been able to retain their excessive power. Furthermore, men in fact use the coercive power of the state to reinforce and consolidate their authority over wives and children.

The argument that nonintervention serves to empower husbands to dominate their wives and children has been particularly useful in the attack upon the claimed neutrality of the state with respect to the family. During the first half of the nineteenth century, state neutrality meant the ratification and reinforcement of social roles within the family that were openly hierarchical. Husbands were expected to control their wives, and wives were expected to obey their husbands. Nineteenth century feminists attacked the state for granting husbands sovereignty within the family, and asserted that the state itself was creating inequality when it endorsed separate social roles and realms of activities for the different members of the family. According to Lucretia Mott, the subjugation of wives by husbands was not apostolic but was "done by law and public opinion." Lucy Stone and Henry Blackwell protested that the marriage laws "confer[red] upon the husband an injurious and unnatural superiority, investing him with legal powers which no honorable man would exercise, and which no man should possess."

     * * *

One response to feminist attacks on the claimed neutrality of the state was the gradual enactment of laws that seemed more neutral. During the late nineteenth century and the twentieth century, much of the law providing for juridical superiority of the male was replaced by statutes and court decisions providing for juridical equality. The effect of this legal change upon the actual subordination of women has been debated, but what is of interest here is the extent to which the assertion of state neutrality between juridically equal husbands and wives is open to the same attacks as is the asserted state neutrality between juridically equal entrepreneurs and workers. The move toward legal equality does represent a change in the mode of explaining or denying the inferior status of women. It can be seen as a shift from a direct to an indirect mode of legitimating the subordination of women. Just as the notion of different, essentially incomparable spheres had replaced the claim that God created women inferior to men, so the notion of separate spheres was supplanted by the claim that men and women were actually equal.

     * * *

I do not advocate replacing the present dichotomies with an all powerful state and an all embracing market any more than I would advocate making women just like men. The state as it now exists must be ended at the same time that civil society as it now exists is ended; and when we transform the contemporary family, we must simultaneously transform the market. * * *

Contract Law, the Free Market, and State Intervention: A Jurisprudential Perspective

STATE, SOCIETY AND CORPORATE POWER 17, 17–23 (Marc R. Tool & Warren J. Samuels eds., 2d ed. 1989).

■ ROBERT B. SEIDMAN

It frequently is argued that the more the state plans, the more power is placed in the hands of the planners. Social engineering begets power, and Lord Acton long ago warned us that power tends to corrupt.

The classical response has been the celebration of the free market economy. Social engineering and planning are perceived as the very opposites of the free market; intervention is the opposite of nonintervention. The legal expression of social engineering is perceived as a set of commands directed by the state to various citizens. The legal expression of the free market is perceived as facilitative law, of which the law of contract is the archetype. As social engineering is the opposite of a free market, so command law is the opposite of facilitative law.

* * *

Many sorts of law on their face are rules expressing how the lawmaker expects the targets of the law to behave, on pain of sanction. Criminal law and tort law fit this model nicely. A rule is promulgated; if a person violates the rule he is punished, either directly as in criminal law, or through the imposition of a judgment for damages.

Many other sorts of rules, however, seem to be cut from a different bolt of cloth. Contract law does not require people to do anything. It merely prescribes that if certain agreements are entered upon, and broken, the courts may be required to levy a sanction. General corporation laws do not require anyone to enter upon a corporation. They provide a facilitative form. If parties wish to enter into a corporate relationship, the law prescribes some of the consequences. Because role occupants are not required to enter upon particular contracts, or to enter into particular organizations, the facilitative form seems to free the role occupant of coercion and to release him from the shadow of overarching power.

Is it true that facilitative law frees the role occupant from coercion? We shall denote the two contrary answers to this question as the classical and the anticlassical views.

THE CLASSICAL PERSPECTIVE

The classical paradigm asserts that facilitative law does free the citizen from state coercion. Long ago Sir Henry Maine said that the movement of all progressive societies heretofore has been from status to contract. By this Sir Henry meant that "the Individual is substituted for the Family, as the unit of which civil laws take account.... Starting, as from one terminus of history, from a condition of society in which all the relations of Persons are summed up in the relations of Family, we seem to have steadily moved towards a phase of social order in which all these relations arise from the free agreement of individuals."

Jurisprudential theories were developed which gave ideological support for the theme of contract. Thomas Hobbes said that the definition of injustice "is no other than the nonperformance of Covenant." Nietzsche, perhaps sarcastically, was even more extravagant: "To breed an animal that is able to make promises—is that not precisely the . . . task which Nature set for herself as regards man"?

Contract is a device for social cooperation. In a highly complex society, people must do many different things. Manufacturers must buy from suppliers, employ labor, sell to customers; landlords must rent to tenants; submanufacturers must contract with manufacturers; wholesalers and retailers and customers must interact with each other to keep the vast engine of the economy moving.

Without planned organization of the interchanges necessitated by the division of labor, it seems preferable for every man to seize his own opportunity. Through contract, the parties to an exchange define the norms of conduct for the occasion. The market becomes a giant communication system, by its "Invisible Hand" advising individuals the sort of norms to demand and accept in order to maximize their personal benefit.

From the point of view of the parties to the contract, they merely exercise a personal freedom to conduct their affairs in accordance with their emergent needs and desires. They exercise freedom by themselves determining the norms to which they will be bound.

The notion that contract law embodies "freedom" is closely intertwined with the ideal type of the market economy. If perfect competition prevails, then, by definition, no individual has the power to affect market price. The availability of other potential bargaining partners, who offer their services or goods on terms and conditions defined not by themselves, but by the Invisible Hand of the market, protect the parties each from arbitrary power in the other.

What ideal type of legal order is apt for this ideal conceptualization of the economic order? Unless one can exclude others from interfering with his possession of things, he will not purchase them. The law of property and of torts purports to guarantee rights of peaceable possession. Unless there are guarantees that the law of marginal utility will not continue to operate after a bargain is struck, promises for future performance become mere pious intentions. The law of contract purports to ensure that promises, once made, will be kept.

The classical view implies a model of the state as a value neutral framework whose task it is to ensure only that in case of dispute these bodies of law are enforced. It presupposes a sharp discontinuity between the private sphere, between state action and state non-action. The former consists of intervention and social engineering; the latter consists of adjudicating disputes arising in the private sector. In this view, the laissez-faire ideal of the state is the very opposite of social engineering. State inaction is markedly different from state action.

We can summarize the classical perspective in a series of propositions. (1) Facilitative law permits the parties to an interaction to determine their own norms of conduct. (2) The perfect competitive market ensures that neither party has power over the other. (3) The state is a neutral, impartial framework within which bargaining can take place peaceably and conflict can be resolved peaceably. (4) The state, by limiting its function to conflict resolution, does not engage in ordering the society; there is, therefore, a sharp discontinuity between state inaction and state action. (5) Facilitative law therefore ensures "voluntariness."

THE ANTICLASSICAL PERSPECTIVE

The anticlassical paradigm is at issue with the classical on all but the first of these propositions. Facilitative law does permit the parties to the transaction to determine between themselves the norms defining their interchange. Through it, the state delegates to the contracting parties a portion of its sovereign power. The two parties legislate for themselves in the act of bargaining; they lay down rules; the state proceeds to enforce them. "From this point of view the law of contract may be viewed as a subsidiary branch of public law, as a body of rules according to which the sovereign power of the state will be exercised in accordance to the rules agreed upon between the parties to a more or less voluntary transaction."

Parties to bargains are seldom of equal bargaining strength. To the extent that they are not, contract, however it may appear to the parties, is not a matter of freedom of choice, but of command. Is it significantly different to say to a man, "I will pay you a wage if you will work for me?" rather than, "You will get no wage unless you work for me"? Two hundred years ago Lord Chancellor Northington expressed it succinctly: "Necessitous men are not, truly speaking, free men."

At law, to treat unequals notionally as equals is in fact to elevate the stronger to a position of domination. In a bargaining situation, the stronger imposes upon the weaker the norms of conduct which he desires. * * *

The power to create norms of conduct, that is, to legislate, plus the use of state power to enforce them are two of the three familiar attributes of government. The net result of contract law is to transfer to the economically superior classes in the community the most significant powers of the state, all under the fictional disguise of equality and freedom. Facilitative law and "voluntariness" begin with notions of "freedom." They end by subjecting the weaker party to the power of the stronger. Facilitative law manipulates the weaker party, as does planning law or social engineering. The principal difference lies in who does the manipulating.

     * * *

The anticlassical understanding of facilitative law, therefore, focuses upon the framework of institutions within which bargains are struck and upon the power relationships of the parties. A bargain implies "freedom" only in that, *given the available alternatives*, both parties prefer the bargain struck. It is the framework which structures the alternatives available to each party which determines the extent of their volitional freedom.

It is further argued that the model of the value neutral state providing an impartial framework within which conflict can be resolved peaceably is not only empirically but also theoretically impossible. A decision-making structure—and the state is, par excellence, a decision-making structure—cannot be value neutral. The rules that define any decision-making process necessarily limit the range of potential inputs, conversion processes, and feedback functions. These rules, to that degree, predetermine the outputs, that is, the decisions. The state, perceived as a framework for the resolution of conflict, is a decision-making structure. No more than can any other decision-making structure can it be value neutral. * * *

The state must, willy-nilly, favor some and disadvantage others. For the state to stand by and permit the private activity of citizens to determine the configurations of the economy is as much state action as overt intervention. *Cui bono*? is not simply a possible query; it is the most significant question of all.

We can summarize the anticlassical model in a set of propositions. (1) Facilitative law permits the parties to an interaction to determine their own norms of conduct. (2) Facilitative law ensures that the more powerful party to an interchange will impose his desires upon the weaker. Further, the perfectly free market does not and cannot exist as a protection against the imposition of private power. (3) The state, by enforcing private agreements, lends its reserve monopoly of violence to enforce the norms agreed upon by the parties to the interchange. (4) Since every decision-making function is necessarily value laden, the state is not and cannot be a value neutral arbiter. (5) The enforcement of private bargains made under the guise of facilitative law is therefore as much a form of state intervention as more direct commands from the state to citizens. (6) Facilitative law therefore ensures that the state will delegate its power to the more powerful party to the exchange.

* * *

NOTES AND QUESTIONS

1. Structural liberalism across political spectrum. Structural liberalism, as Olsen and Seidman describe it, governs the thinking of political conservatives and libertarians as well as traditional liberals. As chapter 3 explores in more detail, those on the political right typically argue that political freedom and individual happiness require a relatively small public sphere and a large private sphere; those on the political left typically argue the opposite. Political conservatives and liberals also argue over whether there should be some kind of minimum "social safety net" for people at the very bottom of the economy and, if so, the size and composition of this net. Both sides of the debate, however, treat the public sphere and the private sphere as being inherently different; their arguments are over the relative size and priority of these spheres.

2. Jurisprudential critiques of public/private distinction. As Olsen's and Seidman's excerpts indicate, one criticism of the so-called "public/private distinction" is that it conceals normative assumptions about the role of law. Several generations of legal theorists have made this point. For example, in the 1920s, scholars identifying themselves with the Legal Realist movement sharply criticized the view that rules that abridge common law rights, especially property rights, constitute state "intervention" in the market. For the Legal Realists, property rights are already a creation of the state, so changing their distribution is not a special "intervention" in anything. The idea of "laissez-faire" economics—that one should allow the market to "naturally" allocate goods without state intervention—is therefore an illusion; markets themselves are a creation of the state. *See, e.g.,* Robert L. Hale, *Coercion and Distribution in a Supposedly Non–Coercive State*, 38 Pol. Sci. Q. 470 (1923); Morris R. Cohen, *Property and Sovereignty*, 13 Cornell L.Q. 8 (1927); Robert L. Hale, *Rate Making and the Revision of the Property Concept*, 22 Colum. L. Rev. 209 (1922); Note, *Peppercorn Theory of Consideration and the Doctrine of Fair Exchange*, 35 Colum. L. Rev. 1090 (1935).

The critique was picked up in the 1980s by the Critical Legal Studies movement and by the feminist legal theory movement, movements with which Olsen herself was affiliated. CLS scholars attacked dichotomies of all sorts in legal rhetoric, including the public/private distinction, arguing that they inhibited clear thinking about justice and social change. *See, e.g.,* Mark Kelman, A Guide to Critical Legal Studies 103 (1987) (observing that CLS scholars have both reiterated the Realist point that "the state is inextricably involved in the supposedly private realm," and "noted the extent to which coercion and choicelessness can readily exist in the realms traditionally denominated private"). Feminist scholars, like Olsen, criticized the public/private distinction for its tendency to ignore the politics of the family. For more recent versions of the feminist argument, see, Susan Moller Okin, *Justice and Gender: An Unfinished Debate*, 72 Fordham L. Rev. 1537 (2004); Tracy E. Higgins, *Why Feminists Can't (or Shouldn't) Be Liberals*, 72 Fordham L. Rev. 1629 (2004).

A version of this argument applied to contemporary United States constitutional law has been made by Cass Sunstein. Sunstein argues that the justices of the Supreme Court tend to treat common law distributions of wealth labeled "private"—for example, distributions in the form of property and contract rights—as the "baseline" from which to perceive state action. As a result, state-initiated social welfare programs look like "intervention," or "takings." *See also* Gary Peller & Mark Tushnet, *Charles L. Black, Jr.: State Action and a New Birth of Freedom*, 92 Geo. L.J. 779 (2004) (tracing a form of the argument to an essay by Charles Black published in 1967).

———

2.   STRUCTURAL LIBERALISM AND CONSTITUTIONAL LAW

It is often observed that the United States constitutional structure protects some kinds of rights—political and civil rights—but not others, namely social and economic rights. Sometimes this is explained as stemming from the distinction between positive and negative rights: the U.S. Constitution attempts to protect citizens from the abuse of government power, but does not require the government to provide its citizens with anything. Other times, the lack of economic and social rights in the U.S. Constitution is explained as an outgrowth of structural liberalism: the kind of governance appropriate to the market does not include economic and social rights. In any case, political liberals who favor a strong welfare state have frequently found themselves stymied by the lack of constitutional support. Consider the opinion in DeShaney, below, and its relationship to structural liberalism.

———

DeShaney v. Winnebago County Dep't of Soc. Servs.
489 U.S. 189 (1989).

■ CHIEF JUSTICE REHNQUIST delivered the opinion of the Court.

Petitioner is a boy who was beaten and permanently injured by his father, with whom he lived. Respondents are social workers and other local officials who received complaints that petitioner was being abused by his father and had reason to believe that this was the case, but nonetheless did not act to remove petitioner from his father's custody. Petitioner sued respondents claiming that their failure to act deprived him of his liberty in violation of the Due Process Clause of the Fourteenth Amendment to the United States Constitution. We hold that it did not.

I

The facts of this case are undeniably tragic. Petitioner Joshua DeShaney was born in 1979. In 1980, a Wyoming court granted his parents a divorce and awarded custody of Joshua to his father, Randy DeShaney. The father shortly thereafter moved to Neenah, a city located in Winnebago County, Wisconsin, taking the infant Joshua with him. There he entered into a second marriage, which also ended in divorce.

The Winnebago County authorities first learned that Joshua DeShaney might be a victim of child abuse in January 1982, when his father's second wife complained to the police, at the time of their divorce, that he had previously "hit the boy causing marks and [was] a prime case for child abuse." The Winnebago County Department of Social Services (DSS) interviewed the father, but he denied the accusations, and DSS did not pursue them further. In January 1983, Joshua was admitted to a local hospital with multiple bruises and abrasions. The examining physician suspected child abuse and notified DSS, which immediately obtained an order from a Wisconsin juvenile court placing Joshua in the temporary custody of the hospital. Three days later, the county convened an ad hoc "Child Protection Team" consisting of a pediatrician, a psychologist, a police detective, the county's lawyer, several DSS caseworkers, and various hospital personnel to consider Joshua's situation. At this meeting, the Team decided that there was insufficient evidence of child abuse to retain Joshua in the custody of the court. The Team did, however, decide to recommend several measures to protect Joshua, including enrolling him in a preschool program, providing his father with certain counselling services, and encouraging his father's girlfriend to move out of the home. Randy DeShaney entered into a voluntary agreement with DSS in which he promised to cooperate with them in accomplishing these goals.

Based on the recommendation of the Child Protection Team, the juvenile court dismissed the child protection case and returned Joshua to the custody of his father. A month later, emergency room personnel called the DSS caseworker handling Joshua's case to report that he had once again been treated for suspicious injuries. The caseworker concluded that there was no basis for action.

For the next six months, the caseworker made monthly visits to the DeShaney home, during which she observed a number of suspicious injuries on Joshua's head; she also noticed that he had not been enrolled in school, and that the girlfriend had not moved out. The caseworker dutifully recorded these incidents in her files, along with her continuing suspicions that someone in the DeShaney household was physically abusing Joshua, but she did nothing more. In November 1983, the emergency room notified DSS that Joshua had been treated once again for injuries that they believed to be caused by child abuse. On the caseworker's next two visits to the DeShaney home, she was told that Joshua was too ill to see her. Still DSS took no action.

In March 1984, Randy DeShaney beat 4–year–old Joshua so severely that he fell into a life-threatening coma. Emergency brain surgery revealed a series of hemorrhages caused by traumatic injuries to the head inflicted over a long period of time. Joshua did not die, but he suffered brain damage so severe that he is expected to spend the rest of his life confined to an institution for the profoundly retarded. Randy DeShaney was subsequently tried and convicted of child abuse.

Joshua and his mother brought this action under 42 U.S.C. § 1983 in the United States District Court for the Eastern District of Wisconsin against respondents Winnebago County, DSS, and various individual employees of DSS. The complaint alleged that respondents had deprived Joshua of his liberty without due process of law, in violation of his rights under the Fourteenth Amendment, by failing to intervene to protect him against a risk of violence at his father's hands of which they knew or should have known. The District Court granted summary judgment for respondents.

The Court of Appeals for the Seventh Circuit affirmed.[1] * * *

---

1. 812 F.2d 298 (1987).

The Due Process Clause of the Fourteenth Amendment provides that "[n]o State shall . . . deprive any person of life, liberty, or property, without due process of law." Petitioners contend that the State deprived Joshua of his liberty interest in "free[dom] from . . . unjustified intrusions on personal security," by failing to provide him with adequate protection against his father's violence. The claim is one invoking the substantive rather than the procedural component of the Due Process Clause; petitioners do not claim that the State denied Joshua protection without according him appropriate procedural safeguards, but that it was categorically obligated to protect him in these circumstances.

But nothing in the language of the Due Process Clause itself requires the State to protect the life, liberty, and property of its citizens against invasion by private actors. The Clause is phrased as a limitation on the State's power to act, not as a guarantee of certain minimal levels of safety and security. It forbids the State itself to deprive individuals of life, liberty, or property without "due process of law," but its language cannot fairly be extended to impose an affirmative obligation on the State to ensure that those interests do not come to harm through other means. Nor does history support such an expansive reading of the constitutional text. Like its counterpart in the Fifth Amendment, the Due Process Clause of the Fourteenth Amendment was intended to prevent government "from abusing [its] power, or employing it as an instrument of oppression." * * * Its purpose was to protect the people from the State, not to ensure that the State protected them from each other. The Framers were content to leave the extent of governmental obligation in the latter area to the democratic political processes.

Consistent with these principles, our cases have recognized that the Due Process Clauses generally confer no affirmative right to governmental aid, even where such aid may be necessary to secure life, liberty, or property interests of which the government itself may not deprive the individual.[2] * * * As we said in *Harris v. McRae*: "Although the liberty protected by the Due Process Clause affords protection against unwarranted *government* interference . . ., it does not confer an entitlement to such [governmental aid] as may be necessary to realize all the advantages of that freedom."[3] If the Due Process Clause does not require the State to provide its citizens with particular protective services, it follows that the State cannot be held liable under the Clause for injuries that could have been averted had it chosen to provide them. As a general matter, then, we conclude that a State's failure to protect an individual against private violence simply does not constitute a violation of the Due Process Clause.

* * *

---

2. See, *e.g.*, *Harris v. McRae*, 448 U.S. 297, 317–318 (1980) (no obligation to fund abortions or other medical services) (discussing Due Process Clause of Fifth Amendment); *Lindsey v. Normet*, 405 U.S. 56, 74 (1972) (no obligation to provide adequate housing) (discussing Due Process Clause of Fourteenth Amendment); see also *Youngberg v. Romeo*, [457 U.S. 307,] 317 ("As a general matter, a State is under no constitutional duty to provide substantive services for those within its border").

3. 448 U.S., at 317–318 (emphasis added).

■ Justice Blackmun, dissenting.

Today, the Court purports to be the dispassionate oracle of the law, unmoved by "natural sympathy." * * * But, in this pretense, the Court itself retreats into a sterile formalism which prevents it from recognizing either the facts of the case before it or the legal norms that should apply to those facts. As Justice Brennan demonstrates, the facts here involve not mere passivity, but active state intervention in the life of Joshua DeShaney—intervention that triggered a fundamental duty to aid the boy once the State learned of the severe danger to which he was exposed.

The Court fails to recognize this duty because it attempts to draw a sharp and rigid line between action and inaction. But such formalistic reasoning has no place in the interpretation of the broad and stirring Clauses of the Fourteenth Amendment. Indeed, I submit that these Clauses were designed, at least in part, to undo the formalistic legal reasoning that infected antebellum jurisprudence, which the late Professor Robert Cover analyzed so effectively in his significant work entitled Justice Accused (1975).

Like the antebellum judges who denied relief to fugitive slaves, see *id.*, at 119–121, the Court today claims that its decision, however harsh, is compelled by existing legal doctrine. On the contrary, the question presented by this case is an open one, and our Fourteenth Amendment precedents may be read more broadly or narrowly depending upon how one chooses to read them. Faced with the choice, I would adopt a "sympathetic" reading, one which comports with dictates of fundamental justice and recognizes that compassion need not be exiled from the province of judging. Cf. A. Stone, Law, Psychiatry, and Morality 262 (1984) ("We will make mistakes if we go forward, but doing nothing can be the worst mistake. What is required of us is moral ambition. Until our composite sketch becomes a true portrait of humanity we must live with our uncertainty; we will grope, we will struggle, and our compassion may be our only guide and comfort").

Poor Joshua! Victim of repeated attacks by an irresponsible, bullying, cowardly, and intemperate father, and abandoned by respondents who placed him in a dangerous predicament and who knew or learned what was going on, and yet did essentially nothing except, as the Court revealingly observes, *ante*, at 193, "dutifully recorded these incidents in [their] files." It is a sad commentary upon American life, and constitutional principles—so full of late of patriotic fervor and proud proclamations about "liberty and justice for all"—that this child, Joshua DeShaney, now is assigned to live out the remainder of his life profoundly retarded. Joshua and his mother, as petitioners here, deserve—but now are denied by this Court—the opportunity to have the facts of their case considered in the light of the constitutional protection that 42 U.S.C. § 1983 is meant to provide.

State Action Is Always Present

3 Chi. J. Int'l L. 465 (2002).

■ Cass R. Sunstein

What is the place of social and economic guarantees in a democratic constitutional order? Do such guarantees place a special strain on the judiciary? Do they help poor people? What is the relationship between such guarantees and doctrines involving state action and the horizontal application of constitutional norms?

[In his article *State Action, Social Welfare Rights, and the Judicial Role*,[4] Mark Tushnet] casts new light on [these questions] by analyzing a number of cases in which courts have, or have not, taken their constitutions to alter background rules of property, contract, and tort. Tushnet contends that the rise of the activist state, understood as some form of social democracy, unsettles preexisting understandings of the relationship between constitutional norms and the private sector. In the classical liberal state, the constitution does not apply horizontally; there are no economic guarantees; and what counts as state action is relatively clear. But once the state assumes "affirmative obligations," constitutional norms might well be triggered, and the state's failure to alter the background rules of property and contract law might well raise serious constitutional problems. To borrow from Tushnet's summary of his complex account: In a "thin social democratic nation," such as Canada, courts are placed in a new and extremely difficult position, being forced either to "enforce obviously arbitrary lines between what they treat as state action and what they do not," or to work out "the set of entitlements people should have in a thicker social democracy."

Much of what Tushnet says is highly illuminating, but I think that there are several gaps in his discussion. I emphasize two points here. First, the classical liberal state assumes affirmative obligations, and does so no less than the social democratic state. The obligations are different, but they are not less affirmative. The widespread neglect of this point, within the legal and political culture, has led to serious failures in analysis, and the failures are not innocuous. Second, state action is always present. The constitutional question, in any system that has a state action requirement, is not whether there is state action, but whether the relevant state action is unconstitutional. That is a hard question on the merits, but it is not a hard state action question. A thin social democracy may struggle with constitutional issues, but by virtue of its status as a thin social democracy, it ought not to have any special struggle with questions involving state action or horizontal effect. A nation that currently embraces social democracy might create, at the constitutional level, social and economic rights, or it might not. A nation that currently rejects social democracy might offer, at the constitutional level, social and economic rights, or it might not. The legal questions involve the merits.

I now offer some details about these two points.

1. The so called activist state is no more activist than what preceded it. Tushnet speaks of the "rise of the activist state," which he contrasts with the "classical liberal state." In his view, the "activist state . . . is defined by

---

4. 3 CHI. J. INT'L L. 435 (2002).

the fact that it has affirmative obligations." This is the conventional understanding. But the conventional understanding is an unfortunate way of seeing the relevant categories. Most of the so-called negative rights require governmental assistance, not governmental abstention. Those rights cannot exist without public assistance. Consider, for example, the right to private property. As Bentham wrote, "Property and law are born together, and die together. Before laws were made there was no property; take away laws, and property ceases." In the state of nature, private property cannot exist, at least not in the way that it exists in a free society. In the state of nature, any property "rights" must be protected either through self-help—useful to the strong, not to the weak—or through social norms. This form of protection is far too fragile to support a market economy or indeed the basic independence of citizens. As we know it, private property is both created and protected by law; it requires extensive governmental assistance.

The same point holds for the other foundation of a market economy, the close sibling of private property: freedom of contract. For that form of freedom to exist, it is extremely important to have reliable enforcement mechanisms in the form of civil courts. The creation of such mechanisms requires action, not abstention. Nor is the point—the dependence of rights on public assistance—limited to the foundations of a market economy. Take, for example, the right to be free from torture and abuse, perhaps the defining "negative" freedom. Of course it is possible to say this right is a "negative" safeguard against public intrusion into the private domain. But as a practical matter, this right requires a state apparatus willing to ferret out and to punish the relevant rights violations. If the right includes protection against private depredations, it cannot exist simply with governmental abstention. If the right is limited to protection against public abuse of power, it can be satisfied by abstention; but in practice, abstention from torture and abuse must be guaranteed by a public apparatus that will deter and punish misconduct. Some rights require the government to protect against its own rights violations. If we go down the list of conventional private rights, we will see this same point at every turn.

There is a larger implication, with direct relevance to the question of social and economic rights. All constitutional rights have budgetary implications; all constitutional rights cost money. If the government plans to protect private property, it will have to expend resources to ensure against both private and public intrusions. If the government wants to protect people against unreasonable searches and seizures, it will have to expend resources to train, monitor, and discipline the police. If the government wants to protect freedom of speech, it must, at a minimum, take steps to constrain its own agents; and these steps will be costly. It follows that insofar as they are costly, social and economic rights are not unique.

Now it is possible that such rights are unusually costly. To ensure, for example, that everyone has housing, it will be necessary to spend more than must be spent to ensure that everyone is free from unreasonable searches and seizures. But any such comparisons are empirical and contingent; they cannot be made on an a priori basis. We could imagine a society in which it costs a great deal to protect private property, but not so much to ensure basic subsistence.

2. *State action is always present, and the real question involves the merits—the meaning of the relevant constitutional guarantees.* Much discussion of the state action question, and the "horizontal" application of constitutional norms, seems to me confused, because it disregards the extent to which the state is present in the arrangements under challenge.
* * *

NOTES AND QUESTIONS

1.   Constitutional law and "status quo neutrality." Sunstein argues that the assumptions of structural liberalism wrongly influence constitutional decision making. Elsewhere he has criticized what he calls "status quo neutrality":

> [T]he understanding that I mean to challenge defines neutrality by taking, as a given and as the baseline for decision, the status quo, or what various people and groups now have: existing distributions of property, income, legal entitlements, wealth, so-called natural assets, and preferences. A departure from the status quo signals partisanship; respect for the status quo signals neutrality. When government does not interfere with existing distributions, it is adhering to the neutrality requirement, and it rarely needs to justify its decision at all. When it disrupts existing arrangements, it is behaving partially, and is thus subject to constitutional doubt. Current rights of ownership are not seen as a product of law.
>
> Even more than this, the very categories of government "action" and "inaction" are given their content by the status quo. Courts answer the question whether government has acted by reference to existing practices and existing distributions. Decisions that upset those practices and distributions are treated as "action." Decisions that do not are perceived to stay close to nature and thus to amount to no action at all.

CASS R. SUNSTEIN, THE PARTIAL CONSTITUTION 3 (1993).

Is *DeShaney* a reflection of status quo neutrality? If Sunstein is correct that constitutional law should give no special protection to existing distributions, how should courts decide which acts of redistribution are legitimate?

2.   Structural liberalism in United States constitutional jurisprudence. Structural liberalism is reflected in United States constitutional jurisprudence in several ways. First, U.S. constitutional law guarantees rights to poor people but, with a few exceptions, not the financial ability to exercise those rights. *See, e.g.,* Harris v. McRae, 448 U.S. 297, 317–18 (1980) (no constitutional obligation to fund abortions even though the right to abortion is constitutionally protected); Lindsey v. Normet, 405 U.S. 56, 74 (1972) (no constitutional obligation to provide adequate housing); *see also Youngberg*, 457 U.S. at 317 ("As a general matter, a State is under no constitutional duty to provide substantive services for those within its borders"). A partial exception is the Supreme Court jurisprudence requiring state funding for the constitutional right to legal representation for indigent defendants. *But see* David Cole, "A Muted Trumpet," in No EQUAL JUSTICE: RACE AND CLASS IN THE AMERICAN CRIMINAL JUSTICE SYSTEM 63–95 (1999) (arguing that inadequate funding of this right leaves indigent defendants without effective protection from the power of the state).

Second, U.S. constitutional law treats legislative decisions with respect to social welfare as entitled to the greatest judicial deference: thus, although government decisions made on the basis of race and gender receive heightened constitutional scrutiny, government decisions made affecting poverty will be upheld as long as the Court can discern a real or imaginary "rational basis" for them. *See, e.g.,* Dandridge v. Williams, 397 U.S. 471 (1970); San Antonio Indep. Sch. Dist. v. Rodriguez, 411 U.S. 1, 28–29 (1973) (wealth is not a "suspect classification").

Third, U.S. constitutional law subjects legislative actions that alter or threaten to alter common law property rights to heightened scrutiny. *See, e.g.*, Pennsylvania Coal Co. v. Mahon, 260 U.S. 393 (1922) (establishing that government regulations can effect a "taking" of private property, triggering the right to compensation under the Fifth Amendment); RICHARD A. EPSTEIN, TAKINGS: PRIVATE PROPERTY AND THE POWER OF EMINENT DOMAIN (1985) (arguing for broad constitutional protection of existing private property rights). The law of "takings" is complex, however, reflecting the desire to defend state police power to redefine property rights as well as the desire to limit this power. *See* Frank I. Michelman, *Property, Utility, and Fairness: Comments on the Ethical Foundations of "Just Compensation" Law*, 80 HARV. L. REV. 1165 (1967); Stewart Sterk, *The Federalist Dimension of Regulatory Takings Jurisprudence*, 114 YALE L.J. 203 (2004).

In the New Deal period, the Supreme Court famously (or infamously) sought to give constitutional protection to contract rights, striking down labor legislation, price regulation, and restrictions on entry into business in the name of freedom of contract. *See, e.g.,* Lochner v. New York, 198 U.S. 45 (1905) (striking down state regulation of hours in the baking industry). The *"Lochner* era" came to an end with the Court's decision in *West Coast Hotel Co. v. Parrish*, 300 U.S. 379 (1937) (upholding a state law establishing a minimum wage for women). *Lochner* has been criticized by scholars as an attempt to entrench a libertarian or laissez-faire conception of markets and the role of government into the Constitution. *See* Cass R. Sunstein, Lochner's *Legacy*, 87 COLUM. L. REV. 873, 874–75 (1987); CASS R. SUNSTEIN, THE PARTIAL CONSTITUTION (1993). While the Supreme Court in *Lochner* sought to limit government power over markets in the name of economic liberty, the President and some national legislators sought to establish broad economic rights as foundations of the New Deal. See the excerpt from William Forbath, below.

Fourth, U.S. constitutional law limits the protection of constitutional rights to the "public" sphere. As *DeShaney* indicates, actions that occur in the "private" sphere of the family are not perceived as involving state action, even when the state has taken on the task of monitoring and regulating families. *See also* United States v. Morrison, 529 U.S. 598 (2000).

3. **Explaining the public/private distinction in United States constitutional law.** Why does the United States Constitution protect private property rights but not public social welfare rights? There are many responses to this question.

One response is doctrinal. As one casebook on constitutional law observes:

> The Constitution contains several provisions that expressly restrict government's power to interfere with market ordering and the private economic interests of individuals. The fifth and fourteenth amendments, for example, provide that "[n]o person shall [be] deprived of [property] without due process of law." Article I, section 10 provides that "[n]o State shall [pass] any [Law] impairing the Obligation of Contracts." And the fifth amendment provides that "private property" shall not "be taken for public use, without just compensation."

GEOFFREY R. STONE ET AL., CONSTITUTIONAL LAW 813 (3d ed. 1996).

In contrast, the Constitution does not contain any explicit social welfare rights.

A second response points to the structure of the Constitution, which creates procedural obstacles to the significant redistribution of wealth and power. Examining the *Federalist Papers* and James Madison's fear of the propertyless mob, Jennifer Nedelsky argues that "[t]he Framers' preoccupation with property generated a shallow conception of democracy and a system of institutions that allocates political power unequally and fails to foster political participation." JENNIFER NEDELSKY, PRIVATE PROPERTY AND THE LIMITS OF AMERICAN CONSTITUTIONALISM: THE MADISONIAN FRAMEWORK AND ITS LEGACY 1 (1990). The concern is that people without wealth and property are kept at arm's length from political power. Thus, Nedelsky writes, "When we try to understand why Americans, and particularly poor Americans, don't vote, we should remember that the basic structure of our institutions was not designed to encourage their participation." *Id.* at 215.

In a more tendentious vein, Charles Beard has argued that the U.S. Constitution was the product of "special interest" groups concerned to protect their economic privilege. CHARLES A. BEARD, AN ECONOMIC INTERPRETATION OF THE CONSTITUTION OF THE UNITED STATES (Transaction Publishers 1998) (1913). Beard notes that four groups were completely disfranchised from participation in the Constitutional Convention: slaves, indentured servants, men who could not qualify for voting under the property tests imposed by the state constitutions and laws, and women. BEARD, AN ECONOMIC INTERPRETATION OF THE CONSTITUTION OF THE UNITED STATES at 24. He then offers some further observations:

The movement for the Constitution of the United States was originated and carried through principally by four groups of personality interests which had been adversely affected under the Articles of Confederation: money, public securities, manufactures, and trade and shipping.

The first firm steps toward the formation of the Constitution were taken by a small and active group of men immediately interested through their personal possessions in the outcome of their labors.

No popular vote was taken directly or indirectly on the proposition to call the Convention which drafted the Constitution.

A large propertyless mass was, under the prevailing suffrage qualifications, excluded at the outset from participation (through representatives) in the work of framing the Constitution.

The members of the Philadelphia Convention which drafted the Constitution were, with a few exceptions, immediately, directly, and personally interested in, and derived economic advantages from, the establishment of the new system.

The Constitution was essentially an economic document based upon the concept that the fundamental private rights of property are anterior to government and morally beyond the reach of popular majorities.

The major portion of the members of the Convention are on record as recognizing the claim of property to a special and defensive position in the Constitution.

In the ratification of the Constitution, about three-fourths of the adult males failed to vote on the question, having abstained from the elections at which delegates to the state conventions were chosen, either on account of their indifference or their disfranchisement by property qualifications.

The Constitution was ratified by a vote of probably not more than one-sixth of the adult males.

Beard, An Economic Interpretation of the Constitution, supra at 324–25.

Most efforts at making the political process less beholden to economic interests have focused on strengthening campaign finance restrictions. Restrictions on corporate spending, for example, were the subject of *Austin v. Michigan Chamber of Commerce*, 494 U.S. 652 (1990). In that case the Supreme Court upheld a Michigan campaign finance law prohibiting corporations from using corporate treasury funds for independent expenditures in support of or in opposition to candidates in elections for state office. Justice Marshall wrote for the Court:

State law grants corporations special advantages—such as limited liability, perpetual life, and favorable treatment of the accumulation and distribution of assets—that enhance their ability to attract capital and to deploy their resources in ways that maximize the return on their shareholders' investments. These state-created advantages not only allow corporations to play a dominant role in the Nation's

> economy, but also permit them to use "resources amassed in the economic marketplace" to obtain "an unfair advantage in the political marketplace."

Austin, 494 U.S. at 658–59. This advantage was unfair, the Court explained further, because "[t]he resources in the treasury of a business corporation . . . are not an indication of popular support for the corporation's political ideas. They reflect instead the economically motivated decisions of investors and customers. The availability of these resources may make a corporation a formidable political presence, even though the power of the corporation may be no reflection of the power of its ideas." *Id.*, quoting FEC v. Massachusetts Citizens for Life, Inc., 479 U.S. 238, 258 (1986). For the *Austin* Court, the state's interest in curbing this unfair advantage in electoral politics was a compelling state interest overriding the First Amendment.

In Citizens United v. Federal Election Commission, 130 S.Ct. 876 (2010), however, the Court overruled *Austin,* and struck down a federal law prohibiting corporations and unions from using their general treasury funds to make independent expenditures for speech that was an "electioneering communication" or for speech that expressly advocated the election or defeat of a candidate. Writing for the Court, Justice Kennedy rejected the "anti-distortion" rationale that the *Austin* Court had upheld as a compelling state interest. The rule in *Austin,* according to the *Citizens United* Court, interfered with the "open marketplace" of ideas protected by the First Amendment. Justice Kennedy observed further:

> The censorship we now confront is vast in its reach. The Government has "muffle[d] the voices that best represent the most significant segments of the economy." And "the electorate [has been] deprived of information, knowledge and opinion vital to its function." By suppressing the speech of manifold corporations, both for-profit and nonprofit, the Government prevents their voices and viewpoints from reaching the public and advising voters on which persons or entities are hostile to their interests. Factions will necessarily form in our Republic, but the remedy of "destroying the liberty" of some factions is "worse than the disease." Factions should be checked by permitting them all to speak, and by entrusting the people to judge what is true and what is false.

Citizens United at *29 (citations omitted).

In dissent, Justice Stevens wrote:

> The conceit that corporations must be treated identically to natural persons in the political sphere is not only inaccurate but also inadequate to justify the Court's disposition of this case.

> In the context of election to public office, the distinction between corporate and human speakers is significant. Although they make enormous contributions to our society, corporations are not actually members of it. They cannot vote or run for office. Because they may be managed and controlled by nonresidents, their interests may conflict in

fundamental respects with the interests of eligible voters. The financial resources, legal structure, and instrumental orientation of corporations raise legitimate concerns about their role in the electoral process. Our lawmakers have a compelling constitutional basis, if not also a democratic duty, to take measures designed to guard against the potentially deleterious effects of corporate spending in local and national races.

Id. at *53 (Stevens, J., dissenting).

The Supreme Court's decision in *Buckley v. Valeo*, 424 U.S. 1 (1976), striking down limits on the amount a candidate may spend from personal or family funds as violative of the First Amendment, has also been a significant obstacle to campaign finance reform efforts. Critics of the decision in *Buckley* argue that the majority wrongly took the existing distribution of wealth as "natural." Thus, Cass Sunstein argues:

> We should view [*Buckley*] as the modern-day analogue of [*Lochner*]: a decision [that takes] the market status quo as just and prepolitical, and [uses it] to invalidate democratic efforts at reform. Reliance on [existing distributions] is [treated as] government neutrality.... [But] it should be clear that elections based on those distributions are ... subject to a regulatory system, made possible and constituted through law. That law consists, first, in legal rules protecting the present distribution of wealth, and more fundamentally, in legal rules allowing candidates to buy speech rights through markets.

Cass R. Sunstein, *Free Speech Now*, 59 U. Chi. L. Rev. 255, 291–92 (1992).

A third answer to the puzzle focuses on the contingencies of United States history. For example, Akhil Amar argues below that the constitutional revolution represented by Reconstruction should be understood as having fundamentally altered the allocation of social and economic rights. William Forbath suggests that the promise of economic reconstruction symbolized by the slogan "forty acres and a mule" was never fulfilled, however, because of repeated failures to completely dismantle racial subordination. *See* William E. Forbath, *Caste, Class, and Equal Citizenship*, 98 Mich. L. Rev. 1 (1999).

A fourth answer to the question why the U.S. Constitution protects common law property rights but not social welfare rights points to the centrality of ideology. American political ideology contains a strong libertarian strand, which stresses skepticism toward, if not fear of, "big government" and perceives a strong connection between freedom, property rights, and a weak national government. Consider the excerpt by Mary Ann Glendon, below, in this light. For an ideological analysis that examines the American focus on property rights as the key to individual liberty, *see* David Abraham, *Liberty Without Equality: The Property–Rights Connection in a "Negative Citizenship" Regime*, 21 Law & Soc. Inquiry 1 (1996).

3.   STRUCTURAL LIBERALISM IN "PRIVATE" LAW

Un–Making Law: The Classical Revival in the Common Law

28 SEATTLE U. L. REV. 1 (2004).

■ JAY M. FEINMAN

The common law—the law of contracts, torts, and property—is in the throes of a potentially remarkable transformation. The transformation is pervasive; many changes already have been adopted, more are in process, and still more have been proposed. If they all come to pass, the law will have experienced a once-in-a-century remaking. More precisely, we may be observing the "un-making" of law, to use Stephen Sugarman's phrase, as the principal common-law developments of the twentieth century are rolled back. In this sense, the changes are both radical and regressive, representing a classical revival, instituting in the twenty-first century common law a barely updated version of the classical law that reigned in the Gilded Age at the end of the nineteenth century. Even more broadly, the changes in the law and the vision that animates them are part of a more general transformation of American government and society.

This article describes the possibility of a classical revival in the common law and situates the revival in its historical context. * * *

* * * This remarkable fact is best understood in this context: The un-making of the common law is part of the effort by conservatives and business interests to elevate the market and diminish the government.

I.   ORIGINS: CLASSICAL LEGAL THOUGHT AND CRITIQUE

Contracts, torts, and property have ancient origins, but most of their history is barely relevant to understanding modern law. The story really begins with classical legal thought, the body of law usually seen as dominant from 1870 to 1920. * * * Classical legal thought is the thesis, and the combination of sociological jurisprudence, legal realism, and related Progressive ideas comprise a critique that is the antithesis of classicism. Thesis and antithesis are resolved to a considerable extent in the synthesis of modern law, the law that begins to take shape after World War II and achieves its mature form in the 1970s. Because in this resolution the critique supplemented and modified classical law but did not supplant it altogether, this modern body of law is often called "neoclassical law."

A.   Classical Law

Classical legal thought once was seen as the age of *Lochner*, in which a conservative bench and bar reformulated the law to serve the interests of the new corporate oligarchs. More recent scholarship has shown that picture to be incomplete or misleading; although the effects of classical jurisprudence may have served big business, the motivations of its authors were more complex, including the important development of an autonomous legal science and the preservation of traditional values against emerging monopoly capitalism. In any case, the inquiry here is less about causes and consequences and more about the body of classical law as a coherent whole against which later critics would react, the essential elements of which are being revived in our time. This section briefly summarizes the content, structure, and method of classical law.

[Thomas] Grey defines the three essential characteristics of classical legal thought:

> First, it must be *determinate*, its judgments following from the application of norms to facts, without the exercise of discretion or contestable judgment. Second, it must be *systematic*, forming a coherent structure of relatively abstract concepts and principles. Finally, it must be *autonomous*, deriving its norms from distinctively legal sources, rather than from the contestable claims of religion, philosophy, or political economy.

The substantive vision of classical legal thought is a world of independent individuals, each of whom acts within a broad sphere of legal autonomy to pursue his own self-interest. The role of government is precisely defined and narrowly circumscribed. The legislature has limited authority to regulate narrowly and traditionally defined harmful activities. The courts, applying a complete, coherent, and formal body of law, police the boundaries of legislative authority and define the ground rules for interaction among private individuals, namely, the rules of contract, tort, and property.

Classical contract law described a broad realm in which individuals could exercise their autonomy by consenting to agreements with other autonomous individuals. Individuals could accept the liability of an enforceable contract by exercising consent and could be free from liability unless consent had been exercised. The entire body of contract doctrine flowed from this single principle. * * *

While contract law defined a broad scope of individual autonomy, tort law encompassed a much narrower realm in which the law recognized liability for harm wrongfully committed. Tort liability, unlike contract liability, was not created by the consent of the parties, but neither was it imposed by the courts. Instead, tort law was corrective justice through which the law provided recompense when one person caused injury by invading the preexisting right to bodily security held by another person. For liability to be imposed, corrective justice required that the defendant must have been at fault and must have caused the injury. In classical tort law, each of these elements had a fixed meaning. * * *

The law of property was more of an agglomeration, because of its antique categories and doctrinal variety. Nevertheless, a core concept of classical property law developed. Blackstone's concept of property as "sole and despotic dominion" was dephysicalized and commodified. Where once property had largely been associated with land, the generalization of the market in classical law led to an understanding of property as "everything which has exchangeable value," as Justice Swayne wrote in dissent in the *Slaughterhouse Cases*. Property was defined by the ability to be exchanged, and the purpose of property was to be exchanged. An individual's right to own property included the creation, exchange, and accumulation of wealth of all kinds, from dynastic trusts to corporate wealth. The state could control property rights only in limited ways, under traditional doctrines and consistent with the ability of an owner to realize the value of property; classical property law "sanctioned capitalist accumulation, the starkest sort of property-as-wealth . . . and it created a large private domain of unregulated and unregulatable market activity."

The classical ideal was realized through a rigid structure that drew sharp distinctions between realms of authority and areas of law. First, public law was distinguished from private law. Public law encompassed the area in which the legislature could legitimately exercise its regulatory and coercive authority—the police power. Private law, by contrast, was defined and governed by individual rights to own property, to contract, and to take any other action that did not invade the rights of other persons. Because its content flowed from legal rights, private law did not require the kinds of policy choices that the legislature made in public law. Second, within private law, clear lines were drawn between contracts, torts, and property. Each subject had a proper sphere of authority, defined by the subjects' respective organizing principles of consent, fault, and ownership.

In exercising the police power, the legislature could consider political and distributive concerns, so that legislative choice was, in a technical sense, unprincipled. Courts, by contrast, were nonpolitical institutions that did not exercise discretion or make political judgments. They could maintain this posture by applying the distinctive decisional method of formal legal reasoning. A court engaged in legal reasoning began with the few basic propositions that lay at the heart of the common law, such as "an exercise of consent creates a contract;" sometimes these principles were obvious, while in other instances they were defined by induction from an examination of cases. Judges then used inexorable, deductive logic to generate narrower doctrinal rules and decisions in individual cases, all of which were merely specific instances of the basic propositions. Any preexisting rules or decided cases that did not conform to the derived logic were discarded. The task was made simpler by devices such as the prevalence of binary categories. A statement was either a manifestation of willingness to enter into a bargain sufficient to constitute an offer or it was not; there was no intermediate category of, say, a promise which could be relied on even though it was not an offer.

For some, of whom Langdell was the most notable, the primary attraction of classical legal reasoning was its claim to be a scientific method, an application of the rigorous, logical process of induction and deduction that simultaneously developed in the natural and social sciences. For others, the primary attraction of the classical method was political, in the sense that it guaranteed that rights would be defined and protected without the exercise of potentially redistributive choice by the courts.

B. The Critique of Classical Law

The critique of classical legal thought began almost at the moment of classical thought's creation. In *The Common Law* in 1881, Holmes was the theorist and objectivist who outlined much of the structure and content of classical law even as he rejected its conceptualist method. By the late 1890s, in "Privilege, Malice, and Intent" and "The Path of the Law," as pragmatist, skeptic, and empiricist Holmes had begun the process of undermining classical law's integrity.

Holmes was followed by successive waves of pragmatists, Progressives, sociological jurisprudents, and legal realists through the 1930s who revealed in detail the weaknesses of classical law. The divergence in intellectual approach and political orientation among the critics was great. The dispute between Roscoe Pound and Karl Llewellyn is the most famous, but any movement, or even succession of movements, that includes Cardozo, Frank, Corbin, Moore, Sturges, and Fuller will be very diverse. What each of these critics minimally shared was distaste for at least some elements of classical thought, commonly the grand classical claims to abstraction, autonomy, and rigor.

From the perspective of the subsequent developments, a useful entry point in seeing how classical law collapsed is by examining the most arcane, scholastic effort at critique of the twentieth century. Wesley Newcomb Hohfeld attempted to construct a new taxonomy of legal relationships in his exquisite tables of "Jural Correlatives" and "Jural Opposites," but the destructive effect of his work was more important than the reconstruction. Hohfeld explained that general concepts such as ownership were descriptive rather than normative, that they were in fact composed of many different legal relations, and that the concepts were two-sided, so that obligation rather than entitlement could be described as the basis of legal relationships. To say that one owns property, for example, simply summarizes a set of legal relationships between the owner and non-owners. The relationships can be specified more precisely, as in the right to exclude and the privilege to enter, or the relationships can be reversed, focusing on the obligations they impose on the non-owner rather than the benefits they bestow on the owner; a duty to not trespass is the consequence of a right to exclude. The lawyer economist Robert Hale applied and contextualized the analysis, dissecting "liberty," "property," "freedom," and "coercion" to show that these concepts represented the exercise of legal power, not the absence of it, and so lacked the axiomatic content ascribed to them by classical law. Property, for example, consisted of a set of Hohfeldian interests that enabled an owner to exercise the power of the state in withholding access to the property from others unless they bargained on his terms. "The law has delegated to him a discretionary power over the rights and duties of others." Similarly, bargains are not free contracts but rather mutual coercions set against a background of market inequality established by legal entitlements. By the time the critique had crested in 1930, Felix Cohen would summarize much of the classical method as "transcendental non-sense," or the use of such empty concepts to reach circular results.

Under this view, courts in common-law cases were engaged in the allocation of rights, not the application of rights, and in that respect they were as much public law entities engaged in distributional judgments as the legislature. Contract, property, and tort law all necessarily involve discretion in imposing legal liability. Nor could the discretion be vitiated by a formal, rule-based body of doctrine, because the traditional concepts were incapable of providing that degree of formality. The inadequacy of language and the complexity of facts made the ideal unrealizable; rules could not be both precise and comprehensive, so judges, not rules, decided the cases. Therefore the public-private distinction in general and the organizing principles of the common law subjects in particular were incapable of carrying the weight the classicists attributed to them.

If the common law involved policy choices, its individualist, market-oriented principles were at least incomplete, if not invalid. The critics offered to supplement or replace those principles from two directions. The first direction, grounded in their scientific and functionalist bent, was empirical. Law ought to attend to the realities of the world, complex as they might be. The principles of individualism and the market were found wanting when tested against the circumstances of lack of personal choice in an imperfect world, concentrations of economic power, and networks of social relations. The second direction, grounded as much in the critics' Progressive politics as in their academic approach, focused on the collectivist concern of social welfare as an antidote to excessive individualism. Here, too, concern for instrumental policymaking to achieve Progressive social objectives required departure from the classical ideal. In each of the subjects, the critique demonstrated that the classical method and substance needed to be discarded in favor of a more complex, functional analysis.

* * *

C. The Critique Consolidated

The critique of classical legal thought flourished in the 1920s and early 1930s, undermining the classical claims to abstraction, coherence, and autonomy. The critique initially had its greatest impact in the legal academy, but it also made its way into the mainstream of the law. * * *

* * *

The core concept of classical law was individual autonomy, derived from abstract principle and embodied in the right to own property, the right to contract, and the right to act without being subject to unwarranted tort liability. The critique demonstrated that the concept of autonomy was at best incomplete and at worst illusory. Neoclassical law began by balancing individual autonomy and non-individualist considerations of social welfare. Neoclassical tort law, for example, merged corrective justice principles in an individual case with social interests in compensation and accident prevention.

A particularly important area for this balancing is the market. Market transactions in the real world are often not characterized by the exercise of autonomy, but are plagued by inequality and market failures. For example, the market may not provide low-income workers and consumers with meaningful choices to realize basic human needs. Moreover, the market is not the measure of all things. Non-market values such as community, collective responsibility, and protection of the disadvantaged also are important. Accordingly, the law regulates and intervenes in market transactions. Contract law, for example, balances assent with fairness norms derived from commercial practice and from the broader society. Under neoclassical law, this approach was unavoidable. Law constructs social relations, including market relations, through its doctrines, by prescribing terms of ownership and exchange. Therefore, law is necessarily constitutive and regulatory.

Neoclassical courts had to immerse themselves in the world they regulated. In the decision of individual cases, courts need to construct detailed accounts of the events and context to reach proper conclusions. Each case is also representative of a larger area of social process, and courts, now engaged overtly in regulating that social process, need a broad understanding of it. Once engaged in that kind of detailed contextual inquiry, potentially in every case and actually in many cases, courts are faced with choices about social policy. Courts as much as legislatures necessarily and appropriately engage in policymaking when they formulate and apply doctrine, typically in the form of vague standards that leave play for contextual and policy inquiries in future cases. For example, where the original Restatements were typically cast as syllogistic rules, the second Restatements are replete with standards made up of "factors to be considered."

Therefore, by the 1970s, the full effects of the critique, in revised form, were finally felt in the law. The generalization of negligence and the rise of products liability in torts, consumerism and the adoption of flexible rules in contracts, and a regulatory property law best exemplified by the revolution in landlord-tenant law, created in a mature form the kind of law for which the critics of classicism, in their reformist mode, had been striving. The second round of Restatements solidified many of the developments. By 1980, neoclassical law had arrived.

II.   The Transformation of Contract, Tort, and Property Law

The contemporary changes adopted, underway, and proposed in the common law subjects are diverse and broad-ranging, but they share a common core. Despite a century of critique and neoclassical development, the changes attempt to revive elements of the classical common law. This part highlights some of the most significant developments in each of the subjects.

A.   Contract Law

Two major developments in neoclassical contract law were the contextualization of previously abstract doctrine and the recognition of the necessity of regulating market transactions. In the 1960s and 1970s, these developments culminated in a wave of progressive legislation and well-known judicial decisions. Statutes such as the Uniform Commercial Code and the Truth in Lending Act mandated more disclosure of contract terms. The U.C.C. also expanded formation doctrines. A contract could be found based on the bargain in fact, even though the moment of its formation was undetermined and previously essential terms such as price and quantity were missing. Courts also expanded on the process of contract interpretation; insurance contracts in particular were interpreted according to the reasonable expectations of the subordinate party, and a relaxed parol evidence rule undermined the primacy of written agreements. Courts also recognized the full complexity of contractual settings; promissory estoppel expanded to provide a remedy for reliance (and, arguably, even reasonable expectations without reliance) created by promises that failed the traditional standards of assent and consideration. And courts felt free to review the fairness of contracts, especially between parties of unequal bargaining power; unconscionability enabled courts to strike down oppressive contract terms, from the cross-collateral clause in a consumer installment sale in *Williams v. Walker–Thomas Furniture Co.* to the arbitration provision signed by an experienced concert promoter in *Graham v. Scissor Tail, Inc.*

The classical revival challenges these developments, arguing that the law has departed from the core principle governing contract law: Courts should simply enforce the contracts people make. In this view, neoclassical contract law makes two mistakes.

First, it diminishes personal freedom, of which freedom of contract is an essential element in a market economy. As Judge Kozinski of the Ninth Circuit writes,

> Perhaps most troubling, the willingness of courts to subordinate voluntary contractual arrangements to their own sense of public policy and proper business decorum deprives individuals of an important measure of freedom. The right to enter into contracts—to adjust one's legal relationships by mutual agreement with other free individuals—was unknown through much of history and is unknown even today in many parts of the world. Like other aspects of personal autonomy, it is too easily smothered by government officials eager to tell us what's best for us.

Second, because parties are the best judges of their own interest, and because the market, left to its own devices, will produce the best results for society, detrimental results are likely to happen when courts interfere with contracts. Richard Epstein explains the superiority of the enforcement of contracts over legal intervention:

> [Contract] law can facilitate (not compel, but facilitate) sizable productive interactions which will continue to expand over time and transactions until they embrace all individuals who possess the minimum capacity to engage in contracting at all. The system goes forward in a benevolent fashion because the exchanges are mutually beneficial.... The background knowledge of the uniform incentives moving self interested parties is a more reliable guide to their interests than any public vetting of their deal.

The solution to these problems is to revert to a simple model of contract based on an ideal market, strictly enforcing the bargains that parties make, not reading beyond the four corners of a document in enforcing a contract, and certainly not evaluating the bargains for fairness. The model is so simple that it can ignore the complexities of the modern world. * * *

As a result, law under the classical revival emphasizes abstraction over contextualization. In general, this means less attention to the factual details of a particular case or of the class of cases of which it is representative and more attention to the complexities of real-world contracting as a means of better understanding and regulating the parties' contract. Contract law also becomes more abstract in a particular way. The process of abstraction moves the principles of contract to more closely resemble those of an ideal market, and the market model achieves primacy as the source of contract doctrine.

Under the classical revival, formality reigns at two levels. First, the contract doctrine itself becomes more formal; ostensibly clear, rigid rules are favored over flexible standards. Second, the substance of the rules favors formality in contracting practices. Written contracts (including standard form contracts) are favored over oral contracts; the interpretation of contracts looks primarily to their plain meaning; and parties are given great freedom to define the terms of their relationships without examination or intervention by the law. The practical consequence of the implementation of this vision is that businesses can use contract law more effectively to control relationships with their customers and employees because they can more easily dictate the terms of dealing, avoid being legally bound except on their own terms, avoid review by the courts of the fairness of those terms, and control how disputes are resolved under their contracts. The sections that follow illustrate the principles and their consequences by discussing formation doctrines, including approaches to form contracts and rolling contracts; the decline of reliance; the parol evidence rule; and the enforcement of mandatory arbitration clauses.

* * *

A useful summary of the structure of the classical revival is provided by an article by William Powers, Jr., *Border Wars*, 72 TEX. L. REV. 1209, 1210–11 (1994), in which Powers discusses the bad faith tort in the context of the larger "border wars" between contract law and tort law. Powers defines the "basic paradigms" of private law, each of which has a "prime directive" or central organizing principle:

- The tort or negligence paradigm reflects the basic norm that people should act reasonably under the circumstances. If people do not act reasonably, this norm demands that they should then compensate those whom they foreseeably injure. . . .

- [T]he property paradigm gives individuals entitlements to do as they please with their own property. . . .

- The contract paradigm expresses the basic norm that individuals should be able to agree between and among themselves how to allocate resources. Contract law does not itself give entitlements or independently evaluate the reasonableness of each party's conduct; instead, it establishes a structure within which individuals can voluntarily bargain and reach their own agreements.

Each paradigm assigns authority for development of the content of the law to a different institution. The contract and property paradigms assign responsibility to individuals through actions in the private market. Tort, on the other hand, assigns power to courts and juries.

When the paradigms potentially overlap, conflicts between them can be resolved by a resort to their purposes, which are reflected in the structure of the common law under the classical revival. * * *

* * *

2. Method

The challenges to neoclassical private law include a new orientation to legal method as well as to substance and structure. The method is more formal than neoclassical law, and there has been much academic discussion of this "new formalism" in both public and private law. But formalism is too broad a term to capture what is going on in the new approach to legal method.

Classical legal thought defined the problem of legal method as keeping legal reasoning (the decision from legal doctrine, as done in courts) distinct from policy-oriented legislative reasoning. Classical law resolved this problem through a legal method that was autonomous and determinate: courts could deductively apply legal rules and principles without regard for their social consequences to produce certain results in particular cases. The critique of classical legal thought undermined the claims of autonomy and determinacy. Critics demonstrated that the classical structure, principles, and method were inadequate to the task of producing a formal legal system. Courts necessarily engaged in the allocation of rights, not just the application of rights, and so were engaged in the making of public policy.

Some of the most policy-oriented of the critics were unconcerned by this similarity and urged the courts to embrace a legislative role. But that path was too extreme for most legal scholars, ordinary judges, and lawyers and, ultimately, the social and political environment in which they operated. Accordingly, as neoclassical law matured it developed a distinctive legal method that preserved a role for doctrine and a relatively autonomous legal method. Under neoclassical law, ordinary cases are handled by a deductive method in which doctrinal principles are applied straightforwardly to sets of facts. The principles are adequate for ordinary cases, but not for unusual cases, and it is recognized that even in the ordinary cases their application is always provisional. The principles are based on policy, they are typically cast as standards rather than rules, and they require detailed factual determinations, all of which leaves considerable but not unlimited room for judicial discretion.

The classical revival rejects the neoclassical resolution of the problem of legal method. It attempts to solve the problem by reinstating elements of the classical approach in a revised form—an "anti-antiformalism"—it being not so much classical formalism as a formalist reaction to the critique and its neoclassical progeny.

This method has its roots in the substance of the classical revival. The core of the substance is an idealized market in which autonomous individuals contract to maximize their wealth. This resembles the classical ideal of the market, but it gives more room for state intervention to maintain the conditions under which the market can operate by enforcing legal rules that support the market and, to a very limited extent, to correct market failures and provide remedies in non-market transactions.

This substance has methodological consequences. First, there is a preference for determinate rules over standards. Rules clarify the rights and obligations of market participants; this facilitates market transactions by enabling parties to plan more effectively and by reducing the opportunities for judicial interference. Second, the rules are such that they require less extensive factual inquiry. In particular cases, courts may engage in considerable discussion of the facts, but the purpose of doing so is to provide, as it were, the middle term of a syllogism: if certain facts are present, then a result follows from the rule. This contrasts with neoclassical law, in which fact finding serves as part of the balancing process in the application of a standard and as a basis for policy making in the formulation of rules, subrules, and exceptions to rules.

These forms of rule preference permit a relatively effective deductive process to operate at several levels. Rules are derived from market principles, sub rules are derived from more general rules, and individual results are derived from the sub rules. As a result, courts have less discretion in defining rules of law and juries have less discretion in applying them.

So far this description resembles the method of classical legal thought, with a shift in emphasis from rights derived from abstract, quasi-natural principle to rights derived from the ideal market. But there is an important difference. Policy was largely absent in classical law, but after decades of critique and neoclassical law, it is hard for the challenge to neoclassical law to forsake that development entirely. Policy is part of the challenge, but in particular ways.

First, the policy arguments are constrained by the market-oriented substance. Neoclassical law embodied a conflict of policies, which can be captured as market versus non-market or individualist versus collectivist; that is what made it neoclassical. Not so in the current challenges; the policies argued are substantially weighted in support of the ideal market. If neoclassical policy argument reflects a form of pluralist, interest group politics, the policy argument of its challengers reflects a kind of universalism or social absolutism, in which only market concerns deserve substantial weight because they benefit everyone.

Second, policy tends to be applied wholesale rather than retail. In neoclassical law, policy arguments were applied quite particularly, on individual issues of doctrine. In the recent challenges, the tendency is more to make policy arguments in support of market solutions generally, and the arguments simply resonate at the level of particular doctrinal issues. This is formalist reasoning in the sense that the market norms are presumed to generate sub-rules in a relatively direct fashion and with particular results. Grey nicely sums up this element of the new formalism as "treating doctrinal elaboration as a search for coherent structures of general concepts and principles, rather than as a process of gap-filling sublegislation ancillary to particularized dispute resolution."

III. CONCLUSION: THE CLASSICAL REVIVAL IN CONTEXT

Grant Gilmore famously remarked that there are alternating tides in law, just as in art, architecture, music, and fashion—classicism to romanticism, formality to flexibility, and back again. One might consider the changes in the common law to be little more than a reflection of political fashion in the current, more conservative era that follows the liberalism of the 1960s and 1970s. In context, however, the classical revival is remarkable.

In historical context, the revival represents a conceptual regress. Despite alternating styles, law has generally been assumed to progress over time. Rules and decisions will always be inadequate and mistakes will always be made, but at least they will be new mistakes, not repetitions of past errors. The appropriate metaphor for legal development is a spiral, back and forth but continually upward. The classical revival, in its reinstatement of an ostensible formality and reliance on principles assumed to be fundamental, simply updates positions that the critique of classical legal thought demonstrated to be flawed almost a century ago. The movement is radical, not conservative, in rejecting that demonstration. Justice Scalia asserts that there are categorical rules of property; Hohfeld knew better in 1917. Tort reformers argue for a simple principle of fault as the basis of personal injury law; Leon Green showed in 1928 that no simple principle existed. Judge Alex Kozinski claims that we need to restore the "sanctity of contract;" Robert Hale explained why that was a bankrupt concept in 1943. Professor Epstein states there are simple rules that can govern a complex world; Hohfeld, Green, Hale, and other scholars, and Benjamin Cardozo, Roger Traynor, and scores of other judges have known better for generations.

This error is puzzling as an intellectual matter, but its origins are very clear if the classical revival is seen in its contemporary context. The unmaking of the common law is consistent with the contemporary campaign by political conservatives and business interests to reshape American government, law, and society.

Ronald Reagan proclaimed the principal item on the agenda of this campaign most baldly in his first inaugural address: "Government is not the solution to our problems; government is the problem." If government is the problem, then the solution is to reduce the reach of government. Anti-tax activist Grover Norquist declared the movement's ambition to be cutting the size of federal, state, and local government in half, to "get it down to the size where we can drown it in the bathtub." Many government programs can be reduced or eliminated altogether; others will be cut by shifting responsibility from the federal government to the states and from government to the market. Publicly supported retirement and health care will be replaced by private investment accounts instead of Social Security and HMOs and private prescription insurance instead of Medicare. Public support of education will be replaced by voucher-funded school choice. Public welfare, already reformed "as we know it" under centrist Democrat Bill Clinton, will be supplanted by voluntary, faith-based initiatives. Tax cuts will starve government across the board.

In this vision, government is the problem because it interferes with individual freedom, particularly the individual freedom to pursue self-interest through the market. Conservatives idealize and worship the market as the single social institution that produces efficient, just, and democratic results: "One market under God," as Thomas Frank has styled it.

The master narrative of the vision of market centrality is Reagan-esque: Once upon a time there was a golden age when a man (always a man) could stand on his own two feet, his rights inviolate. Individual liberty, personal responsibility, and economic opportunity were the foundations of American life. Society was organized and controlled by two institutions: the market and the state. The market was primary; through it, people could maximize their potential, realize their dreams, and rise or fall on their own merits. The state was subordinate; beyond its minimal functions of guaranteeing physical security, providing public goods, and protecting individual rights, government offered only the possibility of unwise and pernicious interference in the social order created by the market.

The narrative is hardly new or unique. Judge Posner traces the ideology's roots to the classical liberalism of John Stuart Mill:

> [T]he government's role is to provide an unobtrusive framework for private activities. Government provides certain goods, such as national defense and (in some versions) education, that private markets will not provide in sufficient quantities. But beyond that it merely protects a handful of entitlements (property rights and some personal liberties) that are necessary to prevent markets from not working at all or from running off the rails.

But the breadth of the market fervor in the modern conservative era is striking. "More than anything else," said Reagan, "I want to see the United States remain a country where someone can get rich." In this narrative, the ideal state of affairs was corrupted by liberal politicians and judges who expanded the role of government and thereby disrupted the natural and just order of things. When government spread beyond its proper role of protecting individual rights and preserving market competition through fixed rules known in advance, it began down "The Road to Serfdom," as Austrian economist Friedrich Hayek entitled his 1944 book which became an instant best-seller in the United States.

The mainstream discourse of conservatism seldom makes explicit the place of the common law in this picture, but a vision of the common law is central to the conservative ideology, and the conservative ideology is central to contemporary changes in the common law. The ideal of individual freedom and limited government and the classical revival conceptions of property, contract, and tort law are mutually reinforcing. The protection of absolute private property is "the foundation from which America's prosperity was launched." The "sanctity of contract" also is a condition of freedom, according to Judge Kozinski. The role of courts, therefore, is simply to enforce the contracts the parties appear to have made, not to assess their reasonableness or fairness: "Like other aspects of personal autonomy, [freedom of contract] is too easily smothered by government officials eager to tell us what's best for us." Tort law supplements property and contract law in the relatively few cases of wrongful acts that cause injury. The Reagan Administration's Tort Policy Working Group called fault "the only vehicle in tort law capable of distinguishing wrongful (or undesirable) from beneficial (or desirable) conduct," but the fault principle has been corrupted by activist judges and grasping lawyers.

The radical conservative, business-oriented agenda in property, contract, and tort law fits well with the broader ideology of individualism and the free market. This ideology also promotes an understanding of the common law as nonpolitical. The common law is portrayed exclusively as a realm of corrective justice, righting wrongs between individuals according to objective principles of law, as contrasted with the political choices made in electoral politics and in legislation. In this understanding, the choice of common-law rules that favor the conservative conception of private property, freedom of contract, and limited tort law is not a political choice; indeed, it is hardly a choice at all. Instead, the substance of the common law and the process of judicial decision-making reside as a neutral background against which "real" political conflicts are played out. The common law, like the interstate highway system, is simply part of the natural, nonpolitical infrastructure of society. In this way, conservatives attempt to withdraw from the realm of politics the allocation of economic, political, and social values by the common law.

But like the interstate highway system, the conservative vision of the common law is neither natural nor nonpolitical. Instead, it furthers the economic interests of big business and the political interests of conservative politicians, and it promotes an ideology in support of those interests. Contemporary conservatives are "rolling back the twentieth century," returning America to the Gilded Age, with George W. Bush playing the part of William McKinley. Classical legal thought reigned in the Gilded Age, and the classical revival in the common law presents the same challenge to what throughout the twentieth century became the mainstream of American law as conservatism generally presents to the mainstream of American government.

NOTES AND QUESTIONS

1. Historical origins of structural liberalism. Legal scholar Bernard Harcourt traces structural liberalism to eighteenth-century French political economists François Quesnay, the Marquis of Mirabeau, Dupont de Nemours, Le Mercier de Rivière, and others. Harcourt credits these thinkers with the idea of "natural order": "the notion of an economic system that is autonomous and achieves equilibrium *without government intervention.*" Bernard E. Harcourt, "Neoliberal Penality: The Birth of Natural Order, the Illusion of Free Markets," John M. Olin Law & Economics Working Paper No. 433, Public Law and Legal Theory Working Paper No. 238, p.26, available at http://ssrn.com/abstract=1278067 (September 2008). Harcourt argues further:

> It is the idea of *natural order* that renders coherent and makes possible the belief in self-adjusting and self-sustaining markets. The idea of self-stabilizing internal flows that function best when left alone—this conceptualization of natural orderliness, of spontaneous equilibrium, of natural harmony in the economic realm, is what allowed eighteenth century thinkers to reimagine social reality, and it is what facilitates the understanding we have today.

Id. (italics in original).

> By 1776, Harcourt argues:

> Natural order reigned in the economic domain—in agriculture and commerce—and thereby obviated the need for "police." The sphere of public economy came to be viewed as an autonomous, self-adjusting system regulated by natural laws that, if left alone, produced a *net product.* The only way for the state to participate in the wealth of the nation was not to administer and police, but instead to pull out of the sphere of agricultural production and stop intervening in commerce and trade.

Id. at 31–32. Harcourt asserts, "The same notion resurfaces in the work of Adam Smith and Jeremy Bentham, and, today, in the work of contemporary neoliberal thinkers, such as Richard Posner or Richard Epstein." *Id.* at 34. At the same time, Harcourt argues, the idea of natural order "leads inexorably to a penal sphere that is, on the one hand, marginalized, but on the other hand unleashed and allowed to expand without any limitation. Since some men's passions are out-of-order and these men cannot appreciate the natural order, the legal despot has full and unlimited discretion to repress and punish. Man-made, positive law serves only one legitimate function: to punish those who violate the natural order." *Id.* at 37. Thus, for Harcourt the modern criminal justice system, invested heavily in discipline and punishment, is the flip side of economic laissez-faire.

2.   The Chicago School and neoliberalism. If structural liberalism has deep historical roots, Jay Feinman nevertheless points to President Ronald Reagan, first elected in 1980, as a key promoter of the "classical revival." Bernard Harcourt similarly identifies the 1980s as an important historical moment in the evolution of what he calls "neoliberalism," but he finds an intellectual source: the "Chicago School" of economics, founded by Milton Friedman and George Stigler.

> For the educated reader of the *New York Times*, the tenets of the Chicago School are usefully summarized by the economics columnist, David Leonhardt, in the following terms: "The Chicago School believes that markets—that is, millions of individuals making separate decisions—almost always function better than economies managed by governments. In a market system, prices adjust whenever there is a shortage or a glut, and the problem soon resolves itself. Just as important, companies constantly compete with each other, which helps bring down prices, improves the quality of goods, and ultimately lifts living standards." * * *

> In contrast to the more extreme rhetoric of the Chicago School—for instance, the argument that the free market is practically always more efficient—market liberals suggest that government intervention tends to be less efficient; that it is generally the case that market mechanisms work better, in part because of lower transaction costs, but also because market participants are better information gatherers and tend to be more invested in the ultimate outcome; and that government agencies suffer from greater principal-agent problems, are less nimble at adjusting to changing market conditions, and become more entrenched and subject to interest group capture. These are familiar arguments and, together, they tend to promote a loose default position that favors market mechanisms over "regulation"—a tilt in favor of markets.

Bernard E. Harcourt, *id*. at 14, 15. We will examine the Chicago School, and its critics, more closely in chapters 3 and 4.

3.   Free markets as an article of faith? Harcourt notes that belief in the virtue of free markets is proclaimed by nearly all public figures in the United States, as well as by ordinary citizens responding to pollsters in the United States.

> In a Financial Times/Harris Poll opinion poll conducted September 6 and 17, 2009, 49% of respondents in the United States answered affirmatively—in contrast to 17% who responded negatively—to the question "Do you think a free-market, capitalist economy (an economic system in which prices and wages are determined by unrestricted competition between businesses, with limited government regulation or fear of monopolies) is the best economic system or not?" In another poll, a twenty-nation poll conducted by the Program on International Policy Attitudes (PIPA) at the University of Maryland, researchers found that an average of 71% of respondents in the United States agree with the statement that "The free enterprise system and free

market economy is the best system on which to base the future of the world;'' only 24% of respondents disagreed with that statement.''

Id. at 16. Do you think that the Great Recession has changed these poll numbers?

B.   RESTRUCTURING STRUCTURAL LIBERALISM

As Sunstein and others argue, the U.S. Constitution's allocation of rights is not the only possible allocation. The United Nations International Covenant on Economic, Social and Cultural Rights represents a different approach. As the Glendon excerpt below suggests, the United States Constitution predates the Covenant, but more recently written constitutions, such as the Constitution of South Africa, show the influence of the Covenant. Compare the South African Constitution, excerpted below, to the United States Constitution and to the Covenant.

The United States also has a ''social citizenship'' tradition. Consider the speech by President Franklin D. Roosevelt below, along with the commentary by William Forbath.

International Covenant on Economic, Social and Cultural Rights

United Nations.

Article 6

1.   The States Parties to the present Covenant recognize the right to work, which includes the right of everyone to the opportunity to gain his living by work which he freely chooses or accepts, and will take appropriate steps to safeguard this right.

2.   The steps to be taken by a State Party to the present Covenant to achieve the full realization of this right shall include technical and vocational guidance and training programmes, policies and techniques to achieve steady economic, social and cultural development and full and productive employment under conditions safeguarding fundamental political and economic freedoms to the individual.

Article 7

The States Parties to the present Covenant recognize the right of everyone to the enjoyment of just and favourable conditions of work which ensure, in particular:

(a) Remuneration which provides all workers, as a minimum, with:

(i) Fair wages and equal remuneration for work of equal value without distinction of any kind, in particular women being guaranteed conditions of work not inferior to those enjoyed by men, with equal pay for equal work;

(ii) A decent living for themselves and their families in accordance with the provisions of the present Covenant;

(b) Safe and healthy working conditions;

(c) Equal opportunity for everyone to be promoted in his employment to an appropriate higher level, subject to no considerations other than those of seniority and competence;

(d) Rest, leisure and reasonable limitation of working hours and periodic holidays with pay, as well as remuneration for public holidays. * * *

ARTICLE 8

1.   The States Parties to the present Covenant undertake to ensure:

(a) The right of everyone to form trade unions and join the trade union of his choice.* * *

ARTICLE 9

The States Parties to the present Covenant recognize the right of everyone to social security, including social insurance. * * *

ARTICLE 11

1.   The States Parties to the present Covenant recognize the right of everyone to an adequate standard of living for himself and his family, including adequate food, clothing and housing, and to the continuous improvement of living conditions. * * *

2.   The States Parties to the present Covenant, recognizing the fundamental right of everyone to be free from hunger, shall take, individually and through international cooperation, the measures, including specific programmes, which are needed:

(a) To improve methods of production, conservation and distribution of food by making full use of technical and scientific knowledge, by disseminating knowledge of the principles of nutrition and by developing or reforming agrarian systems in such a way as to achieve the most efficient development and utilization of natural resources;

(b) Taking into account the problems of both food-importing and food-exporting countries, to ensure an equitable distribution of world food supplies in relation to need.* * *

ARTICLE 13

1.   The States Parties to the present Covenant recognize the right of everyone to education. They agree that education shall be directed to the full development of the human personality and the sense of its dignity, and shall strengthen the respect for human rights and fundamental freedoms. They further agree that education shall enable all persons to participate effectively in a free society, promote understanding, tolerance and friend-

ship among all nations and all racial, ethnic or religious groups, and further the activities of the United Nations for the maintenance of peace.

2. The States Parties to the present Covenant recognize that, with a view to achieving the full realization of this right:

(a) Primary education shall be compulsory and available free to all;

(b) Secondary education in its different forms, including technical and vocational secondary education, shall be made generally available and accessible to all by every appropriate means, and in particular by the progressive introduction of free education;

(c) Higher education shall be made equally accessible to all, on the basis of capacity, by every appropriate means, and in particular by the progressive introduction of free education;

(d) Fundamental education shall be encouraged or intensified as far as possible for those persons who have not received or completed the whole period of their primary education;

(e) The development of a system of schools at all levels shall be actively pursued, an adequate fellowship system shall be established, and the material conditions of teaching staff shall be continuously improved.

* * *

Rights in Twentieth–Century Constitutions

59 U. CHI. L. REV. 519, 523–26, 535–36 (1992).

■ MARY ANN GLENDON

A renowned European legal historian recently compiled a list he described as representing the "basic inventory" of rights that have been accepted by "most western countries" at the present time. The list includes, first and foremost; human dignity; then personal freedom; fair procedures to protect against arbitrary governmental action; active political rights (especially the right to vote); equality before the law; and society's responsibility for the social and economic conditions of its members. An American reader of this list is apt to be struck both by the omission of property rights, and by the inclusion of affirmative welfare obligations. Yet the list cannot be faulted as description of the law on the books of "most western countries." Welfare rights (or responsibilities) have become a staple feature of post-war international declarations and have been accorded a place beside traditional political and civil liberties in the national constitutions of most liberal democracies. It is the eighteenth-century American Constitution that, with the passage of time, has become anomalous in this respect.

As Gerhard Casper has pointed out, these differences regarding the rights that are accorded constitutional status in various countries are not merely a function of the age of the documents establishing those rights. To a great extent, the differences are legal manifestations of divergent, and deeply rooted, cultural attitudes toward the state and its functions. Historically, even eighteenth- and nineteenth-century continental European constitutions and codes acknowledged state obligations to provide food, work, and financial aid to persons in need. And continental Europeans today, whether of the right or the left, are much more likely than Americans to assume that governments have affirmative duties actively to promote the well-being of their citizens. The leading European conservative parties, for example, accept the subsidization of child-raising families, and the funding of health, employment, and old age insurance at levels most Americans find scarcely credible. By contrast, it is almost obligatory for American politicians of both the right and the left to profess mistrust of government.

These divergent attitudes toward the state have found constitutional expression in what are sometimes called "negative" and "positive" rights. The American Bill of Rights is frequently described as a charter of "negative" liberties, protecting certain areas of individual freedom from state interference. Judge Posner has succinctly stated the position: "The men who wrote the Bill of Rights were not concerned that the federal government might do too little for the people, but that it might do too much to them." The Supreme Court, while willing to accord procedural due process protection to statutory welfare entitlements, has consistently declined to recognize constitutional welfare rights. * * *

These statements contrast markedly with the attitudes of the post World War II European constitution makers who supplemented traditional negative liberties with certain affirmative social and economic rights or obligations. The idea of government underlying the "positive rights" in European constitutions has a complex history. In part, it represents a transposition to the modern state of the feudal notion that an overlord owed certain protection to his dependents in exchange for their service and loyalty. More proximately, it reflects the programs of the major European political parties—one large group animated by Christian social thought, and another by socialist or social democratic principles. As Casper has observed, it was only natural that peoples accustomed to the notion of a state with affirmative responsibilities would carry that idea forward when they added bills of rights to their constitutions.

* * *

In view of the long-standing American rights tradition, and the recent history of expansive judicial protection of a broad spectrum of individual and minority rights, [a] third aspect of American distinctiveness may at first glance seem puzzling. I refer to the dubious distinction of the United States as the only liberal democracy that has not ratified a number of important human rights instruments, notably the two United Nations Covenants on Civil and Political Rights, and on Economic, Social and Cultural Rights. This reticence, no doubt, is due in large part to our prudent unwillingness to submit to the jurisdiction of international organizations dominated by critics of the United States. But, particularly where economic and social rights are concerned, our reluctance is also attributable to our prevailing ideas about which sorts of needs, goods, interests, and values should be characterized as fundamental rights. Another likely reason is that the American civil litigation system is not well equipped to handle the potential consequences of characterizing a new set of interests as fundamental rights.

* * *

[E]very country in the democratic world is experiencing a tension between the two ideals that are linked together in the deceptively bland title of this symposium—a regime of rights and a welfare state. Every country is grappling with a set of problems that are in a general way similar: how to provide needed social aid without undermining personal responsibility; how to achieve the optimal mix of markets and central planning in a mixed economy; and how to preserve a just balance among individual freedom, equality, and social solidarity under constantly changing circumstances. The problem of "the Bill of Rights in the Welfare State" is nothing less than the great dilemma of how to hold together the two halves of the divided soul of liberalism—our love of individual liberty and our sense of a community for which we accept a common responsibility.

Below the surface of that dilemma lies a more serious one. Neither a strong commitment to individual and minority rights, nor even a modest welfare commitment like the American one, can long be sustained without the active support of a citizenry that is willing to respect the rights of others; that is prepared to accept some responsibility for the poorest and most vulnerable members of society; and that is prepared to accept responsibility, so far as possible, for themselves and for their dependents.

* * *

Constitution of the Republic of South Africa

Chapter 2—Bill of Rights

Rights

7. (1) This Bill of Rights is a cornerstone of democracy in South Africa. It enshrines the rights of all people in our country and affirms the democratic values of human dignity, equality and freedom.

    (2) The state must respect, protect, promote and fulfill the rights in the Bill of Rights.

    (3) The rights in the Bill of Rights are subject to the limitations contained or referred to in section 36, or elsewhere in the Bill.

Application

8. (1) The Bill of Rights applies to all law, and binds the legislature, the executive, the judiciary and all organs of state.

(2) A provision of the Bill of Rights binds a natural or a juristic person if, and to the extent that, it is applicable, taking into account the nature of the right and the nature of any duty imposed by the right.

(3) When applying a provision of the Bill of Rights to a natural or juristic person in terms of subsection (2), a court

    a. in order to give effect to a right in the Bill, must apply, or if necessary develop, the common law to the extent that legislation does not give effect to that right; and

    b. may develop rules of the common law to limit the right, provided that the limitation is in accordance with section 36(1).

(4) A juristic person is entitled to the rights in the Bill of Rights to the extent required by the nature of the rights and the nature of that juristic person.

Equality

9. (1) Everyone is equal before the law and has the right to equal protection and benefit of the law.

(2) Equality includes the full and equal enjoyment of all rights and freedoms. To promote the achievement of equality, legislative and other measures designed to protect or advance persons, or categories of persons, disadvantaged by unfair discrimination may be taken.

(3) The state may not unfairly discriminate directly or indirectly against anyone on one or more grounds, including race, gender, sex, pregnancy, marital status, ethnic or social origin, colour, sexual orientation, age, disability, religion, conscience, belief, culture, language and birth.

(4) No person may unfairly discriminate directly or indirectly against anyone on one or more grounds in terms of subsection (3). National legislation must be enacted to prevent or prohibit unfair discrimination.

(5) Discrimination on one or more of the grounds listed in subsection (3) is unfair unless it is established that the discrimination is fair.

* * *

Environment

24. Everyone has the right—

a. to an environment that is not harmful to their health or well being; and

b. to have the environment protected, for the benefit of present and future generations, through reasonable legislative and other measures that

i. prevent pollution and ecological degradation;

ii. promote conservation; and

iii. secure ecologically sustainable development and use of natural resources while promoting justifiable economic and social development.

Property

25. (1) No one may be deprived of property except in terms of law of general application, and no law may permit arbitrary deprivation of property.

(2) Property may be expropriated only in terms of law of general application

a. for a public purpose or in the public interest; and

b. subject to compensation, the amount of which and the time and manner of payment of which have either been agreed to by those affected or decided or approved by a court.

(3) The amount of the compensation and the time and manner of payment must be just and equitable, reflecting an equitable balance between the public interest and the interests of those affected, having regard to all relevant circumstances, including

a. the current use of the property;

b. the history of the acquisition and use of the property;

c. the market value of the property;

d. the extent of direct state investment and subsidy in the acquisition and beneficial capital improvement of the property; and

e. the purpose of the expropriation.

(4) For the purposes of this section

a. the public interest includes the nation's commitment to land reform, and to reforms to bring about equitable access to all South Africa's natural resources; and

b. property is not limited to land.

(5) The state must take reasonable legislative and other measures, within its available resources, to foster conditions which enable citizens to gain access to land on an equitable basis.

(6) A person or community whose tenure of land is legally insecure as a result of past racially discriminatory laws or practices is entitled, to the extent provided by an Act of Parliament, either to tenure which is legally secure or to comparable redress.

(7) A person or community dispossessed of property after 19 June 1913 as a result of past racially discriminatory laws or practices is entitled,

to the extent provided by an Act of Parliament, either to restitution of that property or to equitable redress.

(8) No provision of this section may impede the state from taking legislative and other measures to achieve land, water and related reform, in order to redress the results of past racial discrimination, provided that any departure from the provisions of this section is in accordance with the provisions of section 36(1).

(9) Parliament must enact the legislation referred to in subsection (6).

Housing

26. (1) Everyone has the right to have access to adequate housing.

(2) The state must take reasonable legislative and other measures, within its available resources, to achieve the progressive realisation of this right.

(3) No one may be evicted from their home, or have their home demolished, without an order of court made after considering all the relevant circumstances. No legislation may permit arbitrary evictions.

Health care, food, water and social security

27. (1) Everyone has the right to have access to

a.   health care services, including reproductive health care;

b.   sufficient food and water; and

c.   social security, including, if they are unable to support themselves and their dependants, appropriate social assistance.

(2) The state must take reasonable legislative and other measures, within its available resources, to achieve the progressive realisation of each of these rights.

(3) No one may be refused emergency medical treatment.

* * *

Education

29. (1) Everyone has the right

a.   to a basic education, including adult basic education; and

b.   to further education, which the state, through reasonable measures, must make progressively available and accessible.

(2) Everyone has the right to receive education in the official language or languages of their choice in public educational institutions where that education is reasonably practicable. In order to ensure the effective access to, and implementation of, this right, the state must consider all reasonable educational alternatives, including single medium institutions, taking into account

a.   equity;

b.   practicability; and

    c. the need to redress the results of past racially discriminatory laws and practices.

(3) Everyone has the right to establish and maintain, at their own expense, independent educational institutions that

    a. do not discriminate on the basis of race;

    b. are registered with the state; and

    c. maintain standards that are not inferior to standards at comparable public educational institutions.

(4) Subsection (3) does not preclude state subsidies for independent educational institutions.

* * *

Limitation of rights

36. (1) The rights in the Bill of Rights may be limited only in terms of law of general application to the extent that the limitation is reasonable and justifiable in an open and democratic society based on human dignity, equality and freedom, taking into account all relevant factors, including

    a. the nature of the right;

    b. the importance of the purpose of the limitation;

    c. the nature and extent of the limitation;

    d. the relation between the limitation and its purpose; and

    e. less restrictive means to achieve the purpose.

(2) Except as provided in subsection (1) or in any other provision of the Constitution, no law may limit any right entrenched in the Bill of Rights.

* * *

Enforcement of rights

38. Anyone listed in this section has the right to approach a competent court, alleging that a right in the Bill of Rights has been infringed or threatened, and the court may grant appropriate relief, including a declaration of rights. The persons who may approach a court are-

    a. anyone acting in their own interest;

    b. anyone acting on behalf of another person who cannot act in their own name;

    c. anyone acting as a member of, or in the interest of, a group or class of persons;

    d. anyone acting in the public interest; and

    e. an association acting in the interest of its members.

Interpretation of Bill of Rights

39. (1) When interpreting the Bill of Rights, a court, tribunal or forum

    a.   must promote the values that underlie an open and democratic society based on human dignity, equality and freedom;

    b.   must consider international law; and

    c.   may consider foreign law.

(2) When interpreting any legislation, and when developing the common law or customary law, every court, tribunal or forum must promote the spirit, purport and objects of the Bill of Rights.

(3) The Bill of Rights does not deny the existence of any other rights or freedoms that are recognised or conferred by common law, customary law or legislation, to the extent that they are consistent with the Bill.

———

Justiciable Social Rights as a Critique of the Liberal Paradigm

38 TEX. INT'L L.J. 763, 779–93 (2003).

■ JEANNE M. WOODS

* * *

V.   SOUTH AFRICAN SOCIAL RIGHTS JURISPRUDENCE

A.   Soobramoney: *The Utilitarian Calculus*

The 1996 South African Constitution contains an extensive panoply of socio-economic rights and duties. In contrast to previous efforts to constitutionalize social rights, the Constitution contains a unique bill of rights that integrates social rights with the more traditional fundamental freedoms. The absence of a structural hierarchy of rights effectively merges the public and private spheres, engaging the state in the formerly private endeavor of securing the social and economic pre-conditions to the full realization of human freedom. The state is obligated to "take reasonable legislative and other measures, within its available resources, to achieve the progressive realization of each of these rights." This constitutional formulation of the state's duty reflects the collective character of social rights, whose realization requires the resources and effort of the whole society.

The Constitutional Court was presented with its first opportunity to interpret this language barely a year after the 1996 Constitution took effect, posing an unenviable challenge to a new judiciary with precious little precedent to guide it. *Soobramoney v. Minister of Health* involved a forty-one year old unemployed diabetic who suffered from chronic renal failure, necessitating regular kidney dialysis. Because Mr. Soobramoney suffered from a combination of serious ailments rendering his condition irreversible, the treatment was calculated to prolong his life but would not cure him. He had exhausted his personal funds and sought treatment at the state hospital in Durban. Due to an insufficient number of dialysis machines in the public health sector, however, the hospital rationed their use, limiting them to patients who were eligible for a kidney transplant. Under the guidelines developed by the hospital, Mr. Soobramoney was ineligible for a transplant because of his complicated medical history. The plaintiff invoked several provisions of the South African Constitution, claiming violations of his rights to life, health, and emergency medical treatment.

In the Court's first pronouncement on social rights, it affirmed their integral connection to human dignity, freedom, and equality, without which the aspirations of the new constitutional dispensation would "have a hollow ring." Noting, however, that in Section 27(2) the state's duty with regard to health care was circumscribed by the "available resources" the Court read additional limiting language into the provision, restating the obligation of the state as "dependent upon the resources available *for such purposes.*" Thus, the Court indicated that it would not consider the state's resources as a whole, but in effect limited the state's duty to whatever resources it had already allocated to health care in general, and dialysis treatment in particular.

The Court also declined to give serious consideration to the plaintiff's right to life claim, reasoning that resort to the right to life in Section 11 was obviated by Section 27's specific protection of health care. Cautioning that its "purposive" approach to constitutional interpretation may not always require a "generous" construction of the rights afforded by the Constitution, the Court narrowly construed the right to emergency medical treatment in Section 27(3), holding it to be a negative right that does not confer affirmative obligations on the state, and declining to impute any positive obligations from the right to life in Section 11. The Court defined an "emergency" as an urgent, sudden occurrence for which advance preparation was not possible and a constitutional violation as state denial of available treatment, implying that there must be some misconduct or improper motive for the denial, such as racial discrimination. In the Court's view, such a narrow construction was necessary in order to conserve the resources needed to effectuate the state's overall health care obligations.

The Court's analysis under Sections 27(1) and (2) was similarly circumspect. It rejected the claim that the positive right to health required the state to make additional resources available for dialysis treatment, emphasizing that the regional health budget was already overspent, and that a dramatic increase of the health budget would be required to accommodate all similarly situated patients in South Africa, which would imperil other state social obligations. Applying a reasonableness test to the guidelines imposed by the hospital administration, the Court announced what appeared to be an overly deferential standard of review with regard to social rights, cautioning that it would "be slow to interfere with rational decisions taken in good faith by the political organs and medical authorities whose responsibility it is to deal with such matters."

Expressing sympathy for the appellant (who died three days after the decision), the Court acknowledged "[t]he hard and unpalatable fact ... that if the appellant were a wealthy man he would be able to procure [dialysis] treatment from private sources...." The Court nonetheless reasoned that the state has to manage its limited resources, and that "[t]here will be times when this requires it to adopt a holistic approach to the larger needs of society rather than to focus on the specific needs of particular individuals within society."

Thus, the Court adopted a utilitarian perspective advancing the health of the population as a whole versus "doing everything for each individual patient until you run out of funds and everybody else gets nothing." Such reasoning is extremely problematic in a rights context. The point of giving policy choices the priority status of fundamental rights is to avoid the utilitarianism inherent in majority decision making. Utilitarianism in this context is premised on a presumption of fixed and limited resources. While such a presumption is contained in the language of the constitutional provision itself, it is troubling that the Court arbitrarily embellished this language with the additional qualification that the resources be available "for such purposes."

In a concurring opinion, Justice Sachs asserted that "the rationing of access to life prolonging resources is ... integral to ... a human rights approach to health care." He proposed a "new analytical framework" for collective rights, which substituted interdependence for autonomy as its bedrock principle:

> Traditional rights analyses ... have to be adapted so as to take account of the special problems created by the need to provide a broad framework of constitutional principles governing the right of access to scarce resources and to adjudicate between competing rights bearers. When rights by their very nature are shared and inter-dependent, striking appropriate balances between the equally valid entitlements or expectations of a multitude of claimants should not be seen as imposing limits on those rights ... but as defining the circumstances in which the rights may most fairly and effectively be enjoyed.

Soobramoney may be understood especially in light of the Court's subsequent jurisprudence, discussed below as a first step in defining the minimum normative core of the social rights guaranteed by the South African Constitution. Under this analysis, the relief sought by Mr. Soobramoney required access to a level of health care that exceeded the minimum core of the right to health. Similarly, although the majority opinion did not reach this issue, the case suggests that the minimum core of the right to life does not require the state to provide extraordinary life support measures that would not lead to a cure of the patient's illness.

Nevertheless, both the majority and concurring opinions beg the question whether the collective right to health actually conflicted with the individual's right to health and life in this context, that is, whether the state should be allowed to treat dialysis as an extraordinary resource that must be rationed for the poor in a country whose white citizens enjoy one of the highest standards of living in the world. The majority opinion made no mention of the resources available in the private sector, nor did it suggest that the state should do anything further to respond to the epidemic of kidney disease. In acknowledging that a person's wealth determined whether he would live or die, yet failing to interpret the constitutional rights to health and life to avoid this outcome, the Court missed an important opportunity to give meaning to the new social contract, suggesting a retreat from the challenge of justiciable social rights.

B. Grootboom: *Collective Remedies for Legislative Commands*

The Constitutional Court's decision in *Government of the Republic of South Africa v. Grootboom* reassured social rights advocates that it was indeed willing to adjudicate positive rights claims. Contrary to the complaint that justiciable social rights remove policy choices from the legislative prerogative, the South African Constitutional Court demonstrated that violations of these rights can be remedied by a court without intruding unduly on legislative discretion.

The case arose under Section 26 of the South African Constitution which provides, in pertinent part:

(1) Everyone has the right to have access to adequate housing.

(2) The state must take reasonable legislative and other measures, within its available resources, to achieve the progressive realization of this right.

As part of the legacy of apartheid, millions of Black South Africans live in intolerable conditions. To alleviate the acute shortage of adequate housing in the country, the South African government developed an ambitious long term plan to build quality housing. However, a desperate need for emergency housing existed, which was not addressed in the plan. The Court found that this omission was a fatal constitutional flaw and ordered the Constituent Assembly to develop a program to accommodate those in desperate need with temporary shelter short of the sophisticated dwellings contemplated by the government plan.

The case was brought by a group of families who lived in Wallacedene, a squatter camp in the Western Cape, in what the Court described as "appalling conditions." When their situation became intolerable, they were forced to move out and settled on private land that had been earmarked for public housing. They were evicted by the government in a brutal manner reminiscent of the forced removals of the apartheid era: their shacks and belongings were destroyed, and the families were left homeless.

The Court found that the plaintiffs' housing situation was exacerbated by extreme poverty, noting that "a quarter of the households in Wallacedene had no income at all.... In some cases, their shacks are permanently flooded during the winter rains, others are severely overcrowded and some are perilously close to busy roads." The case was appealed by the government to the Constitutional Court after a lower court ordered the state to accommodate the families in basic shelter until permanent housing could be provided.

While commending the "major achievement" represented by the government's comprehensive housing program, the Court determined that the plan was not a reasonable effort to promote the constitutional right of access to adequate housing, because it excluded a significant segment of the population—those in desperate need. Noting that the United Nations Committee on Economic, Social and Cultural Rights has formulated the concept of a state's "minimum core obligation," the Court stated that it was possible to ascertain the meaning of this standard in international law and apply it to the rights enumerated in the South African Constitution: "Minimum core obligation is determined generally by having regard to the needs of the most vulnerable group that is entitled to the protection of the right in question." A reasonable measure must therefore address the needs of this group.

In developing this concept the Court gave more teeth to the reasonableness standard than it appeared willing to do in *Soobramoney*. While giving assurances that it would not substitute its judgment on the wisdom of legislative measures for that of the political branches, the Court outlined the parameters of reasonableness in terms of the minimum core obligation: A reasonable legislative program "must be balanced and flexible and make appropriate provision for attention to housing crises and to short, medium and long term needs." It must take into account "[t]hose whose needs are the most urgent and whose ability to enjoy all rights therefore is most in peril. . . ." Mere statistical success is not enough.

Similarly, the Court found added normative weight in the criterion in Section 26(2) of "progressive realization," a phrase that was not part of the analysis in *Soobramoney*, although it is also contained in the health care provision. Under this standard, consistent with the meaning that term is given in international law, the measures promulgated by the state must be calculated to realize the rights in question for everyone incrementally. Again, the Court cited the analysis of the Committee on Economic, Social and Cultural Rights, which declared that the requirement of progressive realization of the right to housing "imposes an obligation to move as expeditiously and effectively as possible towards that goal."

Accordingly, the Court found that the government's program lacked the requisite momentum:

> The absence of this component [emergency shelter] may have been acceptable if the nationwide housing programme would result in affordable houses for most people within a reasonably short time. However the scale of the problem is such that this simply cannot happen. Each individual housing project could be expected to take years. . . . The result is that people in desperate need are left without any form of assistance with no end in sight.

Emphasizing that the state has "the obligation to devise, fund, implement and supervise measures to provide relief to those in desperate need," the Court ordered the government to create a program that includes "reasonable measures . . . to provide relief for people who have no access to land, no roof over their heads, and who are living in intolerable conditions or crisis situations." The opinion observed that the right to housing protects not only the most vulnerable in society, but people at all economic levels of society. However, the Court ruled that there was no positive individual right to housing on demand.

Grootboom represents a major milestone in the vindication of justiciable social rights. The decision has enriched the jurisprudence on the meaning of two fundamental concepts in international human rights law: that of minimum core obligation and progressive realization. Significantly, the case illustrates that because of the collective character of social rights these standards do not necessarily impose limitations on rights, but can be stringent criteria by which a court can measure states' compliance.

At the same time, the decision evidences the possibilities of judicial restraint. While undertaking the novel task of discovering the normative content of a constitutional right that is subject to the unusual condition of resource availability, the Court utilized textbook judicial methods to determine the reasonableness of a legislative measure. If its intervention could be labeled redistributive, it merely redistributed resources within the government program; the Court did not disturb the legislative determination of what resources were available. Thus, while the protection of fundamental rights required the judiciary to exercise a policy choice, the Court left to the legislature the ultimate policy decision of how much of the state's resources to commit to the right to housing.

The Court's ruling does, however, represent a victory for the organized efforts of housing rights advocacy groups, which could prompt the legislature to reconsider the adequacy of its housing budget. By highlighting the priority status of the right to housing and the plight of those deprived of that right, judicial review serves as a catalyst for social change.

C. Treatment Action Campaign: *Negative Rights and Positive Remedies*

In *Minister of Health v. Treatment Action Campaign*, the South African Constitutional Court revisited the issue of the scope of the right to health in the context of the tragic AIDS epidemic—a public health crisis of enormous proportions. The government appealed a High Court ruling finding it in breach of its constitutional obligation with respect to the right to health. In the decision, the High Court cited estimates that 10% of the South African population is HIV-positive, including 24% of pregnant women. Approximately 70,000 infants are infected annually through mother-to-child transmission. Clinical trials showed that the anti-retroviral drug Nevirapine could significantly reduce this risk if administered during labor. The manufacturer of the drug had offered to supply it to South African health authorities free of charge for five years. However, the Health Ministry instituted a limited pilot program administering the drug to pregnant women at a few selected public health clinics throughout the country.

The petitioners, apparently learning the lessons of *Soobramoney* and *Grootboom*, did not argue that every pregnant woman had a right to be provided Nevirapine on demand, but they challenged the government's failure to design a comprehensive nationwide program. They further argued that the state should not prohibit the administration of the drug by doctors and other health care professionals in the public health sector so long as patients have given informed consent to treatment. The High Court's opinion, authored by Justice Botha, focused on Section 27(2) of the Constitution, framing the issue as whether the limited treatment program constituted a reasonable governmental measure to ensure the progressive realization of the right to health.

Citing *Grootboom*, the Court identified the factors to be considered in making a determination of reasonableness: (1) provision of appropriate financial and human resources; (2) reasonable implementation of the plan; and (3) the inclusion of all relevant segments of society. While acknowledging that the standard of progressive realization contemplates that the right to health care would not be achievable immediately, the Court pointed out that the program lacked an "unqualified commitment to reach the rest of the population in any given time or at any given rate." In view of the enormity of the threat to human life and health, the Court ruled that the phased implementation of the Nevirapine program was discriminatory. It reasoned that the state violated the negative obligation to desist from impairing the right to health care implicit in Section 27(1) by prohibiting the use of Nevirapine outside the pilot sites, and that the government had no justification for not making the drug widely available to the public. Moreover, the Court determined that the state had also violated the positive obligation in Section 27(2) to achieve the progressive realization of the right, concluding that "[t]he programme of the respondents lacks the impetus that is required for a programme that must move progressively. If there is no time-scale, there must be some other built-in impetus to maintain the momentum of progression. . . . That does no justice to the exigency of the case."

On appeal the Constitutional Court affirmed the essential elements of the High Court's ruling. Declaring that economic and social rights are "[c]learly" justiciable, the Court added that "when it is appropriate to do so, courts . . . must . . . use their wide powers to make orders that affect policy as well as legislation." In citing its earlier decision in *Soobramoney* in support of justiciability, the Court implicitly distinguished that case on its facts, opining that the plaintiff had simply failed to make out a violation of the right to health.

In preliminary comments, the Court sought to clarify its elaboration of the concept of "minimum core" in *Grootboom*, rejecting an argument by amici that this principle vests everyone with an individual right to the satisfaction of basic needs. Rather, the Court explained, the concept of minimum core provides a standard by which to assess the reasonableness of a governmental measure. Under this standard, the government program must address the needs of the most vulnerable in society, "[t]hose whose needs are the most urgent and whose ability to enjoy all rights therefore is most in peril. . . ."

The case before it required the Court to consider the claim of a uniquely vulnerable group—infants threatened with the transmission of HIV/AIDS from their mothers at birth—that the government violated the negative dimension of their right to health by confining the use of Nevirapine to the pilot sites. It found that the allegedly prohibitive costs cited by the government as justification for its policy were associated with the development of a comprehensive long-term program, not with the provision of a single dose of the drug to mothers and their babies at birth. Dismissing concerns raised by the government regarding the efficacy and safety of the drug as unsupported by the evidence, the Court ruled that the government had breached its obligation under Sections 27(1) and (2) by its insistence that Nevirapine be administered only under the most optimal conditions. Thus, the government's program would not achieve the progressive realization of the right to health care mandated in Section 27(2) of the constitution, because it entailed "waiting for a protracted period before taking a decision on the use of Nevirapine beyond the research and training sites...."

After concluding that restricting access to Nevirapine in public health centers was unreasonable, the Court considered the implications of this determination for the government's AIDS policy, emphasizing the need for "a concerted national effort to combat the HIV/AIDS pandemic." It ruled that the government's policy "fails to meet constitutional standards because it excludes those who could reasonably be included where such treatment is medically indicated to combat mother to child transmission of HIV." While reiterating that this ruling does not grant everyone the right to individual treatment on demand, the court stressed that "[e]very effort must ... be made to [achieve this goal] as soon as reasonably possible." In the meantime, "[t]he policy will have to be that Nevirapine must be provided where it is medically indicated at those hospitals and clinics within the public sector where facilities exist for testing and counselling."

The Court acknowledged that since the case was first brought, the government had made significant adjustments in its AIDS policy, relaxing its rigid restrictions on the availability of Nevirapine, making substantial additional funds available for HIV treatment, and establishing comprehensive programs to combat mother-to-child transmission in three of the nine provinces in the country. Nevertheless, the Court found that additional relief was necessary, and ordered the government to "devise and implement within its available resources a comprehensive and co-ordinated programme to realise progressively the rights of pregnant women and their newborn children to have access to health services to combat mother-to-child transmission of HIV" which must include counseling, testing, and treatment.

The government was further ordered "without delay" to (a) remove the restrictions on Nevirapine; (b) make it available at public hospitals and clinics when medically indicated; (c) provide counselors at these sites; and (d) expand the availability of testing and counseling facilities throughout the public health sector to "facilitate and expedite the use of Nevirapine for the purpose of reducing the risk of mother-to-child transmission of HIV." Thus, while taking pains to insist that it was not creating a private right of action, the Court's ruling nonetheless requires the government to provide specific medical treatment to a specific population.

This ruling highlights the speciousness of Erica De Wet's distinction between traditional individual rights and social rights framed as constitutional commands addressed to state, which she calls "objective legal norms." Because in her view only individual entitlements are rights, De Wet does not regard legislative commands as generating correlative enforceable rights, since they do not, in terms, entitle individuals to relief on demand. Nevertheless, as this case illustrates, a court order enforcing a constitutional legislative command ultimately will benefit specific individuals. The perceived dilemma she posits is resolved if social rights are understood as collective rights, for which individual remedies are not necessarily the most efficacious response.

D.   Reconciling the Results

The South African case law has evolved from the rejection of individual rights claims for life-preserving dialysis treatment, to recognition of collective rights to comprehensive government programs to address urgent social needs for housing and health care. Permeating these decisions is the influence of the two often-countervailing components of the social construction of rights: ideology and practice. On the one hand, pervasive individualist norms, such as the public/private dichotomy and the principle of free choice, inhibit the expansion of rights analysis beyond traditional first generation liberties. On the other, popular movements stimulate legal developments that can lead to more encompassing definitions of rights.

Both kidney disease and AIDS are serious, life-threatening harms. However, the AIDS epidemic has all of the characteristics of a classic "public" health crisis: a communicable disease that threatens the entire population. As such, AIDS more readily falls within the traditional scope of liberal state responsibility. In contrast, kidney disease, no matter how widespread, is seen as a "private" misfortune; its victims, while generating sympathy, may even be deemed "undeserving" of an urgent public response by having made bad lifestyle choices. Notably, in *Treatment Action Campaign*, the beneficiaries of constitutional relief were not the infected mothers, but the innocent—hence "deserving"—infants to whom the disease was transmitted *in utero*. Hopefully, these mothers will survive long enough to care for their children.

The fact that public housing has long been imbued with assumptions of government responsibility may also explain the *Grootboom* Court's willingness to intercede. Mass homelessness evokes the specter of rampant crime, disease, and public unrest. Interestingly, the court in this case identified individuals and other agents, as well as the state, as duty-holders of the right to housing. In contrast, in *Soobramoney* the Constitutional Court was markedly unwilling to recognize any duty in the private sector for the provision of dialysis treatment, despite the fact that the identical language on which it relied to eliminate the public/private distinction is contained in the section on the right to health.

Finally, the Court more readily acknowledged rights and correlative state duties where there was a history of political struggle demanding their recognition. Both the housing and AIDS cases took place against the backdrop of tenacious local and international movements on those issues. In light of the huge domestic and international outcry over the South African government's handling of the AIDS crisis, the Court was apparently unwilling to presume the good faith of the authorities, as it had in *Soobramoney*. With each case, the Court has been more willing to question the adequacy of the government's allocation of resources to pressing social needs.

VI. Toward a Global Sense of Community

The new South African jurisprudence demonstrates that there are no institutional obstacles to the realization of collective rights where the political will exists to enforce them. The cases also show that the full protection of social rights cannot be achieved without a reevaluation and reconstruction of liberal rights discourse.

According to economist Michel Chossudovsky, the world's poor countries, with 85.2% of the population, share only 21.5% of its income, while rich nations—14.8% of the population—account for 78.5%. As the chasm widens between the planet's privileged minority and its impoverished masses, the need for international recognition of collective rights has never been more apparent. Such a development is needed to fulfill the promise of universality proclaimed by human rights discourse. As Felice points out, in many cultures "the concept of collective human rights . . . has an historical basis that runs far deeper . . . than does the Western concept of individual rights." Moreover, individual rights are inadequate to protect disempowered groups when collective rights have not been realized.

The argument that a scarcity of resources renders social rights unattainable is unpersuasive. It is well documented that the world's abundant resources are sufficient to meet minimum core needs. World poverty is a function not of scarcity, but of distribution. [Michael] Walzer defines the available resources of the community as "the past and present product, the accumulated wealth of its members—not some 'surplus' of that wealth. . . . Socially recognized needs are the first charge against the social product; there is no real surplus until they have been met." He criticizes the inherently undemocratic nature of the right to unlimited accumulation in the face of dire need: "Men and women who appropriate vast sums of money for themselves while needs are still unmet act like tyrants, dominating and distorting the distribution of security and welfare."

To Walzer's definition I would add that the available resources include not just the wealth produced within a given state but that of the global community as a whole. This conception flows not only from the recognition of humanity's interdependence in the age of globalization but from elementary principles of justice: the international slave trade, colonialism, apartheid, physical and cultural genocide of indigenous peoples and continued inequities in North–South relations provide ample grounds to support an inclusive definition of available resources. Moreover, these historical experiences are constitutive of the human person in the twenty-first century. They are part of our collective identity. They are who we are. The rapid globalization of the economy and communications, as well as objective threats to global human welfare—such as nuclear war, environmental degradation, and the AIDS epidemic—lend urgency to the need for a collective conceptualization of the self that transcends geographical boundaries.

Thus, the available resources of South Africa include not only the monies directly at the disposal of the state; they include the immense wealth in the hands of the white minority—riches wrung from the suffering of the African people. It is possible that when the total resources of the country are taken into account, kidney dialysis could be considered a component of the minimum core right to health. Moreover, many rich nations are heavily indebted to the Black majority of South Africa for their government's economic, political, diplomatic, and military support of the apartheid regime. Similarly, the available resources of the "Third World" include those of the industrialized nations whose development was made possible by colonial exploitation.

Despite its theoretical weaknesses, the collective right of peoples to development offers a potential conceptual framework within which the issue of scarcity of resources can be addressed. Originally formulated by Senegalese jurist Keba M'Baye, the United Nations General Assembly adopted the Declaration on the Right to Development in 1986. The Declaration defines the right to development in both individual and collective terms. It is "an inalienable human right by virtue of which every human person and all peoples are entitled to participate in, contribute to, and enjoy economic, social, cultural and political development, in which all human rights and fundamental freedoms can be fully realized."

Critics correctly point out that the Declaration is vague as to the juridical basis and normative content of the right to development, including the identity of the rights-holders and duty-holders. Tanzanian scholar Issa Shivji criticizes the concept as essentially a demand for charity "based on an illusory model of co-operation and solidarity." When seen as part of the global demand for economic, social, and cultural rights, however, the right to development has the potential to surmount welfarist constraints. As William Felice argues, the right to development establishes an emerging principle in international law that "there is a collective international responsibility for the human condition."

VII.   CONCLUSION

In order for human rights discourse to evolve in the twenty-first century, the eighteenth-century fiction of natural, self-evident rights must give way to the realization that all rights are social constructs. They are the product of collective struggles: particular demands made on organized society in particular historical times and places. They represent values that, as a result of these struggles, society has agreed to prioritize. Critical scholars have deconstructed, denounced, and defended rights discourse, and have vigorously debated the efficacy of reifying fundamental values in legal form. Nevertheless, rights ideology is a powerful transformative force and a potent weapon in the hands of the dispossessed. Just as individual rights-talk served as a catalyst in the democratic revolutions of Europe and the United States, so too will the demand for second-and third-generation rights play a galvanizing role in the ongoing struggle of the world's impoverished millions to realize fully the dream of human dignity.

———

The Economic Bill of Rights

Excerpt from January 11, 1944, message to Congress on the State of the Union.

■ FRANKLIN D. ROOSEVELT

It is our duty now to begin to lay the plans and determine the strategy for the winning of a lasting peace and the establishment of an American standard of living higher than ever before known. We cannot be content, no matter how high that general standard of living may be, if some fraction of our people—whether it be one-third or one-fifth or one-tenth—is ill-fed, ill-clothed, ill-housed, and insecure.

This Republic had its beginning, and grew to its present strength, under the protection of certain inalienable political rights—among them the right of free speech, free press, free worship, trial by jury, freedom from unreasonable searches and seizures. They were our rights to life and liberty.

As our nation has grown in size and stature, however—as our industrial economy expanded—these political rights proved inadequate to assure us equality in the pursuit of happiness.

We have come to a clear realization of the fact that true individual freedom cannot exist without economic security and independence. "Necessitous men are not free men." People who are hungry and out of a job are the stuff of which dictatorships are made.

In our day these economic truths have become accepted as self evident. We have accepted, so to speak, a second Bill of Rights under which a new basis of security and prosperity can be established for all—regardless of station, race, or creed.

Among these are:

The right to a useful and remunerative job in the industries or shops or farms or mines of the nation;

The right to earn enough to provide adequate food and clothing and recreation;

The right of every farmer to raise and sell his products at a return which will give him and his family a decent living;

The right of every businessman, large and small, to trade in an atmosphere of freedom from unfair competition and domination by monopolies at home or abroad;

The right of every family to a decent home;

The right to adequate medical care and the opportunity to achieve and enjoy good health;

The right to adequate protection from the economic fears of old age, sickness, accident, and unemployment;

The right to a good education.

All of these rights spell security. And after this war is won we must be prepared to move forward, in the implementation of these rights, to new goals of human happiness and well being.

America's own rightful place in the world depends in large part upon how fully these and similar rights have been carried into practice for our citizens.

———

The New Deal Constitution in Exile

51 DUKE L.J. 165, 176–222 (2001).

■ WILLIAM E. FORBATH

* * * On the hustings, in radio addresses, and in more sustained debates, speeches, and writings, the lawmakers and [President Franklin D. Roosevelt] argued not simply that Congress had the *power* under the Constitution, rightly understood or amended, to regulate agriculture, industry, and labor. They argued that citizens had fundamental economic and social rights under the Constitution, rightly understood or amended; and Congress, therefore, had the *duty* to exercise its power to govern economic and social life in a way that sought to secure those rights. Making these arguments, New Dealers drew on a half-century-old tradition of constitutional discourse that I have dubbed the "social citizenship" tradition. It provided them not only a rights rhetoric, but also a constitutional narrative, modes of interpretation, and conceptions of the allocation of interpretive authority.

The narrative, of course, was about a "changing," "living" Constitution; more specifically, it was about constitutional change and continuity in an industrialized America. * * *

In Congress, after [*Schechter Poultry Corp. v. United States*, 295 U.S. 495 (1935), (invalidating a provision of the National Industrial Recovery Act of 1933 as beyond the power of Congress)] in May 1935, and, with growing intensity, after [*Carter v. Carter Coal Co.*, 298 U.S. 238 (1936) (, invalidating a provision of the Bituminous Coal Conservation Act of 1935 as beyond the power of Congress)] in May 1936, proposals for constitutional amendments multiplied. "[H]aving in mind the Supreme Court's [decision in *Schechter*]," scores of New Deal congressmen would declare that "the time has come to extend the Bill of Rights to embrace such guarantees as 'the right to honest work,' an industry wide 'minimum standard of hours, wages, and fair competition,' and the like."

* * *

Accompanying these substantive ideas was a set of views about the allocation of interpretive and enforcement authority. It was clear that "[s]omebody should determine whether an act of Congress is repugnant to the Constitution." Only on rare occasions, however, and only in respect of certain constitutional provisions was the Court the proper somebody. The Constitution was a "statesman's document," whose general "abstract phrases" were best "interpreted in the legislative laboratory where and when the statute [was] being made." Until the late nineteenth century, New Dealers pointed out, the houses of Congress, the president, and the people at the polls were (almost) the sole wielders of a constitutional veto over congressional statutes.

Now that Congress had affirmative obligations as well as duties of self-restraint in respect of rights protection, this allocation of interpretive authority to Congress was all the more imperative. The right to work, "the equal right ... to a share of the Nation's employment asset"—these were modern rights that the Constitution, rightly understood, both authorized and obliged Congress to protect, and advocates insisted on the right of Congress "to determine for itself the meaning of [the Constitution's general rights protecting] provisions" in recognizing a modern social right to work. To those who insisted on "the traditional legal habit of looking upon rights as negative," these advocates first objected that seventeenth-and eighteenth-century ideas had imparted a rigidity that ill-served "legislators who must implement" the Constitution. * * * To be sure, social rights did not lend themselves to judicial enforcement, but judicial enforcement was not always the proper test of a right.

* * *

From the first New Deal onward, the president set himself a task of constitutional narration and interpretation, to elaborate and win the nation's support for a "redefinition of [inherited constitutional] rights in terms of a changing and growing social order." Thus, Roosevelt situated those rights in terms of their eighteenth century meaning. Quoting Jefferson, he evoked an agrarian past when America had "no paupers. The great mass of our population [was] of laborers ... [and m]ost of the laboring class possess[ed] property...." For these smallholder-citizens, the rights "involved in acquiring and possessing property," together with the ballot and the freedom to live by one's "own lights," ensured liberty and equality.

Well into the nineteenth century, Roosevelt's grand rights-interpreting narrative continued, roughly comparable conditions endured. If industrial concentration and industrial depressions tore away from many Americans the kind of economic independence and decent work that underwrote republican citizenship, still the frontier remained open, land remained cheap, and the scale of commerce and production in much of the nation remained small and local. So, for almost a century, in pre-industrial and industrializing America, the "old and sacred possessive [common law] rights" of property and labor, enshrined in the Court's Constitution, retained much of their social meaning for the "welfare and happiness" of ordinary Americans.

By the end of the nineteenth century, however, the frontier had closed, free land was "no more," and "our industrial combinations had become great uncontrolled and irresponsible units of power within the State." These new conditions robbed the old rights of their original meaning. All Americans understood this social historical sea change, Roosevelt suggested, and all had access to the insight that new contexts demanded new meanings lest old texts be distorted and old values lost.

* * * A mature industrial society could not be governed by a laissez-faire Constitution, insulating industry and finance from the modern claims of liberty and equality. America needed an "economic constitutional order." The terms of our basic rights "are as old as the Republic," but new conditions demand new readings. * * * A right "to make a living—a living decent according to the standard of the time" was at the heart of the new interpretation of the constitutional promise of liberty that Roosevelt had expounded throughout the 1936 election campaign.

* * *

[T]he social citizenship tradition held that lawmakers, and not the courts, were the appropriate interpreters and guardians of an important subset of fundamental rights, including the rights to social provision, decent labor standards, and decent work. It was patent to generations of populists and progressives that the courts not only would not, but also could not and should not translate the general rights-declaring provisions of the Reconstruction Amendments into specific guarantees of social and economic rights in industrial America. That required redistributive legislation and administrative machinery and a broad national political will to support them. The only important contribution the courts could make to this essentially political and legislative task was to allow the process to go forward. * * *

II. THE COUNTERREVOLUTION AND THE DEFEAT OF SOCIAL CITIZENSHIP

* * * To understand the present exile of the "right to live" and to make a living, we must examine the fate of the New Deal mandate.

A. *The Solid South, the Counterrevolution, and the Fracturing of Social Citizenship*

That fate was decided by the sway of Jim Crow over the politics of New Deal lawmaking. The nation's betrayal of Reconstruction prevented the legislative enactment of the New Deal vision of national citizenship. Measures instituting rights to decent work and social provision for all Americans enjoyed broad support, yet they expired in Congress. Thanks to their numbers, their seniority, and their control over key committees, southern Democrats had a hammerlock on Congress. The Solid South's national representatives generally supported the New Deal until the late 1930s. They demanded, however, that New Deal social provision and labor standards respect states' rights, by resting on state, and not national, administration and standard setting. Also, they insisted that key bills exclude the main categories of southern labor, else Congress would fall guilty of doing what it had done so often in the past, using legislation to "overcome the splendid gifts of God to the South." 'If southern agricultural labor were covered, how "were they going to get blacks to pick and chop cotton when Negroes [on federal work programs] were receiving . . . more than twice as much as they had ever been paid." The outrage to "our region" also "outrage[d] the Constitution," by threatening to "set up a dangerous and all powerful board . . . in Washington" in "utter violation of States' rights, local self-government, [and] local self-determination of our own sociological and economic problems."

At stake was the South's labor market, with its unique fusion of class and caste relations and its low wages. Social Security is a prime illustration of the Solid South's sway over reforms affecting that market. Roosevelt's Committee on Economic Security fashioned the administration's proposals to appease the Southern Bourbons. The Committee's blueprints adopted state-level autonomy—though with national minimum standards—in both unemployment insurance and assistance for the needy aged, dependent children, and blind. Only the old age benefits program would be purely federal. Nonetheless, when the blueprints arrived in Congress, the Dixiecrats demanded more from the sponsors of the administration bill. National standards for unemployment and old age insurance also vanished and the core principle of a national commitment to include all employed persons in the unemployment and old-age insurance schemes was abandoned. Finally, the Dixiecrats expelled agricultural and domestic workers from the nation's core social insurance programs, thereby expelling the majority of black Americans, who worked in these two sectors.

So it went across the array of core reforms. Whether the arena was agricultural or industrial recovery, industrial relations or labor standards, broad, inclusive bills—bills with national rather than local standards and administration—enjoyed solid support from the northern Democrats (and from disenfranchised southern blacks and poor whites). But the bills failed. For his first term, Roosevelt seemed entirely willing to oblige his party's powerful southern bloc and the "racial civilization" they prized. Then, however, as the 1936 election approached and business opposition to the New Deal intensified, Roosevelt grew more attentive to two crucial constituencies: the insurgent new industrial unions of the CIO and the black voters of the large cities of the North. As these groups began to bulk large in his 1936 reelection bid, Roosevelt's social and economic rights talk grew more universal and robust—and the southern attacks began. Governor Talmadge of Georgia called a "Grass Roots" convention to uphold the Constitution against "Negroes, the New Deal and . . . Karl Marx." For his part, Senator Carter Glass of Virginia challenged the white South to show "spirit and courage enough to face the new Reconstruction era that northern so called Democrats are menacing us with."

In the fall of 1937, after the Court had handed down *West Coast Hotel Co. v. Parrish* and *Jones & Laughlin*, and its steadfastness in upholding the old Constitution seemed to be crumbling, the New Deal's foes in Congress were galvanized. The old Constitution found a new redoubt, and

the counterrevolution authored a manifesto. A group of conservative southern Democrats in the Senate met with like-minded Republican senators to
consider a more formal alliance against the New Deal. If the judicial
safeguards for state sovereignty and individual liberty were eroding, they
agreed, they must invest renewed vigor in the century-old Constitution of
congressional constitutional precedent and practice. They drafted a "statement of principles"—-it became known as the "Conservative Manifesto"
that reaffirmed their devotion to the Constitution of states' rights ("the
vigorous maintenance of States' rights, home rule, and local self-government"), liberty of contract (and the "common law principles of free men"),
and the property rights of the owners of capital ("the constitutional
guaranties of the rights . . . of property"). The attempt at forming a new
conservative party foundered, but the coalition and its role as bulwark for
the old Constitution held firm and prevailed.

The conservative coalition managed to cripple or undo administration
measures in the areas of labor reform and social insurance. World War II,
in turn, brought labor shortages and a burgeoning of national governmental controls on local and state economies. With this, southern congressmen
openly joined ranks with the minority-party Republicans to thwart
Roosevelt's executive reorganization plan, to gut the administration's 1945
Full Employment Bill, and to abolish the National Resources Planning
Board (NRPB).

The conservative coalition's accomplishments in destroying these agencies and thwarting these measures meant that Roosevelt's famous "second,
economic Bill of Rights" would find no enduring legislative and institutional embodiments, and the maturation of the idea of legislated fundamental
rights would cease. * * *

The constitutional bad faith—the willful blindness toward the Reconstruction Amendments' condemnation of racial caste—that for half a century enabled both parties and all three branches of the federal government to
condone or support Jim Crow and disenfranchisement produced the anomaly of a reactionary core, the Solid South, at the heart of Roosevelt's New
Deal liberal coalition. In the face of the Fifteenth Amendment's bar on
race-based disenfranchisement, the southern state governments disenfranchised black citizens through such racially "neutral" measures as the poll
tax and literacy tests. From the Southern oligarchs' perspective, these had
the additional benefit of also disenfranchising a majority of the region's
poor and working class whites, which enabled the Dixiecrat oligarchy to
choose the bulk of the South's congressional delegation. The upshot was
the derailing of the New Deal "revolution" by a Dixiecrat-led counterrevolution.

Put simply, the absence of *political* citizenship led to the defeat of
social citizenship in America. Not only were most black Americans excluded
from the benefits of the main New Deal programs, but this constitutional
bad faith at black America's expense also deprived all Americans of the
institutional foundations and political constitutional legacy of social citizenship. Broad social and economic rights talk fell into disuse after the decisive

defeats that the New Deal agenda suffered in the 1940s. Blocked by the Dixiecrats at every legislative crossroad, the CIO, social citizenship's only powerful, organized constituency, gradually abandoned its efforts to "complete the New Deal."

* * *

White America and the federal government's abandonment of Reconstruction did more than deprive black Americans of civil and political rights for almost another century. By allowing the emergence and consolidation of the Solid South, this constitutional bad faith prevented all Americans from securing the boon of social citizenship. From the perspective of this history, the New Deal constitutional legacy that is under attack today by restorationist scholars and judges is a marred one. The vast expansion of national governmental power has been constitutionally enshrined, but the reason for its expansion has not.

Nevertheless, this history may yield a constitutional imperative that binds citizens and lawmakers, the true authors and interpreters of the political Constitution. If this history proves persuasive, then perhaps the New Deal constitutional revolution was left unfinished. Its expansion of national authority rested on an unkept promise, and the fate of this promise of social citizenship was decided by the nation and government's complicity with Jim Crow. If I am right about these historical matters, then the question of social citizenship was concluded illegitimately and must be reopened. Even further, those who defend the main contours of congressional power under the New Deal Constitution may be obliged to make good faith efforts to enact the social citizenship rights it promised. The Court will not do anything to mend the broken constitutional links between racial and economic justice, but we can.

* * *

Forty Acres and a Mule: A Republican Theory of Minimal Entitlements

13 HARV. J.L. & PUB. POL'Y 37 (1990).

■ AKHIL REED AMAR

Let me begin by mapping out what, for this Federalist Society audience, I take to be common ground. Pure socialism is bad. A system of private property, at least up to a point, is good. A regime in which the state controlled all resources would threaten both individual liberty and true democracy. * * *

I will now move from this common ground to stake out a position that for this group may seem far less obvious. Private property is such a good thing that every citizen should have some. Indeed, a minimal entitlement to property is so important, so constitutive, and so essential for both individual and collective self-governance that to provide each citizen with that minimal amount of property, the government may legitimately redistribute property from other citizens who have far more than their minimal share. But wait—there's more. The notion of minimal entitlements is not simply constitutive, it is constitutional—not just constitutionally permissible, meaning that the government *may* distribute or redistribute to insure every citizen a minimal stake in society, but constitutionally obligatory. The government *must* do so. * * *

Now that I have your attention, let me explain. There is a tradition deep in American constitutional law that I shall refer to as the "R/republican tradition," with both a lowercase and a capital "R." This tradition was a driving force behind a number of significant political movements that helped shape the American political experience. These include Abraham Lincoln's Republican party in the 1860s (and before it the Free Soil party), Thomas Jefferson's Democratic Republicans at the turn of the Nineteenth Century, and before that, the ideological platform of a group of commonwealth writers, most prominently James Harrington, in England in the Seventeenth and Eighteenth Centuries.

In this R/republican tradition, there is a recognition that for one truly to be a citizen in a democracy and to participate in the democratic process, one needs a minimum amount of independence. Economic independence is necessary if the citizen is to be able to deliberate on the common good, the *res publica*, the thing public. (Hence the word republicanism.) According to this tradition, the problem of poor people is that, in a real way, they have no wills of their own. You may give them the right to vote, but they will alienate that right. They will sell it either to rich people or to foreign tyrants. They lack some minimal stake in society sufficient to connect their own personal interests with that of the larger public interest. * * *

I suggest that there are two basic ways of dealing with the R/republican notion that in order for a democracy to work, people must have a stake in society. The first way is the dark side—the exclusionary side—of the R/republican vision. It is the Athenian solution, and I would suggest the original American solution. That solution is to enslave people, to ruthlessly disfranchise people who do not have property, to adopt poll taxes and property qualifications. * * *

This original R/republican solution was radically modified by the Civil War and the Thirteenth Amendment. The solution to the problem is no longer the Athenian solution of enslavement. It is now an inclusionary solution, a solution that says We the People of the United States will not allow a degraded caste of people to exist in our society. It is a solution that provides people with inalienable property rights in their own persons. Moreover, I suggest, it is a vision that, especially under section two of the Thirteenth Amendment, * * * provides for forty acres and a mule. It is a vision that provides a right to sustenance and shelter: minimum sustenance, minimum shelter.

    * * *

When the Reconstruction Amendments are viewed as a whole, a radically different vision of society emerges. Precisely because the Fifteenth Amendment gave former slaves the right to vote, and the Fourteenth Amendment made them citizens by dint of their birth, we should interpret the Thirteenth Amendment to guarantee each American a certain minimum stake in society. Otherwise, We the People of the United States really failed to set the slaves free—free from economic dependence. Without guaranteeing independence, it would have been both futile and dangerous under R/republican principles to have extended the rights of equal citizenship and equal votes to freedmen. * * *

* * * I have not, at least here, argued that this Thirteenth Amendment vision of forty acres and a mule is judicially enforceable under section one of the Thirteenth Amendment. There may very well be a variety of institutional limitations on courts that make them unsuitable for the task. Rather, I would like to stress the obligation—not only a moral obligation, but a legal, a *constitutional* obligation—of Congress, under section two of the Thirteenth Amendment. Congress has both a constitutional right and a constitutional duty to implement this vision.

NOTES AND QUESTIONS

1. Social citizenship and economic and social rights. The term social citizenship was discussed in a famous essay by T.H. Marshall written in the 1940s. T.H. MARSHALL, *Citizenship and Social Class, in* SOCIOLOGY AT THE CROSSROADS 67 (1963). Marshall argued that the concept of citizenship was steadily broadening in order to ensure a fully participatory democracy, and that as part of this evolution the liberal state would expand its recognition of rights claims. Marshall envisioned a progression from civil rights (the classical eighteenth-century rights limiting the exercise of state power against citizens, such as freedom of speech and association) to political rights (rights, like the right to vote and to run for public office, that guarantee the citizen's technical ability to participate in a democratic government) to, finally, social rights, which would include "the whole range from the right to a modicum of economic welfare and security to the right to share to the full in the social heritage and to live the life of a civilized being according to the standards prevailing in the society." *Id.* at 74.

C.B. Macpherson makes a similar distinction between civil rights, which are rights against the state, and social rights, which are "claims for benefits to be guaranteed by the state." C.B. MACPHERSON, *Problems of Human Rights in the Late Twentieth Century, in* THE RISE AND FALL OF ECONOMIC JUSTICE AND OTHER ESSAYS 25 (1985).

Compare Roosevelt's *Economic Bill of Rights* to the United Nations' *International Covenant on Economic, Social and Cultural Rights*, and to the South African Constitution. What are the similarities and differences? Which rights identified in these texts are civil rights, which are political rights, and which are social rights?

2. Judicial role in enforcing economic and social rights. As both the Woods excerpt and the Forbath excerpt suggest, the implementation of social rights, including economic rights, may look very different than the implementation of political and civil rights. What is the role of the courts in enforcing social rights? Would an economic bill of rights in the United States necessarily change the relationship between the branches of government? Would it change what we mean by a right in the first place? Would a gradualist approach to fundamental rights, represented by South African constitutional law, be alien to United States legal culture? Would it be helpful or hurtful to political and legal movements for social change?

3. Race, class, and political economy. What is the relationship between race and class? Much ink has been spilled on this question. For example, some Marxists have insisted that racial exploitation is merely a cover for capitalist exploitation, while others have insisted that racial exploitation has a psychological and social dynamic that is independent of economic relations. *See* Martha R. Mahoney, *Class and Status in American Law: Race, Interest, and the Anti–Transformation Cases*, 76 S. CAL. L. REV. 799 (2003); Frances Lee Ansley, *Stirring the Ashes: Race, Class and the Future of Civil Rights Scholarship*, 74 CORNELL L. REV. 993 (1989). It seems generally agreed, however, that whether or not race and class exploitation are autonomous or one a subset of the other, they are certainly intertwined in United States history. Both Amar and Forbath suggest, for instance, that African American subordination and resistance are tied to the political economy. Is this true of other racialized groups?

4. Racial liberation movements and economic development movements: some convergences. Scott Cummings traces the history of community economic development back to the famous dialogues between W.E.B. DuBois and Booker T. Washington. Although DuBois emphasized political action and Washington emphasized private investments in human capital and business development, both men saw economic development as key to black empowerment in the post-slavery era, and both championed the development of black businesses. Scott L. Cummings, *Community Economic Development as Progressive Politics: Toward a Grassroots Movement for Economic Justice*, 54 STAN. L. REV. 399, 410–11 (2001).

Many years later, another grassroots movement for black economic justice was spearheaded by women rather than men. The National Welfare Rights Organization (NWRO) was led by African American women, such as Johnnie Tillmon, who implemented local organizing campaigns designed to educate women receiving Assistance to Dependent Children (ADC), a program that was later renamed Aid to Families with Dependent Children (AFDC), about their rights to grants for food, rent, clothing, and furniture, and to force welfare offices to pay them. *See* GUIDA WEST, THE NATIONAL WELFARE RIGHTS MOVEMENT: THE SOCIAL PROTEST OF POOR WOMEN (1981). The hope was that "a mass welfare drive would expand benefits to millions of eligible persons and ultimately force the federal government to drastically reorganize the welfare—possibly through the imposition of a national guaranteed minimum income." Cummings, *supra* at 418.

Legal scholars as well as organizers looked forward to a constitutional right to welfare, *see, e.g.,* Frank I. Michelman, *The Supreme Court 1968 Term—Foreword: On Protecting the Poor Through the Fourteenth Amendment*, 83 HARV. L. REV. 7 (1969), and at its peak, the NWRO claimed 22,000 dues paying members nationwide. Cummings, *supra*, at 419. The NWRO eventually collapsed, however, and in the 1980s President Ronald Reagan would use the image of black "welfare queens" as a central rallying point for the destruction of AFDC and other means-tested entitlement programs. *Id.* at 422. AFDC was ultimately abolished by President Clinton, who replaced the program with Temporary Assistance for Needy Families (TANF).

Analyzing the failure of the NRWO, some scholars argue that the effort of African American women to demand political inclusion based on a right to welfare conflicted with a long-standing ideology that identified female economic prosperity with marriage and dependency on a man earning a "family wage," not the state. *See* RICKIE SOLINGER, BEGGARS AND CHOOSERS: HOW THE POLITICS OF CHOICE SHAPES ADOPTION, ABORTION, AND WELFARE IN THE UNITED STATES (2001); LINDA GORDON, PITIED BUT NOT ENTITLED: SINGLE MOTHERS AND THE HISTORY OF WELFARE, 1890–1935 (1994). Others argue that the welfare rights movement was politically vulnerable and ultimately failed because it was not tied to the principle of the inherent dignity and value of wage work, a principle deeply embedded in United States conceptions of citizenship. *See* William E. Forbath, *Constitutional Welfare Rights: A History, Critique and Reconstruction*, 69 FORDHAM L. REV. 1821 (2001).

Another debate among historians concerning the convergence of the struggle for black liberation and the struggle for economic justice involves the Civil Rights Movement of the 1960s. Forbath argues that Civil Rights Movement leaders such as Martin Luther King, Jr. had a well-developed agenda for economic justice, but that it floundered, like the New Deal era agenda, on the rock of racial subordination. *See* William E. Forbath, *Caste, Class, and Equal Citizenship*, 98 MICH. L. REV. 1 (1999). Risa Goluboff argues that the National Association for the Advancement of Colored People Legal Defense and Education Fund (commonly called the "NAACP Inc. Fund" or "Inc. Fund") must bear a share of the blame for the contemporary understanding of rights against racial discrimination as not comprehending economic rights. Goluboff argues that the Inc. Fund subordinated the complaints of black tenant farmers and sharecroppers, whose problems involving involuntary servitude, peonage, and wage ceilings were profoundly linked to the political economy of the South, to cases in which workers, "because they were black, were denied privileges extended to white workers in the same unions, the same jobs, the same companies, the same industries." Risa L. Goluboff, *"We Live's in a Free House Such As It Is": Class and the Creation of Modern Civil Rights*, 151 U. PA. L. REV. 1977, 2012 (2003). According to Goluboff, "As NAACP lawyers contemplated their attack on racial inequality in the 1940s, labor-related inequality as experienced by African Americans working in southern agriculture stood outside their framework." *Id.* at 2010.

Scholars also have questioned whether African Americans have been well served by their historic alliance with the political left. David Bernstein suggests that the traditional "liberal," pro-union, pro-civil rights position has disserved Chinese American and African American agricultural, service, and industrial workers, who would have been benefitted more from adherence to laissez-faire ideology and anti-union political movement. *See* David Bernstein, Lochner, *Parity, and the Chinese Laundry Cases*, 41 WM. & MARY L. REV. 211 (1999); David E. Bernstein, *The Law and Economics of Post–Civil War Restrictions on Interstate Migration by African–Americans*, 76 TEX. L. REV. 781 (1998); David Bernstein, *The Davis–Bacon Act: Vestige of Jim Crow*, 13 NAT'L BLACK L.J. 276 (1994). *But see* Kendall Thomas, *Rouge et Noir Reread: A Popular Constitutional History of the Angelo Herndon Case*, *in* CRITICAL RACE THEORY: THE KEY WRITINGS THAT FORMED THE MOVEMENT 465 (Kimberlé Crenshaw et al. eds., 1995) (describing the solidarity between African American radicals and the Communist Party).

5. Basing economic rights in Reconstruction Constitution. Do the Reconstruction Amendments provide, as Akhil Amar suggests, an imaginative resource for rethinking economic rights? For another attempt to use antislavery constitutionalism as a foundation for economic justice and anti-subordination vision generally, see Peggy Cooper Davis, *Neglected Stories and Progressive Constitutionalism*, 4 WIDENER L. SYMP. J. 101 (1999).

CHAPTER 4

Classic Market Theory and Law and Economics

A. Classic Market Theory

Economics is the study of how scarce resources—land, capital, and labor—can best be allocated to satisfy human wants. Although it would be impossible to cover the whole of economic theory in a single chapter, this section describes some basic assumptions about human nature, the organization of society, and the role of government that have influenced the development of our modern economic and legal systems.

Economic analyses can be divided into two types: *positive* and *normative*. Positive economics attempts to describe in a rigorous way how markets operate, without judging whether the outcomes are good or bad. Normative economics takes the pursuit of greater efficiency as the primary good in governance, and frequently argues that governance through markets is superior to governance by direct state regulation. As you read the excerpts below, ask yourself which arguments are positive and which are normative, and why it makes a difference. Ask yourself, also, in what ways contemporary economic analysis has diverged from the work of Adam Smith.

Both strands of economic analysis—positive and normative—owe a central debt to the work of Adam Smith (1723–1790). Smith was a popular, absent-minded professor of moral philosophy—a field that at the time incorporated theology, ethics, justice, and political economy—at Scotland's University of Glasgow. Smith is called the "father of modern economics" because "[he] was the first to explain in detail the role of human beings in the development of markets and how these markets function to solve the basic economic problems that confront any society: what goods to produce, how to produce them, and to whom they should be distributed."

From the sixteenth through the nineteenth centuries, European nations generally solved these problems through mercantilism, an economic system in which the government regulated and dictated economic activity. Mercantilism used tools such as monopolies, subsidies, tariffs, and restrictive labor policies to build up a nation's gold and silver reserves, the theoretical source of economic power. Despite the restrictive regulations mercantilism involved, the English economy was expanding, in part through illegal market activities.

Smith's emphasis on the role of people in economic development was pioneering. His work defined the classical school of economics, which explains the economy in the context of human behavior. *The Theory of Moral Sentiments* (1759) explored the ethics and principles motivating human behavior and argued that people are mainly driven by self-interest, tempered by an "impartial spectator," or conscience. In the *Wealth of Nations* (1776), his most famous work, Smith used his theory of human nature to show how individuals acting in their own self-interest, unregulated by the state, could nevertheless collectively maximize the wealth of all. Smith argued that "[s]elf interest leads to market exchange, which fosters the division of labor, which leads in turn to specialization, expertise, dexterity, and improved machinery and ultimately creates greater wealth." Most famously, Smith described the results of this system of undirected market exchange as "the invisible hand": even purely self-interested behavior can result in a better life for all, as if an invisible hand had ordered the result.

Smith's assumption, shared by most contemporary economists, that people are chiefly motivated by self-interest is a controversial one. The following excerpt examines in more detail Smith's beliefs about human nature.

Adam Smith's View of Man

19 J.L. & ECON. 529 (1976).

■ R. H. COASE

* * * It is sometimes said that Adam Smith assumes that human beings are motivated solely by self-interest. Self-interest is certainly, in Adam Smith's view, a powerful motive in human behaviour, but it is by no means the only motive. I think it is important to recognise this since the inclusion of other motives in his analysis does not weaken but rather strengthens Adam Smith's argument for the use of the market and the limitation of government action in economic affairs.

* * * In *The Theory of Moral Sentiments*, man's actions are influenced by benevolence. In the *Wealth of Nations*, this motive is apparently absent. This view is supported by a much-quoted passage: "It is not from the benevolence of the butcher, the brewer, or the baker, that we expect our dinner, but from their regard to their own interest. We address ourselves, not to their humanity but to their self-love, and never talk to them of our own necessities but of their advantages." What is not quoted is something which Adam Smith says earlier in the same paragraph: "In civilized society [man] stands at all times in need of the co-operation and assistance of great multitudes, while his whole life is scarce sufficient to gain the friendship of a few persons." This puts a completely different complexion on the matter. For that extensive division of labour required to maintain a civilized standard of living, we need to have the co-operation of great multitudes, scattered all over the world. There is no way in which this co-operation could be secured through the exercise of benevolence. Benevolence, or love, may be the dominant or, at any rate, an important factor within the family or in our relations with colleagues or friends, but as Adam Smith indicates, it operates weakly or not at all when we deal with strangers. Benevolence is highly personal and most of those who benefit from the economic activities in which we engage are unknown to us. * * *

Looked at in this way, Adam Smith's argument for the use of the market for the organisation of economic activity is much stronger than it is usually thought to be. The market is not simply an ingenious mechanism, fueled by self-interest, for securing the co-operation of individuals in the production of goods and services. In most circumstances it is the only way in which this could be done. Nor does government regulation or operation represent a satisfactory way out. A politician, when motivated by benevolence, will tend to favour his family, his friends, members of his party, inhabitants of his region or country (and this whether or not he is democratically elected). Such benevolence will not necessarily redound to the general good. And when politicians are motivated by self-interest unalloyed by benevolence, it is easy to see that the results may be even less satisfactory.

The great advantage of the market is that it is able to use the strength of self-interest to offset the weakness and partiality of benevolence, so that those who are unknown, unattractive, or unimportant, will have their wants served. But this should not lead us to ignore the part which benevolence and moral sentiments do play in making possible a market system. Consider, for example, the care and training of the young, largely carried out within the family and sustained by parental devotion. If love were absent and the task of training the young was therefore placed on other institutions, run presumably by people following their own self-interest, it seems likely that this task, on which the successful working of human societies depends, would be worse performed. At least, that was Adam Smith's opinion: "Domestic education is the institution of nature—public education the contrivance of man. It is surely unnecessary to say which is likely to be the wisest." Again, the observance of moral codes must very greatly reduce the costs of doing business with others and must therefore facilitate market transactions. As Adam Smith observes, "Society . . . cannot subsist among those who are at all times ready to hurt and injure one another. . . ."

Adam Smith allows for a good deal of folly in human behaviour. But this does not lead him to advocate an extensive role for government. Politicians and government officials are also men. Private individuals are constrained in their folly because they personally suffer its consequences: "Bankruptcy is perhaps the greatest and most humiliating calamity which can befall an innocent man. The greater part of men, therefore, are sufficiently careful to avoid it." But, of course, men who bankrupt a city or a nation are not necessarily themselves made bankrupt. Adam Smith, therefore, continues: "Great nations are never impoverished by private, though they sometimes are by public prodigality and misconduct." As he later observes: "[Kings are and ministers] are themselves, always, and without any exception, the greatest spend thrifts in the society. Let them look well after their own expence, and they may safely trust private people with theirs. If their own extravagance does not ruin the state, that of their subjects never will."

* * *

It is wrong to believe, as is commonly done, that Adam Smith had as his view of man an abstraction, an "economic man," rationally pursuing his self-interest in a single-minded way. Adam Smith would not have thought it sensible to treat man as a rational utility-maximiser. He thinks of man as he actually is—dominated, it is true, by self-love but not without some concern for others, able to reason but not necessarily in such a way as to reach the right conclusion, seeing the outcomes of his actions but through a veil of self-delusion. No doubt modern psychologists have added a great deal, some of it correct, to this eighteenth-century view of human nature. But if one is willing to accept Adam Smith's view of man as containing, if not the whole truth, at least a large part of it, realisation that his thought has a much broader foundation than is commonly assumed makes his argument for economic freedom more powerful and his conclusions more persuasive.

———

As the Coase excerpt above suggests, Smith's theory was influential in part because it sought to provide a better policy solution than mercantilism to the problem of production and exchange in a mass society. Smith showed how a system of competition, under which producers competed to offer the highest quality goods at the lowest possible prices, could encourage the efficient allocation of resources without the need to resort to government coercion. The excerpt that follows updates Smith's basic insight.

———

The Advantages of a Free–Enterprise Price System

INVISIBLE HAND 64–68 (Adrian Klaasen ed., 1965).

■ W. ALLEN WALLIS

* * *

Suppose you were asked how to organize [the population of the United States] to utilize the resources available to them for their material satisfactions. You can imagine you have a fairly detailed inventory of the natural resources of the country, of the people and their knowledge, energies and abilities and of their wants. Imagine that all these resources are as unorganized as a set of chessmen just poured out of their box and awaiting organization on the chessboard. [The next issue concerns deciding how to organize the supply to meet the demand.]

[O]ne of the first things you are going to need is some way of establishing goals and measuring achievement. Which of the many things wanted are going to be produced, in what quantities, and with what priorities?

After you establish these goals and priorities, you will need a method of assigning the various pieces of capital, the various natural resources and the various people to particular activities. Each will have several alternative uses; you will need a method of deciding which use to assign it or him to, and of coordinating the resources assigned to cooperate in each task.

Then, third, you will have to have some system for dividing the product among the people: who gets how much of what, and when?

Fourth, you will probably realize that for one reason or another your system [will create mismatches between supply and demand]. You will need some system of adjustment to [account for these mismatches], until your method of measuring achievement and your method of allocating resources can get the basic situation corrected.

A fifth kind of problem you may worry about is that of providing for the expansion and improvement of your capital, equipment and technological knowledge.

These five functions have to be provided for when you establish any organization, even a small and relatively simple one. When we consider the large and complex organization of an entire economy, what are some of the alternative ways of arranging for them?

The most obvious way to arrange things is the way an army does. You set up a commander or a general staff. They decide on goals, they decide who shall do what to attain them, they decide how to apportion the product; and they issue orders accordingly. Another method is that used in beehives and ant colonies, in which caste and custom determine who does what. Things go on in the same way, generation after generation.

A third way is to introduce money and let each person decide what activities that others will pay for he will engage in, and what things that others offer for money he will buy. This is a method that no one really invented. It requires careful and sometimes complicated analysis to discover how it will really work. Indeed, it was only with the recognition that this is in fact a method of organizing society that the scientific study of economics began, back in 1776.

Under this system, goals are set by the money offers of individuals for goods and services. Resources are allocated to one activity or another by the desires of their owners for money income. Goods are distributed to individuals according to their willingness and ability to pay the prices. Thus prices become the crucial organizing element in such an economy. Indeed, this system is often called the "price system."

The price system has two outstanding features. First, it is by all odds the most efficient system of social organization ever conceived. It makes it possible for huge multitudes to cooperate effectively, multitudes who may hardly know of each other's existence, or whose personal attitudes toward one another may be indifference or hostility. Second, it affords a maximum of individual freedom and a minimum of coercion. And since people can cooperate effectively in production even when their attitudes on other issues are hostile, there is no need for unity and conformity in religion, politics, recreation and language—or even in patriotism and goodwill, except in the very broadest senses.

       * * *

       ————

NOTES AND QUESTIONS

1.   Markets, price theory, and the invisible hand. Are there times when price theory fails to adequately serve the communication function Wallis identifies? Are there technical obstacles in some situations to using the price system for the allocation of goods? Theories of "market failure," discussed in the next chapter, take up these questions.

2.   Smith and professional economists. For many modern economists, Smith was a great economist, perhaps the greatest ever. Adam Smith was not truly an economist as we understand that discipline today. Smith laid many of the foundations of modern economics with the *Wealth of Nations*, "but not for another century did economics truly become established as . . . a separate discipline." Skousen, *supra* at 195. As an academic, Smith was appointed professor of Logic at the University of Glasgow in 1751, and transferred to the chair of moral philosophy in 1752. ROBIN PAUL MALLOY & JERRY EVENSKY, ADAM SMITH AND THE PHILOSOPHY OF LAW AND ECONOMICS 34 (1994). As a moral philosopher, Smith drew on the work of contemporary thinkers such as Hume, Franklin, and Montesquieu when writing both *The Theory of Moral Sentiments* and the *Wealth of Nations*. SKOUSEN, *supra* at 38, 41–42.

3.   Economic analysis and the rational actor. Although Adam Smith's understanding of "economic man" incorporated benevolence, altruism, and sympathy, the tradition of "neoclassical" economics that followed in his footsteps focused on modeling self-interested behavior rather than other-directed behavior. In contemporary terms, economic analysis adopts some version of "rational choice" theory: individuals enter a market with specific preferences, and they act so as to satisfy those preferences to the greatest extent possible at the lowest possible cost. Rational choice theory has been much criticized; these critiques will be taken up in the next chapter.

4.   Modern evolution of classic market theory: victory of neoclassical theory. Historian Michael Bernstein notes that an important debate within the discipline of economics took place around the turn of the twentieth century. On the one hand were:

> those determined to preserve for economics a pride of place, grounded in rigorous theory, among the social sciences. For these scholars it was clear that, in the words of the eminent Alfred Marshall, "the raison d'être of economics as a separate science [wa]s that it deal[t] chiefly with the part of [people's] action which [wa]s most under the control of

measurable motives." It was necessarily the case, therefore, that economists had to employ "selective principles" in order to understand human behavior. Utilizing "a series of deductions from the fundamental concept of scarcity," the discipline's practitioners were thus in a position to engage in truly "analytical" studies that were, given a "correspondence [between] original assumptions and the facts," realistic approximations of social conduct. While history, institutions, law, and ideology could provide more detailed and nuanced explanations of actual economic events, the core analytical principles of economic explanation remained distinct.

Michael A. Bernstein, A Perilous Progress: Economists and Public Purpose in Twentieth-Century America 45–46 (2001).

For these scholars, the discipline of economics could provide an "objective science of society." *Id.* at 45. These "neoclassical" economists were drawn to rigorous mathematical models of economic behavior.

On the other side of the debate were the "institutionalists," a group of economists, many of them involved in public policy work for the federal government, who sought a broader scope for economics. Institutionalist economics was rooted in the work of Thorstein Veblen, who in the late 1890s and early 1900s attacked neoclassical theory for its excessive abstraction from the real world of economic behavior and posited that the search for social "status"—not just the desire for financial profit—motivated much of economic production, by spurring the desire for conspicuous consumption. According to Bernstein:

> [T]he institutionalists conceived of economics as a far more catholic field in which any claims to realism rested perforce on broadly construed disciplinary boundaries. Indeed, both [Wesley] Mitchell and Veblen themselves had aggressively attacked the manner in which neoclassical investigators ignored human activity that could not be understood simply as the "rational" and calculating response of individuals to the constraints of the market. To their minds "such institutions as the market, trade, contract, property, and competition" were themselves the product of political, cultural, and historical circumstances all of which were worthy of the economist's attention.

Id. at 46.

Accordingly, the institutionalists were empiricist rather than theoretical and mathematical in their bent. Ultimately, however, it was the neoclassicists who won the battle and ascended to power over the institutionalists.

5. Cold War and discipline of economics. Michael Bernstein argues that "[i]n its theoretical and methodological trajectory, the American economics profession was decisively affected by the pressures, constraints, and opportunities afforded by the Cold War preoccupations of the federal government, colleges and universities, and private foundations and 'think tanks.' " *Id.* at 94. During World War II, mathematically-driven developments in economics such as "activity analysis" and "linear programming" made it possible for economists to help the War Department plan resource allocation and distribution plans (for example, to calculate the most efficient supply shipments). During the Cold War, the federal government, both directly and through organizations such as the RAND Corporation (originally Project RAND under the supervision of the Air Force) and the National Science Foundation, generously supported research into "game theory" and other mathematical approaches to the problem of modeling competitive behavior. Game theory, for example, demonstrated how strategic behavior could be modeled mathematically, and these models could be applied to problems such as nuclear deterrence. Macroeconomic theory was also appealing to government funders because of the promise that it could be directly applied to the project of sustaining the American economy and preserving and protecting the nation's security. For example, in 1954, the staff of the Council of Economic Advisers initiated "a series of wide-ranging discussions on the matter of 'emergency economic stabilization' in the event of a nuclear exchange." *Id*. at 104. The idea was that "in the event of a nuclear attack civil defense authorities should be given the power to set wages, prices, and rents—as well as to ration goods and services. To be effective, plans for such a contingency would need to be set up in advance." *Id*.

The issues of national security and national prosperity were intertwined, and both of them seemed uniquely suited to economists' strengths. Bernstein observes:

> High rates of growth, robust levels of employment, and stable prices were the standards by which a capitalist society could demonstrate its advantages over command economies premised upon socialist or communist designs. As the emblematic "Kitchen Debate" between Soviet premier Nikita Khrushchev and Vice President Richard Nixon had suggested in 1959, winning the Cold War involved more than husbanding a credible nuclear deterrent, deploying fleets, garrisons, and air wings around the world, and utilizing special forces in counterinsurgency campaigns. It also required that an economic system deliver the goods to the people. Prosperity was an essential weapon in the struggle for the hearts and minds of any society.

Id. at 107.

By the 1950s, argues Bernstein, "No longer the study of 'the nature and causes of the wealth of nations' (as Adam Smith had claimed), or 'a critical analysis of capitalist production' (as Karl Marx suggested), economics had become the formal study of 'the adaptation of scarce means to given ends.'" *Id*. at 95. The means to this study should be apolitical and objective. Thus, "[g]one from a rising number of nationally ranked graduate programs in economics, by the late 1950s, were agendas that acquainted the student with the work of a Thorstein Veblen, a Joseph Schumpeter, or a Karl Polanyi—not to mention a Karl Marx. In their place were 'core' course sequences that emphasized neoclassical theory, most often in its mathematical representations." *Id*. at 123. Although the 1960s and 1970s saw a challenge by a "New Left" within the economics profession—which formed organizations such as the Union for Radical Political Economics (URPE), and identified and attacked logical inconsistencies at the heart of neoclassical economics—neoclassical economics continued to define the discipline up to the end of the twentieth century.

6. Economic theory and the rise and fall of Keynesian macroeconomics. As we have seen, Adam Smith wrote primarily against the "mercantilism" of his time, a system in which the state heavily controlled economic behavior, often by granting monopolies in crucial trading industries to particular organizations and individuals. Smith's metaphor of the invisible hand suggested that a market free of such government intervention would provide more prosperity for everyone, and that such a market would be self-regulating. In 1936, however, an Englander named John Maynard Keynes [1883–1946], published a book called *The General Theory of Employment, Interest, and Money* [hereafter the *General Theory*] that paved the way for a new discipline of "macroeconomics." Keynes was many things during his illustrious career: "a brilliant student at England's most famous prep school; an equally brilliant student and then professor at Kings College in Cambridge; a financier who made a fortune for himself, and, later for Kings College by overseeing its endowment fund; president of a life-insurance company; patron of the arts; husband of a famous Russian ballerina; member of the influential 'Bloomsbury set' of intellectuals; esteemed official of the British Treasury; board member of the Bank of England; and the principal designer of the international financial system after World War II." Charles Sackrey & Geoffrey Schneider, Introduction to Political Economy 80–81 (3d ed. 2002).

Keynes's innovation begins with the "business cycle": over time, national economies tend to experience periods of growth, followed by periods of seeming economic collapse, involving sudden drops in wages, mass unemployment, and drastically reduced spending power (known as recessions). The most famous of these in the United States was, of course, the Great Depression, which followed the stock crash of 1929. Classical economists argued that during these depressions, falling wages would lower costs and prices and invite a greater demand for goods and services. Thus, downturns in the business cycle are always self-correcting. Keynes argued, however, that "a *general* fall in wages . . . would likely cause an eventual *decline* in the demand for goods and services that workers buy, rather than an increase encouraged by the lower prices." *Id.* at 92. Moreover, falling wages could reduce the optimism of capitalists and encourage them to reduce investment in new equipment. The result would be a downward spiral for the economy rather than a self-correcting equilibrium. As a policy matter, then, Keynes argued that an active rather than passive government response to recessions and depressions was required:

> [A]s investment and consumption spending fell, the government should take up the slack in demand by borrowing money to increase its own expenditures * * * And it didn't matter for what those expenditures were made. As this spending worked its way through the economy, it would ultimately produce a better outlook for businesses, which meant

more investment on capital goods. * * * [T]his would start the whole process moving back upward to recovery and economic growth.

Id. at 97.

Keynesian theory and policy quickly became mainstream. The massive government spending involved in the United States' participation in World War II appeared to prove Keynes right about the ability of governments to take action against economic recessions, and the Cold War period saw the adoption of Keynesian macroeconomic policy on a broad scale. Sackrey and Schneider observe:

> A symbolic highpoint of the influence of Keynes occurred in 1963, when in a speech at Yale University John Kennedy used the idea of the Keynesian multiplier to justify the cut in personal income taxes he was urging on the Congress as a way to cause a sluggish economy to grow faster. The essentially Keynesian basis of domestic U.S. economic policy remained in place for about 25 years, and, in 1971, an economic conservative, Richard Nixon, argued that "we are all Keynesians now."

Id. at 98.

> Nevertheless, the rise of Keynesian macroeconomics was followed by a fall. Beginning in the late 1960s, the American national economy began to experience persistent and growing inflation. In the early 1970s, the Organization of Petroleum Exporting Countries (OPEC) announced a plan to dramatically cut petroleum production, setting off a series of global economic shocks. Soon the American economy was experiencing high inflation and high unemployment at the same time—a situation, nicknamed "stagflation," thought to be impossible by professional economists. Real incomes fell dramatically and capital investments stagnated, and Keynesian theorists seemed helpless to address the problem. Into the breach stepped new macroeconomic theories. The "new classical" economists argued that government interventions in the market were futile because economic actors would always be able to anticipate and adjust their behavior to such interventions. "Supply-side" economists argued that the country's economic woes were caused by high levels of government spending, high taxation of income, and extensive governmental regulation of economic affairs. Excessive income taxation, it was argued, stifled productive effort, for example, by discouraging overtime work. It robbed individuals of the fruits of enterprise and risk-bearing. Finally, it distorted economic decision making so as to slow growth and create the very fiscal pressure that contributed to the problems of "stagflation" in the first instance. The solution would involve a radical reduction in taxes, a systematic shrinking of government spending programs and, thus, federal agency budgets, and the elimination of costly regulatory measures.

MICHAEL A. BERNSTEIN, A PERILOUS PROGRESS, *supra* at 164.

These scholarly arguments were supported by a new turn in electoral politics against "big government." Ronald Reagan's decisive 1980 victory over Jimmy Carter for the presidency symbolized a new consensus in the electorate that government did not work, that private businesses should be as free of regulation as possible, and that taxes should be cut in order to reward individual initiative and let the "invisible hand" do its work. Although few professional economists agreed with the excesses of "Reaganomics," a general mood in favor of laissez-faire economics, deregulation, and "privatization" now characterized the electorate and dominated thought in the Beltway.

As we explore more fully in chapter 6, the Great Recession of 2008 has accelerated and deepened the sharp critiques of neoclassical economics.

B.   Libertarianism

Created Equal

Free to Choose: A Personal Statement 128–49 (1980).

■ Milton Friedman & Rose Friedman

"Equality," "liberty"—what precisely do these words from the Declaration of Independence mean? Can the ideals they express be realized in practice? Are equality and liberty consistent one with the other, or are they in conflict?

Since well before the Declaration of Independence, these questions have played a central role in the history of the United States. The attempt to answer them has shaped the intellectual climate of opinion, led to bloody war, and produced major changes in economic and political institutions. This attempt continues to dominate our political debate. It will shape our future as it has our past.

In the early decades of the Republic, equality meant equality before God; liberty meant the liberty to shape one's own life. The obvious conflict between the Declaration of Independence and the institution of slavery occupied the center of the stage. That conflict was finally resolved by the Civil War. The debate then moved to a different level. Equality came more and more to be interpreted as "equality of opportunity" in the sense that no one should be prevented by arbitrary obstacles from using his capacities to pursue his own objectives. That is still its dominant meaning to most citizens of the United States.

Neither equality before God nor equality of opportunity presented any conflict with liberty to shape one's own life. Quite the opposite. Equality and liberty were two faces of the same basic value—that every individual should be regarded as an end in himself.

A very different meaning of equality has emerged in the United States in recent decades—equality of outcome. Everyone should have the same level of living or of income, should finish the race at the same time. Equality of outcome is in clear conflict with liberty. The attempt to promote it has been a major source of bigger and bigger government, and of government-imposed restrictions on our liberty.

EQUALITY BEFORE GOD

When Thomas Jefferson, at the age of thirty-three, wrote "all men are created equal," he and his contemporaries did not take these words literally. They did not regard "men"—or as we would say today, "persons"—as equal in physical characteristics, emotional reactions, mechanical and intellectual abilities. * * *

The clue to what Thomas Jefferson and his contemporaries meant by equal is in the next phrase of the Declaration—"endowed by their Creator with certain unalienable rights; that among these are Life, Liberty, and the pursuit of Happiness." Men were equal before God. Each person is precious in and of himself. He has unalienable rights, rights that no one else is entitled to invade. He is entitled to serve his own purposes and not to be treated simply as an instrument to promote someone else's purposes. "Liberty" is part of the definition of equality, not in conflict with it.

Equality before God—personal equality—is important precisely because people are not identical. Their different values, their different tastes, their different capacities will lead them to want to lead very different lives. Personal equality requires respect for their right to do so, not the imposition on them of someone else's values or judgment. Jefferson had no doubt that some men were superior to others, that there was an elite. But that did not give them the right to rule others.

If an elite did not have the right to impose its will on others, neither did any other group, even a majority. Every person was to be his own ruler—provided that he did not interfere with the similar right of others. Government was established to protect that right—from fellow citizens and from external threat—not to give a majority unbridled rule. * * *

Similarly, Alexis de Tocqueville, the famous French political philosopher and sociologist, in his classic *Democracy in America*, written after a lengthy visit in the 1830s, saw equality, not majority rule, as the outstanding characteristic of America. "In America," he wrote,

> the aristocratic element has always been feeble from its birth; and if at the present day it is not actually destroyed, it is at any rate so completely disabled, that we can scarcely assign to it any degree of influence on the course of affairs. The democratic principle, on the contrary, has gained so much strength by time, by events, and by legislation, as to have become not only predominant but all-powerful. There is no family or corporate authority....

> America, then, exhibits in her social state a most extraordinary phenomenon. Men are there seen on a greater equality in point of fortune and intellect, or, in other words, more equal in their strength, than in any other country of the world, or in any age of which history has preserved the remembrance.

* * *

It is striking testimony to the changing meaning of words that in recent decades the Democratic party of the United States has been the chief instrument for strengthening that government power which Jefferson and many of his contemporaries viewed as the greatest threat to democracy. And it has striven to increase government power in the name of a concept of "equality" that is almost the opposite of the concept of equality Jefferson identified with liberty and Tocqueville with democracy.

    * * *

EQUALITY OF OPPORTUNITY

Once the Civil War abolished slavery and the concept of personal equality—equality before God and the law—came closer to realization, emphasis shifted, in intellectual discussion and in government and private policy, to a different concept—equality of opportunity.

Literal equality of opportunity—in the sense of "identity"—is impossible. One child is born blind, another with sight. One child has parents deeply concerned about his welfare who provide a background of culture and understanding; another has dissolute, improvident parents. One child is born in the United States, another in India, or China, or Russia. They clearly do not have identical opportunities open to them at birth, and there is no way that their opportunities can be made identical.

Like personal equality, equality of opportunity is not to be interpreted literally. Its real meaning is perhaps best expressed by the French expression dating from the French Revolution: *Une carriere ouverte aux les talents*—a career open to the talents. No arbitrary obstacles should prevent people from achieving those positions for which their talents fit them and which their values lead them to seek. Not birth, nationality, color, religion, sex, nor any other irrelevant characteristic should determine the opportunities that are open to a person—only his abilities.

On this interpretation, equality of opportunity simply spells out in more detail the meaning of personal equality, of equality before the law. And like personal equality, it has meaning and importance precisely because people are different in their genetic and cultural characteristics, and hence both want to and can pursue different careers.

Equality of opportunity, like personal equality, is not inconsistent with liberty; on the contrary, it is an essential component of liberty. If some people are denied access to particular positions in life for which they are qualified simply because of their ethnic background, color, or religion, that is an interference with their right to "Life, Liberty, and the pursuit of Happiness." It denies equality of opportunity and, by the same token, sacrifices the freedom of some for the advantage of others.

Like every ideal, equality of opportunity is incapable of being fully realized. The most serious departure was undoubtedly with respect to the blacks, particularly in the South but in the North as well. Yet there was also tremendous progress—for blacks and for other groups. The very concept of a "melting pot" reflected the goal of equality of opportunity. So also did the expansion of "free" education at elementary, secondary, and higher levels—though, as we shall see in the next chapter, this development has not been an unmixed blessing.

The priority given to equality of opportunity in the hierarchy of values generally accepted by the public after the Civil War is manifested particularly in economic policy. The catchwords were free enterprise, competition, laissez-faire. Everyone was to be free to go into any business, follow any occupation, buy any property, subject only to the agreement of the other parties to the transaction. Each was to have the opportunity to reap the benefits if he succeeded, to suffer the costs if he failed. There were to be no arbitrary obstacles. Performance, not birth, religion, or nationality, was the touchstone.

One corollary was the development of what many who regarded themselves as the cultural elite sneered at as vulgar materialism—an emphasis on the almighty dollar, on wealth as both the symbol and the seal of success.

* * *

Another corollary, of course, was an enormous release of human energy that made America an increasingly productive and dynamic society in which social mobility was an everyday reality. Still another, perhaps surprisingly, was an explosion in charitable activity. This explosion was made possible by the rapid growth in wealth. It took the form it did—of nonprofit hospitals, privately endowed colleges and universities, a plethora of charitable organizations directed to helping the poor—because of the dominant values of the society, including, especially, promotion of equality of opportunity.

Of course, in the economic sphere as elsewhere, practice did not always conform to the ideal. Government *was* kept to a minor role; no major obstacles to enterprise were erected, and by the end of the nineteenth century, positive government measures, especially the Sherman Anti–Trust Law, were adopted to eliminate private barriers to competition. But extralegal arrangements continued to interfere with the freedom of individuals to enter various businesses or professions, and social practices unquestionably gave special advantages to persons born in the "right" families, of the "right" color, and practicing the "right" religion. However, the rapid rise in the economic and social position of various less privileged groups demonstrates that these obstacles were by no means insurmountable.

In respect of government measures, one major deviation from free markets was in foreign trade, where Alexander Hamilton's *Report on Manufactures* had enshrined tariff protection for domestic industries as part of the American way. Tariff protection was inconsistent with thoroughgoing equality of opportunity * * * and, indeed, with the free immigration of persons, which was the rule until World War I, except only for Orientals. Yet it could be rationalized both by the needs of national defense and on the very different ground that equality stops at the water's edge—an illogical rationalization that is adopted also by most of today's proponents of a very different concept of equality.

EQUALITY OF OUTCOME

That different concept, equality of outcome, has been gaining ground in this century. It first affected government policy in Great Britain and on the European continent. Over the past half-century it has increasingly affected government policy in the United States as well. In some intellectual circles the desirability of equality of outcome has become an article of religious faith: everyone should finish the race at the same time. As the Dodo said in *Alice in Wonderland*, "*Everybody* has won, and *all* must have prizes."

For this concept, as for the other two, "equal" is not to be interpreted literally as "identical." No one really maintains that everyone, regardless of age or sex or other physical qualities should have identical rations of each separate item of food, clothing, and so on. The goal is rather "fairness," a much vaguer notion—indeed, one that it is difficult, if not impossible, to define precisely. "Fair shares for all" is the modern slogan that has replaced Karl Marx's, "To each according to his needs, from each according to his ability."

This concept of equality differs radically from the other two. Government measures that promote personal equality or equality of opportunity enhanced liberty; government measures to achieve "fair shares for all" reduce liberty. If what people get is to be determined by "fairness," who is to decide what is "fair"? As a chorus of voices asked the Dodo, "But who is to give the prizes?" "Fairness" is not an objectively determined concept once it departs from identity. "Fairness," like "needs," is in the eye of the beholder. If all are to have "fair shares," someone or some group of people must decide what shares are fair—and they must be able to impose their decisions on others, taking from those who have more than their "fair" share and giving to those who have less. Are those who make and impose such decisions equal to those for whom they decide? Are we not in George Orwell's *Animal Farm*, where "all animals are equal, but some animals are more equal than others"?

In addition, if what people get is determined by "fairness" and not by what they produce, where are the "prizes" to come from? What incentive is there to work and produce? How is it to be decided who is to be the doctor, who the lawyer, who the garbage collector, who the street sweeper? What assures that people will accept the roles assigned to them and perform those roles in accordance with their abilities? Clearly, only force or the threat of force will do.

The key point is not merely that practice will depart from the ideal. Of course it will, as it does with respect to the other two concepts of equality as well. The point is rather that there is a fundamental conflict between the *ideal* of "fair shares" or of its precursor, "to each according to his needs," and the *ideal* of personal liberty. This conflict has plagued every attempt to make equality of outcome the overriding principle of social organization. The end result has invariably been a state of terror: Russia, China, and, more recently, Cambodia offer clear and convincing evidence.

* * *

The far less extreme measures taken in Western countries in the name of equality of outcome have shared the same fate to a lesser extent. They, too, have restricted individual liberty. They, too, have failed to achieve their objective. It has proved impossible to define "fair shares" in a way that is generally acceptable, or to satisfy the members of the community that they are being treated "fairly." On the contrary, dissatisfaction has mounted with every additional attempt to implement equality of outcome.

Much of the moral fervor behind the drive for equality of outcome comes from the widespread belief that it is not fair that some children should have a great advantage over others simply because they happen to have wealthy parents. Of course it is not fair. However, unfairness can take many forms. It can take the form of the inheritance of property—bonds and stocks, houses, factories; it can also take the form of the inheritance of talent—musical ability, strength, mathematical genius. The inheritance of property can be interfered with more readily than the inheritance of talent. But from an ethical point of view, is there any difference between the two? Yet many people resent the inheritance of property but not the inheritance of talent.

Look at the same issue from the point of view of the parent. If you want to assure your child a higher income in life, you can do so in various ways. You can buy him (or her) an education that will equip him to pursue an occupation yielding a high income; or you can set him up in a business that will yield a higher income than he could earn as a salaried employee; or you can leave him property, the income from which will enable him to live better. Is there any ethical difference among these three ways of using your property? Or again, if the state leaves you any money to spend over and above taxes, should the state permit you to spend it on riotous living but not to leave it to your children?

The ethical issues involved are subtle and complex. They are not to be resolved by such simplistic formulas as "fair shares for all." Indeed, if we took that seriously, youngsters with less musical skill should be given the greatest amount of musical training in order to compensate for their inherited disadvantage, and those with greater musical aptitude should be prevented from having access to good musical training; and similarly with all other categories of inherited personal qualities. That might be "fair" to the youngsters lacking in talent, but would it be "fair" to the talented, let alone to those who had to work to pay for training the youngsters lacking talent, or to the persons deprived of the benefits that might have come from the cultivation of the talents of the gifted?

* * *

Still another facet of this complex issue of fairness can be illustrated by considering a game of chance, for example, an evening at baccarat. The people who choose to play may start the evening with equal piles of chips, but as the play progresses, those piles will become unequal. By the end of the evening, some will be big winners, others big losers. In the name of the ideal of equality, should the winners be required to repay the losers? That would take all the fun out of the game. Not even the losers would like that.

They might like it for the one evening, but would they come back again to play if they knew that whatever happened, they'd end up exactly where they started?

This example has a great deal more to do with the real world than one might at first suppose. Every day each of us makes decisions that involve taking a chance. Occasionally it's a big chance as when we decide what occupation to pursue, whom to marry, whether to buy a house or make a major investment. More often it's a small chance, as when we decide what movie to go to, whether to cross the street against the traffic, whether to buy one security rather than another. Each time the question is, who is to decide what chances we take? That in turn depends on who bears the consequences of the decision. If we bear the consequences, we can make the decision. But if someone else bears the consequences, should we or will we be permitted to make the decision? * * *

The system under which people make their own choices—and bear most of the consequences of their decisions—is the system that has prevailed for most of our history. It is the system that gave the Henry Fords, the Thomas Alva Edisons, the George Eastmans, the John D. Rockefellers, the James Cash Penneys the incentive to transform our society over the past two centuries. It is the system that gave other people an incentive to furnish venture capital to finance the risky enterprises that these ambitious inventors and captains of industry undertook. Of course, there were many losers along the way—probably more losers than winners. We don't remember their names. But for the most part they went in with their eyes open. They knew they were taking chances. And win or lose, society as a whole benefited from their willingness to take a chance.

The fortunes that this system produced came overwhelmingly from developing new products or services, or new ways of producing products or services, or of distributing them widely. The resulting addition to the wealth of the community as a whole, to the well-being of the masses of the people, amounted to many times the wealth accumulated by the innovators. Henry Ford acquired a great fortune. The country acquired a cheap and reliable means of transportation and the techniques of mass production. Moreover, in many cases the private fortunes were largely devoted in the end to the benefit of society. The Rockefeller, Ford, and Carnegie foundations are only the most prominent of the numerous private benefactions which are so outstanding a consequence of the operation of a system that corresponded to "equality of opportunity" and "liberty" as these terms were understood until recently.

* * *

There is no inconsistency between a free market system and the pursuit of broad social and cultural goals, or between a free market system and compassion for the less fortunate, whether that compassion takes the form, as it did in the nineteenth century, of private charitable activity, or, as it has done increasingly in the twentieth, of assistance through government—provided that in both cases it is an expression of a desire to help others. There is all the difference in the world, however, between two kinds of assistance through government that seem superficially similar: first, 90 percent of us agreeing to impose taxes on ourselves in order to help the bottom 10 percent, and second, 80 percent voting to impose taxes on the top 10 percent to help the bottom 10 percent—William Graham Sumner's famous example of B and C deciding what D shall do for A. The first may be wise or unwise, an effective or an ineffective way to help the disadvantaged—but it is consistent with belief in both equality of opportunity and liberty. The second seeks equality of outcome and is entirely antithetical to liberty.

WHO FAVORS EQUALITY OF OUTCOME?

There is little support for the goal of equality of outcome despite the extent to which it has become almost an article of religious faith among intellectuals and despite its prominence in the speeches of politicians and the preambles of legislation. The talk is belied alike by the behavior of government, of the intellectuals who most ardently espouse egalitarian sentiments, and of the public at large.

* * *

For intellectuals, the clearest evidence is their failure to practice what so many of them preach. Equality of outcome can be promoted on a do-it-yourself basis. First, decide exactly what you mean by equality. Do you want to achieve equality within the United States? In a selected group of countries as a whole? In the world as a whole? Is equality to be judged in terms of income per person? Per family? Per year? Per decade? Per lifetime? Income in the form of money alone? Or including such nonmonetary items as the rental value of an owned home; food grown for one's own use; services rendered by members of the family not employed for money, notably the housewife? How are physical and mental handicaps or advantages to be allowed for?

However you decide these issues, you can, if you are an egalitarian, estimate what money income would correspond to your concept of equality. If your actual income is higher than that, you can keep that amount and distribute the rest to people who are below that level. If your criterion were to encompass the world—as most egalitarian rhetoric suggests it should—something less than, say, $200 a year (in 1979 dollars) per person would be an amount that would correspond to the conception of equality that seems implicit in most egalitarian rhetoric. That is about the average income per person worldwide.

What Irving Kristol has called the "new class"—government bureaucrats, academics whose research is supported by government funds or who are employed in government financed "think tanks," staffs of the many so-called "general interest" or "public policy" groups, journalists and others in the communications industry—are among the most ardent preachers of the doctrine of equality. Yet they remind us very much of the old, if unfair, saw about the Quakers: "They came to the New World to do good, and ended up doing well." The members of the new class are in general among the highest paid persons in the community. And for many among them, preaching equality and promoting or administering the resulting legislation has proved an effective means of achieving such high incomes. All of us find it easy to identify our own welfare with the welfare of the community.

Of course, an egalitarian may protest that he is but a drop in the ocean, that he would be willing to redistribute the excess of his income over his concept of an equal income if everyone else were compelled to do the same. On one level this contention that compulsion would change matters is wrong—even if everyone else did the same, his specific contribution to the income of others would still be a drop in the ocean. His individual contribution would be just as large if he were the only contributor as if he were one of many. Indeed, it would be more valuable because he could target his contribution to go to the very worst off among those he regards as appropriate recipients. On another level compulsion would change matters drastically: the kind of society that would emerge if such acts of redistribution were voluntary is altogether different—and, by our standards, infinitely preferable—to the kind that would emerge if redistribution were compulsory.

Persons who believe that a society of enforced equality is preferable can also practice what they preach. They can join one of the many communes in this country and elsewhere, or establish new ones. And, of course, it is entirely consistent with a belief in personal equality or equality of opportunity and liberty that any group of individuals who wish to live in that way should be free to do so. Our thesis that support for equality of outcome is word-deep receives strong support from the small number of persons who have wished to join such communes and from the fragility of the communes that have been established.

* * *

CONSEQUENCES OF EGALITARIAN POLICIES

In shaping our own policy, we can learn from the experience of Western countries with which we share a common intellectual and cultural background, and from which we derive many of our values. Perhaps the most instructive example is Great Britain, which led the way in the nineteenth century toward implementing equality of opportunity and in the twentieth toward implementing equality of outcome.

Since the end of World War II, British domestic policy has been dominated by the search for greater equality of outcome. Measure after measure has been adopted, designed to take from the rich and give to the poor. Taxes were raised on income until they reached a top rate of 98 percent on property income and 83 percent on "earned" income, and were supplemented by ever heavier taxes on inheritances. State-provided medical, housing, and other welfare services were greatly expanded, along with payments to the unemployed and the aged. Unfortunately, the results have been very different from those that were intended by the people who were quite properly offended by the class structure that dominated Britain for centuries. There has been a vast redistribution of wealth, but the end result is not an equitable distribution.

Instead, new classes of privileged have been created to replace or supplement the old: the bureaucrats, secure in their jobs, protected against inflation both when they work and when they retire; the trade unions that profess to represent the most downtrodden workers but in fact consist of the highest paid laborers in the land—the aristocrats of the labor movement; and the new millionaires—people who have been cleverest at finding ways around the laws, the rules, the regulations that have poured from Parliament and the bureaucracy, who have found ways to avoid paying taxes on their income and to get their wealth overseas beyond the grasp of the tax collectors. A vast reshuffling of income and wealth, yes; greater equity, hardly.

The drive for equality in Britain failed, not because the wrong measures were adopted—though some no doubt were; not because they were badly administered—though some no doubt were; not because the wrong people administered them—though no doubt some did. The drive for equality failed for a much more fundamental reason. It went against one of the most basic instincts of all human beings. In the words of Adam Smith, "The uniform, constant, and uninterrupted effort of every man to better his condition"—and, one may add, the condition of his children and his children's children. Smith, of course, meant by "condition" not merely material well-being, though certainly that was one component. He had a much broader concept in mind, one that included all of the values by which men judge their success—in particular the kind of social values that gave rise to the outpouring of philanthropic activities in the nineteenth century.

When the law interferes with people's pursuit of their own values, they will try to find a way around. They will evade the law, they will break the law, or they will leave the country. Few of us believe in a moral code that justifies forcing people to give up much of what they produce to finance payments to persons they do not know for purposes they may not approve of. When the law contradicts what most people regard as moral and proper, they will break the law—whether the law is enacted in the name of a noble ideal such as equality or in the naked interest of one group at the expense of another. Only fear of punishment, not a sense of justice and morality, will lead people to obey the law.

When people start to break one set of laws, the lack of respect for the law inevitably spreads to all laws, even those that everyone regards as moral and proper—laws against violence, theft, and vandalism. Hard as it may be to believe, the growth of crude criminality in Britain in recent decades may well be one consequence of the drive for equality.

* * *

We in the United States have not gone as far as Britain in promoting the goal of equality of outcome. Yet many of the same consequences are already evident—from a failure of egalitarian measures to achieve their objectives, to a reshuffling of wealth that by no standards can be regarded as equitable; to a rise in criminality, to a depressing effect on productivity and efficiency.

Capitalism and Equality

Everywhere in the world there are gross inequities of income and wealth. They offend most of us. Few can fail to be moved by the contrast between the luxury enjoyed by some and the grinding poverty suffered by others.

In the past century a myth has grown up that free market capitalism—equality of opportunity as we have interpreted that term—increases such inequalities, that it is a system under which the rich exploit the poor.

Nothing could be further from the truth. Wherever the free market has been permitted to operate, wherever anything approaching equality of opportunity has existed, the ordinary man has been able to attain levels of living never dreamed of before. Nowhere is the gap between rich and poor wider, nowhere are the rich richer and the poor poorer, than in those societies that do not permit the free market to operate. That is true of feudal societies like medieval Europe, India before independence, and much of modern South America, where inherited status determines position. It is equally true of centrally planned societies, like Russia or China or India since independence, where access to government determines position. It is true even where central planning was introduced, as in all three of these countries, in the name of equality.

* * *

In 1848 John Stuart Mill wrote: "Hitherto it is questionable if all the mechanical inventions yet made have lightened the day's toil of any human being. They have enabled a greater population to live the same life of drudgery and imprisonment, and an increased number of manufacturers and others to make fortunes. They have increased the comforts of the middle classes. But they have not yet begun to effect those great changes in human destiny, which it is in their nature and in their futurity to accomplish."

No one could say that today. You can travel from one end of the industrialized world to the other and almost the only people you will find engaging in backbreaking toil are people who are doing it for sport. To find people whose day's toil has not been lightened by mechanical invention, you must go to the non-capitalist world: to Russia, China, India or Bangladesh, parts of Yugoslavia; or to the more backward capitalist countries—in Africa, the Mideast, South America; and until recently, Spain or Italy.

Conclusion

A society that puts equality—in the sense of equality of outcome—ahead of freedom will end up with neither equality nor freedom. The use of force to achieve equality will destroy freedom, and the force, introduced for good purposes, will end up in the hands of people who use it to promote their own interests.

On the other hand, a society that puts freedom first will, as a happy by-product, end up with both greater freedom and greater equality. Though a by-product of freedom, greater equality is not an accident. A free society releases the energies and abilities of people to pursue their own objectives. It prevents some people from arbitrarily suppressing others. It does not prevent some people from achieving positions of privilege, but so long as freedom is maintained, it prevents those positions of privilege from becoming institutionalized; they are subject to continued attack by other able, ambitious people. Freedom means diversity but also mobility. It preserves the opportunity for today's disadvantaged to become tomorrow's privileged and, in the process, enables almost everyone, from top to bottom, to enjoy a fuller and richer life.

NOTES AND QUESTIONS

1.   Operation of government and market in Wealth of Nations. In his second book, *Wealth of Nations*, Adam Smith advocated a limited role for government in economic life. Nevertheless, Smith advocated government authority to ensure the provision of four basic necessities:

1.   The need for a well-financed militia for national defense

2.   A legal system to protect liberty, property rights, and to enforce contracts and payment of debts

3.   Public works—roads, canals, bridges, harbors, and other infrastructure projects

4.   Universal public education to counter the alienating and mentally degrading effects of specialization (division of labor) under capitalism

MARK SKOUSEN, THE MAKING OF MODERN ECONOMICS 33 (2001).

Additionally, Smith identifies three characteristics necessary for a self-regulating economics system:

1.   Freedom: the right to produce and exchange products, labor, and capital

2.   Self-interest: the right to pursue one's own business and to appeal to the self interest of others

3.   Competition: the right to compete in the production and exchange of goods and services

Id. at 22.

2.   Friedman's political philosophy. Milton Friedman is associated with the libertarian school of political philosophy. According to this school, the best government is the smallest, least intrusive government possible, "consistent with the maximum freedom for each individual to follow his own ways, his own values, as long as he doesn't interfere with anybody else who's doing the same." *Uncommon Knowledge, Take it to the Limits: Milton Friedman on Libertarianism* (American Public Television broadcast, Feb. 10, 1999), *available at* http://www.uncommonknowledge.org/99winter/324.htm/.

Friedman does not justify his advocacy of a free market society by some external referent like wealth maximization. Instead he says that:

> A free society, I believe, is a more productive society than any other. . . . But that is not why I am in favor of a free society. I believe and hope that I would favor a free society even if it were less productive than some alternative. . . . I favor a free society because my basic value is freedom itself.

ROBIN PAUL MALLOY & JERRY EVENSKY, ADAM SMITH AND THE PHILOSOPHY OF LAW AND ECONOMICS 160 (1994).

3. Libertarianism and law and economics. Friedman's libertarian political philosophy is often associated with the law and economics movement discussed *infra* at 210. As one commentator put it "law and economics scholars will—with only rare exceptions—take positions comparable with libertarian conservatives." Michael McConnell, *The Counter–Revolution in Legal Thought,* 41 POL'Y REV. 18, 24 (1987). For more on libertarianism, especially as it relates to law and economics see this text, *infra* at 211.

4. Friedman's equality.

    a. Friedman's negative definitions of equality. Friedman, when introducing what he asserts are distinct stages in the progression of equality, defines what each stage was not. For example, Friedman states that Thomas Jefferson "did not regard men . . . as equal in physical characteristics, emotional reactions, mechanical and intellectual abilities." FRIEDMAN, *supra*, at 211. Why does Friedman do this? Does he mean to imply that the only alternative interpretation of equality to the one he ascribes to the founding fathers is literal physical equality? If there are other possible interpretations of the Declaration of Independence, why should we choose Friedman's? For example, Charles Black asserts that the Declaration of Independence can be read as guaranteeing every person a right to a livelihood. Charles Black, *Further Reflections on the Constitutional Justice of Livelihood*, 86 COLUM. L. REV. 1103 (1986) (arguing that the right to pursuit of happiness and the elimination of poverty are not simply matters of compassion. Black argues that these rights can be derived from the preamble to, and Ninth Amendment of, the Constitution and the Declaration of Independence). Given that there are alternative readings of the Declaration of Independence that are vastly more persuasive than the literal equality Friedman addresses, should his refusal to address those alternatives make us skeptical about his main claims?

    b. Friedman's use of straw-men when discussing equality of outcome. When discussing personal equality and equality of opportunity, Friedman cites admired historical and cultural figures such as Jefferson, de Tocqueville, and Lincoln. When discussing equality of outcome, Friedman cites the Dodo from *Alice in Wonderland* and Karl Marx. If, as Friedman claims is the case, "equality of outcome . . . has become almost an article of religious faith among intellectuals," why did Friedman not cite a supporter of equality of outcome who is both nonfictional and non-discredited? FRIEDMAN, *supra* at 215. A possible example of an individual who believed in equality of outcome would be Martin Luther King, Jr. who stated that a political alliance between organized labor and African Americans could bring about the American dream which King interpreted as "a dream of equality of opportunity, of privilege and property widely distributed, a dream of a nation where all our gifts and resources are held not for ourselves but as instruments of service for the rest of humanity. . . ." STEPHEN B. OATES, LET THE TRUMPET SOUND: A LIFE OF MARTIN LUTHER KING, JR. 187 (1994). Does the fact that Friedman chose to attribute equality of outcome to a fictional dodo rather than the infinitely more persuasive Dr. King detract from the persuasiveness of his conclusions?

c. Effect of Dr. King on Friedman's piece. Including the views of Dr. King would have had three effects on Friedman's piece. First, because Dr. King believed that his dream was the realization of the American dream, including his views would have demonstrated that Friedman's assertion that equality of outcome is a radical departure from traditions of liberty is highly questionable. Second, including the voice of Dr. King, or any minority leader, would have drawn attention to the fact that, to minorities, formal equality is inadequate because it ignores the handicaps placed upon them by private discrimination, both past and present. *See* MARTIN LUTHER KING, JR., WHY WE CAN'T WAIT 134 (1964); T. Alexander Aleinikoff, *A Case for Race–Consciousness*, 91 COLUM. L. REV. 1060 (1991). This insufficiency of formal equality would have led to the third effect of including Dr. King, tying wealth redistribution to Friedman's second duty of government, "establishing an exact administration of justice." MILTON FRIEDMAN & ROSE FRIEDMAN, *The Role of Government, in* FREE TO CHOOSE: A PERSONAL STATEMENT 27, 29 (1980). Dr. King stated that American society had done "something special *against* the Negro for hundreds of years [and] must . . . do something special *for* him, in order to equip him to compete on a just and equal basis." WHERE DO WE GO FROM HERE (quoted in OATES, *supra* note 2b, at 426). Linking wealth redistribution to justice would have been anathema to a libertarian like Friedman. For a history of the development of affirmative action, including its origins as a compensatory measure, *see* Erin E. Byrnes, *Unmasking White Privilege to Expose the Fallacy of White Innocence: Using a Theory of Moral Correlativity to Make the Case for Affirmative Action Programs in Education*, 41 ARIZ. L. REV. 535 (1999).

5. Equality and liberty. Friedman sees equality of outcome as antithetical to liberty, but he claims equality of opportunity to be a companion to liberty. How do barriers to equality interfere with liberty? What can be done to remove those barriers?

a. Private barriers. In *Capitalism and Freedom*, Friedman said, "[T]he preserves of discrimination in any society are the areas that are most monopolistic in character, whereas discrimination against groups of particular color or religion is least in those areas where there is the greatest freedom of competition." MILTON FRIEDMAN (WITH THE ASSISTANCE OF ROSE D. FRIEDMAN), CAPITALISM AND FREEDOM 109 (1962). The invisible hand of the market ideally promotes society's welfare through competition and self-interest, and equality of opportunity ideally allows such competition by rendering characteristics such as birth, race, and sex irrelevant. Friedman resigns himself to the fact that equality of opportunity is an ideal which cannot be fully realized while he applauds government efforts to legally reinforce the ideal of competition. If supposedly irrelevant characteristics in reality impede equality of income, and therefore its partner liberty, what justifies government intervention to remove some private barriers to competition but not others? What similarities and differences exist between the concentration of wealth and monopolistic trade practices?

> The Sherman Anti–Trust Act is a "positive government measure . . . adopted to eliminate private barriers to competition." The Act outlaws monopolies and contracts, combinations, or conspiracies to restrain trade. Sherman Antitrust Act, 15 U.S.C. §§ 1–7 (2000). At common law, contracts in restraint of trade were void and unenforceable, but in 1890 Congress deemed such contracts illegal and created a civil action for damages. Denison Mattress Factory v. Spring–Air Co., 308 F.2d 403, 407 (5th Cir. 1962). In 1910, the Supreme Court affirmed the dissolution of the Rockefellers' Standard Oil Company, which controlled approximately ninety percent of the petroleum trade, and stock was transferred back to the many subsidiary companies. Standard Oil Co. v. United States, 221 U.S. 1 (1911). By controlling the petroleum trade, Standard Oil had been able to fix prices and restrain trade, violating the principles of the price system. Antitrust law gave the Court the tools to promote a competitive oil market. *Id.* at 33. If the triumphs of antitrust law over obstacles to competition are favorable in this situation, can we ignore other private obstacles to competition, such as race and gender inequality, because they are "not insurmountable"? If measures such as the Fourteenth Amendment and the Civil Rights Acts have not completely eliminated such barriers, what else can be done to improve competition?

b. Equality of access. Friedman compares the unfairness of inherited property to inherited talent, and he uses access to musical training for an untalented child instead of a musically gifted child to illustrate the impossibility of fairness. But suppose that the talented child was too poor to afford private music lessons and lived in an impoverished school district that had cut the music program for financial reasons, as so many schools have been forced to do, and his musical talent was never developed. And suppose the untalented child, whose family was wealthy, had unlimited access to music lessons, which did little to improve her skill. While we cannot, and probably would not want to, evenly distribute talents and interests throughout the population, it is at least possible that resources could be distributed in such a manner that makes them available to all. Perhaps equality of outcome is not possible or desirable, but meaningful freedom to choose demands true equality of access.

6. The "other Milton Friedman"? In a 2006 article in the New York Times, economist Robert Frank observed that the "patron saint of small-government conservatism" was also "the architect of the most successful social welfare program of all time." Robert H. Frank, *The Other Milton Friedman: A Conservative With a Social Welfare Program*, N.Y. TIMES, Nov. 23, 2006, at C3. Frank was referring to a proposal Friedman called the "negative income tax," designed to enable all citizens to meet their basic economic needs. Under the negative income tax scheme, every citizen would receive an annual cash payment from the I.R.S. If the payment were $6,000 per person, a family of four with no market income would therefore receive $24,000. For each dollar earned, however, the payment would be reduced by some fraction. If the fraction were 50 percent, then, a family of four earning $12,000 a year "would receive a net supplement of $18,000 (the initial $24,000 less the $6,000 tax on its earnings)." *Id.*

Frank observes that the negative income tax was never adopted in the end out of concern that it might reduce the incentive to work. "With a payment of $6,000 per person, for example, rural communes of 30 would have a pooled annual payment of $180,000, which they could supplement by growing vegetables and raising animals." *Id.* However, Congress instead adopted the earned-income tax credit, "essentially the same program except that only people who were employed received benefits." The EITC has been hailed by many as one of the most efficient anti-poverty schemes ever devised. Frank concludes, "By all accounts, Mr. Friedman was a generous and compassionate man, someone more keenly aware of good luck's contribution to individual prosperity than many of his disciples. Careful students of his work will be inspired not to dismantle the social safety net but to make it more effective." *Id.*

C. LAW AND ECONOMICS

The Uses of History in Law and Economics
4 THEORETICAL INQUIRIES L. 659 (2003).

■ RON HARRIS

   * * *

[T]he official, internal history of the field begins in Chicago. * * * [M]ost stress as the immediate origins, both in terms of time and substance, the contributions of two economists: Ronald Coase and Gary Becker, circa 1960. Coase, in his seminal 1960 article [*The Problem of Social Cost*, 3 J.L. & ECON. 1 (1960)], reintroduced transaction costs (after doing so for the first, relatively unnoticed, time twenty-three years earlier in the context of his *The Nature of the Firm*), but this time with direct reference to the relevance of legal liability rules in a world with transaction costs. Becker, after completing his doctoral dissertation in 1955 (published in 1957), extended the realm of neo-classical theory by employing it in the analysis of non-market behavior. His starting point was racial discrimination; he then proceeded to the family (until then a black box for economists), and, by the late 1960s, arrived at crime and punishment. Thus the work of Coase and Becker planted the roots of the modern incarnation of law and economics in Chicago and in the neo-classical tradition.

* * *

Both Coase and Becker, the intellectual founders of law and economics, were economists by training and much more interested in the study of economics than law. Ironically, the new field of law and economics that their work launched focused mainly on the law. Both noted this a few years ago at a [University of] Chicago Law School round table on the future of law and economics. Becker noted, "I am certainly not an expert in law and economics. . . . [A] relatively small fraction of my time over the years has been spent on this subject." Coase confessed, "[N]ow an economist isn't really interested in this part of Law and Economics—the use of economics to analyze the law—at least this economist isn't." Despite the fact that Coase and Becker laid the theoretical foundations of law and economics and occupy a mythical position in its official history, they were not awarded the Nobel Prize for their contribution to this field, but, rather, for their work in economics in general. Nor did they operate in the field of law and economics as later defined by Posner, and they failed to shift the field's research agenda to studying the effects of the law on the economy or the economy on the law.

It was Richard Posner who, in fact, set and shaped the boundaries of the Chicago School of Law and Economics, limiting them to the economic analysis of the law. This school of thought marginalized and may even have prevented other potential connections between law and economics. The boundaries set by Posner and his colleagues held strong for at least three decades. A discussion of the reasons for this is beyond the scope of this article. I believe that it is related to Posner's personal interest and eminent position in the field. Limiting the boundaries of law and economics made sense for a newly formed field, as it enabled concentrating on research resources and rapidly advancing learning on a narrow front. Moreover, law and economics was institutionalized as a discipline in law schools rather than in economics departments. By analyzing legal rules and providing prescriptions for legal reforms, law and economics scholars could participate in the major areas of discourse within legal academia. They could even demonstrate the power of their coherent and rigorous theory over the confused intuitions of other legal scholars. This further expanded their sphere of activity within the law schools. Only in the last decade has research transgressing these boundaries begun to appear.

In sum, on the assumption that law has no methodology of its own to contribute to the study of economics, three potential outcomes of the interaction between the disciplines of economics and law appeared around 1960: 1) the study of the effects of law on the economy; 2) the study of the effects of the economy on legal change; and 3) the application of economic methodology to the analysis of law. Until recently, only the third of these possible research agendas was considerably advanced within the field of law and economics. The narrow scope of the newly created field partly explains its ahistorical nature and its lack of interaction with economic and legal history.

In addition to developing a normatively-based policy analysis, Posner and colleagues developed a positive branch of law and economics. The two were unified in the framework of the theory of the common law's tendency toward efficiency. This theory deals with the effects of law on economic growth or the effects of economic growth on the law. It also can be understood as encompassing both the positive and normative research agendas by creating identification between them, at least insofar as the common law is concerned. * * * [R]efining and defending this general theory of the common law's tendency toward efficiency consumed a great deal of the time and energy of law and economics scholars and impinged on their interest in positive theories. Instead, they were occupied with proposing and examining theoretical mechanisms that might explain the tendency toward efficiency in the common law. * * * This weak start at positive research further removed law and economics scholars from engaging in the first two research agendas, which seemed important to both Coase and Becker. The interest in these two agendas was developed outside law and economics in fields such as New Institutional Economics, Historical New Institutional Economics, and the Wisconsin School of Legal History. Only recently has law and economics expanded its agenda to include these two issues.

More specifically, Chicago law and economics scholars claimed to be interested not only in legal rules but also in how legal incentives affect individuals' behavior. However, their research did not focus on studying the behavior of individuals, and the behavior of societies and basic social structures and trends was entirely beyond the scope of their research agenda. The behavior of individuals was assumed to be affected by changes in legal rules that affected individual incentives. Law and economics aimed at changing behavior but, in fact, studied rules and their change. As its other name, economic analysis of the law, implies, law and economics mainly aspired to normatively evaluate legal rules and prescribe their modification. Only rarely, when legal rules functioned within a market setting, as in the case of anti-trust and securities regulation, did Chicago law and economics scholars inquire into the behavior of individual agents more closely. It was more often the case that the legal rules were analyzed in non-market settings and the behavior of individuals was assumed rather than studied. * * *

From its inception, Chicago law and economics involved the application of neo-classical tools, which reached a powerful phase in the 1950s and 1960s in the Chicago School of Economics. Neo-classical economics at [the University of Chicago] was remarkably ahistorical. The detachment of economics from change over real time, and thus from history, began with the marginalist revolution and [Alfred Marshall], continued with Keynes, and culminated in Chicago in the 1950s.

For economics, the 1950s was a decade of high theory. It was one of markets, allocation, and equilibrium; of abstraction and deduction; of marginalism and incremental change; of optimization and mathematization. It was one in which the basic assumptions of neo-classical theory still held strong. This decade was a low point in economic theory in terms of interest in history and change over real time. Theory was mainly static, not dynamic. Insofar as dynamic elements played a role in economic theory, they were reflected in shifts of curves, moves from point to point along curves, or leaps from one equilibrium to the next, over a single time period. Time was not discussed in terms of months or years or decades; the flow of time was not treated differently for different historical eras. Not only was change over time neglected, but there was also a perception that the past of any given system had no bearing on its present and certainly not on its future. Since any given current regime of functions, allocations, and equilibria is not burdened by its past, it can serve as a good starting point for future predictions. An economic theoretician thus did not have to reconstruct the passage of time, as did historians—and some sociologists, anthropologists, political scientists, lawyers, literary critics, and philosophers. Imagining change was confined to the two-dimensional classroom world of blackboard curves and to figures in books. This static state of economic theory thus hindered the development of a history-conscious law and economics.

This was the economic theory applied in the late 1960s and early 1970s by Richard Posner and his colleagues at the University of Chicago Law School. By that point, law and economics had acquired all its familiar characteristics: reliance on the neo-classical assumption that individuals are rational maximizers; equating change in legal rules with change in relative prices; and adoption of Kaldor–Hicks efficiency ("potential Pareto efficiency," in more obscure terms) in the sense of wealth maximization as a standard of evaluation.

The ahistorical neoclassical characteristics of law and economics dominated the field. Well into the 1980s and beyond, law and economics was still engaged in adapting price theory to non-market legal behavior as part of a wider project of the expansion of economics. It focused on the application of price theory to the specific contours of the law: judge-made law and legislation; property, contracts, and torts; liability rules; and remedies. Law and economics scholars were engaged in intense normative and policy debates with critics from rival jurisprudential and doctrinal schools. These debates revolved around the imperialistic tendencies of economics, its unrealistic assumptions (e.g., of rationality), and its ideological bias in favor of efficiency considerations at the expense of distributive considerations. As long as the debates at the normative and policy level were intense, law and economics scholars were not likely to find much time or motivation to turn to the study of history.

* * *

In the first edition of *Economic Analysis of Law* (1972), what Posner termed "the economic logic of the common law" was the first theoretical argument in law and economics to draw the attention of scholars in the emerging field of the history of law. * * * Posner based his thesis that common law exhibits a tendency toward efficiency on a few historical examples from nineteenth-century America, including: enterprise liability for faulty products; industrial accidents; railroad-crossing accidents; damage caused by train engine sparks; and the impossibility doctrine in contracts. He claimed that these examples, when viewed in the framework of his positive theory of common law, confirm his thesis. These examples also serve to counter arguments that common law is either irrelevant to economic growth or encourages economic growth by subsidizing big business and increasing social inequality.

Posner did not base his claims on thorough historical research, but he most decidedly challenged historians. His positive theory of the law was historical in nature. It purported to explain how law changes over time. This explanation was too deterministic for most legal historians. It subjected their micro-historical interpretations to his macro theory and, in a sense, made them secondary to it. Furthermore, he used concrete examples rooted in time and place that are central to the work of many American legal historians. In doing so, he called into dispute concrete historical studies. It is not surprising that several legal historians, in response to this challenge, criticized Posner for misunderstanding the history of legal doctrines and their social and economic effects. In each of the editions of *Economic Analysis of Law*, Posner's discussion of the positive theory of common law's tendency toward efficiency grew in length, increasing from the four-and-a-half pages in the first edition to six-and-a-half pages in the 1977 second edition to nine-and-a-half pages in the 1986 third edition. * * * These increases in length were not the result of more historical studies conducted to test or confirm the theory. Rather, greater space was devoted to criticizing legal historians for not understanding economic theory, including the theory of the common law's tendency toward efficiency and the concept of efficiency. Legal historians became more critical of Posner, and Posner became more critical of legal historians, particularly those who viewed the law as subsidizing business, redistributing wealth, and oppressing the weak.

Posner had to answer not only to legal historians, but also to other legal scholars, even some with an economic orientation. These legal scholars questioned his thesis on a theoretical rather than empirical-historical level. What in the common law, they asked, could lead it to produce efficient rules? Some law and economics scholars tried to support Posner's claim and counter the growing criticism against it, by explaining its theoretical logic. Some suggested that judges are the agents who steer the common law toward efficiency; even if they are not aware that they maximize efficiency, they behave as if they are doing so. Justice and common sense considerations lead to efficient judgments. Other scholars saw litigants in general (losing litigants or repeat litigants) as the agents of the drive toward efficiency: inefficient rules will be rooted out by ongoing litigation. By the mid–1980s, the debate over the tendency of the common law toward efficiency, both on the historical and theoretical levels, had exhausted itself.

* * *

Though not one of the first fields within economics to apply theoretical novelties, over time, law and economics adopted extensions and modifications of the basic models of price theory to account for, among other things, transaction costs, risk sensitivity, and information a symmetry. A main new feature of research in the 1980s and early 1990s was the addition of game theory tools to the law and economics analysis. Another was the gradual opening up of law and economics to public choice analysis. * * * Law and economics has become more empirical and more comparative in recent years. * * *

Contrary to these trends in economic theory and the research agenda of law and economics, some Chicago law and economics scholars still view price theory as the sole economic tool for analyzing the law. They believe that despite its imperfections, it cannot be successfully replaced by any other theoretical framework. Moreover, they argue that the use of multiple theoretical frameworks will cause incoherence and complications, which would result in less rigorous tools, more limited applicability, and less insightful conclusions. They view the future of their field as developing along three main trajectories: first, sophistication within the neo-classical price theory paradigm, by employing heavier mathematical, game theoretic, and micro tools; second, expansion into the relatively neglected areas of public law; and third, the filling in of the remaining gaps in the analysis of private law. * * *

The Economic Approach to Law

The Problems of Jurisprudence 353–92 (1990).

■ Richard A. Posner

* * *

The Approach

The basic assumption of economics that guides the version of economic analysis of law that I shall be presenting is that people are rational maximizers of their satisfactions—*all* people (with the exception of small children and the profoundly retarded) in all of their activities (except when under the influence of psychosis or similarly deranged through drug or alcohol abuse) that involve choice. Because this definition embraces the criminal deciding whether to commit another crime, the litigant deciding whether to settle or litigate a case, the legislator deciding whether to vote for or against a bill, the judge deciding how to cast his vote in a case, the party to a contract deciding whether to break it, the driver deciding how fast to drive, and the pedestrian deciding how boldly to cross the street, as well as the usual economic actors, such as businessmen and consumers, it is apparent that most activities either regulated by or occurring within the legal system are grist for the economic analyst's mill. It should go without saying that nonmonetary as well as monetary satisfactions enter into the individual's calculus of maximizing (indeed, money for most people is a means rather than an end) and that decisions, to be rational, need not be well thought out at the conscious level—indeed, need not be conscious at all. Recall that "rational" denotes suiting means to ends, rather than mulling things over, and that much of our knowledge is tacit.

Since my interest is in legal doctrines and institutions, it will be best to begin at the legislative (including the constitutional) level. I assume that legislators are rational maximizers of their satisfactions just like everyone else. Thus nothing they do is motivated by the public interest as such. But they want to be elected and reelected, and they need money to wage an effective campaign. This money is more likely to be forthcoming from well-organized groups than from unorganized individuals. The rational individual knows that his contribution is unlikely to make a difference; for this reason and also because voters in most elections are voting for candidates rather than policies, which further weakens the link between casting one's vote and obtaining one's preferred policy. The rational individual will have little incentive to invest time and effort in deciding whom to vote for. Only an organized group of individuals (or firms or other organizations—but these are just conduits for individuals) will be able to overcome the informational and free-rider problems that plague collective action. But such a group will not organize and act effectively unless its members have much to gain or much to lose from specific policies, as tobacco farmers, for example, have much to gain from federal subsidies for growing tobacco and much to lose from the withdrawal of those subsidies. The basic tactic of an interest group is to trade the votes of its members and its financial support to candidates in exchange for an implied promise of favorable legislation. Such legislation will normally take the form of a statute transferring wealth from unorganized taxpayers (for example, consumers) to the interest group. If the target were another interest group, the legislative transfer might be effectively opposed. The unorganized are unlikely to mount effective opposition, and it is their wealth, therefore, that typically is transferred to interest groups.

* * * [B]ecause of the costs of transactions within a multi-headed legislative body, and the costs of effective communication through time, legislation does not spring full-grown from the head of the legislature; it needs interpretation and application, and this is the role of the courts. They are agents of the legislature. But to impart credibility and durability to the deals the legislature strikes with interest groups, courts must be able to resist the wishes of current legislators who want to undo their predecessors' deals yet cannot do so through repeal because the costs of passing legislation (whether original or amended) are so high, and who might therefore look to the courts for a repealing "interpretation." The impediments to legislation actually facilitate rather than retard the striking of deals, by giving interest groups some assurance that a deal struck with the legislature will not promptly be undone by repeal. An independent judiciary is one of the impediments.

Judicial independence makes the judges imperfect agents of the legislature. This is tolerable not only for the reason just mentioned but also because an independent judiciary is necessary for the resolution of ordinary disputes in a way that will encourage trade, travel, freedom of action, and other highly valued activities or conditions and will minimize the expenditure of resources on influencing governmental action. Legislators might appear to have little to gain from these widely diffused rule-of-law virtues. But if the aggregate benefits from a particular social policy are very large and no interest group's ox is gored, legislators may find it in their own interest to support the policy. Voters understand in a rough way the benefits to them of national defense, crime control, dispute settlement, and the other elements of the night watchman state, and they will not vote for legislators who refuse to provide these basic public services. It is only when those services are in place, and when (usually later) effective means of taxation and redistribution develop, that the formation of narrow interest groups and the extraction by them of transfers from unorganized groups become feasible.

The judges thus have a dual role: to interpret the interest-group deals embodied in legislation and to provide the basic public service of authoritative dispute resolution. They perform the latter function not only by deciding cases in accordance with preexisting norms, but also—especially in the Anglo–American legal system—by elaborating those norms. They fashioned the common law out of customary practices, out of ideas borrowed from statutes and from other legal systems (for example, Roman law), and out of their own conceptions of public policy. The law they created exhibits, according to the economic theory that I am expounding, a remarkable (although not total—remember the extension of the rule of capture to oil and gas) substantive consistency. It is as if the judges wanted to adopt the rules, procedures, and case outcomes that would maximize society's wealth.

I must pause to define "wealth maximization," a term often misunderstood. The "wealth" in "wealth maximization" refers to the sum of all tangible and intangible goods and services, weighted by prices of two sorts: offer prices (what people are willing to pay for goods they do not already own); and asking prices (what people demand to sell what they do own). If A would be willing to pay up to $100 for B's stamp collection, it is worth $100 to A. If B would be willing to sell the stamp collection for any price above $90, it is worth $90 to B. So if B sells the stamp collection to A (say for $100, but the analysis is qualitatively unaffected at any price between

$90 and $100—and it is only in that range that a transaction will occur), the wealth of society will rise by $10. Before the transaction A had $100 in cash and B had a stamp collection worth $90 (a total of $190); after the transaction A has a stamp collection worth $100 and B has $100 in cash (a total of $200). The transaction will not raise measured wealth—gross national product, national income, or whatever—by $10; it will not raise it at all unless the transaction is recorded, and if it is recorded it is likely to raise measured wealth by the full $100 purchase price. But the real addition to social wealth consists of the $10 increment in *nonpecuniary* satisfaction that A derives from the purchase, compared with that of B. This shows that "wealth" in the economist's sense is not a simple monetary measure, and explains why it is a fallacy (the Earl of Lauderdale's fallacy) to think that wealth would be maximized by encouraging the charging of monopoly prices. The wealth of producers would increase but that of consumers would diminish—and actually by a greater amount, since monopoly pricing will induce some consumers to switch to goods that cost society more to produce but, being priced at a competitive rather than a monopoly price, appear to the consumer to be cheaper. The fallacy thus lies in equating business income to social wealth.

Similarly, if I am given a choice between remaining in a job in which I work forty hours a week for $1,000 and switching to a job in which I would work thirty hours for $500, and I decide to make the switch, the extra ten hours of leisure must be worth at least $500 to me, yet GNP will fall when I reduce my hours of work. Suppose the extra hours of leisure are worth $600 to me, so that my full income rises from $1,000 to $1,100 when I reduce my hours. My former employer presumably is made worse off by my leaving (else why did he employ me?), but not more than $100 worse off, for if he were, he would offer to pay me a shade over $1,100 a week to stay—and I would stay. (The example abstracts from income tax.)

Wealth is *related* to money, in that a desire not backed by ability to pay has no standing—such a desire is neither an offer price nor an asking price. I may desperately desire a BMW, but if I am unwilling or unable to pay its purchase price, society's wealth would not be increased by transferring the BMW from its present owner to me. Abandon this essential constraint (an important distinction, also, between wealth maximization and utilitarianism—for I might derive greater utility from the BMW than its present owner or anyone else to whom he might sell the car), and the way is open to tolerating the crimes committed by the passionate and the avaricious against the cold and the frugal.

The common law facilitates wealth-maximizing transactions in a variety of ways. It recognizes property rights, and these facilitate exchange. It also protects property rights, through tort and criminal law. (Although today criminal law is almost entirely statutory, the basic criminal protections—for example, those against murder, assault, rape, and theft—have, as one might expect, common law origins.) Through contract law it protects the process of exchange. And it establishes procedural rules for resolving disputes in these various fields as efficiently as possible.

The illustrations given thus far of wealth-maximizing transactions have been of transactions that are voluntary in the strict sense of making everyone affected by them better off, or at least no worse off. Every transaction has been assumed to affect just two parties, each of whom has been made better off by it. Such a transaction is said to be Pareto superior, but Pareto superiority is not a necessary condition for a transaction to be wealth maximizing. Consider an accident that inflicts a cost of $100 with a probability of .01 and that would have cost $3 to avoid. The accident is a wealth-maximizing "transaction" (recall Aristotle's distinction between voluntary and involuntary transactions) because the expected accident cost ($1) is less than the cost of avoidance. (I am assuming risk neutrality. Risk aversion would complicate the analysis but not change it fundamentally.) It is wealth maximizing even if the victim is not compensated. The result is consistent with Learned Hand's formula, which defines negligence as the failure to take cost-justified precautions. If the only precaution that would have averted the accident is not cost-justified, the failure to take it is not negligent and the injurer will not have to compensate the victim for the costs of the accident.

* * *

The wealth-maximizing properties of common law rules have been elucidated at considerable length in the literature of the economic analysis of law. Such doctrines as conspiracy, general average (admiralty), contributory negligence, equitable servitudes, employment at will, the standard for granting preliminary injunctions, entrapment, the contract defense of impossibility, the collateral-benefits rule, the expectation measure of damages, assumption of risk, attempt, invasion of privacy, wrongful interference with contract rights, the availability of punitive damages in some cases but not others, privilege in the law of evidence, official immunity, and the doctrine of moral consideration have been found—at least by some contributors to this literature—to conform to the dictates of wealth maximization. * * * It has even been argued that the system of precedent itself has an economic equilibrium. Precedents are created as a by-product of litigation. The greater the number of recent precedents in an area, the lower the rate of litigation will be. In particular, cases involving disputes over legal as distinct from purely factual issues will be settled. The existence of abundant, highly informative (in part because recent) precedents will enable the parties to legal disputes to form more convergent estimates of the likely outcome of a trial, and as noted in previous chapters, if both parties agree on the outcome of trial they will settle beforehand because a trial is more costly than a settlement. But with less litigation, fewer new precedents will be produced, and the existing precedents will obsolesce as changing circumstances render them less apt and informative. So the rate of litigation will rise, producing more precedents and thereby causing the rate of litigation again to fall.

This analysis does not explain what drives judges to decide common law cases in accordance with the dictates of wealth maximization. Prosperity, however, which wealth maximization measures more sensitively than purely monetary measures such as GNP, is a relatively uncontroversial policy, and most judges try to steer clear of controversy: their age, method of compensation, and relative weakness vis-à-vis the other branches of government make the avoidance of controversy attractive. It probably is no accident, therefore, that many common law doctrines assumed their modern form in the nineteenth century, when laissez-faire ideology, which resembles wealth maximization, had a strong hold on the Anglo–American judicial imagination * * *.

It may be objected that in assigning ideology as a cause of judicial behavior, the economist strays outside the boundaries of his discipline; but he need not rest on ideology. The economic analysis of legislation implies that fields of law left to the judges to elaborate, such as the common law fields, must be the ones in which interest-group pressures are too weak to deflect the legislature from pursuing goals that are in the general interest. Prosperity is one of these goals, and one that judges are especially well equipped to promote. The rules of the common law that they promulgate attach prices to socially undesirable conduct, whether free riding or imposing social costs without corresponding benefits. By doing this the rules create incentives to avoid such conduct, and these incentives foster prosperity. In contrast, judges can, despite appearances, do little to redistribute wealth. A rule that makes it easy for poor tenants to break leases with rich landlords, for example, will induce landlords to raise rents in order to offset the costs that such a rule imposes, and tenants will bear the brunt of these higher costs. Indeed, the principal redistribution accomplished by such a rule may be from the prudent, responsible tenant, who may derive little or no benefit from having additional legal rights to use against landlords—rights that enable a tenant to avoid or postpone eviction for nonpayment of rental—to the feckless tenant. That is a capricious redistribution. Legislatures, however, have by virtue of their taxing and spending powers powerful tools for redistributing wealth. So an efficient division of labor between the legislative and judicial branches has the legislative branch concentrate on catering to interest-group demands for wealth distribution and the judicial branch on meeting the broad-based social demand for efficient rules governing safety, property, and transactions. Although there are other possible goals of judicial action besides efficiency and redistribution, many of these (various conceptions of "fairness" and "justice") are labels for wealth maximization, or for redistribution in favor of powerful interest groups; or else they are too controversial in a heterogeneous society, too ad hoc, or insufficiently developed to provide judges who desire a reputation for objectivity and disinterest with adequate grounds for their decisions.

Finally, even if judges have little commitment to efficiency, their inefficient decisions will, by definition, impose greater social costs than their efficient ones will. As a result, losers of cases decided mistakenly from an economic standpoint will have a greater incentive, on average, to press for correction through appeal, new litigation, or legislative action than losers of cases decided soundly from an economic standpoint—so there will be a steady pressure for efficient results. Moreover, cases litigated under inefficient rules tend to involve larger stakes than cases litigated under efficient rules (for the inefficient rules, by definition, generate social waste), and the larger the stakes in a dispute the likelier it is to be litigated rather than settled; so judges will have a chance to reconsider the inefficient rule.

Thus we should not be surprised to see the common law tending to become efficient, although since the incentives to judges to perform well along any dimension are weak (this is a by-product of judicial independence), we cannot expect the law ever to achieve perfect efficiency. Since wealth maximization is not only a guide in fact to common law judging but also a genuine social value and the only one judges are in a good position to promote, it provides not only the key to an accurate description of what the judges are up to but also the right benchmark for criticism and reform. If judges are failing to maximize wealth, the economic analyst of law will urge them to alter practice or doctrine accordingly. In addition, the analyst will urge—on any legislator sufficiently free of interest-group pressures to be able to legislate in the public interest—a program of enacting only legislation that conforms to the dictates of wealth maximization.

Besides generating both predictions and prescriptions, the economic approach enables the common law to be reconceived in simple, coherent terms and to be applied more objectively than traditional lawyers would think possible. From the premise that the common law does and should seek to maximize society's wealth, the economic analyst can deduce in logical—if you will, formalist—fashion (economic theory is formulated nowadays largely in mathematical terms) the set of legal doctrines that will express and perfect the inner nature of the common law, and can compare these doctrines with the actual doctrines of common law. After translating from the economic vocabulary back into the legal one, the analyst will find that most of the actual doctrines are tolerable approximations to the implications of economic theory and so are formalistically valid. * * *

The project of reducing the common law—with its many separate fields, its thousands of separate doctrines, its hundreds of thousands of reported decisions—to a handful of mathematical formulas may seem quixotic, but the economic analyst can give reasons for doubting this assessment. Much of the doctrinal luxuriance of common law is seen to be superficial once the essentially economic nature of the common law is understood. A few principles, such as cost-benefit analysis, the prevention of free riding, decision under uncertainty, risk aversion, and the promotion of mutually beneficial-exchanges, can explain most doctrines and decisions. Tort cases can be translated into contract cases by re-characterizing the tort issue as finding the implied pre-accident contract that the parties would have chosen had transaction costs not been prohibitive, and contract cases can be translated into tort cases by asking what remedy if any would maximize the expected benefits of the contractual undertaking considered ex ante. The criminal's decision whether to commit a crime is no different in principle from the prosecutor's decision whether to prosecute; a plea bargain is a contract; crimes are in effect torts by insolvent defendants because if all criminals could pay the full social costs of their crimes, the task of deterring antisocial behavior could be left to tort law. Such examples suggest not only that the logic of the common law really is economics but also that the teaching of law could be simplified by exposing students to the clean and simple economic structure beneath the garb of legal doctrine.

If all this seems reminiscent of Langdell; it differs fundamentally in being empirically verifiable. The ultimate test of a rule derived from economic theory is not the elegance or logicality of the derivation but the rule's effect on social wealth. The extension of the rule of capture to oil and gas was subjected to such a test, flunked, and was replaced (albeit through legislative rather than judicial action) by efficient rules. The other rules of the common law can and should be tested likewise.

* * *

CRITICISMS OF THE NORMATIVE THEORY

The question whether wealth maximization *should* guide legal policy, either in general or just in common law fields (plus those statutory fields where the legislative intent is to promote efficiency—antitrust law being a possible example), is ordinarily treated as separate from the question whether it *has* guided legal policy, except insofar as the positive theory may be undermined by the inadequacies of the normative theory. Actually the two theories are not as separable as this, illustrating again the lack of a clear boundary between "is" and "ought" propositions. One of the things judges ought to do is follow precedent, although not inflexibly; so if efficiency is the animating principle of much common law doctrine, judges have some obligation to make decisions that will be consistent with efficiency. This is one reason why the positive economic theory of the common law is so contentious.

The normative theory has been highly contentious in its own right. Most contributors to the debate over it conclude that it is a bad theory, and although many of the criticisms can be answered, several cannot be, and it is those I shall focus on.

The first is that wealth maximization is inherently incomplete as a guide to social action because it has nothing to say about the distribution of rights—or at least nothing we want to hear. Given the distribution of rights (whatever it is), wealth maximization can be used to derive the policies that will maximize the value of those rights. But this does not go far enough, because naturally we are curious about whether it would be just to start off with a society in which, say, one member owned all the others. If wealth maximization is indifferent to the initial distribution of rights, it is a truncated concept of justice.

Since the initial distribution may dissipate rapidly, this point may have little practical significance. Nor is wealth maximization completely silent on the initial distribution. If we could compare two otherwise identical nascent societies, in one of which one person owned all the others and in the other of which slavery was forbidden, and could repeat the comparison a century later, almost certainly we would find that the second society was wealthier and the first had abolished slavery (if so, this would further illustrate the limited effect of the initial distribution on the current distribution). Although it has not always and everywhere been true, under modern conditions of production slavery is an inefficient method of organizing production. The extensive use of slave labor by the Nazis during World War II may seem an exception—but only if we disregard the welfare of the slave laborers.

This response to the demand that wealth maximization tell us something about the justice of the initial distribution of rights is incomplete. Suppose it were the case—it almost surely *is* the case—that some people in modern American society would be more productive as slaves than as free persons. These are not antisocial people whom we want to punish by imprisoning (a form of slavery that is tolerated); they are not psychotic or profoundly retarded; they just are lazy, feckless, poorly organized, undisciplined people—people incompetent to manage their own lives in a way that will maximize their output, even though the relevant output is not market output alone but also leisure, family associations, and any other sources of satisfaction to these people as well as to others. Wealth would be maximized by enslaving these people, provided the costs of supervision were not too high—but the assumption that they would not be too high is built into the proposition that their output would be greater as slaves than as free persons, for it is net output that we are interested in. Yet no one thinks it would be right to enslave such people, even if there were no evidentiary problems in identifying them, the slave masters could be trusted to be benign, and so on; and these conditions, too, may be implicit in the proposition that the net social output of some people would be greater if they were slaves.

It is no answer that it would be inefficient to enslave such people unless they consented to be enslaved, that is, unless the would-be slave-master met the asking price for their freedom. The term *"their* freedom" assumes they have the property right in their persons, and the assumption is arbitrary. We can imagine assigning the property rights in persons (perhaps only persons who appeared likely to be unproductive) to the state to auction them to the highest bidder. The putative slave could bid against the putative master, but would lose. His expected earnings, net of consumption, would be smaller than the expected profits to the master, otherwise enslavement would not be efficient. Therefore he could not borrow enough—even if capital markets worked without any friction (in the present setting, even if the lender could enslave the borrower if the latter defaulted!)—to outbid his master-to-be.

This example points to a deeper criticism of wealth maximization as a norm or value: like utilitarianism, which it closely resembles, or nationalism, or Social Darwinism, or racialism, or organic theories of the state, it treats people as if they were the cells of a single organism; the welfare of the cell is important only insofar as it promotes the welfare of the organism. Wealth maximization implies that if the prosperity of the society can be promoted by enslaving its least productive citizens, the sacrifice of their freedom is worthwhile. But this implication is contrary to the unshakable moral intuitions of Americans, and . . . conformity to intuition is the ultimate test of a moral (indeed of any) theory.

    * * *

I have said nothing about the conflict between wealth maximization and equality of wealth, because I am less sure of the extent of egalitarian sentiment in our society than that of individualistic sentiment (by "individualism" I mean simply the rivals to aggregative philosophies, such as utilitarianism and wealth maximization). Conflict there is, however, and it points to another important criticism of wealth maximization even if the critic is not an egalitarian. Imagine that a limited supply of growth hormone, privately manufactured and sold, must be allocated. A wealthy parent wants the hormone so that his child of average height will grow tall; a poor parent wants the hormone so that his child of dwarfish height can grow to normal height. In a system of wealth maximization the wealthy parent might outbid the poor parent and get the hormone. This is not certain. Amount of wealth is only one factor in willingness to pay. The poor parent might offer his entire wealth for the hormone, and that wealth, although meager, might exceed the amount of money the wealthy parent was willing to pay, given alternative uses to which he could put his money. Also, altruists might help the poor parent bid more than he could with only his own resources. The poor might actually be better off in a system in which the distribution of the hormone were left to the private market, even if there were no altruism. Such a system would create incentives to produce and sell the hormone sooner, and perhaps at a lower price, than if the government controlled its distribution; for the costs of production would probably be lower under private rather than public production, and even a monopolist will charge less when his costs fall.

But what seems impossible to maintain convincingly in the present ethical climate is that the wealthy parent has the *right* to the hormone by virtue of being willing to pay the supplier more than the poor parent can; more broadly, that consumers have a right to purchase in free markets. These propositions cannot be derived from wealth maximization. Indeed, they look like propositions about transactional freedom rather than about distribution only because I have assumed that the growth hormone is produced and distributed exclusively through the free market. An alternative possibility would be for the state to own the property right in the hormone and to allocate it on the basis of need rather than willingness to pay. To argue against this alternative (socialist medicine writ small) would require an appeal either to the deeply controversial idea of a natural right to private property, or to purely instrumental considerations, such as the possibility that in the long run the poor will be better off with a free market in growth hormone—but to put the question *this* way is to assume that the poor have some sort of social claim by virtue of being poor, and thus to admit the relevance of egalitarian considerations and thereby break out of the limits of wealth maximization.

A stronger-seeming argument for the free-enterprise solution is that the inventor of the hormone should have a right to use it as he wishes, which includes the right to sell it to the highest bidder. But this argument seems stronger only because we are inclined to suppose that what has happened is that *after* the inventor invented it the government decided to rob him of the reward for which he had labored. If instead we assume that Congress passes a law in 1989 which provides that after the year 2000 the right to patent new drugs will be conditioned on the patentee's agreeing to limit the price he charges, we shall have difficulty objecting to the law on ethical, as distinct from practical, grounds. It would be just one more restriction on free markets.

* * * Although the advocate of wealth maximization can argue that to the productive should belong the fruits of their labor, the argument can be countered along the lines [that] production is really a social rather than individual effort[] to which it can be added that wealth may often be due more to luck (and not the luck of the genetic lottery, either) than to skill or effort. Furthermore, if altruism is so greatly admired, as it is by conservatives as well as by liberals, why should not its spirit inform legislation? Why should government protect only our selfish instincts? To this it can be replied that the spirit of altruism is voluntary giving. But the reply is weak. The biggest reason we value altruism is that we *desire* some redistribution—we may admire the altruist for his self-sacrifice but we would not admire him as much if he destroyed his wealth rather than giving it to others—and we think that voluntary redistribution is less costly than involuntary. If redistribution is desirable, some involuntary redistribution may be justifiable, depending on the costs, of course, but not on the principle of the thing.

There is a still deeper problem with founding wealth maximization on a notion of natural rights. The economic perspective is thoroughly (and fruitfully) behaviorist. "Economic man" is not, as vulgarly supposed, a person driven by purely pecuniary incentives, but he is a person whose behavior is completely determined by incentives; his rationality is no different from that of a pigeon or a rat. The economic task from the perspective of wealth maximization is to influence his incentives so as to maximize his output. How a person so conceived could be thought to have a *moral* entitlement to a particular distribution of the world's goods—an entitlement, say, to the share proportional to his contribution to the world's wealth—is unclear. Have marmots moral entitlements? Two levels of discourse are being mixed.

* * *

The strongest argument for wealth maximization is not moral, but pragmatic. Such classic defenses of the free market as chapter 4 of Mill's *On Liberty* can easily be given a pragmatic reading. We look around the world and see that in general people who live in societies in which markets are allowed to function more or less freely not only are wealthier than people in other societies but have more political rights, more liberty and dignity, are more content (as evidenced, for example, by their being less prone to emigrate)—so that wealth maximization may be the most direct route to a variety of moral ends. The recent history of England, France, and Turkey, of Japan and Southeast Asia, of East versus West Germany and North versus South Korea, of China and Taiwan, of Chile, of the Soviet Union, Poland, and Hungary, and of Cuba and Argentina provides striking support for this thesis.

Writing in the early 1970s, the English political philosopher Brian Barry doubted the importance of incentives. "My own guess," he said, "is that enough people with professional and managerial jobs really like them (and enough others who would enjoy them and have sufficient ability to do them are waiting to replace those who do not) to enable the pay of these jobs to be brought down considerably ... I would suggest that the pay levels in Britain of schoolteachers and social workers seem to offer net rewards which recruit and maintain just enough people, and that this provides a guideline to the pay levels that could be sustained generally among professionals and managers." He rejected the "assumption that a sufficient supply of highly educated people will be forthcoming only if lured by the anticipation of a higher income afterwards as a result," adding that "it would also be rash to assume that it would be an economic loss if fewer sought higher education." He discussed with approval the Swedish experiment at redistributing income and wealth but thought it hampered by the fact that "Sweden still has a privately owned economy." He worried about "brain drain" but concluded that it was a serious problem only with regard to airline pilots and physicians; and a nation can do without airlines and may be able to replace general practitioners "with people having a lower (and less marketable) qualification." (Yet Barry himself was soon to join the brain drain, and he is neither a physician nor an airline pilot.) He proposed "to spread the nastiest jobs around by requiring everyone, before entering higher education or entering a profession, to do, say, three years of work wherever he or she was directed. (This would also have educational advantages.) To supplement this there could be a call-up of say a month every year, as with the Swiss and Israeli armed forces but directed towards peaceful occupations."

At least with the benefit of hindsight we can see that Barry wrote a prescription for economic disaster. It may be impossible to lay solid philosophical foundations under wealth maximization, just as it may be impossible to lay solid philosophical foundations under the natural sciences, but this would be a poor reason for abandoning wealth maximization, just as the existence of intractable problems in the philosophy of science would be a poor reason for abandoning science. We have reason to believe that markets work—that capitalism delivers the goods, if not the Good—and it would be a mistake to allow philosophy to deflect us from the implications, just as it would be a mistake to allow philosophy to alter our views of infanticide.

A sensible pragmatism does not ignore theory. The mounting evidence that capitalism is more efficient than socialism gives us an additional reason for believing economic theory (not every application of it, to be sure). The theory in turn gives us greater confidence in the evidence. Theory and evidence are mutually supporting. From the perspective of economic theory, brain drain is not the mysterious disease that Barry supposes it to be; it is the rational response to leveling policies by those whose incomes are being leveled downward.

* * *

My pragmatic judgment is, moreover, a qualified one. All societies depart from the precepts of wealth maximization. The unanswered question is how the conditions in these societies would change if the public sector could somehow be cut all the way down to the modest dimensions of the night watchman state that the precepts of wealth maximization seem to imply. That is a difficult counterfactual question (it seems that no society's leadership has both the will and the power to play the guinea pig in an experiment with full-fledged wealth maximization) * * *. Until it is answered, we should be cautious in pushing wealth maximization; incrementalism should be our watchword.

The fact that wealth maximization, pragmatically construed, is instrumental rather than foundational is not an objection to its use in guiding law and public policy. It may be the right principle for that purpose even though it is right only in virtue of ends that are not solely economic. At least it may be the right default principle, placing on the proponent of departures from wealth maximization the burden of demonstrating their desirability.

Even if my observations on comparative economic performance in the Third World and elsewhere are correct, do such matters belong in a book on jurisprudence? They do. The object of pragmatic analysis is to lead discussion away from issues semantic and metaphysical and toward issues factual and empirical. Jurisprudence is greatly in need of such a shift in direction. Jurisprudence needs to become more pragmatic.

Common Law Revisited

The case for using wealth maximization as a guiding principle in common law adjudication is particularly strong. The common law judge operates within a framework established by the Constitution, which, by virtue of a number of the amendments, not only rules out of bounds the ethically most questionable applications of wealth maximization but largely eliminates the problems of incompleteness and indeterminacy that result from the uncertain relationship between wealth maximization and the initial distribution of rights. That initial distribution is more or less a given for the common law judge. A related point is that such a judge operates in a domain where distributive or egalitarian considerations can play at best only a small role. The judge whose business is enforcing tort, contract, and property law lacks effective tools for bringing about an equitable distribution of wealth, even if he thinks he knows what such a distribution would be. He would be further handicapped in such an endeavor by the absence of consensus in our society on the nature of a just distribution, an absence that undermines the social acceptability of attempts to use the judicial office to achieve distributive goals. A sensible division of labor has the judge making rules and deciding cases in the areas regulated by the common law in such a way as to maximize the size of the social pie, and the legislature attending to the sizes of the slices.

The case is strongest in those common law areas where the relevant policies are admitted to be economic. Suppose the idea of an implied warranty of habitability—which entitles a tenant to sue his landlord if the premises fall below the standards of safety and comfort specified in the local housing code—is defended, as normally it is defended, on the ground that it is needed to protect tenants from deception and over reaching by landlords and will not lead to a reduction in the stock of housing available to poor people or to higher rentals than the poor are willing and able to pay. If research demonstrates that these assumptions are incorrect, the proponent, if fair-minded, will have to withdraw the proposal. In this example, in principle (for the necessary research is difficult to conduct), legal questions can be made determinate by the translation of a legal question into a social-scientific one in a setting of common ends, and therefore the valid Benthamite project of placing law on a more scientific basis can be advanced without injury to competing values.

If it could be shown or if it is conceded that common law decision making is indeed not an apt field for efforts to redistribute wealth, then it may be possible to ground wealth maximization (as used to guide such decision making) in a more powerful normative principle of economics, the Pareto principle. A transaction is Pareto superior when it makes at least one person better off and no one worse off. A simple contract approximates a Pareto-superior transaction. Neither party would sign the contract unless he thought he would be better off as a result. So, assuming adequate information (which does not mean assuming omniscience) and no adverse effects on third parties, the contract will be Pareto superior. At least this will be so on an ex ante basis, for as things turn out one of the parties (perhaps both) may be made worse off by the contract. This possibility is inevitable if there is uncertainty, and uncertainty is inevitable.

The ethical appeal of the Pareto principle is similar to that of unanimity. If everyone affected by a transaction is better off, how can the transaction be socially or ethically bad? There are answers to this question, yet a Pareto-superior transaction makes a powerful claim for ethical respect because it draws on intuitions that are fundamental to both utilitarianism and Kantian individualism-respect for preferences, and for persons, respectively. It may seem paradoxical to derive a norm of wealth maximization from the principle of Pareto superiority, when the hallmark of the latter is compensation of all potential losers (for remember that no one must be made worse off by the transaction if it is to be Pareto superior), while wealth maximization requires only that the winners' gains exceed the losers' losses. But if, as in the contract example, compensation is permitted to be ex ante, the paradox disappears.

The difference between the ex ante and ex post perspectives is fundamental, and failure to attend to it underlies much confused thinking about markets and transactional competence. Because many choices are made, unavoidably, under conditions of uncertainty, a fair number must turn out badly. Ex post, they are regarded as mistaken and engender regret, yet ex ante they may have been perfectly sensible. Suppose I have a choice between two jobs. One would pay me $50,000 every year with certainty the other either $500,000 a year (with a 90 percent probability) or nothing (with a 10 percent probability). The expected income in the first job is $50,000 and in the second $450,000. (Notice the use of Bayesian probability, mentioned in Chapter 6.) The second, however, involves uncertainty. If I am risk averse—and let us assume I am—I will value an uncertain expectation at less than its actual equivalent. Hence the second job will not really be worth $450,000 to me, and let us suppose it will be worth only one-third as much—$150,000. Still, that is more than $50,000, so I will take the second job. But I am unlucky, the 10 percent chance materializes, and my income is zero. I would be less (or more) than human if I did not regret my choice, rail against my fate, berate myself for having chosen stupidly. But in fact I made the right choice—and would make it again, given the same uncertainty as before.

Consider now the case where negligence is the more efficient principle, in a wealth-maximizing sense, than strict liability because when all the costs and benefits are toted up the negligence regime turns out to produce the greater excess of benefits over costs. If so, the sum of liability and accident insurance premiums will be lower in the negligence regime and all drivers will be better off ex ante, although ex post, of course, some may do better in a regime of strict liability. Actually, not all will be better off even ex ante. Some people who are more prone to be injured than to injure will be worse off, since negligence favors injurers relative to strict liability, and some who are more prone to injure than to be injured will be better off. The "losers" will lose little, though—a matter of slightly higher insurance premiums. And both the "winners" and the vast majority of drivers who are neither disproportionately likely to injure than to be injured nor vice versa will be better off. Complete unanimity will be unattainable, but near unanimity can be presumed and the few losers will hardly be degraded, their autonomy wrecked, or their rights destroyed by having to pay a few dollars a month more in automobile insurance premiums.

I am painting with slightly too rosy a palette. Some people will lack the knowledge, intelligence, and foresight to buy insurance (I am putting to one side the deliberate risk takers); some may not be able to afford adequate insurance; and insurance that pays off as generously as common law damages may not be available in the market. When a person becomes a victim of a serious accident in which the injurer is not at fault, it may spell a financial disaster not attributable to the choices or the deserts of the victim—a disaster that strict liability could have avoided. An alternative, of course, is social insurance—the famous safety net. If cases of catastrophic uninsured nonnegligent accidental injury are rare, social insurance may be a better solution than a strict liability system that would require compensation through the tort system in all accident cases.

The essential point is that the availability of insurance, private or social, is necessary to back wealth maximization with the ethical weight of the Pareto principle. Once it is so backed, however, wealth maximization provides an ethically adequate guide to common law decision making—indeed a superior guide to any other that has been suggested. And the adequacy of private and public insurance markets, on which this conclusion depends, is an empirical, a studiable, issue.

No doubt most judges (and lawyers) think that the guiding light for common law decision making should be either an intuitive sense of justice or reasonableness, or a casual utilitarianism. But these may all be the same thing, and if pressed such a judge would probably have to admit that what he called utilitarianism was what I am calling wealth maximization. Consider whether a thief should be permitted to defend himself at trial on the ground that he derived greater pleasure from the stolen item than the pain suffered by the owner. The answer obviously is no, but it is offered more confidently by the wealth maximizer than by the pure utilitarian. The former can point out that the thief is bypassing the market system of exchange and that the pleasure he derives from the good he has stolen has no social standing because his desire for the good is not backed by willingness to pay. These are separate points. The thief might be willing to pay if he had to—that is, he might value the good more than its owner—yet prefer theft because it is a cheaper way for him to acquire the good. So theft might be utility maximizing, although this is unlikely because a practice of theft would result in enormous, utility-reducing expenditures on protection of property.

Since utility is more difficult to estimate than wealth, a system of wealth maximization may seem a proxy for a utilitarian system, but it is more; its spirit is different. Wealth maximization is an ethic of productivity and social cooperation—to have a claim on society's goods and services you must be able to offer something that other people value—while utilitarianism is a hedonistic, unsocial ethic, as the last example showed. And an ethic of productivity and cooperation is more congruent with the values of the dominant groups in our society than the pure utilitarian ethic would be. Unfortunately, wealth maximization is not a pure ethic of productivity and cooperation, not only because even lawful efforts at maximizing wealth often make some other people worse off, but more fundamentally because luck plays a big role in the returns to market activities. What is worse, it is always possible to argue that the distribution of productivity among a population is itself the luck of the genetic draw, or of upbringing, or of where one happens to have been born, and that these forms of luck have no ethical charge. There are counterarguments, of course, but they are not decisive. So, once again, the foundations of an overarching principle for resolving legal disputes are rotten, and one is driven back to the pragmatic ramparts.

* * *

NOTES AND QUESTIONS

1. Increase of wealth through theft. Posner claims that society's wealth will not be increased by transferring a BMW to an individual who can not pay for it, even if that individual would enjoy the BMW more than anyone who could pay for it. However, is this true? If, for example, the BMW is worth $50,000 to A and $60,000 to B, then transferring the BMW from A to B will increase society's wealth by $10,000, regardless of whether B pays for the BMW or not. If B pays nothing, then A will be $50,000 worse off from having his car stolen, but B will be $60,000 better off for having stolen the car, a net gain to society of $10,000. This transfer, in which society's wealth is maximized even though one party to the transfer is left worse off, is based on the idea of Kaldor–Hicks efficiency which states that a transaction is efficient if "the winners win more than the losers lose." Guido Calabresi, *The Pointlessness of Pareto: Carrying Coase Further*, 100 Yale L.J. 1211, 1221 (1991).

Posner's reliance on economic theory was dramatically transformed in response to the collapse of global financial markets during the subprime real estate bubble in 2008. His new views are contained in A Failure of Capitalism, The Crisis of '08 and the Descent Into Depression.

2. Place of the poor in law and economics. In Posner's view, society's wealth is generated not through money but through individual preferences. *See* the stamp collection example discussed *supra* at note 2. However, Posner distinguishes law and economics from utilitarianism by stating that only those preferences backed by money should "count." Does this reliance on money, which admittedly does not increase society's wealth not have the effect of simply shutting the poor out of the law and economics equation? Is Posner explicitly calling on the law to treat the rich (who have the money to back up their preferences in the market) differently from the poor (who, under Posner's framework, can only have preferences for the necessities of life, and sometimes not even those)? Additionally, Posner states that slavery is inefficient and that Nazi use of slave labor only looks efficient when the welfare of the slaves is ignored. Posner, *supra* at 239. But, since slave laborers in Nazi Germany had no money, do we not have to ignore their preferences? How can Posner's statement about paying attention to the welfare of slaves be squared with his assertion that "a desire not backed by ability to pay has no standing?"

3. Relationship between price and wealth. Under Posner's analysis, the price of a commodity actually has no relationship to the wealth generated by its exchange. To use his stamp collection example from pages 233–234, if B paid $1,000,000 for A's stamp collection, then society would be better off because A would have gained $1,000,000 and lost $90.00, while B would have lost $1,000,000 and gained $100. In all cases, because B values the stamp collection more highly than A and money is fungible, society's wealth is maximized by the exchange, even if it is blatantly unfair to either A or B. This is a direct result of the wealth maximizing properties of Kaldor–Hicks efficiency, discussed in Calabresi, *supra*.

4. **Inefficiency of tort.** Posner claims that the common law "establishes procedural rules for resolving disputes . . . as efficiently as possible." THE PROBLEMS OF JURISPRUDENCE, *supra* at 357. However, tort law is notoriously inefficient at resolving disputes and several alternative statutory systems such as no-fault insurance and worker's compensation might provide better methods of adjudication. In particular, no-fault auto insurance might return over 90 percent of premium dollars in the form of benefits, compared with only 50 percent for liability insurance. DAN B. DOBBS & PAUL T. HAYDEN, TORTS AND COMPENSATION: PERSONAL ACCOUNTABILITY AND SOCIAL RESPONSIBILITY FOR INJURY 898 (4th ed. 2001). How can such inefficiency in the tort system be squared with Posner's claims about the procedural benefits of the common law?

5. **Effect of family privilege.**

    a. **Intergenerational persistence of wealth.** Posner's claim that the initial distribution of wealth will dissipate within three generations is almost certainly incorrect. The study by Becker and Tomes on which he based his statements on has since been criticized for, among other things, estimating an individual's lifetime income from one year's income. Gary Solon, *Intergenerational Income Mobility in the United States*, 82 AM. ECON. REV. 393, 395 (1992); *see also* BHASHKAR MAZUMDER, FEDERAL RESERVE BANK OF CHICAGO, THE MIS–MEASUREMENT OF PERMANENT EARNINGS: NEW EVIDENCE FROM SOCIAL SECURITY EARNINGS DATA (2001), *available at* http://www.chicagofed. org/publications/workingpapers/papers/Wp2001–24.pdf (critiquing the use of short-term averages of earnings as a proxy for permanent earnings). Newer research indicates that the actual requirement for regression to the mean is between four and six generations. Alan B. Krueger, *The Apple Falls Close to the Tree, Even in the Land of Opportunity*, N.Y. TIMES, Nov. 14, 2002, at C2.

    b. **Effect of legacy on meritocracy.** In 1998, nine students from Groton boarding school in Massachusetts applied for admission to Stanford University; only one was admitted. Her SAT score was lower than seven of the eight other Groton grads who applied to Stanford and both her SAT scores and class rank were significantly lower than the class ranks and test scores of the vast majority of students admitted to Stanford. However, she had something other students' didn't have: a father who was chairman of Stanford's board and who had given $25,000,000 to Stanford in 1992. Does the policy of preferential admission of the children of alumnae and donors cast doubt on Posner's arguments about the rapid dissipation of the initial distribution of wealth? Even if a free market would lead to dissipation of the initial wealth distribution, do policies like legacy admissions serve to maintain the initial distribution of wealth, perhaps indefinitely? For more, see Daniel Golden, *College Ties*: *For Groton Grads, Academics Aren't Only Keys to Ivy Schools*, WALL ST. J., Apr. 25, 2003, at A1.

6. Morality in law and economics. Is law and economics amoral? Judge Posner notes that "it would be possible in a system unflinchingly dedicated to wealth maximization to come up with results that would be deeply, perhaps universally, offensive." Richard Posner, *Law and Economics is Moral, in* ADAM SMITH AND THE PHILOSOPHY OF LAW AND ECONOMICS 174 (Rubin Paul Malloy & Jerry Evensky eds., 1994). One such specific proposal is child trafficking which Posner believes is a form of transaction that would be wealth maximizing and would repair a serious imbalance in the supply and demand for babies for adoption.

> We have in this country an enormous production of illegitimate births and, on the other hand, a terrible shortage of babies for adoption. This is clearly a disequilibrium, and it results in part from refusing to allow an explicit trade in babies.

Id. at 173.

Should the fact that law and economics can justify such schemes which even Posner admits are "deeply, perhaps universally, offensive" undermine the persuasive authority of law and economics?

7. Libertarianism and persuasive power of law and economics. In its statement of principles, the Libertarian party of the United States declares that:

> People should not be forced to sacrifice their lives and property for the benefit of others. They should be left free by government to deal with one another as free traders; and the resultant economic system, the only one compatible with the protection of individual rights, is the free market.

LIBERTARIAN PARTY, STATEMENT OF PRINCIPALS, *available at* http://www.lp.org/issues/platform_all.shtml#sop.

This economic position seems to mirror the law and economics of Judge Posner which recommends that the legal system act as much like the free market as possible when resolving disputes. Indeed, many of the thinkers most closely associated with law and economics, including Judge Posner himself, identify as libertarians. Given the conservative nature of libertarianism, does this association undermine claims of Law and Economics as a value-neutral method of jurisprudence?

8. Contradictions between libertarianism and utilitarianism. Ayn Rand, an influential libertarian thinker, stated:

> Parasites, moochers, looters, brutes and thugs can be of no value to a human being—nor can he gain any benefit from living in a society geared to their needs, demands and protection, a society that treats him as a sacrificial animal and penalizes him for his virtues in order to reward them for their vices, which means: a society based on the ethics of altruism.

AYN RAND, THE VIRTUE OF SELFISHNESS 32 (1964).

Such sentiments are very similar to the consequence of the money requirement in law and economics which results in the preferences of the destitute having zero weight. Thus, it seems that libertarianism and law and economics are a perfect match for one another. However, on closer examination, is there not a contradiction between libertarianism, which focuses on the primacy of the individual, and law and economics, which bases its normative appeal on the good of the community? Some libertarians, like Posner, support economic individualism only to the extent that it is the most effective way of providing for the well-being of everyone. Others, like Rand, seem to favor a devil take the hindmost approach to the marketplace. For more on this tension, see Gary Lawson, *Efficiency and Individualism*, 42 DUKE L.J. 53 (1992) (explaining difficulties relating to interpersonal comparisons of utility and addresses the tension between individualism and social wealth); Larry Alexander & Maimon Schwarzschild, *The Uncertain Relationship Between Libertarianism and Utilitarianism*, 19 QUINNIPIAC L. REV. 657 (2000) (tracing the development of the jurisprudence of Epstein and noting the contradiction between his early libertarian philosophy and his later utilitarian bent.); Heidi Li Feldman, *Law and Economics: Libertarianism with a Twist*, 94 MICH. L. REV. 1883 (1996) (questioning Epstein's attempt to justify a libertarian state through rule utilitarianism).

1. LAW AND ECONOMICS IN JUDICIAL REASONING

a. An Early Precursor

Learned Hand's opinion in *U.S. v Carroll Towing Co.* is a classic of tort law. It is recognized for introducing an algebraic representation (negligence $=PL > B$) of the economic cost benefit test to replace the more vague and general common law standard of "reasonable care." In the arguments of the law and economics movement, the Hand formulation is taken as an expression of the goal of economic efficiency. The Hand formulation fits neatly into both the positive and normative claims of law and economics. The positive argument is that the common law has been constructed so as to pursue efficiency as its goal. This argument has been vigorously contested by torts scholars who have argued that many nineteenth-century tort cases are quite inconsistent with the efficiency interpretation. *See* Gary T. Schwartz, *The Character of Early American Tort Law*, 36 UCLA L. REV. 641 (1989); Gary T. Schwartz, *Tort Law and the Economy in Nineteenth–Century America: A Reinterpretation*, 90 YALE L.J. 1717 (1981).

Other scholars have disputed the normative claim, that tort law *should* pursue efficiency and wealth maximization as primary goals. *Carroll Towing Company* is often used to support the normative position as well. The cost benefit approach to personal injury rules is designed to allow the party whose activities will inflict injury to continue to do so, as long as the burden of taking precaution exceeds the combined probability of injury multiplied by the gravity of injury should it occur. Legal philosopher Jules Coleman argued that corrective justice, rather than economic efficiency, explains the arc of tort common law developments. JULES COLEMAN, RISK AND WRONGS, 374–82 (1992).

Now, read this familiar case and decide whether it supports either the Posnerian positive or normative efficiency claims.

United States v. Carroll Towing Co.

159 F.2d 169 (2d Cir.1947).

■ L. HAND, Circuit Judge.

* * *

On June 20, 1943, the Conners Company chartered the barge, "Anna C." to the Pennsylvania Railroad Company at a stated hire per diem, by a charter of the kind usual in the Harbor, which included the services of a bargee, apparently limited to the hours 8 A.M. to 4 P.M. On January 2, 1944, the barge, which had lifted the cargo of flour, was made fast off the end of Pier 58 on the Manhattan side of the North River, whence she was later shifted to Pier 52. At some time not disclosed, five other barges were moored outside her, extending into the river; her lines to the pier were not then strengthened. At the end of the next pier north (called the Public Pier), lay four barges; and a line had been made fast from the outermost of these to the fourth barge of the tier hanging to Pier 52. The purpose of this line is not entirely apparent, and in any event it obstructed entrance into the slip between the two piers of barges. The Grace Line, which had chartered the tug, "Carroll," sent her down to the locus in quo to "drill" out one of the barges which lay at the end of the Public Pier; and in order to do so it was necessary to throw off the line between the two tiers. On board the "Carroll" at the time were not only her master, but a "harbormaster" employed by the Grace Line. Before throwing off the line between the two tiers, the "Carroll" nosed up against the outer barge of the tier lying off Pier 52, ran a line from her own stem to the middle bit of that barge, and kept working her engines "slow ahead" against the ebb tide which was making at that time. The captain of the "Carroll" put a deckhand and the "harbormaster" on the barges, told them to throw off the line which barred the entrance to the slip; but, before doing so, to make sure that the tier on Pier 52 was safely moored, as there was a strong northerly wind blowing down the river. The "harbormaster" and the deckhand went aboard the barges and readjusted all the fasts to their satisfaction, including those from the "Anna C." to the pier.

After doing so, they threw off the line between the two tiers and again boarded the "Carroll," which backed away from the outside barge, preparatory to "drilling" out the barge she was after in the tier off the Public Pier. She had only got about seventy-five feet away when the tier off Pier 52 broke adrift because the fasts from the "Anna C," either rendered, or carried away. The tide and wind carried down the six barges, still holding together, until the "Anna C" fetched up against a tanker, lying on the north side of the pier below—Pier 51—whose propeller broke a hole in her at or near her bottom. Shortly thereafter: i.e., at about 2:15 P.M., she careened, dumped her cargo of flour and sank. The tug, "Grace," owned by the Grace Line, and the "Carroll," came to the help of the flotilla after it broke loose; and, as both had syphon pumps on board, they could have kept the "Anna C" afloat, had they learned of her condition; but the bargee had left her on the evening before, and nobody was on board to observe that she was leaking. The Grace Line wishes to exonerate itself from all liability because the "harbormaster" was not authorized to pass on the sufficiency of the fasts of the "Anna C" which held the tier to Pier 52; the Carroll Company wishes to charge the Grace Line with the entire liability because the "harbormaster" was given an over-all authority. Both wish to charge the "Anna C" with a share of all her damages, or at least with so much as resulted from her sinking. The Pennsylvania Railroad Company also wishes to hold the barge liable. The Conners Company wishes the decrees to be affirmed.

The first question is whether the Grace Line should be held liable at all for any part of the damages. The answer depends first upon how far the "harbormaster's" authority went, for concededly he was an employee of some sort. Although the judge made no other finding of fact than that he was an "employee," in his second conclusion of law he held that the Grace Line was "responsible for his negligence." Since the facts on which he based this liability do not appear, we cannot give that weight to the conclusion which we should to a finding of fact; but it so happens that on cross-examination the "harbormaster" showed that he was authorized to pass on the sufficiency of the facts of the "Anna C." He said that it was part of his job to tie up barges; that when he came "to tie up a barge" he had "to go in and look at the barges that are inside the barge" he was "handling"; that in such cases "most of the time" he went in "to see that the lines to the inside barges are strong enough to hold these barges"; and that "if they are not" he "put out sufficient other lines as are necessary." That does not, however, determine the other question: i.e., whether, when the master of the "Carroll" told him and the deckhand to go aboard the tier and look at the fasts, preparatory to casting off the line between the tiers, the tug master meant the "harbormaster" to exercise a joint authority with the deckhand. As to this the judge in his tenth finding said: "The captain of the Carroll then put the deckhand of the tug and the harbor master aboard the boats at the end of Pier 52 to throw off the line between the two tiers of boats after first ascertaining if it would be safe to do so." Whatever doubts the testimony of the "harbormaster" might raise, this finding settles it for us that the master of the "Carroll" deputed the deckhand and the "harbormaster," jointly to pass upon the sufficiency of the "Anna C's" fasts to the pier. The case is stronger against the Grace Line than Rice v. The Marion A. C. Meseck, was against the tug there held liable, because the tug had only acted under the express orders of the "harbormaster." Here, although the relations were reversed, that makes no difference in principle; and the "harbormaster" was not instructed what he should do about the fast, but was allowed to use his own judgment. The fact that the deckhand shared in this decision, did not exonerate him, and there is no reason why both should not be held equally liable, as the judge held them.

We cannot, however, excuse the Conners Company for the bargee's failure to care for the barge, and we think that this prevents full recovery. * * * As we have said, the deckhand and the "harbormaster" jointly undertook to pass upon the "Anna C's" fasts to the pier; and even though we assume that the bargee was responsible for his fasts after the other barges were added outside, there is not the slightest ground for saying that the deckhand and the "harbormaster" would have paid any attention to any protest which he might have made, had he been there. We do not therefore attribute it as in any degree a fault of the "Anna C" that the flotilla broke adrift. Hence she may recover in full against the Carroll Company and the Grace Line for any injury she suffered from the contact with the tanker's propeller, which we shall speak of as the "collision damages." On the other hand, if the bargee had been on board, and had done his duty to his employer, he would have gone below at once, examined the injury, and called for help from the "Carroll" and the Grace Line tug. Moreover, it is clear that these tugs could have kept the barge afloat, until they had safely beached her, and saved her cargo. This would have avoided what we shall call the "sinking damages." Thus, if it was a failure in the Conner Company's proper care of its own barge, for the bargee to be absent, the company can recover only one third of the "sinking" damages from the Carroll Company and one third from the Grace Line. For this reason the question arises whether a barge owner is slack in the care of his barge if the bargee is absent.

* * *

It appears from the foregoing review that there is no general rule to determine when the absence of a bargee or other attendant will make the owner of the barge liable for injuries to other vessels if she breaks away from her moorings. However, in any cases where he would be so liable for injuries to others obviously he must reduce his damages proportionately, if the injury is to his own barge. It becomes apparent why there can be no such general rule, when we consider the grounds for such a liability. Since there are occasions when every vessel will break from her moorings, and since, if she does, she becomes a menace to those about her; the owner's duty, as in other similar situations, to provide against resulting injuries is a function of three variables: (1) The probability that she will break away; (2) the gravity of the resulting injury, if she does; (3) the burden of adequate precautions. Possibly it serves to bring this notion into relief to state it in algebraic terms: if the probability be called P; the injury, L; and the burden, B; liability depends upon whether B is less than L multiplied by P: i.e., whether $B < PL$. Applied to the situation at bar, the likelihood that a barge will break from her fasts and the damage she will do, vary with the place and time; for example, if a storm threatens, the danger is greater; so it is, if she is in a crowded harbor where moored barges are constantly being shifted about. On the other hand, the barge must not be the bargee's prison, even though he lives aboard; he must go ashore at times. We need not say whether, even in such crowded waters as New York Harbor a bargee must be aboard at night at all; it may be that the custom is otherwise, as Ward, J., supposed in "The Kathryn B. Guinan," supra; and that, if so, the situation is one where custom should control. We leave that question open; but we hold that it is not in all cases a sufficient answer to a bargee's absence without excuse, during working hours, that he has properly made fast his barge to a pier, when he leaves her. In the case at bar the bargee left at five o'clock in the afternoon of January 3rd, and the flotilla broke away at about two o'clock in the afternoon of the following day, twenty-one hours afterwards. The bargee had been away all the time, and we hold that his fabricated story was affirmative evidence that he had no excuse for his absence. At the locus in quo-especially during the short January days and in the full tide of war activity-barges were being constantly "drilled" in and out. Certainly it was not beyond reasonable expectation that, with the inevitable haste and bustle, the work might not be done with adequate care. In such circumstances we hold—and it is all that we do hold—that it was a fair requirement that the Conners Company should have a bargee aboard (unless he had some excuse for his absence), during the working hours of daylight.

    * * *

b.   Modern Cases

It is easy to forget that Professor Posner is also a judge whose views on law and economics extend beyond the realm of theory into the judicial arena. In this Seventh Circuit opinion, we see two University of Chicago law and economics scholars, Judges Easterbrook and Posner, carve out a separate rationale in a concurrence in a case in which they agree with the holding. Can you identify the tenets of law and economics legal theory upon which their opinion is based? What is the difference between the views of Judges Cudahy and Posner and Easterbrook? Do you agree with the Posner/Easterbrook analysis of the disparate impact of the rent control ordinance on the "poor" and the "middle class"?

In the second case in this section, Judge Posner is using law and economics reasoning to define the standard applicable under the common law as restated in the American Law Institute Restatement of the Law of Torts section 520 on strict liability for ultrahazardous activity liability. Like *Chicago Board of Realtors, Indiana Harbor* is strictly a question of law for the judge to decide what legal standard is applicable to resolve the dispute. In *Indiana Harbor*, Posner explores the relationship between two tort liability regimes: negligence, as we have discussed in *U.S. v. Carroll Towing Company* above, and strict liability. He decides that strict liability is inappropriate for the shipper/manufacturer of a highly flammable chemical that leaked while in a Chicago railyard near occupied homes. One component of the Restatement test for whether an activity is abnormally dangerous or ultrahazardous is whether the activity is unusual or inappropriate in the area in which the accident occurred. Consider Posner's opinion, that:

> ... It is no more realistic to propose to reroute the shipment of all hazardous materials around Chicago than it is to propose the relocation of homes adjacent to the Blue Island switching yard to more distant suburbs. It may be less realistic. Brutal though it may seem to say it, *the inappropriate use* to which land *is* being put in the Blue Island yard and neighborhood may be, not the transportation of hazardous chemicals, but *residential living*. The analogy is to building your home between the runways at O'Hare.

Indiana Harbor Belt R.R. Co. v. American Cyanamid Co., 916 F.2d 1174, 1181 (7th Cir. 1990) (emphasis added).

———

Chicago Board of Realtors, Inc. v. City of Chicago

United States Court of Appeals, Seventh Circuit, 819 F.2d 732 (1987).

■ POSNER, CIRCUIT JUDGE, concurring.

[In 1986, the Chicago City Council passed a Residential Landlord and Tenant ordinance. It codified the "implied warrant of habitability," which is a doctrine of property law that requires landlords to provide a baseline of quality in the housing they let, a duty which is independent of the tenant's obligation to pay rent. The ordinance was upheld against a challenge by property owners who questioned its constitutionality. In his opinion for the court, Judge Cudahy ruled that the ordinance was sufficiently specific and reasonable under the government's police power.

In the concurrence that follows, Judge Posner, joined by Judge Easterbrook, laid out a policy analysis of the ordinance.]

We agree with Judge Cudahy's opinion as far as it goes, and we therefore join it. But in our view it does not go far enough. It makes the rejection of the appeal seem easier than it is, by refusing to acknowledge the strong case that can be made for the unreasonableness of the ordinance. It does not explain how the district judge's denial of a preliminary injunction against such an interference with contract rights and economic freedom can be affirmed without violating the contract clause and the due process clause of the Constitution. So we are led to write separately, and since this separate opinion commands the support of two members of this panel, it is also a majority opinion.

The new ordinance rewrites present and future leases of apartments in Chicago to give tenants more legal rights than they would have without the ordinance. It requires the payment of interest on security deposits; requires that those deposits be held in Illinois banks; allows (with some limitations) a tenant to withhold rent in an amount reflecting the cost to him of the landlord's violating a term in the lease; allows a tenant to make minor repairs and subtract the reasonable cost of the repair from his rent; forbids a landlord to charge a tenant more than $10 a month for late payment of rent (regardless of how much is owing); and creates a presumption (albeit rebuttable) that a landlord who seeks to evict a tenant after the tenant has exercised rights conferred by the ordinance is retaliating against the tenant for the exercise of those rights.

The stated purpose of the ordinance is to promote public health, safety, and welfare and the quality of housing in Chicago. It is unlikely that this is the real purpose, and it is not the likely effect. Forbidding landlords to charge interest at market rates on late payment of rent could hardly be thought calculated to improve the health, safety, and welfare of Chicagoans or to improve the quality of the housing stock. But it may have the opposite effect. The initial consequence of the rule will be to reduce the resources that landlords devote to improving the quality of housing, by making the provision of rental housing more costly. Landlords will try to offset the higher cost (in time value of money, less predictable cash flow, and, probably, higher rate of default) by raising rents. To the extent they succeed, tenants will be worse off, or at least no better off. Landlords will also screen applicants more carefully, because the cost of renting to a deadbeat will now be higher; so marginal tenants will find it harder to persuade landlords to rent to them.

Those who do find apartments but then are slow to pay will be subsidized by responsible tenants (some of them marginal too), who will be paying higher rents, assuming the landlord cannot determine in advance who is likely to pay rent on time. Insofar as these efforts to offset the ordinance fail, the cost of rental housing will be higher to landlords and therefore less will be supplied—more of the existing stock than would otherwise be the case will be converted to condominia and cooperatives and less rental housing will be built.

The provisions of the ordinance requiring that interest on security deposits be paid and that those deposits be kept in Illinois banks are as remote as the provision on late payment from any concern with the health or safety of Chicagoans, the quality of housing in Chicago, or the welfare of Chicago as a whole. Their only apparent rationale is to transfer wealth from landlords and out-of-state banks to tenants and local banks—making this an unedifying example of class legislation and economic protectionism rolled into one. However, to the extent the ordinance seeks to transfer wealth from landlords to tenants it could readily be undone by a rent increase; the ordinance puts no cap on rents. Cf. Coase, *The Problem of Social Cost*, 3 J. Law & Econ. 1 (1960).

The provisions that authorize rent withholding, whether directly or by subtracting repair costs, may seem more closely related to the stated objectives of the ordinance; but the relation is tenuous. The right to withhold rent is not limited to cases of hazardous or unhealthy conditions.

And any benefits in safer or healthier housing from exercise of the right are likely to be offset by the higher costs to landlords, resulting in higher rents and less rental housing.

The ordinance is not in the interest of poor people. As is frequently the case with legislation ostensibly designed to promote the welfare of the poor, the principal beneficiaries will be middle-class people. They will be people who buy rather than rent housing (the conversion of rental to owner housing will reduce the price of the latter by increasing its supply); people willing to pay a higher rental for better-quality housing; and (a largely overlapping group) more affluent tenants, who will become more attractive to landlords because such tenants are less likely to be late with the rent or to abuse the right of withholding rent—a right that is more attractive, the poorer the tenant. The losers from the ordinance will be some landlords, some out-of-state banks, the poorest class of tenants, and future tenants.* * *

A growing body of empirical literature deals with the effects of governmental regulation of the market for rental housing. The regulations that have been studied, such as rent control in New York City and Los Angeles, are not identical to the new Chicago ordinance, though some—regulations which require that rental housing be "habitable"—are close. The significance of this literature is not in proving that the Chicago ordinance is unsound, but in showing that the market for rental housing behaves as economic theory predicts: if price is artificially depressed, or the costs of landlords artificially increased, supply falls and many tenants, usually the poorer and the newer tenants, are hurt. * * * The single proposition in economics from which there is the least dissent among American economists is that "a ceiling on rents reduces the quantity and quality of housing available." * * *

Indiana Harbor Belt R.R. Co. v. American Cyanamid Co.

916 F.2d 1174 (7th Cir. 1990).

■ POSNER, CIRCUIT JUDGE.

American Cyanamid Company * * * is a major manufacturer of chemicals, including acrylonitrile, a chemical used in large quantities in making acrylic fibers, plastics, dyes, pharmaceutical chemicals, and other intermediate and final goods. On January 2, 1979, at its manufacturing plant in Louisiana, Cyanamid loaded 20,000 gallons of liquid acrylonitrile into a railroad tank car that it had leased from the North American Car Corporation. * * * [The car was brought to] the Blue Island railroad yard * * * in the Village of Riverdale, which is just south of Chicago and part of the Chicago metropolitan area.

* * * Several hours after it arrived, employees of the switching line noticed fluid gushing from the bottom outlet of the car. The lid on the outlet was broken. After two hours, the line's supervisor of equipment was able to stop the leak by closing a shut-off valve controlled from the top of the car. No one was sure at the time just how much of the contents of the car had leaked, but it was feared that all 20,000 gallons had, and since acrylonitrile is flammable at a temperature of 30° Fahrenheit or above, highly toxic, and possibly carcinogenic (*Acrylonitrile*, 9 International Toxicity Update, no. 3, May–June 1989, at 2, 4), the local authorities ordered the homes near the yard evacuated.* * *

[The plaintiff] asserts that the transportation of acrylonitrile in bulk through the Chicago metropolitan area is an abnormally dangerous activity, for the consequences of which the shipper (Cyanamid) is strictly liable to the switching line, which bore the financial brunt of those consequences because of the decontamination measures that it was forced to take.* * *

The question whether the shipper of a hazardous chemical by rail should be strictly liable for the consequences of a spill or other accident to the shipment en route is a novel one in Illinois, despite the switching line's contention that the question has been answered in its favor by two decisions of the Illinois Appellate Court that the district judge cited in granting summary judgment.* * *

The parties agree that the question whether placing acrylonitrile in a rail shipment that will pass through a metropolitan area subjects the shipper to strict liability is, as recommended in Restatement (Second) of Torts § 520, comment *l* (1977), a question of law, so that we owe no particular deference to the conclusion of the district court. They also agree * * * that the Supreme Court of Illinois would treat as authoritative the provisions of the Restatement governing abnormally dangerous activities. The key provision is section 520, which sets forth six factors to be considered in deciding whether an activity is abnormally dangerous and the actor therefore strictly liable.

The roots of section 520 are in nineteenth-century cases. [In *Guille v. Swan*, 19 Johns. (N.Y.) 381 (1822) a] man took off in a hot-air balloon and landed, without intending to, in a vegetable garden in New York City. A crowd that had been anxiously watching his involuntary descent trampled the vegetables in their endeavor to rescue him when he landed. The owner of the garden sued the balloonist for the resulting damage, and won. Yet the balloonist had not been careless. In the then state of ballooning it was impossible to make a pinpoint landing.

Guille is a paradigmatic case for strict liability. (a) The risk (probability) of harm was great, and (b) the harm that would ensue if the risk materialized could be, although luckily was not, great (the balloonist could have crashed into the crowd rather than into the vegetables). The confluence of these two factors established the urgency of seeking to prevent such accidents. (c) Yet such accidents could not be prevented by the exercise of due care; the technology of care in ballooning was insufficiently developed. (d) The activity was not a matter of common usage, so there was no presumption that it was a highly valuable activity despite its unavoidable riskiness. (e) The activity was inappropriate to the place in which it took place—densely populated New York City. The risk of serious harm to others (other than the balloonist himself, that is) could have been reduced by shifting the activity to the sparsely inhabited areas that surrounded the city in those days. (f) Reinforcing (d), the value to the community of the activity of recreational ballooning did not appear to be great enough to offset its unavoidable risks.

* * * The baseline common law regime of tort liability is negligence. When it is a workable regime, because the hazards of an activity can be avoided by being careful (which is to say, nonnegligent), there is no need to switch to strict liability. Sometimes, however, a particular type of accident cannot be prevented by taking care but can be avoided, or its consequences minimized, by shifting the activity in which the accident occurs to another locale, where the risk or harm of an accident will be less ((e)), or by reducing the scale of the activity in order to minimize the number of accidents caused by it ((f)). * * * By making the actor strictly liable—by denying him in other words an excuse based on his inability to avoid accidents by being more careful—we give him an incentive, missing in a negligence regime, to experiment with methods of preventing accidents that involve not greater exertions of care, assumed to be futile, but instead relocating, changing, or reducing (perhaps to the vanishing point) the activity giving rise to the accident. * * * The greater the risk of an accident ((a)) and the costs of an accident if one occurs ((b)), the more we want the actor to consider the possibility of making accident-reducing activity changes; the stronger, therefore, is the case for strict liability. Finally, if an activity is extremely common ((d)), like driving an automobile, it is unlikely either that its hazards are perceived as great or that there is no technology of care available to minimize them; so the case for strict liability is weakened.

The largest class of cases in which strict liability has been imposed under the standard codified in the Second Restatement of Torts involves the use of dynamite and other explosives for demolition in residential or urban areas.* * *

Against this background we turn to the particulars of acrylonitrile. Acrylonitrile is one of a large number of chemicals that are hazardous in the sense of being flammable, toxic, or both; acrylonitrile is both, as are many others.* * *

[W]e can get little help from precedent, and might as well apply section 520 to the acrylonitrile problem from the ground up. To begin with, we have been given no reason * * * for believing that a negligence regime is not perfectly adequate to remedy and deter, at reasonable cost, the accidental spillage of acrylonitrile from rail cars * * * More important, although acrylonitrile is flammable even at relatively low temperatures, and toxic, it is not so corrosive or otherwise destructive that it will eat through or otherwise damage or weaken a tank car's valves although they are maintained with due (which essentially means, with average) care. No one suggests, therefore, that the leak in this case was caused by the *inherent* properties of acrylonitrile. It was caused by carelessness—whether that of the North American Car Corporation in failing to maintain or inspect the car properly, or that of Cyanamid in failing to maintain or inspect it, or that of the Missouri Pacific when it had custody of the car, or that of the switching line itself in failing to notice the ruptured lid, or some combination of these possible failures of care. Accidents that are due to a lack of care can be prevented by taking care; and when a lack of care can * * * be shown in court, such accidents are adequately deterred by the threat of liability for negligence.

It is true that the district court purported to find as a fact that there is an inevitable risk of derailment or other calamity in transporting "large quantities of anything." 662 F.Supp. at 642. This is not a finding of fact, but a truism: anything can happen. The question is, how likely is this type of accident if the actor uses due care? For all that appears from the record of the case or any other sources of information that we have found, if a tank car is carefully maintained the danger of a spill of acrylonitrile is negligible. If this is right, there is no compelling reason to move to a regime of strict liability, especially one that might embrace all other hazardous materials shipped by rail as well. This also means, however, that the amici curiae who have filed briefs in support of Cyanamid cry wolf in predicting "devastating" effects on the chemical industry if the district court's decision is affirmed. If the vast majority of chemical spills by railroads are preventable by due care, the imposition of strict liability should cause only a slight, not as they argue a substantial, rise in liability insurance rates, because the incremental liability should be slight. The amici have momentarily lost sight of the fact that the feasibility of avoiding accidents simply by being careful is an argument against strict liability.

    * * *

The district judge and the plaintiff's lawyer make much of the fact that the spill occurred in a densely inhabited metropolitan area. Only 4,000 gallons spilled; what if all 20,000 had done so? Isn't the risk that this might happen even if everybody were careful sufficient to warrant giving the shipper an incentive to explore alternative routes? Strict liability would supply that incentive. But this argument overlooks the fact that, like other transportation networks, the railroad network is a hub-and-spoke system. And the hubs are in metropolitan areas. Chicago is one of the nation's largest railroad hubs. In 1983, the latest year for which we have figures, Chicago's railroad yards handled the third highest volume of hazardous-material shipments in the nation. East St. Louis, which is also in Illinois, handled the second highest volume. * * * With most hazardous chemicals (by volume of shipments) being at least as hazardous as acrylonitrile, it is unlikely—and certainly not demonstrated by the plaintiff—that they can be rerouted around all the metropolitan areas in the country, except at prohibitive cost. Even if it were feasible to reroute them one would hardly expect shippers, as distinct from carriers, to be the firms best situated to do the rerouting.* * *

The difference between shipper and carrier points to a deep flaw in the plaintiff's case. * * * [H]ere it is not the actors—that is, the transporters of acrylonitrile and other chemicals—but the manufacturers, who are sought to be held strictly liable. * * * A shipper can in the bill of lading designate the route of his shipment if he likes, 49 U.S.C. § 11710(a)(1), but is it realistic to suppose that shippers will become students of railroading in order to lay out the safest route by which to ship their goods? Anyway, rerouting is no panacea. Often it will increase the length of the journey, or compel the use of poorer track, or both. When this happens, the probability of an accident is increased, even if the consequences of an accident if one occurs are reduced; so the expected accident cost, being the product of the probability of an accident and the harm if the accident occurs, may rise. * * * It is easy to see how the accident in this case might have been prevented at reasonable cost by greater care on the part of those who handled the tank car of acrylonitrile. It is difficult to see how it might have been prevented at reasonable cost by a change in the activity of transporting the chemical. This is therefore not an apt case for strict liability.

We said earlier that Cyanamid, because of the role it played in the transportation of the acrylonitrile—leasing, and especially loading, and also it appears undertaking by contract with North American Car Corporation to maintain, the tank car in which the railroad carried Cyanamid's acrylonitrile to Riverdale—might be viewed as a special type of shipper (call it a "shipper-transporter"), rather than as a passive shipper. But neither the district judge nor the plaintiff's counsel has attempted to distinguish Cyanamid from an ordinary manufacturer of chemicals on this ground, and we consider it waived. Which is not to say that had it not been waived it would have changed the outcome of the case. The very fact that Cyanamid participated actively in the transportation of the acrylonitrile imposed upon it a duty of due care and by doing so brought into play a threat of negligence liability that, for all we know, may provide an adequate regime of accident control in the transportation of this particular chemical.

In emphasizing the flammability and toxicity of acrylonitrile rather than the hazards of transporting it, as in failing to distinguish between the active and the passive shipper, the plaintiff overlooks the fact that ultrahazardousness or abnormal dangerousness is, in the contemplation of the law at least, a property not of substances, but of activities: not of acrylonitrile, but of the transportation of acrylonitrile by rail through populated areas. * * * Natural gas is both flammable and poisonous, but the operation of a natural gas well is not an ultrahazardous activity. * * * Whatever the situation under products liability law (section 402A of the Restatement), the manufacturer of a product is not considered to be engaged in an abnormally dangerous activity merely because the product becomes dangerous when it is handled or used in some way after it leaves his premises, even if the danger is foreseeable. * * * The plaintiff does not suggest that Cyanamid should switch to making some less hazardous chemical that would substitute for acrylonitrile in the textiles and other goods in which acrylonitrile is used. Were this a feasible method of accident avoidance, there would be an argument for making manufacturers strictly liable for accidents that occur during the shipment of their products (how strong an argument we need not decide). Apparently it is not a feasible method.

The relevant activity is transportation, not manufacturing and shipping. This essential distinction the plaintiff ignores. But even if the [defendant] is treated as a transporter and not merely a shipper, [the plaintiff] has not shown that the transportation of acrylonitrile in bulk by rail through populated areas is so hazardous an activity, even when due care is exercised, that the law should seek to create—perhaps quixotically—incentives to relocate the activity to nonpopulated areas, or to reduce the scale of the activity, or to switch to transporting acrylonitrile by road rather than by rail. * * * It is no more realistic to propose to reroute the shipment of all hazardous materials around Chicago than it is to propose the relocation of homes adjacent to the Blue Island switching yard to more distant suburbs. It may be less realistic. Brutal though it may seem to say it, the inappropriate use to which land is being put in the Blue Island yard and neighborhood may be, not the transportation of hazardous chemicals, but residential living. The analogy is to building your home between the runways at O'Hare.

* * *

The case for strict liability has not been made. Not in this suit in any event. We need not speculate on the possibility of imposing strict liability on shippers of more hazardous materials, such as [bombs], any more than we need differentiate (given how the plaintiff has shaped its case) between active and passive shippers. We noted earlier that acrylonitrile is far from being the most hazardous among hazardous materials shipped by rail in highest volume. Or among materials shipped, period.* * *

The judgment is reversed (with no award of costs in this court) and the case remanded for further proceedings, consistent with this opinion, on the plaintiff's claim for negligence.

90–Day Hazmat Ban Is Passed; Measure Will Bar Shipments in D.C.

WASHINGTON POST, Feb. 2, 2005, at B01.

■ ERIC M. WEISS and SPENCER S. HSU

The D.C. Council yesterday approved a temporary ban on shipments of hazardous materials through the nation's capital, becoming the first jurisdiction in the nation to halt such cargo in response to the threat of terrorism. Council members, who approved the 90–day emergency legislation 10 to 1, said reassurances from federal officials were not enough to safeguard residents. Mayor Anthony A. Williams (D) said through a spokesman that he will sign the bill as soon as possible.

Although the legislation does not require congressional review, the council is also considering a bill for a permanent ban, which would be subject to review by Congress.

The D.C. action sets up a potential legal battle with rail giant CSX Corp., which owns and operates the major freight line that runs through the city, passing within four blocks of the U.S. Capitol. Senior federal officials opposed the action, noting that they have pushed CSX to voluntarily reroute dangerous materials. But the officials have declined to make public exactly what safeguards are being taken.

"This is the nation's capital, and we need the toxics out," said council member Kathy Patterson (D–Ward 3), the measure's chief sponsor.

A CSX rail line in the District moves 8,500 chemical cars a year through the city, though only a fraction of those chemicals are toxic when inhaled. The legislation bans the most dangerous types of material, including certain classes of explosives, flammable gases and poisonous gases and materials. It also requires all rail and truck firms carrying other hazardous materials to obtain permits from the city's Transportation Department. Ban advocates say they expect about 5 to 10 percent of rail shipments to fall under the prohibition.

A chief U.S. Naval Research Laboratory scientist projected that in a worst-case scenario, a release of chlorine from a 90–ton tanker car during a Fourth of July celebration on the Mall could kill 100 people a second and 100,000 in 30 minutes.

Council member Carol Schwartz (R–At Large) cast the only vote against the measure. Marion Barry (D–Ward 8) was at a funeral and did not vote.

Schwartz, who is chairman of the council's public works committee, said CSX officials privately assured her that the company has been rerouting the most dangerous cargo since the Madrid train bombing in March. Therefore, she said, the legislation is unnecessary and would trigger a legal battle.

"We are better served by cooperating with the feds rather than by confronting them," Schwartz said.

The U.S. Department of Homeland Security and the U.S. Department of Transportation issued separate statements suggesting that federal and industry officials have taken safety measures that go beyond the D.C. ban but declined to say what material is being rerouted.

"We will also continue to explore other options that might be available with regards to routes for transporting hazardous materials through the national Capital region," the Department of Transportation said.

The Transportation Security Administration last year conducted a security study and hazardous material response plan for 42 miles of rail corridor in the Washington area. It is implementing a $7 million long-term plan for low-tech measures such as fencing and added patrols as well as more sophisticated safeguards, including intrusion detection systems and video surveillance.

The rail industry and transportation lawyers have closely watched the D.C. legislation. Although the consensus of legal analysts is that the law would not pass a federal court challenge, it feeds a national debate about the power of communities to control the flow of toxic shipments, spurred by the Sept. 11, 2001, terrorist attacks and by recent rail accidents.

Spokesman Robert T. Sullivan said CSX had grave reservations about the bill but stopped short of promising a legal challenge.

"We will review it again and make a determination about exactly what to do," Sullivan said. "But when you get into cities dictating how commodities can move, it frustrates interstate commerce."

Industry groups reiterated that shipping hazardous materials by rail is generally safer than using trucks. They noted that chemicals such as chlorine are used to purify half of the nation's water systems and predicted that a D.C. ban would set off a series of prohibitions that would cripple the U.S. rail system.

A coalition of environmental, labor and civic groups, mobilized to pass the ban, called it a landmark.

"This is probably the most important vote D.C. Council members will ever take," said Rick Hind, legislative director of the Greenpeace Toxics Campaign, which mounted a two-year lobbying effort to pass the ban with Friends of the Earth and the local Sierra Club.

Ultimately, whether the city will be allowed to implement a permanent ban may be decided by Congress, which has been reluctant to impose new restrictions on the rail industry since 2001, analysts said.

"Congress may feel compelled to say there are certain circumstances where we shouldn't let materials like this go close to particular sites," said James B. Reed, transportation program director for the National Council of State Legislatures. "But under existing law, it would probably be preempted under a court challenge." On May 3, 2005, the District of Columbia Court of Appeals ruled in favor of the railway, granting an injunction enforcing the HazMat ban. The court found that although under the Federal Rail Safety Act a city could adopt a more protective standard than the Federal Rule, the action must however be limited to eliminating "an essentially local safety or security hazard." In addition the local provision must not "burden interstate commerce." The court found that protecting the Capitol building was not an "essentially local hazard" and that the city ordinance burdened interstate commerce. The injunction sought by the CSX Railway Co. was therefore granted. CSX Transportation, Inc. v. Anthony Williams, 406 F.3d 667 (D.C.Cir.2005). This case is still pending in the courts as of 2010, although it is yet unclear how the Obama administration stands on this issue. The Bush administration strongly supported CSX's position.

NOTES AND QUESTIONS

1.   Role for judges in deciding economic common law cases. In *The Economic Approach to Law*, THE PROBLEMS OF JURISPRUDENCE 353–92 (1990), Posner argues that:

The judge whose business is enforcing tort, contract, and property law lacks effective tools for bringing about an equitable distribution of wealth, even if he thinks he knows what such a distribution would be. He would be further handicapped in such an endeavor by the absence of consensus in our society on the nature of a just distribution, an absence that undermines the social acceptability of attempts to use the judicial office to achieve distributive goals. *A sensible division of labor has the judge making rules and deciding cases in the areas regulated by the common law in such a way as to maximize the size of the social pie,* and the legislature attending to the sizes of the slices.

Richard A. Posner, *The Economic Approach to Law, in* The Problems of Jurisprudence (1990) (emphasis added).

Does this decision upholding the landlord tenant ordinance "increase the size of the social pie?"

2. Importance of empirical support for economic assumptions. In the following excerpt *Posner* next takes up a hypothetical, not unlike the *Chicago Board of Realtors* case above, in which a common law judge is asked to rule on the validity of a landlord-tenant ordinance:

The case is strongest in those common law areas where the relevant policies are admitted to be economic. Suppose the idea of an implied warranty of habitability—which entitles a tenant to sue his landlord if the premises fall below the standards of safety and comfort specified in the local housing code—is defended, as normally it is defended, on the ground that it is needed to protect tenants from deception and over reaching by landlords and will not lead to a reduction in the stock of housing available to poor people or to higher rentals than the poor are willing and able to pay. If research demonstrates that these assumptions are incorrect, the proponent, if fair-minded, will have to withdraw the proposal.

Posner, *supra* at 388.

Posner argues that "[a] growing body of empirical literature deals with the effects of governmental regulation of the market for rental housing." *Chicago Bd. of Realtors*, 819 F.2d at 742. However, does Posner base his majority opinion in *Chicago Board of Realtors* on the existence of empirical research showing the characteristics of the rental housing market in Chicago in response to a housing ordinance with the features of the Chicago ordinance? Does comparing Chicago with New York and Los Angeles, where studies were done but the ordinances are different, meet a judge's burden of persuasion to develop the empirical basis for economic reasoning in an action seeking an injunction?

3. Is economic reasoning precedent? What is the basis for Posner's agreement with the holding of the Cudahy opinion, if he disagrees with Cudahy's conclusion that the ordinance is Constitutional? Consider this passage from the Posner/Easterbrook concurrence:

It does not explain how the district judge's denial of a preliminary injunction against such an interference with contract rights and economic freedom can be affirmed without violating the contract clause and the due process clause of the Constitution. So we are led to write separately.

Id. at 741.

Since the ordinance was ultimately upheld, is the economic reasoning just a rhetorical flourish in the case—an "advisory opinion"—not a common law precedent based upon economic reasoning, even though it is a "majority opinion?"

Is the key piece of economic reasoning that might qualify as precedent found in this passage of the Posner opinion?:

> Their only apparent rationale is to transfer wealth from landlords and out-of-state banks to tenants and local banks—making this an unedifying example of class legislation and economic protectionism rolled into one. However, to the extent the ordinance seeks to transfer wealth from landlords to tenants it could readily be undone by a rent increase; the ordinance puts no cap on rents. Cf. Coase, *The Problem of Social Cost*, 3 J. LAW & ECON. 1 (1960).

Id. at 742.

Thus, Posner can support the legislation despite his misgivings about its constitutionality or efficiency because landlords retain wealth-maximizing options to control the price of rental housing in response to any of the intrusive features of the ordinance.

————

2.   THE PROBLEM OF INCOMPATIBLE PROPERTY USES: THE ROLES FOR PRIVATE BARGAINING AND JUDICIAL INJUNCTIONS

A central tenet of the law and economics approach to legal reasoning has been the Coase Theorem. The theorem asserts that when there are no barriers to transactions between parties, the affected parties will bargain so as to obtain an efficient allocation of resources regardless of how the legal rule or decision would assign the rights initially. The major assumption of this theorem is that there are no transactions costs. What happens when transactions costs are substantial—does that change the assessment of whether the bargaining has produced an efficient outcome?

We now examine the problem of how to structure the remedies for property owners whose uses are incompatible. Where one owner's use presents continuing invasions of the rights of others, either because of pollution, noise, particulate discharge, or because the adjoining structure blocks the light or view of the other property owner, the question in law and economic terms is: for the efficient distribution of property value, does it ultimately matter whether the court grants the injunction or not? Will the parties seek to bargain in the shadow of the court decision, so that the party who values the right the most will buy the right to engage in the incompatible use from the party who values it less?

Boomer v. Atlantic Cement Co.

257 N.E.2d 870 (N.Y. 1970).

■ BERGAN, JUDGE.

Defendant operates a large cement plant near Albany. These are actions for injunction and damages by neighboring land owners alleging injury to property from dirt, smoke and vibration emanating from the plant. A nuisance has been found after trial, temporary damages have been allowed; but an injunction has been denied.

The public concern with air pollution arising from many sources in industry and in transportation is currently accorded ever wider recognition accompanied by a growing sense of responsibility in State and Federal Governments to control it. Cement plants are obvious sources of air pollution in the neighborhoods where they operate.

But there is now before the court private litigation in which individual property owners have sought specific relief from a single plant operation. The threshold question raised by the division of view on this appeal is whether the court should resolve the litigation between the parties now before it as equitably as seems possible; or whether, seeking promotion of the general public welfare, it should channel private litigation into broad public objectives.

* * *

It seems apparent that the amelioration of air pollution will depend on technical research in great depth; on a carefully balanced consideration of the economic impact of close regulation; and of the actual effect on public health. It is likely to require massive public expenditure and to demand more than any local community can accomplish and to depend on regional and interstate controls.

A court should not try to do this on its own as a by-product of private litigation and it seems manifest that the judicial establishment is neither equipped in the limited nature of any judgment it can pronounce nor prepared to lay down and implement an effective policy for the elimination of air pollution. This is an area beyond the circumference of one private lawsuit. It is a direct responsibility for government and should not thus be undertaken as an incident to solving a dispute between property owners and a single cement plant—one of many—in the Hudson River valley.

The cement making operations of defendant have been found by the court at Special Term to have damaged the nearby properties of plaintiffs in these two actions. That court, as it has been noted, accordingly found defendant maintained a nuisance and this has been affirmed at the Appellate Division. The total damage to plaintiffs' properties is, however, relatively small in comparison with the value of defendant's operation and with the consequences of the injunction which plaintiffs seek.

The ground for the denial of injunction, notwithstanding the finding both that there is a nuisance and that plaintiffs have been damaged substantially, is the large disparity in economic consequences of the nuisance and of the injunction. This theory cannot, however, be sustained without overruling a doctrine which has been consistently reaffirmed in several leading cases in this court and which has never been disavowed here, namely that where a nuisance has been found and where there has been any substantial damage shown by the party complaining an injunction will be granted.

The rule in New York has been that such a nuisance will be enjoined although marked disparity be shown in economic consequence between the effect of the injunction and the effect of the nuisance.

* * *

Although the court at Special Term and the Appellate Division held that injunction should be denied, it was found that plaintiffs had been damaged in various specific amounts up to the time of the trial and damages to the respective plaintiffs were awarded for those amounts. The effect of this was, injunction having been denied, plaintiffs could maintain successive actions at law for damages thereafter as further damage was incurred.

The court at Special Term also found the amount of permanent damage attributable to each plaintiff, for the guidance of the parties in the event both sides stipulated to the payment and acceptance of such permanent damage as a settlement of all the controversies among the parties. The total of permanent damages to all plaintiffs thus found was $185,000. This basis of adjustment has not resulted in any stipulation by the parties.

This result at Special Term and at the Appellate Division is a departure from a rule that has become settled; but to follow the rule literally in these cases would be to close down the plant at once. This court is fully agreed to avoid that immediately drastic remedy; the difference in view is how best to avoid it.

One alternative is to grant the injunction but postpone its effect to a specified future date to give opportunity for technical advances to permit defendant to eliminate the nuisance; another is to grant the injunction conditioned on the payment of permanent damages to plaintiffs which would compensate them for the total economic loss to their property present and future caused by defendant's operations. For reasons which will be developed the court chooses the latter alternative.

If the injunction were to be granted unless within a short period—e.g., 18 months—the nuisance be abated by improved methods, there would be no assurance that any significant technical improvement would occur.

The parties could settle this private litigation at any time if defendant paid enough money and the imminent threat of closing the plant would build up the pressure on defendant. If there were no improved techniques found, there would inevitably be applications to the court at Special Term for extensions of time to perform on showing of good faith efforts to find such techniques.

Moreover, techniques to eliminate dust and other annoying by-products of cement making are unlikely to be developed by any research the defendant can undertake within any short period, but will depend on the total resources of the cement industry Nationwide and throughout the world. The problem is universal wherever cement is made.

* * *

On the other hand, to grant the injunction unless defendant pays plaintiffs such permanent damages as may be fixed by the court seems to do justice between the contending parties. All of the attributions of economic loss to the properties on which plaintiffs' complaints are based will have been redressed.

The nuisance complained of by these plaintiffs may have other public or private consequences, but these particular parties are the only ones who have sought remedies and the judgment proposed will fully redress them. The limitation of relief granted is a limitation only within the four corners of these actions and does not foreclose public health or other public agencies from seeking proper relief in a proper court.

It seems reasonable to think that the risk of being required to pay permanent damages to injured property owners by cement plant owners would itself be a reasonable effective spur to research for improved techniques to minimize nuisance.

* * *

■ Jasen, Judge (dissenting).

I agree with the majority that a reversal is required here, but I do not subscribe to the newly enunciated doctrine of assessment of permanent damages, in lieu of an injunction, where substantial property rights have been impaired by the creation of a nuisance.

It has long been the rule in this State, as the majority acknowledges, that a nuisance which results in substantial continuing damage to neighbors must be enjoined. * * * To now change the rule to permit the cement company to continue polluting the air indefinitely upon the payment of permanent damages is, in my opinion, compounding the magnitude of a very serious problem in our State and Nation today.

* * *

The harmful nature and widespread occurrence of air pollution have been extensively documented. Congressional hearings have revealed that air pollution causes substantial property damage, as well as being a contributing factor to a rising incidence of lung cancer, emphysema, bronchitis and asthma.

* * *

I see grave dangers in overruling our long-established rule of granting an injunction where a nuisance results in substantial continuing damage. In permitting the injunction to become inoperative upon the payment of permanent damages, the majority is, in effect, licensing a continuing wrong. It is the same as saying to the cement company, you may continue to do harm to your neighbors so long as you pay a fee for it. Furthermore, once such permanent damages are assessed and paid, the incentive to alleviate the wrong would be eliminated, thereby continuing air pollution of an area without abatement.

* * *

It is not my intention to cause the removal of the cement plant from the Albany area, but to recognize the urgency of the problem stemming from this stationary source of air pollution, and to allow the company a specified period of time to develop a means to alleviate this nuisance.

* * *

Fontainebleau Hotel Corp. v. Forty–Five Twenty–Five, Inc.

114 So.2d 357 (Fla.Dist.Ct.App.1959).

■ PER CURIAM

This is an interlocutory appeal from an order temporarily enjoining the appellants from continuing with the construction of a fourteen-story addition to the Fontainebleau Hotel, owned and operated by the appellants. Appellee, plaintiff below, owns the Eden Roc Hotel, which was constructed in 1955, about a year after the Fontainebleau, and adjoins the Fontainebleau on the north. Both are luxury hotels, facing the Atlantic Ocean. The proposed addition to Fontainebleau is being constructed twenty feet from its north property line, 130 feet from the mean high water mark of the Atlantic Ocean, and 76 feet 8 inches from the ocean bulkhead line. The 14–story tower will extend 160 feet above grade in height and is 416 feet long from east to west. During the winter months, from around two o'clock in the afternoon for the remainder of the day, the shadow of the addition will extend over the cabana, swimming pool, and sunbathing areas of the Eden Roc, which are located in the southern portion of its property.

In this action, plaintiff-appellee sought to enjoin the defendants-appellants from proceeding with the construction of the addition to the Fontainebleau (it appears to have been roughly eight stories high at the time suit was filed), alleging that the construction would interfere with the light and air on the beach in front of the Eden Roc and cast a shadow of such size as to render the beach wholly unfitted for the use and enjoyment of its guests, to the irreparable injury of the plaintiff; further, that the construction of such addition on the north side of defendants' property, rather than the south side, was actuated by malice and ill will on the part of the defendants' president toward the plaintiff's president; and that the construction was in violation of a building ordinance requiring a 100–foot setback from the ocean. * * *

The defendants' answer denied the material allegations of the complaint, pleaded laches and estoppel by judgment.

The chancellor heard considerable testimony on the issues made by the complaint and the answer and, as noted, entered a temporary injunction restraining the defendants from continuing with the construction of the addition. His reason for so doing was stated by him, in a memorandum opinion, as follows:

> "In granting the temporary injunction in this case the Court wishes to make several things very clear. The ruling is not based on any alleged presumptive title nor prescriptive right of the plaintiff to light and air nor is it based on any deed restrictions nor recorded plats in the title of the plaintiff nor of the defendant nor of any plat of record. It is not based on any zoning ordinance nor on any provision of the building code of the City of Miami Beach nor on the decision of any court, nisi prius or appellate. It is based solely on the proposition that no one has a right to use his property to the injury of another. In this case it is clear from the evidence that the proposed use by the Fontainebleau will materially damage the Eden Roc. There is evidence indicating that the construction of the proposed annex by the Fontainebleau is malicious or deliberate for the purpose of injuring the Eden Roc, but it is scarcely sufficient, standing alone, to afford a basis for equitable relief."

This is indeed a novel application of the maxim *sic utere tuo ut alienum non laedas*. This maxim does not mean that one must never use his own property in such a way as to do any injury to his neighbor. * * * In Reaver v. Martin Theatres, 52 So.2d 682, under this maxim, it was stated that 'it is well settled that a property owner may put his own property to any reasonable and lawful use, so long as he does not thereby deprive the adjoining landowner of any right of enjoyment of his property *which* is *recognized and protected by law, and so long as his use is not such a one as the law will pronounce a nuisance.*' [Emphasis supplied.]

No American decision has been cited, and independent research has revealed none, in which it has been held that—in the absence of some contractual or statutory obligation—a landowner has a legal right to the free flow of light and air across the adjoining land of his neighbor. Even at common law, the landowner had no legal right, in the absence of an easement or uninterrupted use and enjoyment for a period of 20 years, to unobstructed light and air from the adjoining land.* * *

There being, then, no legal right to the free flow of light and air from the adjoining land, it is universally held that where a structure serves a useful and beneficial purpose, it does not give rise to a cause of action, either for damages or for an injunction under the maxim *sic utere tuo ut alienum non laedas*, even though it causes injury to another by cutting off the light and air and interfering with the view that would otherwise be available over adjoining land in its natural state, regardless of the fact that the structure may have been erected partly for spite.* * *

We see no reason for departing from this universal rule. If, as contended on behalf of plaintiff, public policy demands that a landowner in the Miami Beach area refrain from constructing buildings on his premises that will cast a shadow on the adjoining premises, an amendment of its comprehensive planning and zoning ordinance, applicable to the public as a whole, is the means by which such purpose should be achieved. (No opinion is expressed here as to the validity of such an ordinance, if one should be enacted pursuant to the requirements of law. Cf. City of Miami Beach v. State ex rel. Fontainebleau Hotel Corp., Fla.App.1959, 108 So.2d 614, 619; certiorari denied, Fla.1959, 111 So.2d 437.) But to change the universal rule—and the custom followed in this state since its inception—that adjoining landowners have an equal right under the law to build to the line of their respective tracts and to such a height as is desired by them (in the absence, of course, of building restrictions or regulations) amounts, in our opinion, to judicial legislation.* * *

    * * *

The record affirmatively shows that no statutory basis for the right sought to be enforced by plaintiff exists. The so-called Shadow Ordinance enacted by the City of Miami Beach at plaintiff's behest was held invalid in City of Miami Beach v. State ex rel. Fontainebleau Hotel Corp., supra. It also affirmatively appears that there is no possible basis for holding that plaintiff has an easement for light and air, either express or implied, across defendants' property, nor any prescriptive right thereto—even if it be assumed, arguendo, that the common-law right of prescription as to 'ancient lights' is in effect in this state. And from what we have said heretofore in this opinion, it is perhaps superfluous to add that we have no desire to dissent from the unanimous holding in this country repudiating the English doctrine of ancient lights.

    * * *

While the chancellor did not decide the question of whether the setback ordinance had been violated, it is our view that, even if there was such a violation, the plaintiff would have no cause of action against the defendants based on such violation. The application of simple mathematics to the sun studies filed in evidence by plaintiff in support of its claim demonstrates conclusively that to move the existing structure back some 23 feet from the ocean would make no appreciable difference in the problem which is the subject of this controversy. * * * The construction of the 14–story addition is proceeding under a permit issued by the city pursuant to the mandate of this court in City of Miami Beach v. State ex rel. Fontainebleau Hotel Corp., supra, which permit authorizes completion of the 14–story addition according to a plan showing a 76–foot setback from the ocean bulkhead line. Moreover, the plaintiff's objection to the distance of the structure from the ocean appears to have been made for the first time in the instant suit, which was filed almost a year after the beginning of the construction of the addition, at a time when it was roughly eight stories in height, representing the expenditure by defendants of several million dollars. In these circumstances, it is our view that the plaintiff has stated no cause of action for equitable relief based on the violation of the ordinance—assuming, arguendo, that there has been a violation.

Since it affirmatively appears that the plaintiff has not established a cause of action against the defendants by reason of the structure here in question, the order granting a temporary injunction should be and it is hereby reversed with directions to dismiss the complaint.

Reversed with directions.

————

NOTES AND QUESTIONS

1. Courts or markets. One of the key insights of the Coase Theorem is that the market solution to conflicts such as those present in *Boomer* and *Fontainebleu* will ultimately prevail over any judicial determination of the respective rights. This can be understood as a normative commentary on the respective benefits of these two mechanisms for resolving disputes. Is this preference for markets consistent with the libertarian commitments of the law and economics school in which government actors are given a marginal role in allocating economic resources?

2. The deal. Did the court impose a deal on the parties by granting an injunction against the cement plant, conditioned on the plant paying its neighbors the amount of permanent damages determined by the court? If the court imposed a deal, is this inconsistent with the Coase Theorem? Once the court granted the conditional injunction, what would you expect the bargaining between the parties to include?

3. No transactions costs. The Coase Theorem assumes that there are no transactions costs. Imagine a scenario in which there *are* transactions costs. What might the costs include if the court had granted the permanent injunction in *Boomer*, and the plant had chosen to initiate a series of Coasian bargains with the plaintiffs, seeking to buy the right to pollute?

Might the costs include legal expenses such as the cost of retaining lawyers and drafting documents to support the agreements allowing the plant to pollute? If these costs ever exceed the value to the defendant of the right to pollute, would you expect the Coasian bargain to take place?

What if one or more of the plaintiffs has a strong moral opposition to environmental and personal injury damage caused by pollution? This plaintiff becomes a "hold out" who flatly refuses to compromise. The hold out says, "I will not sell my lungs to you for any price." What might the impact of a hold out be on the hypothetical exchange? Does the principled hold out have monopoly power in this situation? Can the hold out demand that the plant be shut down? Does it matter what motivation the hold out has to oppose the bargain? Is a mercenary who simply wants to exact an exorbitant settlement in the same position as the environmentally conscious hold out? What if the hold out demands that the defendants set up a fund for free private education and health care for as long as it operates in that community? What would you expect to be the limit of the defendants' willingness to respond to these third party directed demands?

3.   THE PROBLEM OF REDISTRIBUTION

An especially thorny and controversial issue for law and economics theory has been the problem of economic inequality and what its response should be, if any, to the social and economic effects of the vast wealth disparities among market participants. One answer, given by the neoclassical modern economists such as Friedman, Becker, and Coase has been to regard the distribution of wealth in society as the product of market competition, and therefore not a suitable target for government intervention. In this view, as forcefully argued by Milton Friedman in the essay "Created Equal," above, central government-controlled economic equality in the distribution of wealth is antithetical to liberty. Friedman observes:

> In some intellectual circles the desirability of equality of outcome has become an article of religious faith: everyone should finish the race at the same time. As the Dodo said in *Alice in Wonderland*, 'Everybody has won, and *all* must have prizes."
>
> * * *
>
> Everywhere in the world there are gross inequities of income and wealth. They offend most of us. Few can fail to be moved by the contrast between the luxury enjoyed by some and the grinding poverty suffered by others.
>
> In the past century a myth has grown up that free market capitalism—equality of opportunity as we have interpreted that term—increases such inequalities, that it is a system under which the rich exploit the poor.
>
> Nothing could be further from the truth.

MILTON FRIEDMAN & ROSE FRIEDMAN, *Created Equal*, in FREE TO CHOOSE 134, 146 (1980).

Libertarian aims include expanding the zone of individual autonomy and reducing the zone of governmental control. For libertarians, economic inequality, though regrettable, is unavoidable—even natural.

More recently, modern law and economics scholars have tried to grapple directly with the problem of fairness, defined as some form of redistribution, and the conflict between fairness and efficiency, defined as maximizing market forces without government intervention. Law and economics scholars Kaplow and Shavell have framed these arguments in complex detail in *Fairness Versus Welfare*, 114 HARV. L. REV. 961 (2001) in which they argue that legal policy should be concerned with the effect of such policies on the well-being of individuals, and not with notions of fairness that extend beyond the welfare of the individual to "notions of fairness, such as corrective justice and retributive justice...." *Id.* at 1381. Instead, Kaplow and Shavell argue that people's welfare can be built into the very structure of efficiency analysis. Their theoretical approach is known as "welfare economics." For an argument that Kaplow and Shavell have cheated by incorporating an extremely broad definition of "welfare," see Michael B. Dorff, *Why Welfare Depends on Fairness: A Reply to Kaplow and Shavell*, 75 S.Cal. L.Rev. 847 (2002).

In what follows, law and economics scholar Mitchell Polinsky offers a more accessible account of the tension between efficiency and equity. What solution does Polinsky ultimately identify as the acceptable avenue for attending to questions of fairness, however defined? Does this position differ markedly from the libertarian position articulated by Friedman?

———

Efficiency and Equity

An Introduction to Law and Economics 7–10 (3d ed. 2003).

■ A. Mitchell Polinsky

For the purposes of this book, the term *efficiency* will refer to the relationship between the aggregate benefits of a situation and the aggregate costs of the situation; the term *equity* will refer to the distribution of income among individuals. In other words, efficiency corresponds to "the size of the pie," while equity has to do with how it is sliced. Economists traditionally concentrate on how to maximize the size of the pie, leaving to others—such as legislators—the decision how to divide it. The attractiveness of efficiency as a goal is that, under some circumstances described below, everyone can be made better off if society is organized in an efficient manner.

Is There a Conflict?

An important question is whether there is a conflict between the pursuit of efficiency and the pursuit of equity. If the pie can be sliced in any way desired, then clearly there is no conflict—with a bigger pie, everyone can get a bigger piece. If, however, in order to create a bigger pie, its division must be quite unequal, then, depending on what constitutes an equitable division of the pie, there may well be a conflict between efficiency and equity. It may be preferable to accept a smaller pie (less efficiency) in return for a fairer division (more equity).

The potential conflict between efficiency and equity can be illustrated by a simple example. Suppose that the government must decide whether to build a dam and that the Dean of Stanford Law School and I are the only two individuals affected by it. Currently, without the dam, the Dean has $65 and I have $35, so total income is $100. The dam would cost $30 to build, consisting of $30 worth of my labor but none of the Dean's. The dam would create benefits worth $40, all of which would go to the Dean because the only feasible location for building the dam happens to be on her property. Should the dam be built?

On efficiency grounds, the dam clearly should be built because it creates benefits of $40 and costs only $30, thereby creating net benefits of

$10. But the equity effects need to be considered as well. Before the dam is built, the Dean has $65 and I have $35. After the dam is built, the Dean will have $105 (including the $40 benefit) and I will have $5 (after subtracting my $30 cost). Whether these distributional consequences are desirable depends on what constitutes a fair distribution of income. Suppose that the most equitable distribution of income involves the Dean receiving 60 percent of income and my receiving 40 percent. If the dam is not built, then the Dean should have $60 and I should have $40. If the dam is built and total income rises by $10, the Dean should have $66 and I should have $44.

But suppose, regardless of whether the dam is built, it is impossible to redistribute income between the two of us. Therefore, the choice is between the Dean's having $65 and my having $35 if the dam is not built, and the Dean's having $105 and my having $5 if the dam is built. Building the dam is more efficient but less equitable. How this conflict between efficiency and equity should be resolved depends on how important efficiency is relative to equity. If promoting equity is very important, it might be more desirable to sacrifice some efficiency for more equity by not building the dam (in other words, "damn" the Dean).

Alternatively, suppose it is possible to costlessly redistribute income between the Dean and me. Then, given the preferred distribution of income, if the dam is not built, $5 would be transferred from the Dean to me, so that she would end up with $60 and I would have $40. If the dam is built, $39 would be transferred from the Dean to me, so that she would end up with $66 and I would have $44. Clearly, since total income is distributed according to the percentages desired and we both are better off with the dam, the dam should be built. There is no conflict between efficiency and equity.

Note that, if it is possible to redistribute income at no cost, the dam should be built regardless of what constitutes an equitable distribution of income. If, for example, an egalitarian income distribution is desired, then without the dam the Dean and I each have $50 and with the dam we each could have $55. If, alternatively, equity required that everything should go to the Dean, the dam should be built because she then could have $110 rather than $100.

The dam example illustrates two important general observations. If income cannot be costlessly redistributed, there may be a conflict between efficiency and equity. Whether there is in fact a conflict depends on the specific distributional consequences of pursuing efficiency and on what constitutes an equitable distribution of income. However, if income can be costlessly redistributed, there is no conflict between efficiency and equity. This is true regardless of the specific distributional consequences of pursuing efficiency and regardless of what constitutes an equitable distribution of income. In other words, if income can be costlessly redistributed, it is always preferable to maximize the size of the pie because the pie can be sliced in any way desired.

Whether income can be costlessly distributed is discussed [below]. Although the conclusion there is that income redistribution is generally costly, it is argued nonetheless that efficiency should be the principal criterion for evaluating the legal system. This argument rests on the observations, explained at length [below], that it is often impossible to redistribute income through the choice of legal rules and that, even when it is possible, redistribution through the government's tax and transfer system may be cheaper and is likely to be more precise. In other words, the potential conflict between efficiency and equity when income redistribution is costly should be considered in the design of the government's tax and transfer system, but not generally in the choice of legal rules. Thus, *for purposes of discussing the legal system*, a reasonable simplifying assumption is that income can be costlessly redistributed.

* * *

Before proceeding, it is worth mentioning several other standard assumptions of economic analysis that will be made in analyzing the efficiency of legal rules. First, all benefits and costs can be measured in terms of a common denominator—dollars. It is important to emphasize that this assumption is made for expositional simplicity. It is not essential to economic analysis and does not exclude considerations that might be thought of as noneconomic—such as the protection of life and limb. Second, individuals themselves determine the dollar values to place on their benefits and costs. This is known as the assumption of *consumer sovereignty*. It is an acceptable assumption if one believes that individuals generally know what is best for themselves. Third, the values that individuals place on their benefits and costs are "stable" in the sense that these values are not affected by changes in public policy. For example, an individual's evaluation of the desirability of cleaner air is assumed not to depend on whether the legal system establishes a right to clean air. This is known as the assumption of *exogenous preferences*. Finally, individuals (and, when relevant, firms) maximize their benefits less their costs. This is known as the assumption of *utility maximization* (or, when firms are involved, profit maximization).

————

Efficiency and Equity Reconsidered

Introduction to Law and Economics 147–56 (3d ed. 2003).

■ A. Mitchell Polinsky

The discussion of efficiency and equity [above] showed that there is no conflict between these goals if income can be redistributed costlessly. In essence, this is because any inequity in the distribution of income caused by the pursuit of efficiency could be corrected at no cost. The assumption that redistribution was costless was made at the end of that chapter. We now consider this assumption, first with respect to the redistribution of income by means of government's tax and transfer system and then with respect to redistribution by the choice of legal rules.

REDISTRIBUTION BY TAXES AND TRANSFERS

In general, the redistribution of income by taxes and transfers is costly in the following sense. * * * If the price of a good equals its cost of production, only those individuals who value the good more than its cost will purchase it. This was seen to be efficient. The good used to illustrate this point * * * was a lawnmower that cost $100 to produce. Suppose that rich people are more likely to purchase lawnmowers than poor people because they are more likely to live in houses than in apartment buildings. Then, by imposing an excise tax on purchases of lawnmowers, the government would raise more tax revenue from the rich than from the poor. Assuming that the revenue is spent in a way that does not disproportionately favor the rich—say it benefits everyone equally—then the net effect of the tax would be to redistribute income from the rich to the poor. However, an inevitable byproduct of this redistribution is that the price of lawnmowers will be "distorted"—that is, the effective price of lawnmowers, including the tax, will exceed their cost of production. As a consequence, too few lawnmowers will be bought. For example, if the excise tax is $10 per lawnmower, then everyone who values a lawnmower more than the production cost of $100 but less than $110 will not purchase one, an inefficient outcome given that they value the good more than its cost of production. In general, to redistribute income by excise tax it is necessary to sacrifice some efficiency with respect to consumption decisions. This loss of efficiency is a cost of redistributing income.

The same kind of problem applies to income taxes, although not in as obvious a way. To see the distortion from income taxes, first note that leisure is commodity desired by consumers just like any other commodity. The "price" of an hour of leisure is the income forgone by not working that hour. For example, suppose that the wage rate in the widget industry is $25 per hour. * * * If widget workers did not have to pay income taxes, then they would give up $25 to consume an hour of leisure. Thus, those individuals who valued another hour of leisure more than $25 would "buy" more leisure by working an hour less. But suppose widget workers faced a 20 percent income tax. Then for every hour worked, they would pay $5 to the government and retain $20. The "price" of leisure therefore would fall to $20 per hour. Now individuals who value leisure more than $20 per hour will work less. Assuming that the $25 per hour wage reflects a worker's contribution to the value of the widgets produced, the income tax will cause an inefficient consumption decision regarding leisure. For example, a worker who values leisure at $21 per hour will work less even though the value of the worker's time in terms of widget production is $25 per hour. As in the case of the excise tax, the income tax distorts the price of some commodity—in this case leisure—and causes inefficient consumption decisions. Thus, it too imposes a cost in order to redistribute income.

Redistributing income by transfers rather than by taxes does not avoid the problem of distorting consumption decisions. For instance, suppose the government subsidizes the price of electricity for low-income individuals. Then the individuals who receive the subsidy will face an effective price of electricity that is below the cost of producing electricity and they therefore will buy too much of it relative to what is efficient. In general, any kind of tax or transfer used to redistribute income will distort the price of some commodity and will have this kind of efficiency cost.

CAN LEGAL RULES REDISTRIBUTE INCOME?

Given the cost of redistributing income by taxes and transfers, the question naturally arises whether the legal system should be used to redistribute income. That legal rules *can* be used to redistribute income was suggested by the discussion * * * of the distributional aspects of the Coase Theorem. In the example * * * of the factory polluting the residents, * * * when there were no transaction costs, the choice between the right to pollute and the right to clean air redistributed income by the $150 cost of the smokescreen (the least-cost solution to the conflict). It does not follow from that discussion, however, that legal rules always affect the distribution of income. To understand why, it will be useful to distinguish between legal disputes in which the parties are in some kind of contractual relationship, including a market relationship, and disputes in which the parties are, in effect, "strangers" prior to the dispute. The breach of contract and products liability examples would be characterized as *contractual disputes*, while the nuisance law, automobile accident, and pollution control examples would be described as *disputes between strangers*. (The products liability example is one of the first type because the victim is a consumer; it would be of the second type if the victim were a third party). It will be shown below that legal rules often cannot redistribute income in contractual disputes, whereas legal rules always can redistribute income in disputes between strangers.

To see why it is frequently difficult, if not impossible, to use legal rules to redistribute income in contractual disputes, consider * * * breach of contract. * * * [T]he seller of widgets might want to breach the contract with the initial buyer if an offer from a third party materialized. Suppose it is desirable for equity reasons to redistribute income from the seller to the buyer. Giving the buyer the remedy of expectation damages makes the buyer as well off if the contract is breached as he would have been had it been performed. Giving the buyer the remedy of reliance damages or restitution damages makes the buyer worse off if the contract is breached. However, because the contract price the buyer and seller negotiate depends on what the remedy is, it does not follow that the buyer is better off with the expectation remedy. Clearly, the seller will demand a higher price and the buyer will be willing to pay more if the buyer receives a larger payment in the event of a breach, the buyer may not be any better off with the expectation remedy. In general, the parties will take any distributional effects of breach of contract remedies into account when they negotiate the contract price; thus, how the joint benefits of entering into the contract are shared between the parties depends primarily, if not exclusively, on their relative bargaining strengths, not on the remedies available to them.

An analogous observation can be made about the products liability application when the victim of the product accident is a consumer of the good. Suppose, for example, that it is desirable for equity reasons to redistribute income from producers to consumers. * * * [U]nder the rule of negligence, producers will meet the standard of care, and, therefore, consumers will bear their own losses. But under the rule of strict liability, consumers will be fully compensated for their losses (assuming, if there is a defense of contributory negligence, they meet the standard of care applicable to them). Consumers will not, however, be better off as a class under strict liability because, in a competitive long-run equilibrium, the price of the good will rise by an amount equal to the producers' expected liability. In general, then, whenever the parties to a dispute are in some kind of contractual or market relationship, it may be difficult, if not impossible, to use the legal system to redistribute income.

To see why legal rules can be used to redistribute income in disputes between strangers, reconsider the discussion of automobile accidents * * *. In the simplest version of the example employed there, the pedestrian's expected accident losses depended solely on whether the driver chose to drive slowly, moderately, or rapidly. Under a negligence rule, the pedestrian will bear her own losses because the driver will choose to meet the standard of care—to drive moderately—whereas under a strict liability rule the driver will have to compensate the pedestrian for her losses. Because there is no contractual or market relationship between the parties, there is no contract price or market price that can be adjusted when legal rules change. Thus, shifting from one liability rule to the other will redistribute income by the amount of the expected losses.

Analogous observations can be made with respect to the nuisance law and pollution control applications. In the nuisance example * * *—of a polluting factory next to a single resident—the choices of the entitlement and the remedy for protecting the entitlement have distributional consequences. Given the entitlement, a party generally is better off if it is protected by an injunctive remedy rather than by a damage remedy (with liability equal to actual damages); although the damage remedy guarantees that the protected party will be fully compensated for damages, the injunctive remedy gives that party the right to hold out for more. And under either remedy, a party obviously is better off if the entitlement is more favorable to the party.

In the pollution control example * * * in which the pollution victims are third parties, the distributional effects of choosing between strict liability and negligence to control the polluting industry are similar to those discussed in the automobile accident context. Under negligence, the victims bear their own losses, whereas under strict liability, the producers—and ultimately consumers of the product—bear these losses. In general then, whenever the parties to a dispute are "strangers"—that is, not in a contractual or market relationship—the choice of legal rules will have distributional consequences.

SHOULD LEGAL RULES BE USED TO REDISTRIBUTE INCOME?

Having now identified the types of situations in which the legal system is most likely to have distributional effects, we can return to the question of whether legal rules *should* be used in these situations to promote distributional equity. The answer to this question depends in part on the "cost" of using legal rules to redistribute income relative to the cost of using taxes or transfers.

There are two senses in which redistribution through the legal system may be costly. The first relates to the administration costs of using the legal system. Suppose, for example, that the consumers of the goods produced by some polluting industry are high-income individuals, while the victims living near the polluting factories are low-income individuals. By making the firms strictly liable for the pollution damages, income will be transferred from rich people to poor people. A similar transfer could be accomplished by taxing high-income individuals and transferring the proceeds to low-income persons. The tax and transfer system is a *much* less expensive way to redistribute income than is the legal system. Roughly speaking, to transfer a dollar through a private lawsuit from a defendant to a plaintiff costs on average about a dollar in administrative costs of both parties and costs of the court system. To transfer a dollar through the tax and transfer system costs only a fraction of this amount.

Legal redistribution also may be costly in a second sense: Inefficient rules may have to be chosen in order to achieve the desired result. For example, * * * driver-pedestrian accidents in which both parties are risk averse and the pedestrian cannot affect expected losses. It was seen that negligence is efficient because the driver will meet the standard of care and the pedestrian will be able to buy a first-party accident insurance policy with full coverage; strict liability may not be efficient because of the moral hazard problem (which could result in the driver not being able to buy a liability insurance policy with full coverage and/or in the driver not taking appropriate care). But if drivers are wealthier than pedestrians, strict liability may be preferable to negligence on equity grounds. The loss of efficiency from using strict liability rather than negligence is a "cost" of redistributing income from drivers as a class to pedestrians as a class.

There may be instances in which redistribution through the legal system is not costly in this sense. For example, suppose that in some types of nuisance disputes the parties can be expected to bargain in a cooperative way. Then, * * * any entitlement will lead to the efficient outcome, whether protected by an injunctive remedy or a damage remedy. Thus, the choices of the entitlement and the remedy can be used to redistribute income without causing an inefficient resolution of the nuisance dispute. In general, however, not all legal rules will be efficient, so it often may be necessary to choose an inefficient legal rule in order to promote equity.

An additional consideration in deciding whether to use the legal system to promote distributional equity is the "precision" of legal redistribution. Legal rules will not be able to redistribute income systematically unless the status of the parties in a certain type of dispute corresponds closely to the groups between which redistribution is desired. For example, in automobile accidents involving drivers and pedestrians, there probably is not a close correspondence between the income of a party and whether that party is a driver or a pedestrian. It may be that higher income persons are more likely to be drivers than pedestrians, but certainly there are many low-income drivers and high-income pedestrians. Thus, liability rules regarding driver-pedestrian accidents are not very precise instruments for accomplishing income redistribution. In nuisance and pollution control disputes, there may be a closer correspondence between the income of a party and whether that party is victim or an injurer. The purchasers of the goods produced by some polluting industry may be mainly higher-income people, while the victims of the pollution may be primarily lower-income persons. Thus, in some kinds of disputes, the choice of a legal rule might contribute towards the implementation of distributional goals.

Even where there is a close correspondence between the status of the parties in a certain kind of dispute and the groups between which redistribution is desired, legal rules still might not be able to achieve redistribution as systematically as an income tax system. This is because redistribution through the legal system only may occur when a dispute arises, and not all members of a given income class will be involved in a dispute. For instance, even if the goods produced by a polluting industry were consumed exclusively by rich persons and the pollution victims were all poor people, not every rich person necessarily purchases this commodity and not every poor person lives near a factory in this industry. Thus, the legal rule used to control the pollution dispute will, as best, redistribute income from a subset of one income class to a subset of another. In sum, the legal system is not nearly as precise as the tax system in redistributing income.

The initial discussion of efficiency and equity * * * showed that, if it is costly to redistribute income, there may be a tradeoff between efficiency and equity. In other words, it may be desirable to choose an inefficient policy in order to promote the desired distribution of income. [This discussion] has shown that income redistribution generally *is* costly, whether it is accomplished by the tax and transfer system or by the legal system. Nonetheless, several reasons have been suggested * * * why the choice of legal rules should be based primarily on efficiency considerations. In some circumstances—contractual dispute—legal rule often will have little or no effect on the distribution of income. In situations in which the legal system does have distributional consequences—disputes between strangers—legal rules still should be based primarily on efficiency considerations because legal rules generally are more costly than taxes and transfers as means of redistributing income and less precise. Thus, the justification for the assumption made * * * that income could be redistributed without cost * * * is not only that this simplified the subsequent exposition by allowing us to focus on the efficiency analysis of legal rules. As this chapter has shown, the justification also is that, even when the cost of redistributing income is taken into account, there are reasons why the efficiency analysis should be of principal importance.

4. Politics

Public Choice and the Future of Public–Choice–Influenced Legal Scholarship

50 Vand. L. Rev. 647 (1997) (reviewing Maxwell L. Stearns, Public Choice and Public Law: Readings and Commentary (1997)).

■ David A. Skeel, Jr.

* * *

At a general level, the distinctive characteristic of public choice is its "use of economic tools to deal with the traditional problems of political science." Perhaps the most basic of these tools is the assumption of individual rationality. In contrast to much traditional political analysis, public choice assumes that all of the relevant players tend to act in their own self-interest, and explores the implications of self-interest for the legislative and other institutional decisionmaking processes.

The public choice literature thus can, and in my view should, be seen as including any analysis that incorporates or explicitly challenges the self-interestedness premise in addressing institutional decisionmaking processes. The literature that fits within this definition consists of two principal branches. The first can be described as interest group analysis, and the second is social choice.

The central insight of interest group analysis is that concentrated interest groups often benefit at the expense of more widely scattered groups, even if the diffuse group has much more at stake overall. Although this insight is now so familiar that it seems obvious to many, it was far from obvious when it emerged in the public choice literature. Whereas many theorists assumed that interest group competition tends to produce public-regarding legislation, public choice suggested that self-interested behavior by each of the relevant actors could lead to strikingly different outcomes.

The reasoning is as follows. For a self-interested voter, taking the time to inform herself and to vote intelligently is an unattractive proposition, since the likelihood that her vote will affect the outcome of an election is minuscule. Although voters as a group would benefit if each took the time to vote intelligently, ordinary voters simply do not have an incentive to do so. By contrast, because the members of a concentrated interest group have more at stake with respect to the issues that concern them, they tend both to inform themselves and to participate actively in the political process.

The interest group branch of public choice suggests that the distinction between ordinary voters and concentrated interest groups is not lost on legislators. Self-interested legislators are likely to focus principally on getting reelected, since legislators who fail to do so quickly become ex-legislators. Because interest groups are better informed than ordinary voters, and serve as an important source of political funding, legislators have a tremendous incentive to be responsive to interest group perspectives.

Like the interest group literature itself, I have focused principally on the advantages interest groups have in the legislative process. But this analysis, and in particular its self-interest assumption, also has generated important insights into related areas such as the incentives of agency bureaucrats and * * * the nature of the judicial process.

The second branch of public choice is social choice. At the heart of much of the recent social choice literature is Kenneth Arrow's famous impossibility theorem. Arrow's Theorem demonstrates that it is impossible to design a system that will always both aggregate the preferences of a group of decisionmakers in a rational fashion, and satisfy a short list of fairness requirements. If there is a particular kind of inconsistency, referred to as multipeakedness, across the preferences of a group of decisionmakers (each of whose individual preferences is wholly consistent), the voting procedure will cycle endlessly among the possible outcomes unless one or more of the fairness requirements is relaxed.

To see this, assume that Voter 1 prefers outcome A to B, and B to C; Voter 2's preferences are B, C, A; and Voter 3's ranking is C, A, B. In a pairwise vote between A and B, outcome A would prevail (with Voter 1 and Voter 3 voting for A). Outcome C would prevail over A in a similar vote (on the strength of votes from Voter 2 and Voter 3). But, in a third vote between C and B, B would prevail, despite the fact that it loses to outcome A, which C defeats. On closer consideration, it quickly becomes clear that none of the three options can defeat the other two in pairwise voting, and that any voting outcome is thus unstable. This cycling occurs because the preferences are "multipeaked." Preferences are multipeaked only if the decisionmakers not only disagree about which choice is best (or second best or worst), but also disagree about the relationship among the choices. If their preferences were arrayed from smallest to largest, or conservative to liberal, the problem would disappear. Cycling would not occur even if the decisionmakers each chose a different first choice.

Much of the recent literature has focused on the trade-off posed by the possibility of multipeaked preferences. A voting institution that adheres to Arrow's fairness criteria will cycle endlessly in these circumstances, but relaxing one or more of the requirements introduces the possibility of path dependence and path manipulation. To give a familiar example, Congress's prohibition against reconsidering an outcome that has been defeated in an earlier vote counteracts the risk of cycling. In the illustration above, for instance, outcome C would prevail under this rule, since outcome B could not be reintroduced after it lost to outcome A. Yet the cost of eliminating cycling is that the order of voting determines the outcome-the result is path dependent. The rule, therefore, vests significant power in anyone who has the ability to manipulate the order of the voting.

The discussion thus far suggests a rough rule of thumb for distinguishing between the interest group and social choice branches of public choice. Many of the important contributions of interest group theory stem from the insight that not all voters are equal due to the organizational advantages enjoyed by members of a concentrated group. Social choice, on the other hand, explores the dynamics of voting under conditions where voters are at least initially assumed to have an equal voice. In fact, the literature on cycling shows that voting pathologies can emerge even if each voter participates fully.

Despite this distinction, it is important to emphasize that the line between interest group theory and social choice is a rough one, and it quickly blurs in both directions. The two branches of public choice analysis share a common history, and commentators often employ both in their efforts to understand a particular voting institution. Consider the extensive literature on logrolling. From a social choice perspective, logrolling may act as a solution to cycling concerns, since legislators avoid cycling by trading votes on matters they are relatively indifferent about for votes on matters about which they care deeply. Interest group theory raises questions as to whether the "solution" is an attractive one, however, given that logrolling could enhance interest groups' ability to obtain private benefits from the legislative process.

An additional source of confusion is that the term public choice is used in two ways. I have characterized public choice as a general term comprising both interest group theory and social choice, and many commentators do likewise. But other commentators use public choice more narrowly, as a synonym for interest group analysis. When a commentator indicates that she will tell a "public choice story" about a given issue, it is often this narrower definition that she has in mind.

B. Related Concepts

Having explored in some detail what we mean when we talk about public choice, we still must consider how several related modes of analysis interact with public choice. Two of the most important are game theory and collective action theory. I will focus on these, then conclude with a brief description of the emerging literature employing "positive political theory."

Game theory refers to the economic analysis of strategic interaction— the choices that individuals make when they recognize the outcome depends in part on the decisions made by others. The "game" in game theory, then, is the interaction between two or more independent decisionmakers, each of whom attempts to account for the actions of the others. Game theoretic analysis formalizes this interaction by precisely specifying the players involved, the information available to each at any given point, and the different outcomes that would result from each set of "moves" the players might make.

The most familiar game theory insight is the prisoners' dilemma. In the prisoners' dilemma, two prisoners who have committed a crime and cannot communicate with one another must each decide whether to confess. Although the prisoners would be better off if neither confessed than if both confessed, the best outcome results from confessing when the other prisoner refuses to do so. As a result, both have an incentive to confess and the game often results in the least desirable outcome—two confessions.

The irony of the prisoners' dilemma—that the actions of individuals behaving in their own best interests can produce outcomes that are undesirable for all of them—has led to valuable insights in a wide range of areas. One of the most important is in public choice. Recall the interest group insight that diffuse groups tend to fare poorly in the legislative process. The principal reason for this is that while the members of a diffuse group might be better off if each participated in an informed fashion, each member has little incentive to do so. In other words, diffuse groups tend to face a debilitating prisoners' dilemma problem. Interest group analysis thus depends in important respects on a concept taken straight from game theory.

In contrast, the central insight in social choice theory, Arrow's Theorem, does not involve game theory in its initial formulation. The principled voting requirement precludes voters from considering the preferences and likely actions of other voters, thus ruling game theoretic interactions out of bounds. Yet once we move beyond the initial formulation—as we must, given that *no* institution can both satisfy the fairness requirements and guarantee rational outcomes—strategic interaction quickly reenters the picture. The agenda control and strategic voting concerns that have animated much of the social choice literature are classic examples of strategic interaction, and are particularly amenable to game theoretic analysis.

As should be clear by now, game theory is a useful tool in any context where we wish to consider the nature of strategic interaction between two or more decisionmakers. Because strategic interaction is integral to much of public choice, it is not surprising that we find so much game theoretic analysis in the public choice literature. The second term we need to fit into our picture is collective action—not to be confused with the misleadingly similar term "collective choice." As with game theory, we can see the relevance of collective action theory most easily by focusing on the interest group branch of public choice. Recall that the prisoners' dilemma from game theory is a useful tool for explaining the barriers that often prevent large groups from acting in concert. The collective action literature starts from precisely the same insight, that free riding prevents many groups from acting collectively.

Collective action theorists take the obstacles to collective action as their starting point, and ask how it is that some groups do succeed in acting collectively. These theorists have identified two factors that seem particularly important to successful group action. First, smaller groups have a significant advantage as compared to large ones, both because members may have a larger individual stake in successful action and because members can more easily police one another against free riding. Second, groups that have access to "selective incentives"—that is, mechanisms for rewarding or punishing members for contributing or failing to contribute to the collective action—are more likely to prove effective.

A moment's reflection will make clear that collective action analysis is central to the distinction between concentrated and diffuse groups in interest group analysis, and to any effort to predict which groups will prove successful in legislative and other decisionmaking processes. The collective action literature is less immediately relevant to social choice, since social choice tends to focus on the voting decisions made by isolated individuals within a decisionmaking process. Yet as soon as we move beyond stylized assumptions about the voting process, and integrate interest group questions such as why some voters vote and others don't into our social choice analysis, collective action concerns come back into play.

In attempting to relate game theory and collective action to public choice, it is tempting to suggest that the former apply broadly to aspects of legislative, market, and judicial behavior, whereas public choice is uniquely concerned with the legislative process. Yet this would be a mistake. Although public choice has focused primarily on legislative behavior, it increasingly has been employed to explore courts and markets as well * * *.

Before we turn to the applications of public choice, however, we should briefly consider one final term: positive political theory. Positive political theory uses game theory to explore relationships among decisionmaking institutions such as Congress, administrative agencies, and the courts. It differs from public choice in that it focuses on the strategic interactions among political decisionmaking institutions, and on institutional structures, rather than on the individuals who comprise the institutions. Positive political theory does take account of the problems of multi-individual decisionmaking that preoccupy collective action theory and the two branches of public choice. But it does so indirectly. Positive political theory incorporates these considerations into its characterization of an institution. It then takes intra-institution concerns as a given, in a sense, in order to emphasizes strategic interactions between and among institutions.

In short, this new perspective makes direct use of game theoretic analysis; though it has a different focus than either branch of public choice, it is closely connected to both.

III. Public Choice and the Legal Literature

As is usually the case when legal academics draw on nonlegal insights, public choice did not enter legal discourse until well after it had captured the attention of economists and political scientists. It was not until the mid–1970s that legal scholars first explored the implications of public choice, even though many of the seminal insights of both interest group theory and social choice had been in place for over a decade. Since then, public choice has taken the legal literature by storm. In this Part, I will briefly describe the diffusion of public choice into the legal literature. I then will speculate as to the future of public-choice-influenced legal scholarship.

A. Law and Public Choice: The First Wave

The first wave of public choice inquiry in the legal literature can be seen as a classic illustration of legal academics sticking to their area of comparative advantage. Whereas much of the extant economic and political science public choice literature focused on the legislative process, legal academics asked what the implications of public choice are for the legal system.

The first wave took as its starting point the social choice and interest group insights that the legislative process cannot guaranty outcomes that are both fair and rational, and that concentrated interest groups will exert disproportionate influence over the process. The obvious issue raised by the prospect of legislative dysfunction was the proper role for judges to play. How should public choice affect our view of the nature of statutory interpretation and, more generally, of judicial review?

Three commentators prompted a vigorous debate on this question by offering distinct visions of statutory interpretation in a post-public choice world. The starkest proposal was that of Judge Frank Easterbrook. Judge Easterbrook suggested that courts not only should recognize the role of interest groups in the political process, but that they also should enforce any interest group bargains reflected in the legislative product. Rather than trying to "correct" the process in some way, judges should interpret statutes in accordance with the realities of how they were enacted. Judge Richard Posner initially staked out a position similar to Judge Easter-brook's, though he subsequently shifted his focus to a perspective less obviously tied to the insights of public choice.

Professor Jonathan Macey responded to Judge Easterbrook and to Judge Posner's initial position by proposing a more independent, and more aggressive, role for courts. While agreeing that courts should enforce clear interest group bargains, Professor Macey contended that courts should refuse to enforce "implicit" bargains-that is, interest group deals that legislators disguise by defending the provision in question in public-regarding terms. Professor Macey contended that by refusing to enforce implicit bargains, courts could raise the costs to interest groups of obtaining private interest legislation, and in doing so moderate the influence of interest groups.

In addition to their political conservatism, each of the commentators shared a view that the pessimistic insights of public choice do, in fact, accurately describe the legislative process. Not surprisingly, this perspective prompted a backlash of sorts. Most prominently, Daniel Farber and Philip Frickey acknowledged that the public choice account of legislation is accurate in important respects, but contended that many of the dire conclusions of public choice are overstated. In their view, judges should simply police the political process for obvious defects, and should otherwise let the political process run its course.

Although generally sympathetic to public choice, William Eskridge shared some of Professors Farber and Frickey's concerns as to its limitations. Professor Eskridge's model of statutory interpretation called for judges to show solicitude for underrepresented minorities when they exercise judicial review. Cass Sunstein has used public choice insights in somewhat similar fashion, and has argued that courts should interpret statutes and the Constitution so as to curb interest group excesses.

Despite the sophistication of the debate, nearly all of the proposals suffered from a single, obvious weakness: in striking contrast to their sober portrayal of legislators, the proposals tended to assume that judges are somehow above the fray and can be wholly objective in interpreting the statutes that come before them. Yet there is no reason to believe that the judicial process is immune from interest group activity and the other kinds of distortions that characterize legislation. Once we subject judges to the same public choice scrutiny previously reserved for legislators, it becomes much more difficult to blithely assume that statutory interpretation can counteract the problems of legislative decisionmaking.

Interestingly, the literature on the evolution of the common law has proceeded on a somewhat analogous track, with overly optimistic early accounts giving way to more realistic assessments of the judicial process. Starting in the early 1970s, Judge Posner contended that common law rules tend to become efficient over time, due in large part to judges' unarticulated preference for efficient, rather than inefficient, rules. Other commentators argued for the efficiency of the common law on other grounds. Yet the differential interests of different kinds of litigants, and other biases in the cases that go to trial, suggest that any tendency toward common law efficiency is likely to be, at most, a weak one.

The first wave of public choice scholarship has thus complicated, rather than simply clarified, our understanding of the roles of legislators and judges. The extent to which interest group influence and the distortions identified by social choice undermine the legislative process remains unclear. In addition, the ability of the judiciary to counteract these influences on legislative decisions is open to question. The obvious next step is to engage in a more nuanced comparison of decisionmaking institutions. As we shall see, this raises intriguing questions as to the future of public-choice-influenced legal scholarship.

B. Catching the Next Wave

It seems safe to say, as I have just noted, that the next wave of public choice scholarship will reflect an increasing interest in comparative institutional analysis. Rather than simply identifying the flaws of a particular institution, public-choice-influenced legal scholars will consider the comparative attributes of each of the relevant institutions.

Evidence of just such a trend already exists. A recent book by Neil Komesar contends that there is an urgent need for comparative institutional analysis in order to counteract the distortions of single institution analysis in law-and-economics scholarship. Professor Komesar's transaction costs model emphasizes the interests that affected individuals or groups have, their costs of participation, and how these factors change as we shift our focus among markets, the legislative process, and the judicial system.

With the enhanced sensitivity to comparative institutional analysis, we can expect to see increasingly sophisticated applications of public choice insights in the legal literature. Ironically, however, existing comparative analysis has tended to fall into precisely the same trap that its advocates criticize: the assumption that there exists an objective, unbiased context where institutional distortions can be corrected. Thus, comparative analysis often begins with a nuanced assessment of the respective institutions, then shifts to a prescriptive mode whose proposals depend on implementation by an unbiased decisionmaker. Most frequently, the analysis awards this status to courts, whose limitations are ignored when it comes time to act on the insights of the comparative analysis.

It is easy enough to see the reason for this oversight. Because legal scholarship is at its heart prescriptive, comparative analysts feel a natural urge to progress from descriptive analysis to proposals for change. In doing so, however, they face a strong temptation to forget the real world limitations of the institutions with which they are concerned.

The obvious antidote to this problem is to pursue the analysis all the way down—that is, to resist the temptation to address correctives to a hypothetically unbiased decisionmaker. Yet this poses an intriguing dilemma for future public choice scholarship. Given the typically prescriptive nature of legal scholarship, what role can the next wave of public choice literature, with its enhanced sensitivity to institutional limitations, play? To what can such a relentlessly descriptive an analysis aspire to do?

BEYOND CLASSIC MARKET THEORY– INTERNAL CRITIQUES

In recent years, the field of law and economics has exploded with new theoretical and methodological developments and political challenges that call into question various aspects of the classic market theory introduced in the previous chapter. This chapter examines three intellectual challenges to classic market theory raised by scholars working within the tradition of economic analysis.

These new developments reflect turmoil within the discipline of economics itself. Cracks in the edifice of classic market theory had been visible for quite some time. In 2008, however, American financial markets suffered a sudden and catastrophic meltdown, touched off by a collapse in the market for mortgage-backed securities, and the American crisis quickly became a global one. (We take a closer look at this crisis in Chapter 2.) In the recession that followed, some economists pointed fingers at classic market theory itself.

This chapter explores three critiques of classic market theory: critiques of price theory, particularly as applied to macroeconomic phenomena; critiques of the rational choice theory of human behavior; and critiques of existing measures of economic wellbeing.

First, price theory has been subject to increasing critique as scholars recognize the differences between the functioning of markets in the imaginary world of perfect competition assumed by neoclassical economics and the functioning of markets in the real world. One direction the literature on the economic analysis of law has taken concerns the question of when markets "fail" and the role that law and government should play in responding to "market failure." The neoclassical vision of frictionless markets has been challenged by "transaction cost economics," which relaxes traditional neoclassical economics' assumption that economic interaction is costless, and by "institutional economics," which recognizes that markets function differently depending on the organizational context in which bargaining takes place. At the level of national economies, the classic image of markets as tending toward equilibrium has been challenged by economists who study "bubbles," as well as by Keynesians and post-Keynesians who argue that government regulation is indispensable to counterbalance market instability. Finally, scholars who study the "care sector" of the economy point out that it makes up a large percentage of total economic activity, yet classic economic analysis ignores this sector because it does not occur within a formal market.

Second, the "rational choice" theory of human behavior on which neoclassical economics relies has been challenged from a number of different directions. Behavioral economics argues that people are influenced in their economic decisions not only by prices and their own internal preferences, but by cognitive errors and shortcuts that are inherent in human psychology. Social norms theorists argue that economic actors are also influenced in their preferences by the wants, needs, values, and rules of their reference group. Behavioral economists as well as evolutionary economists, who argue that some economic behavior is biologically driven, conclude that humans are sometimes the prisoners of their own bad judgment. Social norms theorists hope to rescue them with carefully-engineered social policy.

Finally, traditional neoclassical economics relies on standard indicators of success. The most well known example is GDP, or gross domestic product, but other standard economic indicators are used to measure phenomena such as unemployment, poverty, and inflation. These indicators, however, may not always successfully measure what they set out to measure. They may be based on faulty assumptions or bad data. Indicators may also be put to improper uses. For example, GDP is frequently used as an indicator of national well-being, despite being ill-suited for this purpose. Finally, economic indicators may be misleading based on what they fail to take into account. For example, standard indicators assume that natural resources are costless and infinite, and that economies are capable of growing forever. As the planet reaches certain ecological limits, those assumptions become increasingly problematic.

From another angle, new research in psychology and neuroscience suggests that economic well-being has a complicated relationship with subjective well-being. Is economic growth a good in and of itself, or is it only valuable as a proxy for human happiness? What should we do when and if more money does not make us happier?

A.   THE CRISIS IN ECONOMIC THEORY

The Financial Crisis Blame Game

BusinessWeek, October 18, 2008.
http://www.businessweek.com/investor/content/oct2008/pi20081017_950382.html.

■ BEN STEVERMAN AND DAVID BOGOSLAW

[I]t was a series of bad ideas, surprising linkages, and all-too-predictable blunders that came together to send the U.S. financial system, and then the entire world economy, into a serious credit crunch and global stock panic. That's not to say that it couldn't have been prevented.

A Sign: Soaring Home Price-to-Income Ratio

First, there was a bubble in the U.S. housing market as home prices hit unsustainable levels. We should have recognized a bubble when we saw it: Just a few years before, another market bubble collapsed—in technology stocks. And all the signs were there in housing.

If you ever drove through row after row of new tract homes sprouting from the California desert and wondered, "How can all these people afford $500,000 houses?" the answer was, they couldn't. For the two decades until 2001, the national median home price went up and down, but it remained between 2.9 and 3.1 times the median household income, according to the Harvard Joint Center for Housing Studies. By 2004, however, the ratio of home prices to income hit 4.0, and by 2006 the ratio was 4.6. Or consider this statistic: in 2006, at the height of the bubble, more than four in every 10 California households owning a home spent 30% or more of their incomes on housing.

"As a system, we were pressing beyond what the economics were suggesting people could afford," says Michael Strauss, chief economist at Commonfund. Nonetheless, nearly everyone in the system had a "false sense of security that housing prices would always go up."

That included home buyers and real estate and mortgage professionals.

Another Sign: The Securitization Monster

But what turned a nasty housing downturn into an extinction-level event for the whole economy was a Wall Street innovation called securitization.

With interest rates low, investors around the world were eager for places to put their money that offered substantial returns. While the federal funds rate was at 6.5% for much of 2000, by the end of 2001 Federal Reserve Chairman Greenspan had lowered the rate to below 2%. It remained there until late 2004. In 2003, the yield on the one-year Treasury bill dipped well below 2%, its lowest level in the past 40 years. Securitization, and the new investment products it could spawn, seemed to be the answer for a Wall Street seeking a bigger payoff.

Through securitization, Wall Street firms would buy up mortgages, bundle them together, and sell them off to investors. These mortgage-backed securities were highly complex and hard to price accurately. But selling them offered returns for financial firms far above those of safer investments. And with home prices continuing to rise, many, including ratings agencies, assumed that assets backed by U.S. mortgages were safe.

"The development of the securitization pipeline [meant] there was a lot of pressure to create the loans," says University of Kansas finance professor George Bittlingmayer. Mortgages were given to buyers with low credit scores—so-called subprime borrowers—and other high-risk borrowers, with little concern that they wouldn't be able to pay the loans off. The easy money, in turn, contributed to an "upward spiral" of home prices, Bittlingmayer says—"until the bubble collapsed."

Most of the mortgage brokers who originated these loans weren't "bad people," Bittlingmayer adds. "They were doing what the system was asking them to do."

Wall Street was eager to buy up, bundle, and securitize the mortgages. Washington, in turn, had urged the mortgage industry to give more loans to low-income home buyers. During the Clinton and Bush Administrations, "there was a push to try to put homes within reach of everyone," says Larry Tabb, founder and chief executive of the TABB Group, a capital markets research and advisory firm.

No "Skin in the Game"

That led some lawmakers to overlook serious problems at federally chartered mortgage giants Fannie Mae (FNM) and Freddie Mac (FRE). Major players in the securitization process, both were taken over by the government in early September after it became clear the firms wouldn't have enough capital to cover mounting losses from defaulting mortgages.

"Everybody thought they were passing on the risk to someone else through securitization," Aggarwal says. When the housing bubble collapsed, the folly of the securitization process and the mortgage craze became apparent.

The problem was that investment banks didn't have "skin in the game," says Dan Lufkin, one of the founders of Donaldson, Lufkin & Jenrette. Banks "made plenty of money putting [mortgage-backed securities] out on the marketplace. But they could explode a day later and you are not impacted one single iota."

That means that unlike the old-fashioned community savings and loan officer who poured over your pay stubs to make sure you'd make the monthly payments, Wall Street had little incentive to ensure the quality of the underlying loans in its mortgage-backed securities. Credit agencies awarded high ratings to mortgage-backed securities, giving investors more confidence that they were safe investments.

All the large Wall Street investment banks were enthusiastic participants in the securitization process. But two firms, Lehman Brothers and Bear Stearns, were most aggressive about their mortgage investments. According to Thomson Reuters (TRI), Lehman issued more U.S. mortgage-backed securities than any other firm in 2007, $95.8 billion out of an industry total of $922.1 billion. Bear Stearns had the top spot in 2006, issuing $100 billion in U.S. mortgage-backed securities out of an industry total above $1 trillion. Both firms' reliance on the mortgage business helped lead to their failures in 2008.

"A Lot of Smoke and Mirrors"

With all the brainpower on Wall Street—and many of those who created securitized products had doctorates in math or physics—few made the connection between the trillions of dollars in real estate assets held by financial firms and what would happen if the value of those assets suddenly dropped.

But this might not have created a serious economic crisis without other ingredients.

Wall Street had become increasingly sophisticated in the past few decades, and this complexity made the entire system extremely fragile. In addition to securitizing mortgages and other assets, financial firms created a vast array of other products, called derivatives. The buying and selling of these obligations, such as credit default swaps, was supposed to be "a way of reducing risk, not adding risk," Strauss says.

However, "there was a lot of smoke and mirrors," says Bob Ried, president of Ried Thunberg ICAP, a financial research firm. For example, because the products were highly complex, there was no central market-place, making it difficult to know how much they were worth.

Ironically, the huge number of derivative contracts between institu-tions actually increased the chances that problems at one firm would ripple through the financial system, causing a chain reaction of losses. That's what prompted Berkshire Hathaway (BRKA) Chief Executive and legend-ary investor Warren Buffett to call derivatives "financial weapons of mass destruction" in 2003.

Too Much Leverage

Another big risk that financial firms took was in borrowing heavily. Many firms were employing leverage—debt used in investing—of 30 to 40 times their core holdings. Previously, the SEC had kept firms to leverage ratios of 10 to 15 times their core holdings, but the agency loosened the rules for investment banks in 2004. With leverage, "you can make fantastic income when things are going the right direction," Tabb says. "When things go against you, it unwinds very quickly."

Why did Wall Street ever take such dangerous risks?

The big reason, obviously, is greed. Wall Street bankers were taking home a lot of money by making these gambles. The chief executive of Lehman, Richard Fuld Jr., for example, earned $34.4 million in 2007. "Once this business model gets going, it's very hard to stop," Tabb says. Firms had hired risk managers who should have spoken up, but they were not supposed to "get too much in the way of generating revenue."

Many also have criticized the way Wall Streeters are paid. "People [were] compensated on the returns they got, and so there was a motivation to take more risk," Aggarwal says. In the record year of 2006, Wall Street executives took home bonuses totaling $23.9 billion, according to the New York State Comptroller's Office. Wall Street traders were thinking of the bonus at the end of the year, not the long-term health of their firm, Tabb says.

The whole system—from mortgage brokers to Wall Street risk manag-ers—seemed tilted toward making short-term risks while ignoring long-term obligations. The most damning evidence is that most of the people at the top of the banks didn't really understand how those credit default swaps and other instruments worked.

"Regulators Didn't Regulate"

Finally, all this risk-taking by firms added up to a big gamble for the entire financial system, which only became fully apparent as the crisis unfolded. Because no firm knew of other firms' exposures to toxic assets or complex derivatives, it was difficult to predict how problems would flow through the system. "It's very hard to tell the risks various parties are exposed to," says Bittlingmayer. "We don't have transparency."

As the crisis approached, few in government spotted these problems. And no one in a position of power moved to prevent them.

"The regulators as a whole didn't regulate," Ried says. Some officials, often at the state or even city level, did warn of the risk but were ignored. Ried blames regulators for relying on a "free market philosophy" that "just let things go."

But Wall Street also made it worth Congress' while to look the other way. According to the Center for Responsive Politics, the securities and investment industry, including donors at Goldman Sachs (GS), Morgan Stanley (MS), Merrill Lynch (MER), Lehman, and Bear Stearns, gave $97.7 million to federal political candidates for the 2004 election, and another $70.5 million for the 2006 congressional election.

A big reward for Wall Street came in 1999, when Congress passed, and President Bill Clinton signed, legislation loosening New Deal-era bank rules, including the Glass–Steagall Act creating strict separation between investment banks and commercial banks. Commercial banks, which rely on deposits for funding, were allowed to encroach on investment banks' turf. That, in turn, spurred investment banks to take on even more leverage and risk to survive.

"Investment banks started operating more like hedge funds," Aggarwal says.

In the End, Basic Bad Banking

The complexity of the people, actions, and instruments behind the meltdown are truly mind-boggling. But strip things down to their essence and you are left with some surprisingly simple notions.

Investment banks and corporations engaged in basic bad banking, says Robert Ellis of the financial consulting firm Celent. They broke a cardinal rule: "Never borrow short to lend or invest long." Firms were relying on short-term funding sources for long-term obligations. When the crisis froze up short-term markets, these institutions ran dangerously short of cash.

Even more basic was the mistake of taking too much risk. More risk allows for bigger payoffs for participants, but it put the whole system in jeopardy.

Finally, even as problems were becoming apparent, few spoke up. Maybe it was because everyone assumed that someone smarter than them understood how it all worked.

"There were so many financial incentives and political incentives that were aligned toward making this work," Tabb says. "It was very difficult to stop it."

————

NOTE: TURMOIL IN THE DISCIPLINE OF ECONOMICS

The Great Recession of 2008 also prompted an upheaval among economists. The title of an article by Paul Krugman in the New York Times Magazine says it all: *How Did Economists Get It So Wrong?* N.Y.TIMES MAGAZINE, Sept. 6, 2009. Krugman charged that mainstream economists had blinded themselves to "the very possibility of catastrophic failures in a market economy," so sure were they that "stocks and other assets were always priced just right." *Id.* Krugman's diagnosis was that "the economics profession went astray because economists, as a group, mistook beauty, clad in impressive-looking mathematics, for truth.... [I]n love with the old, idealized version of an economy in which rational individuals interact in perfect markets, this time gussied up in fancy equations," economists ignored the gap between theory and reality. "They turned a blind eye to the limitations of human rationality that often lead to bubbles and busts; to the problem of institutions that run amok; to the imperfections of markets—especially financial markets—that can cause the economy's operating system to undergo sudden, unpredictable crashes; and to the dangers created when regulators don't believe in regulation." *Id.*

James K. Galbraith, building on Krugman's accusations, noted that in fact, not all economists got it wrong. But economists who study the nature and causes of financial collapses have been relegated to the margins of the profession: "[T]he lines of discourse that take up these questions have been marginalized, shunted to the sidelines within academic economics.... The scholars who betray their skepticism by taking an interest in them are discouraged from academic life—or if they remain, they are sent out into the vast diaspora of lesser state universities and liberal arts colleges. There, they can be safely ignored." James K. Galbraith, "Who Are These Economists, Anyway?" Thought & Action, The NEA Higher Education Journal 85, 87 (Fall 2009). Galbraith identifies several different tribes of these exiled economists: Marxian economists, such as Robert Brenner and David Harvey; economists that specialize in "bubble detection," such as Dean Baker at the Center for Economic and Policy Research in Washington, D.C.; macroeconomists who focus on national accounts, such as Randall Wray of the Levy Institute at Bard College; followers of Hyman Minsky, whose work explored the paradox that stability in financial markets breeds instability as confident and complacent investors seek higher and higher rates of return; and economists working at the intersection of organizational analysis, law, and economics, such as Gary Dymski and William K. Black, who observed and documented the interaction between weak regulation and fraud and corruption in financial markets leading up to the crash. *Id.* Galbraith ends by quoting his own 2002 article, "How the Economists Got It Wrong:"

> Leading active members of today's economics profession ... have formed themselves into a kind of Politburo for correct economic thinking. As a general rule—as one might generally expect from a gentleman's club—this has placed them on the wrong side of every important policy issue, and not just recently but for decades. They predict disaster when none occurs. They deny the possibility of events that then happen. . . . They oppose the most basic, decent and sensible reforms, while offering placebos instead. They are always surprised when something untoward (like a recession) occurs. And when finally they sense that some position cannot be sustained, they do not reexamine their ideas. . . . Rather, they simply change the subject.

Galbraith, *id.* at 95, quoting James K. Galbraith, "How the Economists Got It Wrong," The American Prospect, February 2002, available at http://www.prospect.org/cs/articles?article=how_the_economists_got_it_wrong.

B.   BEYOND PERFECT MARKETS

Krugman's New York Times article above prompted the following rejoinder from Casey Mulligan, of University of Chicago, Economics Department. This debate among macroeconomists reveals the depth of differences among economists about the efficacy of New Classical economic predictions before the economic and financial collapse of 2008–09.

———

Is Macroeconomics Off Track?

The Economists' Voice, Vol. 6(10).

■ CASEY B. MULLIGAN

Should macroeconomists begin again, particularly those at Chicago, Minnesota, Rochester and other freshwater schools? These days, commentators tell us that we should scrap all that we hold dear—neoclassical growth models, asset pricing models, and the efficient market hypothesis alike. And not just run-of-the-mill journalists. No less than the Nobel Laureate Paul Krugman argued this September in the New York Sunday Magazine that we are "mistaking beauty for truth," dismissing "the Keynesian vision of what recessions are all about," falling "in love with the vision of perfect markets," and blaming entire recessions on laziness. Krugman and others are getting carried away. Allow me to defend neoclassical growth models, by providing some examples of the application of these models to the current recession, and to previous recessions. The reader can then evaluate whether Krugman's accusations are at all accurate.

The Neoclassical Growth Model

The neoclassical growth model is an aggregate model with two basic tradeoffs: (1) current versus future and (2) market versus non-market allocations of labor. Resources are allocated over time via decisions to accumulate a homogeneous capital good, rather than consuming in the current period. People allocate their time between the market and non-market sectors via employment and hours decisions. The model has a few equilibrium conditions. Three conditions denoted (Y), (L), and (K) relate to current consumption and work: (Y) output is produced according to capital and labor inputs, (L) the supply of labor equals its demand, and (K) the supply of capital (consumption foregone) equals its demand. The remaining two conditions are versions of (Y) and (L) for the future period. Stated this way, the model seems to be based on the assumption that markets always clear. But twenty years of applying the model has not exactly been a love affair with perfect markets. My practice and others is to include a residual in each of the conditions: a 'productivity shock' in condition (Y), a 'labor market distortion' in condition (L), and an 'investment' or 'capital market-distortion' in condition (K), which means that I expect there may be significant market imperfections or other unpredictabilities. The not-so-subtle truth is that we often suspect that markets are not functioning efficiently: one of my papers on the topic has the title "A Century of Labor-Leisure Distortions."

Three Diagnostics

In its most basic form, the neoclassical growth model has neither money nor fiscal policy. Nevertheless, it provides some diagnostics as to how public policy variables might be affecting the private sector. In this approach, the first step uses the macroeconomic data to suggest which of the conditions—(Y) or (L) or (K)—has the most variable residual. Much like microeconomists ask "was it supply or demand?", as Lawrence Katz and Kevin Murphy have done with changes in relative wages, we users of the neoclassical growth model ask "Was it productivity? Labor supply? Labor demand? Capital supply? Or Capital demand?" We doubt that the complexity of the larger economy will ever be understood without some means of compartmentalizing the various behaviors, and the three 'equilibrium conditions' are our means of doing so. While a variety of tools would be appropriate for understanding the roles of monetary and fiscal policy, the neoclassical growth model's decomposition offers some suggestions as to which approaches might help the most. For example, we might think differently about monetary policy if it depressed the labor market by inadvertently raising real wages, rather than depressing capital accumulation by adding frictions to capital markets.

Not All Recessions Are the Same

Well before the current recession began, this approach led to the conclusion that recessions have various causes, and therefore that no one government policy could fix all recessions, or be blamed for all of them. I have long been of the opinion that the labor supply residual, rather than productivity or investment shocks, was the most important of the three residuals in the Great Depression. Despite the current recession's capital market theatrics, it again seems that much of the action is with the labor supply residual. For both 1929–33 and 2008–9, labor supply residuals seem key because employment was low while total factor productivity and real pre-tax wages were high (or, in 1929–33, at least not commensurately low): my story, then, is not so different from the business cycle described by General–Theory–Keynes himself. In this regard, results like mine, and those in recent papers by Lee Ohanian, Robert Shimer, and Robert Hall are quite consistent with "the Keynesian vision of what recessions are all about": something made real wages high and employment low. But long ago we recognized that many other recessions cannot be characterized that way: real wages and employment frequently cycle together as Mark Bils has found. In these other cases, the "productivity shock"—the shock emphasized in the seminal work of Fin Kydland and Edward Prescott—seems to be pretty important. There was a good reason why old-time Keynesian models fell into disrepute soon after the 1970s stagflation.

Examination of Incentives

Given the recent time series for real wages and productivity, I doubt many of us are looking for an adverse productivity shock. But we do ask how individual incentives might be consistent with those patterns. It's this type of reasoning that led Lee Ohanian to blame some of the Great Depression on Hoover's industrial policy. When it came to this recession, the neoclassical decomposition quickly led me to look further at public policies—absent from some of the other recessions—that might have caused the supply of labor to shift relative to its demand. Like others, I noticed that the federal minimum wage was hiked three consecutive times. I also turned up a major policy (the Treasury and FDIC plans for modifying mortgages) that creates marginal income tax rates in excess of 100 percent. Much research remains to be done, and undoubtedly other users of the neoclassical growth model will make convincing cases for the roles of monetary and other factors. Paul Krugman's scorn is all we have to suggest that marginal tax rates in excess of 100 percent are not worthy of attention, and that today's low employment is not even partly a consequence of public policy. But, regardless of how economists ultimately interpret today's recession, it will be notable for the basic fact that total factor productivity advanced while employment fell, and for the initial reception suffered by the basic facts in a politicized marketplace for ideas.

———

If It Were a Fight, They Would Have Stopped It in December of 2008

© The Berkeley Electronic Press, *The Economists' Voice,* www.bepress.com/ev April, 2010.

■ ROBERT J. BARBERA

In the December 2009 issue of *The Economists' Voice*, University of Chicago Professor Casey Mulligan rejected Paul Krugman's rebuke of fresh water economics and reaffirmed his faith in the New Classical Economics. His defense was short. He offered up a super stylized macro model and pointed out that inclusion of a distortion term for his capital and labor market equilibrium conditions allow him to comfortably explain the 2008–2009 recession. Really?

As a Wall Street economic practitioner, I am decidedly unconvinced. Practitioners and theorists, I think, are in agreement that a theory is supposed to help us understand how the world works. If a theory of gravity concludes that apples freed from trees tend to float to the heavens, one need not understand the math to reject the construct. And that is why, after the brutal events of the past year, I naïvely thought we would be able to end debate about the plausibility of real business cycle theory.

It is worth looking back at Professor Mulligan's op-ed piece in *The New York Times* from October of 2008. There, Professor Mulligan dismissed the notion of contagion in the financial sector. He looked for pension funds, university endowments, and newly created and capitalized banks to fill the lending gap: Although banks perform an essential economic function— bringing together investors and savers—they are not the only institutions that can do this. Pension funds, university endowments, venture capitalists and corporations all bring money to new investment projects without banks playing any essential role. The average corporation gets about a quarter of its investment funds from the profits it has after paying dividends—and could double or even triple that amount by cutting its dividend, if necessary.

What's more, it's not as if banking services are about to vanish. When a bank or a group of banks go under, the economy wide demand for their services creates a strong profit motive for new banks to enter the market-place and for existing banks to expand their operations. (Bank of America and J. P. Morgan Chase are already doing this.)

He went on to dismiss the importance of financial market gyrations:

Economic research has repeatedly demonstrated that financial-sector gyrations like these are hardly connected to non-financial sector performance. Studies have shown that economic growth cannot be forecast by the expected rates of return on government bonds, stocks or savings deposits.

A much better predictive tool, he asserted, was the marginal product of capital: When the profit per dollar of capital invested in the economy is higher than average, future rates of economic growth also tend to be above average. The same cannot be said about rates of return on the S. & P. 500, or any other measurement that commands attention on Wall Street.

He pointed out that "the marginal product of capital was more than 10 percent per year." Strong gains for the marginal product of capital thus favored good growth in 2009.

The crisis in banks, Professor Mulligan concluded, was really only a concern for the hapless few who work for banks:

> So, if you are not employed by the financial industry (94 percent of you are not), don't worry. The current unemployment rate of 6.1 percent is not alarming, and we should reconsider whether it is worth it to spend $700 billion to bring it down to 5.9 percent.

Reality check

The facts on the ground, however, refused to cooperate. In the fourth quarter of 2008, as Professor Mulligan penned his words, 1.68 million payroll jobs were lost and the unemployment rate jumped by a full percentage point, to 7.2 percent. Needless to say, more than 90 percent of the job losers worked outside the financial sector. All of this carnage was already looming when Professor Mulligan wrote his *Times* essay. The conclusion I am forced to come to is that the new classical economics framework seems to be an impediment not only to prediction, but to description.

To be sure, a single forecasting error is not sufficient grounds to dismiss either a framework or a forecaster. Indeed, if getting a prediction wrong was all it took for dismissal, the unemployment rate among forecasters would be awfully close to 100 percent. At the same time, if unwavering faith in a framework blinds you to both the potential for crisis and to its actual *arrival*, you have a big problem.

Worse still, if you and your framework have the ear of policymakers, you might well become a problem for all of us. To put it bluntly, it is dangerous to pretend that bank runs cannot happen—especially when you are knee deep in one.

Isn't it reasonable for *all economists* to acknowledge that the events of the past year were a whopping big *natural experiment*? In the aftermath of the failed Lehman Brothers rescue effort two very distinct storylines appeared. Shouldn't we all care about which narrative carried the day?

Keynesian economists, comfortable with the elaborations of Hyman Minsky and Charles Kindleberger, declared in late 2008 that we were experiencing a "Minsky moment." All the classic Minsky/Kindleberger signs were there: Bank run dynamics in the repo market and a collapsing commercial paper market. Panic hoarding of cash by companies on Main Street was destined to follow. This would produce a slashing of orders and sharp rise in joblessness. A massive bank rescue effort might well prevent a depression from happening again. But a tough recession was baked in the cake.

New classical economists could not have disagreed more. "Forget the banks," they explained; pension funds and insurance companies will wisely step in and prevent a contagion. Companies will continue to see their profits rise, and will be comfortable depending on internally generated funds for working capital. Economists need only focus on the heady marginal product of capital in place in 2007 and 2008. On that basis they should be willing to argue that 2009 would surprise on the upside. Faith in unfettered markets and the New Classical tradition would be rewarded when 2009 turns out to be fine.

Not a pretty picture

The results of course have come in.

A modern day bank run unfolded in the repo market. The contagion infected risky asset markets in areas far removed from housing or banking. Pension funds, university endowments and banks were engulfed in the crisis and in no mood to step up as lenders. Companies hoarded cash and were universally unwilling to depend on internally generated funds. The result was a global plunge of activity and employment. A worldwide rescue of banks ensued. And then, in classic Kindlebergian form, an unmistakable revival in risky asset markets. And most recently, signs of economic recovery.

Professor Mulligan, of course, interprets the past year very differently. Undaunted by his fantastic forecasting error, his December 2009 essay recasts the story of 2008–2009. For Mulligan, notwithstanding "the current recession's capital market theatrics . . . much of the action is with the labor supply residual." What caused the labor supply shock? Mulligan notes "that the minimum wage was hiked three consecutive times." But the important point to remember, as I see it, is not what Professor Mulligan asserted last month, but instead what he counseled in late 2008. Sadly for him and for all of us, everything he expected to happen did not come to pass. Everything he dismissed as unlikely actually happened in spades.

Am I missing something? I am sure that many real-business-cycle zealots think I have missed almost everything. But for the majority of economists, those who use theory to try and make sense of the world, shouldn't we all agree that the new classical framework failed in spectacular fashion last year?

Irrational exuberance

For me, the hard part in all of this is to figure out how anyone is still willing to make a *rational* case for new classical economics. My best explanation arrives via my own experience as a baseball fan. I have been a Mets fan since 1963, surrounded by an extended family of Yankee fans. This exercise in masochism has caused me untoward humiliation and embarrassment for decades. But my commitment occurred in my formative years, and I just can't bring myself to acknowledge the longstanding and readily observable superiority of the Yankee tradition. It is not rational for me to remain a Mets fan. But my emotional attachment wins out over my rational self.

Is it rational for real-business-cycle enthusiasts to defend a model that missed the biggest economic event of our lifetimes? Or are emotions getting the better of them? Letters commenting on this piece or others may be submitted at http://www.bepress.com/cgi/submit.cgi?context=ev.

———

Consumer Sovereignty: A Unified Theory of Antitrust and Consumer Protection Law

65 ANTITRUST L.J. 713, 723–28 (1997).

■ NEIL W. AVERITT & ROBERT H. LANDE

It is axiomatic that perfect competition, the perfect functioning of a competitive market, will maximize the welfare of consumers. Markets that diverge significantly from perfect competition may not do so. If a market's characteristics differ dramatically from those required for perfect competition, a condition termed "market failure" can exist. The overall level of consumer welfare may then be far below what it otherwise would be, and wealth that Congress assigned to consumers may be "unfairly" acquired by firms with market power.

Although economists generally agree on the fundamental concept of perfect competition, there is no universally agreed upon list of factors that define perfect competition or whose absence may lead to market failure. But the disagreements generally arise only over taxonomic matters—views of which concepts are implicit in others, which are assumed as necessary predicates or subsets of one another and are caused by other factors that themselves prevent markets from functioning optimally.

A leading scholar of the subject, Edwin Mansfield, believes that perfect competition requires four conditions: product homogeneity, relatively small buyers and sellers, mobile resources, and perfect information. Jack Hirshleifer has considered the converse situation and provided a list of three possible imperfections that can prevent a market from functioning perfectly: imperfect information, time lags, and transaction [costs]. Significant problems in any of these areas can cause competition to be suboptimal.

Additional market failures are added to some other lists. These further potential problems include coerced decisionmaking, barriers to the entry of new firms, circumstances of natural monopoly, positive or negative externalities, and situations involving "public goods," "free riders," "prisoner's dilemmas," "lemons," and adverse selection. Despite disputes over taxonomy, this basic list of factors that can plausibly cause competition to become suboptimal is relatively noncontroversial.

Far more controversial is the question of just how often market failures occur and, therefore, how often remedial action under the antitrust or consumer protection statutes might be appropriate. This controversy may be illustrated by the role of imperfect information, perhaps the most important single market failure. Even Chicago School adherents concede that information often is imperfect. Much of what separates "post-Chicago" antitrust from Chicago School antitrust, however, are differing beliefs concerning the frequency and degree to which information is imperfect, the implications this has for competition, and whether government intervention is likely to correct the situation more optimally or more rapidly than the market.

Proponents of post-Chicago views are perhaps more inclined than the Chicago School to believe that important informational and other market failures may exist because they have come to believe that there are a number of ways in which such failures, perhaps small in themselves, can interact with and reinforce each other. In the final analysis, there is no substitute for close study of the facts of individual cases.

––––––

NOTES AND QUESTIONS

1. Price theory, imperfect markets, and "rents." While the concept of supply and demand is widely known and frequently discussed, non-economists may not understand the precise meaning of the terms. JEFFERY L. HARRISON, LAW AND ECONOMICS IN A NUTSHELL 7 (2d ed. 2000). Demand is the range of prices and the amount of a good or service consumers are willing and able to purchase in a given market at a given time, not including those potential consumers who cannot or will not pay for the good or service. *Id.* Supply is the range of prices and the amount of the good or service available for sale at each price in a given market at a given time. *Id.* at 11. The equilibrium price combines supply and demand to establish the price and quantity toward which the market tends to gravitate. *Id.* at 14.

This model assumes perfect market competition in which the sellers are price takers, passively reacting to the market-determined price. A perfect market depends on such factors as multiple suppliers with homogenous products, availability of information about prices and other relevant considerations, easiness for suppliers to enter the industry, and no single supplier large enough to affect prices by increasing or decreasing its output. An imperfect market exists if such a factor is absent and therefore a seller is able to raise prices above those of a competitive market. *Id.* at 20–22. Under perfect conditions, competitors will make a normal profit, or the minimum profit necessary to stay in business. If competition is imperfect, however, the seller may be able to make an economic profit (or "rent"), which is profit in excess of a normal profit. Competition is therefore important in determining prices. *Id.* at 24–26.

2. Market failures and "government intervention." The concept of market failure is popularly used by scholars and policymakers to indicate when government mechanisms, rather than market mechanisms, should allocate a resource. As the excerpts above indicate, there may be many situations in which markets can be said to fail. In the legal literature, market failures are popularly pointed to as a reason for antitrust law, consumer protection law, and environmental law. Antitrust law responds to the market failures represented by oligopoly and monopoly power; consumer protection law responds to the market failures traceable to asymmetrical information between consumers and firms; and environmental law responds to the market failures caused by the negative externalities of pollution and the positive externalities of clean air and water.

But, assuming that government action is necessary, what should the government do? Debates have raged in the legal and economic literature for some time about whether market failures are better addressed by "command and control" government regulation, or whether government should seek to create more "marketlike" structures for bargaining. For example, rather than telling factory owners how much of which toxic substances they may emit into the environment, governments could create a system of tradeable emission permits, allowing firms to bargain with one another for the right to pollute. For a discussion of the more fundamental problems environmental pollution poses to traditional economic analysis, see section C below.

3.   New theories of market failure: informational economics. Market failures have long been assumed to exist with respect to certain "public goods" such as environmental cleanliness and police and fire protection. More recently, economists such as Joseph Stiglitz and George Akerlof have argued that "market failure" is not limited to these kinds of goods, but is pervasive throughout all kinds of markets. These economists identify asymmetric information as a source of market failure. Consider the excerpt by Joseph Stiglitz (who won a Nobel Prize for his work) below.

———

Keynesian Economics and Critique of First Fundamental Theorem of Welfare Economics

Market Failure or Success: The New Debate 41, 48–57, 58 (2004) (Tyler Cowen & Eric Crampton eds.).

■ Joseph E. Stiglitz

[Stiglitz begins by arguing that traditional neoclassical economics assumes that there is perfect information and that there is a complete set of markets for everything that can be exchanged.]

The assumption that there is a complete set of markets, including a complete set of risk and futures markets is important in the standard competitive paradigm but unrealistic. * * *

The incompleteness of markets can itself be explained by transaction costs, an important component of which is information costs. There are costs associated with establishing a market. If there were markets for each of the millions of commodities, each of the billions of contingencies, each of the infinity of future dates, then so much of societies' resources would be absorbed in organizing these transactions that there would be little left over to be bought and sold on each of these markets!

Once we recognize the myriad events that affect us, we recognize the impossibility of having even a complete set of risk markets (insurance against all contingencies). Each firm is affected not only by the events that affect the industry but by idiosyncratic events—the illness of its president, a breakdown in one of its machines, the departure of a key salesperson. The firm itself can buy insurance for many of the risks it faces, such as that its trucks get into accidents or that its factories burn down, but most of the risks it faces cannot be insured against. The notion that there be markets for each of these risks is mind-boggling. * * *

Consider * * * the market for labor. Each individual is different, in myriad ways. A complete set of markets would entail there being a different market for each type of labor—a market for Joe Stiglitz's labor, which is different from the market for Paul Samuelson's labor, which in turn is different from the market for plumbers, which in turn is different from the market for unskilled labor, and so on. If we are careful in defining markets for homogenous commodities (Joe Stiglitz's labor delivered at a particular date, in a particular state, at a particular location), then there is only one trader on one side of the market (Joe Stiglitz). If we expand the markets to embrace all theoretical economists, then it is obviously more competitive. But we have had to drop the assumptions that commodities are homogenous and that the set of markets is incomplete; there is not a separate market for each homogenous commodity. * * *

[B]eyond that, asymmetries of information greatly limit the opportunities to trade, a notion captured in the familiar maxim: I wouldn't want to buy something from someone who is willing to sell it to me. Of course the old principles concerning differences in preferences and comparative advantage providing motives for trade still remain valid, but there is another motive for trading, which can be put baldly as "cheating." While in traditional exchanges both parties are winners, I can get you to pay more for something than it is worth—to buy a used car that is a lemon—I win and you lose. Farmers have a strong incentive to sell their crops on futures markets, but most do not avail themselves much of this opportunity, and for good reason. Those markets are dominated by five large trading companies, who have every incentive to be more informed than the small farmer. The differential information means the farmer is at a disadvantage; the trading companies can make a profit off the farmer's relative ignorance. Knowing this, a choice is made to bear the risk rather than pay the price.

Asymmetries of information give rise to market imperfections in many markets, other than the insurance market, futures markets, and the market for used cars. Consider, for instance, the market for "used labor," workers who already have a job. Their present employer normally has more information concerning their abilities than do prospective employers. A prospective employer knows that if it makes an offer to attract an employee from another firm, the other firm will match it, if the worker is worth it, and will not if the worker is not. Thus, again, the prospective employer is in a heads you win, tails I lose situation: it is only successful in hiring the new employee if it has offered higher wages than the current (well-informed) employer thinks the worker is worth. To be sure, there are instances when the prospective employee's productivity at the new firm will be higher than at the old job—the employee is better matched for the job—or where there are other (nonpecuniary) reasons why the individual may wish to move (to be near relatives, or get away from them). As a result there is *some* trade in the used labor market, but apart from younger workers who are trying to get well matched with a firm, these markets tend to be thin. * * *

Asymmetries of information give rise to two problems, referred to as the (adverse) selection and the incentive or moral hazard problems. Both are seen most clearly in the context of insurance markets, but they arise in a variety of other contexts as well. The first problem results in firms being unable to obtain insurance on their profits: clearly the firm is more informed about its prospects than any insurance firm could be, and the insurance firm worries that if the firm is willing to pay the premium, it is getting too good of a deal. That is, there is a high probability that the insurance firm will have to pay off on the policy.

Moral hazard also leads to limited insurance. The more complete the insurance coverage, the less incentive individuals or firms have to take actions that ensure that the insured-against event does not occur. Because the actions that would be required to reduce the likelihood of the insured-against event occurring are often not observable (and/or it cannot be verified that the insured took the requisite actions), the payment of the insurance cannot be made contingent on the individual or firm taking those actions. Thus health insurance firms would like those they insure not to smoke or to be in places where they suffer the consequences of "second-hand smoke," that is, smoking by others. But insurance firms cannot observe these actions, and hence cannot require those they insure not to smoke.

The provision of *complete* insurance would greatly attenuate incentives, so much so in many cases that for the insurance firm to break even would require charging such a high premium that the policy would be unattractive. Thus, in general, whenever there is moral hazard, there will be incomplete insurance. * * *

It should be clear of course that for traders to have incentives to gather information required that information not be perfectly disseminated in the market. If, simply by looking at market prices, those who do not spend money to acquire information can glean all the information that the informed traders who have spent money to acquire information have, then the informed traders will not have any informational advantage; they will not be able to obtain any return to their expenditures on information acquisition. Accordingly, *if there were a complete set of markets, information would be so well conveyed that investors would have no incentives to gather information.* (Of course with all participants having the same [zero] information, incentives to trade would be greatly reduced.) To put the matter differently, the assumptions of "informed" markets and "a complete set of markets" may be mutually exclusive. * * *

The problems with the assumption of a complete set of markets run deeper. [Elsewhere] I emphasize the importance of innovations, but it is hard to conceive of there being markets for contingencies (states) that have not yet been conceived of: surely an event such as the discovery of the principles underlying atomic energy and the subsequent development of commercial atomic power is an event of immense economic importance, in particular for owners of other energy resources. Yet how could markets in these risks—or in the risks associated with lasers or transistors—have existed before the underlying concepts had been developed? This is a fundamental incoherence between the ideas of a complete set of markets and notions of innovation. * * *

Another critique of the fundamental theorem of welfare economics is that it *assumes* that there is perfect competition, that every firm is a price taker. Most markets are in fact not perfectly competitive. One reason is that when information is imperfect and costly, markets will normally not be perfectly competitive. Imperfect information confers on firms a degree of market power. Though there is competition, it is not the perfect competition of textbook economics, * * * it is *more* akin to monopolistic competition. * * * Because of imperfect information, if a firm raises its price, not all the firm's customers will immediately be able to find a firm that charges a lower price for the same commodity: indeed customers may well infer that other firms have raised their prices as well. By the same token, if it lowers its price, it does not instantly garner for itself all the customers from the higher-priced stores. Search is costly, and so those in the market rarely know the prices being charged by all the firms selling every good in which they are interested.

The imperfections of competition arise not only, however, from imperfect information but also from fixed costs, many of which are information-related costs. There are fixed costs that arise directly in production—the overhead costs of running a firm—and fixed costs associated with acquiring information about how to produce. This means that there is unlikely to be a very large number of firms producing every quality of every good at every location at every date in every state of nature. As we have noted before, with even small fixed costs, many of these "markets" will have relatively few suppliers. * * *

Finally, we think of one of the great virtues of market economies is its ability to "solve" information problems efficiently. Yet when information is costly, firms act to take advantage of that. In doing so, they may *create* noise—they create, sometimes deliberately, information problems for consumers.

Temporary price reductions ("sales"), though we normally do not view them from this perspective, create price dispersion. Costly search gives firms good reason to charge different prices, or to temporarily reduce prices. Low-priced firms can gather themselves a larger customer base, but the high-priced firms can still survive, serving only those who have high search costs and who have not had the good fortune to find a low-priced firm. The high-priced firms compensate for the smaller scale of their sales with a higher profit (price) per sale. * * *

Thus, while price dispersion gives rise to search and other activities directed at reducing the "noise" of the market, and search limits the extent to which prices may differ in the market, the fact of the matter is that the existence of imperfect information—costly search—is what creates the price dispersion in the first place. The price dispersion itself arises, in part, not in response to exogenous changes in economic circumstances, or the differences in economic circumstances facing different firms, but endogenously, as part of the market equilibrium where each firm recognizes the consequences of the fact that search is costly. * * *

These results * * * reduce the confidence we have in the presumption that markets are efficient. There are two important differences between the new market failures, based on imperfect and costly information and incomplete markets, and the older market failures associated with, for instance, public goods and pollution externalities: the older market failure were, for the most part, easily identified and limited in scope, requiring well-defined government interventions. Because virtually all markets are incomplete and information is always imperfect—moral hazard and adverse selection problems are endemic to all market situations—the market failures are pervasive in the economy. * * *

The new information paradigm has revealed that "market failures" are indeed pervasive in the economy. They appear in virtually every transaction among private parties in the economy, and while they may be small in each case, cumulatively they are important. Moreover the market failures are not like those concerning air pollution, for which a well-defined and effective government policy can often easily be designed. This pervasiveness of failures, while it reduces our confidence in the efficiency of market solutions, also reduces our confidence in the ability of the government to correct them. Most important from our perspective, neither the theory nor the practice of socialism paid any attention to these problems.

———

The Failure of Market Failure

18 J. Pol'y Anal. & Mgt. 558–64, 571, 572 (1999).

■ Richard O. Zerbe Jr. & Howard E. McCurdy

The question of the proper role of government in the marketplace is an old and fundamental one. Public officials throughout the world grapple with this issue, deciding which public services to provide or how to regulate the activities of individuals and firms, a task made more urgent by recent efforts to privatize public responsibilities and "reinvent" government. In the search for objective standards by which such decisions can be made, public officials have increasingly turned to the concept of market failure. Use of the market failure concept is widespread, both in teaching curricula and in practicing government circles.

* * *

The concept of market failure initially appeared as a means of explaining in economic terms why the need for government expenditures should arise. It constituted, according to its presenters, "a normative judgment about the role of government and the ability of markets to establish mutually beneficial exchanges."

* * *

* * * In one leading textbook on the new science of policy analysis, David Weimer and Aidan Vining reach a conclusion that appears frequently in the literature: "When is it legitimate for government to intervene in private affairs? In the United States, the normative answer to this question has usually been based on the concept of *market failure*—a circumstance where the pursuit of private interest does not lead to an efficient use of society's resources or a fair distribution of society's goods." Textbooks on microeconomics and public finance commonly present the concept of market failure as a general justification for government intervention.

As it matured, the market failure concept took on an additional characteristic—that of a diagnostic tool by which policymakers learned how to objectively determine the exact scope and type of intervention. Expansion of this normative concept into a diagnostic tool appeared in conjunction with the growth of policy analysis as a field of study and university training. One scholar argues: "The welfare theorem lets [us] classify inefficiencies as due to monopoly externalities, and so on. This helps us to understand and perhaps to solve such inefficiencies just as a doctor's diagnosis . . . is part of treatment."

* * *

What began as a simple attempt to provide a normative explanation for the existence of government expenditures has developed into a quasi-scientific full-scale diagnostic test with the prescription of cures. Some textbooks even present tables that allow students to identify appropriate interventions for different types of market and government failures. This appears to be a powerful and attractive model. It looks scientific. It seems to provide an objective test for governmental intervention. It appears to be something that can be usefully taught in schools.

Inevitably, such concepts and teachings find their way into public policy. Recently the U.S. government issued Executive Order 12866 [1993], which requires federal officials to conduct an economic analysis as a means of determining the need for proposed regulations. Guidelines for carrying out this order require officials to make a finding of "whether the problem constitutes a significant market failure" as a prerequisite for recommending government intervention. The guidelines further provide instructions for identifying types of failures, comparing potential interventions, and guarding against "unintentional harmful effects on the efficiency of market outcomes." The resulting regulatory impact analyses make reference to a variety of market failure concepts. * * *

An extensive flowering of the market failure concept has occurred in the field of law. The number of law review articles and court decisions using the concept run into the thousands, with 239 references turned up by a search of law reviews for the 12 months between June 1995 and June 1996 alone. These references occur not just in monopoly, antitrust, and environmental issues, but appear to span virtually the entire corpus of law. References are found, for example, in family law articles, in connection with setting product standards, in references to the plight of refugees, in connection with health care, and with regard to problems of creating markets in less developed countries, as well as in securities law, the creation of financial derivatives, moral legal theory, contracts, occupational injuries, controls on credit card interest rates, intellectual property, discrimination in insurance markets, the information superhighway, and zoning. Similarly, court decisions that refer to market failure and to externalities are made with great frequency.

Long before social scientists applied diagnostic skills to public affairs, doctors of medicine guessed that diseases of the body could be traced to imbalances in bodily "humors." By the 18th century, this fit of deductive reasoning had been elevated to the level of a diagnostic procedure. The approach led doctors to prescribe a variety of ineffective and often dangerous remedies, such as bleeding or purging. It eventually was replaced by more scientifically valid approaches, such as the discovery of antibiotics and the theory of germs. The theory of market failures, this paper will show, is little better grounded than the outdated belief in bodily humors.

A fundamental problem with the concept of market failure, as economists occasionally recognize, is that it describes a situation that exists everywhere. While the ubiquity of market failures seems well accepted, the consequences of this observation are not. * * *

Market failures are thought to occur when the market fails to produce public goods, or inadvertently produces externalities, or gives rise to natural monopolies, or disenfranchises parties through information asymmetries, or creates undesirable income distributions. All of these forms are types of externalities, since each consists of nonmonetary effects not taken into account in the decisionmaking process, which is the classic definition of externalities. Hence, when we charge that the market failure concept has certain shortcomings, we mean to apply this statement to all forms of externalities including nonmarket failures by government institutions.

The core argument against market failure analysis is derived from the study of transactions. Externalities arise when parties engage in transactions. The effect of transactions on market behavior was first analyzed in the 1930s, beginning with an examination of brokerage charges and other costs of exchange. This quickly expanded into an analysis of the relationship between property rights and the cost of transactions. The property rights approach began with an article by R.H. Coase, now well known in the discipline of economics. Coase argued that individuals form firms because use of the price system is not costless. In other words, entrepreneurs create firms in an effort to reduce the transaction costs associated with using the price system. This approach developed mainly after Coase's 1960 article on "The Problem of Social Cost" * * *.

The property rights approach is important because it defines the condition under which externalities entirely disappear. Transaction costs in this respect are defined as *the resources necessary to transfer, establish, and maintain property rights.* As property rights become more extensive and complete, transaction costs approach zero. In a similar fashion, as transaction costs decline, property rights become more complete as it is cheaper to defend them or transfer property.

Only when property rights are perfect do transaction costs vanish. In a zero transaction cost world, with well-specified rights, there would be markets for everything and all markets would clear, producing efficient outcomes for any collective problem that parties chose to resolve. This condition is expressed by the so-called "weak form" of the Coase Theorem.[3] * * *

No such world, of course, can ever exist. This realization is critical to understanding why the market failure model fails. * * *

    * * *

Market failures may be defined as departures from the optimum with respect to an operating price system that is costless. The existence of unpriced but nonzero transaction costs means that some trades are not created—trades that would be undertaken if the cost of the unpriced transactions were zero (or less than the net monetary impact to be gained). Failure to undertake these trades creates a market failure.

Market failures disappear only when the cost of operating the price system is zero. In the real world, however, this never occurs. People incur costs resolving, transferring, and maintaining property rights. This occurs wherever transactions take place. Unpriced transaction costs, as a consequence, appear everywhere. Since unpriced transaction costs are ubiquitous, this gives rise to a situation in which externalities and hence market failures can be found wherever transactions occur.

How then does an analyst distinguish between externalities that require government attention and those that do not? The market failure approach owes much of its success to the fact that sophisticated users have focused on the provision of goods with large net benefits where government has an advantage with respect to transaction costs. For example, market failure analysts have focused on goods with high exclusion costs, such as clean air. These are goods for which the government can better exploit its advantage in coercion to effect substantial per unit reductions in transaction costs and in which the potential markets—clean air and water, police and fire services, and the like—are large. The choice of these markets, however, is essentially ad hoc (aside from their transaction cost features).

---

3. The first formal statement of the Coase Theorem did not appear until 1966, when George Stigler offered that "the Coase Theorem . . . asserts that under perfect competition private and social costs will be equal." Since this original formulation, the theorem has been stated in numerous ways, including: "if one assumes rationality, no transaction costs, and no legal impediments to bargaining, *all* misallocations of resources would be fully cured in the market by bargains" and "if transaction costs are zero the structure of the law does not matter because efficiency will result in any case." Paradoxically, the Coase Theorem has spawned a huge literature dealing with the artificial world of zero transaction costs, but Coase meant to emphasize real world analysis.

Going beyond these obvious cases, the market failure concept can also be applied to situations that most analysts would consider trivial and not worthy of government attention, which analysts recognize and tend to avoid. When a neighbor fails to plant more flowers even though this would increase property values in the neighborhood by more than the cost of planning, an externality and a market failure exist. The highway driver who drives too slowly fails to consider the time costs he or she imposes on other drivers, thereby creating an externality. (Since the government owns the highway we should probably say that a nonmarket failure exists.) Wherever moral hazard or adverse selection may be found, externalities arise. Companies providing fire insurance worry that policyholders will ignore efficient fire prevention measures; flood insurance may induce people to build in flood plains; government insurance for savings and loan companies may induce investments that are too risky; and * * * colleges granting tenure to professors may find they work too little thereafter.

Externalities exist anytime there is inefficiency in the law affecting markets. A law that encourages inefficient breach of contract produces an externality, as does a tort law that sets the penalty for reckless driving so low that too much reckless driving occurs. A person who inadvertently issues a fraudulent check may not take into account the burden he or she imposes on other users of checks. Suppose that buying a car involves title transfer fees imposed by the state. If these fees are set too high, some trades will not be made. The car manufacturer will produce too few cars, just as a monopolist would.

As these situations suggest, analysts in search of externalities and market failures can find them anywhere they look, providing a universal justification for any sort of government intervention that one might want to undertake. Supporters of the market failure concept avoid this problem by focusing on failures that are "big." In its worst form, this amounts to little more than the substitution of the ideological biases of the analyst.
* * *

* * *

The issue of government intervention is largely an empirical and not a theoretical one. As Nelson says, "there is no satisfactory normative theory regarding the appropriate roles of government in a mixed economy." No theory captures the variety of institutional arrangements that people have developed to resolve collective problems. The market failure concept is not inherently empirical and as such cannot provide answers to empirical questions.

The most important empirical question is this: What are the net benefits (if any) of any particular institutional arrangement? The only general statement that can be made about government intervention on Kaldor–Hicks efficiency grounds is that government should intervene where the costs of intervention are less than the benefits. No simple diagnostic scheme can indicate whether the costs of intervention will be less than the benefits for any general class of cases. Empirical analysis invites the analyst to consider the particular costs that govern each case.

* * *

For thinking about intervention decisions, the transaction cost concept provides analysts with insights into the relationship between government and the marketplace not otherwise apparent. It provides insights into the accumulation of institutional arrangements that exist in practice and it avoids the endless quest for "failures" either in the private or public sector that provide a basis for government intervention. The transaction cost concept is correct in principle, we believe, although not all of its facets have been worked out.

The transaction cost concept invites the analysis to answer a key question: What are the transaction costs that affect the search for collective solutions, and in each case how are those costs affected by government laws and actions?

The transaction cost approach does tend to restore law to a more central role in the study of government. The strengthening of private property rights often lowers transaction costs and thereby permits private parties to achieve collective solutions in situations where the costs of litigation and bargaining would otherwise be prohibitive. In such cases, government intervention through the strengthening of private property rights may improve the market. Such markets are inefficient not because of any inherent "failures," but because the government has neglected to provide the appropriate institutional framework.

* * *

Transaction cost analysis calls attention to the characteristics of government that give it an advantage relative to other institutions in its ability to lower transaction costs. There is one such advantage: the power of coercion. A classic definition of government is that of an institution that monopolizes the use of force or coercive powers over a given territory. The government may change laws and use force to compel compliance with them; it may force payment for goods through taxation and it may use police powers to forbid or compel actions. The most general statement about government intervention is that it should perform those functions for which its powers of coercion give it an absolute advantage. This is also a positive prediction about what government will do, since in failing to perform these functions government sacrifices both wealth and power. What are the important market failures to which its advocates refer? They are simply instances in which government action can lower transaction costs sufficiently to produce significant welfare gains.

* * *

Better empirical analysis, more attention to net benefits, and a deeper understanding of transaction costs would all help to improve the process of policy analysis. Continued reliance on the market failure concept will not.

———

NOTES AND QUESTIONS

1.   The failure of market failure. As Zerbe and McCurdy note, lawyers use the concept of "market failure" frequently, because it is a starting point for the justification of government regulation. Some legal scholars have deliberately embraced a definition of market failure that is broader than the economists'. Consider, for example, intellectual property scholar Wendy Gordon's notion of market failure:

> Briefly, the category of "market malfunction" identifies instances where economic norms appropriately govern, but which display imperfect market conditions (such as significant externalities). This is the category most law and economics scholars mean by "market failure." By comparison, the category of "inherent limitation" refers to circumstances where even under perfect market conditions we cannot rely on markets to function as socially satisfactory institutions for the distribution of resources. These are the many instances where market norms themselves fail to provide fully suitable criteria for resolving a dispute, instances where we do not want money to determine what happens.

> It is often said that babies should not be treated as commodities, nor should adult bodies. There may be occasions when works of authorship, too, involve values that should not be subject solely to monetary forces. As will appear below, policies regarding commodification can help us distinguish when a court should treat a given copyright interaction as appropriately governed by market norms, and when instead the court should treat such norms as fully or partly inadequate.

Wendy J. Gordon, *Excuse and Justification in the Law of Fair Use: Transaction Costs Have Always Been Only Part of the Story,* 50 J. COPYRIGHT SOC'Y U.S.A. 149, 152 (2003).

Does Gordon's conception of market failure support Zerbe and McCurdy's argument that "market failure" is a conclusion, not a description? What might be Gordon's response to Zerbe and McCurdy's suggestion that transaction cost analysis be substituted for market failure analysis?

2.   Transaction cost economics, the theory of the firm, and the economic analysis of law. One use to which transaction cost economics, or TCE, has been put, as the Zerbe and McCurdy excerpt suggests, is to provide a different way of thinking about the question of what mix of facilitative ("market") mechanisms and coercive ("government") mechanisms for the allocation of resources and production of goods will best further social welfare. Another use to which TCE has been put is in explaining why corporate actors, or "firms," exist in markets, and what the possibilities and limitations of firms are vis-à-vis economic production and distribution. *See, e.g.,* Alan J. Meese, *Intrabrand Restraints and the Theory of the Firm,* 83 N.C. L. REV. 5 (2004) (using TCE to justify antitrust law); Reuven S. Avi–Yonah, *Corporations, Society, and the State: A Defense of the Corporate Tax,* 90 VA. L. REV. 1193 (2004) (using TCE to justify corporate taxation).

3.   Beyond the market and the firm. Are there ways to organize economically productive activity outside markets and firms as we know them? What prospects do the "information economy" and technologies such as the Internet offer to projects of democracy and economic justice? In the excerpt below, Yochai Benkler offers one perspective.

————

Freedom in the Commons: Towards a Political Economy of Information

52 Duke L.J. 1245, 1250–58, 1259–61, 1262, 1265–66, 1267–69, 1272, 1273–74, 1276 (2003).

■ Yochai Benkler

A.   How We Got Here

For over 150 years, new communications technologies have tended to concentrate and commercialize the production and exchange of information, while extending the geographic and social reach of information distribution networks. When large-volume mechanical presses and the telegraph were introduced, newspapers changed from small-circulation, local efforts, into mass media—intended to reach ever larger and more dispersed audiences. Of practical necessity, as the size of the audience and its geographic and social dispersion increased, public discourse adapted to an increasingly one-way model. Information and opinion flowed from ever more capital-intensive commercial and professional producers to consumers who, over time, became passive and undifferentiated. This model was easily adopted and amplified by radio, television, and later, cable and satellite communications.

The Internet presents the possibility of a radical reversal of this long trend. It is the first modern communications medium that expands its reach by decentralizing the distribution function. Much of the physical capital that embeds the intelligence in the network is diffused and owned by end users. Network routers and servers are not qualitatively different from the computers that end users use, unlike broadcast stations or cable systems that are vastly different from the televisions to which they transmit. What I hope to persuade you of today is that this basic change in the material conditions of information and cultural production and distribution can have quite substantial effects on how we perceive and pursue core values in modern liberal societies. * * *

For the moment, I will suggest that we call the combination of these two trends—the radical decentralization of intelligence in our communications network and the centrality of information, knowledge, culture, and ideas to advanced economic activity—the *networked information economy.* By "networked information economy," I mean to describe an emerging *stage* of what in the past has been called more generally "the information economy" or "the information society." I would use the term in contradistinction to the earlier stage of the information economy, which one could call the "*industrial* information economy."

The "information economy," conjuring up the Big Five (accounting firms or recording companies, your choice), began as a response to the dramatic increase in the importance of usable information as a means of controlling our economy. James Beniger's study of what he called *The Control Revolution* showed how the dramatic increase in physical production and distribution capabilities in the nineteenth century created a series of crises of control over the material world—crises resolved through the introduction of more efficient modes of producing and using information to control physical processes and the human behavior that relates to them. Ranging from the introduction of telegraph to control the rolling stock of railroads, which, as Chandler has shown, made Western Union the first nationwide prototype for modern corporate organization, to the invention of double-entry bookkeeping, scientific management, and brand advertising, that economy was largely driven by a concern with control of material flows into, through, and out of the new, unmanageably productive factories. The "cultural" offshoots of that moment—Hollywood, the broadcast networks, and the recording industry—were also built around maintaining control over the use and transmission paths of their products. For the first time, music or performance could be captured in a thing, a thing that could be replicated millions of times, and which therefore had to be made to capture the attention and imagination of millions. This first stage might best be thought of as the "industrial information economy."

"The networked information economy" denotes a new stage of the information economy, to succeed this older industrial stage. It is a stage in which we can harness many more of the richly diverse paths and mechanisms for cultural transmission that were muted by the capital structure of communications, a capital structure that had led to the rise of the concentrated, controlled form, whether commercial or state-run. The most important aspect of this new stage is the possibility it opens for reversing the control focus of the information economy. In particular, it permits the reversal of two trends in cultural production, trends central to the project of control: concentration and commercialization. Although the claim that the Internet leads to some form or another of "decentralization" is not new, the fundamental role played in this transformation by the emergence of nonmarket, nonproprietary production and distribution is often overlooked, if not willfully ignored. * * *

Certain characteristics of information and culture lead us to understand them as "public goods" in the technical economic meaning of the term, rather than as pure "private goods" or standard "economic goods." Economists usually describe "information" as "nonrival." The analytic content of the term applies to all cultural forms, and it means that the marginal cost of producing information, knowledge, or culture is zero. Once a scientist has established a fact, or once Tolstoy has written *War and Peace*, neither the scientist nor Tolstoy need spend a single second on producing additional *War and Peace* manuscripts or studies for the one-hundredth, one-thousandth, or one-millionth user. Economists call such goods "public," because a market will never produce them if priced at their marginal cost—zero. Given that welfare economics claims that a market is producing a good efficiently only when it is pricing the good at its marginal cost, a good that can *never* be sold both at a positive price and at its marginal cost is fundamentally a candidate for substantial nonmarket production.

Information has another quirky characteristic in the framework of mainstream welfare economics—it is both the input and the output of its own production process. This has important implications that make property rights and market-based production even less appealing as the exclusive mechanisms for information and cultural production than they would have been if the sole quirky characteristic of information were the public goods problem. These characteristics form the standard economic justification for the substantial role of government funding, nonprofit research, and other nonproprietary production in our information production system, and have been understood as such at least since Nobel Laureate Kenneth Arrow identified them in this context four decades ago.

The standard problems that economics reveals with purely market-based production of information and culture have now been coupled with a drastic decline in the physical capital costs associated with production and distribution of this public good. As I mentioned, one primary input into information or cultural production is pre-existing information, which is itself a public good. The other inputs are human creativity and the physical capital necessary to generate, fix, and communicate transmissible units of information and culture—like a recording studio or a television network. Ubiquitously available cheap processors have radically reduced the necessary capital input costs. What can be done now with a desktop computer would once have required a professional studio. This leaves individual human beings closer to the economic center of our information production system than they have been for over a century and a half. And what places human beings at the center is not something that is homogeneous and largely fungible among people—like their physical capacity to work or the number of hours they can stay awake. Those fungible attributes of labor were at the center of the industrial model that Fredrick Taylor's scientific management and Henry Ford's assembly line typified. Their centrality to industrial production in the physical economy was an important basis for concentration and the organization of production in managed firms. In contrast, human beings are central in the networked information economy because of attributes in which they differ widely—creativity, wisdom, taste, social experience—as well as their effort and attention. And human beings use these personal attributes not only in markets, but also in nonmarket relations. From our homes to our communities, from our friendships to our play, we live life and exchange knowledge and ideas in many more diverse relations than those mediated by the market. In the physical economy, these relationships were largely relegated to spaces outside of our production system. The promise of the networked information economy and the digitally networked environment is to bring this rich diversity of living smack into the middle of our economy and our productive lives.

In the physical economy, we settled more or less on two modes of making production decisions. The first was the market. The second was corporate hierarchy. Markets best coordinated some economic activities, while managers were better at organizing others. The result was that most individuals lived their productive life as part of corporate organizations, with relatively limited control over how, what, or when they produced; and these organizations, in turn, interacted with each other largely through markets. We came to live much of the rest of our lives selecting from menus of goods, heavily advertised to us to try to fit our consumption habits to the decisions that managers had made about investment in product lines.

B.   Examples of Change

What is emerging in the networked information economy is a wider scope for two very different phenomena. The first is a much-expanded role for nonmarket enterprises familiar to us from the real world—both professional, like National Public Radio, nonprofit academic research, philharmonic orchestras, or public libraries, and nonprofessional, like reading groups or fan clubs. The second phenomenon is radical decentralization, which can be seen at the simplest level in the information available on the World Wide Web from an amazing variety of individuals and networks of individuals. The most radically new and unfamiliar element in this category is *commons-based peer production* of information, knowledge, and culture, whose most visible instance has been free software. Here, digital networks seem to be permitting the emergence of radically new relationships between individuals and their information environment, and, more dramatically, radically new roles that individuals play in the production process.

The role of nonmarket enterprises in information and cultural production has always been great, though appreciation for its centrality has waned over the past two decades. Think, most obviously, of science and news. In science, perhaps more than in any other cultural form, the nonprofit academic enterprise, funded by government grants, philanthropy, and teaching, has been the center of basic science, while market-based research was at the periphery. In most fields, the best scientists make the most fundamental advances in academic settings. Firms then take this science, refine it, and then apply it. They do very valuable and important work, but the core of the scientific enterprise has been people who forgo monetary rewards and work instead for glory, immortality, or the pure pleasure of learning something new. If you think of news, the story is more mixed, with commercial providers like the *New York Times* or CNN playing a tremendously important role. Still, public professional producers—like NPR or PBS in the United States, or the BBC in the United Kingdom—play a crucial role, far beyond what we usually see in, for example, automobile or wheat production.

The difference that the digitally networked environment makes is its capacity to increase the efficacy, and therefore the importance, of many more, and more diverse, nonmarket producers. A Google search for "presidential debates," for example, shows CNN as the first commercial site to show up, but it is tenth on the list, while C–SPAN, a nonprofit funded by commercial cable providers shows up fifth. Both are preceded and surrounded by nonmarket organizations, like the Commission on Presidential Debates, a museum, an academic site, and a few political action sites. If you search for "democracy" in Google, PBS is the first media organization to show up, at ninth place, and no commercial entity shows up until a story in *The Atlantic* magazine some ninety-five links into the search. A number of the most highly ranked sites are nonprofit sites devoted to disseminating information about candidates. Consider for example what DemocracyNet, the League of Women Voters website, created for the city-council elections in Raleigh, North Carolina in 2001. What one sees as compared to, say, the local television news broadcasts—is a facility that allows individuals to post questions in writing to the candidates and that allows the candidates to respond directly. For example, we see each candidate's response to the question of whether or not there should be a living-wage ordinance. The site does not provide pages on pages of analysis—one might see a line or two, although some candidates may have written more in response to questions that are more central to their agenda. But you actually see the difference between the candidates on this particular question. * * * The point here is that because of the low capital costs, a nonprofit organization is capable of providing information down to the level of city council elections that is richer than anything we have gotten from the commercial broadcast media. There is, then, both an increase in the number of nonmarket producers and an increase in their effectiveness.

The networked information economy departs more dramatically from the industrial information economy in the possibilities it opens for radically decentralized collaborative production, a phenomenon I call "peer production." Peer production describes a process by which many individuals, whose actions are coordinated neither by managers nor by price signals in the market, contribute to a joint effort that effectively produces a unit of information or culture. Now this is not completely new. Science is built by many people contributing incrementally—not operating on market signals, not being handed their research marching orders by their dean—but independently deciding what to research, bringing their collaboration together, and creating science. The *Oxford English Dictionary* was created in roughly the same way in the nineteenth century—laboriously and over many years. But what we see in the networked information economy is a dramatic increase in the importance and the centrality of information produced in this way.

Free software has become the quintessential instance of peer production in the past few years. Over 85 percent of emails are routed using the sendmail software that was produced and updated in this way. Over the past six years the Apache web server software has risen from being nonexistent to capturing over 60 percent of the market in server software. Choosing the server software that runs one's site is not a situation in which a few hundred or a few thousand dollars will cause a company to adopt a particular application, but superior performance will, and it is in such a market that we see tremendous adoption of software produced by peer production. Similarly, Windows NT and Sun's Solaris are steadily losing ground to the GNU/Linux operating system, which is produced in this way and already runs on some 30 percent of servers connected to the Web.

While free software is the most visible instance of peer production, in fact, peer production is ubiquitous in the digitally networked environment. We see it happening all around. Think of the web itself. Go to Google, and plug in any search request. The particular collection of information you see did not exist before you actually ran the search, and now it exists on your search page. How was it produced? One nonprofit, another person who is a hobbyist, a third company that has as part of its business model to provide certain information for free—all sorts of individuals and groups, small and large, combine on your Google results page to provide you the information you wanted.

But we also see this phenomenon occur less diffusely as well. The Mars "clickworkers" project was an experiment run by NASA that allowed 85,000 people to collaborate on mapping Mars craters. People looked at images of Mars's surface online and mapped craters, and after six months, when NASA did an analysis comparing the results from the Internet to the mapping done by the trained Ph.D.s they had used previously, they described the outcomes as "practically indistinguishable." Massive multiplayer online games, like EverQuest or Ultima Online, are another example. There, thousands or tens of thousands of people play a game whose effect is to tell a story together, instead of going to the movies and receiving the story as a finished good.

Or compare "Wikipedia" (www.wikipedia.com), an online encyclopedia produced by distributed contributors, to encyclopedia.com, produced by Columbia Encyclopedia. Look up the term "copyright" on encyclopedia.com and you see "right granted by statute to the author," etc., and there is a bit of analysis, and some discussion of the Berne Convention, for example, and so on. Now we go to Wikipedia, enter the same search term, and we see a similar copyright discussion. One might agree or disagree with it, as one might, as a professional, agree or disagree with any short encyclopedia definition. But it is there, it is plausible, it may even be better than the definition offered in encyclopedia.com, and it is collaboratively produced by about 2000 volunteers. * * *

C. The Impact of the Change

In all these communities of production, individuals band together, contributing small or large increments of their time and effort to produce things they care about. They do so for a wide range of reasons—from pleasure, through socially and psychologically rewarding experiences, to economic calculation aimed at receiving consulting contracts or similar monetary rewards. At this point, what is important to see is that these efforts mark the emergence of a new mode of production, one that was mostly unavailable to people in either the physical economy (barring barn raising and similar traditional collective efforts in tightly knit communities) or in the industrial information economy. In the physical world, capital costs and physical distance—with its attendant costs of communication and transportation—mean that most people cannot exercise much control over their productive capacities, at least to the extent that to be effective they must collaborate with others. The digitally networked environment enables more people to exercise a greater degree of control over their work and productive relationships. In doing so, they increase the productivity of our information and cultural production system beyond what an information production system based solely on the proprietary industrial model could produce.

     *   *   *

A. Democracy

[I]n the mass-mediated environment only a tiny minority of players gets to participate in political public discourse and to affect decisionmaking directly. As Howard Jonas, chairman of a growing telecommunications company, incautiously described his ambitions, "Sure I want to be the biggest telecom company in the world, but it's just a commodity. . . . I want to be able to form opinion. By controlling the pipe, you can eventually get control of the content." The high cost of mass media communications translates into the high cost of a seat at the table of public political debate, a cost that renders individual participation all but impossible. The digitally networked environment makes it possible for many individuals and groups of similar beliefs to band together, express their views, organize, and gain much wider recognition than they could at a time when gaining recognition required acceptance by the editors of the mass media. * * *

What radical decentralization of information production promises is the correction of some of the main maladies of the electronic mass media—the centralization of power to make meaning, the increased power of corporate interest in influencing the agenda, and the inescapable sound-bite character of the discussion.

The second democratic deficit of the mass-mediated communications environment concerns what some, like Niva Elkin Koren and William Fisher, have called "semiotic democracy," a term originally developed by John Fiske to describe the extent to which a medium permits its users to participate in structuring its message. In the mass media model, a small group of actors, focused on maintaining and shaping consumer demand, has tremendous sway over the definition of meaning in society—what symbols are used and what they signify. The democracy implicated by this aspect is not political participation in formal governance, but rather the extent to which a society's constituents participate in making sense of their society and their lives. In the mass media environment, meaning is made centrally. Commercial mass media owners, and other professional makers of meaning who can buy time from them, largely define the terms with which we think about life and develop our values. Television sitcoms, Barbie dolls, and movies define the basic set of symbols with which most of us can work to understand our lives and our society. In the pervasively networked environment, to the contrary, meaning can be produced collaboratively, by anyone, for anyone. Again, as with public political discourse, this will result in a more complicated and variegated, perhaps less coherent, story about how we should live together as constituents of society. But it will be a picture that we made, not one largely made for us and given to us finished, prepackaged, and massively advertised as "way cool."

B.   AUTONOMY

Autonomy, or individual freedom, is the second value that I suggest can be substantially served by increasing the portion of our information environment that is a commons and by facilitating nonmarket production. * * *

First, the mass media model, and its core of an owned and controlled communications infrastructure, provides substantial opportunities for individuals to be manipulated by the owners of the media. That is, for any number of business reasons, media owners can decide to disclose or reveal information to their consumers, or change the efficacy with which certain information is available to certain users. When they do so, they can, if they choose to, shape the options that individuals know about.

       * * *

Second, decentralization of information production and distribution has the capacity qualitatively to increase both the range and diversity of information individuals can access. In particular, the commercial mass media model has generally presented a relatively narrow range of options about how to live, and these options have been mostly variations on the mainstream. This is so largely because the economies of that model require large audiences to pay attention to anything distributed, constraining the content to that which would fit and attract large audiences. Decentralization of information production, and in particular expansion of the role of nonmarket production, makes information available from sources not similarly constrained by the necessity of capturing economies of scale. This will not necessarily increase the number of different ways people will actually live, but it will increase the number of different ways of living that each one knows about, and thereby enhance their capacity to choose knowledgeably.

A different type of effect of commons-based nonmarket production, in particular peer production, on autonomy is relevant only within a narrower set of conceptions of autonomy—those usually called "substantive." These are conceptions of autonomy that recognize that individuals are always significantly constrained—by genes, environment, and social and economic constraints—and consider the institutions of a society in terms of their effect on the relative role that individuals can play in planning and pursuing their own life plan. The networked information economy promises the possibility of an expansion of elements of autonomous choice into domains previously more regimented by the decisions of firm managers in the market. In particular, the shift can alter two central organizational constraints on how our lives are shaped—the organization of production and the organization of consumption. Much of our day-to-day time is occupied with, and much of our well being shaped by, production and consumption, work and play. In the twentieth century, the economics of mass production led to a fairly regimented workday for most people, at the end of which most people went into a fairly regimented pattern of consumption and play at the mall or in front of the television set. Autonomy in these domains was largely limited to consumer sovereignty—that is, the ability to select finished goods from a range of products available in usefully reachable distribution channels.

Peer production and otherwise decentralized nonmarket production can fundamentally alter the producer/consumer relationship with regard to culture, entertainment, and information. We are seeing the emergence of a new category of relationship to information production and exchange—that of "users." Users are individuals who are sometimes consumers, sometimes producers, and who are substantially more engaged participants, both in defining the terms of their productive activity and in defining what they consume and how they consume it. To the extent that people spend more of their production and consumption time in this ambiguous category of "user," they can have a greater autonomy in self-defining their productive activity, and in making their own consumption goods. The substantive capacity of individuals to control how their life goes—day to day, week to week—would increase to cover aspects of life previously unavailable for self-governance by individuals seeking to put together an autonomously conceived and lived life.

C. Justice

Finally, as we think about the relationship between the structure of information and cultural production and liberal society, there is the question of how the transition to more commons-based production will affect social justice, or equality. Here in particular it is important to retain a cautious perspective as to how much can be changed by reorganizing our information production system. Raw poverty and social or racial stratification will not be substantially affected by these changes. Education will do much more than a laptop and a high speed Internet connection in every home, though these might contribute in some measure to avoiding increasing inequality in the advanced economies, where opportunities for both production and consumption may increasingly be known only to those connected.

For some individuals and societies, where access to capital, not education, is a primary barrier to development, however, there is some promise that a substantial commons in the information economy will provide valuable opportunities.

* * *

Building * * * a commons would * * * add a more competitive layer of goods and services from market-based sources, as well as nonmarket sources, thereby providing a wider range of information and cultural goods at lower cost. On the consumption side this has an unusual flavor as an argument within a social-democratic framework. Proposing a mechanism that will increase competition and decrease the role of government-granted and regulated monopolies is not exactly the traditional social-democratic way. But lower prices are a mechanism for increasing the welfare of those at the bottom of the economic ladder, and in particular, competition in the provision of a zero-marginal-cost good, to the extent it eventually drives the direct price of access and use to zero, will have this effect. More important-ly, access to such resources, free of the usual capital constraints, will permit easier access to production opportunities for some in populations tradition-ally outside the core of the global economy—particularly in developing nations. Such access could provide, over the long term, somewhat greater equity in the distribution of wealth globally, as producers in peripheral economies take these opportunities to compete through a globally connect-ed distribution medium, access to which is relatively unaided by wealth endowments. * * *

CONCLUSION

We are at a moment in our history at which the terms of freedom and justice are up for grabs. We have an opportunity to improve the way we govern ourselves—both as members of communities and as autonomous individuals. We have an opportunity to be more just at the very core of our economic system. The practical steps we must take to reshape the bound-aries of the possible in political morality and to improve the pattern of liberal society will likely improve productivity and growth through greater innovation and creativity. Instead of seizing these opportunities, however, we are sleepwalking. We shuffle along, taking small steps in the wrong direction, guided by large political contributions, lobbyists, and well-fi-nanced legal arguments stretching laws written for a different time, policy arguments fashioned for a different economy. The stakes are too high, however, for us to take our cues from those who are well adapted to be winners in the economic system of the previous century. The patterns of press culture became settled for five hundred years within fifty years of Gutenberg's invention; radio had settled on the broadcast model within twenty-five years of Marconi's invention. Most of the major decisions that put the twentieth century broadcast culture in place were made in the span of six years between 1920 and 1926. The time to wake up and shape the pattern of freedom and justice in the new century is now.

NOTES AND QUESTIONS

1. Institutional economics. Another offshoot of Coase's work, in addi-tion to transaction cost economics, has been the development of "institu-tional economics," also referred to as "new institutional economics," or NIE, to distinguish it from an early-twentieth-century movement con-cerned with thick description of existing markets. The distinctive feature of NIE is its interest in the "rules of the game" that structure market behavior. As Alan Meese explains:

> [A]ll economic cooperation takes place against a backdrop of numerous "rules of the game" produced and enforced by the State. The law of contract empowers individuals and firms to make enforceable promises

to each other, and such promises are the basis of cooperation. The law of property, including that of intellectual property, vests exclusive control of most resources in particular persons or entities and thus facilitates cooperative bargaining between potential users. Property law also facilitates the enforcement of bargains, by making self-help possible. (A franchisor can "terminate" a franchisee because trademark law allows the franchisor to exclude others from use of its trademark.) Finally, the law of tort facilitates bargains by, for instance, deterring fraudulent statements and thus ensuring that parties need not take wasteful precautions to verify a trading partner's representations.

These "rules of the game" include more than just generally-applicable common law rules of contract, property, and tort. They also include statutory provisions and common law rules that facilitate the creation and operation of various types of business organizations such as partnerships, limited liability companies, and corporations. Each such business code, backed up by common law rules of agency and fiduciary duties, creates a distinctive series of presumptive or "default" rules that enable individuals to select and tailor that form of organization that best suits the particular enterprise they have chosen. Thus, when a firm acts, either alone or in concert, it does so because the State has recognized its authority to do so. When combined with other background "rules of the game," such rules (hopefully) minimize the cost of creating and running a business organization.

Taken together, these various rules—contract, property, tort, and the law of business entities—all create what economists call the "institutional framework." When they construct such frameworks, states recognize and facilitate the innumerable forms of cooperation that characterize the modern economy. As noted at the outset, some such cooperation takes place between firms, other cooperation occurs within them. By changing this framework, states can in turn alter the cost of entering and preserving relationships, thus affecting the allocation of resources and the nature and amount of social output. Indeed, what economists and others call a "private" market is in fact a social institution, constructed by innumerable background rules, created or enforced by the State.

Of course, cooperation between economic actors is not always a good thing. Society in general and consumers in particular should not rejoice if Ford and General Motors cooperate when setting prices or if Microsoft and Dell cooperate to exclude Netscape from its most efficient channel of distribution. As a result, an institutional framework that simply enforces all commercial contracts will not suffice to maximize social welfare. A society that wishes to reap the most possible gains from economic activity must therefore construct an institutional framework that minimizes the cost of beneficial cooperation while deterring that cooperation which injures society.

Alan J. Meese, *Intrabrand Restraints and the Theory of the Firm*, 83 N.C. L.Rev. 5, 11–14 (2004).

2. Peer production, freedom, and democracy. Benkler argues that the "networked information economy" makes possible important transformations in the American (and perhaps the global) political economy, including advances for democracy, autonomy, and social justice. Is his argument persuasive? The newspaper publishing industry, the book industry, and the music industry have all been decimated by the technological changes Benkler extols. See, e.g., Emily Henry, *Life After Death: Newspapers and the Re–Invention of Paper Technology*, Online Journalism Rev., June 19, 2009, available at http://www.ojr.org/ojr/people/emilyhenry/ 200906/1753/ (discussing not only the death of newspapers but of literary and investigative journalism); Boris Kachka, *The End*, New York Magazine, Sept. 14, 2008, available at http://nymag.com/news/media/50279/ (discussing the death of the book publishing industry); Michael Stroud, "An Industry Death Knell?" Wired Magazine, Jan. 11, 2000, available at http://www. wired.com/culture/lifestyle/news/2000/01/33559 (discussing the death of the music industry). Or are these birth pains of the new economy Benkler sees? For a perspective similar to Benkler's, see Lewis Hyde, The Gift: Imagination and the Erotic Life of Property (3d ed. 1983).

What about the threat of re-centralization, arguably posed by giant corporations such as Google? Are there privacy and control concerns when "users" are willing to share so much private information on the web? Where should the line be drawn between protecting intellectual property rights and preserving a "cultural commons" on which new artists can draw? And does the new networked information economy promote democracy, autonomy, and justice, or does it isolate us in virtual echo chambers in which we only listen to ourselves and our friends?

The field of intellectual property law and policy has lately been consumed by a vigorous argument over whether and to what extent information should be treated as similar to real property, and how to balance protection of existing creators with encouragement to future creators. Much of the passion and uncertainty come from the nonrivalrous and input/output nature of intellectual property; as Benkler argues, these characteristics make conventional "markets" seem inappropriate. On the property rights analogy, see, e.g., Mark A. Lemley, *What's Different About Intellectual Property?*, 83 Tex. L. Rev. 1097 (2005) (arguing against the real property analogy); Frank H. Easterbrook, *Intellectual Property is Still Property*, 13 Harv. J.L. & Pub. Pol'y 108, 112 (1990) (maintaining that a "right to exclude in intellectual property is no different in principle from the right to exclude in physical property"); Rochelle Cooper Dreyfuss, *We Are Symbols and Inhabit Symbols, So Should We Be Paying Rent? Deconstructing the Lanham Act and Rights of Publicity*, 20 Colum.-VLA J.L. & Arts 123, 140 (1996) (speaking of the "privatization" of words and symbols). On the line between protecting existing intellectual property and encouraging the production of new cultural products, see, e.g., Lawrence Lessig, Free Culture: The Nature and Future of Creativity (2005) (arguing that copyright law grants too many protections to holders at the expense of innovation); Jessica Litman, *The Public Domain*, 39 Emory L.J. 965 (1990) (arguing that the default position for creative work should be the public domain); Wendy J. Gordon, *Render Copyright Unto Caesar: On Taking Incentives Seriously*, 71 U. Chi. L. Rev. 75 (2004).

The Unpaid Care Work/Paid Care Connection

The Levy Economics Institute Working Paper No. 541, (July 2008), pp. 13–1418, 2008. Available at http://ssrn.com/abstract=1176661.

■ Rania Antonopoulos

Among the contributions of gender-aware economic analysis is the reexamination of the function households play at the macroeconomic level of investigation. For our purposes it is worth noting that, traditionally, households have been presumed to supply labor to the business sector in return for income, which they either consume or save. This, as feminist economists have pointed out, is a rather limited view, as it conceals the fact that households are also linked to the rest of the economy through their *production* capacity in so far as they produce goods and provide services through unpaid work. * * *

Our starting point is that household production expands the available pool of necessities human beings rely on for their physical and social reproduction. At one level then, household unpaid (care) work supplements the goods and services bought with income from the market and those made available through public-sector provisioning. * * * [Estimates of the size of the household sector] range from an additional 20 percent to 60 percent of GDP, highlighting the contribution of this hidden sector of the economy and, in particular, women's contributions to economic well-being.

But even more important than assigning monetary value to the contributions of household production, awareness of unpaid labor's value leads to the recognition that the three sectors—households, markets, and government (and for some developing countries, the NGO sector)—are structurally interlinked at the economic level. Accepting such a vision implies that while investigating questions related to growth, as well as fiscal, monetary, international trade, and financial sector policies, the household *production* sector should not be viewed as an add-on or afterthought, but rather as one of the fundamental building blocks. From a policy point of view, how people divide their time between paid and unpaid work ought to be used to understand the impact of macro policies on those performing unpaid work, as well as those that operate mostly within formal markets. * * *

Unpaid work activities entail everyday routine household maintenance work, such as cooking, cleaning, shopping, doing the laundry, caring for children, etc. Viewed from the point of view of classical economics, this work lowers the cost of labor; at the macro level this allows for a smaller wage fund and thus, a larger pool of profits, which facilitates the process of accumulation at any given time. Unpaid time spent on these activities can then be thought of as a "subsidy" to the business sector, as a transfer, a "gift" if you may, from one institution—the household/family—to the institution of the market. That unpaid work may be important at a personal level, both to the giver and to the receiver, does not alter the fact that in its absence, in order to maintain the same standard of living for employees and their families a higher real wage would be necessary, with consequences for cost structures and wage-profit rates. At the same time, the "subsidies" unpaid work provides result in lower overall levels of labor force participation, income that could have been generated, and lower levels of effective demand for goods and services that could be providing employment and generating further economic activity, especially in employment-intensive sectors. * * *

The provisioning of a different linkage of unpaid work and the rest of the economy exists through its connection to public sector goods provisioning. For example, unpaid work provides care to the homebound, chronically ill, or those in need of protracted treatment; care is provided in hospitals due to lack of nurse-aides, sanitation personnel, cooks, etc., or at home due to shortened hospital stays dictated by the structural adjustment policies of the late 1980s and 1990s. Time-use data and satellite accounts allow for estimations of the volume of unpaid work directed to the provisioning of goods and service delivery that the public sector should be making available: health, education, transportation, water, sanitation, and childcare. It is time spent performing unpaid work in these areas that we will refer to as "subsidies" to *public-sector provisioning*. Included in these activities are the delivery of raw foodstuff, cooking, serving and cleaning up for (school) children's nutrition enhancement programs, fetching and carrying water, fossil fuels for sanitation and energy use in households, and childcare and eldercare provisioning for one's own family and community, to give just some examples.

This work places an enormous time-tax on some people asymmetrically—particularly on women, and especially on poor women and children in developing countries—which limits other aspects of social engagement. * * * Internalized as one's "destiny," the inviolable obligations of unpaid work deprive some of their "rights" and citizenship by *de facto* segregation. * * *

The fundamental gender-based division of labor between production of commodities and unpaid work devoted to the reproduction of human beings has resulted in women being concentrated in economic activities with low earnings, insecure and irregular jobs, and where there is little protection through labor laws. * * * Women are consistently found to be in this line of work anywhere between 150 to 380 percent more than men. * * *

[Antonopoulos notes that women are overrepresented as family workers; in informal work, including home-based piecework; in part-time work; and in irregular employment. Where women do work for wages, they are concentrated in service sector jobs that reflect traditional gender roles, such as community, social, and personal services. These jobs pay less and have fewer benefits than the professional service jobs occupied mainly by men.]

[W]hether women are engaged in paid work or not, they spend: (a) more time in unpaid care work than men and (b) more total time in paid and unpaid work combined. In other words, their lower time allocation in paid work is more than compensated in unpaid work contributions.

* * * [T]he unequal distribution of paid and unpaid work between women and men is accompanied by a different inequality—that of persistent wage differentials. * * * [W]hile women's total workload is higher than men's, their earnings are lower than that of men. * * *

The paid care sector tends to evolve alongside the unpaid care sector. In many countries, paid care work is highly female-dominated, as well as being low-status and low-paid compared to other forms of paid work involving similar levels of skill and training. Race and ethnicity are also important markers in occupational hierarchies, with disadvantaged ethnic and racial groups often over-represented as frontline caregivers.

One common pattern observed across the globe is the fact that domestic work is one of the major sources of employment for women. * * * The intersection of unpaid and paid work becomes more evident when one recognizes the particularities of paid domestic work, which tend not only to be undervalued and unregulated jobs with the lowest pay and low status, but also embedded in expectations of being on call twenty-four hours a day.
* * *

Trying to keep up with the responsibilities of care work and the paid domestic work adds to the hardship of the conditions of domestic work. Women who cannot delegate domestic work burdens at their own places frequently devote themselves to household work and stay at home without earnings if they can afford staying home. * * *

When the responsibility is delegated, unless there is an active state involvement in some sort of public policy to support families, it is passed off to relatives and other family members—either to grandmothers or to the daughters. * * *

Either because of the demand for cheap labor in destination countries or due to lack of available job opportunities in the country of birth (with expectations of finding better-paying jobs) or for both reasons, millions of women move across borders. However, given the basic gender division of labor in destination countries, women migrants are often restricted to traditionally "female" occupations—such as domestic work, care work, nursing, work in the domestic services, and sex work—that are frequently unstable jobs marked by low wages, the absence of social services, and poor working conditions.

Discrimination in labor legislation and laws against domestic workers, a majority of which are women, adds to their vulnerability. On top of the fact that they are isolated from their own families and communities, women [migrants] are more subject to deprivation, hardship, violence, theft, fraud, or abuse. * * *

This said, it has been argued that migration can offer economic opportunities, financial independence, and decision-making power for women to escape restrictions. In addition, it is also argued that migration through remittances can play a significant role in poverty reduction and growth in developing countries, benefiting the countries of origin. Estimations show that in 2005 remittances were as high as $300 billion, which corresponds to almost three times the $104 billion from the world's combined foreign aid budgets. * * *

Since care work is traditionally a woman's responsibility back in their countries of birth and/or in country of destination, when one considers the intersection of unpaid care work and paid care work, one should recognize that without any support to the migrant families, remittances alone are not sufficient to redistribute the burden of their workload. Supporting families with social provisioning for their children becomes extremely vital. Sometimes the children are left behind because the working conditions for the women do not permit them to have accompanying family members, so more frequently they are left with grandparents or other relatives, subsidizing the system of global care chain.

As a result of all these patterns, women tend to be in sectors/industries and occupations that remain unprotected. In the context of globalization, it makes it harder for them to realize their fundamental rights as workers, even in countries where such rights exist in law and are enforced. The problem is not only the existence of the laws and their enforcement, but also the differential ability of men and women to realize these fundamental rights (such as freedom of association, the right to bargain over conditions of work, etc., as well as the absence of forced labor). * * *

The role of the modern liberal state was historically circumscribed within the era immediately following the Great Depression. At that time, a welfare-promoting (activist) Keynesian state came into existence in many parts of the world, making it part and parcel of the state's responsibility to provide goods, services, and employment for those unable to do so within the market system. An equally significant development, in parallel, was the emergence of a new kind of public sphere. Since the market was understood as the institution that provides goods and services, as well as the necessary income to purchase them, the privatized economic relations of the marketplace were brought under the auspices of public authority. Securing the adequate functioning of the market amounted to establishing and safeguarding institutions and rights that allowed citizens to enter and freely negotiate contracts, own property, and, in general, participate in economic life as free agents. * * *

Coming in the aftermath of the Great Depression, this social contract implied a central role for the state, over a citizen's life-cycle, that aimed to reconcile market functioning and social cohesion in three domains: (a) when the private sector did not have an incentive or the ability to provide basic goods and services in sufficient quantities and prices to satisfy basic needs, i.e. infrastructure, education, and healthcare, the state would undertake the public provisioning of such goods and services and citizens were entitled to these; (b) in view of the cyclical nature of market economies, Keynesian—state activist in nature—governance took stronghold, i.e., stepping in and implementing countercyclical and economic stabilization policies; and (c) when the market failed to provide jobs, democratic liberal states were to augment social protection programs and unemployment insurance, as well as direct job provisioning. They were, as in the New Deal program, part of the liberal democracy's charge and were envisioned as entitlements, not charitable (statist) contributions. They also provided a framework within which the state enabled individuals to pursue economic goals while providing the space for group interest protection and daily life negotiations. * * *

Is the state responsible for such provisioning or should other institutions participate in such provisioning, such as the market and business-supported benefits for their own workers? The 1980s and 1990s provided an answer in the form of neoliberal policies. The role of the state was to be minimized through the selling of public assets and drastic reductions in public services; expanded and highly unregulated entrepreneurial freedom was presumed to result in economic growth that would, in a more efficient manner, take care of all citizens' needs that the newly diminished role of the state would no longer provide. * * *

At present, the Washington Consensus has opened up space for policy reversals in which government spending is seen, in many instances, as necessary and desirable. If there is renewed policy space, what will be the best possible arrangements for such provisioning from the point of view of reducing unpaid care work burdens?

NOTES AND QUESTIONS

1. Is care work "work"? As Antonopoulos notes, care work has traditionally been invisible to economic analysis, in part because of structural liberalism (examined in Chapter 2). Feminist theorists, however, have struggled to put the analysis of care work back into the work of mainstream economics. Feminist legal theorists have observed that the state plays an important role in keeping care work assigned to the "private" sphere of the family (and women) rather than the "public" sphere of the market (and men). See, e.g., Joan Williams, Unbending Gender: Why Family and Work Conflict and What to Do About It 64–81 (2000); Martha Albertson Fineman, The Neutered Mother, The Sexual Family and Other Twentieth Century Tragedies 87–89 (1995); Nancy Folbre, The Invisible Heart: Economics and Family Values 83–108, 131–35 (2001); Katharine B. Silbaugh, *Commodification and Women's Household Labor*, 9 Yale J.L. & Feminism 81, 112–15 (1997). For a collection of articles considering the way care work is delivered; the legal and social responses to the delivery of care work; the class, immigration, and racialized aspects of the delivery of care; and the impact of care work on women's economic and social position, see Symposium, *Conceptions of Care Work*, 76 Chi.-Kent L. Rev. 1389 (2001) (collecting articles).

C.   BEYOND THE "RATIONAL ACTOR"

In addition to identifying the limits of price theory, contemporary economists and scholars of the economic analysis of law have begun to question another fundamental assumption of neoclassical market theory: the "rational actor." The literature on "social norms" evolved to explain the puzzle that people often engage in behavior that is from a neoclassical perspective "irrational": for example, people vote even though the likelihood of their vote making a difference is very small, and drivers stop at stoplights in the middle of the night even when their chances of being caught by the police are very low. Legal scholars became interested in social norms as an alternative to legal rules: Are legal rules really necessary in some situations? Can, and should, the state change "norms" to prevent unwanted behavior ex ante rather than simply punishing that behavior ex post? The social norms literature does not directly dispute the notion that people act rationally, but it makes accounts of the "inputs" spurring market behavior—"preferences"—more complex.

More recently, a literature in "behavioral economics" has emerged, drawing on cognitive psychology to suggest that economic behavior is influenced not only by social norms, but also by inherent quirks of human cognition. Legal scholars have put behavioral economics to use in a number of fields to explain why rules intended to cause certain kinds of behavior may fail to work properly, or may have unintended consequences.

Social Norms and Social Roles

96 COLUM. L. REV. 903, 904–14, 959–61, 967–68 (1996).

■ CASS R. SUNSTEIN

I.   TALES OF RATIONALITY AND CHOICE

A.   *Ultimatums and Fairness*

Economists have invented a game: the ultimatum game. The people who run the game give some money, on a provisional basis, to the first of two players. The first player is told to offer some part of the money to the second player. If the second player accepts that amount, he can keep what is offered, and the first player gets to keep the rest. But if the second player rejects the offer, neither player gets anything. Both players are informed that these are the rules. No bargaining is allowed. Using standard assumptions about rationality, self-interest, and choice, economists predict that the first player should offer a penny and the second player should accept.

This is not what happens. Offers usually average between 30% and 40% of the total. Offers of less than 20% are often rejected. Often there is a 50–50 division. These results cut across the level of the stakes and across diverse cultures.

B. Littering

Why do people litter? Why don't they throw things out instead? Social psychologist Robert Cialdini tried to find out. He placed flyers under the windshield wipers of cars and waited to see what drivers would do with them. Cialdini made arrangements so that before reaching their cars, some people would see someone (a Cialdini associate) walk past them, pick up from the street a bag from a fast-food restaurant, and throw it in the trash can. Of the group who both saw the responsible behavior and noticed the flyers, almost none threw them on the street. In the control experiment, with no one showing responsible behavior, over 1/3 of the drivers threw the flyers on the street. * * *

E. John Jones

John Jones lives in California. Here is a description of some aspects of his behavior.

1. He buys smoke alarms and installs them in three rooms in his house.

2. He loves chocolate and ice cream, and eats a lot of both. He also eats a fair amount of frozen foods; he makes sure that they are "lean" whenever he has a choice. According to his doctor, he is slightly over his ideal weight.

3. On warm days, he likes to ride his bicycle to and from work, and he enjoys riding his bicycle on busy city streets, even though he has heard about a number of collisions there.

4. He is happily married. He tries to share the work around the house, but he doesn't much like domestic labor. He does less than his share. He acknowledges that this is both true and unfair, and he supports many policies that are conventionally described as "feminist."

5. He buckles his seat belt whenever he is in a car. His own car is a Volvo, and he bought it partly because it is said to be an especially safe car.

6. He is not worried about the risk of an earthquake in California. On some days, he says that he doesn't think that an earthquake is very likely; on other days, he claims to be "fatalistic about earthquakes."

7. He does not recycle. He considers recycling a personal "irritation." He is mildly embarrassed about this, but he has not changed his behavior.

8. He considers himself an environmentalist; his votes reflect his enthusiasm for environmentalism. He supports aggressive regulation designed to encourage conservation and to protect people from risks to their life and health. In fact he is in favor of mandatory recycling, notwithstanding his own failure to recycle.

9. In his own mind, his resources fall in various mental "compartments." Some money is reserved for retirement. Some money is saved for charitable donations. Some money is kept for vacation. Some money is for monthly bills. His forms of mental accounting are very diverse. He is fully aware of this.

Is Jones inconsistent or irrational? Is Jones risk-averse or risk-inclined? What is Jones's dollar valuation of a human life, or of his own life?

F. The Point of this Article

My goal in this article is to challenge some widely held understandings of rationality, choice, and freedom, and to use that challenge to develop some conclusions about human behavior and the appropriate uses and domain of law. I particularly seek to understand and defend the place of law in "norm management."

I urge that behavior is pervasively a function of norms; that norms account for many apparent oddities or anomalies in human behavior; that changes in norms might be the best way to improve social well-being; and that government deserves to have, and in any case inevitably does have, a large role in norm management. As I will suggest, norm management is an important strategy for accomplishing the objectives of law, whatever those objectives may be. One of my goals is to show how this is so. * * *

Existing social norms encourage much risk-taking behavior; and almost all of these risks of death could be much reduced with different norms. Consider smoking, diet/activity, alcohol, firearms, sexual behavior, motor vehicles, and illicit drugs as causes of death. In all these cases, new norms could save lives. A regulatory policy that targets social norms may well be the cheapest and most effective strategy available to a government seeking to discourage risky behavior. It may complement or work more efficiently than existing regulatory approaches.

Social norms are also part and parcel of systems of race and sex equality. If norms changed, existing inequalities would be greatly reduced. It is thus transparently important to see whether shifts in social norms, brought about through law, might operate to save lives and otherwise improve human well-being.

But part of my motivation is theoretical. It involves a conceptual puzzle. In the last decade there has been an intense debate about whether and to what extent law should try to change people's "preferences." But the term "preferences" is highly ambiguous, and it is not clear what the participants in this debate are actually disputing when they say that "preferences" should or should not be respected by law. I attempt to clarify possible meanings of the term. I also suggest that when the idea of a "preference" is unpacked, it becomes plain that the term is often too abstract and coarse-grained to be a reliable foundation for either normative or positive work. We will thus find reason to doubt the elaborate edifice of social science based on the notion of "preference." The ultimate task is to separate positive, descriptive, and normative inquiries more sharply and, in the process, to try to untangle different motivational states and their influences on choices.

More particularly, I aim to make a set of conceptual or descriptive points:

1. Existing social conditions are often more fragile than might be supposed, because they depend on social norms to which—and this is the key point—people may not have much allegiance. What I will call norm entrepreneurs—people interested in changing social norms—can exploit this fact. If successful, they produce what I will call norm bandwagons and norm cascades. Norm bandwagons occur when small shifts lead to large ones, as people join the "bandwagon"; norm cascades occur when there are rapid shifts in norms. Successful law and policy try to take advantage of learning about norms and norm change.

2. Sometimes people do not behave as economists predict. Many important and well-known anomalies in human behavior are best explained by reference to social norms and to the fact that people feel shame when they violate those norms. Thus when people deviate from economic predictions—when they appear not to maximize their "expected utility"—it is often because of norms.

3. There is no simple contrast between "rationality" or "rational self-interest" and social norms. Individual rationality is a function of social norms. The costs and benefits of action, from the standpoint of individual agents, include the consequences of acting inconsistently with social norms. Many efforts to drive a wedge between rationality and social norms rest on obscure "state of nature" thinking, that is, on efforts to discern what people would like or prefer if social norms did not exist. Those efforts are doomed to failure. * * *

John Jones, the protagonist of the fifth tale, is in one way quite usual: There is an evident and pervasive difference between people's choices as consumers and their choices as citizens. This is because people are choosing quite different things. In their private capacity, people may watch silly situation comedies; but they may also support, as citizens, the use of government resources to assist public broadcasting. Some people seek stringent laws protecting the environment or endangered species even though they do not use the public parks or derive material benefits from protection of endangered species—and even though in their private behavior, they are unwilling to do much to protect environmental amenities. The mere existence of certain environmental goods seems to be highly valued by political participants, even if they are not willing to back up the valuation with dollars in private markets. Of course many people give to organizations that support environmental protection. But what people favor as political participants can be different from what they favor as consumers. It is in part for this reason that democratic outcomes are distinct from those that emerge from markets.

In fact a good deal of empirical work shows that people's judgments about politics are not a product of their self-interest, narrowly understood. People without health care are not more likely to support laws creating a right to health care; people recently victimized by crime are not more likely to support aggressive policies against crime. Norms and values are instead the principal determinant of political judgment.

The disjunction between political and consumption choices presents a puzzle. Would it make sense to say that consumer behavior is a better or more realistic reflection of "actual" preferences than is political behavior? In light of the fact that choices depend on context, and do not exist in the abstract, the very notion of a "better reflection" of "actual" preferences is a confusing one; there is no such thing as an "actual" (in the sense of unitary or acontextual) preference in these settings. The difference might be explained by the fact that political behavior reflects judgments made for a collectivity. For this reason it reflects a variety of social norms that are distinctive to the context of politics.

Because of the governing norms, citizens may seek to implement individual and collective aspirations in political behavior but not in private consumption. As citizens, people may seek the aid of the law to bring about a social state that they consider to be higher than what emerges from market ordering. People may, in their capacity as political actors, attempt to promote altruistic or other-regarding goals, which diverge from the self-interested preferences sometimes characteristic of markets. Political decisions might also vindicate metapreferences or second-order preferences. People have wishes about their wishes, and sometimes they try to vindicate those second-order wishes, including considered judgments about what is best, through law. And norms with respect to public discussion may impose "taxes" on public statements of various sorts—perhaps requiring them to be "laundered," perhaps inducing conformity by punishing certain dissident views that might be reflected in other spheres.

In all of these ways, the norms at work in democratic arenas can produce different choices from those produced by markets. It would be wrong to say that the market choices are more "real" or "true." The question of which choices should govern for purposes of law and policy depends on a range of contextual issues that cannot be resolved by reference to notions of "choice" and "preference" alone. * * *

Norms relate to some broader issues as well. Often it is said that the common law, and a liberal regime dedicated to freedom, take "preferences" as they are and do not seek to change them. But the term "preferences" is highly ambiguous. If the term is meant to refer to "choices," it should be understood that choices are very much a function of context, including governing norms, meanings, and roles. Certainly the particular choices made by people in markets—in their capacity as consumers or laborers—do not suggest global or acontextual valuations of relevant goods. If the term "preferences" is meant to refer not to choices but to the motivational and mental states behind choices, it is important to recognize that those mental states include assessments of social norms, the expressive meaning of acts, and the expectations associated with a dazzling variety of social roles. Norms and roles affect both public action and public talk, in ways that can much disguise how people think privately. This point has large implications. In many settings, it would be best to dispense with the idea of "preferences," and to shift instead to more concrete ideas, including intrinsic value, reputational effects, and effects on self-conception.

We have also seen that norms can be far more fragile than they appear. Hence "norm entrepreneurs" can help solve collective action problems, and hence "norm bandwagons" and cascades are common. Sometimes law interacts with the efforts of norm entrepreneurs, facilitating or blunting their efforts, and sometimes law ratifies or accelerates—or halts—norm bandwagons and cascades.

While social life would be impossible without norms, meanings, and roles, individual people have little control over these things. The result can be severe limits on human well-being and autonomy. Certainly there is a problem with existing norms when all or almost all people would seek a change. There may well be a problem when reputational incentives lead people to do what they would otherwise refuse to do, at least if the relevant norms deny people the preconditions for autonomy or otherwise undermine well-being. In fact lives are shortened and unjustified inequalities are perpetuated by the existence of many current norms.

People need collective help if they want to change norms, meanings, or roles. Collective help may be futile or counterproductive; it may be illegitimately motivated. But these matters require an inquiry into the particular context. The issue should not be foreclosed by resort to confusing claims about the need to respect private choice.

———

A Behavioral Approach to Law and Economics

50 Stan. L.Rev. 1471 (1998).

■ Christine Jolls, Cass Sunstein, and Richard A. Thaler

Our goal in this article is to advance an approach to the economic analysis of law that is informed by a more accurate conception of choice, one that reflects a better understanding of human behavior and its well-springs. We build on and attempt to generalize earlier work in law outlining behavioral findings by taking the two logical next steps: proposing a systematic framework for a behavioral approach to economic analysis of law, and using behavioral insights to develop specific models and approaches addressing topics of abiding interest in law and economics. * * * The unifying idea in our analysis is that behavioral economics allows us to model and predict behavior relevant to law with the tools of traditional economic analysis, but with more accurate assumptions about human behavior, and more accurate predictions and prescriptions about law.* * *

We suggest that an approach based on behavioral economics will help with the three functions of any proposed approach to law: positive, prescriptive, and normative. The positive task, perhaps most central to economic analysis of law and our principal emphasis here, is to explain both the effects and content of law. How will law affect human behavior? What will individuals' likely response to changes in the rules be? Why does law take the form that it does? A superior understanding of human behavior will improve answers to such questions.

The prescriptive task is to see how law might be used to achieve specified ends, such as deterring socially undesirable behavior. Much of conventional economic analysis is concerned with this sort of question. Explicit consideration of behavioral factors can improve the prescriptions offered by the analyst. For instance, instead of focusing only on the actual probability of detecting criminal behavior in considering whether offenders will be deterred, the analyst might also want to consider the perceived probability of detection and how it might differ in systematic and predictable ways from the actual probability.

The normative task is to assess more broadly the ends of the legal system. In conventional economic analysis, normative analysis is no different from prescriptive analysis, since the goal of the legal system is to maximize "social welfare," usually measured by people's revealed preferences, and prescriptive (in our sense of the term) analysis also focuses, for the conventional economist, on how to maximize social welfare. But from the perspective of behavioral economics, the ends of the legal system are more complex. This is so because people's revealed preferences are a less certain ground on which to build; obviously issues of paternalism become central here.

Each of these three strands of our project is deeply constructive. Behavioral economics is a form of economics, and our goal is to strengthen the predictive and analytic power of law and economics, not to undermine it. Behavioral economics does not suggest that behavior is random or impossible to predict; rather it suggests, with economics, that behavior is systematic and can be modeled. * * *

A.   Homo Economicus and Real People

The task of behavioral law and economics, simply stated, is to explore the implications of actual (not hypothesized) human behavior for the law. How do "real people" differ from homo economicus? We will describe the differences by stressing three important "bounds" on human behavior, bounds that draw into question the central ideas of utility maximization, stable preferences, rational expectations, and optimal processing of information. People can be said to display bounded rationality, bounded willpower, and bounded self-interest.

All three bounds are well documented in the literature of other social sciences, but they are relatively unexplored in economics * * *. Each of these bounds represents a significant way in which most people depart from the standard economic model. * * *

1.   Bounded rationality.

Bounded rationality, an idea first introduced by Herbert Simon, refers to the obvious fact that human cognitive abilities are not infinite. We have limited computational skills and seriously flawed memories. People can respond sensibly to these failings; thus it might be said that people sometimes respond rationally to their own cognitive limitations, minimizing the sum of decision costs and error costs. To deal with limited memories we make lists. To deal with limited brain power and time we use mental shortcuts and rules of thumb. But even with these remedies, and in some cases because of these remedies, human behavior differs in systematic ways from that predicted by the standard economic model of unbounded rationality. Even when the use of mental shortcuts is rational, it can produce predictable mistakes. The departures from the standard model can be divided into two categories: judgment and decisionmaking. Actual judgments show systematic departures from models of unbiased forecasts, and actual decisions often violate the axioms of expected utility theory.

A major source of differences between actual judgments and unbiased forecasts is the use of rules of thumb. As stressed in the pathbreaking work of Daniel Kahneman and Amos Tversky, rules of thumb such as the availability heuristic—in which the frequency of some event is estimated by judging how easy it is to recall other instances of this type (how "available" such instances are)—lead us to erroneous conclusions. People tend to conclude, for example, that the probability of an event (such as a car accident) is greater if they have recently witnessed an occurrence of that event than if they have not. What is especially important in the work of Kahneman and Tversky is that it shows that shortcuts and rules of thumb are predictable. While the heuristics are useful on average (which explains how they become adopted), they lead to errors in particular circumstances. This means that someone using such a rule of thumb may be behaving rationally in the sense of economizing on thinking time, but such a person will nonetheless make forecasts that are different from those that emerge from the standard rational-choice model.

Just as unbiased forecasting is not a good description of actual human behavior, expected utility theory is not a good description of actual decisionmaking. While the axioms of expected utility theory characterize rational choice, actual choices diverge in important ways from this model * * *. The model offered by Kahneman and Tversky, called prospect theory, seems to do a good job of explaining many features of observed behavior * * *.

2. Bounded willpower.

In addition to bounded rationality, people often display bounded willpower. This term refers to the fact that human beings often take actions that they know to be in conflict with their own long-term interests. Most smokers say they would prefer not to smoke, and many pay money to join a program or obtain a drug that will help them quit. As with bounded rationality, many people recognize that they have bounded willpower and take steps to mitigate its effects. They join a pension plan or "Christmas Club" (a special savings arrangement under which funds can be withdrawn only around the holidays) to prevent undersaving, and they don't keep tempting desserts around the house when trying to diet. In some cases they may vote for or support governmental policies, such as social security, to eliminate any temptation to succumb to the desire for immediate rewards. Thus, the demand for and supply of law may reflect people's understanding of their own (or others') bounded willpower; consider "cooling off" periods for certain sales and programs that facilitate or even require saving.

3. Bounded self-interest.

Finally, we use the term bounded self-interest to refer to an important fact about the utility function of most people: They care, or act as if they care, about others, even strangers, in some circumstances. (Thus, we are not questioning here the idea of utility maximization, but rather the common assumptions about what that entails.) Our notion is distinct from simple altruism, which conventional economics has emphasized in areas such as bequest decisions. Self-interest is bounded in a much broader range of settings than conventional economics assumes, and the bound operates in ways different from what the conventional understanding suggests. In many market and bargaining settings (as opposed to nonmarket settings such as bequest decisions), people care about being treated fairly and want to treat others fairly if those others are themselves behaving fairly. As a result of these concerns, the agents in a behavioral economic model are both nicer and (when they are not treated fairly) more spiteful than the agents postulated by neoclassical theory. * * *

4. Applications.

* * *

When is each bound likely to come into play? Any general statement will necessarily be incomplete, but some broad generalizations can be offered. First, bounded rationality as it relates to judgment behavior will come into play whenever actors in the legal system are called upon to assess the probability of an uncertain event. We discuss many examples below, including environmental legislation * * *, negligence determinations * * *, and risk assessments * * *. Second, bounded rationality as it relates to decisionmaking behavior will come into play whenever actors are valuing outcomes; a prominent example here is loss aversion and its corollary, the endowment effect, which we discuss in connection with bargaining behavior * * *, mandatory contract terms * * *, prior restraints on speech * * *, and risk assessments * * *. Bounded willpower is most relevant when decisions have consequences over time; our example is criminal behavior * * *, where the benefits are generally immediate and the costs deferred. Finally, bounded self-interest (as we use the term) is relevant primarily in situations in which one party has deviated substantially from the usual or ordinary conduct under the circumstances; in such circumstances the other party will often be willing to incur financial costs to punish the "unfair" behavior. Our applications here include bargaining behavior * * * and laws banning market transactions * * *.

B. Testable Predictions

Behavioral and conventional law and economics do not differ solely in their assumptions about human behavior. They also differ, in testable ways, in their predictions about how law (as well as other forces) affects behavior. To make these differences more concrete, consider the three "fundamental principles of economics" set forth by Richard Posner in his Economic Analysis of Law, in a discussion that is, on these points, quite conventional. * * * To what extent would an account based on behavioral law and economics offer different "fundamental principles"?

The first fundamental principle for the conventional approach is downward-sloping demand: Total demand for a good falls when its price rises. This prediction is, of course, valid. There are few if any documented cases of Giffen goods (goods that are consumed more heavily at high prices, due to the fact that the price increase makes people unable to afford goods that are even pricier than the good in question). However, confirmation of the prediction of downward-sloping demand does not suggest that people are optimizing. As Becker has shown, even people choosing at random (rather than in a way designed to serve their preferences) will tend to consume less of a good when its price goes up as long as they have limited resources. This behavior has also been demonstrated with laboratory rats. Thus, evidence of downward-sloping demand is not evidence in support of optimizing models.

The second fundamental principle of conventional law and economics concerns the nature of costs: "Cost to the economist is 'opportunity cost,'" and "'[s]unk' (incurred) costs do not affect decisions on prices and quantity." Thus, according to traditional analysis, decisionmakers will equate opportunity costs (which are costs incurred by foregoing opportunities— say, the opportunity to sell one's possessions) to out-of-pocket costs (such as costs incurred in buying possessions); and they will ignore sunk costs (costs that cannot be recovered, such as the cost of nonrefundable tickets). But each of these propositions is a frequent source of predictive failures. The equality of opportunity costs and out-of-pocket costs implies that, in the absence of important wealth effects, buying prices will be roughly equal to selling prices. This is frequently violated, as is well known. Many people holding tickets to a popular sporting event such as the Super Bowl would be unwilling to buy tickets at the market price (say $1000), yet would also be unwilling to sell at this price. Indeed, estimates of the ratio of selling prices to buying prices are often at least two to one, yet the size of the transaction makes it implausible in these studies to conclude that wealth effects explain the difference. * * *

The traditional assumption about sunk costs also generates invalid predictions. Here is one: A theater patron who ignores sunk costs would not take into account the cost of a prepaid season pass in deciding whether to "rou[se] [him]self . . . to go out" on the evening of a particular performance; the decision would be made purely on the basis of the benefits and costs from that moment forward. However, in a study of theater patrons, some of whom were randomly assigned to receive discounted prices on prepaid passes, the patrons who received discounts were found to attend significantly fewer performances than those who did not receive discounts, despite the fact that (due to random assignment) the benefit-cost ratio that should have mattered—benefits and costs going forward—was the same on average in the two groups. In short, sunk costs mattered; again, the standard prediction proved invalid.

The third fundamental principle of conventional law and economics is that "resources tend to gravitate toward their most valuable uses" as markets drive out any unexploited profit opportunities. When combined with the notion that opportunity and out-of-pocket costs are equated (see fundamental principle two), this yields the Coase theorem—the idea that initial assignments of entitlements will not affect the ultimate allocation of resources so long as transaction costs are zero. Many economists and economically oriented lawyers think of the Coase theorem as a tautology; if there were really no transaction costs (and no wealth effects), and if an alternative allocation of resources would make some agents better off and none worse off, then of course the agents would move to that allocation. Careful empirical study, however, shows that the Coase theorem is not a tautology; indeed, it can lead to inaccurate predictions. That is, even when transaction costs and wealth effects are known to be zero, initial entitlements alter the final allocation of resources. These results are predicted by behavioral economics, which emphasizes the difference between opportunity and out-of-pocket costs.

Consider the following set of experiments conducted to test the Coase theorem; let us offer an interpretation geared to the particular context of economic analysis of law. The subjects were forty-four students taking an advanced undergraduate course in law and economics at Cornell University. Half the students were endowed with tokens. Each student (whether or not endowed with a token) was assigned a personal token value, the price at which a token could be redeemed for cash at the end of the experiment; these assigned values induce supply and demand curves for the tokens. Markets were conducted for tokens. Those without tokens could buy one, while those with tokens could sell. Those with tokens should (and do) sell their tokens if offered more than their assigned value; those without tokens should (and do) buy tokens if they can get one at a price below their assigned value. These token markets are a complete victory of economic theory. The equilibrium price was always exactly what the theory would predict, and the tokens did in fact flow to those who valued them most.

However, life is generally not about tokens redeemable for cash. Thus another experiment was conducted, identical to the first except that now half the students were given Cornell coffee mugs instead of tokens. Here behavioral analysis generates a prediction distinct from standard economic analysis: Because people do not equate opportunity and out-of-pocket costs for goods whose values are not solely exogenously defined (as they were in the case of the tokens), those endowed with mugs should be reluctant to part with them even at prices they would not have considered paying to acquire a mug had they not received one.

Was this prediction correct? Yes. Markets were conducted and mugs bought and sold. Unlike the case of the tokens, the assignment of property rights had a pronounced effect on the final allocation of mugs. The students who were assigned mugs had a strong tendency to keep them. Whereas the

Coase theorem would have predicted that about half the mugs would trade (since transaction costs had been shown to be essentially zero in the token experiments, and mugs were randomly distributed), instead only fifteen percent of the mugs traded. And those who were endowed with mugs asked more than twice as much to give up a mug as those who didn't get a mug were willing to pay. This result did not change if the markets were repeated. This effect is generally referred to as the "endowment effect"; it is a manifestation of the broader phenomenon of "loss aversion"—the idea that losses are weighted more heavily than gains—which in turn is a central building block of Kahneman and Tversky's prospect theory.

What are we to make of these findings? There are at least three important lessons. First, markets are indeed robust institutions. Even naive subjects participating at low stakes produce outcomes indistinguishable from those predicted by the theory when trading for tokens. Second, when agents must determine their own values (as with the mugs), outcomes can diverge substantially from those predicted by economic theory. Third, these departures will not be obvious outside an experiment, even when they exist and have considerable importance. That is, even in the mugs markets, there was trading; there was just not as much trading as the theory would predict. These lessons can be applied to other markets; we offer some examples below.

The foregoing discussion illustrates the point with which we began this section: The difference between conventional and behavioral law and economics is not just a difference in the validity of the assumptions about human behavior. While the assumptions of unbounded rationality, willpower, and self-interest are unrealistic, the force of behavioral economics comes from the difference in its predictions (for example, fewer trades for mugs than for tokens). In this sense, our analysis is consistent with the precept originally proposed by Milton Friedman: Economics should not be judged on whether the assumptions are realistic or valid, but rather on the quality of its predictions. * * *

D.   Parsimony

A possible objection to our approach is that conventional economics has the advantage of simplicity and parsimony. At least—the objection goes—it provides a theory. By contrast, a behavioral perspective offers a more complicated and unruly picture of human behavior, and perhaps that picture will make prediction more difficult, precisely because behavior is more complicated and unruly. Everything can be explained in an ex post fashion—some tool will be found that is up to the task—but the elegance, generalizability, and predictive power of the economic method will be lost. Shouldn't analysts proceed with simple tools? We offer two responses: First, simplicity and parsimony are indeed beneficial; it would be highly desirable to come up with a model of behavior that is both simple and right. But conventional economics is not in this position, for its predictions are often wrong. We will encounter many examples in addition to those already discussed.

Second, to the extent that conventional economics achieves parsimony, it often does so at the expense of any real predictive power. Its goal is to provide a unitary theory of behavior, a goal which may be impossible to achieve. By itself the notion of "rationality" (the centerpiece of traditional analysis) is not a theory; to generate predictions it must be more fully specified, often through the use of auxiliary assumptions. Indeed, the term "rationality" is highly ambiguous and can be used to mean many things. A person might be deemed rational if her behavior (1) conforms to the axioms of expected utility theory; (2) is responsive to incentives, that is, if the actor changes her behavior when the costs and benefits are altered; (3) is internally consistent; (4) promotes her own welfare; or (5) is effective in achieving her goals, whatever the relationship between those goals and her actual welfare. We observe departures from most of these definitions; thus, with respect to (1), scholars have documented departures from expected utility theory for nearly fifty years, and prospect theory seems to predict behavior better. With respect to (4) and (5), people's decisions sometimes do not promote their welfare or help them to achieve their own goals; and with respect to (3), behavioral research shows that people sometimes behave in an inconsistent manner by, for example, indicating a preference for X over Y if asked to make a direct choice, but Y over X if asked to give their willingness to pay for each option. Many of our examples will thus show that people are frequently not rational if the term is understood to mean (1), (3), (4), or (5). As for (2), without some specification of what counts as a cost and a benefit, the idea of responsiveness to incentives is empty. If rationality is used to mean simply that people "choose" what they "prefer" in light of the prevailing incentives, then the notion of rationality offers few restrictions on behavior. The person who drinks castor oil as often as possible is rational because she happens to love castor oil. Other self-destructive behavior (drug addiction, suicide, etc.) can be explained on similar grounds. It is not even clear on this view whether rationality is intended as a definition of "preference" or as a prediction.

If such a notion of rationality allowed for good predictions, then perhaps there would be no reason for complaint; the problem, however, is that so high a degree of flexibility leaves the theory with few a priori restrictions. A theory with infinite degrees of freedom is no theory at all.

* * *

We believe that a behavioral approach imposes discipline on economic theorizing because assumptions cannot be imported at will. In a behavioral approach, assumptions about behavior should accord with empirically validated descriptions of actual behavior. For example, in the case of "fairness," specifically defined and empirically verified patterns of behavior are used to generate predictions in new contexts. ("Fairness" is not, on this view, simply a catch-all to explain any observed behavior.) This is the approach we advocate for economic analysis of law. This approach, we believe, produces a better understanding of law and a better set of predictions about its effects.

———

NOTES AND QUESTIONS

1. Bounded rationality: data. Theorists of bounded rationality have identified a host of cognitive quirks of human beings that, Jolls, Sunstein, and Thaler argue, undermine the concept of the neoclassical "rational actor." These include the following:

(1) Complex decisions and "satisficing." Traditional economic theory would suggest that the more information that should be provided to people, the better they will be able to satisfy their preferences. But in fact people have limited abilities to process information and limited time in which to do so. Thus, when faced with very complex consumer decisions (Which cell phone plan should I adopt? Which health care insurance plan should I adopt?), people adopt decision-making shortcuts, and they look for a "good enough" outcome, rather than the "optimal" outcome.

(2) People tend systematically to make mistakes about probabilities relating to representativeness and risk. People assume that memorable events are more common than they are. For example, most people believe that homicides and car accidents kill more Americans than diabetes and stomach cancer, presumably because of the greater media coverage provided to the former two, although the two diseases kill far more people.

(3) People tend to interpret the world in self-serving ways. That is, even if they intellectually recognize the probabilities of certain events, they predict that good things will disproportionately happen to them and bad things will disproportionately happen to other people. For example, newlyweds are likely to represent the odds of their divorce as zero or close to zero, even though it is common knowledge that half of all marriages end in divorce.

(4) People employ "hindsight bias" to interpret events in the past as having been inevitable.

(5) People exhibit the "endowment effect": they place a higher monetary value on items they own than on those that they do not own. Thus, people tend to demand more money to have an item taken away from them than they would pay to acquire the same item.

2. Bounded rationality: reliability of the theory. The theory of bounded rationality rests on experimental findings, usually involving students and other test subjects paid to participate in a research study. Should these findings be extrapolated to the real world?

Are these findings culture-specific, or might they vary cross-culturally? Consider, for example, Robin Paul Malloy's attempt to demonstrate the famous "prisoner's dilemma" to a group of Chinese legal scholars, lawyers, and officials:

Using the classic scenario, I informed all players that they had just committed a serious criminal offense, such as a robbery. I told them they and their partner had both been arrested and that the police would deal with each of them individually. Then I separated the teams and isolated each player from the other member of his or her team.

* * *

In this classic arrangement, self-interest is supposed to lead each player to snitch on the other so that we end up with a less than optimal strategy being selected. Clearly both players are best off when they each remain silent, but the incentive structure of the game motivates the rational self-interested player to cooperate with the police. This is because neither player wants to be left "holding the bag," so to speak, in the event that the other player uses a cooperation strategy in order to pin the crime on his or her accomplice.

In all six teams, each composed of players who did not know each other prior to attending this training program, every single player opted to remain silent. Thus, not one of the twelve players was convicted and no one acted in the way that traditional law and economic approaches would predict. When we took class time to discuss the outcome I explained how the pay-off matrix was supposed to encourage them to snitch on each other. Participants in the exercise responded that they understood the costs and the incentives presented by the matrix. They said that they understood that the incentive structure encouraged them to cooperate with the police but none of them gave credence to the incentives. They interpreted the incentive structure from within a community understanding in which no one in China trusts the police. Any incentive structure offered by the police would, therefore, not be expected to be honored. The best course of action when dealing with the police, I was told, was to say nothing.

ROBIN PAUL MALLOY, LAW AND MARKET ECONOMY: REINTERPRETING THE VALUES OF LAW AND ECONOMICS 12–13 (2000).

3.   Bounded rationality: implications. Does the idea of bounded rationality destroy the foundations of neoclassical economics? Or might neoclassical economics find a way to mathematically model bounded rationality in a way that preserves the basic theory? Most behavioral economists, like Jolls, Sunstein, and Thaler, wish not to displace neoclassical economics entirely, but only to supplement it.

Within the legal academy, a movement called "socioeconomics" has emerged which seeks to bring insights from the social sciences into law and economics. Socioeconomists draw not only on cognitive psychology, as behavioral economics does, but also on sociology, anthropology, and cultural studies. See, e.g., Lynne Dallas, *Law and Public Policy: A Socioeconomic Approach* (2005); Jeffrey L. Harrison, *Law and Socioeconomics*, 49 J. LEGAL EDUC. 224 (1999); Morality, Rationality, and Efficiency: New Perspectives on Socio–Economics (Richard M. Coughlin ed., 1991); Socio–Economics: Toward a New Synthesis (Amitai Etzioni & Paul R. Lawrence eds., 1991); Richard M. Coughlin, *Whose Morality? Which Community? What Interests? Socio–Economic and Communitarian Perspectives*, 25 J. SOCIO-ECON. 135 (1996).

4. The empire strikes back. Although the behavioral economists argue that they do not come to bury traditional law and economics but to praise it, traditional law and economics scholars have resisted behavioral economics. For a response by Richard Posner to the Jolls, Sunstein, and Thaler article excerpted above, see Richard A. Posner, *Rational Choice, Behavioral Economics, and the Law*, 50 Stan. L.Rev. 1551 (1998); see also Mark G. Kelman, *Behavioral Economics as Part of a Rhetorical Duet: A Response to Jolls, Sunstein, and Thaler*, 50 Stan. L.Rev. 1577 (1998); Christine Jolls, Cass R. Sunstein, and Richard Thaler, *Theories and Tropes: A Reply to Posner and Kelman*, 50 Stan. L.Rev. 1593 (1998). For a debate over whether traditional law and economics or behavioral economics provides a better approach to the problem of consumer contracts, see "Consumer Contracts: Behavioral Economics vs. Neoclassical Economics, An Exchange Between Oren Bar–Gill and Richard Epstein," New York University Law and Economics Working Papers (2007), available at http://lsr.nellco.org/nyu_lewp/91.

5. Bounded rationality and public policy. How should law and public policy respond to the fluidity of people's preferences and the theory of bounded rationality? In the excerpt that follows, updating his earlier work on social norms, Cass Sunstein (writing with Richard Thaler) concludes that some form of government paternalism is both inevitable and desirable.

———

Libertarian Paternalism Is Not an Oxymoron

70 U. Chi. L. Rev. 1159, 1159–66, 1184–86, 1188–90, 1199–1201, 1202 (2003).

■ Cass R. Sunstein & Richard H. Thaler

＊ ＊ ＊

Consider two studies of savings behavior:

- Hoping to increase savings by workers, several employers have adopted a simple strategy. Instead of asking workers to elect to participate in a 401(k) plan, workers will be assumed to want to participate in such a plan, and hence they will be enrolled automatically unless they specifically choose otherwise. This simple change in the default rule has produced dramatic increases in enrollment.

- Rather than changing the default rule, some employers have provided their employees with a novel option: *Allocate a portion of future wage increases to savings.* Employees who choose this plan are free to opt out at any time. A large number of employees have agreed to try the plan, and only a few have opted out. The result has been significant increases in savings rates. ＊ ＊ ＊

We propose a form of paternalism, libertarian in spirit, which should be acceptable to those who are firmly committed to freedom of choice on grounds of either autonomy or welfare. Indeed, we urge that libertarian paternalism provides a basis for both understanding and rethinking a number of areas of contemporary law, including those aspects that deal with worker welfare, consumer protection, and the family. In the process of defending these claims, we intend to make some objections to widely held beliefs about both freedom of choice and paternalism. Our emphasis is on the fact that in many domains, people lack clear, stable, or well-ordered preferences. What they choose is strongly influenced by details of the context in which they make their choice, for example default rules, framing effects (that is, the wording of possible options), and starting points. These contextual influences render the very meaning of the term "preferences" unclear.

Consider the question whether to undergo a risky medical procedure. When people are told, "Of those who undergo this procedure, 90 percent are still alive after five years," they are far more likely to agree to the procedure than when they are told, "Of those who undergo this procedure, 10 percent are dead after five years." What, then, are the patient's "preferences" with respect to this procedure? Repeated experiences with such problems might be expected to eliminate this framing effect, but doctors too are vulnerable to it. Or return to the question of savings for retirement. It is now clear that if an employer requires employees to make an affirmative election in favor of savings, with the default rule devoting 100 percent of wages to current income, the level of savings will be far lower than if the employer adopts an automatic enrollment program from which employees are freely permitted to opt out. Can workers then be said to have well-defined preferences about how much to save? This simple example can be extended to many situations involving the behavior of workers and consumers.

As the savings problem illustrates, the design features of both legal and organizational rules have surprisingly powerful influences on people's choices. We urge that such rules should be chosen with the explicit goal of improving the welfare of the people affected by them. The libertarian aspect of our strategies lies in the straightforward insistence that, in general, people should be free to opt out of specified arrangements if they choose to do so. To borrow a phrase, libertarian paternalists urge that people should be "free to choose." Hence we do not aim to defend any approach that blocks individual choices.

The paternalistic aspect consists in the claim that it is legitimate for private and public institutions to attempt to influence people's behavior even when third-party effects are absent. In other words, we argue for self-conscious efforts, by private and public institutions, to steer people's choices in directions that will improve the choosers' own welfare. In our understanding, a policy therefore counts as "paternalistic" if it attempts to influence the choices of affected parties in a way that will make choosers better off. Drawing on some well-established findings in behavioral economics and cognitive psychology, we emphasize the possibility that in some cases individuals make inferior decisions in terms of their own welfare—decisions that they would change if they had complete information, unlimited cognitive abilities, and no lack of self-control. In addition, the notion of libertarian paternalism can be complemented by that of *libertarian benevolence*, by which plan design features such as default rules, framing effects, and starting points are enlisted in the interest of vulnerable third parties. We shall devote some discussion to this possibility.

* * * In its most cautious forms, libertarian paternalism imposes trivial costs on those who seek to depart from the planner's preferred option. But the approach we recommend nonetheless counts as paternalistic, because private and public planners are not trying to track people's anticipated choices, but are self-consciously attempting to move people in welfare-promoting directions. Some libertarians are likely to have little or no trouble with our endorsement of paternalism for private institutions; their chief objection is to paternalistic law and government. But as we shall show, the same points that support welfare-promoting private paternalism apply to government as well. It follows that one of our principal targets is the dogmatic anti-paternalism of numerous analysts of law, including many economists and economically oriented lawyers. We believe that this dogmatism is based on a combination of a false assumption and two misconceptions.

The false assumption is that almost all people, almost all of the time, make choices that are in their best interest or at the very least are better, by their own lights, than the choices that would be made by third parties. This claim is either tautological, and therefore uninteresting, or testable. We claim that it is testable and false, indeed obviously false. In fact, we do not think that anyone believes it on reflection. Suppose that a chess novice were to play against an experienced player. Predictably the novice would lose precisely because he made inferior choices—choices that could easily be improved by some helpful hints. More generally, how well people choose is an empirical question, one whose answer is likely to vary across domains. As a first approximation, it seems reasonable to say that people make better choices in contexts in which they have experience and good information (say, choosing ice cream flavors) than in contexts in which they are inexperienced and poorly informed (say, choosing among medical treatments or investment options). So long as people are not choosing perfectly, it is at least possible that some policy could make them better off by improving their decisions.

The first misconception is that there are viable alternatives to paternalism. In many situations, some organization or agent must make a choice that will affect the behavior of some other people. There is, in those situations, no alternative to a kind of paternalism—at least in the form of an intervention that affects what people choose. * * * As a simple example, consider the cafeteria at some organization. The cafeteria must make a multitude of decisions, including which foods to serve, which ingredients to use, and in what order to arrange the choices. Suppose that the director of the cafeteria notices that customers have a tendency to choose more of the items that are presented earlier in the line. How should the director decide in what order to present the items? To simplify, consider some alternative strategies that the director might adopt in deciding which items to place early in the line:

1. She could make choices that she thinks would make the customers best off, all things considered.

2. She could make choices at random.

3. She could choose those items that she thinks would make the customers as obese as possible.

4. She could give customers what she thinks they would choose on their own.

Option 1 appears to be paternalistic, but would anyone advocate options 2 or 3? Option 4 is what many anti-paternalists would favor, but it is much harder to implement than it might seem. Across a certain domain of possibilities, consumers will often lack well-formed preferences, in the sense of preferences that are firmly held and preexist the director's own choices about how to order the relevant items. If the arrangement of the alternatives has a significant effect on the selections the customers make, then their true "preferences" do not formally exist.

Of course, market pressures will impose a discipline on the self-interested choices of those cafeteria directors who face competition. To that extent, those directors must indeed provide people with options they are willing to buy. A cafeteria that faces competition and offers healthy but terrible-tasting food is unlikely to do well. Market-oriented libertarians might urge that the cafeteria should attempt to maximize profits, selecting menus in a way that will increase net revenues. But profit maximization is not the appropriate goal for cafeterias granted a degree of monopoly power—for example, those in schools, dormitories, or some companies. Furthermore, even those cafeterias that face competition will find that some of the time, market success will come not from tracking people's ex ante preferences, but from providing goods and services that turn out, in practice, to promote their welfare, all things considered. Consumers might be surprised by what they end up liking; indeed, their preferences might change as a result of consumption. And in some cases, the discipline imposed by market pressures will nonetheless allow the director a great deal of room to maneuver, because people's preferences are not well-formed across the relevant domains.

* * * [F]or government, the risks of mistake and overreaching are real and sometimes serious. But governments, no less than cafeterias (which governments frequently run), have to provide starting points of one or another kind; this is not avoidable. As we shall emphasize, they do so every day through the rules of contract and tort, in a way that inevitably affects some preferences and choices. In this respect, the anti-paternalist position is unhelpful—a literal nonstarter.

The second misconception is that paternalism always involves coercion. As the cafeteria example illustrates, the choice of the order in which to present food items does not coerce anyone to do anything, yet one might prefer some orders to others on grounds that are paternalistic in the sense that we use the term. Would anyone object to putting the fruit and salad before the desserts at an elementary school cafeteria if the result were to increase the consumption ratio of apples to Twinkies? Is this question fundamentally different if the customers are adults? Since no coercion is involved, we think that some types of paternalism should be acceptable to even the most ardent libertarian. * * *

Once it is understood that some organizational decisions are inevitable, that a form of paternalism cannot be avoided, and that the alternatives to paternalism (such as choosing options to make people worse off) are unattractive, we can abandon the less interesting question of whether to be paternalistic or not, and turn to the more constructive question of how to choose among the possible choice-influencing options. To this end we make two general suggestions. First, programs should be designed using a type of welfare analysis, one in which a serious attempt is made to measure the costs and benefits of outcomes (rather than relying on estimates of willingness to pay). Choosers should be given more choices if the welfare benefits exceed the welfare costs. Second, some results from the psychology of decisionmaking should be used to provide ex ante guidelines to support reasonable judgments about when consumers and workers will gain most by increasing options. We argue that those who are generally inclined to oppose paternalism should consider these suggestions uncontroversial.

* * *

In the domain of employee behavior, there are many imaginable illustrations. Employees might be automatically enrolled in a 401(k) plan, with a right to opt out, but employers might require a waiting period, and perhaps a consultation with an adviser, before the opt-out could be effective. Thaler and Benartzi have proposed a method of increasing contributions to 401(k) plans that also meets the libertarian test. Under the Save More Tomorrow plan, * * * employees are invited to sign up for a program in which their contributions to the savings plan are increased annually whenever they get a raise. Once employees join the plan, they stay in until they opt out or reach the maximum savings rate. In the first company to use this plan, the employees who joined increased their savings rates from 3.5 percent to 11.6 percent in a little over two years (three raises). Very few of the employees who join the plan drop out. We believe that this is successful libertarian paternalism in action. In fact, the ideas of automatic enrollment and Save More Tomorrow provide quite promising models for increasing saving; they might well be more effective than imaginable economic incentives, as for example through decreased taxes on savings.

The same sort of strategy might be used in many domains. Moving from paternalism to protection of third parties, employers (or the state) might seek to increase charitable giving from workers. Is it possible to produce a form of libertarian benevolence, and if so, how might this be done? Moral suasion may or may not succeed, but compare a system of Give More Tomorrow. Because workers appear quite willing to part with a fraction of their future raises, such a system, like Save More Tomorrow, would be highly appealing to many people. In fact the ideas explored here might well be used to produce significant increases in charitable donations (of course, there are obvious complexities about institutional design and appropriate default beneficiaries). * * *

We are now in a position to categorize a diverse set of paternalistic interventions: minimal paternalism, required active choices, procedural constraints, and substantive constraints.

a) Minimal paternalism. Minimal paternalism is the form of paternalism that occurs whenever a planner (private or public) constructs a default rule or starting point with the goal of influencing behavior. So long as it is costless or nearly costless to depart from the default plan, minimal paternalism is maximally libertarian. This is the form of paternalism that we have described as inevitable.

b) Required active choices. Unsure of what choices will promote welfare, a planner might reject default plans or starting points entirely and force people to choose explicitly (what we have described as the strategy of required active choices). This approach finds an analogue in information-eliciting default rules in contract law, designed to give contracting parties a strong incentive to say what they want. To the extent that planners force people to choose whether or not people would like to choose, there is a paternalistic dimension to their actions. ("Choosing is good for both freedom and welfare," some appear to think, whether or not people agree with them!) We think that the argument for requiring choices stands or falls largely on the welfare consequences.

c) Procedural constraints. A slightly more aggressive form of paternalism occurs when the default plan is accompanied by procedural constraints designed to ensure that any departure is fully voluntary and entirely rational. When procedural constraints are in place, it is not costless to depart from the default plan. The extent of the cost, and the aggressiveness of the paternalism, will of course vary with the extent of the constraints. The justification for the constraints will depend on whether there are serious problems of bounded rationality and bounded self-control; if so, the constraints are justified not on the ground that the planner disagrees with people's choices, but because identifiable features of the situation make it likely that choices will be defective. Such features may include an unfamiliar setting, a lack of experience, and a risk of impulsiveness. The Age Discrimination in Employment Act is our principal example here.

d) Substantive constraints. Alternatively, a planner might impose substantive constraints, allowing people to reject the default arrangement, but not on whatever terms they choose. On this approach, the planner selects the terms along which the parties will be permitted to move in their preferred directions. The Model Termination Act and the Fair Labor Standards Act are illustrations. The extent of the departure from libertarianism will be a function of the gap between the legally specified terms and the terms that parties would otherwise reach. Here too the justification for the constraint depends on bounded rationality and bounded self-control.

e) A thin line. A planner might reject freedom of choice on the ground that those who reject the default plan will err all or almost all of the time. Such a planner will impose significant costs on those who depart from the plan. As we have said, there is a thin line between non-libertarian paternalists and libertarian paternalists who impose high costs, procedural or substantive, on those who reject the plan. Almost all of the time, even the non-libertarian paternalist will allow choosers, at some cost, to reject the proposed course of action. Those who are required to wear motorcycle helmets can decide to risk the relevant penalty, and to pay it if need be. Employers and employees might agree to sub-minimum wage work and risk the penalties if they are caught. In this particular sense, penalties are always prices.

* * *

The argument for libertarian paternalism seems compelling to us, even obvious, but we suspect that hard-line anti-paternalists, and possibly others, will have objections. We respond to three possible objections here.

The first objection is that by advocating libertarian paternalism, we are starting down a very slippery slope. Once one grants the possibility that default rules for savings or cafeteria lines should be designed paternalistically, it might seem impossible to resist highly non-libertarian interventions. Critics might envisage an onslaught of what seem, to them, to be unacceptably intrusive forms of paternalism, from requiring motorcycle riders to wear helmets, to mandatory waiting periods before consumer purchases, to bans on cigarette smoking, to intrusive health care reforms of many imaginable kinds. In the face of the risk of overreaching, might it not be better to avoid starting down the slope at all?

There are three responses. First, in many cases there is simply no viable alternative to paternalism in the weak sense, and hence planners are forced to take at least a few tiny steps down that slope. Recall that paternalism, in the form of effects on behavior, is frequently inevitable. In such cases, the slope cannot be avoided. Second, the libertarian condition, requiring opt-out rights, sharply limits the steepness of the slope. So long as paternalistic interventions can be easily avoided by those who seek to adopt a course of their own, the risks emphasized by anti-paternalists are minimal. Third, those who make the slippery slope argument are acknowledging the existence of a self-control problem, at least for planners. But if planners, including bureaucrats and human resource managers, suffer from self-control problems, then it is highly likely that other people do too.

A second and different sort of objection is based on a deep mistrust of the ability of the planner (especially the planner working for the government) to make sensible choices. Even those who normally believe that everyone chooses rationally treat with deep skepticism any proposal that seems to hinge on rational choices by bureaucrats. Part of the skepticism is based on a belief that bureaucrats lack the discipline imposed by market pressures; part of it is rooted in the fact that individuals have the welfare-promoting incentives that are thought to come from self-interest; part of it is rooted in the fear that well-organized private groups will move bureaucrats in their preferred directions. We happily grant that planners are human, and thus are both boundedly rational and subject to the influence of objectionable pressures. Nevertheless, as we have stressed, these human planners are sometimes forced to make choices, and it is surely better to have them trying to improve people's welfare rather than the opposite. In emphasizing the important effect of plan design on choice (a point under-appreciated by economists, lawyers, and planners), we hope to encourage plan designers to become more informed. And by arguing for a libertarian check on bad plans, we hope to create a strong safeguard against ill-considered or ill-motivated plans. To the extent that individual self-interest is a healthy check on planners, freedom of choice is an important correc-tive.

A third objection would come from the opposite direction. Enthusiastic paternalists, emboldened by evidence of bounded rationality and self-control problems, might urge that in many domains, the instruction to engage in only libertarian paternalism is too limiting. At least if the focus is entirely or mostly on welfare, it might seem clear that in certain circum-stances, people should not be given freedom of choice for the simple reason that they will choose poorly. In those circumstances, why should anyone insist on libertarian paternalism, as opposed to unqualified or non-libertari-an paternalism?

This objection raises complex issues of both value and fact, and we do not intend to venture into difficult philosophical territory here. Our basic response is threefold. First, we reiterate our understanding that planners are human, and so the real comparison is between boundedly rational choosers with self-control problems and boundedly rational planners facing self-control problems of their own. It is doubtful that the comparison can sensibly be made in the abstract. Second, an opt-out right operates as a safeguard against confused or improperly motivated planners, and in many contexts, that safeguard is crucial even if it potentially creates harm as well. Third, nothing we have said denies the possibility that in some circumstances it can be advisable to impose significant costs on those who reject the proposed course of action, or even to deny freedom of choice altogether. * * * Our only qualification is that when third-party effects are not present, the general presumption should be in favor of freedom of choice, and that presumption should be rebutted only when individual choice is demonstrably inconsistent with individual welfare.

                    * * *

In our view, libertarian paternalism is not only a conceptual possibility; it also provides a foundation for rethinking many areas of private and public law. We believe that policies rooted in libertarian paternalism will often be a big improvement on the most likely alternative: inept neglect.

NOTES AND QUESTIONS

1. Behavioral economics and macroeconomics. Much of the focus in behavioral economics so far is on microeconomics. What light might behav-ioral economics shed on macroeconomic issues? Economists George Akerlof and Robert Shiller argue that "animal spirits" must be taken into account when analyzing the behavior of national economies. They describe five different aspects of animal spirits: (1) confidence, and the feedback mechanisms between bearish or bullish attitudes and the economy that amplify disturbances; (2) fairness concerns, which affect the setting of wages and prices; (3) the problem of corrupt and antisocial behavior, which distorts market mechanisms; (4) "money illusion," or the fact that people do not understand inflation and deflation and so do not take it into account when bargaining; and (5) the importance of stories, including stories about the economy, which affect economic decisionmaking. George A. Akerlof and Robert J. Shiller, ANIMAL SPIRITS: HOW HUMAN PSYCHOLOGY DRIVES THE ECONOMY, AND WHY IT MATTERS FOR GLOBAL CAPITALISM 5–6 (2009).

2.   Bounded rationality: Glass half full or half empty? Sunstein and Thaler seem quite optimistic about government's ability to make people better off while still respecting their preferences. Edward McCaffery and Jonathan Baron come to a gloomier conclusion: that democracy, at least in the form of democratic tax policy, does not work quite as well as one might have hoped. McCaffery and Baron ran a series of experiments asking their subjects to make choices about tax policy, and found that the cognitive effects outlined by behavioral economists, particularly the class of effects called "focusing effects" or "isolation effects," profoundly affected their subjects' choices. As McCaffery and Baron explain:

> People tend to isolate or focus on a narrow choice problem before them, ignoring relevant information and otherwise failing to integrate their logically connected judgments and decisions into a coherent whole. An early example of this in the literature is Thaler's "mental accounts." Thaler found that many, perhaps most people treat the source of funds as relevant to their use, even though money is fungible. People who are normally frugal and even risk averse would spend lottery proceeds on luxury items or binge purchases. In doing so, they viewed their windfall gains in isolation and failed to integrate their newfound wealth with all their liabilities and assets.

> The isolation effect is central to our findings on the political psychology of redistribution. We found that subjects are hard pressed to integrate multiple tax systems, in the disaggregation bias discussed below, or to integrate the tax and spending dimensions of public finance to achieve constant levels of redistribution, in the privatization effect that we also discuss. The seemingly harmless tendency to separate out matters in one's mind can lead to disturbing anomalies in one's acceptance of global public finance systems.

Edward J. McCaffery and Jonathan Baron, *The Political Psychology of Redistribution*, 52 UCLA L.REV. 1745, 1751 (2005). Their conclusions are set out in the excerpt that follows.

The Political Psychology of Redistribution

52 UCLA L.REV. 1745 (2005).

■ EDWARD J. MCCAFFERY AND JONATHAN BARON

There is a tendency to conclude that if tax and other public finance systems appeal to popular perceptions, so much the better, because there will be psychological gains from putting the pain of tax in its most pleasing light. We believe that this happy tale is wrong—dangerously wrong—for several reasons.

First, * * * even psychologically pleasing taxes have real effects. In particular, pleasing taxes can be inefficient, violating the first prong of the optimal welfare-economics analysis. The corporate tax is a leading example of a popular hidden tax. Although the tax seems to please people because it does not strike them as a "tax"—or at least not one that they personally pay—a corporate tax has real effects on prices and other allocative decisions. If the distorting costs of the tax are higher than those of any alternative equal revenue-raising measure, then, ceteris paribus, society is paying a real welfare cost for its psychological preferences. In such a case, the first prong of the optimal welfare economics approach cannot be followed because people will not accept efficiency-enhancing or wealth-maximizing reforms on account of their cognitive errors.

Second, and perhaps worse, equity can suffer from cognitive errors as well. Equity can be pitted against efficiency in a tradeoff not mandated by the optimal welfare-economics approach. Psychologically pleasing hidden taxes, such as corporate income ones, generally will not be as progressive as subjects themselves desire taxes to be in the abstract. If the isolation or disaggregation effect were not so widespread, this equity effect may not matter all that much, although the efficiency losses noted in the prior paragraph would still occur. Society could have as many regressive taxes or surcharges as it desired, as long as it had a single system, such as the personal income tax, in which to redistribute. We have seen, however, that ordinary subjects have a hard time understanding extreme progressivity in any single system, viewed in isolation. This fact counsels against the earned income tax credit's strategy of using a negative income tax bracket to offset positive taxes elsewhere, because the negative tax becomes salient and draws fire. The reformer concerned with redistribution needs to look at all tax systems individually because the polity will not adequately integrate them. The same tension is evident in the privatization effect. The two-part optimal welfare-economics analysis suggests that efficiency alone should dictate whether the government provides a good or service. But because ordinary subjects have a difficult time integrating the effect of spending cuts or government downsizing on the residual tax system, bottom-line redistribution can suffer on account of even an efficiency-enhancing reform. The paretian constraint will not hold with privatization; the rich will get richer, the poor, poorer.

These two findings—that equity and efficiency can both suffer on account of prevalent heuristics and biases—constitute major ethical challenges to the status quo, and to traditional welfare economics. They are thus our principal concerns. Consistent with many other researchers in diverse disciplines, we have found that most subjects want at least moderate redistribution, viewed as a baseline matter. Yet citizen support for redistribution can change with the institutional setting. This is puzzling and troubling. And thinking about public finance raises still other concerns.

Third, for example, the resolution of public finance matters can be fragile and volatile, as equivalent frames can shift public opinion. Instability in public finance systems is itself a bad because it alone reduces welfare. Cognitive psychology suggests that people's preference shifts or reversals can obtain with no change in the underlying substance, so it is not a matter of people seeing the light and adopting "better" resolutions of public finance issues. People will simply choose more progressivity if they can be led to think in percentage terms, and less in dollar terms. They will choose policies that can be understood as bonuses, and then reject the same policies when they come to see them as penalties. This back and forth, on purely formal grounds, is problematic.

Fourth, given the importance of framing and related effects, politics will reward rhetoric over substance. "Great communicators" will be prized, not because they advocate "better" policies, but because they make their policies sound better to voters. This diverts political resources from the potentially welfare-enhancing study of substantive policy effects to the purely formal rhetorical presentation of matters. This leads to the next concern, which is especially great.

Finally, and perhaps most disturbingly, a skilled politician or political party can manipulate public opinion and get a public finance system in place that conflicts with prevalent democratic preferences. Suppose for example that a politician or party wanted to reverse course, and to reduce the degree of redistribution prevailing throughout public finance systems. Our research provides an eerie roadmap for success. Our findings suggest that a policy position to lessen social redistribution would likely lose in a straight up or down vote because a majority of people favor at least moderate redistribution. The rhetorically skilled politician, however, could effect a collective preference reversal. She might first choose hidden taxes, with a regressive incidence, and raise money through a series of relatively flat surcharges not labeled as taxes. People would likely support these, and a surplus might even result. Larger surpluses might follow from selective "privatization" of government goods and services, reducing the need for taxes. Cuts could then be made to the most salient tax—the income tax—which would continue to reflect moderate progressivity, even as its importance in the overall budget declined. Indeed, the politician could take this a step further, and separate out the topics of tax and spending cuts, cutting taxes now and postponing spending cuts until later. The resulting deficit would curtail government growth, and it could lead to replacement taxes less progressive than the initial baseline; ultimately, the pressures of the deficit and tax aversion would lead to support for even category spending cuts. The net result would be a smaller government and less dependence on the single remaining progressive tax system, a tax system that would continue to have only moderate levels of progressivity. Overall, the series of steps would lead to dramatically less redistribution than the people themselves wanted at the outset, and along the way there would be many "losers," concentrated in the lower-income classes. The cumulative changes would fail to meet the basic paretian constraint. Of course, the astute observer might notice that this is what has been done in the United States, under Republican Party leadership, beginning with Ronald Reagan in 1981.

D.   BEYOND TRADITIONAL MEASURES OF ECONOMIC WELL-BEING

In February 2008, Nicholas Sarkozy, President of the French Republic, asked renowned economists Joseph Stiglitz and Amartya Sen to convene a Commission on the Measurement of Economic Performance and Social Progress. The Commission's subsequent report, released in 2009 ("the Sarkozy report"), acknowledged that a central but often neglected problem in economic analysis is the problem of statistical measurement. What do economic indicators such as Gross Domestic Product (GDP) really measure? And what is the relationship between economic indicators and ultimate social goals, such as environmental sustainability and human happiness?

The Sarkozy report noted that there are several possible problems with statistical indicators. First, the concepts underlying the indicators may be correct, but the measurement process may be imperfect. Second, there may be disagreement about the concepts themselves. Third, overall statistics may mask underlying problems, as when rising inequality causes certain subgroups to be worse off even while the economy as a whole is growing. Fourth, commonly used indicators may simply fail to measure certain relevant issues, as when measures of growth do not take into account increased resource depletion and environmental pollution. Fifth and finally, sometimes indicators are perfectly adequate for what they set out to measure, but are misused or misunderstood.

The Sarkozy report paid particular attention to GDP, and its report adds credibility to economists and other scholars who have long criticized its use as a proxy for economic well-being. In addition to noting particular problems with GDP, however, the report also called for better measures of quality of life and of economic sustainability.

Report by the Commission on the Measurement of Economic Performance and Social Progress

Available at http://www.stiglitz-sen-fitoussi.fr/documents/rapport_anglais.pdf.

■ JOSEPH E. STIGLITZ, AMARTYA SEN, AND JEAN-PAUL FITOUSSI

Chapter 1: Classical GDP Issues

Gross domestic product (GDP) is the most widely used measure of economic activity. There are international standards for its calculation, and much thought has gone into its statistical and conceptual bases. But GDP mainly measures market production, though it has often been treated as if it were a measure of economic wellbeing. Conflating the two can lead to misleading indications about how well-off people are and entail the wrong policy decisions.

One reason why money measures of economic performance and living standards have come to play such an important role in our societies is that the monetary valuation of goods and services makes it easy to add up quantities of a very different nature. When we know the prices of apple juice and DVD players, we can add up their values and make statements about production and consumption in a single figure. But market prices are more than an accounting device. Economic theory tells us that when markets are functioning properly, the ratio of one market price to another is reflective of the relative appreciation of the two products by those who purchase them. Moreover, GDP captures all final goods in the economy, whether they are consumed by households, firms or government. Valuing them with their prices would thus seem to be a good way of capturing, in a single number, how well-off society is at a particular moment. Furthermore, keeping prices unchanged while observing how quantities of goods and services that enter GDP move over time would seem like a reasonable way of making a statement about how society's living standards are evolving in real terms.

As it turns out, things are more complicated. First, prices may not exist for some goods and services (if for instance government provides free health insurance or if households are engaged in child care), raising the question of how these services should be valued. Second, even where there are market prices, they may deviate from society's underlying valuation. In particular, when the consumption or production of particular products affects society as a whole, the price that individuals pay for those products will differ from their value to society at large. Environmental damage caused by production or consumption activities that is not reflected in market prices is a well-known example.

There is yet another problem. While talking about the concepts of "prices" and "quantities" may be straightforward, defining and measuring how they change in practice is an altogether different matter. As it happens, many products change over time—they disappear entirely or new features are added to them. Quality change can be very rapid in areas like information and communication technologies. There are also products whose quality is complex, multi-dimensional and hard to measure, such as medical services, educational services, research activities and financial services. Difficulties also arise in collecting data in an era when an increasing fraction of sales take place over the internet and at sales as well as discount stores. As a consequence, capturing quality change correctly is a tremendous challenge for statisticians, yet this is vital to measuring real income and real consumption, some of the key determinants of people's well-being. * * *

For market prices to be reflective of consumer's appreciation of goods and services, it is also necessary that consumers are free to choose and that they dispose of the relevant information. It takes little imagination to argue that this is not always the case. Complex financial products are an example where consumer ignorance prevents market prices from playing their role as carriers of correct economic signals. The complex and ever-changing bundles of services offered by telecommunications companies are another case in point where it is difficult to ensure the transparency and comparability of price signals.

All of the above considerations imply that price signals have to be interpreted with care in temporal and spatial comparisons. * * *

This Chapter suggests five ways of dealing with some of the deficiencies of GDP as an indicator of living standards. First, emphasize well-established indicators other than GDP in the national accounts. Second, improve the empirical measurement of key production activities, in particular the provision of health and education services. Third, bring out the household perspective, which is most pertinent for considerations of living standards. Fourth, add information about the distribution of income, consumption and wealth to data on the average evolution of these elements. Finally, widen the scope of what is being measured. In particular, a significant part of economic activity takes place outside markets and is often not reflected in established national accounts. However, when there are no markets, there are no market prices, and valuing such activities requires estimates ("imputations"). These are meaningful, but they come at a cost. * * *

Chapter 2: Quality of Life

Quality of life is a broader concept than economic production and living standards. It includes the full range of factors that influences what we value in living, reaching beyond its material side. While some extensions of economic accounting (discussed in Chapter 1) allow including some of the elements that shape quality of life in conventional measures of economic well-being, every approach based on resources (or on people's command over commodities) remains limited in important ways. First, resources are means that are transformed into well-being in ways that differ across people: individuals with greater capacities for enjoyment or greater abilities for achievement in valuable domains of life may be better off even if they command fewer economic resources. Second, many resources are not marketed, and even when they are, prices will differ across individuals, making it problematic to compare real income across people. Finally, many of the determinants of human well-being are aspects of people's life-circumstances: they cannot be described as resources with imputable prices, even if people do make trade-offs among them. These arguments by themselves are sufficient to suggest that resources are an insufficient metric for quality of life. Which other metric should be used instead of assessing quality of life depends on the philosophical perspective taken.

While a long tradition of philosophical thought has addressed the issues of what gives life its quality, recent advances in research have led to measures that are both new and credible. This research suggests that the need to move beyond measures of economic resources is not limited to developing countries (the traditional focus of much work on "human development" in the past) but is even more salient for rich industrialized countries. These measures, while not replacing conventional economic indicators, provide an opportunity to enrich policy discussions and to inform people's view of the conditions of the communities where they live. More importantly, the new measures now have the potential to move from research to standard statistical practice. While some of them reflect structural conditions that are relatively invariant over time but that differ systematically across countries, others are more responsive to policies and more suitable for monitoring changes over shorter periods of time. Both types of indicator play an important role in evaluating quality of life.

Three conceptual approaches have retained the attention of the Commission as useful in thinking about how to measure quality of life.

The first approach, developed in close connection with psychological research, is based on the notion of subjective well-being. A long philosophical tradition views individuals as the best judges of their own conditions. This approach is closely linked to the utilitarian tradition but has a broader appeal due to the strong presumption in many streams of ancient and modern culture that enabling people to be "happy" and "satisfied" with their life is a universal goal of human existence.

The second approach is rooted in the notion of capabilities. This approach conceives a person's life as a combination of various "doings and beings" (functionings) and of his or her freedom to choose among these functionings (capabilities). Some of these capabilities may be quite elementary, such as being adequately nourished and escaping premature mortality, while others may be more complex, such as having the literacy required to participate actively in political life. The foundations of the capability approach, which has strong roots in philosophical notions of social justice, reflect a focus on human ends and on respecting the individual's ability to pursue and realize the goals that he or she values; a rejection of the economic model of individuals acting to maximize their self-interest heedless of relationships and emotions; an emphasis on the complementarities between various capabilities; and a recognition of human diversity, which draws attention to the role played by ethical principles in the design of the "good" society.

The third approach, developed within the economics tradition, is based on the notion of fair allocations. The basic idea, which is common to welfare economics, is that of weighting the various non-monetary dimensions of quality of life (beyond the goods and services that are traded in markets) in a way that respects people's preferences. This approach requires choosing a particular reference point for each of the various non-monetary dimensions, and obtaining information on people's current situations and on their preferences with respect to these points. This approach avoids the pitfall of basing evaluations on an "average" willingness-to-pay that may disproportionately reflect the preferences of those who are better-

off in society and focuses instead on equality among all of its members.
* * *

Chapter 3: Sustainable Development and Environment

* * * [T]he capacity of future generations to have standards of well-being at least equal to ours depends upon our passing them sufficient amounts of all the assets that matter for well-being. If we denote by "W" the "extended wealth" index used to quantify this stock of resources, measuring sustainability amounts to testing whether this global stock or some of its components evolve positively or negatively, i.e. computing its or their current rates of change, dW or dWi. If negative, this means that downward adjustments in consumption or well-being will be required sooner or later. This is exactly what one should understand by "non-sustainability."

* * * Returning to fundamentals means asking precisely what would be required to measure the above-mentioned dW indices in a satisfactory way. Assuming away the measurement problems at first, we have to be more specific about several concepts: What is to be sustained? How do the various assets that will be passed on to future generations affect this measure of well-being? And how should they be weighted against each other?

It is clearly this last question that is more problematic and tends to crystallize opposition between the proponents of money indicators and physical indicators. Is there actually some prospect of evaluating everything in money units, or should we accept that this is possible only up to a certain point?

If all assets were traded on perfect markets by perfectly forward-looking agents fully taking into account the welfare of future generations, one could argue that their current prices reflect the discounted streams of their future contributions to future well-being. But many assets are not traded at all, and even for those that are it is unlikely that current prices fully reflect this future-oriented dimension, due to market imperfections, myopia and uncertainty. This implies that a true measure of sustainability requires a dW index in which assets are valued not at market prices, but rather using imputed "accounting prices" based on some objective physical or economic modeling of how future damage to the environment will affect well-being, just as it requires an exact evaluation of how current additions to the stock of human or physical capital are likely to improve or help maintain well-being in the future. * * *

Measuring sustainability with a single dW index can work only under two strong assumptions: one is that future eco-environmental developments can be predicted perfectly, and the second is that there is perfect knowledge about how these developments are going to affect well-being. These two assumptions are clearly at odds with our real world situation. Debates on eco-environmental perspectives are dominated by ignorance and uncertainty about future interactions between the two spheres, and by a lack of consensus about the very definition of the objective function.

Let's briefly develop the first point. The future is fundamentally uncertain. Uncertainty takes many forms, some of them amenable to probability computation, while many others are much more radical. This affects not only the parameters of any models that one may try to use to project eco-environmental interactions, but also the structure of the models themselves, the measurement of current stocks, and even the list of the natural assets for which current and future stocks need to be taken into account. Most of the debate concerning long-term environmental change reflects different beliefs about future eco-environmental scenarios. There is no reason why sustainability measurement should escape such difficulties. * * *

The problem then is to present such an index in a compelling way. Monetary indices have the advantage of using units that speak to everyone. In addition, they can be related to other monetary quantities: this is what we do when we compute extended savings rates, and the orders of magnitude of such savings rates can be understood easily. On the other hand, a tonnage of CO_2 emissions is not a very informative number if we do not have some reference for how many tons can be emitted each year without severe consequences for the climate. Other physical indicators have been advocated by climate specialists, * * * [b]ut it is difficult for non-experts to take such indicators on board. It is essential to find more suggestive ways to highlight such figures if we want the indicator to have an impact on the debate. One of the major successes of the ecological footprint has been its ability to express pressure on the environment in an easily understandable unit. * * *

In addition to raising technological issues, measuring sustainability with a single index number would confront us with severe normative questions. The point is that there can be as many indices of sustainability as there are normative definitions of what we want to sustain. In standard national accounting practice, the normative issue of defining preferences is generally avoided through the assumption that observed prices reveal the true preferences of people. No explicit normative choice is therefore to be made by the statistician. But as soon as we recognize that market prices cannot be trusted, alternative imputed prices must be computed, whose values will strongly depend upon normative choices.

Can we solve this normative problem? One could attempt to solve it empirically by trying to infer the definition of well-being from current observations of how people value environmental factors compared to economic ones, using contingent valuations or direct measures of the impact of environmental amenities on indices of subjective well-being. But can the contingent evaluations and subjective measures established today in our specific eco-environmental settings be used to predict the valuations of future generations in eco-environmental settings that may have become very different? It could be argued that our descendants may become very sensitive to the relative scarcity of some environmental goods to which we pay little attention today because they are still relatively abundant, and that this requires that we immediately place a high value on these items just because we think that our descendants may wish to do so.

Another example of these normative issues is the question of determining how sustainability indices should aggregate individual preferences. This depends on how distributional considerations are taken into account in our measures of current well-being. For instance, if we consider that the headline indicator of current well-being must be the total disposable income of the bottom 80% of the population, or of the bottom 50%, rather than global disposable income, then sustainability indicators should be adapted to such an objective function. * * * In a world where inequalities within countries naturally tend to increase, messages concerning sustainability will differ depending on the goal that we set ourselves. Specific attention to distributional issues may even suggest enlarging the list of capital goods that matter for sustainability: the "sustainability" of well-being for the bottom x% of the population may imply some specific investment in institutions that offer efficient help in protecting this population from poverty. * * *

In order to measure sustainability, what we need are indicators that tell us the sign of the change in the quantities of the different factors that matter for future well-being. Putting the sustainability issue in these terms compels recognition that sustainability requires the simultaneous preservation or increase in several "stocks": quantities and qualities not only of natural resources but also of human, social and physical capital. Any approach that focuses on only a part of these items does not offer a comprehensive view of sustainability.

NOTES AND QUESTIONS

1. Adjusting GDP: What counts? The problems with GDP identified by the Sarkozy report are not new. Simon Kuznets, the Nobel Prize-winning economist who initially helped the U.S. Department of Commerce structure GNP (gross national product, the predecessor of GDP) in the early twentieth century, himself warned that it should not be used as a measure of general welfare. In particular, Kuznets noted that not all commodities currently produced, exchanged, and consumed are a source of final satisfaction to their users. Rather, some are "intermediate goods" that are necessary in order to enjoy some other good. Work clothes and commuting expenses are examples of intermediate goods that might better be treated as expenses of production and not as final consumption that bring subjective satisfaction to their users. Yet intermediate goods are not distinguished from final goods in GNP and GDP.

The German economist Christian Leipert named a particular class of intermediate goods "defensive goods," and defined these as "expenditures ... made to eliminate, mitigate, neutralize, or anticipate and avoid damages and deterioration that industrial society's process of growth has caused to living, working, and environmental conditions." Christian Leipert, *Social Costs of the Economic Process and National Accounts: The*

Example of Defensive Expenditures, 3 J. Interdisciplinary Econ. 27, 28 (1989). Leipert identified six areas in which major defensive costs arise: the environment, transportation, housing, personal security, health, and the workplace. In his view, for example, money spent on auto repairs and medical treatments resulting from highway accidents should not count in GNP as consumption, but as costs. Applying his adjusted GNP measure to the West German economy in the mid–1980s, Leipert found that defensive expenditures made up over ten percent of GNP.

Another problem with GNP and GDP is that neither measure takes into account asset depreciation, whether of human or natural resource assets. For example, these measures do not recognize depreciation in labor capacity caused by domestic violence, workplace injuries, or prolonged unemployment. Nor do GNP and GDP recognize that natural resources may be depleted or exhausted by economic activity. Thus, in 1984 the World Resources Institute compared the economic situation of Indonesia with and without taking account of resource extraction, and argued that the depletion of forests, soils, and petroleum resources constituted 17.3 percent of GDP. Official economic reports left this depletion invisible. See Richard W. England, *Measurement of Social Well–Being: Alternatives to Gross Domestic Product*, 25 Ecological Economics 89, 92 (1998).

2. Replacing GDP. Recognizing the many limitations of GDP, some economists and others have proposed alternative measures of economic well-being. One such measure is Robert Eisner's total incomes system of accounts (TISA). As well as responding to the intermediate goods problem, TISA responds to two other problems with GDP. First, GDP implicitly assumes that all social investment is made in the private sector, ignoring government and household investments in education, infrastructure, and technology. Second, GDP ignores productive economic activity that occurs outside of markets, such as housework, home repair and maintenance, and the care of children and the elderly. Imputing economic value to these activities, Eisner found that the household sector's share of GNP in the United States in the late 1980s was one-third. See Robert Eisner, The Total Incomes System of Accounts (1989).

Amartya Sen, one of the authors of the Sarkozy report, argues that economic success should not be an end in itself, but only a means toward optimal quality of life. Sen is also concerned with social inequality, particularly the divide in well-being between the global North and the global South. Building on his argument that research can identify universal human "capabilities," the United Nations Development Programme created the Human Development Index (HDI). The HDI adjusts per capita GDP to recognize the fact that a given amount of money means more to the poor than to the rich. The HDI also includes measures of longevity and access to education. These three indicators comprise a country's "deprivation score."

The HDI reveals that countries with similar GDP may be situated very differently in terms of human development. For example, Sri Lanka, Congo, and Pakistan have similar average incomes, but Sri Lanka receives a much higher HDI rating because its citizens are likely to live substantially longer and be better educated. England at 96.

In 1989, economist Herman Daly and theologian John Cobb sought to incorporate all of these corrections to GDP in an entirely new measure, called the Index of Sustainable Economic Welfare (ISEW). The ISEW recognized social inequality, resource depletion, environmental damage, and household production in addition to the problem of intermediate goods. More recently, a variant of the ISEW called the Genuine Progress Indicator (GPI) has come to be used in policy-making and analysis at national, state, and even local levels. GPI combines measures of economic well-being with measures of environmental and social well-being. See Redefining Progress, The Genuine Progress Indicator 2006: A Tool for Sustainable Development, available at http://www.rprogress.org/publications/2007/GPI% 202006.pdf.

Plotting GPI against GDP, researchers John Talberth, Clifford Cobb, and Noah Slattery of the nonprofit organization Redefining Progress found that in the period from 1950 to approximately 1980, the two measures moved together in a positive direction overall. Beginning in 1980, however, GDP continued to rise while GPI stagnated or even dropped. *Id.* Talberth, Cobb, and Slattery observe:

> [W]hat this implies is that since 1980 or so the marginal benefits associated with growth in personal consumption expenditures, non-market time, and capital services have been offset by the marginal costs associated with income inequality, natural capital depletion, consumer durable expenditures, defensive expenditures, undesirable side effects of growth, and net foreign borrowing. This trend, found in many of the GPI and ISEW studies completed over the past fifteen years or so has been put forth as evidence of a "threshold" effect.

Id. at 19. They quote the Chilean economist Manfred Max–Neef:

> For every society there seems to be a period in which economic growth brings about an improvement in the quality of life, but only up to a point—the threshold point—beyond which, if there is more economic growth, the quality of life begins to deteriorate.

Manfred Max–Neef, *Economic Growth and Quality of Life: A Threshold Hypothesis*, 15 ECOLOGICAL ECONOMICS 115, 117 (1995).

Cass Sunstein has argued that the U.S. government should issue an annual "quality of life" report:

> I cannot give a full account of the appropriate ingredients of such a report. But it seems clear that the report should include, among other things, per capita income, poverty, housing, unemployment, average weekly earnings, inflation, child mortality, longevity, subjection to violent crime, literacy, and educational attainment. The report should also specify minimum standards for such things as income, education, health, and housing. The report should allow for comparison across regions, between men and women, and among different racial and ethnic groups.

Cass R. Sunstein, *Well–Being and the State*, 107 HARV. L.REV. 1315, 1324 (1993–94).

3. Toward the pursuit of happiness? Advances in neuroscience and psychology have made it more feasible than ever before to directly investigate and measure subjective happiness. Economist Richard Layard argues that the burgeoning "science of happiness" means that GDP and similar purely economic measures no longer need serve as objective proxies for happiness. Plotting survey research against GDP, Layard finds that the data support Max–Neef's observation: Economic growth makes people in poor countries happier, but the happiness of people in rich countries does not track their wealth. Indeed, according to surveys of satisfaction and happiness, people in the West have not gotten any happier in the last fifty years, despite steady rises in GDP. Meanwhile, alcoholism, depression, and crime have risen. Layard argues that policymakers should return to the philosophy of utilitarianism, which seeks the greatest happiness for the greatest number of people, and discard the pursuit of endless economic growth. According to Layard, utilitarianism suggests that rich countries should redistribute some of their wealth to poor countries, seek economic stability rather than growth, and encourage their citizens through tax policy to work less and play more. See Richard Layard, HAPPINESS: LESSONS FROM A NEW SCIENCE (2005).

The nation of Bhutan anticipated Layard's advice. Beginning in the 1980s, the king of Bhutan coined the phrase "Gross National Happiness" to describe his nation's chief economic measure. Long before the phrase took hold, however, Bhutan had been pursuing a policy of economic development that placed its people's happiness over their wealth. Stefan Priesner argues that Bhutan's long political and geographic isolation from the rest of the world and its deeply entrenched Buddhist values produced a unique culture that allowed the Bhutanese to reject Western recipes for development. Stefan Priesner, "Gross National Happiness: Bhutan's Vision of Development and Its Challenges," in Partha Nath Mukerji and Chandan Sengupta (eds.), *Indigeneity and Universality in Social Science: A South Asian Response* 212 (2004). For the Bhutanese, "[T]he overarching goal of every aspect of life, including economics, is not seen in the multiplication of material wants, which can be satisfied by consumption, but in the purification of the human character. The objectives of market economics, that is, increasing consumption and accelerating growth are thus only relevant as means to an entirely different end—human well-being." *Id.* at 222–23. Priesner observes, however, that a younger generation of policy-makers and politicians may yet adopt Western notions of endless growth as a good in itself.

4. Ecological devastation, measuring risk, and the problem of future generations. Accounting for the services provided by the earth to all human life and the depletion of natural resources presents thorny problems of valuation. Even more daunting, however, is the task of estimating the cost to future generations of present actions. The seemingly mathematical notion of "discount rate" turns out to have troubling philosophical and political implications. As Douglas Kysar explains:

> When evaluating a particular investment decision, economists typically reduce expected costs and benefits to present value using a discount rate, or a percentage factor that adjusts the amount of a value over time. For instance, using a discount rate of 10%, an investment yielding $110 in year two is worth only $100 in year one. If the investment costs $105 to make in year one, it is not an economic choice. Such reasoning holds well in the context of paper investment decisions. However, when the expected yield consists of saved lives, preserved ecosystem services, and other nontangible benefits to present and future generations, it is not altogether obvious that the same analysis should apply. * * *

> Frequently, discount rates are determined based on the prevailing real rate of interest charged in capital markets. However, positive interest rates, which can be said to represent the growth potential of man-made capital, are a poor indicator of the growth potential of natural capital. The fact that capital may grow in a bank at 10% per year does not necessarily imply that an old growth forest will regenerate at an equal rate. A timber company adopting a 10% discount rate to determine harvesting schedules will "rationally" clear forests faster than they can regrow, essentially liquidating the natural capital of the forest rather than consuming only its annual income. * * *

> Besides encouraging unsustainable investment strategies, discounting can also discourage ecologically desirable government regulations. Because society must often pay the costs of environmental regulation long before the benefits accrue, discounting of future costs and benefits frequently counsels against the adoption of environmentally-protective measures. Daniel Farber and Paul Hemmersbaugh provide an extreme illustration by positing the case of two alternative designs for a nuclear waste repository. The designs will cost the same amount and will both be paid for entirely in the first year. If the first design is adopted, no workers will be killed during construction but one billion people will be killed in five hundred years due to a radiation leak from the repository. If the second design is adopted, between one and two workers will likely be killed during construction but no leaks and therefore no deaths will occur in five hundred years. Using a discount rate of 5%, the regulator selecting between designs "will choose the first option because one billion lives 500 years hence have a lower present value than one life today." * * *

> On the standard approach, if a proposed regulation would save the lives of one billion people five hundred years from now, the value of those lives is discounted to a present value. In essence, economists attempt to measure what it is worth to society now to save the lives of a billion people in the future. As Farber and Hemmersbaugh demonstrate, it turns out not to be worth very much. However, the use of the present generation's valuation of the worth of a future generation's

lives is a normative judgment that should not be obscured by arithmetic. As Lisa Heinzerling powerfully put it, "Generating numbers that are ultimately irrelevant to the questions to be resolved does more than waste precious regulatory resources. It changes the apparent nature of the decision itself, and permits politics and ideology to hide behind a mask of technical expertise."

Douglas A. Kysar, *Sustainability, Distribution, and the Macroeconomic Analysis of Law*, 43 B.C. L.Rev. 1 (2001). Should decisions about preserving the environment then turn on purely moral intuitions? How can sensible public policymaking take place without resort to numbers?

5. Ecological sustainability, economic activity, and the primacy of humans. In order to be "sustainable," the activities that make up the global economy must remain within the carrying capacity of the earth for the foreseeable future. Like the question of discounted risk, the issue of sustainability is rife with value judgments and political questions, as well as the problem of the unknowable future. Nonetheless, in order to plan sensibly for the future, measures of sustainability must be developed and used, despite their inherent flaws.

One measure that has gained popularity in recent years is "ecological footprint" (EF). EF is a standardized measure of the earth's biological carrying capacity required to support humanity's resource use and waste production. Ecological footprint analysis (EFA) compares this measure with the earth's ability to renew its capacity over time. According to some estimates, humanity's EF currently exceeds the carrying capacity of the earth by 23 percent. Redefining Progress, "Refining the Ecological Footprint" (2006), available at http://www.rprogress.org/publications/2006/RefiningEF_2006.pdf.

Like its cousin the carbon footprint, EF is based on arguable assumptions. For instance, some critics argue that EF is overly optimistic about the possibility of technological innovation. The nonprofit organization Redefining Progress acknowledges a number of technical problems with EF, such as its approach to carbon sequestration rates, but also offers a different kind of critique: EF is overly anthropocentric. Researchers Jason Venetouli and John Talberth argue in a Redefining Progress report that EF counts biocapacity only in terms of parts of the earth that can be directly used by people. Under EF, uninhabited areas such as mountains, deserts, tundra, ice sheets, and oceans could be ecologically devastated with no adverse consequences to sustainability. EF also counts only human beings as users of the planet. Thus, humans could appropriate 100 percent of the earth's biocapacity and still count their economic activity as sustainable. Refining the Ecological Footprint, supra.

6. Economic "business as usual" and the crisis of climate change. Is traditional economic analysis not only unhelpful, but actually an impediment to the ability of policymakers and citizens to respond appropriately to the threat of climate change? Julie Nelson raises this question:

Some will argue that standard, marginalist CBA [cost-benefit analysis] or cost-effectiveness analysis can still play a central role in determining the most efficient way to reach goals, once proper climate change goals have been set by social and ethical discussion. There are reasons, however, to doubt that this is the most effective way to use economists' energies right now, if we are to deal adequately with the climate crisis.

The first reason is that the core assumptions of the models themselves emphasize concerns that may, at this point in history, be more distracting than helpful. Efficiency, central to such modeling, is, in the present case, of second order importance at best. The models emphasize small changes, monetary valuation, individual self-interest, and individual utility from consumption—all of which tend to take us in exactly the wrong direction. A narrow focus on marginalist modeling may dangerously serve to distract economists, policy-makers', and the public's attention from the more important questions of equity, large changes, and community. * * *

Second, the fact that models are extremely sensitive to the specification of assumptions, and very dependent on projections of radically uncertain future events, makes them very easy to misuse in policy evaluation. For example, there is a disturbing tendency on the part of some environmental groups to want, from economists, "studies" that show that preventing climate change will be "good for the economy" in terms of GDP growth, and will not change people's lives very much. * * * No one who takes the long-run climate change science seriously believes that the problem would be adequately addressed by the rather modest sorts of legislation currently considered politically viable. No one who takes issues of global environmental justice seriously believes that the patterns of consumption, transportation, and residence of those in the rich parts of the world can continue more or less unchanged. * * *

The "better model" strategy relies on the * * * political assumptions that people are self-interested and rational, and take measured steps towards well-thought-out goals. It assumes that policymaking is actually a reasoned process in which legislators try to decide what is best for their constituents. While as academics (or at least readers of academic journals) we are often biased towards thinking of people as rational, considerable evidence tells us that this is not how important policies are enacted. * * * What we need in regard to climate change is not another model, but a mobilization on the order of going to war . . . only much bigger.

Julie A. Nelson, *Between a Rock and a Soft Place: Ecological and Feminist Economics in Policy Debates*, 69 Ecological Econ. 1, 5–6 (2008).

7. Bounded rationality, self-interest, and ecological economics. Does economic theory explain why ecological economics remains at present a marginal rather than a central stream within the discipline of economics? That is, are politicians and policymakers concerned with their own short-term self-interest over an altruistic concern for the earth or for future generations? Does behavioral economics also provide some insight? Are politicians and policymakers afflicted with problems relating to bounded rationality when it comes to environmental issues?

8. The fall of neoclassical theory? Douglas Kysar concludes in his article that "macroeconomics rests on what is arguably now a discredited world-view." Kysar, *Sustainability, Distribution, and the Macroeconomic Analysis of Law*, note 4 above. Do you agree? What can be done about it?

Based on the critiques outlined in this chapter, what useful insights, if any, remain from classical market theory? Do the critiques outlined in this chapter challenge Adam Smith's original insights, or only the narrowing of his work by neoclassical economists?

CHAPTER 6

BEYOND CLASSIC MARKET THEORY: EXTERNAL CRITIQUES

As the influence of the first wave of law and economics scholarship grew in the legal academy, so did the depth and breadth of criticism directed to its organizing concepts. As we have seen in chapter 5, these criticisms now span a broad range of perspectives. There are scholars, generally friendly to the project of infusing economics into law, who use cognitive psychology and other social sciences to relax some of the assumptions of neoclassical economics. Other scholars, such as ecological economists, are also friendly to the discipline, but work at the very limits of economic analysis.

In this chapter, we examine criticisms by scholars who are not so friendly to classical economic analysis. In this category there are scholars committed to moral or humanistic analysis, who reject the normative premise that wealth maximization is a coherent value for evaluating the legal rules that govern the distribution of material goods in a democracy. There are scholars whose principal concerns are phenomena, like racism and sexism, that have been neglected or ignored by economic analysis. And there are scholars who view the entire project of first-wave law and economics as pure right-wing ideology. As Anita Bernstein's review of the first wave of law and economics shows, these outside challengers have sometimes used colorful language to report their findings that the central tenets of law and economics were "incoherent," "dubious in the extreme," "garbage in and garbage out," and a "cult."

In this chapter we explore several of the most powerful external challenges to first-wave law and economics. First, we examine the most extreme attack on first-wave law and economics, the claim that it is nothing more than an apology for laissez-faire economic policy. Second, we examine various strands of the central external objection to economic analysis, which is that it is incomplete as a rhetoric for social ordering without a moral analysis centered on justice. One moral attack on traditional economic analysis is the commodification challenge to markets. This argument insists that some aspects of social life are inappropriate for market ordering, not because markets fail but because they succeed too well—crowding out human impulses toward altruism, social justice, and community in favor of self-interest. A second example of a problem where scholars armed with moral theory have rejected economic analysis is social oppression. For scholars who believe that racial subordination is a central conundrum in contemporary legal thought and in society, for instance, the rational choice model of human behavior is unpersuasive. A third moral attack on economic analysis comes from political theory. Here, scholars from Marxists to civic republicans have argued that economic analysis reduces political values relating to solidarity, democracy, justice, and fairness to add-ons. From this perspective, the welfare economist's premise that a society should build wealth first and worry about distributional problems later is wrong-headed.

In the first section of the chapter we present a broadly-stated conflict between materialist and humanist values; at the end of the chapter, in section C, we present two attempts to think beyond the conflict and to incorporate both materialist and humanist values in economic thinking.

A. THE CASE AGAINST (LAW AND) ECONOMICS

Whatever Happened to Law and Economics?
64 MD. L. REV. 101 (2005).

■ ANITA BERNSTEIN

* * * "Every fresh contribution to the economic analysis of tort law," wrote Ernest Weinrib in 1989, "adds a new storey to an edifice whose bottom has long since disappeared into the sand."

* * * Then came Leonard Jaffee * * *: "So, I have two big gripes against Law and Economics. One is that it's sick and spreads sickness. The other's that it doesn't work in ways it claims, or do what it pretends." * * * According to David Gray Carlson, "[t]here are two types of law-and-economics: one that is dubious and another that is dubious in the extreme." In her 2004 book, *The Triumph of Venus*, Jeanne Schroeder, who'd majored in economics in college, declared that "most law-and-economic proposals are classic cases of GIGO (garbage in—garbage out): nonfalsified theories are applied to untested assumptions in order to produce nonverifiable conclusions. Law-and-economics has all the characteristics of a cult."

These attacks arrayed in the background, I make here a somewhat different claim: that law and economics is no longer amenable to critique. This movement, in my view, is not an edifice whose bottom has disappeared into the sand. Instead it is not an edifice at all. In past decades, it did take shape as a unique structure; the Chicago school bore distinctive characteristics. A scholar generating new work in law and economics during this "edifice" era would borrow precepts from neoclassical economics and apply them to the law, in an effort either to describe, in material terms, how law affects and responds to aggregations of human beings ("positive" law and economics) or to propose measures designed to improve these consequences ("normative" or "prescriptive" law and economics). Many practitioners, Richard Posner foremost among them, dealt in both description and prescription. The combination brought to law the most philosophical strand in microeconomic theory, welfare economics.

Today the Chicago edifice shares attention with other types of law and economics. Anyone reading this far has undoubtedly heard that law and economics contains multitudes—an array of literatures, sub-movements, and schools of thought. Perhaps it does. Certainly a scholar trained in both economics and law has the vocabulary to combine the two disciplines in ways that would not hew to the descriptions of Chicago-style welfare economics, or to any other fraction of the genre. But observers with no stake in the cliché about diversity can see how well it serves insiders, who get from it a basis to say that their movement is big *and* a ready retort to semi-disavow anything in it that provokes criticism: "Well, that's one of the other schools." Law and economics can claim pluralism when pluralism suits, monolithic unity when pluralism threatens to splinter its power.

This inclination within the movement to have it both ways impels me to take a second look at its premise that law and economics is distinct from all other disciplines yet eclectic and pluralistic, the academy's big tent. The two postures are not only in tension with each other but perhaps also, I start to suspect, questionable in isolation. For law and economics to be valid, two conditions must obtain: law and economics needs a foundation of meaningful concepts and a boundary to fence out what it rejects or does not believe. If these two elements are missing, then its distinctive aspects may be unsound and its variations, offshoots, and alliances may be incoherent. In this Article I explore this question of foundations under, and boundaries around, the movement.

* * * [M]y rhetorical question, *Whatever happened . . . ?* broaches an argument that although a generation ago law and economics stood—as an edifice, if you like—it no longer endures. The movement was done in by a blend of some claims that were wrong with other claims that came across in legal circles as too right—and also too trivial to reject. Law and economics combined too little accuracy with too much: While ill founded, dubious, or tautological premises were eroding its credibility, other notions from the movement, consistent with what diverse thinkers and audiences believed, blurred the line between law and economics on one hand and everything else in jurisprudence on the other. Withdraw the mistakes and exaggerations from law and economics and what you get is either positive scholarship declaring 5 to be the sum of 3 and 2, or some indistinguishable share of the centrist, forward-looking quasi-utilitarian mélange of advice to policy-minded lawyers that now dominates the legal academy, unconfined to any sector.

During the last decade, members of the movement labored to stop the fall. Unable to do much about errors, they worked on the second front, the crisis of too much acceptance, mainly by trying to claim successful outsider movements as their own, rather than reacting to them as threats or challenges. When psychology dealt blows to the ideal of a rational actor, for instance, economic analysts invoked the label of "behavioral economics" to describe claims that were directly contrary to neoclassical dogma. Led by Robert Ellickson, they used the word "norms" to summarize phenomena inconvenient to the edifice. This capacious label not only could obscure what did not fit the neoclassical model, but also aid a contention that human behaviors deviating from the paradigm—behaviors that reveal altruism, expenditures that appear to waste rather than accrete money, refusals to cheat or defect in games, and the like are consistent with law and economics, rather than refutations of its core premises. This cooptation strategy reached a height in 2002 with the publication of *Fairness Versus Welfare*, a book from two scholars identified with the law and economics movement who declared victory by asserting that Welfare accounted for everything that jurisprudence pursues, except for a handful of silly vestigial claims which the authors disparaged as Fairness. This putative victory, however, would be better described as submergence into a larger whole. Part of the law and economics edifice has disappeared into the sand; part has joined the sand itself.

So much for Weinrib's edifice; Jeanne Schroeder had a different one-word critique. Schroeder called law and economics a "cult" in order to rebuke it for falling short of scientific standards. Yet cults are characterized by more than just clinging to a dogma that gets reality wrong. They are social groups. They contain members who disdain nonmembers, and who have been known to enjoy thinking that outsiders feel hostility towards them. I quote Schroeder's insult with approval even though one might debate her charges of falsity—as a concise description of a movement done in by the twin stabbings of excessive inaccuracy and trivial accuracy. Stripped of its distinctive intellectual features, no longer able to give descriptions or policy recommendations that could not have come from sources outside the movement, law and economics now functions mainly as a faculty club with opaque, arbitrary criteria for membership.

Where do *The Costs of Accidents* and Guido Calabresi fit in this picture? Away from the missteps. Calabresi's book, in contrast to the one by Kaplow and Shavell, focuses on Welfare without perceiving it as a prizefighter that has beaten or should beat a straw man, hapless Fairness. It draws readers in with its clarity and reason, never trying to exclude or intimidate anyone. It is a model, indeed, of what law and economics scholarship can contribute in the eras following refutation of its core tenets: a wide social science that invites participants to consider the common good.

I. Errors: What Has Crumbled, What Has Never Been

Consider how the tenets and distinguishing features of law and economics are faring at the thirty-fifth anniversary of *The Costs of Accidents*.

A. *Three Precepts*

1. Rational Choice.—On the first page of *Economic Analysis of Law*, Richard Posner declared a first axiom: "man is a rational maximizer of his ends in life." This individual knows what he wants and chooses means to reach his goals. The world through economists' eyes begins here, at the point where an individual makes a choice among alternatives. Rational choice is the "first and most basic" of "the critical early moves" in law and economics. Only if individuals can know what they want and act instrumentally on their desires can the other central precepts of the discipline—among them preferences, opportunities, and a consciousness of scarcity—make sense.

Moreover, Posner continues,

> the concept of rationality used by the economist is objective rather than subjective, so that it would not be a solecism to speak of a rational frog. Rationality means little more to an economist than a disposition to choose, consciously or unconsciously, an apt means to whatever ends the chooser happens to have.

According to this construction of rationality, the chooser will not lose the designation of "rational" just because her choices are self-destructive, perverse, opaque, inconsistent, unstable over time, resistant to Arrovian ordinal ranking, or dependent on the unpredictable choices that others make. Her choices can even defy the downward-sloping demand curve. As Arthur Leff noted decades ago, when

> a society dentist raises his prices and thereby increases his gross volume of business, it is no violation of the principle of the inverse relation between price and quantity. It only proves that buyers now perceive that they are buying something else which they now value more highly, "society dentistry" say, rather than "mere" dentistry.

Because "whatever ends the chooser happens to have" emerge from her behavior rather than from her own testimony or other expression, any means in this "objective" sense can be "apt."

One critique of Chicago-style law and economics argues that rational choice according to this school remains vulnerable to challenges that philosophy has long been expressing, perhaps "since the fourth century B.C." For openers, explains philosopher and classics scholar Martha Nussbaum, law and economics regards preferences as "exogenous, i.e., not significantly shaped by laws and institutions," whereas "the endogeneity of preferences has been recognized by almost all the major writers on emotion and desire in the history of Western philosophy." To speak of choice as if it originated entirely inside the actor is simply wrong. Furthermore, individuals do not simply make choices: they value their power to do so. People "do not typically view as equivalent two states of the world, one produced by their own agency and the other not." Ends, which law and economics sees as fixed, actually vary over time and through discourse; human beings deliberate about them. The concept of "preferences" sloppily throws together what philosophers have kept separated as five distinct phenomena: "belief, desire, perception, appetite, and emotion."

Along with old writings that cast the economists' version of rational choice into question, newer ones have refuted this concept through experimentation and revision. The neoclassical conception of rationality had fancied that human beings make choices within a preference ordering that is complete and transitive, subject to perfect and costlessly acquired information. Reality began to sully the premise. In the mid-twentieth century

Herbert Simon established a beachhead for empiricism in economics with his identification of "bounded rationality," whereby a subject makes the best choices she can, given her limited "knowledge and computational capacities and skills." Simon's work brought about behavioral economics, the branch of microeconomics that focuses on the choices individuals make rather than the processes of their decisionmaking. "Choice," manifested in behaviors rather than the trail of conscious strategy that precedes them, came to subsume "rational": if some actor did it, then we'll say she made a choice in pursuit of her own ends.

* * * [T]his outcome cannot sit well in law and economics because of how much it gives away. * * * Posner "assumes that adding an account of 'nonrationality' in market relations would be tantamount to abandoning theory entirely in favor of a mere all-inclusive description of empirical behavior lacking any explanatory or predictive power." He concludes that "behavioral economics merely describes human actions [and does a poor job of doing so] but has no theory of action." * * *

* * * [T]he dilemma for law and economics is clear. Neoclassical assertions of rationality—abstract, laboratory-crystalline, severed from ordinary experience—stray too far from empirical fact to explain or predict much. Posner's "rational frog" expresses this limitation succinctly: we believe the frog pursues her own ends, but we have nothing but her behavior to look at when we seek support for that belief. To the extent that economic analysts accept variety in human behavior, especially behavior that defies well-ordered pursuit of transparent ends, they became less able to explain and predict because they have conceded that human behavior is either random or, alternatively, obedient to some logic alien to the rational actor model, and thus beyond their ken.

Economic analysts regret this defeat and hope they can undo it. "Deviations from the rational-actor assumption can and should be incorporated into economic analysis," declares the Harvard law and economics website. The cooptation strategy cannot, however, readily accommodate material so contrary to a first principle of economic analysis.

2. Efficiency vs. Wealth Maximization vs. Welfare.—What do, or should, individuals or societies or legal systems choose to pursue? Economic analysts have shuttled between terms to describe the goal. Two leading contenders have been "efficiency" (or sometimes allocative "efficiency") and "wealth maximization." A third term, "welfare," has arisen more recently. None is stable. * * *

If "efficiency" stands in for utilitarianism, Posner argued, then efficiency is inferior to wealth maximization as a description of what individuals and societies pursue, or should be understood as pursuing. Utilitarianism, in Posner's rendering, seeks a "surplus of pleasure over pain," but gives its followers no guidance as to whose pleasure counts (are animals included?), no distinction between average and total happiness, and no metric to evaluate success and failure. Wealth maximization as an alternative ideal avoids these difficulties by insisting on "value in dollars or dollar equivalents." In Posner's summation: The only kind of preference that counts in a system of wealth maximization is thus one that is backed up by money—in other words, that is registered in a market. * * *

The reliance on prices adds other complications to the wealth maximization criterion. * * * Price is a function of demand, and demand will vary in response to preexisting distributions of wealth. It is thus idle—or instead politically significant, . . . —to contemplate wealth maximization without attention to how much wealth each maximizer already has. With a dollar the only metric and with the marginal utility of money a sure fact, wealth maximization "has the result of weighting the preferences of wealthy persons more heavily than the preferences of poorer persons"—that is, the rich get extra ballots in the form of dollars they don't need to save. *Tant pis* for wealth maximization.

Following this critique of the wealth-maximization criterion, "welfare" has arisen as a kind of successor to the old precursor of wealth maximization, "efficiency." Louis Kaplow and Steven Shavell have led the charge among economic analysts to promote this word as summation of what societies and individuals pursue. To many, welfare seems more capacious, perhaps more humanistic, than "efficiency" or any other word standing in for utilitarianism. Yet because it does not repair what "wealth maximization" once purported to fix—that is, vagueness, indeterminacy, disagreements about measurement—"welfare" carries economic analysts back to their old condition of not being able to describe what they seek.

We see here a dilemma similar to that which haunts the economist's view of rational choice. The movement can cling to "efficiency" and remain vulnerable to criticisms about tautology, circularity, vagueness, and evasion of pertinent political questions. Alternatively, it can focus on "wealth maximization," a path that adds misdescription to the mix and cannot escape similar perils of tautology. Or try "welfare," which in application cannot be distinguished from efficiency and its perils.

3. Faith in Markets.—Following *The Problem of Social Cost*, both descriptive and normative strands of law and economics evinced some enthusiasm for what they called "the market." Coase had recharacterized costs. Whereas earlier thinking, following Pigou, had seen costs as detriments that one entity imposes on another, to Coase costs were instead phenomena that obstructed market functions. The market, always central in all of microeconomics, took on after Coase even more fundamental importance to its cousin law and economics. Efficiency, for instance, could be defined as the outcome that a free market would produce. In this normative sense, the existence of a market makes efficiency (or wealth maximization) possible.

The normative truism about markets making wealth has not much occupied law and economics. In an alternative, descriptive sense, however, law and economics has seen markets wherever human beings deal with one another, including venues far from commercial transactions. Marriage and family formation take place in markets, according to Gary Becker and others. Individuals negotiate their sexual relations as trades. Scarce body parts like kidneys, say economists, could profitably become the objects of regulated exchange. The adoption of infants takes place within a market whether we like it or not, said Posner in the famously career-thwarting paper he wrote with Elisabeth Landes. Gestational surrogacy for pay is a service that American law has long been condoning. * * * In a recent essay, Claire Hill defends the faith-in-markets perspective within law and economics, and urges "skeptics" who don't want to see markets applied to "the personal sphere" to reconsider their position.

Yet even if "the market" can shed light on "the personal sphere," the law and economics project of identifying unseen markets—in human bodies and intimate associations and the like—seems to have run its course. At the risk of signing a death certificate before the patient has died, and thus compelling myself to lie next to Morton Horwitz and Owen Fiss, I will venture to say that today "the market" does not account for much novelty or centrality in this field, neither its normative nor its more recent descriptive versions. Coase's masterpiece, always amenable to divergent readings, now sounds like a warning that markets always fail, rather than a promise that exchange will work perfectly after the friction of transaction costs has been removed.

Accompanying this decline of the market in law and economics scholarship, a generation of writings skeptical of this institution has taken critical hold. The most important external criticism of the market appears in literature on "incommensurability" and "commodification." Work in this genre rejects the market insofar as this artifact assigns a cash value to anything capable of being transferred from one possessor to another. The leading scholar in this field identifies her thesis, first expressed in her title *Market-Inalienability*, as directly hostile to law and economics, whose "methodological archetype" she calls "universal commodification."

* * *

* * * "[M]arket failure" has become almost as familiar a phrase in law and economics as "the market" itself. Same recipe as the one that cooked up "behavioral economics": When truisms fail, or get refuted, reassert ownership of all material under question by adding a layer of counter-jargon. * * *

II. What Little Remains of Law and Economics

Now that rational choice, utilitarianism, efficiency, wealth maximization, markets, predictive power, and coherence have been questioned, abandoned, or smudged beyond recognition, the list of essential features defining law and economics gets shorter. I offer here all I could come up with: only three items, and even that small total contains some redundancy.

A. *The Policymaker Ascendant*

The insightful critic Jeanne Schroeder has noticed something central to law and economics that seems to have escaped members of the movement and other observers: "Law and economics is a policy science," whereas some other sectors of jurisprudence have no desire to form policy or, as Schroder puts it, "give advice to the government." Not everyone writing scholarship about the law takes the perspective of the legislator or a judge. One important contributor, the "speculative theorist or critical legal scholar," instead focuses on "the position of the governed—those who are subjected to the law." * * *

* * *

Here, then, we see a piece of what remains in law and economics: an inclination to address governing entities more than governed individuals as ends of inquiry in themselves. Desires or resistances of human beings enter policymaking only in the aggregate. While the critical legal scholar works to "free the legal subject from manipulation by the law," the policymaker works to articulate the best manipulation.

* * *

* * * [A]s soon as law and economics lost its distinctive character (thanks to too much refutation and too much acceptance), its adherents lost their basis for dividing the legal academy into members and nonmembers. Nevertheless their inclination to sort people into two piles without transparent criteria for division—the kind of dichotomous sorting that a Jeanne Schroder-style "cult" would do—remains. Unconstrained by genuine criteria for membership, decisionmakers in the academy and beyond—to the extent that law and economics extends beyond law schools—are now free to substitute prejudices for standards.

The most widely suspected prejudice is of political conservatism. Consider the possibility that

> facile assumptions have been carefully chosen to push forward a politically conservative agenda. Viewed in this light, the choreography is unsurpassed. First, equate utility with ability to pay, but assume away the issue of initial wealth distribution and bargaining inequalities. Next, combine with the inevitability of common-law efficiency. The result is a bias away from government regulation toward a nineteenth-century, almost Lochneresque, laissez-faire conception of the primacy of private law. The ability of good rhetoric to make this all appear natural is remarkable.

* * *

IV.   CONCLUSION: WHERE NOW?

* * * Writers frequently depict law and economics as an aging giant. Their metaphors of decline and old age perhaps rush too fast to judgment: In addition to premature proclamations of death, and wishful thinking that the movement had "peaked," the literature on law and economics includes a 1991 claim about a "mid-life crisis." I have already fretted about hurrying to entomb law and economics. That said, this birthday of a great book, marking indeed "a generation of influence," does invite thought about the state of the movement it helped inaugurate.

Conceding that dichotomous thinkers within the law and economics movement might be inclined to classify the reflections in this Article as hostile to their cause, I maintain that the Article has depicted law and economics as evolving, rather than entirely refuted or spent. This Article has indeed argued that the core tenets of the movement are refuted and spent. It has also contended that law and economics has failed to rescue itself by its tactic of trying to claim for itself various refutations of these tenets. But my reflections find a paradox in law and economics: the movement while deteriorating has been thriving. It reached heights scaled by no other jurisprudential school. Its success has consisted mainly of telling lawyers, lawmakers, and legal scholars how and why they must keep their eye on the welfare ball when making policy—but it has also fostered other triumphs: the importation of interdisciplinary findings into law and across campuses; the insistence on (if not quite the achievement of) empirical research as integral to legal policy; and the touch of science—whose perils and pretensions I have noted but that also can spur lawyers to reach for more rigorous work.

* * *

———

NOTES AND QUESTIONS

1. Scientific discipline or cult? Bernstein makes two distinct, but related arguments: First, that law and economics cannot sustain its claim to scientific rigor. Second, that its adherents maintain their influence through policing membership in the genre according to prospective members' willingness to advance a politically conservative agenda. This, she concludes, is a cult—a secular belief system rooted in libertarianism.

    a. Scientific Discipline? As we discussed in chapter 1, law and economics distinguishes itself from other genres of legal thought by claiming to be objective and scientific. Posner asserts that: "the concept of rationality used by the economist is objective rather than subjective . . ." If, as Bernstein argues, the scientific foundations of law and economics have "disappeared into the sand," what is left of its contribution to modern legal thought?

    b. Cult. Is Bernstein's argument on this point internally contradictory? On one hand, she argues that law and economics has preserved itself by inclusion: "Unable to do much about errors, [law and economics scholars] worked on the second front, the crisis of too much acceptance, mainly by trying to claim successful outsider movements as their own, rather than reacting to them as threats or challenges. When psychology dealt blows to the ideal of a rational actor, for instance, economic analysts invoked the label of 'behavioral economics' to describe claims that were directly contrary to neoclassical dogma." Bernstein, *supra*, at 104. On the other hand, she claims that they have preserved their intellectual identity by exclusion.

Yet cults . . . are social groups. They contain members who disdain nonmembers, and who have been known to enjoy thinking that outsiders feel hostility towards them. . . . [L]aw and economics now functions mainly as a faculty club with opaque, arbitrary criteria for membership. . . .

Unconstrained by genuine criteria for membership, decisionmakers in the academy . . . are now free to substitute prejudices for standards.

The most widely suspected prejudice is of political conservatism.

Id. at 105, 129.

Can both criticisms be true?

2. Law and economics as political ideology. Another claim made by external critics of law and economics is that, as Bernstein suggests, it is not "objective" but rather provides scientific-appearing justifications for conservative and libertarian political leanings. (We explored the connection between Milton Friedman's economics and his politics in chapter 3.) Martha McCluskey argues that the first wave of law and economics was a political project, or at least closely aligned with a political project:

In the 1970s, a number of wealthy right-wing activists organized to make theory a basic part of their political strategy. One leader of this political campaign, former Republican Treasury Secretary William E. Simon, wrote two best-selling books outlining a strategy which he then implemented as a longtime president of the John M. Olin Foundation. Simon argued that '[t]he alliance between the theorists and men of action in the capitalist world is long overdue in America. It must become a veritable crusade if we are to survive in freedom.' Simon further argued that corporate profits needed to 'rush by [the] multimillions' to provide 'intellectual refuges for the non-egalitarian scholars and writers . . . [who] must be given grants, grants and more grants in exchange for books, books and more books.' Simon explained that the goal must not just be to take sides in existing controversies, but to open up the 'basic premises of these controversies' for debate and to produce a new 'counterintelligentsia' capable of setting the terms of the debate. * * * Simon's work built on a similar well publicized call for right-wing theory by Lewis Powell in 1971, shortly before his appointment to the Supreme Court. Working with the Chamber of Commerce, Powell advocated an organized system of financial support for conservative scholars, media, educational textbooks, and public speakers who could promote American free enterprise and develop an attack on political 'liberals.' * * *

Legal theory was at the center of this radical vision to mobilize intellectuals for the right. By the end of the twentieth century, the Olin Foundation, under William E. Simon's leadership, had made an 'investment' of around $50 million in 'law-and-economics' scholarship. Looking back at that foundation's history, the succeeding executive director James Piereson attributed its success in maximizing political 'dividends' to its strategic 'investment in ideas.' According to Piereson, the Olin Foundation was designed to heed a 'call to arms' in 'defense of capitalism.' Right-wing leaders realized that this defense of 'commercial civilization' required a 'full-blown engagement with the world of ideas' that would discuss not just business but 'deeper cultural assumptions' about the 'rule of law, religion, the family and the evolution of our political institutions.' * * *

Following their view of theory as part of foundation-shaking, consciously revolutionary political mission, the right-wing foundations have enhanced the institutional connections between scholarship and practical politics through two methods that differ from their 'more genteel' centrist and 'liberal' counterparts. First, the new conservative foundations solidified and sustained a strong ideological direction in the scholarship they funded by rejecting the governance structure common among long-established centrist groups like the Ford Foundation, which tended to disperse control among a large and diverse group of board members and staff with a broader range of viewpoints and backgrounds than their founders. Instead, wealthy conservative activists structured their foundations to centralize control among a small, interlocking group of business executives sharing a sharply focused political vision. * * *

In a second tactic for bridging the gap between scholarship and politics, the new right-wing funding for intellectuals has included substantial resources devoted to marketing theoretical work to popular media, lobbyists, grassroots activists, lawyers, politicians, and judges. Scholarship, in this view, is not a collegial quest for truth or pleasure (and not simply a way to provide a nice middle-class income and lifestyle for academics). Instead, leading contemporary right-wing activists have viewed intellectual work as part of a strategic business plan that can produce large returns for their donors in a tough competition for power and profit. * * *

As a particularly important part of their plan for ensuring theory's impact, conservative 'venture capital[ists]' developed a large network of interconnected think tanks. In the 1990s, these right-wing think tanks spent over one billion dollars, and had become 'the key generator and purveyor of public ideas,' according to a study by liberal philanthropists. One of these, the Heritage Foundation, explains its power by noting that ' "traditional" think tanks cling to the notion that their work will leave its imprint on Washington through a process of osmosis. Heritage efforts are deliberate and straightforward.' Twenty percent of the Heritage Foundation's 2002 spending, for example, went to media and government relations and another twenty-one percent went to educational programs. Similarly, the conservative John M. Olin Foundation funds not only the production of ideas in think tanks, law schools, law professors, law students, and Law and Economics theory workshops, but also spends lavishly to disseminate and implement these ideas through conservative publications, public interest law firms, judicial training, and, through their board members and senior staff, Republican political candidates. * * *

[T]he Olin Foundation has made the development of the Law and Economics branch of legal theory a long-term priority over the last twenty years. A founding organizer of this right-wing legal theory reflected that the field might have fizzled out in the late 1970s or early 1980s if John M. Olin had not decided to use his gun and chemical company wealth to fund academic fellows who could promote a conservative economic vision. After Olin's death, the John M. Olin Foundation continued and expanded its 'enormous' financial support for Law and Economics scholarship with the effect of producing an 'organized program in every major law school in the country (and several in Canada)' by 1986, along with numerous journals, textbooks, and conferences. By the 1990s, this support had continued to develop into a prominent professional society and a specialized law school (George Mason), with the result that '[n]o other intellectual paradigm in legal education could begin to match the power of law and economics.'

Martha T. McCluskey, *Thinking With Wolves: Left Legal Theory After the Right's Rise*, 54 BUFF. L.REV. 1191, 1213–22 (2007). Is the source of a movement's funding relevant to the truth of its ideas? Does McCluskey's narrative fail to account for the history of the discipline of economics, which predates law and economics?

3. Policy science? Legal scholar Jeanne Schroeder suggests that "law and economics is policy science ... [that] seeks to give advice to the government." Jeanne L. Schroeder, *Rationality in Law and Economics Scholarship*, 79 OR. L. REV. 147, 151 (2000). If this observation is convincing, would this make law and economics an oxymoron: a movement to reduce the sphere of government power, whose primary function now is giving advice to the government?

B.   NORMATIVE CRITIQUES OF ECONOMIC ANALYSIS

The normative challenges to law and economics span a broad range of contentions. Scholars have challenged virtually all of the central concepts and techniques of modern law and economics, including rational choice, efficiency, cost benefit analysis, wealth maximization, and the relationship between preferences expressed as monetary units and democratic participation in markets and governance.

What all the critics share, however, despite their different targets, is a commitment to moral analysis as prior to economic analysis. "Justice" is a major theme of the external critics of law and economics. For these scholars, the question "What is just?" must come before "What is efficient?"

James Boyd White sets the stage for examining justice challenges to economic analysis by suggesting that economic analysis comes with a set of values which he describes as "materialist." In contrast, White argues for "humanist" values, which for him revolve around "fundamental moral and political equality among human beings," White's moral critique of economic analysis sets the stage for the more specific criticisms that follow.

1. ECONOMIC ANALYSIS AND MORAL ANALYSIS: AN INTRODUCTION TO THE TENSIONS

Economics and Law: Two Cultures in Tension

54 TENN. L. REV. 161, 166–67, 172–73, 174–75, 178, 182–83, 184–85, 191–93 (1986).

■ JAMES BOYD WHITE

* * *

Many people think of economics solely as a scientific, conceptual, and cognitive system, apparently unaware that there are any other dimensions of meaning in economic talk. But all expression is loaded with values, ethical and otherwise; all expression defines a self and another and proposes a relation between them; all expression remakes its language; in these senses all expression proposes the creation of a community and a culture. All expression, in short, is ethical, cultural, and political, and it can be analyzed and judged as such. To claim that economics is a science is perhaps to claim that it cannot be judged in such terms. But "sciences" are cultures too, with their own created worlds and values. One way to describe my aim * * *, then, is to say that it reverses the usual flow: we are used to economic analyses of this or that aspect of our common life—voting, the family, war, etc. I propose here to begin what I would call a rhetorical or cultural analysis of a certain kind of economics.

* * *

IV. ECONOMICS AS A SYSTEM OF VALUES

We can start with the question of value. In its purest form economics claims to be a value-free social science. But as I suggested earlier I think it in fact enacts a set of values, including political ones, values to which the speaker of the language cannot avoid finding himself at least in part committed.

A. In the World

Think, for example, of the way in which economics defines the economic actor and the processes by which he functions. He is for the most part assumed to be an individual of indeterminate age, sex, race and cultural background, but of adequate competence at manipulating economic relations. He acts as one who is both perfectly aware of his own wishes and wholly rational—in the special sense in which that term is used, to mean "calculating"—in his pursuit of them. He exists as an individual, not as part of a community, except insofar as he establishes contractual or exchange relations with others. He is assumed to be motivated by self-interest, which in turn is defined in terms of competition, acquisition, and dominion, at least in relation to resources and other actors, for in the process of exchange the self is reduced to those desires.

Of course a particular individual may have other values—indeed the economist insists that he must, calling them "tastes" or "preferences"— perhaps including a "taste" for altruism, for peace and quiet, for heavy metal music, for appreciating nature unspoiled, for beautiful or ugly art, and so forth. These values will drive his participation in the exchange process, or his decision to withdraw from it. But in either case they are themselves valued by the method of exchange: either by an actual exchange that takes place or by a hypothetical or imagined exchange that is forgone (or in a more complicated case by a combination of exchanges made and forgone). In both cases these external values are converted by the discourse into the acquisitive or instrumental values—the desire to extend the dominion of the will—that all economic actors are assumed to have, for this is the only kind of value about which economics can directly talk.

With respect to the external values in their original form, the system is purportedly "value neutral." That is, it regards individual values as simply exogenous to the system itself. Economics of course recognizes that these values exist, but it demeans them by calling them "tastes" or "preferences," names that imply that no serious conversation can proceed on such subjects and economics itself is by definition not about those values, but about the process by which they are reflected in the activity of exchange. This means that economics cannot, in principle, talk about any value other than the acquisitive or instrumental one that it universalizes. (Indeed it does not talk about this value either, but merely assumes and acts upon it.) This is not to be "value free," as its apologists claim, but to make self-interest the central, indeed almost the only, value, for it is the only one that can be talked about in these terms. To come at it the other way, it is to claim that all values can be talked about, at least for some purposes, as if they were selfish, quantifiable, and interchangeable.

* * *

Yet economics is troubling not only for the self-interested values it directly asserts, but also for the very neutrality, the "value freedom," that it claims. It is in principle neutral on all questions of value that are external to the acquisitive and competitive ones enacted in the exchange game, which it lumps together as "tastes" or "preferences" among which no distinctions can be drawn. But this is to be silent on all the great questions of human life: questions of beauty and ugliness in art and music, sincerity and falsity in human relations, wisdom and folly in conduct and judgment, and the greatest of all questions, which is how we ought to lead our lives. Economic analysis assumes as a given the existence of "tastes" or "preferences" which drive the system, but economics as a language can provide no way of talking about these values, whether in oneself or another, no way of thinking about which to prefer and which not. To the extent that economics does reach out for these questions it may be worse than silent, for silence after all can be a mode of controlling a discourse. When economics tries to speak about these matters it does so in the only way it knows how to speak, in purely quantitative terms and on the assumption that all human transactions can be reduced to the model of exchange.

* * *

For the purposes of economic analysis all human wishes and desires are thus reduced to the same level, as though no principled choices could be made among them, as though it didn't matter what choices one made. This in turn means that it is impossible to talk in these terms about our most important choices as individuals and communities, or about the education of mind or heart, for any impulse that we or others may happen to have is as good, valid, and entitled to respect as any other.

* * * We must and do have preferences, as the economist knows; and these necessarily commit those who have them to the inquiry of better and worse, as well as to that of greater and less. To refuse to engage in this inquiry—to privatize it—as economics in its neutral phase necessarily does, is to deny an essential and necessary aspect of human life. To reduce all value to self-interest, as it does the rest of the time, is intellectually and ethically intolerable. How could one educate one's children or oneself to live in a world that was neutral on all the great questions of life, except that it reduced them to acquisition, competition, and calculation?

* * *

The second ground upon which the market is justified is that not of its gross effects but of its fairness. In one version this justification rests upon the ethical standing of voluntary action and holds that the results of the market process are justified with respect to every actor because the choices by which the market works are voluntary. In another version, it becomes the affirmative celebration of autonomy or liberty: whether or not it is efficient, the market is good because it gives the widest possible range to freedom of choice and action. Here the claim moves beyond justifying market results by the voluntary character of the choices upon which they rest to the point of asserting autonomy as the central social and political value. The obvious trouble with this line of defense, in both of its forms, is that it assumes that all exchanges are for all actors equally voluntary and equally expressive of autonomy, a position that common sense denies.

* * *

The market purports to rest upon an assumption of the equality of all the actors in the system. In fact, it rests upon a different assumption, namely, the equality of every dollar in the system. Since some players have many more dollars, and through this fact are at a competitive advantage, it is a system that actively supports inequality among its actors.

It is not too much to say, I think, that the modern celebration of the market as the central social institution—the most fair, the most respecting of autonomy, and the most efficient—threatens to destroy the single greatest achievement of Western political culture: the discovery that a community can govern itself through a rule of law that attempts to create a fundamental moral and political equality among human beings. The great phrase in the Declaration of Independence—"all men are created equal"—is partly a theological statement about the conditions under which we are created and partly a political statement about the obligation of the government to acknowledge, indeed to create or recreate, that equality. This value is the heart of what is meant both by equality under law and by our democratic institutions more generally, resting as they do on the premise that each person's vote is worth exactly what everyone else's is. The ideology of the market, if it prevailed in its desire to convert all institutions into markets, would destroy this set of political relations and would create another in its stead, based upon the dollar.

* * *

The market ideology claims to be radically democratic and egalitarian because it leaves every person free to do with her own what she will. But this freedom of choice is not equally distributed among all people. The market is democratic not on the principle of one person one vote, but on the far different principle of one dollar, one vote. One could hardly make a greater mistake than to equate, as so much modern public talk carelessly does, the "free market" with democracy.

There are two distinct points here. First, the exchange transactions that the market celebrates are not entitled to the special respect claimed for them as free and voluntary, and hence fair, unless each person has roughly the same amount of money and the same competence and freedom in its use, which is demonstrably not the case. The accumulations of wealth it permits thus cannot be justified by the fairness of the transactions by which the accumulation occurs. Second, if the advocates of the market succeeded in converting other institutions into markets, the result would be to transfer to those who have wealth not only the economic power that inescapably follows it but also the political power that in our democratic tradition the people have claimed for themselves and have exercised through the institutions of self-government. This would validate and institutionalize private economic power held by one person over another, of the rich over the poor. If we were to yield entirely to its claims, we would gradually find our traditional government, which operates by collective deliberation on a premise of fundamental equality of citizens, replaced by a private-sector government of the few over the many, wholly unregulated by collective judgment.

* * *

VI.   ECONOMICS AS A SYSTEM OF ECONOMIC ANALYSIS
D.   Erasing Community

For similar reasons this kind of economics has the greatest difficulty in reflecting the reality of human community and the value of communal institutions. Its necessary tendency seems to be to destroy the idea of public action, indeed the idea of community itself. This is partly because this methodology tends to resolve all communities and organizations into the individual human actors who constitute them, partly because commitment to the market system leads one to think that everything that can be made the subject of the market should be. The idea is that every economic actor should pay for what he wants, and should not have to pay for what he doesn't want. But this tends to destroy our public institutions, all of which extend benefits far beyond those who would pay (if they were reduced to markets) or who do pay (when they are supported by taxes). Such institutions reflect a communal judgment that we need to educate ourselves and each other, that our "tastes" are not all of equal value but need to be formed, and formed well rather than badly. Public universities, libraries, orchestras, museums, parks—all these would fall before the ideology that denies the existence and reality of community and reduces all institutions, all human production, to the language of the market.

Think here of the way economists explain why people who will probably never visit, say, the Everglades or an art museum are happy to have their taxes used to maintain them. The economist says it is because the actor wants to maintain the option of visiting them some day, and calls this an "option demand." But may it not be that the voter simply takes pleasure in what other people have and in what other people can do, in belonging to a community that is good for all its members? Or that he respects their desires and wants a community based on that kind of mutual respect? This possibility is systematically denied by the assumption of economic talk, that individuals and communities are in principle incapable of generosity, or more precisely, that "altruism" can adequately be talked about as a species of selfishness.

The language of self and self-interest not only fails to reflect the reality of community and of shared interests, it draws attention away from those aspects of life and devalues them. To continue to talk on these assumptions, even hypothetically, is to encourage "self-interest" in an ethical sense and to erode the commitments we have to each other that underlie such essential practices of citizenship as the willingness to pay taxes, to work for the local school, or to serve in the army, upon which everything depends. To adopt the economic view would in fact threaten the very existence of community, for on these premises no one would conceivably die or seriously risk his life for his community: at the point of danger one's self-interest in survival would outweigh all other self-interests. And to speak of all "tastes" as if they were equivalent is to invite oneself and others to think that they are, and to confirm the premises of our culture, already drummed into the mind by the consumer economy, that the consumer is king, that whatever you happen to want is a good that you should seek to satisfy, that no distinction can be drawn between the beautiful and ugly, the wise and foolish, and so on. It is to confirm a vulgar view of democracy that makes the preference or will supreme, as if we functioned by instant referendum. It erases the sense that a democracy is a mode of communal self-constitution and self-education that may have higher ends than the satisfaction of wants, namely the creation of a community of a certain sort, at once based upon a set of responsibilities and offering us a set of opportunities for civic and social action.

* * *

NOTES AND QUESTIONS

1. When rational is wrong. White argues that the central defect of law and economics is that it is a scholarly discipline that masks its commitment to materialism with scientific precepts that do not withstand close scrutiny of their value-laden premises that elevate materialism over fairness.

The challenge for scholars working with both economics and the injuries of subordination is to create an alternative to the economic vocabulary for understanding how humans accumulate the resources to fulfill their basic needs. Since Adam Smith, the vocabulary of rationality has been dominant. In the following, Charles Pouncy argues for a "robust expression" of the "concept of economic justice" as an alternative to the neoclassical lexicon:

> Economic justice is not a concern of neoclassical theory. Neoclassical theory is not designed to achieve economic justice, and in fact intervenes to prevent it.
>
> *Id.* at 23.
>
> Neoclassical theory intervenes in consensus reality to support the notion of colorblind economics, an economic system in which markets negate the impact of irrational criteria, such as race, in economic decision-making.
>
> *Id.* at 28.
>
> Neoclassical theory works in concert with the preservative nature of law to prevent the development of a jurisprudence of economic justice.
>
> *Id.*
>
> Racism and classism are insulated from approbation by . . . economic rationality.
>
> *Id.* at 17.
>
> When we combine the belief that the individual is the proper unit of economic analysis and that individuals base their decisions on their perception of their own best interests, then discrimination and racism are transformed from indicia of hatred or irrational hatred to good business decisions.
>
> *Id.* at 20.

Charles R.P. Pouncy, *Economic Justice and Economic Theory: Limiting the Reach of Neoclassical Ideology*, 14 U. FLA. J. L. & PUB. POL'Y 11, 11 (2002). Is Pouncy persuasive in his critique? How should we go about making decisions about production, distribution, and exchange based on "justice"? If the individual is not the proper unit of economic analysis, what is?

2. Effect of terminology on White's critique. White states that "all systems of discourse commit their users to values . . . [and that] economics is [not] wrong to do what it does." James Boyd White, *Economics and Law: Two Cultures in Tension*, 54 TENN. L. REV. 161, 176 (1986). If all White wishes is for economics to acknowledge that it is no different from other systems of discourse, does his critique of law and economics have any value? Would the problems White identifies with law and economics be solved by acknowledging that law and economics has values without making any substantive changes to the discipline? Would White be satisfied with such a solution?

3. The pernicious nature of law and economics. At the close of his article, White states that "to continue to talk on . . . [law and economics'] assumptions, even hypothetically, is to encourage 'self interest' in an ethical sense and to erode the commitments we have to each other that underlie such essential practices of citizenship as the willingness to pay taxes, to work for the local school, or to serve in the army, upon which everything depends. To adopt the economic view would in fact threaten the very existence of community . . ." *Id.* at 192. If White is correct about the dire consequences of even hypothesizing in an economic framework, how can he assert that economics is not wrong to "do what it does?" *Id.* at 176.

2. ECONOMIC ANALYSIS AND THE CRITIQUE FROM SUBORDINATION

Why Markets Don't Stop Discrimination

Free Markets and Social Justice 3–9, 151–63 (1997).

■ Cass R. Sunstein

Free markets are often defended as an engine of economic productivity, and properly so. But they are also said to be required for social justice, and here things become far more complex. Certainly there are connections between free markets and social justice. A system aspiring to social justice aspires to liberty, and a system of free markets seems to promise liberty, because it allows people to trade goods and services as they wish. In fact, a system of free markets seems to promise not merely liberty but equality of an important sort as well, since everyone in a free market is given an equal right to transact and participate in market arrangements. This form of equality should not be trivialized or disparaged. For example, race and sex discrimination has often consisted of exclusions of certain classes of people from the market domain. In both South America and the United States, discriminatory practices frequently took the form of incursions on free markets in employment. * * *

This * * * is not, however, a simple celebration of free markets, and it raises a number of questions about economic analysis of law in its conventional form. Free markets can produce economic inefficiency and (worse) a great deal of injustice. Even well-functioning economic markets should not be identified with freedom itself. Freedom is a complex notion, to say the least, and free markets can sharply limit freedom as that term is usually understood. In fact, free markets depend on a range of coercive legal interventions, including the law of property, which can be a serious intrusion on the freedom of people who lack ownership rights. And it should not be necessary to emphasize that important forms of equality—including race and sex equality—can be undermined, not promoted, by free markets. Race discrimination is often fueled by market forces.

Moreover, economics—at least as it is used in the conventional economic analysis of law—often works with tools that, while illuminating, may be crude or lead to important errors. Consider, for example, descriptive or "positive" economics. The economic analysis of law has been built on a certain conception of human rationality, in which people are seen as "rational profit-maximizers." For some purposes, this is a helpful foundation. Certainly it is true that most people try, most of the time, to find ways of promoting their own ends. But it is not always clear in what sense human beings can be said to be "rational" or "profit-maximizers." The motivational foundations of human behavior have enormous complexity. Sometimes people do not seem at all rational. Sometimes they are ignorant and sometimes they seem to defeat their own goals. * * *

* * * If we turn to the evaluative side—to questions about what the law should be or do—economic analysis of law encounters equally serious problems. In its usual form, economics offers an inadequate understanding of social welfare. Often it is concerned with the satisfaction of existing preferences. This is far from an unworthy goal; the frustration of peoples' preferences can lead to misery and injustice. But in any society, existing preferences should not be taken as natural or sacrosanct. They are a function of context. Sometimes they are a product of deprivation, injustice, or excessive limits in available opportunities.

Moreover, the economists' conception of social welfare is too "flat," insofar as it evaluates diverse social goods along the same metric. People care about things not just in terms of amounts, but also in different ways. Some human goods, like cash, are simply for use. But people value things for reasons other than use. They respect other people; sometimes they love each other; they see some things, like a painting or a beach, as objects of awe and wonder. A well-functioning legal system attempts to make space for people's diverse valuation of diverse human goods. This point bears on the uses and the limits of free markets. * * *

I argue that under plausible assumptions and in many settings, markets will not stop discrimination and that reliance on competitive pressures would be a grave mistake for a government intending to eliminate discriminatory practices. Indeed, markets are often the problem rather than the solution. They guarantee that discrimination will persist. Enthusiasm for markets as an anti-discrimination policy is at best wishful thinking.

I. Why Markets Produce Discrimination: Standard Accounts

As a provisional matter, let us define discrimination as a decision by a market actor to treat one person differently from another because that person is black or female. It is irrelevant for present purposes whether the differential treatment is based on hostility, fear, taste, unconscious devaluation, selective empathy and indifference, employer self-interest, unwarranted generalizations, or an accurate perception of facts about group members.* * *

On one view, the notion that competitive markets act against discrimination, so defined, might seem odd or even idiosyncratic. In the history of the United States as well as other nations, markets and discrimination have accompanied one another at numerous points and in numerous places. Surely, governmentally imposed discrimination, because of its centralized character, has especially egregious effects; but to point to the comparative strength of collective controls is not to say that decentralized markets work in the opposite direction. Indeed, there is good empirical evidence that government programs have succeeded in reducing discrimination produced by the market. The enactment of civil rights legislation appears to have led to increases in black and female employment in various sectors. At least in general, the disputed question has to do not with the direction of change but with the degree of the improvement.

Moreover, study after study has shown that the market often devalues the products and enterprises of both blacks and women. This should not be surprising. In a system with a significant amount of race and sex prejudice, covert and overt, conscious and unconscious, the "willingness to pay" criterion—as it is reflected in the purchasing and selling decisions of employers, employees, consumers, and others—will ensure that those subject to discriminatory attitudes will be at a comparative disadvantage in the market. At least this is so when the participation of disfavored groups is highly visible, as indeed it often is. In this context, the most natural initial judgment is that if discrimination is the problem, markets are hardly the solution.

But the judgment, as stated, seems too crude. Suppose a set of companies in a competitive industry—call them "D companies"—decides not to sell to or employ an identifiable segment of the community; suppose too that the D companies must compete with nondiscriminators engaged in the same line of work ("ND companies"). In the long run, the D companies should be at a significant disadvantage. They will be unable to draw on as large a pool of workers; they will be unable to sell to as large a group of purchasers. In practice, their discriminatory behavior will place a tax on their operations. To say the least, businesses that impose on themselves a tax not faced by their competitors are unlikely to fare well.

As patrons and prospective employees drift to ND companies, the D companies will be driven out. Eventually, the consequences should be nothing short of disastrous for discrimination in general. It is this understanding that accounts for the plausible claim that an effective antidiscrimination policy consists of reliance on decentralized markets.

Notwithstanding its plausibility (and even, in some settings, its accuracy), I want in this section to make three arguments against this claim. In setting out these arguments, I make no claim to special originality. All of them can be found, at least in some form, in standard economic discussions of the problem.

Third Parties

An influential approach to the problem of discrimination, captured in the account just offered, attributes the phenomenon to employers' "taste" for discrimination. On this view, employers discriminate because they do not like to associate with blacks, women, or others. The engine that drives discrimination is employer preferences—not economic self-interest, narrowly defined. Indeed, economic self-interest is in conflict with employers' taste for discrimination. This idea has a degree of truth to it; certainly, it explains many practices by employers. But sometimes discrimination is caused by employer practices that result precisely from economic self-interest, rather than from the employer's noneconomic goals. The reason is that third parties are frequently in a position to impose financial punishments on nondiscriminatory employers. Suppose, for example, that purchasers or fellow employees refuse to buy from or work for a company that does not discriminate. Third parties can pressure employers in the direction of discrimination, even if employers would, other things being equal, choose not to discriminate or have no particular view about whether to discriminate or not. Ironically, it is the failure to discriminate that operates as a tax on the employer's business, rather than vice versa. And when this is so, reliance on competitive pressures will force employers to behave in a discriminatory manner if they wish to survive.

The phenomenon is hardly unusual. Consider, for example, a shopkeeper whose customers do not like dealing with blacks or women; a commercial airline whose patrons react unfavorably to female pilots; a university whose students and alumni prefer a primarily male or white faculty; a law firm whose clients prefer not to have black lawyers; or a hospital whose patients are uncomfortable with female doctors or black nurses. The persistence of private segregation in major league baseball is a familiar example of this phenomenon.

In all of these cases, market pressures create rather than prevent discrimination. An employer who wants to act nondiscriminatorily will be punished, not rewarded. Indeed, an employer who wants not to be a discriminator will be engaging in what is, from his point of view, a form of affirmative action. From his point of view, discrimination is in fact neutral, in the sense that it is a quite ordinary form of profit-maximization through catering to consumer demand. From his point of view, a refusal to discriminate is also economically harmful to him; if he is a nondiscriminator, it is not for the sake of profits, but in order to promote the long-range goal of race and sex equality. If discrimination is to be eliminated, it may well be as a result of legal rules forbidding discrimination from continuing.

Ideas of precisely this sort played a role in the passage of the Civil Rights Act of 1964. Many restaurants and hotels sought regulation constraining their own behavior by outlawing discrimination. Their goal was to obtain the force of the law to overcome the effects of private racism (in the form of violence as well as competitive sanctions). They sought to overcome, through law, the discrimination-producing consequences of market pressures. They sought to "hide behind the law" to do what, in a sense, they wanted to do: to behave nondiscriminatorily. Without the force of law, they would encounter third-party pressures, including social norms * * *, that would push them in the direction of discrimination.

On this account, it remains necessary to explain why third parties are not themselves hurt by their "taste." At least part of the reason lies in the fact that third parties often are not market actors in the ordinary sense—that is, they will not suffer competitive injury in markets if they indulge their discriminatory preferences. Consider, for example, ordinary people who prefer not to fly in airplanes piloted by blacks or women (or having black or male stewards). At least in many cases, the harm suffered by people who indulge their prejudice—perhaps higher prices of some form or another—will not drive them out of any "market," but instead, and more simply, will make them somewhat poorer. For a customer, a racist or sexist taste operates like any other taste, such as the taste for high-sugar cereals, luxury cars, or fancy computers; the taste may increase prices, but market pressures need not make the taste disappear.

In a competitive market that contains private racism and sexism, then, the existence of third-party pressures can create significant spheres of discrimination. To be sure, sometimes the participation of blacks or women (or the handicapped) is invisible; in any case, racism and sexism are currently not so widespread as to make it costly for all employers to act in a nondiscriminatory fashion. Because of their decentralized character, markets are usually far less effective than governmental controls in perpetuating discrimination, as the experience in South Africa has (at least sometimes) showed. Moreover, third-party effects will probably produce a degree of occupational segregation instead of, or as well as, discrimination. But discriminatory practices in many areas are likely to persist over time precisely because of the market, which by its very nature registers consumer preferences, including discriminatory ones.

There is an additional problem here. Suppose that society includes a number of traders who want to interact with blacks or women as well as a number of traders who do not. Suppose, too, that it is difficult for traders who are themselves indifferent to race and sex distinctions to tell which traders are discriminators (a frequent phenomenon in competitive markets). If these conditions are met, discrimination is likely to be a rational strategy for traders. New companies will do poorly if they refuse to discriminate. All this suggests that markets will frequently have great difficulty in breaking down discrimination, if discriminatory tastes are even somewhat widespread.

Statistical or Economically Rational Discrimination

I have referred to the common-sense understanding that employers treat blacks and women differently because of hostility or prejudice on their part—an idea that often accompanies the claim that markets are an enemy of discrimination. This form of hostility or prejudice is frequently described as "irrational." But the category of irrational prejudice is an ambiguous one. Perhaps we can understand it to include (a) a belief that members of a group have certain characteristics when in fact they do not, (b) a belief that many or most members of a group have certain characteristics when in fact only a few do, and (c) reliance on fairly accurate group-based generalizations when more accurate classifying devices are relatively inexpensive and available. In all of these cases, it is possible to say that someone is acting on the basis of irrational prejudice.

Suppose instead, however, that discriminatory behavior is a response to generalizations or stereotypes that, although quite overbroad and from one point of view invidious, provide an economically rational basis for employment decisions. Such stereotypes may be economically rational in the sense that it is cheaper to use them than it is to rely on more fine-grained approaches, which can be expensive to administer. Stereotypes and generalizations, of course, are a common ingredient of day-to-day market decisions. There are information costs in making distinctions within categories, and sometimes people make the category do the work of a more individualized and often far more costly examination of the merits of the particular employee.

Such categorical judgments are not only pervasive; they are entirely legitimate in most settings. We all depend on them every day. Employers rely on "proxies" of many sorts, even though those proxies are overbroad generalizations and far from entirely accurate. For example, test scores, employment records, level of education, and prestige of college attended are all part of rational employment decisions. Emphasis on these factors is a common form of stereotyping; at least in ordinary circumstances, it would be odd to say that such factors reflect hostility or prejudice of the sort that the law should ban. People may use stereotypes not because they are very accurate, but because they are less costly to use than any more individualized inquiry.

There can be no question that at least in some contexts, race and sex operate as similar proxies. In various ways, blacks differ from whites and women differ from men; there are "real differences" between the two groups. * * * Indeed, in light of past and present discrimination against blacks and women, it would be shocking if group-based differences were not present. Women, for example, are more likely than men to be the primary caretakers of children and more likely to leave the employment market because of that role. Along every indicator of social welfare—poverty, education, employment, vulnerability to private (or public) violence, participation in violent crime—blacks are less well-off than whites. And in light of those differences, it is fully possible that in certain settings, race- and sex-based generalizations are economically rational as proxies for relevant characteristics. Indeed, it is fully possible that race or sex is, in some contexts, every bit as accurate a signaling device as, say, test score, education, and previous employment. (Notably, the use of those proxies may itself have discriminatory consequences and indeed might be counted as a form of discrimination. But I put this point to one side for now.)

If race or sex can be a good signaling device, an employer might discriminate not because he hates or devalues blacks or women, or has a general desire not to associate with them, or is "prejudiced" in the ordinary sense, but because he believes (on the basis either of plausible assumptions or actual experience) that the relevant stereotypes have sufficient truth to be a basis for employment decisions. For example, an employer might believe that women are more likely to leave a high-pressure job than men, or that they are less suited for physically demanding employment; he might think that blacks are less likely to have the necessary training. With respect to the handicapped, the same scenario is of course readily predictable: "Real differences" call for differential treatment. As I understand it here, statistical discrimination occurs when the employer does not harbor irrational hatred or discriminatory feelings, but instead acts according to stereotypes of the sort that are typically relied on by market actors, and that are no less false than ordinary stereotypes. * * *

One might agree with all this and still acknowledge what seems undoubtedly true: Discrimination sometimes persists because it is economically rational to rely on a race-or sex-based generalization. And if this is so—if discrimination of this sort is a significant part of modern practice—then markets will be the furthest thing from a corrective. If discrimination is rational, then discriminatory behavior is rewarded in the marketplace. Efforts to view people through more finely tuned (and hence more expensive) devices than stereotypes will be punished.

Moreover, if discrimination is rooted in economically rational stereotypes, it remains necessary to ask what is wrong with it. The (apparent) social consensus that prejudice is irrational tends to downplay the difficulty of finding firm moral foundations for antidiscrimination law. Contemporary American law consistently condemns discrimination even if it is fully rational—that is, if it is as accurate as other generalizations typically used in the labor market. It is no defense to a claim of race or sex discrimination that the practice under attack is reasonable stereotyping. And because contemporary law singles out one kind of rational stereotyping and bans it, the distinction between affirmative action and antidiscrimination norms is extremely thin and perhaps invisible in principle. This is because in some settings, an antidiscrimination norm itself operates to bar economically rational behavior in the interest of long-term social goals. It does so selectively; in the interest of producing a racially improved future, the law forbids rational racial stereotyping when it allows stereotyping of most other kinds. An antidiscrimination norm even requires innocent victims—for example, customers who must pay higher prices—to be sacrificed in the interest of that goal.

Indeed, the distinction between affirmative action and antidiscrimination is crisp only to those who see discrimination as always grounded in hostility and irrationality, which it clearly is not. * * *

However we may think about this more adventurous claim, the central point remains. Markets will not drive out discrimination precisely to the extent that discrimination consists of economically rational stereotyping.

The Effects of Discrimination on Human Capital

Suppose that there is widespread discrimination for any number of reasons: employers have a taste for discrimination; third parties impose pressures in discriminatory directions; race or sex is used as a proxy for productivity (whether or not productivity includes the losses produced by the reactions of third parties). If any of these things is so, markets will perpetuate discrimination for yet another reason, one having to do with harmful effects on investment in human capital.

The central point here is that the productivity of blacks or whites and women or men is endogenous to, or a product of, the existence of discrimination in the labor market. Since this is so, it is a mistake to see productivity within any social group as static or independent of decisions by employers. Such decisions will have important dynamic effects on the choice of blacks and whites or women and men to invest in human capital. Decisions about education, training, drug use, trade-offs between work and leisure, and employment programs will be affected by existing patterns of discrimination. In a market that contains such discrimination, blacks and women will invest relatively less in such programs. Indeed, lower investments on their part are perfectly rational. As market actors, women should invest less than men in training to be (say) pilots, economists, politicians, or lawyers if these professions discriminate against women and thus reward their investment less than that of men.

The result can be a vicious circle or even spiral. Because of existing discrimination, the relevant groups will probably invest less in human capital; because of this lower investment, the discrimination will persist or perhaps increase because its statistical rationality itself increases; because of this effect, investments will decrease still further; and so on. Markets are the problem, not the solution.

Undoubtedly, this picture is too bleak in many settings. Proxies not rooted in sex and race have frequently evolved and employers have used them; such proxies are ordinarily far more accurate, and employers who use them sometimes prosper. More generally, the extraordinary persistence of blacks and women in attempting to enter professions dominated by whites and men is one of the most striking phenomena of the post–World War II period. Blacks and women frequently appear to invest huge amounts of human capital even in sectors that treat them inhospitably. In fact, some people respond to discrimination by increasing rather than decreasing their investments in human capital. * * * But there can be little question that discrimination does have a large effect on human capital in many contexts, and that the discouraging reception, known to be accorded to blacks and women, perpetuates the exclusion of both groups from certain sectors of the economy. And when this is so, reliance on markets as an antidiscrimination policy is badly misconceived.

In General: Reinforcing Effects

The three arguments thus far—coupled with the existence of race- and sex-based hostility or devaluation on the part of employers—build on standard economic accounts of discrimination. It is notable that none of the various effects unambiguously reflects a market failure in the conventional sense. The incorporation of racist or sexist preferences is efficient, if the efficiency criterion is based on private willingness to pay; so, too, with profit-maximizing reactions to the desires of third parties and with statistical discrimination. In all of these cases, governmental interference will probably produce an efficiency loss, at least in the short term.

The only possible exception is the effect of discrimination on human capital. In that case, it is possible to conceive of discrimination as producing a serious externality, in the form of harmful effects on outsiders—prospective labor market entrants—with corresponding efficiency losses. But it is important to note that there is an optimal level of investment in human capital, and it is not entirely clear why and to what extent existing investments that are adaptive to employer behavior in the labor market should be seen as suboptimal. In fact any generalization that is used in the labor market will have a signaling effect that will shift investments in human capital, and it is not easy to develop a model revealing which signals produce suboptimal investments. In general, then, markets will perpetuate discrimination for reasons that are unrelated to the market failures that provide traditional economic grounds for legal intervention.

Moreover, and crucially, each of these effects reinforces the others in potentially powerful ways. If there is ordinary prejudice, it will interact with statistical discrimination so as to produce more of both. People tend to notice events consistent with their prejudice and disregard events that are inconsistent with them, and the result will be more in the way of both prejudice and statistical discrimination. If third parties attempt to promote discrimination, they will increase the existence of both prejudice and statistical discrimination. Employers will hire fewer blacks and women, who in turn will appear less frequently in desirable positions, with consequent reinforcing effects on both prejudice and statistical discrimination.

In addition, if there is prejudice and statistical discrimination, and if third parties promote discrimination, victims of discrimination will decrease their investments in human capital. Such decreased investments will be a perfectly reasonable response to the real world. And if there are decreased investments in human capital, then prejudice, statistical discrimination, and third-party acts will also increase. Statistical discrimination will become all the more rational; prejudice will hardly be broken down but, on the contrary, strengthened; consumers and employers will be more likely to be discriminators. * * *

By this point the fact that markets often perpetuate discrimination should present no puzzle at all. Markets can be an ally of discrimination.* * * And all this follows from quite conventional economic approaches to the problem.

II.   Markets and Discrimination: Noneconomic Accounts

In this section, I provide two additional arguments against the view that markets will prevent discrimination. Neither of them is standard within economics, but both of them have considerable explanatory power.

Preference and Belief Formation

In economic theory, preferences and beliefs are usually taken as given—an approach that is often helpful in building models for understanding social life. But in the context of discrimination, and elsewhere as well, this approach will cause both descriptive and normative problems.* * *

In the setting at hand, the problem is that private preferences, on the part of both discriminators and their victims, tend to adapt to the status quo, and to do so in a way that makes significant change hard to achieve. The reduction of cognitive dissonance is a powerful motivating force: People attempt to bring their beliefs and perceptions in line with existing practice. The victims of inequality may well try to reduce dissonance by adapting their preferences to the available opportunities. * * *

There is of course extremely powerful evidence in the psychological literature for the thesis that human beings try to reduce dissonance. Some work here reveals that people who engage in cruel behavior change their attitudes toward the objects of their cruelty and thus devalue them. Observers tend to do the same. The phenomenon of blaming the victim has clear motivational foundations. The notion that the world is just, and that existing inequalities are deserved or desired, plays a large role in the formation of preferences and beliefs. The reduction of cognitive dissonance thus operates as a significant obstacle to the recognition that discrimination is a problem, or even that it exists. Adaptation of beliefs to a social status quo can also affect social norms. The social norms governing women's work may be quite hard to change; the social meaning of being female, or being black, may be nearly intractable.

This problem can be tied quite tightly to the operation of a market economy, whose participants are self-consciously involved in catering to existing tastes and in perpetuating and reinforcing them. Markets, partly because of this effect, are an engine of productivity and respect for individual autonomy in most circumstances; but in this setting, they sometimes perpetuate inequality. This is especially true in the context of sex discrimination, where advertising and consumption powerfully reinforce existing stereotypes, with consequences for the development of preferences and beliefs. Consider, for example, the multiple ways in which the beauty industry, broadly understood, attempts to define and to commodify femininity, in efforts to reach men and women alike. Women as well as men have often adapted their preferences and beliefs to a system of sex inequality.

The inevitable effect of a discriminatory status quo on preferences and beliefs is related to the phenomenon, noted previously, of decreased investment in human capital. In both cases, the response to discrimination is endogenous rather than exogenous and has the consequence of perpetuating existing inequalities. But with respect to preferences and beliefs, the effect is especially pernicious. Here the consequence is not merely to shift investments in self-development but, instead, to make people believe that the existing regime, including discrimination, presents no problem at all.

Once preferences and beliefs are affected, the likelihood of social change through markets diminishes dramatically. Here, as well, there is a mutually reinforcing effect among the various sources of market discrimination. The effect of discrimination on preferences and beliefs fortifies existing prejudice, produces a decrease in investment in human capital, leads to more in the way of statistical discrimination, and increases the unwillingness of third parties to deal with blacks and women.

Baselines and Discrimination Law

Almost by definition, markets incorporate the norms and practices of advantaged groups. Conspicuous examples include the many ways in which employment settings, requirements, and expectations are structured for the able-bodied and for traditional male career patterns. Here the market, dependent as it is on the criterion of private willingness to pay, is extremely unlikely to eliminate discrimination (understood as such by reference to widespread [sic] intuitions). To say that the refusal to provide flexible time, child care, or building access for the disabled does not count as "discrimination" is to rely on an exceptionally narrow conception of what discrimination is—a conception that is repudiated in much of current American law, that is inconsistent with an approach that is alert to discriminatory purposes or effects, and that in any case will do very little about existing inequalities.

In these circumstances, a legal system committed to an antidiscrimination principle might in some cases restructure market arrangements so as to put members of disadvantaged groups on a plane of greater equality—not by allowing them to be "like" members of advantaged groups, but by changing the criteria themselves, at least when those criteria do not have a firm independent justification. Consider the conventional test of American discrimination law: Is the member of the disadvantaged group "similarly situated" to the member of the advantaged group? That is: Have women, who are otherwise the same as men, or disabled people, who are otherwise the same as the able-bodied, been treated differently from men or the able-bodied? The problem with this test is that it itself reflects inequality, since it takes the norms and practices of the advantaged groups as the baseline against which to measure equality. And here market ordering, dependent as it is on the criterion of private willingness to pay, will inevitably present a problem.

Ideas of this sort underlie recent efforts to ban discrimination on the basis of pregnancy and disability. As in the case of statistical discrimination, these forms of discrimination are perfectly rational from the standpoint of employers and others. The argument for legal controls is that, in these settings, the criteria used in private markets are hardly prepolitical or natural, have neither good moral status nor powerful independent justification, and at the least should be overridden when their predictable consequences are exclusion or second-class citizenship for certain social groups.

In the case of disability, for example, the handicapped face a wide range of obstacles to participation in both public and private spheres. These obstacles are not a function of "handicap" itself (a most ambiguous concept; what would handicap mean in an entirely different world?) but instead are the inevitable consequence of humanly created barriers, including stairs, doors, and standards in general made by and for the able-bodied. The market in these circumstances is wholly nonresponsive. In light of the humanly created barriers, the market itself may not much value the contributions of handicapped people, which are by hypothesis relatively low if measured by normal productivity standards, understood as these are through the lens of willingness to pay. Discrimination of this sort may well require a legal remedy. And though the specification of the content of that remedy is a difficult question, markets will not respond, even in the long run.

The point, then, is that the valuation of the market will be a reflection of prevailing norms and practices, and those norms and practices sometimes are what an antidiscrimination principle is designed to eliminate or reduce. When this is so, reliance on markets will be unsuccessful. The rationale for antidiscrimination laws in these cases becomes more controversial, complex, and difficult. Certainly the cost of change is highly relevant; an effort to restructure the world would not be worthwhile if it impoverished most or many people. But my basic point remains: Private markets will not stop discrimination.

III.   What's Wrong with Discrimination

* * *

It follows that the claim of discrimination, best understood, is not for prevention of certain irrational acts, or of "prejudice," but instead for the elimination, in places large and small, of something in the nature of a caste system. Hence the antidiscrimination principle is best conceived as an anticaste principle. The concept of caste is hard to define, and I will have to be tentative and somewhat vague about it. I do not mean at all to suggest that the caste-like features of current practices are precisely the same, in nature or extent, as those features of genuine caste societies. I do mean to say that the similarities are what make the current practices a reason for collective concern.

The motivating idea behind an anticaste principle is that without very good reason, legal and social structures should not turn differences that are irrelevant from the moral point of view into social disadvantages. They certainly should not be permitted to do so if the disadvantage is systemic. A systemic disadvantage is one that operates along standard and predictable lines in multiple important spheres of life and that applies in realms—such as education, freedom from private and public violence, wealth, political representation, and political influence—that are deeply implicated in basic participation as a citizen in a democratic society.

In the areas of race and sex discrimination, and of disability as well, the problem is precisely this sort of systemic disadvantage. A social or biological difference has the effect of systematically subordinating the relevant group and of doing so in multiple spheres and along multiple indices of social welfare: poverty, education, political power, employment, susceptibility to violence and crime, and so forth. That is the caste system to which the legal system is attempting to respond.

————

NOTES AND QUESTIONS

1.   Role of storytelling in disrupting racial discrimination. Sunstein argues that market forces alone cannot eliminate racial discrimination; indeed, markets can perpetuate and entrench discrimination. Only government intervention can correct the kind of systemic disadvantage that caste systems produce. Critical race theorists, however, have argued that government interventions are also subject to "capture" by caste systems. This claim lies at the heart, for instance, of the critical race theory critique of equal protection clause jurisprudence. See Ian Haney Lopez, *Institutional Racism: Judicial Conduct and a New Theory of Racial Discrimination*, 109 Yale L.J. 1717 (2000). Indeed, critical race theorists argue, as Rachel Moran puts it, that "[e]ven in the realm of feeling, seemingly the most interior aspect of personal life, people are trapped within a sociopolitical economy of emotion, one that replicates boundaries of race and gender." Rachel F. Moran, *The Elusive Nature of Discrimination* (Book Review), 55 Stan. L.Rev. 2365, 2416 (2003).

What then is to be done? Moran suggests that "storytelling," a hallmark of critical race theory, can make a difference: "In contrast to psychological studies that keep victims at a safe and objective distance, narrative has the power to make unique human connections. Stories can transport white readers across the color line momentarily, so that they begin to appreciate the individual experiences of nonwhites." *Id.* at 2396.

Economists George Akerlof and Robert Shiller incorporate shared stories into their theory of "animal spirits" to help explain why racial minorities, particularly African Americans, are persistently poor. They argue that white and black market behavior is organized around different "stories."

> Sociology Michele Lamont's *The Dignity of Working Men* has shown what [these different stories] mean in real life. Lamont interviewed both white and black working-class males. * * * She wanted to know their story. What motivates them to get up in the morning and go to work? Her interviewees all face the same problem. None of them is doing more than moderately well in meeting the ideals of American society. In terms of money, they are not earning much. In terms of prestige, they command little respect. To maintain their dignity, to go about their difficult and demanding jobs with so little reward, they must have a view of the world and how they fit into it.

Of course not all white and all black workers say the same thing; there is considerable variation. But nevertheless, according to Lamont, there is a modal story that seems to describe the group's view of itself. Let's first view the world according to whites. In their view the world is a tough place. It is highly competitive. But capitalism is the best of all possible systems, and they fit into it. They are proud to be independent contributors to this system. Despite all these difficulties they manage to take care of themselves and of their families, and they take great pride in that. They assume individual responsibility for their fate, and also for their relative success and failure. In addition they think they are better people, more concerned with values and less concerned with money, than those who are higher on the social scale. This is the life that they have chosen, and they are responsible for living with it. Their view of the world is, remarkably, a page out of Milton and Rose Friedman's *Free to Choose*.

In contrast, the African Americans Lamont interviewed have a slightly different story. Like the whites, the working-class blacks also take pride in their self-reliance. But their self-reliance is manifested under yet more difficult circumstances than that of the whites. They did not just receive an unlucky draw from the cards of capitalism. The whites tend to believe that they live in a just society, and that their relatively low status in it is the result of mere bad luck, or perhaps of their own choices. But for African Americans their lack of success has to be viewed as the result of being *them* rather than *us*. *They* deal out the rewards in society, such as jobs and pay. *We* are the recipients. Indeed, relative to the whites, the African Americans must be especially self-reliant, since they must deal with the hostile world of *them* as well as the congenial world of *we*. This gives African Americans a view of solidarity among themselves. It also gives them a sense that there are underdogs and that those underdogs should be helped. Lack of success is not just the result of bad luck in situations in which everyone has an equal chance, or choices of a different lifestyle. That is central to their self-image of who they are and who they ought to be.

In Lamont's interviews race plays a central role for the blacks, as might have been expected, but also for the whites. The whites, priding themselves on their self-reliance, define themselves in opposition to blacks, and especially blacks who are on welfare. In contrast, blacks define themselves in contrast to whites, who they think are stingy and unfair. * * *

We see then that African Americans have a problem that white Americans do not. They must work in a world in which they have been dealt a bad hand in terms of the resources of their parents and the resources of their neighborhoods. They must also play this bad hand in a world that is psychologically stacked against them. The dealer cheated. It takes extra psychological work to manage in a world that cannot be seen as morally just and fair.

George A. Akerlof and Robert J. Shiller, ANIMAL SPIRITS: HOW HUMAN PSYCHOLOGY DRIVES THE ECONOMY, AND WHY IT MATTERS FOR GLOBAL CAPITALISM 159–61 (2009).

How effective might changing the stories that are told about race be in altering market behavior? Altering government behavior? Family and intimate behavior? How easy or difficult might be this task?

Moran notes that anti-subordinationist storytelling carries dangers as well:

> Unlike conventional psychological studies, narrative must struggle to avoid essentializing racial experience by creating the impression that one person's account is emblematic of an entire group's experience. Paradoxically, the very stories that are designed to be individuating and idiosyncratic can, when imbued with larger symbolic significance, become a new source of stereotypes.

Moran, *id.* at 2396–97.

2. Can law and economics and critical race theory be combined?

As the work of Akerlof and Shiller suggests, economists interested in explaining the persistence of racial discrimination may need to reach beyond the standard analytical tools of economics. In the mid 1990s, legal scholar, Edward L. Rubin urged the combination of critical race theory and law and economics. Rubin perceived enough common ground between these two, often antagonistic, schools of legal reasoning to suggest that they could be combined:

> [C]ontemporary law and economics and outsider scholarship share a common ground—the effort to locate law, social policy, and social change in a closely analyzed institutional context. What is particularly promising about the effort is that institutional analysis has also become a major theme in the academic fields that gave rise to both these schools. To develop a new synthesis of discourse for legal scholarship, ideas from all these fields must be incorporated, for most scholars agree that law can no longer sustain itself as an autonomous discipline. Whether these complex and disparate elements can actually be integrated is an open question—there is nothing inevitable about the process—but synthesis seems like an appealing alternative to the currently fragmented state of legal scholarship.

Edward L. Rubin, *The New Legal Process, the Synthesis of Discourse, and the Microanalysis of Institutions*, 109 HARV. L. REV. 1393, 1394 (1996).

In the early 2000s, a critical race theorist, Devon Carbado and an economist, Mitu Gulati, endorsed Rubin's proposal for collaboration and synthesis between the two schools, and began to write together, devising an account of how corporate employees of color manage their racial identities that draws on both bodies of work. See, e.g, Devon W. Carbado and Mitu Gulati, *The Law and Economics of Critical Race Theory*, 112 YALE L.J. 1757, 1761 (2003) (book review); Devon W. Carbado and Mitu Gulati, *Working Identity*, 85 CORNELL L. REV. 1259 (2000).

3.   ECONOMIC ANALYSIS AND THE CRITIQUE FROM COMMODIFICATION

Justice and the Market Domain

MARKETS AND JUSTICE 165–89 (John W. Chapman & J. Roland Pennock eds., 1989).

■ MARGARET JANE RADIN

I.   INTRODUCTION: THE METAPHOR OF THE WALL

It has been traditional to view some aspects of social life as inappropriate for the market. We speak of a metaphorical wall between the market and other realms of social life, much as we speak of a wall between church and state. There is a traditional understanding that important political activities, like voting, are on the nonmarket side of the wall. There is also an understanding that certain special kinds of interactions between persons are on the nonmarket side of the wall—that is, are morally required to be kept there—even if some people desire to "marketize" them. It is this latter understanding that I wish to explore and question here. Does justice require that we delineate and protect a nonmarket domain? In general, how might a theory of social justice take into account the question of the domain of the market?

A traditional liberal view is that the market appropriately encompasses most desired transactions between people, with a few special exceptions. Those few exceptions—for example, the way we acquire a spouse or a child—are morally and legally protected from the market. I want to suggest that the traditional view is wrong in granting too much ground to the market. The metaphor of a wall between a market and nonmarket realm is inapposite because it wrongly suggests a large realm of pure free-market transactions to which special kinds of personal interactions form a special exception. It wrongly suggests that a laissez-faire market regime is prima facie just.

* * *

In order to frame this discussion it is necessary to notice that there is another way to deny the appositeness of the wall metaphor, and that is to say that in principle there is no limit to the market. Someone who holds this view thinks of the market as encompassing the social world. She thinks not only that social justice does not require us to protect a nonmarket domain, but also that social justice requires a universal market structure. This is the approach taken by some of the contemporary theorists who bring economics to bear on political and legal theory. Hence, it is possible to see an imaginary battle being waged. The traditional liberal view, asserting that there must be a realm of personal interactions walled off from the market, is striving to hold some territory against the oncoming forces of economics and the notion that everything is grist for the market mill.

In my view, both sides are wrong, and so is the battle. Instead of trying to defend the small piece of ground representing the list of special non-market personal interactions, it would be better to try to reclaim for peaceful co-existence some of the territory the traditional liberal view concedes to the market. The traditional liberal view is wrong because it assumes that not much is on the nonmarket side of the wall, and the battle lines prevent us from appreciating the nonmarket aspects of many of our market relations. They prevent us from seeing fragments of a nonmarket social order embedded or latent in the market society. They prevent us from thinking about social justice in terms of fostering this latent co-existent nonmarket order.

II. Universal Commodification vs. the Wall

A. *The Market as Methodological Archetype*

Let us first consider a sketch of an archetype representing the economic view, and then consider the reasons given by its opponents for walling off a few special things from the market. Some law-and-economics theorists can be understood to endorse a methodological archetype that is sometimes referred to as market-imperialism, but which I prefer to call universal commodification. Under universal commodification, all things desired or valued—from personal attributes to good government—are goods or commodities. Commodities are usually pictured as objects separate from the self and social relations. Hence, universal commodification is a form of objectification. It assimilates personal attributes, relations, and desired states of affairs to the realm of objects. Universal commodification implies that all things can and should be separable from persons and exchanged through the free market, whenever some people are willing to sell and others are willing to buy. All human attributes are conceived of as possessions bearing a value characterizable in money terms, and all human interactions are conceived as exchanges understandable in terms of gains from trade.

The language in which this conceptual scheme is couched is the rhetoric of the market. Under universal commodification, the human universe of social interaction—from government to love and sexuality—is conceived and described in the rhetoric of trading objects for money. Hobbes conceived of the value of a person in market rhetoric: "the *Value* or WORTH of a man, is as of all other things, his Price; that is to say, so much as would be given for the use of his Power." In Hobbes's conception, everything about a person that others need, desire, or value is a possession that is priced. The Hobbesian person fits into the archetype of universal commodification. The Hobbesian conception of the political order likewise conceives of politics in market rhetoric. Modern Hobbesians view political activity as fully describable in terms of "rent seeking" by those who can achieve monetary gain from the capture of portions of Leviathan's power.

* * *

For one who is willing to conceive of everything (corneas for transplant, sexuality, babies for adoption) in market rhetoric, the only explanation for why some things might be held out of the market is market failure: free riders and holdouts, administrative costs, information costs, and so on. Judge Richard Posner, for example, apparently views a ban on selling oneself into slavery as justified by information costs. Finding no apparent market failures that would suggest noncommodification of children, he suggests that a free market in babies would be a good idea.

B.   *Three Attempts to Maintain the Wall*

Those who advocate the traditional wall to claim a few things for a domain that is in principle off limits to the market rely on reasons other than market failure. Three prevalent kinds of arguments are deployed in trying to keep something—babies, blood, kidneys—on the nonmarket side of a metaphorical wall. The first is an argument based upon the degradation and invasion of personhood occasioned by allowing sales. The second is an argument based upon creating or preserving opportunities for altruism. The third is a slippery slope argument that I call a domino theory, claiming that to allow sales for some people who choose them will foreclose nonmarket sharing for those who don't choose the market regime. * * *

* * * [T]hese arguments have been aimed at shoring up a wall between the market and nonmarket domains, but in fact they undermine the wall metaphor. These arguments fail to capture what is wrong about universal commodification.

Personhood prophylaxis. The first strand of argument is often thought of in connection with organ transplants, especially from living people. The argument holds that we must prevent poor people from being forced to sell their kidneys and corneas. The general idea is that it is somehow degrading to be selling off one's body parts, and that this is an injury to personhood that society should prevent. Thus I characterize the argument as aimed at personhood prophylaxis. In this strand of argument it is also thought that in some sense such sales are the result of coercion and do not represent a voluntary act on the seller's part.

Of course, it is problematic whether this kind of action that results from poverty should count as coerced. Does poverty "coerce" someone into selling a kidney, or does someone, because she is poor, choose to sell a kidney? A hard choice is not a non-choice. But the main problem with the personhood prophylaxis form of argument is that it seems cruelly smug. Under what circumstances do people need money badly enough to sell a kidney? Perhaps to feed, clothe, and house their children, or to support elderly or handicapped relatives. It may appear to observers that selling a kidney is degrading, but if these are the circumstances, it seems more degrading instead to have to endure the state of affairs that the sale was supposed to ameliorate.

* * *

Preserving opportunities for altruism. According to the second strand of argument, something should be held off the market when permitting sales would foreclose, or fail to create, opportunities for altruism that ought to be open. With regard to human blood, for example, Richard Titmuss claimed that altruism is encouraged if society permits only donation, and discouraged if society permits both gifts and sales. In the Titmuss style of argument, altruism is encouraged by donation rather than sale because giving is thought to be communitarian and to emphasize interdependence, whereas market transactions are thought to be individualistic and to emphasize isolation. A donor's experience in being responsible for saving a stranger's life is said to bring us closer together, cement our community, in a way that buying and selling cannot. Interdependence is also emphasized by the possibility of reciprocity. A donor's sense of obligation today could be partially founded on the recognition that she might well need to become a recipient tomorrow. A recipient's sense of gratitude and acknowledgment of dependence upon others' altruism rather than upon her own wealth creates solidarity and interdependence.

According to this argument, altruism is foreclosed if both donations and sales are permitted. If sales are not allowed, donations have no market value and remain unmonetized. If sales are allowed, then even gifts have a market equivalent. My giving a pint of blood is like giving $50 of my money. According to this argument, such monetization discourages giving. We are more willing to give health, perhaps life itself, to strangers than we are to give them $50 of our money.

* * *

Even accepting a need to find gift objects that must remain completely unmonetized, it still seems that the argument about opportunities for altruism is more general than its proponents have thought. Many kinds of gift objects or volunteer services that can be given on a one-shot basis and do not require much special training might still fit the argument: gifts of old clothes or books; services like reading to blind people, being a subject for experimentation, driving voters to the polls, census-taking, and so on. Why do we not think of keeping these things completely unmonetized? Maybe those who make the argument about opportunities for altruism would further try to cabin it by suggesting that, in addition to being things that can be given on a one-shot basis, the things that must be kept unmonetized are extremely important, perhaps meaning the difference between life or death, to the recipient. But such an attempt to cabin the argument must fail, because it is unclear why the level of importance should matter in this way. There seems to be no reason why we must make altruism dramatic in order to preserve it.

The domino theory. The third strand of argument, the domino theory, holds that there is a slippery-slope leading from toleration of any sales (of something) to an exclusive market regime (for that thing). Although it is a necessary supposition of the argument about opportunities for altruism, the domino theory is more often brought up in connection with prostitution and sale of babies. The domino theory implicitly makes two claims: first, as a background normative premise, that it is important for a nonmarket regime to exist; and second, as an empirical premise, that a nonmarket regime cannot co-exist with a market regime. The market drives out the nonmarket version, hence the market regime must be banned.

The domino theory covers more than just the territory supposedly conducive to altruism, since those who argue that sexuality must remain nonmonetized do not argue that the reason is so that it may be altruistically given. Indeed, as I suggested earlier, it seems that the concept of altruism already presupposes more distance, remoteness, or impersonality between people than we wish to countenance in our ideals of sexuality. Those who are against monetized sex are probably against altruistic sex also.

Preserving opportunities for altruism does not, then, seem to be the main reason for asserting that noncommercial sex must remain possible. Nor does it seem to be the main reason at work in the inclination to ban baby selling, although it can play a part, as my earlier discussion indicated. Rather, it appears that the uncommodified version must remain possible because commodification somehow destroys or deeply disfigures the possible value of sex itself or the value of the baby itself.

With babies this does not seem difficult to understand. Superficially, at least, it seems to fail to treat children as persons to make them all realize that they have a definite commercial value, and that this is all their value amounts to, even if their parents did not choose to sell them or did not obtain them by purchase; the domino theory asserts that this will be the result of permitting sales for those who choose them. Is it similarly an injury to personhood to commercialize sex? If noncommercial sex becomes impossible, as we are here assuming, the argument that the answer is yes asserts that we shall all be deprived of a significant form of human bonding and interrelation. If disrespect for personhood has an individualistic flavor, perhaps this would be better put as disrespect for humanity or human relations. Under this analysis, noncommercial sex is a component of human flourishing, like the need for opportunities to express altruism. Commercial friendship is a contradiction in terms, as is commercial love. If opportunities for noncommercial friendship and love were not available, we would not be human. The argument we are reviewing asks us to see sexuality analogously.

But let us finally focus on the domino part of the theory. Is it the case that if some people are allowed to sell babies or sexual services, those things will be thereby commercialized for everyone? The argument that the answer is yes assumes that once the fact of market value enters our discourse, it must be present in, and dominate, every transaction. The fact of pricing brings with it the conceptual scheme of commodification. We cannot know the price of something and know at the same time that it is priceless. Once something has a price, money must be a part of the interaction, and the reason or explanation for the interaction, when that something changes hands. A sale cannot simultaneously be a gift. If our children know that the going rate of babies is $10,000, they will know that they are worth $10,000. They will know that they are worth as much as an economy car, but not as much as a house. Worse, if they know that the market price of "good" babies is $10,000, whereas the price of "medium-grade" babies is only $8,000, they will be anxiously comparing themselves with the "good" grade of child in hopes that they measure up. One can fill in the analogous argument regarding sexuality.

III.   Incomplete Commodification:

The Metaphor of Coexistence

A.   Coexistence of Market and Nonmarket Interaction

The domino theory assumes that we cannot both know the price of something and know that it is priceless. We cannot have a sale that is also, and "really," a gift. Is this assumption correct? * * *

Because this is a market society, most people must be paid for their work if they are to live, yet the kind of work we all hope to have—I think—is that which we would do anyway, without money, if somehow by other means our necessities of life were taken care of. Our ideals about work—at least for many of us—do not turn on capitalist rationality. What we hope to get out of working is not all money, nor understandable in money terms (unless the archetype of universal commodification describes our conceptual scheme).

Inspired by Hannah Arendt, I think it is helpful here to introduce a distinction between work and labor, though it is not the same one she had in mind. It is possible to think of work as always containing a noncommodified human element; and to think of the fully commodified version as labor. I think we can understand the difference between working and laboring the way we understand the difference between playing notes and playing music. Laborers play notes, workers play the music. * * *

Many people have the sense, however, that these ideals about work are declining. As market rationality takes over, there is less and less room for working with care. Many kinds of work are becoming impersonal, some say. (Health care is a primary example.) What does it mean to say they are becoming impersonal? That seems to be simply to say that market rhetoric fully characterizes the process of interaction between seller and buyer. This is to say that to the participants in the interaction the services or things are completely commodified. The relation between health-care provider and patient, for example, is no different from that between the proverbial seller and buyer of widgets.

Putting it this way suggests that complete noncommodification—complete removal from the market—is not the only alternative to complete commodification. Incomplete commodification is also possible. Incomplete commodification describes a situation in which things are sold but the interaction between the participants in the transaction cannot be fully or perspicuously described as the sale of things. If many kinds of sales retain a personal aspect even though money changes hands, those interactions are not fully described as sales of commodities. There is an irreducibly non-market or nonmonetized aspect of human interaction going on between seller and recipient; to them the things sold are incompletely commodified. That there should be the opportunity for work to be personal in this sense does seem to be part of our conception of human flourishing—which is why those who see increasing depersonalization deplore it. Complete commodification of work—pure labor—does violence to our notion of what it is to be a well-developed person.

B.   Incomplete Commodification and the Ideals of Personhood and Community

Now it may be clear why I think it gives up the ball game to argue that certain specific items (for example, blood) must remain completely noncommodified so as to keep open opportunities for altruism, especially if those who argue this way hope that these sporadic opportunities may lead the way to a less commodified society. The way to a less commodified society is to see and foster the nonmarket aspect of much of what we buy and sell, rather than to erect a wall to keep a certain few things completely off the market and abandon everything else to market rationality.

If social justice would be improved by a less commodified society, then, rather than walling off a few transactions from the pure free market, we should seek to deepen and consolidate the nonmarket countercurrents that cut across the market. One way that we already do this to some extent is, of course, with regulation. At least, that is one way of interpreting what regulation means. Such an interpretation would be consistent with prevalent critiques of liberal notions of the individual and society. * * *

Incomplete commodification as an expression of a nonmarket order co-existent with a market order can be related to this shift in conception of the ideals of personhood and community. The kinds of goods that deviate most from laissez-faire are those related to human beings' homes, work, food, environment, education, communication, health, bodily integrity, sexuality, family life, and political life. For these goods it is easiest to see that preservation and fostering of the nonmarket aspect of their provision and use is related to human flourishing and social justice—to personhood and community as reconceived to meet the critique of liberalism. Once we accept that pervasive incomplete commodification is related to appropriate ideals of personhood and community, it is clear why the arguments for piecemeal noncommodification of specific items are unsatisfactory. It seems that the values of personhood and community require not that certain specific exceptional things be insulated by a wall while everything else is governed by market forces; rather, it seems that the values of personhood and community pervasively interact with the market and alter many goods from their pure free-market form.

* * *

IV.   Some Ramifications for a Theory of S.C. Justice

* * *

B.   Incomplete Commodification and the Form of a Theory of Justice

* * *

Positing the propriety of pervasive coexistence of market and non-market aspects to human interactions is an alternative both to theories that imply or can be understood to countenance universal commodification and to "wall" theories of social justice like Walzer's. Incomplete commodification would be reflected both in a theory of overall distributive fairness and a theory of proper treatment of individuals. Key principles for both these aspects of justice in such an alternative theory are that who should get what things of value depends upon the appropriate relation between persons and things, and between persons and other people.

For example, if we accept as appropriate a close connection between persons and their housing, then housing should be socially provided in such a way not only that everyone may have the shelter necessary for physical survival, but also that everyone may have the continuity of residence (often) necessary for proper self-development. Housing, both rented and owned, is appropriately incompletely commodified: it has special nonmarket significance to participants in market interactions regarding it, and it is appropriately socially regulated in recognition of the propriety of this self-investment. This is not because, as Walzer might have it, housing belongs to the "sphere" of security and welfare, in which distribution should be according to the principle of need, rather than to the "sphere" of money and commodities, in which distribution is appropriately according to the principle of free exchange. Rather it is because, although we value the efficiency of the market, at the same time housing must be incompletely commodified in recognition of its connection with personhood.

Who gets what depends upon appropriate relations between persons and other people, and not just between persons and things. People engaged in market interactions are not just acquiring things, they are relating to each other. A theory of social justice should recognize that these interactions often are (and ought to be able to be) valued for themselves and specifically, and not merely instrumentally and fungibly. As critics of Rawls (for example) have often noted, many kinds of solidarity and interrelations between people are central to our conception of human flourishing and hence must not be excluded from a theory of social justice.

* * *

D. Further Implication for Justice as Respect for Personhood
* * *

The dilemma of commodification. First, there is the observation that the prophylactic personhood argument—that people should not be allowed to sell their organs, etc., because that is degrading to personhood—calls attention to a more pervasive problem of social justice. If people are so desperate for money that they are trying to sell things we think cannot be separated from them without significant injury to personhood, we do not cure the desperation by banning sales. Nor do we avoid the injury to personhood. Perhaps the desperation is the social problem we should be looking at, rather than the market ban. Perhaps worse injury to person-hood is suffered from the desperation that caused the attempt to sell a kidney or cornea than would be suffered from actually selling it. The would-be sellers apparently think so. Then justice is not served by a ban on "desperate exchanges."

These considerations change the arena of argument from considerations of appropriateness to the market to explicit considerations of social justice. If neither commodification nor non-commodification can put to rest our disquiet about harm to personhood in conjunction with certain specific kinds of transactions—if neither commodification nor non-commodification can satisfy our aspirations for a society exhibiting equal respect for persons—then we must rethink the larger social context in which this dilemma is embedded. We must think about wealth and power redistribution.

* * *

If it appears that we cannot respect personhood either with commodification or non-commodification, given the surrounding social circumstances, for example with organ-selling, and if we agree that this means we ought to change the surrounding circumstances, we are still faced with the question of whether or not we should permit commodification while we try to do that. If we opt to permit sales for those who choose, as the libertarian and radical might both recommend, we risk complete commodification—if the domino theory correctly predicts the resulting social consciousness, given the level of commodification already present. Complete commodification makes the supposed goal of greater respect for persons in a less commodified future even less imaginable. But perhaps this risk is not as bad as the degradation of personhood and reinforcement of powerlessness brought about by the regime of enforced non-commodification. Obviously, I have no handy algorithm for making this decision.

Regulation and community. A second connection between justice and my discussion of the arguments surrounding the wall metaphor is the question of nonefficiency justification for regulation—that is, socially mandated deviations from the laissez-faire market regime for many things that are bought and sold. If everything is appropriately fully commodified unless efficiency dictates otherwise, then exceptions from the laissez-faire regime are justified only where the market for some reason cannot achieve efficient outcomes. This in fact is the position of many economists on regulation. It makes many types of regulation (for example, residential rent control) difficult to justify; when these types of regulation are frequently imposed anyway by the political order, they are seen as obvious examples of selfish rent-seeking by powerful interest groups. But as I have argued above, there is another way to view regulation of many things that are important to human personhood and community, and that is as incomplete commodification. If we stubbornly intuit that these things that are very important to human life, health, and self and community development ought not to be completely monetized, then regulation that does not (theoretically) meet an efficiency test is in principle justified. Then the response of the political order in imposing the constraints on commodification may be seen as a good-faith working out of community values, so that persons and the community may properly flourish, rather than interest-group rent-seeking.

Can market rhetoric be unjust? The third question that I would like to raise here has to do with whether social justice (as respect for persons) and the rhetoric of universal commodification are connected. I think that conceiving of politics as mere rent-seeking, and essential human attributes as mere scarce commodities, expresses and fosters a conception of human flourishing inferior to that expressed and fostered by a discourse that recognizes personhood and community as essentially unmonetized and not fungible. But is it unjust to think of these aspects of human life in terms of commodities? Does Richard Posner act unjustly in trying to convince us that the right way to think of children is as commodities, and that the right way to think of much that legislatures do is in terms of rent-seeking?

————

Commodification and Women's Household Labor

9 Yale J.L. & Feminism 81 (1997).

■ Katharine Silbaugh

I.   Introduction

A woman washes a kitchen floor. She puts the mop away and drives to the corner market. She consults a shopping list, and purchases groceries from it, carefully choosing the least expensive options. A four-year-old child is tugging at her leg while she does this, and she tries to entertain him, talking to him about the mopped floor, the grocery items. When she returns from the store, she prepares lunch from what she has brought home with her. She and the child both eat lunch. After lunch, she and the child collect laundry and she runs a load. She takes the garbage out to the curb. Then she reads him a story. They play a game where she comes up with a word, and he tries to name its opposite. Sometimes there is no opposite, and that is particularly funny to both of them. She has done housework.

There is no way to tell from this description whether these activities were market or non-market, whether her work is a commodity or not. Would it help to categorize her work if you knew the location? Is this her home? Suppose that she is a paid domestic worker, and this housework is a commodity. She leaves her employer's home. She goes home and does exactly the same thing there, but this time she is preparing dinner. The second child is her own. Whether these activities are viewed as a commodity is contextual, not activity-based.

Should we think and talk about unpaid domestic labor—housework—using market, or economic, language? * * *

I want to reject current categorical thinking about women's home activity. I argue that economic understandings are very useful, and that they do not and need not supply a complete understanding of human activities. I will make the case that economic understandings are representations of a given activity, as are sentimental or emotional understandings, and that they can and should co-exist. Margaret Jane Radin, the foremost legal scholar who has addressed commodification concerns, has also argued that multiple understandings can co-exist. Her goal, however, is to bring non-market understandings to market activities, in search of a less commodified society.

This Article questions that goal. My central argument is that the entirely emotional understanding of home labor is itself an impoverished one. If one conceded that the use of economic rhetoric could habituate people to thinking about a topic differently, as critics of economic language assert, that would not necessarily make the case *against* the use of such rhetoric in all contexts. I make the uncommon case here for the value of bringing market understandings to non-market activities where they can co-exist with non-economic conceptions. The broader implication of the thesis is that we should not assume that analyses that can remake relations are always doing a disservice, especially where those relations are already fraught with problematic analyses. In certain contexts it may be a very conservative claim that economic analysis is bad *because* it has the power to change the way we view something.

My claim is that gender equality requires us to take the economics of home labor seriously. This argument turns on a comparison between wage labor and home labor, which are similar both in content and in many of the motivations that drive workers. I argue that the difference in the treatment between them may be difference based on gender. I discuss the tendency to raise commodification concerns when women's interests are at stake, and question whether resistance to market reasoning in these contexts is a form of resistance to women's economic power. I then examine some legal doctrines touching on home labor that could benefit from economic analysis. If importing economic reasoning into these areas transforms our understanding of them, I posit that women would *benefit* from that transformation. I conclude that as long as so many of women's activities remain non-market and as long as women's economic welfare is a concern of feminists, economic analysis of non-market activities is affirmatively desirable. My objective is to show what can be gained by allowing economics to inform, without dominating, the discourse on policy and doctrine surrounding home labor. Concern over women's lives becoming entirely commodified seems by comparison an abstract worry.

II.   THE COMMODIFICATION OBJECTION: SETTING
OUT THE CASE AGAINST ECONOMICS

* * *

A.   *The Basic Problem with Commodification*

* * *

The commodification critique applies to an *analysis* of the economy of the home and the family labor that occurs there, as well as to the actual purchase and sale of that labor. To [philosopher Elizabeth] Anderson, market norms have an "expressive significance" as well as a practical one, and can thus infect non-market conceptions of women's labor. The argument posits that talk matters: you can pervert the personalness of something by talking about it as if it were fungible. Identifying an "economy," meaning a set of implicit valuations and exchanges, is possible even where "real markets" are either prohibited or practically impossible to imagine: organs for transplantation, sexual contacts, candidates for marriage partnerships, religious convictions, love, or a person's politics. Although in many cases this is just talk, to a commodification skeptic, that talk itself does damage to the integrity of the attribute in question: sexuality, love, marriage, health.

James Boyd White has made this case most powerfully, arguing that expression is never transparent, but instead constitutes and transforms the reality it describes. * * * In passing, he applies this critique to an economic understanding of home labor, noting that:

> The segmentation of the exchange model tends to misvalue the work we do for ourselves, which is most of the traditional work of women.... This is especially true of people who raise their own children. Such work cannot be segmented into functions and then made the material of the market process, actual or hypothetical, for what the child requires is the sustained presence of, and interaction with, a loving and respectful person, something no alternative can supply. Similarly, housework has a different meaning when one is maintaining one's own home rather than acting as a servant for others.

To those who see a difference between real and rhetorical markets, the difference tends to be treated as one of degree. Under this view, it might not hurt personhood as much to talk about markets in certain attributes as it does to create such markets, but talk certainly doesn't *help*. By condemning talk as well as trades, skeptics take away the opportunity to make the affirmative case for the benefits of an economic perspective. For legal analysts, this conflation of actual buying and selling and market analysis proves problematic * * *.

* * *

C. *Feminism and Economic Skepticism*

Feminists rank high among those who are skeptical of economists. This skepticism proceeds on two fronts in the domestic labor context. The two parts are a negative reaction to economics as a way to describe home activities, and an affirmatively positive response to love and affections as a descriptively accurate way of understanding and explaining productivity in the home.

1. *Offense at Economics*

Some feminists have a visceral dislike for economic analysis. While there are many reasons for this, I believe two are most strongly at play. The first is situational: Many feminists don't trust the current practitioners of economic analysis. The second is more substantive: Many feminists do not accept the implicit notion of fungibility at play in economic analysis.

The problem of distrust may come from two characteristics of economic discourse. The first is a driving, relentless essentialism among economists. Much economic literature reads like much more than a useful tool with which to explain certain phenomenon. It instead reads like the *raison d'être* of that phenomenon, its beginning and end. Everyone has her favorite example of a social phenomenon being mercilessly pushed into an economic model producing logically clean but absurd explanations: adoption, marriage, heroic rescues, voting, altruism, religion, childbirth, sexuality. This kind of relentless essentialism among economists leaves reasonable people with what appears to be a decision to either embrace the whole absurd end of the spectrum or jump ship entirely. I will argue that it is fully possible and desirable to use economics to assist in understanding a social phenomenon without turning away from other possible explanations or understandings. But this does not describe much of the dominant economic analysis practiced in the *legal* academic community. The idea of extending this sort of essentialism into the social relations surrounding family labor seems to carry the risk of damaging the complex context of dependencies and moral and emotional commitments made there.

The second reason many feminists distrust practitioners of economic analysis is that they often employ assumptions with suspect origins. Moreover, although these are almost always identified at the outset as assumptions, by the end of the equation they seem to have assumed the status of fact. In legal discourse, when an assumption is used in an economic model, we usually see the burden of proof implicitly shifted to critics of the model to disprove the factual assumption despite the frequent lack of evidence in favor of the assumption from the outset. There is the well-known joke about the economists on a desert island with a case of food in tin cans. They begin their plan for opening the cans by saying, "First, let's assume a can opener." It's funny when it's a can opener. It is not so funny, or at least it shouldn't be, when the empirically unsupported assumption is that women want children more than men do, that women have higher inherent value when they are young and men are worth more when they are older, that husbands and wives in most cases have the perfect trust and agency necessary to treat them as a single economic unit (individuals are selfish and self-interested but family heads are altruistic), or that rapists would pay for sex somehow if they had the necessary wealth of money, power, or looks themselves. Having those assumptions implicitly raised to the level of facts over the course of an economic analysis is particularly problematic.

I think of the implicit elevation of assumption to fact as "assumption slippage." It must be noted that this slippage is a dynamic process: Readers of economic texts, particularly in the legal community, are participants in its occurrence as much if not sometimes more than economic authors. Much of the most prominent economic analysis of family and gender relations, particularly that associated with Gary Becker, relies on very questionable assumptions that appear to come right out of the pages of *The*

Total Woman and from there they help to build economic rationalizations for very conventional mid-twentieth century middle class suburban gender relations. * * * Assuming altruistic heads of households reduces the need to worry about disparate human capital investments made within the family. The assumption that women desire children more than men do provides an explanation for what otherwise might be tricky distributional results that occur within families. If these are to be the assumptions on which an economic analysis of home labor is to proceed, many people do not want any part of it. * * *

The next level of concern over economic analysis does not center solely on the supposed "priors" of its practitioners. It is a more substantive criticism: A rejection of the suggestion that many attributes of family life and work are fungible, and thus that the study of value can proceed by observing choices people make. Fungibility is the idea that goods, services, or attributes can be placed on a single metric of value and then traded off against one another on that metric. Fungible things can be replaced by something else that falls in the same place on the metric, such as similar services by a different person, or simply money measured in the right amount, without regret. On this account, economics is entirely concerned with theoretically measurable maximized choice among alternatives, rather than being concerned with the personal experience of choice, methods of provisioning in general (whether by voluntary exchange, gift-giving, or coercion), or with the process of developing what economists call preferences. Radin concedes that whether we think the fact of choice between alternatives proves fungibility, as many economists believe, or instead prove nothing about fungibility, is largely a matter of intuition. Joseph Raz argues that the meaning we give to a choice is its conventional understanding, and if that does not include a trade along a single metric, then no such fungibility can be inferred. Raz taps into many people's response to the talk of fungibility when thinking about marriage, romantic partners, and family work choices that are implicit in an economic analysis of home labor.

There is a similar negative response to the notion of bargaining within marriage or within family relations, which is an important element of an economic understanding of home labor. Though a bargaining model is often thought of as an improvement on Becker's notion of an altruistic head of household which can justify a failure to examine interspousal conflict, the bargaining model itself draws a negative response from many. While many would acknowledge much day-to-day bargaining within the family, it is also thought that a bargaining analysis fails to capture the altruistic behavior layered alongside self-interested behavior in family relations. It is difficult to predict much about behavior if one can rely neither on complete self-interest nor on complete altruism, and a bargaining analysis of family labor puts forward assumptions about family behavior to which many respond negatively. * * *

2. *Women as Non-commodifiable: Questioning the Origins of an Idea*

Does concern about the comparison between wage labor and home labor commodification grow out of an implicit assumption that there is something intrinsically different about home labor? We might want to ask whether it is coincidental, or instead highly relevant, that that intrinsic difference at play in analysis also cuts along gender lines: women's work, hereby, would be essentially non-marketable. Consider the problems with assuming that women are inclined to make gifts of attributes of their personalities. Women serve, men sell. It is a familiar notion about which many feminists have been skeptical.

a. The Gender Line: Cashless Women

At a practical level, women should at least be wary of anti-commodification arguments, because these arguments arise when women receive money for something, not when women are paying money for something. The argument is used most frequently in legal discourse when talking about women receiving money for surrogate parenting and sexual contact, and herein for household labor. While Radin extends the argument into gender neutral territories, such as housing, most of the commodification red flags are raised by her and by others when discussing *women's* commodification.

One might respond that the emphasis of the anticommodification argument is that some aspect of women's personhood is going to be sold, not that women are about to receive money. It is the sale that is objectionable, not that women may end up with cash. Consider, though, that it is not uncommon to find people who approve of altruistic transfer in these same areas, for example, human egg donation and surrogacy. In fact, the current fee caps in both of these fields reflect that ideal in practice: donors are not supposed to be *too* motivated by money, so fees are held down to ensure that there is a partially altruistic motivation for donating. In these cases, it seems arguable that the difference that a woman *experiences* may simply be whether money comes to her, and how much, as compared to other wage labor that she might similarly perform from partially altruistic motivation. This difference occurs in the name of non-commodification. It is worth asking whether Anderson's concern about exploitation due to the commodification of women's reproductive capacity might just as easily turn into exploitation from non-commodification, not just in a "nonideal" world. Here the mixed motivations of women are exploited by highlighting the altruistic aspects of those motives in a discriminatory fashion. Only *women's* mixed motives relating to feminine activities are highlighted and offered as justification for leaving women without cash. Mixed motivations in the labor force at large do not require regulatory practices aimed at keeping wages down.

Social practices also exist where the characterization of the problem as "withholding money from women" seems even more apt at the practical level than "preventing the sale of women," given the particular form that current decommodification takes. Prostitutes and pimps have a relationship that results where prohibition on sale ensures that although a female attribute is being sold, a woman is not getting most of the money. * * * Few would argue that the current form of the criminalization of prostitution is intended or designed for the protection of prostitutes, and so the lack of connection between non-commodification (and its female cashless-ness) and sale is hardly remarkable. But in the reproductive areas of surrogacy and egg donation, non-commodification ideals drive the policy of leaving women relatively cashless despite their (partial?) sale.

We do not usually see the anticommodification argument raised as forcefully when things typically associated with male personhood are being sold. While it may be that women's personhood is more at risk for being inappropriately objectified and commercialized, we should at least consider an alternative understanding of why commodification concerns focus on women's issues. It may have as much to do with notions of femininity and a desire to elevate a romantic essentialism about femininity as it does with a desire to protect women's integrity. Consider Anderson's argument that women's reproductive labor is inappropriately alienated by surrogacy be-cause a surrogate mother must "divert [her labor] from the end which the social practices of pregnancy rightly promote—an emotional bond with her child." It is not clear why the end which Anderson prefers for women's labor must be extinguished by money, but it is clear that her argument leaves women without money for their labor. If a reinscription of the public-private spheres ideology on which market rhetoric thrives occurs around women's home labor, it may depend on a particular notion of femininity that has as one of its characteristics cashless women.

NOTES AND QUESTIONS

1. Personhood. Although in the first excerpt above Radin favors incom-plete commodification over the anti-commodification "wall" approach, she has also argued elsewhere that some items, which are "personal," should not be bought or sold because the exchange of such items can damage the personhood of individuals. See Margaret Jane Radin, *Market–Inalienability*, 100 HARV. L.REV. 1849, 1854–55 (1987). Radin explains that certain aspects of life are integral to human beings, and to attach a dollar value to these life aspects would dehumanize them:

> I believe that a better view of personhood should understand many kinds of particulars—one's politics, work, religion, family, love, sexuali-ty, friendships, altruism, experiences, wisdom, moral commitments, character, and personal attributes—as integral to the self. To under-stand any of these as monetizable or completely detached from the person * * * is to do violence to our deepest understanding of what it is to be human.

MARGARET JANE RADIN, CONTESTED COMMODITIES 56 (1996).

Is this view inconsistent with Radin's rejection of the "wall" approach? What items would Radin consider to be essential to "human flourishing" or "personhood"?

Is human body tissue an item too personal to be part of the market? In *Moore v. Regents of the University of California*, 793 P.2d 479 (Cal. 1990), the California Supreme Court encountered this issue. There, the court rejected a patient's claim that his property rights had been violated when his physician and other medical employees made commercial use of the patient's surgically removed spleen without first requesting his permission or sharing the profits. Would Radin disagree with the decision because such a case may provide an incentive for destitute people to sell their organs, thereby injuring their personhood? Or would Radin argue that banning sales of organs fails to cure individuals' desperation for resources, and that legislators should look at the poverty problem itself rather than the market for organs in determining whether some items are essential to personhood?

Based on the *Moore* decision, should the sale of human organs be regulated on the free market?

For an intriguing analysis of the moral and ethical dilemmas of the growing underground market for human body parts, see Michele Goodwin, BLACK MARKETS: THE SUPPLY AND DEMAND OF BODY PARTS, Cambridge University Press (2006).

For more on notions of personhood, please see Sarah E. Waldeck, *Encouraging a Market in Human Milk*, 11 COLUM. J. GENDER & L. 361 (2002); Zachary M. Garsek, *Napster Through the Scope of Property and Personhood: Leaving Artists Incomplete People*, 19–SPG ENT. & SPORTS LAW. 1 (2002); Radhika Rao, *Property, Privacy and the Human Body*, 80 B.U. L. REV. 359 (2000).

2. Altruism. Some scholars suggest that making all products market alienable discourages individuals from making donations, for example, the market for blood samples. Price incentives offered by markets would decrease opportunities for philanthropy and cause the supply of blood donations to diminish. Could a market for blood and a blood donation be mutually exclusive? Would the existence of a market take away individuals' "right to give?" *See* RICHARD M. TITMUSS, THE GIFT RELATIONSHIP: FROM HUMAN BLOOD TO SOCIAL POLICY 198, 237 (1971).

3. Incomplete commodification and women. Radin has explored commodification in the markets in babies or in sexual services. She argues that when sexual and reproductive activities are "commodified," there is a "threat to the personhood of women, who are the 'owners of these commodities.'" However, noncommodification of reproductive and sexual services can also hurt women's personhood. Radin calls this dilemma faced by women the "double bind":

> The threat to personhood from commodification arises because essential attributes are treated as severable fungible objects, and this denies the integrity and uniqueness of the self. But if the social regime prohibits this kind of commodification, it denies women the choice to market their sexual or reproductive services, and given the current feminization of poverty and lack of avenues for free choice for women, this also poses a threat to the personhood of women. The threat from enforced noncommodification arises because narrowing women's choices is a threat to liberation, and because their choices to market

sexual or reproductive services, even if nonideal, may represent the best alternatives available to those who would choose them.

Thus the double bind: both commodification and noncommodification may be harmful.

Margaret Jane Radin, *The Pragmatist and the Feminist*, 63 S. CAL. L. REV. 1699, 1699–1700 (1990).

Katharine Silbaugh wonders why it is activities associated with women, such as childbearing and sex work, that frequently spark an anti-commodification critique. Is there buried sexism in presuming that women should labor for love, not money, and that women's personhood is uniquely at risk when their activities are commodified? Is this another area where "changing stories" might be helpful?

For more on commodification, please see Margaret J. Radin, *Rent Control and Incomplete Commodification: A Rejoinder*, 17 PHIL. & PUB. AFF. 80 (1988); Michelle B. Bray, Note, *Personalizing Personality: Toward a Property Right in Human Bodies*, 69 TEX. L. REV. 209, 241 (1990); Barbara Rothman, *Reproductive Technology and the Commodification of Life, in* EMBRYOS, ETHICS AND WOMEN'S RIGHTS 95 (Elaine Baruch et al. eds., 1988); Elizabeth Anderson, *Is Women's Labor a Commodity?*, 19 PHIL. & PUB. AFF. 71 (1990).

4. ECONOMIC ANALYSIS AND THE CRITIQUE FROM DEMOCRACY

Pricing the Priceless

150 U. Pa. L. Rev. 1553 (2002).

■ FRANK ACKERMAN

■ LISA HEINZERLING

Many analytical approaches to setting environmental standards require some consideration of costs and benefits. Even technology-based regulation, maligned by cost-benefit enthusiasts as the worst form of regulatory excess, typically entails consideration of economic costs. Cost-benefit analysis differs, however, from other analytical approaches in the following respect: it demands that the advantages and disadvantages of a regulatory policy be reduced, as far as possible, to numbers, and then further reduced to dollars and cents. In this feature of cost-benefit analysis lies its doom. Indeed, looking closely at the products of this pricing scheme makes it seem not only a little cold, but a little crazy as well.

Consider the following examples, which we are not making up. They are not the work of a lunatic fringe, but, on the contrary, they reflect the work products of some of the most influential and reputable of today's cost-benefit practitioners. We are not sure whether to laugh or cry; we find it impossible to treat these studies as serious contributions to a rational discussion.

Several years ago, states were in the middle of their litigation against tobacco companies, seeking to recoup the medical expenditures they had incurred as a result of smoking. At that time, W. Kip Viscusi—a professor of law and economics at Harvard and the primary source of the current $6.3 million estimate for the value of a statistical life—undertook research concluding that states, in fact, saved money as the result of smoking by their citizens. Why? Because they died early! They thus saved their states the trouble and expense of providing nursing home care and other services associated with an aging population.

Viscusi didn't stop there. So great, under Viscusi's assumptions, were the financial benefits to the states of their citizens' premature deaths that, he suggested, "cigarette smoking should be subsidized rather than taxed."

Amazingly, this cynical conclusion has not been swept into the dustbin where it belongs, but instead recently has been revived: the tobacco company Philip Morris commissioned the well-known consulting group Arthur D. Little to examine the financial benefits to the Czech Republic of smoking among Czech citizens. Arthur D. Little International, Inc., found that smoking was a financial boon for the government—partly because, again, it caused citizens to die earlier and thus reduced government expenditure on pensions, housing, and health care. This conclusion relies, so far as we can determine, on perfectly conventional cost-benefit analysis.

* * *

* * *

Private businesses, striving to make money, only produce things that they believe someone is willing to pay for. That is, firms only produce things for which the benefits to consumers, measured by consumers' willingness to pay for them, are expected to be greater than the costs of production. It is technologically possible to produce men's business suits in brightly colored polka dots. Nonetheless, successful producers suspect that no one is willing to pay for such products, and usually stick to, at most, minor variations on suits in somber, traditional hues. If some firm did happen to produce a polka-dotted business suit, no one would be forced to buy it; the producer would bear the entire loss resulting from the mistaken decision.

Government, in the view of many critics, is in constant danger of drifting toward producing polka-dot suits—and making people pay for them. Policies, regulations, and public spending do not face the test of the marketplace; there are no consumers who can withhold their dollars from the government until it produces the regulatory equivalent of navy blue and charcoal gray. There is no single quantitative objective for the public sector comparable to profit maximization for businesses. Even with the best of intentions, critics suggest, government programs can easily go astray for lack of an objective standard by which to judge whether or not they are meeting citizens' needs.

Cost-benefit analysis sets out to do for government what the market does for business: add up the benefits of a public policy and compare them to the costs. The two sides of the ledger raise very different issues.

A. Estimating Costs

The first step in a cost-benefit analysis is to calculate the costs of a public policy. For example, the government may require a certain kind of pollution control equipment, for which businesses must pay. Even if a regulation is less detailed and only sets a ceiling on emissions, it results in costs that can be at least roughly estimated through research into available technologies and business strategies for compliance.

The costs of protecting human health and the environment through the use of pollution control devices and other approaches are, by their very nature, measured in dollars. Thus, at least in theory, the cost side of cost-benefit analysis is relatively straightforward. In practice, as we shall see, it is not quite that simple.

The consideration of the costs of environmental protection is not unique to cost-benefit analysis. Development of environmental regulations has almost always involved consideration of economic costs, with or without formal cost-benefit techniques. What is unique to cost-benefit analysis, and far more problematic, is the other side of the balance, the monetary valuation of the benefits of life, health, and nature itself.

B. Monetizing Benefits

Since there are no natural prices for a healthy environment, cost-benefit analysis requires the creation of artificial ones. This is the hardest part of the process. Economists create artificial prices for health and environmental benefits by studying what people would be willing to pay for them. One popular method, called "contingent valuation," is essentially a form of opinion poll. Researchers ask a cross section of the affected population how much they would be willing to pay to preserve or protect something that can't be bought in a store.

Many surveys of this sort have been done, producing prices for things that appear to be priceless. For example, the average American household is supposedly willing to pay $257 to prevent the extinction of bald eagles, $208 to protect humpback whales, and $80 to protect gray wolves. These numbers are quite large: since there are about 100 million households in the country, the nation's total willingness to pay for the preservation of bald eagles alone is ostensibly more than $25 billion.

An alternative method of attaching prices to unpriced things infers what people are willing to pay from observation of their behavior in other markets. To assign a dollar value to risks to human life, for example, economists usually calculate the extra wage—or "wage premium"—that is paid to workers who accept riskier jobs. Suppose that two jobs are comparable, except that one is more dangerous and better paid. If workers understand the risk and voluntarily accept the more dangerous job, then they are implicitly setting a price on risk by accepting the increased risk of death in exchange for increased wages.

What does this indirect inference about wages say about the value of a life? A common estimate in recent cost-benefit analyses is that avoiding a risk that would lead, on average, to one death is worth roughly $6.3 million. This number, in particular, is of great importance in cost-benefit analyses because avoided deaths are the most thoroughly studied benefits of environmental regulations.

C. Discounting the Future

One final step in this quick sketch of cost-benefit analysis requires explanation. Costs and benefits of a policy frequently occur at different times. Often, costs are incurred today, or in the near future, to prevent harm in the more remote future. When the analysis spans a number of years, future costs and benefits are discounted, or treated as equivalent to smaller amounts of money in today's dollars.

Discounting is a procedure developed by economists in order to evaluate investments that produce future income. The case for discounting begins with the observation that $100 received today is worth more than $100 received next year, even in the absence of inflation. For one thing, you could put your money in the bank today and earn interest by next year. Suppose that your bank account earns 3% interest per year. In that case, if you received the $100 today rather than next year, you would earn $3 in interest, giving you a total of $103 next year. Likewise, in order to get $100 next year you only need to deposit $97 today. So, at a 3% discount rate, economists would say that $100 next year has a present value of $97 in today's dollars. * * *

Cost-benefit analysis routinely uses the present value of future benefits; that is, it compares current costs, not to the actual dollar value of future benefits, but to the smaller amount you would have to put into a hypothetical savings account today to obtain those benefits in the future. This application of discounting is essential, and indeed commonplace, for many practical financial decisions. If offered a choice of investment opportunities with payoffs at different times in the future, you can (and should) discount the future payoffs to the present in order to compare them to each other. The important issue for environmental policy, as we shall see, is whether this logic also applies to outcomes far in the future, and to opportunities—like long life and good health—that are not naturally stated in dollar terms.

II. The Case for Cost–Benefit

Before describing the problems with cost-benefit analysis, it will be useful to set forth the arguments in favor of this type of analysis. Many different arguments for cost-benefit analysis have been offered over the years. Most of the arguments fall into one of two broad categories. First, there are economic assertions that better results can be achieved with cost-benefit analysis. Second, there are legal and political claims that a more objective and open government process can emerge through this kind of analysis.

A.   Better Results

Economics frequently focuses on increasing efficiency—on getting the most desirable results from the least resources. How do we know that greater regulatory efficiency is needed? For many economists, this is an article of faith: greater efficiency is always a top priority, in regulation or elsewhere. Cost-benefit analysis supposedly furthers efficiency by ensuring that regulations are only adopted when benefits exceed costs and by helping direct regulators' attention to those problems for which regulatory intervention will yield the greatest net benefits.

But many advocates also raise a more specific argument, imbued with a greater sense of urgency. The government, it is said, often issues rules that are insanely expensive, out of all proportion to their benefits—a problem that could be solved if proposed regulations were screened through cost-benefit analysis. Thus much of the case for cost-benefit analysis depends on the case against current regulation.

Scarcely a congressional hearing on environmental policy occurs in which fantastic estimates of the costs of federal regulations do not figure prominently. Economists routinely cite such estimates as proof of the need for more economic analysis. Browse the websites of any of a variety of think tanks, and you will find numerous references to the extravagant costs of regulation. * * *

From this perspective, cost-benefit analysis emerges as both a money-saver and a life-saver. By subjecting regulations to a cost-benefit test, we would not only stop spending hundreds of millions or billions of dollars to save a single life, we could also take that money and spend it on saving even more lives through different life-saving measures. * * *

B.   Objectivity and Transparency

A second important set of arguments holds that cost-benefit analysis would produce a better regulatory process—one that is more objective and more transparent, and thus more accountable to the public.

The holy grail of administrative law is agency decision making based on objective standards. The idea is to prevent an agency either from making arbitrary decisions or, more invidiously, from benefiting politically-favored groups through its decisions. Cost-benefit analysis has been offered as a means of constraining agency discretion in this way.

Another important goal, said to be promoted by cost-benefit analysis, is the transparency of administrative procedures. Decisions about environmental protection are notoriously complex. They reflect the input of biologists, toxicologists, epidemiologists, economists, engineers, lawyers, and other experts whose work is complicated and arcane. The technical details of these decisions often conceal crucial judgments about how much scientific uncertainty is too much, which human populations should be protected from illness and even death, and how important the future is relative to the present.

In order for the public to be part of the process of decision making about the environment, these judgments must be offered and debated in language accessible to people who are not biologists, toxicologists, or other kinds of experts. Many advocates of cost-benefit analysis believe that their methodology provides such a language. Relatedly, they assert that cost-benefit analysis renders decision making transparent insofar as it requires decision makers to reveal all of the assumptions and uncertainties reflected in their decisions. * * *

As we have seen, cost-benefit analysis involves the creation of artificial markets for things—like good health, long life, and clean air—that are not bought and sold. It also involves the devaluation of future events through discounting.

So described, the mindset of the cost-benefit analyst is likely to seem quite foreign. The translation of all good things into dollars and the devaluation of the future are inconsistent with the way many people view the world. Most of us believe that money doesn't buy happiness. Most religions tell us that every human life is sacred; it is obviously illegal, as well as immoral, to buy and sell human lives. Most parents tell their children to eat their vegetables and do their homework, even though the rewards of these onerous activities lie far in the future. Monetizing human lives and discounting future benefits seem at odds with these common perspectives.

The cost-benefit approach also is inconsistent with the way many of us make daily decisions. Imagine performing a new cost-benefit analysis to decide whether to get up and go to work every morning, whether to exercise or eat right on any given day, whether to wash the dishes or leave them in the sink, and so on. Inaction would win far too often—and an absurd amount of effort would be spent on analysis. Most people have long-run goals, commitments, and habits that make such daily balancing exercises either redundant or counterproductive. The same might be true of society as a whole undertaking individual steps in the pursuit of any goal, set for the long haul, that cannot be reached overnight—including, for example, the achievement of a clean environment.

Moving beyond these intuitive responses, we offer in this Section a detailed explanation of why cost-benefit analysis of environmental protection fails to live up to the hopes and claims of its advocates. There is no quick fix, because these failures are intrinsic to the methodology, appearing whenever it is applied to any complex environmental problem. * * *

A. Dollars Without Sense

Recall that cost-benefit analysis requires the creation of artificial prices for all relevant health and environmental impacts. To weigh the benefits of regulation against the costs, we need to know the monetary value of preventing the extinction of species, preserving many different ecosystems, avoiding all manner of serious health impacts, and even saving human lives. Without such numbers, cost-benefit analysis cannot be conducted.

Artificial prices have been estimated for many, though by no means all, benefits of regulation. As discussed, preventing the extinction of bald eagles reportedly goes for somewhat more than $250 per household. Preventing retardation due to childhood lead poisoning comes in at about $9000 per lost IQ point in the standard view, or as low as $1100 per point in Lutter's alternative. Saving a life is ostensibly worth $6.3 million.

This quantitative precision, achieved through a variety of indirect techniques for valuation, comes at the expense of accuracy and sometimes, common sense. Though problems arise in many areas of valuation, we will focus primarily on the efforts to attach a monetary value to human life, both because of its importance in cost-benefit analysis and because of its glaring contradictions. * * *

1.   There Are No "Statistical" People

What can it mean to say that saving one life is worth $6.3 million? Human life is the ultimate example of a value that is not a commodity and does not have a price. You cannot buy the right to kill someone for $6.3 million, nor for any other price. Most systems of ethical and religious belief maintain that every life is sacred. If analysts calculated the value of life itself by asking people what it is worth to them (the most common method of valuation of other environmental benefits), the answer would be infinite, as "no finite amount of money could compensate a person for the loss of his life, simply because money is no good to him when he is dead."

The standard response is that a value like $6.3 million is not actually a price on an individual's life or death. Rather, it is a way of expressing the value of small risks of death; for example, it is one million times the value of a one in a million risk. If people are willing to pay $6.30 to avoid a one in a million increase in the risk of death, then the "value of a statistical life" is $6.3 million.

Unfortunately, this explanation fails to resolve the dilemma. It is true that risk (or "statistical life") and life itself are distinct concepts. In practice, however, analysts often ignore the distinction between valuing risk and valuing life. Many regulations reduce risk for a large number of people and avoid actual death for a much smaller number. A complete cost-benefit analysis should, therefore, include valuation of both of these benefits. However, the standard practice is to calculate a value only for "statistical" life and to ignore life itself. * * *

2.   People Care About Other People

Another large problem with the standard approach to valuation of life is that it asks individuals (either directly through surveys or indirectly through observing wage and job choices) only about their attitudes toward risks to themselves.

A recurring theme in literature suggests that our deepest and noblest sentiments involve valuing someone else's life more highly than our own: think of parents' devotion to their children, soldiers' commitment to those whom they are protecting, lovers' concern for each other. Most spiritual beliefs call on us to value the lives of others—not only those closest to us, but also those whom we have never met.

This point echoes a procedure that has become familiar in other areas of environmental valuation. Economists often ask about existence values: how much is the existence of a wilderness area or an endangered species worth to you, even if you never will experience it personally? If this question makes sense for bald eagles and national parks, it must be at least as important when applied to safe drinking water and working conditions for people we don't know.

What is the existence value of a person you will never meet? How much is it worth to you to prevent a death far away? The answer cannot be deduced solely from your attitudes toward risks to yourself. We are not aware of any attempts to quantify the existence value of the life of a stranger, let alone a relative or a friend, but we are sure that most belief systems affirm that this value is substantial (assuming, of course, that the value of life is a number in the first place).

3. Voting Is Different from Buying

Cost-benefit analysis, which relies on estimates of individuals' preferences as consumers, also fails to address the collective choice presented to society by most public health and environmental problems.

Valuation of environmental benefits is based on individuals' private decisions as consumers or workers, not on their public values as citizens. However, policies that protect the environment are often public goods and are not available for purchase in individual portions. In a classic example of this distinction, the philosopher Mark Sagoff found that his students, in their role as citizens, opposed commercial ski development in a nearby wilderness area, but, in their role as consumers, would plan to go skiing there if the development were built. There is no contradiction between these two views: as individual consumers, the students would have no way to express their collective preference for wilderness preservation. Their individual willingness to pay for skiing would send a misleading signal about their views as citizens.

It is often impossible to arrive at a meaningful social valuation by adding up the willingness to pay expressed by individuals. What could it mean to ask how much you are personally willing to pay to clean up a major oil spill? If no one else contributes, the clean-up will not happen regardless of your decision. As the Nobel Prize-winning economist Amartya Sen has pointed out, if your willingness to pay for a large-scale public initiative is independent of what others are paying, then you probably have not understood the nature of the problem. Instead, a collective decision about collective resources is required.

In a similar vein, the philosopher Henry Richardson argues that reliance on the cost-benefit standard forecloses the process of democratic deliberation that is necessary for intelligent decision making. In his view, attempts to make decisions based on monetary valuation of benefits freeze preferences in advance, leaving no room for the changes in response to new information, rethinking of the issues, and negotiated compromises that lie at the heart of the deliberative process.

Cost-benefit analysis turns public citizens into selfish consumers and interconnected communities into atomized individuals. In this way, it distorts the question it sets out to answer—how much do we, as a society, value health and the environment?

4. Numbers Don't Tell Us Everything

A few simple examples illustrate that numerically equal risks are not always equally deserving of regulatory response. The death rate is roughly the same (somewhat less than one in a million) from a day of downhill skiing, from a day of working in the construction industry, or from drinking about twenty liters of water containing fifty parts per billion of arsenic—the old regulatory limit that was recently revised by the EPA. This does not mean that society's responsibility to reduce risks is the same in each case.

Most people view risks imposed by others, without an individual's consent, as more worthy of government intervention than risks that an individual knowingly accepts. On that basis, the highest priority among our three examples is to reduce drinking water contamination—a hazard to which no one has consented. The acceptance of a risky occupation such as construction is at best quasi-voluntary; it involves somewhat more individual discretion than the "choice" of public drinking water supplies even though many people go to work under great economic pressure and with little information about occupational hazards. In contrast, the choice of risky recreational pursuits such as skiing is entirely discretionary; obviously, no one is forced to ski. Safety regulation in construction work is thus more urgent than regulation of skiing, despite the equality of numerical risk.

In short, even for ultimate values such as life and death, the social context is decisive in our evaluation of risks. Cost-benefit analysis assumes the existence of generic, acontextual risk and thereby ignores the contextual information that determines the manner in which many people, in practice, think about real risks to real people.

5. Artificial Prices Are Expensive

Finally, the economic valuation called for by cost-benefit analysis is fundamentally flawed because it demands an enormous volume of consistently updated information, which is beyond the practical capacity of our society to generate.

All attempts at valuation of the environment begin with a problem: the goal is to assign monetary prices to things that have no prices because they are not for sale. One of the great strengths of the market is that it provides so much information about real prices. For any commodity that actually is bought and sold, prices are communicated automatically, almost costlessly, and with constant updates as needed. To create artificial prices for environmental values, economists have to find some way to mimic the operation of the market. Unfortunately, the process is far from automatic, certainly not costless, and has to be repeated every time an updated price is needed.

As a result, there is constant pressure to use outdated or inappropriate valuations. Indeed, there are sound economic reasons for doing so: no one can afford constant updates, and significant savings can be achieved by using valuations created for other cases. * * *

B.   Trivializing the Future

* * *

Cost-benefit analysis systematically downgrades the importance of the future in two ways: through the technique of discounting and through predictive methodologies that take inadequate account of the possibility of catastrophic and irreversible events. * * *

C.   Exacerbating Inequality

The third fundamental defect of cost-benefit analysis is that it tends to ignore, and therefore has the effect of reinforcing, patterns of economic and social inequality. Cost-benefit analysis consists of adding up all the costs of a policy, adding up all the benefits, and comparing the totals. Implicit in this innocuous-sounding procedure is the controversial assumption that it does not matter who gets the benefits and who pays the costs. Both benefits and costs are measured simply as dollar totals; those totals are silent on questions of equity and distribution of resources.

In our society, concerns about equity frequently do, and should, enter into debates over public policy. There is an important difference between spending state tax revenues to improve the parks in rich communities and spending the same revenues to clean up pollution in poor communities. The value of these two initiatives, measured using cost-benefit analysis, might be the same in both cases, but this does not mean that the two policies are equally urgent or desirable.

The problem of equity runs even deeper. Benefits are typically measured by willingness to pay for environmental improvement, and the rich are able and willing to pay for more than the poor. Imagine a cost-benefit analysis of siting an undesirable facility, such as a landfill or incinerator. Wealthy communities are willing to pay more for the benefit of not having the facility in their backyards; thus, the net benefits to society as a whole will be maximized by putting the facility in a low-income area. (Note that wealthy communities do not actually have to pay for the benefit of avoiding the facility; the analysis depends only on the fact that they are willing to pay.)

This kind of logic was made (in)famous in a 1991 memo circulated by Lawrence Summers (former Secretary of the Treasury and current President of Harvard University) when he was the chief economist at the World Bank. Discussing the migration of "dirty industries" to developing countries, Summers' memo explained:

> The measurements of the costs of health impairing pollution depend [] on the foregone earnings from increased morbidity and mortality. From this point of view a given amount of health impairing pollution should be done in the country with the lowest cost, which will be the country with the lowest wages. I think the economic logic behind dumping a load of toxic waste in the lowest wage country is impeccable and we should face up to that.

After this memo became public, Brazil's then-Secretary of the Environment Jose Lutzenburger wrote to Summers:

> Your reasoning is perfectly logical but totally insane ... Your thoughts [provide] a concrete example of the unbelievable alienation, reductionist thinking, social ruthlessness and the arrogant ignorance of many conventional "economists" concerning the nature of the world we live in.

If decisions are based strictly on cost-benefit analysis and willingness to pay, most environmental burdens will end up being imposed on the countries, communities, and individuals with the least resources. This theoretical pattern bears an uncomfortably close resemblance to reality. Cost-benefit methods should not be blamed for existing patterns of environmental injustice; we suspect that pollution is typically dumped on the poor without waiting for formal analysis. Still, cost-benefit analysis rationalizes and reinforces the problem, allowing environmental burdens to flow downhill along the income gradients of an unequal world. It is hard to see this as part of an economically optimal or politically objective method of decision making.

In short, equity is an important criterion for evaluation of public policy, but it does not fit into the cost-benefit framework. The same is true of questions of rights and morality principles that are not reducible to monetary terms. * * *

D. Less Objectivity and Transparency

A fourth fundamental flaw of cost-benefit analysis is that it is unable to deliver on the promise of more objective and more transparent decision making. In fact, in most cases the use of cost-benefit analysis is likely to deliver less objectivity and less transparency.

For the reasons we have discussed, there is nothing objective about the basic premises of cost-benefit analysis. Treating individuals solely as consumers, rather than as citizens with a sense of moral responsibility to the larger society, represents a distinct and highly contestable world view. Likewise, the use of discounting reflects judgments about the nature of environmental risks and citizens' responsibilities toward future generations that are, at a minimum, debatable. Because value-laden premises permeate cost-benefit analysis, the claim that cost-benefit analysis offers an "objective" way to make government decisions is simply bogus.

Furthermore, as we have seen, cost-benefit analysis relies on a byzantine array of approximations, simplifications, and counterfactual hypotheses. Thus, the actual use of cost-benefit analysis inevitably involves countless judgment calls. People with strong, and clashing, partisan positions naturally will advocate that discretion in the application of this methodology be exercised in favor of their positions, further undermining the claim that cost-benefit analysis is objective.

Perhaps the best way to illustrate how little economic analysis has to contribute, objectively, to the fundamental question of how clean and safe we want our environment to be is to refer again to the controversy over cost-benefit analysis of the EPA's regulation of arsenic in drinking water. As Cass Sunstein has recently argued, the available information on the benefits of arsenic reduction supports estimates of net benefits from regulation ranging from less than zero up to $560 million or more. The number of deaths avoided annually by regulation is, according to Sunstein, between zero and 112. A procedure that allows such an enormous range of different evaluations of a single rule is certainly not the objective, transparent decision rule that its advocates have advertised.

These uncertainties arise from the limited knowledge of the epidemiology and toxicology of exposure to arsenic as well as the controversial series of assumptions required for valuation and discounting of costs and (particularly) benefits. As Sunstein explains, a number of different positions, including most of those heard in the recent controversy over arsenic regulation, could be supported by one or another reading of the evidence.

Some analysts might respond that this enormous range of outcomes is not possible if the proper economic assumptions are used—if, for example, human lives are valued at $6 million apiece and discounted at a five percent yearly rate (or, depending on the analyst, other favorite numbers). But these assumptions beg fundamental questions about ethics and equity, and one cannot decide whether to embrace them without thinking through the whole range of moral issues they raise. Yet once one has thought through these issues, there is no need then to collapse the complex moral inquiry into a series of numbers. Pricing the priceless merely translates our inquiry into a different, and foreign, language—one with a painfully impoverished vocabulary.

For many of the same reasons, cost-benefit analysis also generally fails to achieve the goal of transparency. Cost-benefit analysis is a complex, resource-intensive, and expert-driven process. It requires a great deal of time and effort to attempt to unpack even the simplest cost-benefit analysis. Few community groups, for example, have access to the kind of scientific and technical expertise that would allow them to evaluate whether, intentionally or unintentionally, the authors of a cost-benefit analysis have unfairly slighted the interests of the community or some of its members. Few members of the public can participate meaningfully in the debates about the use of particular regression analyses or discount rates which are central to the cost-benefit method.

The translation of lives, health, and nature into dollars also renders decision making about the underlying social values less rather than more transparent. As we have discussed, all of the various steps required to reduce a human life to a dollar value are open to debate and subject to uncertainty. However, the specific dollar values kicked out by cost-benefit analysis tend to obscure these underlying issues rather than encourage full public debate about them.

―――――

Democratic Estates

Harvard Public Law Working Paper No. 08–42 (2009).
http://ssrn.com/abstract=1278136.

■ Joseph W. Singer

In thinking about property and property law, we cannot confine ourselves to the techniques of economic theory or cost-benefit analysis. Rather, we must look to basic moral and political theory for the normative frameworks that economic theory lacks. Although economic analysis of property rights appears to be the dominant approach in law schools these days, the underlying moral theory on which it is based is generally regarded by moral and political philosophers as fatally flawed—at least unless it is supplemented or cabined by normative analyses of other kinds, such as considerations of justice, fairness, obligations, and ethics. The only form of utilitarian analysis that has strong support among moral theorists these days is a morally-constrained utilitarianism; preference-based theories are generally deemed defective unless they focus on idealized preferences—what preferences would be if perfectly informed and chosen in a suitable decision setting. Moral theorists espouse a variety of ways of thinking about right conduct but almost all of them ask us to consider the ways in which our actions affect others and the extent to which we could justify our actions to those affected by them. Cost-benefit analysis fails to meet this basic test because its fails to respect the separateness of persons, each of whom is entitled to be treated with equal concern and respect.

Moreover, political theorists wrestle with the question of how to structure a society of free and equal persons with differing conceptions of the good. Liberty and justice in such a society can only be established by fair ground rules for exercising political and economic power. Political and moral theory, as well as sophisticated economic theory, requires us to judge the legitimacy of individual interests and the shape of basic institutional structures. We do not take preferences merely as given, partly because some preferences are illegitimate in a democracy and partly because preferences are shaped by law and custom. Moreover, markets are not states of nature; they are regulated by law and the legal rules defining property rights are a major element of that regulation. One cannot ask what the market solution to a problem is without first defining the legal parameters of market institutions and economic relationships. It is circular to ask economic analysis to define property rights when one needs to define property rights first to determine what market transactions will emerge. There is no escape from the need to use some other form of analysis, such as political and moral theory, to define and shape the basic structure of society. Political theory supports the idea of creating a democracy that respects fundamental human rights. This institutional setting forms the background within which the market can operate, not the reverse.

The democratic model of property recognizes that property serves plural values and that law should reflect those multiple values. Property gives us freedom and stability, provides a source of wealth and well-being, the bases for creative work and useful investment. Property provides a place to create family life, to nurture friendships, to rest, and to have fun. Property allows us to be good neighbors and good citizens and it promotes various human values, including privacy, the freedom to associate with others, religious liberty, tranquility and peace of mind. It is a mistake to try to reduce values to a single metric such as wealth, utility, well-being, welfare, or even liberty. We care about qualitative distinctions among values, not just the extent to which our preferences are satisfied. * * *

What are the normative features of property law in a free and democratic society? We value autonomy; individuals must have the freedom to determine the shape of their own lives, in a manner consistent with a similar freedom for others. Thus, they cannot be forced to remain on the family homestead, impressed into the family business against their will. We value mobility; people should not be "tied to the land" and prevented from moving to another place, taking another job, forming new family and friendships and business relations. Thus, we view restraints on alienation of property with a highly skeptical eye. We value widespread distribution of property and realistic potential for access to ownership. Thus, we enact laws to promote equal opportunity. We create public schools and we prohibit discrimination in housing, employment, and public accommodations. We value freedom of contract but we also ensure that market participants comply with minimum standards for economic and social relationships. Thus, we have consumer protection statutes, the implied warranty of habitability, workplace safety laws. We feel obligations to each other in times of need, so we have unemployment compensation, Social Security, Medicare, disaster relief. * * * Different property rules and regulations serve different purposes and some serve multiple purposes. The plural values we hold underlie those regulations and definitions of property rights. * * *

What implications does the democratic model of property have for specific cases? Consider the question of whether a tenant has the right to post a sign supporting Obama or McCain in the front yard of a rented house. How should we think about this question?

Efficiency theorists suggest we should figure out the result that maximizes satisfaction of preferences as measured by market values. If the tenant values the right to post signs on the property, she should bargain for it; if the landlord refuses, we have evidence the costs to the landlord outweigh the benefits to the tenant. Transaction costs are not likely to be high here, nor are externalities since the tenant can support her preferred candidate in other ways. And we can expect no different result if we created a default rule that individuals have a right to post such signs; landlords who do not like this will simply bargain around it. And we can save both bargaining and information costs by limiting the rights of tenants and letting them know that if they want access to someone else's land, they need to bargain for the terms they want. This leaves the specification of rights to the private market place (the bargaining of the parties) rather than the inefficient litigation process whereby judges try to approximate the welfare-maximizing result.

Libertarians will make similar but even stronger arguments. Owners have no duty to rent to tenants and they have the right to determine the terms on which tenants access their land. The law should not prevent the parties from making the contracts that serve their mutual interests. Liberal egalitarians may be worried about denying tenants the right to engage in expressive speech but it is not clear that they have a good answer to the question of why the tenant's right to post a sign is more important than the landlord's right to keep the property free of such signs, especially if the landlord supports a different candidate for president. They may argue that tenants have unequal bargaining power and that if tenants had sufficient market power, they would be unlikely to give up the right to engage in the political process in this manner. But this argument assumes that we know what bargains would occur in the absence of unequal market power, and such predictive claims are hard to back up; they seem much more based on substantive judgments about the relative importance of the parties' interests than a real prediction of what bargains would be reached if property were distributed differently. In other words, this "prediction" seems to mask or be based on a *judgment* about which interest is more important in a democratic society. Such a judgment goes beyond considerations of distributive justice; it requires discussion of qualitative differences among interests and the legitimate contours of the good society.

Radin's personality theory does allow us to discuss qualitative distinctions; the right to put up a political sign is associated with core elements of personality and humanity and we could argue that individuals should not be forced to give up such rights. This suggests that the tenant's personal interest in posting the sign outweighs the landlord's fungible interest in protecting the market value of the property. At the same time, landlords may have personal interests in the appearance of their property, especially if the property is owner-occupied. And, like tenants, landlords have personal interests in not having their property used to support candidates they do not support. Why should the tenant's interest outweigh the landlord's interest? The answer might be that the landlord can put up a sign on his own house. He does not have the right to also put up signs on property he has rented to others; nor may he deprive tenants of similar rights. This requires, however, a substantive judgment that landlords should not be allowed to treat rental property the same as they treat their homes. What is the basis of this conclusion? It rests on a notion of equality but it also depends on an assumption about the liberties that property law both enables and constrains.

The personality theory asks us to look at how property is connected to personality, but it also suggests that we consider whether it is *legitimate* for landlords to claim the right to treat their business property in the same way they treat their personal property. A landlord, for example, may wish to discriminate on the basis of race in his choice of tenants; this may even go to the core of his sense of himself. Racially segregated property is not fungible with integrated property in the mind of a racist landlord. But our system outlaws this arrangement regardless of the strength of the land-lord's preference. We do so because we judge this arrangement to be beyond the contours of allowable social relationships in a free and democratic society.

In contrast to traditional approaches, the democratic model of property focuses our attention on the need to make normative judgments about the appropriate contours of property relationships in a free and democratic society. We may do this on a number of levels. We would first ask whether denying someone the right to put up a political sign on her property violates *basic norms* governing social, political, and economic relationships in a polity that treats each person with equal concern and respect. Even if we do not consider this to be a basic human right (whether or not based in the first amendment or other aspects of constitutional law), we should still consider whether such a regulation should be imposed as a matter of *consumer protection law*, either because it protects justified expectations or because it accords with settled convictions about rights that ought to go along with possession of land. * * *

There are various ways to think through and justify alternative resolutions to these questions. None of them gives us a mechanical decision procedure to generate an outcome. They include, for example, exercises in framing the issue, telling the story, balancing the parties' interests, defining the values of a free and democratic society, asking what rule we would favor if we did not know whether we would be the landlord or the tenant, considering the legitimate scope of obligations we have to others as equal human beings, considering our national history and customs and the availability of alternative means of expressing political support for candidates. We must also consider the consequences of adopting one rule over another. Will people get around the rule by creating new property rights we have not yet imagined? Will we make things worse for people by depriving them of the power to give up this right? Will we be depriving people of the power to create a living space free of political campaigning?

NOTES AND QUESTIONS

1. Beyond cost-benefit analysis? Ackerman and Heinzerling's attack on cost-benefit analysis draws force from several of the attacks we have examined in this chapter, including the anti-commodification critique and the anti-subordination critique. Does their attack, however, add up to a case for eliminating cost-benefit analysis entirely, or simply recognizing its limits? Is their attack on cost-benefit analysis an attack on economic analysis generally? If so, is it persuasive?

2.   Economic analysis and democratic deliberation: the theory of civic republicanism. One of the many items in the Ackerman and Heinzerling case against cost-benefit analysis is the argument that it subverts or undermines the project of building and sustaining equal citizenship and participatory democracy. Singer makes this argument in a more sustained way. These scholars and others draw on a theory of politics known as "civic republicanism." Civic republicanism rejects the "liberal" ideal of politics, in which interest groups lobby and negotiate to further their individual interests, and instead endorses a view of politics in which citizens should come together to discuss and argue about the common good. This view of participatory politics is premised on the notion that American society is based on a social contract, under which a nation's people agree to participate and support each other through a government mechanism.

> It is as if we made a contract with the state, or more properly with each other, that we would live together according to certain rules, which are also—according to our best rational calculations—in our own interest as well. In return for our obedience to the rules, everyone else will obey them too (or be threatened and forced to do so).

Robert C. Solomon, A Passion for Justice: Emotions and Origins of the Social Contract 55 (1990). This theory draws on the political theory of John Locke. See The Social Contract: Essays By Locke, Hume and Rousseau 56–57 (Greenwood Press 1980) (Sie Ernest Barker ed., 1947).

From a civic republican perspective, political actors can, and should, advise each other to attain a degree of separation from popular preferences and subject their preferences to extensive analysis. By detaching themselves from the heavy influence of interest groups and sharing ideas with one another, government officials can reach more rational and collective decisions for the common good. Both political participation and deliberation are needed for a strong body politic, but deliberation is needed to manage and mitigate the heavy pressures exerted by intermediary organizations to influence public policies. Though the two notions go hand in hand, deliberation differs from mere political participation in that it helps strengthen the political process:

> If the common good is entirely a matter of an agency's decisionmaking procedure, participation and deliberation will often, but not always, be complementary, and citizens who participate in agency decisions will be afforded all of the advantages of a deliberative process. Likewise, deliberation depends upon participation because for the common good to prevail throughout the process, members of the affected community must be allowed to participate directly in its deliberations. * * * * * *

As a conceptual matter, deliberation is quite separable from participation. Participation helps to ensure that agency decisions are responsive to the will of the public, transparent, and open. Deliberation, by contrast, removes decision events from the immediate influence of the public, slowing down the political process and giving it a deeper legitimacy; it ensures that collective decisions are something more than the consensus of "mere majorities." While participation encourages breadth in the agency decisionmaking process, deliberation is more concerned with depth.

Jim Rossi, *Participation Run Amok: The Costs of Mass Participation for Deliberative Agency Decisionmaking*, 92 Nw. U. L. REV. 173, 211, 212 (1997).

Rossi is arguing that because deliberation lessens the pace of political procedures, government officials are less likely to be influenced by the clout of factions in making policy. With deliberation, politicians can make their own rational decisions, effectively working for a greater common good:

> Deliberative democracy presumes that the public interest is more than the result of a contest between competing private interests. Politics is understood to be a process in which private interests are subordinated in "an ongoing process of collective self-determination." Because the self is understood to be "socially situated," it is only partially knowable apart from knowledge of others. As a result, a political process based merely on inputting private preferences is unsatisfactory because the political process must also shape preferences in order to permit the " 'intersubjective' constitution of individual selves."
>
> * * *
>
> [Cass] Sunstein understands the administrative process to be deliberative. The administrator's superior technical sophistication makes it possible for agency policy to be governed by reason, not power. The expert administrator for Sunstein, though, is less Platonic guardian than informed citizen—a person whose superior knowledge facilitates deliberative democratic performance. Their technical expertise enables participants in the administrative process with "disparate views" to push past their unreflective, personal preferences and find consensus.

Note, *Civic Republican Administrative Theory: Bureaucrats as Deliberative Democrats*, 107 HARV. L. REV. 1401, 1402–03, 1406–07 (1994). Because government officials have the requisite technical knowledge to render reasonable decisions, their choices should be viewed as legitimate. Conversely, ordinary citizens may lack the civic competence to make reasonable recommendations to officials who produce policy:

> Civic competence is a central preoccupation of people who want citizens to base political choices on a broad and accurate understanding of their consequences. Such desires, however, are dashed by evidence that citizens spend little time and effort engaging in politics. The finding that many Americans cannot answer common survey questions about a wide range of political phenomena, for example, dampens many observers' confidence in civic competence.

Arthur Lupia, *Deliberation Disconnected: What It Takes to Improve Civic Competence*, 65 SUM. LAW & CONTEMP. PROBS. 133, 133–34 (2002). Does this mean that politicians are more likely than lesser competent ordinary citizens to issue legitimate policies?

Where does economic analysis fit in this picture? Should cost-benefit analysis be one of the tools of democratic deliberation? Or is it inimical to such deliberation?

3.   Is civic republicanism possible in a mass society? Civic republicans emphasize the need for participation in order for citizens to have some control over policies that affect their lives. However, in order for individuals to participate in the political process, the size of the republic must be limited—a large republic runs the risk of decreasing the relationship between citizens and their representatives and reduces opportunities for participation. Criticizing Cass Sunstein, who has been a prominent proponent of civic republicanism, Karan Bhatia briefly describes the need for a small republic:

> Sunstein uses the terms "citizenship" and "participation" interchangeably. Participation in government serves several functions in the republican calculus. Obviously, it is instrumental to deliberation. Equally important, Sunstein argues, participation nurtures feelings of empathy, virtue, and community essential to a healthy republic. The importance of citizen participation makes representation at best a necessary evil in a republican scheme. This explains why republics are commonly thought of as small and decentralized.

Bhatia, *supra*, at 1310. With a small republic, citizens will have a better chance to deliberate and work towards a common good; sharing similar views regarding institutions and foundations, individuals can reach agreements relatively easily. Is it correct to assume that a small republic would encourage political participation? What are some ways in which a small republic may be an impediment to an efficient government system?

Inclusion of citizenship highlights the need for deliberation and participation. Though citizenship and discussion among community members are appealing, it may be too idealistic to assume that all individuals will participate and reach a consensus in making policy decisions:

> Once again, the civic republicans are faced with an insoluble dilemma. On the one hand, if the community is truly organic, every citizen must have a say in the community's discussions and must participate in the process in order to develop the properly virtuous attitudes and values. On the other hand, if the community forces citizens to participate against their will, a strongly motivated minority will be able to manipulate the political process by obtaining support for their favored policies from unwilling participants in exchange for an agreement to support the unwilling participants in some later policy dispute. Unless the civic republicans make the unrealistic and utopian presumption that all citizens agree about important policy matters before political deliberation begins, their organic community dissolves into a system

> indistinguishable from the one whose problems civic republicanism is supposed to cure.

Gey, *supra* at 820. Gey's disagreement with Sunstein centers in on the fact that many citizens can be apathetic regarding political participation, making the possibility of every citizen taking part in the political process quite futile. However, if every citizen is forced to partake in deliberative decision-making, political bargaining and the struggle between interest groups may intensify, which is an unattractive pluralistic notion. Gey, *supra*, at 820. Is Gey correct that Sunstein's view of complete political participation by community members runs the risk of increasing the force of influential interest groups?

Vanderbilt University Professor of Law Suzanna Sherry would probably agree with Gey's views. She asserts that most citizens are not prepared enough to participate politically, and that unless deliberation is limited to a select few elites, Sunstein's idealized system may try to change the values of ordinary citizens:

> First, the neo-republican ideal of deliberative democracy borders on the utopian. The vast majority of Americans are neither inclined nor equipped to engage in the kind of sustained, reasoned deliberation contemplated by the republicans. Moreover, republican suggestions for promoting rational deliberation may actually have the effect of "undermining public political participation, especially among poorer groups." The republican revival will not go beyond a small corps of elite law professors if it does not face up to the citizenry's lack of interest. However, neither of the two most promising ways of coming to terms with that problem is politically acceptable to most neo-republicans: either we could acknowledge that real political participation will necessarily be limited to the few because only the few are civic minded enough to participate, or we might attempt to change the values of the many so that they too are interested in participating in our rational political discussions. The first solution conflicts with the egalitarianism of modern republicans, and the second with their unwillingness to abandon the ethical relativism of modern liberalism.

Suzanna Sherry, *Responsible Republicanism: Educating for Citizenship*, 62 U. CHI. L. REV. 131, 137–38 (1995). Is Sherry correct in asserting that Sunstein's model may alter citizens' choices and values? What are some mechanisms by which the government can change citizens' views so they could partake in the deliberation process?

For more discussion on citizenship in the civic republican model, please refer to Kathryn Abrams, *Law's Republicanism*, 97 YALE L.J. 1591 (1988); Frank I. Michelman, *Law's Republic*, 97 YALE L.J. 1493 (1988); J. David Hoeveler, Jr., *Original Intent and the Politics of Republicanism*, 75 MARQ. L. REV. 863 (1992); Daniel Rodgers, *Republicanism: The Career of a Concept*, 79 J. AM. HIST. 11, 12–13 (1992); G. Edward White, *Reflections on the "Republican Revival": Interdisciplinary Scholarship in the Legal Academy*, 6 YALE J.L. & HUM. 1, 13, 22 (1994); JOYCE ABBLEBY, LIBERALISM AND REPUBLICANISM IN THE HISTORICAL IMAGINATION (1992); Adrian Oldfield, *Citizen-*

ship and Community: Civic Republicanism and the Modern World, in THE CITIZENSHIP DEBATES: A READER, 75–92 (Gerson Shafir ed., 1998).

4. Radical political theory. Civic republicanism is not the only possible lens through which to elevate democratic values over efficiency values. According to radical theory, which studies the socio-historic process of the political economy under capitalism, capitalism cannot meet the needs of the people collectively. Centuries of capitalism have failed to provide everyone with health care, a living wage, and a secure livelihood. Neither the conservative free market nor liberal welfare conceptions of capitalism meet the needs of society. Like Friedman, most economists identify a human capital gap, which can be overcome by increased education and technological training, as the main cause of wage and opportunity disparities. Radical theorists reject this conception. They conclude that, so long as the present capitalist economic system exists, differentials in pay, income, and employment opportunities will exist for women, minorities, and the disabled. "Neither the market nor civil rights laws can undermine the structure of inequality nor prevent its reproduction." We must return to basic questions that neoclassical economists claim the price system answered: What purposes should our economy serve? "What is work, who controls it, and what is its purpose?"

The fall of the Soviet Union brought with it an intellectual disintegration of Marxist theory. However, Johns Hopkins University geographer, David Harvey writes eloquently of the history of postmodernity. Harvey argues that postmodernist culture is an extension of the "basic rules of capitalistic accumulation." In the following passage, Harvey summarizes the major insights of Marx and Engels.

The Condition of Postmodernity: An Enquiry Into the Origins of Cultural Change
Blackwell (1989) at 99–106.

■ DAVID HARVEY

In *The Communist Manifesto* Marx and Engels argue that the bourgeoisie has created a new internationalism via the world market, together with "subjection of nature's forces to man, machinery, application of chemistry to agriculture and industry, steam navigation, railways, electric telegraphs, clearing of whole continents for cultivation, canalization of rivers, whole populations conjured out of the ground." It has done this at great cost: violence, destruction of traditions, oppression, reduction of the valuation of all activity to the cold calculus of money and profit. Furthermore:

> Constant revolutionizing of production, uninterrupted disturbance of all social relations, everlasting uncertainty and agitation, distinguish the bourgeois epoch from all earlier times. All fixed, fast-frozen relationships, with their train of venerable ideas and opinions, are swept away, all new-formed ones become obsolete before they can ossify. All

that is solid melts into air, all that is holy is profaned, and men at last are forced to face with sober sense the real conditions of their lives and their relations with their fellow men. Karl Marx, The Communist Manifesto.

But what is special about Marx is the way he dissects the origin of this general condition.

Marx begins *Capital*, for example, with an analysis of commodities, those everyday things (food, shelter, clothing, etc.) which we daily consume in the course of reproducing ourselves. Yet the commodity is, he avers, "a mysterious thing" because it simultaneously embodies both a use value (it fulfils a particular want or need) and an exchange value (I can use it as a bargaining chip to procure other commodities). This duality always renders the commodity ambiguous for us; shall we consume it or trade it away? But as exchange relations proliferate and price-fixing markets form, so one commodity typically crystallizes out as money. With money the mystery of the commodity takes on a new twist, because the use value of money is that it represents the world of social labour and of exchange value. Money lubricates exchange but above all it becomes the means by which we typically compare and assess, both before and after the fact of exchange, the value of all commodities. * * *

The advent of a money economy, Marx argues, dissolves the bonds and relations that make up "traditional" communities so that "money becomes the real community." We move from a social condition, in which we depend directly on those we know personally, to one in which we depend on impersonal and objective relations with others. As exchange relations proliferate, so money appears more and more as "a power external to and independent of the producers," so what "originally appears as a means to promote production becomes a relation alien" to them. Money concerns dominate producers. Money and market exchange draws a veil over, "masks" social relationships between things. This condition Marx calls "the fetishism of commodities." * * *

The conditions of labour and life, the sense of joy, anger, or frustration that lie behind the production of commodities, the states of mind of the producers, are all hidden to us as we exchange one object (money) for another (the commodity). We can take our daily breakfast without a thought for the myriad people who engaged in its production. All traces of exploitation are obliterated in the object (there are no finger marks of exploitation in the daily bread). We cannot tell from contemplation of any object in the supermarket what conditions of labour lay behind its production. The concept of fetishism explains how it is that under conditions of capitalist modernization we can be so objectively dependent on "others" whose lives and aspirations remain so totally opaque to us. * * *

As commodity producers seeking money, * * * we are dependent upon the needs and capacity of others to buy. Producers consequently have a permanent interest in cultivating "excess and intemperance" in others, in feeding "imaginary appetites" to the point where ideas of what constitutes social need are replaced by "fantasy, caprice, and whim." The capitalist producer increasingly "plays the pimp" between the consumers and their sense of need, excites in them "morbid appetites, lies in wait for each of [their] weaknesses—all so that he can demand the cash for this service of live." Pleasure, leisure, seduction, and erotic life are all brought within the range of money power and commodity production. Capitalism therefore "produces sophistication of needs and of their means on the one hand, and a bestial barbarization, a complete, unrefined, and abstract simplicity of need, on the other." Advertising and commercialization destroy all traces of production in their imagery, reinforcing the fetishism that arises automatically in the course of market exchange.

Furthermore, money, as the supreme representation of social power in capitalist society, itself becomes the object of lust, greed, and desire. Yet here, too, we encounter double meanings. Money confers the privilege to exercise power over others—we can buy their labour time or the services they offer, even build systematic relations of domination over exploited classes simply through control over money power. Money, in fact, fuses the political and the economic into a genuine political economy of overwhelming power relations * * *. The common material languages of money and commodities provide a universal basis within market capitalism for linking everyone into an identical system of market valuation and so procuring the reproduction of social life through an objectively grounded system of social bonding. Yet within these broad constraints, we are "free," as it were, to develop our own personalities and relationships in our own way, our own "otherness," even to forge group language games, provided, of course, that we have enough money to live on satisfactorily. Money is a "great leveler and cynic," a powerful underminer of fixed social relations, and a great "democratizer." As a social power that can be held by individual persons it forms the basis for a wide-ranging individual liberty, a liberty that can be deployed to develop ourselves as free-thinking individuals without reference to others. Money unifies precisely *through* its capacity to accommodate individualism, otherness, and extraordinary social fragmentation. * * *

Participation in market exchange presupposes a certain division of labour as well as a capacity to separate (alienate) oneself from one's own product. The result is an estrangement from the product of one's own experience, a fragmentation of social tasks and a separation of the subjective meaning of a process of production from the objective market valuation of the product. A highly organized technical and social division of labour, though by no means unique to capitalism, is one of the founding principles of capitalist modernization. This forms a powerful lever to promote economic growth and the accumulation of capital, particularly under conditions of market exchange in which individual commodity producers (protected by private property rights) can explore the possibilities of specialization within an open economic system. This explains the power of economic (free market) liberalism as a founding doctrine for capitalism. It is precisely in such a context that possessive individualism and creative entrepreneurialism, innovation, and speculation, can flourish, even though this also means a proliferating fragmentation of tasks and responsibilities, and a necessary transformation of social relations to the point where producers are forced to view others in purely instrumental terms. * * *

Capitalists when they purchase labour power necessarily treat it in instrumental terms. The labourer is viewed as a "hand" rather than as a whole person * * *, and the labour contributed is a "factor" (notice the reification) of production. The purchase of labour power with money gives the capitalist certain rights to dispose of the labour of others without necessary regard for what the others might think, need, or feel. The omnipresence of this class relation of domination, offset only to the degree that the labourers actively struggle to assert their rights and express their feelings, suggests one of the founding principles upon which the very idea of "otherness" is produced and reproduced on a continuing basis in capitalist society. The world of the working class becomes the domain of that "other," which is necessarily rendered opaque and potentially unknowable by virtue of the fetishism of market exchange. And I should also add parenthetically that if there are already those in society (women, blacks, colonized peoples, minorities of all kinds) who can readily be conceptualized as the other, then the conflation of class exploitation with gender, race, colonialism, ethnicity, etc. can proceed apace with all manner of invidious results. Capitalism did not invent "the other" but it certainly made use of and promoted it in highly structured ways. * * *

The "coercive laws" of market competition force all capitalists to seek out technological and organizational changes that will enhance their own profitability vis-à-vis the social average, thus entraining all capitalists in leap-frogging processes of innovation that reach their limit only under conditions of massive labour surpluses. The need to keep the labourer under control in the workplace, and to undercut the bargaining power of the labourer in the market (particularly under conditions of relative labour scarcity and active class resistance), also stimulates capitalists to innovate. Capitalism is necessarily technologically dynamic, not because of the mythologized capacities of the innovative entrepreneur (as Schumpeter was later to argue) but because of the coercive laws of competition and the conditions of class struggle endemic to capitalism.

The effect of continuous innovation, however, is to devalue, if not destroy, past investments and labour skills. *Creative destruction* is embedded within the circulation of capital itself. Innovation exacerbates instability, insecurity, and in the end, becomes the prime force pushing capitalism into periodic paroxysms of crisis. Not only does the life of modern industry become a series of periods of moderate activity, prosperity, over-production, crisis, and stagnation, "but the uncertainty and instability to which machinery subjects the employment, and consequently the conditions of existence, of the operatives become normal." Furthermore:

"All means for the development of production transform themselves into means of domination over, and exploitation of, the producers' they mutilate the labourer into a fragment of a man, degrade him to the level of an appendage of a machine, destroy every remnant of charm from his work and turn it into a hated toil; they estrange from him the intellectual potentialities of the labour-process in the same proportion as science is incorporate in it as an independent power; they distort the conditions under which he works, subject him during the labour-process to a despotism the more hateful for its meanness; they transform his life-time into working-time, and drag his wife and child beneath the wheels of the Juggernaut of capital." Karl Marx, CAPITAL, vol. 1, at 604 (1955,c1952). Edited by Friedrich Engels. (Translated from the 3d German ed. by Samuel Moore and Edward Aveling. Rev., with additional translation from the 4th German ed., by Marie Sachey and Herbert Lamm) Imprint Chicago, Encyclopaedia Britannica.

A Future for Socialism

EQUAL SHARES: MAKING MARKET SOCIALISM WORK 7–12 (Erik Olin Wright ed., 1996).

■ JOHN ROEMER

1. Introduction

The demise of the Communist system in the Soviet Union and Eastern Europe has caused many to believe that socialism cannot exist, either in the present world or as an ideal. I shall argue that it can, but that it requires some revision of standard views of what constitutes socialism. If one thought socialism were coextensive with the Soviet model, then clearly it would be dead. I shall defend the idea of market socialism.

The term "market socialism" comes to us from what has been called the socialist calculation debate of the 1930s, in which the two principal protagonists were Oscar Lange and Friederich Hayek. Lange argued that what economists now call neoclassical price theory showed the possibility of combining central planning and the market; while Hayek retorted that planning would subvert at its heart the mechanism which is the source of capitalism's vitality. Hayek's criticisms of Lange's market socialism, and more recently those of Janos Kornai, are for the most part on the mark. But the experiences of capitalism, as well as of socialism, since 1945, suggest ways of reformulating the concept of market socialism in response to the Hayekian critique of its intellectual ancestor. This reformulation is my task.

Economic theory does not yet enable us to write a complete balance sheet of the benefits and costs of the market mechanism. During the 1930s, when Lange and Hayek wrote about market socialism, the Soviet Union was undergoing rapid industrialization. There was, apparently, full employment in that country, while workers and machines were massively idle in the industrialized capitalist world. Hayek therefore wrote from a defensive position, while Lange may well have felt that his proposal was fine-tuning for a socialist system that was, inevitably, the face of the future. Today, the tables are turned. Yet both the pro-socialists of the 1930s and the pro-capitalists of today jump too quickly to conclusions, for we understand fully the effects of markets only in very special circumstances.

Economic theory can explain how, if all economic actors are small relative to the market and cannot individually affect prices, if externalities are absent, and if there is a sufficient number of insurance and financial markets, the equilibrium in a market economy will engender an allocation of resources that is Pareto efficient—that is, efficient in the sense that no other allocation of resources exists which could render everyone simultaneously better off. But this kind of static efficiency may be relatively unimportant compared to the dynamic efficiency with which markets are often credited—that they produce innovations in technology and commodities more effectively than any other economic mechanism could. Although we seem to have much evidence of market dynamism, we have no adequate economic theory of it; nor do we have a controlled experiment which would permit a skeptical scientist confidently to assert that markets are superior to planning in this dynamic sense. The real-life experiments are severely polluted, from a scientific viewpoint: the most dynamic economies of the 1960s onwards (Japan and the East Asian tigers) have used markets with a good dose of planning, and the Communist economies not only had planning and the absence of markets but also political dictatorship, a background condition an experimental designer would like to be able to alter.

The social scientist must, therefore, be more agnostic about the effects of the market than are elementary economics textbooks and the popular press. Indeed, contemporary economic theory has come to see markets as operating within the essential context of non-market institutions, most notably: firms; contract law; the interlinking institutions between economic institutions and other actors, such as between the firm and its stockholders; and the state. Large capitalist firms are centrally planned organizations (in which internal transactions are not mediated by a price system), usually run by managers hired to represent the interests of shareholders. This they do imperfectly, as their own interests do not typically coincide with the interests of shareholders. Contract law is an essential supplement to the market: long-term contracts are, indeed, instruments which render it costly for parties to them to return to the market during the life of the contract. Furthermore, in different capitalist economies different kinds of non-market institutions have evolved. We do have somewhat of a real-life experiment which can help in evaluating alternative economic mechanisms. Germany and Japan, for example, have very different institutions through which owners of firms monitor their managements from those in the United States and the United Kingdom.

In short, the market does not perform its good deeds unaided; it is supported by a myriad cast of institutional characters which have evolved painstakingly over time, and in a variety of ways, in various market economies. My central argument is that these institutional solutions to the design problems of capitalism also suggest how the design problems of socialism may be solved in a market setting.

To see why this may be so, I will first quickly, and necessarily inadequately, summarize the theory of income distribution of Hayek, more generally, of the Austrian school of economics. According to this view, the distribution of income in a market economy is, in the long run, determined by the relative scarcity of various factors of production, principally human talents, including entrepreneurial talent. Property rights should, in the long run, be viewed as themselves derivative of talent. Firms are indeed just the means through which entrepreneurs capitalize their talent; in turn, it is profits from firms which enable their owners to purchase real estate and other natural resources, so that, in the long run, natural resources, too, are owned by talented people or their descendants. Furthermore, any attempt to interfere with the operation of markets—that is, with the institution that maximizes the freedom to compete in the economic sphere—will only reduce overall welfare, as it will inevitably result in conditions which inhibit entrepreneurs from bringing their talents fully into play.

Were this 'naturalistic' view correct, egalitarians would have little remedy for inequality other than education, serving to develop the talents of as many as possible, and perhaps inheritance taxes. What I believe the institutional view of capitalism that I have outlined shows, however, is that the advanced capitalist economy is in large part the product of large, complex institutions, whose operation depends upon the combined efforts of many 'ordinary' people—ordinary in the sense that their talents are not of the rare variety that the Hayekian view envisions, but result from training and education. The wealth of society is not due primarily to rugged and rare individuals, but is reproducible, according to blueprints which are quite well understood. The market is necessary to implement competition and to economize on information, but not so much to cultivate the inspiration of rare geniuses.

A particular way in which the modern view of capitalism suggests a future for socialism is in its understanding of the firm as a nexus of principal-agent relationships. * * * Indeed the mechanisms that have evolved (or been designed) under capitalism that enable owners to control management can be transported to a socialist framework.

In contrast to the "thin" Hayekian and neoclassical views, which see markets as a minimal structure organizing competition among talented individuals, the modern 'thick' view sees markets as operating within the context of complex, man-made institutions, through which all individual contributions become pasteurized and refined. These two views of the market are, I suggest, substantially different, and the latter 'thick' view, unlike the former, is amenable to the coexistence of markets and socialism. Income distribution, in particular, is more malleable under the thick view; the door is opened to reducing inequality substantially, short of massive education, as the reallocation of profits will, if properly done, have little or no deleterious effect on economic efficiency.

In what follows, I will try to flesh out these vague claims.

2. What Socialists Want

I believe socialists want:

1. equality of opportunity for self-realization and welfare;

2. equality of opportunity for political influence; and

3. equality of social status

By self-realization, I mean the development and application of one's talents in a direction that gives meaning to one's life. This is a specifically Marxian conception of human flourishing, and is to be distinguished, for instance, from John Rawls's notion of fulfillment of a plan of life, which might consist in enjoying one's family and friends, or eating fine meals, or counting blades of grass. These activities do not count as self-realization, this being a process of self-transformation that requires struggle in a way that eating a fine meal does not. One does, however, derive welfare from enjoying one's family and eating fine meals, and so I do attribute value to these activities in the socialist's reckoning, for (1) requires equality of opportunity for self-realization and welfare.

That equality of *opportunity* for self-realization and welfare is the goal, rather than equality of self-realization and welfare, requires comment. Were equality of welfare the goal rather than equality of opportunity for welfare, then society would be mandated to provide huge resource endowments to those who adopt terribly expensive and unrealistic goals. Suppose I, a poor athlete, come to believe that my life has been worthless unless I reach the top of Mount Everest on foot. This may require a large amount of money, to hire sufficient Sherpas and other support services to make that journey possible. Equality of opportunity for welfare, on the other hand, puts some responsibility on me for choosing welfare-inducing goals that are reasonable. It is certainly tricky to decide what allocation of resources will give all people an equal opportunity for welfare or self-realization, but I hope the principle is clear from this example. What distinguishes socialists or leftists from conservatives is, in large part, the view of how deeply one must go in order to equalize opportunities. Conservatives believe in going not very deeply: if there is no discrimination in hiring and everyone has access to education through a public school system or vouchers, then the conservative standard of equality of opportunity is met. Socialists believe that those guarantees only touch the surface. Equality of opportunity requires special compensation or subsidy for children who have grown up in homes without access to privilege. Most generally, equality of opportunity requires that people be compensated for handicaps they suffer, induced by factors over which they have no control. * * *

It is, however, impossible to maximize three objectives at once. That is, the kind of social organization that maximizes the equal level of opportunity for self-realization may well induce highly unequal levels of political influence.

There are two responses to this problem. The first says: there is a form of society in which all three objectives are equalized simultaneously, when 'the free development of each becomes the condition for the free development of all,' or some such thing. I think this is an unsubstantiated and utopian claim. The second response says that one must admit the possibility of trade-offs among the three objectives. This, in fact, is what most of us do. For instance, a lively debate has taken place in the socialist movement on the question: 'Which is primary, democracy or equality?' Is equality of opportunity for political influence more important that equality of opportunity for self-realization and welfare? Socialists have different answers to this question. For example, Western socialists assign more importance to equality of opportunity for political influence than most Soviet socialists did. Some socialists did not support the Sandinistas because of the lack of press freedom and democracy in Nicaragua.

I will not offer here any particular preference order over the three equalisanda. I shall be concerned only with investigating the possibility of equalizing income without any unacceptable loss in efficiency. Indeed, I believe raising the income of the poor is the most important single step to improving their opportunities for self-realization and welfare.

————

NOTES AND QUESTIONS

1. Marx and moral critique. Marx is famous for predicting a workers' revolution that would be the instrument of capitalism's self-destruction. To the contrary, capitalism appears to be here to stay (at least until it outruns the capacity of the earth to sustain it). Marx's more lasting legacy may be his moral critique of capitalism. As described by Harvey, is Marx an anti-commodificationist? Is he an anti-subordinationist?

2. Markets and socialism. Is Roemer's argument that the decentralized economy of private markets can be reconciled with the central planning that is characteristic of socialism? What changes would be required to make such a major conversion of the political economy of the United States?

3. Equality of opportunity. Roemer is careful to avoid making an explicit argument for equality of outcome. Would his carefully articulated definition of equal opportunity meet with approval from Milton Friedman? Reconsider Friedman's essay, *Created Equal, in* Free to Choose: A Personal Statement at p. 153.

4. The "R" word: redistribution. Progressive philosopher and activist Cornel West argues that:

> The historic role of American progressives is to promote redistributive measures that enhance the standard of living and quality of life for the have-nots and have-too-littles. Affirmative action was one such redistributive measure that surfaced in the heat of battle in the 1960s among those fighting for racial equality.
>
> * * *
>
> In American politics, progressives must not only cling to redistributive ideals, but must also fight for those policies that—out of compromise and concession—imperfectly conform to those ideals. Liberals who give only lip service to these ideals, trash the policies in the name of

realpolitik, or reject the policies as they perceive a shift in the racial bellwether give up precious ground too easily. And they do so even as the sand is disappearing under our feet on such issues as regressive taxation, layoffs or takebacks from workers, and cutbacks in health and child care.

CORNEL WEST, RACE MATTERS 63, 65 (1993).

What are the most significant differences between affirmative action and the market socialism that Roemer advocates? Does Roemer address the social, cultural, and psychological phenomena of commodification, alienation, and fetishism that Harvey conveys as the major Marxist criticisms of capitalism?

C.   TOWARD ECONOMIC JUSTICE?

Reclaiming Corporate Law in a New Gilded Age

2 Harv. Rev. L. & Pol'y 1 (2008).

■ KENT GREENFIELD

Corporate law matters. Traditionally seen as the narrow study of the relationship between managers and shareholders, corporate law has frequently been relegated to the margins of legal discussion and political debate. The marginalization of corporate law has been especially prevalent among those who count themselves as progressives. While this has not always been true, in the last generation or so progressives have focused on constitutional law and other areas of so-called public law, and have left corporate law to adherents of neoclassical law and economics. To the extent that the behavior of businesses has been a matter of concern, that concern has been aimed at adjusting the rules of environmental law, administrative law, employment law, and the like.

The time has come to reclaim corporate law as a topic of wide debate and progressive concern. Instead of being a narrow discipline with limited implications, corporate law determines the rules governing the organization, purposes, and limitations of some of the largest and most powerful institutions in the world. By establishing the obligations and priorities of companies and their management, corporate law affects everything from employees' wage rates (whether in Bakersfield or Bangalore), to whether companies will try to skirt environmental laws, to whether they will tend to look the other way when doing business with governments that violate human rights. Corporate law also determines whether corporations will look at the long term or the short term, whether they will see themselves as owing any responsibilities to stakeholders other than shareholders, and indeed whether they consider themselves to be constrained by law at all.

There are reasons to challenge the dominant vision of corporate law in the United States. Adjustments in corporate law not only could stifle the worst impulses of the corporation but also could create room for businesses to be a more positive social force, primarily by creating and more broadly distributing financial surplus.

Indeed, the main thesis of this article is that corporate law is much more important than most progressives realize. Corporate law can be part of the wider task of regulating corporations in particular and business in general. The rules that govern corporations should more expressly take into account the fact that corporations are collective enterprises that demand investment from a number of different sources. These investments come in various forms: inflows of capital from shareholders and creditors; cash inflows from customers; infrastructural support from governments and communities; and effort, intelligence, and direction from employees. Whereas corporate law presently focuses on the financial investments of shareholders only, it could, and should, be adjusted to take into account the contributions of 'non-equity investors.' Adjusted in this way, corporate law will make it more possible for corporations to serve their purpose of facilitating the creation of wealth, broadly defined and distributed. Instead of shareholder primacy being the lodestar for corporate decisionmaking, corporations should be governed by the maxim of 'abundance for all.' * * *

Traditionally, large corporations were seen as quasi-public institutions with social responsibilities that came as a condition of their charter. But beginning just over a century ago, states began to bestow increasing power on corporations and to remove many of the previous limits on their size and authority. Corporations came to be seen as supremely private entities, whose primary purpose was making money. Corporations now enjoy legal benefits—including limited liability of shareholders, a perpetual existence separate from their creators and investors, and legal and constitutional personhood—that help ensure their power and maximize the likelihood of their success. Corporations are also the beneficiaries of a huge array of public resources, including the very fabric of the securities markets, infrastructural support ranging from sewers to educational facilities, and regulatory and judicial protection of their intellectual property. Various public sources also contribute billions of dollars in "corporate welfare" for a variety of purposes, including state and local tax incentives to affect factory location decisions and federal government subsidies to support international marketing.

These public supports of corporations are important and valuable, and not just to the corporations themselves. Corporations provide one of society's most powerful engines of wealth creation, and the nation as a whole enjoys more abundance because of them.

A. Externalities

But corporations have their pathologies as well, and these pathologies are partially a function of their advantages. We endow the corporation with the authority and ability to create wealth; but without constraints, it can be overly single-minded in the pursuit of profit. As an artificial entity, it has no conscience of its own. Because corporate investors are separated from managerial decisionmakers, their consciences are not easily brought to bear. The company has every incentive to externalize costs onto those whose interests are not included in the firm's financial calculus. The firm can do this in many ways. It can refuse to provide health benefits to its employees, leaving Medicare or Medicaid to pick up the tab. It can save on production costs by skirting environmental laws. It can sell shoddy products to one-time purchasers, produce goods in sweatshops, or underfund employees' pension funds. In fact, because of the corporation's tendency to create benefits for itself by pushing costs onto others, the corporation could aptly be called an "externality machine." * * *

B. Shareholder Primacy

The pathologies of the corporate form are not limited to the creation of externalities. In a sense, the corporation's core pathology is its core mission: to advance the interests of shareholders first and foremost. In Milton Friedman's famous explanation, the responsibility of directors is to conduct the business in accordance with the "desires" of the shareholders, "which generally will be to make as much money as possible." This means that the corporation looks after the interests of other contributors to the firm (employees, communities, creditors, etc.) only to the extent that doing so advances shareholder interest, or to the extent those other contributors have sufficient market power to prompt the corporation to consider their interests. * * *

The costs of shareholder primacy are immense. Shareholder primacy means that corporations not only will—but should—take care of the environment, workers, community, or ethics only when doing so serves the shareholders in the end. In the words of the Delaware Supreme Court, a corporate "board may have regard for various constituencies in discharging its responsibilities, provided there are rationally related benefits accruing to the stockholders."

Consider the situation in which a board of directors of a public company makes a decision that benefits its employees financially but imposes real, long-term costs on shareholders. Also assume that the board makes that decision because it has determined that benefits to the employees would far outweigh the costs to shareholders. Even though such a decision would maximize the return to the firm's stakeholders as a whole and thus would maximize the social welfare resulting from such a decision, such a decision would violate existing law. The directors might be able to protect themselves from suit through the elasticity of the business judgment rule, but only if they lie about their motivation and suggest that they are really acting in the long-term interests of the shareholders. While that might be a plausible argument some of the time, it will clearly be a reach in other situations. The shareholder plaintiff law firms, and eventually the courts, will catch on. Moreover, the market will punish the managers severely. The stock price will fall, making the company a target for takeover. Companies whose managers act as if they have duties to stakeholders other than shareholders are squeezed out of the market.

Shareholder primacy not only narrows management's view of their responsibilities, it also squeezes that view temporally, incentivizing a focus on the short term. Shareholders increasingly expect high returns quarter to quarter, and if they do not get such returns they punish the companies that fail to provide them. Shareholders do not have loyalty to the companies whose stock they hold. Indeed, other than through initial public offerings, few shareholders actually invest their money in the companies whose stock they own; the vast majority of shareholders buy their stock on the secondary market, from another stockholder who at some earlier point (months or minutes before) had also purchased shares in the secondary market. If a stock is not performing in the short term, there will always be a more appealing company. Not surprisingly, the average stock turnover for Fortune 500 companies is over 100% a year, and is even greater for smaller companies. Short-termism is made worse by the size and power of institutional shareholders such as mutual funds, pension funds, hedge funds, banks, and insurance companies, which now own more than 60% of all public corporate equities and have their own incentive to maximize the value of their portfolio in the short term.

Shareholder primacy restricts management, keeping it focused on the short term and on shareholder interest. Any company that wants to take the long-term view—or thinks it important to take into account the interests of other firm stakeholders—will be punished in the securities markets. Shareholder primacy thus guarantees that any talk from management about social responsibility will likely be for show; it will mean that legal requirements intended to protect other stakeholders will be seen as costs rather than commands; it will mean that any externality that does not translate into a corporate cost will be disregarded. Non-shareholder stakeholders are left to depend on mechanisms outside corporate law to protect their interests. These mechanisms primarily appear in the form of express contracts or government regulation, both seriously imperfect.

C. Corporations and Economic Inequality

* * *

Shareholder primacy is relevant to the discussion on inequality because the requirement that managers look to maximize shareholder wealth provides disproportionate benefits to those who are already financially well-off. The capital wealth in the United States is controlled by a tiny fraction of the American population, so a rule requiring corporations to be managed to the benefit of shareholders amounts to a rule that corporations should be managed to benefit the rich. The significance of this rule is hard to overstate. The richest one-tenth of 1% of Americans receive over a third of the nation's total capital income, while the bottom 80% of Americans control less than 13%. * * *

Such a disproportionate benefit obviously leads to wealth and income disparity—the rich are seizing an increasing percentage of corporate profits. But the situation vis-à-vis inequality is even worse than this one set of statistics can show, because the source of these profits is in part a transfer from labor. This of course is exactly what one would expect to find in an economy where the largest income-producing sector of the economy—the corporate business sector—operates under a duty to shift as much of its profit as possible toward its shareholders. The statistics bear this out. In 2005, the share of all corporate income that went to labor had fallen to its lowest levels since the late 1960s, and capital's share of corporate income (that is, profits earned by shareholders or retained as earnings) had risen to levels not seen in nearly forty years. Moreover, capital investors have seen their return per dollar of investment improve. In 2005, return to capital was at its highest level in thirty-six years, except for the year 1997. And because of the lowering of taxes on corporate profits, the after-tax return on capital was even higher and more historically dramatic. This expansion of capital's share in corporate income has apparently had real effects on wages. The Economic Policy Institute estimated that if the return to capital was the same in 2005 as it had been in 1979, then wages in the corporate sector would be 5% higher. In other words, in comparison to a generation ago, employees are transferring $235 billion more per year to capital than they were in the late 1970s.

On the national level, these trends result in a greater percentage of total personal income going to owners of capital and a lower percentage going to those who earn income through wages. Not only have the rich seized a greater proportion of capital income, capital income itself is a greater percentage of personal income than it was a generation ago. If the economy is a pie, the rich are getting a larger and larger percentage of the capital income piece, which is itself growing. The disparity effect is thus worsened. As economists Lawrence Mishel, Jared Bernstein, and Sylvia Allegretto suggest, "[s]ince the rich are the primary owners of income-producing property, the fact that the assets they own have commanded an increasing share of total income automatically leads to income growth that is concentrated at the top." * * *

There is a final way in which corporate law creates economic inequality. As discussed above, the business judgment rule gives executives large discretion in managing the firm. Senior management have used this flexibility to increase their compensation to unprecedented levels. * * *

The data bear out the anecdotal evidence of enormous increases in executive compensation. In 1965, the CEOs of major U.S. companies earned 24 times that of an average worker. By 2005, this ratio had ballooned to 262 times the average worker. "In other words, in 2005 a CEO earned more in one workday (there are 260 in a year) than what the average worker earned in 52 weeks." The median CEO saw his total compensation increase 186% between 1992 and 2005, while the median worker saw wages rise by only 7%. The average CEO of a Fortune 500 company now makes nearly $10 million per year, and CEO compensation now amounts to roughly 10% of corporate profits. * * *

While the increase in CEO and executive salaries by itself adds to economic inequality, the collusion between executives and Wall Street creates a snowball effect. Neither has an incentive to slow the push for more and more income for themselves—shareholders keep getting theirs, managers keep getting theirs, and those who gain their livelihood from wage work are left further and further behind. Managers are not compensated for how they benefit their employees or the communities where they do business. Money spent for those things is regarded as costs, not profits, and those mere accounting conventions reveal the underlying assumption within corporate law that shareholders are the only owners and it is their fortunes that count.

III. CORPORATIONS, AND CORPORATE LAW, AS PART OF A SOLUTION

* * *

In arguing that adjustments to corporate law could be an important regulatory tool in addressing issues of stagnant wages and economic inequality, the underlying assumptions must be clear. First, and perhaps the most fundamental, is that corporate law is not an area of law governed by rights of ownership in the traditional sense. The view of shareholders as owners was once championed by a few traditionalists who derived shareholder rights from a rights-based view of the private nature of corporations. Under this view, shareholders are seen as the owners of the firm, and the corporation is their individual property. Their control is to be respected. Managers are agents, and the correct law to apply is the law of property and trusts. Managers are to serve their principals. The proper stance of government is one of deference, with minimal or no governmental regulation.

The defects with this model are numerous and pervasive. Despite its residual popular appeal, the model does not find legitimacy in the reality of the corporate world today. Shareholders do not have a complete bundle of rights to make them owners in the traditional sense: they do not have the right to gain access to the company's place of business, the right to exclude others from the property, the right to decide upon the use of the property on a day-to-day basis, or practically any other right usually associated with the ownership of a piece of property. Moreover, little distinguishes the contributions shareholders make to the firm from those of other stakeholders. To say that shareholders are the only "owners" is to say that there is something inherent in the act of contributing money to buy shares—or in the definition of "ownership" of shares—that distinguishes that act from the contribution of money to buy bonds issued by the company, the supply of raw materials to be refined by the company, or the investment of human labor to be used by the company. * * *

This leads to this article's second major premise: corporations, and therefore corporate law, are created in the interest of society as a whole. Corporations are state creations, and no rational state would willfully allow for the creation of institutions as powerful as corporations unless there was a belief that, on balance, society would be better off. To be clear, this does not necessarily mean that the internal rule of decisionmaking within the corporation should be that the managers always act to maximize the benefit to society. But it does mean that whatever rule society constructs for corporate decisionmaking—whether one of shareholder primacy, stakeholder balance, or societal protection—the ultimate goal is to create social welfare, broadly defined.

Even though it would seem obvious that corporations should be created only if they, on balance, create more benefit than harm, this principle is largely absent in corporate law doctrine, judicial opinions, corporations casebooks, and business courses in both law and business schools. Occasionally one will come across a source that does consider the corporation's responsibility to society, but for the most part, judges and mainstream corporate law scholars take shareholder primacy as the guiding principle and ignore the interests of the public, unless those interests are something the company should take into account in an instrumental way to maximize shareholder value.

Of course, "social welfare" is an elastic term that is difficult to define with precision. What is crucial, however, is the importance of defining social benefits and costs broadly. Benefits include not only profit to the shareholders but also workers' earnings, the stability a company brings to communities in which it does business, the quality and importance of the company's products or services, and more. Costs include pollution, depletion of scarce resources, harmful effects of the company's products or services, and mistreatment of employees. Ultimately, the social value of a company is not measurable by looking at shareholder return alone, which is hardly the best proxy for broader measures. Shareholder return may at times be consistent with social welfare, but it is often uncorrelated with social welfare and may at times be negatively correlated with social welfare.

The argument that corporations are intended to benefit society does not depend on an expectation of benevolence from corporations. It relies rather on another premise: corporations are distinctively able to contribute to social welfare by creating financial prosperity. Public corporations bring together a number of characteristics that distinguish them from other kinds of businesses and that make them particularly successful in making money. These traits include easy transferability of shares, limited liability, specialized and centralized management, and a perpetual existence separate from their shareholders. These and other characteristics create a potentially powerful money-making institution, which occupies a special place in our society. The corporation should not be expected to act altruistically in the same way as churches, families, schools, or social service organizations do. Corporations are institutions with a distinctive purpose, which is to create wealth. If they stop creating wealth, they are failures.

It follows, then, that a corporation that does nothing more than create wealth for its shareholders, employees, and communities is providing an important social service. Even if the corporation does nothing else to advance social welfare, assuming its benefits to society outweigh the cost of the externalities it casts upon the society, the corporation has satisfied its purpose for existence. It may be a good thing if a business provides meaning for people who work there, finds a cure for cancer, or funds the local symphony. These things all add to the positive side of the social benefit "ledger," but these benefits are extras. A company that is otherwise a neutral, lukewarm actor in society can still be counted as a success if it creates wealth for society. Indeed, care should be taken that over-regulation of corporations does not destroy their ability to contribute to society by building its wealth.

Importantly, the wealth that matters includes not only monetary gain by shareholders but also gains to other stakeholders. We must include the value to employees of their jobs and the social worth of the goods or services sold, as well as the multiplier effect on other businesses that provide raw materials, transport the end product to market, or sell sandwiches to the employees at lunchtime. * * *

In this light, the next underlying premise becomes clear: the socially optimal amount of regulation of corporations is not zero. The free market is a figment of imaginations, and only of outlandish ones at that. Even the most shareholder-centric scholars acknowledge that public policy demands regulation of the corporation; they just believe that it should come in the form of external, rather than internal, regulation. Corporations will not, through their own generosity, internalize the external costs of their decisions or keep an eye on the social harms they produce. We use law to grant corporations the characteristics that make them capable of generating great wealth, but we also need to constrain them with law. Whether corporate law should be adjusted to take into account the interests of non-equity investors—those other than shareholders who contribute to the firm— should therefore turn on whether such an adjustment would tend to create more social welfare, broadly defined, not on whether it is inconsistent with the so-called free market.

Finally, the use of the term "non-equity" investor as a way to characterize stakeholders embodies the last premise of this article: corporations are collective entities, demanding a variety of investments from a variety of sources. This last premise is simply a statement of one of the important implications of the first—that corporations are not an entity wherein "ownership" makes much sense. Shareholders own their shares, of course, but as Margaret Blair and Lynn Stout write, "shareholders are not the only group that provides essential, specialized inputs into public corporations." Bondholders own their bonds, suppliers "own" their inventory, governments "own" their infrastructure, and workers own their labor. All of these contribute something essential to the firm, and none does so altruistically. They all contribute to the firm because they believe they will gain more by allowing the corporation to collect and use their inputs than if they keep them to themselves. Indeed, the notion that corporations depend on multiple stakeholders is implicit in most theories of the firm.

B. Corporate Law as Public Policy

* * *

[Let us] examine how adjustments in corporate governance could efficiently bring about gains in societal wealth. The corporation is immensely successful in creating wealth, but because of the narrow fixation on shareholder benefit embedded in the market, social norms, and corporate law, non-equity investors (employees, communities, etc.) are often shortchanged in the distribution of the wealth they help create. Even though the corporation is a collective enterprise when it comes to inputs, the distribution of outputs is determined by a body—the board—dominated by representatives of only two stakeholders: the shareholders and the senior management. Changing this arrangement has the potential not only to improve the corporation's ability to create wealth, but also to address serious and enduring social and economic ills. Almost certainly, if senior managers were required to consider the interests of the firm more broadly—to include the well-being of all investors, equity or non-equity—in their decisionmaking calculus, the firm would be more successful in satisfying the social goal of creating wealth, broadly defined.

Stakeholder concerns could be added to the firm's decisionmaking calculus in a couple of ways. First, the fiduciary duties of management could simply be expanded to include a requirement that the management owe a fiduciary duty to the firm as a whole, rather than to the shareholders alone. Once the fiduciary duties extend to the entire firm, and the firm is seen as a collective enterprise, then managers cannot meet their duties by fixating solely on the interests of shareholders.

A more powerful change would come through acknowledging that a duty to the firm as a whole—which includes a duty to a range of stakeholders—would be best effected by providing some mechanism for non-shareholder stakeholders to elect their own representatives to the board. While the duties of care and loyalty are crucial, they have little connection to the problem of fair allocation of the corporate surplus. The best way for the board to make such decisions is to have all important stakeholders represented. The specifics will be difficult but not impossible: employees could elect a proportion of the board, communities in which the company employs a significant percentage of the workforce could propose a representative for the board, and long-term business partners and creditors could be represented as well. For specific ideas as to mechanisms for choosing stakeholder directors, one could look at the procedures used in various European countries that have boards with non-shareholder representatives.

The specific mechanisms of election do not matter as much as does the notion that the board itself should hear more than a shareholder perspective only. As they participate on the board, all stakeholder representatives will have the incentive to build and maintain profitability in order to sustain the company over time. Moreover, the board will be the locus of the real negotiations among the various stakeholders about the allocation of the corporate surplus. Even though board members might be selected for their positions in different ways and from different constituencies, each would be held to fiduciary duties to the firm as a whole. Decisions that affect major stakeholders would no longer be made cavalierly, without someone on the board being able to anticipate and articulate the likely impact such a decision would have on the workers, creditors, and other interested stakeholders.

The benefits of stakeholder representation on corporate boards could be significant. First, this change would likely benefit society broadly by distributing corporate wealth more fairly. It is reasonable to expect stakeholder boards to behave differently from shareholder boards. The market will be a constraint, to be sure, but one of the goals of the board will be to allocate the surplus so as to maintain the firm as a going concern. Shareholders will get their proportion, but so will others. In a sense, this conception would use the corporation not only as a mechanism for creation of wealth but for its distribution as well.

There may be a comparative advantage to using stakeholder governance over other kinds of regulatory efforts. Current public policy tools that redistribute wealth and income tend to either take effect after the initial distribution of financial wealth (e.g., taxes, welfare policy) or benefit only those at the lowest rung of the economic ladder (e.g., the minimum wage). These mechanisms are notoriously inefficient. A stakeholder-oriented corporate governance system would operate at the initial distribution of the corporate surplus and would benefit stakeholders up and down the economic hierarchy and earlier in the wealth creation process.

This is not as jarring as it might seem at first. In the United States, and indeed in most industrialized countries, one of the most important tasks of the state is to redistribute a portion of private wealth and income. Mechanisms include the tax and welfare system, the minimum wage, and Social Security. At base, this article proposes simply that the structure of corporate law be adjusted to better serve this purpose as well. * * *

Not only will adjustments in corporate governance create beneficial effects, but these benefits may be achieved at a much lower cost than through other regulatory initiatives, because stakeholder governance will benefit corporations themselves over time. Because corporations are a collective effort, the key to sustainability is for those who contribute to the firm to believe that the firm can be trusted. Broadening stakeholder representation will help build this trust, ensuring that all stakeholders will be willing to invest in the firm whether by way of financial investments, or investments in terms of labor or expertise. For example, workers who believe they are treated fairly tend to work harder, be more productive, obey firm rules more often, and be more loyal to their employers. This, in turn, is likely to make those firms more profitable than they would have been absent such fair treatment.

If stakeholder governance would help firms be more profitable, why do so few firms voluntarily adopt it? One answer is that some firms already try to share wealth created by the collective action of their stakeholders, and some firms even recognize that they owe an obligation to treat all their stakeholders fairly. The more general answer is that, in all likelihood, firms simply do not see the potential long-term profitability of stakeholder governance. Boards are elected by shareholders, and the law makes shareholders supreme. Few directors or managers have the incentive to push their firms to take what must seem like a huge short-term risk—reallocating a greater portion of the corporate surplus to non-shareholder stakeholders—for gains that seem abstract. Moreover, since many shareholders are interested only in the short term (as described earlier), the likelihood of long-term benefits is immaterial. No one has the incentive to make the first move. The law must overcome this "stickiness" of the status quo.

Another reason why stakeholder governance would be beneficial to the firm is that it would improve managerial decisionmaking. The success of corporations comes about in part because of the abilities of a highly talented group decisionmaker, the board, at the top of the hierarchy. The benefits of group decisionmaking, however, are drastically diminished, and sometimes undermined completely, when the group is too homogeneous. In fact, more and more studies show that good decisionmaking requires a diversity of viewpoints. * * *

If homogeneity is a flaw, then corporate boards are indeed suboptimally constituted. At present, corporate boards are among the least diverse institutions in America. A 2002 survey found that 82% of the director positions on Fortune 1000 companies were held by white men while only 14% were held by women, 3% by African–Americans, 2% by Asian–Americans, and 2% by Hispanics.

These statistics reference only racial and gender diversity, but the point is likely even stronger when it comes to diversity of perspective and background. This homogeneity is a function of legal decisions—giving the right to elect board members to shareholders and the right to nominate to the board itself. But this could be changed through law as well. Adding perspectives other than those of rich, white men will almost certainly improve the quality of business decisions made by the board. * * *

The notion that decisions produced by a finely wrought process of dialogue and compromise are better than decisions made unilaterally by a uniform group of individuals is widely accepted by institutions other than corporate boards. Legislative bodies, administrative agencies, school faculties, and nonprofit boards recognize that a diversity of viewpoints increases the likelihood of groups welcoming dissent, hearing important perspectives, and vetting decisions more fully. In fact, greater diversity in perspectives and backgrounds within the boardroom will lessen the risk over time that the board will engage in the defects and systematic mistakes of "groupthink." Notwithstanding the unique attributes of the corporation and the intense competitive environment in which it operates, perhaps the same is true in corporate governance. * * *

Corporations are creatures of law, and they are regulated pervasively by various aspects of the legal system. Law is essential to make the corporation successful as an institution that collects various inputs and uses them to create wealth. At present, corporate law takes a very narrow view of the obligations of corporate management, and this legal choice has resulted in a number of social costs, including stagnant wages and increasing economic inequality.

Corporate law reform thus represents an area of significant promise in addressing issues of social concern. If corporate management owed fiduciary duties to the firm as whole, or if corporate decisionmaking bodies included representatives of various stakeholders, the unique and powerful capabilities of the corporation could be put to use to create wealth and to distribute it broadly, and to do so more efficiently than through existing regulatory options.

————

Roadmap to a New Economics: Beyond Capitalism and Socialism

Tikkun Magazine.
http://www.tikkun.org/article.php/nov_dec_09_eisler.

■ RIANE EISLER

When thinking of a new economics, let's not think of stocks, bonds, derivatives, or other financial instruments. Let's think of children. Let's ask what kind of economic policies and practices are good for children. Let's ask what's needed so all children are healthy, get a good education, and are prepared to live good lives. More fundamentally, let's ask what kind of economic system helps, or prevents, children from realizing their great potentials for consciousness, empathy, caring, and creativity—the capacities that make us fully human. * * *

The Failures of Capitalism and Socialism

In the wake of the global economic meltdown that began in 2008 has come an outcry against capitalism, especially against its latest stage of "neoliberalism" with its massive deregulation of powerful moneyed interests. Critics point not only to the havoc wreaked by deregulating banks and other financial institutions but also to the gargantuan size and power of multinational corporations; the widening gap between haves and have-nots, both between and within nations, caused by the globalization of "free markets"; and the decimation of our natural environment by irresponsible business practices. Some argue that capitalism must be replaced with socialism because historically capitalism has been unjust, violent, and exploitive of both people and nature.

But this argument reflects yet another old way of thinking that we must re-examine and transcend: classifying societies in terms of conventional categories such as socialist vs. capitalist, religious vs. secular, rightist vs. leftist, Eastern vs. Western, industrial vs. postindustrial, and so forth. None of these categories describes the totality of a society's beliefs and institutions—from the family, education, and religion, to politics and economics. Since these old categories focus only on particular aspects of a society, they are useless for understanding what a more equitable, sustainable, and caring system really looks like.

The social categories of *partnership system* and *domination system* reveal the core configurations of societies that support two very different kinds of relations. The domination system supports relations of top-down rankings: man over man, man over woman, race over race, religion over religion, nation over nation, and man over nature. The partnership system supports the relations we want and urgently need at this critical juncture of history: relations of mutual respect, accountability, and benefit.

If we re-examine the critique of capitalism as unjust, violent, and exploitive, from this perspective we see that, in reality, it is a critique of the structures, relationships, and values inherent in domination systems—be they ancient or modern, Western or Eastern, feudal, monarchic, or totalitarian. Long before capitalist billionaires amassed huge fortunes, Egyptian pharaohs and Chinese emperors hoarded their nations' wealth. Indian potentates demanded tributes of silver and gold while lower castes lived in abject poverty. Middle Eastern warlords pillaged, plundered, and terrorized their people. European feudal lords killed their neighbors and oppressed their subjects.

A domination system of top-down rankings has also characterized the two large-scale modern applications of socialism: the former Soviet Union and China. Both turned out to be authoritarian and violent. And while they alleviated some economic disparities, they were hardly egalitarian. * * *

This does not mean we should discard everything from capitalism and socialism. We need both markets and central planning. But to effectively address our problems, we have to go much deeper, to matters that conventional economic analyses and theories ignore. * * *

Economics, Societies, and Values

Economics is above all about *values*. So to change economics, we must also look at cultural beliefs about what is valuable or not valuable. And one of the distinctions between partnership and domination systems is what is and is not considered of economic value.

In both the Soviet Union and China, socialism was imposed in cultures that oriented closely to the configuration of the domination system. The core configuration of this system consists of top-down rankings in the family and state or tribe maintained by physical, psychological, and economic control; the ranking of the male half of humanity over the female half, and with this, the devaluation by both men and women of anything stereotypically considered feminine; and a high degree of culturally accepted abuse and violence—from child- and wife-beating to pogroms, terrorism, and chronic warfare.

A close orientation to this configuration can be found in societies that have little in common when looked at through the lenses of conventional social and economic categories such as communist or capitalist, Eastern or Western, secular or religious, and so forth. For example, viewed from the perspective of conventional categories, Hitler's Germany (a technologically advanced, Western, rightist society), the Taliban of Afghanistan and fundamentalist Iran (two Eastern, religious societies), and the would-be regime of the rightist-fundamentalist alliance in the United States seem totally different. But all have the same basic dominator configuration. * * *

The partnership system has a very different configuration. Its core elements are a democratic and egalitarian structure in both the family and state or tribe; equal partnership between women and men; and a low degree of violence, because it's not needed to maintain rigid rankings of domination.

No society is either a pure partnership or domination system. But the degree to which it is affects everything: from the society's guiding system of values to the construction of all its institutions—from the family, education, and religion to politics and economics.

Economics and Caring

Nordic nations such as Sweden, Norway, and Finland are the contemporary countries that have moved most closely to the partnership side of the partnership-domination continuum. They have more equality in both the family and the state; a higher status of women (approximately 40 percent of their national legislators are female); and concerted efforts to leave behind traditions of violence (they pioneered the first peace studies and the first laws prohibiting physical discipline of children in families, and have a strong men's movement to disentangle "masculinity" from its equation with domination and violence).

Supported by their more partnership-oriented social configuration, these nations developed economic policies that combine positive elements of socialism and capitalism—but go beyond both to an economics in which caring for people and nature is a top priority. These nations have government-supported child care, universal health care, stipends to help families care for children, elder care with dignity, and generous paid parental leave.

These more caring policies, in turn, made it possible for these nations to move from extreme poverty (famines in the early twentieth century) to societies with a generally high standard of living for all. Today these nations not only rank high in the United Nations annual Human Development Reports in measures of quality of life; they are also in the top tiers of the World Economic Forum's annual global competitiveness reports.

Nordic countries don't have the huge gaps between haves and have-nots characteristic of dominator-oriented nations. While they're not ideal societies, they have succeeded in providing a generally good living standard for all. They have low poverty and crime rates and high longevity rates. Their children score high on international tests. And studies show that workers in these nations are more satisfied and happier than people in countries such as the United States where the gross national product is higher.

Nordic nations also pioneered environmentally sound industrial approaches such as the Swedish "Natural Step." And some of the first experiments in industrial democracy came from Sweden and Norway, as did studies showing that a more participatory structure, where workers play a part in deciding such basic matters as how to organize tasks and what hours to work, can be extremely effective.

Moreover, Nordic nations have a long history of business cooperatives, jointly owned and democratically controlled enterprises that have included, as one of their guiding principles, concern for the community in which they operate. Their cooperatives have also been heavily involved in renewable energy projects. For example, many Swedish housing cooperatives are switching to alternative energy sources to help meet Sweden's goal of oil independence by 2015.

The Nordic nations' success has sometimes been attributed to their relatively small and homogeneous populations. But in smaller, even more homogeneous societies such as some oil-rich Middle–Eastern nations where absolute conformity to one religious sect and one tribal or royal head is demanded, we find large gaps between haves and have-nots and other inequities characteristic of the domination system.

So we have to look at other factors to understand why the Nordic nations moved out of poverty to develop a prosperous, more caring and equitable economic system in a relatively short time. Once we do, we see that what made these nations successful was their move toward the partnership configuration, which made it possible for them to become what they sometimes call themselves: "caring societies."

The core components of this configuration are mutually supporting and reinforcing. And one of its core components, in contrast to the domination system, is equality between the male and female halves of humanity. So women can, and do, occupy the highest political offices in the Nordic world. And this higher status of Nordic women has had important consequences for the values that guide Nordic policies.

In domination-oriented systems, men are socialized to distance themselves from women and anything stereotypically considered feminine. But in partnership-oriented cultures, men can give more value to caring, caregiving, nonviolence, and other traits and activities deemed inappropriate for men in dominator societies because they're associated with "inferior" femininity. So, along with the higher status of Nordic women, many men and women back more caring policies—policies that give value and visibility to the work of caring for people and nature.

With the ascendancy of neoliberalism and the globalization of unregulated capitalism, over the last decades of the twentieth century Nordic nations too began to move somewhat toward more privatization. Nonetheless, they have been able to maintain most of their caring policies and hence their high rankings in international surveys of quality of life—ranging from infant mortality rates (where the United States by contrast fell behind every industrialized nation and even behind poor ones like Cuba) to human rights and environmental ratings.

The basic reason is that these nations continue their massive investment of resources in caring for people and nature. Indeed, these nations contribute a larger percentage of their gross domestic product than other developed nations to caring international programs: programs working for fair economic development, environmental protection, and human rights. * * *

Economic Policy, Poverty, and the Hidden System of Gendered Values

Many people, including politicians, think it's OK to have big government deficits to fund prisons, weapons, and wars—all stereotypically associated with men and "real masculinity." But when it comes to funding caring for people—for child care, health care, early childhood education, and other such expenditures—they say there's not enough money.

If we look back just a few hundred years, we see this devaluation of the "feminine" in stark relief. At that time, Western culture still looked like some of the most repressive societies do today. The norm was an authoritarian structure in both the family and the state. Wars and religious persecutions were chronic. And women and anything associated with them were so devalued that some theologians seriously doubted that women have immortal souls.

There has obviously, since then, been movement toward the partnership system—albeit against enormous resistance and periodic regressions. But the gendered system of valuations we inherited is still extremely resistant to change—so much so that when men embrace traits considered "soft" or "feminine" they are tarred with derisive terms such as "effeminate" and "sissy." Another symptom of this devaluation of women and anything associated with them is that discrimination against the female half of humanity is still generally seen as "just a women's issue"—to be addressed after more important problems are solved.

So while politicians often say their goal is ending, or at least decreasing, poverty and hunger, they hardly ever mention a staggering statistic: women represent 70 percent of those in our world who live in absolute poverty, which means starvation or near starvation. Also ignored in conventional discussions of poverty is that globally, women earn an average of two-thirds to three-fourths as much as men for the same work in the market economy and that most of the work women do in families—including child care, health and elder care, housekeeping, cooking, collecting firewood, drawing and carrying water, and subsistence farming—is not remunerated.

This is by no means to say that only women suffer economically from our domination heritage. Men also suffer, and this is particularly true of the men at the bottom of the domination pyramid. Yet women are still the most oppressed, the "slaves of the slaves," as John Lennon wrote.

Even in the rich United States, woman-headed families are the lowest tier of the economic hierarchy. In addition, according to the U.S. Census Bureau, the poverty rate of women over sixty-five is almost twice that of men over sixty-five.

The fact that worldwide poverty and hunger disproportionately affect women is neither accidental nor inevitable. It is the direct result of political and economic systems that still have a strong dominator stamp. For example, the fact that older women are so much more likely to live in poverty than older men, even in an affluent nation like the United States, is not only due to wage discrimination in the market economy; it is also largely due to the fact that these women are, or were for much of their lives, caregivers—and this work is neither paid nor later rewarded through social security or pensions.

Again, this is not to say that economic inequities based on gender are more important than those based on class, race, or other factors. These inequalities are all inherent in domination systems. But a basic template for the division of humanity into "superiors" and "inferiors" that children in dominator families internalize early on is a male-superior/female-inferior model of our species. And this template can then be applied to ranking race over race, religion over religion, and so forth.

Economics through a New Lens

When societies move toward the partnership side of the partnership-domination continuum (and it's always a matter of degree), women and the "feminine" are not devalued. And this benefits not only women but also men and children of both genders.

We have empirical evidence of this—although once again it is ignored in conventional economic and social analyses.

The study "Women, Men, and the Global Quality of Life," conducted by the Center for Partnership Studies, compared statistical measures on the status of women using measures of quality of life such as infant mortality, human rights ratings, and environmental ratings from eighty-nine nations. We found that in significant respects the status of women can be a better predictor of quality of life than can gross domestic product.

Other studies also verify this relationship between the status of women and a society's general quality of life. The World Values Survey is the largest international survey of attitudes and how they correlate with economic development and political structure. For the first time, in 2000 this survey focused attention on attitudes about gender. Based on data from 65 societies representing 80 percent of the world's population, it found a strong relationship between support for gender equality and a society's level of political rights, civil liberties, and quality of life.

There are many reasons for a correlation of the status of women with a higher or lower quality of life for all. One, of course, is that women make up half of any population. But the reasons go much deeper, to the still largely unrecognized and undiscussed dynamics of domination systems. Here are just two examples:

Dominator Male Preference:

In some world regions, the ranking of males over females is so ingrained that parents (both mothers and fathers) not only deny girls access to education and give them less health care but also often feed girls less than boys. These practices obviously have extremely adverse consequences for girls and women. But giving less food to girls and women also adversely impacts the development of boys.

It is well known that children of malnourished women are often born with poor health and below-par brain development. So this gender-based nutritional and health care discrimination robs *all* children, male or female, of their birthright: their potential for optimal development. This in turn affects children's and later adults' abilities to adapt to new conditions, tolerance of frustration, and propensity to use violence—which in their turn impede solutions to chronic hunger, poverty, and armed conflict, and with this, chances for a more humane, prosperous, and peaceful world for all.

Dominator Intra–Household Resource Allocation:

The above is just one consequence of something else left out of conventional economic analyses: the patterns of intra-household resource allocation characteristic of domination systems.

There is empirical evidence across diverse cultures and income groups that women have a higher propensity than men to spend on goods that benefit children and enhance their capacities. How much higher this propensity is was shown by Duncan Thomas in his report "Intra–Household Resource Allocation." He found that in Brazil, $1 in the hands of a Brazilian woman has the same effect on child survival as $18 in the hands of a man. Similarly, Judith Bruce and Cynthia B. Lloyd found that in Guatemala an additional $11.40 per month in a mother's hands would achieve the same weight gain in a young child as an additional $166 earned by the father.

Of course, there are men even in rigidly male-dominated cultures who give primary importance to meeting their families' needs. Typically, however, men in these cultures are socialized to believe it's their prerogative to use their wages for non-family purposes, including drinking, smoking, and gambling, and that when women complain, they are nagging and controlling. As Dr. Anugerah Pekerti, chair of World Vision, Indonesia, notes, many fathers seem to have no problem putting their immediate desires above the survival needs of their children.

Yet traditional economic theories, capitalist and socialist, are based on the assumption that the male head of household will expend the resources he controls for the benefit of all family members. Not only that, development aid programs still allocate enormous funds to large-scale projects in which women have little or no say—and from which poor women and children derive few if any benefits. Even microlending or "village loan" programs that largely target women generally provide only minimal amounts—often at exorbitant interest rates. And the bulk of large bank loans go to businesses owned by male elites or to male "heads of household."

* * *

This economic double standard, and with it the subordination of the stereotypically feminine to the stereotypically masculine, not only hurts women; it hurts us all. It hurts men in a myriad ways—from the psychological pain of having to disassociate themselves from the "feminine," including their own mothers, to the economic and political consequences of devaluing and subordinating women and anything associated with them. * * *

Endings and Beginnings

* * *The current economic meltdown and the meltdown of the ice caps are not isolated events: both are symptoms of the domination system reaching its logical end.

We must build economic structures, rules, policies, and practices that support caring for ourselves, others, and nature in *both* the market and the nonmarket economic sectors. At the same time, we must accelerate the shift to partnership cultures and structures worldwide so that anything stereotypically considered "soft" or "feminine"—such as caring and caregiving—is no longer devalued.

Market rules—both locally and globally—must be changed to reward caring business practices and penalize uncaring ones. To make these changes we must show that this benefits not only people and nature but also business.

Hundreds of studies show the cost-effectiveness of supporting and rewarding caring in the market economy. To give just one example, companies that regularly appear on the *Working Mothers* or Fortune 500 lists of the best companies to work for—that is, companies with good health care, child care, flextime, parental leave, and other caring policies—have a higher return to investors.

On the national policy level, we already saw how in Nordic nations, caring policies played a major role in their move from dire poverty to a high quality of life for all. Other examples abound, such as reports of the enormous financial benefits that have come from investing in parenting education and assistance (as shown by the Canadian Healthy Babies, Healthy Children program) and investing in high-quality early childhood education (as shown by follow-up studies of the U.S. Abecedarian Project).

There are many ways of funding this investment in our world's human infrastructure—which should be amortized over a period of years, as is done for investments in material infrastructure, such as machines and buildings. One way is to shift funding from the heavy investment in weapons and wars characteristic of domination systems. Another is through the savings a society gains when it no longer has to pay the immense costs of *not* investing in caring and caregiving: the huge expenditures of taxpayer money on crime, courts, prisons, lost human potential, and environmental damage. Taxes on financial speculation and other harmful activities, such as making and selling junk food, can also fund investment in caring for people and our natural habitat.

Good care for children will ensure we have the flexible, innovative, and caring people needed for the postindustrial workforce. Both psychology and neuroscience show that whether these capacities develop largely hinges on the quality of care children receive.

Educating and remunerating people for caregiving will help close the "caring gap"—the worldwide lack of care for children, the elderly, and the sick and infirm. And it will eventually lead to a redefinition of "productivity" that gives visibility and value to what really makes us healthy and happy—and in the bargain leads to economic prosperity and ecological sustainability.

Economic systems are human creations. They can be changed. We must build a political movement to pressure policymakers to make these changes—or change the policymakers. We must see to it that our world's governments make a massive investment in parenting education, paid parental leave, and innovative measures such as tax credits for caregivers and social security credit for the first years of caring for a child (as is already done in Norway).

We can all be leaders in building a social and economic system that really meets human needs—not only our material ones but also our emotional and spiritual ones. * * * If we join together, we can build these foundations and create a future in which all children can realize their great potentials for consciousness, empathy, caring, and creativity—the capacities that make us fully human.

NOTES AND QUESTIONS

1. Corporate governance as civic republicanism. There is a large literature on the social responsibility of corporations. Greenfield, however, is not arguing for corporations to voluntarily act in a more benevolent fashion, but to rewrite the basic structure of corporations to make their actions serve a broader range of interests. Does his proposal have some of the same flaws as civic republicanism? Are there likely to be differences in information, access to participation, and inclination to deliberate among the various stakeholders?

2. Imagining new economic systems. What strains of external critique can you identify in Eisler's article? Does she utilize the argument from commodification? The argument from domination? The argument from political theory?

How would Eisler get us from here to there? See Riane Eisler, THE REAL WEALTH OF NATIONS: CREATING A CARING ECONOMICS (2007).

CHAPTER 7

WEALTH AND INEQUALITY

Introduction

As Deborah Malamud has observed:

Class is all but invisible in contemporary American social discourse. At most, it is a fleeting image, a rarely detected underlayer to the complex texture of race, ethnicity, and gender that captures our society's attention. For many, America stands as the model of the classless society, one in which most people think of themselves as middle class (or at least as potentially so, with hard work and a little luck) and in which middle-classness is the socioeconomic face of "American-ness." The recognized exception, the chronic poor, is seen as an aberration rather than evidence of a general system of class in the United States.

Similarly, American law does not recognize class. Constitutional equal protection doctrine and antidiscrimination statutes are the major mechanisms through which American law recognizes and redresses hierarchy in American society. Both are silent on the question of class. Welfare law advocates have utilized litigation and other mechanisms to argue that "the poor" is a legally significant group, that "poverty" is a suspect classification, and that welfare benefits are "new property" entitled to protection. Scholars have exhibited interest in addressing the question of how the law contributes both to the creation of cycles of poverty and to the social construction of poverty. But the very location of this work within poverty advocacy and theory has meant that it has drawn attention not to class as a general social phenomenon but to the aberrational nature of poverty and our social tolerance for it. Thus poverty is marked, middle-classness unmarked; poverty is figure, middle-classness ground. Poverty needs social, culture, and legal explanation. Middle-classness does not.

Deborah C. Malamud, *"Who They Are—Or Were": Middle–Class Welfare in the Early New Deal*, 151 U. Pa. L. Rev. 2019, 2019 (2003).

In this chapter, we will attempt to make visible the invisible category of class. Part A examines the difficulties in conceptualizing and measuring "class." Part B provides some historical perspectives on the law's role in shaping the class structure and relations we have today. Part C looks at income and wealth inequality at present and points at future trends.

A. DEFINING "CLASS"

Martha Mahoney notes that social and political theory has been dominated by two different concepts of class. One concept of class—"status-class"—draws on the work of sociologist Max Weber, and "analyzes economic participation through a focus on distribution and the market and emphasizes status as an important aspect of structural inequality." In contrast, economist and theorist Karl Marx's concept of class "emphasizes class relations in a system of production and the exploitation of labor by capital." A class analysis in the Weberian tradition, then, might divide American society into upper, middle, and lower classes (looking for indicia of stratification); a class analysis in the Marxist tradition might divide American society into capitalists and workers (looking for relations of power and exploitation). Another way to distinguish the two theories of class is to note that Weberian theories take a "snapshot" of existing class relations; Marxist theories attempt to explain historically how classes emerge and evolve.

To the extent that Americans are comfortable thinking about class relations at all, they usually focus on status. The excerpt that follows points out some of the difficulties in measuring and analyzing status-class.

————

Class–Based Affirmative Action: Lessons and Caveats

74 TEX. L. REV. 1847, 1852–93 (1996).

■ DEBORAH C. MALAMUD

Two basic models of economic inequality compete in the American ideological marketplace, each with two major versions. * * *

One view—which I will call economic individualism—depicts the American economic order as completely open to economic mobility for those individuals with the gumption to pursue it. The economic individualist view admits (as it must) that at any given moment individuals occupy a wide range of positions on a continuum of economic attainment. But this distribution is seen as a result of, rather than a constraint on, free market forces. So long as there is sufficient mobility by individuals, the inequalities in the rewards accorded to different positions are of no theoretical or political importance.

A more moderate version of economic individualism—and the only form of economic individualism that an advocate of class-based affirmative action could embrace—is what one might call pro-interventionist economic individualism. Here, it is admitted that past economic position is a constraint on future economic position; for example, that lack of economic resources can interfere with an individual's capacity to make the investments in human capital necessary for advancement. It is thus perceived as necessary to make a modest level of economic assistance available on the basis of need at certain key junctures of personal economic development—financial aid for college, for example. Once modest assistance is given, previous experiences of economic disadvantage are deemed no longer relevant to future success.

The other major perspective on economic inequality posits the existence of class—a structured system of inequality (as opposed to a simple unequal distribution of economic outcomes among individuals) that is intrinsic to the economic realm and that is not fundamentally altered by the economic mobility of individuals. What distinguishes class perspectives from individualist perspectives on economic inequality is that class perspectives are inherently social (as opposed to individual) and diachronic (as opposed to synchronic). Class is social in the dual sense that the class system is inherent in and perpetuated by the structure of economic relations in the society and that shared class position has the potential for being mobilized as the basis for both group identity and political action. Class is diachronic in the triple sense that class position is (1) intergenerationally transmitted, (2) mediated through the strategic behavior of social actors over time, and (3) incapable of being understood without reference to patterns of change in the economic organization of the society.

Finally, there is an alternative version of a belief in class, which builds on the meaning of class just described, but goes beyond it. In this view, class is said to interact with race, gender, and ethnicity (and perhaps other elements of social identity, such as place of residence) in interlocking and mutually defining structures, and it is their interaction that is seen to shape both consciousness and life chances. * * *

II.   MEASURING ECONOMIC INEQUALITY

A.   *The Shape of Economic Inequality: Continua, Categories, and Conflicts*

On the broadest level, economic inequality can be represented in one of three ways. Under one view, relative economic advantage is represented as *gradational*: as a continuous sliding scale of relative economic position, rank ordered according to one or more specified criteria. The continuum may then be divided for convenience into categories (such as "lower class," "lower middle class," "upper middle class," etc.) by assigning labels to certain ranges on the continuum. But the validity of the gradational model does not turn on any notion that the theorist's groupings identify groups of people with similar patterns of consciousness and action.

Under the *categorical* approach, economic space is divided in a noncontinuous manner on the basis of the criterion that is, according to the relevant theory, the most significant indicator of economic status. The classic example of a categorical approach is the importance placed by some scholars on the distinction between blue-collar (manual) and white-collar (nonmanual) employment. It is generally contended that the theorists' categories capture "native" distinctions—in other words, that they describe patterns of affinity and difference that motivate social action. Thus, the fact that the values and behavior patterns of some skilled blue-collar workers appear to be closer to those of white-collar workers than to those of their unskilled blue-collar brethren is, for a categorical theorist (but not for a gradational theorist), a challenge to the theory or evidence of a flaw in methodology.

Finally, under what [Erik Olin] Wright calls the *relational* approach, the groups that matter for the analysis of economic inequality are identified not merely by patterns of affinity and difference, but also by their intrinsically antagonistic social relations with other economic groups. Just as the elements within such classic pairings as "parent and child" and "master and servant" take their meaning only in relationship to each other, relational perspectives see each economic grouping as existing only with reference to and in tension with the others. Different terms are used to describe the field in which economic groups operate (for example, "the market" or "relations of production") and the nature of the tension among them (for example, "domination," "hegemony," "exploitation," or "exclusion")—terminologies that often do a better job of identifying putative alliances with Weberian, neo-Marxist, or classical Marxist social theory than of describing different social realities. But what identifies an approach as relational is its emphasis on the structured nature of group relations and on the intrinsically antagonistic nature of group interests. * * *

B. Whose Economic Inequality?: Individual Versus Household or Family as the Relevant Unit of Analysis

In discussing economic inequality, one cannot go far without confronting the question of whose economic position is to be measured. Many studies use the individual worker as the unit of analysis. But in any household or family with more than one worker, each worker's economic position is potentially modified by that of the others—not only as to the availability of second (or third) incomes, but in *all* the many ways in which economic position affects life chances. * * *

Family and *household* are not the same concept. Family may or may not involve blood or marital ties, as work on gay and lesbian kinship demonstrates. Divorce creates families and households of numerous shapes, and decision rules must be developed to determine the economic saliency of noncustodial parents, of custodial stepparents, of the subsequent spouses of noncustodial parents, and so forth. Even in the absence of divorce (or widowhood), families may not fit the nuclear family image: family-based households often include other relatives whose economic experiences can be quite salient to all members of the household well beyond the effects of any income-sharing that may take place. Substituting the "traditional" nuclear family for the isolated individual as the unit for measuring class position is thus only a small step in the right direction, and it creates myriad problems of its own. Furthermore, class not only is shaped by family and household composition, but at times also shapes family and household composition. Measuring class position with reference to the nuclear family mirrors middle class kinship ideology, but fails both to accord validity to other classes' conceptions of family life (a flaw on the level of cultural adequacy) and to make available for measurement the wide range of relationships upon which individuals are empowered to draw for resources under these alternative conceptions (a flaw on the level of technical adequacy).

Furthermore, household or family is important in the dimension not only of space (the sharing of the space of a common household), but also in the dimension of time. For example, it is undisputed that at least to some extent, the economic characteristics of a person's family of origin shape that person's economic prospects and attainment over the life span. There is room for debate over the extent to which this is true, the length of time for which it is true, and the mechanisms that cause it to be true. But for our present purposes, what matters is the existence of *"intergenerational* inertia,"* because of which the intergenerational family is the appropriate unit for understanding a family's economic status.

The complexity of "family" as a unit existing in time and space is well demonstrated by an example used by Frank Parkin. Picture two families, in each of which the father is a blue-collar worker and the mother is a high school graduate who is not employed outside the home. In one family, the mother is the child of a blue-collar worker: she has married within her own class. In the other, the mother is the child of a white-collar worker, meaning that she has "married down." According to a study cited by Parkin, the son of the within-class marriage has a forty-two percent chance of going to college, while the son of the mother who "married down" has an eighty percent chance of going to college. In the dimension of space, it is the child's interaction with his nonworking mother that is determinative of his college prospects. In the dimension of time, the key to understanding the child's life chances lies in the grandparental generation. Without considering the economic status of the high school boys in light of their families viewed in the dimensions of time and space, the boys would appear to be similarly situated. In reality, they are not.

C.   Trajectory

Sophisticated analyses of economic inequality take into consideration not merely a *snapshot* of an individual's (or household's or family's) economic circumstances, but a longer view. Jobs that require significant investments in human capital tend to have rising trajectories. In contrast, some occupations are quintessential "young man's (or woman's) games"—such as sports, dance, or physically dangerous service or industrial jobs—in which work opportunities and earnings decline over time. Furthermore, Pierre Bourdieu correctly points out that in periods of economic change, there exists a "collective trajectory"—the mobility of an entire occupation, class fragment, or class—that does much to shape both political attitudes and the class's capacity to maintain its socioeconomic position. At the extreme, rising or falling group trajectories can destabilize basic elements of the class structure. In all of these aspects, economic position must be understood as playing out over time. There can be doubt as to whether the downwardly mobile family (intra- or inter-generational) is better or worse off than the upwardly mobile family at the point at which their trajectories cross. But it is clear that a snapshot is an oversimplification of the true position of economically mobile families.

D. Measuring Relative Economic Status: The Constituent Elements of Economic Inequality

Up to this point, I have mentioned in passing a number of factors that shape the economic situations of individuals and families: occupation, income, education, orientation toward educational attainment, and numerous extra-economic characteristics (including race and gender). When I have asked students to identify their "class," they have referred to a good number of these factors and some others. But each factor raises its own problems of definition and measurement, and their interactions are complex. I am pessimistic about the capacity of the legal system to capture enough of these complexities to achieve anything resembling a culturally adequate account; and even technical adequacy may be beyond its reach.

1. Wealth.—I mention wealth first precisely because it is so invisible in most studies of economic inequality: indeed, it is common to think of "socioeconomic status" as a product of earned income, occupation, and education, with no regard to wealth at all. Perhaps wealth is ignored because Americans are far more private about their wealth than about their incomes. As one working man said to Paul Fussell, classes "can't be [defined by] money, . . . because nobody ever knows that about you for sure."

"Wealth" in the sense of ownership of productive assets is no longer at the core of theories of economic inequality. But that is no justification for ignoring wealth as an element of economic status. Wealth is "distributed far less equally than income" in American society. Wealth barriers are strongly resistant to intergenerational mobility, and inequalities in wealth have greatly increased in the United States since the mid–1970s.

Wealth has a major impact on life chances, in that it diminishes the dependency of an individual's economic well-being upon occupation, income, educational attainment, or any of the other conventionally measured elements of relative economic position. Even the expectation of future wealth is highly significant in assessing an individual's economic circumstances. For example, a recent college graduate who expects to inherit wealth in the near future can accept a "meaningful" low-paying job in social services, the humanities, or the arts and can even create the appearance that he is living on his salary. But he knows that if he ever wants to buy a house, he need not save in advance for a down payment (an obstacle that would be insurmountable for nonwealthy people of his income); he knows that he need not save money for retirement, limit himself to jobs that provide health benefits, or worry that his choices will render him unable to afford to raise children. Wealth is thus a source of personal economic freedom in a broader sense: it is the freedom to take risks, to make mistakes, to be cushioned from market forces. To fail to consider wealth is to understate the extent both of economic inequality in the United States and of its intergenerational transmission. * * *

2.   *Occupation.*—Occupation is of central importance to the sociological study of class; indeed, it is common for studies that claim to be about "social mobility" to in fact be solely concerned with occupational mobility. For classical Marxist theory, class is largely determined by position in relations of production, and the locus of attention is therefore on occupation. Marxism is not alone in stressing occupation: so do numerous other neo-Weberian, neo-Marxist, and structuralist theories. Where these theories disagree is on *why* occupation is so central to class. For classical Marxists, occupation matters because the all-important exploitative relationship between capital and labor is most clearly experienced through work. For social scientists in a Weberian tradition, occupation plays an important role in shaping life chances, although it may well not be the central line of political cleavage in a society. For any number of social scientists, in contrast, there is no perceived necessity to theorize the centrality of occupation; instead, occupation is used as a convenient proxy for other important criteria (for example, income, human capital investment, or likelihood of participation in internal labor markets) or for their combined effects.

The central tool of occupation-based class analysis is some sort of scheme for grouping and ranking occupations. These scales are works of social construction on a number of different levels, in which some principled basis must be found for decisionmaking—from the level of deciding how many occupational "classes" there are, to defining and labeling them, to assigning "jobs" to them.

Occupations might be ranked according to one or more of a number of criteria, some of which are the "social prestige" or honor they command, the quantity and quality of credentials or training necessary to perform them, the degree of supervisory or managerial authority they involve, the amount of autonomy they afford, and their income-earning potential. Shortcuts might be used—such as the white-collar versus blue-collar distinction—on the theory that they capture interrelationships of a number of the important criteria. The rankings can be designed to give priority to one criterion (for example, white-collar versus blue-collar employment) and then consider other criteria for purposes of secondary fine-tuning. But unless the ranking system is to be unworkably complex, choices must be made that are bound to produce unnuanced results. Indeed, the results often seem counterintuitive or downright wrong to lay sensibilities (and perhaps to expert sensibilities as well). For example, where collar color plays a central role in the occupational hierarchy, it is considered "upward mobility" to move, via deindustrialization, from a position as a skilled machinist to one as a file clerk. * * *

The picture within categories is no more compelling. Take, for example, the category "service class"—the "top" category—in the occupational scheme of Erikson and Goldthorpe. The category is defined not in terms of the "service sector," but rather in terms of the authors' distinction

between "service relationships" and relationships governed by labor contracts—with the former involving the exercise of "delegated authority or
specialized knowledge and expertise" and therefore requiring the employees to be accorded a fair measure of autonomy. This means, of course, that
the category is (as it should be) theory-driven, based on the view that
autonomy and discretion are central to the definition of class relations. But
even given the authors' theoretical approach, the category includes occupations that vary widely in respects that are theory-relevant. For example, it
includes "supervisors of non-manual workers" in the same category as
"large proprietors" and "higher-grade professionals"—meaning that Bill
Gates of Microsoft is grouped together with the Microsoft employees who
have the power to hire and fire secretaries. All professionals and high-level
technicians are included in the top category as well (meaning, for example,
that a high school teacher and a physician would be in the same category).

These problems of aggregation have important consequences. Frank
Parkin has observed that "there is what might be called a social and
cultural 'buffer zone' " between classes and that "[m]ost mobility, being of
a fairly narrow social span, involves the movement into and out of th[ese]
zone[s] rather than movement between the class extremes." This means
that the ability to detect mobility between groups crucially depends on
where the lines between the groups are drawn.

Even after "occupations" have been defined and ranked, the work of
social construction continues. The "occupations" found in social scientific
occupational scales are not necessarily the "jobs" that people are hired to
do, which are in turn not necessarily the "jobs" that people actually do.
The process of assigning a person's "job" (in either sense) to one of a
restricted number of "occupational" categories is a complex process, one
that produces inevitable distortions. Take the job of "secretary," routinely
classified in occupational scales as "white-collar clerical." Then consider
the differences between a member of a secretarial pool in a medium-sized
company and a secretary for a Supreme Court Justice or for the CEO of a
major corporation. Or, for another example, consider the job of "professor,"
likely to be classified as "professional/managerial" in most scales. Then
examine the differences between a professor who strings together part-time
and temporary teaching jobs and a tenured professor at a major research
university. In both of these comparisons, both individuals in the pair would
be classified as having the same "occupation," but there are likely to be
gaps between them in prestige, autonomy, job-related social networks, job
benefits, and other aspects of life and work (beyond differences in income)
that would go uncaptured by their occupational classification. The latter
example points, in particular, to the dangers of occupational schemes that
do not reflect the important concerns of segmented labor market theory.

Finally, the problems inherent in systems of occupational classification
go far deeper than mere problems of measurement. As Frank Parkin notes,

> Sociological models are almost bound to take on something of the
> imprint of the age in which they are put together; and the model of
> class recommended in a period of general affluence and economic

growth is likely to look a strange and awkward thing in a period haunted by the anxieties of inflation, recession, and economic stagnation.

Many of the leading occupational frameworks have an anachronistic quality to them: they are based on theories that no longer match the realities of work. With the demise of private-sector unions, there are likely to be fewer reasons in the future to be concerned about the class placement of good blue-collar jobs. Privatization is putting pressure on the line between public and private employment. Overseas outsourcing and decreasing stability of tenure in white-collar work, including such highly trained "knowledge" work as computer programming, is increasing the commonality of job conditions across the collar color line. Cost-containment pressures are limiting the autonomy of the traditional professions. The middle classes are far from becoming an undifferentiated proletariat. But the field is wide open for social scientists to theorize the emerging economic order (or orders)—and, in particular, to theorize the elements of comparative advantage among the different segments of the middle classes. * * *

3. *Income.*—Many scholars focus on income rather than on occupation as the major force in determining relative economic advantage. So do many lay people. For a number of reasons, income-based measures are particularly compatible with the economic individualist perspective. A stress on income suggests that the "goodies" that constitute relative economic advantage (for example, knowledge, education, cultural refinement, residence in safe suburbs, etc.) are commodities that can be purchased with money. An income measure is (at least potentially) agnostic as to the source of income and therefore tacitly rejects the theoretical position that the labor process is at the center of economic relations. Finally, mobility studies that focus on income tend to show higher rates of intergenerational economic mobility in the United States than do occupation-based studies.

Income-based measures also have the practical advantage that the measurement of income is more straightforward than the construction and implementation of occupational hierarchies. But income measurement presents a number of methodological problems that are capable of generating troublesome inaccuracies, both in measuring individual cases and in depicting economic mobility.

First among the issues in income measurement is the question of whose income it is appropriate to measure. Many studies of income inequality look solely at the incomes of individual earners—in part because this information is easily obtained (from employers and from tax returns, for example). But households routinely pool income, so that the more accurate measure of economic position is "family" or "household" income—the measurement of which is complex. Even at the level of the individual, conventional measures of income tend to understate the economic position of high-income individuals and families by excluding the value of employee benefits (for example, pensions and health benefits). And high-income taxpayers have the greatest opportunities to shelter income from taxation, which means that relying on tax returns as the source of income data understates their economic advantage.

Once a measure of income is agreed upon, there remains the question of how (if at all) to determine which income levels correspond to meaningful "breaks"—whether for purposes of a gradational or a categorical scheme. The first question is whether the breaks are to be determined in absolute terms, in relative terms, or in terms of the purchasing power of the income. Another important question is the number of groupings to use. A fairly common approach is to divide individuals into quintiles according to income and then study mobility between quintiles. But mobility between two adjacent quintiles—the most common form of mobility—may not be much mobility at all: it may simply represent a trading of positions between those with income locations at the quintile boundaries. As is the case with occupations, aggregation is necessary for the sake of simplicity, but the data loss inherent in aggregation makes the data harder to interpret—and may well overstate the degree of income mobility in this country. * * *

* * * Education is most often quantified as the number of years studied or the highest degree attained. But to treat education as a commodity in this fashion is to miss differences that are palpably relevant in work and in life. On the college level, for example, educational attainment is routinely judged in real life by type of school (four-year college versus community college, accredited versus unaccredited, day versus night program, and so forth); quality of school (often measured by selectivity or by academic reputation); content of study (with superiority of attainment measured for different purposes along a number of potentially conflicting dimensions ranging from raw difficulty to likelihood of producing cultural literacy); grades and honors; outside enrichment activities (overseas studies, for example); and numerous other more subjective judgments about the student's "character" as reflected through her curricular choices. * * *

5. Consumption.—It was turn-of-the-century economist Thorstein Veblen who most colorfully pointed to patterns of consumption as definitive of class aspiration and class position. Just as inflation can be measured by the relative cost of a fixed "basket" of food items, middle class status is often described as the possession of a "basket" of middle class goods. When middle class status is so defined, mobility into the middle classes is made easier to the extent that the items in the basket are easy to identify (through advertising, popular culture, and so forth) and easy to afford (as the Levittowns democratized suburbanization for white urbanites).

At first glance, it would seem easy to create a quick material index to capture the key elements of middle class material consumption. The consumption choice that most defines ascent into the middle classes is home ownership—which is why federal tax policy subsidizes home ownership and why the fact that young people cannot afford homes is viewed as a breach of faith with the middle class. A conventional consumption index might include such elements as home ownership; type of home (stand-alone versus townhouse versus mobile home); location (with suburban rating highest, except for the most exclusive city homes); home size; the ownership of cars (divided by old and new); the purchase of private primary or secondary education; number and kind of home electronics (with class ascending as the ratio of computers and cellular phones to televisions increases); the eating of meals outside of the home; and perhaps the nature of preferred leisure activities. Such a list—reworked as required by location (for example, the lack of home ownership and cars for many affluent New Yorkers)—could provide broad brush strokes to draw a line between lower and middle classes.

But as anyone with a good ear for the culture knows, these elements of consumption are not so much measures of class unity as they are fields for the social process (and processing) of distinction. Houses can be large because they have many bedrooms (for many children) or because they offer grand spaces for entertaining. Their grounds can be groomed "just right," too poorly, or too well ("If there's no crabgrass at all, we can infer an owner who spends much of his time worrying about slipping down a class or two...."). The living room can be furnished from antique markets or from Sears. Cars can be utilitarian objects or displays of wealth and taste; they can be old in order to demonstrate patrician nonconcern with material values or because the family cannot afford new. Food cooked at home can be traditional or gourmet. The gulfs in consumption within the "middle class" category are, in short, huge. The advertising industry knows this, and it markets goods not to some broad aggregate "middle class," but to very carefully defined segments within it, defined as much by class aspiration and cultural orientation as by income.

The literature on consumption-based markers of class identity always generates laughter because it so sharply points out the anxiety of our attempts to manipulate social status. But consumption is no laughing matter. The material world is a minefield for the class-mobile, and every dollar spent a potentially fatal misstep. Consumption choices shape opportunities for conversation and for the formation of friendships and professional networks. (If tennis is the game of choice at your office, being a top-notch bowler does you no good; and try inviting your boss to dinner if your only table is in the kitchen.) They are, at the very least, the most easily observed markers of who you are and where you fit into the social hierarchy; they may in fact be an important part of the constitution of the self.

In sum, consumption is central to our (often unarticulated) cultural understandings of class. * * *

6.   *Consciousness.*—Categorical and relational models of class are built upon the claim that the "classes" they describe have the potential for some degree of consciousness of themselves as classes. Class consciousness is important to students and practitioners of politics and for Marxist theorists, for whom the capacity of groups to organize and take action on the basis of class is all-important. It is also important to culturally oriented class theorists, for whom the system of *beliefs* about economic inequality is an important component of the system of economic inequality. And under-

standing the consciousness of social actors is necessary if their dignity is to be respected. * * *

7. *Interactions Among the Elements of Economic Inequality.*—The various measures of economic inequality I have reviewed are not independent of one another, but cannot freely substitute for one another. The acquisition of credentials may have some value in and of itself, but its greatest value is in securing a job that utilizes those credentials (or purports to utilize them) and brings one into contact with coworkers who have attained similar or greater educational levels. Access to high culture is limited by lack of income, but high income alone does not guarantee the "right" kind of understanding and the entree into cultured circles that goes with it. Within prestigious occupations, status declines in relation to the relative status of one's clients. Impressive attainments of cultural capital are of little use without the income and occupation to put them to work and the education to announce their presence on the surface of a resume. Resources can be rendered far less meaningful in their impact by coming too early or too late in the lifespan. Yet there is *some* measure of tolerance for gaps in the personal economic armor, *some* capacity for substitution.

What this means is that the relationships among the elements of economic privilege are not simply additive or multiplicative. They are structural. The factors contributing to relative economic advantage exist in a delicate balance and interact in space and time, as is generally true of the elements of society and culture. Their effects are likely to be nonhomogeneous—meaning that the analysis of important socioeconomic factors and their interrelationships must be "disaggregated," with an eye to spotting relevant discontinuities. No easily administered, quantitative, composite index of the elements of economic inequality can capture their complex interrelationships.

To the extent that social scientific studies can simultaneously recognize and order the complexities of class, theory allows them to do so. At some point, it is necessary to stress one element and de-emphasize the others—to decide, for example, whether class or economic inequality is or is not fundamentally grounded in the realm of work. That is the role of theory. But the corollary of the centrality of theory is that in shopping for a measurement method and in deciding which factors form the core of relative economic advantage, the legal system will be buying a social theory—whether it admits it or not, and whether it wants one or not. * * *

8. *Outside Interactions: Race, Gender, and the Danger of False Claims of "Holding Class Constant."*—Up until this point, we have discussed class as though it were a hermetically sealed category, impervious to other forms of inequality. But it is not. Just as economic variables interact, there are important interactions between each of those elements (and their interactions) and "outside" elements, such as race and gender.

Gender issues in class analysis are obscured (or perhaps underscored) by the fact that studies of social mobility commonly look only at the experience of men. The reason is that one of the most vexing problems in research on class and economic inequality is how to determine the economic position of women—both their individual status and their contributions as wage-earners and domestic producers to the economic status of their households and families. It should be obvious that ignoring the economic participation of women distorts the picture of household or family economic status in important ways. * * * Indeed, there is ample evidence that the interactions among economic factors differ for men and women, that women are less able than men to take personal advantage of inherited and earned economic and social capital, and that occupational schemes developed for men are less accurate for women.

Theorizing and measuring the economic status of members of racial and ethnic minority groups pose problems of equal magnitude. I will limit myself to only a few illustrations of the many ways in which strategies for the transmission of economic advantage from parents to children have historically been less successful for blacks than for whites.

Part of the problem is that black upward mobility is so recent a phenomenon for many black families. In a study of intergenerational elements of educational attainment in the black middle class, Zena Smith Blau found that when black and white families of seemingly similar socioeconomic status (measured by the occupational status of the higher ranking parent and both parents' educational attainment) were compared, black families "in fact, possess fewer resources than those white families." The key difference was that white parents' own socioeconomic status translated into a more privileged social milieu. This means, Blau concluded, that parental occupational and educational gains in white families "are more readily translated into access to middle-class influences and role models than is usually the case for black families." There is also evidence, from Coleman, that although "black parents . . . show a greater interest in their child's education and greater aspirations for his success in education than do white parents of the same economic level," the interests of black, Hispanic, and Native American parents do not translate as well into improved academic performance for the child.

More generally, the past and present effects of discrimination mean that blacks and whites who appear to have the same occupation, education, or residential situation when a simple metric is used may well not occupy the same status in reality. When black families live in the suburbs, they tend to live in predominantly black suburbs that lie closer to the inner city and that are less advantaged in their public and private services. Blacks are more likely to be employed in the public sector, where civil-service employment rules diminish the ability of parents to use their influence to provide jobs for children in their community. Although patterns of segregation are breaking down, black professionals are historically more likely to serve within the black community, which means that having professionals in the family opens up a less advantaged social network for blacks than for whites. Blacks in the professions remain more likely than whites to be employed in occupations at the lower end of the category in credentials, prestige, and income. Blacks have less wealth than whites of the same income level. And skin color remains a powerful obstacle to the translation of wealth, occupation, income, education, and cultural capital into even the most basic dignity in public life. As one Jewish carpenter explained to an ethnographer in Brooklyn, New York, my hometown: "The problem is that we see blacks as a mass. It is unfortunate. We can't tell the difference between a black pimp and a black mailman. When I look at a white man, I can tell what social class he is, but if he is colored, I can't tell." There is little gain to be had from class mobility if its public indicia are overwhelmed by the more socially salient reality of race.

These examples demonstrate that if an overly simplistic measurement of class is used, systematic differences in the present and historical economic condition of blacks will be ignored, and the socioeconomic privilege of middle class blacks will be overstated. It is highly likely, given the complexity of the phenomenon, that even the most earnest efforts at designing an adequate metric will fail. And the result of failure will likely be that the law's official discourse will falsely proclaim that in the contest for economic equality, class has been "held constant"—and that if blacks still lose, their loss must be because of some postulated lack of individual or collective merit. That is a significant danger for anyone concerned with racial justice in this country.

NOTES AND QUESTIONS

1. Class position. How would you describe your class position? What was your parents' class position when you were growing up? Has it changed over time? Of the factors Malamud lists as relevant to the determination of a person's "class," which do you think are the most determinative? Is class a relevant category in American life?

2. The American Dream. A central ideology of American democracy and markets is that economic mobility is fully open to all citizens with talent and a strong work ethic. The asserted classlessness of American society remains a cherished characterization of the opportunity structure here. Americans venerate our tradition of individual achievement. Opposition to the accumulation of great wealth and the hereditary privileges associated with such concentrations of political, social, and economic power have been a feature of American political rhetoric since the founding of the nation.

Political scientist Jennifer Hochschild uses a quote from former President Bill Clinton to encapsulate the "American Dream":

> The American Dream that we were all raised on is a simple but powerful one—if you work hard and play by the rules you should be given a chance to go as far as your God-given ability will take you.

President Bill Clinton, Speech to Democratic Leadership Council, 1993.

> In one sentence, President Clinton has captured the bundle of shared, even unconsciously presumed, tenets about achieving success that make up the ideology of the American Dream. Those

tenets answer the questions: *Who* may pursue the American Dream? In *what* does the pursuit consist? *How* does one successfully pursue the dream? *Why* is the pursuit worthy of our deepest commitment?

The answer to "who" in the standard ideology is "everyone, regardless of ascriptive traits, family background, or personal history." The answer to "what" is "the reasonable anticipation, though not the promise, of success, however it is defined." The answer to "how" is "through actions and traits under one's control." The answer to "why" is "true success is associated with virtue."

JENNIFER L. HOCHSCHILD, FACING UP TO THE AMERICAN DREAM: RACE, CLASS, AND THE SOUL OF THE NATION 18 (1995).

How does belief in the American Dream shape attitudes toward class?

3. The immigrant story. Related to the American Dream is another central ideology in American life, one that relates to the possibility of group rather than individual class mobility. The United States is a nation of immigrants, and many Americans can tell stories of a great-grandfather or grandfather who came to this country with "nothing" and was able to "work his way up," eventually passing wealth along to his children. Nathan Glazer puts this kind of story into a larger framework:

> [T]he American polity has * * * been defined by a steady expansion of the definition of those who may be included in it to the point where it now includes all humanity; * * * the United States has become the first great nation that defines itself not in terms of ethnic origin but in terms of adherence to common rules of citizenship; * * * no one is now excluded from the broadest access to what the society makes possible; and * * * this access is combined with a considerable concern for whatever is necessary to maintain group identity and loyalty.

Nathan Glazer, *The Emergence of an American Ethnic Pattern, in* FROM DIFFERENT SHORES: PERSPECTIVES ON RACE AND ETHNICITY IN AMERICA 13, 14 (Ronald Tataki ed., 1987).

Is the immigrant story of individual and group social and economic mobility despite ethnic difference a story that can be told about all groups? Robert Blauner argues that there is a key historical difference between "colonized" and "immigrant" minorities. As he sets forth his argument, he identifies three assumptions on which it rests:

> The first assumption is that racial groups in America are, and have been, colonized peoples; therefore their social realities cannot be understood in the framework of immigration and assimilation that is applied to European ethnic groups. The second assumption is that the racial minorities share a common situation of oppression, from which a potential political unity is inferred. The final assumption is that there is a historical connection between the third world abroad and the third world within.

Robert Blauner, *Colonized and Immigrant Minorities, in* FROM DIFFERENT SHORES: PERSPECTIVES ON RACE AND ETHNICITY IN AMERICA 149, 149 (Ronald Takaki ed., 1987).

4. Genetic Ability and Intergenerational Earnings? Haoming Liu and Jinli Zeng argue that the correlation between genetics and earnings is stronger than most people would suspect. They found that the earning correlation between fathers and children would be halved if their biological link is removed. Haoming Liu and Jinli Zeng, *Genetic Ability and Intergenerational Earnings Mobility*, Springer–Verlag, August 3, 2007. What do you believe; do you believe that class is a result of in-borne ability and needs or your surroundings? Why or why not?

5. *San Antonio Independent School District v. Rodriguez*. Malamud is pessimistic about American law's ability to adequately deal with issues of class. As you read *San Antonio Independent School District v. Rodriguez*, think about how Justice Powell is trying to conceptualize wealth discrimination. Does he adequately distinguish this case from the precedents he discusses? Does "class" fit into the ways lawyers think about "discrimination"? How might Malamud conceptualize the issues faced by the litigants in the case?

B. THE CONSTITUTION: WEALTH AND CLASS

San Antonio Independent School District v. Rodriguez
411 U.S. 1 (1973).

■ MR. JUSTICE POWELL delivered the opinion of the Court.

This suit attacking the Texas system of financing public education was initiated by Mexican–American parents whose children attend the elementary and secondary schools in the Edgewood Independent School District, an urban school district in San Antonio, Texas. They brought a class action on behalf of schoolchildren throughout the State who are members of minority groups or who are poor and reside in school districts having a low property tax base. * * *

I

The first Texas State Constitution, promulgated upon Texas' entry into the Union in 1845, provided for the establishment of a system of free schools. Early in its history, Texas adopted a dual approach to the financing of its schools, relying on mutual participation by the local school districts and the State. As early as 1883, the state constitution was amended to provide for the creation of local school districts empowered to levy ad valorem taxes with the consent of local taxpayers for the "erection ... of school buildings" and for the "further maintenance of public free schools." Such local funds as were raised were supplemented by funds distributed to each district from the State's Permanent and Available School Funds. * * *

Until recent times, Texas was a predominantly rural State and its population and property wealth were spread relatively evenly across the State. Sizable differences in the value of assessable property between local school districts became increasingly evident as the State became more industrialized and as rural-to-urban population shifts became more pronounced. The location of commercial and industrial property began to play a significant role in determining the amount of tax resources available to each school district. These growing disparities in population and taxable property between districts were responsible in part for increasingly notable differences in levels of local expenditure for education.

In due time it became apparent to those concerned with financing public education that contributions from the Available School Fund were not sufficient to ameliorate these disparities. * * *

Recognizing the need for increased state funding to help offset disparities in local spending and to meet Texas' changing educational requirements, the state legislature in the late 1940's undertook a thorough evaluation of public education with an eye toward major reform. In 1947, an 18–member committee, composed of educators and legislators, was appointed to explore alternative systems in other States and to propose a funding scheme that would guarantee a minimum or basic educational offering to each child and that would help overcome interdistrict disparities in taxable resources. The Committee's efforts led to the passage of the Gilmer–Aikin bills, named for the Committee's co-chairmen, establishing the Texas Minimum Foundation School Program. Today, this Program accounts for approximately half of the total educational expenditures in Texas.

The Program calls for state and local contributions to a fund earmarked specifically for teacher salaries, operating expenses, and transportation costs. The State, supplying funds from its general revenues, finances approximately 80% of the Program, and the school districts are responsible—as a unit—for providing the remaining 20%. The districts' share, known as the Local Fund Assignment, is apportioned among the school districts under a formula designed to reflect each district's relative taxpaying ability. * * *

In the years since this program went into operation in 1949, expenditures for education—from state as well as local sources—have increased steadily.

* * *

The school district in which appellees reside, the Edgewood Independent School District, has been compared throughout this litigation with the Alamo Heights Independent School District. This comparison between the least and most affluent districts in the San Antonio area serves to illustrate the manner in which the dual system of finance operates and to indicate the extent to which substantial disparities exist despite the State's impressive progress in recent years. Edgewood is one of seven public school districts in the metropolitan area. Approximately 22,000 students are enrolled in its 25 elementary and secondary schools. The district is situated in the core-city sector of San Antonio in a residential neighborhood that has little commercial or industrial property. The residents are predominantly of Mexican–American descent: approximately 90% of the student population is Mexican–American and over 6% is Negro. The average assessed property value per pupil is $5,960—the lowest in the metropolitan area—and the median family income ($4,686) is also the lowest. At an equalized tax rate of $1.05 per $100 of assessed property—the highest in the metropolitan area—the district contributed $26 to the education of each child for the 1967–1968 school year above its Local Fund Assignment for the Minimum Foundation Program. The Foundation Program contributed $222 per pupil for a state-local total of $248. Federal funds added another $108 for a total of $356 per pupil.

Alamo Heights is the most affluent school district in San Antonio. Its six schools, housing approximately 5,000 students, are situated in a residential community quite unlike the Edgewood District. The school population is predominantly "Anglo," having only 18% Mexican–Americans and less than 1% Negroes. The assessed property value per pupil exceeds $49,000, and the median family income is $8,001. In 1967–1968 the local tax rate of $.85 per $100 of valuation yielded $333 per pupil over and above its contribution to the Foundation Program. Coupled with the $225 provided from that Program, the district was able to supply $558 per student. Supplemented by a $36 per-pupil grant from federal sources, Alamo Heights spent $594 per pupil.

    * * *

The District Court held that the Texas system discriminates on the basis of wealth in the manner in which education is provided for its people. Finding that wealth is a "suspect" classification and that education is a "fundamental" interest, the District Court held that the Texas system could be sustained only if the State could show that it was premised upon some compelling state interest. On this issue the court concluded that "[n]ot only are defendants unable to demonstrate compelling state interests . . . they fail even to establish a reasonable basis for these classifications."

Texas virtually concedes that its historically rooted dual system of financing education could not withstand the strict judicial scrutiny that this Court has found appropriate in reviewing legislative judgments that interfere with fundamental constitutional rights or that involve suspect classifications. If, as previous decisions have indicated, strict scrutiny means that the State's system is not entitled to the usual presumption of validity, that the State rather than the complainants must carry a "heavy burden of justification," that the State must demonstrate that its educational system has been structured with "precision," and is "tailored" narrowly to serve legitimate objectives and that it has selected the "less drastic means" for effectuating its objectives, the Texas financing system and its counterpart in virtually every other State will not pass muster. The State candidly admits that "[n]o one familiar with the Texas system would contend that it has yet achieved perfection." Apart from its concession that educational financing in Texas has "defects" and "imperfections," the State defends the system's rationality with vigor and disputes the District Court's finding that it lacks a "reasonable basis."

This, then, establishes the framework for our analysis. We must decide, first, whether the Texas system of financing public education operates to the disadvantage of some suspect class or impinges upon a fundamental right explicitly or implicitly protected by the Constitution, thereby requiring strict judicial scrutiny. If so, the judgment of the District Court should be affirmed. If not, the Texas scheme must still be examined to determine whether it rationally furthers some legitimate, articulated state purpose and therefore does not constitute an invidious discrimination in violation of the Equal Protection Clause of the Fourteenth Amendment.

II

The District Court's opinion does not reflect the novelty and complexity of the constitutional questions posed by appellees' challenge to Texas' system of school financing. In concluding that strict judicial scrutiny was required, that court relied on decisions dealing with the rights of indigents to equal treatment in the criminal trial and appellate processes, and on cases disapproving wealth restrictions on the right to vote. Those cases, the District Court concluded, established wealth as a suspect classification. Finding that the local property tax system discriminated on the basis of wealth, it regarded those precedents as controlling. It then reasoned, based on decisions of this Court affirming the undeniable importance of education, that there is a fundamental right to education and that, absent some compelling state justification, the Texas system could not stand.

We are unable to agree that this case, which in significant aspects is *sui generis*, may be so neatly fitted into the conventional mosaic of constitutional analysis under the Equal Protection Clause. Indeed, for the several reasons that follow, we find neither the suspect-classification nor the fundamental-interest analysis persuasive.

A

The wealth discrimination discovered by the District Court in this case, and by several other courts that have recently struck down school-financing laws in other States, is quite unlike any of the forms of wealth discrimination heretofore reviewed by this Court. Rather than focusing on the unique features of the alleged discrimination, the courts in these cases have virtually assumed their findings of a suspect classification through a simplistic process of analysis: since, under the traditional systems of financing public schools, some poorer people receive less expensive educations than other more affluent people, these systems discriminate on the basis of wealth. This approach largely ignores the hard threshold questions, including whether it makes a difference for purposes of consideration under the Constitution that the class of disadvantaged "poor" cannot be identified or defined in customary equal protection terms, and whether the relative—rather than absolute—nature of the asserted deprivation is of significant consequence.

* * *

The case comes to us with no definitive description of the classifying facts or delineation of the disfavored class. Examination of the District Court's opinion and of appellees' complaint, briefs, and contentions at oral argument suggests, however, at least three ways in which the discrimination claimed here might be described. The Texas system of school financing might be regarded as discriminating (1) against "poor" persons whose incomes fall below some identifiable level of poverty or who might be characterized as functionally "indigent," or (2) against those who are relatively poorer than others, or (3) against all those who, irrespective of their personal incomes, happen to reside in relatively poorer school districts. Our task must be to ascertain whether, in fact, the Texas system has been shown to discriminate on any of these possible bases and, if so, whether the resulting classification may be regarded as suspect.

The precedents of this Court provide the proper starting point. The individuals, or groups of individuals, who constituted the class discriminated against in our prior cases shared two distinguishing characteristics: because of their impecunity they were completely unable to pay for some desired benefit, and as a consequence, they sustained an absolute deprivation of a meaningful opportunity to enjoy that benefit. In *Griffin v. Illinois* and its progeny, the Court invalidated state laws that prevented an indigent criminal defendant from acquiring a transcript, or an adequate substitute for a transcript, for use at several stages of the trial and appeal process. The payment requirements in each case were found to occasion *de facto* discrimination against those who, because of their indigency, were totally unable to pay for transcripts. And the Court in each case emphasized that no constitutional violation would have been shown if the State had provided some "adequate substitute" for a full stenographic transcript.
* * *

Likewise, in *Douglas v. California*, a decision establishing an indigent defendant's right to court-appointed counsel on direct appeal, the Court dealt only with defendants who could not pay for counsel from their own resources and who had no other way of gaining representation. *Douglas* provides no relief for those on whom the burdens of paying for a criminal defense are relatively speaking, great but not insurmountable. Nor does it deal with relative differences in the quality of counsel acquired by the less wealthy.

Williams v. Illinois and *Tate v. Short* struck down criminal penalties that subjected indigents to incarceration simply because of their inability to pay a fine. Again, the disadvantaged class was composed only of persons who were totally unable to pay the demanded sum. Those cases do not touch on the question whether equal protection is denied to persons with relatively less money on whom designated fines impose heavier burdens. The Court has not held that fines must be structured to reflect each person's ability to pay in order to avoid disproportionate burdens. Sentencing judges may, and often do, consider the defendant's ability to pay, but in such circumstances they are guided by sound judicial discretion rather than by constitutional mandate.

Finally, in *Bullock v. Carter* the Court invalidated the Texas filing-fee requirement for primary elections. Both of the relevant classifying facts found in the previous cases were present there. The size of the fee, often running into the thousands of dollars and, in at least one case, as high as $8,900, effectively barred all potential candidates who were unable to pay the required fee. As the system provided "no reasonable alternative means of access to the ballot", inability to pay occasioned an absolute denial of a position on the primary ballot.

Only appellees' first possible basis for describing the class disadvantaged by the Texas school-financing system—discrimination against a class of definably "poor" persons—might arguably meet the criteria established in these prior cases. Even a cursory examination, however, demonstrates that neither of the two distinguishing characteristics of wealth classifications can be found here. First, in support of their charge that the system discriminates against the "poor," appellees have made no effort to demonstrate that it operates to the peculiar disadvantage of any class fairly definable as indigent, or as composed of persons whose incomes are beneath any designated poverty level. Indeed, there is reason to believe that the poorest families are not necessarily clustered in the poorest property districts. A recent and exhaustive study of school districts in Connecticut concluded that "[i]t is clearly incorrect . . . to contend that the 'poor' live in 'poor' districts. . . . Thus, the major factual assumption of *Serrano*—that the educational financing system discriminates against the 'poor'—is simply false in Connecticut." Defining "poor" families as those below the Bureau of the Census "poverty level," the Connecticut study found, not surprisingly, that the poor were clustered around commercial and industrial areas—those same areas that provide the most attractive sources of property tax income for school districts. Whether a similar pattern would be discovered in Texas is not known, but there is no basis on the record in this case for assuming that the poorest people—defined by reference to any level of absolute impecunity—are concentrated in the poorest districts.

Second, neither appellees nor the District Court addressed the fact that, unlike each of the foregoing cases, lack of personal resources has not occasioned an absolute deprivation of the desired benefit. The argument here is not that the children in districts having relatively low assessable property values are receiving no public education; rather, it is that they are receiving a poorer quality education than that available to children in districts having more assessable wealth. Apart from the unsettled and disputed question whether the quality of education may be determined by the amount of money expended for it, a sufficient answer to appellees' argument is that, at least where wealth is involved, the Equal Protection Clause does not require absolute equality or precisely equal advantages. Nor indeed, in view of the infinite variables affecting the educational process, can any system assure equal quality of education except in the most relative sense. Texas asserts that the Minimum Foundation Program provides an "adequate" education for all children in the State. * * *

For these two reasons—the absence of any evidence that the financing system discriminates against any definable category of "poor" people or that it results in the absolute deprivation of education—the disadvantaged class is not susceptible of identification in traditional terms.

As suggested above, appellees and the District Court may have embraced a second or third approach, the second of which might be characterized as a theory of relative or comparative discrimination based on family income. Appellees sought to prove that a direct correlation exists between the wealth of families within each district and the expenditures therein for education. That is, along a continuum, the poorer the family the lower the dollar amount of education received by the family's children. * * *

If, in fact, these correlations could be sustained, then it might be argued that expenditures on education—equated by appellees to the quality of education—are dependent on personal wealth. Appellees' comparative-discrimination theory would still face serious unanswered questions, including whether a bare positive correlation or some higher degree of correlation is necessary to provide a basis for concluding that the financing system is designed to operate to the peculiar disadvantage of the comparatively poor, and whether a class of this size and diversity could ever claim the special protection accorded "suspect" classes. These questions need not be addressed in this case, however, since appellees' proof fails to support their allegations or the District Court's conclusions. * * *

This brings us, then, to the third way in which the classification scheme might be defined—*district* wealth discrimination. Since the only correlation indicated by the evidence is between district property wealth and expenditures, it may be argued that discrimination might be found without regard to the individual income characteristics of district residents. Assuming a perfect correlation between district property wealth and expenditures from top to bottom, the disadvantaged class might be viewed as encompassing every child in every district except the district that has the most assessable wealth and spends the most on education. Alternatively, as suggested in Mr. Justice Marshall's dissenting opinion, * * * the class might be defined more restrictively to include children in districts with assessable property which falls below the statewide average, or median, or below some other artificially defined level.

However described, it is clear that appellees' suit asks this Court to extend its most exacting scrutiny to review a system that allegedly discriminates against a large, diverse, and amorphous class, unified only by the common factor of residence in districts that happen to have less taxable wealth than other districts. The system of alleged discrimination and the class it defines have none of the traditional indicia of suspectness: the class is not saddled with such disabilities, or subjected to such a history of purposeful unequal treatment, or relegated to such a position of political powerlessness as to command extraordinary protection from the majoritarian political process. * * *

[The Court turns to the question of whether education is a fundamental right protected by the Constitution.]

Lindsey v. Normet, decided only last Term, firmly reiterates that social importance is not the critical determinant for subjecting state legislation to strict scrutiny. The complainants in that case, involving a challenge to the procedural limitations imposed on tenants in suits brought by landlords under Oregon's Forcible Entry and Wrongful Detainer Law, urged the Court to examine the operation of the statute under "a more stringent standard than mere rationality." The tenants argued that the statutory limitations implicated "fundamental interests which are particularly important to the poor," such as the "need for decent shelter" and the "right to retain peaceful possession of one's home." MR. JUSTICE WHITE'S analysis, in his opinion for the Court is instructive:

> "We do not denigrate the importance of decent, safe and sanitary housing. But the Constitution does not provide judicial remedies for every social and economic ill. We are unable to perceive in that document any constitutional guarantee of access to dwellings of a particular quality or any recognition of the right of a tenant to occupy the real property of his landlord beyond the term of his lease, without the payment of rent.... *Absent constitutional mandate*, the assurance of adequate housing and the definition of landlord-tenant relationships are legislative, not judicial, functions."

Similarly, in *Dandridge v. Williams*, the Court's explicit recognition of the fact that the "administration of public welfare assistance ... involves the most basic economic needs of impoverished human beings," provided no basis for departing from the settled mode of constitutional analysis of legislative classifications involving questions of economic and social policy.
* * *

[The Court concludes that education is not a fundamental right and that the Texas system survives the rational basis test.]

■ MR. JUSTICE MARSHALL, with whom MR. JUSTICE DOUGLAS concurs, dissenting.

* * * In my view, * * * it is inequality—not some notion of gross inadequacy—of educational opportunity that raises a question of denial of equal protection of the laws. I find any other approach to the issue unintelligible and without directing principle. Here, appellees have made a substantial showing of wide variations in educational funding and the resulting educational opportunity afforded to the schoolchildren of Texas. This discrimination is, in large measure, attributable to significant disparities in the taxable wealth of local Texas school districts. This is a sufficient showing to raise a substantial question of discriminatory state action in violation of the Equal Protection Clause.

NOTES AND QUESTIONS

1. Economic inequality. One issue that bears both on how we measure class and on our understanding of the American Dream is the issue of economic inequality. In this section, we look at readings that investigate economic inequality along two of the dimensions of class described by Malamud—income and wealth.

2. The right to education under state constitutions. Forty-eight out of the fifty states have education clauses in their state constitutions. *See* Michael Heise, *State Constitutions, School Finance Litigation, and the "Third Wave": From Equity to Adequacy*, 68 TEMPLE L. REV. 1151, 1163 (1995). *See* Paul L. Tractenberg, *Using the Law to Advance the Public Interest: Rutgers Law School and Me*, 51 RUTGERS L. REV. 1001, 1011–12 (Rutgers Law Review Symposium 1999); Susan H. Bitensky, *Theoretical Foundations for a Constitutional Right to Education Under the U.S. Constitution: A Beginning to the End of a National Education Crisis*, 86 Nw. U. L. REV. 550 (1992); Molly McUsic, *The Use of Education Clauses in School Finance Reform Litigation*, 28 HARV. J. ON LEGIS. 307 (1991); James S. Liebman, *Three Strategies for Implementing Brown Anew, in* RACE IN AMERICA: THE STRUGGLE FOR EQUALITY 112, 120–21 (Herbert Hill & James E. Jones, Jr. eds., 1993).

C. CLASS AND INEQUALITY—HISTORICAL PERSPECTIVES

1. INCOME INEQUALITY, IS IT THE RIGHT MEASURE?

Black Wealth/White Wealth: New Perspectives on Racial Inequality

■ MELVIN L. OLIVER & THOMAS M. SHAPIRO 12–13, 13–15, 16–18 (1995).

Disparities in wealth between blacks and whites are not the product of haphazard events, inborn traits, isolated incidents or solely contemporary individual accomplishments. Rather, wealth inequality has been structured over many generations through the same systemic barriers that have hampered blacks throughout their history in American society: slavery, Jim Crow, so-called de jure discrimination, and institutionalized racism. How these factors have affected the ability of blacks to accumulate wealth, however, has often been ignored or incompletely sketched. * * *

The close of the Civil War transformed four million former slaves from chattel to freedmen. Emerging from a legacy of two and a half centuries of legalized oppression, the new freedmen entered Southern society with little or no material assets. With the north's military victory over the South freshly on the minds of Republican legislators and white abolitionists, there were rumblings in the air of how the former plantations and the property of Confederate soldiers and sympathizers would be confiscated and divided among the new freedmen to form the basis of their new status in society. The slave's often-cited demand of "forty acres and a mule" fueled great anticipation of a new beginning based on land ownership and a transfer of skills developed under slavery into the new economy of the South. Whereas slave muscle and skills had cleared the wilderness and made the land productive and profitable for plantation owners, the new vision saw the freedmen's hard work and skill generating income and resources for the former slaves themselves. W.E.B. DuBois, in his *Black Reconstruction in America*, called this prospect America's chance to be a modern democracy.

Initially it appeared that massive land redistribution from the Confederates to the freedmen would indeed become a reality. Optimism greeted Sherman's March through the South, and especially his Order 15, which confiscated plantations and redistributed them to black soldiers. Such wartime actions were eventually rescinded and some soldiers who had already started to cultivate the land and build new lives were forced to give up their claims. Real access to land for the freedman had to await the passage of the Southern Homestead Act in 1866, which provided a legal basis and mechanism to promote black landownership. In this legislation public land already designated in the 1862 Homestead Act, which applied only to non-Confederate whites but not blacks, was now opened up to settlement by former slaves in the tradition of homesteading that had helped settle the West. The amount of land involved was substantial, a total of forty-six million acres. Applicants in the first two years of the Homestead Act were limited to only eighty acres, but subsequently this amount increased to 160 acres. The Freedmen's Bureau administered the program, and there was every reason to believe that in reasonable time slaves would be transformed from farm laborers to yeomanry farmers.

This social and economic transformation never occurred. The Southern Homestead Act failed to make newly freed blacks into a landowning class or to provide what Gunnar Myrdal in *An American Dilemma* called "a basis of real democracy in the United States." Indeed, features of the legislation worked against its use as a tool to empower blacks in their quest for land. First, instead of disqualifying former Confederate supporters as the previous act had done, the 1866 legislation allowed all persons who applied for land to swear that they had not taken up arms against the Union or given aid and comfort to the enemies. This opened the door to massive white applications for land. One estimate suggests that over three-quarters (77.1 percent) of the land applicants under the act were white. In addition, much of the land was poor swampland and it was difficult for black or white applicants to meet the necessary homesteading requirements because they could not make a decent living off the land. What is more important, blacks had to face the extra burden of racial prejudice and discrimination along with the charging of illegal fees, expressly discriminatory court challenges and court decisions, and land speculators. While these barriers faced all poor and illiterate applicants, Michael Lanza has stated in his *Agrarianism and Reconstruction Politics* that "The freedmen's badge of color and previous servitude complicated matters to almost incomprehensible proportions."

Gunnar Myrdal's *An American Dilemma* provides the most cogent explanation of the unfulfilled promise of land to the freeman in an anecdotal passage from a white Southerner. Asked, "Wouldn't it have been better for the white man and the Negro" if the land had been provided? The old man remarked emphatically:

> "No, for it would have made the Negro 'uppity.'" . . . and "the real reason . . . why it wouldn't do, is that we are having a hard time now keeping the nigger in his place, and if he were a landowner, he'd think he was a bigger man than old Grant, and there would be no living with him in the Black District. . . . Who'd work the land if the niggers had farms of their own?"

Nevertheless, the extent of black landowning was remarkable given the economically deprived backgrounds from which the slaves emerged. * * *

The suburbanization of America was principally financed and encouraged by actions of the federal government, which supported suburban growth from the 1930s through the 1960s by way of taxation, transportation, and housing policy. Taxation policy, for example, provided greater tax savings for businesses relocating to the suburbs than to those who stayed and made capital improvements to plants in central city locations. As a consequence, employment opportunities steadily rose in the suburban rings of the nation's major metropolitan areas. In addition, transportation policy encouraged freeway construction and subsidized cheap fuel and mass-produced automobiles. These factors made living on the outer edges of cities both affordable and relatively convenient. However, the most important government policies encouraging and subsidizing suburbanization focused on housing. In particular, the incentives that government programs gave for the acquisition of single-family detached housing spurred both the development and financing of the tract home, which became the hallmark of suburban living. While these governmental policies collectively enabled over thirty-five million families between 1933 and 1978 to participate in homeowner equity accumulation, they also had the adverse effect of constraining black Americans' residential opportunities to central-city ghettos of major U.S. metropolitan communities and denying them access to one of the most successful generators of wealth in American history—the suburban tract home.

This story begins with the government's initial entry into home financing. Faced with mounting foreclosures, President Roosevelt urged passage of a bill that authorized the Home Owners Loan Corporation (HOLC). According to Kenneth Jackson's *Crabgrass Frontier*, the HOLC "refinanced tens of thousands of mortgages in danger of default or foreclosure." Of more importance to this story, however, it also introduced standardized appraisals of the fitness of particular properties and communities for both individual and group loans. In creating "a formal and uniform system of appraisal, reduced to writing, structured in defined procedures, and implemented by individuals only after intensive training, government appraisals institutionalized in a rational and bureaucratic framework a racially discriminatory practice that all but eliminated black access to the suburbs and to government mortgage money." Charged with the task of determining the "useful or productive life of housing" they considered to finance, government agents methodically included in their procedures the evaluation of the racial composition or potential racial composition of the community. Communities that were changing racially or were already black were deemed undesirable and placed in the lowest category. The categories, assigned various colors on a map ranging from green for the most desirable, which included new, all-white housing that was always in demand, to red, which included already racially mixed or all-black, old, and undesirable areas, subsequently were used by Federal Housing Authority (FHA) loan officers who made loans on the basis of these designations.

Established in 1934, the FHA aimed to bolster the economy and increase employment by aiding the ailing construction industry. The FHA ushered in the modern mortgage system that enabled people to buy homes on small down payments and at reasonable interest rates, with lengthy repayment periods and full loan amortization. The FHA's success was remarkable: housing starts jumped from 332,000 in 1936 to 619,000 in 1941. The incentive for home ownership increased to the point where it became, in some cases, cheaper to buy a home than to rent one. As one former resident of New York City who moved to suburban New Jersey pointed out, "We had been paying $50 per month rent, and here we come up and live for $29.00 a month." This included taxes, principal, insurance, and interest.

This growth in access to housing was confined, however, for the most part to suburban areas. The administrative dictates outlined in the original act, while containing no antiurban bias, functioned in practice to the neglect of central cities. Three reasons can be cited: first, a bias toward the financing of single-family detached homes over multifamily projects favored open areas outside of the central city that had yet to be developed over congested central-city areas; second, a bias toward new purchases over repair of existing homes prompted people to move out of the city rather than upgrade or improve their existing residences; and third, the continued use of the "unbiased professional estimate" that made older homes and communities in which blacks or undesirables were located less likely to receive approval for loans encouraged purchases in communities where race was not an issue.

While the FHA used as its model the HOLC's appraisal system, it provided more precise guidance to its appraisers in its *Underwriting Manual*. The most basic sentiment underlying the FHA's concern was its fear that property values would decline if a rigid black and white segregation was not maintained. The *Underwriting Manual* openly stated that "if a neighborhood is to retain stability, it is necessary that properties shall continue to be occupied by the same social and racial classes" and further recommended that "subdivision regulations and suitable restrictive covenants are the best way to ensure such neighborhood stability." The FHA's recommended use of restrictive covenants continued until 1949, when, responding to the Supreme Court's outlawing of such covenants in 1948 (*Shelley v. Kraemer*), it announced that "as of February 15, 1950, it would not insure mortgages on real estate subject to covenants."

Even after this date, however, the FHA's discriminatory practices continued to have an impact on the continuing suburbanization of the white population and the deepening ghettoization of the black population. While exact figures regarding the FHA's discrimination against blacks are not available, data by county show a clear pattern of "redlining" in central-city counties and abundant loan activity in suburban counties.

The FHA's actions have had a lasting impact on the wealth portfolios of black Americans. Locked out of the greatest mass-based opportunity for wealth accumulation in American history, African Americans who desired and were able to afford home ownership found themselves consigned to central-city communities where their investments were affected by the "self-fulfilling prophecies" of the FHA appraisers: cut off from sources of new investment their homes and communities deteriorated and lost value in comparison to those homes and communities that FHA appraisers deemed desirable. One infamous housing development of the period— Levittown—provides a classic illustration of the way blacks missed out on this asset-accumulating opportunity. Levittown was built on a mass scale, and housing there was eminently affordable, thanks to the FHA's and VHA's accessible financing, yet as late as 1960 "not a single one of the Long Island Levittown's 82,000 residents was black."

————

Race, Gender & Work: A Multicultural Economic History of Women in the United States

(1991).

■ TERESA AMOTT & JULIE MATTHEI

Chapter 4—The Soul of the *Tierra Madre*: Chicano Women

Much of the complex economic history of the Chicana/o people centers on struggles over land and national boundaries. The earliest ancestors of today's Chicanas were members of many different Indian nations who inhabited the lands now known as Mexico and the U.S. Southwest, including the Aztec, Pueblo, and Tlaxcalán. Beginning in the sixteenth century, these indigenous peoples were conquered by Spanish invaders. Sexual relations, many of them forced, between Spanish men and indigenous (and African slave) women soon produced a *mestiza/o* population. Through colonization and settlement, the Spanish extended their territories north. The vast country of Mexico was formed after independence from Spain in 1821, stretching from what we know today as Guatemala up through Texas, California, Arizona, Colorado, New Mexico, and Nevada, and even into parts of Oregon, Utah, and Idaho.

In the early nineteenth century, Anglo settlers from the deep South migrated to Texas, sowing the seeds for a war between Mexico and the United States that eventually led to the annexation of almost half of Mexico's territories in 1848. From then up until the present, Mexican citizens have migrated to the United States in search of work, and many have become U.S. citizens. * * *

As a result of this history, the economics and politics of the U.S. Chicana population are inextricably linked to those of Mexico. * * *

* * * [In Mexico, t]he period between 1834 and 1846 has been called the "Golden Age of the ranchos" because land became increasingly concentrated in the hands of a few wealthy ranchers, all of them of Spanish ancestry (or claiming to be). Next in the class hierarchy were *mestiza/o* small ranchers and farmers. Following them were *mestiza/o* artisans, skilled workers, laborers, and seasonal workers in the cattle industry. Lowest of all were the Indians, the chief source of manual labor.

The new country quickly became engaged in a bitter struggle with Anglo settlers in what we know now as Texas, culminating in the Mexican–American War of 1846. Anglo settlers began arriving in Mexico's northern territories in the early 1800s, granted land first by the Spanish government and later by Mexico, which encouraged migration to the sparsely settled area. Most Anglo settlers came to farm or raise cattle, but starting in 1829, an increasing number brought slaves from the deep South to work cotton plantations. Although there were some landed Mexicans in Texas, by the 1830s, Anglo Texans outnumbered Mexicans by five to one. To discourage slavery and stem further Anglo immigration, Mexico prohibited importation of slaves in 1830. In 1835, Anglo Texans, chafing under these restrictions, began the Texas Revolt to free themselves from Mexican rule. After losses at the Alamo and Goliad, they defeated Mexican forces in 1837 and set up the Lone Star Republic. In 1845, Texas became part of the United States. One researcher documented the transfer of land ownership from Mexicans to Anglos in Nueces County, Texas in the 1800s: "at the beginning of the Texas Revolt in 1835 every foot of land in Nueces County was held under Mexican land grants, two years prior to the Civil War all but one had passed out of Mexican hands, and by 1883 none was held by Mexicans."

* * * The [Mexican–American] war ended with the Treaty of Guadalupe Hidalgo in 1848, in which Mexico was forced to give up more than half her territory—including California, New Mexico, Utah, Nevada, Colorado, and Arizona—in exchange for $15 million. In the annexation, the United States acquired lands populated by over 80,000 Spanish-speaking people, most of them *mestiza/o* and *criolla/o*. The quarter of a million Indian peoples in these lands now faced U.S. rather than Mexican efforts to subordinate or exterminate them.

While the language of the Treaty contained protections for Mexican land titles and water rights, the United States government made no attempt to safeguard these rights. Thus the annexation of Mexican territories placed annexed Mexicans in a vulnerable position. As Anglo settlers flooded into the Southwest, they took over the lands and wealth of the

Mexican inhabitants, reducing most of the Mexican population in the Southwest to a landless, politically disempowered group.

Some of the *ricos* were able to protect their landholdings by intermarrying with Anglo newcomers. In San Antonio, for instance, marriage records between 1837 and 1860 show that one daughter from almost every *rico* family had married an Anglo. Such marriages were attractive to Anglo men since daughters as well as sons inherited property in Mexican families.

But many other Mexicans, particularly those with smaller landholdings or subsistence plots, lost their lands through a variety of devices familiar to us from the history of American Indians. Anglo domination of the political and judicial systems, along with the use of force and violence, ensured Anglo economic domination. For instance, when floods, drought, or economic downturns made it difficult for Mexican ranchers to pay taxes imposed by the Anglo-controlled government, their lands were quickly sold to Anglos. California passed a law in 1851 that encouraged squatters to take over Mexican lands. Lynching was also a common tool employed by Anglos to terrorize Mexicans into leaving their lands. Some estimate that more Mexicans were lynched between 1850 and 1930 than African Americans during the same period.

* * *

During the second half of the nineteenth century, the southwestern economy expanded rapidly. Subsistence farming began to give way to huge ranches and cash crops as railroads made it possible for southwestern products to reach eastern markets. Displaced Mexicans found jobs as seasonal agricultural workers, domestic workers, or miners in isolated, company-controlled towns.

* * *

Chapter 7—Climbing Gold Mountain: Asian American Women

From 1840 through World War II, Asian immigrants—first Chinese, then Japanese, and finally Filipinas/os—were recruited as a low-wage second-class labor force by employers in the western United States and Hawaii. The U.S. legal system denied Asian immigrants the legal rights which had been accorded their European counterparts, relying on the 1790 naturalization law that restricted the privilege of citizenship to "free white persons." When the law was revised after the Civil War to make African Americans eligible for citizenship, the phrase "persons of African descent" was added, and the law continued to bar Asian immigrants from naturalizing. Unable to become citizens, Asian immigrants remained permanent "aliens" (non-citizens), and whites were able to pass numerous laws which restricted their rights simply by referring to their alien status. For example, in the early twentieth century California passed laws which prevented Asian immigrants from purchasing land. However, children of immigrant Asians were allowed to become citizens and escape these restrictions if they were born in the United States.

On the West Coast, where the vast majority of Asians lived, whites bolstered their own relative economic status at the expense of Asian immigrants. White employers achieved higher profits by using Asians as low-wage replacements for white workers and as strikebreakers. White workers resented the threat Asians appeared to pose to wages and unionizing efforts. Self-employed whites felt threatened by Asian successes in small business.

To defend their economic positions, whites formed broad-based movements to restrict Asian immigration and even to send migrants back to Asia. Filipino historian Paul Valdez wrote of the anti-"Oriental" movement of the 1920s, "They used to pass out leaflets saying that the Japanese were taking the lands from the Americans, the Chinese were taking the businesses, and the Filipinos were taking the women." Under these pressures, white-controlled federal and state governments passed close to 50 laws specifically aimed at restricting and subordinating Asian immigrants between 1850 and 1950. These sentiments culminated in laws excluding further immigration. Chinese immigration was cut off in 1882 and 1892; Japanese in 1907–08 and 1924; Indian in 1917; and Filipina/o in 1934.

Whites also discriminated against second-generation Asians who, unlike white ethnics, could not disguise their ethnicity by speaking English and adopting European American ways. These barriers to upward mobility in the labor market compelled many Asian Americans to seek advancement through self-employment in family-based businesses—for the Chinese, laundries and restaurants; for the Japanese, truck farming; and for the Koreans, grocery stores.

2. WEALTH, CLASS AND ECONOMIC MOBILITY—THE INTERGENERATIONAL EFFECTS

In what follows, three writers—two influential Princeton economists, Alan B. Krueger and Paul Krugman, as well as conservative *New York Times* columnist, David Brooks—explore the emerging problem of decreasing economic mobility and pinched opportunity structures arising from inherited economic status across all socio-economic groups. Their research and arguments pose a direct challenge to that part of our national story that depends on belief in the power of individual effort, merit, and achievement. If parent-child wealth correlations are as strong as these economists argue, it reveals a largely hidden force that will preserve economic inequality for a long time. This force could be described as the new "invisible hand," shaping markets and posing a threat to the democratic distribution of political power.

The Sticky Ladder

N.Y. TIMES, Jan. 25, 2005, at A19.

■ DAVID BROOKS

In his Inaugural Address President Bush embraced the grandest theme of American foreign policy—the advance of freedom around the world. Now that attention is turning to the State of the Union address, it would be nice if he would devote himself as passionately to the grandest theme of domestic policy—social mobility.

The United States is a country based on the idea that a person's birth does not determine his or her destiny. Our favorite stories involve immigrants climbing from obscurity to success. Our amazing work ethic is predicated on the assumption that enterprise and effort lead to ascent. "I hold the value of life is to improve one's condition," Lincoln declared.

The problem is that in every generation conditions emerge that threaten to close down opportunity and retard social mobility. Each generation has to reopen the pathways to success.

Today, for example, we may still believe American society is uniquely dynamic, but we're deceiving ourselves. European societies, which seem more class driven and less open, have just as much social mobility as the United States does.

And there are some indications that it is becoming harder and harder for people to climb the ladder of success. *The Economist* magazine gathered much of the recent research on social mobility in America. The magazine concluded that the meritocracy is faltering: "Would-be Horatio Algers are finding it no easier to climb from rags to riches, while the children of the privileged have a greater chance of staying at the top of the social heap."

Economists and sociologists do not all agree, but it does seem there is at least slightly less movement across income quintiles than there was a few decades ago. Sons' income levels correlate more closely to those of their fathers. The income levels of brothers also correlate more closely. That suggests that the family you were born into matters more and more to how you will fare in life. That's a problem because we are not supposed to have a hereditary class structure in this country.

But we're developing one. In the information age, education matters more. In an age in which education matters more, family matters more, because as James Coleman established decades ago, family status shapes educational achievement.

At the top end of society we have a mass upper-middle class. This is made up of highly educated people who move into highly educated neighborhoods and raise their kids in good schools with the children of other highly educated parents. These kids develop wonderful skills, get into good colleges (the median family income of a Harvard student is now $150,000), then go out and have their own children, who develop the same sorts of wonderful skills and who repeat the cycle all over again.

In this way these highly educated elites produce a paradox—a hereditary meritocratic class.

It becomes harder for middle-class kids to compete against members of the hypercharged educated class. Indeed, the middle-class areas become more socially isolated from the highly educated areas.

And this is not even to speak of the children who grow up in neighborhoods in which more boys go to jail than college, in which marriage is not the norm before child-rearing, in which homes are often unstable, in which long-range planning is absurd, in which the social skills you need to achieve are not even passed down.

In his State of the Union address, President Bush is no doubt going to talk about his vision of an ownership society. But homeownership or pension ownership is only part of a larger story. The larger story is the one Lincoln defined over a century ago, the idea that this nation should provide an open field and a fair chance so that all can compete in the race of life.

Today that's again under threat, but this time from barriers that are different than the ones defined by socialists in the industrial age. Now, the upper class doesn't so much oppress the lower class. It just outperforms it generation after generation. Now the crucial inequality is not only finance capital, it's social capital. Now it is silly to make a distinction between economic policy and social policy.

We can spend all we want on schools. But if families are disrupted, if the social environment is dysfunctional, bigger budgets won't help.

President Bush spoke grandly and about foreign policy last Thursday, borrowing from Lincoln. Lincoln's other great cause was social mobility. That's worth embracing too.

Economic Scene; The Apple Falls Close to the Tree, Even in the Land of Opportunity

N.Y. TIMES, Nov. 14, 2002, at C1.

■ ALAN B. KRUEGER

It seems increasingly apparent that the secret to success is to have a successful parent. Consider some prominent examples: George H. W. Bush and George W. Bush; Bobby Bonds and Barry Bonds; Henry Fonda and Jane Fonda; Estee Lauder and Ronald Lauder; Julio Iglesias and Enrique Iglesias; Sam Walton and Jim, John, S. Robson and Alice Walton.

As more recent and better data have become available, economists have marked up their estimate of the impact of parents' socioeconomic status on their children's likelihood of economic success.

It turns out that the famous line attributed to Andrew Carnegie—"from shirt-sleeves to shirt-sleeves in three generations"—is an understatement. Five or six generations are probably required, on average, to erase the advantages or disadvantages of one's economic origins.

This represents a marked departure from past thinking. In the 1980s, when Gary S. Becker of the University of Chicago pioneered the economic theory of intergenerational transmission of economic status, it was believed that the correlation between a father's and son's income was only around 0.15—less than half the correlation between fathers' and sons' heights.

The early studies suggested that if a father's income was twice the average, his son's expected income would be 15 percent above average, and his grandson's just 2 percent above average. This is fast "regression to the mean," a concept Sir Francis Galton used to describe the progression of offspring toward the average height.

Landmark studies published by Gary Solon of the University of Michigan and David J. Zimmerman of Williams College in The American Economic Review a decade ago, however, led economists to revise substantially upward the estimate of the similarity of fathers' and sons' incomes. They noted that income fluctuated for idiosyncratic reasons from year to year—an employee could lose a job, for example—so estimates that depended on a single year were based on "noisy" data. Also, the samples previously analyzed represented only a narrow slice of the population at different points in individual careers. These factors caused the correlation in annual incomes to understate the correlation in "lifetime" incomes.

Averaging earnings over five years produced a correlation of around 0.40 for fathers' and sons' earnings—the same as the correlation between their heights. If people's incomes were represented by their heights, the similarity in income between generations would resemble the similarity observed in the heights of fathers and sons.

New studies by Bhashkar Mazumder of the Federal Reserve Bank of Chicago suggest that the similarity in income is even greater. Using Social Security records, he averaged fathers' earnings over 16 years (1970 through 1985) and sons' earnings over four years (1995 through 1998), and found that around 65 percent of the earnings advantage of fathers was transmitted to sons. The wider window provides a better reflection of lifetime earnings.

Also, the samples previously analyzed represented only a narrow slice of the population at different points in individual careers. These factors caused the correlation in annual incomes to understate the correlation in "lifetime" incomes.

The relationship between fathers' and daughters' earnings was just as strong.

So that grandson (or granddaughter) mentioned previously could expect to earn 42 percent more than average. After five generations, the earnings advantage would still be 12 percent.

Furthermore, the degree of persistence across generations is strong for both rich and poor. Thomas Hertz of American University finds that a child born in the bottom 10 percent of families ranked by income has a 31 percent chance of ending up there as an adult and a 51 percent chance of ending up in the bottom 20 percent, while one born in the top 10 percent has a 30 percent chance of staying there and a 43 percent chance of being in the top 20 percent.

In another study, David I. Levine of Berkeley and Dr. Mazumder found that the impact of parental income on adult sons' income increased from 1980 to the early 1990s.

Why is there such a strong connection between parents' socioeconomic status and their children's? A large part of the answer involves intergenerational transmission of cognitive ability and educational level.

But these factors can "explain at most three-fifths of the intergenerational transmission of economic status," Samuel Bowles and Herbert Gintis of the University of Massachusetts wrote in the latest issue of The Journal of Economic Perspectives. They suggest that the intergenerational transmission of race, geographical location, height, beauty, health status and personality also plays a significant role.

Arthur S. Goldberger of the University of Wisconsin has long questioned whether knowledge of the "heritability" of income is of much use. Even if the father-son correlation is high because traits that affect earning power are inherited, well-designed interventions could still be cost effective and improve the lot of the disadvantaged.

To take an extreme example, the correlation in incomes between fathers and sons was high in South Africa under apartheid because race is an inherited trait. The abolition of apartheid reduced the correlation. The organization of society matters.

Perhaps the only legitimate use of the intergenerational correlation in income is to characterize economic mobility. The data challenge the notion that the United States is an exceptionally mobile society. If the United States stands out in comparison with other countries, it is in having a more static distribution of income across generations with fewer opportunities for advancement.

Anders Bjorklund of Stockholm University and Markus Jantti of the University of Tampere in Finland, for example, find more economic mobility in Sweden than in the United States. Only South Africa and Britain have as little mobility across generations as the United States.

Luke Skywalker and Darth Vader are an unusual father-son pair; in most families, the apple does not fall so far from the tree.

————

The Sons Also Rise

N.Y. TIMES, Nov. 22, 2002, at A27.

■ PAUL KRUGMAN

America, we all know, is the land of opportunity. Your success in life depends on your ability and drive, not on who your father was.

Just ask the Bush brothers. Talk to Elizabeth Cheney, who holds a specially created State Department job, or her husband, chief counsel of the Office of Management and Budget. Interview Eugene Scalia, the top lawyer at the Labor Department, and Janet Rehnquist, inspector general at the Department of Health and Human Services. And don't forget to check in with William Kristol, editor of The Weekly Standard, and the conservative commentator John Podhoretz.

What's interesting is how little comment, let alone criticism, this roll call has occasioned. It might be just another case of kid-gloves treatment by the media, but I think it's a symptom of a broader phenomenon: inherited status is making a comeback.

It has always been good to have a rich or powerful father. Last week my Princeton colleague Alan Krueger wrote a column for The Times surveying statistical studies that debunk the mythology of American social mobility. "If the United States stands out in comparison with other countries," he wrote, "it is in having a more static distribution of income across generations with fewer opportunities for advancement." And Kevin Phillips, in his book "Wealth and Democracy," shows that robber-baron fortunes have been far more persistent than legend would have it.

But the past is only prologue. According to one study cited by Mr. Krueger, the heritability of status has been increasing in recent decades. And that's just the beginning. Underlying economic, social and political trends will give the children of today's wealthy a huge advantage over those who chose the wrong parents.

For one thing, there's more privilege to pass on. Thirty years ago the C.E.O. of a major company was a bureaucrat—well paid, but not truly wealthy. He couldn't give either his position or a large fortune to his heirs. Today's imperial C.E.O.'s, by contrast, will leave vast estates behind—and they are often able to give their children lucrative jobs, too. More broadly, the spectacular increase in American inequality has made the gap between the rich and the middle class wider, and hence more difficult to cross, than it was in the past.

Meanwhile, one key doorway to upward mobility—a good education system, available to all—has been closing. More and more, ambitious parents feel that a public school education is a dead end. It's telling that Jack Grubman, the former Salomon Smith Barney analyst, apparently sold his soul not for personal wealth but for two places in the right nursery school. Alas, most American souls aren't worth enough to get the kids into the 92nd Street Y.

Also, the heritability of status will be mightily reinforced by the repeal of the estate tax—a prime example of the odd way in which public policy and public opinion have shifted in favor of measures that benefit the wealthy, even as our society becomes increasingly class-ridden.

It wasn't always thus. The influential dynasties of the 20th century, like the Kennedys, the Rockefellers and, yes, the Sulzbergers, faced a public suspicious of inherited position; they overcame that suspicion by demonstrating a strong sense of noblesse oblige, justifying their existence by standing for high principles. Indeed, the Kennedy legend has a whiff of

Bonnie Prince Charlie about it; the rightful heirs were also perceived as defenders of the downtrodden against the powerful.

But today's heirs feel no need to demonstrate concern for those less fortunate. On the contrary, they are often avid defenders of the powerful against the downtrodden. Mr. Scalia's principal personal claim to fame is his crusade against regulations that protect workers from ergonomic hazards, while Ms. Rehnquist has attracted controversy because of her efforts to weaken the punishment of health-care companies found to have committed fraud.

The official ideology of America's elite remains one of meritocracy, just as our political leadership pretends to be populist. But that won't last. Soon enough, our society will rediscover the importance of good breeding, and the vulgarity of talented upstarts.

For years, opinion leaders have told us that it's all about family values. And it is—but it will take a while before most people realize that they meant the value of coming from the right family.

NOTES AND QUESTIONS

1. The inequality conundrum. In a 2007 article, Roger Lowenstein noted in the New York Times Magazine that people in the highest quintile of income in the United States keep getting richer, much faster and much more than people in lower quintiles:

> In 2004, according to the Congressional Budget Office's latest official analysis, households in the lowest quintile of the country were making only 2 percent more (adjusted for inflation) than they were in 1979. Those in the next quintile managed only an 11 percent rise. And the middle group was up 15 percent. Do you sense a pattern? The income of families in the fourth quintile—upper-middle-class folks with an average yearly income of $82,000—rose by 23 percent. Only when you get to the top quintile were the gains truly big—63 percent.

Roger Lowenstein, *The Inequality Conundrum,* N.Y. TIMES, Jun. 10, 2007, sec. 6 (magazine), at 11. Lowenstein suggests that the problem is not that the rich have too much money, but that "so many have been stuck for so long at the bottom and in the middle." Other countries, Lowenstein notes, reduce inequality with higher taxes and higher transfer payments; a poor person in Belgium, for example, is better off than a poor person in the United States, even though the United States is richer than Belgium. For Lowenstein, however, a better solution to the conundrum is education, so that more people can move up the "skills ladder." He notes, for example, that "College grads make more than 40 percent more than high-school grads. Those with postgraduate degrees earn twice as much." *Id.*

Can more education really solve the inequality problem? Or is this reasoning subject to the "Lake Wobegon effect"? That is, if everyone in the United States had a postgraduate degree, would it follow that everyone would be in the upper quintile of income? Or by definition, does somebody in the United States have to take the worst-paying jobs?

2.   Economic inequality becoming an even bigger problem? Eugene Robinson of the Washington Post argues that economic inequality is becoming an even greater problem in the twenty-first century because now only 6 percent of children who are born in the lowest quintile in America ever reach the highest quintile. Robinson argues that this truth is destroying the myth of rags to riches in this country. Eugene Robinson, *Tattered Dream, Who'll Tackle the Issue of Upward Mobility?*, THE WASHINGTON POST, Nov. 23, 2007, at A39. Do you believe that this is true? Or do you believe that rags to riches was always a myth, and that this time period is no different than any other time period in American history?

3.   How much do family incomes go up and down in America? Steven J. Rose and Scott Winship explore in "Ups and Downs: Does The American Economy Still Promote Upward Mobility?" how much American incomes can change from year to year. They discovered that over a two year period, roughly 45 percent of working-age adults have their real family incomes increase or decrease by more than 25 percent, a rate that has been relatively unchanged since 1969. Of those families experiencing a loss in 1994, a fifth (19 percent) recovered within one year and another third (31 percent) recovered with four years. One-third, however, failed to recover even after ten years.

The risk of experiencing a large income drop over two years have been and remains lowest for those under age 46, whites, college graduates, and couples who get married or move in together. It remains unclear, however, if these good bounce back numbers remain true in the aftermath of the Great Recession of 2008–2009. Steven J. Rose and Scott Winship, *Ups and Downs, Does the American Economy Still Promote Upward Mobility?*, Economic Mobility Project, June 2009.

4.   A lack of anger? Before the Great Recession of 2008–2009, Doug Henwood wrote in an article for *The Nation* magazine that despite the growth in economic inequality and despite the fact that the "New Wealthy" were providing very little for working families, there was very little anger at the very rich, unlike in previous times in American history. Doug Henwood, *Our Glided Age*, THE NATION, June 11, 2008. Do you believe this has now changed because of the Great Recession of 2008–2009? If so, how much has it changed? How is this change expressed?

5.   The GINI coefficient. One example of how much the inequality in the United States has grown recently is to look at the GINI coefficient, which is a classic measurement of the inequality in society. In the United States, the GINI coefficient has grown from 0.395 in 1974 to 0.463 in 2007. By this measure, the United States is less unequal than many developing countries, but well above Denmark, Finland, and Sweden. *A Special Report on the Rich*, The Economist, April 4, 2009.

———

TABLE 2. **More Than 50 Percent of Taxpayers in the Bottom Quintile Moved to Higher Quintile Within Ten Years**

Income Mobility Relative to the Total Tax
Filing Population, 1996 to 2005

1996 Income Quintile	Lowest	Second	Middle	Fourth	Highest	Total	Top 10%	Top 5%	Top 1%
Lowest	42.4	28.6	13.9	9.9	5.3	100.0	2.3	1.3	0.2
Second	17.0	33.3	26.7	15.1	7.9	100.0	3.0	1.2	0.1
Middle	7.1	17.5	33.3	29.6	12.5	100.0	4.2	1.4	0.3
Fourth	4.1	7.3	18.3	40.2	30.2	100.0	8.6	2.7	0.3
Highest	2.6	3.2	7.1	17.8	69.4	100.0	43.4	22.5	4.4
Top 10%	2.6	2.2	4.9	11.8	78.6	100.0	61.1	37.6	8.3
Top 5%	2.6	1.8	3.9	8.6	83.1	100.0	71.6	54.4	15.2
Top 1%	3.2	1.3	2.2	4.9	88.4	100.0	82.7	75.0	42.6
All Income Groups	13.2	16.8	19.6	23.3	27.1	100.0	13.4	6.4	1.2

Source: Income Mobility in the U.S. from 1996 to 2005, U.S. Department of the Treasury, November 13, 2007.

TABLE 2.1. **How Did the Absolute Incomes of the Top 1 Percent in 1996 Change by 2005?**

1996 Income Percentile	Mean Income				Median Income		
	1996	2005	% Change		1996	2005	% Change
0.1 to 1%	654,953	801,672	22.4		557,503	412,433	−26.0
0.01 to 0.1%	2,854,752	3,150,686	10.4		2,375,946	1,180,878	−50.3
Top 0.01%	17,518,043	14,391,130	−17.8		11,592,130	4,102,806	−64.6
All Income Groups	70,420	97,206	38.0		48,684	60,487	24.2

TABLE 2.2. **"Like Parent, Like Child—Recent Studies Find That There Is Less Income Mobility from One Generation to Another than Previously Believed."**

Table: Children's Chances of Experiencing Both Absolute and Relative
Mobility, by Parents Family Income
(percent in each category)

Parents Family Income Rank	Bottom Quintile	Second Quintile	Middle Quintile	Fourth Quintile	Top Quintile	All Families
Upwardly Mobile: Higher Income and up 1 or more quintiles	58	52	36	26	n/a	34
Riding The Tide: Higher income and same quintile	24	20	23	32	34	27

Falling despite the Tide: Higher income and down 1 quintile	n/a	1	7	9	10	5
Downwardly mobile: Lower income and lower/same quintile	18	26	34	33	57	33
Total all children's families	100	100	100	100	100	100

Source: Income Mobility in the U.S. from 1996 to 2005, U.S. Department of the Treasury, November 13, 2007.

————

For Richer

N.Y. TIMES, Oct. 20, 2002, § 6 (magazine), at 62.

■ PAUL KRUGMAN

THE DISAPPEARING MIDDLE

When I was a teenager growing up on Long Island, one of my favorite excursions was a trip to see the great Gilded Age mansions of the North Shore. Those mansions weren't just pieces of architectural history. They were monuments to a bygone social era, one in which the rich could afford the armies of servants needed to maintain a house the size of a European palace. By the time I saw them, of course, that era was long past. Almost none of the Long Island mansions were still private residences. Those that hadn't been turned into museums were occupied by nursing homes or private schools.

For the America I grew up in—the America of the 1950's and 1960's—was a middle-class society, both in reality and in feel. The vast income and wealth inequalities of the Gilded Age had disappeared. Yes, of course, there was the poverty of the underclass—but the conventional wisdom of the time viewed that as a social rather than an economic problem. Yes, of course, some wealthy businessmen and heirs to large fortunes lived far better than the average American. But they weren't rich the way the robber barons who built the mansions had been rich, and there weren't that many of them. The days when plutocrats were a force to be reckoned with in American society, economically or politically, seemed long past.

Daily experience confirmed the sense of a fairly equal society. The economic disparities you were conscious of were quite muted. Highly educated professionals—middle managers, college teachers, even lawyers—often claimed that they earned less than unionized blue-collar workers. Those considered very well off lived in split-levels, had a housecleaner come in once a week and took summer vacations in Europe. But they sent their kids to public schools and drove themselves to work, just like everyone else.

But that was long ago. The middle-class America of my youth was another country.

We are now living in a new Gilded Age, as extravagant as the original. Mansions have made a comeback. Back in 1999 this magazine profiled

Thierry Despont, the "eminence of excess," an architect who specializes in designing houses for the superrich. His creations typically range from 20,000 to 60,000 square feet; houses at the upper end of his range are not much smaller than the White House. Needless to say, the armies of servants are back, too. So are the yachts. Still, even J.P. Morgan didn't have a Gulfstream.

As the story about Despont suggests, it's not fair to say that the fact of widening inequality in America has gone unreported. Yet glimpses of the lifestyles of the rich and tasteless don't necessarily add up in people's minds to a clear picture of the tectonic shifts that have taken place in the distribution of income and wealth in this country. My sense is that few people are aware of just how much the gap between the very rich and the rest has widened over a relatively short period of time. In fact, even bringing up the subject exposes you to charges of "class warfare," the "politics of envy" and so on. And very few people indeed are willing to talk about the profound effects—economic, social and political—of that widening gap.

Yet you can't understand what's happening in America today without understanding the extent, causes and consequences of the vast increase in inequality that has taken place over the last three decades, and in particular the astonishing concentration of income and wealth in just a few hands. To make sense of the current wave of corporate scandal, you need to understand how the man in the gray flannel suit has been replaced by the imperial C.E.O. The concentration of income at the top is a key reason that the United States, for all its economic achievements, has more poverty and lower life expectancy than any other major advanced nation. Above all, the growing concentration of wealth has reshaped our political system: it is at the root both of a general shift to the right and of an extreme polarization of our politics.

NOTES AND QUESTIONS

1.   Other factors influencing income inequality. Besides intergenerational economic position, what are other factors that could explain income inequality in America?

2.   Intergenerational economic mobility: racial implications. The above-cited study by Charles and Hurst portrays the strong correlation between individuals' parents' incomes and their own economic futures. Are such findings consistent for all demographic groups? In other words, are members of one ethnic or racial group more likely to break free of their parents' economic status than members of another demographic group?

American University professor of economics Tom Hertz encountered this question in a study of economic mobility. Using data compiled from the Panel Study of Income Dynamics, consisting of a sample of 6,723 black and white families observed over thirty-two years and in two generations, Hertz found that African Americans are more likely to remain in lower income brackets than their white counterparts. The study revealed that blacks' rate of persistence at low-income levels was 42 percent, while their rate of persistence at high income levels was only 4 percent. On the other hand, for whites, the rate of persistence at the bottom was approximately half that at the top (17 percent versus 30 percent). Adjusted for age, the study revealed blacks' persistence to remain in a lower income bracket was 41 percent, while whites' persistence to remain at the bottom was 25 percent. Also, for white families, extreme upward mobility is more likely than downward mobility (14 percent versus 9 percent), but the reverse is true for blacks—blacks have a 35 percent chance of substantially sliding down the income scale, and only have a 4 percent chance of substantially moving up the scale. These findings all point to the conclusion that black families have a significantly lower rate of upward mobility from the bottom income bracket than do whites. Tom Hertz, *Rags, Riches and Race: The Intergenerational Mobility of Black and White Families in the United States, in* UNEQUAL CHANCES: FAMILY BACKGROUND AND ECONOMIC SUCCESS (Samuel Bowles, et al. eds., 2005).

What are the reasons for income differences among demographic groups?

3. Intergenerational economic mobility: gender implications. One recent study argues that family structure has become an important mechanism for the reproduction of inequality. According to Sara McLanahan and Christine Percheski, increases in income inequality may lead to increases in single motherhood, which in turn decreases intergenerational economic mobility by affecting children's material resources and the parenting they experience. These family structure changes exacerbate racial inequalities, as African–American women are more likely to be single mothers. Moreover, as mothers incur more child-related costs and fewer fathers experience family life with children, gender inequalities increase as well. See Sara McLanahan and Christine Percheski, *Family Structure and the Reproduction of Inequalities*, 34 ANN. REV. SOC. 257 (2008).

4. Income inequality and the Great Recession. How has the 2008 financial meltdown affected trends in income inequality? A study by the Pew Charitable Trusts concluded that overall the American economy continues to promote upward absolute mobility, and that recovery from income losses is comparable to that of past periods. Nevertheless, the study found that, "Nearly a quarter of American adults experience a large ten-year drop in income, and they have only a fifty-fifty chance of recovery within the subsequent ten years. The evidence implies that in the current downturn, more people will experience large short-term income losses than large gains." Stephen J. Rose and Scott Winship, Economic Mobility Project, *Ups and Downs: Does the American Economy Still Promote Upward Mobility?* (June 2009), at http://www.economicmobility.org.

If the overall picture of income mobility has not changed very much over the last forty years, there are nonetheless winners and losers. Some have suggested that after the recession the rich have ceased getting richer, and may even be getting poorer. See David Leonhardt and Geraldine Fabrikant, New York Times, *Rise of the Super–Rich Hits a Sobering Wall,*

New York Times, Aug. 20, 2009, http://www.nytimes.com/2009/08/21/business/economy/21inequality.html?pagewanted=1&fta=y.

For those already on the bottom rung of the economic ladder, the effects of the Great Recession are far more serious. Columnist Bob Herbert of the New York Times cited a study finding that households with annual incomes of $12,499 or less had an unemployment rate in the fourth quarter of 2009 of 30.8 percent, "more than five points higher than the overall jobless rate at the height of the Depression." Bob Herbert, "The Worst of the Pain," New York Times, Feb. 9, 2010, http://www.nytimes.com/2010/02/09/opinion/09herbert.html.

The Great Recession has apparently affected groups differentially by race and gender, as well. Barbara Ehrenreich and Dedrick Muhammad argue:

> For African Americans—and to a large extent, Latinos—the *recession* is over. It occurred between 2000 and 2007, as black employment decreased by 2.4 percent and incomes declined by 2.9 percent. During the seven-year long black recession, one third of black children lived in poverty and black unemployment—even among college graduates—consistently ran at about twice the level of white unemployment. That was the black recession. What's happening now is a *depression*.

> Black unemployment is now at 14.7 percent, compared to 8.7 for whites. In New York City, black unemployment has been rising four times as fast as that of whites. Lawrence Mishel, president of the Economic Policy Institute, estimates that 40 percent of African Americans will have experienced unemployment or underemployment by 2010, and this will increase child poverty from one-third of African–American children to slightly over half. No one can entirely explain the extraordinary rate of job loss among African Americans, though factors may include the relative concentration of blacks in the hard-hit retail and manufacturing sectors, as well as the lesser seniority of blacks in better-paying, white collar, positions.

Barbara Ehrenreich and Dedrick Muhammed, *The Destruction of the Black Middle Class*, Barbara's Blog, August 4, 2009, http://ehrenreich.blogs.com/barbaras_blog/2009/08/the-destruction-of-the-black-middle-class.html.

Interestingly, the Great Recession has improved women's position relative to men's. In 2009, women outnumbered men on U.S. payrolls for the first time. Economist Casey Mulligan explains:

> Construction and manufacturing are male-intensive industries and were industries with particularly large percentage employment losses during this recession. Over the past 24 months, the number of female payroll employees fell 2.6 million, while the number of men fell 5.8 million.

> In fact, almost all of the gains in women's relative employment over the last 20 years occurred during the three recessions [1990–91, 2001, and 2008–10].

Casey B. Mulligan, *In a First, Women Surpass Men on U.S. Payrolls,* Economix Blog, New York Times, Feb. 5, 2010, http://economix.blogs. nytimes.com/2010/02/05/in-historical-first-women-outnumber-men-on-us-payrolls/.

———

3. WEALTH INEQUALITY
Race, Gender and Wealth

Lifting as We Climb: Women of Color, Wealth, and America's Future

Insight Center for Community Economic Development.

■ MARIKO CHANG, PH.D.

The Wealth Gap for Women of Color

Because Americans ... equate success with working hard. The corollary is that those who have not succeeded have either not worked hard enough or have their own behaviors to blame. As a result, women of color are often the targets of negative stereotypes and media images. In truth, past and current institutional factors play a significant role in positioning women of color at the bottom of the economic ladder.

1. Prior Institutional Factors

> * * * The benefits of citizenship, open to Europeans, was forbidden to Asian immigrants. The exclusion of Social Security coverage for a whole generation of farm workers, laborers, and domestic workers, kept Latino and black elders in poverty.

Advantage and disadvantage is passed from generation to generation often with a cumulative effect, thereby contributing to the current racial wealth gap.

Laws against interracial marriage also helped cement the historical legacy of wealth inequality between groups. In addition, there were particular historical impacts on women of different races. For instance, the "transfer" of land from Native Americans took away a source of wealth that many Native American women once controlled; land was traditionally passed down along matrilineal lines, but U.S. policy divided their land and distributed it to men only, creating a rift between Native men and women that still waits re-bridging.

Mexicans, like Native women, could inherit and own property. However, this changed in the 1800s after the Treaty of Guadalupe Hidalgo that annexed from Mexico what is now most of the Southwestern states. When Mexican women property owners married white men, U.S. laws accorded ownership of the land to their husbands. These and other historical policies have been well-documented in *The Color of Wealth: The Story Behind the U.S. Racial Divide.*

* * * women of color were not only affected by historical policies directed at persons of color, they were affected by policies that restricted opportunities for women to own and build wealth. Before states passed married women's property acts, married women could not control property, even property that they owned prior to marriage. And, until passage of the Equal Credit Opportunity Act of 1974, it was extremely difficult for women to obtain credit in their own name because lenders could deny applications on the basis of sex or marital status. * * *

Until the passage of the 1963 Equal Pay Act and Title VII of the 1964 Civil Rights Act, women could be denied a job or promotion simply because they were women and employers could pay women less than men doing the same job or could fire women for getting married or becoming pregnant. * * *

2.   Current Institutional Factors

Wage Disparities

In 2007, the gender wage ratio for annual earnings of full-year workers reached an all-time high of 78%, but fell to 77% in 2008 (the most recent year available). The pay gap affects all women, but it is not uniform for women of different racial and ethnic groups. * * *

Men and women of color, with the exception of Asians, have lower median earnings than whites. Black and Hispanic women are particularly likely to be employed in jobs and industries with lower pay. But women of color experience the cumulative earnings disadvantage of being both a person of color and a woman.

When compared to men of their same race or ethnicity, the largest gender pay gap is between white men and white women, with women earning only 72.6% of the pay of their male counterparts. In contrast, Black and Hispanic women earn 87.1%, Asian women earn 80%, Native American women earn 83%, and Native Hawaiian and Other Pacific Islanders earn 82% of the pay of their same-race male counterparts. One reason why the pay gap is larger between white men and women than it is between men and women of color is that men of color have lower salaries than white men. . . .

Government Benefits Impact the Ability to Build Wealth

Public Assistance

The government provides financial safety nets for the most economically vulnerable. Because women of color have such low incomes and low wealth, they are more likely to need economic assistance. But public assistance programs such as Temporary Assistance to Needy Families (TANF) negatively affect recipients' ability to build wealth.

The asset limits of such public assistance programs have come under criticism for making it more difficult for people to build assets over the long run, thereby actually increasing their economic vulnerability.

For instance, owning a vehicle worth more than $5,000 disqualifies a person from being eligible for benefits in fifteen states. Yet many recipients need a reliable vehicle to apply for jobs or get to their place of employment, and research indicates that owning a vehicle increases the probability of employment, hours worked, and earnings. In addition to restrictions on value of vehicles owned, every state except Ohio has limits on countable assets ("cash on hand," money held in checking and savings accounts, etc.) to ensure that public assistance is going to those who need it most. * * *

Social Insurance

Social insurance programs such as Social Security, unemployment insurance and workers compensation also impact the wealth gap for women of color. Because Social Security benefits are linked to earnings and years of employment, women of color receive lower benefits because of their lower earnings. In addition, like white women, women of color often reduce their work hours to care for others, which further decreases their income and contributes to lower benefits during retirement. Women of color are also more likely to be employed as domestic or agricultural workers, where employer compliance with reporting income and withholding Social Security taxes is weaker

Marital Status

Marital status also affects Social Security benefits. Married persons can collect benefits based on their own or their spouse's employment and earnings record, whichever is higher. Because white women are more likely to marry and remain married, they more often have the ability to choose between benefits based on their own employment record or the record of their likely higher earning spouse. In 2008, 57% of black women aged 65 and over were entitled to benefits only as workers, 20% were dually entitled, and 22% entitled only as a wife or widow of a worker. For non-white women of other races, 46% were entitled only as workers, 13% were dually entitled, and 42% were entitled only as the wife or widow of a worker. In contrast, 40% of white women were entitled as workers only, 31% were dually entitled, and 28% were entitled only as a wife or widow of a worker.

Women who are entitled to benefits only as workers (as is the case most often for women of color) receive lower average benefits because women generally earn less than men. Nevertheless, even though women of color receive lower Social Security benefits based on employment, Social Security is a critically important benefit for women of color since they are less likely to have other sources of income during retirement. Black women in particular rely heavily on Social Security. For more than 25% of black women ages 65 and over, Social Security is their *only* source of income * * *

Parenthood

The rising numbers of women (and to a lesser extent, men) who are raising children on their own [has a direct impact on wealth]. Since 1970, the percentage of children living in single-parent families has more than doubled. Adoption is also increasingly common for singles. Women of color (except Asian or Pacific Islanders) are also much more likely to be single parents. Women of color are generally younger when they have their first child and have more children, on average, than white non-Hispanic women (although this may be less true in the future as fertility rates have been declining for teens of all races, especially black teens). Due to the economic instability in their communities, women of color are more likely to be grandparenting or taking in the children of relatives than their white counterparts.

NOTES AND QUESTIONS

1. Ledbetter v. Goodyear Tire and Rubber Co. and the Congressional Response. In 2007, the Supreme Court ruled in favor of Goodyear Tire in an Employment Discrimination Case on the basis of gender, *Ledbetter v. Goodyear Tire and Rubber, Co.*, 550 U.S. 618 (2007). In the case, Ms. Ledbetter argued that she was the victim of pay discrimination due to her gender, which is a violation of both Title VII and the Equal Pay Act. Goodyear argued that Ms. Ledbetter only had 180 days from her first paycheck with the company to file the initial complaint, and that time had already passed. Ms. Ledbetter argued that every time she received a paycheck that 180 day clock started all over again. The Supreme Court, in a 5–4 decision, agreed with Goodyear, and said the clock had already run out on Ms. Ledbetter's timeframe to file the complaint under the Equal Pay Act. Congress responded to this decision in 2009 by passed the Lilly Ledbetter Fair Pay Act, which essentially overturned the Supreme Court decision and allowed the 180 days to run from any check received from the company. The Lilly Ledbetter Fair Pay Act of 2009, P.L. 111–2, 111th Congress, 2009.

2. What has happened in the last 40 years of the women's movement? Stephanie Luce and Mark Brenner describe the changes that have occurred in the women's movement in the last 40 years in the article, "Women and Class: What Has Happened in Forty Years?" They note several positive changes, but also note several challenges that continue to be present for women in the workforce. First, they note that now more women are present in the workforce than ever before. Next, they note, however that minority women continue to suffer an education gap, despite being more present in the workforce than ever before. In addition, they note that more women than men are still responsible for the raising of children and that lower wages for women continue to persist. The explanation that the authors give for these continuing issues are racial discrimination and women working towards individual goals instead of the betterment of the women's movement as a whole. Stephanie Luce and Mark Brenner,

Women and Class: What Has Happened in Forty Years?, 58 Monthly Review 80 (2006).

3.   A gender-based pay gap continues to exist? A BusinessWeek article from 2008 says that women graduates from undergraduate colleges in all fields except business expect to get paid less than men. *Grads Still See A Gender Based Pay Gap*, BUSINESSWEEK, June 30, 2008, 12. Is that what you believe? Do you believe that women still get unfairly underpaid in all job fields? Do you believe that the recession has changed this dynamic in any way? Why or why not?

————

Wealth and Inequality in America

BLACK WEALTH/WHITE WEALTH: A NEW PERSPECTIVE ON RACIAL INEQUALITY 53–90 (1997).

■ MELVIN L. OLIVER & THOMAS M. SHAPIRO

[A] thorough analysis of economic well-being and social and racial equality must include a wealth dimension. A lack of systematic, reliable data on wealth accumulation, however, partly explains the general absence of such an analysis until now. * * *

The bulk of our analysis and discussion of wealth is drawn from the Survey of Income and Program Participation. SIPP is a sample of the U.S. population that interviews adults in households periodically over a two-and-a-half-year period. A new panel is introduced every year. Data for this study came from the 1987 Panel. Household interviews began in June 1987, and the same households were reinterviewed every four months through 1989. The full data set of eight interviews was available for 11,257 households. * * *

What is wealth? How does one define it? What indicators of wealth are the best ones to use? Definitional and conceptual questions about wealth have produced a diverse and sometimes confusing set of approaches to the topic. Indeed, a major difficulty in analyzing wealth is that people define it in different ways with the result that wealth measures lack comparability. After working with the literature for several years, we decided to measure wealth by way of two concepts. The first, *net worth* (NW) conveys the straightforward value of all assets less any debts. The second, *net financial assets* (NFA), excludes equity accrued in a home or vehicle from the calculation of a household's available resources.

Net worth gives a comprehensive picture of all assets and debts; yet it may not be a reliable measure of *command over future resources* for one's self and family. Net worth includes equity in vehicles, for instance, and it is not likely that this equity will be converted into other resources, such as prep school for a family's children. Thus one's car is not a likely repository in which to store resources for future use. Likewise, viewing home equity as a reasonable and unambiguous source of future resources for the current generation raises many vexing problems. Most people do not sell their homes to finance a college education for their children, start a business, make other investments, buy medical care, support political candidates, or pay lobbyists to protect their special interests. Even if a family sells a home, the proceeds are typically used to lease or buy replacement housing. An exception to the general rule may involve the elderly. Mortgage payments, especially in times of high housing inflation, may be seen as a kind of "forced savings" to be cashed in at retirement or to pass along to one's children.

* * * The specific difference between net worth and net financial assets is that equity in vehicles and homes is excluded from the latter, although debts are subtracted from NFA. In contrast to net worth, net financial assets consist of more readily liquid sources of income and wealth that can be used for a family's immediate well-being. Because the distinction between net worth and net financial assets is somewhat controversial and still open to debate, we usually present both measures. Generally, in our view, however, net financial assets seem to be the best indicator of the current generation's command over future resources, while net worth provides a more accurate estimate of the wealth likely to be inherited by the next generation.

Let us now turn to the substantive questions at the heart of our study. How has wealth been distributed in American society over the twentieth century? What about the redistribution of wealth that took place in the decade of the eighties? And finally, what do the answers to these questions imply for black-white inequality?

The 1980s and Beyond Bigger Shares for the Wealthy

Available information concerning wealth in the twentieth century, until very recently, comes mainly from national estate-tax records for the very wealthy collected between 1922 and 1981, and from sporadic cross-sectional household surveys starting in 1953. Drawing from these data bases, we track trends in the distribution of wealth, paying particular attention to whether inequality is falling, remaining stable, or rising, into the late 1980s and early 1990s.

Estate-tax data show consistently high wealth concentrations throughout the early part of the twentieth century. According to Edward Wolff's "The Rich Get Increasingly Richer," the top 1 percent of American households possessed over 25 percent of total wealth between 1922 and 1972. Beginning in 1972, however, the data indicate a significant decline in wealth inequality. The share of the top percentile declined from 29 percent to 19 percent between 1972 and 1976. While this decline was unexpected, it was not permanent. In fact in the next five-year period, from 1976 to 1981, a sharp renewal of wealth inequality occurred. Between 1976 and 1981 the share of the richest 1 percent expanded from 19 to 24 percent.

The standard theory explaining wealth inequality associates the phenomenon with the process of industrialization. Stable, low levels of inequality characterize preindustrial times; the onset of modern economic growth is characterized by rapid industrialization, which ushers in a sharp increase in inequality; and then advanced, mature industrial societies experience a gradual leveling of inequality and finally long-term stability. This explanation highlights industrialization as a universal, master trend in the evolution of market economies. The twentieth century in particular is said to represent a clear pattern, specifically from 1929 on, when, according to Jeffrey Williamson's and Peter Lindert's *American Inequality*, wealth imbalance "seems to have undergone a permanent reduction." One must question the persistence of this reduced inequality into the 1990s, especially in light of growing income inequalities.

Estimates of household wealth inequality from two relatively consistent sources of household survey data, the 1962 Survey of Financial Characteristics of Consumers and the Surveys of Consumer Finances conducted in the 1980s, furnish more recent information. Responses to these surveys indicate that wealth inequality remained relatively fixed between 1962 and 1983. The top 3 percent of wealth holders held 32 percent of the wealth in 1962 and 34 percent in 1983. The Gini coefficient, which measures equality over an entire distribution rather than as shares of the top percentile, rose slightly, from 0.73 in 1962 to 0.74 in 1983. The Gini ratio is a statistic that converts levels of inequality into a single number and allows easy comparisons of populations. Gini figures range from 0 to 1. A low ratio indicates low levels of inequality; a high ratio indicates high levels of inequality. Thus Ginis closer to 0 illustrate more distributional equality, while figures closer to 1 indicate more inequality. While the Gini coefficient is a very useful summary measure of inequality, it is probably most helpful and meaningful as a way of comparing distributions of wealth between time periods, given its sensitivity to small changes and its clear indication of the direction of change.

What happened during the 1980s? Quite simply, the very rich increased their share of the nation's wealth. One leading economist dubbed the resulting wealth imbalance an "unprecedented jump in inequality to Great Gatsby levels." Notably, inequality had risen very sharply by 1989, with the wealthiest 1 percent of households owning 37.7 percent of net worth. An examination of net financial assets suggests even greater levels of inequality. In 1983 the top 1 percent held 42.8 percent of all financial assets, a figure that increased to 48.2 percent in 1989. The Gini coefficient reflects this increase in inequality, rising 0.04 during the period. Wealth inequality by the end of the 1980s closely approximated historically high levels not seen since 1922.

Our review of other wealth indicators and studies corroborates the finding that wealth is reconcentrating. It also goes a way toward revealing the relationship between trends toward wealth concentration and growing inequality and [a] lower standard of living * * *. The evidence presented by Edward Wolff in "The Rich Get Increasingly Richer" and by others using [Survey of Consumer Finances] data suggests that while the concentration of wealth decreased substantially during the mid–1970s, it increased sharply during the 1980s. In particular the *mean* net worth of families grew by over 7 percent from 1983 to 1989. However, *median* net worth grew much more slowly than mean wealth, at a rate of 0.8 percent. According to

Wolff, this discrepancy "implies that the upper-wealth classes enjoyed a disproportionate share [of wealth]" between 1983 and 1989. Wolff's median net financial assets declined 3.7 percent during this period. Thus the typical family disposed of fewer liquid resources in 1989 than in 1983. In stark contrast, the wealth of the "superrich," defined as the top one-half of 1 percent of wealth-holders, increased 26 percent from 1983 to 1989. Over one-half (55 percent) of the wealth created between 1983 and 1989 accrued to the richest one-half of one percent of families, a fact that vividly illustrates the magnitude of the 1980s increase in their share of the country's wealth. Not surprisingly, the Gini coefficient increased sizably during this period, from 0.80 to 0.84. Indeed, U.S. wealth concentration in 1989 was more extreme than at any time since 1929.

SIPP as well as SCF data confirm that the wealth pie is being resliced, and that the wealthy are getting larger pieces of it. In a 1994 update on its ongoing SIPP study, the Census Bureau reports that the median net worth of the nation's households dropped 12 percent between 1988 and 1991. The drop in median wealth is associated with a sharp decline in the middle classes' largest share of net worth: home equity. The median home equity declined by 14 percent between 1988 and 1991 as real estate values fell.

The trends of increasing income and wealth inequality have disrupted long-standing post–World War II patterns. The movement toward income equality and stability expired by the mid–1970s, while the trend toward wealth equality extended into the early 1980s. By 1983 wealth inequality began to rise. The time lag in these reversals is important. Along with declining incomes, a growth in debt burden, and fluctuations in housing values and stock prices, the actions of government—and the Reagan tax cuts of the early 1980s—can only be viewed as prime causes of the increase in wealth inequality.

How has this redistribution of wealth in favor of the rich affected the middle class? Examining wealth groups by ranking all families into wealth fifths provides one way to get at this question. The average holdings of the lower-middle and bottom wealth groups (fifths) declined in real terms by 30 percent. The wealth of the middle group remained unchanged, while that of the upper-middle group increased by slightly less than 1 percent a year. The average wealth of the top group increased by over 10 percent. Combining this with previous information showing a decline in median net financial assets strengthens the argument that the economic base of middle-class life is becoming increasingly fragile and tenuous.

During the 1980s the rich got much richer, and the poor and middle classes fell further behind. One obvious culprit was the Reagan tax cuts. These cuts provided greater discretionary income for middle-and upper-class taxpayers. However, most middle-class taxpayers used this discretionary income to bolster their declining standards of living or decrease their debt burden instead of saving or investing it. Although Reagan strategists had intended to stimulate investment, the upper classes embarked on a frenzy of consumer spending on luxury items. Wolff's "The Rich Get Increasingly Richer" explains the redistribution of wealth in favor of the rich during the 1980s as resulting more from capital gains reaped on existing wealth than from increased savings and investment. He attributes 70 percent of the growth in wealth over the 1983–1989 period to the appreciation of existing financial assets and the remaining 30 percent to the creation of wealth from personal savings. Led by rapid gains in stocks, financial securities, and liquid assets, existing investments grew at an impressive rate at a time when it was difficult to convert earnings into personal savings.

One asset whose value grew dramatically during the eighties was real estate. Home ownership is central to the average American's wealth portfolio. Housing equity makes up the largest part of wealth held by the middle class, whereas the upper class and wealthy more commonly own a greater degree of their wealth in financial assets. The percentage of families owning homes peaked in the mid–1970s at 65 percent and has subsequently declined by a point or two. Forty-three percent of blacks own homes, a rate 65 percent lower than that of whites. Housing equity constitutes the most substantial portion of all wealth assets by far. SIPP results clearly demonstrate this assertion: housing equity represented 43 percent of median household assets in 1988. It is even more significant, however, in the wealth portfolios of blacks than of whites, accounting for 43.3 percent of white wealth and 62.5 percent of black assets. This initial glance at the role of housing in overall wealth carries ramifications for subsequent in-depth analysis. Thus, owning a house—a hallmark of the American Dream—is becoming harder and harder for average Americans to afford, and fewer are able to do so. The ensuing analysis of racial differences in wealth requires a thorough investigation of racial dynamics in access to housing, mortgage and housing markets, and housing values.

The eighties ushered in a new era of wealth inequality in which strong gains were made by those who already had substantial financial assets. Those who had a piece of the rock, especially those with financial assets, but also those with real estate, increased their wealth holdings and consolidated a sense of economic security for themselves and their families. Others, a disproportionate share of them black, saw their financial status improve only slightly or decline.

In *Warm Hearts and Cold Cash* Marcia Millman notes that for most of this century, the primary legacy of middle-class parents to children has been "cultural" capital, that is, the upbringing, education, and contacts that allowed children to get a good start in life and to become financially successful and independent. Now some parents have more to bestow than cultural capital. In particular, middle-class Americans who started rearing families after World War II have amassed a huge amount of money in the value of their homes and stocks that they are now in the process of dispatching to the baby boom generation through inheritances, loans, and gifts. Millman says this money is "enormously consequential in shaping the lives of their adult children."

Much of this wealth was built by their parents between the late 1940s and the late 1960s when real wages and saving rates were higher and housing costs were considerably lower. For the elderly middle class, the escalation of real estate prices over the last twenty years has been a significant boon. * * *

Access to Assets

The potential for assets to expand or inhibit choices, horizons, and opportunities for children emerged as the most consistent and strongest common theme in our interviews. Since parents want to invest in their children, to give them whatever advantages they can, we wondered about the ability of the average American household to expend assets on their children. This section thus delves deeper into the assets households command by (1) considering the importance of home and vehicle equity in relation to other kinds of assets; (2) inspecting available financial assets for various groups of the population; and (3) looking at children growing up in resource-deficient households. We found a strong relationship between the amount of wealth and the composition of assets. Households with large amounts of total net worth control wealth portfolios composed mostly of financial assets. Financial investments make up about four-fifths of the assets of the richest households. Conversely, home and vehicle equity represents over 70 percent of the asset portfolio among the poorest one-fifth of American households, one in three of which possesses zero or negative financial assets.

Table 4.5 reports households with zero or negative net financial assets for various racial, age, education, and family groups. It shows that one-quarter of white households, 61 percent of black households, and 54 percent of Hispanic households are without financial resources. A similar absence of financial assets affects nearly one-half of young households; circumstances steadily improve with age, however, leaving only 15 percent of those households headed by seniors in a state of resource deficiency. The educational achievement of householders also connects directly with access to resources, as 40 percent of poorly educated household heads control no financial assets while over 80 percent of households headed by a college graduate control some NFA. Findings reported in this table also demonstrate deeply embedded disparities in resource command between single and married-couple parents. Resource deprivation characterizes 62 percent of single-parent households in comparison to 37 percent of married couples raising children.

TABLE 4.5 Who is on the Edge?

	Households with 0 or Negative NFA*	Households without NFA* for 3 months**	Households without NFA* for 6 months**
Sample	31.0%	44.9%	49.9%
Race			
White	25.3	38.1	43.2
Black	60.9	78.9	83.1
Hispanic	54.0	72.5	77.2

	Households with 0 or Negative NFA*	Households without NFA* for 3 months**	Households without NFA* for 6 months**
Age of Householder			
15–35	48.0	67.0	72.8
36–49	31.7	45.0	50.7
50–64	22.1	32.0	36.2
65 or older	15.1	26.4	30.6
Education			
Less than high school	40.3	55.5	60.0
High school degree	32.2	48.0	63.2
Some college	29.9	45.3	61.4
College degree	18.9	26.8	31.2
Family Type* * *			
Single parent	61.9	79.2	83.2
Married Couple	36.9	53.8	59.9

* Net financial worth
** NFA reserves to survive at the poverty line of $968 per month
*** Includes only households with children

Besides looking at resource deprivation, table 4.5 also sets criteria for "precarious-resource" circumstances. Households without enough NFA reserves to survive three months at the poverty line ($2,904) meet these criteria. Nearly 80 percent of single-parent households fit this description. Likewise 38 percent of white households and 79 percent of black households live in precarious-resource circumstances.

Among our interviewees, parents with ample assets planned to use them to create a better world for their children. Those without them strategized about acquiring some and talked about their "wish list." Parents talked about ballet lessons, camp, trips for cultural enrichment or even to Disney World, staying home more often with the children, affording full-time day care, allowing a parent to be home after day care. The parents discussed using assets to provide better educational opportunities for their children. Kevin takes great pride in paying for his son's college and being able to offer him advanced training. Stacie wants to be able to afford private school for Carrie. Ed and Alicia told us about the private school choices and dilemmas facing their children.

FIGURE 4.2 Percent of Children in Resource–Deficient Households, by Race

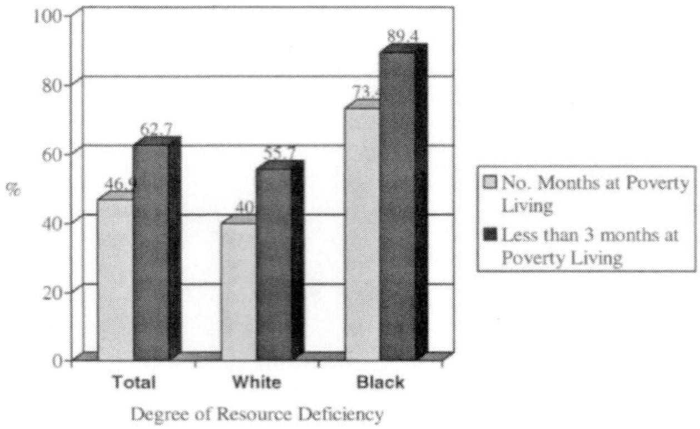

Degree of Resource Deficiency

Figure 4.2 looks at the percentage of children in resource-poor households by race. It provides information both on households with no net financial assets and on those with just enough assets to survive above the poverty line for at least three months. Close to one-half of all children live in households with no financial assets and 63 percent live in households with precarious resources, scarcely enough NFA to cushion three months of interrupted income.

A further analysis of this already disturbing data discloses imposing and powerful racial and ethnic cleavages. For example, 40 percent of all white children grow up in households without financial resources in comparison to 73 percent of all black children. Most telling of all perhaps, only 11 percent of black children grow up in households with enough net financial assets to weather three months of no income at the poverty level. Three times as many white kids live in such households.

According to Richard Steckel and Jayanthi Krishnan, cross-sectional measures of wealth acquisition and inequality may disguise underlying changes in wealth status. Analyzing surveys from 1966 and 1976, Steckel and Krishnan found that changes in marital status were associated with changes in wealth. The largest increase in wealth occurred for single women who later married. Other groups who experienced increases in wealth included households headed by the young, those with at least twelve years of schooling, and individuals who married. The greatest loss in wealth occurred among households headed by older individuals, single men, and those experiencing marital disruption.

SUMMARY

Financial wealth is the buried fault line of the American social system. The wealth distribution portrait drawn in this chapter has disclosed the existence of highly concentrated wealth at the top; a pattern of steep resource inequality; the disproportionate asset reserves held by various demographic groups; the precarious economic foundation of middle-class life; and how few financial assets most American households can call upon. This chapter has also provided documentation concerning the relationship between income inequality and wealth inequality. At one level, income makes up the largest component of potential wealth. At the same time, however, distinctive patterns of income and wealth inequality exist. Put another way, substituting what is known about income inequality for what is not known about wealth inequality limits, and even biases, our understanding of inequality. A thorough understanding of inequality must therefore pay more attention to resources than has been paid in the past.

Perhaps no single piece of information conveys the sense of fragility common to those on the lowest rungs of the economic ladder as the proportion of children who grow up in households without assets. Reducing all life's chances for success to economic circumstances no doubt overlooks much, but resources nonetheless provide an accurate measure of differential access to educational, career, health, cultural, and social opportunities. In poignantly reciting the hopes they have for their children, parents recognize the importance of resources. Our interviews show how parents use assets to bring these hopes to life, or wish they had ample assets so they could bring them to life. Nearly three-quarters of all black children, 1.8 times the rate for whites, grow up in households possessing no financial assets. Nine in ten black children come of age in households that lack sufficient financial reserves to endure three months of no income at the poverty line, about four times the rate for whites.

Racial disparities in net worth

Single women of color are the biggest group of Americans with either zero or negative net worth. A breakdown:

PERCENTAGE OF HOUSEHOLDS WITH ZERO OR NEGATIVE NET WORTH
AGES 18-64, 2007

KEY
Married, cohabitating
Single female
Single male

WHITE, NON-HISPANIC: 15, 23, 23
BLACK: 28, 46, 33
HISPANIC: 31, 45, 38

Source: Center for Community Economic Development   James Hilston/Post-Gazette

NOTES AND QUESTIONS

1.   Some data on poverty rates. During the era of Gunnar Myrdal's classic study of American society, *An American Dilemma*, the majority of African Americans in the United States lived in the South; white supremacy relegated blacks to an inferior socioeconomic status; and social, political, and economic opportunity for African Americans was virtually non-existent. Ronald F. Ferguson, *Shifting Challenges: Fifty Years of Economic Change Toward Black–White Earnings Equality*, in AN AMERICAN DILEMMA REVISITED: RACE RELATIONS IN A CHANGING WORLD 76 (Obie Clayton, Jr. ed., 1996). Though almost sixty years have passed since Myrdal's commentary on the socioeconomic status of African Americans during the period between the Great Depression and World War II, grave economic inequalities continue to plague minorities, maintaining a systematic socioeconomic hierarchy in society. *Id.*, at xxiii.

Sociologists Melvin L. Oliver and Thomas M. Shapiro conclude that several variables account for wealth differences among racial and ethnic communities, including geographic region, educational attainment, the number of workers in the household, marital status, gender, and age.[16] As we have just discussed, intergenerational wealth effects are stronger than was once thought to be the case.

For the poor, low economic and social mobility are locks in disadvantage. A study by the Economic Mobility Project, a research initiative led by the Pew Charitable Trusts, examined the economic fortunes of a large group of families over time, comparing the income of parents in the late 1960s with the income of their children in the late 1990s and early 2000s. The study found that 42 percent of children born to parents in the bottom wealth quintile remain in the bottom as adults, while 36 percent of children born to parents in the top wealth quintile remain at the top as adults. Although only 7 percent of children born to parents in the bottom wealth quintile make it to the top in adulthood, more than 60 percent do move out of the bottom. However, the study also found that 23 percent of those born into the top quintile who do not get a college degree nevertheless stay at the top as adults—a slightly higher percentage than the number of college graduates from the bottom quintile who manage to climb to the top. One of the authors thus concluded that the nation's educational system does not do enough to help poor children overcome their family background. See Press Release, "Economic Mobility Project Releases Comprehensive Study of Income Mobility in the U.S.," Feb. 20, 2008, <http://www.pewtrusts.org/news_room_detail.aspx?id=35524>.

The Pew study also found racial disparities in economic fortunes. Only 31 percent of black children born to middle-income families make more than their parents' family income, compared to 68 percent of white children born to similar families. Even more disturbingly, almost half (45 percent) of black children born into middle-income families end up falling to the

---

16. MELVIN L. OLIVER & THOMAS M. SHAPIRO, *Wealth and Inequality*, in BLACK WEALTH/WHITE WEALTH: A NEW PERSPECTIVE ON RACIAL INEQUALITY 67–90 (1997).

bottom of the income distribution, as compared to 16 percent of white children. Economic Mobility Project, Summary of Key Findings: "Getting Ahead or Losing Ground: Economic Mobility in America," http://www.pew trusts.org/uploadedFiles/wwwpewtrustsorg/Reports/Economic_Mobility/ EMP_EconomicMobilityinAmerica_KeyFindings.pdf. (2007).

Hidden Cost of Being African American

HIDDEN COST OF BEING AFRICAN AMERICAN 141 (2004).

■ THOMAS M. SHAPIRO

In the 20 largest metropolitan areas, where 36 percent of all African Americans live, segregation pervades basic dimensions of community life. The residential color line means that blacks have greater difficulty overcoming problems associated with poor communities, especially crime, violence, housing abandonment, unstable families, poorer health and higher mortality, environmental degradation, and failing schools. No other group experiences segregation to the extent that blacks do. In many geographical areas, two decades of rising income inequality and budget cuts have produced a concentration of poverty that further compounds problems of segregation. Poor black neighborhoods are crowded, highly concentrated, and isolated far more severely than neighborhoods where poor whites, Latinos, or Asians live.

TABLE 2.2.

1984 RESIDENCE	1994 RESIDENCE			
	PREDOMINATELY WHITE AREA	RACIALLY MIXED AREA	PREDOMINATELY BLACK AREA	TOTAL
WHITE FAMILIES				
PREDOMINATELY WHITE AREA	95.6%	4.4%	-	100.0% (456)
RACIALLY MIXED AREA	40.2%	58.8%	1.0%	100.0% (97)
PREDOMINATELY BLACK AREA	-	-	-	100.0%
TOTAL	85.9% (475)	13.9% (77)	0.2% (1)	100.0% (553)
BLACK FAMILIES				
PREDOMINATELY WHITE AREA	66.7%	33.3%	-	100.0% (21)
RACIALLY MIXED AREA	6.5%	79.0%	14.5%	100.0% (214)

PREDOMINATELY BLACK AREA	8.5%	56.4%	66.3%	100.0% (166)
TOTAL	8.5% (34)	56.4% (226)	35.2% (141)	100% (401)

SOURCE: *Id.* at 138.

Sheryll Cashin argues that "housing [is] the last plank in the civil rights revolution . . . [s]egregated residential housing contributes to pervasive inequality in this country." SHERYLL CASHIN, THE FAILURES OF INTEGRATION: HOW RACE AND CLASS ARE UNDERMINING THE AMERICAN DREAM 3 (2004) infra at 484.

———

The Price of Segregation—Unconventional Wisdom: New Facts From the Social Sciences

WASH. POST, Dec. 28, 1997, at C5.

■ RICHARD MORIN

THE PRICE OF SEGREGATION

FOR SALE: Three-bedroom, two-bath ranch-style house. Near good schools and good neighbors. Low taxes, low crime. Located in a white neighborhood.

How much would you pay for this house? If you're white, a new study of housing prices suggests that you'll pay, on average, about thirteen percent more than if the same house were located in a racially integrated part of town.

That's the premium that whites appear to be willing to pay to live in the typical segregated white neighborhood, say Harvard economists David Cutler, Edward Glaeser and Jacob Vigdor.

And it's this extra cost that's now primarily either responsible for keeping America's neighborhoods predominantly black or white decades after legal segregation officially ended, Cutler argues.

To measure just how much whites will pay to live in white neighborhoods, Cutler and his colleagues collected a mountain of data on every neighborhood in three American cities: Cleveland, Atlanta and Sacramento. They selected these cities because they were "representative of the urban experience of the past century." The information they gathered included Census data, neighborhood characteristics and federal reports on housing prices back to 1940, the first year such information was collected.

They found that the whiter the neighborhood, the higher the housing prices. "We can say that the premium that a white pays in a segregated city (such as Cleveland) in 1990 is 18 percent, while the premium that a white pays in a relatively integrated city (such as Sacramento) in 1990 is 12 percent," Glaeser said.

These researchers also said [they] were able to track the shifting patterns of residential segregation, from a system enforced by laws to one sustained by market forces.

Through the 1950s, segregation was enforced by law and the "collective actions taken by whites to exclude blacks from their neighborhoods."

Real estate covenants written into deeds in some neighborhoods barred homeowners from selling or renting to blacks (or Jews or sometimes even unmarried people). When laws and covenants didn't work, Cutler said "whites took bats, broke some windows and threw things at the house to run off black families who dared to move into white neighborhoods, as well as to warn other African–Americans to stay out. You can't do that anymore."

Now, Cutler said it's sticker shock that is keeping many African–Americans out.

————

The Failures of Integration, How Race and Class are Undermining the American Dream

Public Affairs, New York, at 4 (2004).

■ Sheryll Cashin

Housing—where we live—is fundamental in explaining American separatism. Housing was the last plank in the civil rights revolution, it is the realm in which we have experienced the fewest integration gains. When it comes to integration, housing is also the realm in which Americans most seem to agree that separation is acceptable. We may accept, even desire, integrated workplaces and integrated public spheres. But when it come to our private life space, more visceral personal needs of comfort and security take precedence—especially for families with children. In this context, for many, integration is simply irrelevant or perceived as a threat to more fundamental concerns. * * *

How do you decide where to live? Eleven years ago, I bought a lovely bungalow in Shepherd Park, in integrated, albeit a majority-black, upper-middle-class neighborhood in the northwest quadrant of Washington, D.C. My goal at the time was to acquire a house in the best and safest neighborhood I could afford. The race or class of my would-be neighbors was not at the forefront of my thinking. But many communities were beyond consideration. As a committed urbanite and a hater of traffic living outside the Beltway was out of the question. As a black woman with a strong racial identity, I found the overwhelmingly white neighborhoods west of Rock Creek Park, such as Georgetown, American University Park, and Bethesda, inherently unattractive. I was not prepared, even if investment wisdom counseled otherwise, to make the profound personal sacrifice of living totally among 'others' with whom I could not identify and who likely could not identify with me. Implicit in my choice about where to live was the understanding that I wanted to be among more than just a smattering of black people. If I had been forced to describe my ideal neighborhood, I suppose I would have said it was an integrated one.

NOTES AND QUESTIONS

1. Note on wealth and income inequalities. Why do parents and children have similar wealth? Availability of economic resources accounts for some of the correlation, but Charles and Hurst conclude spending patterns and comparable portfolio investment decisions between parents and their children have a considerable impact on the relationship between parents' wealth and their offspring's. They argue that when parents make investment choices, they set an example for their children to follow. For example, a mother who owns a company can advise her children on the tools necessary to succeed in running an enterprise and may pass on the company to her children. In addition, a wealthy parent may allow his children to take on investment decisions, such as stock ownership, early in life. Kerwin Kofi Charles & Erik Hurst, *The Correlation of Wealth Across Generations* (National Bureau of Economic Research (NBER), Working Paper 9314, Oct. 2002), *at* http://www.nber.org/papers/w9314. *See also* Dalton Conley, The Pecking Order: Which Siblings Succeed and Why (2004).

Can Charles and Hurst's conclusion be extended to a large demographic group? For example, is it possible for children to learn about and mimic spending patterns and investment decisions from not only their parents, but also from members of their own ethnic community? The Federal Reserve Board issued a Survey of Consumer Finances in 1998, reporting that the net wealth of the typical African American household was $15,500 that year; this figure is less than one-quarter that of the net wealth of the typical American household (including blacks)—$71,000. The study also revealed considerable differences in self-reported financial behavior between African American families and all families about investments, spending and income, savings tendencies, and risk aversion. Black households are much more likely than all households to have a shorter fiscal planning perspective, spend more rather than less of their earnings, not save and not save consistently, and be less willing to take monetary risks when saving or investing.

Is it possible that African Americans persistently remain in the lower wealth brackets because members of the black community share similar ill-advised spending behaviors? Other factors influence the difference in wealth between black families and other families; for example, fewer African American households reported having received an inheritance, and black inheritors reported receiving lower bequests. Stephen Brobeck, Executive Director of the Consumer Federation of America, believes financial education is needed to aid the black community in revamping their financial behavior in order to increase wealth. However, he maintains that financial education should be shaped to meet the cultural needs of the African–American community:

[F]inancial education needs to recognize important ethnic and cultural differences. Obviously, this education can be most effective if it uses language with which targeted populations are comfortable. But it also may be more effective if the education appeals to unique ethnic identities. For example, a Black American Saves initiative may well have more appeal to African Americans than does a more generalized America Saves initiative. Stephen Brobeck, *Black American Personal Wealth: Current Status* (Consumer Federation of America, Aug. 2002), *at* http://www.americasaves.org/back_page/BlackWealthReport082902.doc.

A recent study, "The Lives and Times of the Baby Boomers" by Duke sociology professors Angela M. O'Rand and Mary Elizabeth Hughes, suggests that the children of African American "baby boomers" are not doing as well as their parents. *See* Darryl Fears, *Black Baby Boomers' Income Gap Cited; Study Says That, Economically, Generation Has Not Improved Over Its Parents'*, WASH. POST, Dec. 17, 2004, at A02.

2. Wealth distribution and residential segregation. Though segregation is no longer enforced by explicitly racist laws, residential segregation is still prevalent. Due to the stark differences in wealth among racial groups, richer white families live in more affluent areas, while poorer minorities often live in meager surroundings. Though the proposition that racial segregation in housing is driven by income differences makes sense, it fails to consider other facts, like the dependency of housing prices on the racial makeup of the neighborhood. Harvard economists David Cutlen, Edward Glaeser, and Jacob Vigdor performed a study in 1997 and found that on average a white individual is willing to pay 13 percent more for a house not located in a racially integrated part of town. The study intimated that because whites are willing to pay a premium to live in the typical segregated white neighborhood, housing prices are higher in white areas.

3. College admissions. Educational attainment is one variable that aids in determining an individual's socioeconomic position in American society. For this reason, the prominence of one's college background plays an influential role in developing cultural capital. Parents invest tremendous amounts of time and resources in preparing their children for college by sending them to prestigious secondary schools, hoping their children's academic excellence will ensure them a prosperous lifestyle in the future.

One impressive institution, the Groton School in Massachusetts, sends countless students to prestigious colleges and universities each year. One would assume that remarkable achievement at such a school would ensure successful results in the college admissions process. However, in a society where familial status and networking are significant factors in attaining success, scholastic honors do not always guarantee a ticket to a top university. Several affluent children of universities' alumni and celebrities often have lower academic scores and still have the opportunity to study at the nation's top colleges. These students have what college admissions officers call a "hook"—criteria for preferential treatment. Henry Park, a 1998 graduate of Groton, had no "hook" to get accepted to several leading institutions. Park's parents, middleclass Korean immigrants from New Jersey, went to college in Korea and sacrificed their finances to pay Groton's $33,000 per year tuition and room and board. However, Mr. Park was ranked fourteenth in his class, earned a 1560 on his SAT, and demonstrated mathematical prowess. How do schools like those that rejected Mr. Park—Harvard, Yale, Brown, and Columbia—justify their choices in admitting less qualified students? Some assert that favoring children of alumni and prospective donors helps to ensure the growth of their institutions through the funding of scholarships, faculty salaries, and other projects by alumni parents. They further contend that children of celebrities "enhance an institution's visibility." Daniel Golden, *For Groton Grads, Academics Aren't Only Keys to Ivy Schools*, WALL ST. J., Apr. 25, 2003, at A1.

The college admissions process has serious implications for low-income and minority students. Considering most prestigious universities have relatively few minority alumni and low-income families do not have the means to contribute to colleges, many promising students are excluded from the elite academic realm. Consequently, they will attend less prestigious schools and have trouble attaining prominent occupations in the job market. In turn, these students will fail to pass to their children the capital necessary to succeed and the socioeconomic caste in society will endure through time. Economic distribution will continue to dwindle and wealth inequalities will consistently prevail.

Is it unjust for colleges to use legacy or donation criteria in deciding to offer a student admission? Some deem that the legacy preference unfairly favors wealthy applicants:

The reason for the legacy preference appears to be primarily economic. Harvard and Yale, along with many other academic institutions, argue that the financial support provided by alumni is critical to their fiscal health. The assumption is that alumni will stop donating to fundraising campaigns if colleges reject their children. If economics were the primary basis for admission, however, why should the wealthiest applicants always not be accepted over all others? The very purpose of a need-blind admissions policy as expounded by both Harvard and Yale is to admit students regardless of their ability to pay or their financial background. Yet by preferring legacies over other applicants based upon economic reasons, both schools are admitting that the financial resources of an applicant's family do matter. Thus, need-blind admissions are a misnomer, for economic considerations apparently are of great importance in the admissions process. John D. Lamb, *The Real Affirmative Action Babies: Legacy Preferences at Harvard and Yale*, 26 COLUM. J.L. & SOC. PROBS. 491, 517–18 (1993).

Do you agree with Lamb that admissions are not truly need-blind because admissions officers take financial issues into account when evaluating applications?

Are the legacy preferences unconstitutional? Can students like Mr. Park bring an equal protection claim against schools like Harvard and Yale for denying them admission and admitting lesser qualified students whose parents donated a gymnasium to the institution? Though no cases address the legitimacy of a private institution's admissions preference for children of alumni, a North Carolina court upheld a preference for out-of-state legacies at the University of North Carolina at Chapel Hill. There, the plaintiff asserted that she was denied equal protection when the school rejected her while accepting legacies and in-state applicants. Because the plaintiff was not part of a suspect class and no fundamental criteria were involved, the state was only required to show a rational basis for its preferential treatment. The court held that because out-of-state alumni offer considerable financial support for the school, the university's preferential treatment was a rational basis and not unconstitutional. *Rosenstock v. Governors of Univ. of N.C.*, 423 F.Supp. 1321, 1322–27 (M.D.N.C. 1976). For more on affirmative action, see chapter 13.

4. Race and extreme inequality. In an article for The Nation, Dedrick Muhammad describes how extreme inequality continues to exist between minority communities and white communities. In 2005, the median per capita income in the United States stood at $16,629 for blacks and $28,946 for whites. At this slow progress, Muhammad states, minorities will not achieve income equality for 537 years. In addition, African–American families in the United States have median net worth of $20,600, only 14.6 percent of the $140,700 median net white worth. Between 1983 and 2004, median black and Latino wealth inched up from 7 percent to 10 percent of median white wealth. At this rate, minorities will not achieve wealth equality for 634 years. Muhammad also states that the Subprime Mortgage Crisis and the Economic Crisis will hit minorities disproportionately hard, causing them to fall even further behind whites in wealth and income. Dedrick Muhammad, *Race and Extreme Inequality*, THE NATION, June 30, 2008, p. 26.

5. Estate tax. The estate tax, also referred to by opponents as the death tax, is a means of limiting the impact of intergenerational transmission of wealth and redistributing wealth through government spending. Only about 2 percent of deaths result in estate tax liability due to exemptions and other provisions, and the average estate paid taxes of 17 percent. Iris J. Lay & Joel Friedman, *Estate Tax Repeal: A Costly Windfall for the Wealthiest Americans* (Center on Budget and Policy Priorities, rev. Feb. 6, 2001), *available at* http://www.cbpp.org/5-25-00tax.htm.

People in the highest 20 percent of the income distribution at the time of their death pay 99 percent of estate taxes. And 91 percent of decedents had annual incomes over $190,000. *Id.* Opponents to the estate tax claim that farms and small businesses bear the weight of the tax, but these estates in fact make up a small proportion of taxable estates and could be given additional relief without repealing the entire estate tax. *Id.* The complete repeal of the estate tax will cost the government about $60 billion annually; the wealthiest people in the country would receive windfalls, often in the millions of dollars; and income such as unrealized capital gains would never be taxed. *Id.*

Despite the potentially devastating effects, there is bipartisan political support for repealing the estate tax. The Economic Growth and Tax Relief Reconciliation Act of 2001 phases out the estate tax between 2002 and 2009, but it includes a sunset provision that would reinstate the estate tax in 2011 unless further legislation extends the repeal. Agnes C. Powell, *Hocus–Pocus: The Federal Estate Tax—Now You See It, Now You Don't,* NAT'L BUS. ASS'N MAG. 21 (Oct. 2001).

The repeal of the estate tax would greatly increase the intergenerational transmission of wealth, further restraining economic mobility and leading to cutbacks of government funded programs. What could prevent further legislation limiting redistribution of wealth? What alternative means of wealth redistribution could close the economic gap between rich and poor, and between black and white?

6.   Race and taxes. Thomas and Mary Edsall argue in *Chain Reaction: The Impact of Race, Rights and Taxes on American Politics* that political party voting alignment with regards to tax policy is linked to issues of race. Specifically, they contend that "race has become a powerful wedge, breaking up what had been the majoritarian economic interests of the poor, working, and lower-middle classes in the traditional liberal coalition." THOMAS BYRNE EDSALL & MARY D. EDSALL, CHAIN REACTION: THE IMPACT OF RACE, RIGHTS AND TAXES ON AMERICAN POLITICS 4 (1991). The general polarization between the two parties that has taken place on issues of race has been reflected in the fashioning of a "Republican populism" in which conservative politicians have devised a strategy "to persuade working and lower-middle class voters to join an alliance with business interests and the affluent." *Id.* at 13. Central to this strategy has been opposition to programs designed to benefit racial minorities, such as busing and affirmative action, along with a commitment to reduced spending and curtailed government programs, and rejection of welfare and social programs which have been portrayed as benefiting minorities to the detriment of working-class whites. *Id.* at 13–19. The Edsalls detect a new definition of taxes, in which they are not understood as resources for the funding of government, but rather as a hand-out from those who work to those who do not, the latter group implicitly being racial minorities. *Id.* at 214. See also Woojin Lee & John Roemer, *Racism and Redistribution in the United States: A Solution to the Problem of American Exceptionalism*, Cowles Foundation for Research in Economics, Discussion Paper No. 1462 (2004).

In a progressive tax system, tax burdens rise with incomes. Dana Milbank & Jonathan Weisman, *Middle Class Tax Shares Set to Rise: Studies Say Burden of Rich to Decline*, WASH. POST, Jun. 4, 2003, at A1. Although progressivity is evident in much of the tax system, cuts on dividends, capital gains, and estate taxes lower the burden on the wealthiest Americans, actually increasing the burden on the middle class. *Id.* How will the tax cuts affect economic equality? Will those households identified by Oliver and Shapiro as "on the edge," and therefore least equipped to handle the economic downturn, benefit from the tax cuts? Is a progressive tax system fair, or should the poor and wealthy contribute comparable portions of their income?

7.   Financial behavior. A thriving couple in *Wealth and Inequality in America* credited their financial success to the values instilled in them by their families. Could differences in financial behaviors (such as financial planning horizons, spending compared to income, saving habits, and financial risk taking in investments) explain the wealth disparities between African Americans and other Americans? Stephen Brobeck, *Black American Personal Wealth: Current Status* (Consumer Federation of America, Aug. 2002), *available at* http://www.americasaves.org/back_page/BlackWealth Report082902.doc. According to the Consumer Federation of America, differences in financial behaviors between black Americans and all other Americans "virtually disappear" when comparing similar wealth levels. *Id.* Discrepancies in financial behavior between African Americans and the nation as a whole can be attributed to the concentration of wealth-poor people—45 percent of black Americans compared with 25 percent of all Americans. While education efforts should continue to recognize ethnic and cultural differences, effective financial education should focus on the behavior of the wealth-poor. *Id.*

8.   Us vs. them? In the article, "Why is There Special Poverty Among Minorities?", it is stated that the African–American poverty rate, despite advances, still remains at 23.6 percent in 2006, triple the white rate and that the black unemployment rate remains double of that for whites. The author hypotheses, based on interviews with both black and white working class people, that blacks still consider themselves to be the "them," or the outsiders in this society, and that causes some of the problems with poverty and unemployment. Do you believe this is true, why or why not?

9.   The lingering effects of racial classification. Jennifer Hochschild and Vesla Weaver in the article "Policies of Racial Classification and The Politics of Racial Inequality," argue that the lingering affects of racial classification is in and of itself a structure for inequality. They also suggest that being a member of a disfavored race, either now or previously, can shape one's life chances independent of one's economic standing. In addition, they also suggest that this lingering classification is still shown in social policy such as education, Social Security, housing subsidies, and criminal justice and that without racial classification and the lingering effects of it, these policies might have developed in a different way. Jennifer Hochschild and Vesla Weaver, *Policies of Racial Classification and The Politics of Racial Inequality*, included in Joe Soss, Jacob S. Hacker and Susan Mettler, REMAKING AMERICA: DEMOCRACY AND PUBLIC POLICY IN AN AGE OF INEQUALITY 159–182 (2007).

10.   Separation causing poverty? In the article, "Race, Class, and Neighborhoods," Mary Pattillo argues that whites separating themselves from blacks in the cities, the idea usually termed as "white flight," has been a great cause of continuing poverty in the United States. She says that this is because white flight has allowed whites to insulate themselves with better schools, less crime, and better social programs. She even argues, using the example of Oakland, California, that when blacks themselves become wealthier, they attempt to separate themselves from poor blacks and other poor minorities as well. Mary Pattilo, *Race, Class, and Neighborhoods,* included in Annette Lareau, SOCIAL CLASS, HOW DOES IT WORK? (2008). Do you believe this is true, why or why not?

11.   Katrina caused by remants of civil war class divisions? In the article, "Hard Truth in the Big Easy: Race and Class in New Orleans, Pre- and Post Katrina," Kristen Lavelle and Joe Feagin argue that the resulting racial tension and disproportionate suffering of blacks and other minorities after Hurricane Katrina was the result of ingrained racism and a class split between Creoles (light skinned minorities), Blacks, and Whites that dates back to the Civil War in New Orleans. Do you believe that was the cause of all of the black suffering in New Orleans after Katrina? Why or why not?

Your Stake in America

41 ARIZ. L. REV. 249 (1999).

■ BRUCE ACKERMAN & ANNE ALSTOTT

America has become a three-class society. More than twenty-five percent of its children now graduate from a four-year college and move into the ranks of the symbol-using class. Their increasing prosperity stands in sharp contrast to the grim picture of life at the bottom. The lowest twenty percent inhabit a world of low wages, dead-end jobs, and high unemployment despite the economic boom.

Then there is the vast majority. Over the past quarter century, they have endured a long period of economic stagnation. Despite optimistic rhetoric from the right, economic growth has bypassed these forgotten Americans. The richest twenty percent has captured virtually all of the growth in the nation's wealth since the early 1980s. While income trends have been somewhat less extreme, family income for the vast middle is only modestly higher than in 1973. Even treading water has been tough. Real wages for men have declined by nearly fifteen percent, and it is only the massive entry by women into the workplace that has taken up the slack.

Trickle-down economics has utterly failed and will continue to fail in the globalizing economy of the future. The past is prologue: By 1995, the top one percent owned 38.5% of the nation's disposable wealth, up from 33.8% in 1983. During the 1990s, the share of total income earned by the top twenty percent has risen to its highest point since 1947.

Our politics has not caught up with this three-class reality. On the one hand, we heap large subsidies on the college-bound. On the other, we target the underclass with diminishing amounts of assistance. However, we have done little to aid the vast middle. While the rich have been showered with tax breaks, the middle has been treated to a series of symbolic gestures signifying nothing. The 1997 "middle-class tax cut" hid a darker agenda. The average family took home a few hundred dollars in new tax credits for children and education, but the rich gained thousands of dollars from the capital gains tax cut and other goodies.

The result is simmering resentment and a ready reception of the protectionist nostrums of Ross Perot and Pat Buchanan. The current boom will hold these economic nationalists in check for a while, but it is past time to search for a more constructive response to economic inequality. How can we use the benefits of globalization to ensure that every American gets a fair start in life?

This is the question we set for ourselves in our new book The Stakeholder Society. Stakeholding seeks justice by rooting it in capitalism's preeminent value: the importance of private property. It points the way to a society that is more democratic, more productive, and more free. Bear with us, and you will see how a single innovation once proposed by Tom Paine can achieve what a thousand lesser policies have failed to accomplish.

The basic proposal is straightforward. As young Americans rise to maturity, they should claim a stake of $80,000 as part of their birthright as citizens. This stake should be financed by an annual wealth tax, equal to two percent of every individual's wealth in excess of $80,000. The tie between wealth-holding and stake-holding expresses a fundamental social responsibility. Every American has an obligation to contribute to a fair starting point for all.

Stakeholders are free. They may use their money for any purpose they see fit: to start a business or pay for higher education, to buy a house or raise a family or save for the future. But they must take responsibility for their choices. Their triumphs and blunders are their own.

At the end of their lives, stakeholders have a special responsibility. Since the $80,000 was central in starting them off in life, it is only fair for them to repay it at death if this is financially possible. The stakeholding fund, in short, will be enriched each year by the ongoing contributions of property-owners, and by a final payback at death.

Stakeholding really does bring power back to the people. It marks a radical break with the elitist tradition of social engineering. We do not need a host of experts to minister to ordinary Americans. Give citizens their stakes and let them inaugurate a new age of freedom.

This call can unify a badly fractured nation. Even many Americans in the top twenty percent may recognize its power. Do they really want their own children to live in gated communities locked away from the rest of American life?

The stakeholder society is no utopia, but it does provide an alternative to our current moral drift. Perhaps we will never fully realize the American Dream of equal opportunity. But without that dream, this country will become a very ugly place.

NOTES AND QUESTIONS

1. Ackerman & Alstott's proposal. Do you think the stakeholder idea effectively addresses the problems of inequality outlined in this section? Will it do what the authors think it will? Is it politically feasible?

2. The stakeholder society and African American reparations. Does Ackerman & Alstott's proposal address racialized disparities in wealth? What can minority groups do to overcome obstacles to economic opportunity? Claud Anderson of The Harvest Institute (a think tank whose goal is to reform the social and economic aspects of African American life) offers several suggestions to African Americans to escape financial inequality, including mastering the principles of capitalism and group economics, vertically integrating industries and businesses, expanding business in minority communities, and increasing black leadership. CLAUD ANDERSON, BLACK LABOR WHITE WEALTH: THE SEARCH FOR POWER AND ECONOMIC JUSTICE 188 (1994). Another notable recommendation by Anderson is for African Americans to ask the government for reparations: "Reparation payments should be directed into black communities ... to repair the socioeconomic damages that the dominant society and government have inflicted in 16 generations of black Americans." *Id.* at 182. Is Anderson's request too radical? If only five or six generations are needed to eradicate the indicia of slavery, why is Anderson asking for *sixteen* generations to be compensated? *See* Emma Coleman Jordan, *A History Lesson: Reparations for What?*, 58 N.Y.U. ANN. SURV. AM. L. 1,557 (2003). *See also*, ROY L. BROOKS, ATONEMENT AND FORGIVENESS: A NEW MODEL FOR BLACK REPARATIONS (2004).

3. A reward for being a citizen? Another author, Philippe Van Parijs, argues in his article, "Basic Income: A Simple and Powerful Idea for the Twenty–First Century," that a person in the United States should get a certain amount of money just for being a citizen of the United States. He states in the article that it would be funded both by progressive taxes and investment of these taxes into investment funds, such as mutual funds. It would be given to stem the consequences of poverty and unemployment and it would be given to everybody, regardless of income or social standing. Philippe Van Parijs, *Basic Income: A Simple and Powerful Idea for the Twenty–First Century*, Politics Society, 2004, p. 32. What do you think of this idea? Do you think it is better that Ackerman's idea or worse? Is there any difference between the two ideas? Why or why not?

4. Stakeholding and inequality. Why do income and wealth inequality matter? After all, capitalism is premised on the notion of competition, and not everyone can be a winner. Do Ackerman and Alstott explain why we should care about rising inequality?

D. THE GREAT RECESSION OF 2008–2009 AND ECONOMIC INEQUALITY

The Consumer Debt Crisis and the Reinforcement of Class Position

40 Loy. U. Chi. L.J. 557 (2009).

■ LOIS R. LUPICA

Introduction

Consumers are indebted to a degree never before seen in history. While consumer over-indebtedness has been many years in the making, only recently has this crisis attracted widespread public attention. The precipitous collapse of iconic financial institutions and the corresponding seizure of the financial markets in the United States, for the first time, have drawn widespread public attention to the operation of the financial system and its connection to and relationship with consumer debt.

This public attention has resulted in initiatives launched in various directions to identify the "causes" of the debt crisis in an effort to develop effective solutions. Intense scrutiny has uncovered a multitude of structural and cultural causes of consumer over-indebtedness, with a focus on consumer behavior, lender practices, market incentives, and the public and private policies sustaining them. For example, shifts in consumptive norms, erosion of the value of frugality and long-term savings, financial ignorance and illiteracy, faulty judgment, and an increasing tolerance toward debt have all been identified as consumer-driven causes of over-indebtedness.

The business behaviors and practices of front-line consumer lenders have similarly been identified as contributors to the problem. Too-liberal credit solicitations, confusing and exploitive lending rates and terms, and inadequate underwriting standards have all contributed to the current high levels of indebtedness.

Finally, taking advantage of new technologies, the globalized financial markets have fallen prey to the lure of new opportunities for immense profits, which served to increase tolerances for ever-higher levels of risk. The past two decades have seen the financial markets' record growth and markedly creative (and in hindsight, catastrophic) transformation, fueled in large part by a steady and growing stream of consumer debt.

An appraisal of these "causes" offers a chilling picture of how we got to this point of crisis. Limiting consideration to these apparent and obvious causes of over-indebtedness, however, results in an incomplete picture. A comprehensive map sketching the full measure of factors contributing to the collapse of consumers' "debt-supported house of cards" reveals that the fundamental underlying cause of the consumer debt crisis is found in the incentives that have shaped the very structure of the consumer marketplace. The drivers of consumption and the policy-makers supporting them created a condition, opportunistically or deliberately, in which high levels of consumer debt became necessary to sustain and support the growth and transformation of the financial markets. The markets affirmatively, aggressively, and insistently encouraged an ever-more rapid and high-risk consumer lending and borrowing cycle, which in turn both fueled and was fueled by ever-increasing levels of consumption and debt. Consumers acquiesced to the efforts made to persuade them to buy and borrow more. Over the past few decades, these dynamics became the established order, thus resulting in widespread consumer over-indebtedness...

The "Causes" of the Consumer Debt Crisis

A.   The Creation of Wants

1.   The Rise of Consumerism: The Traveling English Fair, the Parisian Arcades, and Current Day Cathedrals of Consumption

During the middle and late nineteenth century, industrialization and advances in transportation gave rise to a number of new consumer markets. One such market was the English traveling fair. The fair became a place for the aristocratic, merchant, and plebian classes to gather, sample wares, and be entertained. At the fair—"domains of transgression where place, body, group identity and subjectivity interconnected"—the "high and low" met and "ideology and fantasy conjoined." These fairs provided a forum for merchants to shape consumers' desires and an opportunity for consumers of various strata to develop associations with the merchant class. These marketplaces provided one of the first opportunities for classes to intersect and proved to be socially and culturally transformative. As described, "part of the transgressive excitement of the fair for the subordinate classes was not its 'otherness' to official discourse, but rather the disruption of provincial habits and local tradition by the introduction of certain cosmopolitanism, arousing desires and excitements for exotic and strange commodities."

The nineteenth century Parisian arcade similarly became a central province for the gathering of the populace. Like the English fairs, these arcades were described as "the original temple of commodity capitalism"— giving rise to desires, while at the same time creating frustration and a sense of failure in some at their inability to attain the objects of these desires.

Furthermore:

The dreams created by the new means of consumption can be seen as creating a "false consciousness" among consumers in much the same way that such a consciousness was created among the proletariat in the heyday of producer capitalism. Adrift in a dreamworld of consumption, people are unable to see what is happening to them as well as the realities of the economic system in which they are immersed.

The wares on display in these fairs and arcades were viewed with fascination and reverence and had the effect of transforming desire structures across the social and economic spectrum. Shopping (and browsing) became universally accessible entertainment.

At the same time, a parallel rise in consumerism took place in the United States. The development of the telegraph and railroad networks enabled communication and rapid transportation, thus fostering the emergence of integrated markets for consumer goods. Industrialization led to further economic growth, rising income, and new patterns of production and consumption. By the early 1900s, mass production of consumer goods, advertising, and new merchandising environments, such as department stores and mail order houses, became well established.

The post-World War II economy saw industrialized development on an even larger scale, coupled with rising household prosperity. As suburban communities flourished, with them came the proliferation of the ubiquitous American shopping mall. In lieu of a town fair or marketplace, malls in post-modern culture have provided a place for the citizenry to gather, consume, and be entertained in a sanitized, homogenized environment. Amusement and consumption of goods and services became the core of the enterprise, and retailers prospered by deliberately blurring the line between these activities. At malls, the focus of marketing efforts became the creation and fulfillment of consumptive fantasies. Furthermore:

In an earlier era, it was the means of production that were predominant, but today it is the means of consumption that have gained ascendancy. The shopping mall has replaced the factory as the defining structure of the age in developed societies. Like it or not, the future of such societies lies mainly in consumption and the means that allow, encourage, and even coerce us to consume.

Not only have malls and other "bricks and mortar" shopping destinations become defining features of America's cultural landscape, new media and information technologies have offered ever-more varied means of consumption and have further contributed to recent seismic shifts in consumptive norms. The Internet has brought retail activity into the home and expanded the hours purchases can be made, thus making shopping increasingly efficient. Goods' quality, prices, and availability can be instantly compared, and purchases can be made impulsively and instantaneously. The "think about it" time has evaporated. In the absence of time to consider and reconsider purchasing decisions, greater emotional rather than measured decision-making has become the norm.

In addition, consumers have been subject to ever-greater manipulation through advertising. Consumers' natural purchasing susceptibility has been exacerbated by the ubiquitous media barrage of words and images presenting narratives of a living standard that many aspire to but few can genuinely achieve, all relaying the not-so-subliminal message to consume. Lured by the account of a life enhanced by the acquisition of "more" and fueled by readily available credit, consumers have come to believe the picture of the mythic "middle class America" as genuinely attainable. This conviction masks the truth that the kitchens featured in Williams Sonoma, the clothes at Abercrombie & Fitch, the bedroom set in Pottery Barn, and the electronics gaudily displayed at Best Buy are far beyond the reach of the vast majority of consumers. Entreaties to buy, and to buy more, appear so crass—so perceptibly manipulative—yet the brilliance of the advertising is revealed by the classic consumer response: the calculating nature of the message advertised is recognized, understood, and "seen through," at the same time it is responded to.

For many consumers, the ability to fulfill consumptive desires as quickly as they are created has resulted in an apparent cultural homogenization—consumers can dress alike, drive the latest model car, use the same cell phones, and listen to identical MP3 players—notwithstanding vast disparities in income and wealth levels. In many communities, difference is made invisible—hidden behind the chimera of material satisfaction. The diabolical genius of the private and public policies that encourage consumption and credit use is that they appear to be the exact opposite of what they are—policies that foster the illusion of classlessness, even as they directly create and reinforce sharp and severe class divisions. Thus, the homogenization efforts become the very force that produces greater societal stratification—meaning greater disparities in wealth, which means compromised social, economic, and political power for those on the lower end of the strata.

The public and private policies that support the illusion of classlessness mask the hegemonic forces that affect consumers in the retail and credit marketplace. The simultaneous consent and resistance to these forces commonly exhibited by consumers is the product of "the systematic (but not necessarily or even usually deliberate) engineering of mass consent to the established order. No hard and fast line can be drawn between the mechanisms of hegemony and the mechanisms of coercion. . . . In any given society, hegemony and coercion are interwoven."

It is inadequate, however, to suggest simply that mere coercion is the only force driving consumers' enthusiastic embrace of consumerism and corresponding incurrence of debt. While retailers and consumer credit providers have certainly benefited from the creation and satisfaction of consumptive yearnings to the detriment of consumers, consumers are not acting under blind duress: the dynamic is far more insidious and nuanced. In the liminal space between desire and resistance, consumers have voluntarily adopted and realized the illusion of a middle class identity in their willingness to acquire "stuff" at any cost. Consumers know that carrying a balance on a credit card makes all purchases more expensive and that using home equity funds to go on a Disneyland vacation can mean financing it over thirty years. Nevertheless, the acquisition yields significant benefits for consumers: an identity in addition to the "stuff."

2.   The Rise of the Consumer Credit Industry: Deregulation and Credit's Democratization

Despite a largely unregulated environment, banks issued comparatively conservative credit products until as recently as the late 1980s. For example, most credit cards continued to offer fixed interest rates, charged annual fees, and were marketed to borrowers with strong credit histories. It was not until the early 1990s that the consumer banking industry found the good-credit-risk market close to saturated. New entrants into the consumer credit supply market, including pay day lenders, rent-to-own centers, and other non-bank lenders, put increasing pressure on traditional banks to increase their market share in order to maintain profitability. The proliferation of the high-cost non-bank lenders began at the same time the traditional banking industry was becoming increasingly consolidated.

In response to these competitive pressures, banks' card issuers took measures to expand their target markets to include less affluent households. Citicorp credit card division's decision to alter its business model is reflective of industry practice at that time:

> After increasing the finance charges on its credit cards, Citicorp sought to expand the social frontiers of its credit card portfolio by soliciting lower-income households. This was an important marketing shift because the early focus on more affluent, middle-class households produced large numbers of unprofitable, albeit low-risk, convenience users. Bankers had hoped that a larger proportion of these cardholders would revolve a portion of these purchases or occasionally forget to pay their credit card bills. Instead, they soon realized that they were stuck with costly deadbeat clients, who zealously paid off their charges within the specified grace period. As inflation rates climbed to double digits, the architects of [this business model] encountered a crucial institutional crossroads: continue losing even more money on large numbers of low-risk, middle-class clients or increase their lending to higher-risk, lower-income households that previously had been avoided.

Credit card issuers further sought to increase profits by raising interest rates and charging higher fees and penalties following the Supreme Court's decision in Smiley v. Citibank. The Court held that late payment, over-limit, cash advance, returned check, membership, and other fees fell within the definition of "interest"—making their proliferation, as well as industry profits, virtually unhindered by regulation.

The consumer credit industry has continued to modify its business model and marketing practices with the persistent goal of expanding demand and increasing profits. In addition, the credit products currently offered more widely are far more expensive than they were twenty years ago and "[the credit card industry] has shifted from a lending and underwriting paradigm to a sales paradigm; penalties, fees, and default interest at rates that were illegal a generation ago are no longer regrettable outcomes to be avoided but central to the business model."

Credit cards have become as ubiquitous as cash and are used ever-more commonly. According to the Federal Reserve, Americans are now carrying $943.5 billion in revolving credit card debt, up 6.8% from a year ago:

> Between 1989 and 2001: Credit card debt among very low-income families grew by an astonishing 184 percent. But middle-class families were also hit hard—their credit card debt rose by 75 percent. Very low-income families are most likely to be in credit card debt: 67 percent of cardholding families with incomes below $10,000 are affected. Moderate-income families are not far behind: 62 percent of families earning between $25,000 and $50,000 suffer from credit card debt.

Moreover, in the first quarter of 2008, consumers financing the purchase of a new car through an auto finance company had an average outstanding balance of $28,174, with a loan-to-value ratio of 94% and maturity of 62.6 months. In 2003, mortgage originations and refinancings hit a decade high, with $3.802 trillion of housing-backed loans made. These high debt levels have been incurred at a time where household savings levels are at an all-time low, leaving many without a safety net in the event of an unexpected expense or interruption in income. Enormous pressure has been brought to bear on consumers to buy instead of save, and to borrow, rather than wait.

A similar culture of free borrowing has been encouraged by the mortgage banking industry. Aided by rising real estate values, consumers have taken advantage of the mortgage market's liquidity, borrowing against their homes to a greater degree than before seen in history. Seemingly under the impression that the market's rising valuations would continue forever, liberal mortgage underwriting, low introductory variable rate products, and low-and no-documentation loans with high loan-to-value ratios led many consumers to buy more house than they could afford and carry larger mortgages than could be repaid. The present day escalation in the number of housing foreclosures—the very issue that brought public attention to the crisis of consumer over-indebtedness—is a consequence of the normalization of lax underwriting, overly optimistic value projections, the conversion of unsecured debt into home-secured debt, and the lure of low introductory rates for adjustable rate mortgages, as well as the escalation of subprime and predatory lending.

The credit industry has created the pressure to borrow and knows where consumers' social, economic, and psychological vulnerabilities lie. It knows that consumers tend to discount the long- and short-term consequences of credit use, due to the temporal disconnect between the charge and receipt of a bill. This discounting and underestimation extends to a number of features of credit use, including present and future balances, the importance of interest rates, the likelihood of a late payment, the speed at which interest accrues, the implications of merely making the minimum payment due; as well as the likelihood of exceeding credit limits, and credit products have been designed to opportunistically exploit these susceptibilities. As observed:

> The averse [sic] consequences for using credit cards is abstract (i.e., a printed bank statement) and delayed, and thus is likely to have less of an impact on behavior. High interest rates and penalties are present when payments are delinquent, often making it difficult to reduce the total amount of debt for individuals who do make payments. Thus, although not inevitable, credit cards allow for disadvantageous allocation of funds by allowing immediate impulsive purchasing at high long-term cost.

Simply put, the credit industry knows that the classic economic model of the rational market actor does not prove to be an accurate description of consumer behavior in practice.

Moreover, the "consumer protection" regulatory model currently in place is premised on the concepts of disclosure and private enforcement. With few meaningful limits placed on the cost of credit, disclosure has proven to offer little consumer protection; the display of onerous credit terms in the context of aggressive marketing has not corrected the information asymmetries in access to information that characterize the consumer lending market. Moreover, with recourse for abuses available only on the basis of individual consumer transactions rather than on systemic flaws in the operation of the market itself, consumers with relatively small claims and truncated access to information are excluded from regulatory protections. Myriad reported cases have illuminated the barriers consumers face in seeking a remedy for harms caused by creditor behavior or industry practices. Defending consumers' affirmative responses to offers of credit as part of the supply and demand cycle places the risk of loss solely and squarely on consumers. Thus, it is not surprising that consumer financiers, in accounting for consumers' systematic biases, have reported record profits in recent years—profits which have been directly correlated to record levels of consumer over-indebtedness.

———

Testimony of Sheila Crowley, MSW, Ph.D., President of the National Low Income Housing Coalition, Financial Services Committee, United States House of Representatives

July 9, 2009

What the National Housing Trust Fund Will Do

To recap the purpose and structure of the National Housing Trust Fund, primarily it is intended to produce, preserve, and rehabilitate rental homes that are affordable for extremely and very low income households. HUD will distribute funds to states using a formula that is based on the need for rental homes affordable for this income group. States will make grants to qualifying public, non-profit, or for profit entities that will produce and operate the rental homes. All the funds must benefit households with incomes at or below 50% of the area median; at least 75% of the funds must benefit households with incomes at or below 30% of the area median. At least 90% of the funds must be used for rental homes.

This is the first federal rental housing production program that is specifically targeted to extremely low income households since the Section 8 program was established in 1974. The goal for the NHTF set by the NHTF campaign and articulated in H.R. 2895 is to build or preserve 1.5 million rental homes over 10 years.

HUD is now completing the interim regulations for the NHTF as required by statute for implementation this fall. The version of the NHTF legislation that ultimately was enacted did not have the level of specificity on the structure of the program that was found in H.R. 2895. Therefore, the NHTF campaign has submitted suggestions to HUD on how to shape the regulations to reflect some of the decision-making that went into the drafting of H.R. 2895. (A copy of letter to former Secretary Preston is attached.) Because the regulations have not yet been made public, I cannot comment today on whether additional legislation is needed to clarify or augment Congressional intent on how the NHTF should and will operate.

. . . The companies take next as the country works its way through the mortgage crisis and recession that they will be again be able to make contributions to the NHTF. But Fannie and Freddie's contributions were never intended to be the sole source of revenue. Indeed, the legislation allows Congress to direct any appropriations, transfers or credits into the NHTF. The level of contributions from Fannie and Freddie enacted in HERA would not have generated the level of funding needed to reach the goal of 1.5 million rental homes.

Use of TARP dividends for the NHTF is a welcome proposal from our perspective. According to the GAO, by June 12, 2009 Treasury had received approximately $6.2 billion in dividend payments from financial and other institutions that received TARP funds. The Troubled Asset Relief Program, $700 billion in taxpayer dollars used to prevent the failure of major private, for profit institutions caught up in the mortgage crisis, is controversial, but ultimately probably a necessary intervention. Nonetheless, it is difficult for ordinary American citizens to understand how TARP has or will help us weather the recession and not lose economic ground. For people who are truly suffering in the recession, TARP is most likely seen as a bail-out of the very people who are to blame for getting us into this mess.

The notion of "TARP for Main Street" offers some balance and fairness to federal response to the country's economic crisis. Indeed, I would recommend that the Committee and Congress lay claim now to the all current and future dividends that TARP yields for "Main Street" purposes, including the NHTF.

The National Housing Trust Fund Is Needed Now More Than Ever

For years, NLIHC and others have documented the shortage of rental homes that are affordable to the lowest income households. The mortgage crisis and recession have only made the problem worse.

Unfortunately a shorthand analysis of the current housing market causes some to believe that because the country has an excess supply of housing, housing production is unnecessary. This simplistic analysis does not account for the mismatch between housing supply and housing need in the U.S. housing market today. The latest *State of the Nation's Housing* report by the Joint Center on Housing Studies at Harvard documents both the high housing vacancy rate and the growing rates of housing cost burdens (paying more than 30% of income for housing). Unfortunately, the housing that has been produced in recent years seems to be more in line with what Americans desire than what we need and can afford.

A new analysis done for HUD shows that the number of rental housing units increased by between 3.3 and 3.7% between 2005 and 2007. However, all the growth occurred in units affordable to households with incomes at 51% of the area median income or more. The number of units affordable to these households grew by 16% or 2,791,000 rental homes. For households with incomes of over 100% of the area median, the number of affordable units grew by 34%. At the same time, the number of units affordable to very low and extremely low income households (50% area median income or less) fell by 7% during the same period for a loss of 1,526,000 homes.

With the growth in unemployment and foreclosures continuing unabated, the demand for affordable rental homes remains high. At the same time that delinquencies in multifamily loans are growing at an alarming rate.

The ultimate consequence of the failure of our housing market is that some portion of the population will end up with no home at all. Reports of new homelessness are showing up with some regularity now. The *New York Times* ran a story this week about the surge in homelessness now that school is out. Families hold on in tenuous housing situations as long as they can so that kids can finish out the school year. We know that the rate of poverty increases as unemployment increases and that for ten people in poverty in given year, one will become homeless. Earlier this year when the unemployment rate was expected to reach 9%, 800,000 new people a year were predicted to become homeless. Unemployment has now of course exceeded 9% and shows no signifigant sign of letting up.

Congress has taken some measures to intervene to prevent such a precipitous increase in homelessness. Recently enacted legislation to make sure that renters are not evicted without reasonable notice when their landlords are foreclosed on will give renters some time to find new homes that hopefully they can afford, although that will be harder for lower income households. We deeply appreciate the work of committee members Mr. Ellison, Ms. McCarthy, and Mr. Capuano on the renter protection legislation. Also important is the $1.5 billion in the American Recovery and Reinvestment Act that is funding the new Rapid Rehousing and Homelessness Prevention Program at HUD.

But in the absence of new resources that will expand the supply of homes that people who are elderly, disabled, employed in the low wage force, or out of work all together can afford, we will see a growth in homelessness that rivals the recession of the early 1980s. We made the mistake back then of thinking it was a temporary problem that could be addressed by providing temporary shelter, instead of providing permanent housing. We know better now and should not repeat the same mistake.

———

NOTES AND QUESTIONS

1.   More Sheila Crowley testimony. Sheila Crowley also testified to the Financial Services Committee on the United States House of Representatives on April 10, 2008 and suggested four ideas to solve the housing crisis: provide renter protection, provide emergency assistance through TARP, and provide assistance to the states to help with the housing crisis. She additionally recommended that the program should be administered by HUD and that the data on the state assistance should be very detailed and that there should be increased accountability in the housing market, especially on issues related to fair housing. *Testimony of Sheila Crowley,*

President of the National Low Income Housing Coalition, Financial Services Committee, U.S. House of Representatives, April 10, 2008.

2.   Government testimony. On July 9, 2009, William Apgar, the Senior Advisor to HUD Secretary Shaun Donovan, supported Crowley's position and suggested similar steps to be taken to fix the housing crisis such as: aid for states, rental assistance, and taking some TARP money and putting it towards the housing crisis. *Testimony of William Apgar, Senior Advisor to HUD Secretary Shaun Donovan,* House Financial Services Committee, Hearing For "TARP For Main Street Act of 2009," July 9, 2009.

————

Borrowing While Black: Applying Fair Lending Laws to Risk–Based Mortgage Pricing

60 S.C. L. Rev. 677 (2009).

■ ALAN M. WHITE

Introduction

As a wave of foreclosures sweeps across the nation, black and Hispanic families are seeing billions in accumulated housing wealth evaporate as a consequence of their overrepresentation in the high cost, high risk sub-prime mortgage sector. While the mortgage market after the crisis will never be the same as it was, price discrimination will endure, as will the essential and as yet unfulfilled goal of fair lending laws—ensuring that minority families can borrow on equal terms with white families.

In the contemporary United States mortgage loan market, the predominant fair lending issue is no longer denial of loan applications; it is instead the fact that minority homeowners pay much more in interest rates and are much more likely to get risky subprime mortgages that lead to foreclosure. On the one hand, minority homebuyers and homeowners still have less collateral and weaker credit history than whites. On the other hand, time after time, studies have controlled for those variables and found that objective credit qualifications cannot explain away the racial price gap.

The mortgage industry protests that in the past decade automated underwriting has removed the human factor and, hence, the possibility to discriminate. Loan applicants, appraisers, and credit bureaus provide mortgage application information that is entered into a computerized underwriting model. The underwriting model generates both an approval decision and a price (interest rate, fees, etc.). Racial disparities that remain, the industry argues, must be the product of legitimate cost-based considerations.

There are at least three reasons why this benign story turns out to be false. First, lenders do not put all mortgage applicants through the same underwriting and pricing analysis. Instead, they use different pricing structures by dividing applications among different business channels and product groups. Minority applicants are overrepresented in higher priced channels and loan product categories and as customers of higher priced lenders. Second, pricing is not purely computer-generated because mortgage brokers retain the discretion to increase interest rates to certain borrowers in order to increase the brokers' compensation. Third, the pricing models benefit and penalize borrowers through a series of adjustments to a base interest rate, and these adjustments are not necessarily tied directly and measurably to the lender's underlying costs for origination, servicing, and credit losses.

Fair lending law, including regulations and bank supervisor examining guidelines, must take account of this new terrain in the mortgage market. Disparate impact analysis, properly and rigorously applied, could help reduce the price discrimination that is partly responsible for the persisting homeownership wealth gaps between blacks and whites in the United States.

In Part II of this Article, I review the significance of mortgage pricing to minority homeowners. I also examine the research on disparities in loan approval and loan pricing and whether the disparities represent discrimination. In Part III, I explain in detail how mortgage pricing works and how it disadvantages minorities. Finally, in Part IV, I advocate for application of fair lending laws to price discrimination using a disparate impact test that takes account of lender steering of minorities into different products, lender delegation of pricing discretion to brokers, and lender use of risk-based pricing of dubious validity that may not accurately reflect credit risk and costs.

II.   BLACKS AND HISPANICS PAY MORE FOR MORTGAGES

A.   The Wealth Gap and the Importance of Interest Rates

Blacks and Hispanics still arrive at the economic starting line far behind their white counterparts because of the persistent and large wealth gap in America. In 2004, the median nonwhite or Hispanic household had a net worth of $24,800; in comparison, non-Hispanic whites had a net worth of $140,700, a ratio of nearly 6:1. The wealth gap is much wider than the gap in incomes, which was roughly 2:1 in 2004. 29.4% of black families have zero or negative net worth, compared with 13.0% of white families.

The smaller wealth endowment of minority families is also much more concentrated in home values and equity. The availability of mortgages obviously limits opportunities even to begin acquiring home wealth. More importantly in the contemporary market, mortgage terms have a huge impact on wealth accumulation. A higher interest rate will delay wealth accumulation and reduce the home value that a family can acquire, diverting more income towards interest and away from debt reduction. In addition, nontraditional loan terms, some of which allow for payment of interest only or even negative amortization, completely defeat the goal of wealth accumulation. Finally, aggressive selling of cash-out refinancing mortgages prevents wealth growth by promoting continual draining of what little equity the borrower accumulates. Thus, to reduce the wealth gap, minority homeowners need mortgage products that are inexpensive and fully amortizing.

2. Efforts to Explain Disparities
Based on Credit Risk or Cost

The Federal Reserve Board (FRB) staff tried to determine whether legitimate, nonracial factors could account for the racial disparities in the HMDA price data. Unfortunately, HMDA reports do not include all relevant creditworthiness information. However, the FRB staff were able to control for income, assets, and a credit score proxy and found that other variables could explain some, but not all, of the racial disparities.

In particular, the FRB staff found that controlling for income, loan size, and other borrower-related factors accounted for about 25% of the disparities, and that controlling for lender identity accounted for another 45%, leaving the remaining 30% of the disparity unexplained by available variables. It is important to note that the FRB staff could control for neither credit scores or credit histories nor for whether the interest rate was fixed or adjustable, two factors that are likely to explain some of the disparities. This pattern—large pricing disparities that are only slightly reduced by accounting for borrower characteristics, but significantly reduced by considering which lenders borrowers use—is consistent in the four years of data currently available (2004–2007). Even after controlling for both borrower factors and the concentration of minorities in the portfolios of high cost lenders, the FRB staff's analysis still showed blacks twice as likely as whites to get subprime mortgages.

The story that emerges from the FRB staff's analysis is that minorities pay higher interest rates for mortgages partly because some lenders charge higher interest rates than others, and minority borrowers disproportionately end up with loans from those lenders. The racial segregation among lenders, however, could not fully explain the price disparities.

The FRB staff studies did not include robust controls for borrower credit qualifications apart from income and loan size. Other researchers have tried to fill that gap. Bocian, Ernst, and Lee supplemented HMDA data for 2004 with credit scores and other relevant underwriting variables from a proprietary database to see how much of the racial price disparities could be explained. This study did not control for lender identity and used a sample of mortgages made by subprime lenders only. Bocian, Ernst, and Lee found that after controlling for mortgage product type, credit score, loan-to-value, and other variables, blacks were 6.1% to 34.3% more likely than whites to receive a higher rate subprime mortgage, and Latinos were 28.6% to 44.6% more likely to receive a higher rate mortgage.

Evidence that minorities are steered toward subprime lenders emerges, for example, when looking at borrowers with high credit scores and marginal loan-to-value ratios. These are borrowers who typically would have qualified in 2004 for either a prime or subprime higher cost mortgage. In that category, 21.3% of blacks received higher cost loans, compared with 14.5% of Hispanics and 7.5% of whites.

The FRB staff analysis and the Bocian, Ernst, and Lee study measured discrimination in pricing as a binary variable—whether a lender placed a borrower in a higher cost (i.e., subprime) mortgage or not. The fact that lenders do not report APRs for mortgages below the high cost threshold seriously limits the HMDA data on APRs. Thus, studies based on HMDA data cannot evaluate possible discrimination along the entire mortgage price spectrum.

Dr. Marsha Courchane assembled a proprietary database from a large group of lenders that included APRs for all mortgages, prime and subprime, as well as a full range of explanatory variables that could contribute to the racial price differences in the mortgage market. This permitted her to treat the APR price outcome as a continuous variable; she could measure the effect of race on price directly, rather than via the proxy of whether or not the mortgage is subprime.

III. WHY DO BLACKS AND HISPANICS PAY MORE? HOW MORTGAGE PRICES ARE SET

A. Assignment of Homeowners to Channels, Lenders, and Products

There are many different ways for a consumer to apply for a mortgage. The mortgage market in the 2000s is segmented into various channels by which money from investors and depositors turns into loans for home-owners. These range from traditional banks which intermediate their own customers' deposits and other customers' mortgage loans to specialized mortgage brokers and lenders who originate mortgages solely in order to sell them on the secondary market. The secondary market in turn packages mortgages for distribution by investment banks, who convert them into securities that are sold to individual and institutional investors. Banks are highly regulated and supervised by Federal banking agencies, while mortgage brokers and investment banks making mortgages using the originate-to-distribute model are not.

Minority borrowers are far more likely to receive loans through less regulated and higher priced channels than white borrowers. Dr. Courchane's pricing study reveals that a significant factor causing minorities to pay higher mortgage rates is their greater likelihood of getting a mortgage through a broker rather than by dealing directly with lenders. She also concluded that one-half to two-thirds of the pricing disparity between whites and minority borrowers results from the greater likelihood that minority borrowers end up getting mortgages from subprime lenders. This may be a result of minorities' historical distrust of banks, their willingness to trust mortgage brokers active in local communities, or a variety of other factors. Whatever the cause, the result is that minority borrowers are not randomly distributed among lenders or channels. They are more likely to borrow from lenders that specialize in subprime mortgages, regardless of their credit, and more likely to borrow through brokers interacting with wholesale lenders.

Mortgage brokers have considerably more price discretion than loan officers working for banks and retail lenders. They can choose products and pricing from a variety of different wholesale lenders in a market that is not transparent to consumers. Perhaps not surprisingly, researchers have found that mortgages originated through brokers have higher rates and fees than loans originated through other channels, controlling for borrower credit, property value, and loan terms.

Even once a broker or borrower has selected a particular lender who will receive the application, discrimination in the preapplication and application stages can result in minority borrowers with equal credit quality receiving inferior (i.e., higher priced) products in several ways. First, marginal borrowers who are white are likely to receive assistance in improving their application and information about a number of different loan products, while marginal black borrowers may be discouraged from applying at all, or at least will be given less information than their white counterparts. Thus, the odds of a particular black mortgage seeker finding the most competitively priced and suitable loan are reduced because blacks essentially face higher search costs than whites.

Second, mortgage lenders and brokers may perceive blacks as less price sensitive, perhaps due to the belief that discrimination by other market participants limits their shopping options, or perhaps due to other implicit biases. Consequently, lenders and brokers tend to quote higher estimated interest rates, fees, and closing costs to blacks than to comparable whites.

How a Low Wage Economy With Weak Labor Laws Brought Us the Mortgage Credit Crisis

29 Berkeley J. Emp. & Lab. L. 455 (2008).

■ DAMON A. SILVERS

We are living through a profound global financial crisis. That crisis has many proximate causes in the governance and deregulation of Wall Street. We have seen the astounding bailout of Bear Stearns using $30 billion plus in public money—Bear Stearns—an investment bank, an enterprise that prided itself on being in the business of cowboy capitalism, business without a safety net.

But the real roots of the crisis do not lie on Wall Street. The cause of the crisis can be found in the long-term weakening of the real American economy in an era of globalization—in closed factories, outsourced high tech jobs and low wage jobs with no benefits, and in the unsustainable effort to maintain middle class living standards through borrowing. It is to be found in the reality of lives like that of Kimberly Somsel of Westland Michigan, a member of the AFL–CIO's community affiliate Working America, an unemployed single mother of two battling breast cancer and facing foreclosure due to a ballooning "2 and 28" loan payment. She is selling the family car and her furniture just to get by. Five houses on her block are threatened with foreclosure.

Powerful voices in our country say that public resources should be there for Bear Stearns, but not for Kimberly Somsel, to keep the champagne flowing on Wall Street, but not to build a future for Michigan. But there is another way—a return to a high wage economy driven by productive investment in the United States. This way requires not that we retreat from the global economy, but that we insist that the globalized economy have real rules that work for working people. At the center of these rules must be labor market regulation, and in particular, regulation that empowers workers to speak for themselves by acting together. But rules are not enough. The United States must pursue a real national economic strategy in a globalized world economy.

For thirty years, America's economic elites and their political allies have pursued a combination of economic and social policies designed to produce a low wage economy. These policies—our labor laws and our broader system of labor market regulation, our tax policies and our approach to globalization, have yielded decades of stagnant wages and rising economic inequality.

But at the same time, policymakers of both parties have sought, with some success, to maintain high levels of consumer spending. The pursuit of the contradiction of a low wage, high spending economy has systematically destroyed the various ways we individually and collectively save and invest. Instead of an income driven economy, we have become an economy driven by asset bubbles fueled by cheap debt. The ultimate unsustainability of this strategy has brought us to our current economic crisis.

Getting Ahead or Losing Ground: Economic Mobility in America

The Brookings Institution, February 2008.

■ JULIA ISSACS, ISABEL V. SAWHILL, AND RON HASKINS

For more than two centuries, economic opportunity and the prospect of upward mobility have formed the bedrock upon which the American story has been anchored. Indeed, a desire to escape from the constraints of more class-based societies was the driving force luring many of our ancestors to this New World, and millions of immigrants continue to flood our borders in search of the American Dream. Americans continue to believe that all one needs to get ahead is individual effort, intelligence, and skills: coming from a wealthy family is far from a necessity to achieve success in America.

Many Americans are even unconcerned about the historically high degree of economic inequality that exists in the United States today, because they believe that big gaps between the rich and the poor and, increasingly, between the rich and the middle class, are offset by a high degree of economic mobility. Economic inequality, in this view, is a fact of life and not all that disturbing as long as there is constant movement out of the bottom and a fair shot at making it to the top.

In short, much of what the public believes about the fairness of the American economy is dependent on the generally accepted notion that there is a high degree of mobility in our society. Are those beliefs justified? Is there actually a high degree of mobility in the United States? Is America still the land of opportunity? With new data and analysis, this volume addresses these questions by measuring how much economic mobility actually exists in America today.

In sum, the research reviewed in this volume leads us to the view that the glass is half empty and half full. The American Dream is alive if somewhat frayed. Most people are better off than their parents, but slower and less broadly shared economic growth has made the economy more of a zero-sum game than it used to be, with very high stakes for the winners. Some subgroups, such as immigrants, are doing especially well. Others, such as African Americans, are losing ground. Americans have generally been tolerant of unequal outcomes in the past, even as gaps between the rich and the poor have risen, since most believe that opportunities to get ahead are abundant and that hard work and skill are well rewarded.

We find considerable fluidity in American society. One's family background as a child, measured in terms of either income or wealth, has a relatively modest effect on one's subsequent success as an adult, especially if one grew up in middleclass circumstances. Those at the top or bottom of the ladder are somewhat less mobile. In addition, there is no evidence that opportunity has increased in a way that might offset the slower and less broadly shared growth of income and wealth that families have experienced. Nor is there evidence that the United States is in any way exceptional when compared to other advanced countries. Indeed, a number of advanced countries provide more opportunity to their citizens than does the United States.

UNDERSTANDING ECONOMIC MOBILITY

Broadly defined, economic mobility describes the ability of people to move up or down the economic ladder within a lifetime or from one generation to the next. Most of the chapters in this volume measure mobility in the United States in terms of family income; however, wealth also plays an important role in the story, a topic examined in Chapter IV. Mobility also has a time dimension. One can talk about mobility over a lifetime, between generations, or over a short period such as a year or two. Unlike analyses that investigate shorter-term fluctuations or volatility in incomes, this volume focuses mainly on intergenerational mobility—the extent to which children move up or down the income ladder relative to their parents. This intergenerational focus is intended to capture the spirit of the American Dream, in which each generation is expected to do better than the one that came before.

We also need to distinguish between changes in income across a generation that are the result of absolute and relative mobility and differentiate both of these from changes in income that are due to rising or falling inequality. Imagine the economy as a ladder upon which we are all perched at some level. This ladder may be getting taller, boosting every-one's incomes, as the result of economic growth. In this volume, we refer to this as *absolute mobility*. At the same time, the rungs on the ladder may be getting closer together or further apart as incomes become more or less equally distributed.

We call this a change in the degree of income inequality. Finally, the ability of people to move from one rung to another may be changing as well, depending on the extent of opportunity. We call this a change in *relative mobility*. Much prior research and public discourse has focused on the rate of economic growth or on the fact that income inequality has been increasing in recent decades. Much less has been written about relative mobility since it requires following what happens to specific individuals' incomes over their life course or over several generations. But knowing more about the degree of relative mobility in the United States is essential to judging the fairness of our society.

To illustrate the importance of relative mobility, consider three hypo-thetical societies with *identical* distributions of wealthy, poor, and middle-class citizens.

- **The Meritocratic Society:** In this society those who work the hardest and have the greatest talent, regardless of class, gender, race, or other less-germane characteristics, have the highest income.

- **The Fortune Cookie Society:** In this society, where one ends up bears no relation to talent or energy, and is purely a matter of luck.

- **The Class–Stratified Society:** In this society, family background is all-important—children end up in the same relative position as their parents. Mobility between classes is small to nonexistent.

Given a choice between the three, most people would choose to live in a meritocracy, which is, by its nature, fairer and more just. In a meritocracy, success is dependent on individual action whereas in a class-stratified or fortune cookie society, they are buffeted by forces beyond people's control. Even if the level of income inequality were identical in each of these societies, most people would judge them quite differently. In fact, most individuals might well prefer to live in a meritocracy with more income inequality than in a class-stratified or fortune cookie society with a more equal income distribution. It is worth noting, however, that even in a meritocracy people are born with different genetic endowments and are raised in different family environments over which they have no control, raising fundamental questions about the fairness of even a perfectly func-tioning meritocracy.

These circumstances of birth may be the ultimate inequalities in any society. That said, a meritocracy with a high degree of relative mobility is clearly better than the alternatives. In what follows we give special empha-sis to relative mobility, but since changes in an individual family's fortunes also reflect what is happening to economic growth (absolute mobility) and how broadly that growth is shared (changes in income inequality), we first examine all three sources of change and then return to how, in combination, they have affected the economic well-being of individual Americans.

Economic Growth

A growing economy ensures that each generation is better off than the previous one. Economic growth is an important source of upward mobility. A middle-class family in 2008 has access to many goods and services that were either not available in the past (computers, cell phones, microwaves) or were considered luxuries (air travel, air conditioning, television).

But economic growth and the upward absolute mobility it brings families has slowed. From 1947 to 1973, the rate of growth of the typical family's income was unusually rapid, roughly doubling in a generation's time. However, since 1973 the increase over a generation's time has been much smaller, about 20 percent, as noted in Chapter II. In other words, the tide lifting all boats has weakened with the result that improvements for the youngest generation have not kept pace with what their parents and grandparents experienced. Underlying this trend have been changes in the earnings of both men and women. Especially surprising is the finding that men in their 30s today are earning less than did the men of their father's generation (men who were in their 30s in the 1970s).

As documented in Chapter V, in 2004 the inflation-adjusted incomes of men in their 30s were 12 percent less, on average, than the incomes of men in their father's generation at the same age. Clearly this group of younger men has not benefited from the economic "up-escalator" that has historically ensured that each generation would do better than the last. And yet in spite of declining incomes for young men, family incomes have continued to rise over the past several decades, albeit slowly. Families are better off because more women have gone to work, and the rise in women's earnings has outpaced the decline for men. No longer can the typical family depend on a single earner to move them up the economic ladder.

However, a number of factors complicate the interpretation of these and other data on family incomes. The first is the declining size of the American family which means that the average family has fewer people to support and thus is financially better off for this reason alone. The second is the time squeeze and extra costs for child care or other work-related expenses associated with the loss of a full-time homemaker within the family. The third is the growing importance of non-cash benefits, such as health insurance provided by employers or the government. The fourth is our focus on what is happening to the *typical* family, whose fortunes may improve little in a period when most of the gains from growth are going to people who are concentrated at the top of the distribution. Finally, there has been a substantial decline in marriage rates over the past generation. If having two earners is critical to the economic success of many of today's families, then this decline, by depriving many families of a second earner, has reduced economic mobility. Thus, family size and structure both play a critical role in the mobility story, with the growth of the two-earner family being the primary factor that has saved the typical family from downward mobility. All of these complexities should be kept in mind as one reads this volume, but none of them should, in our view, overturn the basic conclusion that family income growth has slowed. In the process, income inequality and relative mobility have become increasingly important sources of the changing fortunes of individual families.

Inequality

As suggested above, one reason the average family has not fared better in recent decades is economic growth has not been broadly shared. Inequality of both income and wealth has been increasing, as documented in Chapters II and IV. Inequality of family incomes fell until the late 1960s but has risen steadily ever since. Wealth is even more unevenly distributed than income, and the concentration of assets at the top of the income distribution has been growing at least since 1989.

––––––

NOTES AND QUESTIONS

1.   The Great Recession: Hard on the working poor. The working poor struggled a great deal before the recession with stagnant wages, a lack of health care, no pension, and very little vacation and/or off time. Michael A. Fletcher and Jon Cohen, *Hovering Above Poverty, Grasping For Middle Class*, THE WASH. POST, Aug. 3, 2008, A1. Author Barbara Ehrenreich argues that this recession has been even harder on the working poor that it has been on everyone else and has made these previous problems worse:

> "The recession of the '80s transformed the working-class into the working poor, as manufacturing jobs fled to the third world, forcing American workers into the low-paying service and retail sectors. The current recession is knocking the working poor down another notch-from low-wage employment and inadequate housing toward erratic employment and no housing at all. Comfortable people have long imagined that American poverty is far more luxurious than the third world variety, but the difference is rapidly narrowing."

Barbara Ehrenreich, *Too Poor to Make The News*, N.Y. TIMES, June 14, 2009, pg. 10.

David J. Lynch argues that this recession is driving old industrial towns into poverty even further than previous recessions. David J. Lynch, *Labor Marker Takes Toll on Industrial Towns Across USA*, USA TODAY, July 8, 2009. In addition, a field that employs a great deal of the working poor, the home maintenance business (carpentry, carpet repair, etc.) has been devastated by the recession. Iain Levison, *The Blow the Working Class Saw Coming*, THE WASH. POST, Feb. 15, 2009, B1. This has led to more of the working poor taking on second jobs and renting out rooms in their homes to make ends meet during the recession. Michael A. Fletcher, *Life's Basics More of A Stretch, Stagnating Pay Squeezes Low–Wage Workers*, THE WASH. POST, Oct. 17, 2008, D1.

2. People of color and the economic crisis. African Americans, were struggling even before the recession began. Between 2000 and 2006, African Americans saw their median family income fall by 2.9 percent. In addition, during the first part of the twenty-first century, wages of African Americans were only growing at a rate of 0.2 percent. 1 in 4 African Americans were living in poverty in 2006 and nearly 1 million African Americans became uninsured in the period between 2000–2006. Then, when the economic crisis began, African Americans began to lose jobs and homes at a faster rate than whites. U.S. Congress Joint Economic Committee, *African–American Families Are Being Squeezed*, August 1, 2008. In addition, minorities, who received a disproporately high number of sub-prime loans, were hit hardest by the foreclosure crisis. Michael Powell and Janet Roberts, *Minorities Hit Hardest As New York Foreclosures Rise*, N.Y. TIMES, Metropolitan Desk, page 1. What do you believe this resulted from, racism or the fact that minorities make up a disproportionate number of the poor and working poor people in this country? What is your reason for supporting the conclusion that you do?

3. Inflation before the recession: Did it contribute to its severity? Right before the Great Recession began in the Fall of 2008, there was a great deal of inflation of basic needs, such as food and gasoline, due to a sharp rise in commodities prices, especially oil, in the 2007–2008 period. Neil Irwin and Alejandro Lazo, *Inflation Hits the Poor Hardest; No Income Group Is Untouched, But Staples Are Rising Fastest*, THE WASH. POST, Mar. 21, 2008, A1. Did this inflation cause the recession to be worse than it would have been or did it have no effect? Why or why not?

4. Investors making it difficult to renegotiate mortgages. This economic crisis began with a housing crisis, and since these homes were not financed with conventional loans through a savings and loan or thrift, and instead through unregulated originators who took their fees and passed the loans on to an economic inequality conveyor belt of securitizations. The lenders themselves do not generate the money for the loans, investors do. Investors, therefore, have not had any interest in modifying their agreement with loan servicers, which are called PSAs (Pooling Services Agreements) to allow for modifications. This has made the process for obtaining the needed modifications to these loans a very slow process and has allowed mortgages to remain to be a serious impediment to economic recovery. Gretchen Morgenson, *More Home Foreclosures Loom As Owners Face Mortgage Maze*, N.Y. TIMES, Aug. 6, 2007, Business Section, pg. 1.

5. Communities responding to the mortgage crisis. Some communities, such as Long Island, New York, have responded to the mortgage crisis independent of government intervention. Long Island has responded by banding together with neighbors having difficulties and offering housing counseling and prepurchase seminars. They have even begun to renovate foreclosed homes to prevent decay in the neighborhood. Robin Finn, *Long Island: Prevention and Intervention*, N.Y. TIMES, July 19, 2009, Metropolitan Desk, pg. 8. Do you think that this is a good sign or a bad sign that people are beginning to try to fix the housing crisis on their own? Why or why not? What actions should the government take to promote community involvement, if any?

6. Immigration tension. The economic downturn has led to more criticism of illegal immigration and more calls to restrict illegal immigration into the United States. One extreme example of this tension is the Arizona law "which proponents and critics alike said was the broadest and strictest immigration measure in generations, would make the failure to carry immigration documents a crime and give the police broad power to detain anyone suspected of being in the country illegally." "Arizona Enacts Stringent Law on Immigration" Randal C. Archibold, N.Y. TIMES, Apr. 23, 2010. See also, *Immigration Riddle*, N.Y. Times Editorial Page, Dec. 30, 2008, pg. 24. What do you think? Do you think, due to the serious unemployment problem in the United States, that the United States should crack down on illegal immigration? Why or why not?

7. The mortgage mess in New Jersey. The mortgage crisis did not have to be as bad as it was in New Jersey, but some people with prime mortgages were convinced to refinance into subprime mortgages to gain more money that they could spend and put back into the economy. Kareem Fahim, *As Job Nears End, Loss of Home Looms*, N.Y. TIMES, May 17, 2009, New Jersey Weekly Desk, May 17, 2009, pg. 13. New Jersey working class families, including both white and minority families have been hit especially hard by the housing crisis due to family illnesses, loss of jobs, poor investments, and fraud. In addition, they have also been hurt because of the fact that a great deal of rental properties in New Jersey have gone into foreclosure. Even the building that Cory Booker, the Mayor of Newark, rents an apartment has had problems paying its mortgage. Kareem Fahim and Janet Roberts, *Foreclosures, With No End in Sight,* N.Y. TIMES, New Jersey Weekly Desk, pg. 1.

CHAPTER 8

LIFE IN A CLASS SOCIETY

A. DOWN AND OUT

Foreclosure Forces Ex–Homeowners to Turn to Shelters

NEW YORK TIMES, October 19, 2009.

■ PETER GOODMAN

The first night after she surrendered her house to foreclosure, Sheri West endured the darkness in her Hyundai sedan. She parked in her old driveway, with her flower-print dresses and hats piled in boxes on the back seat, and three cherished houseplants on the floor. She used her backyard as a restroom.

The second night, she stayed with a friend, and so it continued for more than a year: Ms. West—mother of three grown children, grandmother to six and great-grandmother to one—passed months on the couches of friends and relatives, and in the front seat of her car.

But this fall, she exhausted all options. She had once owned and overseen a group home for homeless people. Now, she succumbed to that status herself, checking in to a shelter.

"No one could have told me that in a million years: I'd wake up in a homeless shelter," she said. "I had a house for homeless people. Now, I'm homeless." Growing numbers of Americans who have lost houses to foreclosure are landing in homeless shelters, according to social service groups and a recent report by a coalition of housing advocates.

Only three years ago, foreclosure was rarely a factor in how people became homeless. But among the homeless people that social service agencies have helped over the last year, an average of 10 percent lost homes to foreclosure, according to "Foreclosure to Homelessness 2009," a survey produced by the National Coalition for the Homeless and six other advocacy groups.

In the Midwest, foreclosure played a role for 15 percent of newly homeless people, according to the survey, reflecting soaring rates of unemployment—Ohio's reached 10.8 percent in August—and aggressive lending to people with damaged credit. At a shelter for women and children run by the West Side Catholic Center in Cleveland, where Ms. West now lives, foreclosure accounted for zero arrivals in 2007, the center's executive director, Gerald Skoch, said. Last year, two cases emerged. This year, the number has already reached four. Many take refuge with families and friends, occupying extra bedrooms, basements and attics. But such hospitality rarely lasts.

So, as lean times endure and paychecks disappear, homeless shelters are absorbing those who have run out of alternatives. By December, she will exhaust the shelter's 90–day limit, so she is hurrying to line up a house to rent while arranging a subsidy through the West Side Catholic Center.

She is still shaken by the past and anxious about the future, but she is again looking ahead. "I do want to eventually own a house again," she said. "That's the American dream. That's what everybody wants."

People and Families in Poverty by Selected Characteristics, 2008 and 2007

The following table shows the percent and number of people living in poverty in the United States in 2007 and 2008. Data is broken up by race, income, region, age, nativity, and type of household.

Characteristic	2008		2007	
	Number (thousands)	**Percent[1]**	**Number (thousands)**	**Percent[1]**
INDIVIDUALS				
Total	39,829	13.2%	37,276	12.5%
Family status				
In families	28,564	11.5	26,509	10.8
Householder	8,147	10.3	7,623	9.8
Related children under 18	13,507	18.5	12,802	17.6
Related children under 6	5,295	21.3	5,101	20.8
In unrelated subfamilies	555	46	577	38.1
Reference person	207	45.7	222	36.5
Children under 18	341	47.8	332	40.5
Unrelated individual	10,710	20.8	10,189	19.7
Male	4,759	18.9	4,348	17.1
Female	5,951	22.6	5,841	22.2
Race[2] and Hispanic origin				
White	26,990	11.2	25,120	10.5
Non–Hispanic	17,024	8.6	16,032	8.2
Black	9,379	24.7	9,2378	24.5
Asian	1,576	11.8	1,349	10.2
Hispanic[3]	10,987	23.2	9,890	21.5
Age				
Under 18	14,068	19.0	13,324	18.0
18–64	22,105	11.7	20,396	10.9
65 and over	3,656	9.7	3,556	9.7
Nativity				
Native	33,293	12.6	31,126	11.9
Foreign born	6,536	17.8	6,150	16.5
Naturalized citizen	1,577	10.2	1,426	9.5

Characteristic	2008		2007	
	Number (thousands)	Percent[1]	Number (thousands)	Percent[1]
Not a citizen	4,959	23.3	4,724	21.3
Region				
Northeast	6,295	11.6	6,166	11.4
Midwest	8,120	12.4	7,237	11.1
South	15,862	14.3	15,501	14.2
West	9,552	13.5	8,372	12.0
Work experience				
All workers (16 years and older)	27,216	11.5	25,297	10.8
Worked full-time, year-round.	2,754	2.6	2,768	2.5
Not full-time, year-round	7,331	13.5	6,320	12.7
Did not work at least one week	17,131	22.0	16,208	21.5
FAMILIES				
Total	8,147	10.3	7,623	9.8
Type of Family				
Married couple	3,261	5.5	2,849	4.9
Female householder, no husband present	4,163	28.7	4,078	28.3
Male householder, no wife present	723	13.8	696	13.6

1. Percentage of total population.
2. Data for American Indians and Alaska Natives are not shown separately.
3. Hispanics may be of any race.
Source: U.S. Census Bureau, *Income, Poverty, and Health Insurance Coverage in the United States*

Figure 3
Mortgage delinquency rates rise with cooling of house prices

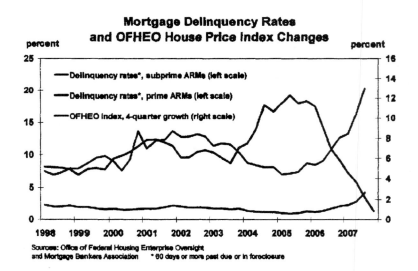

Mortgage Delinquency Rates and OFHEO House Price Index Changes

Sources: Office of Federal Housing Enterprise Oversight and Mortgage Bankers Association   * 60 days or more past due or in foreclosure

NOTES AND QUESTIONS

1. The rise of foreclosures after the collapse of the housing bubble during the Great Recession. Foreclosure starts rose in 2007. Federal Reserve Board staff estimates that foreclosure starts in 2007 totaled about 1.5 million, up 50 percent from 2006 levels, which themselves were up 53 percent from 2005 levels. More than half of the foreclosure starts in 2007 were on subprime mortgages, even though subprime loans accounted for only about 13 percent of the 54.5 million mortgages outstanding as of the end of 2007. The rise in foreclosures likely contributed materially to the number of vacant unsold existing homes, estimated to have been above 2 million at the end of 2007. The foreclosure crisis grew even more serious in 2008 and 2009. In 2009, 3.4 million foreclosures occurred. Even in 2010, 2.4 million foreclosures were expected. New York Times; Federal Reserve, Synopses of Selected Research on Housing, Mortgages, and Foreclosures, September 1, 2008.

2. Loss of wealth due to financial crisis. The wealthy in the world have lost $10 trillion due to the economic crisis. Robert Frank, World's Wealthy Have Lost $10 Trillion Due To Financial Crisis. A 2008 study by United for a Fair Economy found African–Americans and Latinos could lose $213 billion in wealth due to the financial crisis when it finally reaches its conclusion. By 2009, home ownership in minority communities had already dropped 2–3 percent from a couple of years before.

3. Increase in poverty due to Great Recession. 2,500 more families dropped into poverty from 2005 to 2008. The entire poverty rate increased by .6 percent between 2005 and 2008. In addition, the median income dropped 3.4 percent from 2005 to 2008. Census Poverty Data. 2008.

———

Just Trying to Survive

Rosa Lee: A Mother and Her Family in Urban America 39–47 (1996).

■ Leon Dash

Rosa Lee guided her eleven-year-old grandson through the narrow aisles of a thrift shop in suburban Oxon Hill, Maryland, past the crowded racks of secondhand pants and shirts, stopping finally at the row of children's jackets and winter coats. Quickly, the boy selected a mock-leather flight jacket with a big number on the back and a price tag stapled to the collar.

"If you want it," Ross Lee said, "then you're going to have to help me get it."

"Okay, Grandmama," he said nervously. "But do it in a way that I won't get caught."

Like a skilled teacher instructing a new student, Rosa Lee told her grandson what to do. "Pretend you're trying it on. Don't look up! Don't look around! Don't laugh like it's some kind of joke! Just put it on. Let Grandma see how you look."

The boy slipped off his old, coat and put on the new one. Rosa Lee whispered, "Now put the other one back on, over it." She pushed down the new jacket's collar so that it was hidden.

"What do I do now?" he asked.

"Just walk on out the door," Rosa Lee said. "It's your coat."

Four days later, Rosa Lee is recounting this episode for me, recreating the dialogue by changing her voice to distinguish between herself and her grandson. It is January 1991. By now, I have spent enough time with Rosa Lee that her shoplifting exploits no longer surprise me.

The previous November, Rosa Lee took her eight-year-old granddaughter into the same thrift shop on a Sunday morning to steal a new winter coat for the girl one week after they were both baptized in a Pentecostal church. On the Sunday of the shoplifting lesson, Rosa Lee had decided she did not want to take her granddaughter back to the church because her winter coat was "tacky and dirty."

In the thrift shop, Rosa Lee told her granddaughter to take off her coat and hang it on the coatrack. Next, she told the grinning child to put on the attractive pink winter coat hanging on the rack.

"Are we going to take this coat, Grandma?" asked the skinny little girl.

"Yes," Rosa Lee told her. "We are exchanging coats. Now walk out the door."

A month later, a week before Christmas, Rosa Lee was searching for something in a large shopping bag in her bedroom and dumped the contents onto the bed. Out spilled dozens of bottles of expensive men's cologne and women's perfume, as well as leather gloves with their sixty-dollar price tags still attached. She leaves the tags on when she sells the goods as proof of the merchandise's newness and quality.

"Did you get all this in one trip?" I ask.

"Oh, no," she says. "This is a couple of weeks' worth."

In Rosa Lee's younger years especially, shoplifting was a major source of income, supplementing her welfare payments and the money she made during fifteen years of waitressing at various nightclubs. With eight children to feed and clothe, stealing, she says, helped her survive. Later on, when she began using heroin in the mid–1970s, her shoplifting paid for drugs.

She stole from clothing stores, drugstores, and grocery stores, stuffing items inside the torn liner of her winter coat or slipping them into one of the oversized black purses that she carries wherever she goes. When her children were young—the ages of the grandson and granddaughter—she taught them how to shoplift as well.

"Every time I went somewhere to make some money, I would take my children," she said. "I would teach them or they would watch me. 'Just watch what Mama does. I'm getting food for y'all to eat.'"

In supermarkets, she could count on her children "to distract the security guard while I hit the meat freezer. The guards would always watch groups of children before they'd watch an adult."

Her favorite targets were the department stores. One of her two older brothers, Joe Louis Wright, joked with me one day that Rosa Lee "owned a piece" of Hecht's and had put Lansburgh's out of business. "Man, she would get coats, silk dresses," he recalled. "A cloth coat with a mink collar. She got me a mohair suit. Black. Three-piece. I don't know how the hell she'd get them out of there."

Her stealing has caused divisions and hard feelings in her family, and is one reason why Rosa Lee's relationships with several of her brothers and sisters are strained. They see Rosa Lee's stealing as an extreme and unjustified reaction to their impoverished upbringing. And her sons Alvin and Eric have always refused to participate in any of their mother's illegal activities.

Rosa Lee has served eight short prison terms for various kinds of stealing during the past forty years, dating back to the early 1950s. Her longest stay was eight months for trying to steal a fur coat from a Maryland department store in 1965. She says that she went to prison rehabilitation programs each time but that none had much of an effect on her. "I attended those programs so it would look good on my record when I went before the parole board," she says. "What they were talking about didn't mean anything to me. I didn't have the education they said would get me a job. I couldn't read no matter how many programs I went to."

Nothing seems to deter her from shoplifting, not even the specter of another jail term. On the day she directed her grandson in stealing the flight jacket, she was four days away from sentencing at the city's Superior Court for stealing the bedsheets from Hecht's the previous summer.

"I'm just trying to survive," she says.

Rosa Lee had chosen her clothes carefully for her appearance before Commissioner John Treanor in November. She wanted to look as poor as possible to draw his sympathy.

She wore an ill-fitting winter coat, gray wool overalls and a white wool hat pulled back to show her graying hair. She had removed her upper dental plate to give herself a toothless look when she smiled. "My homey look," she calls it. "No lipstick. No earrings. No nothing!"

Rosa Lee did not expect to go home that day. She saw a heavyset female deputy U.S. marshal move into place behind the defense table when the courtroom clerk called her name. It was a certain sign that Treanor had already decided to "step her back" and send her to jail. She hastily handed me her purse with all her documents.

"Hold on to these papers for me, Mr. Dash," she whispered. "Looks like I'm going to get some jail time. Tell my children where I'm at. You better come see me!"

Her lawyer's statements matched her downtrodden look. Rosa Lee's life was a mess, Elmer D. Ellis told Treanor. She was addicted to heroin, a habit she had developed in 1975. She was HIV positive. She was caring for three grandchildren because their mother was in jail.

Rosa Lee told Treanor that she was trying hard to turn herself around. She was taking methadone every day to control her heroin addition and had turned again to the church. "I got baptized Sunday, me and my three grandchildren," she said, her voice breaking. "And I'm asking you from the bottom of my heart, give me a chance to prove that I'm taking my baptize seriously, 'cause I know I might not have much longer."

Tears ran down her cheeks. "I'm asking you for a chance, please," she begged Treanor. "I know I have a long record."

Rosa Lee was stretching the truth. Yes, she had been baptized, and yes, she was taking methadone. But no, she wasn't caring for her grandchildren alone. Their mother's jail term had ended in July, and she had returned to Rosa Lee's two-bedroom apartment to take care of the children, with help from Rosa Lee.

Treanor looked unimpressed with Rosa Lee's performance. He glowered at her, and Rosa Lee braced for the lecture she knew was coming. Both had played these roles before.

"Every time you pump yourself full of drugs and spend money to do it," he said, "you're stealing from your grandchildren. You're stealing food from their plates, clothes from their backs, and you're certainly jeopardizing their future. You're going to be the youngest dead grandmother in town. And you're going to have three children that will be put up for adoption or going out to some home or some junior village or someplace."

That had been Rosa Lee's opening. "Can I prove to you that my life has changed?"

"Yeah, you can prove it to me, very simply," Treanor answered. "You can stay away from dope. Now I'll make a bargain with you.... You come back here the end of January and tell me what you've been doing, and then we'll think about it. But you're looking at jail time. You're looking at the cemetery."

Rosa Lee had won. Treanor postponed the sentencing. The marshal, who had moved in closer behind Rosa Lee at the start of Treanor's lecture, moved back. Treanor, red-faced with anger, called a ten-minute recess and hurriedly left the bench. Ellis shook Rosa Lee's hand.

Rosa Lee came over to me, her cheeks still tearstained but her face aglow. "Was I good?" she asked.

"Yeah," I said, startled at her boldness.

"Thank you," she said, smiling.

The marshal walked up to Rosa Lee. She too was smiling. She had escorted Rosa Lee and her daughters to the jail several times in the not-so-distant past. "You were going to jail, honey," she said to Rosa Lee. "You stopped him with those three grandchildren. He didn't want to have to deal with making arrangements for those children if he had sent you to jail. Is their mama still over the jail?"

"Yes, she is," Rosa Lee lied, putting on a sad face.

Five days before the hearing Rosa Lee was teaching her grandchild how to shoplift. Through most of November and December, Rosa Lee stole cologne, perfume, gloves, and brightly colored silk scarves to sell to people who used them as Christmas presents. The day before her court appearance, she and a fellow drug-clinic patient, Jackie, were shoplifting in a drugstore one block from the Superior Court building shortly after they had drunk their morning meth.

When she returns for sentencing on January 22, a transformed Rosa Lee enters the courthouse. She looks good. She has a clean report from the methadone clinic. She stopped injecting heroin and cocaine in November, after her last seizure. She seems to have done everything Commissioner Treanor asked.

She always dresses well, but she has outdone herself today: she's wearing a two-piece, white-and-gray cotton knit suit with tan leather boots and a tan pocketbook. A gold-colored watch on a gold-colored chain hangs around her neck, both items she stole from the drugstore.

Before they enter Treanor's courtroom, Elmer Ellis has a word with Rosa Lee. "Please don't cry, Mrs. Cunningham," her lawyer says gently. "If you start crying again, you're only going to make Treanor angry." Rosa Lee laughs and agrees not to cry.

"What would you like to say, Mrs. Cunningham?" Treanor asks Rosa Lee when she stands in front of him.

"Well, Your Honor, I know I haven't been a good person. I know it," she begins.

Treanor cuts her off. His demeanor is softer, his words more sympathetic than in November. "Wait a minute, now. Why do you say that? . . . You're taking care of those three grandchildren, isn't that right?"

"Yes, Sir," Rosa Lee says, keeping up the pretense.

"All right," he says. "Now you've raised one family, and now you have another one."

"Yes, Sir," she says.

"Which is really too much to ask of anybody, so I don't think you should sell yourself short. You're doing the Lord's work. Your daughter's in jail for drugs, right?"

"Yes, sir," Rosa Lee says.

"And you have or have had a bad drug problem yourself."

"Yes, Sir."

Then Treanor launches into another lecture about drugs. He doesn't ask Rosa Lee why she steals. "You steal to support your habit," he says. "It's as plain as the nose on your face."

But it isn't that plain. Rosa Lee began stealing long before she became a drug addict.

Finally, Treanor announces his decision: no jail. Instead, he gives her a suspended sentence and one year of probation with drug counseling. "Now, don't come back here," he says.

Rosa Lee sometimes puts on a public mask, the way she wants the world to see her. She fudges a little here, omits a little there, even when she is trying to be candid about her behavior. By her account, her stealing started when she was a teenager. It was her eldest brother, Ben Wright, who told me that Rosa Lee's stealing started when she was nine years old. Her target: the lunch money that her fourth-grade classmates at Giddings Elementary School kept in their desks.

"JESUS, BEN!" Rosa Lee shouts when I ask her about it.

"What's the matter?" I laugh. "You said I could interview Ben."

It is a late afternoon in January, not long after her court appearance. We are talking in my car, which is parked outside Rosa Lee's apartment. We watch the teenage crack dealers come and go, making the rounds of the low-rent housing complex. Two of Rosa Lee's grandchildren are playing nearby on a patch of dirt where the grass has been worn away. The sun is beginning to sink behind the buildings as she tells me about her first theft.

The year was 1946, and Giddings's imposing red-brick building at Third and G streets, S.E., was a bustling part of the District's then-segregated education system. The school served black children living in Capitol Hill neighborhoods; some, like Rosa Lee, came from poor sharecropping families who had moved to Washington during the Depression, and they did not have the new clothes and spending money that their better-off classmates did.

Rosa Lee's father, Earl Wright, never made much money. He worked for a paving contractor as a cement finisher but he was never given that title; instead, he was always classified as a "helper" and paid a lower wage. Eventually, drinking became the primary activity of his life. Rosa Lee's mother, Rosetta Lawrence Wright, brought in most of the family's money, working as a domestic on Capitol Hill during the day.

"She used to call it 'day work,' " remembers Rosa Lee. "That's what she used to do down in the country" in North Carolina. "Clean white people's houses."

Rosetta also sold dinners from the family's kitchen in the evening and on weekends, always for cash. "She wanted cash because she was getting a welfare check for us," says Rosa Lee. The welfare payments began several years before her father's death because he spent all his time drinking and did not work. After he died, Rosetta had four additional children by another man. "Back in those days, they gave you a check for each child. Seventeen dollars a check. You never want the welfare to know how much money you got. They'll cut the check."

Ben contends that his sister's memory is faulty, that the family did receive monthly deliveries of surplus government food in this period, as did all of the poorest families in Washington, but his mother did not receive a monthly welfare stipend.

Whatever the truth, Rosa Lee and Ben agree that their family—there were eleven children in all—was poor. For much of her childhood, they lived in a ramshackle wooden row house within a mile of the Capitol, since replaced with a public housing project. None of the houses they rented over the years had electricity. The toilet for each dwelling was an outhouse along the edge of the property in the back yard. Water came from a standpipe spigot in the center of the yard.

"I hated them!" says Rosa Lee of the houses, her mouth turning down in a grimace. "No privacy. People knew what you were doing when you went into" the outhouse. "No bathtub. I was always afraid of the kerosene lamps. I was scared they'd turn over and we'd all burn up in those houses."

Other girls came to school with change to buy "brownie-thins"— penny-a-piece cookies that the teachers sold to go with free milk at lunch. Rosa Lee's family was too poor to spare even a few pennies. Rosa Lee was determined to steal her classmates' money so she too could buy cookies. And she did. She knew it was wrong to steal from her classmates' desks, she says. But she couldn't stand being poor, either.

Rosa Lee soon found that she had plenty of opportunities to steal, if she were daring enough. During the summer of 1948, a sinewy Rosa Lee was the only girl among the many "roughneck" boys selling the *Baltimore–Washington Afro–American* newspaper door-to-door on Tuesday and Thursday evenings. She was eleven. The newspaper sales were timed to catch middle-class black people—low-level federal and city civil servants—when they had just come from work.

Rosa Lee was not concerned about tough neighborhood bullies taking her money or trying to force her off the blocks where an *Afro* seller was sure to be successful. "Rosa Lee would fight quick," remembers Ben. "Fight anybody! Beat up most girls and a good many boys. I don't remember ever having to stick up for her."

Selling the *Afro* also gave Rosa Lee a chance to slip into neighborhood row houses and rifle through the pocketbooks that women often left on the dining room table or the living room couch. Washington was a safer place in those days, and Rosa Lee discovered that many families would leave their front screen doors unlatched while they chatted in their back yards, trying to cool off on hot summer evenings after returning home from work.

"I would walk down Fourth Street," says Rosa Lee, in front of the row houses across from Mount Joy Baptist Church, where her family worshipped. "I would go and knock on their screen door. '*Afro!* Anybody want an *Afro?*' I would open the screen door and if no one answered, I'd go in. I could look through the house and see them out back," she remembers. "Some people would leave their pocketbooks on the chair in the front room or on their table. I would go into so many peoples' houses." * * *

———

Mathematics

BLACK ON BOTH SIDES (Priority Records 1999).

■ MOS DEF

* * *

Yo, it's one universal law but two sides to every story

Three strikes and you be in for life, mandatory

* * *

Young soldiers tryin' to earn they next stripe

When the average minimum wage is $5.15

You best believe you gotta find a new ground to get cream

The white unemployment rate, is nearly more than triple for black

so frontliners got they gun in your back

Bubblin' crack, jewel theft and robbery to combat poverty

and end up in the global jail economy

Stiffer stipulations attached to each sentence

Budget cutbacks but increased police presence

And even if you get out of prison still livin'

join the other five million under state supervision

This is business, no faces just lines and statistics

from your phone, your zip code, to S–S–I digits

The system break man child and women into figures

Two columns for who is, and who ain't niggaz

Numbers is hardly real and they never have feelings

but you push too hard, even numbers got limits

Why did one straw break the camel's back? Here's the secret:

the million other straws underneath it—it's all mathematics.

* * *

———

Homelessness and the Issue of Freedom

39 UCLA L. Rev. 295, 299–302 (1991).

■ Jeremy Waldron

Estimates of the number of homeless people in the United States range from 250,000 to three million. A person who is homeless is, obviously enough, a person who has no home. One way of describing the plight of a homeless individual might be to say that there is no place governed by a private property rule where he is allowed to be.

In fact, that is not quite correct. Any private proprietor may invite a homeless person into his house or onto his land, and if he does there *will* be some private place where the homeless person is allowed to be. A technically more accurate description of his plight is that there is no place governed by a private property rule where he is allowed to be whenever *he* chooses, no place governed by a private property rule from which he may not at any time be excluded as a result of someone else's say-so. As far as being on private property is concerned—in people's houses or gardens, on farms or in hotels, in offices or restaurants—the homeless person is utterly and at all times at the mercy of others. And we know enough about how this mercy is generally exercised to figure that the description in the previous paragraph is more or less accurate as a matter of fact, even if it is not strictly accurate as a matter of law.

For the most part the homeless are excluded from *all* of the places governed by private property rules, whereas the rest of us are, in the same sense, excluded from *all but one* (or maybe all but a few) of those places. That is another way of saying that each of us has at least one place to be in a country composed of private places, whereas the homeless person has none.

Some libertarians fantasize about the possibility that *all* the land in a society might be held as private property ("Sell the streets!"). This would be catastrophic for the homeless. Since most private proprietors are already disposed to exclude him from their property, the homeless person might discover in such a libertarian paradise that there was literally *nowhere* he was allowed to be. Wherever he went he would be liable to penalties for trespass and he would be liable to eviction, to being thrown out by an owner or dragged away by the police. Moving from one place to another would involve nothing more liberating than moving from one trespass liability to another. Since land is finite in any society, there is only a limited number of places where a person can (physically) be, and such a person would find that he was legally excluded from all of them. (It would not be entirely mischievous to add that since, in order to exist, a person has to be *somewhere*, such a person would not be permitted to exist.)

Our society saves the homeless from this catastrophe only by virtue of the fact that some of its territory is held as collective property and made available for common use. The homeless are allowed to *be*—provided they are on the streets, in the parks, or under the bridges. Some of them are allowed to crowd together into publicly provided "shelters" after dark (though these are dangerous places and there are not nearly enough shelters for all of them). But in the daytime and, for many of them, all through the night, wandering in public places is their only option. When all else is privately owned, the sidewalks are their salvation. They are allowed to *be* in our society only to the extent that our society is communist.

This is one of the reasons why most defenders of private property are uncomfortable with the libertarian proposal, and why that proposal remains sheer fantasy. But there is a modified form of the libertarian catastrophe in prospect with which moderate and even liberal defenders of ownership seem much more comfortable. This is the increasing regulation of the streets, subways, parks, and other public places to restrict the activities that can be performed there. What is emerging—and it is not just a matter of fantasy—is a state of affairs in which a million or more citizens have no place to perform elementary human activities like urinating, washing, sleeping, cooking, eating, and standing around. Legislators voted for by people who own private places in which they can do all these things are increasingly deciding to make public places available only for activities other than these primal human tasks. The streets and subways, they say, are for commuting from home to office. They are not for sleeping; sleeping is something one does at home. The parks are for recreations like walking and informal ball-games, things for which one's own yard is a little too confined. Parks are not for cooking or urinating; again, these are things one does at home. Since the public and the private are complementary, the activities performed in public are to be the complement of those appropriately performed in private. This complementarity works fine for those who have the benefit of both sorts of places. However, it is disastrous for those who must live their whole lives on common land. If I am right about this, it is one of the most callous and tyrannical exercises of power in modern times by a (comparatively) rich and complacent majority against a minority of their less fortunate fellow human beings.

———

NOTES AND QUESTIONS

1. Illicit activity as means for survival. Traditionally, the majority of African American women have been obliged, by necessity, to work outside the home to support their families. LEITH MULLINGS, ON OUR OWN TERMS: RACE, CLASS, AND GENDER IN THE LIVES OF AFRICAN AMERICAN WOMEN 90 (1997). Due to severe levels of unemployment of black men, the labor force participation rate of black females has become approximately equal to that of black males. *Id*. Though black women comprise a considerable proportion of the labor force, women like Rosa Lee still face several obstacles to achieve economic stability and must therefore resort to either government assistance and/or illicit activity to support their families. In a study performed in Central Harlem in 1990, for example, 54.7 percent of women eligible to work were not in the labor force, with 28.9 percent of individuals residing in Harlem receiving Aid to Families with Dependent Children. *Id*.

at 91 (citing *Persons 16 Years and Over by Labor Force Status and Sex, New York City, Boroughs and Community Districts.* (New York: Department of City Planning, no. 317, 1990)). Furthermore, that study found that more than half of all households in Harlem headed by females that include children under age eighteen have incomes below the poverty line. *Id.* (citing *Socioeconomic profiles: A Portrait of New York City's Community Districts from the 1980 and 1990 Census of Population and Housing* (New York: Department of City Planning)). Faced with poor odds of achieving economic stability, and in "just trying to survive," what can women like Rosa Lee do but break the law to support their families?

University of Pennsylvania Professor of Law Regina Austin explains that though illegal activity may be disparaged, it may be the only means for underprivileged African Americans to survive in America:

> [F]or some poor blacks, breaking the law is not only a way of life: it is the only way to survive. Thus, what is characterized as economic deviance in the eyes of a majority of people may be viewed as economic resistance by a significant number of blacks. Regina Austin, *"An Honest Living": Street Vendors, Municipal Regulation, and The Black Public Sphere*, 103 YALE L.J. 2119, 2119 (1994).

Austin reaches this conclusion based on her study of black street vendors in major cities like New York, Washington, D.C., and Philadelphia. These vendors are part of an informal economy where merchants work without a license and in violation of applicable regulations and sales tax laws. Though illegal, street vending by black workers gives people jobs, supplies African Americans with their preferred products, contributes to the maintenance of African American culture, and assists individuals in gaining the necessary capital and knowledge to operate a business in the formal sector. Because of street vending's benefits for afflicted black communities, Austin stresses that such activity should not immediately be written off, and should instead be respected:

> As blacks in America, we must not fall into the trap of automatically equating legitimacy with legality. Just because an enterprise is small, informal, and illegal does not mean that it is not valuable or that it should be disparaged. *Id.* at 2130.

Based on her comments, how do you think Austin would react to Rosa Lee's illegal behavior? Would she disagree with Rosa Lee's actions because stealing, like street vending, does not achieve legitimate objectives such as promoting African American black entrepreneurial activity?

2. **Sociology of deviance.** Are lawbreakers innately inclined to transgress social norms, or are they simply reacting to society's imposed institutions? In other words, are individuals like Rosa Lee instinctively prone to deviate from societal standards, or are they simply products of their insolvent, unstable environments? Howard S. Becker addressed these questions in *Outsiders: Studies in the Sociology of Deviance*, and proposed the premise that deviant peoples violate rules because social groups establish laws whose breach constitutes deviance, and by applying those laws and

penalties to an "offender." Becker defines an outsider as an individual who others deem deviant and therefore unworthy of inclusion in society's "normal" social functions.

Would Howard Becker maintain that Rosa Lee is an outsider—one who is judged by law-abiders and stands outside of conventional social groups? Is she more likely to be labeled as an outsider because she is an African American? Becker elaborates on the implications of being an outsider:

> The degree to which an act will be treated as deviant depends also on who commits the act and who feels he has been harmed by it. Rules tend to be applied more to some persons than others. Studies of juvenile delinquency make the point clearly. Boys from middleclass areas do not get as far in the legal process when they are apprehended as do boys from slum areas. The middle-class boy is less likely, when picked up by the police, to be taken to the station; less likely when taken to the station to be booked; and it is extremely unlikely that he will be convicted and sentenced. This variation occurs even though the original infraction of the rule is the same in the two cases. Similarly, the law is differentially applied to Negroes and whites. It is well known that a Negro believed to have attacked a white woman is much more likely to be punished than a white man who commits the same offense; it is only slightly less well known that a Negro who murders another Negro is much less likely to be punished than a white man who commits murder.

HOWARD S. BECKER, OUTSIDERS: STUDIES IN THE SOCIOLOGY OF DEVIANCE 12–13 (1973).

Consider Becker's proposition and Rosa Lee's case. Recall that Rosa Lee was acquitted when she returned to court for a shoplifting charge. Though she is African American and a "deviant outsider," she was able to receive approval from the judge and continue to maintain her freedom. However, was Rosa Lee not trying to portray herself as an "insider" by wearing more respectable attire and emotionally appealing to the judge?

3. "Underclass" and "culture of poverty." Since the 1970s, conservative scholars and critics have attempted to highlight the role of "culture" in maintaining poverty, arguing that poverty becomes intergenerational when poor people lack self-discipline, initiative, and "soft skills" required for success in the working world. These arguments played a large part in welfare reform from the 1970s through the turn of the twenty-first century. A similar debate has gone on about the so-called "underclass," identified as a group of people (Marx would have called them an "industrial reserve army") so chronically lacking regular employment that they can be seen as having effectively been marginalized from the economy altogether. In the late 1980s, the media spent a lot of time worrying about the "underclass," which was said to epitomize all the cultural deviance (lack of initiative, dependency, and so on) exhibited by the poor more generally, and which was thought to be a breeding ground for street crime. For scholarly discussions of the "underclass," *see, e.g.,* WILLIAM JULIUS WILSON, THE TRULY DISADVANTAGED: THE INNER CITY, THE UNDERCLASS, AND PUBLIC POLICY (1987);

CHRISTOPHER JENCKS, RETHINKING SOCIAL POLICY: RACE, POVERTY, AND THE UNDERCLASS (1992).

Is it "culture" or material conditions that account for the large gaps that remain in family income, wages, and employment between African Americans and whites? For a "cultural" explanation, *see, e.g.,* STEPHEN THERNSTROM & ABIGAIL THERNSTROM, AMERICA IN BLACK AND WHITE (1997); for a "material" explanation, *see, e.g.,* MICHAEL K. BROWN, ET AL., WHITEWASHING RACE: THE MYTH OF A COLOR-BLIND SOCIETY 66–103 (2003). Does a material explanation account for the behavior of people like Rosa Lee?

4. *"Underclass"* and prison industrial complex. Some might argue that to the extent that an underclass exists, it is, ironically, the effect as much as the cause of state policy. The "war on drugs" and the "war on crime" more generally have created an incarceration crisis for many poor communities. African American and Latino men are incarcerated for long periods at dramatic rates, which creates a social ripple effect of poverty: ex-felons find it difficult to get jobs when they get out of prison; the removal of these men from families and neighborhoods places extra economic and social stress on the people left behind. This social disorganization, in turn, leads to more crime in the increasingly impoverished and dangerous neighborhoods of inner cities. *See* Tracey Meares, *Social Organization and Drug Law Enforcement,* 35 AM. CRIM. L. REV. 191 (1998); Dorothy Roberts, *The Social and Moral Cost of Mass Incarceration in African American Communities,* 56 STAN. L. REV. 1271 (2004).

Some scholars argue that this vicious circle is coupled with another vicious circle: the increasing dependency of strapped towns and counties on prisons as economic engines, which leads to the increased political power of prison guards and prison officials unions, which leads in turn to a continuation of punitive criminal justice policies. *See* Stephen C. Thaman, *Is America a Systematic Violator of Human Rights in the Administration of Criminal Justice?* 44 ST. LOUIS L.J. 999 (2000). Another element in the continuing appeal of punitive policies, some scholars argue, is the declining influence of criminal justice experts: criminal justice policy today tends to be seen as a populist issue and not an issue about which experts should have any particular say. In this environment, politicians promising to be "tough on crime" and prosecutors dominate the legislative process. *See* Franklin Zimring, *Populism, Democratic Government, and the Decline of Expert Authority: Some Reflections on "Three Strikes" in California,* 28 PAC. L.J. 243 (1996); William Stuntz, *The Pathological Politics of Criminal Law,* 100 MICH. L. REV. 505 (2001).

5. Crime, class, and race. The United States mass incarceration policy does not seem to have been either effective at stopping crime nor economically efficient. Why, then, has it persisted? Some scholars argue that punitive criminal justice policy serves ideological functions that are more powerful than their economic or social functions. *See, e.g.,* JEFFREY REIMAN, THE RICH GET RICHER AND THE POOR GET PRISON: IDEOLOGY, CLASS, AND CRIMINAL JUSTICE (7th ed. 2003); MICHAEL TONRY, MALIGN NEGLECT: RACE, CRIME, AND

Punishment in America (1996); David Cole, No Equal Justice: Race and Class in the American Criminal Justice System (2000).

6. Homelessness and criminal justice policy. Like "the underclass," "the homeless" are frequently a target of fear and loathing in American culture; like the poor generally, some make an effort to distinguish the innocent or involuntary homeless from those who have "chosen" their situation; and like poverty generally, homelessness and crime are closely connected in the public mind, resulting in, ironically, more criminalization. *See* Christopher Jencks, The Homeless (1995); Peter H. Rossi, Down and Out in America: The Origins of Homelessness (1991). For a lively discussion of how not only law but architecture and urban planning are affected by the desire to make homeless people invisible in city spaces, see Mike Davis, City of Quartz: Excavating the Future in Los Angeles (1992).

B. Relations of (Re)production

The Working Poor: Invisible in America

39–44 50, 64–67 (2004).

■ David K. Shipler

Christie did a job that this labor-hungry economy could not do without. Every morning she drove her battered '86 Volkswagen from her apartment in public housing to the YWCA's child-care center in Akron, Ohio, where she spent the day watching over little children so their parents could go to work. Without her and thousands like her across the country, there would have been fewer people able to fill the jobs that fueled America's prosperity. Without her patience and warmth, children could have been harmed as well, for she was more than a baby-sitter. She gave the youngsters an emotionally safe place, taught and mothered them, and sometimes even rescued them from abuse at home.

For those valuable services, she received a check for about $330 every two weeks. She could not afford to put her own two children in the day-care center where she worked.

Christie was a hefty woman who laughed more readily than her predicament should have allowed. She suffered from stress and high blood pressure. She had no bank account because she could not keep enough money long enough. Try as she might to shop carefully, she always fell behind on her bills and was peppered with late fees. Her low income entitled her to food stamps and a rental subsidy, but whenever she got a little pay raise, government agencies reduced the benefits, and she felt punished for working. She was trapped on the treadmill of welfare reform, running her life according to the rules of the Personal Responsibility and Work Opportunity Reconciliation Act of 1996. The title left no doubt about what Congress and the White House saw as poverty's cause and solution.

Initially the new law combined with the good economy to send welfare caseloads plummeting. As states were granted flexibility in administering time limits and work requirements, some created innovative consortiums of government, industry, and charity to guide people into effective job training and employment. But most available jobs had three unhappy traits: They paid low wages, offered no benefits, and led nowhere. "Many who do find jobs," the Urban Institute concluded in a 2002 report, "lose other supports designed to help them, such as food stamps and health insurance, leaving them no better off—and sometimes worse off—than when they were not working."

Christie considered herself such a case. The only thing in her wallet resembling a credit card was a blue-green piece of plastic labeled "Ohio" and decorated with a drawing of a lighthouse projecting a beam into the night. Inside the "O" was a gold square—a computer chip. On the second working day of every month, she slipped the card into a special machine at Walgreen's, Save–A–Lot, or Apple's, and punched in her identification number. A credit of $136 was loaded into her chip. This was the form in which her "food stamps" were now issued—less easy to steal or to sell, and less obvious and degrading in the checkout line.

The card contained her first bit of income in every month and permitted her first expenditure. It could be used for food only, and not for cooked food or pet food. It occupied the top line in the balance sheet she kept for me during a typical October.

"2nd Spent 136.00 food stamps," she wrote. So the benefit was all gone the day she got it. Three days later she had to come up with an additional $25 in cash for groceries, another $54 on October 10, and $15 more on the twelfth. Poor families typically find that food stamps cover only one-half to three-quarters of their grocery costs.

Even the opening balance on the card was chipped away as Christie inched up in salary. It makes sense that the benefit is based on income: the less you need, the less you get. That's the economic side. On the psychological side, however, it produces hellish experiences for the beneficiaries. Every three months Christie had to take half a day off from work (losing half a day's wages) and carry an envelope full of pay stubs, utility bills, and rent receipts to be pawed over by her ill-tempered caseworker, who applied a state-mandated formula to figure her food stamp allotment and her children's eligibility for health insurance. When Christie completed a training course and earned a raise of 10 cents an hour, her food stamps dropped by $10 a month.

That left her $6 a month ahead, which was not nothing but felt like it. Many former welfare recipients who go to work just say good riddance to the bureaucracies that would provide food stamps, medical coverage, and housing. Some think wrongly that they're no longer eligible once they're off welfare; others would rather forfeit their rights than contend with the hassle and humiliation. Quiet surrender ran against Christie's grain, however. She was smart and insistent, as anyone must be to negotiate her way through the system. She never flinched from appealing to higher authority.

When she once forgot to put a utilities bill in her sheaf of papers, her caseworker withheld her food stamps. "I mailed it to her the next day," Christie said. Two weeks passed, and the card remained empty. Christie called the caseworker. "She got really snotty," Christie remembered. " 'Well, didn't I tell you you were supposed to send some documentation?' "

"I was like, 'Have you checked your mail?' " No, as it turned out, the caseworker's mail had piled up unread. "She was like, 'Well, I got people waiting up to two, three months on food stamps.' And she didn't get back with me. I had to go to her supervisor." The benefits were then restored.

It is easy to lose your balance having one foot planted tentatively in the working world and the other still entwined in this thicket of red tape. Managing relations with a boss, finding reliable child care, and coping with a tangle of unpaid bills can be daunting enough for a single mother with little such experience; add surveillance by a bureaucracy that seems more prosecutor than provider, and you have Christie's high blood pressure.

While she invoked the system's rules to get her due, she also cheated—or thought she did. Living with her surreptitiously was her boyfriend, Kevin, the father of her son. She was certain that if the Housing Authority knew, she would be evicted, either because he was a convicted felon (two years for assault) or because his earning power, meager though it was, would have lifted her beyond eligibility. So slight are the margins between government assistance and outright destitution that small lies take on large significance in the search for survival.

Kevin looked like a friendly giant—a solid 280 pounds, a shaved head, and a small earring in his right ear. His income was erratic. In decent weather he made $7.40 an hour working for a landscaper, who rewarded him with a free turkey to end the season at Thanksgiving—and then dumped him onto unemployment for the winter. He wanted to drive a truck or cut meat. He had received a butcher's certificate in a training course during imprisonment, but when he showed the document from the penitentiary, employers didn't rush to put a knife in his hand.

The arithmetic of Christie's life added up to tension, and you had to look hard through her list of expenditures to find fun or luxury. On the fifth she received her weekly child support check of $37.66 from Kevin (she got nothing from her daughter's father, who was serving a long prison sentence for assault). The same day, she put $5 worth of gas in her car, and the next day spent $6 of her own money to take the day-care kids to the zoo. The eighth was payday, and her entire $330 check disappeared in a flash. First, there was what she called a $3 "tax" to cash her check, just one of several such fees for money orders and the like—a penalty for having no checking account. Immediately, $172 went for rent, including a $10 late fee, which she was always charged because she never had enough to pay by the first of the month. Then, because it was October and she had started to plan for Christmas, she paid $31.47 at a store for presents she had put on layaway, another $10 for gasoline, $40 to buy shoes for her two kids, $5 for a pair of corduroy pants at a secondhand shop, another $5 for a shirt, $10 for bell-bottom pants, and $47 biweekly car insurance. The $330 was gone.

She had no insurance on her TVs, clothes, furniture, or other household goods.

Utilities and other bills got paid out of her second check toward the end of the month. Her phone usually cost about $43 a month, gas for the apartment $34, electricity $46, and prescriptions between $8 and $15. Her monthly car payment ran $150, medical insurance $72, and cable TV $43. Cable is no longer considered a luxury by low-income families that pinch and sacrifice to have it. So much of modern American culture now comes through television that the poor would be further marginalized without the broad access that cable provides. Besides, it's relatively cheap entertainment. "I just have basic," Christie explained. "I have an antenna, but you can't see anything, you get no reception." And she needed good reception because she and Kevin loved to watch wrestling.

One reason for Christie's tight budget was the abundance of high-priced, well-advertised snacks, junk food, and prepared meals that provide an easy fallback diet for a busy working mother—or for anyone who has never learned to cook from scratch. Besides the staples of hamburgers, and chicken, "I buy sausages," Christie said, "I buy the TV dinners 'cause I might be tired some days and throw it in the oven—like Salisbury steaks and turkey and stuff like that. My kids love pizza. I get the frozen pizzas.... I buy my kids a lot of breakfast things 'cause we're up early and we're out the door. You know, those cereal bars and stuff like that, they're expensive! You know? Pop Tarts, cereal bars, Granola." The cheaper breakfasts, like hot cereal, came only on weekends, when she had time. "They eat the hot cereal, but during the week we're on the go. So I give them cereal in the bag. My son likes to eat dry cereal, so I put him some cereal in the lunch bag. Cocoa Puffs. They got Cocoa Dots." She laughed. "Lucky Charms. He's not picky. My daughter's picky." Those candylike cereals soak up dollars. At my local supermarket, Lucky Charms cost dearly: $4.39 for a box of just 14 ounces, while three times as much oatmeal goes for nearly the same price, $4.29. * * *

Her mother, "Gladys," had dropped out of high school, spent years on welfare, and nurtured the fervent dream of seeing her three children in college. The ambition propelled two of them. Christie's brother became an accountant, and her sister, a loan officer. But Christie never took to higher education. She began reluctantly at the University of Akron, lived at home, and finally got fed up with having no money. The second semester of her sophomore year, she went to work instead of to school, a choice that struck her then as less momentous than it turned out to be.

"She didn't take things as serious as they really were," Gladys complained. "Now she sees for herself how serious this is." Just how serious depended on what she wanted to do. She loved working with children but now discovered that without a college degree she would have trouble getting hired at a responsible level in the Head Start preschool program, much less as a teacher in a regular school; she was limited to a YWCA day-care center whose finances were precarious. Since 95 percent of the Y's children came from low-income families, the fees were essentially set by the center's main source of income, Ohio's Department of Human Services, which paid $99 to $114 a week for full-time care. Given the center's heavy expenses, the rates were not enough to pay teachers more than $5.30 to $5.90 an hour.

Christie's previous jobs had also imprisoned her close to the minimum wage as a hostess-cashier at a Holiday Inn, a cashier at Kmart, a waitress in a bar, a cook and waitress and cashier in various restaurants. She had become a veteran of inadequate training programs designed to turn her into a retail salesperson, a bus driver, and a correctional officer, but the courses never enabled her and her classmates to pass the tests and get hired. She had two words to explain why she had never returned to college. "Lazy. Lazy."

It was strange that she thought of herself as lazy, because her work was exhausting, and her low wage required enormous effort to stay afloat. * * *

The new millennium arrived in a crescendo of American riches. The nation wallowed in luxury, burst with microchips, consumed with abandon, swaggered globally. Everything grew larger: homes, vehicles, stock portfolios, life expectancy. Never before in the sweep of human history had so many people been so utterly comfortable.

Caroline Payne was not one of them. A few weeks after New Year's Day, she sat at her kitchen table and reflected on her own history. Two of her three goals had been achieved: She had earned a college diploma, albeit just a two-year associate's degree. And she had gone from a homeless shelter into her own house, although it was mostly owned by a bank. The third objective, "a good-paying job," as she put it, still eluded her. Back in the mid–1970s, she earned $6 an hour in a Vermont factory that made plastic cigarette lighters and cases for Gillette razors. In 2000, she earned $6.80 an hour stocking shelves and working cash registers at a vast Wal–Mart superstore in New Hampshire. * * *

Anyone who walked all the way around the outside of the Wal–Mart superstore on Route 103 would walk a mile, Caroline said. The place was immense. It sold everything from lawn mowers to ground beef, underpricing smaller stores that were struggling to survive in the center of town. Its 300 to 330 employees, who came and went seasonally, wore Wal–Mart's uniform of blue smocks and friendly smiles, trained as they were to be surprisingly helpful to customers.

Mark Brown, the manager, could pay his people more without raising prices, he conceded. He sat at a table in the store's snack bar, watching the part of the grocery section he could see, listening to the public address system's call for help at the registers, his eyes darting around this corner of his fiefdom like a school principal waiting for the next catastrophe. He was thirty-one, but he looked as young as a college kid and spoke with the twang of his native southeast Missouri. He had come from another store in Georgia and was learning to ski here in New Hampshire.

His employees started at $6.25 an hour, earned an extra dollar at night and another 25 cents "for going to the front end," which meant working one of the twenty-four cash registers. And if he started them at $8 an hour, say, instead of $6.25, how would that change the economics of the store? "Hmmmm. I don't think it would change at all." He wouldn't have to raise prices? "No. We've got a corporate pricing structure. And the way we do things, we go out and we check our competition every single week. Every department manager in this store goes out once a week and checks competition, and that's what determines our prices. We have a core price structure that we set regionally, by areas. Definitely the base price here would be probably higher than what it is in Arkansas, where there's a cheap cost of living. So it would be higher here, but it would still be standard to this area. And then after they give us that base, then we go out and check our competition, and if we're gettin' beat, we lower our prices."

So there's enough profit to absorb an increase from $6.25 to $8? "There would be, because if we were having to raise our wages, then evidently everybody else would be too, and if we make sure we're low enough, our competitors' customers are gonna shop with us." Would wage increases have any effect at all? "We'd have to cut corners on other things like, you know, we may not be able to put all the pretty balloons up all over the store. The non-necessities we'd have to cut back on."

Three days later Wal–Mart Stores, Inc., announced a net income of $5.58 billion for 1999, up 26 percent from the previous year.

Caroline was bouncing from one department to another, from one shift to another, but her pay stayed within a narrow range, beginning at $6.25, going to $6.80, sometimes up to $7.50 if she worked at night. So unpredictable were her hours that she couldn't work a second job, which would have helped her cash flow. She kept applying to higher positions and kept hearing that she needed a bit more experience. * * *

In more depressed parts of the country and during recessions,* * * some Wal–Mart managers were accused of forcing employees to work before punching in or after punching out to avoid paying overtime as required by law. "Wal–Mart management doesn't hold itself to the same standard of rectitude it expects from its low-paid employees," wrote Barbara Ehrenreich, who worked at a Wal–Mart in Minnesota while researching her book *Nickel and Dimed*. "When I applied for a job at Wal–Mart in the spring of 2000, I was reprimanded for getting something 'wrong' on this test: I had agreed only 'strongly' to the proposition, 'All rules have to be followed to the letter at all times.' The correct answer was 'totally agree.' Apparently the one rule that need not be slavishly adhered to at Wal–Mart is the federal Fair Labor Standards Act, which requires that employees be paid time and a half if they work more than forty hours in a week." Workers were warned against "time theft," which meant "doing anything other than working during company time, anything at all," she reported. "Theft of *our* time is not, however, an issue."

Caroline never had the overtime problem in her New Hampshire store, but in six Southern states employees filed a class-action suit against the company for ordering them off the clock as their weekly time approached forty hours. Their attorney calculated the benefits to the firm: If each of 250 hourly wage "associates" in a single store worked just one hour of unpaid overtime a week, that would total 250 unpaid hours a week, 1,000 a month, 12,000 a year—and there were over 300 Wal–Mart stores in Texas, producing savings in that state alone of more than $30 million that should have been paid to employees.

Caroline did not suffer from any violations of law, as far as she could tell, but her career went nowhere. Mark Brown, the manager who liked her, got transferred to Pennsylvania, dimming her prospects for advancement. So after a year and a half at Wal–Mart, she signed up with a temp agency, which found her a $7.50–an-hour daytime job Monday through Friday assembling wallpaper sample books. And she had the pleasure of telling Wal–Mart's assistant manager that she was leaving for higher pay.

Down and Out in Discount America

The Nation, Dec. 16 2004, http://www.thenation.com/doc.mhtml?i=20050103&s=feather stone.

■ LIZA FEATHERSTONE

On the day after Thanksgiving, the biggest shopping day of the year, Wal–Mart's many progressive critics—not to mention its business competitors—finally enjoyed a bit of schadenfreude when the retailer had to admit to "disappointing" sales. The problem was quickly revealed: Wal–Mart hadn't been discounting aggressively enough. Without low prices, Wal–Mart just isn't Wal–Mart.

That's not a mistake the big-box behemoth is likely to make again. Wal–Mart knows its customers, and it knows how badly they need the discounts. Like Wal–Mart's workers, its customers are overwhelmingly female, and struggling to make ends meet. Betty Dukes, the lead plaintiff in *Dukes v. Wal–Mart*, the landmark sex-discrimination case against the company, points out that Wal–Mart takes out ads in her local paper the same day the community's poorest citizens collect their welfare checks. "They are promoting themselves to low-income people," she says. "That's who they lure. They don't lure the rich. . . . They understand the economy of America. They know the haves and have-nots. They don't put Wal–Mart in Piedmonts. They don't put Wal–Mart in those high-end parts of the community. They plant themselves right in the middle of Poorville."

Betty Dukes is right. A 2000 study by Andrew Franklin, then an economist at the University of Connecticut, showed that Wal–Mart operated primarily in poor and working-class communities, finding, in the bone-dry language of his discipline, "a significant negative relationship between median household income and Wal–Mart's presence in the market." Although fancy retailers noted with chagrin during the 2001 recession that absolutely everybody shops at Wal–Mart—"Even people with $100,000 incomes now shop at Wal–Mart," a PR flack for one upscale mall fumed— the Bloomingdale's set is not the discounter's primary market, and probably never will be. Only 6 percent of Wal–Mart shoppers have annual family incomes of more than $100,000. A 2003 study found that 23 percent of Wal–Mart Supercenter customers live on incomes of less than $25,000 a year. More than 20 percent of Wal–Mart shoppers have no bank account, long considered a sign of dire poverty. And while almost half of Wal–Mart Supercenter customers are blue-collar workers and their families, 20 percent are unemployed or elderly.

Al Zack, who until his retirement in 2004 was the United Food and Commercial Workers' vice president for strategic programs, observes that appealing to the poor was "Sam Walton's real genius. He figured out how to make money off of poverty. He located his first stores in poor rural areas and discovered a real market. The only problem with the business model is that it really needs to create more poverty to grow." That problem is cleverly solved by creating more bad jobs worldwide. In a chilling reversal of Henry Ford's strategy, which was to pay his workers amply so they could buy Ford cars, Wal–Mart's stingy compensation policies—workers make, on average, just over $8 an hour, and if they want health insurance, they must pay more than a third of the premium—contribute to an economy in which, increasingly, workers can only afford to shop at Wal–Mart.

To make this model work, Wal–Mart must keep labor costs down. It does this by making corporate crime an integral part of its business strategy. Wal–Mart routinely violates laws protecting workers' organizing rights (workers have even been fired for union activity). It is a repeat offender on overtime laws; in more than thirty states, workers have brought wage-and-hour class-action suits against the retailer. In some cases, workers say, managers encouraged them to clock out and keep working; in others, managers locked the doors and would not let employees go home at the end of their shifts. And it's often women who suffer most from Wal–Mart's labor practices. *Dukes v. Wal–Mart*, which is the largest civil rights class-action suit in history, charges the company with systematically discriminating against women in pay and promotions. * * *

SOLIDARITY ACROSS THE CHECKOUT COUNTER

Given the poverty they have in common, it makes sense that Wal–Mart's workers often express a strong feeling of solidarity with the shoppers. Wal–Mart workers tend to be aware that the customers' circumstances are similar to their own, and to identify with them. Some complain about rude customers, but most seem to genuinely enjoy the shoppers.

One longtime department manager in Ohio cheerfully recalls her successful job interview at Wal–Mart. Because of her weight, she told her interviewers, she'd be better able to help the customer. "I told them I wanted to work in the ladies department because I'm a heavy girl." She understands the frustrations of the large shopper, she told them: " 'You know, you go into Lane Bryant and some skinny girl is trying to sell you clothes.' They laughed at that and said, 'You get a second interview!' "

One plaintiff in the *Dukes* lawsuit, Cleo Page, who no longer works at Wal–Mart, says she was a great customer service manager because "I knew how people feel when they shop, so I was really empathetic."

Many Wal–Mart workers say they began working at their local Wal–Mart because they shopped there. "I was practically born in Wal–Mart," says Alyssa Warrick, a former employee now attending Truman State University in Missouri. "My mom is obsessed with shopping.... I thought it would be pretty easy since I knew where most of the stuff was." Most assumed they would love working at Wal–Mart. "I always loved shopping there," enthuses *Dukes* plaintiff Dee Gunter. "That's why I wanted to work for 'em."

Shopping is traditionally a world of intense female communication and bonding, and women have long excelled in retail sales in part because of the identification between clerk and shopper. Page, who still shops at Wal–Mart, is now a lingerie saleswoman at Mervyn's (owned by Target). "I do enjoy retail," she says. "I like feeling needed and I like helping people, especially women."

Betty Dukes says, "I strive to give Wal–Mart customers one hundred percent of my abilities." This sentiment was repeated by numerous other Wal–Mart workers, always with heartfelt sincerity. Betty Hamilton, a 61-year-old clerk in a Las Vegas Sam's Club, won her store's customer service award last year. She is very knowledgeable about jewelry, her favorite department, and proud of it. Hamilton resents her employer—she complains about sexual harassment and discrimination, and feels she has been penalized on the job for her union sympathies—but remains deeply devoted to her customers. She enjoys imparting her knowledge to shoppers so "they can walk out of there and feel like they know something." Like Page, Hamilton feels she is helping people. "It makes me so happy when I sell something that I know is an extraordinarily good buy," she says. "I feel like I've done somebody a really good favor."

The enthusiasm of these women for their jobs, despite the workplace indignities many of them have faced, should not assure anybody that the company's abuses don't matter. In fact, it should underscore the tremendous debt Wal–Mart owes women: This company has built its vast profits not only on women's drudgery but also on their joy, creativity and genuine care for the customer.

WHY BOYCOTTS DON'T ALWAYS WORK

Will consumers return that solidarity and punish Wal–Mart for discriminating against women? Do customers care about workers as much as workers care about them? Some women's groups, like the National Organization for Women and Code Pink, have been hoping that they do, and have encouraged the public not to shop at Wal–Mart. While this tactic could be fruitful in some community battles, it's unlikely to catch on nationwide. A customer saves 20–25 percent by buying groceries at Wal–Mart rather than from a competitor, according to retail analysts, and poor women need those savings more than anyone.

That's why many women welcome the new Wal–Marts in their communities. *The Winona* (Minnesota) *Post* extensively covered a controversy over whether to allow a Wal–Mart Supercenter into the small town; the letters to the editor in response offer a window into the female customer's loyalty to Wal–Mart. Though the paper devoted substantial space to the sex discrimination case, the readers who most vehemently defended the retailer were female. From the nearby town of Rollingstone, Cindy Kay wrote that she needed the new Wal–Mart because the local stores didn't carry large-enough sizes. She denounced the local anti-Wal–Mart campaign as a plot by rich and thin elites: "I'm glad those people can fit into and afford such clothes. I can barely afford Shopko and Target!"

A week later, Carolyn Goree, a preschool teacher also hoping for a Winona Wal–Mart, wrote in a letter to the *Post* editor that when she shops at most stores, $200 fills only a bag or two, but at Wal–Mart, "I come out with a cart full top and bottom. How great that feels." Lacking a local Wal–Mart, Goree drives over the Wisconsin border to get her fix. She was incensed by an earlier article's lament that some workers make only $15,000 yearly. "Come on!" Goree objected. "Is $15,000 really that bad of a yearly income? I'm a single mom and when working out of my home, I made $12,000 tops and that was with child support. I too work, pay for a mortgage, lights, food, everything to live. Everything in life is a choice. . . . I am for the little man/woman—I'm one of them. So I say stand up and get a Wal–Mart."

Sara Jennings, a disabled Winona reader living on a total of $8,000, heartily concurred. After paying her rent, phone, electric and cable bills, Jennings can barely afford to treat herself to McDonald's. Of a recent trip to the LaCrosse, Wisconsin, Wal–Mart, she raved, "Oh boy, what a great treat. Lower prices and a good quality of clothes to choose from. It was like heaven for me." She, too, strongly defended the workers' $15,000 yearly income: "Boy, now that is a lot of money. I could live with that." She closed with a plea to the readers: "I'm sure you all make a lot more than I. And I'm sure I speak for a lot of seniors and very-low-income people. We *need* this Wal–Mart. There's nothing downtown."

From Consumers to Workers and Citizens

It is crucial that Wal–Mart's liberal and progressive critics make use of the growing public indignation at the company over sex discrimination, low pay and other workers' rights issues, but it is equally crucial to do this in ways that remind people that their power does not stop at their shopping dollars. It's admirable to drive across town and pay more for toilet paper to avoid shopping at Wal–Mart, but such a gesture is, unfortunately, not enough. As long as people identify themselves as consumers and nothing more, Wal–Mart wins.

The invention of the "consumer" identity has been an important part of a long process of eroding workers' power, and it's one reason working people now have so little power against business. According to the social historian Stuart Ewen, in the early years of mass production, the late nineteenth and early twentieth centuries, modernizing capitalism sought to turn people who thought of themselves primarily as "workers" into "consumers." Business elites wanted people to dream not of satisfying work and egalitarian societies—as many did at that time—but of the beautiful things they could buy with their paychecks.

Business was quite successful in this project, which influenced much early advertising and continued throughout the twentieth century. In addition to replacing the "worker," the "consumer" has also effectively displaced the citizen. That's why, when most Americans hear about the Wal–Mart's worker-rights abuses, their first reaction is to feel guilty about shopping at the store. A tiny minority will respond by shopping elsewhere—and only a handful will take any further action. A worker might call her union and organize a picket. A citizen might write to her congressman or local newspaper, or galvanize her church and knitting circle to visit local management. A consumer makes an isolated, politically slight decision: to shop or not to shop. Most of the time, Wal–Mart has her exactly where it wants her, because the intelligent choice for anyone thinking as a consumer is not to make a political statement but to seek the best bargain and the greatest convenience.

To effectively battle corporate criminals like Wal–Mart, the public must be engaged as citizens, not merely as shoppers. What kind of politics could encourage that? It's not clear that our present political parties are up to the job. Unlike so many horrible things, Wal–Mart cannot be blamed on George W. Bush. The Arkansas-based company prospered under the state's native son Bill Clinton when he was governor and President. Sam Walton and his wife, Helen, were close to the Clintons, and for several years Hillary Clinton, whose law firm represented Wal–Mart, served on the company's board of directors. Bill Clinton's "welfare reform" has provided Wal–Mart with a ready workforce of women who have no choice but to accept its poverty wages and discriminatory policies.

Still, a handful of Democratic politicians stood up to the retailer. California Assemblywoman Sally Lieber, who represents the 22nd Assembly District and is a former mayor of Mountain View, was outraged when she learned about the sex discrimination charges in *Dukes v. Wal–Mart*, and she smelled blood when, tipped off by dissatisfied workers, her office discovered that Wal–Mart was encouraging its workers to apply for public assistance, "in the middle of the worst state budget crisis in history!" California had a $38 billion deficit at the time, and Lieber was enraged that taxpayers would be subsidizing Wal–Mart's low wages, bringing new meaning to the term "corporate welfare."

Lieber was angry, too, that Wal–Mart's welfare dependence made it nearly impossible for responsible employers to compete with the retail giant. It was as if taxpayers were unknowingly funding a massive plunge to the bottom in wages and benefits—quite possibly their own. She held a press conference in July 2003, to expose Wal–Mart's welfare scam. The Wal–Mart documents—instructions explaining how to apply for food stamps, Medi–Cal (the state's healthcare assistance program) and other forms of welfare—were blown up on posterboard and displayed. The morning of the press conference, a Wal–Mart worker who wouldn't give her name for fear of being fired snuck into Lieber's office. "I just wanted to say, right on!" she told the assemblywoman.

Wal–Mart spokespeople have denied that the company encourages employees to collect public assistance, but the documents speak for themselves. They bear the Wal–Mart logo, and one is labeled "Wal–Mart: Instructions for Associates." Both documents instruct employees in procedures for applying to "Social Service Agencies." Most Wal–Mart workers I've interviewed had co-workers who worked full time for the company and received public assistance, and some had been in that situation themselves. Public assistance is very clearly part of the retailer's cost-cutting strategy. (It's ironic that a company so dependent on the public dole supports so many right-wing politicians who'd like to dismantle the welfare state.)

Lieber, a strong supporter of the social safety net who is now assistant speaker pro tempore of the California Assembly, last year passed a bill that would require large and mid-sized corporations that fail to provide decent, affordable health insurance to reimburse local governments for the cost of providing public assistance for those workers. When the bill passed, its opponents decided to kill it by bringing it to a statewide referendum. Wal–Mart, which just began opening Supercenters in California this year, mobilized its resources to revoke the law on election day this November, even while executives denied that any of their employees depended on public assistance.

Citizens should pressure other politicians to speak out against Wal–Mart's abuses and craft policy solutions. But the complicity of both parties in Wal–Mart's power over workers points to the need for a politics that squarely challenges corporate greed and takes the side of ordinary people. That kind of politics seems, at present, strongest at the local level.

Earlier this year, labor and community groups in Chicago prevented Wal–Mart from opening a store on the city's South Side, in part by pushing through an ordinance that would have forced the retailer to pay Chicago workers a living wage. In Hartford, Connecticut, labor and community advocates just won passage of an ordinance protecting their free speech rights on the grounds of the new Wal–Mart Supercenter, which is being built on city property. Similar battles are raging nationwide, but Wal–Mart's opponents don't usually act with as much coordination as Wal–Mart does, and they lack the retail behemoth's deep pockets.

With this in mind, SEIU president Andy Stern has recently been calling attention to the need for better coordination—and funding—of labor and community anti-Wal–Mart efforts. Stern has proposed that the AFL–CIO allocate $25 million of its royalties from purchases on its Union Plus credit card toward fighting Wal–Mart and the "Wal–Martization" of American jobs. * * *

Such efforts are essential not just because Wal–Mart is a grave threat to unionized workers' jobs (which it is) but because it threatens all American ideals that are at odds with profit—ideals such as justice, equality and fairness. Wal–Mart would not have so much power if we had stronger labor laws, and if we required employers to pay a living wage. The company knows that, and it hires lobbyists in Washington to vigorously fight any effort at such reforms—indeed, Wal–Mart has recently beefed up this political infrastructure substantially, and it's likely that its presence in Washington will only grow more conspicuous.

The situation won't change until a movement comes together and builds the kind of social and political power for workers and citizens that can balance that of Wal–Mart. This is not impossible: In Germany, unions are powerful enough to force Wal–Mart to play by their rules. American citizens will have to ask themselves what kind of world they want to live in. That's what prompted Gretchen Adams, a former Wal–Mart manager, to join the effort to unionize Wal–Mart. She's deeply troubled by the company's effect on the economy as a whole and the example it sets for other employers. "What about our working-class people?" she asks. "I don't want to live in a Third World country." Working people, she says, should be able to afford "a new car, a house. You shouldn't have to leave the car on the lawn because you can't afford that $45 part."

————

NOTES AND QUESTIONS

1. Wal–Mart as avatar of new economy. Simon Head notes the phenomenal success of Wal–Mart:

> Within the corporate world Wal–Mart's preeminence is not simply a matter of size. In its analysis of the growth of U.S. productivity, or output per worker, between 1995 and 2000—the years of the "new economy" and the high-tech bubble on Wall Street—the McKinsey Global Institute has found that just over half that growth took place in two sectors, retail and wholesale, where, directly or indirectly, Wal–Mart "caused the bulk of the productivity acceleration through ongoing managerial innovation that increased competition intensity and drove the diffusion of best practice." This is management-speak for Wal–Mart's aggressive use of information technology and its skill in meeting the needs of its customers.
>
> In its own category of "general merchandise," Wal–Mart has taken a huge lead in productivity over its competitors, a lead of 44 percent in 1987, 48 percent in 1995, and still 41 percent in 1999, even as competitors began to copy Wal–Mart's strategy. Thanks to the company's superior productivity, Wal–Mart's share of total sales among all the sellers of "general merchandise" rose from 9 percent in 1987 to 27 percent in 1995, and 30 percent in 1999, an astonishing rate of growth which recalls the rise of the Ford Motor Company nearly a century ago. McKinsey lists some of the leading causes of Wal–Mart's success. For example, its huge, ugly box-shaped buildings enable Wal–Mart "to carry a wider range of goods than competitors" and to "enjoy labor economies of scale."

McKinsey mentions Wal–Mart's "efficiency in logistics," which makes it possible for the company to buy in bulk directly from producers of everything from toilet paper to refrigerators, allowing it to dispense with wholesalers. McKinsey also makes much of the company's innovative use of information technology, for example its early use of computers and scanners to track inventory, and its use of satellite communications to link corporate headquarters in Arkansas with the nationwide network of Wal–Mart stores. Setting up and fine-tuning these tracking and distribution systems has been the special achievement of founder Sam Walton's (the "Wal" of Wal–Mart) two successors as CEOs, David Glass and the incumbent Lee Scott.

Simon Head, *Inside the Leviathan,* 51 N.Y. Rev. Books 80 (2004), *available at* http://www.nybooks.com/archives. Wal–Mart's success has also, however, crucially relied on its ability to keep wages and benefits low. Like Featherstone, Head argues for stronger and better enforced labor laws, asserting that "Wal–Mart has reached back beyond the New Deal to the harsh, abrasive capitalism of the 1920s." *Id.*

2. Wal–Mart and gender discrimination. In the summer of 2004, a federal district court certified a sex discrimination class action against Wal–Mart on behalf of 1.6 million women who had worked at Wal–Mart since December 26, 1998. The plaintiffs in *Dukes v. Wal–Mart,* 222 F.R.D. 137 (N.D. Cal. 2004), the largest private civil rights case in United States history, alleged that Wal–Mart discriminated against its female employees in making promotions, job assignments, pay decisions and training, and retaliated against women who complained about such practices. *See* http://www.walmartclass.com.

3. Markets in poverty. Many services as well as goods are targeted to the poverty market. As David Shipler describes in his book, *The Working Poor: Invisible in America* (2004), tax preparers, check-cashing outlets, credit card companies, and mortgage and other loan providers often market their services to poor people. Services to the poor, however, tend to cost more money than the same services to the middle-class or the wealthy. The "subprime" market is a lucrative one because the customers have few options, urgent need, and often little information about their rights. Shipler offers an example of how poverty costs money:

> Say you're short of cash, and the bills are piling up, along with some disconnection notices. Payday is two weeks away, and your phone and electricity will be shut off before then. The guy at the local convenience store, who has a booth for cashing checks, throws you a lifeline. If you need $100 now, you write him a check for $120, postdated by two weeks. He'll give you the $100 in cash today, hold your check until your wages are in your bank account, and then put the check through. Or you can give him the $120 in cash when you get it, and he'll return your check. Either way, 20 percent interest for two weeks equals 1.438 percent a day, or 521 percent annually. * * *

Furthermore, the loans are not technically loans in some states, because there's a check. And if a check bounces, more severe penalties apply than those for unrepaid loans. Borrowing $300, for instance, an Indiana woman paid a $30 fee and wrote a check for $330. When the check bounced, her bank and the payday loan establishment charged $80 in fees. Then the lender took her to court, won triple damages of $990, lawyer's fees of $150, and $60 in court costs. The total charge on the $300 loan: $1,310.

SHIPLER, THE WORKING POOR, *supra* at 18–19.

4.   Health care and bankruptcy. A recent study found that about half of personal bankruptcy filers interviewed cited "medical causes" as the reason for their filing bankruptcy. Among those whose illnesses led to bankruptcy, out-of-pocket costs averaged $11,854 since the start of illness; 75.7 percent had insurance at the onset of illness. David U. Himmelstein et al., *Market Watch: Illness and Injury as Contributors to Bankruptcy*, HEALTH AFFAIRS, Feb. 2, 2005, http://content.healthaffairs.org/cgi/content/full/hlthaff.w5.63/DC1. The authors of the study concluded that "Even middle-class insured families often fall prey to financial catastrophe when sick." *Id.*

5.   Downward mobility of the white-collar middle class in the financial crisis. Sustained unemployment following the financial collapse of 2008 has delivered persistent unemployment hovering at 10 percent in 2010. This unemployment pattern, unlike previous unemployment cycles, has produced downward mobility among college graduates. The financial crisis and the collapse of the housing bubble erased home equity, retirement savings, and put pressure on college opportunity for families dependent on home equity to finance college opportunity for their children.

Journalist Barbara Ehrenrich, captures the alienation and frustration relying on the same undercover technique she used to chronicle the experiences of low wage workers, when she worked as a white collar worker in the corporate sector. Her books, BAIT AND SWITCH: THE FUTILE PURSUIT OF THE AMERICAN DREAM (2005) (white collar workers) and NICKELED AND DIMED ON NOT GETTING BY IN AMERICA (2001) (blue collar workers).

———

Nanny Diaries and Other Stories: Imagining Immigrant Women's Labor in the Social Reproduction of American Families[1]

52, 809, 813, 814–22, 832–47 (2003).

■ MARY ROMERO

Wanted: One young woman to take care of four-year-old boy. Must be cheerful, enthusiastic, and selfless—bordering on masochistic. Must relish sixteen-hour shifts with a deliberately nap-deprived preschooler. Must love getting thrown up on, literally and figuratively, by everyone

———

[1]. For further discussion of the racial, national and class dimensions of the U.S. domestic labor market, see chapter 12 at pp. 934–936.

in his family. Must enjoy the delicious anticipation of ridiculously erratic pay. Mostly, must love being treated like fungus found growing out of employer's Hermes bag. Those who take it personally need not apply.

Introduction

Two former nannies employed on the Upper East Side of Manhattan offer this want advertisement as an illustration of employers' expectations and working conditions awaiting potential employees. Although it is a fictionalized account of their total six-year experience as nannies while attending college, Emma McLaughlin and Nicola Kraus's *The Nanny Diaries: A Novel* has spurred significant attention from the media. * * *
* * *

II. *The Nanny Diaries*: Reality or Fantasy?

Given the media attention and public discourse generated by the novel, it is worth asking the question: How representative is *The Nanny Diaries?*
* * *

Given the large number of undocumented immigrants and United States workers employed "off the books," workers with temporary or permanent visas, and the broad category that the Department of Labor and the Census classify as domestic service, precise numbers of domestics and nannies are difficult to obtain. Assessing the United States Bureau of Labor Statistics, Human Rights Watch estimates that 800,000 private household workers were officially recorded in 1998, of which 30% were immigrant women. Regions exporting the largest number of women to labor as domestic servants are Asia, Africa, Latin America, and Eastern Europe. Research conducted on domestics in the United States include immigrants from Latin America, the Caribbean, and the Philippines.

A distinctive characteristic of domestic service in the United States is the race and ethnic differences between employer and employee. The intersection of class, race, and ethnicity has been a prominent component to the study of African–American, Chicana and Japanese–American domestics. Racial distinctions remain a striking feature identifying caregivers from their charges and employers. Reflecting on the playground scene in Central Park depicted in *The Nanny Diaries*, one onlooker contrasted the faces of children and caretakers:

> There are also adults there, but curiously, the faces of the two groups (adults and children) don't match. For every white child in a stroller, there is a black woman leaning down, to guide a juice box into their mouth. If she isn't black, she is Hispanic or Asian. The women are the children's nannies. In many cases, they are stepping in for white parents, who are working full-time.

Apparent differences between native-born and immigrant women of color employed as maids and nannies are education and previous work experience. African–American, Chicana and Japanese–American women rarely have more than a high school education. A growing number of

Latina and Caribbean immigrants are high school and college graduates, and some have held white-collar positions in their homeland. Helma Lutz noted the international trend toward older and better educated third-world immigrant women in her survey of research on the globalization of domestic service. Unlike younger and single European immigrant women at the turn of the twentieth century, these women work to cope with financial crisis, to support families, and to educate their children. Thus, Nan's race, marital status, and citizenship are not characteristic of many women employed as nannies in the United States. With the exception of European women immigrating to the United States with J–1 visas to work as *au pairs* while pursuing their education, most immigrant women are not part-time college students. Nan's career trajectory is obviously destined for a professional or managerial position; whereas, older immigrant working mothers find little if any social mobility. For these women, domestic service is best described as a ghetto occupation rather than a bridging occupation.

Nan informs the reader of the existing continuum of childcare arrangements which she designates as three types of nanny gigs: (1) "a few nights a week for people who work all day and parent most nights;" (2) " 'sanity time' a few afternoons a week to a woman who mothers most days and nights;" and (3) "provide twenty-four/seven 'me time' to a woman who neither works nor mothers." Embedded in this classification are live-in positions (twenty-four hours a day, seven days a week) and day workers that might work solely for one employer full-time or for a number of employers. Employers make arrangements with agencies, franchises, collectives, or directly with the employee. Employees working on their own include some that are bonded and considered self-employed, and others working in the underground economy. However, the actual distinctions are reflected in the working conditions: hours of employment, wages, lack of benefits, and the inclusion of all household work alongside childcare.

Researchers and labor advocates reporting wages for immigrant women over the last decade point to the variability in the market. Grace A. Rosales found wages ranging from $100 to $400 a week in Los Angeles. In her study of immigrant women employed as domestics and nannies in Los Angeles, Pierrette Hondagneu–Sotelo states that many Latina live-in workers do not receive minimum wage, whereas day workers averaged a higher wage of $5.90 an hour. Doreen Mattingly interviewed current and former Latina domestics in San Diego during the same period and found the average hourly rate for day workers was $8.02 and for live-ins was $2.72. Rhacel Salazar Parreñas reports that Filipina women migrating to Los Angeles earned an average of $425 a week for providing elderly care and $350 a week for live-in housekeeping and childcare. In a survey conducted in 2000, the Center for the Childcare Workforce in Washington, D.C., found that half of childcare providers earned less than $4.82 an hour and worked 55 hours a week. Human Rights Watch reviewed 43 egregious cases among domestic workers with special visas in the United States, and found a median hourly rate of $2.14.

Variation in wages and working conditions among employees points to the hierarchical structure in domestic service reinforced by employers' preferences. Obviously the hierarchy was not completely lost by McLaughlin and Kraus. In a reading at a Barnes & Noble bookshop, Kraus acknowledged the privileged subject position she and her colleague experienced: "We were the Hermès bags of nannies. . . . [A]s white, middle-class and university-educated nannies they [she and McLaughlin] were able to avoid the seamier elements of the industry." Latina and Caribbean immigrants are more vulnerable in the labor market than European immigrants. Skills do appear to be taken into consideration under certain circumstances. For instance, in her study of language between nannies and children in Los Angeles, Patricia Baquedano–López concluded that speaking English and a high school education were assets that domestics used in their negotiations with employers.

McLaughlin and Kraus portray a typical day of nanny tasks as "spent schlepping Grayer to French class, music lessons, karate, swimming, school and play dates." Although consistent with the image of Maria Rainer, the governess that Captain Von Trapp hired to care for his children in the film *The Sound of Music*, most employers with a live-in nanny assign employees a wide range of household tasks. While the distinction between housekeepers and nannies is frequently used to distinguish workers employed primarily to care for children, housekeepers may occasionally be asked to assist in childcare and nannies may be expected to cook, wash dishes, "pick-up," and do other household work directly related to the care of children. A consistent complaint among nannies is the expectation that they do housework and cook, alongside caring for children. Distinctions between domestic workers or private household workers and nannies are blurred in the everyday reality of employees as they engage in a broad range of household and caregiving activities, including cleaning, cooking, laundry, nursing the sick, supervising, playing with children, and grocery shopping.

Obviously, the most lucrative and sought after positions are the ones that make a clear distinction between tasks and recognize employees' skills, expertise, and experience. Immigrant women, particularly those who are undocumented, are more likely to be hired for live-in, as well as day work, positions that do not have clearly defined job descriptions. These nannies are unlikely to have much authority over the children or in planning activities. Instead, they find themselves at the beck and call of children as they serve and wait on them. Given the number of immigrant women nannies that McLaughlin and Kraus saw in the park, it is not surprising that they wrote, "[E]very playground has at least one nanny getting the shit kicked out of her by an angry child." *San Francisco Chronicle* reporter Adair Lara differentiated job descriptions offered to non-immigrant women: "At the other end of the spectrum, a professional nanny often works weekends, engages the child in imaginative play, knows CPR. . . . She will want her hours guaranteed, will expect a bonus, and might be persnickety about doing more than the dishes and the baby's laundry."

Nan's life implies that work as a nanny is filled with new learning opportunities and adventures, from learning to cook exotic foods for Grayer to vacationing among the rich and famous. This depiction does not capture the overwhelming sense of isolation reported by immigrant women, particularly among live-in workers. Since Lucy Salmon's sociological study at the turn of the century, extreme isolation continues to be cited among live-in workers as one of the worst aspects of the job. Isolation from relatives, friends, and other domestic workers removes them from gaining resources to find employment elsewhere. Separation from their own children is frequently identified as a major force in developing strong emotional attachment to their charges. Domestics' loneliness is not countered by stimulating tasks. In the transformation of domestic labor from the unpaid work of mothers to low-wage work, physical demands are increased and more creative aspects are eliminated. The transformation from unpaid to paid childcare results in assigning immigrant nannies to the least pleasant tasks. Childcare advocates Suzanne W. Helburn and Barbara R. Bergmann describe the division as follows: "The parents try to reserve the more interesting child-rearing tasks for themselves. They do the storytelling and reading, supervise homework, and organize outings and parties in order to spend 'quality time' with their children."

Like the public discourse generated by the Nannygate scandals over the last decade, *The Nanny Diaries* examined the impact on employers and their children rather than on the employees and their children. Editorials and book reviews focus on employer rights to privacy, poor parenting, and the suffering and deprivation of "the poor little rich boy, Grayer." Since the novel's fictionalized couple who hired the nanny was portrayed as a cheating husband and an unemployed trophy wife, the stage is set against a public debate over the needs of working parents. Labor issues are contextualized as interpersonal gender relationships between women (and their competing expectations and emotions in doing "women's work") and the difficulty of employees identifying as a servant. Reference to immigrant nannies are curtailed to discussions concerning the impact that their limited English skills and cultural differences have on children under their care.

However, when immigrant women speak for themselves, the following list of labor issues are similar to the concerns expressed by workers in the United States: low wages, unpaid hours, lack of decent standards, absence of health insurance and other employee benefits, and constant supervision. In the case of live-in domestics, employer abuses include violations of their human rights. Grievances reported in Bridget Anderson and Philzacklea's international study that are also found in the United States include:

> denial of wages in cases of dismissal following trial or probation periods, refusal by employers to arrange legal resident status (for tax reasons, etc.); control and sexual harassment; pressure to do additional work (for friends and colleagues); excessive workloads, especially where in addition to caring for children and elderly people they are responsi-

ble for all other household chores; and finally the very intimate relationship between the domestic helpers and their employers.

Human Rights Watch cites the following additional employer abuses in the United States: "basic telephone privileges, prohibiting them from leaving employers' homes unaccompanied, and forbidding them to associate or communicate with friends and neighbors." "To prevent domestic workers from leaving exploitative employment situations, employers confiscate the workers' passports and threaten them with deportation if they flee. In the most severe cases of abuse, migrant domestic workers—both live-in and day workers—have reported instances of sexual assault, physical abuse, and rape." Health hazards posed by cleaning chemicals "causing everything from skin irritation and rashes to serious respiratory problems from inhaling toxic fumes" is another grievance reported by human rights and labor advocates.

* * *

IV.   IMMIGRANT NANNY CARE AND THE REPRODUCTION OF PRIVILEGE

Globalization of childcare is based on income inequality between women from poor countries providing low-wage care work for families in wealthier nations. Even with the low wages and variability in the market cited above, hiring a nanny is recognized as the most expensive childcare option. Researchers recognize this reality: "The grim truth is that some women's access to the high-paying, high-status professions is being facilitated through the revival of semi-indentured servitude. Put another way, one woman is exercising class and citizenship privilege to buy her easy way out of sex oppression." The largest number of domestic workers are located in areas of the country with the highest income inequality among women. In regions with minimal income inequality, the occupation is insignificant. Particular forms of domestic labor that affirm and enhance employers' status, shift the burden of sexism to low-wage women workers, and relegate the most physically difficult and dirty aspects of domestic labor. However, little attention has been given to the ways that privilege is reproduced through childcare arrangements and the significance that third-world immigrant women's labor plays in the reproduction of privilege.

Intensive and competitive mothering revolves around individuality, competition, and the future success of their children. Competition and individualism are values embedded in children's activities. Annette Lareau refers to this version of child rearing as "concerted cultivation" geared toward "deliberate and sustained effort to stimulate children's development and to cultivate . . . cognitive and social skills." Concerted cultivation aims to develop children's ability to reason by negotiating with parents and placing value on children's opinions, judgments, and observations. Family leisure time is dominated by organized children activities, such as sports, clubs, and paid lessons (e.g., dance, music, tennis). Most children's time is adult-structured rather than child-initiated play. "Play is not just play anymore. It involves the honing of 'large motor skills,' 'communication skills,' 'hand-eye coordination,' and the establishment of 'developmentally appropriate behavior.' "

Qualities of intensive and competitive mothering are at odds with demanding careers. Everyday practices of intensive mothering [require] immense emotional involvement, constant self-sacrificing, exclusivity, and a completely child-centered environment. These mothering activities are financially draining and time-consuming. Mothers with disposable income use commodities to fulfill areas of intensive and competitive mothering that they find themselves falling short of. In *The Mother Puzzle*, Judith D. Schwartz argues that advertising companies use guilt as significant child leverage:

> Companies who are marketing to our guilt inevitably start marketing the guilt itself in order to keep us shopping. This toy will help your child develop motor skills (implicit message: his motor skills will suffer without it). This line of clothing is made of the softest cotton (implicit message: other, less expensive fabrics may be abrasive).

By the 1990s, "babies and children were firmly entrenched as possessions that necessitated the acquisition of other commodities (and that became more valuable with further investment in goods and services)." Advertisers targeted the new "Skippies" market (school *k*ids with *i*ncome and *p*urchasing *p*ower). Quoting *People* magazine, Schwartz characterizes parents of these "gourmet children" as "rapaciously grabbing kudos for their kids with the same enterprise applied to creating fortunes on Wall Street." She suggests that, "Teaching values to our children has been replaced by building value into them ... by preparing them to compete and giving them what we think they need to do so."

Hiring a live-in immigrant worker is the most convenient childcare option for juggling the demands of intensive mothering and a career. Purchasing the caretaking and domestic labor of an immigrant [woman] commodificates reproductive labor and reflects, reinforces, and intensifies social inequalities. The most burdensome mothering activities (such as cleaning, laundry, feeding babies and children, and chauffeuring children to their various scheduled activities) are shifted to the worker. Qualities of intensive mothering, such a sentimental value, nurturing, and intense emotional involvement, are not lost when caretaking work is shifted to an employee. Employers select immigrant caretakers on the basis of perceived "warmth," "love for children," and "naturalness in mothering." Different racial and ethnic groups are stereotyped by employers as ideal employees for housework, childcare, or for live-in positions. Stereotyping is based on a number of individual characteristics—race, ethnicity, class, caste, education, religion, and linguistic ability—and results in a degree of "otherness" for all domestic servants. However, such a formalization of difference does not always put workers in the subordinate position, and employers' preferences can vary from place to place. Janet Henshall Momsen notes that, "Professionally-trained British nannies occupy an élite niche in Britain and North America." Interviewing employers in Los Angeles and New York City, Julia Wrigley observed Spanish-speaking nannies were identified by employers for their ability to broaden the cultural experience of their children, particularly in exposing them to a second language in the home.

Employers referenced the growing Latino population in their community and the long-term benefits of their children learning Spanish. However, the socialization to race and culture politics may be the most significant consequence of the current commodification of reproductive labor.

The primary mission of reproductive labor in contemporary mothering is to assure their children's place in society. This is partially accomplished through socialization into class, gender, sexual, ethnic and race hierarchies. Employment of immigrant women as caregivers contributes to this socialization. Reinforced by their parents' conceptualization of caretaking as a "labor of love," children learn a sense of entitlement to receiving affection from people of color that is detached from their own actions. Children learn to be "consumers of care" rather than providers of caregiving. Caretaking without parental authority does not teach children reciprocal respect but rather teaches that the treatment of women of color as "merely means, and not as ends in themselves." The division of labor between mother and live-in caretaker domestic stratifies components of reproductive labor and equates burdensome, manual and basic maintenance labor with immigrant women of color. This gendered division of labor serves to teach traditional patriarchal privilege. Privilege is learned as they acquire a sense of entitlement to having a domestic worker always on call to meet their needs.

Stratified reproductive labor of a live-in immigrant domestic assures "learned helplessness and class prejudice in the child," and teaches "[dependence], aggressiveness, and selfishness." Systems of class, racial, ethnic, gender and citizenship domination are taught to children by witnessing "the arbitrary and capricious interaction of parents and servants or if they are permitted to treat domestic servants in a similar manner." As children move from their homes located in class (and frequently racially) segregated neighborhoods to schools (also likely to be segregated), power relationships and the larger community's class and racial etiquette are further reinforced. "As care is made into a commodity, women with greater resources in the global economy can afford the best-quality care for their family." If mothering is directed toward assuring their child's social and economic status in society—a society that is racist, capitalist, and patriarchal—then her goals are strengthened by employing a low wage, full-time or live-in immigrant woman. Conditions under which immigrant women of color are employed in private homes is structured by systems of privilege and, consequently, employers' children are socialized into these norms and values.

V.   Prolongation of Immigrant Women Subordination

Paid reproductive labor in the United States is structured along local, national and international inequalities, positioning third-world immigrant women as the most vulnerable workers. Careworkers are sorted by the degree of vulnerability and privilege. Consequently, paid domestic labor is not only structured around gender but is stratified by race and citizenship status, relegating the most vulnerable worker to the least favorable working conditions and placing the most privileged in the best positions. A major initiative in the American childcare movement is addressing low wages in the childcare industry. However, the plight of live-in caregivers and immigrant women as a specific group is rarely addressed. The solution of hiring a live-in domestic, used by a relatively privileged group, is a component of reproductive labor in the United States, and serves to intensify inequalities between women: first, by reinforcing childcare as a private rather than public responsibility; and second, by reaping the benefits gained by the impact of globalization and restructuring on third-world women. The globalization of domestic service contributes to the reproduction of inequality between nations in transnational capitalism and cases reported of domestic servitude is increasingly characterized as global gender apartheid.

Devaluation of immigrant women in the international division of labor begins in the home as unpaid labor; then is further devalued in the segregated labor forces within third-world countries used by wealthier nations for cheap labor. Women are relegated to low-wage factory work in textiles and electronics industries with no opportunities available for better-paid positions. Migrating and working as domestics becomes the primary strategy for sustaining households for both poor and middle-class women. The demand for low-wage migrant workers expands the pool of cheap labor that unemployment and welfare regulations are unable to maintain. Theorists have traditionally argued that women's unpaid domestic labor in the home served as a reserve labor force. Applying this qualification to immigrant domestic workers, the employment of third-world women becomes a significant source for reproducing a labor reserve, similar to the function of the unemployed and underemployed. Saskia Sassen states this proposition in the following question: "Does domestic service—at least in certain locations—become one of the few alternatives and does it, then, function, as a privatized mechanism for social reproduction and maintenance of a labor reserve?" The transnational export of women from global south to the rich industrialized countries of the north has resulted in promoting domestics as a major "export product." Transnational division of labor is determined "simultaneously by global capitalism and systems of gender inequality in both sending and receiving countries of migration."

A prominent feature of globalized reproductive labor is commodification. Parreñas argues that, "Commodified reproductive labor is not only low-paid work but declines in market value as it gets passed down the international transfer of caretaking." However, Anderson argues that the commodification process in globalization is not limited to the labor but is extended to the worker. In her work on the global politics of domestic labor, she points out that employers "openly stipulate that they want a particular type *person* justifying this demand on the grounds that they will be working in the home." Having hired the preferred racialized domestic caretaker on the basis of personal characteristics rather than former experience or skills, the emotional labor required is not recognized by the employer but the worker's caring "brings with it no mutual obligations, no entry into a community, no 'real' human relations, only money."

Employers' hiring preferences for employees who are a particular race, ethnicity, and nationality contributes to the hierarchical chain of domestic caretakers. Hondagneu–Sotelo notes that African Americans are no longer the preferred employee in Los Angeles homes because [they] are portrayed as "bossy" and with "terrifying images associated with young black men." Similar images are applied to Caribbean women in New York and are cautioned against coming "across in interviews as being in any way aggressive." Latina immigrants in Los Angeles are perceived as "responsible, trustworthy, and reliable" workers as well as "exceptionally warm, patient, and loving mothers." In the case of Filipina women, Dan Gatmaytan argues that their labor is distinctively featured in international division of labor as "docile and submissive," and thus, ideally packaged to be imported "by other countries for jobs their own citizens will not perform and for wages domestic citizens would not accept." Parreñas's findings suggest that employers view Filipinas as providing a "higher-quality" service because they speak English and generally have a higher education than Latina immigrants.

However, without state regulations of labor and immigration policies, employers' preferences are irrelevant in the racialization of reproductive labor in the United States. Joy Mutanu Zarembka, director of the Campaign for Migrant Domestic Workers' Rights, argues that the estimated four thousand special visas issued annually for third-world immigrant women contributes to commodification of these workers into a "maid to order" in the United States. Three visas perpetuating the subordination of immigrant women of color as live-in domestic workers are:

A–3 visas to work for ambassadors, diplomats, consular officers, public ministers, and their families; G–5 visas to work for officers and employees of international organizations or of foreign missions to international organizations and their families; and B–1 visas to accompany U.S. citizens who reside abroad but are visiting the United States or assigned to the United States temporarily for no more than four years, or foreign nations with nonimmigrant status in the United States.

In contrast to special visas given primarily to third-world immigrant women, the J–1 visa is increasingly used to bring young and middle-class European immigrant women as nannies or *au pairs* with "educational and cultural exchange" their primary purpose. Under this visa, each nanny receives an orientation session and is placed in geographical locations near other nannies. After her placement, she attends an orientation session and "receives information on community resources, educational opportunities and contacts for a local support network." Counselors have monthly sessions with each employer and nanny to "report any problems and resolve disputes." "In contrast, with the G–5, A–1 and B–1 domestic worker programs, there are no official orientations, no information, no contact numbers, no counselors, and no educational programs. In practice, as well, there is often no freedom—many are systematically (though illegally) forbidden from contacting the outside world."

Human Rights Watch further asserts that special visas intensify workers' vulnerability to abuse and facilitate the violation of other human rights. Procedures, guidelines, laws, and regulations governing special domestic worker visas construct circumstances that tolerate and conceal employer abuses, and restrict workers' rights. Among the problems cited by Human Rights Watch are the lack of INS follow-up monitoring or investigations to verify employer compliance with employment contracts, and the Department of Labor's lack of involvement with administrating these visas. Consequently, no governmental agency is responsible for enforcing contracts. Zarembka asserts that the secrecy of the whereabouts of G–5, A–3 and B–1 workers makes "them some of the most vulnerable and easily exploited sectors of the American workforce" and violation of human rights is silenced by their invisibility. In addition to low wages, long hours, and the lack of both privacy and benefits that are common among live-in conditions, immigrant women experience other abuses. They include passport confiscation, limited freedom of movement and ability to communicate with others, employer threats of deportation, assault and battery, rape, servitude, torture, and trafficking. Changing employers under live-in conditions has always been difficult for workers, and for women with employment-based visas, they are faced with weighing "respect for their own human rights and maintaining their legal immigration status." For similar reasons, women are reluctant to report abuse because they fear losing their jobs, deportation, unfamiliarity with the American legal system, social and cultural isolation, and fear that "their retaliation powerful employers will retaliate against their families in their countries of origin."

Exclusion from a number of labor policies contribute to the hardships immigrant women experience as live-in domestics. They are excluded from overtime provisions provided in the Fair Labor Standard Act, from the right to organize, strike, and bargain collectively in the National Labor Relations Act, and from regulations in the Occupational Safety and Health Act. "In practice, too, live-in domestic workers are rarely covered by Title VII protections against sexual harassment in the workplace, as Title VII only applies to employers with fifteen or more workers."

Third-world immigrant domestics experience first hand the inequalities of caregiving as they provide labor for parents in rich industrialized countries while leaving their own children. Sarah Blaffer Hrdy equates mothers leaving their children with relatives in their homelands to European infants left in foundling homes or sent to wet nurses during the eighteenth century: "Solutions differ, but the tradeoffs mothers make, and the underlying emotions and mental calculations, remain the same." Anderson notes that immigrant women's care for their children is limited "in the fruits of hard labour, in remittances, rather than in the cuddles and 'quality time' that provide so much of the satisfaction of care." Transnational mothering cannot provide the "physical closeness, seen as healthy and 'normal' in the Western upbringing of a child, are not given, because most of the women are not allowed to take their children with them." These conditions reduce mothering to the basic function of economic support. In her research on Filipina women in Rome and Los Angeles,

Parrenas observed the impact of economic ties rather than affective ties between mother and child departed from each over a long period of time. The use of material good, financial assistance, and school tuition result in commodifying family relationships and motherhood. Inequalities in the distribution and quality of domestic labor and caregiving is a cost borne by the children of live-in workers. The absence of retirement benefits pension assures that workers will not be able to contribute financially to their children's future, but rather will need their assistance.

VI. CONCLUSION

Before the September 11 attacks, the Federation for American Immigration Reform (FAIR), Patrick Buchanan, Pete Wilson and others vilified immigrants as the cause of all problems in the United States. Homeland security has further fanned the flames of xenophobia and support for vilifying immigrants. Yet, within the intimacy of many American homes, immigrant women (primarily Latina and Caribbean immigrants) continue to provide assisted reproductive labor that fulfills the basic tasks of maintaining families of dual career couples and contribute to middle-upper- and upper-class lifestyles. Popular culture functions to normalize the hiring of immigrant women by depicting domestic service as a bridging occupation that offers social mobility, opportunities to learn English, and other cultural skills that assist in the assimilation process. The characterization of nannies and private household workers in *The Nanny Diaries*, as well as in films and sitcoms, serves to reduce the significance of immigrant women in fulfilling childcare needs in the United States and to erase issues of employee rights from the American imagination. Instead, employers are classified as good or bad: good employers who are benevolent and provide immigrant women with a modernizing experience, or bad employers who are rich couples ignoring their children. Popular culture does not contextualize paid reproductive labor. Economic, political and legal structures surrounding the migration of Latina, Caribbean and Filipina women are ignored along with the circumstances that relegate their labor to low-wage dead-end jobs. Consequently, we can maintain our illusions of Latina domestics as sexually out of control and utterly colorful spitfire, the self-deprecating accented smart-mouthed, or the rosary-praying maid. We can continue to see these images and sing out, "Yes, that's what maids are like."

     * * *

Centering immigration on questions of "belonging" (and related concepts, e.g., assimilation, ethnic differences, and ethnic loyalty) blinds us to inquiries into the role of immigration in sustaining systems of privilege and perpetuating myths and ideologies central to national identity. Immigration and labor regulations reproduce race, class, gender and citizenship inequalities and privileges. In the case of immigrant women employed as private household workers or caregivers, the social reproduction of inequalities begins in the employer's home. Managing the contradictions of intimacy and vilification of immigrants through cultural images that falsify employee-employer relationships, allows Americans to reap the benefits of retaining a vulnerable labor force unprotected from exploitation while arguing humanitarian positions. The popular version of nannies depicted in *The Nanny Diaries* assists in normalizing privilege and erases issues of economic injustice. Our complacency in the subordination of immigrant women is once again obtained by our fascination with chatty gossip on sex, drugs, money, and family values of the wealthy on Park Avenue. Moreover, our illusion that there is no greater state of being than Americans is further enhanced by denying the privileges gained by third-world assisted social reproduction.

The Hidden Injuries of Class

79–87 (1972).

■ RICHARD SENNETT & JONATHAN COBB

Josiah Watson Grammar School is an old red-brick building with a simple but well-kept playground. It is a large school, in the midst of an urban neighborhood of mostly three-decker houses. In the community surrounding the school live groups of Irish, Italian, and old-stock New Englanders, but almost all are manual laborers. The median family income in the neighborhood is about $8000—neither poor nor affluent.

The rooms at the Watson School evoke the interiors of the children's homes: old, rather run down, and yet clean, almost austere. In each schoolroom the only decorations consist of an American flag, a bound set of maps, and a plaque with the Pledge of Allegiance. The school desks are new—tubular steel legs holding up flat wooden boxes. In them, children's supplies are neatly arranged, even for the littlest children. The teachers take a certain pride in this, but they apologize to the visitor for the tops scratched with the obscene words, drawings, and initials that children always seem to inflict on such objects.

The classes in Watson School, even as low as the second grade, jolt the outsider who has lost touch with the institutional life of children. Everything that goes on in the second-grade class, from reading preparedness to play with toys, is directed by the teacher. She takes great pains to see that the children act "good and proper." The visitor who is aware of his own presence in these classrooms at first thinks this show of discipline, this constant commanding and watching, is the teacher's response to that presence. After the teacher relaxes and forgets he is there, however, the discipline continues. It varies among the teachers from harsh to loving; but all those in charge of classrooms at the Watson School act like conductors who must bring potentially unruly mobs of musicians under their direction. As the principal remarks, "It is by establishing authority that we make this school work."

In Watson School, teachers restrict the freedom of the children because these figures of authority have a peculiar fear of the children. It is the mass who seem to the teachers to threaten classroom order, by naughty or unruly behavior; only a few are seen as having "good habits" or the right attitude. As one teacher explained, "These children come from simple laborers' homes where the parents don't understand the value of education." Yet in the early grades the observer noticed few examples of disruptive behavior. He sensed among the six-and seven-year olds a real desire to please, to accept the teacher's control and be accepted by her. One pathetic incident, although extreme, stands out. In the middle of a reading-preparedness class, a child wet his pants because he was absorbed in his lesson. "What can you do with children like that?" the teacher later remarked in a tone of disgust.

What happens is that the teachers act on their expectations of the children in such a way as to *make* the expectations become reality. Here is how the process worked in one second-grade class at Watson School—unusual in that it was taught by a young man. In this class there were two children, Fred and Vincent, whose appearance was somewhat different from that of the others: their clothes were no fancier than the other children's, but they were pressed and seemed better kept; in a class of mostly dark Italian children, these were the fairest-skinned. From the outset the teacher singled out these two children, implying that they most closely approached his own standards for classroom performance. He never praised them openly by comparison to the other children, but a message that they were different, were better, was spontaneously conveyed. As the observer watched the children play and work over the course of the school year, he noticed these two boys becoming more serious, more solemn, as the months passed. Obedient and never unruly from the first, by the end of the year they were left alone by the other children.

By then they were also doing the best work in the class. The other children had picked up the teacher's hidden cues that their performance would not be greeted with as much enthusiasm as the work of these two little boys. "It's not true of the other children that they generally have less potential," the teacher remarked. "It's a question of not developing their ability like Fred and Vincent. I know you're right, I tend to encourage them more despite myself, but I—it's obvious to me these little boys are going to make something of themselves."

In the Watson School, by the time the children are ten or eleven the split between the many and the few who are expected to "make something of themselves" is out in the open; the aloofness developing in the second grade has become open hostility by the sixth. Among the boys, this hostility is expressed by images which fuse sex and status. Boys like Fred and Vincent are described by the "ordinary" students as effeminate and weak, as "suck-ups." The kids mean by this both that the Freds and Vincents are getting somewhere in school because they are so docile, and that only a homosexual would be so weak; the image of a "suck-up" crystallizes this self-demeaning, effeminate behavior that to them marks off a student whom the institution can respect.

What has happened, then, is that these children have directed their anger at their schoolmates who are rewarded as individuals rather than at the institution which is withholding recognition of them. Indeed, the majority of boys in the fifth and sixth grades are often not consciously in conflict with the school at all. Something more complex is happening to them.

These "ordinary" boys in class act as though they were serving time, as though schoolwork and classes had become something to wait out, a blank space in their lives they hope to survive and then leave. Their feeling, apparently, is that when they get out, get a job and some money, *then* they will be able to begin living. It is not so much that they are bored in school—many in Watson School like their classes. It is rather that they have lost any expectation that school will help them, that this experience will change them or help them grow as human beings.

One teacher in this school, an enthusiastic young woman who liked to work with "ordinary" students, said her greatest problem was convincing the students that they could trust her. The other teachers and the principal disapprove of her because she runs her class in an informal manner. They feel she lets the students "get away with anything," "that she can't keep discipline." Permissiveness is a vice, order a necessity, in the minds of the other teachers; they believe that most of their charges, due to family class background and past school performances, will resist following the rules which to an educated adult seem so logical and beneficial. It is not that these teachers are intentionally mean, but that they unwittingly set in motion in the classroom a vicious circle that produces exactly the kind of behavior they expect.

There is a counterculture of dignity that springs up among these ordinary working-class boys, a culture that seeks in male solidarity what cannot be found in the suspended time that comprises classroom experience. This solidarity also sets them off from the "suck-ups." Hanging around together, the boys share their incipient sexual exploits, real and imagined; sex becomes a way to compete within the group. What most cements them as a group, however, is the breaking of rules—smoking, drinking, or taking drugs together, cutting classes. Breaking the rules is an act "nobodies" can share with each other. This counterculture does not come to grips with the labels their teachers have imposed on these kids; it is rather an attempt to create among themselves badges of dignity that those in authority can't destroy.

A full circle: outsider observers—parents, teachers, and others—who see only the external aspects of this counterculture, are confirmed in their view that "hanging around" is destructive to a child's self-development. Dignity in these terms exacts a toll by the standards of the outer world.

The division of children, in schools like Watson, into groups with a shared sense of loyalty and individuals alone but "getting somewhere," characterizes many levels of education; it is not something unique to, say, college-bound youth as opposed to vocational school boys. Studies of trade schools show the same phenomenon occurring: boys who are good at car mechanics in school start to feel cut off from others, even though the possession of those skills might make them admired by their less-skilled peers outside of school. It is an institutional process that makes the difference, a question of mere toleration versus active approval from those in power.

The drama played out in the Watson School has as its script the assigning and the wearing of badges of ability like those described earlier, worn by adults. The teachers cast the Freds and Vincents into the role of Andrew Carnegie's virtuous man. Ability will make these children into individuals, and as individuals they will rise in social class. The mass find themselves in a role similar to that which Lipset assigns to adult workers: their class background allegedly limits their self-development, and the counterculture of compensatory respect they create reinforces, in a vicious circle, the judgments of the teachers.

The teacher has the *power* to limit the freedom of development of his or her students through this drama. But why is he or she moved to act in this repressive way? This question is really two questions: it is first a matter of a teacher legitimizing in his own mind the power he holds, and second, a matter of the students taking that power as legitimate.

The teachers are in a terrible existential dilemma. It is true that they are "prejudiced" against most of their students; it is also true that they, like all human beings, want to believe in the dignity of their own work, no matter how difficult the circumstances in which they have to work seem to them. If a teacher believed that every single student would perpetually resist him, he would have no reason to go on teaching—his power in the classroom would be empty. A teacher needs at least a responsive few in order to feel he has a *reason* to possess power. The few will confirm to him that his power to affect other people is real, that he can truly do good. To sort out two classes of ability, then, in fear of the "lower" class of students, is to create a meaningful image of himself as an authority rather than simply a boss.

It is true that an analysis at this level of teachers, or other power figures dealing with working-class people, is by itself inadequate. A teacher may be having an existential crisis, but that doesn't explain why images of social class and classes of ability have come to fuse in his mind, nor does it explain how useful, how convenient, this crisis of self-legitimacy is in keeping the present class structure going. Still, it is important to keep before ourselves the experiential reality facing a person who has power over others. The teachers at Watson did not think of themselves as tools of capitalism, or even as repressive. They felt they had to legitimize their own work's dignity in the face of working-class students; and making a moral hierarchy on the basis of ability—however artificially and unjustifiably— was the natural means they used.

The perceptions the children had of the teachers similarly concerned not their power, but their legitimacy.

The observer is playing marbles with Vinny, a third-grader, described by his teacher as an "unexceptional average student who tolerates school," and Vinny begins absentmindedly to arrange the marbles in sets by color.

The observer points out to him that he is doing something like what the teacher had asked him to do in arithmetic hour and he hadn't then been able to do. Vinny replies, "I didn't want to give her no trouble"—an answer the observer notes without, at the time, understanding what Vinny meant. In a class on grammar, Stephanie gives a past participle incorrectly; the teacher asks her to try again, but while she is thinking, one of the bright children interrupts with the right answer. The teacher—the experimental and "permissive" woman already described—tells the bright child to shut up and gives Stephanie another answer to work out. Stephanie looks at her in total surprise, wondering why the teacher should still care about whether *she* can learn to do it, if the right answer has already been provided. Max, an obnoxious fifth-grade bully, has somehow formed an interest in writing doggerel rhymes. During a composition hour he reads one, but when he finishes, the teacher makes no reply, merely smiles and calls on the next pupil. Asked later how he felt, Max looks a little crestfallen and says with characteristic grace, "Lookit, shithead, she ain't got time to waste on me."

NOTES AND QUESTIONS

1. "Globalization" at top and bottom of economy. Saskia Sassen argues that "globalization" has produced both transnational marginalized labor classes and transnational privileged classes: while the elite of "global cities" such as New York, Hong Kong, and Paris are increasingly inter-twined through networks of education and training, the "underclass" in such cities are also intertwined, through networks of migration and the demand for low-end service work. Saskia Sassen, *Toward a Feminist Analytics of the Global Economy,* 4 IND. J. GLOBAL LEGAL STUD. 7 (1996). Sassen argues that migration (legal and illegal), which is often treated as only a problem for the government sector to be solved through immigration law, should be seen as intimately connected to trade policy and economic policy more generally.

How might the increasing income and wealth inequality brought about by globalization affect women as a group? Sassen is hopeful that the globalizing economy, as it pulls more women into wage work, will empower them within their families and in the public sector. *Id.* at 27. At the same time, she acknowledges that women are "constituted as an invisible and disempowered class of workers in the service of the strategic sectors constituting the global economy." *Id.* at 26.

2. Modern-day slavery. The very lowest caste of contemporary workers is made up of those whose labor power is forcibly expropriated by others. Kevin Bales argues that slavery is alive and well today, although it takes different legal and social forms than the "old" slavery:

> *My best estimate of the number of slaves in the world today is 27 million.*

This number is much smaller than the estimates put forward by some activists, who give a range as high as 200 million, but it is the number I feel I can trust * * *. The biggest part of that 27 million, perhaps 15 to 20 million, is represented by *bonded labor* in India, Pakistan, Bangladesh, and Nepal. Bonded labor or debt bondage happens when people give themselves into slavery as security against a loan or when they inherit a debt from a relative * * *. Otherwise slavery tends to be concentrated in Southeast Asia, northern and western Africa, and parts of South America (but there are some slaves in almost every country in the world, including the United States, Japan, and many European countries). There are more slaves alive today than all the people stolen from Africa in the time of the transatlantic slave trade. Put another way, today's slave population is greater than the population of Canada, and six times greater than the population of Israel.

These slaves tend to be used in simple, nontechnological, and traditional work. The largest group work in agriculture. But slaves are used in many other kinds of labor: brickmaking, mining or quarrying, prostitution, gem working and jewelry making, cloth and carpet making, and domestic service; they clear forests, make charcoal, and work in shops. Much of this work is aimed at local sale and consumption, but slave-made goods reach into homes around the world. Carpets, fireworks, jewelry, and metal goods made by slave labor, as well as grains, sugar, and other foods harvested by slaves, are imported directly to North America and Europe. In addition, large international corporations, acting through subsidiaries in the developing world, take advantage of slave labor to improve their bottom line and increase the dividends to their shareholders.

Kevin Bales, Disposable People: New Slavery in the Global Economy 8–9 (1999).

Bales argues that the new slavery differs from the old slavery in several ways. Among these differences are the following: slaveholders no longer assert legal ownership over their slaves; slaveholders do not contribute to the maintenance costs of their slaves; ethnic differences between slaveholding and slave classes are less important than they were in, for example, American slavery; slaves produce very high profits; the relationship between slaveholder and slave tends to be short-term rather than long-term; and there is a surplus rather than a shortage of potential slaves. *Id.* at 15.

The International Labor Organization defines "forced labor" as "all work or service which is exacted from any person under the menace of any penalty and for which the said person has not offered himself voluntarily." International Labor Organization, Convention Concerning Forced Labor (No. 29). Using this definition, a team of researchers at the University of California at Berkeley, working with a nonprofit antislavery organization, examined the nature and scope of forced labor in the United States from January 1998 to December 2003. According to their report:

Over the past five years, forced labor operations have been reported in at least ninety U.S. cities. These operations tend to thrive in states with large populations and sizable immigrant communities, such as California, Florida, New York, and Texas—all of which are transit routes for international travelers.

Forced labor is prevalent in five sectors of the U.S. economy: prostitution and sex services (46%), domestic service (27%), agriculture (10%), sweatshop/factory (5%), and restaurant and hotel work (4%) * * *. Forced labor persists in these sectors because of low wages, lack of regulation and monitoring of working conditions, and a high demand for cheap labor. These conditions enable unscrupulous employers and criminal networks to gain virtually complete control over workers' lives.

HUMAN RIGHTS CENTER & FREE THE SLAVES: FORCED LABOR IN THE UNITED STATES 1 (2004), *available at* http://www.hrcberkeley.org/download/hiddenslaves_report.pdf. (posted September 2004) (last visited, Mar. 6, 2005). The researchers estimated that approximately 10,000 people are working as forced laborers in the United States at any given time. *Id.*, at 10.

In the United States, slavery and human trafficking are subject to the federal Victims of Trafficking and Violence Protection Act of 2000, § 107, 22 U.S.C. § 7105 (2004). The act, among other things, establishes mandatory restitution from convicted traffickers, and an amendment allows survivors to sue their captors for civil damages for violations of the statute. *See* Trafficking Victims Protection Reauthorization Act of 2003, 18 U.S.C. § 1595 (2004) (civil damages provision). The act also provides social services and immigration status to victims of a "severe form of trafficking" who cooperate with law enforcement to prosecute the traffickers.

3. Women, prostitution, and sex work: abolitionists versus labor activists. Feminists have long argued over whether prostitution and other forms of sex work should be abolished as forms of violence against women, or legalized and regulated as just another kind of labor. Jane Larson argues that the dichotomy is unhelpful and that prostitution, like sweatshop labor, child labor, and various forms of bonded and indentured labor, should be examined more closely to help us think more generally about what kinds of labor are acceptable and why:

Instead of fruitless debates about the "essential nature" of the commodity relation of prostitution, I urge instead a common project aimed at defining the material, moral, and legal differences between free and unfree labor, describing with empirical depth and range what conditions of work characterize commercial sex in its various forms and locales, and measuring the sex industry against the free labor standard. What is force and compulsion in the sex labor setting? Is the definition of force such that the exchange of money refutes the claim of compulsion, or can the liberal concern for substantive freedom in labor relations translate into international standards? What working conditions render prostitution a per se unacceptably exploitative practice for children? Is it different for adults? Why or why not? What kinds of discrimination on the basis of sex or race are unacceptable? Does the demographic constitution of the market for sexual labor demonstrate such discrimination? If prostitution is one of women's best economic options, how does this shape other economic opportunities for women? Does female prostitution violate the equality ideal?

Jane E. Larson, *Prostitution, Labor, and Human Rights,* 37 U.C. DAVIS L. REV. 673, 698–99 (2004).

4. Public education and construction of failure. Cobb and Sennett were concerned primarily with the education and socialization of the sons of white working class "ethnic" immigrants. Other scholars have found that public education similarly sets up African American and Latino/a working class children, especially boys, to fail. For example, Theresa Glennon observes:

> First, African American boys are much more likely to be identified as disabled or delinquent than other children, including African American girls. Second, they are more likely than other children to be placed in educational, mental health, and juvenile justice programs that exert greater external control and deliver fewer services despite identified needs. Third, these negative experiences lead African American boys to stay away from or exit these institutional settings.

Theresa Glennon, *Knocking Against the Rocks: Evaluating Institutional Practices and the African American Boy,* 5 J. HEALTH CARE L. & POL'Y 10, 11 (2002). Glennon argues that these disparities are a result of racism.

Sociologist John Ogbu found another dynamic among African American children similar to that identified by Sennett and Cobb: black students both underperform and pressure one another to underperform by associating school success with "acting white." Signithia Fordham & John U. Ogbu, *Black Students' School Success: Coping with the "Burden of Acting White,"* 18 URB. REV. 176 (1986). Ogbu and Fordham's findings have been controversial in African American communities.

––––––––

The Overworked American: The Unexpected Decline of Leisure

17–24 (1991).

■ JULIET B. SCHOR

Time squeeze has become big news. In summer 1990, the premiere episode of Jane Pauley's television show, "Real Life," highlighted a single father whose computer job was so demanding that he found himself at 2:00 A.M. dragging his child into the office. A Boston-area documentary featured the fourteen-to sixteen-hour workdays of a growing army of moonlighters. CBS's "Forty–Eight Hours" warned of the accelerating pace of life for everyone from high-tech business executives (for whom there are only two types of people—"the quick and the dead") to assembly workers at Japanese-owned automobile factories (where a car comes by every sixty seconds). Employees at fast-food restaurants, who serve in twelve seconds, report that the horns start honking if the food hasn't arrived in fifteen. Nineteen-year-olds work seventy-hour weeks, children are "penciled" into their parents' schedules, and second-graders are given "half an hour a day to unwind" from the pressure to get good grades so they can get into a good college. By the beginning of the 1990s, the time squeeze had become a national focus of attention, appearing in almost all the nation's major media outlets. * * *

The time squeeze surfaced with the young urban professional. These high achievers had jobs that required sixty, eighty, even a hundred hours a week. On Wall Street, they would regularly stay at the office until midnight or go months without a single day off. Work consumed their lives. And if they weren't working, they were networking. They power-lunched, power-exercised, and power-married. As the pace of life accelerated, time became an ever-scarcer commodity, so they used their money to buy more of it. Cooking was replaced by gourmet frozen foods from upscale delis. Eventually the "meal" started disappearing, in favor of "grazing." Those who could afford it bought other people's time, hiring surrogates to shop, write their checks, or even just change a light bulb. They cut back on sleep and postponed having children. ("Can you carry a baby in a briefcase?" queried one Wall Street executive when she was asked about having kids.)

High-powered people who spend long hours at their jobs are nothing new. Medical residents, top corporate management, and the self-employed have always had grueling schedules. But financiers used to keep bankers' hours, and lawyers had a leisured life. Now bankers work like doctors, and lawyers do the same. A former Bankers Trust executive remembers that "somebody would call an occasional meeting at 8 A.M. Then it became the regular 8 o'clock meeting. So there was the occasional 7 A.M. meeting.... It just kept spreading." On Wall Street, economic warfare replaced the clubhouse atmosphere—and the pressure forced the hours up. As women and new ethnic groups were admitted into the industry, competition for the plum positions heightened—and the hours went along. Twenty-two-year-olds wear beepers as they squeeze in an hour for lunch or jogging at the health club.

What happened on Wall Street was replicated throughout the country in one high-income occupation after another. Associates in law firms competed over who could log more billable hours. Workaholics set new standards of survival. Even America's sleepiest corporations started waking up; and when they did, the corporate hierarchies found themselves coming in to work a little earlier and leaving for home a little later. As many companies laid off white-collar people during the 1980s, those who remained did more for their monthly paycheck. A study of "downsizings" in auto-related companies in the Midwest found that nearly half of the two thousand managers polled said they were working harder than two years earlier.

At cutting-edge corporations, which emphasize commitment, initiative, and flexibility, the time demands are often the greatest. "People who work for me should have phones in their bathrooms," says the CEO from one aggressive American company. Recent research on managerial habits reveals that work has become positively absorbing. When a deadline approached in one corporation, "people who had been working twelve-hour days and Saturdays started to come in on Sunday, and instead of leaving at midnight, they would stay a few more hours. Some did not go home at all, and others had to look at their watches to remember what day it was." The recent growth in small businesses has also contributed to overwork. When Dolores Kordek started a dental insurance company, her strategy for survival was to work harder than the competition. So the office was open from 7 A.M. to 10 P.M. three hundred and sixty-five days a year. And she was virtually always in it.

This combination of retrenchment, economic competition, and innovative business management has raised hours substantially. One poll of senior executives found that weekly hours rose during the 1980s, and vacation time fell. Other surveys have yielded similar results. By the end of the decade, overwork at the upper echelons of the labor market had become endemic—and its scale was virtually unprecedented in living memory.

If the shortage of time had been confined to Wall Street or America's corporate boardrooms, it might have remained just a media curiosity. The number of people who work eighty hours a week and bring home—if they ever get there—a six-figure income is very small. But while the incomes of these rarefied individuals were out of reach, their schedules turned out to be downright common. As Wall Street waxed industrious, the longer schedules penetrated far down the corporate ladder, through middle management, into the secretarial pool, and even onto the factory floor itself. Millions of ordinary Americans fell victim to the shortage of time.

The most visible group has been women, who are coping with a double load—the traditional duties associated with home and children and their growing responsibility for earning a paycheck. With nearly two-thirds of adult women now employed, and a comparable fraction of mothers on the job, it's no surprise that many American women find themselves operating in overdrive. Many working mothers live a life of perpetual motion, effectively holding down two full-time jobs. They rise in the wee hours of the morning to begin the day with a few hours of laundry, cleaning, and other housework. Then they dress and feed the children and send them off to school. They themselves then travel to their jobs. The three-quarters of employed women with full-time positions then spend the next eight and a half hours in the workplace.

At the end of the official workday, it's back to the "second shift"—the duties of housewife and mother. Grocery shopping, picking up the children, and cooking dinner take up the next few hours. After dinner there's clean-up, possibly some additional housework, and, of course, more child care. Women describe themselves as "ragged," "bone-weary," "sinking in quicksand," and "busy every waking hour." For many, the workday rivals those for which the "satanic mills" of the Industrial Revolution grew justly infamous: twelve-or fourteen-hour stretches of labor. By the end of the decade, Ann Landers pronounced herself "awestruck at the number of women who work at their jobs and go home to another full-time job ... How do you do it?" she asked. Thousands of readers responded, with tales ranging from abandoned careers to near collapse. According to sociologist Arlie Hochschild of the University of California, working mothers are exhausted, even fixated on the topic of sleep. "They talked about how much they could 'get by on': ... six and a half, seven, seven and a half, less, more ... These women talked about sleep the way a hungry person talks about food."

By my calculations, the total working time of employed mothers now averages about 65 hours a week. Of course, many do far more than the average—such as mothers with young children, women in professional positions, or those whose wages are so low that they must hold down two jobs just to scrape by. These women will be working 70 to 80 hours a week. And my figures are extremely conservative: they are the lowest among existing studies. A Boston study found that employed mothers *average* over 80 hours of housework, child care, and employment. Two nationwide studies of white, married couples are comparable: in the first, the average week was 87 hours; in the second, it ranged from 76 to 89, depending on the age of the oldest child.

One might think that as women's working hours rose, husbands would compensate by spending less time on the job. But just the opposite has occurred. Men who work are also putting in longer hours. The 5:00 Dads of the 1950s and 1960s (those who were home for dinner and an evening with the family) are becoming an "endangered species." Thirty percent of men with children under fourteen report working fifty or more hours a week. And many of these 8:00 or 9:00 Dads aren't around on the weekends either. Thirty percent of them work Saturdays and/or Sundays at their regular employment. And many others use the weekends for taking on a second job.

A twenty-eight-year-old Massachusetts factory worker explains the bind many fathers are in: "Either I can spend time with my family or support them—not both." Overtime or a second job is financially compelling: "I can work 8–12 hours overtime a week at time and a half, and that's when the real money just starts to kick in.... If I don't work the OT my wife would have to work much longer hours to make up the differences, and our day care bill would double.... The trouble is, the little time I'm home I'm too tired to have any fun with them or be any real help around the house." Among white-collar employees the problem isn't paid overtime, but the regular hours. To get ahead, or even just to hold on to a position, long days may be virtually mandatory.

Overwork is also rampant among the nation's poorly paid workers. At $5, $6, or even $7 an hour, annual earnings before taxes and deductions range from $10,000 to $14,000. Soaring rents alone have been enough to put many of these low earners in financial jeopardy. For the more than one-third of all workers now earning hourly wages of $7 and below, the pressure to lengthen hours has been inexorable. Valerie Connor, a nursing-home worker in Hartford, explains that "you just can't make it on one job." She and many of her co-workers have been led to work two eight-hour shifts a day. According to an official of the Service Employees International Union in New England, nearly one-third of their nursing-home employees now hold two full-time jobs. Changes in the low end of the labor market have also played a role. Here is less full-time, stable employment. "Twenty hours here, thirty hours there, and twenty hours here. That's what it takes to get a real paycheck," says Domenic Bozzotto, president of Boston's hotel and restaurant workers union, whose members are drowning in a sea of work. Two-job families? Those were the good old days, he says. "We've got four-job families." The recent influx of immigrants has also raised hours. I.N. Yazbeck, an arrival from Lebanon, works ninety hours a week at three jobs. It's necessary, he says, for economic success.

This decline of leisure has been reported by the Harris Poll, which has received widespread attention. Harris finds that since 1973 free time has fallen nearly 40 percent—from a median figure of 26 hours a week to slightly under 17. Other surveys, such as the 1989 Decision Research Corporation Poll, also reveal a loss of leisure. Although these polls have serious methodological drawbacks, their findings are not far off the mark. A majority of working Americans—professionals, corporate management, "working" mothers, fathers, and lower-paid workers—*are* finding themselves with less and less leisure time.

————

Life.com

The Berkeley Monthly, October 1999.

■ Clive Thompson

The elevator door slides open and Jess slides in, looking slightly rumpled. Tara sizes her up.

"Didn't get much sleep last night?"

"You can tell?"

"Well, you're wearing the same clothes as yesterday."

Jess laughs. Her music show, Freq, broadcast live over the internet here at the new-media house Pseudo, went late last night and the staff wound up hanging around till dawn. Now it's 10:30 a.m. and she's back from breakfast to make some calls and set up meetings.

"At some point I'm gonna have to shower," she mutters as she wanders off to her desk.

Tara and I tour the studios, strolling through Pseudo's odd mix of high camp and high tech. The office is a study in chaos and energy, each room reflecting the peculiar pop-cultural animus of the twenty-somethings who work here. There's the room for the women's net shows, done up in late-'70s drag with a rainbow-colored bead-curtain entrance. There's a group of goateed musicians hanging out in one room, holding keyboards and a computer monitor. Who are they? "I have no idea," Tara says.

"Sorry," she apologizes at one point, yawning. "I'm a bit burnt out today."

I'm not surprised. In new media it's difficult to find anyone who can boast a full night's rest. Later in the day I visit a 23–year–old acquaintance at a website design firm across town and find him collapsed on a sofa in the staff room.

Late night? "Yeah." He's been setting up a database for a website that's set to go live in two days. The deadline looms and the client—a major corporation—is getting twitchy. Some deeply caffeinated all-nighters will be called for.

"It's intense but it's going pretty well," he says, his hair out of whack with a minor case of bed-head. "I figure I have another two days like this. But it's cool. It's a really cool project."

He pours himself a thick coffee in the well-stocked kitchen and heads back to his workstation, plopping down beside some two dozen other coders and designers clacking away at their keyboards as a stereo pumps out ambient techno in an endless loop. Most of them figure they'll be here until 4 in the morning.

Working till sunup, destroying your eyesight, playing Quake on the company lan, hanging out in a funky office with your dog: in the modern digital workplace this sort of stuff is de rigueur. Indeed, for young Turks in new media—software, website development or the amorphous zone of "content"—aggressively casual and freewheeling is the signature office style.

On the surface it has to do with making work seem a lot more fun and thus a lot less like work. It is, as it were, the master narrative of the New Work, which we could sketch out like this: young digital employees have thrown off the 9–to–5 straitjacket in which their parents so miserably toiled. No more suits, no more rigid corporate hierarchies, no more dull, repetitive tasks. Today work means getting to wear your Star Wars T-shirt, sport multiple piercings and hang out in an office with homey perks: massage-therapist visits, pets, wacky furniture, toys and lots of beer. The staff dines together and parties together. It works hard, sure, but it plays hard too, and usually at the same time. And the workers aren't chained to one job. Instead they hop at will from company to company, forcing hapless employers to scramble after them, offering ever more perks and stock options to lure their portable, highly paid talents. These kids hold all the cards.

It's a story that has fascinated the media. Reporters covering the industry regularly marvel at the scenes of controlled chaos and pop-cultural riot. In Mountain View [California], Netscape staff members are willing to quit if they can't bring their dogs to work. *USA Today* once breathlessly noted that the office at Organic Online "has been the scene of a dance party, complete with disc jockeys, for 400 people."

Which is precisely the problem.

The studied hipness of new media is a rather devious cultural illusion. Those ultracool offices cover up a seldom-discussed truth: that the jobs themselves often demand intense work and devotion for relatively low pay and zero security. By making work more like play, employers neatly erase the division between the two, which ensures that their young employees will almost never leave the office.

High-tech employees hang out at work long after the city has gone to bed. They'll kill themselves over deadlines, putting in up to 80 hours a week. Then they'll smile and thank their lucky stars that they're part of the digital revolution, the cultural flashpoint of the '90s. For employers, of course, it's a sweet deal—you can't buy flexibility like that. As more than one worker has told me, a website design company can almost always hold a meeting at 2 o'clock on a Saturday afternoon because, well, everyone's there. Where else would they be?

New-media companies are notorious for employee burnout and nanosecond turnover. It's not surprising: given the insane hours, the payoffs are rather slim. We're hit relentlessly with media hype about digital workers' high pay, desirability and stock options. But none of these myths holds up under statistical scrutiny. The vast majority of new-media workers in New York, for example, make less than junior accountants, enjoy the job security of fast-food workers and have a laughably small chance of getting offered any stock anytime anywhere. As for programmers, most are paid surprisingly little and hurled overboard as soon as they hit their mid–30s.

Enamored of its distorted image, the digital workforce is reluctant to accept the facts. "People do not want to face reality," says Bill Lessard, a veteran of the industry who runs NetSlaves, a website that compiles true tales of new-media burnout. "Someone will tell you, 'Oh, I'm a producer.' But they're just a schmuck who's working 90 hours a week. You give these companies body and soul and you really get nothing back."

These workers are touted as the most renegade, the most entrepreneurial generation in years. Yet they are, in traditional labor terms, amazingly compliant. Chained to their keyboards, working far longer hours than they're paid for and blurring the boundaries between their jobs and their lives, digital employees paradoxically present the kind of servile workforce that would have pleased Henry Ford, Nelson Rockefeller and probably Chairman Mao.

When I visit Fred Kahl he's busy designing a computer game based on the TV cartoon "Space Ghost." I peer over his shoulder at the screen, where Fred is fiddling with a sequence: Space Ghost chasing the arch-villain Lokar, who is impersonating Santa Claus. In a few days this will air on the website of the Cartoon Network, one of the major clients of Funny Garbage, the new-media design firm that Kahl works for.

It's hard to deny that new-media workplaces are, aesthetically anyway, extremely pleasant places to be. Kahl shows me around Funny Garbage—a firm respected for its right-brained, creative web animations—and it's not unlike wandering through a gallery of '70s kitsch. Workstations are cluttered with retro-pop toys and icons. One of the company's founders, 33–year–old Peter Girardi, has three different video-game systems in his office.

This is not to suggest that everyone is horsing around. Over by the animation computers, three designers are hunkering down for a long haul, even though it's already past 5 o'clock on a Friday night. By 9, staff members will likely launch into a Quake tournament on the company lan. ("I had to stop," Kahl says. "I almost destroyed my wrists.") In this context, it's easy to see how work and life inexorably bleed into each other. It's also easy to see how new-media employers can capitalize on the confusion. For people involved in digital culture, a highly wired office—replete with digital toys and fueled by a T1 connection—can be a more inviting place to hang out than a cramped apartment or a bar or club.

In fact, sometimes work offers even better partying than a club.

One of Psuedo's longest-serving staff members, a 29–year–old programmer named Joey Fortuna, remembers arriving on his first day four years ago to find the office in a fantastic mess from a party held the night before. Pseudo CEO Josh Harris staggered in from his on-site apartment wearing nothing but boxer shorts and instantly set Fortuna to work, even though Fortuna had never written a line of code in his life.

To get up to speed on HTML, Fortuna—like most of the staff—put in months of 12–hour days. In 1996 he spent Christmas Day writing code for a video-publishing database. "It was just insane!" he says. "I was working all the time. I lived here. But I didn't mind. It was like a clubhouse."

He gestures around the loft, pointing to its kooky mix of high-and low-tech. "You know, it's ironic," he grins, "but in the last century this used to be a sweatshop."

If there's an archetypal success story in new media it's probably that of Jeff Dachis and Razorfish. In spring 1995, Dachis and his friend Craig Kanarick, both in their late 20s, founded the website design company in their living rooms. Last year they had 350 employees in eight offices and did $30 million in business.

Companies like Razorfish have built the mythos of gold-rush success in new media: start a firm in your garage, wow senior executives at Fortune 500 companies, then take occasional breaks from your PlayStation to watch the dough roll in. "The trappings of power have changed," wrote *Time* magazine in an October 1997 survey of the "cyber-elite."

But here too the hype outstrips the reality. True, there are dozens of fantastic entrepreneurial successes. But when you look at the statistics the New Work starts to look like an old story: low pay, no security and those who no longer suit the company profile pitched instantly overboard.

In 1997 the New York New Media Association did a study of the local scene. It discovered that high-tech jobs paid an average of $37,212. That's middling at best for a city as expensive as New York. It's also far outpaced by the average salaries in other media: advertising, $71,637; periodicals, $69,849; TV broadcasting, $85,938.

The churn rate in new-media jobs is amazingly high. The New York study found that almost half the work in new media is freelance or part time. More than two-thirds of all freelance contracts last fewer than six months, most are three-month stints. Part-time jobs are growing four-times faster than full-time positions.

In place of decent pay and regular work, new media offers the lure of instant wealth—the fabled stock options that turned the creators of Amazon.com or TheGlobe.com into overnight multimillionaires. It's a seductive tale, and those who have won the game have won huge. Berkeley's Adam Sah, who was in on the ground floor at Inktomi, cashed in some stocks when the company went public. The years of 400–hour months paid off. "It wasn't fun," he says, "but it did turn out all right for me."

Sah previously worked at Microsoft, which pretty much invented the stock-options trick, knowing that the lure of the market is one of the few things that will motivate coders to impale themselves upon unshippable products with unmeetable deadlines. "It's amazing what people will do for money," Sah laughs wryly.

The stock payoff, though, is about as chimerical as you can get. There are no stats on new-media stock cash-ins but high-tech hunters counsel their clients that the chance of getting lucrative options are slim.

"To cash in on stock you have to stick around for several years at a company," says Alex Santic, head of Silicon Valley Connections, one of the first headhunting firms to specialize in new media. "But few people really want to. They want to move on after a year. They get lured in by the promise of stock but rarely see it through." Indeed, as the New York new-media study found, the only folks who own substantial equity are management and founders—worker bees have a statistically insignificant slice of the pie.

Perhaps the most persistent myth of recent years, though, is that of the "programmer shortage." According to this tale, the geeks now run the show. There isn't enough programming talent to go around, so companies are fighting tooth and nail over warm bodies. Mainstream media have taken up the story like a mantra. "Business leaders say the shortage has reached near-crisis proportions," wrote the *Washington Post* in an article detailing—with a sort of horrified fascination—the incredible perks offered to lure programmers, from "signing bonuses like professional athletes" to $70–an-hour rates for temp work.

Again, the facts contradict the hype. Last year Norman Matloff, a professor of computer science at UC Davis, released one of the few studies ever done on the programmer job market. He surveyed the hiring practices of software and new-media firms and concluded that there was, in fact, no shortage of programmers. Companies were hiring only two to four percent of the people they interviewed, a rate far below that for other types of engineers.

Older programmers, meanwhile, are ruthlessly squeezed out. Age discrimination, Matloff says, is "amazingly rampant." He found that after age 35 and increasingly as they get older, programmers are ditched in favor of the fresh-scrubbed kids released each year from technical colleges. By their early 40s fewer than one-fifth of all trained programmers are still working in the field. One 47–year–old programmer Matloff talked to was fluent in C++, Perl, Unix and a host of other languages, but when he went looking for a new job he landed only two interviews in 15 months of searching. Another man had been programming since 1976. "I can't get so much as an interview," he told Matloff. "I now earn about $24,000 a year in retail sales and management."

When you look at the facts you begin to realize the incredible power of new-media workplace culture. It sells a lifestyle of liberation and autonomy that is wildly out of sync with reality. Then you begin to realize why those Quake marathons, those cappuccino machines in the staff kitchen and all those dogs at work are important. Absent decent pay and a commitment from your boss, maybe a game of Quake is the best you can get.

———

The Law and Economics of Critical Race Theory

112 YALE L.J. 1757, 1789–93, 1795–96, 1797–99, 1801–14 (2003) (reviewing CROSSROADS, DIRECTIONS, AND A NEW CRITICAL RACE THEORY (Francisco Valdes et al. eds., 2002)).

■ DEVON W. CARBADO & MITU GULATI

A starting point for thinking about workplace discrimination is to raise the question of whether today's workplace is buttressed by institutionalized racial norms. With respect to explicit racial norms, the answer is no: That would violate antidiscrimination law. But do implicit racial norms structure today's workplace culture? [Critical race theory, or CRT] answers this question affirmatively, pointing to workplace practices like English-only rules and grooming regulations (e.g., rules prohibiting employees from braiding their hair) that restrict the expression of particular identities and, in so doing, marginalize them.

There is, however, a subtle form of institutional discrimination to which CRT scholars have not paid attention. This discrimination derives from a commitment on the part of many employers, particularly employers who use teams to manage their workplace culture to achieve trust, fairness, and loyalty (TFL). Why? TFL reduces transaction costs. Empirical evidence suggests that the effectiveness of teams is enhanced when employers engender TFL among their employees. Employees who perceive that they are a part of a "TFL community" work hard, cooperate, police each other, and share valuable information. Based on this evidence, scholars have argued that law should be structured to facilitate the creation of TFL workplaces. In addition to its efficiency gains, TFL values seem normatively appealing.

TFL's normative surface appeal helps to explain why the institutional discrimination story we articulate below has not yet been told. Central to our story is not the fact that employers are invested in TFL but rather how they go about realizing that investment—by aggressively promoting homogeneity. Evidence suggests that, at least in the short term, a manager with a demographically homogeneous work team has a better chance of producing TFL than one with a diverse team. If, as is often suggested, managers focus primarily on short-term results, there is an incentive for managers to seek demographically homogeneous teams.

The relationship between the pursuit of demographic homogeneity and racial discrimination is direct. In short, workplaces organized to achieve homogeneity are likely to discriminate because homogeneity norms, by their very nature, reflect a commitment to sameness (favoring people perceived to be members of the in-group ("insiders")) and a rejection of difference (disfavoring people perceived to be members of the out-group ("outsiders")). Coupled with the fact that, within most professional settings, whites are insiders and nonwhites are outsiders, the relationship between discrimination and homogeneity becomes clear.

The foregoing suggests that race-neutral workplace norms institutionalize insider racial preference. Is this a reason for concern? The answer is not obviously yes. One might argue that, even to the extent that there are incentives for employers to create and maintain homogeneous workplaces, the threat of antidiscrimination sanctions undermines that incentive. Richard Epstein famously worried about exactly this effect of antidiscrimination law. According to Epstein, part of the problem with antidiscrimination law is that it compromises workplace efficiency by preventing employers from establishing homogeneous workplace cultures. One might conclude, then, that given the threat of legal sanctions, the institutionalized racism problem we have identified is theoretical—not real.

Moreover, there are institutional legitimacy concerns that militate against the establishment of homogenous workplaces. White-only work forces can create public relations problems. Perhaps not surprisingly, there is no employer-driven movement afoot to have antidiscrimination laws repealed because they prohibit employers from establishing demographically homogenous workplaces. To the contrary, even a cursory examination of the management and organizational behavior literature reveals (at least rhetorically) an institutional commitment to manage, and not to eliminate, heterogeneity. Thus, all seems well: Law prevents institutions from privileging homogeneity, and institutions perceive the pursuit of homogeneity to be problematic.

Our claim, however, is that all is not well. Neither antidiscrimination law nor the affirmative pursuit of diversity operates as a meaningful barrier to, or substantially undermines the incentives for employers to achieve, workplace homogeneity. Epstein need not worry. To be sure, the law prohibits blatant racial animus in hiring and promotion. But that is a minimal barrier to the managerial pursuit of racial homogeneity. To move from a phenotypic conception of race to a performative conception is to find that, to a significant extent, judges can (and, we surmise, do) apply antidiscrimination law to actually *protect* the pursuit of racial homogeneity. They do so by failing to capture employment discrimination based on *intraracial* distinctions—distinctions employers make among people within a particular racial group.

Driving these distinctions is a question about racial stereotypes and racial salience. Other things being equal, employers prefer nonwhites whose racial identity is not salient and whose identity performance is inconsistent with stereotypes about their racial group. In other words, employers screen for racial palatability. With respect to Asian Americans, for example, employers determine whether, notwithstanding phenotypic difference, a particular Asian American is (based on how she performs her identity) sufficiently like insiders to be successfully assimilated into a homogenized workplace.

To date, there are no Title VII cases that render a racial palatability discrimination claim cognizable. Thus, employers can make these kinds of intraracial distinctions with legal impunity. And to the extent employers engage in this practice, their associated institutional legitimacy remains intact because the practice anticipates and produces at least some work-place racial integration. Finally, because the racial diversity employers achieve by making intraracial distinctions is literally skin deep, it comfortably coexists with their commitment to homogeneity.

The foregoing sets forth a theory of institutional racism—that it is a function of an investment on the part of employers to realize the efficiency gains of homogeneity. Because many institutions operate under what we call a *diversity constraint*—a constraint that requires the firm to hire at least some nonwhites—employers will determine which nonwhites to hire on evidence of racial palatability. The more racially palatable employers perceive a potential employee to be, the less concerned they will be over the possibility that that potential employee will (racially) disrupt workplace homogeneity. * * *

B.   *The Incentive for Employers To Pursue Homogeneity*
     * * *

1.   *Theories*

There are at least three theories suggesting that employers are motivated to pursue homogeneity: social identity theory, similarity-attraction theory, and statistical judgments theory.

Social identity theory suggests that people have an affinity for those they perceive to be part of their in-group. In concrete terms, people are more likely to demonstrate TFL (which, again, is shorthand for trust, fairness, and loyalty) to those they perceive to be members of their in-group. Conversely, they are more likely to discriminate against those they perceive to be members of an out-group. Race, being both socially salient and facially visible, is one of the primary categories along which people make initial in-group and out-group categorizations. One explanation is that people assume that those of a similar race are likely to share similar values and to have had similar experiences. As a result, racial outsiders are vulnerable to discrimination from their racial insider colleagues. To avoid this distrust and dislike (which will likely undermine workplace efficiency by increasing transaction costs), employers will want to hire people who are similar to insiders.

The similarity-attraction theory is largely analogous. It posits that people are attracted to those who are similar. The theory is that race is one of the primary categories used to determine similarity and that this similarity, in turn, translates into attraction. * * *

The final theory suggesting that employers are motivated to pursue homogeneity is statistical judgments theory. Most often attributed to economics (though also central to psychology), this theory claims that racial differences often activate *statistical judgments* about likely behavioral tendencies. These statistical judgments are a type of mental shortcut, a resource-saving device. For example, white workers may see a new black colleague as likely to be lazy, untrustworthy, disloyal (especially to her white colleagues), frequently angry (perhaps as a result of oversensitivity about race), and difficult to communicate with (due to her likely having different values, different interests, and different cultural and experiential points of reference). Under this theory, whether an insider-employer will hire a black person turns on the currency of the foregoing statistical judgments. The stronger the statistical judgment, the stronger the employer's perception that a prospective black employee will not fit into the institution.

These theories suggest that there is a disincentive for employers to hire outsiders and a corresponding incentive for employers to hire insiders. Difference engenders distrust, dislike, disconnection, disidentification, and disassociation. Each of these characteristics (and certainly all of them together) undermines a necessary condition for the effective operation of teams—cooperative behavior—and therefore increases the transaction costs of managing the workplace.

2. *Empirical Evidence*

a. *The Basic Story*

In addition to the theoretical literature, there is empirical evidence predicting that racially heterogeneous teams are likely to be less effective than homogenous ones. Studies consistently show what the above theories suggest: Racial heterogeneity undermines trust and cooperation. Team members in heterogeneous teams tend not to communicate as well as team members in homogeneous teams. Turnover rates in heterogeneous teams are higher. And managerial attempts to spur innovation by diversifying their teams have "met with mixed success."

b. *The More Complicated Account*

Recent scholarship on diversity management suggests that the empirical story about workplace homogeneity may be more complicated than we have thus far described. The complication is that heterogeneity can operate as a double-edged sword. To appreciate how this is so, it is helpful to conceptualize heterogeneity/diversity as operating in a two-stage process. At stage one, superficial differences in terms of variables like race cause distrust, difficulties in communication, and a reluctance to cooperate. However, under the right conditions of intergroup contact—equal status, opportunities for self-revelation, egalitarian norms, and tasks that require cooperative interdependence—diverse team members can, at stage two, gain each other's trust, begin to see commonalities, work cooperatively, and realize the benefits of working as a diverse team. Central to this theory is the notion that there are meaningful things an employer can do at stage one—the initial contact stage—to facilitate cooperative behavior at stage two. * * *

C. *Summary*

There is theoretical and empirical evidence suggesting that employers are motivated to pursue homogeneity: Put simply, homogeneous workplaces facilitate trust, loyalty, and cooperative behavior. The story with respect to heterogeneous work teams is different. First, at an institutional level, heterogeneity is difficult and costly to manage. Second, the most cost-effective way for individual supervisors to manage heterogeneity is to "socialize away" outsider difference. Thus, it is more accurate to characterize this strategy as eliminating, rather than managing, heterogeneity. Third, even assuming that heterogeneity can be effectively managed, the benefits of a heterogeneous workplace are speculative, and they are realized primarily over the long term.

Acknowledging the homogeneity incentive is helpful to CRT in at least two ways. First, it provides critical race theorists with a different perspective on colorblindness. The homogeneity incentive exists because of the transaction costs of heterogeneity. Like colorblindness, then, the homogeneity incentive requires the submersion of racial difference. Second, the existence of the homogeneity incentive supports CRT's claim that an employer's preference for racial sameness won't always be motivated by racial animus. One of the most important ideas in CRT is that racism is not just a function of individual bad actors. From here, CRT advances one of two arguments: (1) that discrimination is unconscious and (2) that discrimination is institutional. The homogeneity incentive provides an additional base from which to theorize about the latter. It demonstrates that institutional discrimination can exist in the absence of racial animosity. * * *

IV. HOW EMPLOYERS RESPOND TO THE HOMOGENEITY INCENTIVE

Given antidiscrimination laws and social norms disfavoring racial exclusivity, institutions are unlikely to respond to the homogeneity incentive by hiring only insiders. They will hire outsiders as well. The claim we advance is that employers will use specific mechanisms to screen outsiders for evidence of racial palatability. These mechanisms select "but for outsiders"—outsiders who, but for their racial phenotype, are very similar to the insiders—and they select against "essential outsiders"—outsiders whose personal characteristics are consistent with the image of the prototypical outsider. * * *

A.   *The "Race–Neutral" Response to the Homogeneity Incentive*

1.   *The Basic Idea: Selection and Socialization*

Broadly speaking, there are two mechanisms employers can use to respond to the homogeneity incentive: "selection" and "socializing" mechanisms. Selection mechanisms operate at the hiring and the promotion stages. Here, an employer screens individuals for particular characteristics that function as proxies for determining whether a given individual (1) is willing to be homogenized into the workplace culture *and* (2) has the capacity to do so. Socializing mechanisms, in turn, are used to initiate and integrate the individual into the workplace. In other words, socializing mechanisms are the rites of passage that structure a new employee's experiential travels through the workplace after selection mechanisms are used to bring her into the firm. Constituting this passage are numerous rituals through which the individual is expected to demonstrate her commitment to homogeneity. More particularly, she must effectively prove that the employer made the right selection decision. Due to space constraints, we do not elaborate further on socialization mechanisms. We focus on selection, identifying four selection mechanisms employers can use to screen potential employees for evidence of performative (and not simply phenotypic) homogeneity.

2.   *The Selection Mechanisms*

Four interrelated selection mechanisms that we draw out of the theory and evidence on homogeneity are: similarity, comfort, differentiation, and respectable exoticism.

a.   *Similarity*

This mechanism is intuitive. The question is whether the individual exhibits personal characteristics suggesting she is similar to employees already at the firm. The more an individual appears to be similar to existing employees, the more likely an employer is to conclude that the individual has the potential to be assimilated. The potential employee's response to standard interview questions can signal her potential for assimilation to employers. Consider, for example, Johnny, who is being considered for a mid-level associate position at an elite corporate law firm. A senior partner has asked Johnny to "tell us a little bit about yourself." Johnny's response includes the following:

> *I enjoy tennis and golf, though I confess that both need improvement. I like a good Gore Vidal novel; in fact, I'm in the process of rereading* Julian, *which, by the way, I highly recommend. I'm not a huge sports fan, but I try to make time to watch a good basketball game—usually with colleagues and friends. I wasn't always fond of theater, but two years ago my wife took me to see* The Tin Man, *and I've been sold on theater—both high and low—ever since. I enjoy Italian cinema, the old Fellini stuff as well as some of the more contemporary productions. And*

every so often, I truly enjoy a good B movie—not a B movie masquerading as an A movie, but a B movie that knows it's a B movie. I love going to the museum with my kids. We try to go twice a month. You'd be surprised at the interpretational skills of a six-year old.

This response provides the employer with signals about Johnny's socialized identity, information that the employer can use to make a determination as to whether Johnny is sufficiently like the firm's existing employees. Johnny plays tennis and golf, the preferred sports of corporate America. The fact that both need improvement suggests that he is available to play both sports with his colleagues and not likely to be unduly competitive when he does so. In this way, both games can function as sites for socialization. Johnny's response also indicates that he is not an avid sports fan, but that he enjoys a good basketball game. Here, Johnny signals respectable (but not hyper-) masculinity and a willingness to participate in group-based spectator sport rituals. Johnny is married with kids, which reveals his heterosexuality and possibly a certain traditionalism. He appears to be cultured (he reads Gore Vidal, watches Italian cinema, attends the theater, and visits museums), but he is not overly elitist or pompous (he enjoys the occasional B movie and attends low-brow (and just barely high-brow) theater). Finally, the fact that Johnny's wife successfully socialized him into the theater, an experience that he was not predisposed to enjoy, suggests that he will likely not resist the firm's socialization efforts.

Not every institution will select for the foregoing qualities: Similarity selection mechanisms will vary from institution to institution. The point here is twofold: (1) Most employers will have a set of characteristics that they perceive to define their workplace, and (2) without much difficulty, employers can screen for these qualities in interviews.

> b. *Comfort*

Related to similarity is comfort. Here, employers want to know whether incumbent employees will be comfortable working with the prospective hire. Again, they can select for comfort (or at least select against discomfort) by considering a prospective employee's response to standard interview questions. Stipulate once more that Johnny is interviewing for a job with an elite corporate law firm. The partner asks Johnny: "Tell us what kind of firm you're looking for." Johnny responds:

I am looking for a firm doing high-level, sophisticated corporate work. Quite frankly, most of the firms I am interviewing with seem to fall in that category—certainly your firm does. What becomes important for me, then, is firm culture. I am looking for a firm that values and respects difference. I guess I believe that people shouldn't have to lose themselves at work. They should be permitted to be who they are. I was happy to learn that your firm recently adopted a casual Friday policy.

I am also looking for a firm within which junior associates have a voice—that is, an opportunity to comment on the institutional governance of the firm, for example, the firm's billing, hiring, and pro bono policies. That sort of participation helps to make junior associates invested in the firm.

Employers could interpret Johnny's response in a number of ways. But if they are screening for comfort, a given employer may have concerns about whether Johnny "fits." Johnny's view is that individuals should be permitted to be themselves and that a firm should value difference. However, difference can be uncomfortable or discomforting. To employ what many would consider an extreme example, the firm would likely be uncomfortable with Johnny coming to work as a cross-dresser. If Johnny does cross dress, the firm would expect him to do so (if at all) outside of the workplace.

Recall that Johnny wants a voice in institutional governance and provides an indication of the kinds of issues he hopes to engage. Johnny's representations here might send a positive signal—specifically, that he wants to become a part of the firm. To the extent the employer is selecting for comfort, however, the employer could interpret Johnny's comments to suggest that he will likely make the firm uncomfortable about its hiring, pro bono, and billing practices, among other institutional governance matters.

c. *Differentiation*

Employers are most likely to utilize the differentiation mechanism when they perceive themselves to be making a "risky hire." Here, prospective employees are in a *category* that is presumed to be incapable of homogenization (or that is disinterested in socialization). Imagine that Johnny is seeking an entry-level job with a law firm. He is a third-year law student at State Law School, which is a third-tier law school. He is on law review and has an A-grade point average. His letters of recommendation are effusive; his writing sample is strong.

The firm has never hired a law student from State Law School, in part because the school is insufficiently elite and because most of the students at State Law School are from working-class backgrounds. The firm therefore assumes that these students are likely to have difficulty fitting into an elite corporate law firm. The firm might not be right for them (read: they might not be right for the firm). Given this concern, whether the employer hires Johnny will be a function of whether Johnny can differentiate himself from the category within which he is situated—that is, State law students. Consider the following exchange between Johnny and a senior partner.

Partner: Good of you to stop by. Come in and have a seat. It seems that I've left your resume elsewhere in the office. You wouldn't happen to have an extra copy, would you?

Johnny: Yes, in fact I do.

Partner: Oh yes . . . I am beginning to remember this resume. I see that you went to Harvard undergrad and that you rowed crew. How did we do this year? I graduated Harvard in '75.

Johnny: We lost to Yale, second year in a row, no pun intended. I suppose if we're going to lose to any school, it ought to be Yale. Their heavyweight eight was selected to represent the country at the World Championships in London.

Partner: So you did really well at Harvard—Magna in history, 3.7 GPA, member of the debating team. I suspect that you had a lot of options when you applied to law school.

Johnny: I was fortunate to have a few. In addition to State, NYU, Columbia, and Michigan said yes. Harvard and Stanford placed me on a waiting list. Yale said no.

Partner: I didn't get into Yale, either. What's more, I've lived to tell the tale. You will, too. But, seriously, you had all these options. I'm curious as to how you made your decision.

Johnny: Well, to a considerable extent my decision was a financial one. I couldn't afford to attend any of the other schools. And I didn't want to burden my parents anymore than I had to. Besides, I hoped that if I distinguished myself at State, I would have many of the same opportunities as if I had attended, say, Michigan.

Partner: So, Johnny, tell me about how you're thinking about law firms. Big law firms are not for everyone, and as you know, we're a pretty big law firm.

Johnny: I had the good fortune of clerking for two summers at Bronton, Stevely & Kellog in Chicago.

Partner: Yes, yes, an excellent firm.

Johnny: I had a good time there. People got along well. They had interests similar to mine. I got the sense that the attorneys there felt that they were part of a larger community. Your firm describes itself in precisely that way. Most of my classmates run away from big firms. Why go through that haze, some ask?

Partner: They consider big firms a haze?

Johnny: Some do. Most simply believe that big firms treat individuals as fungible commodities. That's not my assumption but it is the predominant assumption on campus.

Partner: What's your view, then? Let me guess: You love big firms?

Johnny: Of course. Kidding aside, I'd say that, whether it's a big firm or a small firm, the question is really twofold: whether the individual is committed to becoming a part of a team and whether the firm provides him with the opportunity to play ball.

The foregoing reflects enough differentiation on Johnny's part to effectively remove him from, or at least situate him on the periphery of, the outsider group (again, students at State Law School). Presumably, few law students at State attended Harvard. Johnny's Harvard education is significant in at least three respects. First, it signifies Johnny's intellectual capacity. Second, the fact that Johnny graduated from Harvard (and rowed crew) suggests that he has the potential for socialization. Finally, Johnny's Harvard education places Johnny and the partner in a community that has significant cultural capital—the community of Harvard alumni. That the partner recognizes this shared community is evident in his question: "How did we do this year?"

Nor would many students at State have had the opportunity to attend NYU, Michigan, and Columbia or to clerk at an elite corporate law firm. Here, too, Johnny is different. Finally, Johnny is also different in terms of his strong academic performance and the fact that he does not have a bias against big-firm practice. In short, after completing the interview with Johnny, the partner could tell himself that, although, as a formal matter, Johnny belongs to the group of State Law students, in a substantive sense, he is different. It is this kind of information that the differentiation selection mechanism is designed to ascertain.

d. *Respectable Exoticism*

Certain differences do not threaten firm homogeneity. To the extent that a given difference is both exotic (not an awful lot of people are likely to have it) and respectable (the difference is not overdetermined by a negative social meaning), firms can commodify this difference to their advantage. Thus, while hiring too many immigrants might compromise a firm's commitment to homogeneity, hiring an immigrant of royal lineage might not produce that effect. Immigrant difference that is located in the context of royal identity can be marketed—for example, to employees who might feel special because they have a royal coworker.

Another example of respectable exoticism might be an ex-NBA player in a corporate context. Note, however, that while a firm's homogeneity might tolerate one such individual, it may not be able to tolerate several. The incentive for the employer to utilize the exotic difference selection perhaps is not as strong as the employer's incentive to utilize similarity, comfort, or differentiation. In this respect, it might be more accurate to say that a firm will not select against respectable exoticism than it would be to say that the firm will actively select for that characteristic.

B. *Explicitly Racializing the Discussion: Combining CRT Insights*

The preceding discussion does not identify the racial effects of selection mechanisms. These effects can be demonstrated by adopting CRT's methodology of racializing the analysis. To borrow from Jerome Culp, we "raise ... the race question" and, in the process, make a number of empirical assumptions about race. While we think the assumptions are plausible, the analysis is necessarily tentative and meant only to be illustrative of the type of analysis that might be performed.

1. *How Likely Is It That Johnny Will Be a Racial Minority?*

How likely is it that "Johnny" will be a racial minority? Consider, for example, the Johnny who is a student at State Law School. Recall that this Johnny attended Harvard College and rowed crew. Rowing crew often means that one attended an elite East Coast prep school, and the number of minorities who fit in this category will be small. Further, although Johnny is at State Law School, he had the option of attending first-tier law schools. Not many students of color at a third-tier law school will have had that opportunity. In short, few minorities will have the kind of cultural capital reflected in Johnny's background.

2. *Assuming That the Johnny at State Law School Is Black, Will He Be "Selected"?*

Our hypothetical assumes that an elite corporate firm would select a person like Johnny, notwithstanding the fact that Johnny does not fit the standard profile (that is, a person who has attended a first-tier law school). But if Johnny is black, this issue is far from clear. Few elite corporate firms hire blacks from schools other than those in the first-tier—more specifically, in the top ten. This may be (at least in part) due to two assumptions. The first is an assumption about affirmative action and intellectual competence—namely, that given race-based admission preferences, "smart blacks" should end up at first-tier schools. The second is an assumption about race and class—namely, that a black person at State Law School is likely to be working class and thus may have difficulty fitting into the law firm. While both assumptions can be rebutted, doing so would require an employer to engage in more intensive (read: more costly) screening of Johnny.

3. *As a General Matter, What Kind of Person of Color Is Johnny Likely to Be?*

Except for respectable exoticism, each of the selection mechanisms described above is designed to ascertain the extent to which a prospective employee is different from firm insiders. The outsiders likely to be the least different from the firm's insiders are those on (or who perform their identity as if they are on) the periphery of their outsider group identity. These "most peripheral outsiders" are likely to have grown up in predominantly white neighborhoods and to have attended elite (and predominantly white) high schools, colleges, and law schools. Employers can use these background characteristics as proxies for whether, and to what extent, outsider candidates will fit comfortably into a predominantly white workplace.

But there is a more direct method the employer can use to determine whether an outsider has the capacity to work within a homogenized workplace. There is evidence suggesting that particular types of outsiders are, from an employer's perspective, likely to cause fewer problems in the operation of a team dominated by insiders than are other types of outsiders. Racial outsiders who are "extroverted" and effective at "self-monitoring" are more likely to succeed than those who are not. Good self-monitors assess how others perceive them and adjust their behavior accordingly; extroverts project a strong and identifiable self-identity. Presumably, the reason these types of outsiders cause minimal disruption is that they actively engage in "impression management." That is, they are constantly interacting with others, sending signals about themselves, and reacting to the impressions that others have of them. An employer's selection decision likely will take account of how well outsiders manage impressions about their racial identity (that is, at least in part, how well they disprove racial stereotypes).

4. *How Do People of Color Signal Racial Differentiation?*

The point of differentiation strategies is to convey one of three ideas—that one does not identify as an outsider, that one is a different kind of outsider, or that what others think of outsiders is wrong. To convey the first idea, that one does not identify as an outsider, an employee would engage in disidentification or disassociation strategies—strategies that signal that the employee does not really identify with his outsider group. Imagine that, in the context of an interview with an elite firm, a partner says this to Johnny: "I have to tell you, Johnny, racial diversity at our firm is not good. We do our best. But the numbers are what they are—not pretty." That statement offers Johnny an "opportunity" to articulate his relationship to his outsider identity. To disidentify and disassociate, Johnny can say: "I appreciate your telling me this, but I am more interested in learning about how your firm cultivates and trains junior associates." Johnny's response could also reflect even stronger evidence of outsider disidentification and disassociation. He might have said: "I appreciate your telling me this, but I just don't believe in identity politics. Diversity is fine and good, but people are people." The point is that the earlier response is enough differentiation to suggest to the employer that Johnny is not a "race man."

To convey the second idea of differentiation, that one is a different kind of outsider, the outsider could adopt an individualized stereotype negation strategy. Here, the outsider would attempt to convey to the employer that stereotypes about his outsider identity do not apply to him. Imagine that the employer asks Johnny what he does with his spare time and Johnny responds: "Fishing, golfing, and catching up on foreign cinema." The employer could interpret this response to suggest that Johnny is not an ordinary black man (who, based on stereotypes, would have responded: "Watching basketball, playing basketball, and listening to hip-hop."). To the extent the employer does not perceive Johnny to be a black male prototype, the employer is less likely to attribute negative stereotypes of black men to Johnny.

Johnny can convey the final idea of differentiation—that others' assumptions about outsiders are wrong—through generalized stereotype negation. Under this strategy, Johnny attempts to persuade the employer that stereotypes about the employee's outsider group are inaccurate. This strategy is difficult and risky to perform when one is interviewing for a job. For instance, after articulating what he likes to do in his spare time (fishing, golfing, and catching up on foreign cinema), Johnny could add something like: "Not all black men like basketball. Moreover, most of the stereotypes about blacks are simply inaccurate. Consider, for example, crime. . . ." It is unlikely that, in the context of an interview, Johnny would engage the employer in this way: The statement presupposes that the employer harbors stereotypes about blacks, a presupposition that could engender racial discomfort on the part of the employer ("This black guy thinks I am a racist."). Further, even if Johnny did make such a statement to the employer, it is unlikely that the employer would be persuaded by it. For generalized stereotype negation to work, there needs to be a level of trust, and sustained interaction, between the outsider and the employer.

Performing each of the foregoing differentiation strategies constitutes a form of work—identity work. Among other problems with this work, it can compromise one's sense of identity.

> 5. *What Are the Racial Community Costs of Differentiation Strategies?*

One of the problems with the first two differentiation strategies (disidentification/disassociation and individual stereotype negation) is that they are individually oriented. To the extent that an employee feels pressured to perform these strategies, he privileges his individual advancement over that of his group. Differentiation strategies are a response to an institutionalized problem—the employer's investment in homogeneity. So long as the homogeneity incentive drives employment decisions, there is little room for racial diversification. Society ends up with minimal (or token) outsider economic advancement into the workplace. The incentives for the outsider group, therefore, should be to engage in a collective struggle to change the system to tolerate (if not welcome) greater expression and representation of outsider identities. The first two differentiation strategies undermine that goal. They encourage outsiders to disidentify with, and disassociate from, the collective interests of the outsider group. In this sense, the problem with homogeneity is not simply that it drives employers to hire only certain kinds of outsiders, but also that the outsiders whom the employer hires are not likely to lift as they climb.

To summarize, the employer's pursuit of a homogenous workforce is likely to produce the following effects (subject to the assumptions made):

- Given the negative presumption that applies to the ability and willingness of outsiders to satisfy the homogeneity requirement (and the positive presumptions that apply to whites), the quantum of cultural capital (or the price of entry) that employers require of outsiders is likely to be higher than that for their white counterparts.

- Within the outsider community, only the elite are likely to possess the quantum of cultural capital necessary to gain entry. Employers seeking to satisfy the diversity constraint will affirmatively pursue this small subset of minorities.

- The strategies that an individual outsider employee is likely to pursue, such as differentiation, may hurt the collective cause of her minority group and compromise her sense of self. The collective cause may be better served by a struggle to reduce and remove barriers, as opposed to a competition among outsiders for a few slots (and which requires outsider homogenization).

* * *

NOTES AND QUESTIONS

1. "Lean" production and new, ruthless economy. Changes in technology have permitted a steady rise in economic productivity for the United States in recent years. These changes, however, collectively have made labor much more insecure. William Greider discusses the case of labor unions and the manufacturing sector:

> Starting in the 1970s, U.S. companies gravitated toward a different strategy in which global price pressures were offset by extracting more from labor. Corporations discarded their long postwar truce with unions and began moving jobs, first to the low-wage South and then offshore. They closed factories and demanded wage contracts that depressed wages. They mobilized both political and economic power to weaken labor's bargaining position.

> American corporate managers might point out that they themselves were driven to these defensive actions by the global economic forces. The "virtuous circle" of the 1950s and 1960s had also been sustained by the existence of industrial oligopolies—a few big companies that dominated major sectors like autos, steel and aircraft and were powerful enough to set prices and wages in a clubby, arbitrary fashion. The rise of foreign producers, especially from Japan, broke up that comfortable arrangement forever.

> As firms shifted production to lower-wage workers, organized labor lost members and became steadily less able to discipline managements. The decline in wages was not confined to union members, however, but was more general. Retail sales workers, for instance, experienced a much sharper fall than manufacturing. In 1970, wages constituted 67 percent of all personal income in the United States, a ratio that had held constant for decades. By 1994, wages were less than 58 percent of total incomes. In 1960, wages were about 26 percent of total sales. By 1994, they were about 20 percent.

WILLIAM GREIDER, ONE WORLD, READY OR NOT: THE MANIC LOGIC OF GLOBAL CAPITALISM 77 (1997). Greider argues that these trends are symptomatic of a larger phenomenon: "wage arbitrage." Wage arbitrage "moves the production and jobs from a high-wage labor market to another where the labor is much cheaper. The producers thus reduce their costs and enhance profits by arbitraging these wage differences, usually selling their finished products back into the high-wage markets." *Id.* at 57. Since labor is much less mobile than capital, wage arbitrage means the upper hand in bargaining power for capital in particular disputes. Unions, which are usually organized within national boundaries, become vulnerable to the threat of moving jobs to lower-wage countries.

2. Law firms as internal labor markets. For an extended application of economic theory to explain the hiring and promotion practices of large law firms, see David B. Wilkins & G. Mitu Gulati, *Reconceiving the Tournament of Lawyers: Tracking, Seeding, and Information Control in the Internal Labor Markets of Elite Law Firms*, 84 VA. L. REV. 1581 (1998).

3. **Winner-take-all markets.** Some economists argue that a new feature of contemporary labor markets is the existence of the "winner take all" market. In such markets there are many competitors for a very few extremely lucrative slots. The entertainment industry provides many examples: as reality shows like *American Idol* dramatically illustrate, the possibility of fame and fortune in the entertainment world draws many more people than could possibly succeed. As the economists argue, and as *American Idol* also illustrates, winner-take-all markets are socially wasteful because the possibility of extremely high rewards (coupled with the cognitive quirks identified by bounded rationality theory) draws people who would do better for themselves and the rest of society if they put their time and energy elsewhere. Winner-take-all markets also contribute to income inequality, since a very small number of players make a huge amount of money and the rest make very little. Robert Frank and Philip Cook argue that changes in tax policy, tort reform, health care finance, educational finance, and antitrust policy, among other reforms, could promote both efficiency and equity by reducing the spread and impact of winner-take-all markets. *See* ROBERT H. FRANK & PHILIP J. COOK, THE WINNER-TAKE-ALL SOCIETY 211–31 (1995).

4. **Women and emotional labor.** For an excellent discussion of gender, intimacy and economic relations *see*, Jill Hasday, *Intimacy and Economic Exchange*, 119 HARV. L.REV. 491 (2005). Hasday argues that both anti-commodification and pro-market scholars agree that the law forms a boundary between intimate economic exchanges and non-intimate exchange. However, she concludes that the law already permits substantial exchange among intimates. However she concludes that "efforts to denote the sanctity of intimate relationships through the regulation of economic exchange appear to systematically perpetuate and exacerbate distributive inequality for women and the poor. These distributive consequences suggest a need to reexamine and reform how the legal system establishes the specialness of an intimate relationship." Arlie Russell Hochschild, in *The Managed Heart: Commercialization of Human Feeling* (20th anniversary edition 2003), argues that women in the workplace often face demands not placed on men, that they display certain kinds of emotions, usually cheeriness and nurturance. ARLIE RUSSELL HOCHSCHILD, THE MANAGED HEART: COMMERCIALIZATION OF HUMAN FEELING (20th anniv. ed. 2003). Thus, women may be asked to smile, will be expected to be peacemakers in workplace disputes, and are expected to defer to the emotional needs and desires of men. Hochschild argues that the requirement of emotional labor also tends to fall upon occupations that have been heavily feminized, such as secretaries and nurses, without regard to the sex of the people in those occupations. *See also* ARLIE RUSSELL HOCHSCHILD, COMMERCIALIZATION OF INTIMATE LIFE: NOTES FROM HOME AND WORK (2003). Does Carbado and Gulati's analysis suggest a similar burden of emotional labor on racial minorities in the workplace?

5. **Impression management.** Carbado and Gulati's analysis is indebted to the work of sociologist Erving Goffman, who coined the phrase "impression management" to describe how individuals attempt to control how they

are seen by others, while those others in turn attempt to discern the "real" self behind the front. *See, e.g.*, Erving Goffman, *The Arts of Impression Management, in* The Presentation of Self in Everyday Life 208–37 (1959). Goffman emphasizes that everyone in social life is constantly engaged in impression management, both in private and in public settings, and uses the metaphor of the dramatic performance throughout his analysis:

> In this report, the individual was divided by implication into two basic parts: he was viewed as a *performer*, a harried fabricator of impressions involved in the all-too-human task of staging a performance; he was viewed as a *character*, a figure, typically a fine one, whose spirit, strength, and other sterling qualities the performance was designed to evoke. The attributes of a performer and the attributes of a character are of a different order, quite basically so, yet both sets have their meaning in terms of the show that must go on. * * *

> A correctly staged and performed scene leads the audience to impute a self to a performed character, but this imputation—this self—is a *product* of a scene that comes off, and is not a *cause* of it. The self, then, as a performed character, is not an organic thing that has a specific location, whose fundamental fate is to be born, to mature, and to die; it is a dramatic effect arising diffusely from a scene that is presented, and the characteristic issue, the crucial concern, is whether it will be credited or discredited.

Id. at 252–53.

C. Class and Consumption

The Overspent American: Why We Want What We Don't Need

80–91 (1998).

■ Juliet B. Schor

While television has long been suspected as a promoter of consumer desire, there has been little hard evidence to support that view, at least for adult spending. After all, there's not an obvious connection. Many of the products advertised on television are everyday low-cost items such as aspirin, laundry detergent, and deodorant. Those TV ads are hardly a spur to excessive consumerism. Leaving aside other kinds of ads for the moment (for cars, diamonds, perfumes), there's another counter to the argument that television causes consumerism: TV is a *substitute* for spending. One of the few remaining free activities, TV is a popular alternative to costly recreational spending such as movies, concerts, and restaurants. If it causes us to spend, that effect must be powerful enough to overcome its propensity to save us money.

Apparently it is. My research shows that the more TV a person watches, the more he or she spends. The likely explanation for the link between television and spending is that what we see on TV inflates our sense of what's normal. The lifestyles depicted on television are far different from the average American's: with a few exceptions, TV characters are upper-middle-class, or even rich.

Studies by the consumer researchers Thomas O'Guinn and L.J. Schrum confirm this upward distortion. The more people watch television, the more they think American households have tennis courts, private planes, convertibles, car telephones, maids, and swimming pools. Heavy watchers also overestimate the portion of the population who are millionaires, have had cosmetic surgery, and belong to a private gym, as well as those suffering from dandruff, bladder control problems, gingivitis, athlete's foot, and hemorrhoids (the effect of all those ads for everyday products). What one watches also matters. Dramatic shows—both daytime soap operas and prime-time drama series—have a stronger impact on viewer perceptions than other kinds of programs (say news, sports, or weather).

Heavy watchers are not the only ones, however, who tend to overestimate standards of living. Almost everyone does. (And almost everyone watches TV.) In one study, ownership rates for twenty-two of twenty-seven consumer products were generally overstated. Your own financial position also matters. Television inflates standards for lower-, average-, and above-average-income students, but it does the reverse for really wealthy ones. (Among those raised in a financially rarefied atmosphere, TV is almost a reality check.) Social theories of consumption hold that the inflated sense of consumer norms promulgated by the media raises people's aspirations and leads them to buy more. In the words of one Los Angeles resident, commenting on this media tendency, "They try to portray that an upper-class lifestyle is normal and typical and that we should all have it."

Television also affects norms by giving us real information about how other people live and what they have. It allows us to be voyeurs, opening the door to the "private world" inside the homes and lives of others. * * *

Another piece of evidence for the TV-spending link is the apparent correlation between debt and excessive TV viewing. In the Merck Family Fund poll, the fraction responding that they "watch too much TV" rose steadily with indebtedness. More than half (56 percent) of all those who reported themselves "heavily" in debt also said they watched too much TV.

It is partly because of television that the top 20 percent of the income distribution, and even the top 5 percent within it, has become so important in setting and escalating consumption standards for more than just the people immediately below them. Television lets *everyone* see what these folks have and allows viewers to want it in concrete, product-specific ways. Let's not forget that television programming and movies are increasingly filled with product placements—the use of identifiable brands by characters. TV shows and movies are more and more like long-running ads. * * *

Part of what keeps the see-want-borrow-and-buy sequence going is lack of attention. Americans live with high levels of denial about their spending patterns. We spend more than we realize, hold more debt than we admit to, and ignore many of the moral conflicts surrounding our acquisitions. The importance of denial for dysfunctional consumers has been well document-ed. We've all heard the stories about people who drive around in cars full of unpaid credit card bills, who sneak into the guest room at 2:00 A.M. to make a QVC purchase, or who quietly slip off at lunchtime for a quick trip to the mall. What is not well understood is that the spending of many normal consumers is also predicated on denial. (How many times have you heard someone say, "Oh, I'm not materialistic, I'm just into books and CDs—and travel"?) * * *

Nowhere is denial so evident as with credit cards. Contrary to econo-mists' usual portrayal of credit card debtors as fully rational consumers who use the cards to smooth out temporary shortfalls in income, the finding of the University of Maryland economist Larry Ausubel was that people greatly underestimate the amount of debt they hold on their cards— 1992's actual $182 billion in debt was thought to be a mere $70 billion. Furthermore, most people do not expect to use their cards to borrow, but, of course, they do. Eighty percent end up paying finance charges within any given year, with just under half (47 percent) always holding unpaid balances.

Not paying attention to what we spend is also very common. How many of us really keep track of where the cash from the ATM goes? Most Americans don't budget. And they don't watch. Many "fritter," as this downshifter recalled: "All I know is at the end of the month I never had anything left. And so I have to say I spent it all. I don't know what I frittered away. I really don't know what I spent the money on." * * *

Finally, denial also helps us navigate the moral conflicts associated with consumption. Most of our cherished religious and ethical teachings condemn excessive spending, but we don't really know what that means. We have a sense that money is dirty and a nagging feeling that there must be something better to do with our hard-earned dollars than give them to Bloomingdale's. As our salaries and creature comforts expand, many of us keep alive our youthful fantasies of doing humanitarian work, continuing the inner dialogue between God and Mammon. Not looking *too* hard helps keep that inner conflict tolerable. Squarely facing the fact that you spent $6,000 on your wardrobe last year and gave less than one-third of that sum to charity is a lot harder than living with a vague sense that you need to start spending less on clothes and giving away more money. * * *

In many places, private school is becoming a part of the upper-middle- (and even middle-) class standard of living—a requisite element in the basic package. Parents worry that without it their children will fall behind. Fears about education become magnified because they tap into larger, more deep-seated anxieties. Class position seems to be at stake. And, of course, as the middle and upper-middle classes abandon the public schools, the class divisions widen. Public school becomes tainted with a lower-class image. As another mother in the Los Angeles study explained, the public schools work well for her "housekeeper's child," who will have language problems, but not for her children. "Our concern with the public schools is really the safety issue. I have blond-haired, blue-eyed children who are not very physical and not very aggressive, and I worry about interactions on playgrounds."

At the same time, these parents have to deal with the complications of schooling alongside the super-wealthy. The same woman who is afraid of the public school playgrounds also worries about her children being at the bottom of the economic ladder in their private school. "The wealth of these kids is just mind-boggling. You put them in an environment in which we cannot compete, nor do we *want* them to compete and have those kinds of values. I don't want them to come home and say, 'Why don't we live in a ten-bedroom house?' " * * *

We have no problem acknowledging the "conspicuous consumption" of the early twentieth century that [Thorstein] Veblen wrote about. Middle class Americans shake their heads at what inner-city youths do to obtain expensive sneakers or gold chains. We can even get passionate about the dangers of status symbols in the Third World. Many Americans boycotted Nestle for promoting infant formula, the often deadly status alternative to breast milk. (Nestle and other companies had women in "modern" white uniforms doling out free supplies of formula in hospitals, leading to sickness, malnutrition, and even death among "bottle babies.") Many Americans deplore the entry of soft drinks and fast-food outlets into poor countries because they contribute to comerciogenic malnutrition: the poor spend their few pesos on soft drinks or French fries, forgoing nutritious food and becoming sick in the process. On the lighter side, we can chuckle at Peruvian Indians carrying rocks painted like transistor radios, Chinese who keep the brand tags on their designer sunglasses, Brazilian shanty-town dwellers with television antennae but no TV's, or the Papua New Guineans who substitute Pentel pens for boars' nose pieces. Third World status consumption seems straightforward, unambiguous in motive.

We have more trouble seeing the counterparts of these behaviors in the American middle class, and in ourselves.

No Scrubs

TLC, *on* FANMAIL, LA FACE (1999).

■ KEVIN BRIGGS, KANDI BURRUSS, TAMEKA COTTLE

A scrub is a guy that thinks he's fly
And is also known as a buster
Always talkin' about what he wants
And just sits on his broke ass
So (no)

I don't want your number (no)
I don't want to give you mine and (no)
I don't want to meet you nowhere (no)
I don't want none of your time and (no)
Chorus:
I don't want no scrub
A scrub is a guy that can't get no love from me
Hanging out the passenger side
Of his best friend's ride
Trying to holler at me
I don't want no scrub
A scrub is a guy that can't get no love from me
Hanging out the passenger side
Of his best friend's ride
Trying to holler at me

But a scrub is checkin' me
But his game is kinda weak
And I know that he cannot approach me
Cuz I'm lookin' like class and he's lookin' like trash
Can't get wit' no deadbeat ass
So (no)

I don't want your number (no)
I don't want to give you mine and (no)
I don't want to meet you nowhere (no)
I don't want none of your time (no)
Chorus
If you don't have a car and you're walking
Oh yes son I'm talking to you
If you live at home wit' your momma
Oh yes son I'm talking to you (baby)
If you have a shorty but you don't show love
Oh yes son I'm talking to you
Wanna get with me with no money
Oh no I don't want no (oh)

No scrub
No scrub (no no)
No scrub (no no no no no)
No scrub (no no)
No
* * *

———

Dress As Success

Beauty Secrets: Women and the Politics of Appearance 79–80, 83–85, 88–93 (1986).

■ Wendy Chapkis

Appearance talks, making statements about gender, sexuality, ethnicity and class. In a sexually, racially and economically divided society all those visual statements add up to an evaluation of power. Economic power, or class position, is easily suggested by a man's use of the standard business suit. An expensive tailored three-piece suit says authority and privilege quietly but unmistakeably. For a woman to get that kind of attention, she must speak up more loudly. Even dressed in designer everything and costly jewelry her appearance makes a less unambiguous statement than a man's $1,000 suit.

Traditionally, a woman dressed in money has been assumed to be making a statement not about herself, but about a man. Her expensive clothing was thought to signal to the world that her husband or other male provider was so wealthy he could afford a clearly useless luxury in the form of this female. In this Veblenesque* interpretation, the woman herself is relegated to the position of a passive object much like a clothes hanger in someone else's closet. While this may well explain a husband's rationale for paying the bills, conspicuous consumption has a special purpose in a wealthy woman's life, too. * * *

Not only has consuming been one of the few pursuits open to women of a certain class, but being dressed in money demonstrates to the viewing public that the woman's one all important investment—marriage—has paid off nicely. Woman to woman we know that the marriage contract is far from an agreement between peers. At least being well-dressed serves as the visual equivalent of a large pay check.

Women in the role of wife establish social position second hand. A wealthy husband provides access to power for the woman married to him. But this ascribed power has to be made visible. If he has it, you flaunt it—not merely to reflect well on him, but to protect yourself. Dressed in money, a woman looks like someone not to be trifled with despite her sex. She is clearly protected by someone with the ability to do the job.

Increasingly, though, women are finding a need to indicate *personal* financial authority through their dress. Many more women now are breadwinners than in the past. This change is due in part to the women's movement. However, perhaps even more important than feminism is rising male unemployment and inflation making a woman's paycheck indispensable. Higher divorce rates, too, have helped make female financial independence a necessity.

How a woman should indicate professional power through her appearance is still a subject of debate. But all those voices presuming to advise women on how to put together such an image seem to agree on two fundamental things. First, *looking* "successful" is more than half the battle in actually achieving professional success. And second, success is a formula not to be tinkered with—that is, women may now aspire to professional success but should not attempt to redefine it.

---

* Thorstein Veblen, author of *The Theory of the Leisure Class,* published in 1899.

Both these precepts have a particular resonance for women. Haven't we always known that how we look is far more important than what we do or how we do it? And as interlopers in the man-made world of business, we tend toward gratitude if someone even takes the time to explain the rules of the game—we may feel in no position to try to change them. Success in these terms is intensely individual and conformity a useful strategy.

* * *

The carefully composed look of success is not without its fashion competition. New Wave culture and punk style are among the most radical forms of visual dissent. At a very minimum, punk is a statement about consumerism. At least initially, the fashion was put together from hand-made or second hand clothing. Jewelry was to be found or created from inexpensive materials like rubber, plastic and cheap metals.

Punk has also been an explicit message on the state of the economy. If there is a possibility of a job interview in the near future, one probably won't choose a fluorescent green hair dye or a Mohawk haircut. But when unemployment becomes a predictable long-term condition, little is put at risk by looking outrageous. Radically transforming one's personal appearance can be an exercise of personal power in a life that feels out of control. While it may not be possible for an individual to change the reality of high unemployment, housing shortages and poverty, it is possible to transform one's body into a visual shout: "No, I do not accept the goodness of your goals and expectations. No, I will not help you feel secure in your choices. Do I look frightening? Do I look angry? Do I look dangerous? Do you still feel safe in thinking that the system works just fine? Think again."

Not surprisingly, it is not the Punk but the young urban professionals—the so-called Yuppies—who have become the darlings of contemporary media. Their aerobic bodies and expensive dress speak confidently of physical and economic health. The image is above all reassuring. The system works just fine if you play by the rules. We accept the goals and the methods and we will be among the winners.

Success as it is known in the contemporary corporate world is dependent on a division between winners and losers, with a built-in guarantee that more will fail than will be rewarded. Women have always been the structural losers in the system. To be a woman was to be slotted for the position of support staff, both professionally and personally. The reality remains that even today most women will not become senior executives. In fact, most women will not even marry senior executives. The majority of working women will remain on a parallel job ladder which ends in the position of executive secretary or senior administrative assistant.

As anyone with experience in the business world knows, these are the women who run the show, without whom many organizations would come to a standstill. Yet they will never have the money or the authority to accompany the responsibility.

As long as success remains an individual characteristic, only one name will go on the by-line, while research assistants will have to be satisfied with a thank you in the acknowledgements. Secretaries will continue to receive lunch invitations or roses once a year instead of colleague-to-colleague respect and recognition of their partnership in the business endeavor. And women who do make it to a position of recognized power will have to quickly switch class and gender allegiance. Too close an identification with the secretarial crowd, too much empathy with those who come up on the short end of the unequal division of rewards will only be detrimental to one's own climb toward success.

It is arguably an improvement if women as a group are no longer automatically relegated to subordinate positions. But only those who find Jeane Kirkpatrick and Margaret Thatcher shining examples of feminism will believe that this sort of individual success is the same thing as women's liberation.

* * *

In the early days of the contemporary women's movement, women created strategies of empowerment that focused on shared experience and collective labor. However, we also longed for the individual perques of authority and prestige. But we were operating in an economic structure that insured that while our efforts might allow some of us to "make it," all of us would not. Western industrial society is based on competition and scarcity; equality not of condition but of opportunity. Taking on male bastions of power like the corporate world and opening them up to women meant collectively breaking down the barriers to women's participation. We worked for and achieved legislation that guaranteed us access. But once we succeeded in opening the door, we stepped through and realized that the stairway to the top was narrow and already crowded.

Still, now that the opportunity was there, failure became evidence of personal inadequacy not a political problem. Nor was class (known in America as one's "background") a political concern—provided one knew how to hide it. An entire literature developed teaching the common woman how to reach uncommon heights by "applying" herself and dressing for the part. * * *

Once inside and part way up the corporate ladder, the need to disguise your origins becomes imperative. In order to become executive materials, you must look as if you come from executive stock—the upper middle class. Enter John T. Molloy and *Dress for Success*:

> We can increase [a woman's] chances of success in the business world; we can increase her chances of being a top executive; we can make her more attractive to various types of men.

Molloy believes at least as firmly as [Helen Gurley Brown, founder of *Cosmopolitan* magazine] that a woman's business success lies in her own hands. Failure, too, is a personal not a structural problem: "If you have to tell your boss not to send you for coffee, you must have already told him non-verbally that you were ready to go." He quotes "Two extremely successful women" to back him up on this; these women expressed the belief that "The reason most young women wouldn't succeed was because they didn't look like they wanted to succeed."

Dressed in the proper outfit and sporting the proper attitude, the political problem of sexism can be sidestepped. The trick is learning to *accept* reality, not trying to change it. "It is a stark reality that men dominate the power structure. . . . I am not suggesting that women dress to impress men simply because they are men [but rather because men have power] . . . It is not sexism; it is realism."

In the chapter entitled "Does Your Background Hurt You," Molloy dismisses class as a political problem as neatly as he does sex. Women who intend to move into "The power ranks of American society" first must "learn the manners and mores of the inner circle. And the inner circle is most emphatically upper middle class." Not to worry; his advice is exceedingly specific:

> My research showed that a woman wearing a black raincoat is definitely not automatically categorized as lower middle class. Raincoats are important for women, but not as important as they are for men. . . . The country-tweed look is very upper middle class and highly recommended. . . . The blazer, by its very nature, is upper middle class; every woman should have at least one. . . . Office sweaters . . . say lower middle class and loser. Don't wear lower middle class colors such as purple and gold.

Predictably, the colors that test best are "gray, medium range blue, beige, deep maroon, deep rust." And the colors to avoid are "most pastels, particularly pink and pale yellow, most shades of green, mustard, bright anything, any shade that would be considered exotic." What we end up with as acceptable colors in the business world are those commonly associated with men and with the white upper class. This look is then defined as "serious." Serious becomes a question of conformity not creative difference, of masculinity not femininity and of the bland over the exotic, i.e. the foreign or racially "deviant."

Racial difference is indeed problematic to success and must be minimized. The process begins with learning to lose any ethnic accent and avoiding exotic fashions. But people of color serious about success are also advised to do whatever possible to transform even their bodies. In African women's magazines, advertisements promote the skin lightner Clere:

> Clere for your own special beauty. We are a successful people and have to look successful. We use Clere for a lighter, smoother skin. Now, Clere will work its magic for you, and make you more beautiful and successful.

Of course, it is not only among dress for success advisors that one finds these prejudices. They just help make them respectable. Even among articulate critics of sexism and racism in contemporary society there is evidence that these standards have been internalized. * * *

The shift from full-time homemaking to double duty (working both for wages and in the home) has helped create a need for new symbols of identity. Women are discovering that they are expected to have not one, but several conflicting images: the wholesome mother, the coolly professional businesswoman and the sexy mistress. No wonder women turn to the magic of wardrobe and makeup to provide inspiration for their multiple selves: "Springfever by Elizabeth Arden ... New make-up. New inspiration." "I can bring home the bacon, fry it up in a pan and never let you forget you're a man ... En Jolie" "Colors that inspire ... Let L'erin do the talking." You almost can hear the poor woman sigh "gladly."

The cosmetics industry has been carefully studying how best to make use of this bewildering set of demands made upon working women. Women's wages have been a mixed blessing for the beauty trade. In 1983, *Advertising Age*, an industry trade journal, noted with some alarm an increase in the number of women working outside the home:

> Today, 49% of America's mothers with children under six years old are employed as opposed to only 18% in 1960 ... Where women in this group once spent middays at the department store, they are now in the office.... Women who formerly had the time to sample and listen and spend money are no longer shoppers. Even when they do visit the store, they do so as buyers.

The subtle distinction between "shopping" and "buying," *Advertising Age* points out, is that the former implies leisure. This distinction seems to be borne out by figures on grocery store cosmetic sales (cheap and fast). In the U.S., they increased by 35 percent from 1980 to 1982.

Without the leisure to linger and shop, a woman may buy what is handy and in the process discover that what she is buying for convenience is not substantially different than the more expensive brand she used to carefully seek out. *Advertising Age* warns: "This is a dangerous conclusion for the industry."

And indeed after decades of constant growth, the beauty trade is now faced with a leveling off of sales and, in some cases, even a slight decline. Not all product lines have felt the squeeze, though. "Customers seem to be turning away from medium price products," the vice-president for marketing of one of America's largest cosmetic companies notes. "They are buying better goods or switching to generic, low-price products." * * *

Often the expensive and cheap products are not only produced by different divisions of the same conglomerate, but they are made of nearly identical ingredients. Even when we know this to be true, we often will buy the more expensive item because the fantasy it offers is more attractive. Psychologist Erika Freeman explains,

> An item that promises a fantasy by definition must be priced fantastically.... If a cream begins to sell at 50 cents it will not sell as well nor will it be considered as miraculous as a cream that sells for $30.
> * * *

Why do women buy costly beauty products that demonstrably have little purpose other than participation in a fantasy? The purchase of a new cosmetic, the decision to change the color or style of one's hair, the start of a new diet are the female equivalent of buying a lottery ticket. Maybe *you* will be the one whose life is transformed. Despite daily experience to the contrary, we continue to hope that maybe this time, maybe this product, will make a difference in our lives. And if it doesn't, it is still a relatively inexpensive way to visit the mysterious orient of Shiseido, the elite circle of Chanel, the smouldering, sensuous world of Dior. Everything that is so difficult to attain in real life is promised for the price of a new perfume or eye shadow.

———

NOTES AND QUESTIONS

1. Thorstein Veblen and social meaning of consumption. Thorstein Veblen (1857–1929) was an American economist whose work focused on the embeddedness of economic activity in a larger social world in which the desire for prestige in the eyes of others is as central as the desire for purely material gain. Two of the concepts he elaborated—"conspicuous consumption" and "pecuniary emulation"—illustrate this focus. Veblen argued that wealthy people desire to signal to others that they are wealthy, and that buying and displaying luxury goods is an important means by which this is done. Thus, "Conspicuous consumption is how the wealthy demonstrate their wealth, and thus their success in war or in business. By purchasing the finest houses, autos, suits, and shoes—all visible and public signs of financial success—they gain the respect and admiration of their peers and subordinates." Janet Knoedler, *Thorstein Veblen and the Predatory Nature of Contemporary Capitalism, in* Introduction to Political Economy 66 (Charles Sackrey & Geoffrey Schneider (eds.), (3d ed. 2002)).

Veblen also argued that people in all economic classes make consumption decisions based not only on their rational desire for goods and services to make their life better, but out of envy of those who are more successful. This desire to be like and to be seen as like those with more money and social success he named "pecuniary emulation":

> [T]he standard of expenditure which commonly guides our efforts is not the average, ordinary expenditure already achieved; it is an ideal of consumption that lies just beyond our reach ... The motive is emulation—the stimulus of an invidious comparison which prompts us to outdo those with whom we are in the habit of classing ourselves ... [e]ach class envies and emulates the class next above it in the social scale, while it rarely compares itself with those below or with those who are considerably in advance.

Thorstein Veblen, The Theory of the Leisure Class 81 (Houghton Mifflin Co. 1973) (1899).

2. Crisis of over-production and creation of desire. Economic historians argue that after 1890, as modern forms of industrial production began to take shape and more and more mass-produced goods began to flood American markets, American business interests began a campaign to change consumption patterns away from patterns of thrift, self-denial, and self-reliance. As William Leach argues:

> From the 1890s on, American corporate business, in league with key institutions, began the transformation of American society into a society preoccupied with consumption, with comfort and bodily well-being, with luxury, spending, and acquisition, with more goods this year than last, more next year than this. American consumer capitalism produced a culture almost violently hostile to the past and to tradition, a future-oriented culture of desire that confused the good life with goods. It was a culture that first appeared as an alternative culture—or as one moving largely against the grain of earlier traditions of republicanism and Christian virtue—and then unfolded to become the reigning culture of the United States. It was the culture that many people the world over soon came to see as *the* heart of American life.

WILLIAM LEACH, LAND OF DESIRE: MERCHANTS, POWER, AND THE RISE OF A NEW AMERICAN CULTURE, xiii (1993); *see also* STUART EWEN, CAPTAINS OF CONSCIOUSNESS: ADVERTISING AND THE SOCIAL ROOTS OF THE CONSUMER CULTURE (2001).

Consumer culture is partly a response to what Veblen identified as an incipient crisis within capitalist societies: the threat of overproduction, too many goods chasing too few buyers. As William Greider puts it:

> As economist Thorstein Veblen taught several generations ago, the problem of capitalist enterprise is always the problem of supply: managing the production of goods in order to maximize profit and the return on invested capital. * * *

> The great virtue of capitalism—the quality that always confounded socialist critics and defeated rival economic systems—is its ability to yield more from less. Its efficient organization of production strives to produce more goods from less input, whether the input is capital, labor or raw resources. Assuming markets are stable, the rising productivity increases the profit per unit, the yields that get distributed as returns to invested capital or as rising wages for labor or in lower product prices for consumers and, in the happiest circumstances, all three.

> But this expanding potential to produce more goods also poses the enduring contradiction for capitalist enterprise: how to dispose of the surplus production. You can make more things, but can you sell them? An undisciplined expansion of productive capacity will be self-defeating, even dangerous for a firm, if all it accomplishes are continuing supply surpluses that degrade prices and undermine the rate of return. The problem of surplus capacity drives not only the competition among firms for market shares but also the imperative to discover new markets.

WILLIAM GREIDER, ONE WORLD, READY OR NOT: THE MANIC LOGIC OF GLOBAL CAPITALISM 44–45 (1997).

3. Branding and consumption. As the culture of consumption has matured, advertising strategies have changed as well. In the early 1990s,

American corporations began to shift even more profoundly away from advertising what Karl Marx would have called the use-value of their products, to focus instead on using advertising to create an affective link between their products and the consumer's dreams and fantasies. This new technique relied on "branding," and the advertising of the brand rather than the product. As Naomi Klein observes:

> Overnight, "Brands, not products!" became the rallying cry for a marketing renaissance led by a new breed of companies that saw themselves as "meaning brokers" instead of product producers. What was changing was the idea of what—in both advertising and branding—was being sold. The old paradigm had it that all marketing was selling a product. In the new model, however, the product always takes a back seat to the real product, the brand, and the selling of the brand acquired an extra component that can only be described as spiritual.
>
> * * *
>
> On Marlboro Friday [a day in 1993 when Marlboro announced plans to dramatically reduce its prices in an attempt to compete with bargain cigarette brands], a line was drawn in the sand between the lowly price slashers and the high-concept brand builders. The brand builders conquered and a new consensus was born: the products that will flourish in the future will be the ones presented not as "commodities" but as concepts: the brand as experience, as lifestyle.

NAOMI KLEIN, NO LOGO: TAKING AIM AT THE BRAND BULLIES 21 (1999).

Does the ever-more-ephemeral link between products and the consumer's actual need for them threaten the pursuit of happiness?

———

Uneasy Ryder! Jury Finds Winona Guilty in Shoplift Case

N.Y. DAILY NEWS, Nov. 6, 2002.

THE ASSOCIATED PRESS

BEVERLY HILLS, Calif.—Actress Winona Ryder was convicted Wednesday of stealing $5,500 worth of high-fashion merchandise from Saks Fifth Avenue last year.

The jury found the star of "Girl, Interrupted" guilty of felony grand theft and vandalism but cleared her of burglary.

She faces anywhere from probation to three years in prison. Sentencing is scheduled for Dec. 6.

Ryder showed no emotion as the verdict was announced. She kept her eyes on the jurors as they were asked whether the verdicts were accurate. They said yes.

She whispered to her attorney, Mark Geragos, took a drink of water and looked briefly toward her supporters in the audience.

The jury reached the verdict after 5 1/2 hours of deliberations over two days. The one count on which she was acquitted required a specific intent to go into the store to steal. District attorney's spokeswoman Sandi Gibbons said jurors often believe burglary is a crime of breaking and entering, but it does not require those circumstances.

"We're gratified with the verdicts," Gibbons added.

Ryder, a two-time Oscar nominee who marked her 31st birthday in the defendant's chair, was arrested Dec. 12 as she left the Beverly Hills store, her arms filled with packages.

Ryder did not testify during the two-week trial.

Prosecutors said Ryder came to Saks with larceny on her mind, bringing shopping bags, a garment bag and scissors to snip security tags off items.

"She came, she stole, she left. End of story," Deputy District Attorney Ann Rundle said. "Nowhere does it say people steal because they have to. People steal out of greed, envy, spite, because it's there or for the thrill."

Jurors were shown videotape of Ryder moving through the store laden with goods, and Saks security workers testified that after she was detained she apologetically told them a director had told her to shoplift to prepare for a movie role.

Her attorney denounced the security guards as liars even before the trial began.

At the start of her shopping trip, she paid more than $3,000 for a jacket and two blouses. The defense said Ryder believed the store would keep her account "open" while she shopped and would charge her later. But there was no evidence of an account.

In closing arguments Monday, Geragos suggested that the store, trying to avoid a lawsuit, conspired with employees to invent a story that would make Ryder appear guilty.

Geragos ridiculed the charge that Ryder vandalized merchandise by cutting holes in clothes when removing the security tags.

"This woman is known for her fashion sense," he said. "Was she going to start a new line of 'Winona wear' with holes in it?"

He carried a hair bow, which she allegedly had stolen, over to her, placed it on her head and said: "Can anyone see Ms. Ryder with this on top of her head? Does that make sense?"

Settlement talks between the defense and prosecution failed, but just before trial the district attorney's office agreed to dismiss a drug charge after a doctor said he had given her two pills found in her possession when she was arrested.

The 12–member jury included several people with Hollywood connections, including producer Peter Guber, who presided over Sony Entertainment Pictures when three successful Ryder films were made there.

Ryder has made some two-dozen films since 1986, including "Beetle-juice," "Heathers," "Mermaids," "Little Women," "The Age of Inno-cence," "Edward Scissorhands," "Bram Stoker's Dracula," "Reality Bites" and "Mr. Deeds."

She received her Academy Award nominations for "Little Women" (best actress) and for "The Age of Innocence" (supporting actress).

Ryder was raised by parents who were part of the counterculture revolution in the 1960s. Her godfather was LSD guru Timothy Leary.

In 1993, Ryder posted a $200,000 reward in the kidnap-murder case of a 12–year–old girl, Polly Klaas, in Petaluma, Calif., where the actress grew up. When Ryder was charged with shoplifting, Polly's father, Mark, came to legal proceedings to support her.

In recent years, Ryder has been featured frequently in fashion maga-zines. Her delicate beauty and waiflike persona were on display at the trial along with a wardrobe of appropriate trial clothes—dark sweaters and skirts, soft dresses and, on the climactic day of closing arguments, a cream silk suit with a pleated skirt and short jacket.

NOTES AND QUESTIONS

1. Consumerism and capitalism. Can capitalism survive without ever-expanding production and ever-expanding consumer demand? William Greider argues that a global crisis is on the way:

> The economic luxury hidden in the capitalist process is space—capital-ism's ability to move on and re-create itself, abandoning the old for the new, creating and destroying production, while trailing a broad flume of ruined natural assets in its wake. Because globalization has nar-rowed distances, the luxury has diminished visibly. It is now possible for people to glimpse what was always true: the wasteful nature of their own prosperity. So long as the consequences could be kept afar from the beneficiaries, no one had much incentive—neither producers nor consumers—to face the collective implications.

> The brilliant possibility of "one world" is the emerging recognition that there is not going to be anyplace to hide. If Thailand becomes rich, where will it ship its toxic wastes? To Vietnam? To Africa? When every nation has industrialized, will they all dump their refuse in the ocean, as the so-called civilized societies now do? If the rain forests are shrinking, will someone invent machines to purify the air and generate rainfall? When the automobile conquers China, will the world be choking on the polluted atmosphere?

> The economic dilemma embedded in these questions revolves around price: global producers are caught up in the desperate competition to reduce costs and prices to hold on to market share, yet the earth's imperative asks the economic system to achieve the opposite—to raise

the price of goods so that consumers will begin paying the real production costs of their consumption. The marketplace (including most consumers) is naturally hostile to that imperative since it puts enterprises at immediate disadvantage unless all their competitors in the global system are required to accept the same pricing standards. There is at present no mechanism to achieve such harmony of purpose even if everyone agreed on its wisdom.

The social dilemma grows out of the same facts: If the collective interest requires a transformation of the industrial system's values, the poor will likely be injured more profoundly than the rich since they are the new entrants and least able to pay higher prices for consumption. The developing nations, after all, are emulating the rapacious practices they learned from the advanced economies and are understandably skeptical when high-minded reformers urge them not to repeat the same environmental mistakes—"mistakes" that have made Americans and Europeans quite wealthy. The environmental ethic proposes to alter the basic rules of capitalism at the very moment when some impoverished former colonies are at last enjoying the action.

WILLIAM GREIDER, ONE WORLD, READY OR NOT: THE MANIC LOGIC OF GLOBAL CAPITALISM 446–47 (1997).

2.   The Role of Advertising in Stimulating Desires.—

In Advertising at the Edge of the Apocalypse, Jhally argues that the cumulative cultural effects of advertising can be devastating to mankind:

> In this article I wish to make a simple claim: 20th century advertising is the most powerful and sustained system of propaganda in human history and its cumulative cultural effects, unless quickly checked, will be responsible for destroying the world as we know it. As it achieves this it will be responsible for the deaths of hundreds of thousands of non-western peoples and will prevent the peoples of the world from achieving true happiness. Simply stated, our survival as a species is dependent upon minimizing the threat from advertising and the commercial culture that has spawned it. I am stating my claims boldly at the outset so there can be no doubt as to what is at stake in our debates about the media and culture as we enter the new millennium.
>
> Seeking this understanding will involve clarifying what we mean by the power and effectiveness of ads, and of being able to pose the right question. For too long debate has been concentrated around the issue of whether ad campaigns create demand for a particular product. If you are Pepsi Cola, or Ford, or Anheuser Busch, then it may be the right question for your interests. But, if you are interested in the social power of advertising—the impact of advertising on society—then that is the wrong question.
>
> The right question would ask about the *cultural* role of advertising, not its marketing role. Culture is the place and space where a society tells stories about itself, where values are articulated and expressed, where notions of good and evil, of morality and immorality, are defined. In

our culture it is the stories of advertising that dominate the spaces that mediate this function. If human beings are essentially a storytelling species, then to study advertising is to examine the central storytelling mechanism of our society. The correct question to ask from this perspective, is not whether particular ads sell the products they are hawking, but what are the consistent stories that advertising spins as a whole about what is important in the world, about how to behave, about what is good and bad. Indeed, it is to ask what values does advertising consistently push.

Sut Jhally, *"Advertising at the Edge of the Apocalypse" Critical Studies in Media Commercialism*, New York: Oxford University Press, 2000, 27–39, *available at* http://www.sutjhally.com/onlinepubs/onlinepubs_frame.html (n.d.).

3. Consumerism and fantasy. Can exhortations like Jhally's and Greider's stand up against the entwining of goods, the good life, fantasies, and dreams?

CHAPTER 9

DEFINING FAMILY

Introduction

The systematic application of economic theory to the complex zone of intimate, cultural, religious, and long term relationships that we call the family has had a checkered history. In macroeconomic theory, the economic implications of human fertility were explored by the eighteenth-century population economist, Thomas Malthus, who argued that the population would outstrip food supply, leading to rising poverty. This proposition was spelled out in his 1798 work, An Essay on the Principle of Population, in which he argued:

> Population, when unchecked, increases in a geometrical ratio. Subsistence only increases in an arithmetical ratio. A slight acquaintance with numbers will show the immensity of the first power compared to the second.

He also predicted that fertility would rise and fall in direct correlation with rising and falling incomes. When this early hypothesis was challenged by the dramatic decrease during the late-nineteenth and early-twentieth century in birthrates in industrialized countries with increasing incomes, Malthus's theories fell out of favor and economists of the era concluded that family decision-making was unsuited for useful macroeconomic theory.

In the 1960s, economist Gary Becker turned his attention to the microeconomic dynamics of family decision making. Relying on rational choice theory, once thought to be confined to the marketplace, Becker pursued an ambitious research agenda exploring the dynamics of economic activity within spheres of social interaction, in kinship relations, usually thought to be outside of the market domain. These included his seminal idea of measuring "human capital," investments in education, training, and other prerequisites to market competence.

In Becker's 1981 *Treatise on the Family*, work that is directly related to this chapter in which we consider the social norms and legal rules that define the family, he extended rational choice theory to family behavior, previously thought to be dominated by sentiment and irrationality. One famous application of this idea is the "Rotten Kid Theorem" (RKT). The core idea of the RKT is somewhat counterintuitive. The RKT posits that when parents invest altruistically in their children's early development and education (see chapter 3), the children, no matter how selfish, will act to maximize the collective income of the entire family. Thus, the Rotten Kid Theorem introduces the concepts of interdependent preferences within a family system, and altruism. Both of these variables have a weak, if not nonexistent role in conventional microeconomic markets shaped by strangers. Needless to say, feminist economists have criticized both Becker's assumptions and conclusions.

In the cases that follow, we take up questions often put on the back burner of analysis in both family law and constitutional doctrine: What are the economic imperatives within living units that foster social cohesion for both individuals and society? Do legal rules incorporate social constructs about the "natural," pre-political norms of how a family should be configured? Does state intervention or refusal to intervene create economic incentives or disincentives for caring bonds that flow outside of conventional arrangements? Do legal rules privilege some family cultural practices over others, thus placing an economic burden on already disfavored groups? How are the tensions we referred to earlier between community, equality and individual rights resolved in these cases? Can Mrs. Moore's decision to provide housing for her grandchild be explained by Becker's rational choice theory?

A.   Nuclear Family vs. Extended Family

Moore v. City of East Cleveland, Ohio

Supreme Court of the United States, 431 U.S. 494 (1977).

■ Mr. Justice Powell announced the judgment of the Court, and delivered an opinion in which Mr. Justice Brennan, Mr. Justice Marshall, and Mr. Justice Blackmun joined.

[In an earlier, related case, *Village of Belle Terre v. Boraas*, 416 U.S. 1 (1974), the Supreme Court rejected a challenge to the constitutionality of a zoning ordinance of the Village of Belle Terre, New York, restricting land use to one-family dwellings, and prohibiting occupancy of a dwelling by more than two unrelated persons as a "family," while permitting occupancy by any number of persons related by blood, adoption, or marriage. Justice Douglas, expressing the view of seven members of the court, held that the zoning ordinance (a) was not unconstitutional since it did not violate any right of interstate travel; (b) involved no procedural disparity inflicted on some but not on others; (c) involved no fundamental constitutional right, such as the rights of association or privacy; and (d) was reasonable and bore a rational relationship to a permissible state objective, thus not violating equal protection.

Justice Marshall's dissent argued that the challenged ordinance was unconstitutional. Marshall would have found that it unnecessarily burdened tenants' fundamental rights of association and privacy guaranteed by the First and Fourteenth Amendments. Marshall argued that since the village's legitimate interests in controlling land use and population density could be protected by limiting the number of occupants without discriminating on the basis of such occupants' constitutionally protected choices of life style.]

East Cleveland's housing ordinance, like many throughout the country, limits occupancy of a dwelling unit to members of a single family. § 1351.02.[1] But the ordinance contains an unusual and complicated definitional section that recognizes as a "family" only a few categories of related individuals. § 1341.08.[2] Because her family, living together in her home, fits none of those categories, appellant stands convicted of a criminal offense. The question in this case is whether the ordinance violates the Due Process Clause of the Fourteenth Amendment.

I

Appellant, Mrs. Inez Moore, lives in her East Cleveland home together with her son, Dale Moore, Sr., and her two grandsons, Dale, Jr., and John Moore, Jr. The two boys are first cousins rather than brothers; we are told that John came to live with his grandmother and with the elder and younger Dale Moore after his mother's death.

In early 1973, Mrs. Moore received a notice of violation from the city, stating that John was an "illegal occupant" and directing her to comply with the ordinance. When she failed to remove him from her home, the city filed a criminal charge. Mrs. Moore moved to dismiss, claiming that the ordinance was constitutionally invalid on its face. Her motion was overruled, and upon conviction she was sentenced to five days in jail and a $25 fine. The Ohio Court of Appeals affirmed after giving full consideration to her constitutional claims and the Ohio Supreme Court denied review. We noted probable jurisdiction of her appeal, 425 U.S. 949 (1976).

---

1. All citations by section number refer to the Housing Code of the city of East Cleveland, Ohio.

2. Section 1341.08 (1966) provides:

" 'Family' means a number of individuals related to the nominal head of the household or to the spouse of the nominal head of the household living as a single housekeeping unit in a single dwelling unit, but limited to the following:

"(a) Husband or wife of the nominal head of the household.

"(b) Unmarried children of the nominal head of the household or of the spouse of the nominal head of the household, provided, however, that such unmarried children have no children residing with them.

"(c) Father or mother of the nominal head of the household or of the spouse of the nominal head of the household.

"(d) Notwithstanding the provisions of subsection (b) hereof, a family may include not more than one dependent married or unmarried child of the nominal head of the household or of the spouse of the nominal head of the household and the spouse and dependent children of such dependent child. For the purpose of this subsection, a dependent person is one who has more than fifty percent of his total support furnished for him by the nominal head of the household and the spouse of the nominal head of the household.

"(e) A family may consist of one individual."

II

The city argues that our decision in *Village of Belle Terre v. Boraas, 416 U.S. 1 (1974),* requires us to sustain the ordinance attacked here. Belle Terre, like East Cleveland, imposed limits on the types of groups that could occupy a single dwelling unit. Applying the constitutional standard announced in this Court's leading land-use case, *Euclid v. Ambler Realty Co.,* 272 U.S. 365 (1926),[6] we sustained the Belle Terre ordinance on the ground that it bore a rational relationship to permissible state objectives.

But one overriding factor sets this case apart from *Belle Terre.* The ordinance there affected only *unrelated* individuals. It expressly allowed all who were related by "blood, adoption, or marriage" to live together, and in sustaining the ordinance we were careful to note that it promoted "family needs" and "family values." 416 U.S., at 9. East Cleveland, in contrast, has chosen to regulate the occupancy of its housing by slicing deeply into the family itself. This is no mere incidental result of the ordinance. On its face it selects certain categories of relatives who may live together and declares that others may not. In particular, it makes a crime of a grandmother's choice to live with her grandson in circumstances like those presented here.

When a city undertakes such intrusive regulation of the family, neither *Belle Terre* nor *Euclid* governs; the usual judicial deference to the legislature is inappropriate. "This Court has long recognized that freedom of personal choice in matters of marriage and family life is one of the liberties protected by the Due Process Clause of the Fourteenth Amendment." * * * A host of cases * * * have consistently acknowledged a "private realm of family life which the state cannot enter." * * * Of course, the family is not beyond regulation. * * * But when the government intrudes on choices concerning family living arrangements, this Court must examine carefully the importance of the governmental interests advanced and the extent to which they are served by the challenged regulation. * * *

When thus examined, this ordinance cannot survive. The city seeks to justify it as a means of preventing overcrowding, minimizing traffic and parking congestion, and avoiding an undue financial burden on East Cleveland's school system. Although these are legitimate goals, the ordinance before us serves them marginally, at best.[7] For example, the ordinance permits any family consisting only of husband, wife, and unmarried children to live together, even if the family contains a half dozen licensed

---

Selected footnotes omitted.

6. *Euclid* held that land-use regulations violate the Due Process Clause if they are "clearly arbitrary and unreasonable, having no substantial relation to the public health, safety, morals, or general welfare." 272 U.S., at 395. See *Nectow v. Cambridge,* 277 U.S. 183, 188 (1928). Later cases have emphasized that the general welfare is not to be narrowly understood; it embraces a broad range of governmental purposes. See *Berman v. Parker,* 348 U.S. 26 (1954). But our cases have not departed from the requirement that the government's chosen means must rationally further some legitimate state purpose.

7. It is significant that East Cleveland has another ordinance specifically addressed to the problem of overcrowding. See *United States Dept. of Agriculture v. Moreno,* 413 U.S. 528, 536–537 (1973). Section 1351.03 limits population density directly, tying the maximum permissible occupancy of a dwelling to the habitable floor area. Even if John, Jr., and his father both remain in Mrs. Moore's household, the family stays well within these limits.

drivers, each with his or her own car. At the same time it forbids an adult brother and sister to share a household, even if both faithfully use public transportation. The ordinance would permit a grandmother to live with a single dependent son and children, even if his school-age children number a dozen, yet it forces Mrs. Moore to find another dwelling for her grandson John, simply because of the presence of his uncle and cousin in the same household. We need not labor the point. Section 1341.08 has but a tenuous relation to alleviation of the conditions mentioned by the city.

III

The city would distinguish the cases based on *Meyer* and *Pierce*. It points out that none of them "gives grandmothers any fundamental rights with respect to grandsons," * * * and suggests that any constitutional right to live together as a family extends only to the nuclear family—essentially a couple and their dependent children.

To be sure, these cases did not expressly consider the family relationship presented here. They were immediately concerned with freedom of choice with respect to childbearing, * * * or with the rights of parents to the custody and companionship of their own children, *Stanley v. Illinois, supra,* or with traditional parental authority in matters of child rearing and education. *Yoder, Ginsberg, Pierce, Meyer, supra.* But unless we close our eyes to the basic reasons why certain rights associated with the family have been accorded shelter under the Fourteenth Amendment's Due Process Clause, we cannot avoid applying the force and rationale of these precedents to the family choice involved in this case.

Understanding those reasons requires careful attention to this Court's function under the Due Process Clause. Mr. Justice Harlan described it eloquently:

> "Due process has not been reduced to any formula; its content cannot be determined by reference to any code. The best that can be said is that through the course of this Court's decisions it has represented the balance which our Nation, built upon postulates of respect for the liberty of the individual, has struck between that liberty and the demands of organized society. If the supplying of content to this Constitutional concept has of necessity been a rational process, it certainly has not been one where judges have felt free to roam where unguided speculation might take them. The balance of which I speak is the balance struck by this country, having regard to what history teaches are the traditions from which it developed as well as the traditions from which it broke. That tradition is a living thing. A decision of this Court which radically departs from it could not long survive, while a decision which builds on what has survived is likely to be sound. No formula could serve as a substitute, in this area, for judgment and restraint."

> ". . . [T]he full scope of the liberty guaranteed by the Due Process Clause cannot be found in or limited by the precise terms

of the specific guarantees elsewhere provided in the Constitution. This 'liberty' is not a series of isolated points pricked out in terms of the taking of property; the freedom of speech, press, and religion; the right to keep and bear arms; the freedom from unreasonable searches and seizures; and so on. It is a rational continuum which, broadly speaking, includes a freedom from all substantial arbitrary impositions and purposeless restraints, . . . and which also recognizes, what a reasonable and sensitive judgment must, that certain interests require particularly careful scrutiny of the state needs asserted to justify their abridgment." *Poe v. Ullman*, supra, at 542–543 (dissenting opinion).

Substantive due process has at times been a treacherous field for this Court. There *are* risks when the judicial branch gives enhanced protection to certain substantive liberties without the guidance of the more specific provisions of the Bill of Rights. As the history of the *Lochner* era demonstrates, there is reason for concern lest the only limits to such judicial intervention become the predilections of those who happen at the time to be Members of this Court. That history counsels caution and restraint. But it does not counsel abandonment, nor does it require what the city urges here: cutting off any protection of family rights at the first convenient, if arbitrary boundary—the boundary of the nuclear family.

Appropriate limits on substantive due process come not from drawing arbitrary lines but rather from careful "respect for the teachings of history [and] solid recognition of the basic values that underlie our society." * * * Our decisions establish that the Constitution protects the sanctity of the family precisely because the institution of the family is deeply rooted in this Nation's history and tradition.[12] It is through the family that we inculcate and pass down many of our most cherished values, moral and cultural.

---

12. In *Wisconsin v. Yoder*, 406 U.S. 205 (1972), the Court rested its holding in part on the constitutional right of parents to assume the primary role in decisions concerning the rearing of their children. That right is recognized because it reflects a "strong tradition" founded on "the history and culture of Western civilization," and because the parental role "is now established beyond debate as an enduring American tradition." *Id.*, at 232. In *Ginsberg v. New York*, 390 U.S. 629 (1968), the Court spoke of the same right as "basic in the structure of our society." *Id.*, at 639. *Griswold v. Connecticut, supra,* struck down Connecticut's anticontraception statute. Three concurring Justices, relying on both the Ninth and Fourteenth Amendments, emphasized that "the traditional relation of the family" is "a relation as old and as fundamental as our entire civilization." 381 U.S., at 496 (Goldberg, J., joined by Warren, C.J., and Brennan, J., concurring). Speaking of the same statute as that involved in *Griswold,* Mr. Justice Harlan wrote, dissenting in *Poe v. Ullman*, 367 U.S. 497, 551–552 (1961): "[H]ere we have not an intrusion into the home so much as on the life which characteristically has its place in the home. . . . The home derives its pre-eminence as the seat of family life. And the integrity of that life is something so fundamental that it has been found to draw to its protection the principles of more than one explicitly granted Constitutional right."

Although he agrees that the Due Process Clause has substantive content, Mr. Justice White in dissent expresses the fear that our recourse to history and tradition will "broaden enormously the horizons of the Clause." *Post,* at 549–550. To the contrary, an approach grounded in history imposes limits on the judiciary that are more meaningful than any based on the abstract formula taken from *Palko v. Connecticut*, 302 U.S. 319 (1937), and apparently suggested as an alternative. Cf. *Duncan v. Louisiana, supra,* at 149–150, n.14 (rejecting the

Ours is by no means a tradition limited to respect for the bonds uniting the members of the nuclear family. The tradition of uncles, aunts, cousins, and especially grandparents sharing a household along with parents and children has roots equally venerable and equally deserving of constitutional recognition.[14] Over the years millions of our citizens have grown up in just such an environment, and most, surely, have profited from it. Even if conditions of modern society have brought about a decline in extended family households, they have not erased the accumulated wisdom of civilization, gained over the centuries and honored throughout our history, that supports a larger conception of the family. Out of choice, necessity, or a sense of family responsibility, it has been common for close relatives to draw together and participate in the duties and the satisfactions of a common home. Decisions concerning child rearing, which *Yoder, Meyer, Pierce* and other cases have recognized as entitled to constitutional protection, long have been shared with grandparents or other relatives who occupy the same household—indeed who may take on major responsibility for the rearing of the children.[15] Especially in times of adversity, such as the death of a spouse or economic need, the broader family has tended to come together for mutual sustenance and to maintain or rebuild a secure home life. This is apparently what happened here.[16]

Whether or not such a household is established because of personal tragedy, the choice of relatives in this degree of kinship to live together may not lightly be denied by the State. *Pierce* struck down an Oregon law requiring all children to attend the State's public schools, holding that the Constitution "excludes any general power of the State to standardize its children by forcing them to accept instruction from public teachers only." 268 U.S., at 535. By the same token the Constitution prevents East Cleveland from standardizing its children—and its adults—by forcing all to live in certain narrowly defined family patterns.

Palko formula as the basis for deciding what procedural protections are required of a State, in favor of a historical approach based on the Anglo–American legal tradition). Indeed, the passage cited in MR. JUSTICE WHITE'S dissent as "most accurately reflect[ing] the thrust of prior decisions" on substantive due process, *post,* at 545, expressly points to history and tradition as the source for "supplying . . . content to this Constitutional concept." *Poe* v. *Ullman, supra,* at 542 (Harlan, J., dissenting).

14. See generally B. Yorburg, The Changing Family (1973); Bronfenbrenner, The Calamitous Decline of the American Family, Washington Post, Jan. 2, 1977, p. C1. Recent census reports bear out the importance of family patterns other than the prototypical nuclear family. In 1970, 26.5% of all families contained one or more members over 18 years of age, other than the head of household and spouse. U.S. Department of Commerce, 1970 Census of Population, vol. 1, pt. 1, Table 208. In 1960 the comparable figure was 26.1%. U.S. Department of Commerce, 1960 Census of Population, vol. 1, pt. 1, Table 187. Earlier data are not available.

15. Cf. *Prince* v. *Massachusetts*, 321 U.S. 158 (1944), which spoke broadly of family authority as against the State, in a case where the child was being reared by her aunt, not her natural parents.

16. We are told that the mother of John Moore, Jr., died when he was less than one year old. He, like uncounted others who have suffered a similar tragedy, then came to live with the grandmother to provide the infant with a substitute for his mother's care and to establish a more normal home environment. Brief for Appellant 25.

Reversed.

■ MR. JUSTICE BRENNAN, with whom MR. JUSTICE MARSHALL joins, concurring.

I join the plurality's opinion. I agree that the Constitution is not powerless to prevent East Cleveland from prosecuting as a criminal and jailing[1] a 63–year–old grandmother for refusing to expel from her home her now 10–year–old grandson who has lived with her and been brought up by her since his mother's death when he was less than a year old. I do not question that a municipality may constitutionally zone to alleviate noise and traffic congestion and to prevent overcrowded and unsafe living conditions, in short to enact reasonable land-use restrictions in furtherance of the legitimate objectives East Cleveland claims for its ordinance. But the zoning power is not a license for local communities to enact senseless and arbitrary restrictions which cut deeply into private areas of protected family life. East Cleveland may not constitutionally define "family" as essentially confined to parents and the parents' own children.[3] The plurality's opinion conclusively demonstrates that classifying family patterns in this eccentric way is not a rational means of achieving the ends East Cleveland claims for its ordinance, and further that the ordinance unconstitutionally abridges the "freedom of personal choice in matters of . . . family life [that] is one of the liberties protected by the Due Process Clause of the Fourteenth Amendment." *Cleveland Board of Education v. LaFleur,* 414 U.S. 632, 639–640 (1974). I write only to underscore the cultural myopia of the arbitrary boundary drawn by the East Cleveland ordinance in the light of the tradition of the American home that has been a feature of our society since our beginning as a Nation—the "tradition" in the plurality's words, "of uncles, aunts, cousins, and especially grandparents sharing a household along with parents and children. . . ." *Ante,* at 504. The line drawn by this ordinance displays a depressing insensitivity toward the economic and emotional needs of a very large part of our society.

In today's America, the "nuclear family" is the pattern so often found in much of white suburbia. J. Vander Zanden, Sociology: A Systematic Approach 322 (3d ed. 1975). The Constitution cannot be interpreted, however, to tolerate the imposition by government upon the rest of us of white suburbia's preference in patterns of family living. The "extended family" that provided generations of early Americans with social services

---

1. This is a criminal prosecution which resulted in the grandmother's conviction and sentence to prison and a fine. Section 1345.99 permits imprisonment of up to six months, and a fine of up to $1,000, for violation of any provision of the Housing Code. Each day such violation continues may, by the terms of this section, constitute a separate offense.

3. The East Cleveland ordinance defines "family" to include, in addition to the spouse of the "nominal head of the household," the couple's childless unmarried children, but only one dependent child (married or unmarried) having dependent children, and one parent of the nominal head of the household or of his or her spouse. Thus an "extended family" is authorized in only the most limited sense, and "family" is essentially confined to parents and their own children. Appellant grandmother was charged with violating the ordinance because John, Jr., lived with her at the same time her other grandson, Dale, Jr., was also living in the home; the latter is classified as an "unlicensed roomer" authorized by the ordinance to live in the house.

and economic and emotional support in times of hardship, and was the beachhead for successive waves of immigrants who populated our cities, remains not merely still a pervasive living pattern, but under the goad of brutal economic necessity, a prominent pattern—virtually a means of survival—for large numbers of the poor and deprived minorities of our society. For them compelled pooling of scant resources requires compelled sharing of a household.[5]

The "extended" form is especially familiar among black families.[6] We may suppose that this reflects the truism that black citizens, like generations of white immigrants before them, have been victims of economic and other disadvantages that would worsen if they were compelled to abandon extended, for nuclear, living patterns.[7] Even in husband and wife house-

---

5.   See, *e.g.,* H. Gans, The Urban Villagers 45–73, 245–249 (1962).

"Perhaps the most important—or at least the most visible—difference between the classes is one of family structure. *The working class subculture* is distinguished by the dominant role of the family circle....

"The specific characteristics of the family circle may differ widely—from the collateral peer group form of the West Enders, to the hierarchical type of the Irish, or to the classical three-generation extended family.... What matters most—and distinguishes this subculture from others—is that there be a family circle which is wider than the nuclear family, and that all of the opportunities, temptations, and pressures of the larger society be evaluated in terms of how they affect the ongoing way of life that has been built around this circle." *Id.,* at 244–245 (emphasis in original).

6.   Yorburg, *supra,* n. 4, at 108. "Within the black lower-class it has been quite common for several generations, or parts of the kin, to live together under one roof. Often a maternal grandmother is the acknowledged head of this type of household which has given rise to the term 'matrifocal' to describe lower-class black family patterns." See J. Scanzoni, The Black Family in Modern Society 134 (1971); see also Anderson, The Pains and Pleasures of Old Black Folks, Ebony 123, 128–130 (Mar. 1973). See generally E. Frazier, The Negro Family in the United States (1939); Lewis, The Changing Negro Family, in E. Ginzberg, ed., The Nation's Children 108 (1960).

The extended family often plays an important role in the rearing of young black children whose parents must work. Many such children frequently "spend all of their growing-up years in the care of extended kin.... Often children are 'given' to their grandparents, who rear them to adulthood.... Many children normally grow up in a three-generation household and they absorb the influences of grandmother and grandfather as well as mother and father." J. Ladner, Tomorrow's Tomorrow: The Black Woman 60 (1972).

7.   The extended family has many strengths not shared by the nuclear family.

"The case histories behind mounting rates of delinquency, addiction, crime, neurotic disabilities, mental illness, and senility in societies in which autonomous nuclear families prevail suggest that frequent failure to develop enduring family ties is a serious inadequacy for both individuals and societies." D. Blitsten, The World of the Family 256 (1963).

Extended families provide services and emotional support not always found in the nuclear family:

"The troubles of the nuclear family in industrial societies, generally, and in American society, particularly, stem largely from the inability of this type of family structure to provide certain of the services performed in the past by the extended family. Adequate health, education, and welfare provision, particularly for the two nonproductive generations in modern societies, the young and the old, is increasingly an insurmountable problem for the nuclear family. The unrelieved and sometimes unbearably intense parent-child relationship, where childrearing is not shared at least in part by others, and the loneliness of nuclear family

holds, 13% of black families compared with 3% of white families include relatives under 18 years old, in addition to the couple's own children.[8] In black households whose head is an elderly woman, as in this case, the contrast is even more striking: 48% of such black households, compared with 10% of counterpart white households, include related minor children not offspring of the head of the household.[9]

I do not wish to be understood as implying that East Cleveland's enforcement of its ordinance is motivated by a racially discriminatory purpose: The record of this case would not support that implication. But the prominence of other than nuclear families among ethnic and racial minority groups, including our black citizens, surely demonstrates that the "extended family" pattern remains a vital tenet of our society. It suffices that in prohibiting this pattern of family living as a means of achieving its objectives, appellee city has chosen a device that deeply intrudes into family associational rights that historically have been central, and today remain central, to a large proportion of our population.

Moreover, to sanction the drawing of the family line at the arbitrary boundary chosen by East Cleveland would surely conflict with prior decisions that protected "extended" family relationships. For the "private realm of family life which the state cannot enter," recognized as protected in *Prince v. Massachusetts*, 321 U.S. 158, 166 (1944), was the relationship of aunt and niece. And in *Pierce v. Society of Sisters*, 268 U.S. 510, 534–535 (1925), the protection held to have been unconstitutionally abridged was "the liberty of parents and *guardians* to direct the upbringing and education of children under their control" (emphasis added). See also *Wisconsin v. Yoder*, 406 U.S. 205, 232–233 (1972). Indeed, *Village of Belle Terre v. Boraas*, 416 U.S. 1 (1974), the case primarily relied upon by the appellee, actually supports the Court's decision. The Belle Terre ordinance barred only unrelated individuals from constituting a family in a single-family zone. The village took special care in its brief to emphasize that its ordinance did not in any manner inhibit the choice of *related* individuals to constitute a family, whether in the "nuclear" or "extended" form. This was because the village perceived that choice as one it was constitutionally powerless to inhibit. Its brief stated: "Whether it be the extended family of a more leisurely age or the nuclear family of today the role of the family in raising and training successive generations of the species makes it more important, we dare say, than any other social or legal institution.... *If any freedom not specifically mentioned in the Bill of Rights enjoys a 'preferred position' in the law it is most certainly the family.*" (Emphasis supplied.)

---

units, increasingly turned in on themselves in contracted and relatively isolated settings, is another major problem." Yorburg, *supra,* n. 4, at 194.

8. R. Hill, The Strengths of Black Families 5 (1972).

9. *Id.,* at 5–6. It is estimated that at least 26% of black children live in other than husband-wife families, "including foster parents, the presence of other male or female relatives (grandfather or grandmother, older brother or sister, uncle or aunt), male or female nonrelatives, [or with] only *one* adult (usually mother) present...." Scanzoni, *supra,* n. 6, at 44.

* * * The cited decisions recognized, as the plurality recognizes today, that the choice of the "extended family" pattern is within the "freedom of personal choice in matters of . . . family life [that] is one of the liberties protected by the Due Process Clause of the Fourteenth Amendment." 414 U.S., at 639–640.

* * *

■ Mr. Justice Stevens, concurring in the judgment.

In my judgment the critical question presented by this case is whether East Cleveland's housing ordinance is a permissible restriction on appellant's right to use her own property as she sees fit.

Long before the original States adopted the Constitution, the common law protected an owner's right to decide how best to use his own property. This basic right has always been limited by the law of nuisance which proscribes uses that impair the enjoyment of other property in the vicinity. But the question whether an individual owner's use could be further limited by a municipality's comprehensive zoning plan was not finally decided until this century.

The holding in *Euclid v. Ambler Realty Co.*, 272 U.S. 365, that a city could use its police power, not just to abate a specific use of property which proved offensive, but also to create and implement a comprehensive plan for the use of land in the community, vastly diminished the rights of individual property owners. It did not, however, totally extinguish those rights. On the contrary, that case expressly recognized that the broad zoning power must be exercised within constitutional limits.

In his opinion for the Court, Mr. Justice Sutherland fused the two express constitutional restrictions on any state interference with private property—that property shall not be taken without due process nor for a public purpose without just compensation—into a single standard: "[B]efore [a zoning] ordinance can be declared unconstitutional, [it must be shown to be] clearly arbitrary and unreasonable, *having no substantial relation to the public health, safety, morals, or general welfare.*" *Id.*, at 395 (emphasis added). This principle was applied in *Nectow v. Cambridge*, 277 U.S. 183; on the basis of a specific finding made by the state trial court that "the health, safety, convenience and general welfare of the inhabitants of the part of the city affected" would not be promoted by prohibiting the landowner's contemplated use, this Court held that the zoning ordinance as applied was unconstitutional. * * *

Litigation involving single-family zoning ordinances is common. Although there appear to be almost endless differences in the language used in these ordinances, they contain three principal types of restrictions. First, they define the kind of structure that may be erected on vacant land.[4]

---

4. As this Court recognized in *Euclid,* even residential apartments can have a negative impact on an area of single-family homes.

"[O]ften the apartment house is a mere parasite, constructed in order to take advantage of the open spaces and attractive surroundings created by [a single-family dwelling area]. . . .

Second, they require that a single-family home be occupied only by a "single housekeeping unit." Third, they often require that the housekeeping unit be made up of persons related by blood, adoption, or marriage, with certain limited exceptions.

Although the legitimacy of the first two types of restrictions is well settled, attempts to limit occupancy to related persons have not been successful. The state courts have recognized a valid community interest in preserving the stable character of residential neighborhoods which justifies a prohibition against transient occupancy. Nevertheless, in well-reasoned opinions, the courts of [several states] have permitted unrelated persons to occupy single-family residences notwithstanding an ordinance prohibiting, either expressly or implicitly, such occupancy.

These cases delineate the extent to which the state courts have allowed zoning ordinances to interfere with the right of a property owner to determine the internal composition of his household. The intrusion on that basic property right has not previously gone beyond the point where the ordinance defines a family to include only persons related by blood, marriage, or adoption. Indeed, as the cases in the margin demonstrate, state courts have not always allowed the intrusion to penetrate that far. The state decisions have upheld zoning ordinances which regulated the identity, as opposed to the number, of persons who may compose a household only to the extent that the ordinances require such households to remain nontransient, single-housekeeping units.

There appears to be no precedent for an ordinance which excludes any of an owner's relatives from the group of persons who may occupy his residence on a permanent basis. Nor does there appear to be any justification for such a restriction on an owner's use of his property. The city has failed totally to explain the need for a rule which would allow a homeowner to have two grandchildren live with her if they are brothers, but not if they are cousins. Since this ordinance has not been shown to have any "substantial relation to the public health, safety, morals, or general welfare" of the city of East Cleveland, and since it cuts so deeply into a fundamental right normally associated with the ownership of residential property—that of an owner to decide who may reside on his or her property—it must fall under the limited standard of review of zoning decisions which this Court preserved in *Euclid* and *Nectow*. Under that standard, East Cleveland's

---

[T]he coming of one apartment house is followed by others, interfering by their height and bulk with the free circulation of air and monopolizing the rays of the sun which otherwise would fall upon the smaller homes, and bringing, as their necessary accompaniments, the distributing noises incident to increased traffic and business, and the occupation, by means of moving and parked automobiles, of larger portions of the streets, thus detracting from their safety and depriving children of the privilege of quiet and open spaces for play, enjoyed by those in more favored localities,—until, finally, the residential character of the neighborhood and its desirability as a place of detached residences are utterly destroyed. Under these circumstances, apartment houses, which in a different environment would be not only entirely unobjectionable but highly desirable, come very near to being nuisances." 272 U.S., at 394–395.

unprecedented ordinance constitutes a taking of property without due process and without just compensation.

For these reasons, I concur in the Court's judgment.

■ MR. CHIEF JUSTICE BURGER, with whom MR. JUSTICE STEWART and MR. JUSTICE WHITE join, dissenting.

* * *

"... Courts are forced to add more clerks, more administrative personnel, to move cases faster and faster. They are losing ... time for reflection, time for the deliberate maturation of principles." [Department of Justice Committee on Revision of The Federal Judicial System, Report on the Needs of the Federal Courts 3–4 (1977).]

■ MR. JUSTICE STEWART, with whom MR. JUSTICE REHNQUIST joins, dissenting.

* * *

The *Belle Terre* decision * * * disposes of the appellant's contentions to the extent they focus not on her blood relationships with her sons and grandsons but on more general notions about the "privacy of the home." Her suggestion that every person has a constitutional right permanently to share his residence with whomever he pleases, and that such choices are "beyond the province of legitimate governmental intrusion," amounts to the same argument that was made and found unpersuasive in *Belle Terre*.

To be sure, the ordinance involved in *Belle Terre* did not prevent blood relatives from occupying the same dwelling, and the Court's decision in that case does not, therefore, foreclose the appellant's arguments based specifically on the ties of kinship present in this case. Nonetheless, I would hold, for the reasons that follow, that the existence of those ties does not elevate either the appellant's claim of associational freedom or her claim of privacy to a level invoking constitutional protection.

* * *

The "association" in this case is not for any purpose relating to the promotion of speech, assembly, the press, or religion. And wherever the outer boundaries of constitutional protection of freedom of association may eventually turn out to be, they surely do not extend to those who assert no interest other than the gratification, convenience, and *economy* [emphasis added] of sharing the same residence.

* * *

The appellant also challenges the single-family occupancy ordinance on equal protection grounds. Her claim is that the city has drawn an arbitrary and irrational distinction between groups of people who may live together as a "family" and those who may not. While acknowledging the city's right to preclude more than one family from occupying a single-dwelling unit, the appellant argues that the purposes of the single-family occupancy law would be equally served by an ordinance that did not prevent her from sharing her residence with her two sons and their sons.

This argument misconceives the nature of the constitutional inquiry. In a case such as this one, where the challenged ordinance intrudes upon no substantively protected constitutional right, it is not the Court's business to decide whether its application in a particular case seems inequitable, or even absurd. The question is not whether some other ordinance, drafted more broadly, might have served the city's ends as well or almost as well. The task, rather, is to determine if East Cleveland's ordinance violates the Equal Protection Clause of the United States Constitution. And in performing that task, it must be borne in mind that "[w]e deal with economic and social legislation where legislatures have historically drawn lines which we respect against the charge of violation of the Equal Protection Clause if the law be ' "reasonable, not arbitrary" ' (quoting *Royster Guano Co. v. Virginia*, 253 U.S. 412, 415) and bears 'a rational relationship to a [permissible] state objective.' *Reed v. Reed, 404 U.S. 71, 76."* *Village of Belle Terre v. Boraas*, 416 U.S., at 8. "[E]very line drawn by a legislature leaves some out that might well have been included. That exercise of discretion, however, is a legislative, not a judicial, function." *Ibid.* (footnote omitted).[8]

Viewed in the light of these principles, I do not think East Cleveland's definition of "family" offends the Constitution. The city has undisputed power to ordain single-family residential occupancy. *Village of Belle Terre v. Boraas, supra; Euclid v. Ambler Realty Co.*, 272 U.S. 365. And that power plainly carries with it the power to say what a "family" is. * * *

* * *

For these reasons, I think the Ohio courts did not err in rejecting the appellant's constitutional claims. Accordingly, I respectfully dissent.

■ Mr. Justice White, dissenting.

The Fourteenth Amendment forbids any State to "deprive any person of life, liberty, or property, without due process of law," or to "deny to any person within its jurisdiction the equal protection of the laws." Both provisions are invoked in this case in an attempt to invalidate a city zoning ordinance.

I

The emphasis of the Due Process Clause is on "process." * * * As Mr. Justice Harlan once observed, it has been "ably and insistently argued in

---

8. The observation of Mr. Justice Holmes quoted in the *Belle Terre* opinion, 416 U.S., at 8 n. 5, bears repeating here.

"When a legal distinction is determined, as no one doubts that it may be, between night and day, childhood and maturity, or any other extremes, a point has to be fixed or a line has to be drawn, or gradually picked out by successive decisions, to mark where the change takes place. Looked at by itself without regard to the necessity behind it the line or point seems arbitrary. It might as well or nearly as well be a little more to one side or the other. But when it is seen that a line or point there must be, and that there is no mathematical or logical way of fixing it precisely, the decision of the legislature must be accepted unless we can say that it is very wide of any reasonable mark." *Louisville Gas Co. v. Coleman*, 277 U.S. 32, 41 (dissenting opinion).

response to what were felt to be abuses by this Court of its reviewing power," that the Due Process Clause should be limited "to a guarantee of procedural fairness." *Poe v. Ullman*, 367 U.S. 497, 540 (1961) (dissenting opinion). These arguments had seemed "persuasive" to Justices Brandeis and Holmes, *Whitney v. California*, 274 U.S. 357, 373 (1927), but they recognized that the Due Process Clause, by virtue of case-to-case "judicial inclusion and exclusion," *Davidson v. New Orleans*, 96 U.S. 97, 104 (1878), had been construed to proscribe matters of substance, as well as inadequate procedures, and to protect from invasion by the States "all fundamental rights comprised within the term liberty." *Whitney v. California*, supra, at 373.

* * *

Although the Court regularly proceeds on the assumption that the Due Process Clause has more than a procedural dimension, we must always bear in mind that the substantive content of the Clause is suggested neither by its language nor by preconstitutional history; that content is nothing more than the accumulated product of judicial interpretation of the Fifth and Fourteenth Amendments. This is not to suggest, at this point, that any of these cases should be overruled, or that the process by which they were decided was illegitimate or even unacceptable, but only to underline Mr. Justice Black's constant reminder to his colleagues that the Court has no license to invalidate legislation which it thinks merely arbitrary or unreasonable. And no one was more sensitive than Mr. Justice Harlan to any suggestion that his approach to the Due Process Clause would lead to judges "roaming at large in the constitutional field." *Griswold v. Connecticut, supra*, at 502. No one proceeded with more caution than he did when the validity of state or federal legislation was challenged in the name of the Due Process Clause.

* * *

* * * Here the head of the household may house himself or herself and spouse, their parents, and any number of their unmarried children. A fourth generation may be represented by only one set of grandchildren and then only if born to a dependent child. The ordinance challenged by appellant prevents her from living with both sets of grandchildren only in East Cleveland, an area with a radius of three miles and a population of 40,000. Brief for Appellee 16 n. 1. The ordinance thus denies appellant the opportunity to live with all her grandchildren in this particular suburb; she is free to do so in other parts of the Cleveland metropolitan area. If there is power to maintain the character of a single-family neighborhood, as there surely is, some limit must be placed on the reach of the "family." Had it been our task to legislate, we might have approached the problem in a different manner than did the drafters of this ordinance; but I have no trouble in concluding that the normal goals of zoning regulation are present here and that the ordinance serves these goals by limiting, in identifiable circumstances, the number of people who can occupy a single household. The ordinance does not violate the Due Process Clause.

IV

For very similar reasons, the equal protection claim must fail, since it is not to be judged by the strict scrutiny standard employed when a fundamental interest or suspect classification is involved[.] * * * Rather, it is the generally applicable standard of *McGowan v. Maryland*, 366 U.S. 420, 425 (1961):

> "The constitutional safeguard [of the Equal Protection Clause] is offended only if the classification rests on grounds wholly irrelevant to the achievement of the State's objective. State legislatures are presumed to have acted within their constitutional power despite the fact that, in practice, their laws result in some inequality. A statutory discrimination will not be set aside if any state of facts reasonably may be conceived to justify it."

* * * Under this standard, it is not fatal if the purpose of the law is not articulated on its face, and there need be only a rational relation to the ascertained purpose.

On this basis, as already indicated, I have no trouble in discerning a rational justification for an ordinance that permits the head of a household to house one, but not two, dependent sons and their children.

Respectfully, therefore, I dissent and would affirm the judgment.

NOTES AND QUESTIONS

1. Teachings of history and sanctity of family. What limits can one expect to impose on the murky concepts of substantive due process as applied to government regulation of family life? Justice Powell, writing for the Court, thought that the "appropriate limits on due process come not from drawing arbitrary lines but rather from careful respect for the 'teachings of history [and] solid recognition of the basic values that underlie our society.' " *Moore*, supra at p. 655. *See also* Snyder v. Massachusetts, 291 U.S. 97, 105 (1934); Griswold v. Connecticut, 381 U.S. 479, 501 (1965) (Harlan, J., concurring). Powell goes on to say that the Court's "decisions establish that the Constitution protects the sanctity of the family precisely because the institution of the family is deeply rooted in this Nation's history and tradition." *Moore, supra*, at p. 655.

Is there a cultural consensus about what the "teachings of history" are? Even if we could agree on the definition of the composition of the family, there remain important differences about the norms that should apply within the family system. Disputes about "family values" are a staple of divisive political campaigns today. Families certainly make intensely different decisions as to methods of discipline, breast feeding, intra-family privacy, individual space expectations, the sharing of bathrooms, young children's nakedness in the home, the appropriate age to begin dating, and the willingness of family to discuss biology and emotional components of human sexuality, just to name a few. *See* GILL JAGGER & CAROLINE WRIGHT, CHANGING FAMILY VALUES (eds., 1999).

Has Justice Powell assumed the existence of a stable, widely shared set of values about family in our very diverse society?

Is the model of deference to history likely to produce stagnant or dynamic approaches to constitutional interpretation of state restrictions on family preferences? What should be the role of the legal system in these intra-family debates? What is the role of economic analysis in Justice Powell's approach? What would Fran Olson's arguments about how the law should view the concepts of non-intervention, privacy, and the private/public distinction suggest about Powell's basis of reasoning (see chapter 6)?

2.   Extended family vs. nuclear family. Justices Brennan and Marshall's concurrence focuses on the central role that the extended family has played for immigrant groups throughout American history, as well as African Americans today. The predominance of non-nuclear family structures in America, especially among ethnic and racial minority groups, suggests that the "extended family" pattern remains a vital tenet of our society. *See* ANDREW BILLINGSLEY, CLIMBING JACOB'S LADDER: THE ENDURING LEGACY OF AFRICAN-AMERICAN FAMILIES (1992); Ronald Angel & Marta Tienda, *Determinants of Extended Household Structure: Cultural Pattern or Economic Need?*, 87 AM. J. SOC. 1360 (1982). Under the reasoning in Brennan's concurrence, should associational forms which have been historically utilized by such populations in this country receive special protection?

If a minority group traditionally practiced polygamy in order to aid in pooling resources and to avoid the social problems associated with destitute widows and single motherhood, would Brennan's reasoning protect that group's definition of family? What about in the opposite case of polyandry? What about membership in a potentially criminal organization? *See* Linda Kelly, *Family Planning, American Style*, 52 ALA. L. REV. 943 (2001); Alison Harvison Young, *Reconceiving the Family: Challenging the Paradigm of the Exclusive Family*, 6 AM. U. J. GENDER & L. 505 (1998).

3.   Drawing the line. What sociological theories are and could be employed by the Court to decide where to draw the line defining what is and is not a family? Are courts competent to make use of the often conflicting theories of social science research? Should people not related by blood have similar associational rights as the traditional family? *See* Smith v. Organization of Foster Families, 431 U.S. 816 (1977). What about unmarried parents? *See* Stanley v. Illinois, 405 U.S. 645 (1972). What about people engaging in casual sex? *See* FW/PBS, Inc. v. City of Dallas, 493 U.S. 215 (1990). How would economic theory shape this debate?

4.   Strict scrutiny, rational basis, and *Moore v. East Cleveland*. At the time of *Moore v. East Cleveland*, Fourteenth Amendment Due Process analysis required that if a regulation excluded a suspect class of people, then that regulation must satisfy a "strict scrutiny" test. If the regulation did not discriminate against a suspect class, however, it needed only to pass a much more forgiving "rational basis" standard of review. Though the plurality opinion in *Moore* did not state that the ordinance in question should be subjected to strict scrutiny review, it does seem to be advocating more than a rational basis standard. Does *Moore* create another standard of review between strict scrutiny and rational relationship? If so, does the standard extend past the regulation of families? *See* Robert J. Hopperton, *The Presumption of Validity in American Land–Use Law: A Substitute for Analysis, A Source of Significant Confusion*, 23 B.C. ENVTL. AFF. L. REV. 301 (1996).

5. Race, economics, and family definitions. Brennan and Marshall decry the "cultural myopia" of the plurality. In today's America, the "nuclear family" is the pattern so often found in much of white suburbia. The Constitution cannot be interpreted, however, to tolerate the imposition by government of white suburbia's preference in patterns of living. *See also* PEGGY COOPER DAVIS, NEGLECTED STORIES: THE CONSTITUTION AND FAMILY VALUES (1997); DOROTHY ROBERTS, KILLING THE BLACK BODIES (1998).

On the relevance of racial variation in patterns of family formation, the dissent of Justices Stewart and Rehnquist takes the opposite position than the plurality and concurring opinions:

> The opinion of MR. JUSTICE POWELL and MR. JUSTICE BRENNAN's concurring opinion both emphasize the traditional importance of the extended family in American life. But I fail to understand why it follows that the residents of East Cleveland are constitutionally prevented from following what MR. JUSTICE BRENNAN calls the "pattern" of "white suburbia," even though that choice may reflect "cultural myopia." In point of fact, East Cleveland is a predominantly Negro community, with a Negro City Manager and City Commission.

Moore, *supra* at 537, n.7.

6. Additional reading. For an annotated catalog of cases and articles relating to the definition of "family" in zoning regulations and restrictive covenants, see James L. Rigelhaupt, Jr., *Annotation What Constitutes a "Family" Within Meaning of Zoning Regulation or Restrictive Covenant*, 71 A.L.R.3D 693 (2004). For a description of how housing codes can be used as tools for discrimination, see Ellen J. Pader, *CLUSTER VI: Class, Economics, and Social Rights: Space of Hate: Ethnicity, Architecture and Housing Discrimination*, 54 RUTGERS L. REV. 881 (2002). For an interesting proposal for defining family, see Angie Smolka, Note, *That's the Ticket: A New Way of Defining Family*, 10 CORNELL J. L. & PUB. POL'Y 629 (2001).

B. UNMARRIED HETEROSEXUAL COUPLES

Marvin v. Marvin
557 P.2d 106 (Cal. 1976).

■ JUSTICE TOBRINER delivered the opinion of the court.

During the past 15 years, there has been a substantial increase in the number of couples living together without marrying. Such nonmarital relationships lead to legal controversy when one partner dies or the couple separates. Courts of Appeal, faced with the task of determining property rights in such cases, have arrived at conflicting positions: two cases * * * have held that the Family Law Act (Civ. Code, § 4000 et seq.) requires division of the property according to community property principles, and one decision * * * has rejected that holding. We take this opportunity to resolve that controversy and to declare the principles which should govern distribution of property acquired in a nonmarital relationship.

We conclude: (1) The provisions of the Family Law Act do not govern the distribution of property acquired during a nonmarital relationship; such a relationship remains subject solely to judicial decision. (2) The courts should enforce express contracts between nonmarital partners except to the extent that the contract is explicitly founded on the consideration of meretricious sexual services. (3) In the absence of an express contract, the courts should inquire into the conduct of the parties to determine whether that conduct demonstrates an implied contract, agreement of partnership or joint venture, or some other tacit understanding between the parties. The courts may also employ the doctrine of quantum meruit, or equitable remedies such as constructive or resulting trusts, when warranted by the facts of the case.

In the instant case plaintiff and defendant lived together for seven years without marrying; all property acquired during this period was taken in defendant's name. When plaintiff sued to enforce a contract under which she was entitled to half the property and to support payments, the trial court granted judgment on the pleadings for defendant, thus leaving him with all property accumulated by the couple during their relationship. Since the trial court denied plaintiff a trial on the merits of her claim, its decision conflicts with the principles stated above, and must be reversed.

1. THE FACTUAL SETTING OF THIS APPEAL.

Since the trial court rendered judgment for defendant on the pleadings, we must accept the allegations of plaintiff's complaint as true, determining whether such allegations state, or can be amended to state, a cause of action. * * *

Plaintiff avers that in October of 1964 she and defendant "entered into an oral agreement" that while "the parties lived together they would combine their efforts and earnings and would share equally any and all property accumulated as a result of their efforts whether individual or combined." Furthermore, they agreed to "hold themselves out to the general public as husband and wife" and that "plaintiff would further render her services as a companion, homemaker, housekeeper and cook to . . . defendant."

Shortly thereafter plaintiff agreed to "give up her lucrative career as an entertainer [and] singer" in order to "devote her full time to defendant . . . as a companion, homemaker, housekeeper and cook;" in return defendant agreed to "provide for all of plaintiff's financial support and needs for the rest of her life."

Plaintiff alleges that she lived with defendant from October of 1964 through May of 1970 and fulfilled her obligations under the agreement. During this period the parties as a result of their efforts and earnings acquired in defendant's name substantial real and personal property, including motion picture rights worth over $1 million. In May of 1970, however, defendant compelled plaintiff to leave his household. He continued to support plaintiff until November of 1971, but thereafter refused to provide further support.

On the basis of these allegations plaintiff asserts two causes of action. The first, for declaratory relief, asks the court to determine her contract and property rights; the second seeks to impose a constructive trust upon one half of the property acquired during the course of the relationship.
* * *

2.   *PLAINTIFF'S COMPLAINT STATES A CAUSE OF ACTION FOR BREACH OF AN EXPRESS CONTRACT.*

* * * [W]e established the principle that nonmarital partners may lawfully contract concerning the ownership of property acquired during the relationship. * * * "If a man and woman [who are not married] live together as husband and wife under an agreement to pool their earnings and share equally in their joint accumulations, equity will protect the interests of each in such property."

In the case before us plaintiff, basing her cause of action in contract upon these precedents, maintains that the trial court erred in denying her a trial on the merits of her contention. Although that court did not specify the ground for its conclusion that plaintiff's contractual allegations stated no cause of action, defendant offers some four theories to sustain the ruling; we proceed to examine them.

Defendant first and principally relies on the contention that the alleged contract is so closely related to the supposed "immoral" character of the relationship between plaintiff and himself that the enforcement of the contract would violate public policy. He points to cases asserting that a contract between nonmarital partners is unenforceable if it is "involved in" an illicit relationship. * * * A review of the numerous California decisions concerning contracts between nonmarital partners, however, reveals that the courts have not employed such broad and uncertain standards to strike down contracts. The decisions instead disclose a narrower and more precise standard: a contract between nonmarital partners is unenforceable only *to the extent* that it *explicitly* rests upon the immoral and illicit consideration of meretricious sexual services.

In the first case to address this issue, *Trutalli v. Meraviglia* * * * the parties had lived together without marriage for 11 years and had raised two children. The man sued to quiet title to land he had purchased in his own name during this relationship; the woman defended by asserting an agreement to pool earnings and hold all property jointly. Rejecting the assertion of the illegality of the agreement, the court stated that "The fact that the parties to this action at the time they agreed to invest their earnings in property to be held jointly between them were living together in an unlawful relation, did not disqualify them from entering into a lawful agreement with each other, so long as such immoral relation was not made *a consideration* of their agreement." (Emphasis added.) * * *

In *Bridges v. Bridges, supra,* * * * both parties were in the process of obtaining divorces from their erstwhile respective spouses. The two parties agreed to live together, to share equally in property acquired, and to marry when their divorces became final. The man worked as a salesman and used his savings to purchase properties. The woman kept house, cared for seven children, three from each former marriage and one from the nonmarital relationship, and helped construct improvements on the properties. When they separated, without marrying, the court awarded the woman one-half the value of the property. Rejecting the man's contention that the contract was illegal, the court stated that: "Nowhere is it expressly testified to by anyone that there was anything in the agreement for the pooling of assets and the sharing of accumulations that contemplated meretricious relations as any part of the consideration or as any object of the agreement." * * *

* * * Numerous other cases have upheld enforcement of agreements between nonmarital partners in factual settings essentially indistinguishable from the present case.

* * * Although the past decisions hover over the issue in the somewhat wispy form of the figures of a Chagall painting, we can abstract from those decisions a clear and simple rule. The fact that a man and woman live together without marriage, and engage in a sexual relationship, does not in itself invalidate agreements between them relating to their earnings, property, or expenses. Neither is such an agreement invalid merely because the parties may have contemplated the creation or continuation of a nonmarital relationship when they entered into it. Agreements between nonmarital partners fail only to the extent that they rest upon a consideration of meretricious sexual services. Thus the rule asserted by defendant, that a contract fails if it is "involved in" or made "in contemplation" of a nonmarital relationship, cannot be reconciled with the decisions.

The three cases cited by defendant which have *declined* to enforce contracts between nonmarital partners involved consideration that *was* expressly founded upon an illicit sexual services. In *Hill v. Estate of Westbrook,* * * * the woman promised to keep house for the man, to live with him as man and wife, and to bear his children; the man promised to provide for her in his will, but died without doing so. Reversing a judgment for the woman based on the reasonable value of her services, the Court of Appeal stated that "the action is predicated upon a claim which seeks, among other things, the reasonable value of living with decedent in meretricious relationship and bearing him two children.... The law does not award compensation for living with a man as a concubine and bearing him children.... As the judgment is at least in part, for the value of the claimed services for which recovery cannot be had, it must be reversed."

* * * Upon retrial, the trial court found that it could not sever the contract and place an independent value upon the legitimate services performed by claimant. We therefore affirmed a judgment for the estate. * * *

In the only other cited decision refusing to enforce a contract, * * * the contract "was based on the consideration that the parties live together as husband and wife." * * * Viewing the contract as calling for adultery, the court held it illegal.[6]

The decisions in the *Hill* and *Updeck* cases thus demonstrate that a contract between nonmarital partners, even if expressly made in contemplation of a common living arrangement, is invalid only if sexual acts form an inseparable part of the consideration for the agreement. In sum, a court will not enforce a contract for the pooling of property and earnings if it is explicitly and inseparably based upon services as a paramour. The Court of Appeal opinion in *Hill*, however, indicates that even if sexual services are part of the contractual consideration, any *severable* portion of the contract supported by independent consideration will still be enforced.

The principle that a contract between nonmarital partners will be enforced unless expressly and inseparably based upon an illicit consideration of sexual services not only represents the distillation of the decisional law, but also offers a far more precise and workable standard than that advocated by defendant.

* * * Similarly, in the present case a standard which inquires whether an agreement is "involved" in or "contemplates" a nonmarital relationship is vague and unworkable. Virtually all agreements between nonmarital partners can be said to be "involved" in some sense in the fact of their mutual sexual relationship, or to "contemplate" the existence of that relationship. Thus defendant's proposed standards, if taken literally, might invalidate all agreements between nonmarital partners, a result no one favors. Moreover, those standards offer no basis to distinguish between valid and invalid agreements. By looking not to such uncertain tests, but only to the consideration underlying the agreement, we provide the parties and the courts with a practical guide to determine when an agreement between nonmarital partners should be enforced.

* * * In summary, we base our opinion on the principle that adults who voluntarily live together and engage in sexual relations are nonethe-

---

6. Although not cited by defendant, the only California precedent which supports his position is *Heaps v. Toy* * * * In that case the woman promised to leave her job, to refrain from marriage, to be a companion to the man, and to make a permanent home for him; he agreed to support the woman and her child for life. The Court of Appeal held the agreement invalid as a contract in restraint of marriage (Civ. Code, § 1676) and, alternatively, as "contrary to good morals" (Civ. Code, § 1607). The opinion does not state that sexual relations formed any part of the consideration for the contract, nor explain how—unless the contract called for sexual relations—the woman's employment as a companion and housekeeper could be contrary to good morals.

The alternative holding in *Heaps v. Toy, supra,* finding the contract in that case contrary to good morals, is inconsistent with the numerous California decisions upholding contracts between nonmarital partners when such contracts are not founded upon an illicit consideration, and is therefore disapproved.

less as competent as any other persons to contract respecting their earnings and property rights. Of course, they cannot lawfully contract to pay for the performance of sexual services, for such a contract is, in essence, an agreement for prostitution and unlawful for that reason. But they may agree to pool their earnings and to hold all property acquired during the relationship in accord with the law governing community property; conversely they may agree that each partner's earnings and the property acquired from those earnings remains the separate property of the earning partner.[10] So long as the agreement does not rest upon illicit meretricious consideration, the parties may order their economic affairs as they choose, and no policy precludes the courts from enforcing such agreements.

In the present instance, plaintiff alleges that the parties agreed to pool their earnings, that they contracted to share equally in all property acquired, and that defendant agreed to support plaintiff. The terms of the contract as alleged do not rest upon any unlawful consideration. We therefore conclude that the complaint furnishes a suitable basis upon which the trial court can render declaratory relief. * * * The trial court consequently erred in granting defendant's motion for judgment on the pleadings.

3.   * * *

As we have noted, both causes of action in plaintiff's complaint allege an express contract; neither assert any basis for relief independent from the contract. In *In re Marriage of Cary,* * * * however, the Court of Appeal held that, in view of the policy of the Family Law Act, property accumulated by nonmarital partners in an actual family relationship should be divided equally. Upon examining the *Cary* opinion, the parties to the present case realized that plaintiff's alleged relationship with defendant might arguably support a cause of action independent of any express contract between the parties. The parties have therefore briefed and discussed the issue of the property rights of a nonmarital partner in the absence of an express contract. Although our conclusion that plaintiff's complaint states a cause of action based on an express contract alone compels us to reverse the judgment for defendant, resolution of the *Cary* issue will serve both to guide the parties upon retrial and to resolve a conflict presently manifest in published Court of Appeal decisions.

Both plaintiff and defendant stand in broad agreement that the law should be fashioned to carry out the reasonable expectations of the parties. Plaintiff, however, presents the following contentions: that the decisions prior to *Cary* rest upon implicit and erroneous notions of punishing a party for his or her guilt in entering into a nonmarital relationship, that such decisions result in an inequitable distribution of property accumulated during the relationship, and that *Cary* correctly held that the enactment of

---

10. A great variety of other arrangements are possible. The parties might keep their earnings and property separate, but agree to compensate one party for services which benefit the other. They may choose to pool only part of their earnings and property, to form a partnership or joint venture, or to hold property acquired as joint tenants or tenants in common, or agree to any other such arrangement. * * *

the Family Law Act in 1970 overturned those prior decisions. Defendant in response maintains that the prior decisions merely applied common law principles of contract and property to persons who have deliberately elected to remain outside the bounds of the community property system.[11] *Cary,* defendant contends, erred in holding that the Family Law Act vitiated the force of the prior precedents.

* * * This failure of the courts to recognize an action by a nonmarital partner based upon implied contract, or to grant an equitable remedy, contrasts with the judicial treatment of the putative spouse. Prior to the enactment of the Family Law Act, no statute granted rights to a putative spouse.[13] The courts accordingly fashioned a variety of remedies by judicial decision. Some cases permitted the putative spouse to recover half the property on a theory that the conduct of the parties implied an agreement of partnership or joint venture. * * * Others permitted the spouse to recover the reasonable value of rendered services, less the value of support received. * * * Finally, decisions affirmed the power of a court to employ equitable principles to achieve a fair division of property acquired during putative marriage. * * *

Thus in summary, the cases prior to *Cary* exhibited a schizophrenic inconsistency. By enforcing an express contract between nonmarital partners unless it rested upon an unlawful consideration, the courts applied a common law principle as to contracts. Yet the courts disregarded the common law principle that holds that implied contracts can arise from the conduct of the parties.[16] Refusing to enforce such contracts, the courts

---

11. We note that a deliberate decision to avoid the strictures of the community property system is not the only reason that couples live together without marriage. Some couples may wish to avoid the permanent commitment that marriage implies, yet be willing to share equally any property acquired during the relationship; others may fear the loss of pension, welfare, or tax benefits resulting from marriage * * * Others may engage in the relationship as a possible prelude to marriage. In lower socio-economic groups the difficulty and expense of dissolving a former marriage often leads couples to choose a nonmarital relationship; many unmarried couples may also incorrectly believe that the doctrine of common law marriage prevails in California, and thus that they are in fact married. Consequently we conclude that the mere fact that a couple have not participated in a valid marriage ceremony cannot serve as a basis for a court's inference that the couple intend to keep their earnings and property separate and independent; the parties' intention can only be ascertained by a more searching inquiry into the nature of their relationship.

13. The Family Law Act, in Civil Code section 4452, classifies property acquired during a putative marriage as " 'quasi-marital property,' " and requires that such property be divided upon dissolution of the marriage in accord with Civil Code section 4800.

16. "Contracts may be express or implied. These terms however do not denote different kinds of contracts, but have reference to the evidence by which the agreement between the parties is shown. If the agreement is shown by the direct words of the parties, spoken or written, the contract is said to be an express one. But if such agreement can only be shown by the acts and conduct of the parties, interpreted in the light of the subject matter and of the surrounding circumstances, then the contract is an implied one." * * * Thus, as Justice Schauer observed in *Desny v. Wilder* * * * in a sense all contracts made in fact, as distinguished from quasi-contractual obligations, are express contracts, differing only in the manner in which the assent of the parties is expressed and proved. * * *

spoke of leaving the parties "in the position in which they had placed themselves" * * * just as if they were guilty parties *in pari delicto*.

Justice Curtis noted this inconsistency in his dissenting opinion in *Vallera*, pointing out that "if an express agreement will be enforced, there is no legal or just reason why an implied agreement to share the property cannot be enforced." * * * And in *Keene v. Keene* * * * Justice Peters observed that if the man and woman "were not illegally living together ... it would be a plain business relationship and a contract would be implied."

* * *

Still another inconsistency in the prior cases arises from their treatment of property accumulated through joint effort. To the extent that a partner had contributed *funds* or *property*, the cases held that the partner obtains a proportionate share in the acquisition, despite the lack of legal standing of the relationship. * * * Yet courts have refused to recognize just such an interest based upon the contribution of *services*. As Justice Curtis points out "Unless it can be argued that a woman's services as cook, housekeeper, and homemaker are valueless, it would seem logical that if, when she contributes money to the purchase of property, her interest will be protected, then when she contributes her services in the home, her interest in property accumulated should be protected." * * *

Thus as of 1973, the time of the filing of *In re Marriage of Cary* * * * the cases apparently held that a nonmarital partner who rendered services in the absence of express contract could assert no right to property acquired during the relationship. The facts of *Cary* demonstrated the unfairness of that rule.

Janet and Paul Cary had lived together, unmarried, for more than eight years. They held themselves out to friends and family as husband and wife, reared four children, purchased a home and other property, obtained credit, filed joint income tax returns, and otherwise conducted themselves as though they were married. Paul worked outside the home, and Janet generally cared for the house and children.

In 1971 Paul petitioned for "nullity of the marriage." Following a hearing on that petition, the trial court awarded Janet half the property acquired during the relationship, although all such property was traceable to Paul's earnings. The Court of Appeal affirmed the award.

Reviewing the prior decisions which had denied relief to the homemaking partner, the Court of Appeal reasoned that those decisions rested upon a policy of punishing persons guilty of cohabitation without marriage. The Family Law Act, the court observed, aimed to eliminate fault or guilt as a basis for dividing marital property. But once fault or guilt is excluded, the court reasoned, nothing distinguishes the property rights of a nonmarital "spouse" from those of a putative spouse. Since the latter is entitled to half the " 'quasi marital property' " (Civ. Code, § 4452), the Court of Appeal concluded that, giving effect to the policy of the Family Law Act, a nonmarital cohabitator should also be entitled to half the property accumulated during an "actual family relationship." * * *

    * * *

    * * * The argument that granting remedies to the nonmarital partners would discourage marriage must fail; as *Cary* pointed out, "with equal or greater force the point might be made that the pre–1970 rule was calculated to cause the income-producing partner to avoid marriage and thus retain the benefit of all of his or her accumulated earnings." * * * Although we recognize the well-established public policy to foster and promote the institution of marriage * * * perpetuation of judicial rules which result in an inequitable distribution of property accumulated during a nonmarital relationship is neither a just nor an effective way of carrying out that policy.

    In summary, we believe that the prevalence of nonmarital relationships in modern society and the social acceptance of them, marks this as a time when our courts should by no means apply the doctrine of the unlawfulness of the so-called meretricious relationship to the instant case. As we have explained, the nonenforceability of agreements expressly providing for meretricious conduct rested upon the fact that such conduct, as the word suggests, pertained to and encompassed prostitution. To equate the nonmarital relationship of today to such a subject matter is to do violence to an accepted and wholly different practice.

    We are aware that many young couples live together without the solemnization of marriage, in order to make sure that they can successfully later undertake marriage. This trial period, preliminary to marriage, serves as some assurance that the marriage will not subsequently end in dissolution to the harm of both parties. We are aware, as we have stated, of the pervasiveness of nonmarital relationships in other situations.

    The mores of the society have indeed changed so radically in regard to cohabitation that we cannot impose a standard based on alleged moral considerations that have apparently been so widely abandoned by so many. Lest we be misunderstood, however, we take this occasion to point out that the structure of society itself largely depends upon the institution of marriage, and nothing we have said in this opinion should be taken to derogate from that institution. The joining of the man and woman in marriage is at once the most socially productive and individually fulfilling relationship that one can enjoy in the course of a lifetime.

    We conclude that the judicial barriers that may stand in the way of a policy based upon the fulfillment of the reasonable expectations of the parties to a nonmarital relationship should be removed. As we have explained, the courts now hold that express agreements will be enforced unless they rest on an unlawful meretricious consideration. We add that in the absence of an express agreement, the courts may look to a variety of other remedies in order to protect the parties' lawful expectations.[24]

---

    24. We do not seek to resurrect the doctrine of common law marriage, which was abolished in California by statute in 1895. * * * Thus we do not hold that plaintiff and

The courts may inquire into the conduct of the parties to determine whether that conduct demonstrates an implied contract or implied agreement of partnership or joint venture * * * or some other tacit understanding between the parties. The courts may, when appropriate, employ principles of constructive trust * * * or resulting trust * * *. Finally, a nonmarital partner may recover in quantum meruit for the reasonable value of household services rendered less the reasonable value of support received if he can show that he rendered services with the expectation of monetary reward. * * *[25]

Since we have determined that plaintiff's complaint states a cause of action for breach of an express contract, and, as we have explained, can be amended to state a cause of action independent of allegations of express contract,[26] we must conclude that the trial court erred in granting defendant a judgment on the pleadings.

The judgment is reversed and the cause remanded for further proceedings consistent with the views expressed herein.[27]

■ Mr. Justice Clark, concurring in part and dissenting in part.

The majority opinion properly permit recovery on the basis of either express or implied in fact agreement between the parties. These being the issues presented, their resolution requires reversal of the judgment. Here, the opinion should stop.

This court should not attempt to determine all anticipated rights, duties and remedies within every meretricious relationship—particularly in vague terms. Rather, these complex issues should be determined as each arises in a concrete case.

* * *

The general sweep of the majority opinion raises but fails to answer several questions. First, because the Legislature specifically excluded some parties to a meretricious relationship from the equal division rule of Civil Code section 4452, is this court now free to create an equal division rule? Second, upon termination of the relationship, is it equitable to impose the economic obligations of lawful spouses on meretricious parties when the latter may have rejected matrimony to avoid such obligations? Third, does

---

defendant were "married," nor do we extend to plaintiff the rights which the Family Law Act grants valid or putative spouses; we hold only that she has the same rights to enforce contracts and to assert her equitable interest in property acquired through her effort as does any other unmarried person.

25. Our opinion does not preclude the evolution of additional equitable remedies to protect the expectations of the parties to a nonmarital relationship in cases in which existing remedies prove inadequate; the suitability of such remedies may be determined in later cases in light of the factual setting in which they arise.

26. We do not pass upon the question whether, in the absence of an express or implied contractual obligation, a party to a nonmarital relationship is entitled to support payments from the other party after the relationship terminates.

27. We wish to commend the parties and amici for the exceptional quality of the briefs and argument in this case.

not application of equitable principles—necessitating examination of the conduct of the parties—violate the spirit of the Family Law Act of 1969, designed to eliminate the bitterness and acrimony resulting from the former fault system in divorce? Fourth, will not application of equitable principles reimpose upon trial courts the unmanageable burden of arbitrating domestic disputes? Fifth, will not a quantum meruit system of compensation for services—discounted by benefits received—place meretricious spouses in a better position than lawful spouses? Sixth, if a quantum meruit system is to be allowed, does fairness not require inclusion of all services and all benefits regardless of how difficult the evaluation?

When the parties to a meretricious relationship show by express or implied in fact agreement they intend to create mutual obligations, the courts should enforce the agreement. However, in the absence of agreement, we should stop and consider the ramifications before creating economic obligations which may violate legislative intent, contravene the intention of the parties, and surely generate undue burdens on our trial courts.

By judicial overreach, the majority perform a nunc pro tunc marriage, dissolve it, and distribute its property on terms never contemplated by the parties, case law or the Legislature.

NOTES AND QUESTIONS

1. The choice to marry. Rational Choice Theory relies on the assumption that humans have goals and sets of hierarchically ordered preferences or "utilities." In making a choice between one behavior and another, humans will weigh the utility of the behavior against its costs, including the utility of alternate behaviors and the cost of selecting this behavior over another in terms of utility foregone. In an efficient transaction between two parties, the goal is presumably to increase utility for at least one party without sacrificing utility for either party. *See* MICHAEL ALLINGHAM, RATIONAL CHOICE (1999). How do the arguments of Rational Choice Theory apply to *Marvin v. Marvin*? What are the utilities and costs of opting not to marry and instead choosing to contract as the plaintiff in *Marvin* claims? Has utility been maximized in this transaction, given the foregone utility of the alternate behavior of marriage? *See* Margaret F. Brinig, *Unmarried Partners and the Legacy of* Marvin v. Marvin: *The Influence of* Marvin v. Marvin *on Housework during Marriage*, 76 NOTRE DAME L. REV. 1311 (2001). Which sex is most likely to receive the primary benefit of the express and implied contract rules? *See* Debra S. Betteridge, Note, *Inequality in Marital Liabilities: The Need for Equal Protection When Modifying the Necessaries Doctrine*, 17 U. MICH. J.L. REFORM 43 (1983). Are important differences in the transaction costs likely to arise from the enforcement of the express and implied contract theories?

2. History and tradition? Is the court ignoring legal, cultural, and religious arguments in deciding that parties who are eligible to marry but who choose not to should not be given the economic benefits of marriage? Does the court disregard the "history and tradition" of rewarding compliance with the social and legal norms of marriage? *See* Carol Weisbrod, *Gender–Based Analyses of World Religions and the Law: Universals and Particulars: A Comment on Women's Human Rights and Religious Marriage Contracts,* 9 S. CAL. REV. L. & WOMEN'S STUD. 77 (1999). What is the role of cultural change and what framework of analysis did this court rely upon to assess the relevance of these changes to its decision in this case? How do the rationales employed by the court in *Marvin* relate to those employed in *Moore v. East Cleveland*?

3. Bargaining. How would you expect the pre-cohabitation bargaining dynamic to be affected by this decision? How do differences in gender correspond to differences in bargaining power? *See* Elizabeth S. Anderson, *Women and Contracts: No New Deal,* 88 MICH L. REV. 1792 (1990). Is there any way for a couple to cohabit without automatically pooling their assets, short of writing an extremely unromantic contract explicitly separating their assets? *See* Jennifer K. Robbennolt & Monica Kirkpatrick Johnson, *Therapeutic Jurisprudence: Legal Planning for Unmarried Committed Partners: Empirical Lessons for a Preventive and Therapeutic Approach,* 41 ARIZ. L. REV. 417 (1999). How does the rule announced in *Marvin* affect the cultural and economic status of the parties? Furthermore, does this rule provide disincentives for parties who have a strong competitive position in the marriage market because of beauty, wealth, or social status to ever marry? *See* Amy L. Wax, *Bargaining in the Shadow of the Market: Is There a Future for Egalitarian Marriage?*, 84 VA. L. REV. 509 (1998).

4. Meretricious consideration and prostitution. The holding of *Marvin* is limited to the extent that it does not mandate the enforcement of contracts which are made expressly in consideration of sexual services. Given that the courts, as a rule, do not examine the adequacy of consideration, does the court's decision in *Marvin* open the door to legalized prostitution? If a prostitute were to say to a client, "Those pants don't look good on you, let's get them off," would that "fashion advice" qualify as separate consideration and thus render a contract between prostitute and client enforceable under *Marvin*? What is the implication of the court referring to the relationship of two unwed cohabitants as "meretricious," defined as "of, relating to, or befitting a prostitute; having the character of a prostitute" or "showily or superficially attractive but having in reality no value or integrity." OXFORD ENGLISH DICTIONARY (drafted. 2001), *available at* www.oed.com.

5. Common law marriage. From 1920 to 1930, Charlotte Fixel–Erlanger and Abraham Lincoln Erlanger lived together. Charlotte abandoned her career as an actress to support Abraham and take care of his house. Charlotte and Abraham never married and, when Abraham died in 1930, Charlotte was left out of his will. However, in 1932, after a three-month trial, Charlotte was given rights in Abraham's estate as his common-law wife. *In re Estate of Erlanger*, 145 Misc. 1, 259 N.Y.S. 610 (N.Y. Surr. Ct.

1932). Does *Marvin* do anything more than sanction adultery? Is *Marvin* the beginning of common-law polygamy?

6.   Additional reading. For more information on the law of cohabitation, see generally Ariela R. Dubler, *Wifely Behavior: A Legal History of Acting Married*, 100 COLUM. L. REV. 957 (2000); Katherine C. Gordon, Note, *The Necessity and Enforcement of Cohabitation Agreements: When Strings Will Attach and How to Prevent Them a State Survey*, 37 BRANDEIS L.J. 245 (1998/1999). For more information on associational rights and marriage, see generally Symposium, *Liberty and Marriage–Baehr and Beyond: Due Process in 1998*, 12 BYU J. PUB. L. 253 (1998); David A. Anderson, Note, *Jail, Jail, The Gang's All Here: Senate Crime Bill Section 521, The Criminal Street Gang Provision*, 36 B.C. L. REV. 527 (1995). For information on how *Marvin* extends to same sex couples, see Sharmila Roy Grossman, Comment, *The Illusory Rights of* Marvin v. Marvin *for the Same–Sex Couple versus the Preferable Canadian Alternative—*M. v. H., 38 CAL. W. L. REV. 547 (2002).

C.   SAME–SEX COUPLES

Whorton v. Dillingham

248 Cal.Rptr. 405 (Cal. Ct. App. 1988).

■ JUDGE WORK delivered the opinion of the court.

Donnis G. Whorton appeals a judgment dismissing his action against Benjamin F. Dillingham III after the court sustained a demurrer without leave to amend. Whorton claims property rights based on an oral cohabiters' agreement with which he fully complied but which Dillingham breached after approximately seven years. The trial court found the pleadings showed the contract was unenforceable as expressly and inseparably based on sexual services. We conclude Whorton has alleged consideration for the purported contract substantially independent of sexual services, and reverse the judgment.

I

On appeal from a judgment of dismissal arising from the sustaining of a demurrer, we accept the facts pleaded in the complaint as true. (*Noguera v. N. Monterey County Unified Sch. Dist.* (1980) 106 Cal. App. 3d 64, 66, 164 Cal. Rptr. 808.)

The alleged facts include the following. At the time the parties began dating and entered into a homosexual relationship, Whorton was studying to obtain his Associate in Arts degree, intending to enroll in a four-year college and obtain a Bachelor of Arts degree. When the parties began living together in 1977, they orally agreed that Whorton's exclusive, full-time occupation was to be Dillingham's chauffeur, bodyguard, social and business secretary, partner and counselor in real estate investments, and to appear on his behalf when requested. Whorton was to render labor, skills, and personal services for the benefit of Dillingham's business and investment endeavors. Additionally, Whorton was to be Dillingham's constant companion, confidant, traveling and social companion, and lover, to terminate his schooling upon obtaining his Associate in Arts degree, and to make no investment without first consulting Dillingham.

In consideration of Whorton's promises, Dillingham was to give him a one-half equity interest in all real estate acquired in their joint names, and in all property thereafter acquired by Dillingham. Dillingham agreed to financially support Whorton for life, and to open bank accounts, maintain a positive balance in those accounts, grant Whorton invasionary powers to savings accounts held in Dillingham's name, and permit Whorton to charge on Dillingham's personal accounts. Dillingham was also to engage in a homosexual relationship with Whorton. Importantly, for the purpose of our analysis, the parties specifically agreed that any portion of the agreement found to be legally unenforceable was severable and the balance of the provisions would remain in full force and effect.

Whorton allegedly complied with all terms of the oral agreement until 1984 when Dillingham barred him from his premises. Dillingham now refuses to perform his part of the contract by giving Whorton the promised consideration for the business services rendered.

II

Adults who voluntarily live together and engage in sexual relations are competent to contract respecting their earnings and property rights. Such contracts will be enforced "unless expressly and inseparably based upon an illicit consideration of sexual services...." *(Marvin v. Marvin* (1976) 18 Cal. 3d 660, 672 [134 Cal. Rptr. 815, 557 P.2d 106].) One cannot lawfully contract to pay for the performance of sexual services since such an agreement is in essence a bargain for prostitution. (*Id.* at p. 674, 134 Cal. Rptr. 815, 557 P.2d 106.)

A standard which inquires whether an agreement involves or contemplates a sexual relationship is vague and unworkable because virtually all agreements between nonmarital (and certainly, marital) cohabiters involve or contemplate a mutual sexual relationship. Further, a compact is not totally invalid merely because the parties may have contemplated creating or continuing a sexual relationship, but is invalid only to the extent it rests upon a consideration of sexual services. (*Id.* at pp. 670–671, 134 Cal. Rptr. 815, 557 P.2d 106.) Thus, "even if sexual services are part of the contractual consideration, any *severable* portion of the contract supported by independent consideration will still be enforced." (*Id.* at p. 672, 134 Cal. Rptr. 815, 557 P.2d 106.) For instance, contracting parties may make a variety of arrangements regarding their property rights—i.e., agree to pool their earnings and to hold all property in accord with the law governing community property, or to treat monetary earnings and property as separate property of the earning partner, or to keep property separate but compensate one party for services which benefit the other, or to pool only a part of their earnings and property, etc. (*Id.* at p. 674, fn. 10, 134 Cal. Rptr. 815, 557 P.2d 106.) "So long as the agreement does not rest upon illicit meretricious consideration, the parties may order their economic affairs as they choose, and no policy precludes the courts from enforcing such agreements." (*Id.* at p. 674, 134 Cal. Rptr. 815, 557 P.2d 106.)

Regarding the issue of what constitutes adequate consideration, *Marvin* notes "[a] promise to perform homemaking services is, of course, a lawful and adequate consideration for a contract...." (*Id.* at p. 670, fn. 5, 134 Cal. Rptr. 815, 557 P.2d 106.) *Marvin* expressly rejects the argument that the partner seeking to enforce the contract must have contributed either property or services additional to ordinary homemaking services. (*Ibid.*)

In *Marvin*, the plaintiff alleged the parties orally agreed that while they lived together they would combine their efforts and earnings and would share equally all property accumulated as a result of their efforts, that they would hold themselves out to the general public as husband and wife, that plaintiff would render services as companion, homemaker, housekeeper and cook, that plaintiff would give up her career in order to provide these services full-time, and that in return defendant would provide for all of plaintiff's financial support for the rest of her life. (*Id.* at p. 666.) The court stated:

> "... plaintiff alleges that the parties agreed to pool their earnings, that they contracted to share equally in all property acquired, and that defendant agreed to support plaintiff. The terms of the contract as alleged do not rest upon any unlawful consideration." (*Id.* at pp. 674–675, 134 Cal. Rptr. 815, 557 P.2d 106.)

The holding in *Marvin* suggests the court determined that the contract before it did not *expressly* include sexual services as part of the consideration, and thus, it did not need to reach the issue of whether there were severable portions of the contract supported by independent consideration. The only reference to sexual services in *Marvin's* alleged facts was that the parties agreed to hold themselves out to the public as husband and wife, which apparently the court did not interpret as expressly indicating sexual services were part of the consideration. (See *Alderson v. Alderson* (1986) 180 Cal. App. 3d 450, 462–464, 225 Cal. Rptr. 610 [even though couple engaged in sexual relations and plaintiff perceived this as part of her "role," no evidence that implied agreement between the parties explicitly rested upon a consideration of meretricious sexual services].)

III

Unlike the facts of *Marvin*, here the parties' sexual relationship was an express, rather than implied, part of the consideration for their contract. The contract cannot be enforced to the extent it is dependent on sexual services for consideration, and the complaint does not state a cause of action to the extent it asks for damages from the termination of the sexual relationship.

The issue here is whether the sexual component of the consideration is severable from the remaining portions of the contract.[1] We reiterate the guiding language of *Marvin v. Marvin, supra,* 18 Cal. 3d at page 672, 134 Cal. Rptr. 815, 557 P.2d 106 "[E]ven if sexual services are part of the contractual consideration, any *severable* portion of the contract supported by independent consideration will still be enforced." One test for determining the enforceability of a contract having both lawful and unlawful factors for consideration is stated in the Restatement Second of Contracts, section 183, "If the parties' performances can be apportioned into corresponding pairs of part performances so that the parts of each pair are properly regarded as agreed equivalents and one pair is not offensive to public policy, that portion of the agreement is enforceable by a party who did not engage in serious misconduct." (See also Civ. Code, § 1599: "Where a contract has several distinct objects, of which one at least is lawful, and one at least is unlawful, in whole or in part, the contract is void as to the latter and valid as to the rest.")

Tyranski v. Piggins (1973) 44 Mich. App. 570, 205 N.W.2d 595, 596–597, evaluates the issue of severability as follows:

"Professor Corbin and the drafters of the Restatement of Contracts both write that while bargains in whole or in part in consideration of an illicit relationship are unenforceable, agreements between parties to such a relationship with respect to money or property will be enforced if the agreement is independent of the illicit relationship.

"Neither these authorities nor the large body of case law in other jurisdictions . . . articulate a guideline for determining when the consideration will be regarded as 'independent' and when it is so coupled with the meretricious acts that the agreement will not be enforced. A pattern does, however, emerge upon reading the cases.

"Neither party to a meretricious relationship acquires, by reason of cohabitation alone, rights in the property accumulations of the other during the period of the relationship. But where there is an express agreement to accumulate or transfer property following a relationship of some permanence and *an additional consideration in the form of either money or of services, the courts tend to find an independent consideration.*

"Thus, a plaintiff who can show an actual contribution of money, pursuant to an agreement to pool assets and share accumulations, will usually prevail. Services, such as cooking meals, laundering clothes, 'caring' for the decedent through sickness, have been found to be adequate and independent considerations in cases where there was an express agreement." (Fns. omitted; italics added.)

---

1. Dillingham does not assert *Marvin* is inapplicable to same-sex partners, and we see no legal basis to make a distinction.

In *Tyranski v. Piggins, supra,* 205 N.W.2d at pages 596–597, the plaintiff cleaned the house, did the marketing, cooked the food, did the decedent's personal laundry, acted as his hostess, cared for him when he was sick, and contributed money towards the purchase of a house in which the unmarried plaintiff and the decedent resided. The court held it was proper to enforce the parties' express agreement to convey the house, which was held in the name of the decedent, to the plaintiff.

Of particular significance is the decision in *Latham v. Latham* (1976) 274 Ore. 421, 547 P.2d 144. In *Latham*, the court overruled a demurrer where complainant pleaded an agreement to live with defendant, to care for, and to furnish him with all the amenities of married life. The court recognized the alleged agreement specifically included the sexual services implicit in cohabitation. (*Id.* 547 P.2d at p. 145.) Thus, as here, the sexual aspect of the agreement appeared on the face of the complaint. In overruling a demurrer based on public policy, the court stated it was not validating an agreement in which sexual intercourse was the only or primary consideration, but only one of the factors incident to the burdens and amenities of married life. (*Id.* 547 P.2d at p. 147.)

Thus, the crux of our analysis is whether Whorton's complaint negates as a matter of law, a trier of fact finding he made contributions, apart from sexual services, which provided independent consideration for Dillingham's alleged promises pertaining to financial support and property rights. The services which plaintiff alleges he agreed to and did provide included being a chauffeur, bodyguard, secretary, and partner and counselor in real estate investments. If provided, these services are of monetary value, and the type for which one would expect to be compensated unless there is evidence of a contrary intent. Thus, they are properly characterized as consideration independent of the sexual aspect of the relationship. By way of comparison, such services as being a constant companion and confidant are not the type which are usually monetarily compensated nor considered to have a "value" for purposes of contract consideration, and, absent peculiar circumstances, would likely be considered so intertwined with the sexual relationship as to be inseparable. (Cf. *Walters v. Calderon* (1972) 25 Cal. App. 3d 863, 873, 102 Cal. Rptr. 89 [love and affection do not constitute valuable consideration necessary to support validity of contractual promise].)

We hold that Whorton—based on allegations he provided Dillingham with services of a chauffeur, bodyguard, secretary, and business partner—has stated a cause of action arising from a contract supported by consideration independent of sexual services. Further, by itemizing the mutual promises to engage in sexual activity, Whorton has not precluded the trier of fact from finding those promises are the consideration for each other and independent of the bargained for consideration for Whorton's employment.

We believe our holding does not conflict with that in *Jones v. Daly* (1981) 122 Cal. App. 3d 500, 508, 176 Cal. Rptr. 130, where services provided by the complaining homosexual partner were limited to "lover, companion, homemaker, traveling companion, housekeeper and cook...." The court there found the pleadings unequivocally established that plaintiff's rendition of sex and other services naturally flowing from sexual cohabitation was an inseparable part of the consideration for the so-called cohabitor's agreement. The court stated:

> "According to the allegations of the complaint, the agreement provided that the parties would share equally the earnings and property accumulated as a result of their efforts while they lived together and that Daly would support plaintiff for the rest of his life. *Neither the property sharing nor the support provision of the agreement rests upon plaintiff's acting as Daly's traveling companion, housekeeper or cook as distinguished from acting as his lover.* The latter service forms an inseparable part of the consideration for the agreement and renders it unenforceable in its entirety." (*Jones v. Daly, supra,* 122 Cal. App. 3d at p. 509, 176 Cal. Rptr. 130 italics added.)

Jones is factually different in that the complaining party did not allege contracting to provide services apart from those normally incident to the state of cohabitation itself. Further, Jones's complaint stated the agreement was premised on that they "would hold themselves out to the public at large as cohabiting mates...." (*Id.* at p. 505, 176 Cal. Rptr. 130.) In contrast, Whorton's complaint separately itemizes services contracted for as companion, chauffeur, bodyguard, secretary, partner and business counselor. These, except for companion, are significantly different than those household duties normally attendant to nonbusiness cohabitation and are those for which monetary compensation ordinarily would be anticipated. Most of the numerous cases cited in *Marvin* where nonmarital cohabiters' oral agreements to pool earnings were upheld involved contributions other than normal homemaking services. However, *Marvin* states homemaking services alone are lawful consideration. Accepting Whorton's allegations as true, we cannot say as a matter of law any illegal portion of the contract is not severable so as to leave the balance valid and enforceable, especially where it is alleged the parties contemplated such a result when entering into their agreement.

IV

Statute of frauds

Dillingham asserts the oral agreement is invalid under the statute of frauds, requiring agreements not to be performed within one year or for the sale of an interest in real property to be written. (Civ. Code, § 1624, subds. (a) and (c).) In *Marvin v. Marvin, supra,* 18 Cal. 3d at page 674, footnote 10, 134 Cal. Rptr. 815, 557 P.2d 106, the court noted in cases involving agreements between nonmarital partners, the majority of the agreements were oral and the courts have expressly rejected defenses grounded upon the statute of frauds.

Marvin cites *Cline v. Festersen* (1954) 128 Cal. App. 2d 380, 386, 275 P.2d 149. In *Cline*, the court rejected a statute of frauds argument on the basis of estoppel, reasoning that the nonmarital partner seeking to obtain her promised share of the property had trusted and worked for many years in reliance on the promise, and her partner had never repudiated the agreement. *Cline* relies on the principle that the doctrine of estoppel to assert the statute of frauds should be applied to prevent fraud and unconscionable injury that would result from refusal to enforce oral contracts in certain circumstances—i.e., after one party has been induced by the other seriously to change position in reliance on the contract, or when unjust enrichment would result if a party who has received the benefits of the other's performance were allowed to rely upon the statute.

Whorton alleges he stopped his education earlier than planned to assist Dillingham in his business ventures in exchange for promises of support and sharing of accumulated property. These facts are sufficient to estop Dillingham from raising the statute of frauds by way of demurrer to bar enforcement of the contract.

Statute of limitations

Dillingham meritlessly asserts the action is barred by the statute of limitations.

The general rule is that a cause of action for breach of contract accrues at the time of breach. (See 3 Witkin, Cal. Procedure (3d ed. 1985) Actions, § 375, p. 402.) A *Marvin*-type contract is breached when one partner terminates the relationship. (*Estate of Fincher* (1981) 119 Cal. App. 3d 343, 352, 174 Cal. Rptr. 18.) The statute of limitations for an action upon a contract not founded on a writing is two years. (Code Civ. Proc., § 339, subd. 1.) The complaint states the breach occurred "on or about the latter part of 1984." The complaint was filed in June 1986. The complaint on its face does not show the contract cause of action is barred by the statute of limitations.

For the same reasons, the complaint on its face does not show the three-year fraud limitation has expired.[6]

Additionally, a cause of action based on equitable grounds is not barred, for which the statute of limitations is four years. (*Nelson v. Nevel* (1984) 154 Cal. App. 3d 132, 140–141, 201 Cal. Rptr. 93; Code Civ. Proc., § 343; see generally *Marvin v. Marvin*, supra, 18 Cal. 3d at p. 684, fn. 25, 134 Cal. Rptr. 815, 557 P.2d 106.)

Terminable at will

Finally, Dillingham contends that under *Labor Code section 2922*, the contract was terminable at will.[7] That section has no applicability to the issues here. This case does not involve an employment contract within the purview of the Labor Code, but rather a cohabiters' agreement regarding

---

6. The caption of the complaint does not refer to fraud, stating: "Complaint for damages for breach of express oral contract; breach of implied in fact contract; to impress a constructive trust; for declaratory relief; and for injunctive relief." However, the body of the complaint states facts in support of, and refers to, a fraud cause of action.

7. Labor Code section 2922 states: "An employment, having no specified term, may be terminated at the will of either party on notice to the other. Employment for a specified term means an employment for a period greater than one month."

how two nonmarital partners have agreed to regulate their economic affairs. Of course, one partner has a right to end the relationship, and the only issue is whether the facts support a monetary and/or property award to one of the partners.

* * *

Domestic Partner Ordinance Quashed: Atlanta to Appeal in Second Defeat

ATLANTA J. & CONST., Jan. 1, 1997 at D2.

■ BILL RANKIN

A Fulton County judge Tuesday struck down Atlanta's domestic partnership ordinance, the second try by the city to extend insurance benefits to live-in partners of city employees.

The city is attempting "to incorporate a 'family relationship' it has created, domestic partners, into the definition of a dependent," Superior Court Judge Isaac Jenrette said. This "is now inconsistent with state law."

The city will appeal the ruling, said Nick Gold, spokesman for Mayor Bill Campbell. Six city employees have signed up for the domestic partnership benefits, he said.

"Georgia law is clear—no matter how the city manipulates the language of its ordinance, domestic partners are neither 'family' nor 'dependents,'"said Atlanta lawyer David Reed, who argued the case for the conservative Southeastern Legal Foundation. "The taxpayers and families of Georgia have had enough of this nonsense."

Foundation lawyers have said the ordinance was an unconstitutional attempt by the city to encourage homosexuality and was a waste of taxpayers' money.

The foundation filed the lawsuit Sept. 10, the same day the U.S. Senate approved a bill denying recognition of same-sex marriages. The lawsuit challenged an ordinance passed by the City Council to authorize insurance benefits to the unmarried, live-in partners of city employees.

The new provision is a revised version of a 1993 city ordinance granting benefits for domestic partners. The Georgia Supreme Court struck down that ordinance in 1995, saying the city "exceeded its power ... by recognizing domestic partners as 'a family relationship.' " The court noted that the state uses several definitions for "dependents" when allowing insurance benefits and "domestic partners do not meet any of these statutory definitions."

On Tuesday, Jenrette said the city's new ordinance is fatally flawed for the same reasons.

Teresa Nelson, executive director of the Georgia chapter of the American Civil Liberties Union, expressed disappointment at the ruling.

"There are a number of individuals who have no dependents who are city employees, and they have shared the burden for the coverage of those employees who have dependents," Nelson said. "For those who are in partnership relationships, whether they are heterosexual or homosexual, their dependents have been denied that coverage. The city's ordinance is not a statement of morality. It is a statement of equality."

But Matthew Glavin, president of the Southeast Legal Foundation, said the City Council should realize this is not something it has the authority to do.

"If the City Council or the mayor want this kind of ordinance, they should march up the street to the state Legislature and convince it to change the law to include domestic partners," he said. "Unless they do that, anything they do will be unconstitutional, and we will stop them at every attempt."

NOTES AND QUESTIONS

1. Limits of consideration for homosexual couples. The Court in this case held that "Whorton—based on allegations he provided Dillingham with services of a chauffeur, bodyguard, secretary, and business partner— has stated a cause of action arising from a contract supported by consideration independent of sexual services." Of course, none of those services were provided in *Marvin*, though the services that were provided in *Marvin*—keeping house, functioning as a companion, etc. were also present in *Whorton*. Why, then, would the court choose to focus on these tasks to find consideration, and what are the implications of that decision? *See, e.g.,* Jones v. Daly, 176 Cal.Rptr. 130 (Cal. App. 1981).

2. Impact of *Whorton v. Dillingham*. Is *Whorton* a victory for homosexual rights? After all, the case is specifically premised on the idea of an express contract being enforced even though it was partially based on sexual consideration. Since this holding is completely orientation-neutral, why should *Whorton v. Dillingham* be considered significant? If it is a victory, how far does it extend? *See* Sharmila Roy Grossman, Comment, *The Illusory Rights of* Marvin v. Marvin *for the Same–Sex Couple Versus the Preferable Canadian Alternative—*M. v. H., 38 CAL. W. L. REV. 547, 557 (2002). If homosexual couples are allowed to enter valid marriages in the state in which they reside, does the *Marvin v. Marvin* rationale apply?

3. Additional reading. For additional information on domestic partner ordinances, see generally, Jonathan Andrew Hein, *Caring for the Evolving American Family: Cohabiting Partners and Employer Sponsored Health Care*, 30 N.M. L. REV. 19 (2000); Debbie Zielinski, Note, *Domestic Partnership Benefits: Why not Offer Them to Same–Sex Partners and Unmarried Opposite Sex Partners*, 13 J.L. & HEALTH 281 (1998–99); William V. Vetter, *Restrictions on Equal Treatment of Unmarried Domestic Partners*, 5 B.U. PUB. INT. L.J. 1 (1995).

D. SEX BETWEEN CONSENTING ADULTS

Lawrence v. Texas

Supreme Court of the United States, 539 U.S. 558 (2003).

■ JUSTICE KENNEDY delivered the opinion of the Court.

Liberty protects the person from unwarranted government intrusions into a dwelling or other private places. In our tradition the State is not omnipresent in the home. And there are other spheres of our lives and existence, outside the home, where the State should not be a dominant presence. Freedom extends beyond spatial bounds. Liberty presumes an autonomy of self that includes freedom of thought, belief, expression, and certain intimate conduct. The instant case involves liberty of the person both in its spatial and more transcendent dimensions.

I

The question before the Court is the validity of a Texas statute making it a crime for two persons of the same sex to engage in certain intimate sexual conduct.

In Houston, Texas, officers of the Harris County Police Department were dispatched to a private residence in response to a reported weapons disturbance. They entered an apartment where one of the petitioners, John Geddes Lawrence, resided. The right of the police to enter does not seem to have been questioned. The officers observed Lawrence and another man, Tyron Garner, engaging in a sexual act. The two petitioners were arrested, held in custody over night, and charged and convicted before a Justice of the Peace * * * [of] "deviate sexual intercourse, namely anal sex, with a member of the same sex (man)." App. to Pet. for Cert. 127a, 139a. The applicable state law is Tex. Penal Code Ann. § 21.06(a) (2003). It provides: "A person commits an offense if he engages in deviate sexual intercourse with another individual of the same sex." * * *

* * *

We granted certiorari, 537 U.S. 1044 (2002), to consider three questions:

"1. Whether Petitioners' criminal convictions under the Texas 'Homosexual Conduct' law—which criminalizes sexual intimacy by same-sex couples, but not identical behavior by different-sex couples—violate the Fourteenth Amendment guarantee of equal protection of laws?

"2. Whether Petitioners' criminal convictions for adult consensual sexual intimacy in the home violate their vital interests in liberty and privacy protected by the Due Process Clause of the Fourteenth Amendment?

"3. Whether Bowers v. Hardwick, 478 U.S. 186 (1986), should be overruled?" Pet. for Cert. i.

* * *

II

We conclude the case should be resolved by determining whether the petitioners were free as adults to engage in the private conduct in the exercise of their liberty under the Due Process Clause of the Fourteenth Amendment to the Constitution. For this inquiry we deem it necessary to reconsider the Court's holding in *Bowers*.

There are broad statements of the substantive reach of liberty under the Due Process Clause in earlier cases, * * * but the most pertinent beginning point is our decision in *Griswold v. Connecticut*, 381 U.S. 479 (1965).

In *Griswold* the Court invalidated a state law prohibiting the use of drugs or devices of contraception and counseling or aiding and abetting the use of contraceptives. The Court described the protected interest as a right to privacy and placed emphasis on the marriage relation and the protected space of the marital bedroom. *Id.*, at 485.

After *Griswold* it was established that the right to make certain decisions regarding sexual conduct extends beyond the marital relationship. In *Eisenstadt v. Baird*, 405 U.S. 438 (1972), the Court invalidated a law prohibiting the distribution of contraceptives to unmarried persons. The case was decided under the Equal Protection Clause, *id.*, at 454; but with respect to unmarried persons, the Court went on to state the fundamental proposition that the law impaired the exercise of their personal rights, *ibid*. It quoted from the statement of the Court of Appeals finding the law to be in conflict with fundamental human rights, and it followed with this statement of its own:

> "It is true that in *Griswold* the right of privacy in question inhered in the marital relationship.... If the right of privacy means anything, it is the right of the *individual*, married or single, to be free from unwarranted governmental intrusion into matters so fundamentally affecting a person as the decision whether to bear or beget a child." *Id.*, at 453.

The opinions in *Griswold* and *Eisenstadt* were part of the background for the decision in *Roe v. Wade*, 410 U.S. 113 (1973). As is well known, the case involved a challenge to the Texas law prohibiting abortions, but the laws of other States were affected as well. Although the Court held the woman's rights were not absolute, her right to elect an abortion did have real and substantial protection as an exercise of her liberty under the Due Process Clause. The Court cited cases that protect spatial freedom and cases that go well beyond it. *Roe* recognized the right of a woman to make certain fundamental decisions affecting her destiny and confirmed once more that the protection of liberty under the Due Process Clause has a substantive dimension of fundamental significance in defining the rights of the person.

In *Carey v. Population Services Int'l*, 431 U.S. 678 (1977), the Court confronted a New York law forbidding sale or distribution of contraceptive devices to persons under 16 years of age. Although there was no single opinion for the Court, the law was invalidated. Both *Eisenstadt* and *Carey*, as well as the holding and rationale in *Roe*, confirmed that the reasoning of *Griswold* could not be confined to the protection of rights of married adults. This was the state of the law with respect to some of the most relevant cases when the Court considered *Bowers* v. *Hardwick*.

The facts in *Bowers* had some similarities to the instant case. A police officer, whose right to enter seems not to have been in question, observed Hardwick, in his own bedroom, engaging in intimate sexual conduct with another adult male. The conduct was in violation of a Georgia statute making it a criminal offense to engage in sodomy. One difference between the two cases is that the Georgia statute prohibited the conduct whether or not the participants were of the same sex, while the Texas statute, as we have seen, applies only to participants of the same sex. Hardwick was not prosecuted, but he brought an action in federal court to declare the state statute invalid. He alleged he was a practicing homosexual and that the criminal prohibition violated rights guaranteed to him by the Constitution. The Court, in an opinion by Justice White, sustained the Georgia law. * * *

The Court began its substantive discussion in *Bowers* as follows: "The issue presented is whether the Federal Constitution confers a fundamental right upon homosexuals to engage in sodomy and hence invalidates the laws of the many States that still make such conduct illegal and have done so for a very long time." *Id.*, at 190. That statement, we now conclude, discloses the Court's own failure to appreciate the extent of the liberty at stake. To say that the issue in *Bowers* was simply the right to engage in certain sexual conduct demeans the claim the individual put forward, just as it would demean a married couple were it to be said marriage is simply about the right to have sexual intercourse. The laws involved in *Bowers* and here are, to be sure, statutes that purport to do no more than prohibit a particular sexual act. Their penalties and purposes, though, have more far-reaching consequences, touching upon the most private human conduct, sexual behavior, and in the most private of places, the home. The statutes do seek to control a personal relationship that, whether or not entitled to formal recognition in the law, is within the liberty of persons to choose without being punished as criminals.

This, as a general rule, should counsel against attempts by the State, or a court, to define the meaning of the relationship or to set its boundaries absent injury to a person or abuse of an institution the law protects. It suffices for us to acknowledge that adults may choose to enter upon this relationship in the confines of their homes and their own private lives and still retain their dignity as free persons. When sexuality finds overt expression in intimate conduct with another person, the conduct can be but one element in a personal bond that is more enduring. The liberty protected by the Constitution allows homosexual persons the right to make this choice.

Having misapprehended the claim of liberty there presented to it, and thus stating the claim to be whether there is a fundamental right to engage in consensual sodomy, the *Bowers* Court said: "Proscriptions against that conduct have ancient roots." *Id.*, at 192. In academic writings, and in many of the scholarly *amicus* briefs filed to assist the Court in this case, there are fundamental criticisms of the historical premises relied upon by the majority and concurring opinions in *Bowers*. * * * We need not enter this debate in the attempt to reach a definitive historical judgment, but the following considerations counsel against adopting the definitive conclusions upon which *Bowers* placed such reliance.

At the outset it should be noted that there is no longstanding history in this country of laws directed at homosexual conduct as a distinct matter. Beginning in colonial times there were prohibitions of sodomy derived from the English criminal laws passed in the first instance by the Reformation Parliament of 1533. The English prohibition was understood to include relations between men and women as well as relations between men and men. See, *e.g., King v. Wiseman*, 92 Eng. Rep. 774, 775 (K. B. 1718) (interpreting "mankind" in Act of 1533 as including women and girls). Nineteenth-century commentators similarly read American sodomy, buggery, and crime-against-nature statutes as criminalizing certain relations between men and women and between men and men. See, *e.g.,* 2 J. Bishop, Criminal Law § 1028 (1858); 2 J. Chitty, Criminal Law 47–50 (5th Am. ed. 1847); R. Desty, A Compendium of American Criminal Law 143 (1882); J. May, The Law of Crimes § 203 (2d ed. 1893). The absence of legal prohibitions focusing on homosexual conduct may be explained in part by noting that according to some scholars the concept of the homosexual as a distinct category of person did not emerge until the late 19th century. See, *e.g.,* J. Katz, The Invention of Heterosexuality 10 (1995); J. D'Emilio & E. Freedman, Intimate Matters: A History of Sexuality in America 121 (2d ed. 1997) ("The modern terms *homosexuality* and *heterosexuality* do not apply to an era that had not yet articulated these distinctions"). Thus early American sodomy laws were not directed at homosexuals as such but instead sought to prohibit nonprocreative sexual activity more generally. This does not suggest approval of homosexual conduct. It does tend to show that this particular form of conduct was not thought of as a separate category from like conduct between heterosexual persons.

Laws prohibiting sodomy do not seem to have been enforced against consenting adults acting in private. A substantial number of sodomy prosecutions and convictions for which there are surviving records were for predatory acts against those who could not or did not consent, as in the case of a minor or the victim of an assault. As to these, one purpose for the prohibitions was to ensure there would be no lack of coverage if a predator committed a sexual assault that did not constitute rape as defined by the criminal law. Thus the model sodomy indictments presented in a 19th-century treatise, see 2 Chitty, *supra,* at 49, addressed the predatory acts of an adult man against a minor girl or minor boy. Instead of targeting relations between consenting adults in private, 19th-century sodomy prosecutions typically involved relations between men and minor girls or minor boys, relations between adults involving force, relations between adults implicating disparity in status, or relations between men and animals.

* * * The longstanding criminal prohibition of homosexual sodomy upon which the *Bowers* decision placed such reliance is as consistent with a general condemnation of nonprocreative sex as it is with an established tradition of prosecuting acts because of their homosexual character.

The policy of punishing consenting adults for private acts was not much discussed in the early legal literature. We can infer that one reason for this was the very private nature of the conduct. Despite the absence of prosecutions, there may have been periods in which there was public criticism of homosexuals as such and an insistence that the criminal laws be enforced to discourage their practices. But far from possessing "ancient roots," *Bowers*, 478 U.S., at 192, American laws targeting same-sex couples did not develop until the last third of the 20th century. * * *

It was not until the 1970's that any State singled out same-sex relations for criminal prosecution, and only nine States have done so. * * * Post–*Bowers* even some of these States did not adhere to the policy of suppressing homosexual conduct. Over the course of the last decades, States with same-sex prohibitions have moved toward abolishing them. * * *

In summary, the historical grounds relied upon in *Bowers* are more complex than the majority opinion and the concurring opinion by Chief Justice Burger indicate. Their historical premises are not without doubt and, at the very least, are overstated.

It must be acknowledged, of course, that the Court in *Bowers* was making the broader point that for centuries there have been powerful voices to condemn homosexual conduct as immoral. The condemnation has been shaped by religious beliefs, conceptions of right and acceptable behavior, and respect for the traditional family. For many persons these are not trivial concerns but profound and deep convictions accepted as ethical and moral principles to which they aspire and which thus determine the course of their lives. These considerations do not answer the question before us, however. The issue is whether the majority may use the power of the State to enforce these views on the whole society through operation of the criminal law. "Our obligation is to define the liberty of all, not to mandate our own moral code." *Planned Parenthood of Southeastern Pa. v. Casey*, 505 U.S. 833, 850 (1992).

Chief Justice Burger joined the opinion for the Court in *Bowers* and further explained his views as follows: "Decisions of individuals relating to homosexual conduct have been subject to state intervention throughout the history of Western civilization. Condemnation of those practices is firmly rooted in Judeao–Christian moral and ethical standards." 478 U.S., at 196. As with Justice White's assumptions about history, scholarship casts some doubt on the sweeping nature of the statement by Chief Justice Burger as it pertains to private homosexual conduct between consenting adults. See, *e.g.*, Eskridge, Hardwick and Historiography, 1999 U. Ill. L. Rev. 631, 656. In all events we think that our laws and traditions in the past half century are of most relevance here. These references show an emerging awareness that liberty gives substantial protection to adult persons in deciding how to conduct their private lives in matters pertaining to sex. "History and tradition are the starting point but not in all cases the ending point of the substantive due process inquiry." *County of Sacramento v. Lewis*, 523 U.S. 833, 857 (1998) (KENNEDY, J., concurring).

* * *

In *Bowers* the Court referred to the fact that before 1961 all 50 States had outlawed sodomy, and that at the time of the Court's decision 24 States and the District of Columbia had sodomy laws. 478 U.S., at 192–193. Justice Powell pointed out that these prohibitions often were being ignored, however. Georgia, for instance, had not sought to enforce its law for decades. Id., at 197–198, n. 2 ("The history of nonenforcement suggests the moribund character today of laws criminalizing this type of private, consensual conduct").

The sweeping references by Chief Justice Burger to the history of Western civilization and to Judeo–Christian moral and ethical standards did not take account of other authorities pointing in an opposite direction. A committee advising the British Parliament recommended in 1957 repeal of laws punishing homosexual conduct. The Wolfenden Report: Report of the Committee on Homosexual Offenses and Prostitution (1963). Parliament enacted the substance of those recommendations 10 years later. Sexual Offences Act 1967, § 1.

Of even more importance, almost five years before *Bowers* was decided the European Court of Human Rights considered a case with parallels to *Bowers* and to today's case. * * * The court held that the laws proscribing [consenting homosexual] conduct were invalid under the European Convention on Human Rights. *Dudgeon* v. *United Kingdom*, 45 Eur. Ct. H. R. (1981) P52. Authoritative in all countries that are members of the Council of Europe (21 nations then, 45 nations now), the decision is at odds with the premise in *Bowers* that the claim put forward was insubstantial in our Western civilization.

In our own constitutional system the deficiencies in *Bowers* became even more apparent in the years following its announcement. The 25 States with laws prohibiting the relevant conduct referenced in the *Bowers* decision are reduced now to 13, of which 4 enforce their laws only against homosexual conduct. In those States where sodomy is still proscribed, whether for same-sex or heterosexual conduct, there is a pattern of nonenforcement with respect to consenting adults acting in private. The State of Texas admitted in 1994 that as of that date it had not prosecuted anyone under those circumstances. *State v. Morales*, 869 S.W.2d 941, 943.

Two principal cases decided after *Bowers* cast its holding into even more doubt. In *Planned Parenthood of Southeastern Pa. v. Casey*, 505 U.S. 833 (1992), the Court reaffirmed the substantive force of the liberty protected by the Due Process Clause. The *Casey* decision again confirmed that our laws and tradition afford constitutional protection to personal decisions relating to marriage, procreation, contraception, family relationships, child rearing, and education. *Id.*, at 851. In explaining the respect the Constitution demands for the autonomy of the person in making these choices, we stated as follows:

> "These matters, involving the most intimate and personal choices a person may make in a lifetime, choices central to personal dignity and autonomy, are central to the liberty protected by the *Fourteenth Amendment*. At the heart of liberty is the right to define one's own concept of existence, of meaning, of the universe, and of the mystery of human life. Beliefs about these matters could not define the attributes of personhood were they formed under compulsion of the State." *Ibid.*

Persons in a homosexual relationship may seek autonomy for these purposes, just as heterosexual persons do. The decision in *Bowers* would deny them this right.

The second post–*Bowers* case of principal relevance is *Romer v. Evans*, 517 U.S. 620 (1996). There the Court struck down class-based legislation directed at homosexuals as a violation of the Equal Protection Clause. *Romer* invalidated an amendment to Colorado's constitution which named as a solitary class persons who were homosexuals, lesbians, or bisexual either by "orientation, conduct, practices or relationships," *id.*, at 624 (internal quotation marks omitted), and deprived them of protection under state antidiscrimination laws. We concluded that the provision was "born of animosity toward the class of persons affected" and further that it had no rational relation to a legitimate governmental purpose. *Id.*, at 634.

* * *

Equality of treatment and the due process right to demand respect for conduct protected by the substantive guarantee of liberty are linked in important respects, and a decision on the latter point advances both interests. If protected conduct is made criminal and the law which does so remains unexamined for its substantive validity, its stigma might remain even if it were not enforceable as drawn for equal protection reasons. When homosexual conduct is made criminal by the law of the State, that declaration in and of itself is an invitation to subject homosexual persons to discrimination both in the public and in the private spheres. The central holding of *Bowers* has been brought in question by this case, and it should be addressed. Its continuance as precedent demeans the lives of homosexual persons.

The stigma this criminal statute imposes, moreover, is not trivial. The offense, to be sure, is but a class C misdemeanor, a minor offense in the Texas legal system. Still, it remains a criminal offense with all that imports for the dignity of the persons charged. The petitioners will bear on their record the history of their criminal convictions. * * * We are advised that if Texas convicted an adult for private, consensual homosexual conduct under the statute here in question the convicted person would come within the [sexual-offender] registration laws of a least four States were he or she to be subject to their jurisdiction. * * * This underscores the consequential nature of the punishment and the state-sponsored condemnation attendant to the criminal prohibition. Furthermore, the Texas criminal conviction carries with it the other collateral consequences always following a conviction, such as notations on job application forms, to mention but one example.

* * *

* * * The right the petitioners seek in this case has been accepted as an integral part of human freedom in many other countries. There has been no showing that in this country the governmental interest in circumscribing personal choice is somehow more legitimate or urgent.

The doctrine of *stare decisis* is essential to the respect accorded to the judgments of the Court and to the stability of the law. It is not, however, an inexorable command. *Payne v. Tennessee*, 501 U.S. 808, 828 (1991) ("*Stare decisis* is not an inexorable command; rather, it 'is a principle of policy and not a mechanical formula of adherence to the latest decision'") (quoting *Helvering v. Hallock*, 309 U.S. 106, 119 (1940))). In *Casey* we noted that when a Court is asked to overrule a precedent recognizing a constitutional liberty interest, individual or societal reliance on the existence of that liberty cautions with particular strength against reversing course. 505 U.S., at 855–856; see also *id.*, at 844 ("Liberty finds no refuge in a jurisprudence of doubt"). The holding in *Bowers*, however, has not induced detrimental reliance comparable to some instances where recognized individual rights are involved. Indeed, there has been no individual or societal reliance on *Bowers* of the sort that could counsel against overturning its holding once there are compelling reasons to do so. *Bowers* itself causes uncertainty, for the precedents before and after its issuance contradict its central holding.

The rationale of *Bowers* does not withstand careful analysis. In his dissenting opinion in *Bowers* JUSTICE STEVENS came to these conclusions:

> "Our prior cases make two propositions abundantly clear. First, the fact that the governing majority in a State has traditionally viewed a particular practice as immoral is not a sufficient reason for upholding a law prohibiting the practice; neither history nor tradition could save a law prohibiting miscegenation from constitutional attack. Second, individual decisions by married persons, concerning the intimacies of their physical relationship, even when not intended to produce offspring, are a form of "liberty" protected by the Due Process Clause of the Fourteenth Amendment. Moreover, this protection extends to intimate choices by unmarried as well as married persons." 478 U.S., at 216 (footnotes and citations omitted).

JUSTICE STEVENS' analysis, in our view, should have been controlling in *Bowers* and should control here.

* * *

The present case does not involve minors. It does not involve persons who might be injured or coerced or who are situated in relationships where consent might not easily be refused. It does not involve public conduct or prostitution. It does not involve whether the government must give formal recognition to any relationship that homosexual persons seek to enter. The case does involve two adults who, with full and mutual consent from each other, engaged in sexual practices common to a homosexual lifestyle. The petitioners are entitled to respect for their private lives. The State cannot demean their existence or control their destiny by making their private sexual conduct a crime. Their right to liberty under the Due Process Clause gives them the full right to engage in their conduct without intervention of the government. "It is a promise of the Constitution that there is a realm of personal liberty which the government may not enter." *Casey, supra*, at 847. The Texas statute furthers no legitimate state interest which can justify its intrusion into the personal and private life of the individual.

Had those who drew and ratified the Due Process Clauses of the Fifth Amendment or the Fourteenth Amendment known the components of liberty in its manifold possibilities, they might have been more specific. They did not presume to have this insight. They knew times can blind us to certain truths and later generations can see that laws once thought necessary and proper in fact serve only to oppress. As the Constitution endures, persons in every generation can invoke its principles in their own search for greater freedom.

[Reversed.]

It is so ordered.

■ JUSTICE O'CONNOR, concurring in the judgment.

The Court today overrules *Bowers v. Hardwick*, 478 U.S. 186 (1986). I joined *Bowers*, and do not join the Court in overruling it. Nevertheless, I agree with the Court that Texas' statute banning same-sex sodomy is unconstitutional. See Tex. Penal Code Ann. § 21.06 (2003). Rather than relying on the substantive component of the Fourteenth Amendment's Due Process Clause, as the Court does, I base my conclusion on the Fourteenth Amendment's Equal Protection Clause.

The Equal Protection Clause of the Fourteenth Amendment "is essentially a direction that all persons similarly situated should be treated alike." *Cleburne v. Cleburne Living Center, Inc.*, 473 U.S. 432, 439 (1985); see also *Plyler v. Doe*, 457 U.S. 202 (1982). Under our rational basis standard of review, "legislation is presumed to be valid and will be sustained if the classification drawn by the statute is rationally related to a legitimate state interest." *Cleburne v. Cleburne Living Center, supra*, at 440; see also *Department of Agriculture v. Moreno*, 413 U.S. 528, 534 (1973); *Romer v. Evans*, 517 U.S. 620, 632–633 (1996); *Nordlinger v. Hahn*, 505 U.S. 1, 11–12 (1992).

* * * We have consistently held * * * that some objectives, such as "a bare ... desire to harm a politically unpopular group," are not legitimate state interests. *Department of Agriculture v. Moreno, supra*, at 534. See also *Cleburne v. Cleburne Living Center, supra*, at 446–447; *Romer v. Evans, supra*, at 632. When a law exhibits such a desire to harm a politically unpopular group, we have applied a more searching form of rational basis review to strike down such laws under the Equal Protection Clause.

* * *

The statute at issue here makes sodomy a crime only if a person "engages in deviate sexual intercourse with another individual of the same sex." Tex. Penal Code Ann. § 21.06(a) (2003). Sodomy between opposite-sex partners, however, is not a crime in Texas. That is, Texas treats the same conduct differently based solely on the participants. Those harmed by this law are people who have a same-sex sexual orientation and thus are more likely to engage in behavior prohibited by § 21.06.

The Texas statute makes homosexuals unequal in the eyes of the law by making particular conduct—and only that conduct—subject to criminal sanction. * * * [W]hile the penalty imposed on petitioners in this case was relatively minor, the consequences of conviction are not. As the Court notes, see *ante*, at 15, petitioners' convictions, if upheld, would disqualify them from or restrict their ability to engage in a variety of professions, including medicine, athletic training, and interior design. * * * Indeed, were petitioners to move to one of four States, their convictions would require them to register as sex offenders to local law enforcement. * * *

And the effect of Texas' sodomy law is not just limited to the threat of prosecution or consequence of conviction. Texas' sodomy law brands all homosexuals as criminals, thereby making it more difficult for homosexuals to be treated in the same manner as everyone else. Indeed, Texas itself has previously acknowledged the collateral effects of the law, stipulating in a prior challenge to this action that the law "legally sanctions discrimination against [homosexuals] in a variety of ways unrelated to the criminal law," including in the areas of "employment, family issues, and housing." *State v. Morales*, 826 S.W.2d 201, 203 (Tex. App. 1992).

Texas attempts to justify its law, and the effects of the law, by arguing that the statute satisfies rational basis review because it furthers the legitimate governmental interest of the promotion of morality. * * *

This case raises a different issue than *Bowers:* whether, under the *Equal Protection Clause*, moral disapproval is a legitimate state interest to justify by itself a statute that bans homosexual sodomy, but not heterosexual sodomy. It is not. Moral disapproval of this group, like a bare desire to harm the group, is an interest that is insufficient to satisfy rational basis review under the Equal Protection Clause. See, *e.g., Department of Agriculture v. Moreno, supra*, at 534; *Romer v. Evans*, 517 U.S., at 634–635. Indeed, we have never held that moral disapproval, without any other asserted state interest, is a sufficient rationale under the Equal Protection Clause to justify a law that discriminates among groups of persons.

* * *

Whether a sodomy law that is neutral both in effect and application, see *Yick Wo v. Hopkins*, 118 U.S. 356, 30 L. Ed. 220, 6 S. Ct. 1064 (1886), would violate the substantive component of the Due Process Clause is an issue that need not be decided today. I am confident, however, that so long as the Equal Protection Clause requires a sodomy law to apply equally to the private consensual conduct of homosexuals and heterosexuals alike, such a law would not long stand in our democratic society. * * *

A law branding one class of persons as criminal solely based on the State's moral disapproval of that class and the conduct associated with that class runs contrary to the values of the Constitution and the Equal Protection Clause, under any standard of review. I therefore concur in the Court's judgment that Texas' sodomy law banning "deviate sexual intercourse" between consenting adults of the same sex, but not between consenting adults of different sexes, is unconstitutional.

■ JUSTICE SCALIA, with whom THE CHIEF JUSTICE and JUSTICE THOMAS join, dissenting.

"Liberty finds no refuge in a jurisprudence of doubt." *Planned Parenthood of Southeastern Pa. v. Casey*, 505 U.S. 833, 844, 120 L. Ed. 2d 674, 112 S. Ct. 2791 (1992). That was the Court's sententious response, barely more than a decade ago, to those seeking to overrule *Roe v. Wade*, 410 U.S. 113, 35 L. Ed. 2d 147, 93 S. Ct. 705 (1973). The Court's response today, to those who have engaged in a 17–year crusade to overrule *Bowers v. Hardwick*, 478 U.S. 186, 92 L. Ed. 2d 140, 106 S. Ct. 2841 (1986), is very different. The need for stability and certainty presents no barrier.

Most of the rest of today's opinion has no relevance to its actual holding—that the Texas statute "furthers no legitimate state interest which can justify" its application to petitioners under rational-basis review. *Ante*, at 18 (overruling *Bowers* to the extent it sustained Georgia's anti-sodomy statute under the rational-basis test). Though there is discussion of "fundamental propositions," *ante*, at 4, and "fundamental decisions," *ibid.* nowhere does the Court's opinion declare that homosexual sodomy is a "fundamental right" under the Due Process Clause; nor does it subject the Texas law to the standard of review that would be appropriate (strict scrutiny) if homosexual sodomy *were* a "fundamental right." Thus, while overruling the *outcome* of *Bowers*, the Court leaves strangely untouched its central legal conclusion: "Respondent would have us announce ... a fundamental right to engage in homosexual sodomy. This we are quite unwilling to do." 478 U.S., at 191. Instead the Court simply describes petitioners' conduct as "an exercise of their liberty"—which it undoubtedly is—and proceeds to apply an unheard-of form of rational-basis review that will have far-reaching implications beyond this case. *Ante*, at 3.

* * *

Today's approach to *stare decisis* invites us to overrule an erroneously decided precedent (including an "intensely divisive" decision) *if:* (1) its foundations have been "eroded" by subsequent decisions, *ante*, at 15; (2) it has been subject to "substantial and continuing" criticism, *ibid.*; and (3) it has not induced "individual or societal reliance" that counsels against overturning, *ante*, at 16. The problem is that *Roe* itself—which today's majority surely has no disposition to overrule—satisfies these conditions to at least the same degree as *Bowers*.

* * *

I do not quarrel with the Court's claim that *Romer v. Evans*, 517 U.S. 620, 134 L. Ed. 2d 855, 116 S. Ct. 1620 (1996), "eroded" the "foundations" of *Bowers'* rational-basis holding. See *Romer, supra, at 640–643* (SCALIA, J., dissenting).) But *Roe* and *Casey* have been equally "eroded" by *Washington v. Glucksberg*, 521 U.S. 702, 721, 138 L. Ed. 2d 772, 117 S. Ct. 2258, 117 S. Ct. 2302 (1997), which held that *only* fundamental rights which are " 'deeply rooted in this Nation's history and tradition' " qualify for anything other than rational basis scrutiny under the doctrine of "substantive due process." *Roe* and *Casey*, of course, subjected the restriction of abortion to heightened scrutiny without even attempting to establish that the freedom to abort *was* rooted in this Nation's tradition.

* * * *Bowers*, the Court says, has been subject to "substantial and continuing [criticism], disapproving of its reasoning in all respects, not just as to its historical assumptions." *Ante*, at 15. * * * Of course, *Roe* too (and by extension *Casey*) had been (and still is) subject to unrelenting criticism, including criticism from the two commentators cited by the Court today. See Fried, *supra*, at 75 ("Roe was a prime example of twisted judging"); Posner, *supra*, at 337 ("[The Court's] opinion in *Roe* ... fails to measure up to professional expectations regarding judicial opinions"); Posner, Judicial Opinion Writing, 62 U. Chi. L. Rev. 1421, 1434 (1995) (describing the opinion in *Roe* as an "embarrassing performanc[e]").

* * * It seems to me that the "societal reliance" on the principles confirmed in *Bowers* and discarded today has been overwhelming. Countless judicial decisions and legislative enactments have relied on the ancient proposition that a governing majority's belief that certain sexual behavior is "immoral and unacceptable" constitutes a rational basis for regulation. * * * State laws against bigamy, same-sex marriage, adult incest, prostitution, masturbation, adultery, fornication, bestiality, and obscenity are likewise sustainable only in light of *Bowers'* validation of laws based on moral choices. Every single one of these laws is called into question by today's decision; the Court makes no effort to cabin the scope of its decision to exclude them from its holding. * * * The impossibility of distinguishing homosexuality from other traditional "morals" offenses is precisely why *Bowers* rejected the rational-basis challenge. "The law," it said, "is constantly based on notions of morality, and if all laws representing essentially moral choices are to be invalidated under the Due Process Clause, the courts will be very busy indeed." 478 U.S., at 196.

What a massive disruption of the current social order, therefore, the overruling of *Bowers* entails. * * *

Texas Penal Code Ann. § 21.06(a) (2003) undoubtedly imposes constraints on liberty. So do laws prohibiting prostitution, recreational use of heroin, and, for that matter, working more than 60 hours per week in a bakery. But there is no right to "liberty" under the Due Process Clause, though today's opinion repeatedly makes that claim. * * * The Fourteenth Amendment *expressly allows* States to deprive their citizens of "liberty," *so long as "due process of law" is provided[.]*

Our opinions applying the doctrine known as "substantive due process" hold that the Due Process Clause prohibits States from infringing *fundamental* liberty interests, unless the infringement is narrowly tailored to serve a compelling state interest. *Washington v. Glucksberg*, 521 U.S., at 721. We have held repeatedly, in cases the Court today does not overrule, that *only* fundamental rights qualify for this so-called "heightened scrutiny" protection—that is, rights which are " 'deeply rooted in this Nation's history and tradition,' " *ibid.* See *Reno v. Flores*, 507 U.S. 292, 303 (1993) * * * *United States v. Salerno*, 481 U.S. 739, 751 (1987) * * * See also *Michael H. v. Gerald D.*, 491 U.S. 110, 122 (1989) * * * *Moore v. East Cleveland*, 431 U.S. 494, 503 (1977) (plurality opinion); *Meyer v. Nebraska*, 262 U.S. 390, 399 (1923) * * * All other liberty interests may be abridged or abrogated pursuant to a validly enacted state law if that law is rationally related to a legitimate state interest.

Bowers held * * * that criminal prohibitions of homosexual sodomy are not subject to heightened scrutiny because they do not implicate a "fundamental right" under the Due Process Clause, 478 U.S., at 191–194. * * *

The Court today does not overrule this holding. Not once does it describe homosexual sodomy as a "fundamental right" or a "fundamental liberty interest," nor does it subject the Texas statute to strict scrutiny. Instead, having failed to establish that the right to homosexual sodomy is " 'deeply rooted in this Nation's history and tradition,' " the Court concludes that the application of Texas's statute to petitioners' conduct fails the rational-basis test, and overrules *Bowers*' holding to the contrary, see *id.*, at 196. * * *

　　　　* * *

It is (as *Bowers* recognized) entirely irrelevant whether the laws in our long national tradition criminalizing homosexual sodomy were "directed at homosexual conduct as a distinct matter." *Ante*, at 7. Whether homosexual sodomy was prohibited by a law targeted at same-sex sexual relations or by a more general law prohibiting both homosexual and heterosexual sodomy, the only relevant point is that it *was* criminalized—which suffices to establish that homosexual sodomy is not a right "deeply rooted in our Nation's history and tradition." The Court today agrees that homosexual sodomy was criminalized and thus does not dispute the facts on which *Bowers actually* relied.

* * * [T]he Court makes the claim, again unsupported by any citations, that "[l]aws prohibiting sodomy do not seem to have been enforced against consenting adults acting in private." *Ante*, at 8. The key qualifier here is "acting in private"—since the Court admits that sodomy laws *were* enforced against consenting adults (although the Court contends that prosecutions were "infrequent," *ante*, at 9). I do not know what "acting in private" means; surely consensual sodomy, like heterosexual intercourse, is rarely performed on stage. If all the Court means by "acting in private" is "on private premises, with the doors closed and windows covered," it is entirely unsurprising that evidence of enforcement would be hard to come by. (Imagine the circumstances that would enable a search warrant to be obtained for a residence on the ground that there was probable cause to believe that consensual sodomy was then and there occurring.) Surely that lack of evidence would not sustain the proposition that consensual sodomy on private premises with the doors closed and windows covered was regarded as a "fundamental right," even though all other consensual sodomy was criminalized. * * *

* * *

[A]n "emerging awareness" is by definition not "deeply rooted in this Nation's history and traditions," as we have said "fundamental right" status requires. Constitutional entitlements do not spring into existence because some States choose to lessen or eliminate criminal sanctions on certain behavior. Much less do they spring into existence, as the Court seems to believe, because *foreign nations* decriminalize conduct. The *Bowers* majority opinion *never* relied on "values we share with a wider civilization," *ante*, at 16, but rather rejected the claimed right to sodomy on the ground that such a right was not " 'deeply rooted in *this Nation's* history and tradition,' " 478 U.S., at 193–194 (emphasis added). * * *

* * *

The Texas statute undeniably seeks to further the belief of its citizens that certain forms of sexual behavior are "immoral and unacceptable," *Bowers, supra*, at 196—the same interest furthered by criminal laws against fornication, bigamy, adultery, adult incest, bestiality, and obscenity. *Bowers* held that this *was* a legitimate state interest. The Court today reaches the opposite conclusion. The Texas statute, it says, "furthers *no legitimate state interest* which can justify its intrusion into the personal and private life of the individual," *ante*, at 18 (emphasis added). * * * This effectively decrees the end of all morals legislation. If, as the Court asserts, the promotion of majoritarian sexual morality is not even a *legitimate* state interest, none of the above-mentioned laws can survive rational-basis review.

* * *

[As for Justice O'Connor's Equal Protection Clause analysis, m]en and women, heterosexuals and homosexuals, are all subject to [the statute's] prohibition of deviate sexual intercourse with someone of the same sex. To be sure, § 21.06 does distinguish between the sexes insofar as concerns the partner with whom the sexual acts are performed: men can violate the law only with other men, and women only with other women. But this cannot itself be a denial of equal protection, since it is precisely the same distinction regarding partner that is drawn in state laws prohibiting marriage with someone of the same sex while permitting marriage with someone of the opposite sex.

* * * A racially discriminatory purpose is always sufficient to subject a law to strict scrutiny, even a facially neutral law that makes no mention of race. See *Washington v. Davis*, 426 U.S. 229, 241–242 (1976). No purpose to discriminate against men or women as a class can be gleaned from the Texas law, so rational-basis review applies. That review is readily satisfied here by the same rational basis that satisfied it in *Bowers*—society's belief that certain forms of sexual behavior are "immoral and unacceptable," 478 U.S., at 196. This is the same justification that supports many other laws regulating sexual behavior that make a distinction based upon the identity of the partner—for example, laws against adultery, fornication, and adult incest, and laws refusing to recognize homosexual marriage.

JUSTICE O'CONNOR argues that the discrimination in this law which must be justified is not its discrimination with regard to the sex of the partner but its discrimination with regard to the sexual proclivity of the principal actor.

"While it is true that the law applies only to conduct, the conduct targeted by this law is conduct that is closely correlated with being homosexual. Under such circumstances, Texas' sodomy law is targeted at more than conduct. It is instead directed toward gay persons as a class." *Ante*, at 5.

Of course the same could be said of any law. A law against public nudity targets "the conduct that is closely correlated with being a nudist," and hence "is targeted at more than conduct"; it is "directed toward nudists as a class." But be that as it may. Even if the Texas law *does* deny equal protection to "homosexuals as a class," that denial *still* does not need to be justified by anything more than a rational basis, which our cases show is satisfied by the enforcement of traditional notions of sexual morality.

    * * *

Today's opinion is the product of a Court, which is the product of a law-profession culture, that has largely signed on to the so-called homosexual agenda, by which I mean the agenda promoted by some homosexual activists directed at eliminating the moral opprobrium that has traditionally attached to homosexual conduct. * * *

One of the most revealing statements in today's opinion is the Court's grim warning that the criminalization of homosexual conduct is "an invitation to subject homosexual persons to discrimination both in the public and in the private spheres." *Ante*, at 14. It is clear from this that the Court has taken sides in the culture war, departing from its role of assuring, as neutral observer, that the democratic rules of engagement are observed. Many Americans do not want persons who openly engage in homosexual conduct as partners in their business, as scoutmasters for their children, as teachers in their children's schools, or as boarders in their home. They view this as protecting themselves and their families from a lifestyle that they believe to be immoral and destructive. The Court views it as "discrimination" which it is the function of our judgments to deter. So imbued is the Court with the law profession's anti-anti-homosexual culture, that it is seemingly unaware that the attitudes of that culture are not obviously "mainstream[.]" * * *

* * * [P]ersuading one's fellow citizens is one thing, and imposing one's views in absence of democratic majority will is something else. I would no more *require* a State to criminalize homosexual acts—or, for that matter, display *any* moral disapprobation of them—than I would *forbid* it to do so. What Texas has chosen to do is well within the range of traditional democratic action, and its hand should not be stayed through the invention of a brand-new "constitutional right" by a Court that is impatient of democratic change. It is indeed true that "later generations can see that laws once thought necessary and proper in fact serve only to oppress," *ante*, at 18; and when that happens, later generations can repeal those laws. But it is the premise of our system that those judgments are to be made by the people, and not imposed by a governing caste that knows best.

* * *

■ Justice Thomas, dissenting.

I join Justice Scalia's dissenting opinion. I write separately to note that the law before the Court today "is ... uncommonly silly." *Griswold v. Connecticut*, 381 U.S. 479, 527 (1965) (Stewart, J., dissenting). If I were a member of the Texas Legislature, I would vote to repeal it. Punishing someone for expressing his sexual preference through noncommercial consensual conduct with another adult does not appear to be a worthy way to expend valuable law enforcement resources.

Notwithstanding this, I recognize that as a member of this Court I am not empowered to help petitioners and others similarly situated. My duty, rather, is to "decide cases 'agreeably to the Constitution and laws of the United States.'" *Id.*, at 530. And, just like Justice Stewart, I "can find [neither in the Bill of Rights nor any other part of the Constitution a] general right of privacy," *ibid.*, or as the Court terms it today, the "liberty of the person both in its spatial and more transcendent dimensions," *ante*, at 1.

————

NOTES AND QUESTIONS

1. *Moore* within the context of *Lawrence*. The plurality opinion in *Moore* relied on the primary place that the extended family has traditionally occupied in United States history. This reasoning is similar to that used in *Bowers v. Hardwick*, 478 U.S. 186 (1986), where a history and tradition of intolerance for homosexual conduct was used to support an anti-sodomy law. However, now that *Lawrence v. Texas*, 539 U.S. 558 (2003) has overruled *Bowers*, is the history and tradition argument which was invoked by the plurality in *Moore* on shaky ground? *See* David M. Wagner, *Hints, Not Holdings: Use of Precedent in* Lawrence v. Texas, 18 BYU J. Pub. L.

681 (2004); Susan Austin Blazier, Note, *The Irrational Use of Rational Basis Review in* Lawrence v. Texas, 26 CAMPBELL L. REV. 21 (2004).

2. Justice O'Connor's concurrence.

a. Domestic partners and O'Connor's concurrence in *Lawrence*. In her concurring opinion in *Lawrence v. Texas*, 539 U.S. 558 (2003) (O'Connor, J., concurring), Justice O'Connor notes that the conduct targeted by the Texas sodomy law was "closely correlated with being homosexual," and that this contributed to her decision that that law violated the equal protection clause. Under that rationale, it would seem that the state law that forbids recognition of domestic partners as dependants would also violate the equal protection clause, given that, as long as homosexuals are not allowed to marry, they will be forced into domestic partnership arrangements. Does this mean, under O'Connor's equal protection argument, that the state would be required to extend positive benefits (like domestic partner benefits) to homosexuals if those benefits are extended to heterosexuals?

In May 1992, MCA Corporation announced that it would provide health benefits to employees' same-sex partners, but not heterosexual domestic partners. William V. Vetter, *Restrictions on Equal Treatment of Unmarried Domestic Partners*, 5 B.U. PUB. INT. L.J. 1, 3 (1995). Is this asymmetric treatment of same-sex and opposite domestic partnerships discriminatory, or is some level of asymmetry necessary in order to compensate for the asymmetry in marriage laws between same-sex and opposite-sex couples?

b. Heterosexual domestic partnership. Domestic partnership arrangements are certainly not limited to same-sex couples. Would the "correlated with" approach O'Conner uses to equal protection sweep too broadly and end up refuting legislative intent by requiring domestic partner benefits for all cohabiting couples? However, if you reject a "correlated with" approach to equal protection, what would prevent a legislature from enacting a law which fell much more heavily on some disfavored group but had an ostensibly neutral purpose, like promoting marriage?

3. Morality as a state interest. Justice Scalia's dissent is longer than the opinion of the court itself, yet in eleven pages of dissent, he devotes only two paragraphs to the majority opinion, and those two paragraphs merely observe that no other society has decreed that morality is a sufficient basis for the enactment of a law. Does this mean that Scalia believes that enforcing public morality should be considered a legitimate state interest? *See* TracyLee Schimelfenig, Note, *Recognition of the Rights of Homosexuals: Implications of* Lawrence v. Texas, 40 CAL. W. L. REV. 149, 158–59 (2003). If that is the case, under Scalia's philosophy, can any law *ever* fail a rational basis review, since, presumably, the public elected the legislature and the legislature writes laws that are consistent with the social norms of the society that elected them? In other words, if morality alone is a legitimate state interest, is there anything left of due process?

4. Silly laws and legitimate state interests. Justice Thomas' dissent begins by stating that the Texas anti-sodomy law is "uncommonly silly." Given that Justice Thomas does not believe that enforcing this law is a "worthy" use of government resources, how can he support the idea that it survives a due process attack for lacking a rational relation to a legitimate state interest? Is Thomas' version of due process something closer to "a silly relation to an unworthy government interest?" *See* Kris Franklin, *Homophobia and the "Matthew Shepard Effect": In* Lawrence v. Texas, 48 N.Y.L. Sch. L. Rev. 657, 667 at n.51 (2004).

5.   The limits of *Lawrence*. The holding of the court in this case is that "[t]he Texas statute furthers no legitimate state interest which can justify its intrusion into the personal and private life of the individual." However, this holding raises an interesting question: is the Texas statute unconstitutional because it furthers no legitimate state interest, or because it intrudes into the private life of the individual? If the former is true, then it would seem that all morals-based legislation is illegitimate and, unless it has some ancillary benefits, will most likely be struck down. If the latter is the case, *Lawrence* is a much more limited victory for gay rights, essentially stating that individuals have the right to be homosexual in their bedrooms, but nowhere else.

6.   Response of the church to changing social norms. In response to the decision in *Lawrence v. Texas*, televangelist Pat Robertson issued a national call for Christians to pray for the retirement of Justices O'Connor, Stevens, and Ginsburg. Interview by Paula Zahn with Pat Robertson, *Pat Robertson: Pray For Justices to Retire*, July 17, 2003, *available at* http://www.cnn.com/2003/LAW/07/17/cnna.robertson/. Additionally, the Catholic Church has issued a statement condemning homosexual marriage. Victor L. Simpson, *Vatican Issues Offensive on Gay Marriages*, Associated Press, July 28, 2003.

7.   Additional reading. For additional information on morality laws, see generally Peter M. Cicchino, *Reason and the Rule of Law: Should Bare Assertions of "Public Morality" Qualify as Legitimate Government Interests for the Purposes of Equal Protection Review?*, 87 Geo. L.J. 139 (1998); Steve Sheppard, *The State Interest in the Good Citizen: Constitutional Balance Between the Citizen and the Perfectionist State*, 45 Hastings L.J. 969 (1994). For a look at existing methods of gaining state recognition of same-sex marriages, see Phyllis Randolph Frye & Alyson Dodi Meiselman, *Same–Sex Marriages Have Existed Legally in the United States for a Long Time Now*, 64 Alb. L. Rev. 1031 (2001). For an overview of the evolving definition of family with respect to same-sex unions, see Paula Ettelbrick, *Domestic Partnership, Civil Unions, or Marriage: One Size Does Not Fit All*, 64 Alb. L. Rev. 905 (2001).

E.   A Family Based on Same Sex Marriage

Goodridge v. Department of Public Health

798 N.E.2d 941 (Mass. 2003).

■ Marshall, C.J.

Marriage is a vital social institution. The exclusive commitment of two individuals to each other nurtures love and mutual support; it brings stability to our society. For those who choose to marry, and for their children, marriage provides an abundance of legal, financial, and social benefits. In return it imposes weighty legal, financial, and social obligations. The question before us is whether, consistent with the Massachusetts Constitution, the Commonwealth may deny the protections, benefits, and obligations conferred by civil marriage to two individuals of the same sex who wish to marry. We conclude that it may not. The Massachusetts Constitution affirms the dignity and equality of all individuals. It forbids the creation of second-class citizens. In reaching our conclusion we have given full deference to the arguments made by the Commonwealth. But it has failed to identify any constitutionally adequate reason for denying civil marriage to same-sex couples.

We are mindful that our decision marks a change in the history of our marriage law. Many people hold deep-seated religious, moral, and ethical convictions that marriage should be limited to the union of one man and one woman, and that homosexual conduct is immoral. Many hold equally strong religious, moral, and ethical convictions that same-sex couples are entitled to be married, and that homosexual persons should be treated no differently than their heterosexual neighbors. Neither view answers the question before us. * * *

[In *Lawrence*,] the Court affirmed that the core concept of common human dignity protected by the Fourteenth Amendment to the United States Constitution precludes government intrusion into the deeply personal realms of consensual adult expressions of intimacy and one's choice of an intimate partner. The Court also reaffirmed the central role that decisions whether to marry or have children bear in shaping one's identity. * * *

Barred access to the protections, benefits, and obligations of civil marriage, a person who enters into an intimate, exclusive union with another of the same sex is arbitrarily deprived of membership in one of our community's most rewarding and cherished institutions. That exclusion is incompatible with the constitutional principles of respect for individual autonomy and equality under law.

I

The plaintiffs are fourteen individuals from five Massachusetts counties. * * *

In March and April, 2001, each of the plaintiff couples attempted to obtain a marriage license from a city or town clerk's office. * * * In each case, the clerk either refused to accept the notice of intention to marry or denied a marriage license to the couple on the ground that Massachusetts does not recognize same-sex marriage. Because obtaining a marriage license is a necessary prerequisite to civil marriage in Massachusetts, denying marriage licenses to the plaintiffs was tantamount to denying them access to civil marriage itself, with its appurtenant social and legal protections, benefits, and obligations.

[The District Court ruled in favor of the defendants, concluding "prohibiting same-sex marriage rationally furthers the Legislature's legitimate interest in safeguarding the 'primary purpose' of marriage, 'procreation.' "]

* * *

III

A

The larger question is whether, as the department claims, government action that bars same-sex couples from civil marriage constitutes a legitimate exercise of the State's authority to regulate conduct, or whether, as the plaintiffs claim, this categorical marriage exclusion violates the Massachusetts Constitution. We have recognized the long-standing statutory understanding, derived from the common law, that "marriage" means the lawful union of a woman and a man. But that history cannot and does not foreclose the constitutional question.

The plaintiffs' claim that the marriage restriction violates the Massachusetts Constitution can be analyzed in two ways. Does it offend the Constitution's guarantees of equality before the law? Or do the liberty and due process provisions of the Massachusetts Constitution secure the plaintiffs' right to marry their chosen partner? In matters implicating marriage, family life, and the upbringing of children, the two constitutional concepts frequently overlap, as they do here. * * *

We begin by considering the nature of civil marriage itself. Simply put, the government creates civil marriage. In Massachusetts, civil marriage is, and since pre–Colonial days has been, precisely what its name implies: a wholly secular institution. * * *

Civil marriage is created and regulated through exercise of the police power. * * * In broad terms, it is the Legislature's power to enact rules to regulate conduct, to the extent that such laws are "necessary to secure the health, safety, good order, comfort, or general welfare of the community." * * *

Without question, civil marriage enhances the "welfare of the community." It is a "social institution of the highest importance." * * * Civil marriage anchors an ordered society by encouraging stable relationships over transient ones. It is central to the way the Commonwealth identifies individuals, provides for the orderly distribution of property, ensures that children and adults are cared for and supported whenever possible from private rather than public funds, and tracks important epidemiological and demographic data.

Marriage also bestows enormous private and social advantages on those who choose to marry. Civil marriage is at once a deeply personal commitment to another human being and a highly public celebration of the ideals of mutuality, companionship, intimacy, fidelity, and family. * * *

Tangible as well as intangible benefits flow from marriage. The marriage license grants valuable property rights to those who meet the entry requirements, and who agree to what might otherwise be a burdensome degree of government regulation of their activities. * * *

The benefits accessible only by way of a marriage license are enormous, touching nearly every aspect of life and death. The department states that "hundreds of statutes" are related to marriage and to marital benefits. With no attempt to be comprehensive, we note that some of the statutory benefits conferred by the Legislature on those who enter into civil marriage include, as to property [including: joint Massachusetts income tax filing, automatic rights to inherit the property of a deceased spouse who does not leave a will, and entitlement to wages owed to a deceased employee].

* * *

Where a married couple has children, their children are also directly or indirectly, but no less auspiciously, the recipients of the special legal and economic protections obtained by civil marriage. Notwithstanding the Commonwealth's strong public policy to abolish legal distinctions between marital and nonmarital children in providing for the support and care of minors, * * * the fact remains that marital children reap a measure of family stability and economic security based on their parents' legally privileged status that is largely inaccessible, or not as readily accessible, to nonmarital children. Some of these benefits are social, such as the enhanced approval that still attends the status of being a marital child. Others are material, such as the greater ease of access to family-based State and Federal benefits that attend the presumptions of one's parentage.

It is undoubtedly for these concrete reasons, as well as for its intimately personal significance, that civil marriage has long been termed a "civil right." * * *

Without the right to marry—or more properly, the right to choose to marry—one is excluded from the full range of human experience and denied full protection of the laws for one's "avowed commitment to an intimate and lasting human relationship." * * * Because civil marriage is central to the lives of individuals and the welfare of the community, our laws assiduously protect the individual's right to marry against undue government incursion. Laws may not "interfere directly and substantially with the right to marry." * * *

B

For decades, indeed centuries, in much of this country (including Massachusetts) no lawful marriage was possible between white and black Americans. That long history availed not when the Supreme Court of California held in 1948 that a legislative prohibition against interracial marriage violated the due process and equality guarantees of the Fourteenth Amendment, *Perez v. Sharp*, * * * or when, nineteen years later, the United States Supreme Court also held that a statutory bar to interracial marriage violated the Fourteenth Amendment, *Loving v. Virginia*, * * * As both *Perez* and *Loving* make clear, the right to marry means little if it does not include the right to marry the person of one's choice, subject to appropriate government restrictions in the interests of public health, safety, and welfare. * * * As it did in *Perez* and *Loving,* history must yield to a more fully developed understanding of the invidious quality of the discrimination. * * *

The individual liberty and equality safeguards of the Massachusetts Constitution protect both "freedom from" unwarranted government intrusion into protected spheres of life and "freedom to" partake in benefits created by the State for the common good. * * * Both freedoms are involved here. Whether and whom to marry, how to express sexual intimacy, and whether and how to establish a family—these are among the most basic of every individual's liberty and due process rights. * * * And central to personal freedom and security is the assurance that the laws will apply equally to persons in similar situations. "Absolute equality before the law is a fundamental principle of our own Constitution." * * * The liberty interest in choosing whether and whom to marry would be hollow if the Commonwealth could, without sufficient justification, foreclose an individual from freely choosing the person with whom to share an exclusive commitment in the unique institution of civil marriage.

* * *

The department posits three legislative rationales for prohibiting same-sex couples from marrying: (1) providing a "favorable setting for procreation"; (2) ensuring the optimal setting for child rearing, which the department defines as "a two-parent family with one parent of each sex"; and (3) preserving scarce State and private financial resources. We consider each in turn.

The judge in the Superior Court endorsed the first rationale, holding that "the state's interest in regulating marriage is based on the traditional concept that marriage's primary purpose is procreation." This is incorrect. Our laws of civil marriage do not privilege procreative heterosexual intercourse between married people above every other form of adult intimacy and every other means of creating a family. * * * People who have never consummated their marriage, and never plan to, may be and stay married. * * * While it is certainly true that many, perhaps most, married couples have children together (assisted or unassisted), it is the exclusive and permanent commitment of the marriage partners to one another, not the begetting of children, that is the sine qua non of civil marriage.

Moreover, the Commonwealth affirmatively facilitates bringing children into a family regardless of whether the intended parent is married or unmarried, whether the child is adopted or born into a family, whether assistive technology was used to conceive the child, and whether the parent or her partner is heterosexual, homosexual, or bisexual. If procreation were a necessary component of civil marriage, our statutes would draw a tighter circle around the permissible bounds of nonmarital child bearing and the creation of families by noncoital means. The attempt to isolate procreation as "the source of a fundamental right to marry," * * * overlooks the integrated way in which courts have examined the complex and overlapping realms of personal autonomy, marriage, family life, and child rearing. Our jurisprudence recognizes that, in these nuanced and fundamentally private areas of life, such a narrow focus is inappropriate.

> * * *

The department's first stated rationale, equating marriage with unassisted heterosexual procreation, shades imperceptibly into its second: that confining marriage to opposite-sex couples ensures that children are raised in the "optimal" setting. Protecting the welfare of children is a paramount State policy. Restricting marriage to opposite-sex couples, however, cannot plausibly further this policy. * * * The "best interests of the child" standard does not turn on a parent's sexual orientation or marital status. * * *

The department has offered no evidence that forbidding marriage to people of the same sex will increase the number of couples choosing to enter into opposite-sex marriages in order to have and raise children. There is thus no rational relationship between the marriage statute and the Commonwealth's proffered goal of protecting the "optimal" child rearing unit. Moreover, the department readily concedes that people in same-sex couples may be "excellent" parents. These couples (including four of the plaintiff couples) have children for the reasons others do—to love them, to care for them, to nurture them. But the task of child rearing for same-sex couples is made infinitely harder by their status as outliers to the marriage laws. * * * Given the wide range of public benefits reserved only for married couples, we do not credit the department's contention that the absence of access to civil marriage amounts to little more than an inconvenience to same-sex couples and their children. Excluding same-sex couples from civil marriage will not make children of opposite-sex marriages more secure, but it does prevent children of same-sex couples from enjoying the immeasurable advantages that flow from the assurance of "a stable family structure in which children will be reared, educated, and socialized." * * *

The third rationale advanced by the department is that limiting marriage to opposite-sex couples furthers the Legislature's interest in conserving scarce State and private financial resources. The marriage restriction is rational, it argues, because the General Court logically could assume that same-sex couples are more financially independent than married couples and thus less needy of public marital benefits, such as tax advantages, or private marital benefits, such as employer-financed health plans that include spouses in their coverage.

An absolute statutory ban on same-sex marriage bears no rational relationship to the goal of economy. First, the department's conclusory generalization—that same-sex couples are less financially dependent on each other than opposite-sex couples—ignores that many same-sex couples, such as many of the plaintiffs in this case, have children and other dependents (here, aged parents) in their care. The department does not contend, nor could it, that these dependents are less needy or deserving than the dependents of married couples. Second, Massachusetts marriage laws do not condition receipt of public and private financial benefits to married individuals on a demonstration of financial dependence on each other; the benefits are available to married couples regardless of whether they mingle their finances or actually depend on each other for support.

* * *

It has been argued that, due to the State's strong interest in the institution of marriage as a stabilizing social structure, only the Legislature can control and define its boundaries. * * * The Massachusetts Constitution requires that legislation meet certain criteria and not extend beyond certain limits. It is the function of courts to determine whether these criteria are met and whether these limits are exceeded. In most instances, these limits are defined by whether a rational basis exists to conclude that legislation will bring about a rational result. The Legislature in the first instance, and the courts in the last instance, must ascertain whether such a rational basis exists. To label the court's role as usurping that of the Legislature, * * * is to misunderstand the nature and purpose of judicial review. We owe great deference to the Legislature to decide social and policy issues, but it is the traditional and settled role of courts to decide constitutional issues.

* * *

The history of constitutional law "is the story of the extension of constitutional rights and protections to people once ignored or excluded." * * * As a public institution and a right of fundamental importance, civil marriage is an evolving paradigm. * * * Marriage has survived [many] transformations, and we have no doubt that marriage will continue to be a vibrant and revered institution.

* * *

■ [Greaney, J. concurred in the opinion]

■ [Spina, J. and Sosman, J. dissented, with Cordy, JJ. joining both opinions].

■ Cordy, J. (dissenting, with whom Spina and Sosman, JJ., join).

* * *

Civil marriage is the institutional mechanism by which societies have sanctioned and recognized particular family structures, and the institution of marriage has existed as one of the fundamental organizing principles of human society. * * * Marriage has not been merely a contractual arrangement for legally defining the private relationship between two individuals (although that is certainly part of any marriage). Rather, on an institutional level, marriage is the "very basis of the whole fabric of civilized society," * * * and it serves many important political, economic, social, educational, procreational, and personal functions.

Paramount among its many important functions, the institution of marriage has systematically provided for the regulation of heterosexual behavior, brought order to the resulting procreation, and ensured a stable family structure in which children will be reared, educated, and socialized. * * * Admittedly, heterosexual intercourse, procreation, and child care are not necessarily conjoined (particularly in the modern age of widespread effective contraception and supportive social welfare programs), but an orderly society requires some mechanism for coping with the fact that sexual intercourse commonly results in pregnancy and childbirth. The institution of marriage is that mechanism.

The institution of marriage provides the important legal and normative link between heterosexual intercourse and procreation on the one hand and family responsibilities on the other. * * * The alternative, a society without the institution of marriage, in which heterosexual intercourse, procreation, and child care are largely disconnected processes, would be chaotic.

The marital family is also the foremost setting for the education and socialization of children. Children learn about the world and their place in it primarily from those who raise them, and those children eventually grow up to exert some influence, great or small, positive or negative, on society. The institution of marriage encourages parents to remain committed to each other and to their children as they grow, thereby encouraging a stable venue for the education and socialization of children. * * *

It is difficult to imagine a State purpose more important and legitimate than ensuring, promoting, and supporting an optimal social structure within which to bear and raise children. At the very least, the marriage statute continues to serve this important State purpose. * * *

Taking all of this available information into account, the Legislature could rationally conclude that a family environment with married opposite-sex parents remains the optimal social structure in which to bear children, and that the raising of children by same-sex couples, who by definition cannot be the two sole biological parents of a child and cannot provide children with a parental authority figure of each gender, presents an alternative structure for child rearing that has not yet proved itself beyond reasonable scientific dispute to be as optimal as the biologically based marriage norm. * * *

NOTES AND QUESTIONS

1. **Economic framework for same sex marriage.**

   a. Orderly distribution of property, private support for children's care.

   "It is central to the way the Commonwealth identifies individuals, provides for the orderly distribution of property, ensures that children and adults are cared for and supported whenever possible from private rather than public funds . . ."

   b. Property rights to those who choose to marry.

   "The marriage license grants valuable property rights to those who meet the entry requirements, and who agree to what might otherwise be a burdensome degree of government regulation of their activities."

2. **Justifications for ban on same sex marriage.**

   a. Providing a "favorable setting for procreation"

b. Ensuring the optimal setting for child rearing, which the department defines as "a two-parent family with one parent of each sex"

c. Preserving scarce state and private financial resources

Which of the above listed rationales for banning same-sex marriage are based upon libertarian arguments for limited government and maximum personal autonomy?

3. Neo-classical economics and same sex marriage.

Libertarian economist Milton Friedman has argued that there were four duties of government: (1) to protect citizens from military invasion, (2) to protect citizens from violence by fellow citizens, (3) to create and maintain the public works infrastructure and (4) to provide for "irresponsibles." Does a state or federal ban on same-sex marriage fit into any of these categories?

What position would you guess Milton and Rose Friedman take in the same-sex marriage debates? Would their position be consistent with economic libertarianism? If not, what rationale would they give for any inconsistency?

4. Queer theory arguments against same sex marriage?

Can you imagine what the arguments of gay advocates might be against same sex marriage? For a representative selection of such arguments see WILLIAM H. ESKRIDGE & NAN D. HUNTER, *Families We Choose, in* SEXUALITY, GENDER AND THE LAW 1008–99 (2d ed. 2004), (featuring gay argument and counter arguments for same sex marriage).

Paula Ettelbrick argues that:

> "Marriage runs contrary to two of the primary goals of the lesbian and gay movement: the affirmation of gay identity and culture and the validation of many forms of relationships.... At this point in time, making legal marriage for lesbian and gay couples a priority would set an agenda of gaining rights for a few, but would do nothing to correct power imbalances between those who are married (whether gay or straight) and those who are not. Thus justice would not be gained.... Being queer means pushing the parameters of sex, sexuality, and family, and in the process transforming the very fabric of society.... The thought of emphasizing our sameness to married heterosexuals in order to obtain this 'right' terrifies me. It rips away the very heart and soul of what I believe it is to be a lesbian in this world. It robs me of the opportunity to make a difference. We end up mimicking all that is bad about the institution of marriage in our effort to appear to be the same as straight couples."

Id. at 1098 (excerpted from Paula Ettelbrick, *Since When is Marriage a Path to Liberation*, OUTLOOK, Autumn 1989, at 8–12).

5. The constitutionality of California Proposition 8 banning same–sex marriage.

Perry v. Schwarznegger

In the United States District Court for the
Northern District of California

Decided August 4, 2010

Walker, C.J.

Plaintiffs challenge a November 2008 voter-enacted amendment to the California Constitution ("Proposition 8" or "Prop 8"). Cal Const Art I, § 7.5. In its entirety, Proposition 8 provides: "Only marriage between a man and a woman is valid or recognized in California." Plaintiffs allege that Proposition 8 deprives them of due process and of equal protection of the laws contrary to the Fourteenth Amendment and that its enforcement by state officials violates 42 USC § 1983. Plaintiffs are two couples.

Plaintiffs seek to marry their partners and have been denied marriage licenses by their respective county authorities on the basis of Proposition 8. No party contended, and no evidence at trial suggested, that the county authorities had any ground to deny marriage licenses to plaintiffs other than Proposition 8.

Having considered the trial evidence and the arguments of counsel, the court pursuant to FRCP 52(a) finds that Proposition 8 is unconstitutional and that its enforcement must be enjoined....

In the absence of a rational basis, what remains of proponents' case is an inference, amply supported by evidence in the record, that Proposition 8 was premised on the belief that same-sex couples simply are not as good as opposite-sex couples. FF 78–80. Whether that belief is based on moral disapproval of homosexuality, animus towards gays and lesbians or simply a belief that a relationship between a man and a woman is inherently better than a relationship between two men or two women, this belief is not a proper basis on which to legislate. See Romer, 517 US at 633; Moreno, 413 US at 534; Palmore v Sidoti, 466 US 429, 433 (1984) ("[T]he Constitution cannot control [private biases] but neither can it tolerate them.").

The evidence shows that Proposition 8 was a hard-fought campaign and that the majority of California voters supported the initiative. See Background to Proposition 8 above ...

The arguments surrounding Proposition 8 raise a question similar to that addressed in *Lawrence*, when the Court asked whether a majority of citizens could use the power of the state to enforce "profound and deep convictions accepted as ethical and moral principles" through the criminal code. 539 US at 571.

The question here is whether California voters can enforce those same principles through regulation of marriage licenses. They cannot.

California's obligation is to treat its citizens equally, not to "mandate [its] own moral code." Id (citing Planned Parenthood of Southeastern Pa v Casey, 505 US 833, 850, (1992)). "[M]oral disapproval, without any other asserted state interest," has never been a rational basis for legislation.

Lawrence, 539 US at 582 (O'Connor, J, concurring). Tradition alone cannot support legislation. See Williams, 399 US at 239; Romer, 517 US at 635; Lawrence, 539 US at 579.

Proponents' purported rationales are nothing more than post-hoc justifications. While the Equal Protection Clause does not prohibit post-hoc rationales, they must connect to the classification drawn. Here, the purported state interests fit so poorly with Proposition 8 that they are irrational, as explained above. What is left is evidence that Proposition 8 enacts a moral view that there is something "wrong" with same-sex couples.

The evidence at trial regarding the campaign to pass Proposition 8 uncloaks the most likely explanation for its passage: a desire to advance the belief that opposite-sex couples are morally superior to same-sex couples. FF 79–80. The campaign relied heavily on negative stereotypes about gays and lesbians and focused on protecting children from inchoate threats vaguely associated with gays and lesbians.

CHAPTER 10

CULTURE AND IDENTITY

Introduction

The assumptions of conventional economic theory largely ignore questions of race, class, or other variables that affect individual identity. The rational actor of economics is assumed to be, like the reasonable person of law, a male member of the dominant culture. This assumption allows the values and perspectives of the dominant groups to serve as a crude surrogate for a more refined understanding of other perspectives.

The major consequence of omitting identity from economic reasoning is that economic theory has been unable to provide effective tools for diagnosing some of the most critical issues of economic inequality. This omission is present in both theoretical models and empirical research assumptions. The "thin" accounts of how race, gender, and other identity variables play a role in creating economic distribution are now being vigorously challenged by more robust models that for the first time are explicitly concerned with the economic impact of identity.

In 2003, George Akerlof, a Nobel laureate in economics, and Rachel Kranton, a professor of economics, introduced an important model of economic behavior that explicitly addresses critical questions of race, class and other identity factors and their relationship to the distribution of economic resources.

In this chapter, we begin with Akerlof and Kranton's model that offers a persuasive account of identity and culture in the sphere of economic activity. Next, we take up the insights of social norm theory, which draws upon modern sociological theory and turns attention to the dynamics of social group interaction. Finally, we look at race itself, a major identity variable. In this section, we explore the two competing theories about race and economics, and we look at law professor Ian Ayres' pathbreaking empirical study of evidence of pervasive racial discrimination in the market for the second-largest consumer retail purchase: new cars. Ayres has extended his empirical studies of racial discrimination to include transactions as varied as kidney transplants, taxi tipping practices, and bail setting. From these investigations he has argued, with some success in actual litigation, for a more sensitive test of the disparate impact theory of racial discrimination. Ayres' view does not require proof of discriminatory intent, and relies instead upon statistical disparities that show discriminatory impact upon subordinated groups.

A.   Culture and Identity

Economics and Identity

115 Q. J. Econ. 715 (2000).

■ George A. Akerlof and Rachel E. Kranton

This paper considers how identity, a person's sense of self, affects economic outcomes. We incorporate the psychology and sociology of identity into an economic model of behavior. In the utility function we propose, identity is associated with different social categories and how people in these categories should behave. We then construct a simple game-theoretic model showing how identity can affect individual interactions. The paper adapts these models to gender discrimination in the workplace, the economics of poverty and social exclusion, and the household division of labor. In each case, the inclusion of identity substantively changes conclusions of previous economic analysis.

I.   Introduction

This paper introduces identity—a person's sense of self—into economic analysis. Identity can account for many phenomena that current economics cannot well explain. It can comfortably resolve, for example, why some women oppose "women's rights," as seen in microcosm when Betty Friedan was ostracized by fellow suburban housewives for writing *The Feminine Mystique*. Other problems such as ethnic and racial conflict, discrimination, intractable labor disputes, and separatist politics all invite an identity-based analysis. Because of its explanatory power, numerous scholars in psychology, sociology, political science, anthropology, and history have adopted identity as a central concept. This paper shows how identity can be brought into economic analysis, allowing a new view of many economic problems.

We incorporate identity into a general model of behavior and then demonstrate how identity influences economic outcomes. Specifically, we consider gender discrimination in the labor market, the household division of labor, and the economics of social exclusion and poverty. In each case, our analysis yields predictions, supported by existing evidence, that are different from those of existing economic models. The Conclusion indicates many other realms where identity almost surely matters.

Our identity model of behavior begins with social difference. Gender, a universally familiar aspect of identity, illustrates. There are two abstract social categories, "man" and "woman." These categories are associated with different ideal physical attributes and prescribed behaviors. Everyone in the population is assigned a gender category, as either a "man" or a "woman." Following the behavioral prescriptions for one's gender affirms one's self-image, or identity, as a "man" or as a "woman." Violating the prescriptions evokes anxiety and discomfort in oneself and in others. Gender identity, then, changes the "payoffs" from different actions.

This modeling of identity is informed by a vast body of research on the salience of social categories for human behavior and interaction. We present in the next section a series of examples of identity-related behavior. These examples, and other evidence, indicate that (1) people have identity-based payoffs derived from their own actions; (2) people have identity-based payoffs derived from others' actions; (3) third parties can generate persistent changes in these payoffs; and (4) some people may choose their identity, but choice may be proscribed for others.

The concept of identity expands economic analysis for at least four corresponding reasons.

First, identity can explain behavior that appears detrimental. People behave in ways that would be considered maladaptive or even self-destructive by those with other identities. The reason for this behavior may be to bolster a sense of self or to salve a diminished self-image.

Second, identity underlies a new type of externality. One person's actions can have meaning for and evoke responses in others. Gender again affords an example. A dress is a symbol of femininity. If a man wears a dress, this may threaten the identity of other men. There is an externality, and further externalities result if these men make some response.

Third, identity reveals a new way that preferences can be changed. Notions of identity evolve within a society and some in the society have incentives to manipulate them. Obvious examples occur in advertising (e.g., Marlboro ads). As we shall explore, there are many other cases, including public policies, where changing social categories and associated prescriptions affects economic outcomes.

Fourth, because identity is fundamental to behavior, choice of identity may be the most important "economic" decision people make. Individuals may—more or less consciously—choose who they want to be. Limits on this choice may also be the most important determinant of an individual's economic well-being. Previous economic analyses of, for example, poverty, labor supply, and schooling have not considered these possibilities. * * *

B. *Psychology and Experiments on Group Identification*

The prominence of identity in psychology suggests that economists should consider identity as an argument in utility functions. Psychologists have long posited a self or "ego" as a primary force of individual behavior. They have further associated an individual's sense of self to the social setting; identity is bound to social categories; and individuals identify with people in some categories and differentiate themselves from those in others.

While experiments in social psychology do not show the existence of a "self" or this identification per se, they do demonstrate that even arbitrary social categorizations affect behavior. Consider the Robbers Cave experiment. In its initial week, two groups of boys at a summer camp in Oklahoma were kept apart. During this period, the boys developed norms of behavior and identities as belonging to *their* group. When they met for a tournament in the second week, the eleven-year-old equivalent of war broke out, with name-calling, stereotyping, and fighting. Later experiments show that competition is not necessary for group identification and even the most minimal group assignment can affect behavior. "Groups" form by nothing more than random assignment of subjects to labels, such as even or odd. Subjects are more likely to give rewards to those with the same label than to those with other labels, even when choices are anonymous and have no impact on own payoffs. Subjects also have higher opinions of members of their own group.

Our modeling of identity exactly parallels these experiments. In the experiments ... there are social categories; there is an assignment of subjects to those social categories; finally, subjects have in mind some form of assignment-related prescriptions, else rewards would not depend on group assignment.

C. *Examples of Identity–Related Behavior*

We next present a set of "real-world" examples of four different ways, outlined in the introduction and formalized in our utility function, that identity may influence behavior.

Our *first* set demonstrates that people have identity-related payoffs from their own actions. The impact of an action a_j on utility U_j depends in part on its effect on identity I_j.

Self–Mutilation. The first of these examples is perhaps the most dramatic: people mutilate their own or their children's bodies as an expression of identity. Tattooing, body-piercing (ear, nose, navel, etc.), hair conking, self-starvation, steroid abuse, plastic surgery, and male and female circumcision all yield physical markers of belonging to more or less explicit social categories and groups. In terms of our utility function, these practices transform an individual's physical characteristics to match an ideal. The mutilation may occur because people believe it leads to pecuniary rewards and interactions such as marriage. But the tenacity and defense of these practices indicate the extent to which belonging relies on ritual, and people have internalized measures of beauty and virtue.

Gender and Occupations. Female trial lawyer, male nurse, woman Marine—all conjure contradictions. Why? Because trial lawyers are viewed as masculine, nurses as feminine, and a Marine as the ultimate man. People in these occupations but of the opposite sex often have ambiguous feelings about their work. In terms of our utility function, an individual's actions do not correspond to gender prescriptions of behavior. A revealing study in this regard is Pierce's [1995] participant-observer research on the legal profession. Female lawyers thought of themselves as women, yet being a good lawyer meant acting like a man. Lawyers were told in training sessions to act like "Rambo" and to "take no prisoners." In the office, trial attorneys who did not "win big" were described as "having no balls." Intimidation of witnesses was "macho blasts against the other side." A Christmas skit about two partners dramatized the gender conflict:

[O]ne secretary dressed up as Rachel and another dressed up as Michael. The secretary portraying Michael ... ran around the stage barking orders and singing, "I'm Michael Bond, I'm such a busy man. I'm such a busy man." The other secretary followed suit by barking orders and singing. "I'm Rachel Rosen, I'm such a busy man, I mean woman. I'm such a busy man, I mean woman...." Michael responded to the spoof in stride.... Rachel, on the other hand, was very upset [Pierce, 1995, p. 130].

Female lawyers expressed their ambivalence in many discussions. "Candace," another partner, told Pierce: "I had forgotten how much anger I've buried over the years about what happened to the woman who became a lawyer ... To be a lawyer, somewhere along the way, I made a decision that it meant acting like a man. To do that I squeezed the female part of me into a box, put on the lid, and tucked it away" [Pierce 1995, p. 134].

Alumni Giving. Charitable contributions may yield a "warm glow" [Andreoni 1989], but how do people choose one organization over another? Charity to the organization with the highest marginal return would maximize its economic impact. Yet, at least for higher education, contributions may well reflect identity. Graduates give to *their own* alma mater. Alumni giving could enhance the value of a degree by maintaining an institution's reputation. But this explanation suffers from the collective action problem. And it does not account for student loyalty and identification with an institution, as expressed in such lyrics as "For God, for country, and for Yale."

Mountaineering. Why do people climb mountains? Loewenstein [1998] argues that facing the extreme discomfort and danger of mountaineering enhances an individual's sense of self.

Our *second* set of examples demonstrates that people have identity-related payoffs from others' actions. The effect of an action a_j on utility includes an impact on I_j.

Gender and Occupations. A woman working in a "man's" job may make male colleagues feel less like "men." To allay these feelings, they may act to affirm their masculinity and act against female coworkers. In her study of coal handlers in a power plant, Padavic [1991] interpreted the behavior of her male coworkers in this way. On one occasion, they picked her up, tossed her back and forth, and attempted to push her onto the coal conveyer belt (jokingly, of course). In the case of another worker, no one trained her, no one helped her, and when she asked for help, she was refused assistance that would have been routine for male coworkers.

To further assay the reasons for such behavior, we took a random-sample telephone survey relating a vignette about a female carpenter at a construction company who was "baited and teased" by a male coworker. We see in Table I that among the six possible explanations, 84 percent of the respondents said it was "somewhat likely," "likely," or "very likely" that the male worker behaved in this way because he felt less masculine. This explanation was one of the most popular, and more than three-quarters of the respondents thought that a woman in a man's job "frequently" or "almost always" faces such treatment.

Manhood and Insult. For a man, an action may be viewed as an insult which, if left unanswered, impugns his masculinity. As in the example above, an action a_{-j} *impacts* I_j, which may be countered by an action a_j. Psychologists Nisbett and Cohn [1996] have detected such identity concerns in experiments at the University of Michigan. These experiments, they argue, reveal remnants of the white antebellum Southern "culture of honor" in disparate reactions to insult of males from the U. S. South and North. Their experiments involved variations of the following scenario: an associate of the experimenters bumped subjects in the hallway as they made their way to the experiment. Rather than apologizing, the associate called the subject "asshole." Insulted Southerners were more likely than insulted Northerners and control Southerners to fill in subsequent word-completion tests with aggressive words (for example, g-un rather than f-un), and had raised cortisol levels.

TABLE I

Vignette Concerning Harassment and Evaluation of Possible Explanations

Vignette: Paul is a carpenter for a construction company. The company has just hired Christine, its first female carpenter, for 3 dollars *less* per hour than it pays Paul and the other carpenters. On Christine's first day of work, Paul and two of his coworkers bait and tease Christine, making it difficult for her to do her job.

Try to imagine why Paul behaved as he did. Rate each of the following explanations for Paul's behavior as not-at-all likely, not likely, somewhat likely, likely, or very likely.

Explanation	Fraction somewhat likely, likely, or very likely[a,b]	Average Score[c]
Paul put Christine down because he is afraid that by hiring a woman the company can lower his wage.	.36 (.06)	2.5 (.12)
Paul put Christine down because he does not feel that it is fair that Christine is getting a lower wage.	.13 (.04)	1.7 (.12)
Paul put Christine down because he feels less masculine when a woman is doing the same job.	.84 (.04)	3.4 (.12)
Paul put Christine down because he feels he and his friends will not be able to joke around if a woman is present.	.84 (.04)	3.6 (.12)
Paul put Christine down because he is afraid that other men will tease him if a woman is doing the same job.	.76 (.05)	3.3 (.13)
Paul put Christine down because he is afraid that people will think that his	.64 (.06)	2.9 (.12)

Explanation	Fraction somewhat likely, likely, or very likely[a,b]	Average Score[c]
requires less skill if a woman is doing the same job.		
Paul put Christine down because he is afraid that if he does not, then his male coworkers will start to tease him.	.80 (.05)	3.4 (.13)
Paul put Christine down because he feels that it is wrong for women to work in a man's job.	.77 (.05)	3.2 (.14)

a. Sample size is 70 households. Households were selected randomly from the Fremont, CA phonebook.

b. Standard errors are in parentheses.

c. Average with not-at-all likely = 1, not likely = 2, somewhat likely = 3, likely = 4, very likely = 5.

Most revealing that the insult affected identity, insulted Southerners were also more likely to fear that the experimenter had a low opinion of their masculinity. They will probably never meet the experimenter or the hallway accomplice again; their encounter in the experiment is otherwise anonymous. Their concern about the experimenter then can only be a concern about how they feel about themselves, about their own sense of identity, as perceived through the "mirror of the opinions and expectations of others" [Gleitman 1996, p. 343]. We see the same psychology in other examples.

Changing Groups or Violating Prescriptions. Because of j's *identification* with others, it may affect j's identity when another person in j's social category violates prescriptions or becomes a different person. A common response is scorn and ostracism, which distances oneself from the maverick and affirms one's own self-image. Such behavior occurs daily in school playgrounds, where children who behave differently are mocked and taunted. Those who seek upward mobility are often teased by their peers, as in *A Hope in the Unseen* [Suskind 1998], which describes Cedric Jennings' progress from one of Washington's most blighted high schools to Brown University. The book opens with Cedric in the high-school chemistry lab, escaping the catcalls of the crowd at an awards assembly. Those who try to change social categories and prescriptions may face similar derision because the change may devalue others' identity, as for the housewives in Betty Friedan's suburb.

Our *third* set of examples demonstrates that to some extent people choose their identity; that is, c_j may be partially a choice. Many women in the United States can choose either to be a career woman or a housewife (see Gerson [1986]). Parents often choose a school—public versus private, secular versus parochial—to influence a child's self-image, identification with others, and behavior. The choice of where to live at college can both reflect and change how students think of themselves. Fraternities, sororities, African–American, or other "theme"-oriented dorms are all associated with social groups, self-images, and prescribed behavior. The list can continue. The choice for an immigrant to become a citizen is not only a change in legal status but a change in identity. The decision is thus often fraught with ambivalence, anxiety, and even guilt.

Identity "choice," however, is very often limited. In a society with racial and ethnic categories, for example, those with nondistinguishing physical features may be able to "pass" as a member of another group. But others will be constrained by their appearance, voice, or accent.

Our *fourth* set of examples demonstrates the creation and manipulation of social categories **C** and prescriptions **P**.

Advertising. Advertising is an obvious attempt to manipulate prescriptions. Marlboro and Virginia Slims advertisements, for example, promote an image of the ideal man or woman complete with the right cigarette.

Professional and Graduate Schools. Graduate and professional programs try to mold students' behavior through a change in identity. As a "one-L" Harvard Law School student said: " 'They are turning me into someone else. They're making me different' " [Turow 1977, p. 73]. In medicine, theology, the military, and the doctorate, a title is added to a graduate's name, suggesting the change in person.

Political Identity. Politics is often a battle over identity. Rather than take preferences as given, political leaders and activists often strive to change a population's preferences through a change in identity or prescriptions. Again, examples abound. Fascist and populist leaders are infamous for their rhetoric fostering racial and ethnic divisions, with tragic consequences. Symbolic acts and transformed identities spur revolutions. The ringing of the Liberty Bell called on the colonists' identities as Americans. Gandhi's Salt March sparked an Indian national identity. The French Revolution changed subjects into *citizens*, and the Russian Revolution turned them into *comrades*.

III. Economics and Identity: A Prototype Model

In this section we construct a prototype model of economic interaction in a world where identity is based on social difference. In addition to the usual tastes, utility from actions will also depend on identity. Identity will depend on two social categories—Green and Red—and the correspondence of own and others' actions to behavioral prescriptions for their category.

A. A Prototype Model

We begin with standard economic motivations for behavior. There are two possible activities, Activity One and Activity Two. There is a population of individuals each of whom has a taste for either Activity One or Two. If a person with a taste for Activity One (Two) undertakes Activity One (Two), she earns utility V. An individual who chooses the activity that does not match her taste earns zero utility. In a standard model of utility maximization, each person would engage in the activity corresponding to her taste.

We next construct identity-based preferences. We suppose that there are two social categories, Green and Red. We assume the simplest division of the population into categories; all persons think of themselves and others as Green. We add simple behavioral prescriptions: a Green should engage in Activity One (in contrast to Reds who engage in Activity Two). Anyone who chooses Activity Two is not a "true" Green—she would lose her Green identity. This loss in identity entails a reduction in utility of I_s, where the subscript s stands for "self." In addition, there are identity externalities. If an i and j are paired, Activity Two on the part of i diminishes j's Green identity. j has a loss in utility I_o, where the subscript o denotes "other." After i has committed Activity Two, j may "respond." The response restores j's identity at a cost c, while entailing a loss to i in amount L.

Figure I represents an interaction between an individual with a taste for Activity One ("Person One") and an individual with a taste for Activity Two ("Person Two"). Person One chooses an activity first.

This model can be expressed by ideas central to the psychodynamic theory of personality, found in almost any psychology text. In personality development, psychologists agree on the importance of *internalization* of rules for behavior. Freud called this process the development of the *superego*. Modern scholars disagree with Freud on the importance of psychosexual factors in an individual's development, but they agree on the importance of *anxiety* that a person experiences when she violates her internalized rules. One's *identity*, or *ego*, or *self*, must be constantly "defended against anxiety in order to limit disruption and maintain a sense of unity" [Thomas 1996, p. 284]. In terms of our model, Person Two's internalization of prescriptions causes her to suffer a loss in utility of I_s if she chooses Activity Two. To avoid this anxiety, she may refrain from that activity.

Identification is a critical part of this internalization process: a person learns a set of values (prescriptions) such that her actions should conform with the behavior of some people and contrast with that of others. If Person One has internalized prescriptions via such identifications, another person's violation of the prescriptions will cause anxiety for Person One. In our model, this anxiety is modeled as a loss in utility of I_o. Person One's response, in our language, restores her identity, and in terms of the psychology textbook relieves her anxiety and maintains her sense of unity. Person One no longer loses I_o, although she does incur c.

* * *

IV. IDENTITY, GENDER AND ECONOMICS IN THE WORKPLACE

An identity theory of gender in the workplace expands the economic analysis of occupational segregation. As recently as 1970, two-thirds of the United States' female or male labor force would have had to switch jobs to achieve occupational parity. This measure of occupational segregation remained virtually unchanged since the beginning of the century. Yet, in twenty years, from 1970 to 1990, this figure declined to 53 percent. An identity model points to changes in societal notions of male and female as a major cause.

The model we propose captures the "auras of gender" [Goldin 1990a] that have pervaded the labor market. Occupations are associated with the social categories "man" and "woman," and individual payoffs from different types of work reflect these gender associations. This model can explain patterns of occupational segregation that have eluded previous models. It also directly captures the consequences of the women's movement and affords a new economic interpretation of sex discrimination law.

Identity also provides a microfoundation for earlier models. The "distaste" of men for working with women, as in the crudest adaptations of racial discrimination models [Becker 1971; Arrow 1972], can be understood as due to loss in male identity when women work in a man's job. Similarly women's assumed lower desire for labor force participation (as in Mincer and Polachek [1974], Bulow and Summers [1986], and Lazear and Rosen [1990]) can be understood as the result of their identity as homemakers.

A. *The Model*

There are two social categories, "men" and "women," with prescriptions of appropriate activities for each. A firm wishes to hire labor to perform a task. By the initial prescriptions, this task is appropriate only for men; it is a "man's job." Relative to a "woman's job," women lose identity in amount I_s by performing such work. In this situation, male coworkers suffer a loss I_o. They may relieve their anxiety by taking action against women coworkers, reducing everyone's productivity.

To avoid these productivity losses, the firm may change gender-job associations at a cost. The firm is likely to create a "woman's job" alongside the "man's job," rather than render the whole task gender neutral, when a new job description can piggyback on existing notions of male and female. A well-known historical example illustrates. In the nineteenth century, Horace Mann (as Secretary of Education for Massachusetts) transformed elementary school teaching into a woman's job, arguing that women were "more mild and gentle," "of purer morals," with "stronger parental impulses." Secondary school teaching and school administration remained jobs for men.

The model also indicates why gender-job associations may persist. If associations are sector-wide or economy-wide, and not firm-specific, perfectly competitive firms will underinvest in new job categories. Benefits would accrue to other firms. In the absence of market power or technological change, a shift in social attitudes and legal intervention would be necessary for changes in employment patterns.

The model easily extends to the decision to participate in the labor force. If women's identity is enhanced by work inside the home, they will have lower labor force attachment than men. Historically, female labor force participation rates, relative to male rates, have been both lower and more cyclically variable.

B. *Implications for Labor Market Outcomes*

This identity model explains employment patterns arising from associations between gender and type of work. These patterns go beyond what can be explained by women's assumed lower labor force attachment as in Mincer and Polachek [1974], where women work in occupations that require little investment in firm-specific human capital.

In our model, women will dominate jobs whose requirements match construed female attributes and inferior social status; men eschew them. Historically, three occupations illustrate: secretaries (97.8 percent female in 1970) have often been called "office wives," and elements of sexuality are inscribed in the working relationship (boss = male, secretary = female) [MacKinnon 1979; Pringle 1988]. Secretaries are expected to serve their bosses, with deference, and to be attentive to their personal needs [Davies 1982; Kanter 1977; Pierce 1996]. Elementary school teachers (83.9 percent female), in contrast to secondary school teachers (49.6 percent female), are supposed to care for young children. Nurses (97.3 percent female) are supposed to be tender and care for patients, as well as be deferential to doctors [Fisher 1995; Williams 1989].

In our model, women do not enter male professions because of gender associations. Historically, many male professions have required similar levels of education and training to female professions and could have been amenable to part-time and intermittent work. Contrast nursing and teaching with accounting and law. All require college degrees and certification, and sometimes have tenure and experience-based pay. Only the very top of these professions have required continuity in employment and full-time work.

Rhetoric surrounding job shifts from male to female further demonstrates the salience of gender-job associations. The recruitment of women into "men's jobs" during World War II, for example, was accompanied by official propaganda and popular literature picturing women taking on factory work without loss of femininity [Milkman 1987; Honey 1984; Pierson 1986]. In addition, the jobs were portrayed as temporary; only the wartime emergency excused the violation of the usual gender prescriptions.

C. Effects of the Women's Movement

The model gives a theoretical structure for how the women's movement may have impacted the labor market. The movement's goals included reshaping societal notions of femininity (and masculinity) and removing gender associations from tasks, both in the home and in the workplace. In the model, such changes would decrease women's gains (men's losses) in identity from homemaking, and decrease the identity loss I_s of women (men) working in traditionally men's (women's) jobs, as well as the accompanying externalities I_o. These shifts would increase women's labor force participation and lead to a convergence of male and female job tenure rates. More women (men) would work in previously male (female) jobs.

All these outcomes are observed coincidental with and following the women's movement. Gender-job associations diminished, reflected in changes in language (e.g., firemen became firefighters). In 1998 the median job tenure of employed women over 25 was 0.4 years lower than that of men; in 1968 that gap had been 3.3 years. Changes in sex composition within occupations accounted for the major share of decline in occupational segregation from 1970–1990 [Blau, Simpson, and Anderson, 1998]. Of the 45 three-digit Census occupations that were 0.0 percent female in 1970, only one (supervisors: brickmasons, stonemasons, and tile setters), was less than 1 percent female twenty years later. Many incursions of females into male-dominated professions were very large. Consider again accounting and law. In 1970 (1990) females were 24.6 (52.7) percent of auditors and accountants, and 4.5 (24.5) percent of lawyers. Not only did the proportion of women in men's jobs increase, but so did the proportion of men in women's jobs (albeit much less dramatically). Of the triumvirate of explanations for such increases—technology, endowments, and tastes—elimination makes tastes the leading suspect, since there was no dramatic change in technology or endowments that would have caused such increased mixing on the job. Legal initiatives discussed next reflect such changes in tastes.

D. Gender–Job Associations and Sex Discrimination Law

Legal interpretations of sex discrimination correspond to earlier economic models as well as our own. Title VII of the Civil Rights Act of 1964 makes it unlawful for an employer to discriminate "against any individual . . . with respect to . . . compensation, terms, conditions of employment" or "to [adversely] limit, segregate, or classify his employees . . . because of . . . sex." At its most basic, this law prohibits a discriminatory exercise of "tastes" against women (analogous to Becker [1971] and Arrow [1972]). Courts also interpret Title VII as outlawing statistical discrimination by sex or criteria correlated with sex, even when women on average lack a desirable job qualification. Discriminatory hiring because of women's presumed lower workplace attachment, as in Lazear and Rosen [1990], was precisely the issue addressed in *Phillips v. Martin–Marietta*.

Our model, where sex discrimination occurs because jobs have gender associations, corresponds to a wider interpretation of Title VII. This interpretation is at the forefront of current legal debate and is supported by a number of precedents. In *Diaz v. Pan American World Airways*, the Court outlawed sex bans in hiring. The airline originally pleaded for their prohibition of male flight attendants because women were better at "the nonmechanical aspects of the job." But this association of gender with the job was disallowed on appeal since feminine traits were deemed irrelevant to the "primary function or services offered" (cited in MacKinnon [1979, p. 180]). *Price Waterhouse v. Hopkins* set a precedent for workers already hired. The plaintiff had been denied a partnership after negative evaluations for her masculine deportment. The Supreme Court ruled that "an employer who objects to aggressiveness in women but whose positions require this trait places women in an intolerable and impermissible Catch 22" (cited in Wurzburg and Klonoff [1997, p. 182]). Cases have also involved harassment of women working in men's jobs as, in the terminology of our model, male coworkers protect themselves from loss of identity I_o. *Berkman v. City of New York* reinstated a firefighter who had been dismissed because of substandard work performance. The Court ruled that the interference and harassment by her male coworkers made it impossible for her to perform her job adequately [Schultz 1998, p. 1770]. This expansive interpretation of a "hostile work environment," a category of sexual harassment which is in turn a category of sex discrimination, has been exceptional. Judges have viewed sexual desire as an essential element of sexual harassment. However, Schultz [1998] and Franke [1995] argue that any harassment derived from gender prescriptions has discriminatory implications (as depicted in our model) and are thus violations of Title VII.

V. IDENTITY AND THE ECONOMICS OF EXCLUSION AND POVERTY

This section will consider identity and behavior in poor and socially excluded communities. In an adaptation of the previous model of Greens and Reds, people belonging to poor, socially excluded groups will choose their identity. Greens identify with the dominant culture, while those with Red identity reject it and the subordinate position assigned to those of their "race," class, or ethnicity. From the point of view of those with Green identities, Reds are often making bad economic decisions; they might even be described as engaging in self-destructive behavior. Taking drugs, joining a gang, and becoming pregnant at a young age are possible signs of a Red identity. This aspect of behavior has not been explored in previous models, but it is implicit in Wilson's account of black ghetto poverty [1987, 1996]. It also is implicit in every study that finds significant dummy variables for "race," after adjustment for other measures of socioeconomic status. The Green/Red model of this section offers an explanation for the significance of such dummy variables. Furthermore, it yields a less monolithic view of poverty than current economic theories that emphasize conformity (e.g., Akerlof [1997] and Brock and Durlauf [1995]).

A. *Motivation for Model*

Our model reflects the many ethnographic accounts of "oppositional" identities in poor neighborhoods. MacLeod's [1987] study of teenagers in a Boston area housing project, for example, contrasts the murderous and alcoholic Hallway Hangers to their obedient and athletic peers, the Brothers. In *Learning to Labour* Willis [1977] describes the antagonism between the unruly "lads" and the dutiful "earholes" in a working-class English secondary school. Similarly, Whyte's [1943] description of Boston's Italian North End circa 1940 contrasts the Corner Boys to the College Boys. Yet earlier, turn-of-the century accounts of the Irish in the United States contrast the "lace curtain" Irish of poor districts to their neighbors (see, e.g., Miller [1985]).

Our model further evokes the psychological effects of social exclusion in the colonial experience analyzed by Bhabha [1983] and Fanon [1967], and in the context of African–Americans in the United States by Anderson [1990], Baldwin [1962], Clark [1965], DuBois [1965], Frazier [1957], Hannerz [1969], Rainwater [1970], Wilson [1987, 1996], and others. In these settings, individuals from particular groups can never fully fit the ideal type, the ideal "Green," of the dominant culture. Some in excluded groups may try to "pass" or integrate with the dominant group, but they do so with ambivalence and limited success. A series of autobiographies tells of the pain and anger of discovering that one is not really "Green." Former *New York Times* editor Mel Watkins [1998] titles the chapter on his freshman year at Colgate as "stranger in a strange land." Gandhi [1966], Fanon [1967], Fulwood [1996], Staples [1994], and Rodriguez [1982] all relate strikingly similar experiences of perceived or real rejection and alienation. This social exclusion may create a conflict: how to work within the dominant culture without betraying oneself. As Jill Nelson [1993, p. 10] explains her exhaustion after a long day of interviewing for a job at *The Washington Post*:

> I've also been doing the standard Negro balancing act when it comes to dealing with white folks, which involves sufficiently blurring the edges of my being so that they don't feel intimidated, while simultaneously holding on to my integrity. There is a thin line between Uncle-Tomming and Mau-Mauing. To fall off that line can mean disaster. On one side lies employment and self-hatred; on the other, the equally dubious honor of unemployment with integrity.

These reactions, it must be emphasized, reflect how dominant groups define themselves by the exclusion of others. The creation and evolution of such social differences are the subject of much historical research. Said [1978] documents the emergence of the Western idea of the "Oriental," a concept that had significant implications for colonialism. In the United States Roediger [1991] and other historians show how workers of European descent in the nineteenth century increasingly were defined as "white." Prior to Emancipation, this identity evoked the contrast between white freedom and African-American enslavement. In the model we construct, the key interaction is between such social differences and the adoption of oppositional identities by those in excluded groups.

Lack of economic opportunity may also contribute to the choice of an oppositional identity. Wilson [1987, 1996] underscores the relation between the decline in remunerative unskilled jobs, the loss of self-respect by men who cannot support their families, and the rise in inner city crime and drug abuse. This process is illustrated in microcosm by "Richard" in *Tally's Corner* [Liebow 1967]. Unable to find decent-paying work, he abandoned his family and joined Tally's group of idlers on the street corner. By adopting a different identity, Richard no longer suffered the guilt of a failed provider.

Red activities have negative pecuniary externalities. Richard's wife and children had to find alternative means of support. The prime goal of the "lads" in Willis' secondary school was to get a "laff," through vandalism, picking fights, and returning drunk to school from the local pub. Running a school with lads is difficult. The situation corresponds to the externalities in Benabou's [1993, 1996] models of high schooling costs in poor neighborhoods. Further externalities accrue from drug dealing, crime, and other "pathological" behavior. In our model, there are also identity-based externalities. A Red is angered by a Green's complicity with the dominant culture, while a Green is angered by a Red's "breaking the rules." Again consider Willis' lads and earholes. As the lads define themselves in contrast to the earholes, the earholes define themselves in contrast to the lads. The earholes are even more proestablishment than the teachers—feeling that the teachers should be stricter. The lads, in turn, bait the earholes. This situation is just one (relatively tame) example of how interaction between the two groups generates antagonism on both sides.

B.   Identity Model of Poverty and Social Exclusion

As in the prototype model, there are two activities, One and Two. Activity One can be thought of as "working" and Activity Two as "not working." There is a large community, normalized to size one, of individuals. The economic return to Activity One for individual i is v_i which we assume is uniformly distributed between zero and one, to reflect heterogeneity in the population and to ensure interior solutions. The economic return to Activity Two is normalized to zero.

As for identity, there are two social categories, Green and Red. A Green suffers a loss in identity r, representing the extent to which someone from this community is not accepted by the dominant group in society. Those with the less adaptive Red identity do not suffer this loss. Behavioral prescriptions say that Greens (Reds) should engage in Activity One (Two). Thus, a Green (Red) loses identity from Activity Two (One) in amount I^G_s ($I^R_s il$). Because Reds reject the dominant Green culture, they are also likely to have lower economic returns to Activity One than Greens. A Red individual i will only earn v_i—a from Activity One, as well as suffer the loss I^R_s. There are also identity externalities when Greens and Reds meet. A Green (Red) suffers a loss I^G_o (I^R_o. In addition, Reds who have chosen Activity Two impose a pecuniary externality k on those who have chosen Activity One.

Each person i chooses an identity and activity, given the choices of everyone else in the community. We assume that people cannot modify their identity or activity for each individual encounter. Rather, individuals choose an identity and activity to maximize expected payoffs, given the probabilities of encounters with Greens who choose Activity One, Greens who choose Two, Reds who choose One, and Reds who choose Two.

* * *

D.   Further Lessons from the Model

The model and its solution also afford interpretations of policies designed to reduce poverty and the effects of social exclusion.

First, the model indicates why residential Job Corps programs may succeed while other training programs fail [Stanley, Katz, and Krueger 1998]. According to the model, taking trainees out of their neighborhoods would eliminate, at least for a time, the negative effects of interaction with those with Red identities. Moreover, being in a different location may reduce a trainee's direct loss r from being Green and pursuing Activity One. That is, this loss may be both individual-specific and situational, and leaving a poor neighborhood is likely to generate a lower r than otherwise.

In a somewhat controlled experiment, the U.S. government tried to save money with JOBSTART, which preserved many of the features of Job Corps except the expensive housing of trainees. Follow-up studies of JOB-START show little or no improvement in employment or earnings.

Second, the model affords an interpretation of different education initiatives for minority students. Like Job Corps, the Central Park East Secondary School (CPESS) in East Harlem may succeed because it separates Green students from Red students. Students, for example, must apply to the school, indicating their and their parents' willingness to adopt its rules (see Fliegel [1993] and Meier [1995] for this and other details). Another interpretation of CPESS and other successes (e.g., Comer [1980] in New Haven) parallels the logic of the all-Red equilibrium where some people nonetheless pursue Activity One. The schools take measures to reduce the loss in identity of Red students, I^R_s, in activities such as learning Standard English. Delpit's [1995] award-winning book *Other People's Children* proposes numerous ways to reduce the alienation that minority students may experience in school.

Finally, the model illuminates a set of issues in the affirmative action debate. Much of this debate concerns the success or failure of specific programs (see, e.g., Dickens and Kane [1996]). Yet, more is at stake. The rhetoric and symbolism of affirmative action may affect the level of social exclusion r. On the one hand, Loury [1995] argues that portraying African–Americans as victims, a portrayal necessary to retain affirmative action programs, is costly to blacks. In terms of the model, such rhetoric will increase r and the adoption of Red identities. On the other hand, affirmative action will decrease r, to the extent it is seen as an apology for previous discrimination and an invitation for black admission to the dominant culture. Reversal of affirmative action would negate this effect. To cite a recent example, our analysis suggests that removing affirmative action admissions criteria at the University of California and University of Texas Law Schools could have behavioral implications that far exceed the impact on applicants.

The identity model of exclusion, then, explains why legal equality may not be enough to eliminate racial disparities. If African–Americans choose to be Red because of exclusion and if whites perpetuate such exclusions, even in legal ways, there can be a permanent equilibrium of racial inequality. The negative externalities and their consequences, however, would disappear when the community is fully integrated into the dominant culture, so that $r = \mathbf{a} = 0$, and everyone in the community adopts a Green identity. This, of course, is the American ideal of the melting pot, or the new ideal of a mosaic where difference can be maintained within the dominant culture.

VI. Identity and the Economics of the Household

An identity model of the household, unlike previous models, predicts an asymmetric division of labor between husbands and wives. Theories based on comparative advantage (e.g., Becker [1965] and Mincer [1962]) predict that whoever works more outside the home will work less inside the home, whether it be the husband or the wife. Yet, the data we present below indicate a gender asymmetry. When a wife works more hours outside the home, she still undertakes a larger share of the housework.

Hochschild's [1990] study *The Second Shift* reveals the details of such asymmetries. One of the couples in her study found an ingenious way to share the housework. "Evan Holt," a furniture salesman, took care of the lower half of the house (i.e., the basement and his tools). His wife "Nancy," a full-time licensed social worker, took care of the upper half. She took care of the child. He took care of the dog.

Quantitative evidence from Hochschild's sample and our data analysis suggest that the Holts conform to a national pattern. Figure III shows the low average of husbands' share of housework and its low elasticity with respect to their share of outside work hours. The figure plots shares of housework reported by married men in the Panel Study of Income Dynamics, as computed from answers to the question(s): "About how much time do you (your wife) spend on housework in an average week? I mean time spent cooking, cleaning, and doing other work around the house?" The intent of the question was to exclude child care. The figure plots men's share of housework as a fourth-order polynomial of their share of outside hours, for households by age of youngest child. When men do all the outside work, they contribute on average about 10 percent of housework. But as their share of outside work falls, their share of housework rises to no more than 37 percent. As shown in the figure the presence of children of different ages makes a small difference to the function. Similar results obtain when the independent variable is shares of income rather than shares of outside work hours.

Predicted values from tobit estimation

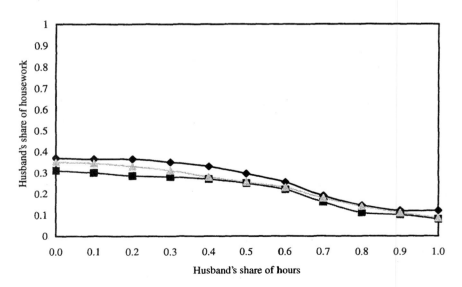

FIGURE III

Husband's Share of Housework versus Their Share of Outside Work Hours

Existing theories do not predict this asymmetry. Consider the following variant based on comparative advantage. Husband and wife both have the same utility function, which is increasing in quantity of a household public good that derives from their joint labor. Utility is decreasing in own labor inputs in outside and home production. We assume equal bargaining power, so that each marriage partner enjoys the same level of utility. With this framework, returns to specialization explain the observed division of labor when a wife has a comparative advantage in home production. Women who put in less than half of the outside work hours put in more than half the housework, as seen in the right-hand side of the graph of Figure III. But this model is inconsistent with the left-hand side of the graph.

Identity considerations can explain the high shares of housework of wives who undertake a large share of outside work hours. Add to the above model two social categories, "men" and "women." Prescriptions dictate that "men" should not do "women's work" in the home and "men" should earn more than their wives. Hochschild's interviews suggest that many men, and some women, hold these prescriptions. In the amended model, the husband loses identity when he does housework and when his wife earns more than half the household income. Equality of utility is restored when the wife undertakes more housework than her husband. Hochschild reports that in the "Tanagawa" household, for example, "Nina" earned more than half the family income, but she worked more than "Peter" at home to assuage his unease with the situation. Eventually, she quit her job.

VII. CONCLUSION

This paper considers how identity affects economic outcomes. Following major themes in psychology and sociology, identity in our models is based on social difference. A person's sense of self is associated with different social categories and how people in these categories should behave. This simple extension of the utility function could greatly expand our understanding of economic outcomes. In a world of social difference, one of the most important economic decisions that an individual makes may be the type of person to be. Limits on this choice would also be critical determinants of economic behavior, opportunity, and well-being.

Identity affects economic behavior in our models through four avenues. First, identity changes the payoffs from one's own actions. We capture this possibility by a value I_s in our models. In our study of gender in the workplace, for example, a woman working in a "man's" job suffers a loss in utility, affecting the labor supply. Second, identity changes the payoffs of others' actions. We capture this externality by a value I_o in our models. A "Red" in our poverty model, for example, is harmed by a member of his own community who complies with the dominant culture. Third, the choice, or lack thereof, of different identities affects an individual's economic behavior. In our poverty model, while individuals could choose between

Green or Red, they could never be a "true" Green. The greater the extent of this social exclusion, the greater the possibility of equilibria in which individuals eschew remunerative activities. Finally, the social categories and behavioral prescriptions can be changed, affecting identity-based preferences. This possibility expanded the scope of employment policy in our model of gender in the workplace and of education policy in our study of social exclusion.

This paper has only scratched the surface of the economic implications of identity. A first tack in future research would be continued analysis of particular settings. Identity is likely to affect economic outcomes, for example, in areas of political economy, organizational behavior, demography, the economics of language, violence, education, consumption and savings behavior, retirement decisions, and labor relations. As in this paper, models that incorporate well-documented existing social categories and prescriptions could yield new results. A second tack in this agenda is comparative, examining identity across space and time. Researchers, for example, could consider why notions of "class" or "race" vary across countries; why might gender and racial integration vary across industries; what might explain the rise and fall of ethnic tensions. Such comparative studies would be a fruitful way to explore the formation of identity-based preferences.

In peroration, this paper explores how to incorporate identity into economic models of behavior. Many standard psychological and sociological concepts—*self-image, ideal type, in-group and out-group, social category, identification, anxiety, self-destruction, self-realization, situation*—fit naturally in our framework, allowing an expanded analysis of economic outcomes. This framework is then perhaps one way to incorporate many different nonpecuniary motivations for behavior into economic reasoning, with considerable generality and a common theme.

Whiteness as Property

106 HARV. L. REV. 1707 (June 1993).

■ CHERYL I. HARRIS

Issues regarding race and racial identity as well as questions pertaining to property rights and ownership have been prominent in much public discourse in the United States. In this article, Professor Harris contributes to this discussion by positing that racial identity and property are deeply interrelated concepts. Professor Harris examines how whiteness, initially constructed as a form of racial identity, evolved into a form of property, historically and presently acknowledged and protected in American law. Professor Harris traces the origins of whiteness as property in the parallel systems of domination of Black and Native American peoples out of which were created racially contingent forms of property and property rights. Following the period of slavery and conquest, whiteness became the basis of racialized privilege—a type of status in which white racial identity provided the basis for allocating societal benefits both private and public in character. These arrangements were ratified and legitimated in law as a type of status property. Even as legal segregation was overturned, whiteness as property continued to serve as a barrier to effective change as the system of racial classification operated to protect entrenched power.

Next, Professor Harris examines how the concept of whiteness as property persists in current perceptions of racial identity, in the law's misperception of group identity and in the Court's reasoning and decisions in the arena of affirmative action. Professor Harris concludes by arguing that distortions in affirmative action doctrine can only be addressed by confronting and exposing the property interest in whiteness and by acknowledging the distributive justification and function of affirmative action as central to that task.

she walked into forbidden worlds

impaled on the weapon of her own pale skin

she was a sentinel

at impromptu planning sessions

of her own destruction . . .

Cheryl I. Harris, *poem for alma*[1]

[P]etitioner was a citizen of the United States and a resident of the state of Louisiana of mixed descent, in the proportion of seven eighths Caucasian and one eighth African blood; that the mixture of colored blood was not discernible in him, and that he was entitled to every recognition, right, privilege and immunity secured to the citizens of the United States of the white race by its Constitution and laws . . . and thereupon entered a passenger train and took possession of a vacant seat in a coach where passengers of the white race were accommodated.

Plessy v. Ferguson[2]

I. INTRODUCTION

In the 1930s, some years after my mother's family became part of the great river of Black migration that flowed north, my Mississippi-born grandmother was confronted with the harsh matter of economic survival for herself and her two daughters. Having separated from my grandfather, who himself was trapped on the fringes of economic marginality, she took one long hard look at her choices and presented herself for employment at a major retail store in Chicago's central business district. This decision would have been unremarkable for a white woman in similar circumstances, but for my grandmother, it was an act of both great daring and

---

1. Cheryl I. Harris, *poem for alma* (1990) (unpublished poem, on file at the Harvard Law School Library).

2. 163 U.S. 537, 538 (1896).

self-denial, for in so doing she was presenting herself as a white woman. In the parlance of racist America, she was "passing."

Her fair skin, straight hair, and aquiline features had not spared her from the life of sharecropping into which she had been born in anywhere/nowhere, Mississippi—the outskirts of Yazoo City. But in the burgeoning landscape of urban America, anonymity was possible for a Black person with "white" features. She was transgressing boundaries, crossing borders, spinning on margins, traveling between dualities of Manichean space, rigidly bifurcated into light/dark, good/bad, white/Black. No longer immediately identifiable as "Lula's daughter," she could thus enter the white world, albeit on a false passport, not merely passing, but *tres*passing.

Every day my grandmother rose from her bed in her house in a Black enclave on the south side of Chicago, sent her children off to a Black school, boarded a bus full of Black passengers, and rode to work. No one at her job ever asked if she was Black; the question was unthinkable. By virtue of the employment practices of the "fine establishment" in which she worked, she could not have been. Catering to the upper-middle class, understated tastes required that Blacks not be allowed.

She quietly went about her clerical tasks, not once revealing her true identity. She listened to the women with whom she worked discuss their worries—their children's illnesses, their husbands' disappointments, their boyfriends' infidelities—all of the mundane yet critical things that made up their lives. She came to know them but they did not know her, for my grandmother occupied a completely different place. That place—where white supremacy and economic domination meet—was unknown turf to her white co-workers. They remained oblivious to the worlds within worlds that existed just beyond the edge of their awareness and yet were present in their very midst.

Each evening, my grandmother, tired and worn, retraced her steps home, laid aside her mask, and reentered herself. Day in and day out, she made herself invisible, then visible again, for a price too inconsequential to do more than barely sustain her family and at a cost too precious to conceive. She left the job some years later, finding the strain too much to bear.

From time to time, as I later sat with her, she would recollect that period, and the cloud of some painful memory would pass across her face. Her voice would remain subdued, as if to contain the still remembered tension. On rare occasions she would wince, recalling some particularly racist comment made in her presence because of her presumed, shared group affiliation. Whatever retort might have been called for had been suppressed long before it reached her lips, for the price of her family's well-being was her silence. Accepting the risk of self-annihilation was the only way to survive.

Although she never would have stated it this way, the clear and ringing denunciations of racism she delivered from her chair when advanced arthritis had rendered her unable to work were informed by those experiences. The fact that self-denial had been a logical choice and had made her complicit in her own oppression at times fed the fire in her eyes when she confronted some daily outrage inflicted on Black people. Later, these painful memories forged her total identification with the civil rights movement. Learning about the world at her knee as I did, these experiences also came to inform my outlook and my understanding of the world.

My grandmother's story is far from unique. Indeed, there are many who crossed the color line never to return. Passing is well-known among Black people in the United States and is a feature of race subordination in all societies structured on white supremacy. Notwithstanding the purported benefits of Black heritage in an era of affirmative action, passing is not an obsolete phenomenon that has slipped into history.

The persistence of passing is related to the historical and continuing pattern of white racial domination and economic exploitation that has given passing a certain economic logic. It was a given to my grandmother that being white automatically ensured higher economic returns in the short term, as well as greater economic, political, and social security in the long run. Becoming white meant gaining access to a whole set of public and private privileges that materially and permanently guaranteed basic subsistence needs and, therefore, survival. Becoming white increased the possibility of controlling critical aspects of one's life rather than being the object of others' domination.

My grandmother's story illustrates the valorization of whiteness as treasured property in a society structured on racial caste. In ways so embedded that it is rarely apparent, the set of assumptions, privileges, and benefits that accompany the status of being white have become a valuable asset that whites sought to protect and that those who passed sought to attain—by fraud if necessary. Whites have come to expect and rely on these benefits, and over time these expectations have been affirmed, legitimated, and protected by the law. Even though the law is neither uniform nor explicit in all instances, in protecting settled expectations based on white privilege, American law has recognized a property interest in whiteness that, although unacknowledged, now forms the background against which legal disputes are framed, argued, and adjudicated.

My Article investigates the relationships between concepts of race and property and reflects on how rights in property are contingent on, intertwined with, and conflated with race. Through this entangled relationship between race and property, historical forms of domination have evolved to reproduce subordination in the present. * * * I examine the emergence of whiteness as property and trace the evolution of whiteness from color to race to status to property as a progression historically rooted in white supremacy and economic hegemony over Black and Native American peoples. The origins of whiteness as property lie in the parallel systems of domination of Black and Native American peoples out of which were created racially contingent forms of property and property rights. I further argue that whiteness shares the critical characteristics of property even as the meaning of property has changed over time. In particular, whiteness and property share a common premise—a conceptual nucleus—of a right to exclude. This conceptual nucleus has proven to be a powerful center around which whiteness as property has taken shape. Following the period of slavery and conquest, white identity became the basis of racialized privilege that was ratified and legitimated in law as a type of status property. After legalized segregation was overturned, whiteness as property evolved into a more modern form through the law's ratification of the settled expectations of relative white privilege as a legitimate and natural baseline.

[I examine] the two forms of whiteness as property—status property and modern property—that are the submerged text of two paradigmatic cases on the race question in American law, *Plessy v. Ferguson* and *Brown v. Board of Education*. As legal history, they illustrate an important transition from old to new forms of whiteness as property. Although these cases take opposite interpretive stances regarding the constitutional legitimacy of legalized racial segregation, the property interest in whiteness was transformed, but not discarded, in the Court's new equal protection jurisprudence.

[I then consider] the persistence of whiteness as property. I first examine how subordination is reinstituted through modern conceptions of race and identity embraced in law. Whiteness as property has taken on more subtle forms, but retains its core characteristic—the legal legitimation of expectations of power and control that enshrine the status quo as a neutral baseline, while masking the maintenance of white privilege and domination. I further identify the property interest in whiteness as the unspoken center of current polarities around the issue of affirmative action. As a legacy of slavery and de jure and de facto race segregation, the concept of a protectable property interest in whiteness permeates affirmative action doctrine in a manner illustrated by the reasoning of three important affirmative action cases—*Regents of the University of California v. Bakke, City of Richmond v. J. A. Croson & Co.,* and *Wygant v. Jackson Board of Education*.

* * *, I offer preliminary thoughts on a way out of the conundrum created by protecting whiteness as a property interest. I suggest that affirmative action, properly conceived and reconstructed, would de-legitimate the property interest in whiteness. I do not offer here a complete reformulation of affirmative action, but suggest that focusing on the distortions created by the property interest in whiteness would provoke different questions and open alternative perspectives on the affirmative action debate. The inability to see affirmative action as more than a search for the "blameworthy" among "innocent" individuals is tied to the inability to see the property interest in whiteness. Thus reconstructed, affirmative action would challenge the characterization of the unfettered right to exclude as a legitimate aspect of identity and property.

II.   The Construction of Race and the Emergence of Whiteness as Property

The racialization of identity and the racial subordination of Blacks and Native Americans provided the ideological basis for slavery and conquest.

Although the systems of oppression of Blacks and Native Americans differed in form—the former involving the seizure and appropriation of labor, the latter entailing the seizure and appropriation of land—undergirding both was a racialized conception of property implemented by force and ratified by law.

The origins of property rights in the United States are rooted in racial domination. Even in the early years of the country, it was not the concept of race alone that operated to oppress Blacks and Indians; rather, it was the *interaction* between conceptions of race and property that played a critical role in establishing and maintaining racial and economic subordination.

The hyper-exploitation of Black labor was accomplished by treating Black people themselves as objects of property. Race and property were thus conflated by establishing a form of property contingent on race—only Blacks were subjugated as slaves and treated as property. Similarly, the conquest, removal, and extermination of Native American life and culture were ratified by conferring and acknowledging the property rights of whites in Native American land. Only white possession and occupation of land was validated and therefore privileged as a basis for property rights. These distinct forms of exploitation each contributed in varying ways to the construction of whiteness as property.

A. Forms of Racialized Property: Relationships Between Slavery, Race, and Property

1. The Convergence of Racial and Legal Status.—Although the early colonists were cognizant of race, racial lines were neither consistently nor sharply delineated among or within all social groups. Captured Africans sold in the Americas were distinguished from the population of indentured or bond servants—"unfree" white labor—but it was not an irrebuttable presumption that all Africans were "slaves" or that slavery was the only appropriate status for them. The distinction between African and white indentured labor grew, however, as decreasing terms of service were introduced for white bond servants. Simultaneously, the demand for labor intensified, resulting in a greater reliance on African labor and a rapid increase in the number of Africans imported into the colonies.

The construction of white identity and the ideology of racial hierarchy also were intimately tied to the evolution and expansion of the system of chattel slavery. The further entrenchment of plantation slavery was in part an answer to a social crisis produced by the eroding capacity of the landed class to control the white labor population. The dominant paradigm of social relations, however, was that, although not all Africans were slaves, virtually all slaves were not white. It was their racial otherness that came to justify the subordinated status of Blacks. The result was a classification system that "key[ed] official rules of descent to national origin" so that "[m]embership in the new social category of 'Negro' became itself sufficient justification for enslaveability." Although the cause of the increasing gap between the status of African and white labor is contested by historians, it is clear that "[t]he economic and political interests defending Black slavery were far more powerful than those defending indentured servitude."

By the 1660s, the especially degraded status of Blacks as chattel slaves was recognized by law. Between 1680 and 1682, the first slave codes appeared, codifying the extreme deprivations of liberty already existing in social practice. Many laws parceled out differential treatment based on racial categories: Blacks were not permitted to travel without permits, to own property, to assemble publicly, or to own weapons; nor were they to be educated. Racial identity was further merged with stratified social and legal status: "Black" racial identity marked who was subject to enslavement; "white" racial identity marked who was "free" or, at minimum, not a slave. The ideological and rhetorical move from "slave" and "free" to "Black" and "white" as polar constructs marked an important step in the social construction of race.

   2. Implications for Property.—The social relations that produced racial identity as a justification for slavery also had implications for the conceptualization of property. This result was predictable, as the institution of slavery, lying at the very core of economic relations, was bound up with the idea of property. Through slavery, race and economic domination were fused.

Slavery produced a peculiar, mixed category of property and humanity—a hybrid possessing inherent instabilities that were reflected in its treatment and ratification by the law. The dual and contradictory character of slaves as property and persons was exemplified in the Representation Clause of the Constitution. Representation in the House of Representatives was apportioned on the basis of population computed by counting all persons and "three-fifths of all other persons"—slaves. Gouveneur Morris's remarks before the Constitutional Convention posed the essential question: "Upon what principle is it that slaves shall be computed in the representation? Are they men? Then make them Citizens & let them vote? Are they property? Why then is no other property included?"

The cruel tension between property and humanity was also reflected in the law's legitimation of the use of Blackwomen's bodies as a means of increasing property. In 1662, the Virginia colonial assembly provided that "[c]hildren got by an Englishman upon a Negro woman shall be bond or free according to the condition of the mother...." In reversing the usual common law presumption that the status of the child was determined by the father, the rule facilitated the reproduction of one's own labor force. Because the children of Blackwomen assumed the status of their mother, slaves were bred through Blackwomen's bodies. The economic significance of this form of exploitation of female slaves should not be underestimated. Despite Thomas Jefferson's belief that slavery should be abolished, like other slaveholders, he viewed slaves as economic assets, noting that their value could be realized more efficiently from breeding than from labor. A letter he wrote in 1805 stated: "I consider the labor of a breeding woman as no object, and that a child raised every 2 years is of more profit than the crop of the best laboring man."

Even though there was some unease in slave law, reflective of the mixed status of slaves as humans and property, the critical nature of social relations under slavery was the commodification of human beings. Productive relations in early American society included varying forms of sale of labor capacity, many of which were highly oppressive; but slavery was distinguished from other forms of labor servitude by its permanency and the total commodification attendant to the status of the slave. Slavery as a legal institution treated slaves as property that could be transferred, assigned, inherited, or posted as collateral. For example, in *Johnson v. Butler,* the plaintiff sued the defendant for failing to pay a debt of $496 on a specified date. Because the covenant had called for payment of the debt in "money or negroes," the plaintiff contended that the defendant's tender of one negro only, although valued by the parties at an amount equivalent to the debt, could not discharge the debt. The court agreed with the plaintiff. This use of Africans as a stand-in for actual currency highlights the degree to which slavery "propertized" human life.

Because the "presumption of freedom [arose] from color [white]" and the "black color of the race [raised] the presumption of slavery," whiteness became a shield from slavery, a highly volatile and unstable form of property. In the form adopted in the United States, slavery made human beings market-alienable and in so doing, subjected human life and person-hood—that which is most valuable—to the ultimate devaluation. Because whites could not be enslaved or held as slaves, the racial line between white and Black was extremely critical; it became a line of protection and demarcation from the potential threat of commodification, and it determined the allocation of the benefits and burdens of this form of property. White identity and whiteness were sources of privilege and protection; their absence meant being the object of property.

Slavery as a system of property facilitated the merger of white identity and property. Because the system of slavery was contingent on and conflated with racial identity, it became crucial to be "white," to be identified as white, to have the property of being white. Whiteness was the characteristic, the attribute, the property of free human beings.

B. Forms of Racialized Property: Relationships Between Native American Land Seizure, Race, and Property

Slavery linked the privilege of whites to the subordination of Blacks through a legal regime that attempted the conversion of Blacks into objects of property. Similarly, the settlement and seizure of Native American land supported white privilege through a system of property rights in land in which the "race" of the Native Americans rendered their first possession rights invisible and justified conquest. This racist formulation embedded the fact of white privilege into the very definition of property, marking another stage in the evolution of the property interest in whiteness. Possession—the act necessary to lay the basis for rights in property—was defined to include only the cultural practices of whites. This definition laid the foundation for the idea that whiteness—that which whites alone possess—is valuable and is property.

Although the Indians were the first occupants and possessors of the land of the New World, their racial and cultural otherness allowed this fact to be reinterpreted and ultimately erased as a basis for asserting rights in land. Because the land had been left in its natural state, untilled and unmarked by human hands, it was "waste" and, therefore, the appropriate object of settlement and appropriation. Thus, the possession maintained by the Indians was not "true" possession and could safely be ignored. This interpretation of the rule of first possession effectively rendered the rights of first possessors contingent on the race of the possessor. Only particular forms of possession—those that were characteristic of white settlement— would be recognized and legitimated. Indian forms of possession were perceived to be too ambiguous and unclear.

The conquest and occupation of Indian land was wrapped in the rule of law. The law provided not only a defense of conquest and colonization, but also a naturalized regime of rights and disabilities, power and disadvantage that flowed from it, so that no further justifications or rationalizations were required. A key decision defending the right of conquest was *Johnson and Graham's Lessee v. M'Intosh,* in which both parties to the action claimed the same land through title descendant from different Indian tribes. The issue specifically presented was not merely whether Indians had the power to convey title, but to whom the conveyance could be made—to individuals or to the government that "discovered" land. In holding that Indians could only convey to the latter, the Court reasoned that Indian title was subordinate to the absolute title of the sovereign that was achieved by conquest because "[c]onquest gives a title which the Courts of the conqueror cannot deny...." If property is understood as a delegation of sovereign power—the product of the power of the state—then a fair reading of history reveals the racial oppression of Indians inherent in the American regime of property.

In *Johnson* and similar cases, courts established whiteness as a prerequisite to the exercise of enforceable property rights. Not all first possession or labor gave rise to property rights; rather, the rules of first possession and labor as a basis for property rights were qualified by race. This fact infused whiteness with significance and value because it was solely through being white that property could be acquired and secured under law. Only whites possessed whiteness, a highly valued and exclusive form of property.

C.   Critical Characteristics of Property and Whiteness

The legal legacy of slavery and of the seizure of land from Native American peoples is not merely a regime of property law that is (mis)informed by racist and ethnocentric themes. Rather, the law has established and protected an actual property interest in whiteness itself, which shares the critical characteristics of property and accords with the many and varied theoretical descriptions of property.

Although by popular usage property describes "things" owned by persons, or the rights of persons with respect to a thing, the concept of property prevalent among most theorists, even prior to the twentieth century, is that property may "consist[] of rights in 'things' that are intangible, or whose existence is a matter of legal definition." Property is thus said to be a right, not a thing, characterized as metaphysical, not physical. The theoretical bases and conceptual descriptions of property rights are varied, ranging from first possessor rules, to creation of value, to Lockean labor theory, to personality theory, to utilitarian theory. However disparate, these formulations of property clearly illustrate the extent to which property rights and interests embrace much more than land and personality. Thus, the fact that whiteness is not a "physical" entity does not remove it from the realm of property.

Whiteness is not simply and solely a legally recognized property interest. It is simultaneously an aspect of self-identity and of personhood, and its relation to the law of property is complex. Whiteness has functioned as self-identity in the domain of the intrinsic, personal, and psychological; as reputation in the interstices between internal and external identity; and, as property in the extrinsic, public, and legal realms. According whiteness actual legal status converted an aspect of identity into an external object of property, moving whiteness from privileged identity to a vested interest. The law's construction of whiteness defined and affirmed critical aspects of identity (who is white); of privilege (what benefits accrue to that status); and, of property (what *legal* entitlements arise from that status). Whiteness at various times signifies and is deployed as identity, status, and property, sometimes singularly, sometimes in tandem.

1. Whiteness as a Traditional Form of Property.—Whiteness fits the broad historical concept of property described by classical theorists. In James Madison's view, for example, property "embraces every thing to which a man may attach a value and have a right," referring to all of a person's legal rights. Property as conceived in the founding era

> included not only external objects and people's relationships to them, but also all of those human rights, liberties, powers, and immunities that are important for human well-being, including: freedom of expression, freedom of conscience, freedom from bodily harm, and free and equal opportunities to use personal faculties.

Whiteness defined the legal status of a person as slave or free. White identity conferred tangible and economically valuable benefits and was jealously guarded as a valued possession, allowed only to those who met a strict standard of proof. Whiteness—the right to white identity as embraced by the law—is property if by property one means all of a person's legal rights.

Other traditional theories of property emphasize that the "natural" character of property is derivative of custom, contrary to the notion that property is the product of a delegation of sovereign power. This "bottom up" theory holds that the law of property merely codifies existing customs and social relations. Under that view, government-created rights such as social welfare payments cannot constitute legitimate property interests because they are positivistic in nature. Other theorists have challenged this conception, and argued that even the most basic of "customary" property rights—the rule of first possession, for example—is dependent on its acceptance or rejection in particular instances by the government. Citing custom as a source of property law begs the central question: whose custom?

Rather than remaining within the bipolar confines of custom or command, it is crucial to recognize the dynamic and multifaceted relationship among custom, command, and law, as well as the extent to which positionality determines how each may be experienced and understood. Indian custom was obliterated by force and replaced with the regimes of common law that embodied the customs of the conquerors. The assumption of American law as it related to Native Americans was that conquest *did* give rise to sovereignty. Indians experienced the property laws of the colonizers and the emergent American nation as acts of violence perpetuated by the exercise of power and ratified through the rule of law. At the same time, these laws were perceived as custom and "common sense" by the colonizers. The Founders, for instance, so thoroughly embraced Lockean labor theory as the basis for a right of acquisition because it affirmed the right of the New World settlers to settle on and acquire the frontier. It confirmed and ratified their experience.

The law's interpretation of those encounters between whites and Native Americans not only inflicted vastly different results on them, but also established a pattern—a *custom*—of valorizing whiteness. As the forms of racialized property were perfected, the value and protection extended to whiteness increased. Regardless of which theory of property one adopts, the concept of whiteness—established by centuries of custom (illegitimate custom, but custom nonetheless) and codified by law—may be understood as a property interest.

2. Modern Views of Property as Defining Social Relations.—Although property in the classical sense refers to everything that is valued and to which a person has a right, the modern concept of property focuses on its function and the social relations reflected therein. In this sense, modern property doctrine emphasizes the more contingent nature of property and has been the basis for the argument that property rights should be expanded.

Modern theories of property reject the assumption that property is "objectively definable or identifiable, apart from social context." Charles Reich's ground-breaking work, *The New Property,* was an early effort to focus on the function of property and note the changing social relations reflected and constructed by new forms of property derived from the government. Property in this broader sense encompassed jobs, entitlements, occupational licenses, contracts, subsidies, and indeed a whole host of intangibles that are the product of labor, time, and creativity, such as intellectual property, business goodwill, and enhanced earning potential from graduate degrees. Notwithstanding the dilution of new property since

Goldberg v. Kelly and its progeny as well as continued attacks on the concept, the legacy of new property infuses the concept of property with questions of power, selection, and allocation. Reich's argument that property is not a natural right but a construction by society resonates in current theories of property that describe the allocation of property rights as a series of choices. This construction directs attention toward issues of relative power and social relations inherent in any definition of property.

3. *Property and Expectations.*—"Property is nothing but the basis of expectation," according to Bentham, "consist[ing] in an established expectation, in the persuasion of being able to draw such and such advantage from the thing possessed." The relationship between expectations and property remains highly significant, as the law "has recognized and protected even the expectation of rights as actual legal property." This theory does not suggest that all value or all expectations give rise to property, but those expectations in tangible or intangible things that are valued and protected by the law are property.

In fact, the difficulty lies not in identifying expectations as a part of property, but in distinguishing which expectations are reasonable and therefore merit the protection of the law as property. Although the existence of certain property rights may seem self-evident and the protection of certain expectations may seem essential for social stability, property is a legal construct by which selected private interests are protected and upheld. In creating property "rights," the law draws boundaries and enforces or reorders existing regimes of power. The inequalities that are produced and reproduced are not givens or inevitabilities, but rather are conscious selections regarding the structuring of social relations. In this sense, it is contended that property rights and interests are not "natural," but are "creation[s] of law."

In a society structured on racial subordination, white privilege became an expectation and, to apply Margaret Radin's concept, whiteness became the quintessential property for personhood. The law constructed "whiteness" as an objective fact, although in reality it is an ideological proposition imposed through subordination. This move is the central feature of "reification": "Its basis is that a relation between people takes on the character of a thing and thus acquires a 'phantom objectivity,' an autonomy that seems so strictly rational and all-embracing as to conceal every trace of its fundamental nature: the relation between people." Whiteness was an "object" over which continued control was—and is—expected. The protection of these expectations is central because, as Radin notes: "If an object you now control is bound up in your future plans or in your anticipation of your future self, and it is partly these plans for your own continuity that make you a person, then your personhood depends on the realization of these expectations."

Because the law recognized and protected expectations grounded in white privilege (albeit not explicitly in all instances), these expectations became tantamount to property that could not permissibly be intruded upon without consent. As the law explicitly ratified those expectations in continued privilege or extended ongoing protection to those illegitimate expectations by failing to expose or to radically disturb them, the dominant and subordinate positions within the racial hierarchy were reified in law. When the law recognizes, either implicitly or explicitly, the settled expectations of whites built on the privileges and benefits produced by white supremacy, it acknowledges and reinforces a property interest in whiteness that reproduces Black subordination.

4. *The Property Functions of Whiteness.*—In addition to the theoretical descriptions of property, whiteness also meets the functional criteria of property. Specifically, the law has accorded "holders" of whiteness the same privileges and benefits accorded holders of other types of property. The liberal view of property is that it includes the exclusive rights of possession, use, and disposition. Its attributes are the right to transfer or alienability, the right to use and enjoyment, and the right to exclude others. Even when examined against this limited view, whiteness conforms to the general contours of property. It may be a "bad" form of property, but it is property nonetheless.

(a) Rights of Disposition.—Property rights are traditionally described as fully alienable. Because fundamental personal rights are commonly understood to be inalienable, it is problematic to view them as property interests. However, as Margaret Radin notes, "inalienability" is not a transparent term; it has multiple meanings that refer to interests that are non-salable, non-transferable, or non-market-alienable. The common core of inalienability is the negation of the possibility of separation of an entitlement, right, or attribute from its holder.

Classical theories of property identified alienability as a requisite aspect of property; thus, that which is inalienable cannot be property. As the major exponent of this view, Mill argued that public offices, monopoly privileges, and human beings—all of which were or should have been inalienable—should not be considered property at all. Under this account, if inalienability inheres in the concept of property, then whiteness, incapable of being transferred or alienated either inside or outside the market, would fail to meet a criterion of property.

As Radin notes, however, even under the classical view, alienability of certain property was limited. Mill also advocated certain restraints on alienation in connection with property rights in land and probably other natural resources. In fact, the law has recognized various kinds of inalienable property. For example, entitlements of the regulatory and welfare states, such as transfer payments and government licenses, are inalienable; yet they have been conceptualized and treated as property by law. Although this "new property" has been criticized as being improper—that is, not appropriately cast as property—the principal objection has been based on its alleged lack of productive capacity, not its inalienability.

The law has also acknowledged forms of inalienable property derived from nongovernmental sources. In the context of divorce, courts have held that professional degrees or licenses held by one party and financed by the labor of the other is marital property whose value is subject to allocation by the court. A medical or law degree is not alienable either in the market or by voluntary transfer. Nevertheless, it is included as property when dissolving a legal relationship.

Indeed, Radin argues that, as a deterrent to the dehumanization of universal commodification, market-inalienability may be justified to protect property important to the person and to safeguard human flourishing. She suggests that non-commodification or market-inalienability of personal property or those things essential to human flourishing is necessary to guard against the objectification of human beings. To avoid that danger, "we must cease thinking that market alienability is inherent in the concept of property." Following this logic, then, the inalienability of whiteness should not preclude the consideration of whiteness as property. Paradoxically, its inalienability may be more indicative of its perceived enhanced value, rather than its disqualification as property.

(b) Right to Use and Enjoyment.—Possession of property includes the rights of use and enjoyment. If these rights are essential aspects of property, it is because "the problem of property in political philosophy dissolves into . . . questions of the will and the way in which we use the things of this world." As whiteness is simultaneously an aspect of identity and a property interest, it is something that can both be experienced and deployed as a resource. Whiteness can move from being a passive characteristic as an aspect of identity to an active entity that—like other types of property—is used to fulfill the will and to exercise power. The state's official recognition of a racial identity that subordinated Blacks and of privileged rights in property based on race elevated whiteness from a passive attribute to an object of law and a resource deployable at the social, political, and institutional level to maintain control. Thus, a white person "used and enjoyed" whiteness whenever she took advantage of the privileges accorded white people simply by virtue of their whiteness—when she exercised any number of rights reserved for the holders of whiteness. Whiteness as the embodiment of white privilege transcended mere belief or preference; it became usable property, the subject of the law's regard and protection. In this respect whiteness, as an active property, has been used and enjoyed.

(c) Reputation and Status Property.—In constructing whiteness as property, the ideological move was to conceptualize white racial identity as an external thing in a constitutive sense—an "object [] or resource [] necessary to be a person." This move was accomplished in large measure by recognizing the reputational interest in being regarded as white as a thing of significant value, which like other reputational interests, was intrinsically bound up with identity and personhood. The reputation of being white was treated as a species of property, or something in which a property interest could be asserted. In this context, whiteness was a form of status property.

The conception of reputation as property found its origins in early concepts of property that encompassed things (such as land and personalty), income (such as revenues from leases, mortgages, and patent monopolies), and one's life, liberty, and labor. Thus, Locke's famous pronouncement, "every man has a 'property' in his own 'person,'" undergirded the assertion that one's physical self was one's property. From this premise, one's labor, "the work of his hands," combined with those things found in the common to form property over which one could exercise ownership, control, and dominion. The idea of self-ownership, then, was particularly fertile ground for the idea that reputation, as an aspect of identity earned through effort, was similarly property. Moreover, the loss of reputation was capable of being valued in the market.

The direct manifestation of the law's legitimation of whiteness as reputation is revealed in the well-established doctrine that to call a white person "Black" is to defame her. Although many of the cases were decided in an era when the social and legal stratification of whites and Blacks was more absolute, as late as 1957 the principle was reaffirmed, notwithstanding significant changes in the legal and political status of Blacks. As one court noted, "there is still to be considered the social distinction existing between the races," and the allegation was likely to cause injury. A Black person, however, could not sue for defamation if she was called "white." Because the law expressed and reinforced the social hierarchy as it existed, it was presumed that no harm could flow from such a reversal.

Private identity based on racial hierarchy was legitimated as public identity in law, even after the end of slavery and the formal end of legal race segregation. Whiteness as interpersonal hierarchy was recognized externally as race reputation. Thus, whiteness as public reputation and personal property was affirmed.

(d) The Absolute Right to Exclude.—Many theorists have traditionally conceptualized property to include the exclusive rights of use, disposition, and possession, with possession embracing the absolute right to exclude. The right to exclude was the central principle, too, of whiteness as identity, for mainly whiteness has been characterized, not by an inherent unifying characteristic, but by the exclusion of others deemed to be "not white." The possessors of whiteness were granted the legal right to exclude others from the privileges inhering in whiteness; whiteness became an exclusive club whose membership was closely and grudgingly guarded. The courts played an active role in enforcing this right to exclude—determining who was or was not white enough to enjoy the privileges accompanying whiteness. In that sense, the courts protected whiteness as any other form of property.

Moreover, as it emerged, the concept of whiteness was premised on white supremacy rather than mere difference. "White" was defined and constructed in ways that increased its value by reinforcing its exclusivity. Indeed, just as whiteness as property embraced the right to exclude, whiteness as a theoretical construct evolved for the very purpose of racial exclusion. Thus, the concept of whiteness is built on both exclusion and racial subjugation. This fact was particularly evident during the period of the most rigid racial exclusion, as whiteness signified racial privilege and took the form of status property.

At the individual level, recognizing oneself as "white" necessarily assumes premises based on white supremacy: It assumes that Black ancestry in any degree, extending to generations far removed, automatically disqualifies claims to white identity, thereby privileging "white" as unadulterated, exclusive, and rare. Inherent in the concept of "being white" was the right to own or hold whiteness to the exclusion and subordination of Blacks. Because "[i]dentity is ... continuously being constituted through social interactions," the assigned political, economic, and social inferiority of Blacks necessarily shaped white identity. In the commonly held popular view, the presence of Black "blood"—including the infamous "one-drop"—consigned a person to being "Black" and evoked the "metaphor ... of purity and contamination" in which Black blood is a contaminant and white racial identity is pure. Recognizing or identifying oneself as white is thus a claim of racial purity, an assertion that one is free of any taint of Black blood. The law has played a critical role in legitimating this claim.

D. White Legal Identity: The Law's Acceptance and Legitimation of Whiteness as Property

The law assumed the crucial task of racial classification, and accepted and embraced the then-current theories of race as biological fact. This core precept of race as a physically defined reality allowed the law to fulfill an essential function—to "parcel out social standing according to race" and to facilitate systematic discrimination by articulating "seemingly precise definitions of racial group membership." This allocation of race and rights continued a century after the abolition of slavery.

The law relied on bounded, objective, and scientific definitions of race—what Neil Gotanda has called "historical race"—to construct whiteness as not merely race, but race plus privilege. By making race determinant and the product of rationality and science, dominant and subordinate positions within the racial hierarchy were disguised as the product of natural law and biology rather than as naked preferences. Whiteness as racialized privilege was then legitimated by science and was embraced in legal doctrine as "objective fact."

Case law that attempted to define race frequently struggled over the precise fractional amount of Black "blood"—traceable Black ancestry—that would defeat a claim to whiteness. Although the courts applied varying fractional formulas in different jurisdictions to define "Black" or, in the terms of the day, "Negro" or "colored," the law uniformly accepted the rule of hypodescent—racial identity was governed by blood, and white was preferred.

This legal assumption of race as blood-borne was predicated on the pseudo-sciences of eugenics and craniology that saw their major development during the eighteenth and nineteenth centuries. The legal definition of race was the "objective" test propounded by racist theorists of the day who described race to be immutable, scientific, biologically determined—an unsullied fact of the blood rather than a volatile and violently imposed regime of racial hierarchy.

In adjudicating who was "white," courts sometimes noted that, by physical characteristics, the individual whose racial identity was at issue appeared to be white and, in fact, had been regarded as white in the community. Yet if an individual's blood was tainted, she could not claim to be "white" as the law understood, regardless of the fact that phenotypically she may have been completely indistinguishable from a white person, may have lived as a white person, and have descended from a family that lived as whites. Although socially accepted as white, she could not *legally* be white. Blood as "objective fact" dominated over appearance and social acceptance, which were socially fluid and subjective measures.

But, in fact, "blood" was no more objective than that which the law dismissed as subjective and unreliable. The acceptance of the fiction that the racial ancestry could be determined with the degree of precision called for by the relevant standards or definitions rested on false assumptions that racial categories of prior ancestors had been accurately reported, that those reporting in the past shared the definitions currently in use, and that racial purity actually existed in the United States. Ignoring these considerations, the law established rules that extended equal treatment to those of the "same blood," albeit of different complexions, because it was acknowledged that, "[t]here are white men as dark as mulattoes, and there are pure-blooded albino Africans as white as the whitest Saxons."

The standards were designed to accomplish what mere observation could not: "That even Blacks who did not look Black were kept in their place." Although the line of demarcation between Black and white varied from rules that classified as Black a person containing "any drop of Black blood," to more liberal rules that defined persons with a preponderance of white blood to be white, the courts universally accepted the notion that white status was something of value that could be accorded only to those persons whose proofs established their whiteness as defined by the law. Because legal recognition of a person as white carried material benefits, "false" or inadequately supported claims were denied like any other unsubstantiated claim to a property interest. Only those who could lay "legitimate" claims to whiteness could be legally recognized as "white," because allowing physical attributes, social acceptance, or self-identification to determine whiteness would diminish its value and destroy the underlying presumption of exclusivity. In effect, the courts erected legal "No Trespassing" signs.

In the realm of *social* relations, racial recognition in the United States is thus an act of race subordination. In the realm of *legal* relations, judicial definition of racial identity based on white supremacy reproduced that race subordination at the institutional level. In transforming white to whiteness, the law masked the ideological content of racial definition and the exercise of power required to maintain it: "It convert[ed] [an] abstract concept into [an] entity."

1. *Whiteness as Racialized Privilege.*—The material benefits of racial exclusion and subjugation functioned, in the labor context, to stifle class tensions among whites. White workers perceived that they had more in

common with the bourgeoisie than with fellow workers who were Black. Thus, W. E. B. Du Bois's classic historical study of race and class, *Black Reconstruction,* noted that, for the evolving white working class, race identification became crucial to the ways that it thought of itself and conceived its interests. There were, he suggested, obvious material benefits, at least in the short term, to the decision of white workers to define themselves by their whiteness: their wages far exceeded those of Blacks and were high even in comparison with world standards. Moreover, even when the white working class did not collect increased pay as part of white privilege, there were real advantages not paid in direct income: whiteness still yielded what Du Bois termed a "public and psychological wage" vital to white workers. Thus, Du Bois noted:

> They [whites] were given public deference ... because they were white. They were admitted freely with all classes of white people, to public functions, to public parks.... The police were drawn from their ranks, and the courts, dependent on their votes, treated them with ... leniency.... Their vote selected public officials, and while this had small effect upon the economic situation, it had great effect on their personal treatment.... White schoolhouses were the best in the community, and conspicuously placed, and they cost anywhere from twice to ten times as much per capita as the colored schools.

The central feature of the convergence of "white" and "worker" lay in the fact that racial status and privilege could ameliorate and assist in "evad[ing] rather than confront[ing] [class] exploitation." Although not accorded the privileges of the ruling class, in both the North and South, white workers could accept their lower class position in the hierarchy "by fashioning identities as 'not slaves' and as 'not Blacks.' " Whiteness produced—and was reproduced by—the social advantage that accompanied it.

Whiteness was also central to national identity and to the republican project. The amalgamation of various European strains into an American identity was facilitated by an oppositional definition of Black as "other." As Hacker suggests, fundamentally, the question was not so much "who is white," *but* "who may be considered white," as the historical pattern was that various immigrant groups of different ethnic origins were accepted into a white identity shaped around Anglo–American norms. Current members then "ponder[ed] whether they want[ed] or need[ed] new members as well as the proper pace of new admissions into this exclusive club." Through minstrel shows in which white actors masquerading in blackface played out racist stereotypes, the popular culture put the Black at " 'solo spot centerstage, providing a relational model in contrast to which masses of Americans could establish a positive and superior sense of identity[,]' ... [an identity] ... established by an infinitely manipulable negation comparing whites with a construct of a socially defenseless group."

It is important to note the effect of this hypervaluation of whiteness. Owning white identity as property affirmed the self-identity and liberty of whites and, conversely, denied the self-identity and liberty of Blacks. The attempts to lay claim to whiteness through "passing" painfully illustrate the effects of the law's recognition of whiteness. The embrace of a lie, undertaken by my grandmother and the thousands like her, could occur only when oppression makes self-denial and the obliteration of identity rational and, in significant measure, beneficial. The economic coercion of white supremacy on self-definition nullifies any suggestion that passing is a logical exercise of liberty or self-identity. The decision to pass as white was not a choice, if by that word one means voluntariness or lack of compulsion. The fact of race subordination was coercive and circumscribed the liberty to self-define. Self-determination of identity was not a right for all people, but a privilege accorded on the basis of race. The effect of protecting whiteness at law was to devalue those who were not white by coercing them to deny their identity in order to survive.

   2.   Whiteness, Rights, and National Identity.—The concept of whiteness was carefully protected because so much was contingent upon it. Whiteness conferred on its owners aspects of citizenship that were all the more valued because they were denied to others. Indeed, the very fact of citizenship itself was linked to white racial identity. The Naturalization Act of 1790 restricted citizenship to persons who resided in the United States for two years, who could establish their good character in court, and who were "white." Moreover, the trajectory of expanding democratic rights for whites was accompanied by the contraction of the rights of Blacks in an ever deepening cycle of oppression. The franchise, for example, was broadened to extend voting rights to unpropertied white men at the same time that Black voters were specifically disenfranchised, arguably shifting the property required for voting from land to whiteness. This racialized version of republicanism—this Herrenvolk republicanism—constrained any vision of democracy from addressing the class hierarchies adverse to many who considered themselves white.

   The inherent contradiction between the bondage of Blacks and republican rhetoric that championed the freedom of all men was resolved by positing that Blacks were different. The laws did not mandate that Blacks be accorded equality under the law because nature—not man, not power, not violence—had determined their degraded status. Rights were for those who had the capacity to exercise them, a capacity denoted by racial identity. This conception of rights was contingent on race—on whether one could claim whiteness—a form of property. This articulation of rights that were contingent on property ownership was a familiar paradigm, as similar requirements had been imposed on the franchise in the early part of the republic.

   For the first two hundred years of the country's existence, the system of racialized privilege in both the public and private spheres carried through this linkage of rights and inequality, and rights and property. Whiteness as property was the critical core of a system that affirmed the hierarchical relations between white and Black.

                              * * *

IV. The Persistence of Whiteness as Property

In the modern period, neither the problems attendant to assigning racial identities nor those accompanying the recognition of whiteness have disappeared. Nor has whiteness as property. Whiteness as property continues to perpetuate racial subordination through the courts' definitions of group identity and through the courts' discourse and doctrine on affirmative action. The exclusion of subordinated "others" was and remains a central part of the property interest in whiteness and, indeed, is part of the protection that the court extends to whites' settled expectations of continued privilege.

The essential character of whiteness as property remains manifest in two critical areas of the law and, as in the past, operates to oppress Native Americans and Blacks in similar ways, although in different arenas. This Part first examines the persistence of whiteness as valued social identity; then exposes whiteness as property in the law's treatment of the question of group identity, as the case of the Mashpee Indians illustrates; and finally, exposes the presence of whiteness as property in affirmative action doctrine.

A. The Persistence of Whiteness as Valued Social Identity

Even as the capacity of whiteness to deliver is arguably diminished by the elimination of rigid racial stratifications, whiteness continues to be perceived as materially significant. Because real power and wealth never have been accessible to more than a narrowly defined ruling elite, for many whites the benefits of whiteness as property, in the absence of legislated privilege, may have been reduced to a claim of relative privilege only in comparison to people of color. Nevertheless, whiteness retains its value as a "consolation prize": it does not mean that all whites will win, but simply that they will not lose, if losing is defined as being on the bottom of the social and economic hierarchy—the position to which Blacks have been consigned.

Andrew Hacker, in his 1992 book *Two Nations,* recounts the results of a recent exercise that probed the value of whiteness according to the perceptions of whites. The study asked a group of white students how much money they would seek if they were changed from white to Black. "Most seemed to feel that it would not be out of place to ask for $50 million, or $1 million for each coming black year." Whether this figure represents an accurate amortization of the societal cost of being Black in the United States, it is clear that whiteness is still perceived to be valuable. The wages of whiteness are available to all whites regardless of class position, even to those whites who are without power, money, or influence. Whiteness, the characteristic that distinguishes them from Blacks, serves as compensation even to those who lack material wealth. It is the relative political advantages extended to whites, rather than actual economic gains, that are crucial to white workers. Thus, as Kimberlé Crenshaw points out, whites have an actual stake in racism. Because Blacks are held to be inferior, although no longer on the basis of science as antecedent determinant, but by virtue of their position at the bottom, it allows whites—all whites—to "include themselves in the dominant circle. [Although most whites] hold no real power, [all can claim] their privileged racial identity."

White workers often identify primarily as white rather than as workers because it is through their whiteness that they are afforded access to a host of public, private, and psychological benefits. It is through the concept of whiteness that class consciousness among white workers is subordinated and attention is diverted from class oppression.

Although dominant societal norms have embraced the idea of fairness and nondiscrimination, removal of privilege and antisubordination principles are actively rejected or at best ambiguously received because expectations of white privilege are bound up with what is considered essential for self-realization. Among whites, the idea persists that their whiteness is meaningful. Whiteness is an aspect of racial identity surely, but it is much more; it remains a concept based on relations of power, a social construct predicated on white dominance and Black subordination.

B. Subordination Through Denial of Group Identity

Whiteness as property is also constituted through the reification of expectations in the continued right of white-dominated institutions to control the legal meaning of group identity. This reification manifests itself in the law's dialectical misuse of the concept of group identity as it pertains to racially subordinated peoples. The law has recognized and codified racial group identity as an instrumentality of exclusion and exploitation; however, it has refused to recognize group identity when asserted by racially oppressed groups as a basis for affirming or claiming rights. The law's approach to group identity reproduces subordination, in the past through "race-ing" a group—that is, by assigning a racial identity that equated with inferior status, and in the present by erasing racial group identity.

In part, the law's denial of the existence of racial groups is predicated not only on the rejection of the ongoing presence of the past, but is also grounded on a basic tenet of liberalism—that constitutional protections inhere in individuals, not groups. As informed by the Lockean notion of the social contract, the autonomous, free-will of the individual is central. Indeed, it is the individual who, in concert with other individuals, elects to enter into political society and to form a state of limited powers. This philosophical view of society is closely aligned with the antidiscrimination principle—the idea being that equality mandates only the equal treatment of individuals under the law. Within this framework, the idea of the social group has no place.

Although the law's determination of any "fact," including that of group identity, is not infinitely flexible, its studied ignorance of the issue of racial group identity insures wrong results by assuming a pseudo-objective posture that does not permit it to hear the complex dialogue concerning the identity question, particularly as it pertains to historically dominated groups.

Instead, the law holds to the basic premise that definition from above can be fair to those below, that beneficiaries of racially conferred privilege have the right to establish norms for those who have historically been oppressed pursuant to those norms, and that race is not historically contingent. Although the substance of race definitions has changed, what persists is the expectation of white-controlled institutions in the continued right to determine meaning—the reified privilege of power—that reconstitutes the property interest in whiteness in contemporary form.

In undertaking any definition of race as group identity, there are implicit and explicit normative underpinnings that must be taken into account. The "riddle of identity" is not answered by a "search for essences" or essential discoverable truth, nor by a search for mere "descriptions and re-descriptions." Instead, when handling the complex issue of group identity, we should look to "purposes and effects, consequences and functions." The questions pertaining to definitions of race then are not principally biological or genetic, but social and political: what must be addressed is who is defining, how is the definition constructed, and why is the definition being propounded. Because definition is so often a central part of domination, critical thinking about these issues must precede and adjoin any definition. The law has not attended to these questions. Instead, identity of "the other" is still objectified, the complex, negotiated quality of identity is ignored, and the impact of inequitable power on identity is masked. These problems are illustrated in the land claim suit brought by the Mashpee, a Massachusetts Indian tribe.

In *Mashpee Tribe v. Town of Mashpee,* the Mashpee sued to recover land that several Indians had conveyed to non-Indians in violation of a statute that barred alienation of tribal land to non-Indians without the approval of the federal government. In order to recover possession of the land, the Mashpee were required to prove that they were a tribe at the time of the conveyance. Although the trial judge admitted to some preliminary confusion about the appropriate definition of "tribe," he ultimately accepted the standard articulated in prior case law that defined tribe as "a body of Indians of the same or similar race, united in a community under one leadership or government, and inhabiting a particular though sometimes ill-defined territory." The Mashpee were held not to be a tribe at the time the suit was filed, so that their claim to land rights based on group identity were rejected.

The Mashpee's experience was filtered, sifted, and ultimately rendered incoherent through this externally constituted definition of tribe that incorporated outside criteria regarding race, leadership, territory, and community. The fact that the Mashpee had intermingled with Europeans, runaway slaves, and other Indian tribes signified to the jury and to the court that they had lost their tribal identity.

But for the Mashpee, blood was not the measure of identity: their identity as a group was manifested for centuries by their continued relationship to the land of the Mashpee; their consciousness and embrace of difference, even when it was against their interest; and, their awareness and preservation of cultural traditions. Nevertheless, under the court's standard, the tribe was "incapable of *legal* self-definition." Fundamentally, then, the external imposition of definition maintained the social equilibrium that was severely challenged by the Mashpee land claims.

The Mashpee case presents new variations on old themes of race and property. Previous reified definitions of race compelled abandonment of racial identity in exchange for economic and social privilege. Under the operative racial hierarchy, passing is the ultimate assimilationist move— the submergence of a subordinate cultural identity in favor of dominant identity, assumed to achieve better societal fit within prevailing norms. The modern definition of "tribe" achieved similar results by misinterpreting the Mashpee's adaptation to be assimilation. The Mashpee absorbed and managed, rather than rejected and suppressed, outsiders; yet the court erased their identity, assuming that, by virtue of intermingling with other races, the Mashpee's identity as a people had been subsumed. The Mashpee were not "passing," but were legally determined to have "passed"—no longer to have distinct identity. This erasure was predicated on the assumption that what is done from necessity under conditions of established hierarchies of domination and subordination is a voluntary surrender for gain.

Beyond the immediate outcome of the case lies the deeper problem posed by the hierarchy of the rules themselves and the continued retention by white-controlled institutions of exclusive control over definitions as they pertain to the identity and history of dominated peoples. Although the law will always represent the exercise of state power in enforcing its choices, the violence done to the Mashpee and other oppressed groups results from the law's refusal to acknowledge the negotiated quality of identity. Whiteness as property assumes the form of the exclusive right to determine rules; it asserts that, against a framework of racial dominance and unequal power, fairness can result from a property rule, or indeed any other rule, that imposes an entirely externally constituted definition of group identity. Reality belies this presumption. In *Plessy,* the Court affirmed the right of the state to define who was white, obliterating aspects of social acceptance and self-identification as sources of validation and identity. The Mashpee were similarly divested of their identity through the state's exclusive retention of control over meaning in ways that reinforced group oppression. When group identity is a predicate for exclusion or disadvantage, the law has acknowledged it; when it is a predicate for resistance or a claim of right to be free from subordination, the law determines it to be illusory. This determinist approach to group identity reproduces racial subordination and reaffirms whiteness as property.

C.   Subjugation Through Affirmative Action Doctrine

The assumption that whiteness is a property interest entitled to protection is an idea born of systematic white supremacy and nurtured over the years, not only by the law of slavery and "Jim Crow," but also by the more recent decisions and rationales of the Supreme Court concerning affirmative action. In examining both the nature of the affirmative action debate and the legal analysis applied in three Supreme Court cases involving affirmative action—*Regents of University of California v. Bakke, City of Richmond v. J. A. Croson Co.,* and *Wygant v. Jackson Board of Education,* it is evident that the protection of the property interest in whiteness still lies at the core of judicial and popular reasoning.

    * * *

VI. Conclusion

Whiteness as property has carried and produced a heavy legacy. It is a ghost that has haunted the political and legal domains in which claims for justice have been inadequately addressed for far too long. Only rarely declaring its presence, it has warped efforts to remediate racial exploitation. It has blinded society to the systems of domination that work against so many by retaining an unvarying focus on vestiges of systemic racialized privilege that subordinates those perceived as a particularized few—the "others." It has thwarted not only conceptions of racial justice but also conceptions of property that embrace more equitable possibilities. In protecting the property interest in whiteness, property is assumed to be no more than the right to prohibit infringement on settled expectations, ignoring countervailing equitable claims that are predicated on a right to inclusion. It is long past time to put the property interest in whiteness to rest. Affirmative action can assist in that task. Affirmative action, if properly conceived and implemented, is not only consistent with norms of equality, but is essential to shedding the legacy of oppression.

NOTES AND QUESTIONS

1. Akerlof, Kranton, and McAdams. The identity payoff model presented in this paper, and the group-status production model presented by McAdams, *infra* at pp. 721–738 and pp. 768–799 both attempt to explain the persistence of economic inequality when classical economic theory states that the free market should eliminate discrimination. However, while the goals of the two papers might be similar, their approaches are quite different. First, McAdams' approach is group based; all individuals are looked upon as basically the same, with differences created by quasi-market forces. By contrast, the model presented by Akerlof and Kranton focuses on individuals and assumes that, even in the absence of markets, some individuals would have a predisposition to be "Red" while others would be "Green." Additionally, McAdams sees discrimination as the result of self-interested behavior on the part of the majority, while Akerlof and Kranton see identity differentiation as arising partially as a survival strategy by the minority. Given these differences between the two explanations for discrimination, is there any way that the Akerlof–Kranton and McAdams positions can be reconciled?

2. Different identities or different settings? Are the "Red" and "Green" cultures of the Akerlof–Kranton model necessarily representative of different identities, or could they be thought of more accurately as different manifestations of the same identity when faced with different circumstances? When Malcolm X began hustling, his mentor gave him the following advice: "[g]et here early ... everything in place ... you never need to waste motion." ALEX HALEY & MALCOLM X, THE AUTOBIOGRAPHY OF MALCOLM X 46 (1965). When Malcolm X became a more successful drug dealer he demonstrated considerable capitalist acumen. He reinvested his profits into his business, developed rational strategies for dealing with law enforcement, and entered new markets when government regulation became too tight. *Id.* at 99–102. Given the effort and business skills required to succeed as a hustler, as well as Malcolm X's success when he was able to find non-criminal employment with the Nation of Islam, does it seem more likely that Malcolm's "Red" identity was different from a mainstream "Green" identity, or that it was simply a "Green" identity expressing itself in "Red" surroundings?

3.   Definition of tribe. This case as discussed in Harris at pp. 759–760, was presented as a contest between history and anthropology, with history winning in the end. However, aren't broad historical and anthropological definitions of the word tribe ultimately beside the point? Shouldn't the definition of tribe be that used by the drafters of the Non–Intercourse Act?

4.   Performative identity. The Indians of Mashpee lost their case because they didn't behave in a way that comported with the jury's view of how an Indian tribe should act, thus their performative identity was not that of a tribe. Isn't this a rather odd way to structure a lawsuit? Modern anti-discrimination laws generally take the opposite approach: the more a minority has assimilated into mainstream culture, the greater chance that minority has of winning an anti-discrimination claim. Devon W. Carbado & Mitu Gulati, *The Law and Economics of Critical Race Theory: Crossroads, Directions, and a New Critical Race Theory*, 112 YALE L.J. 1757, 1822 (2003) (book review). Why is it that in this case, assimilation was (from the standpoint of the outcome of the suit) a bad thing? Does a legal regime which encourages rejection of mainstream culture provide perverse incentives from an anti-discrimination viewpoint?

5.   The point of all this. How did the disposition of this case effect the "tribe?" According to the plaintiffs, the tribe was based on culture, shared traditions, kinship, and other intangible bonds. Would those bonds have been strengthened if the "tribe" had won its suit? Would they have been diluted by the effects of a large settlement? Since the "tribe" was not simply an amalgam of individuals, could it possibly have been aided in any way by a positive verdict? Is it more likely that the "tribe" would have been destroyed by the ascendancy of Tribal Council, Inc., which was organized specifically to provide a structure for interaction with the non-tribal world? Would victory for the corporation have helped the "tribe" of Mashpee?

6.   Taint of whiteness. According to Professor Harris, "[a]t the individual level, recognizing oneself as 'white' necessarily assumes premises based on white supremacy ... privileging 'white' as unadulterated, exclusive, and rare." *Supra* p. 753. Is it constructive to tar all people who recognize themselves as white with the implication of white supremacy? It would seem likely that recognition of the social power of whiteness is necessary in order to try to eliminate discrimination against blacks. How, under Professor Harris' conception of whiteness as property, is it possible for a white person to work against racism, when by acknowledging the social privileges accorded to whiteness, white people assume the premises of white supremacy?

7. Neutrality of affirmative action. Professor Harris asserts that, "[b]ecause affirmative action can only be implemented through conscious intervention and requires constant monitoring and reevaluation, it does not function behind a mask of neutrality in the realm beyond scrutiny." Of course, chattel slavery was also implemented through conscious intervention and required constant monitoring and reevaluation (not to mention terroristic violence). The same is true of Jim Crow segregation. Does this mean that segregation and slavery did not function to distort white expectations because they did not "function behind a mask of neutrality?" Further, how could any meaningful affirmative action program not change black expectations? Will expectations not change if affirmative action is effective and reliable? Is Professor Harris arguing that blacks can never be beneficiaries of racism in the future because they have been its victims in the past?

8. Additional reading. For a comprehensive analysis of the Mashpee case, *see* James Clifford, IDENTITY IN MASHPEE, THE PREDICAMENT OF CULTURE: TWENTIETH-CENTURY ETHNOGRAPHY, LITERATURE AND ART 277–346 (1988). For a non-technical perspective on economics and identity, see Gerald D. Jaynes, *Identity and Economic Performance*, 568 ANNALS AM. ACAD. POL. & SOC. SCI. 128 (2000). For an interesting description of an interaction between cultures, see Ann Southerland, *Complexities of U.S. Law and Gypsy Identity*, 45 AM. J. COMP. L. 393 (1997). For additional information on anthropological issues in the courts, see generally Larry Cata Backer, *Chroniclers in the Field of Cultural Production: Courts, Law and the Interpretive Process*, 20 B.C. THIRD WORLD L.J. 291 (2000); Glen Stohr, Comment, *The Repercussions of Orality in Federal Indian Law*, 31 ARIZ. ST. L.J. 679 (1999). For additional information on Indian tribes in the courts, see generally Jennifer L. Tomsen, Note, *"Traditional" Resource Uses and Activities: Articulating Values and Examining Conflicts in Alaska*, 19 ALASKA L. REV. 167 (2002); Neu Jessup Newton, *Sovereignty and the Native American Nation: Memory and Misrepresentation: Representing Crazy Horse*, 27 CONN. L. REV. 1003 (1995). For additional information on the Mashpee case, see Gerald Torres & Kathryn Milun, *Frontier of Legal Thought III: Translating Yonnondio by Precedent and Evidence: The Mashpee Indian Case*, 1990 DUKE L.J. 625 (1990). For an approach to white privilege outside of the property framework, see Sylvia A. Law, *White Privilege and Affirmative Action*, 32 AKRON L. REV. 603 (1999). For an article that, notwithstanding Harris, espouses the idea of Blackness as property, see Jim Chen, *Affirmative Action: Diversity of Opinions: Embryonic Thoughts on Racial Identity as New Property*, 68 U. COLO. L. REV. 1123 (1997). For a Marxist approach to identity as property, see E. Christi Cunningham, *Identity Markets*, 45 HOW. L.J. 491 (2002). For an analysis of whiteness as property explored through a fictionalized dialogue with a space alien, see Derrick Bell, *Xerces and the Affirmative Action Mystique*, 57 GEO. WASH. L. REV. 1595 (1989).

B.   RACIAL DISCRIMINATION: TWO COMPETING THEORIES AND EMPIRICAL EVIDENCE OF DISPARATE RACIAL IMPACT

A major dispute between scholars who are interested in the problem of persistent racial discrimination is whether the market can be expected to provide a self-correction for racial discrimination that locks members of racial minorities out of participation in basic transactions and therefore wealth accumulation. We return to economics Nobel laureate, Gary Becker for his economic model which treats racial discrimination like any other private preference that can be expressed as a "taste" with monetary value in the marketplace. Legal scholar Richard McAdams draws on sociological theories of group status production to offer an alternative view of the mechanisms fueling persistent racial discrimination. Legal scholar and economist Ian Ayres enters this debate with a powerful new tool: empirical studies of actual marketplace racial dynamics in important transactions.

1.   A RATIONAL CHOICE THEORY OF RACIAL DISCRIMINATION IN THE MARKETPLACE

The Forces Determining Discrimination in the Market Place

THE ECONOMICS OF DISCRIMINATION 13–18 (2d ed. 1971).

■ GARY BECKER

In the socio-psychological literature on this subject one individual is said to discriminate against (or in favor of) another if his behavior toward the latter is not motivated by an "objective" consideration of fact. It is difficult to use this definition in distinguishing a violation of objective facts from an expression of tastes or values. For example, discrimination and prejudice are not usually said to occur when someone prefers looking at a glamorous Hollywood actress rather than at some other woman; yet they are said to occur when he prefers living next to whites rather than Negroes. At best calling just one of these actions "discrimination" requires making subtle and rather secondary distinctions. Fortunately, it is not necessary to get involved in these more philosophical issues. It is possible to give an unambiguous definition of discrimination in the market place and yet get at the essence of what is usually called discrimination.

1.   THE ANALYTICAL FRAMEWORK

Money, commonly used as a measuring rod, will also serve as a measure of discrimination. If an individual has a "taste for discrimination," he must act *as if* he were willing to pay something either directly or in the form of a reduced income, to be associated with some persons instead of others. When actual discrimination occurs, he must, in fact, either pay or forfeit income for this privilege. This simple way of looking at the matter gets at the essence of prejudice and discrimination.

Social scientists tend to organize their discussion of discrimination in the market place according to their disciplines. To the sociologist, different levels of discrimination against a particular group are associated with different levels of social and physical "distance" from that group or with different levels of socioeconomic status; the psychologist classifies individuals by their personality types, believing that this is the most useful organizational principle. The breakdown used here is most familiar to the economist and differs from both of these: all persons who contribute to production in the same way, e.g., by the rent of capital or the sale of labor services, are put into one group, with each group forming a separate "factor of production." The breakdown by economic productivity turns out to be a particularly fruitful one, since it emphasizes phenomena that have long been neglected in literature on discrimination.

By using the concept of a *discrimination coefficient* (this will be abbreviated to "DC"), it is possible to give a definition of a "taste for discrimination" that is parallel for different factors of production, employers, and consumers. The *money* costs of a transaction do not always completely measure *net* costs, and a DC acts as a bridge between money and net costs. Suppose an *employer* were faced with the money wage rate π of a particular factor; he is assumed to act as $\pi(1 + d_i)$ were the net wage rate, with di as his DC against this factor. An *employee*, offered the money wage rate π_i for working with this factor, acts as if $\pi(1-d_j)$ were the *net* wage rate, with dj as his DC against this factor. A *consumer*, faced with a unit money of p for the commodity "produced" by this factor, acts as if the net price were $p(1 + d_k)$ with dk as his DC against this factor. In all three instances a DC gives the percentage by which either money costs or money returns are changed in going from money to net magnitudes: the employer uses it to estimate his net wage costs, the employee his net wage rate, and the consumer the net price of a commodity.

A DC represents a non-pecuniary element in certain kinds of transactions, and it is positive or negative, depending upon whether the non-pecuniary element is considered "good" or "bad." Discrimination is commonly associated with *dis*utility caused by contact with some individuals and this interpretation is followed here. Since this implies that d_i, d_j, and d_k are all greater than zero, to the employer this coefficient represents a non-monetary cost of production, to the employer a non-monetary cost of employment, and to the consumer a non-monetary cost of consumption. "Nepotism" rather than "discrimination" would occur if they were less than zero, and they would then represent non-monetary returns of production, employment, and consumption to the employer, employee, and consumer, respectively.

The quantities πd_i, $\pi j d_j$, and pd_k are the exact money equivalents of these non-monetary costs; for given wage rates and prices, these money equivalents are larger, the larger di, dj, and dk are. Since a DC can take on any value between zero and plus infinity, tastes for discrimination can also vary continuously within this range. This quantitative representation of a taste for discrimination provides the means for empirically estimating the quantitative importance of discrimination.

2. TASTES FOR DISCRIMINATION

The magnitude of a taste for discrimination differs from person to person, and many investigators have directed their energies toward discovering the variables that are most responsible for these differences. I also attempt to isolate and estimate the quantitative importance of some of these variables; the following discussion briefly describes several variables that receive attention in subsequent chapters.

The discrimination by an individual against a particular group (to be called N) depends on the social and physical distance between them and on their relative socioeconomic status. If he works with N in production, it may also depend on their substitutability in production. The relative number of N in the society at large also may be very important: it has been argued that an increase in the numerical importance of a minority group increases the prejudice against them, since the majority begins to fear their growing power; on the other hand, some argue that greater numbers bring greater knowledge and that leads to a decline in prejudice. Closely related to this variable are the frequency and regularity of "contact" with N in different establishments and firms.

According to our earlier definition, if someone has a "taste for discrimination," he must act *as if* he were willing to forfeit income in order to avoid certain transactions; it is necessary to be aware of the emphasis on the words "as if." An employer may refuse to hire Negroes solely because he erroneously underestimates their economic efficiency. His behavior is discriminatory not because he is prejudiced against them but because his is ignorant of their true efficiency. Ignorance may be quickly eliminated by the spread of knowledge, while a prejudice (i.e. preference) is relatively independent of knowledge. This distinction is essential for understanding the motivation of many organizations, since they either explicitly or implicitly assume that discrimination can be eliminated by a wholesale spread of knowledge.

Since a taste for discrimination incorporates both prejudice and ignorance, the amount of knowledge available must be included as a determinant of tastes. Another proximate determinant is geographical and chronological location: discrimination may vary from country to country, from region to region within a country, from rural to urban areas within a region, and from one time period to another. Finally, tastes may differ simply because of differences in personality.

3.   MARKET DISCRIMINATION

Suppose there are two groups, designated by W and N, with members of W being perfect substitutes in production for members of N. In the absence of discrimination and nepotism and if the labor market were perfectly competitive, the equilibrium wage rate of W would equal that of N. Discrimination could cause these wage rates to differ; the market discrimination coefficient between W and N (this will be abbreviated "MDC") is defined as the proportional difference between these wage rates. If π_w and π_n represent the equilibrium wage rates of W and N, respectively, then

$$\text{MDC} = \pi_w - \pi_n \; \pi_w -$$

If W and N are imperfect substitutes, they may receive different wage rates even in the absence of discrimination. A more general definition of the MDC sets it equal to the difference between the ratio of W's and N's wage rate with and without discrimination. In the special case of perfect substitutes, this reduces to the simpler definition given previously, because $\pi 0 w$ would equal $\pi 0_w$.

It should be obvious that the magnitude of the MDC depends on the magnitude of individual DC's. Unfortunately, it is often implicitly assumed that it depends only on them; the arguments proceed as if a knowledge of the determinants of tastes was sufficient for a complete understanding of market discrimination. This procedure is erroneous; many variables in addition to tastes take prominent roles in determining market discrimination, and, indeed, tastes sometimes play a minor part. The abundant light thrown on the other variables by the tools of economic analysis has probably been the major insight gained from using them.

The MDC does depend in an important way on each individual's DC; however, merely to use some measure of the average DC does not suffice. The complete distribution of DC's among individuals must be made explicit because the size of the MDC is partly related to individual *differences* in tastes. It also depends on the relative importance of competition and monopoly in the labor and product markets, since this partly determines the weight assigned by the market to different DC's. The economic and quantitative importance of N was mentioned as one determinant of tastes for discrimination; this variable is also an independent determinant of market discrimination. This independent effect operates through the number of N relative to W and the cost of N per unit of output relative to the total cost per unit of output. Both may be important, although for somewhat different reasons, in determining the weight assigned by the market to different DC's. Reorganizing production through the substitution of one factor for another is a means of avoiding discrimination; the amount of substitution available is determined by the production function.

The MDC is a direct function of these variables and an indirect function of other variables through their effect on tastes. Our knowledge of the economic aspects of discrimination will be considered satisfactory only when these relationships are known exactly. In subsequent chapters I present the results of my own attempts to close some gaps in this knowledge.

* * *

2.   A SOCIOLOGICAL THEORY OF RACIAL DISCRIMINATION IN THE MARKETPLACE

Cooperation and Conflict: The Economics of Group Status Production and Race Discrimination

108 HARV. L. REV. 1003 (1995).

■ RICHARD H. McADAMS

In Shakespeare's history of King Henry V, when the time comes for the young King to ready his troops to battle a much larger French force at Agincourt, he delivers a stirring speech that many regard as a masterpiece of inspirational rhetoric. Rejecting his advisor's lament for more men, he responds: "No, my fair cousin:/ If we are marked to die, we are enow/ To do our country loss: and if to live,/ The fewer men, the greater share of honour." The King proclaims his personal desire for honor, offers safe passage back to England for those who do not wish to fight, and then describes how those who stay will be celebrated on future anniversaries of this day of battle, known as the Feast of St. Crispian:

And Crispin Crispian shall ne'er go by,

From this day to the ending of the world,

But we in it shall be remembered;

We few, we happy few, we band of brothers:

For he to-day that sheds his blood with me

Shall be my brother....

And gentlemen in England, now a-bed,

Shall think themselves accursed they were not here;

And hold their manhoods cheap, whiles any speaks

That fought with us upon Saint Crispin's day.

For those of us who strive to be hard-headed theorists of human behavior, and who use economics and game theory to reveal the consequences of legal rules, our initial response to this speech is likely to be: "What a disaster." The King and his soldiers are about to risk their lives. Yet he denies wanting more men though additional troops would obviously better their odds of surviving and winning. Such a non sequitur can only raise doubts about the clarity of Henry's thinking, which in turn can only increase the chances that his officers will question his commands. And, one might ask, what are the meaning and value of "honor" and "brotherhood"? If Henry wishes to motivate his men, a better strategy would be to spell out the potential material benefits (perhaps promising them more pay) or to remind them of the serious penalties for breaking their promise to fight. Offering to pay their way home, after the enhanced risk of loss has caused Henry's troops to regret their decision to join him in France, is sheer insanity. Finally, those "gentlemen in England now a-bed" will likely count themselves lucky for the opportunity to free-ride on a victory. After all, most of the benefits of victory—the general peace and prosperity of England—cannot be withheld from those who do not fight.

Economics, especially "law and economics," prides itself on the universal application of its method. Yet a theory of human motivation that did not grasp the meaning and power of this speech would be seriously flawed. Military leaders are among the more pragmatic and hard-headed people around and would likely scoff at this economic analysis of Henry's speech. Military rhetoric frequently appeals to honor and brotherhood. If such words prod men and women to risk their lives, one can only imagine how much greater is the power of such words relative to smaller material sacrifices. Consider, for example, the possible economic consequences of the following words:

> Standing in the presence of this multitude, sobered with the responsibility of the message I deliver to the young men of the South, I declare that the truth above all others to be worn unsullied and sacred in your hearts, to be surrendered to no force, sold for no price, compromised in no necessity, but cherished and defended as the covenant of your prosperity, and the pledge of peace to your children, is that the white race must dominate forever in the South, because it is the white race, and superior to that race by which its supremacy is threatened.

A principal purpose of this Article is to illuminate the economic power of this white supremacist oration by Henry Grady and of Henry V's justly celebrated speech, as well as to examine the precise parallel between the two.

Each speech appeals to *group* interests, *group* loyalty, and *group* identity. The ubiquity of social groups says something of their importance: groups include not just firms, trade associations, and families, but groups based on demographic traits such as race, gender, or age, and those based on membership, such as fraternities or sororities, amateur sports teams, gangs, the Rotary or Elks Clubs, or private lunch clubs. Undoubtedly, some or all of these groups, like the firm, serve the individual's interest by minimizing the transaction costs she incurs while acting to satisfy her preference for whatever interest or function the group facilitates. But that explanation offers no insight into the meaning or power of the speeches of Henry V and Henry Grady.

This Article offers an economic theory to explain why individuals make material sacrifices for group welfare. My thesis is that a material view of human motivation underestimates both the level of cooperation that groups elicit from their members and the level of conflict that groups elicit from each other. A single group dynamic connects these added increments of cooperation and conflict: groups achieve solidarity and elicit loyalty beyond what economic analysis conventionally predicts, but solidarity and loyalty within groups lead predictably, if not inevitably, to competition and conflict between groups. The connection is the desire for esteem or status. Groups use intra-group status rewards as a non-material means of gaining material sacrifice from members, but the attendant desire for inter-group status causes inter-group conflict. This theory explains the power of King Henry's speech, which appeals to the individual's identification with the group ("we band of brothers") and effectively describes the status reward by contrasting other members of the group (those gentlemen left in England) who will not share in it. At the same time, the war itself was the product of England's desire for esteem and status—more specifically, Henry's desire for honor—which can only be achieved by conquering France.

This two-fold importance of status is essential to a genuine understanding of race discrimination, which has eluded economics. Discrimination is a means by which social groups produce status for their members, but pivotal to understanding this form of inter-group *conflict* is the role that status plays in generating the intra-group *cooperation* necessary to make discrimination effective. Absent the desire for intra-group status, selfish individuals would not make the material sacrifices that discrimination requires. In this context, Henry Grady's racist speech is an economically explicable (if unusually candid) means of enlisting white troops in the ongoing status warfare, urging them to "compromise[ ] in no [material] necessity" the process of discriminating against, and thereby subordinating, the blacks whose inferior position produces a status gain for whites. The rhetoric helps establish a norm of white behavior, the abrogation of which will lower the in-group status of non-conforming whites.

Race discrimination is the best and most important illustration of what I view as a more general phenomenon of intra-group cooperation and inter-group conflict. Before discussing race, however, I must articulate the general theory—to establish empirically that, because of concern for status, cooperation arises within groups and conflict occurs between groups. Part I sets forth puzzling instances of intra-group cooperation in experimental "dilemma" situations and elsewhere, which are not explained by existing economic theory but are well explained by concern for the esteem of other group members. Part I then proposes a model that describes how 'esteem payments' afford groups a novel means of solving their collective action problems and, finally, how this same mechanism leads inevitably to inter-group status conflict. Part II considers the particular problem of race discrimination—the deficiencies in existing economic theory, the superior ability of a status-production model to explain many race-related phenomena, and the implications of such a model. In particular, if race discrimination is a means of producing group status—if groups are engaged in a form of status "warfare"—then discrimination presents the same case for government prohibition that exists for more traditional government restraints on force and fraud.

I. EXPLAINING "EXCESS" COOPERATION AND CONFLICT:
AN ECONOMIC THEORY OF SOCIAL GROUPS

Current economic theory fails to predict the prevalence of cooperation and conflict in human affairs. Considerable evidence supports David

Hume's observation that "[w]hen men are once inlisted on opposite sides, they contract an affection to the persons with whom they are united, and an animosity against their antagonists: And these passions they often transmit to their posterity." Economics has been slow to address the function of social groups and the means by which they engender levels of loyalty and hostility in apparent defiance of conventional notions of material selfishness. But the psychic motivations that explain these "passions"—and the resulting intra-group cooperation and inter-group conflict—are reconcilable with rational self-interest.

This Part presents the modern evidence that supports Hume's claim. Initially, section A examines the empirical evidence that people cooperate beyond conventionally predicted levels. This "excess" cooperation is explained neither by sophisticated rational choice mechanisms such as reciprocity, nor by unselfish motives such as altruism. Instead, the experimental data indicate that cooperation is related to group membership. Section B advances a theory to account for this data: individuals who seek to maximize the esteem they receive from others have selfish reasons to contribute to group status. Two concepts of "group" are advanced: one defined externally by common characteristics observable by third-parties, and one defined internally by relationships among the members. In each case, there are selfish but non-pecuniary reasons for cooperating with one's group members. Finally, section C suggests reasons that the very mechanisms that increase cooperation within groups also increase conflict between groups, and considers evidence that such status-based "excess" conflict exists.

A.   The Empirical Evidence of "Excess" Cooperation

To understand conflict among social groups, we must first understand how groups elicit cooperation from their members. Game theorists study the strategic interactions of individuals, and their most compelling contribution is their description of the difficulties groups face in procuring the cooperation of members. In contrast to Adam Smith's "invisible hand," which guides society to desirable outcomes though individuals are selfishly motivated, game theory describes "collective action problems"—situations in which individually rational decisions lead to sub-optimal collective outcomes. The classic example is the prisoner's dilemma, but the basic problem exists in more complex situations with more than two parties: each individual faces a choice essentially between cooperation and defection, where the dominant strategy for each individual is defection, but where mutual defection is worse for everyone than mutual cooperation. The interest in studying such "games" is generated by the belief that they represent a fundamental feature of social life. Whether it is the undersupply of "public goods," the overconsumption of common resources, or related difficulties, the problem of collective action is commonly offered as a rationale for government regulation. Conversely, many private economic practices can best be understood as mechanisms for solving collective action problems.

The focus of this section and the next is a particular mechanism for solving collective action problems commonly ignored by legal economists: groups achieve cooperation by allocating intra-group status. To persuade the skeptical that the desire for esteem exists and is necessary to explain important examples of cooperation, I could begin with a number of real-world examples of group cooperation. It is difficult, however, to distinguish subtle motivations in complex, uncontrolled events. Some might plausibly assert that, for any number of reasons, the individual's pecuniary self-interest in such examples happens to conform to the group interest. Others, including some critics of economic analysis, would argue that cooperation indicates the existence, not of a selfish interest in status, but of genuine altruism. Given these difficulties, I turn first to laboratory experiments, which can control for alternative motivations for cooperation.

1. Dilemma Experiments: Evidence of Non–Material Motivations for Cooperation.—Since the 1950s, social scientists have conducted experiments with the prisoner's dilemma game, its multi-party variants, public goods problems, and common resource problems. In each test, experimenters structure monetary payoffs to make defection or free-riding the dominant strategy. Despite the logical force of the monetarily dominant strategy, researchers have not found uniform defection. Many individuals defect, but a significant proportion—one-quarter to two-thirds—chooses to cooperate. After more than two thousand social dilemma experiments, one of the "generally accepted" conclusions is that, when pecuniary incentives appear to compel defection, "many subjects do *not* defect." For those who employ game theory to predict the consequences of legal rules, this residuum of cooperation demands explanation.

One immediate and material explanation is *reciprocity*. When future interactions are likely, reciprocity is possible, and defection may no longer be the dominant strategy. One reciprocal strategy is "tit-for-tat," in which one begins by cooperating and then responds in future rounds by doing whatever the other player did in the previous round. Considerable evidence demonstrates the success of tit-for-tat in preventing mutual defection in iterated prisoner's dilemmas.

Reciprocity does not, however, explain the cooperation observed in the dilemma experiments discussed above. Reciprocity requires future interaction in which players can reciprocate past decisions. Theorists still predict mutual defection for "one-shot" prisoner's dilemmas. Yet a large number of the empirical tests of collective action problems were intentionally designed as "one-shot" games to exclude the opportunity for reciprocity, and these tests have repeatedly found significant amounts of cooperation. In the very circumstance in which there is no material reason to cooperate, there is the undeniable fact of cooperation. Thus, however powerful reciprocity may be in some contexts, a significant residual level of cooperation remains unexplained.

One might note, finally, that the material stakes in these experiments typically involve only a few dollars or less. Though higher stakes might cause people to free-ride, the question is what explains subjects' consistent failure to free-ride when low material stakes suggest they should. After all, entire industries arise to capture stakes of a similar size; what seems low in isolation is vast when aggregated over a large population. Whether we can say the same of the motivations causing this residual cooperation requires us first to discover what those motivations are.

2. *Dilemma Experiments: Evidence of Non–Altruistic Motivations for Cooperation.*—Critics and reformers of economic modeling have pointed to the dilemma experiments described above as proof of altruism or a commitment to principles of fairness. Yet a full review of the psychological research on collective dilemmas refutes this thesis. Some sense of "group identity," rather than altruism or fairness, explains the variations in cooperation researchers have observed. Of particular note are studies revealing that individuals cooperate more frequently in dilemma games than do groups of individuals and studies revealing that discussion increases the level of cooperation in dilemma games.

First, many prisoner's dilemma studies have contrasted games between individual subjects with games between groups of subjects. Holding the payoffs constant, these studies consistently find significantly more cooperation when individuals play individuals than when teams play teams. One study, for example, found that three-person groups defected an average of 8.73 times in twenty rounds, compared to an average of 1.8 defections out of twenty when individuals played each other. This individual-group "discontinuity" is consistent with research finding that the formation of a purely experimental "group" can elicit a bias in favor of in-group members, against out-group members, or both. Psychologists discovered this when they set out to create a base line in which individuals would have no reason to favor their own group. To their surprise, whenever subjects were divided into groups, people consistently evaluated members of their own group more favorably than members of other groups. Summarizing this effect, one pair of researchers stated that "mere awareness of the presence of an out-group is sufficient to provoke intergroup competitive or discriminatory responses on the part of the in-group."

Additional confirmation of the importance of groups is provided by dilemma experiments in which researchers elicited differences in cooperation by symbolically invoking 'real-world' group memberships. In one study, psychologists observed significantly more cooperation from subjects sharing a common resource when they told the subjects that they were being evaluated as a single group against groups not then a part of the experiment (for example, college students versus non-students) than when they told the subjects that they were being evaluated as members of one of two subgroups in the experiment (for example, psychology majors versus economics majors).

These studies appear to confirm David Hume's insight that individuals "have such a propensity to divide into personal factions, that the smallest appearance of real difference will produce them." The experimenter's arbitrary division of subjects into groups is sufficient to "factionalize" them, causing more competitive behavior between groups than between individuals and favoritism for members of one's own 'group.' Neither a general concern for the welfare of others nor a concern for fairness explains why subjects were so much less cooperative with other subjects whom the experimenter placed in a different group.

The second body of studies that challenge the altruism-fairness explanation are those involving discussion. Repeated study shows that permitting communication between the subjects in a prisoner's dilemma situation dramatically increases the level of cooperation; indeed, discussion as much as doubles cooperation rates. Yet "in none of these experiments does group discussion change the fact of defection's dominance"; given the structure of the experiments, there is no reason for any threat or promise to be credible.

To explain this puzzle, researchers varied the conditions of discussion in multi-party prisoner's dilemmas. In one study, the experimenters randomly divided subjects into two groups and placed each group in a separate room. The experimenters permitted ten minutes of discussion in half the groups and no discussion in the others. In addition, half the groups were told that their decisions would affect the payoff for their own group, while the other half were told that their decisions would determine the payoff for the other group and, conversely, that the decisions of the other group would determine the payoff for their group. The results were striking. When subjects believed their decisions would affect the payoffs of members of their own group, discussion increased cooperation from thirty-four percent to sixty-nine percent. But when subjects believed that their decisions affected payoffs for the *other* group, discussion slightly reduced cooperation. The researchers concluded that "discussion does *not* enhance contribution when beneficiaries are strangers." Of course, *all* of these subjects were "strangers" to each other in the sense that they had never met before the experiment and were randomly assigned to the different groups. Yet with ten minutes of discussion about their upcoming decisions, they were, in an important economic sense, no longer strangers. Limited discussion was sufficient to dramatically increase cooperation if and only if the discussants were the beneficiaries of the cooperation.

These findings further demonstrate that altruism and fairness do not fully explain excess cooperation in the prisoner's dilemma. If discussion invoked a general concern for others or for fairness, it should not matter that the beneficiaries are arbitrarily placed in another room. Instead, discussion seems to permit formation of a group identity that creates a special reason for discussants to cooperate. In the transcripts of the subjects' pre-decision discussion, people frequently referred to what "we"—the members of the group—should do. Moreover, where one group knew that its decisions would affect only the other group, there were "frequent statements that the best results would occur if we all keep and they all give to us." The motive seems to fall far short of altruism or fairness. The kind of speech that so effectively increases cooperation tends to be an appeal not to principle, but to solidarity. Thus, successful inspirational rhetoric—like Henry Grady's racist speech—is often centered around repeated invocations of an "us against them" image.

3. *Cooperation Outside the Laboratory: Further Evidence That Groups Matter.*—Although laboratory experiments more easily control for alternative explanations, it is also appropriate to consider two real-world collective action problems: social protest and war. Although law and economics scholars have criticized Title VII, none has attempted to explain why individual blacks participated in the civil rights protests that led to its enactment. Social protests—such as marches, boycotts, and "sit-ins"—are costly to the individual. Although a group may benefit from collective protest, the gains will likely be enjoyed by all members of the group, regardless of whether they participated in the protest. Thus, social movements are rife with collective action problems, which usually prevents such movements from forming or succeeding. Posing this problem, Dennis Chong inquires how the civil rights movement of the 1950s and 1960s succeeded in mobilizing considerable collective action. Given the violence of white resisters, Chong rejects the possibility that material rewards explain the participation, recounting instead the importance of social incentives within small, pre-existing groups such as black churches.

Consider also the high-stakes collective action problems in war. If all soldiers attempt to free-ride on the combat efforts of others, the result is a rout. S.L.A. Marshall argues forcefully that, for the bulk of soldiers, the only thing that stops them from fleeing in the face of fire is the *opinion* of those with whom the soldiers have formed social ties. Marshall's evaluation is based on the fighting effectiveness of "battle stragglers," soldiers separated from their fighting unit who temporarily join an unfamiliar company. He found that individual stragglers had almost no "combat value" in a new unit, while small squads of stragglers "tended to fight as vigorously as any element:"

> Within the group increments the men were still fighting alongside old friends, and though they were now joined to a new parent body, they were under the same compulsion to keep face and share in the common defense. The individual stragglers were simply responding to the first law of nature which began to apply irresistibly the moment they were separated from the company of men whom they knew and who knew them.

Even in the face of death—high stakes indeed—individuals cooperate not merely to secure material rewards, but also to preserve the opinion that group members hold of them. This, of course, is the very dynamic King Henry manipulates in his St. Crispian speech.

B. *Economic Explanations of "Excess" Cooperation: The Production of Inter–Group and Intra–Group Status*

If neither material self-interest nor altruism explains the residuum of cooperation, what can? And why does the level of cooperation vary so significantly with the manner in which individuals are categorized by group? This section proposes an answer: group-based status production. In the experiments discussed above, individuals behave selfishly, not altruistically, but their selfish end is the production of the non-material good of esteem. If individuals seek such non-material ends, members of social groups have another means of solving collective action problems—by allocating esteem to induce members to make contributions to group welfare. Once we add esteem consequences to the material payoffs of individual decisions in such settings, we can explain both the fact and the nature of residual cooperation.

This section argues that human beings seek esteem from others; in aggregate terms, they seek social status. Individuals derive status from groups in two ways: first, individuals gain esteem from strangers based on visible group memberships; and second, within a socially connected group, individuals are especially concerned with the esteem of fellow members. In each case, though for different reasons, status production creates a non-material incentive for group cooperation.

1.   The Individual Preference for Esteem and Status.—If one assumes that individuals behave rationally, the only explanation for the subjects' behavior in the experiments discussed in Part I.A is that the subjects receive benefits from cooperation, or avoid costs from defection, that are not part of the formal, pecuniary payoff structure of the game. One simple way of explaining the cooperation is that the benefit they receive is the esteem of their fellow game-players.

In an earlier article, I described the pervasiveness and power of what I called "negative relative preferences—preferences for approaching or surpassing the consumption level of others." In particular, I offered evidence that people care greatly about achieving a relative social rank or social status. What one gains by attaining 'status,' however, is merely a state of mind—the opinion of others in society—that one is particularly worthy in some way. To understand "excess" cooperation, we should start with precisely this point: that one of the "basic pleasures" people seek in life is the esteem of others.

That people care what others think of them is a parsimonious explanation of many phenomena. The desire for esteem explains, for example, why people are obsessed with the impression their goods make on others. The desire for esteem also underlies the common emotion of embarrassment: individuals feel a momentary but acute pain from loss of esteem at having others observe their missteps or indiscretions. And this desire for esteem helps explain the well-established finding that individuals conform dramatically in the face of a group judgment. Even when there is no material cost to disagreement, individuals appear to fear that dissent will adversely affect how others view them.

Given this behavior, it is not implausible to say that some individuals would cooperate in what is nominally a prisoner's dilemma solely to preserve the minimal esteem strangers (in that community) normally feel for one another. Individuals add the "esteem rewards" and "esteem penalties" to the material payoffs and choose accordingly. Esteem concerns may change the total payoffs enough to make cooperation rational.

2. Members of "Shared–Trait" Groups Cooperate to Produce Inter-Group Status.—To explain the dilemma experiments adequately, an esteem theory must also explain why the level of cooperation varies with "group identity" measures. The concept of "shared-trait groups" explains the existence and variation in the level of cooperation observed in the experiments. By "shared-trait" group, I mean a collection of individuals who have in common some readily observable feature. In American society, people can roughly agree on how to group individuals—for example, by age, by language, or by physical characteristics we refer to as "race." In each case, on the basis of casual observation, one can determine reasonably well whether individuals fall within the category.

Observable traits are important because, when individuals encounter a stranger, they have no other basis for making an esteem judgment. If individuals feel particularly high or low esteem for others with the same trait, they tend to extend that judgment to the stranger. I am not describing irrational prejudice, but a simple application of the economics of information. Given the scarcity of information, it is rational to use cheaper information—proxies—to infer the existence of more expensive, individualized information. The economics literature describes the use of proxies for making decisions of material consequence (such as employment), but proxies can also be used for the allocation of status. Shared-trait group membership is a proxy people use for granting or withholding esteem to individuals they do not know personally.

The use of observable traits as proxies gives individuals a reason to care about the esteem-generating behavior of those with whom they share an observable trait. If an individual shares a trait with others, she expects strangers to extend her the esteem they have for the group that shares the trait. If these third-party observers know only an individual's putative group membership, the individual expects them to judge her entirely on the basis of that membership. She therefore has a selfish concern that the group be highly esteemed in comparison to other groups. Even though the "members" of a group may not know or feel any affinity for each other, third-party categorization gives these members a reason to care about the group's status.

This proxy effect provides a parsimonious explanation of the variation in cooperation observed in the experiments reviewed above: in the laboratory, the experimenter is the third party who categorizes individuals. Any set of subjects the experimenter designates as constituting a group has a "shared trait" for purposes of the experiment. The subjects know that the researcher is observing and evaluating them as members of the group she created. In collective action experiments, the only means of distinguishing successful from unsuccessful groups is the extent to which the group cooperates and achieves the best collective result. Subjects in such experiments may earn additional benefits for cooperating or face additional costs for defecting—thus, esteem consequences may make cooperation a rational strategy.

Further, in the prisoner's dilemma studies, individuals playing the game against individuals cooperated at higher levels than teams playing the same game against teams. With team-play, individuals expect that the esteem they receive depends on the success of the arbitrarily created groups to which they belong. The proxy effect works to raise the payoff of defecting when the other team cooperates (the one way of "beating" the other team) and to lower the payoff of cooperating when the other team defects (thereby "losing"). With individual play, however, either there is no cognizable "group," or the group contains both of the subjects in the game. Thus any proxy effect works toward cooperation. If subjects understand that the experimenter will have other pairs play the game, they may imagine themselves being evaluated as a pair against other pairs, which raises the payoff of mutual cooperation (the best "pair" outcome) and lowers the payoff of mutual defection (the worst "pair" outcome).

To the experiments previously reviewed, we may now add studies on relative deprivation as a cause of social protest. Relative deprivation refers to the fact that individuals react strongly to deprivation when others have what they lack. "Psychologists hypothesize that a central component of people's angry feelings over deprivation is a comparison between themselves and others who have the desired thing." Numerous studies have demonstrated the importance of comparison with others to feelings of relative deprivation and to behavior motivated by such feelings. Most important, many of these studies find that attitudes about inter-group comparisons predict participation in social protest, whereas attitudes about interpersonal comparisons do not. People are more likely to protest when they feel that the group to which they belong is relatively deprived than when they simply feel that they as individuals are relatively deprived.

In sum, laboratory experiments show that, even when the group is an entirely arbitrary construct, individuals seek to acquire esteem from "non-group" members by raising the status of what, in the eyes of those non-group members, is the individuals' group. Outside the laboratory, concern with how one's shared-trait group is regarded also motivates significant action.

3. Members of "Socially Connected" Groups Cooperate to Produce Intra–Group Status.—A second, more conventional understanding of the group posits that the members are, in some manner, socially connected. These socially connected groups are comprised of people who know each other, the paradigm cases being families, networks of friends, or social clubs. Such groups have two noteworthy features, each of which contributes to the group's ability to overcome collective action problems: individuals tend to care especially about the esteem of their fellow group members, and individuals tend to grant esteem to members who contribute to group welfare.

The first feature of socially connected groups is that individuals tend to value the esteem of fellow group members more than they value the esteem of non-members. If we care what others think of us, we care more intensely the more well-informed an opinion is; those with whom we have frequent interaction—group members—know us best. Moreover, the dilemma experiments in which the simple act of discussion generated greater cooperation among discussants indicate that even minimal social connection can significantly increase the concern for the esteem of another. In addition, the very reason many social groups exist is that the members share some skill, trait, or interest; members tend to value the esteem of in-group members more than outsiders because members share a sense of what skills or traits are worth possessing. Finally, there is a self-reinforcing aspect to the concern for intra-group status: we tend to value most the opinion of those we esteem highly, and we prefer to belong to social groups including such people.

Given the especially high concern for esteem from socially connected group members, we can better understand high-stakes cooperation in the collective action problems presented by social protest and war. Military and social protest groups elicit cooperation by rewarding members with esteem or prestige based on how much they contribute to the group's welfare. Yet even if people *seek* intra-group esteem, the question remains why individual group members *provide* intra-group esteem to those who contribute to group welfare. The second noteworthy feature of socially connected groups is that members readily provide esteem to those who benefit the group; even without a central authority, members tend not to free-ride completely on the "esteem payments" of other members.

People provide esteem to members who benefit the group because, up to a point, thinking well of others is not a cost. To the contrary, esteeming others is a valuable "consumption good." A person deprived of this good— who finds no one in the world worth esteeming—is far less happy than one who has located a small collection of worthy souls. Nor is an individual who esteems twenty others necessarily poorer than someone who esteems only ten others to the same degree. To the extent that esteem is not costly, there is no reason to free-ride by withholding esteem from others. Instead, group members tend to allocate esteem in a way that brings them some return by rewarding those who contribute materially to group welfare and, at a secondary level, by rewarding those who allocate esteem in a manner that benefits the group. Imagine, as an analogy, that people have a kind of currency that is useless except for making group members feel better. It would be irrational to keep the currency or to distribute it randomly; one might as well provide it as a reward for those who contribute to group welfare and withhold it to punish those who do not.

Departing briefly from an economic description of human behavior, I can state the point in more realistic psychological terms. "Thinking well of others" is often reflexive rather than deliberate. People who might free-ride on material payments tend not to free-ride on esteem "payments" because they reflexively admire and respect those who benefit the group. Imagine, for example, a chessmaster, a person who not only intensely studies the game, but also socializes predominantly with others who do the same. Taking egoism seriously means that this person will consider chess-playing ability to be an important measure by which others can be judged. Individuals elevate the importance of those traits or skills that they possess. This process helps the individual secure self-esteem. But a consequence of thinking that a particular trait is desirable is to esteem *others* who possess the trait and to esteem them in relation to how much of the trait they possess. It is neither plausible nor coherent for the chessmaster to withhold esteem from other people who excel in chess. Barring an overshadowing negative trait, an individual will more or less *automatically* esteem others who have the traits the individual most values in herself, or the traits the individual would most like to acquire for herself.

Frequently, people reflexively esteem traits or behaviors that increase the welfare of the group. A player's success at chess tournaments raises the prestige of the chess club to which she belongs and earns her esteem within the club. A soldier whose skill or effort saves the lives of his fellow squad members earns their esteem. Moreover, if one who is known to value a particular trait withholds esteem from those who possess it, she risks appearing envious and losing the esteem of others. Especially within a group of people who desire a particular trait, refusing to esteem the trait (or at least to appear to esteem it) calls into question the dissenter's commitment to or understanding of shared values. Of course, some members may nonetheless be envious and refuse to provide esteem. But since esteem is at least partially reflexive, there is less than complete free-riding in allocating esteem, and the group can achieve a significant level of coordination.

Sociological evidence supports the theory that socially connected groups allocate esteem to overcome collective action problems. Socially connected groups, as I have defined them, consist of relatively small numbers of people who know each other. Sociologists have long been interested in how, within larger groups in society, "norms" arise as an important decentralized mechanism of social control. Esteem allocation, it turns out, provides the necessary micro-level explanation for social norms; the functioning of social norms, in turn, demonstrates the full power of intra-group cooperation.

Although economically inclined theorists have mostly ignored norms, one important exception is Robert Ellickson. *In Order Without Law*, Ellickson summarizes and supplements the empirical literature on the success of norms in regulating individual behavior. Ellickson's empirical contribution is his study of norms that govern the resolution of various disputes over livestock between neighbors in Shasta County, California. Like other social norms that arise within "close-knit groups," the Shasta County norms are a means of enhancing group welfare. The norms are a non-legal means by which the group facilitates desirable collective action. To some degree, what Ellickson and others identify as efficient norms are enforced by reciprocity between neighbors who expect to interact indefinitely, and the norms are therefore explicable in material terms. But the unique contribution norms make to cooperation—the additional power of norms beyond reciprocity—is third-party enforcement. What Ellickson has in mind are sanctions administered not by the immediate "victim" of a norm violation, but by "friends, relatives, gossips, vigilantes, and other nonhierarchical third-party enforcers." Third parties sanction—by gossip, scorn, ostracism, or physical retaliation—those who violate the norms or informal rules of the group.

My point, however, is that this informal third-party enforcement cannot exist without the desire for esteem. There is no material incentive to obey norms unless there is a material cost attached to violating them. There is no material cost associated with violation unless someone imposes a material penalty. And there is no material incentive for others to bear the cost of inflicting such a penalty; after all, norm-enforcement is, for the group, a public good, and like all public goods, faces the problem of free-riding. Ellickson says that there is a secondary enforcement norm that compels people to punish those who violate norms and that those who fail to do so will also be sanctioned. But then the question arises why anyone would bear the cost of sanctioning those who failed to sanction a substantive norm violator. As Jon Elster argues, "People do not frown upon others when they fail to sanction people who fail to sanction people who fail to sanction people who fail to sanction a norm violation." As one moves away from the original norm violation, "the cost of receiving disapproval falls rapidly to zero." Yet if the cost of refusing to enforce a norm at any level falls to zero, there is no reason for anyone to enforce the norm, and hence no reason for anyone to follow the norm.

A concern for esteem as an end in itself, however, is sufficient to defend norm enforcement against the infinite regress Elster describes. Elster's argument assumes that mechanisms like gossip, scorn, and ostracism work only to signal who is to be subject to material sanctions and are only as effective as those material sanctions. But if disapproval *itself* exerts a real force, then the gossip, scorn, and ostracism are themselves sufficient to enforce norms; they punish the violator by lowering the esteem she receives from the community. In addition to this direct support, the desire for esteem may produce a secondary enforcement norm that requires material sanctions for violators of the primary norm. To avoid esteem punishment, individuals may have to bear some cost incurred by imposing material sanctions on norm violators. Thus, the considerable body of evidence that shows that social norms govern behavior further supports the significance of esteem motives, especially within socially connected groups.

In sum, individuals care particularly for esteem within socially connected groups. Even without a central authority, individuals tend to provide esteem to those who contribute to the welfare of such groups, and this process of esteem allocation facilitates wider social norms that bring about further cooperation. Of course, group members will still free-ride when their desire for material well-being outweighs their desire for intra-group status, but esteem allocation will ameliorate, if not eliminate, collective action problems.

C. The Consequences of Intra–Group Cooperation: Inter–Group Conflict

Intra-group cooperation increases inter-group conflict. Status is both an additional *means* of ensuring intra-group cooperation and a new *end* of intra-group cooperation, and it contributes in both ways to conflict between groups. Given that social groups often conflict over material resources, the desire for intra-group status means that group members will cooperate more effectively in such disputes, which ensures that groups will be more effective 'combatants' whenever material conflict arises. More important, the very mechanism that facilitates greater intra-group cooperation will ensure a new form of conflict: competition for *inter-group* status. This latter result is the unfortunate and inevitable connection between cooperation and conflict.

Groups sometimes engage in zero-sum competition with other groups. A classic example is lobbying. When interest groups pursue what economists call "rent-seeking" legislation, such as farm subsidies and tax "loopholes," they seek merely to transfer resources from one group to another. Cartels similarly seek to extract the profits of non-competitive pricing from consumers. For lobbying groups and cartels, individual contributions to the group's rent-seeking endeavor tend to be undersupplied; selfish members free-ride on the efforts of other members. But the cooperation secured by intra-group status production means that individuals contribute more heavily than they otherwise would toward their group's effort to win a conflict.

Indeed, intra-group esteem production, and social norms based on such esteem, may provide the only explanations for the success of very large groups in lobbying despite powerful incentives for individuals to free-ride. Judge Richard Posner has conceded some uncertainty, for example, in explaining how farmers cooperate in legislative activities. I propose that the answer is the same for farmers as it is for the ranchers Ellickson studied in Shasta County. Although the occupational status of farmers or ranchers is not as observable as, for example, their race, it is one of the first things strangers detect about them. And within a geographic area, farmers and ranchers tend to be socially connected. Thus, farmers and ranchers have an interest in the status generally accorded their occupation and a means of inducing contributions to that status. Intra-group esteem allocation elicits material contributions to group material welfare, such as monetary contributions to lobbying efforts. For individual farmers and ranchers, the amount contributed may be small, but multiplication by a large number produces considerable political clout.

There is a second reason intra-group esteem allocation increases group conflict. Individuals compete for esteem. One arena of competition is *group status competition*, in which individuals seek to produce status for themselves by raising the status of their groups. Under certain conditions, status is zero-sum, so that satisfaction of the status preferences of one group's members necessarily means non-satisfaction of the status preferences of another group's members.

In another article, I detailed the conditions under which relative preferences "inherently" conflict—that is, the circumstances under which the relative position is genuinely zero-sum. Although I focused there primarily on individual status-seeking, those conditions exist for social groups when members of different groups seek incompatible positions for their groups along some common, observable, and reasonably objective dimension. When these conditions do not hold, group status production is socially benign. But the conditions do hold, for example, when groups compare themselves along the "common dimension" of generalized social status and seek a position of superiority on that scale. Under such circumstances, social status is entirely relative. Investment in such zero-sum competition is therefore socially wasteful; the extent of the investment measures the size of the inefficiency. In particular, note the social waste of an obvious group optimizing strategy: *one way to raise the status of one's group is to invest in lowering the status of other groups.* Thus, the desire for esteem may lead to "subordination" as groups attempt to sabotage each other's general social position.

The status theory of cooperation and conflict may now be summarized. First, individuals seek, as an end, the esteem of others; in aggregate terms, they seek social status. Second, because socially connected group members are a key source of esteem, individuals will make material sacrifices on behalf of the group to gain intra-group status. Conversely, the group will reward such status to those who contribute to its welfare. Third, because another source of status is the larger society beyond one's social groups, one measure of group welfare is its status within society. Consequently, groups will use intra-group status "payments" to encourage members to contribute materially to inter-group status. Finally, because general social status is relative, one group can raise its inter-group status by lowering the status of other groups.

* * *

The novelty of these otherwise non-instrumental beliefs is that the normal economic correctives to false belief formation do not apply. For expressive purposes, a "good" belief is not necessarily an accurate belief, but rather one that is pleasurable to express. Of course, even if a category of beliefs serves only expressive ends, there are some constraints on belief formation. Our cognitive mechanisms may make it difficult for us to believe certain things that are manifestly contradicted by experience. Moreover, we may not experience the full pleasure of expressing our beliefs if others find them palpably false in an uninteresting way.

Most important for our purposes, however, is the constraint of self-esteem. Some beliefs are more pleasant than others. For expressive purposes, people are more likely to adopt beliefs that enhance, rather than degrade, their self-esteem. If the issue is the talent of a celebrity, for example, a person is more likely to think highly of the celebrity if, through some connection—having attended the same school, for example—the celebrity's talent will enhance the individual's self-esteem. If esteem can influence expressive belief formation in this manner, esteem can also affect conventionally instrumental beliefs—beliefs concerning how best to satisfy one's preferences. As long as the gain in esteem from the bias toward esteem-producing beliefs is larger than any instrumental loss from the bias, then such a bias serves the individual's overall interests. There is considerable evidence to support this claim: research shows, for example, that people tend systematically to overevaluate their own performance and characteristics. Such a bias may even be essential to mental well-being. Self-evaluation is clearly an instrumental belief—one needs to know what one's talents and abilities are—yet the need for self-esteem is sufficient to create some deviation from strictly impartial beliefs about oneself.

If esteem production favorably biases one's self-evaluations, esteem production may also cause a positive bias toward the social groups to which one belongs. One may gain pleasure from believing positive things about one's groups. Moreover, groups will reward status to those who hold beliefs that are conducive to group welfare. A favorable bias regarding group members may strengthen intra-group cooperation by increasing the apparent material advantage available from transacting with members rather than non-members.

But groups may encourage and reward beliefs more complex than simple bias. For example, although he does not explain how belief distortion occurs, Richard Posner has invoked such distortion to explain how certain cartels solve collective action problems. According to Posner, the distinguishing feature of certain successful cartels—which he terms "guilds"—is their having an "ideology." A guild is a social as well as an economic institution in which members have adopted a common "personal morality" of loyalty, conformity, and craftsmanship, and which has achieved a certain "mystique" involving the idealization of quality over quantity. The "mutually reinforcing combination" of this morality and mystique comprises "the *ideology* of guild production," which serves the "the self-interest of producers in the cartelization of production."

Posner appears to mean that guild members convince themselves that the public interest is served by the restrictions on market entry and production necessary to cartelize an industry. This analysis implies that a principled concern for the public good has some force in motivating behavior, so that cartel members would be even more likely to free-ride if they realized that cartel pricing is contrary to the public interest. Ideology, however, turns the moral force against free-riding. An ideological commitment to quality allows the guild member to believe that conduct that would undermine the cartel—lowering quality and expanding output—would harm the public. Self-interested self-deception thus serves the cartel's long run interests by curbing the individual's impulse to free-ride on the restraint of others.

Return now to racial beliefs. In Posner's terms, negative stereotypes are part of a racial "guild's" efforts to monopolize production of esteem. Even for beliefs that serve an instrumental purpose (such as evaluating potential employees), the desire for esteem will cause an individual to adopt distorted beliefs about racial groups as long as the esteem benefit exceeds the instrumental cost. Consequently, the status-production model can explain differences in voting behavior between blacks and whites. A person may gain esteem by believing positive things about political candidates from her own group and, at least in a relative sense, negative things about politicians of other races. If people do not vote for instrumental reasons, there is no instrumental check on the accuracy of these beliefs. A small bias may suffice to explain a significant difference in voting behavior because, for different racial groups, the bias works in opposite directions.

If one assumes that this analysis correctly explains the existence and direction of racial bias, the question remains how to explain the *evolution* of white attitudes regarding race. Recall that status production commonly involves the denial that one's motive is status production. When one seeks to gain status by lowering the status of others, it is all the more important to deny that one is degrading others in order to look better by comparison. Consequently, "guild ideology" never acknowledges its self-serving nature. Members of Posner's representative guild do not openly declare, even among themselves, that they desire to restrain competition in order to charge higher prices and earn monopoly profits. Similarly, whites never explain their discriminatory behavior as serving the function of status production. Even in the Jim Crow South, whites attempted to justify segregation not by reference to naked self-interest but by claims that blacks were inherently inferior, that blacks preferred segregation, or that segregation somehow reflected the natural order of things. Toward this end, the Jim Crow doctrine of "separate but equal" was ideal. Separation was a means of expressing contempt; the pretense of equality served to deny the status motivation.

When proponents of a status-driven ideology can no longer confidently deny the status motivation of their beliefs, the ideology fails and proponents must search for another ideology. This insight may explain the evolution of white attitudes toward segregation. Although the exact causal strands are difficult to disentangle, events leading up to and including the modern civil rights movement undermined the ability of whites to believe that their existing racial beliefs were anything other than a self-serving ideology. World War II provided one ideological shock, as revulsion to Nazi claims of racial superiority was difficult to square with rationalization of southern racial practices. Rising levels of black education and job skills put a material strain on racial ideology by raising the attractiveness of black labor and thus the cost of absolute racial exclusion. I suspect the most immediate cause of ideological breakdown occurred during the civil rights movement, when photographs captured segregation extremists using violent means, often against women and children, to suppress peaceful protests. Violence against peaceful demonstrators was, even for some southern supporters of Jim Crow, irrefutable evidence that whites were not (at least morally) superior, that blacks were indisputably unhappy with segregation, and that segregation was not a naturally ordained moral order. One of the constraints I have suggested for non-instrumental beliefs is "palpable falsity"; the events of the 1950s and 1960s made salient to whites the falsity of the belief that intentional racial segregation is something other than selfishly hurtful.

Whatever the causal mechanism, many whites have come genuinely to believe that segregation is wrong. This shift does not mean, however, that a psychological veil of prejudice has simply been lifted from their eyes. The expressive beliefs whites adopt about race can no longer be of the crude form needed to justify segregation, but the quest for the production of status continues. Having abandoned the older ideology, whites still tend to oppose policies and candidates that would increase the social status of blacks. Whites can give up old, extreme stereotypes and still embrace negative views of blacks. Unless one consciously scrutinizes the statistical validity of one's generalizations about other groups—an unlikely scenario— even false stereotypes will rarely be *palpably* false. Thus, one may acknowledge the good faith and intellectual integrity of conservative arguments on political issues concerning race—like busing, affirmative action, and welfare—and still worry that the same status-maximizing bias that first rationalized slavery and then segregation infects much of the public thinking on these matters. It is more pleasant to believe that one lives in a society in which everyone (or at least everyone else) is being treated as well as she deserves, that past transgressions have been righted, and that fairness and justice require no further sacrifice. The evolution of white attitudes, therefore, reflects an ideological adjustment to status production under changed circumstances. The final descriptive virtue of the status-production theory is that it offers some insight into this otherwise puzzling evolution of white attitudes.

C.   Implications of the Status Production Model of Discrimination

The associational model of discrimination has two key implications: market competition will erode discrimination and, partly for that reason, prohibiting race discrimination is inefficient. The status-production model leads to different conclusions on both points.

1.   *The Persistence of Race Discrimination.*—Becker drew an analogy between race discrimination and transportation costs, both of which increase the cost of certain trades. It is uncontroversial that, other things being equal, those who can minimize transportation costs achieve a competitive advantage over those who cannot. If the analogy with discrimination is sound, we should also expect that whites with less intense tastes for discrimination will enjoy a competitive advantage over those with more intense tastes and will tend to dominate a competitive market.

Under the status-production model, discrimination is not the result of costs that discriminators incur from contact with members of other groups, but is a means of producing status. The discriminator does bear a cost in discriminating—forgoing otherwise beneficial trade with the objects of the discrimination—but that cost is an *investment* in the production of status. As long as such investments are cost-effective for the discriminator, the status-production model predicts that race discrimination will persist in the face of market competition. Consequently, the transportation analogy is inapt. Discrimination may exist in a competitive equilibrium for at least three reasons: the power of discriminatory social norms; the existence of reciprocity between whites; and, under certain circumstances, the effect of esteem-producing racial biases. I will examine each of these in turn.

(a) *The Stability of Discriminatory Norms.*—This section presents a theory of discriminatory social norms. I begin with George Akerlof's economic theory of a racial caste system. I then raise and respond to two key objections to Akerlof's theory—that it does not explain why anyone enforces the caste-based norms, and that it does not capture the complexities of modern American society. I conclude that, despite market competition, status production can support a stable system of discriminatory norms.

Akerlof has provided an explanation for the resiliency of the discriminatory customs of a caste society. It is the essence of a caste-system, Akerlof says, that "any transaction that breaks the caste taboos changes the subsequent behavior of uninvolved parties" who may act to punish the caste-breaker. Third party reactions change the calculus for those who have not internalized the norm:

> Those who fail to follow, or even to enforce the caste customs do not gain the profits of the successful arbitrageur but instead suffer the stigma of the outcaste. If the punishment of becoming an outcaste is predicted to be sufficiently severe, the system of caste is held in equilibrium irrespective of individual tastes, by economic incentives; the predictions of the caste system become a self-fulfilling prophecy.

Thus, Akerlof applies to race discrimination the same view of social norm enforcement that Ellickson has applied to property law—because people boycott norm breakers, it often pays to follow norms.

This insight would be trivial, however, if it only applied when *everyone* in society was willing to boycott those who break the caste rules. Surely a few individuals will always be willing to deal with social outcasts (such as other social outcasts or near outcasts). One could argue that, as long as the number of people willing to violate the discriminatory norms exceeds the number of people targeted by the norm, violators need suffer no harm. Further, one might predict that if a few people violate the norm intially, their violation will weaken the norm and induce other violations to follow, eventually leading to the norm's complete unraveling.

Akerlof responds to these arguments with a simple point that depends merely on the existence of transaction costs. Suppose there are search costs for firms seeking buyers or sellers; because of imperfect information about the existence and reputation of buyers and sellers, firms cannot instantly replace existing trading partners but must incur costs inversely proportional to the number of potential trading partners in the relevant geographic market. Under these circumstances, assuming that there are any parties who will boycott "innovators" (those who violate discriminatory norms), the innovators necessarily incur higher search costs in finding trading partners. Thus, each boycotter raises the likely search costs the innovator will incur before locating a trading partner. Further, when the innovator locates a non-boycotter, its higher search costs will place it "in a weaker bargaining position, since the cost of failing to make a trade is greater to [it] than to noninnovators." If the costs of innovation are higher than the benefits, the discriminatory norm will be stable in a competitive market.

There are, however, weaknesses in Akerlof's explanation. First, Akerlof simply posits that some discriminators will boycott those who fail to follow the discriminatory norm. He offers no explanation of why these boycotters are willing to bear such costs. The status-production model does offer such an explanation. The model shows how individuals gain from adhering to and enforcing certain norms, why the kind of norms individuals benefit from enforcing include norms of discrimination, and why the groups for which this process is frequently employed are racial groups. As I argued above, individuals within racial groups benefit from raising the status of their shared traits. One means of contributing to one's racial status is by subordinating members of other races. With sufficient overlap between racial and socially connected groups, whites have a status benefit to exploit and the cooperative means to exploit it.

Consider, however, a second possible weakness in Akerlof's model. A simple caste society is an appropriate starting point, but American society is more complex. Unquestionably, a norm exists against racial discrimination (or at least against certain forms of racial discrimination), and some whites, as well as blacks, boycott those who overtly discriminate. Given this reality, one might reject the Akerlof caste model.

Yet, even with blacks and some whites "counter-boycotting" discriminators, the equilibrium may entail significant discrimination. Discriminators will bear a cost when targeted for a counter-boycott (or other sanction), but unless that cost exceeds the cost that discriminators create for non-discriminators, it will pay to continue discriminating. The relative costs depend largely on the relative size and economic power of the two groups. Because whites constitute a large majority and possess disproportionate wealth, the costs from white boycotts is likely to exceed the costs from black counter-boycotts. At some point, the participation by a sufficient number of whites in the counter-boycott would tip the balance the other way, but this outcome seems unlikely. First, one cannot infer from the fact that opponents of discrimination are more vocal today—when discrimination in various forms is illegal—that white opponents of discrimination exceed supporters. Second, those who rely on the power of white counter-boycotts rely on the force of moral principle (or altruism) to overcome the selfish force of status production. Under existing theory, selfishness is thought to undermine discrimination. But given the status productivity of discrimination, the power of selfishness suggests the more pessimistic outcome.

One might object that discriminatory norms do not exist if any whites are willing to act against them. That some whites will boycott discriminators merely reflects, however, the fact that American whites do not constitute a single group. "Whites" include various ethnic, religious, political, regional, and class subgroups. How much a particular subgroup invests in subordination as a means of producing status will depend on what its various status options are. Low-status whites have fewer options and tend to discriminate more than high-status whites. Further, white condemnation of the blatant racial discrimination common in an earlier era is consistent with a more subtle discriminatory norm. Subordination works only as long as one can deny that one is acting for the purpose of producing status. Whites are less able to deny this function of racial derogation now than in the past; consequently, overt discrimination is no longer as productive of status as it once was. Just as a "nouveau riche" may undermine her own status by engaging in ostentatious and wasteful consumption, a "redneck" or bigot undermines her own status by expressing contempt solely on the basis of race. But, there is still status in wealth if one displays it more deftly, with the appearance of not calculating to make a display. Likewise, there is status to be gained from race discrimination of a more subtle form, especially when one can plausibly deplore its more flagrant manifestations.

One might nevertheless assert that there are significant numbers of whites who oppose even subtle forms of discrimination. One interpretation of this behavior is that high-status whites who condemn low-status whites for their discrimination may gain more by distinguishing themselves from other whites than by investing in the subordination of blacks or other minorities. In fact, certain classes of whites may enjoy free-riding on the status that other whites secure and then further increase their status by subordinating those whites for being discriminatory. A second, more sanguine interpretation begins with Ellickson's claim that norms tend to be efficient, at least from the perspective of the group in which they arise. Ellickson does not discuss norms that span a group as large as an entire society, but a weaker concern for the esteem of strangers might give rise to norms between strangers. If a weak counter-norm arises against discrimination, perhaps it is because discrimination is inefficient from the perspective of the entire society. But because the norm arises at a different and more diffuse level, it can exist alongside more powerful discriminatory norms that arise within or between socially connected groups.

Becker's model does not contemplate the existence of discriminatory social norms. Thus, I cannot be certain how he would respond to the claim I make here. But Robert Cooter, who embraces Becker's prediction that competition will drive out discrimination, does consider social norms. Cooter argues that the proper economic model for discrimination is that of a cartel and that during the Jim Crow era, southern whites advanced their material ends by using law to gain monopoly power in various markets. Like all cartels, whites faced the inherent problem of instability—that is, the incentive for each member to cheat. Cooter agrees that discriminatory social norms countered the incentives to free-ride, but asserts that the effectiveness of the norms probably depended on their being supported by Jim Crow legislation. Thus, Cooter expresses the conventional economic skepticism that the norms that supported the white "cartel" could survive absent such legal restrictions. The material incentives in an unfettered market, in his view, provide a strong lure for individuals to defect from the group enterprise.

The theory of intra-group cooperation and inter-group conflict offers a reason for thinking otherwise. Cooter's skepticism about the independent strength of social norms would be well-founded if the only ends that individuals seek are material. Indeed, I argued previously that social norms add nothing to our understanding of cooperation beyond what can be explained by reciprocity unless people value the esteem of others as an end in itself. Therefore Cooter's argument might be right if the only purpose of the white cartel were to advance the material ends of whites and the only means of inducing cooperation were material rewards. The whole thrust of the status-production model, however, is that the cartel-like behavior of whites serves to maximize the non-material end of status production (the cartel seeks to monopolize social status) and that the cartel employs the non-material means of intra-group status rewards and punishments. If this fundamental point is right, then social norms can support discrimination notwithstanding market competition.

Nevertheless, Cooter's basic insight is quite helpful. Whites do act like a cartel. But whites are more accurately described as the subset of cartels that Posner calls "guilds," that is, cartels with "social cohesiveness." Based on a morality emphasizing loyalty and conformity, these guilds have an "ideology"—a set of beliefs that serves to inhibit free-riding—specifically that blacks tend to be inferior, that whites should not interact with blacks in certain ways, and that whites must "stick together." Posner contends that farmers and lawyers—very large industrial groups—manage to cooperate in legislative lobbying efforts despite incentives to free-ride. Racial groups may similarly succeed. For reasons explained above, the more observable the trait that links a group of people, the more status members have to gain by cooperating and the greater the reason to expect such groups to become socially connected as a means of achieving cooperation. Given that race is more observable than these industrial affinities, there is reason to believe racial groups can better succeed in overcoming their collective action problems despite their large size.

Consider, then, a new economic analogy for race discrimination: not transportation costs, but an analogy to the acquisition of a public reputation. An entrepreneur donates a large sum of money to a local museum, or a corporate president agrees to sponsor a marathon. No doubt, the economically inclined theorist would assert that such behavior occurs not because it serves an individual's "taste" for fame, but because it produces greater profits for entrepreneurs and firms by bolstering their reputation or name recognition. I suspect the main force behind this view, however, is nothing as contingent as empirical data on the profitability of such donations, but an inference that economic actors would not give money away unless it was productive to do so. I merely argue for a similar inference with respect to race discrimination. Discrimination exists because it is productive for its practitioners.

(b) Reciprocity as a Basis for Market Discrimination.—There is a second reason to believe that race discrimination will persist in the face of market competition. Becker's theory does not argue that market competition erodes social discrimination. Yet because social interaction facilitates more commercial reciprocity, social discrimination may cause persistent "market" discrimination.

According to Axelrod's analysis of iterated prisoner's dilemmas, it often pays to seek cooperation through a reciprocal strategy such as tit-for-tat when there is sufficient likelihood of future interaction with another. Axelrod emphasizes that the more likely future interactions are, the more likely it is that those who employ reciprocal strategies will prosper. Thus, to increase the prospects of cooperation with a particular individual, Axelrod advises (consciously) increasing the durability and frequency of interactions with that individual. One time-honored means of implementing Axelrod's strategy is to pursue social interaction with the group of individuals with whom one wishes to cooperate. When prospective business partners eat, talk, or play together, they are not merely acquiring information about each other. Social interaction also supports reciprocity; by joining a social group, one increases the likelihood of future interaction with members of the group. Most important, social interactions may themselves be relatively inexpensive but might increase the chance of cooperation's emerging in a business or market setting, where the benefits of cooperation are greater. Joining a country club, a "businessman's" club, or a particular neighborhood may "lock" one into a particular social group, raising one's ability to cooperate with members in non-social settings.

We can now understand more fully the power of discriminatory norms. Even in the absence of a social norm that restrains market trading with other racial groups, social norms could significantly impede such trades. A norm limited to preventing social contacts with members of another race is sufficient to harm such members economically. Since social contacts affect the probability of reciprocity, the absence of such contacts places the isolated individual or the disfavored group at a comparative disadvantage in economic trades. Consequently, norm-based discrimination in one setting, such as social clubs or housing, may cause discrimination in other settings, such as business or employment. Social clubs that exclude women and minorities thus cause them more harm than simply denying them information about, and the chance to become known to, market players. They deny them the opportunity to make reciprocity work.

(c) The Power of Esteem–Producing Racial Biases.—A final factor that contributes to the persistence of discrimination is racially biased beliefs or stereotypes. As noted above, discriminatory norms invoke rationalization mechanisms; discriminators prefer to have reasons for discriminating other than a bare interest in status production. Indeed, because status production is inconsistent with an overt strategy of subordination, it is important that discriminators have an explanation—an "ideology"—apart from status production. Such an explanation can most easily take the form of negative stereotypes—that the failure of blacks to succeed is their own fault, due to their own shortcomings in ability, integrity, or dependability. This ideology buttresses discriminatory norms. Whatever the social cost of violating the norm, biased evaluations of blacks make it appear that the material benefits of norm violation are less than they are. Self-deception prevents cheating that would undermine the cartel.

Indeed, even if there were no discriminatory social norms, ideologically based racial stereotypes might sustain a stable level of discrimination. One might argue, to the contrary, that absent norms, market competition would discipline whites whose evaluations of blacks were biased. If some white employers fail to perceive black workers accurately, for example, they will lose a competitive advantage to more discerning whites. Yet there is one condition under which stereotypes alone will sustain discrimination—when the material costs of one's miscalculation is zero. In the employment setting, for example, the employer may believe in some cases that the applicants are essentially "tied," that is, they appear to have equal marginal productivities. A white employer would suffer no harm from the decision to hire a white applicant who was tied with a black applicant. Of course, given the white employer's ideology, the employer may not actually perceive the two candidates as being equal, but rather will think that the white candidate is better. The point, however, is that there will be no market correction for such a perception; having white job applicants win all "ties" is a market equilibrium. The question remains how frequently such ties occur in the real world—an interesting empirical question that I, like opponents of Title VII, leave to be answered by others. I simply note that, if such ties were frequent, stereotyping could itself add to the persistence of race discrimination.

In sum, the status-production model provides three reasons to suppose that race discrimination will survive market competition: the power of discriminatory social norms; the existence of reciprocity between whites; and, under certain circumstances, the effect of esteem-producing racial biases.

2.   The Efficiency of Anti–Discrimination Laws.—Many legal economists have contended that federal anti-discrimination laws are efficient only to the extent that they nullify state laws mandating discrimination. These theorists view such laws as inefficient when they prohibit private discrimination because their only function is to frustrate discriminatory preferences. But the new descriptive theory I propose requires a rethinking of this normative claim. The status-production model views anti-discrimination laws as potentially correcting a market failure in which individuals invest in essentially confiscatory behavior. That discrimination is a market failure would not itself prove that government action is desirable. We must consider whether the regulation can correct the failure and whether the benefits of such intervention exceed the costs.

(a) Discrimination as Market Failure: The Theft Analogy.—Welfare economics provides a justification for laws that prohibit theft (and other forms of force and fraud) that is not dependent on discounting the gains to the thief (or other criminals). Even assuming that the transfer accomplished by theft itself causes no wealth loss, because the thief gains what the owner loses, a system that permits theft "results in a very substantial diversion of resources to fields where they essentially offset each other, and produce no positive product." In other words, absent laws against theft, individuals must expend resources merely to protect their property from

seizure. They will also forgo certain wealth-creating activities to protect what they already have and because it may be too costly to protect some forms of wealth from theft. In response, the thief invests in gaining tools and knowledge to circumvent anti-theft practices and technology. These dynamic reactions to the risk of theft result in deadweight losses to society. Less is produced, and part of what is produced (burglar alarms and burglars' tools) provides no greater satisfaction of an individual's preferences, but merely helps the individual to retain or confiscate goods that will satisfy preferences. The net effect is to decrease wealth. The same argument applies for laws against violence. It is, of course, Thomas Hobbes's justification for the state: that the only alternative, the "warre . . . of every man, against every man," is worse.

It follows from the status-production model that a society without discrimination laws permits an unfettered status war of "every group against every group." What is striking about Richard Epstein's *Forbidden Grounds*, which argues for the repeal of laws that prohibit employment discrimination, is not so much his controversial claim that the only role of government is to prevent force or fraud, but that he never considers how laws against race discrimination may fall precisely within this libertarian principle. Status "warfare" may not be as violent as literal combat, but the term is more than just a metaphor. Hobbes identifies competition for honor as one of the three causes of war; he warns that violent conflict results from attempted subordination. Similarly, Hume warned of the tendency of factions to produce "the fiercest animosities." Competition for group status has generated much of America's history of interracial violence, as when whites lynched blacks to preserve their social position or when blacks retaliated against repeated acts of derogation and dishonor.

Of course, laws prohibit such violence. But even with such laws, unregulated status competition mirrors the inefficiency of a regime without laws prohibiting theft. First, racial status preferences inherently conflict. Race discrimination exists because members of (at least) one race seek for their group a status position that is incompatible with the position sought by members of one or more other groups. Even when only one group seeks superiority, if the other group seeks equality, the struggle for social status is zero sum. Consequently, the appropriation of status by subordinating behavior is, like theft, a mere wealth transfer; the gain to the discriminator is at least matched by the loss to the victim. Second, this form of transfer—using discrimination as a mechanism of subordination—generates extremely high costs. By definition, the discriminator makes a material sacrifice (giving up an otherwise favorable trade or engaging in costly behavior) as a means of lowering the status of the victim. The size of the material sacrifice measures the investment that the discriminator makes in status appropriation. This investment determines the initial cost of the process of racial group status production.

But that is not the whole story. As I noted at the outset of this Part, economic analysis of discrimination strikes many non-economists as barren because it fails to acknowledge the full benefit to its practitioners or the full harm to its victims. The status-production model takes as its central premise that whites gain status by discriminating against blacks. To determine the full extent of the investment in, and therefore the costs of, status competition, we must consider the full range of status defense mechanisms employed by victims of discrimination. Such defense mechanisms include the sometimes desperate reactions of those who live as targets of discrimination. These reactions represent further investment in status production and increase the wastefulness of the unregulated process, much like added investment in theft-protection devices constitute waste in a society without theft laws. Of course, the psychological mechanisms at work are vastly more complex. I will attempt merely a brief summary of the reactions within the framework of the status-production model.

First, enraged victims may respond in kind by attempting to disparage and subordinate the original discriminator. Such behavior may take the form of discrimination, which means the victim also makes a wasteful material sacrifice for the sake of status. The victim may, however, lack the opportunity or wealth to respond in kind and may seek a cheaper means of disparagement such as an insult. Violence is the extreme form of such an insult; it inflicts the loss of dignity inherent in an intentional deprivation of bodily integrity. Even if an African American counters with some means other than violence, the original subordinator may resort to violence to ensure the effectiveness of the original insult and to counter any responsive insult. Hobbes identified this escalation over dishonor as a primary source of war.

A second response is to seek to regain status by subordinating someone *other* than the original discriminator. If whites present too difficult a target, other minority groups may be within reach. Thus, the long and unpleasant history of status competition between minority groups exemplifies a predictable response to subordination. The original victim may also focus on vulnerable members of her own group, such as women or those of a different economic class. Evidence suggests, for example, that African Americans discriminate against one another on the basis of the relative lightness or darkness of their skin. Finally, because the original victim may lack any non-violent means of responding to discrimination, some of what appears to be "senseless violence" among discrimination victims may actually be a rational attempt to produce status by subordinating others.

The victim's responses are not limited to subordinating others. The victim may also withdraw from competition—by which status is generally determined—by adopting beliefs that such competitions are without merit. When a subordinated subgroup fails according to the prevailing cultural values, its members may decide to reject those values completely. For example, minorities facing discrimination may decide, rather than be judged by standards of academic or economic success, that education or employment is an overrated "white" value. Like the processes of rationalization, the belief that academics is unimportant may preserve self-esteem; however, such a belief may prove destructive in the long run because it depresses efficient investment in human capital.

Finally, a victim of subordination may wholeheartedly adopt the beliefs of the subordinators, including those that members of her group are deserving of their low status. Such a response might seem unlikely; however, for some it may be easier to accept a lower status with the belief that such a role is natural and proper than to live out such a role every day believing it is arbitrarily imposed. The result, however, is a form of self-loathing.

In sum, many of the effects of discrimination, well-explored in other disciplines, should be of central concern to an economic assessment of the system of race discrimination. In many cases, these effects represent investments that the victims make in defending their status. Combined with the investments made by the original discriminators, these resources represent the deadweight loss of race discrimination. Consequently, considerable evidence demonstrates that race discrimination is a grossly inefficient market failure.

(b) An Efficiency Argument for Anti–Discrimination Laws.—As with laws against theft, the benefit of prohibiting a form of discrimination is to prevent the wasteful investment of resources in such discrimination. When laws prohibit theft, the primary alternative by which the former thief can make material gains is to engage in lawful, productive activity. The argument for laws that prohibit subordination as a means of acquiring status is exactly parallel: by raising the costs of subordination, such laws induce people to switch to socially productive, or at least socially benign, means of acquiring status (either at an individual or a group level). Subordination is not the only means of group status production, and inter-group status production is not the only means of gaining esteem.

A possible distinction from theft, however, is the availability of equally wasteful substitutes to blatant discrimination. A group with a disproportionately large share of political power, economic wealth, and symbols of status will have at its disposal a number of alternative means of subordinating a minority group. Prohibiting one form of subordinating behavior may simply cause a shift to an equally wasteful form of acquiring status. Such a concern, however, may be overstated. After all, common law larceny initially required a trespass in the taking and thus exempted what we now think of as embezzlement and fraud. Even though thieves were free to switch to non-trespassory means of confiscation, the initial prohibition was nonetheless efficient. The opportunities remaining were more limited and costly; a complete substitution would not occur. The same argument can be made for prohibiting private discrimination in certain key areas, such as employment and housing. These forms of discrimination probably represent the most productive means of subordination and therefore induce the greatest 'investment' by whites. As I previously pointed out, employment discrimination offers for whites a double insult to blacks: not only the insult inherent in shunning someone, but also the consequence of lowering black income in a society that accords status to wealth. Similarly, excluding blacks from neighborhoods is not only a very public symbol of subordination, but also denies them the material benefits of reciprocity that may arise among neighbors. Effectively prohibiting employment and housing discrimination would deprive whites of their most productive private means of subordination and would thereby lower the resources invested in this wasteful confiscatory activity.

Second, anti-discrimination laws may lower the investment in status confiscation by increasing the incidence of "cross-membership." *Ceteris paribus*, an individual prefers subordinating a group to which she does not belong to subordinating a group to which she does belong. An individual always bears a cost from subordination of her own group and that cost gives her an incentive to avoid such behavior. In fact, an individual who is a member of group *A* and group *B* might find it in her interest to invest in efforts to prevent members of group *A* from seeking to subordinate group *B*. Therefore, the more "cross-membership" between two groups, the fewer the resources that will be invested by the two groups in subordinating each other.

Laws forbidding race discrimination may increase the occurrence of cross-membership and thereby undermine the effectiveness of racial subordination as a status strategy. Race has been and remains highly correlated with other demographic factors. If a white individual lives in an all-white neighborhood, attends an all-white school, works in an all-white firm, worships at an all-white church, belongs to an all-white amateur sports league, and patronizes all-white hobby clubs, she will never face the problem of cross-membership. If, however, anti-discrimination laws were to integrate neighborhoods, schools, firms, and private clubs, more whites would find themselves in a position in which racial minorities belong to some of *their* groups. Consequently, racial subordination would lower the status of these integrated groups. One response will be for whites to flee the groups that become integrated, but if the costs are too high, as when the law integrates a number of social groups at the same time, the effect might be to lower the effectiveness of racial subordination as a status strategy for many whites.

Finally, anti-discrimination laws may serve to correct the market failure of discrimination by undermining the credibility of rationalizations for discrimination. Several commentators have noted that the law shapes preferences, and that Title VII and other civil rights laws may have reduced the preference for discrimination. The status-production model explains this evolution not as a change in the taste for discrimination, but as a change in the productive capacity of certain forms of subordination. Individuals who seek status require some rationalization for their behavior. Admitting that one seeks to subordinate others for the sake of status conflicts with obtaining such status. Law affects the credibility of any alternative explanation. Take Posner's example of a guild that survives on an ideology of quality to justify restrictions on competition. Consider the long-term effect Posner's critique might have on such ideology were it sufficiently publicized. Exposing the naked self-interest behind platitudes of public concern erodes their effectiveness.

Law is more crude than an intellectual critique, yet it is inherently more public, and can carry more weight. When Jim Crow laws mandated certain forms of segregation, whites confidently spoke of segregation as the natural order of things; when the laws forbade segregation, discriminatory whites had a greater difficulty believing their own ideology. Rationalizations can be fragile things; sometimes they require that dissent be held to a minimum. In the South and elsewhere, Title VII constituted a very powerful 'dissent,' an indication that a large number, perhaps a majority, of Americans no longer believed the explanations of discrimination. If people care about esteem, the law can change behavior merely by signaling on what grounds the majority will henceforth give and withhold esteem.

In sum, law may correct the market failure of discrimination in three ways: by raising the costs and lowering the productive returns of certain forms of subordination; by increasing the racial diversity of socially connected groups, which raises selfish resistance to the subordination strategy; and by symbolizing a consensus that the rationalizations for the subordination strategy are, in fact, mere rationalizations. Whether such laws are efficient depends on the magnitude of these benefits relative to the administrative and opportunity costs of the system that adjudicates discrimination claims. But under the status-production model, the efficiency question is, like it is for the prohibition of theft, an empirical one; one can no longer simply assert that laws prohibiting satisfaction of discriminatory preferences are presumptively inefficient.

One might inquire about the implications of the status-production model of discrimination for affirmative action. In what may seem like an evasion, I believe the model provides no clear answer for affirmative action, but does reveal the consequential tensions the policy represents. The "cross-membership" effect of anti-discrimination laws provides a theoretical foundation for the claim that affirmative action serves to combat discrimination more effectively than a mere non-discrimination policy. Indeed, the benefit of cross-membership might justify a very aggressive affirmative action program. The utility of integrating social groups by race is not limited by any principle of past wrongful discrimination. The status-production model indicates that we can reduce investment in future status subordination by decreasing racial stratification in society.

Conversely, affirmative action creates a "common fate" for those of the same race and thus raises the salience of race. As critics of affirmative action have claimed, this fact may cause whites to identify themselves more fully with their race. The status-production model adds this insight: raising the salience of race may increase the return from racial subordination and enhance the power of whites to elicit intra-group cooperation for the remaining avenues of racial subordination. Affirmative action likely has already had this effect, which offsets the positive effects of cross-membership. However difficult it is to ascertain the present net effect, the more important and difficult question is what the future effects will be. Affirmative action has, so far, done little to integrate effectively American society. Therefore, we have no reason to expect the positive consequences of that policy to have emerged. In the end, the status-production model reveals what I think we knew already: affirmative action is an investment in which we bear certain costs today for the hope of a greater return tomorrow. The model illuminates, but does not resolve, the empirical question of whether the future benefits will outweigh the present costs.

III.   CONCLUSION

Groups inherently tend to elicit a level of cooperation from their members and to incur a level of conflict with other groups. The cooperation, in fact, facilitates the conflict. Intra-group esteem allocation permits groups to overcome certain collective action problems that would otherwise make conflict impossible. At the same time, the desire for esteem provides a new objective of group conflict—competition over social status.

What I have termed the theory of intra-group cooperation and inter-group conflict is merely the logical extension of three other steps in political and economic theory. First, Hobbes, among others, justified the state as necessary to avoid perpetual conflict in the state of nature; thus the state's role is to facilitate peaceful cooperation. Second, economists have persuasively contended that certain forms of peaceful cooperation, such as price-fixing, are detrimental to society. Consequently, the government should act in such cases to prevent cooperation. Third, Ellickson, among others, has written that groups use social norms to solve collective action problems without the centralized coercive power of the state, namely to bring about a cooperative "order without law." The next step, I propose, is to recognize that significant instances of this decentralized cooperation will inevitably be socially destructive and, therefore, that government should obstruct these forms of cooperation. Groups inherently tend to use their powers of decentralized cooperation to produce status through the socially wasteful process of subordination. As with cartels, cooperation in such cases is a social threat that justifies state action.

Aside from these general political implications, the theory of intra-group cooperation and inter-group conflict illuminates the complex problem of race discrimination. Status production explains both the historic and contemporary contours of race discrimination far better than the prevailing associational model of discrimination. Understanding race discrimination as a means of producing status helps us explain its tenacity in the face of market competition and reveals, within an economic model, the full costs of the practice of discrimination. The effort to gain status by taking status away from others, and the responsive measures this effort elicits, are socially wasteful in the same way that confiscation of material property is wasteful. The inefficiency in the system of status competition is measured by the investments each group makes in gaining or protecting its status. Prohibiting the more productive forms of investments can reduce the wastefulness of such actions even if it does not eliminate it.

In criticizing the associational preference model of discrimination, I focused intensively on a single form of discrimination—racial discrimination—and within that category, exclusively on discrimination against African Americans. The points I made in this context, however, apply to other forms of racial and ethnic discrimination. When substantial overlap exists between groups that share publicly observable traits and groups that are socially connected, the theory predicts substantial investment in status production, including the subordination of other groups. With more than two racial and ethnic groups, greater opportunity exists for movement in social position, and there is, therefore, reason to expect greater investment in maintaining or improving status.

* * * * *

Groups matter. Groups form for simple informational reasons, as economics describes in considerable detail: to minimize the transaction costs people incur in the course of satisfying their preferences. Yet the formation of groups has another consequence. People have a loyalty to groups that goes beyond what serves their narrow pecuniary self-interest. I have sought to explain that solidarity in self-interested terms; doing so requires an expanded understanding of self-interest that includes a powerful desire for esteem and status. Given the ubiquity of groups, this broader social science perspective on their function should prove useful in understanding legal issues beyond racial discrimination. For now, I have argued for a sober appreciation that solidarity for some often means enmity for others.

NOTES AND QUESTIONS

1.   Comparing Rational Choice Theory with Group Status Production Theory.

Is it possible to compare the Becker and McAdams Models? What are the starting assumptions of each piece? Does McAdams accept any part of the rational choice heuristic?

2.   Groups vs. individuals.

One possible difference between the Becker and McAdams models is how they treat groups. McAdams is primarily concerned with the operation of intergroup processes for enforcing subordination. In contrast, Becker treats the individual as the central unit of measuring preferences for discrimination. Becker does, however, note that "it has been argued that an increase in the numerical importance of a minority group increases the prejudice against them, since the majority begins to fear their growing power; on the other hand, some argue that greater numbers bring greater knowledge and that leads to a decline in prejudice." To what use does Becker's theory of discrimination put this observation about group size?

3.   Racial discrimination, the moral argument.

If racial discrimination is simply a preference with exactly the same entitlement to expression in the marketplace as a taste for strawberry ice cream, how does rational choice distinguish between morally repugnant choices (child pornography) and morally neutral choices? Does rational choice theory require a normative view of racial discrimination to work?

Becker observes that: "[f]or example, discrimination and prejudice are not usually said to occur when someone prefers looking at a glamorous Hollywood actress rather than at some other woman; yet they are said to occur when he prefers living next to whites rather than Negroes. At best, calling just one of these actions "discrimination" requires making subtle and rather secondary distinctions. Fortunately, it is not necessary to get involved in these more philosophical issues."

What role might Becker's theory of the market dynamics of racial discrimination have played in the development of the market for subprime loans discussed in previous chapters?

4. Adam Smith and Group Status Production Theory.

Recall that Adam Smith argued, p. 202 self interest, modified by benevolence born of conscience, or the influence of the moral spectator are the primary motivations for human economic behavior. Now, compare Smith to McAdams' thesis "that a material view of human motivation underestimates both the level of cooperation that groups elicit from their members and the level of conflict that groups elicit from each other. A single group dynamic connects these added increments of cooperation and conflict: groups achieve solidarity and elicit loyalty beyond what economic analysis conventionally predicts, but solidarity and loyalty within groups lead predictably, if not inevitably, to competition and conflict between groups. The connection is the desire for esteem or status. Groups use intra-group status rewards as a non-material means of gaining material sacrifice from members, but the attendant desire for inter-group status causes inter-group conflict."

––––––

3. AN EMPIRICAL STUDY OF RACIAL DISCRIMINATION

As you read this study of the racial dynamics of new car bargaining consider whether this dynamic was also a feature of the market for subprime loans leading to the financial crisis of 2008.

Fair Driving: Gender and Race Discrimination in Retail Car Negotiations

104 HARV. L. REV. 817 (1991).

■ IAN AYRES

The struggle to eradicate discrimination on the basis of race and gender has a long history in American law. Based on the widely held belief that such discrimination will occur only in markets in which racial or gender animus distorts competition, regulatory efforts have been limited to areas in which interpersonal relations are significant and ongoing, such as housing and employment. In this Article, Professor Ayres offers empirical evidence that seriously challenges faith in the ability of competitive market forces to eliminate racial and gender discrimination in other markets. His Chicago based research demonstrates that retail car dealerships systematically offered substantially better prices on identical cars to white men than they did to blacks and women. Professor Ayres details the nature and startling degree of the discrimination his testers encountered and evaluates various theoretical explanations for their disparate treatment. Based on his conclusions, Professor Ayres explores routes by which "fair driving" plaintiffs might bring suits against dealerships and mechanisms through which regulators might effectively rid the retail car market of such discrimination.

[The] civil rights laws of the 1960s prohibit race and gender discrimination in the handful of markets—employment, housing, and public accommodations—in which discrimination was perceived to be particularly acute. In recent years, lawsuits have increasingly presented claims of more subtle and subjective forms of discrimination within these protected markets. Both legislators and commentators, however, have largely ignored the possibility of discrimination in the much broader range of markets left uncovered by civil rights laws. Housing and employment may be the two most important markets in which people participate, but women and racial minorities may also be susceptible to discrimination when spending billions of dollars on other goods and services. Of these unprotected markets, the market for new cars is particularly ripe for scrutiny because, for most Americans, new car purchases represent their largest consumer investment after buying a home. In 1986, for example, more than $100 billion was spent on new cars in the United States.

This Article examines whether the process of negotiating for a new car disadvantages women and minorities. More than 180 independent negotiations at ninety dealerships were conducted in the Chicago area to examine how dealerships bargain. Testers of different races and genders entered new car dealerships separately and bargained to buy a new car, using a uniform negotiation strategy. The study tests whether automobile retailers react differently to this uniform strategy when potential buyers differ only by gender or race.

The tests reveal that white males receive significantly better prices than blacks and women. As detailed below, white women had to pay forty percent higher markups than white men; black men had to pay more than twice the markup, and black women had to pay more than three times the markup of white male testers. Moreover, the study reveals that testers of different race and gender are subjected to several forms of nonprice discrimination. Specifically, testers were systematically steered to salespeople of their own race and gender (who then gave them worse deals) and were asked different questions and told about different qualities of the car.

At the outset it is difficult to choose how, linguistically, to characterize the results that black and female testers were treated differently from white male testers using the same bargaining strategy. The term "discrimination," although surely a literal characterization, unfortunately connotes to many the notion of animus (even though in antitrust, for example, "price discrimination" is not taken to imply any hatred by sellers). "Disparate treatment," in contrast, connotes to others a strictly technical legal meaning developed in civil rights case law. For the moment, the terms "discrimination" and "disparate treatment" are both used to refer to the result that sellers' conduct was race-and gender-dependent; sellers took race and gender into account and treated differently testers who were otherwise similarly situated. These terms are not meant to imply that salespeople harbored any animus based on race or gender.

In recent years, the Supreme Court has struggled in the employment context to enunciate workable evidentiary standards to govern claims of subtle and possibly unconscious forms of discrimination. Although the 1960s civil rights laws do not reach retail car sales, the finding that car retailers bargain differently with different races might give rise to disparate treatment suits under 42 U.S.C. §§ 1981 and 1982, which originated in the 1866 Civil Rights Act. The test results, by focusing on an unexplored manifestation of disparate treatment, push us to define more clearly what constitutes discrimination generally.

Furthermore, the results highlight a gaping hole in our civil rights laws regarding gender discrimination. Although sections 1981 and 1982 prohibit racial discrimination in contracting and the sale of real and personal property, no federal laws bar intentional discrimination on the basis of gender in the sale of most goods or services. The civil rights laws of the 1960s fail to fill this gap, leaving unregulated a legion of markets in which women contract. Put simply, car dealers can legally charge more or refuse to sell to someone *because* she is a woman. Intentional gender (or race) discrimination of this kind might alternatively be attacked as an "unfair or deceptive" trade practice under state and federal consumer protection laws. In the end, however, courts might perceive that the quintessentially individualized and idiosyncratic nature of negotiation places such disparate treatment entirely outside the purview of either the civil rights or consumer protection laws.

The goal of Congress in passing the Civil Rights Act of 1866 was to guarantee that "a dollar in the hands of a Negro will purchase the same thing as a dollar in the hands of a white man." The standard argument against enacting civil rights laws has been grounded in the conviction that the impersonal forces of market competition will limit race and gender discrimination to the traditionally protected markets, in which there is significant interpersonal contact. Yet the results of this study give lie to such an unquestioning faith in competition: in stark contrast to congressional objectives, this Article indicates that blacks and women simply cannot buy the same car for the same price as can white men using identical bargaining strategies. The price dispersion engendered by the bargaining process implicates basic notions of equity and indicates that the scope of the civil rights laws has been underinclusive. The process of bargaining, already inefficient in many ways, becomes all the more problematic when it works to the detriment of traditionally disadvantaged members of our society.

Part I of this Article describes how the tests of race and gender discrimination were conducted. Part II reports the results of the tests. An analysis of disparate treatment in price, sales tactics, and steering is combined with a regression analysis focusing on the determinants of final offers. Part III explores theoretical explanations of the results. Animus-based theories of disparate treatment are compared with theories of statistical discrimination and tested against the results of the study. Particular attention is paid to the role of competition at both the wholesale and retail level in limiting and channeling the form of race and gender discrimination. Finally, Part IV explores the legal implications of the study. This Part considers whether and how "fair driving" plaintiffs could legally challenge this disparate treatment under consumer protection laws and sections 1981 and 1982. The Article concludes by considering the need for legal reform.

I. METHODOLOGY OF THE TEST

To test whether there is disparate treatment by car retailers on the basis of race or gender, pairs of consumers/testers (for example, a white male and a black female) used the same bargaining strategy in negotiating at new car dealerships. A white male tester was included in each pair of testers. The white male results provide a bench-mark against which to measure the disparate treatment of the non-"whitemale" tester. Three consumer pairs (black female and white male, black male and white male, and white female and white male) conducted approximately 180 tests at ninety Chicago dealerships.

Each tester followed a bargaining script designed to frame the bargaining in purely distributional terms: the only issue to be negotiated was the price. The script instructed the testers to focus quickly on buying a particular car, and testers offered to provide their own financing. The testers elicited an initial price from the dealers and then, after waiting five minutes, the testers responded with an initial counteroffer that equalled an estimate of the dealer's marginal cost. After the tester's initial counteroffer, the salesperson could do one of three things: (1) attempt to accept the tester's offer, (2) refuse to bargain further, or (3) make a lower offer. If the salesperson attempted to accept the tester's offer or refused to bargain further, the test was over (and the tester left the dealership). If the salesperson responded by making a lower offer, the script instructed the tester to wait five minutes and to split the difference. After the tester split the difference, the salesperson again had the same three choices, and the rounds of bargaining continued until the salesperson accepted a tester offer or refused to bargain further. Testers jotted down each offer and counteroffer, as well as options on the car and the sticker price. Upon leaving the dealership, the testers completed a survey recording information about the test.

This design produced results that permit two tests for discrimination. The first, "short test" of discrimination simply compares the dealer's response to the testers' initial question, "How much would I have to pay to buy this car?" The "long test" of discrimination, on the other hand, compares instead the final offers given to testers after the multiple rounds of concessionary bargaining. By focusing on the initial offer, the short test is well controlled because salespeople had little information from which to draw inferences. By focusing on the final offer, the long test isolates more closely the price a real consumer would pay, but it increases the risk that individual differences among the testers influenced the results.

In order to minimize the possibility of non-uniform bargaining, particular attention was paid to issues of experimental control. A major goal of the study was to choose uniform testers and to train them to behave in a standardized manner. Testers were chosen to satisfy the following criteria for uniformity:

1. *Age*: All testers were twenty-four to twenty-eight years old.

2. *Education*: All testers had three or four years of college education.

3. *Dress*: All testers were dressed similarly during the negotiations. Testers wore casual "yuppie" sportswear: the men wore polo or buttondown shirts, slacks, and loafers; the women wore straight skirts, blouses, minimal make-up, and flats.

4. *Economic Class*: Testers volunteered that they could finance the car themselves.

5. *Occupation*: If asked by a salesperson, each tester said that he or she was a young urban professional (for example, a systems analyst for First Chicago Bank).

6. *Address*: If asked by the salesperson, each tester gave a fake name and an address for an upper-class, Chicago neighborhood (Streeterville).

7. *Attractiveness*: Applicants were subjectively ranked for average attractiveness.

The testers were trained for two days before visiting the dealerships. The training included not only memorizing the tester script, but also participating in mock negotiations designed to help testers gain confidence and learn how to negotiate and answer questions uniformly. The training emphasized uniformity in cadence and inflection of tester response. In addition to spoken uniformity, the study sought to achieve tester uniformity in non-verbal behavior.

* * *

Readers should focus, therefore, not merely on statistical significance but also on the *amount* of the reported discrimination. Although perfect control of such complex bargaining is impossible, the amounts of discrimination reported in the next Part cannot be plausibly explained by idiosyncratic divergence from uniform bargaining.

II.   Results of the Test

The results from the tester surveys provide a rich database for investigating how salespeople bargain and whether they treat testers of a different race or gender differently. This Part presents the results of these tests in three sections. The first section reports disparate treatment regarding the prices that dealerships were willing to offer the testers. This section includes an analysis of both initial and final offers as well as refusals to bargain and differences in the bargaining paths (the sequence of offers made in succeeding rounds). In the second section, nonprice dimensions of the bargaining process are analyzed. The tests reveal that salespeople asked testers different types of questions and used different tactics in attempting to sell the cars. Finally, the third section uses multivariate regression analysis to analyze the determinants of the final offers. The regressions reveal a fairly sophisticated seller strategy. In particular, the size of final offers is sensitive not only to the race and gender of both the tester and the salesperson, but also to the information revealed by the tester in the course of bargaining.

A.   Price Discrimination

1.   Final Offers.—The final offer of each test was the lowest price offered by a dealer after the multiple rounds of bargaining. By comparing these final offers with independent estimates of dealer cost, it was possible to calculate the dealer profit associated with each final offer (final offer minus dealer cost). For a sample of 165 tester visits, the average dealer profits for the different classes of tester are presented in Table 1.

TABLE 1: AVERAGE DEALER PROFIT FOR FINAL OFFERS	
White Male	$ 362
White Female	504
Black Male	783
Black Female	1237

Black female testers were asked to pay over three times the markup of white male testers, and black male testers were asked to pay over twice the white male markup. Moreover, race and gender discrimination were synergistic or "superadditive": the discrimination against the black female tester was greater than the combined discrimination against both the white female and the black male tester.

The reliability of these results is buttressed by an analysis of the relative unimportance of individual effects. The average dealer profits on the non-"white male" testers were statistically different from the average profits on the white males at a five percent significance level. The average profits for the three individual white males were, however, not significantly different from each other. This last result lends support to the proposition that the idiosyncratic characteristics of at least the white male testers did not affect the results.

* * *

Dealer discrimination in early rounds will cause disparate concessions by testers that may preclude equal treatment in final rounds. The possibility that early offers matter, however, is not an embarrassment of design. Bargainers engage in time consuming initial rounds of bargaining because they individually believe that these rounds will affect the final price. The tests provide strong evidence that if consumers use the same "split the difference" strategy, they will receive different final offers that are determined by their race and gender. * * *

2. *Initial Offers.*—This study also constructed a test of disparate treatment on the basis of the initial offers sellers made to the testers. * * *

The average dealer profit on offers made to white female testers was not significantly different from the average profit on offers made to white male testers. Sellers, however, offered both black males and black females significantly higher prices: sellers asked black males to pay almost twice the markups they charged white males, and they asked black females to pay two and one-half times that markup.

TABLE 2: AVERAGE DEALER PROFIT FOR FINAL OFFERS	
White Male	$ 818
White Female	829
Black Male	1534
Black Female	2169

3. *Willingness to Bargain.*—Another potentially important form of disparate treatment concerns the sellers' willingness to bargain. Consumers are hurt if the sellers either refuse to bargain or force the consumers to spend more time bargaining to achieve the same price. An analysis of the number of bargaining rounds reveals that the average number of rounds for different types of testers did not differ significantly, as shown in Table 3. The amount of time black male and white female testers spent bargaining (both total and per round) was not statistically longer than the amount spent by white male testers. Although black female testers clearly had to pay the most for cars, it was not because dealers refused to spend time bargaining with them. * * *

TABLE 3: DIFFERENCES IN ROUNDS			
	Average Number of Rounds	Average Length of Test (Minutes)	Average Length per Round (Minutes)
White Male	2.43	35.8	14.8
White Female	2.21	32.9	14.9
Black Male	2.32	49.1	21.2
Black Female	3.08	34.6	11.2

* * *

B.   Nonprice Discrimination

The study also examined other ways in which sellers may have treated the testers differently. Although these other types of disparate treatment do not directly concern the sales price, they could facilitate price discrimination. Moreover, these comparisons suggest something about the racial and sexual perceptions that determine the behavior of salespeople.

  1. *Customer Steering.*—As designed, the script allowed dealerships to steer testers to different types of salespeople or different types of cars. The script instructed testers to go to the center of the showroom and wait for a salesperson to approach them. The salespeople chose the tester, so that the testers could be steered to salespeople of a particular race or gender. In the sample of 119 encounters, sellers paired with testers as reported in Table 4.

  The salesperson's race and gender was not randomly distributed across testers. Instead, sellers steered testers to persons of their own race and gender: white male sellers were more likely to serve white male testers; white female sellers were more likely to serve white female testers; and black male sellers were more likely to serve black testers.

TABLE 4:
STEERING TO PARTICULAR TYPES OF SALESPEOPLE

	Seller Type Percentages		
	White Male	White Female	Black Male
All testers	83.2%	7.5%	9.3%
White Male	89.5	3.5	7.0
White Female	71.4	19.1	9.5
Black Male	83.4	5.5	11.1
Black Female	82.6	4.3	13.1

  In addition, the study was designed to uncover a second type of dealer steering. Upon entering the dealership, the testers told the salesperson that they were interested in buying a certain car model with certain options and then allowed the salesperson to show them specific cars. However, no statistically significant disparate treatment was found. The test results reveal that dealers did not systematically steer different types of testers to cars of different cost.

  2. *Disparate Questioning.*—The testers recorded how often they were asked specific types of questions. Statistical tests were then conducted to evaluate whether sellers asked non-"white male" testers particular questions significantly more or less often than white male testers. These tests indicate the following:

> Sellers asked black female testers *more* often about their occupation, about financing, and whether they were married. Sellers asked black female testers *less* often whether they had been to other dealerships and whether they had offers from other dealers.

> Sellers asked black male testers *less* often if they would like to test drive the car, whether they had been to other dealerships, and whether they had offers from other dealers.

> Sellers asked white female testers *more* often whether they had been to other dealerships. Sellers asked white female testers *less* often what price they would be willing to pay.

These differences may indicate ways that dealers try to sort consumers in order to price discriminate effectively. For example, the fact that salespeople asked black testers less often about whether they had been to other dealerships (or had other offers) may indicate that salespeople do not think that interdealer competition is as much of a threat with black customers as with white customers. Because the price that sellers are willing to offer any customer may be sensitive to that customer's responses, the disparity among who is questioned may facilitate a seller's attempt to price discriminate.

3. Disparate Sales Tactics.—The testers also recorded the different tactics that the salespeople used in trying to sell the car. Test statistics were calculated to evaluate whether particular sales tactics were used significantly more or less often with white male testers than with non-"white male" testers. These tests indicate the following:

> Salespeople tried to sell black female testers *more* often on gas mileage, the color of the car, dependability, and comfort, and asked them more often to sign purchase orders.

> Salespeople tried to sell white female testers more often on gas mileage, the color of the car, and dependability.

> With black male testers, salespeople *more* often offered the sticker price as the initial offer and forced the tester to elicit an initial offer from the seller. Salespeople asked black male testers to sign a purchase order less often.

These tests suggest that salespeople believe women are more concerned with gas mileage, color, and dependability than are men. The tests also indicate that salespeople try to "sucker" black males into buying at the sticker price by offering the sticker price or refusing to make an initial offer until asked.

4. Cost Revelation.—The script also elicited information about the dealers' willingness to reveal their marginal cost to consumers. In half of the bargaining sessions, the testers were told to ask the seller (at the end of the test) what the dealer had paid the car manufacturer. Thirty-five per cent of the sellers represented a specific dollar cost in response to the testers' inquiries. These disclosures, however, were not evenly distributed across the tester groups. Disaggregated by tester type, the disclosure rates indicate that salespeople were less willing to disclose cost data to black testers, especially black female testers, as presented in Table 5.

TABLE 5:
DISCLOSURE OF COST DATA

Tester Type	Percentage of Salespeople Disclosing Cost Figure
All Testers	35%
White Male	47
White Female	42
Black Male	25
Black Female	0

Instead of disclosing their cost information to black testers, the salespeople were more likely to dissemble and claim that they did not know the car's cost. To the extent that such cost disclosure is valuable, the failure to disclose costs to black testers undermines their ability to bargain as effectively as white testers and thus facilitates price discrimination based on race.

Based on this sample, however, it is unclear whether such disclosure would actually put white testers at a competitive advantage. When the seller did reveal his cost, the represented cost was substantially higher than independent estimates of seller cost for the same models, as seen in Table 6. Thus, although salespeople are more likely to disclose cost figures to white testers, they systematically overstate their costs. The greatest misrepresentations were made to white female testers.

* * *

Although the individual interaction variables are not statistically significant, the regressions indicate that the linear constraints in Model Two are binding. * * *

TABLE 6:
SELLER MISREPRESENTATION OF COST DATA

	Average Misrepresentation
White Male Tester	$ 849
White Female Tester	1046
Black Male Tester	752
Black Female Tester	—

White male testers received best deals from white female sellers.

White female testers received best deals from black male sellers.

Black male testers received best deals from white female sellers.

Black female testers received best deals from white male sellers.

The social psychology literature would not suggest this result to be expected. Several studies, for example, have shown that parties tend to bargain more cooperatively with an opponent of their own race and gender than with a person of a different race or gender. The interaction effects revealed in Model Three (although not statistically significant) suggest, however, that salespeople may try to take strategic advantage of consumers' perceptions. This result is especially plausible when combined with the earlier finding that testers were systematically steered to salespeople of the same race and gender. The data thus paints a clear picture: sellers steered testers to salespeople of their own race and gender, who then proceeded to give them the worst deals.

III. Toward a Theoretical Explanation

The preceding Part detailed race and gender discrimination that was not only statistically significant but also surprisingly pronounced. This Part explores possible explanations for why dealers would discriminate in this manner. Only with an accurate understanding of the reasons for dealer behavior can regulators hope to determine what, if any, governmental intervention can effectively protect black and female customers. With this goal in mind, this Part examines two broad theories of discrimination: animus-based theories and theories of statistical discrimination.

A.   Animus–Based Theories of Discrimination

Animus theories of discrimination posit that a certain group is treated differently because that group is disliked or hated. A variety of market participants can interject animus into a market. A dealership, for example, might charge blacks more because the dealership dislikes blacks, because the dealership's employees dislike blacks, or because the dealership's other customers dislike blacks. As originally formulated by Gary Becker, these sources of bigotry could force sellers to charge blacks higher prices as an animus-compensating tax.

The source of bigotry might partially determine the specific form that animus-based discrimination takes. For example, in the fair housing context, consumer animus has led to steering and refusals to bargain. In the "fair driving" context, employee animus against blacks or women might cause salespeople to bargain frivolously. Because testers visited the dealerships during the least busy times of the day, bigoted dealers—with nothing better to do with their time—might have gained satisfaction in frustrating or wasting the time of women or blacks. Finally, the testers also might have experienced "role-based" bigotry: dealers might have discriminated against buyers who acted in ways that diverged from the dealer's expectation. Female testers could have faced prejudice for speaking with "a male voice"; black testers could have faced prejudice for not "staying in their place." In sum, the animus of various market participants can manifest itself as disparate treatment not only in the prices offered but also in other aspects of seller behavior.

* * *

C.   A Tentative Explanation

1.   Statistical Discrimination as an Explanation for Dealer Behavior.—The preceding discussion presented three broad theories of discrimination: animus-based, cost-based, and revenue-based. The fair driving tests, like their fair housing analogues, were designed primarily to identify the existence of disparate treatment—not to determine its cause. As a result, ancillary evidence must be used to determine which of the three competing theories best explains seller behavior. Although more study is warranted, it appears that the revenue-based theory best explains the discrimination that the testers encountered.

The cost-based theories of statistical discrimination are perhaps the weakest. The testers' script was explicitly structured to eliminate cost-based differences among the testers. The testers volunteered that they did not need financing—a potentially major source of disparate dealer cost. Notwithstanding these uniform representations, it is possible that the dealers inferred residual differences among the tester types. As an empirical matter, however, differences in net dealership cost simply do not explain why black female testers paid over three times the markup of white male testers. Moreover, on a cost-based theory, the observed seller inferences about profits from ancillary sales might predict a different pattern of disparate treatment.

Animus theories find more support in the data. The testers, for example, recorded several instances of overtly sexist and racist language by sellers. Nonetheless, animus theories do not appear to explain the magnitude of the discrimination. For example, under a theory of salesperson animus, the seller required a higher price from black females as compensation for having to deal with a black customer whom the seller disliked. The data would then imply that the dealer-required compensation must have been an implausible $900 per hour.

Consumer-based animus also fails to explain adequately disparate treatment by sellers. First, each class of testers received its best treatment from salespeople of a different race and gender and, in many cases, the worst treatment from salespeople of the same race and gender. For example, although all salespeople discriminated against black male testers, black salesmen gave them their worst deals. This result runs counter to the standard notion that a person's bigotry is usually directed at another race. Second, the amount of price discrimination black testers encountered at all dealerships did not vary with the racial makeup of the dealership's customer base. One-third of Chicago dealerships are located in neighborhoods with a greater than ninety percent black population, yet the offers these dealerships made to black testers did not differ from offers black testers received elsewhere. If disparate treatment were caused by white consumers' dislike of blacks, there should be less discrimination by sellers in neighborhoods where most consumers are black. Because the data do not confirm this prediction, the animus theory seems an unlikely explanation for the disparate treatment. Finally, consumer animus is inconsistent with observed salesperson behavior: salespeople did not attempt to reduce the length of bargaining sessions with the non-"white male" testers. If disparate treatment of black consumers were caused by sellers' concern for white consumers' desire not to associate with blacks, dealerships should have discouraged black consumers from bargaining for lengthy periods.

Although any conclusions based on this evidence must remain tentative, the case for revenue-based statistical discrimination is strongest. Despite the large amount of randomness (or unexplained variance) in bargaining outcomes, the dealerships seem to display a great deal of sophistication in bargaining. The systematic steering of customers to salespeople who charge them higher markups may be evidence of revenue-based statistical discrimination. Salespeople of the consumer's race and gender may, for example, be better able to infer that consumer's willingness to pay—and thus more finely tune the price discrimination.

* * *

Yet the conundrum persists as to why race and gender would be proxies for consumers' firm-specific reservation price that disfavor women and blacks. Even accepting that firm-specific willingness to pay is more a function of search costs than of ability to pay, why would blacks and women be disfavored? George Stigler has predicted that consumers with high opportunity costs will search less for a particular good than those consumers with lower opportunity costs. Because white males earn more on average than other tester types, under Stigler's theory a dealer should rationally infer that white males search less than members of other race and gender classes. If race and gender serve as proxies for dealer-specific willingness to pay, these proxies would seem to lead sellers to charge higher prices to white males, and not the lower prices revealed by this study.

Nevertheless, group differences in search costs, information, and aversion to bargaining may explain why profit-maximizing dealers charge white males less. The caricatured assertion that white males have higher opportunity costs (because they forgo higher wages when searching) ignores other effects that on balance may make it more difficult for blacks and women to search for a car. For example, white males may have a greater ability to take time off from work or family responsibilities to search for a car. Moreover, blacks are less likely to have a trade-in car with which to search when purchasing a new car. If, on net, blacks and women experience higher search costs than do white males, revenue-based statistical discrimination might lead dealers to make lower offers to white males. Knowing that blacks and women tend to incur higher search costs, a dealer could "safely" charge members of those groups higher prices, because the dealer would effectively have less competition for members of those groups from other dealers. White men may also have superior access to information about the car market. A large proportion of white men know that automobiles can be purchased for less than the sticker price, and white men may more easily be able to discover the customary size of negotiated discounts from the sticker price.

* * *

2.   *The Reinforcing Role of Dealer Competition.*—Many commentators have argued that competition among sellers will tend to eliminate certain forms of race and gender discrimination against buyers. The following discussion examines how market competition among dealerships may in fact reinforce the opportunities for statistical discrimination.

As a first intuition, competition should quickly eliminate revenue-based statistical discrimination, slowly eliminate animus-based discrimination, and never eliminate cost-based statistical discrimination. Competition should quickly eliminate revenue-based discrimination because rival dealers would immediately move to undercut any supra-competitive prices offered to high-valuing car buyers. Competition should slowly eliminate animus discrimination because bigoted sellers would be at a competitive disadvantage and so would eventually be driven out of the market. By contrast, competition should not eliminate cost-based statistical discrimination because no dealer would have a market-based incentive to offer prices that fall below the best estimates of that dealer's actual costs.

The preceding analysis, however, tentatively suggested just the opposite causal ordering. Cost-based statistical discrimination is the least plausible explanation, and revenue-based statistical discrimination is the most plausible. The simple competitive story thus poses a major challenge to the assertion that revenue-based statistical discrimination caused the disparate treatment. In a large city such as Chicago, with hundreds of car dealerships, how could rival dealerships successfully charge individual consumers significantly more than dealership marginal costs?

    * * *

The dealers' reliance on high-markup buyers lends additional credibility to the notion that dealership disparate treatment of consumers might be a form of revenue-based statistical discrimination. The dealers' search for high-markup buyers may be tailored to focus on specific racial or gender groups. In their quest to locate high-markup buyers, dealers are not guided by the amount that the *average* black woman is willing to pay. Rather, they focus on the proportion of black women who are willing to pay close to the sticker price. Even a small difference in the percentage of high-markup buyers represented by consumers of any one race or gender class may lead to large differences in the way dealers treat that entire class. Thus, the previous explanations of racial-or gender-based differences in search costs, information, or aversion to bargaining need not be true for the average members of a consumer group in order for those differences to generate significant amounts of revenue-based disparate treatment. The Consumer Federation of America recently completed a survey which revealed that thirty-seven percent of consumers do not understand that the sticker price is negotiable. These responses varied greatly across both race and gender. Sixty-one percent of black consumers surveyed did not realize that the sticker price is negotiable, whereas only thirty-one percent of white consumers made this error. This fact by itself could easily explain dramatic disparate treatment by sellers. Profit maximizing dealers may rationally quote higher prices to blacks even if the average black consumer in fact has a lower willingness to pay.

In sum, although simple economic theory suggests that dealer competition should quickly eliminate price dispersion, dealers in the market for new cars nevertheless sell the same car for different prices. Highly concentrated profits give dealers incentives to search for high-markup buyers through the process of bargaining. In particular, the dealers' search for high-markup buyers may reinforce incentives to discriminate on the basis of race or gender. The concentration of profits is a central pathology of retail car sales and one to which we will return below.

IV.   LEGAL IMPLICATIONS

The results of the bargaining tests show that car dealerships treat black and female testers differently than they do white men who use the same bargaining strategy. Whether these findings constitute actionable racial or gender discrimination in a traditional legal sense, however, is a separate matter. The differential treatment of consumers might be seen as a natural consequence of any bargaining process. Market economies sanction such treatment by allowing sellers to pursue high-markup sales through a variety of bargaining methods. The pre-contractual interplay between a potential buyer and seller may seem, in some sense, outside the purview of the law.

This Part argues, however, that the findings presented in this Article constitute compelling evidence of unlawful racial and gender discrimination under both the civil rights and consumer protection laws. In particular, the following section explores whether the car sellers' dealings with black testers constitute unlawful disparate treatment violative of sections 1981 and 1982. Such a claim does not necessarily imply that sellers dislike black or female customers—only that sellers take their customers' race and gender into account when deciding how to bargain. Section B then proposes legal reforms to strengthen sections 1981 and 1982 and to extend their coverage to currently unprotected groups.

A.   Liability Under Sections 1981 and 1982

Sections 1981 and 1982 mandate that all people shall have the same rights "to make and enforce contracts" and to "purchase . . . personal property," respectively, "as is enjoyed by white citizens." Although a racial discrimination suit has never been brought against a retail car dealership under section 1981 or section 1982, there seems little doubt that one or both these laws covers discrimination relating to retail car price bargaining between private parties. In *Jones v. Alfred H. Mayer Co.*, the Supreme Court emphatically stated that section 1982 (and by implication section 1981) applies to acts of private discrimination. Since *Jones*, courts have applied these sections' prohibitions of private discrimination to contexts similar to retail car price bargaining.

Even if car dealership bargaining falls within the scope of sections 1981 and 1982, a fair driving plaintiff would have a number of hurdles to overcome in winning a claim under these statutes. The substantive legal standard under sections 1981 and 1982 is straightforward: plaintiffs claiming disparate treatment must prove that the defendant intentionally discriminated against them and caused them an identifiable injury. Although the Supreme Court has stated that intentional discrimination "can *in some situations* be inferred from the mere fact of differences in treatment," no civil rights case has ever concluded that a showing of disparate treatment was insufficient to establish intentional discrimination. Thus, it appears that courts will find intentional discrimination whenever the defendant's conduct was conditioned on the plaintiff's race. To establish liability in this context, the typical fair driving plaintiff would need to show that the specific car dealer with whom he or she had bargained considered the plaintiff's race in deciding how to bargain.

On the other hand, because of the difficulties in obtaining direct proof that a defendant's conduct was race-dependent, the law has developed a method for allocating the burdens of proof under sections 1981 and 1982 that in effect allows intent to be inferred from indirect evidence. In particular, courts hearing section 1981 or 1982 claims have imported from the title VII context the shifting burdens of proof scheme articulated in *McDonnell Douglas v. Green*.

Applying the *McDonnell Douglas* reasoning to fair driving suits, the plaintiff bears the initial burden of establishing disparate treatment: that sellers took race into account when deciding how to bargain. If the plaintiff can establish a prima facie violation of section 1981 or section 1982, a burden of production shifts to the defendant "to articulate some legitimate, nondiscriminatory reason" for its differential behavior. Finally, if the defendant can offer such a reason, the burden shifts back to the plaintiff to show that the defendant's response is a mere "pretext."

A black tester from the present study who wanted to make out a successful prima facie case against a particular dealership would have to persuade the court of two things. First, she would have to persuade the court that the study was sufficiently controlled—that is, that she and the white tester visiting the defendant's car dealership appeared similar in every objective respect except for the color of their skin. If courts' attitudes in housing cases under sections 1981 and 1982 are any indication, the fair driving tests conducted in this study were more than sufficiently controlled. Although the typical fair housing test is similarly controlled with respect to timing of the tests, it is less controlled with respect to verbal and nonverbal conduct than was the testing in this study.

Second, fair driving plaintiffs would have to persuade the court that the instances of differential treatment are sufficiently numerous so that the results can not be explained by chance. Again, analogy to the fair housing context suggests that the results of one pair of well controlled testers should suffice. Under this standard, the present study could theoretically give rise to dozens of actionable instances of discrimination against individual dealers.

Although comparisons with the fair housing context are generally apposite, courts may be much more reluctant to find the existence of prima facie cases in the fair driving context because society has differing presumptions about the pervasiveness of the two kinds of discrimination. The long and ongoing history of housing discrimination in the United States is so well known and well documented that courts may require relatively less proof. Discrimination in car negotiations may have a similarly long and deep-seated history, but the size and nature of such discrimination may be masked by the processes of bargaining. As a result, a court hearing a fair driving claim may require that the tests be that much more controlled, that the disparity of treatment be that much greater, or that there be that many more instances of disparate treatment by the same dealer.

Once a court finds that a fair driving plaintiff has made out a prima facie case of disparate treatment, the burden shifts to the defendant-dealer to articulate a legitimate, nondiscriminatory explanation for why it treated white buyers and black buyers differently. If the defendant does not directly rebut the plaintiff's evidence of disparate treatment, it might put forward two distinct arguments that the disparate treatment was not "intentional" discrimination. First, the dealer may argue that the disparate treatment was unintentional because the dealer's motive was to make money, not to harm black people. Under this theory, the dealer might openly admit that its behavior flowed from consciously drawn, economically rational inferences based on the race of prospective buyers—revenue-based inferences, for example, about the proportion of blacks willing to pay a higher markup. It is, however, precisely these sorts of inferences—inferences based on the color of a person's skin—that sections 1981 and 1982 do not countenance. As Judge Posner recently held, "[d]iscrimination may be instrumental to a goal not itself discriminatory, just as murder may be instrumental to a goal not itself murderous (such as money); it is not any less—it is, indeed, more clearly—discriminatory on that account."

Alternatively, defendants might claim that their disparate treatment was unintentional in the sense that they were not conscious of it. The D.C. Circuit rejected this argument in *Hopkins v. Price Waterhouse*:

> [Plaintiff demonstrated] that she was treated less favorably than male candidates because of her sex. This is sufficient to establish discriminatory motive; the fact that some or all of the partners at Price Waterhouse may have been unaware of that motivation, even within themselves, neither alters the fact of its existence nor excuses it.

Once a plaintiff has proven that a defendant has treated blacks differently from identically situated whites, it is fair and reasonable to conclude as a matter of law that the dealer at some level of consciousness must have been aware of the testers' race. Such a legal inference conforms with our common moral intuition that a dealer who must consciously decide what initial price to offer every customer who walks through the door must be aware of the skin color of those to whom it consistently offers a higher initial price. Thus, so long as the fair driving plaintiff can persuade the factfinder that sellers treated similarly situated blacks differently from whites, the disparate treatment discussed in this Article violates sections 1981 and 1982.

B. Legal Reform

1. Modernizing Civil Rights Laws.—Lawmakers could respond to bargaining discrimination by expanding the current coverage of the civil rights and consumer protection laws. Most important, Congress could amend sections 1981 and 1982 to extend to women (and other protected classes) the right to be free from discrimination in contracting to buy and sell services as well as goods. Modernized versions of sections 1981 and 1982 could also allow plaintiffs to bring disparate impact suits, currently actionable under title VII, which require no showing of intent. Disparate impact litigation would allow suits to challenge the bargaining practices of sellers that are facially neutral (in the sense that they do not consciously take a buyer's race or gender into account) but have significant discriminatory effects. In sum, creating an additional roman numeraled civil rights "title" to cover the sale of goods and services would provide a remedy for the kinds of discrimination examined in this Article.

Although this Article has argued that the sellers' search for high-markup consumers causes sellers to discriminate against blacks and women, the proposal to extend civil rights protection to the sale of all goods and services is based on the notion that racial and gender-based disparate treatment may well exist in a broader variety of markets. The problem of disparate treatment in new car sales has been perpetuated by the fact that the bargaining process conceals from black and female consumers the prices received by their white male counterparts. Without such information, blacks and women cannot directly learn of disparate treatment. Black and female consumers may also be deprived of this crucial bench-mark in retail markets in which bargaining does not occur. Although uniform stated-pricing eliminates the potential for gender or race discrimination in pricing for most goods, such discrimination may still exist along such different dimensions as product or service quality. Again, although blacks and women can gather information about how other retailers treat them, they face difficulty in learning how retailers treat white men.

The 1960s civil rights laws outlawed discrimination in those markets—most notably housing and employment—in which conspicuous accessible bench-marks disclosed disparate treatment. But the absence of a manifest bench-mark does not imply the absence of discrimination; there is no reason to think that animus or statistical causes of discrimination manifest themselves only in markets in which interracial comparisons of treatment can be readily made. Indeed, as various overt forms of discrimination have become illegal, more subtle and covert manifestations have often replaced them. This Article seeks fundamentally to expand the domain of the civil rights inquiry.

2. Reinvigorating Consumer Protection Laws.—State and federal governments might also attempt to enforce more rigorously consumer protection laws to reduce the type of discrimination revealed in this Article. Indeed, recent Supreme Court decisions hostile to civil rights suits suggest the wisdom of pursuing a remedy under consumer protection laws. In *Patterson v. McLean Credit Union*, for example, the Court, although refusing to apply section 1981 to what it considered "postformation conduct," suggested instead that the victims of discrimination turn to traditional contractual remedies. To the extent that consumer protection laws codify common law remedies such as fraud and duress, they may provide a viable alternative to civil rights remedies. Thus, although consumer protection laws have not yet been used to attack racial disparate treatment as a "deceptive" misrepresentation, this history does not preclude more extensive governmental intervention in the future.

The Federal Trade Commission (FTC) Act and the numerous baby FTC acts passed by the individual states outlaw the use of "unfair or deceptive" trading practices. Utilizing such acts to reach discrimination in bargaining for a new car purchase will require a reconceptualization of what we consider unfair or deceptive. Attacking sellers' disparate treatment in bargaining as being "deceptive" strikes at closely held beliefs about what is appropriate in the normal course of negotiations. The complexity of these beliefs is demonstrated by contrasting the effect of seller misrepresentation in the context of car sales with seller misrepresentation in housing sales. Fair housing cases often gain their moral authority from the egregious nature of seller misrepresentations such as "the apartment is no longer available." In the retail car bargaining context, however, some forms of misrepresentation are broadly accepted. Few would believe, for example, that a seller would be held liable for misrepresenting "I can't reduce the price any further"—even if the seller did reduce the price for another consumer. Seller misrepresentation is present in both the housing market and in the new car market. The distinction in our response turns, if at all, on which types of misrepresentation we deem acceptable.

Nevertheless, consumer protection laws do provide a framework for attacking disparate treatment in bargaining. Courts have construed consumer protection statutes to prohibit implied as well as express misrepresentation. Courts could attack disparate treatment in negotiations for new cars by finding an implied representation that the dealer would not treat black consumers differently from white consumers. In other words, courts may preserve the "essence" of bargaining—by conceding that all consumers should expect inconsistent and unpredictable treatment at the hands of car dealers—but refuse to sanction "discrimination" by rejecting regimes in which the unpredictable behavior is in fact predicated on race or gender.

Such a finding would be completely consistent with freedom of contract. Sellers could avoid making this implicit representation by expressly reserving the right to bargain differently with customers of different races. A judicial or legislative finding of an implicit representation of no racial disparate treatment would simply be "filling a gap" in the parties' contract. Finding an implied representation of no racial disparate treatment is at least as reasonable as finding an implied representation that sellers reserve the right to treat different races differently: few explicit contracts would ever opt for the latter provision. Once lawmakers established a default rule of no disparate treatment, plaintiffs bringing implied misrepresentation cases would then face the same burden as traditional section 1981 plaintiffs: the burden of demonstrating disparate treatment.

The Supreme Court's decision in *Patterson v. McLean Credit Union* strongly supports this analysis. In restricting civil rights protection under section 1981 to discrimination in the formation of a contract, the *Patterson* Court suggested that victims of discrimination should turn to traditional contractual remedies: racial harassment "amounting to a breach of contract under state law is precisely what the language of § 1981 does not cover. That is because, in such a case . . . the plaintiff is free to enforce the terms of the contract in state court." Although the contract at issue was silent as to whether post-formation discrimination was permissible, the court implied that nondiscrimination provisions could be read into state contract remedies. Following the *Patterson* rationale, finding an implicit representation not to treat consumers differently in bargaining because of their race or gender would offer a free market alternative to civil rights interventionism.

3. *Structural Reforms.*—The expansion of traditional civil rights and consumer protection laws is unlikely to completely eliminate disparate treatment in bargaining based on race or gender. Victims of disparate bargaining treatment will most likely be restricted to suing individual dealerships—instead of manufacturers or groups of dealerships. Even if plaintiffs bring class actions and courts consistently grant testers standing to sue, the piecemeal approach of such suits, combined with the protracted nature of litigation, is unlikely to be sufficient to deter race-and gender-dependent behavior.

In light of these conditions, policymakers might consider structural reforms to improve the workings of the market. Structural changes should grow out of specific causal theories of disparate treatment in order quickly and effectively to erase such treatment. For example, if animus is inducing price discrimination, a law that outlawed price discrimination might induce some sellers to refuse to bargain. However, if the disparate treatment is caused by inferences about different consumer demand, then outlawing price discrimination should not generate such refusals. Simply put, to formulate effective intervention, policymakers must understand why sellers discriminate.

The earlier analysis of competition suggested that high-markup customers (and the ensuing concentration of profits) are a central cause of dealer price discrimination. As a result, if policymakers can find a way to reduce significantly the profits on these sucker sales, the manner in which dealerships conduct the retail sale of *all* cars would become dramatically more competitive. Without the pathological effects of highly concentrated profits, dealers would no longer have an incentive to force consumers to expend real and psychic resources in bargaining.

Policymakers could use three different strategies to eliminate high-markup sales. Most directly, courts could strengthen current notions of substantive unconscionability to prohibit high-markup sales. This strategy, however, is unlikely to occur: courts in the past have shown extreme reluctance to distinguish conscionable from unconscionable markups. Although courts voided contracts for unconscionable markups in two well-known cases, *Frostifresh Corp. v. Reynoso* and *American Home Improvement v. MacIver*, few courts since the early 1960s have reached similar holdings. The likelihood of courts taking the dramatic step of expanding this rarely used doctrine becomes even smaller in light of the special nature of bargaining for retail cars and society's solicitude toward such bargaining.

As a second regulatory strategy, policymakers might restrict the amount of price dispersion permissible in the car market. Regulators might, for example, allow dealerships to engage in bargaining, but void sales with markups that are more than twenty percent above the average markup. Unlike direct unconscionability regulation, firms would retain the freedom to set the average markup for any one model as high as the market would bear but would be prohibited from selling similar cars at significantly different prices. At its most extreme, this form of regulation would prohibit bargaining and mandate that dealerships sell at advertised prices. Restraining price dispersion is an attractive form of regulation because it might benefit all would-be car buyers. If the number of high-markup sales is reduced, sellers may find that bargaining (and the transaction costs that it imposes on all consumers) is no longer profitable. Once high-markup consumers are protected, sellers may no longer subject their low-markup consumers to costly and unpleasant bargaining.

Finally and least intrusively, regulators might reduce the number of sales with disparately high markups by mandating various types of disclosure from dealerships to consumers. Dealerships, for example, might be required to reveal the average price for which each make of car is sold. Knowing that the dealership is attempting to charge $3000 more than the average price would allow high-markup consumers to protect themselves. Alternatively, regulation might force dealerships to reveal the size of the markup on each individual transaction. Clay Miller and I have argued elsewhere that markup disclosure could improve both the equity and efficiency of retail car sales: "markup revelation would truncate the bargaining process at each dealership. The possibility of hoodwinking uninformed buyers into purchasing at a high markup would diminish as the excessive profits would be directly revealed."

In sum, mandating disclosure and restraining price dispersion are plausible strategies to reduce the importance that dealerships place on high-markup sales. A central prediction of this Article is that at some point reducing the concentration of dealership profits would rationalize dealership competition by giving individual dealerships an incentive to opt for high-volume, stated-price selling strategies. The relatively unintrusive nature of disclosure and price-dispersion regulation makes them politically and administratively more viable.

Before choosing a strategy to eliminate price dispersion, policy-makers should determine whether a single price equilibrium is "sustainable": that is, whether competitive dealerships that charge a single price could break even and thus survive price dispersion. In markets with high fixed costs, if sellers were required (directly or indirectly through disclosure) to charge a single price, competition might drive that price to a level below sellers' average cost. Such markets have "hollow cores" (because the "core" set of viable single-price equilibriums is empty or "hollow").

If the retail car market has a hollow core, government intervention to eliminate price dispersion would tend to drive dealerships from the market. In such markets, high-markup sales help dealers cover their fixed costs. In the airline industry, for example, the high-markup sales to business travelers may be necessary to meet industry fixed costs. Indeed, business travelers may benefit from the presence of lower-price tourist fares because "cheap" seats defray part of these fixed costs. If regulation eliminated price dispersion and mandated a single fare per route, business travelers might have to pay higher prices than under the current regime. Tourist travelers would stop buying, and the airline would then pass its fixed costs along to the smaller group of business travelers.

Regulator concerns should be allayed, however, because the retail car market does not resemble hollow core markets. Retail car dealerships do not experience significant high fixed costs (especially when compared to many other single price markets such as the market for electronic appliances and stereo equipment). Moreover, it is implausible that white males would (like tourist travelers) stop purchasing in a single price equilibrium. Mandating a single fare for airlines might lead to an inflated price that only businesspeople could afford, but mandating a single price for automobiles would not leave blacks and females alone to shoulder even higher proportions of the retailers' fixed costs.

Although this discussion of potential regulatory strategies is impressionistic, at the very least it suggests that regulators have a variety of choices beyond traditional civil rights and consumer protection remedies to attack the inequalities uncovered in this Article. Naturally, implementing one of these structural interventions would impose enforcement costs that must be weighed against the benefits of regulation. Dealers may attempt to circumvent such regulations in several ways. Nevertheless, in evaluating the efficacy of structural changes, policymakers should pay particular attention to the concentration of profits and the prevalence of high-markup sales.

V. Conclusion

The negotiation of contracts occupies a mysterious and somewhat mythical position in the law and in our society. In *The Wealth of Nations*, Adam Smith opined that people have a natural propensity to "truck and barter" over the sale of goods. Law-and-economic scholars at times extend this insight, suggesting that people will tend to negotiate whenever resources are misallocated: if I want to sit on a crowded subway, I will negotiate with the other passengers for a seat.

Common experience indicates, however, that many people in the United States are averse to bargaining. The frustration that many consumers experience in bargaining for a car is largely attributable to the ludicrously inefficient manner in which cars are marketed. Although Smith and others attach almost mythic qualities to the process of bargaining, this Article has thrown the equity and efficiency of car negotiations into question. The process of retail car negotiations becomes even more problematic when traditionally disadvantaged members of our society effectively pay a bargaining tax whenever they purchase a new car.

Earlier this year, I asked a car dealer during an interview whether the bulk of his profits were concentrated in a few sales. He told me that his dealership made a substantial number of both "sucker" and "non-sucker" sales. He added: "My cousin, however, owns a dealership in a black neighborhood. He doesn't sell nearly as many [cars], but he hits an awful lot of home runs. You know, sometimes it seems like the people that can least afford it have to pay the most." Although it is dangerous to extrapolate from the results of a single study, the amounts of discrimination uncovered, if representative of a larger phenomenon, are truly astounding. A $500 overcharge per car means that blacks annually pay $150 million more for new cars than they would if they were white males. There are substantial reasons to uncover *and eliminate* such discrimination.

———

For further reading, *see also* Peter Siegelman, *Gender and Race Discrimination in Retail Car Negotiations, in* PERVASIVE PREJUDICE?: UNCONVENTIONAL EVIDENCE OF RACE AND GENDER DISCRIMINATION 19 (Ian Ayres ed., 2001).

CHAPTER 11

THE MARKET VALUE OF CULTURE

Introduction

Between culture and commerce lies an ocean of mostly unexplored misunderstandings. In a thousand ways, the captains of commerce and the giants of creative invention live in the perpetual paradox of mutual hostility and mutual dependence. When race and ethnic pluralism are tossed into this already volatile mix, the questions multiply even as the answers diminish in inverse proportion.

This chapter takes up some of the most troublesome issues at the intersection of culture, race, gender, and identity in the marketplace. In what follows we consider four central queries: *First,* can economic behavior be fully understood, without an attentive account of the cultural context in which economic transactions occur? The paucity of attention of neoclassical strands of economic analysis to the cultural variables that we discuss in what follows has produced a largely impotent set of models for predicting many crucial items of economic behavior. These thin models, devoid of cultural context, have dominated the legal discourse about economics. We identify a more complex set of ideas that incorporates culture and its tension with commerce. *Second,* what is the impact of racial dominance on the ownership and control of cultural property? We ask whether the rules of intellectual property support or undermine the growth of economic autonomy for members of culturally subordinated groups. Is the economic structure that frames the labor of musicians, artists, singers, songwriters, actors, and other creators just? *Third,* how does subordination express its effect in the valuation of the human capital components of language, hairstyle, sexual difference, and modes of expressive autonomy in the workplace? *Fourth,* if we reconceptualize the relationship of culture and markets, can we elevate the level of human flourishing for a broader group of citizens?

A. ACCENTS

In this passage, novelist Amy Tan vividly captures the problem of an immigrant mother's effort to communicate her hope for cultural transformation, even while clinging to the project of symbolic and creative preservation of cultural memory. The mother dreams of speaking without an accent.

The old woman remembered a swan she had bought many years ago in Shanghai for a foolish sum. This bird, boasted the market vendor, was once a duck that stretched its neck in hopes of becoming a goose, and now look! It is too beautiful to eat.

Then the woman and the swan sailed across an ocean many thousands of *li* wide, stretching their necks toward America. On her journey she cooed to the swan: 'In America, I will have a daughter just like me. But over there nobody will say her worth is measured by the loudness of her husband's belch. Over there nobody will look down on her, because I will make her speak perfect American English. And over there she will always be too full to swallow any sorrow! She will know my meaning, because I will give her this swan—a creature that became more than what was hoped for.'

But when she arrived in the new country the immigration officials pulled her swan away from her, leaving the woman fluttering her arms and with only one swan feather for a memory. And then she had to fill out so many forms she forgot why she had come and what she had left behind.

Now the woman was old. And she had a daughter who grew up speaking only English and swallowing more Coca–Cola than sorrow. For a long time now the woman had wanted to give her daughter the single swan feather and tell her, "This feather may look worthless, but it comes from afar and carries with it all my good intentions." And she waited, year after year, for the day she could tell her daughter this in perfect American English.

Amy Tan, *Feathers From a Thousand* Li *Away, in* The Joy Luck Club (1989).

Voices of America: Accent, Antidiscrimination Law, and a Jurisprudence for the Last Reconstruction

100 Yale L.J. 1329 (1991).

■ Mari J. Matsuda

I.   Introduction

* * * This Article opens with stories of some of the accents that gave rise to the existing judicial decisions. The influence of the "turn to narrative"—the suggestion that human beings understand and form their worlds through stories—is evident here. These narratives create a doctrinal puzzle. * * * The puzzle is this: Courts recognize that discrimination against accent can function as the equivalent of prohibited national origin discrimination. The fact that communication is an important element of job performance, however, tends to trump this prohibition against discrimination, such that it is impossible to explain when or why plaintiffs will ever win in accent cases. In fact, they almost never do. Much of this section will sound like a positivist's plea for logic.

[This article] attempts to understand the cultural context of accent discrimination by considering the role of speech in society, and the ways in which prejudice and status assumptions are tied inextricably to speech evaluation. Given this sociolinguistic reality, I argue * * * for a doctrinal reconstruction that will apply Title VII to accent cases in a rational way. I criticize the current, conclusory reasoning of most accent decisions, while acknowledging the difficulties courts face. This is positivism plus sociology of law—a kind of thinking I associate with the Yale Law School. It demands that we apply our faculties of reason to the social reality of lived experience.

Having set forth what I believe is a rational and just application of Title VII principles to accent cases, [I will then] consider the ethical implications of accepting or rejecting a doctrinal scheme intended to promote linguistic pluralism. [This article] explores liberal justifications for linguistic tolerance, and * * * considers accent from within the perspective of emerging progressive theories of law, including Critical Legal Studies, Critical Race Theory, and feminist jurisprudence. Utilizing these critical theories, I inquire into the deeper meaning of accent discrimination as situated in structures of subordination. This part is influenced by the critical theorists who have confronted the issue of audience: for whom do we write, and why? I attempt to make explicit my intended and multiple audiences, and my political goals.

* * *

II. THE STORIES

I come from a place that is farther away from any place than any place. The islands of Hawaii, geographically isolated and peopled from all corners of the world, are a linguist's dream. The linguistic and ethnic heritage of the islands is more diverse than that of any other state in the United States. In the voices of the islands one hears traces of Hawaiian, Portuguese, New England English, Japanese, Chinese, Filipino, and Spanish. It is thus no accident that two significant Title VII cases falling in the middle of the doctrinal puzzle of accent discrimination come from Hawaii.

Perhaps in explaining the puzzle, it is best to begin where all cases begin, with a person and the story they bring to court.

A. *Manuel Fragante's Story*

* * *

In 1981 Manuel Fragante took a civil service examination along with over 700 other applicants. He is an intelligent and educated man, and he was not surprised when he received the highest score of all applicants who took the test. Fragante was ranked first on the list of eligibles, but, after a brief interview, he was turned down for the job of clerk in the Division of Motor Vehicles. When he asked why, he learned that he was rejected because of his Filipino accent. Manuel Fragante, combat veteran of two wars and true believer in the rhetoric of equality, promptly contacted a

Filipino American state legislator, who in turn recommended that Fragante visit the run-down office of a neighborhood public interest law firm.

* * *

Because the DMV creates constant demand for new employees, the personnel department sent a specialist to study the job and devise a screening test to help identify a large pool of prospective clerks. This is a well-established procedure used by large employers. The specialist observed clerks on the job. The key skills she identified included alphabetizing, reproducing numbers and letters with accuracy, making change, exhibiting courtesy, and other routine clerical skills. A test was devised to measure these skills.

* * *

This was the premise Manuel Fragante relied on when he took the civil service examination and out-tested his 700 competitors. He was proud of his score and felt assured of the job. While others thought the job was beneath him given his age and experience, he was looking forward to the simplicity of its tasks, to the official feel of working for the government in an air-conditioned building, and to the chance to earn some spending money instead of wasting his time in boring idleness. He found warnings that the job was stressful mildly amusing. Having lived through invasion, war, and economic uncertainty, Manuel Fragante figured he could handle an irate taxpayer complaining about a long wait in line. He thus walked in for his interview with a calm and assured dignity. He knew the job was his.

* * *

Manuel Fragante was passed over for the job. The administrator in charge of hiring recommendations stated, "because of his accent, I would not recommend him for this position." The interviewers heard what any listener would hear in a brief conversation with Mr. Fragante: he speaks with a heavy Filipino accent, one that he is unlikely to lose at his age.

* * *

The linguist sat through the trial and noted the proceedings with interest. Attorneys for both sides suffered lapses in grammar and sentence structure, as did the judge. Mr. Fragante's English, a review of the transcript confirmed, was more nearly perfect in standard grammar and syntax than any other speaker in the courtroom. Mr. Fragante testified for two days, under the stress of both direct and cross-examination. The judge and the examiners spoke to Fragante in English and understood his answers. A court reporter understood and took down his words verbatim. In the functional context of the trial, everyone understood Manuel Fragante's speech. Yet the defendant's interviewers continued to claim Fragante could not be understood well enough to serve as a DMV clerk.

In an irony particularly noticeable to the linguist, lawyers for both sides, as well as the defendant's witnesses, spoke with the accent characteristic of non-whites raised in Hawaii—the Hawaiian Creole accent that would become the subject of another significant Title VII accent case discussed below. * * * The linguist, trained as he was to recognize accents as intriguing differences rather than handicaps, was troubled by the legal result in the *Fragante* case.

* * * The judge was on assignment from Arizona. He listened to four days of testimony and concluded that Manuel Fragante was denied the job *not* because of national origin, but because of legitimate difficulties with his accent. The opinion was somewhat of a puzzle. The judge found, as fact, that Manuel Fragante "has extensive verbal communication skill in English" but paradoxically that he has a "difficult manner of pronunciation" and a "military bearing," and that some listeners would "stop listening" when they hear a Filipino accent. The court made much of the high-stress communication required for the job, and found that speech was a bona fide occupational qualification. Finally, the court applied the *McDonnell Douglas* test, and found no proof of discriminatory intent or subterfuge.

Manuel Fragante was upset by the opinion. Soon after losing out on the DMV job, he was hired by the State of Hawaii as a statistician. Much of his work involved telephone interviews. Fragante felt his employment with the State proved his claim that the city misjudged his accent. He told his attorneys he wanted to press forward with his case.

Fragante lost on appeal before the Ninth Circuit although he did gain the symbolic victory of the court's sympathetic recognition that accent discrimination could violate Title VII. The U.S. Supreme Court denied certiorari.

* * *

B. *The Weather Forecasters*

* * *

In 1985, the National Weather Service advertised for a vacancy in the Honolulu forecast office. Coursework in meteorology, climatology, physics, and mathematics was identified in the vacancy announcement as relevant to the position, as was meteorology experience. James Kahakua, a native Hawaiian, proudly possessed years of experience in meteorology, and a Bachelor of Science degree with coursework in all of the areas identified in the announcement. He applied for a promotion to the open position, but was turned down in favor of a "haole"—or white—newcomer to Hawaii. A speech consultant had rated Kahakua's Creole-tinged speech unacceptable for weather broadcasts. The white applicant had no college degree, and minimal experience in meteorology. He was selected because of his "excellent" broadcasting voice. Kahakua, along with other applicants who felt that the promotion of a neophyte constituted discrimination, sued the Weather Service and lost.

* * *

The district judge, a visitor from Fresno, found that race was not a factor in the promotion. The white candidate was selected because he had "better diction, better enunciation, better pronunciation, better cadence, better intonation, better voice clarity, and better understandability." The judge credited the testimony of speech experts that "standard English is that used by radio and TV announcers" and that "standard English pronunciation should be used by radio broadcasters." The court added, "there is no race or physiological reason why Kahakua could not have used standard English pronunciations." The judge discounted the testimony of the linguist who stated that Hawaiian Creole pronunciation is not incorrect, rather it is one of the many varieties of pronunciation of standard English. The linguist, the judge stated, was not an expert in speech.

C.   *More Stories, More Voices*

In 1988, A. L. Hahn, a young Korean American, ran for city council in Santa Clara, California. The editorial page of the San Jose Mercury News, an award-winning California newspaper, recommended against voting for Hahn, in spite of the paper's general agreement with Hahn on the issues. This seemed odd in an editorial that welcomed change and opened with criticism of the "old guard" of "powerful insiders," arguing against candidates with established real estate and institutional ties. Why would a pro-change editor reject a bright newcomer? The editorial stated:

> *We like Hahn, 34, who was born in South Korea and whose positions on controlling growth are much like our own. Unfortunately, we think his heavy accent and somewhat limited contacts would make it difficult for him to be a councilman.*

* * *

III.   THE DOCTRINAL PUZZLE OF ACCENT AND ANTIDISCRIMINATION LAW

This is the doctrinal puzzle presented by these stories:

1.   Title VII absolutely disallows discrimination on the basis of race and national origin.

2.   A fortiori, Title VII absolutely disallows discrimination on the basis of traits, like accent, when they are stand-ins for race and national origin.

3.   Title VII absolutely allows employers to discriminate on the basis of job ability.

4.   Communication, and therefore accent, employers will insist, are elements of job ability.

The puzzle in accent cases is that accent is often derivative of race and national origin. Only Filipino people speak with Filipino accents. Yet, within the range of employer prerogatives, it is reasonable to require communication skills of employees. The claim that accent impedes job ability is often made with both sincerity and economic rationality. How, then, should Title VII squeeze between the walls of accent as protected trait and speech as job requirement?

This puzzle is evident in every reported case considering accent and Title VII. The courts recognize that discrimination against a trait that is a stand-in for a protected category is prohibited. An employer who says, "I'm not discriminating against people of color, I just don't want to hire people with dark skin," is in violation of Title VII. The EEOC has found that discrimination against an accent associated with foreign birth is the equivalent of discrimination against foreign birth, relying in part on evidence that it is nearly impossible for an adult to eliminate their natural accent. Even the skilled mimics of new accents frequently overcorrect. That is, they blanketly apply stereotypical traits of the acquired accent, even in circumstances in which native speakers would drop the trait. To acquire natural, unself-conscious, and native-sounding speech with a new accent is a feat accomplished easily only by young children, who are still in the process of language acquisition. Given this near-immutability, discrimination against accent is the functional equivalent of discrimination against foreign origin.

* * *

A second complicating factor is the role of speech in the job. In some jobs—say a 911 operator—speech is a critical and central job function. In other jobs, such as a bricklayer or a graphic artist, speech is helpful but not central to the work. In some cases the employer may want a certain accent because of its prestige value—say a French accent in a French restaurant. The range of reasons for wanting speech clarity will vary with the range of jobs.

* * *

Given the pervasive, unconscious bias against low-status accents, it is reasonable to inquire of employers exactly what they mean when they declare an accent nonfunctional for the job. If they mean consciously or unconsciously "I don't like foreign sounds and neither will my customers," they are arguing that discrimination is a justification for discrimination. This kind of tautology is obviously insufficient to surmount Title VII's prohibition against discrimination.

* * *

IV. What is Speech?

* * *

B. *What is Accent?*

Accent, as used in this Article, refers to pronunciation rather than choice of words. A linguist might break down the lay concept of accent into smaller components of phonology, including intonation, stress, and rhythm. While this Article focuses on accent, much of the analysis is also relevant to dialect, or word choice. There are many dialects of English, some more prestigious than others, providing many opportunities for discrimination.

As feminist theorists have pointed out, everyone has a gender, but the hidden norm in law is male. As critical race theorists have pointed out, everyone has a race, but the hidden norm in law is white. In any dyadic relationship, the two ends are equidistant from each other. If the parties are equal in power, we see them as equally different from each other. When the parties are in a relationship of domination and subordination we tend to say that the dominant is normal, and the subordinate is different from normal.

And so it is with accent. Everyone has an accent, but when an employer refuses to hire a person "with an accent," they are referring to a hidden norm of non-accent—a linguistic impossibility, but a socially constructed reality. People in power are perceived as speaking normal, unaccented English. Any speech that is different from that constructed norm is called an accent.

The unstated norm—the so-called standard American accent—is an odd choice for a norm, because only a minority of citizens speak it. Most speakers of North American English have an accent that reflects their regional affiliations, their ethnicity, or their age. An odd recent phenomenon, the geographically dispersed, upper-middle-class, youth-based accent known as "valley" or "sunbelt-speak" is heard increasingly among law students across the country. Because I grew up in a world in which accents tended to attach to races, it seems odd to me as a teacher to hear my students of different races speaking in this new, youth-based accent. (They might characterize a racist decision, for example, as "ruhley" unfair or "see-oh" ridiculous.)

If almost no one speaks with standard pronunciation—or, as they call it in Great Britain, "received pronunciation"—the claim that standardization is important for comprehension loses some force. Variability is the master rule of spoken North American English, and if variability impedes comprehension, then we are already living in the tower of Babel.

We are not. We understand each other, particularly when we are motivated to do so. One of the interesting lessons of sociolinguistics is that comprehension is as much a function of attitude as it is of variability. Human beings can and do adjust to marked variation in pitch, intonation, and pronunciation in ways that scores of computer engineers working in the fields of fuzzy logic and artificial intelligence have been unable to duplicate. The seemingly simple ability of a tiny child to recognize its own name whether spoken at Mom's pitch or at Dad's, is in actuality a complex feat of comprehension. The magnificent switchboard that converts sound to understanding in the human mind can account for gaps, pauses, variations, and distortions of many kinds.

Thus a twentieth-century North American can listen to the long-dead accents in a Shakespeare play and—after perhaps a moment of disorientation—soon follow the dialogue with ease. A traveler to a new region of English-speakers, after a sometimes hilarious miscue, will understand more and more of the local speech, especially if motivated by the need to get a bite to eat or a moment of human company. We have all, at various times, performed the miracle of comprehension across a vast sea of phonological difference.

The ability to comprehend across variations is accompanied by a clumsy inability to alter speech across variations. Most of us feel noticeably uncomfortable and phony when we try to imitate other accents, and few succeed at the task of acquiring a permanent, unself-conscious, new accent.

When the Beatles were an unknown Liverpool band trying to make it in the new world of rock and roll, they inserted "R's" in their pronunciation in order to sound more American. As the British invasion captured the fancy of young whites in America, it became more acceptable to sound British. By the time the Beatles hit superstar status, they had reverted to the "R" dropping that characterized their working class, British backgrounds. The Sergeant Pepper album—which established the Beatles as musicians destined to go down in popular history as more than just another pretty band—is notably authentic in its "R"-lessness.

Meanwhile, back in the midwest, U.S.A.—land of "R" pronunciation so abundant it appears even in words like "wash"—a young white musician named Bob Dylan regularly dropped "R's" in his singing. He did this not because he wanted to sound British, but because he wanted to sound like his idols—the African Americans who regularly dropped "R's" in their creation of the indigenous American art form known as the blues. The boys from Liverpool had made a characteristic imitator's error of overcorrection. In adding R's prodigiously to their early recordings they ended up sounding more like Pat Boone than like their African American inspiration, Little Richard. Bob Dylan, more sophisticated in his understanding of "R" usage in the United States, knew that in the world of contemporary American music, status moved south in more ways than one. Sounding Black, sounding down in the power hierarchy, sounding blue, was the definition of cool among the truly down, downtown, non-"R" pronouncers.

The view of most sociolinguists, grounded as they are in the field of anthropology, is that accent is a societal and cultural creation. It situates people socially and helps them sort through social contexts. Most of us do this unconsciously—we speak differently at work, at play, to children, to authority figures.

Sitting on my porch in Honolulu one day, I was talking long distance to my friend Barb in California. Because I lived in L.A. as a child, it's easy for me to shift into a voice that matches hers when we talk. Shifting closer in accent to someone we like is a common signal of intimacy. As we spoke, the newspaper girl, a thirteen-year-old Tongan–Samoan immigrant, walked by and I called out a friendly greeting and asked her a question.

"Oh, how cute, you're talking local," Barb said over the phone. I laughed, because I hadn't realized I had made a shift, but Barb recognized the melodic, inquiring intonation of "local" Hawaii talk that was so absent when I was speaking to an L.A. friend. Because she has lived in Hawaii and liked it, the accent had a good connotation for her.

Accents sometimes charm us with difference. Barb and I both laugh over the accent of the man who cuts our hair. His is a marked Italian accent, sometimes incomprehensible to both of us. In the West L.A. shop where he works, his accent adds the cachet of difference that recalls an old

Beverly Hills joke about the patient who refused a local anesthetic, insisting instead on the imported.

At other times accents can repel us. In that same West L.A. salon, I overheard a beautiful stylist complaining to a client in Brooklynese, "I can't stand the way I talk, it sounds so low class." Media stereotyping can make some accents sound ignorant or threatening. These evaluations are imposed, not natural. As much as we may believe that certain accents "just sound better" or "sound so harsh," our judgments are mediated judgments. The evidence suggests there is no such thing as an inherently pleasant accent. What sounds "low-class, vulgar, rough" in one culture can sound "interesting, pretty" to someone from another culture unfamiliar with the status position of the accent.

I cling to certain notions of accent attitudes as pure and not culturally generated. I am fond of saying that the Hawaiian language sounds beautiful, as though this were absolutely true rather than true to my ears, in relation to the English I am used to, and in connection with my knowledge of the generous, loving aspects of Hawaiian culture that infuse the language. Similarly, I am fond of saying that a particular person has a beautiful voice or a sexy voice as though that were absolutely true, rather than true as a convocation of Hollywood, Madison Avenue, Motown, and my own desires.

We want to believe, when we say of an accent that it is good, or bad, or easy, or difficult, that we are speaking of facts rather than social constructions. Facts, especially when the alternative conclusion is that our evaluations are produced by bigotry or our own feelings of fear and inadequacy.

While the sociolinguists tell us that accent is a social phenomenon, some experts in the field called "speech" or "communications" hold quite a different view. Books on accents are typically found in two separate places in the libraries: under Sociolinguistics and under Speech Pathology. In the Speech Pathology section, accent is considered a disease in need of a cure. There, chapters on accent are side-by-side with chapters on stuttering and aphasia. Rather than seeing accent as a social phenomenon marking speakers as equidistant from each other, the speech pathology view sees an "accent" as an unfortunate deviation from a standard. This deviation is at once labeled disease and declared curable with a series of exercises and manipulations. This view persists in spite of the evidence that eliminating one's native accent is nearly impossible for most adults.

The presumption behind the speech pathology view is that variability is harmful, both for the speaker and the community. Private accent-elimination classes now exist in some cities to help immigrants sound "less foreign." Speech consultants help employers pick "good" voices. In the *Kahakua* case, the employer's speech consultant discussed the joys of eradicating an ethnic accent in almost sexual tones. Writing of one Japanese American candidate, she stated:

> [H]e needs specific help in the area of developing good speech habits through deleting "pidgin" from his daily vocabulary in order to

insure that Standard English can become his automatic model. This will take disciplined work by means of professional help, but he should make every effort to receive such help. It is my belief that he would experience a most gratifying surge of renewed self-confidence and pride in his accomplishment.

* * *

The language of "control" and "handicap" is typical of the speech pathology view. In referring to the accent as "pidgin" the speech consultant shows unfamiliarity with linguistic terminology. Pidgin is a broken English that is spoken by non-native speakers. Neither speaker evaluated in the passages above was speaking pidgin when evaluated. Both were lifelong, native speakers of English. They were reading a weather report written in standard English. The horrible handicap, subject to control through disciplined study, was simply the local accent native to most non-whites who grow up in Hawaii.

The linguist's evaluation of speakers in the *Kahakua* case differed notably from the speech consultant's. The linguist found that both speakers used an acrolectal variety of Hawaiian Standard English. That is, their speech was quite close to standard mainland pronunciation with certain phonological features characteristic of Hawaiian Creole speakers, such as occasional substitution of the "d" sound for the "th" sound.

The linguist concluded that both speakers

> speak what a large portion of Hawaiian-born, educated, professional people (e.g. the governor and most state legislators) speak: Hawaii Standard English ... both use an acrolectal and highly intelligible English. The HCE [Hawaiian Creole English] features that are observable are phonetic ones that do mark their identity as non-Caucasians, however, they are not accurately viewed as linguistic deficiencies of any kind. Just as one would not fault the southern accent of former President Jimmy Carter or Jim Lehrer (of the McNeil/Lehrer News Hour). . . .

The linguist thus viewed the accents as acceptable and intelligible, while the speech consultant viewed them as handicaps in need of correction. The linguist's view is supported by research that shows that language variability is inevitable and that moderate accent differences rarely impede communication when listeners are motivated and nonprejudiced. The speech consultant's view is supported by a widely held belief that speech standardization is necessary, good, and attainable, and that accent interferes with intelligibility.

* * *

V. TOWARD A DOCTRINAL RECONSTRUCTION

* * *

This doctrinal framework is not intended as a complete guide to the intricacies of Title VII as applied to accent cases. Title VII is one of the most litigated of all federal statutes, and the many significant nuances of Title VII litigation are beyond the scope of this piece. Rather, the intent here is to suggest the critical areas of inquiry that must be part of the analysis of any Title VII accent case, and to suggest why and how a conscientious court would conduct such inquiry.

I suggest that courts should consider four separate questions in accent cases:

1. What level of communication is required for the job?

2. Was the candidate's speech fairly evaluated?

3. Is the candidate intelligible to the pool of relevant, nonprejudiced listeners, such that job performance is not unreasonably impeded?

4. What accommodations are reasonable given the job and any limitations in intelligibility?

* * *

A. *Step One: The Level of Communication Required for the Job*

There are many jobs that people do in silence. In some work places, the level of industrial noise is so high that conversation is impossible. Jobs that rely on visual, manual, and intellectual skills have traditionally comprised the employment of the deaf. The deaf, however, are proving that even jobs that require regular communication can be done by individuals with little or no speech. Our assumption that speech is integral to a job may reflect "hearie" bias.

There are some jobs, however, in which speech is central. Broadcasters and telephone operators, for example, regularly use speech in their jobs.

* * *

The paradigmatic job requiring maximum oral clarity is the 911 operator. Several elements mark the importance of speech in that position:

1. The consequences of miscommunication are grave.

2. Giving and receiving oral communication are a substantial part of the job.

3. The speech interactions are under high stress, where time is of the essence, increasing probability of miscommunication.

4. The interactions are typically one-time calls, such that the caller has little time to adjust in listening and comprehension patterns.

If one or more of these elements is absent, the degree of importance of speech decreases. For example, if time is not of the essence, but clarity of communication is important to avoid grave consequences, forms of communication other than speech—such as writing—may be more appropriate. If interactions are repeated, such that listeners can adjust, again a difference in speech style becomes less of a barrier. Consider, for example, the way in which the regulars at a pier-side fish auction can understand an auctioneer's rapid-fire babble, while newcomers find it incomprehensible.

As one moves farther away from the 911 paradigm, there are a range of jobs in which facility in oral communication is useful but not critical if other job skills are present. Computer programmers, word processors, janitors, dancers, assembly line workers, parking lot attendants, architects, and laboratory technicians, for example, all fall somewhere between the polar opposites of "speech is critical" and "speech is inconsequential."

    * * *

In a range of jobs in which speech seems critical—doctor, bank teller, police officer, teacher, lawyer—consideration of the actual job tasks and needs of patients/customers/clients is useful. Is "bedside manner" the equivalent of oral facility? Not necessarily. Some very articulate doctors have weak skills in empathy. Care, concern, and understanding are communicated by nonspeech—posture, eye contact, touch, and taking the time to listen—as well as speech.

    * * *

The principle that there are gradations of communication skills required in different jobs was recognized by the Ninth Circuit Court of Appeals in *Nanty v. Barrows*. In that case, the employer refused to hire Mr. Nanty, a Native American, for a job as a furniture mover, claiming, among other things, that Nanty was "inarticulate." That claim alone, without any evidence of why articulate speech was essential for the job, was unpersuasive to the court. The applicant was an experienced furniture mover. The court was suspicious of the claim that Mr. Nanty was inarticulate, especially given the fact that the employer had not even conducted an interview. An employer who is serious about the necessity for oral communication will have some job screening mechanism that rationally measures oral skills. The next section discusses applicant screening and fair evaluation.

B. *Step Two: Fair Evaluation*

An employer who claims speech is a critical job function, but who does not fairly evaluate speech of candidates, is behaving irrationally, or discriminatorily, or both. As Justice Rehnquist suggested in the *Furnco* case, we reasonably presume that economic entities act rationally. When they do not—when they prefer less-qualified applicants, for example—it is probable that prejudice is entering into the process. Evaluation of accent is particularly susceptible to bias and distortion, and thus it is appropriate for courts to examine the evaluation process.

    * * *

When we hear a different voice we are likely to devalue it, particularly when it triggers the collective xenophobic unconscious that is the ironic legacy of a nation populated largely by people from other continents. Because misevaluation of speech, and particularly of speech associated with historical targets of discrimination, is common, claims that accent impedes job performance are not credible unless they stem from fair evaluation. An informal answer-a-few-questions interview is less reliable than an evaluation of on-the-job performance, whether simulated or actual. Rather than assuming an accent would be unintelligible over the phone, for example, a candidate might be asked to complete an actual or simulated phone call to see whether breakdowns in communication occur.

Similarly, evaluations that rely on subjective impressions of untrained interviewers are less credible. Interviewers and others making employment decisions can be trained to avoid accent bias. The State of California, for example, has produced a training manual that explains in simple language the danger of bias and prejudice in evaluation of accents.

* * *

C. *Step Three: Comprehension by the Relevant, Nonprejudiced Listener at the Level Required for the Job*

If the employer fairly evaluates the speaker, and if speech is an important job function, then it is reasonable to reject a speaker whose accent impedes intelligibility by the relevant, nonprejudiced listener.

* * *

In public contact jobs, the listener pool is identifiable by region and demography. A bank teller, for example, generally serves clientele from within one city. Having a regional accent, when most of one's clients are from the same region, can enhance rather than impede communication. The point here is that intelligibility is not absolute. It is relational. To whom we speak determines whether our accent helps or hurts communication.

* * *

The testimony of experts familiar with speech interactions in the relevant listener pool is thus entitled to considerable weight in meeting the plaintiff's burden of persuasion. In the *Kahakua* case, the speech pathologist who declared the Creole-accented speech substandard was not from Hawaii, nor did she purport to speak from knowledge of the relevant listener pool. Instead, she used a generic "broadcasting" standard to conclude that a white candidate's accent was superior.

The plaintiff's expert was a linguist whose field of expertise was speech interactions within the relevant listener pool. She testified that the local-accented speech of the plaintiffs was easily intelligible to *all* residents of Hawaii, including white newcomers, and that for the majority of residents who themselves have some level of a local accent, communication was enhanced by speech in that accent.

The court in *Kahakua* apparently applied the speech pathologist's generic standard, rather than the linguist's contextualized standard. The problem with the court's approach is that it imposes a standard on the community without any rationale for choosing the standard. It is not a majoritarian standard, since most Americans speak with an ethnic or regional accent. It is not an intelligibility standard, because there is no evidence that there is a generic accent that is always more intelligible than any other accent in a given listener pool.

The hidden rationale thus becomes a nationalist/monocultural one. That is, holding people in a nation as radically diverse in accents as ours to one standard of pronunciation is a declaration that this is a nation of one voice. In the same way that some insist ours is a Christian nation with Christianity the norm against which all other religions are seen as different, the fiction of a generic American accent implies that this is a white, upper-class nation, and all non-white, ethnic, regional, and lower-class accents are subnormal. Rather than imagining a fictional generic listener, the unbiased court would look to the actual listeners.

* * *

D. *Rejecting the Gift: The Problem of the Prejudiced Listener*

What should we do when members of the relevant listener pool are prejudiced and can't or won't tolerate an accent? In applying Step 3 above, the principles of Title VII require removing prejudiced listeners from analysis of the relevant listener pool.

It is well established under Title VII that bigoted preferences of customers, however real and economically effective, may not govern employment decisions. Even when employers can prove that they will lose customers who prefer not to do business with women, for example, Title VII requires employers to hire qualified women. By holding all employers to this nondiscriminatory standard, Title VII intervenes in the market and disallows an economic advantage to those employers who are otherwise eager to accede to the racist or sexist demands of customers. Title VII was designed to alter business practices in order to eliminate racism and sexism as a factor in hiring, promotion, and setting conditions of work.

* * *

The claim that customers will refuse to do business with employees with ethnic accents raises two problems. First is the problem that customer preference claims are often made without empirical foundation, reflecting false assumptions about the inability of customers to comprehend certain accents. Given the linguistic evidence that comprehension adjustments are relatively easy for motivated listeners, claims of customer preference, at a minimum, should be supported by some evidence of actual refusal to deal.

At the second level is the problem of actual prejudice. Certain accents, to certain listeners, sound "untrustworthy," for example, regardless of the sincerity of the speaker. An employer concerned with establishing customer confidence might be tempted to exclude from the workplace ethnic accents that key customers find untrustworthy. This is not allowed under Title VII. A particular accent sounds untrustworthy, or lazy, or ignorant to a listener when the listener has attached a cultural meaning, typically a racist cultural meaning, to the accent. In matched guise tests, linguists have shown that these cultural meanings rather than any combination of pronunciation or inflection, create the negative impression. Under the matched guise method, listeners hear tapes of the same words spoken by an actor using different accents. The listeners are not told that one person is acting out the different accents. They are then asked to evaluate what they assume are different speakers for qualities such as intelligence, confidence, trustworthiness, and warmth. The use of the same text and same speaker eliminates the role of personality traits or voice quality of the speaker in evaluation. The subjects are also tested separately to determine what racial stereotypes and prejudices they harbor. In repeated studies of this type, there is a high correlation between negative stereotyping of certain races and negative evaluation of accents associated with those races. The listener who thinks X people are lazy will evaluate a speaker with an X accent as lazy. Listeners can even internalize stereotypes about themselves. Members of subordinated groups in one study evaluated speakers of their own accent as "less intelligent" and "more warm" indicating in-group loyalties, as well as internalization of dominant group stereotypes about intellect.

* * *

E. *Step Four: Can the Employee Be Understood with Reasonable Accommodation of Linguistic Difference?*

To determine whether prejudice rather than unintelligibility motivates linguistic discrimination, it is useful to ask whether the employer can make reasonable changes in the workplace that would increase communication within the relevant listener pool. The concept of reasonable accommodation is well developed in the law governing employment of the differently-abled. It asks not that employers go broke in order to accommodate physical differences. Rather, it asks that employers make those alterations which are either costless or impose costs that, while they may cut into short-term returns, will have the long-term benefit of bringing qualified handicapped individuals into the labor force. Wheelchair ramps, braille in elevators, and grab-bars in restroom stalls are all accommodations we have grown accustomed to in recent years. We have made a collective decision that the costs, while not inconsequential, are reasonable in light of the benefits gained.

* * *

There are several specific inquiries that help separate legitimate communication difficulty from biased evaluation. First, as discussed above, expert witnesses can help in identifying the relevant, nonprejudiced listeners, and in determining whether the accent discrepancies are so divergent as to impede communication. Second, accommodations, including assistance to both speakers and listeners in bridging communication gaps, help show that any residual non-understanding reflects a genuine, irremediable intelligibility problem. Finally, the court can inquire into the level of prejudice against the accent. If the accent is one historically subjected to discrimination, for example, this cautions particular scrutiny and special efforts at accommodation in order to avoid the probability of biased evaluations. Again, experts are useful in determining whether there is a demonstrable history of prejudice against a particular accent, and in identifying kinds of phonological differences that actually do impede comprehension.

* * *

G. *Application*

How would the doctrinal reconstruction suggested above apply to the facts of the existing cases? This section will suggest briefly the ways in which the framework of inquiry presented in this Article would have altered the outcome in cases like *Fragante* and *Kahakua*.

1. Fragante *Reconsidered*

* * * The evaluation of *Fragante* was shoddy. Given the care and effort put into the civil service examination process, the cursory interview by untrained office workers seems an irrational allocation of resources. The interviewers who found Fragante's accent "difficult" did not identify any incidences of misunderstanding during the interview. The lack of standard interview questions, the irrationality of the rating sheet, and the absence in the interview process of training or instruction in either speech assessment or the obligation of nondiscrimination, reveal a weak system of evaluation. This weakness is unjustified given the size and the resources of the employer, and the regular turnover in the job. Significantly, the evaluation process did not include a functional component. That is, Fragante's speech was never tested in a real or simulated job setting. There was no evidence other than presumption that Fragante could not communicate with customers at the DMV.

* * *

The trial judge, as well as the employer's interviewers, found Fragante's accent "difficult." There is no distinction in the trial court opinion between "difficult" meaning "foreign, unusual, a strain on my ears because it is not how most people I know talk," and intelligibility at the level necessary to perform job tasks. The failure to make this critical distinction would, at a minimum, require a remand for clarification. The only legitimate inquiry, given the Title VII rule of nondiscrimination, is whether the speaker can communicate at the level required for the job.

The Ninth Circuit opinion in *Fragante* fails to make this distinction. The court found that there was no proof of discriminatory pretext and that the individuals selected in lieu of Fragante "had superior qualifications." The only "superior qualification" on record is speaking without a Filipino accent. The opinion seems to allow the employer to select a favored accent in lieu of a "foreign" accent. If the intent of the court is to prohibit accent discrimination, clarification is required on this point. The court should state unequivocally that once a person's speech is found functional, the employer may not reject it because a competitor's speech is "less foreign."

* * *

Finally, if the courts had considered the possibility of reasonable accommodation, they might well have altered their ultimate conclusions in *Fragante*. If, as the employer claims, customers are frequently frustrated and confused when they visit the DMV, perhaps there are other alterations to procedures, written information, and staffing, that could ease this burden. If a Filipino accent will "turn off" some listeners, those listeners could, perhaps, be directed to another line, or they could ask for a slower repetition of instructions.

* * *

VII.   ACCENT AND ANTISUBORDINATION: A RADICAL CRITIQUE

This Article is written out of contradiction, and this part enters the theoretical world that sees contradiction at the core of meaning in life and law. The contradiction in this Article, the irony of it, is that a self-conscious radical, schooled in the postmodern world, argues from cases, rules, and principles for a result that she sees as liberating. That same system of cases, rules, and principles has enslaved and excluded, taken lives and stilled dissent. That same system of cases, rules, and principles has entrenched ideas of objectivity, neutrality, necessity, and right that have made enslavement, exclusion, murder, and oligarchy seem natural and inevitable. These are the teachings of the feminists, critical legal scholars, and critical race scholars who are the voices of dissent in the world of legal theory. These critical voices constitute the community of scholar-activists whom I consider my colleagues in a most-serious quest for a just world. This part is my tribute to them.

It looks at accent discrimination from within that critical world, to try to understand what is really going on in accent cases, and to suggest an explicitly political justification for the doctrinal position set forth above. If the doctrinal section was "do the logical thing," and the preceding section was "do the liberal thing," I add now, not in jest and not because I reject either logic or liberalism, a section to plead, "do the right thing." This Article is an attempt to do legal scholarship using the tools of critical legal analysis. The method of the following sections follows a pattern emerging within such scholarship:

— First, it attempts to unmask false claims of objectivity, merit, neutrality, and necessity in the rhetoric of accent cases;

— Second, it examines the context of power in which accent cases arise, and draws from an emerging phenomenonology of subordination to understand how accent discrimination fits into broader social, historical, and psychological structures of subordination;

— Third, it is explicit, partisan, and non-neutral in its commitment to the ends of dismantling structures of subordination and promoting radical pluralism;

— Fourth, it understands doctrinal puzzles concerning accent and Title VII as cites of contestation with both ideological and material consequences; and

— Finally, it employs a strategy of legal analysis designed to promote both reformist and radical agendas by exploiting existing tensions in civil rights law. More specifically, by delineating a fair and logical application of Title VII doctrine to accent cases, I hope to affect three constituencies:

    a. Readers—including judges, lawyers, possible litigants, and legal theorists of goodwill—who are committed to the values I draw upon in this Article but who are unclear about how or whether those values should apply in accent cases;

    b. Activists and theorists seeking to form and critique strategies for radical social change; and

    c. Gatekeepers of the established order, whom I hope to reveal as self-interested and politically motivated should they choose to reject a logical argument for accent egalitarianism.

A. *Accent and the Critique of Objectivity*

Which accent is seen as normal, intelligent, most-likely-to-succeed, is a function of power distribution. Thus the key inquiry in understanding accent cases is "what are the power distributions?." Attempting to apply Title VII without asking that question is what allows courts to suggest that employers can pick the best accent out of many, without seeing that "best" points up the racial hierarchy. Unmasking the hidden center reveals accent evaluation for what it is: an exercise in power.

Seeing accent evaluation as an exercise of power helps refute the typical justifications for excluding or repressing certain accents, which include:

1. The inherent superiority of the standard accent. The claim here is that the standard accent is more pure, more eloquent, more expressive, more valuable.

2. The universality of the standard accent. Most people speak it and everyone understands it, therefore it is reasonably designated the national standard.

3. Standardization is efficient. Even if the standard is somewhat arbitrary, having a standard increases communication among diverse speakers. It reduces misunderstanding and saves time.

4. The standard is unifying. Having a standard helps forge a national identity and avoids the balkanizing disarray that comes with language variation.

The concept of positioned perspective, developed by feminists and critical race theorists, and the critique of neutrality associated with Foucault and the critical legal theorists, rejects the idea of a universal measure of accent quality. Add to this critique the empirical work of sociolinguists, and the argument that standard pronunciation is inherently superior and universal disappears. While most people in power speak the standard, the critical technique of challenging false norms as creations of power helps show how the seemingly absolute universality of standard pronunciation is actually an imposed universality.

This leaves the final two arguments of efficiency and unity. The argument that uniformity is efficient presumes that uniformity is attainable and that variability impedes communication. Both claims are historically and empirically false. Uniformity never has been and by all indications never will be the reality of spoken English. Language is a living, moving thing. Linguistic geographers show this graphically in an obscure but fascinating form of cartography that charts the journeys of words and pronunciation over space and time. The names we call things by are born, expand outward gathering more speakers of those names, and die, as other names take over. The word "orts" for scraps of garbage traveled from England to Massachusetts in the time of the colonies, where it thrived and then faded until only one informant in Bar Harbor and one in New Bedford could tell field researchers what it meant. Similarly, "standard pronunciation" varies both regionally in our time and historically over time. The teachers of "correct enunciation" of fifty years ago would hang their heads in sorrow over what passes for correct on Cable News Network today.

* * *

B.   *What Fear Is This? Accent and the Culture of Domination*

* * *

When certain accents are deemed inappropriate for the workplace, for political life, for use in schools and boardrooms, a policing of public and private boundaries occurs. Who may speak, when, and where, is a typical mechanism for distributing power. Who is competent to testify in court, who may speak at political meetings, who is an expert authority—answers to these questions stand at the border between the public realm of power and the private realm of the personal.

As it has become increasingly unacceptable to deny public speech on the basis of race or gender, accent becomes a significant means of maintaining boundaries. The recent push for English-only laws, and the attack on bilingual education, may represent new outlets for racial anxiety now that many traditional outlets are denied. The angry insistence that "they" should speak English serves as a proxy for a whole range of fears displaced by the social opprobrium directed at explicit racism.

* * *

Accents thus construct social boundaries, and social boundaries reinforce accents. The circumstances that perpetuate accents—including residential segregation, tracking systems in schools, and social distancing—are socially created. In distributing social standing according to accent, we distribute according to accents we have, in part, created.

* * *

C.   *Producing Counter–Ideology: Antisubordination Strategies in Law*

* * *

Progressive legal theorists seek to include antisubordination ideology in the law through such strategies as affirmative action, reparations, and restriction of hate speech. All of these legal positions recognize that ours is a non-neutral world in which legal attention to past and present injustice requires rules that work against the flood of structural subordination. Anyone who has swum against the tide knows that it requires effort. Staying still means moving backward.

The accent cases illustrate some of what we know about subordination. We know that subordination has material and ideological dimensions. In the case of accent, the material dimensions include the real denial of life chances: jobs, housing, and educational opportunity may depend on talking the right way. Whether one can speak persuasively before the law—before a police officer or a judge or a legislature or a jury—may determine life or death, freedom or jail, protection or neglect. The ideological dimension of accent discrimination is the creation and maintenance of a belief system that sees some as worthy and others as unworthy based on accent, such that disparities in wealth and power are naturalized.

* * *

Immutability arguments feed into this hierarchical ideology. In arguing for accent tolerance, the rationale of accent as immutable is thus a dangerous one. A more progressive argument is that even if accent is changeable, no citizen should have to alter core parts of identity in order to participate in society. A true antisubordination agenda would apply reasonable accommodation to all differences, whether chosen or immutable, that are historically subject to exploitation or oppression by dominant groups.

In arguing that Title VII should prohibit accent discrimination, the more powerful justification is a notion of radical pluralism, not a notion of charitable concern for the immutably afflicted. Indeed, I am coming to see the antisubordination principle and the radical pluralism principle as necessarily linked.

D. *Accent and Radical Pluralism*

* * *

If language is the nest of culture, and cultural diversity is an absolute good, then linguistic tolerance is a legitimate end of the law. Saying this raises questions of how radical pluralism will work in practice as our imaginations call up much that is ugly when we speak of pluralism, including bitter cultural clashes and domination disguised as cultural expression, to name two.

* * *

In summary, the antisubordination rationale for accent tolerance suggests a radically pluralistic re-visioning of national identity. The only center, the only glue, that makes us a nation is our many-centered cultural heritage. Just as our use of language is rich, varied, interactive, and changeable, so is our national culture. We are the only country in which an Okinawan vendor serves Kosher pastrami and stir-fried vegetables wrapped in a tortilla to young white punk rockers at 3:00 a.m. in the morning. We are the only country in which a white child sleeps blissfully under a quilt lovingly stitched by his aunt, emblazoned with a life-sized portrait of an African American basketball star. We are the only country in which a group of parents planning a little league fundraiser around a transvestite beauty contest would call the ACLU to defend their right to use a public park for the event, and convince a mayor named Hannibal Tavares to change his mind about a permit. From the oversized plaster chickens and donuts that mark our highways to the exquisite wisps of nouvelle Franco–Latin–Japanese cuisine set before our expense-account diners, we are a nation fantastic and wide-ranging in our vernacular and our juxtapositions. From the Grand Ole Opry to neo-metal, from zydeco to the Met, we are a range of tastes and sounds wider than ever before known to the nations of this planet. That is the defining centrality of the American culture I grew up in and love: a broad and delightfully incongruous coming together of difference. In acknowledging plural culture as a strength, and in recognizing and dismantling the false hierarchies that place one culture over another, it may come to pass that we live together in celebration and peace.

E. *To Save Our Own Souls: Law for the Last Reconstruction*

Throughout this Article, I have written to persuade readers of good will to adopt legal rules and ethical positions that promote linguistic pluralism. I have used existing legal doctrine, traditional liberal theory, and new critical theories in this effort. This eclecticism might seem as odd as the kosher burrito and as dangerous as the Ku Klux Klan to those who see impassioned pleas for favored constituencies and eclectic borrowing from many traditions as unprincipled and undisciplined. I believe the antisubordination principle is a principle, and that it can inform our law in a way that is as principled and as disciplined as the ideas of property, equality, and due process that are our constitutional legacy. I have tried to show that accent discrimination is rooted in a culture of dominance fundamentally at odds with the creed of this nation—at odds both with the Enlightenment ideals of liberalism that attended our national birth and the ideal of antisubordination that has constituted the core of our defining struggles against slavery, against fascism, against Jim Crow.

* * *

In suggesting a reconstructed interpretation of Title VII that responds to both liberal and radical critiques, I intended to suggest a model of what law can be and what lawyers can do to work toward justice. The great legal historians of our time have said of Americans that they are users of law. They use it, they believe in it, they constructed a nation around it. Law is part of our culture and it is, therefore, a place to begin in making the changes we need to make.

* * *

VIII.   EPILOGUE: VOICES OF AMERICA

* * *

In recounting the tale of the world's many languages coming to America, I have not forgotten that the journey was often hard. We lost most of our native American languages, as we lost their speakers, in a dark part of our history. Also in darkness, the round sounds of West African languages came to America in the bellies of slave ships. Out of pain and poverty, waves of immigrants came from all corners of the earth. Refugees from war came, survivors of persecution came, all came with their tongues and palates shaping newly-learned English words in ways that echoed their years in other places. That is the American accent, the multiplicity of sound bearing the history of our nation, bearing the struggle of its many-voiced people.

———

NOTES AND QUESTIONS

1. Differences in accents. In her discussion of the accent and the anti-subordination principle, Matsuda argues that the unequal evaluation of differences in accents is directly linked to the framework of racism and ethnic power relationships. Do you have an accent? What is your accent? Is your accent associated with power and authority in our settings? Consider the complaint of a mafia member's child who was in the witness protection program from New Jersey, to Salt Lake City, then Seattle, and asked to "blend in."

2. Preference of some accents to others. Matsuda discusses minorities who were discriminated against for having accents. But she also distinguishes between minority accents and those associated with Europeans. She writes that a plaintiff is most likely to be successful with:

> a slight trace of a European accent, but for the most part ... has adopted the speech patterns associated vaguely with North American television newscasters. She is qualified in every other respect for a job that requires some basic communication ability. Speech, is not however, a major job function.

Matsuda, *supra*, at 1351. This suggests that not all accents are created equal. As the case law demonstrates, a large number of the plaintiffs are members of minority groups. Is it safe to say that a Norwegian or Swedish person would be treated differently upon applying for a communication position than a Hispanic or Filipino? According to Sandra Del Valle, language and accent are not separate from national origin. Because of this, an accent easily marks minorities as the "other." *See* SANDRA DEL VALLE, LANGUAGE RIGHTS AND THE LAW IN THE UNITED STATES: FINDING OUR VOICES 144 (2003).

3. Immutability of accents. Del Valle argues that accents are immutable traits. Foreigners, whether they are Hispanic, European, or Asian, will retain traces of their native origins and language. The immutable nature of accents suggests that it is not a choice when people speak with accents. So, why do courts regard accents differently than they do an Afro? In particular, courts have ruled that employers cannot prohibit Afros because they are an immutable trait of blacks. However, numerous courts have ruled that accents can validly eliminate job applicants from consideration. What concept lies within in the court's distinction? Del Valle asserts that regardless of how vital public speaking is to the position, whenever it is just a small component of the job, courts have allowed employers to eliminate candidates with accents without much debate or question.

4. Can Title VII and the Equal Employment Opportunity Commission interpretation be read as contradictory? As Del Valle argues, Title VII does not ban accent discrimination, but the EEOC bans discrimination based on "cultural or linguistic characteristics." Does that not ban accent discrimination? After all, accents stem from one's cultural background and constitute a linguistic characteristic.

5. The four-pronged test articulated by the Supreme Court in *McDonnell Douglas Corp. v. Green* is not always a clear-cut indicator that discrimination can be successfully proven. The Court laid out these requirements to have a *prima facie* case of discrimination:

1. That the plaintiff belongs to a protected class;

2. That he or she applied and was qualified for the position sought or held;

3. That despite such qualifications, he or she was rejected or fired; and

4. That after his or her rejection, the position sought or terminated from either remained open and the employer continued to seek similarly qualified applicants or was filled by equally or less qualified individuals not of the protected group.

See 411 U.S. 792, 802 (1973). The fact that fulfilling the four-pronged test can be insufficient is exemplified by *Fragante*. The employer felt he spoke with a heavy, Filipino accent that would be difficult to understand. However, it was noted in court that the plaintiff was only asked to repeat his answer on two occasions. Matsuda, *supra* at 1338, n.28.

B.   English–Only Rules

Garcia v. Spun Steak Co.

998 F.2d 1480 (9th Cir. 1993).

■ O'Scannlain, Circuit Judge, delivered the opinion of the court.

* * *

I

Spun Steak Company ("Spun Steak") is a California corporation that produces poultry and meat products in South San Francisco for wholesale distribution. Spun Steak employs thirty-three workers, twenty-four of whom are Spanish-speaking. Virtually all of the Spanish-speaking employees are Hispanic. While two employees speak no English, the others have varying degrees of proficiency in English. Spun Steak has never required job applicants to speak or to understand English as a condition of employment.

Approximately two-thirds of Spun Steak's employees are production line workers or otherwise involved in the production process. Appellees Garcia and Buitrago are production line workers; they stand before a conveyor belt, remove poultry or other meat products from the belt and place the product into cases or trays for resale. Their work is done individually. Both Garcia and Buitrago are fully bilingual, speaking both English and Spanish.

Appellee Local 115, United Food and Commercial Workers International Union, AFL–CIO ("Local 115"), is the collective bargaining agent representing the employees at Spun Steak.

Prior to September 1990, these Spun Steak employees spoke Spanish freely to their co-workers during work hours. After receiving complaints that some workers were using their bilingual capabilities to harass and to insult other workers in a language they could not understand, Spun Steak began to investigate the possibility of requiring its employees to speak only English in the workplace. Specifically, Spun Steak received complaints that Garcia and Buitrago made derogatory, racist comments in Spanish about two co-workers, one of whom is African–American and the other Chinese–American.

The company's president, Kenneth Bertelson, concluded that an English-only rule would promote racial harmony in the workplace. In addition, he concluded that the English-only rule would enhance worker safety because some employees who did not understand Spanish claimed that the use of Spanish distracted them while they were operating machinery, and would enhance product quality because the U.S.D.A. inspector in the plant spoke only English and thus could not understand if a product-related concern was raised in Spanish. Accordingly, the following rule was adopted:

> [I]t is hereafter the policy of this Company that only English will be spoken in connection with work. During lunch, breaks, and employees' own time, they are obviously free to speak Spanish if they wish. However, we urge all of you not to use your fluency in Spanish in a fashion which may lead other employees to suffer humiliation.
>
> * * *

In November 1990, Garcia and Buitrago received warning letters for speaking Spanish during working hours. For approximately two months thereafter, they were not permitted to work next to each other. Local 115 protested the English-only policy and requested that it be rescinded but to no avail.

  * * *

Garcia, Buitrago, and Local 115, on behalf of all Spanish-speaking employees of Spun Steak, (collectively, "the Spanish-speaking employees") filed suit, alleging that the English-only policy violated Title VII. On September 6, 1991, the parties filed cross-motions for summary judgment. The district court denied Spun Steak's motion and granted the Spanish-speaking employees' motion for summary judgment, concluding that the English-only policy disparately impacted Hispanic workers without sufficient business justification, and thus violated Title VII. Spun Steak filed this timely appeal and the EEOC filed a brief amicus curiae and participated in oral argument.

II

As a preliminary matter, we must consider whether Local 115 has standing to sue on behalf of the Spanish-speaking employees at Spun Steak. If Local 115 does not have standing, we will consider the application of the policy only to Garcia and Buitrago, both of whom speak English fluently.

* * * [T]he claim asserted and the relief requested do not require the participation of individual members. Local 115 claims that the policy has a per se discriminatory impact on all Spanish-speaking employees. Further, the union is seeking only injunctive relief on behalf of its members, not damages.

In short, Local 115 has standing.

III

Sections 703(a)(1) and (2) of Title VII provide:

(a) It shall be an unlawful employment practice for an employer—

   (1) to fail or refuse to hire or to discharge any individual, or otherwise to discriminate against any individual with respect to his compensation, terms, conditions, or privileges of employment, because of such individual's race, color, religion, sex or national origin; or

   (2) to limit, segregate, or classify his employees or applicants for employment in any way which would deprive or tend to deprive any individual of employment opportunities or otherwise adversely affect his status as an employee, because of such individual's race, color, religion, sex, or national origin.

42 U.S.C. § 2000e–2(a). It is well-settled that Title VII is concerned not only with intentional discrimination, but also with employment practices and policies that lead to disparities in the treatment of classes of workers. *See, e.g., Griggs v. Duke Power Co.*, 401 U.S. 424, 430–31, (1971). Thus, a plaintiff alleging discrimination under Title VII may proceed under two theories of liability: disparate treatment or disparate impact. *Watson v. Fort Worth Bank & Trust*, 487 U.S. 977, 986–87 (1988). While the disparate treatment theory requires proof of discriminatory intent, intent is irrelevant to a disparate impact theory. *Id. at 988.* "[I]mpact analysis is designed to implement Congressional concern with 'the consequences of employment practices, not simply the motivation." *Rose v. Wells Fargo & Co.*, 902 F.2d 1417, 1424 (9th Cir. 1990) (citations omitted).

A

The Spanish-speaking employees do not contend that Spun Steak intentionally discriminated against them in enacting the English-only policy. Rather, they contend that the policy had a discriminatory impact on them because it imposes a burdensome term or condition of employment exclusively upon Hispanic workers and denies them a privilege of employment that non-Spanish-speaking workers enjoy.

* * *

This case, by contrast, does not fall within the language of section 703(a)(2). While policies that serve as barriers to hiring or promotion clearly deprive applicants of employment opportunities, we cannot conclude that a burdensome term or condition of employment or the denial of a privilege would "limit, segregate, or classify" employees in a way that would "deprive any individual of employment opportunities" or "otherwise adversely affect his status as an employee" in violation of section 703(a)(2). *See Nashville Gas Co. v. Satty*, 434 U.S. 136, 144 (1977) (deprivation of benefits does not fall under § 703(a)(2)). Such claims, therefore, must be brought directly under section 703(a)(1). We have never expressly considered, however, whether disparate impact theory applies to claims under section 703(a)(1), and the Supreme Court has explicitly reserved the issue. *Id.*

* * *

B

To make out a prima facie case of discriminatory impact, a plaintiff must identify a specific, seemingly neutral practice or policy that has a significantly adverse impact on persons of a protected class. *Teal*, 457 U.S. at 446. If the prima facie case is established, the burden shifts to the employer to "demonstrate that the challenged practice is job related for the position in question and consistent with business necessity." 42 U.S.C.A. § 2000e-2(k)(1)(A) (Supp. 1992). In this case, the district court granted summary judgment in favor of the Spanish-speaking employees, concluding that, as a matter of law, the employees had made out the prima facie case and the justifications offered by the employer were inadequate.

1

We first consider whether the Spanish-speaking employees have made out the prima facie case. "[T]he requirements of a prima facie disparate impact case ... are in some respects more exacting than those of a disparate treatment case." *Spaulding v. University of Washington*, 740 F.2d 686, 705 (9th Cir. 1984) (citation omitted). In the disparate treatment context, a plaintiff can make out a prima facie case merely by presenting evidence sufficient to give rise to an inference of discrimination. *McDonnell Douglas Corp. v. Green*, 411 U.S. 792, 802–06 (1973). In a disparate impact case, by contrast, plaintiffs must do more than merely raise an inference of discrimination before the burden shifts; they "must actually prove the discriminatory impact at issue." *Rose*, 902 F.2d at 1421. In the typical disparate impact case, in which the plaintiff argues that a selection criterion excludes protected applicants from jobs or promotions, the plaintiff proves discriminatory impact by showing statistical disparities between the number of protected class members in the qualified applicant group and those in the relevant segment of the workforce. *Wards Cove Packing Co. v.*

Atonio, 490 U.S. 642, 650 (1989). While such statistics are often difficult to compile, whether the protected group has been disadvantaged turns on quantifiable data. When the alleged disparate impact is on the conditions, terms, or privileges of employment, however, determining whether the protected group has been adversely affected may depend on subjective factors not easily quantified. The fact that the alleged effects are subjective, however, does not relieve the plaintiff of the burden of proving disparate impact. The plaintiff may not merely assert that the policy has harmed members of the group to which he or she belongs. Instead, the plaintiff must prove the existence of adverse effects of the policy, must prove that the impact of the policy is on terms, conditions, or privileges of employment of the protected class, must prove that the adverse effects are significant, and must prove that the employee population in general is not affected by the policy to the same degree.

* * *

The crux of the dispute between Spun Steak and the Spanish-speaking employees, however, is not over whether Hispanic workers will disproportionately bear any adverse effects of the policy; rather, the dispute centers on whether the policy causes any adverse effects at all, and if it does, whether the effects are significant. The Spanish-speaking employees argue that the policy adversely affects them in the following ways: (1) it denies them the ability to express their cultural heritage on the job; (2) it denies them a privilege of employment that is enjoyed by monolingual speakers of English; and (3) it creates an atmosphere of inferiority, isolation, and intimidation. We discuss each of these contentions in turn.

* * *

A

The employees argue that denying them the ability to speak Spanish on the job denies them the right to cultural expression. It cannot be gainsaid that an individual's primary language can be an important link to his ethnic culture and identity. Title VII, however, does not protect the ability of workers to express their cultural heritage at the workplace. Title VII is concerned only with disparities in the treatment of workers; it does not confer substantive privileges. *See, e.g., Garcia v. Gloor*, 618 F.2d 264, 269 (5th Cir. 1980), cert. denied, 449 U.S. 1113 (1981). It is axiomatic that an employee must often sacrifice individual self-expression during working hours. Just as a private employer is not required to allow other types of self-expression, there is nothing in Title VII which requires an employer to allow employees to express their cultural identity.

B

Next, the Spanish-speaking employees argue that the English-only policy has a disparate impact on them because it deprives them of a privilege given by the employer to native-English speakers: the ability to converse on the job in the language with which they feel most comfortable. It is undisputed that Spun Steak allows its employees to converse on the job. The ability to converse—especially to make small talk—is a privilege of employment, and may in fact be a significant privilege of employment in an assembly-line job. It is inaccurate, however, to describe the privilege as broadly as the Spanish-speaking employees urge us to do.

* * *

C

Finally, the Spanish-speaking employees argue that the policy creates an atmosphere of inferiority, isolation, and intimidation. Under this theory, the employees do not assert that the policy directly affects a term, condition, or privilege of employment. Instead, the argument must be that the policy causes the work environment to become infused with ethnic tensions. The tense environment, the argument goes, itself amounts to a condition of employment.

i

The Supreme Court in *Meritor Savings Bank v. Vinson*, 477 U.S. at 66, held that an abusive work environment may, in some circumstances, amount to a condition of employment giving rise to a violation of Title VII. The Court quoted with approval the decision in *Rogers v. EEOC*, 454 F.2d 234, 238 (5th Cir. 1971), cert. denied, 406 U.S. 957 (1972):

> [T]he phrase 'terms, conditions or privileges of employment' in [Title VII] is an expansive concept which sweeps within its protective ambit the practice of creating a working environment heavily charged with ethnic or racial discrimination.... One can readily envision working environments so heavily polluted with discrimination as to destroy completely the emotional and psychological stability of minority group workers.

Although *Vinson* is a sexual harassment case in which the individual incidents involved behavior that was arguably intentionally discriminatory, its rationale applies equally to cases in which seemingly neutral policies of a company infuse the atmosphere of the workplace with discrimination. The *Vinson* Court emphasized, however, that discriminatory practices must be pervasive before an employee has a Title VII claim under a hostile environment theory.

* * *

The Spanish-speaking employees in this case have presented no evidence other than conclusory statements that the policy has contributed to an atmosphere of "isolation, inferiority or intimidation." The bilingual employees are able to comply with the rule, and there is no evidence to show that the atmosphere at Spun Steak in general is infused with hostility toward Hispanic workers. Indeed, there is substantial evidence in the record demonstrating that the policy was enacted to prevent the employees from intentionally using their fluency in Spanish to isolate and to intimidate members of other ethnic groups. In light of the specific factual context of this case, we conclude that the bilingual employees have not raised a genuine issue of material fact that the effect is so pronounced as to amount to a hostile environment. * * *

ii

* * *

We do not reject the English-only rule Guideline lightly. We recognize that "as an administrative interpretation of the Act by the enforcing agency, these Guidelines . . . constitute a body of experience and informed judgment to which courts and litigants may properly resort for guidance." *Meritor Sav. Bank*, 477 U.S. 57 at 65 (internal quotations and citations omitted). But we are not bound by the Guidelines. *See Espinoza v. Farah Mfg. Co., Inc.*, 414 U.S. 86, 94 (1973). We will not defer to "an administrative construction of a statute where there are 'compelling indications that it is wrong." *Id.*

* * *

2

Because the bilingual employees have failed to make out a prima facie case, we need not consider the business justifications offered for the policy as applied to them. On remand, if Local 115 is able to make out a prima facie case with regard to employees with limited proficiency in English, the district court could then consider any business justification offered by Spun Steak.

IV

In sum, we conclude that the bilingual employees have not made out a prima facie case and that Spun Steak has not violated Title VII in adopting an English-only rule as to them. Thus, we reverse the grant of summary judgment in favor of Garcia, Buitrago, and Local 115 to the extent it represents the bilingual employees, and remand with instructions to grant summary judgment in favor of Spun Steak on their claims. * * *

REVERSED and REMANDED.

■ BOOCHEVER, CIRCUIT JUDGE, dissenting in part:

I agree with most of the majority's carefully crafted opinion. I dissent, however, from the majority's rejection of the EEOC guidelines. The guidelines provide that an employee establishes a prima facie case in a disparate impact claim by proving the existence of an English-only policy, thereby shifting the burden to the employer to show a business necessity for the rule. *See* 29 C.F.R. § 1606.7(b) (1991) ("An employer may have a rule requiring that employees speak only in English at certain times where the employer can show that the rule is justified by business necessity."). I would defer to the Commission's expertise in construing the Act, by virtue of which it concluded that English-only rules may "create an atmosphere of inferiority, isolation and intimidation based on national origin which could result in a discriminatory working environment." *Id.* § 1606.7(a).

* * *

It is true that EEOC regulations are entitled to somewhat less weight than those promulgated by an agency with Congressionally delegated rulemaking authority. *General Elec. Co. v. Gilbert*, 429 U.S. 125, 141 (1976). Nevertheless, the EEOC guideline is entitled to "great deference" in the absence of "compelling indications that it is wrong." *Espinoza v. Farah Mfg. Co.*, 414 U.S. 86, 94–95 (1973). While one may reasonably differ with the EEOC's position as a matter of policy, I can find no such "compelling indications" in this case. The lack of directly supporting language in § 703(a)(1) or the legislative history of Title VII, relied on by the majority, does not in my opinion make the guideline "inconsistent with an obvious congressional intent not to reach the employment practice in question." *Id.* at 94.

I conclude that if appropriate deference is given to the administrative interpretation of the Act, we should follow the guideline and uphold the district court's decision that a prima facie case was established. I believe, however, that triable issues were presented whether *Spun Steak* established a business justification for the rule, and I would remand for trial of that issue.

––––––

Yniguez v. Arizonans For Official English

69 F.3d 920 (9th Cir. 1995), *vacated by* 520 U.S. 43 (1997).

■ Reinhardt, Circuit Judge:

I.

* * *

State employees who fail to obey the Arizona Constitution are subject to employment sanctions. For this reason, immediately upon passage of Article XXVIII, Yniguez ceased speaking Spanish on the job. She feared that because of Article XXVIII her use of Spanish made her vulnerable to discipline.

In November 1988, Yniguez filed an action against the State of Arizona, Governor Rose Mofford, Arizona Attorney General Robert Corbin, and Director of the Arizona Department of Administration Catherine Eden, in federal district court. She sought an injunction against state enforcement of Article XXVIII and a declaration that the provision violated the First and Fourteenth Amendments of the Constitution, as well as federal civil rights laws.

* * *

II.

* * *

We agree with the district court's construction of Article XXVIII. The article's plain language broadly prohibits all government officials and employees from speaking languages other than English in performing their official duties, save to the extent that the use of non-English languages is permitted pursuant to the provision's narrow exceptions section. * * *

III.

* * *

Arizonans for Official English argues vehemently that First Amendment scrutiny should be relaxed in this case because the decision to speak a non-English language does not implicate pure speech rights. Rather, the group suggests, "choice of language . . . is a mode of conduct"—a *"nonverbal* expressive activity." * * * Accordingly, it compares this case to those involving only "expressive conduct" or "symbolic speech." E.g., *Texas v. Johnson,* 491 U.S. 397 (1989) (burning American flag for expressive reasons); *Tinker v. Des Moines Independent Community School Dist.,* 393 U.S. 503 (1969) (wearing arm band for expressive reasons); *United States v. O'Brien,* 391 U.S. 367 (1968) (burning draft card for expressive reasons). In such cases, the government generally has a wider latitude in regulating the conduct involved, but only when the regulation is not directed at the communicative nature of that conduct. *Johnson,* 491 U.S. at 406.

We find the analysis employed in the above cases to be inapplicable here, as we are entirely unpersuaded by the comparison between speaking languages other than English and burning flags. Of course, speech in any language consists of the "expressive conduct" of vibrating one's vocal chords, moving one's mouth and thereby making sounds, or of putting pen to paper, or hand to keyboard. Yet the fact that such "conduct" is shaped by a language—that is, a sophisticated and complex system of understood meanings—is what makes it speech. Language is by definition speech, and the regulation of any language is the regulation of speech.

* * *

In sum, we most emphatically reject the suggestion that the decision to speak in a language other than English does not implicate pure speech concerns, but is instead akin to expressive conduct. Speech in any language is still speech, and the decision to speak in another language is a decision involving speech alone.

* * *

Arizonans for Official English next contends, incorrectly, that Yniguez seeks an affirmative right to have government operations conducted in foreign tongues. Because the organization misconceives Yniguez's argument, it relies on a series of cases in which non-English-speaking plaintiffs have unsuccessfully tried to require the government to provide them with services in their own language. *See Guadalupe Org. Inc.,* 587 F.2d at 1024 (no right to bilingual education); *Carmona v. Sheffield,* 475 F.2d 738 (9th Cir. 1973) (no right to unemployment notices in Spanish); *Toure v. United States,* 24 F.3d 444 (2d Cir. 1994) (no right to notice of administrative seizure in French); *Soberal–Perez v. Heckler,* 717 F.2d 36 (2d Cir. 1983) (no right to Social Security notices and services in Spanish), *cert. denied,* 466

U.S. 929 (1984); *Frontera v. Sindell,* 522 F.2d 1215 (6th Cir. 1975) (no right to civil service exam in Spanish). These cases, however, hold only that (at least under the circumstances there involved) non-English speakers have no affirmative right to compel state government to provide information in a language that they can comprehend. The cases are inapplicable here.

In the case before us, there is no claim of an affirmative right to compel the state to provide multilingual information, but instead only a claim of a negative right: that the state cannot, consistent with the First Amendment, gag the employees currently providing members of the public with information and thereby effectively preclude large numbers of persons from receiving information that they have previously received. *Cf. Board of Educ. Island Trees Union Free School Dist. No. 26 v. Pico,* 457 U.S. 853, 866–67 (1982). Such a claim falls squarely within the confines of traditional free speech doctrine, and is in no way dependent on a finding of an affirmative duty on the part of the state.

* * *

If this case involved a statewide ban on all uses of languages other than English within the geographical jurisdiction of the state of Arizona, the constitutional outcome would be clear. A state cannot simply prohibit all persons within its borders from speaking in the tongue of their choice. Such a restriction on private speech obviously could not stand. *Meyer v. Nebraska,* 262 U.S. 390, 401 (1923). However, Article XXVIII's restraint on speech is of more limited scope. Its ban is restricted to speech by persons performing services for the government. Thus, we must look beyond first principles of First Amendment doctrine and consider the question of what limitations may constitutionally be placed on the speech of government servants.

* * *

Thus, the Court has made it clear that it is the government's interest in performing its functions efficiently and effectively that underlies its right to exercise greater control over the speech of public employees. * * *

In deciding whether to afford constitutional protection to prohibited employee speech, we must consider both the general interest of the public servant in speaking freely, as described in *Perry* and *Rutan,* and the importance to the public of the speech involved. *See Connick,* 461 U.S. at 149 (considering the public's interest in the speech in determining whether to protect it); *Pickering,* 391 U.S. at 571–72 (same). The employee speech banned by Article XXVIII is unquestionably of public import. It pertains to the provision of governmental services and information. Unless that speech is delivered in a form that the intended recipients can comprehend, they are likely to be deprived of much needed data as well as of substantial public and private benefits. The speech at issue is speech that members of the public desire to hear. Indeed, it is most often the recipient, rather than the public employee, who initiates the dialogue in a language other than English. * * *

For example, monolingual Spanish-speaking residents of Arizona cannot, consistent with the article, communicate effectively with employees of a state or local housing office about a landlord's wrongful retention of a rental deposit, nor can they learn from clerks of the state court about how and where to file small claims court complaints. They cannot obtain information regarding a variety of state and local social services, or adequately inform the service-givers that the governmental employees involved are not performing their duties properly or that the government itself is not operating effectively or honestly. Those with a limited command of English will face commensurate difficulties in obtaining or providing such information. * * * Moreover, as we suggested earlier, the restrictions that Article XXVIII imposes severely limit the ability of state legislators to communicate with their constituents concerning official matters. For example, the provision would preclude a legislative committee from convening on a reservation and questioning a tribal leader in his native language concerning the problems of his community. A state senator of Navajo extraction would be precluded from inquiring directly of his Navajo-speaking constituents regarding problems they sought to bring to his attention. So would his staff. The legislative fact-finding function would, in short, be directly affected.

Arizonans for Official English claims, as it and others did when the initiative was on the ballot, that Article XXVIII promotes significant state interests. The organization enumerates these interests as; protecting democracy by encouraging "unity and political stability"; encouraging a common language; and protecting public confidence. We note at the outset that the sweeping nature of Article XXVIII's restriction on public employee speech weighs significantly in our evaluation of the state's alleged interests. In *National Treasury Employees Union,* the Court explained that when the government seeks to defend a "wholesale deterrent to a broad category of expression by a massive number of potential speakers," 513 U.S. at 466, 115 S.Ct. at 1013, its burden is heavier than when it attempts to defend an isolated disciplinary action. *Id.* Thus, we must examine the state's asserted justifications with particular care.

There is no basis in the record to support the proponents' assertion that any of the broad societal interests on which they rely are served by the provisions of Article XXVIII. * * *

Accordingly, the appellants have not demonstrated that the benefits to be obtained outweigh the burdens imposed on First Amendment rights, particularly given the all-encompassing scope of the restriction they seek to defend. *See National Treasury Employees Union,* 513 U.S. at 469, 115 S.Ct. at 1014 (explaining that the government's "burden is greater" in such cases).

We also reject the justifications for even more basic reasons. Our conclusions are influenced primarily by two Supreme Court cases from the 1920s in which nearly identical justifications were asserted in support of laws restricting language rights. *See Meyer v. Nebraska,* 262 U.S. 390 (1923); *Farrington v. Tokushige,* 273 U.S. 284 (1927). *Meyer* involved a

Nebraska statute that prohibited the teaching of non-English languages to children under the eighth grade level; *Tokushige,* similarly, involved a Hawaii statute that singled out "foreign language schools," such as those in which Japanese was taught, for stringent government control.

Like the Court in *Meyer* and *Tokushige,* we recognize the importance of (1) promoting democracy and national unity and (2) encouraging a common language as a means of encouraging such unity. *See Guadalupe Organization, Inc., supra.* The two primary justifications relied on by the article's proponents are indeed closely linked. We cannot agree, however, that Article XXVIII is in any way a fair, effective, or appropriate means of promoting those interests, or that even under a more deferential analysis its severely flawed effort to advance those goals outweighs its substantial adverse effect on first amendment rights. As we have learned time and again in our history, the state cannot achieve unity by prescribing orthodoxy. * * * (forced "Americanization" violates American tradition of liberty and toleration). Notwithstanding this lesson, the provision at issue here "promotes" English only by means of proscribing other languages and is, thus, wholly coercive. Moreover, the goals of protecting democracy and encouraging unity and stability are at most indirectly related to the repressive means selected to achieve them. Next, the measure inhibits rather than advances the state's interest in the efficient and effective performance of its duties. Finally, the direct effect of the provision is not only to restrict the rights of all state and local government servants in Arizona, but also to severely impair the free speech interests of a portion of the populace they serve.

* * *

V.

* * *

We affirm the district court's judgment that Article XXVIII of the Arizona Constitution is facially overbroad and violates the First Amendment, and that the article is unconstitutional in its entirety. We reverse and remand the district court judgment insofar as it denies Yniguez an award of nominal damages.

AFFIRMED IN PART, REVERSED IN PART AND REMANDED.

* * *

■ FERNANDEZ, CIRCUIT JUDGE, with whom CHIEF JUDGE WALLACE and JUDGES HALL and KLEINFELD join, dissenting:

* * * Maria–Kelley F. Yniguez does not like Article XXVIII as a matter of policy. I can understand and sympathize with that. It is when she goes beyond the realm of policy and seeks to show that the Article violates the First Amendment to the United States Constitution that she goes astray. It is there that we part company.

She, in effect, proceeds from the fundamentally flawed assumption that while performing government business an official or employee has much the same freedom as a private citizen. That leads her into a thicket of incorrect assumptions and assertions about the nature of her speech rights, the nature of language, and the rights and duties of the State when it chooses to speak for itself. As a result, she has left the proper analytical pathway and become hopelessly lost in a forest of her own hopes.

* * * Certainly, if the State can require teaching in a particular language, it can itself choose to use a particular language to express the content of what it has to say.

In fine, the people of the State of Arizona did not violate the First Amendment when they adopted Article XXVIII. For good or ill, it was a question "for the people to decide." *Id.*

Therefore, I respectfully dissent.

NOTES AND QUESTIONS

1.   English-only rules as route to socioeconomic mobility? Arizona Representative Dave Carson (R–Prescott) was the key supporter of the bill in 1987. *See* RAYMOND TATALOVICH, NATIVISM REBORN: THE OFFICIAL ENGLISH LANGUAGE MOVEMENT AND THE AMERICAN STATES 131 (1995). Tatalovich, Carson, and his supporters argued English-only rules would serve as a positive impetus to draw Hispanics out of the "language and economic ghettoes" of Arizona. *Id.* at 132. The bill's supporters regarded English-only rules as a barrier against social and economic segregation in the state. But, it did not seem to take into account the tools needed when immigrants did not understand English. The notion that English is needed to combat segregation and marginalization is reasonable but it ignores the fact that people need the tools, i.e., English fluency, to participate in the marketplace.

2.   Bilingual education initiatives and counterinitiatives—the first rung on the ladder. In the primary and secondary public school arena, advocates of bilingual education have made the argument that children from homes in which English is a second language will secure the full benefit of educational opportunity only if they are given a graduated educational experience, in which they are taught in both their primary language and English in the same curriculum. The opponents of bilingual education, like the English-only advocates for government communication, insist that English is the official language, and that other languages should be banished to the margins of authoritative discourse.

For an explanation of the dynamics of these two political positions, see Charu A. Chandrasekhar, Comment, *The Bay State Buries Bilingualism: Advocacy Lessons from Bilingual Education's Recent Defeat in Massachusetts*, 24 CHICANO-LATINO L. REV. 4 (2003). Chandrasekhar argues that:

> by a vote of 68 to 32 percent, Massachusetts voters endorsed Question 2, a ballot initiative sponsored by anti-bilingual education activist Ron Unz that eviscerates bilingual education and erodes parents' and teachers' rights. . . . The successful passage in Massachusetts

of Question 2 marked another legislative triumph for Unz, who previously crafted Propositions 227 and 203 (successful bills similar to Question 2 banning bilingual education as an instructional method in California and Arizona, respectively).

3. Effectiveness of the EEOC when English-only rules are applied in the workplace. *Garcia* illustrates the success employers can have by enforcing English-only rules. This was especially the case in *Garcia* because the court placed emphasis on the fact that bilingual employees would not be negatively impacted by an English-only rule. In particular, the court argued bilingual employees have the freedom and choice to switch to English while in the workplace. It was noted that only one of Spun Steak's employees did not speak English. The *Garcia* ruling suggests that the EEOC's guidelines cannot be assumed to be automatically applied in English-only environments.

4. Additional reading. *See* Drucilla Cornell & William W. Bratton, *Deadweight Costs & Intrinsic Wrongs of Nativism: Economics, Freedom and Legal Suppression of Spanish*, 84 CORNELL L. REV. 595, 629–34 (1999).

C. CULTURAL PROPERTY

Protecting Folklore of Indigenous Peoples: Is Intellectual Property the Answer?

30 CONN. L. REV. 1 (1997).

■ CHRISTINE HAIGHT FARLEY

INTRODUCTION

What can the Navajos do to prevent non-Navajos from using Navajo rug patterns to produce rugs overseas using cheap materials and labor, thereby undercutting the Navajos themselves in a market for their famous rugs? What can the Australian Aboriginal peoples do when their sacred and secret imagery is reproduced on carpets they did not make, and sold to non-Aboriginals, who will inevitably walk on them? Do these communities have any legal rights to these pieces of their culture? Does the law provide any means for them to take back their culture or to prevent further poaching?

Due to the increasingly widespread commercial appropriation of indigenous images, patterns, designs, and symbols, indigenous rights groups have turned to intellectual property schemes for protection. But indigenous art and folklore present many problems for intellectual property protection, and existing western legal mechanisms may be ill-suited to protect certain types of indigenous art.

* * *

[T]he Article begins by recounting a recent incident of commercial use of indigenous art in order to both illustrate the harm caused by this phenomenon and to suggest the challenges in achieving meaningful protection. Part II of this Article describes the particular situation of the indigenous populations and the growing trend toward commercialization and commodification of their art forms. It also explains the particular nature of indigenous art and why this use is so troubling to them. Part III provides an in-depth analysis of the obstacles to copyright protection of folklore, including the duration of the rights, the originality requirement, the fixation requirement, the individual nature of the rights, the fair use exception, the economic focus of the remedies, and considers possible ways of overcoming these obstacles. Part IV evaluates international proposals to develop *sui generis* rights to protect folklore. Part V appraises the possibility of coupling copyright with other laws to achieve protection of folklore. It analyzes moral rights, public domain statutes, and unfair competition laws. Finally, Part VI assesses these strategies with regard to the particular motivations of the indigenous peoples and concludes that the existing intellectual property regime is well-suited to protect those groups who want to participate in and control the marketing of their arts and crafts. But for those who want to preclude any use of their imagery, the existing intellectual property regime is deficient. Application of intellectual property laws, whose underlying logic is to facilitate dissemination, is fundamentally inappropriate to prevent sacred indigenous images from circulation and re-use.

I. A Case of Pirating Cultural Heritage

The Australian carpet incident alluded to earlier presents an excellent illustration of the harm caused by the commercial poaching of indigenous art. In 1991, Mr. Bethune, an Australian entrepreneur, went into the business of importing hand-knotted, wool carpets into Australia. After a failed attempt to sell carpets with traditional Oriental designs, he decided to have Australian Aboriginal designs reproduced on the carpets, which he thought would generate more interest. After selecting ten designs from reproductions of Aboriginal artists' paintings, Bethune instructed a factory in Vietnam to produce carpets copying these designs, only making them "less busy." In all, he had 266 carpets manufactured. These carpets were sold for up to $4,252 each. Each carpet was affixed with a swing tag that read:

> These unique wall hangings and rugs have been designed by Aboriginal artists from areas throughout Australia. These artists are paid royalties on every carpet sold.... As carpet weaving is not a tradition of the Aboriginal people, the rugs are produced in Vietnam where we can combine the artistic skills of the Aboriginal people with the weaving traditions of the Vietnamese.... [W]e have achieved a blending of the talents of these peoples to produce original artistic creations. Each carpet is a unique piece of art.

But Bethune had no agreement with the Aboriginal artists whose paintings he copied. He neither had their authorization to reproduce the designs, nor did he pay them any royalties.

    * * *

The artists whose paintings were copied sued Bethune, his company, and its two directors in federal court for copyright infringement. They claimed they had a valid copyright in the paintings and that Bethune had violated their exclusive rights under the Australian Copyright Act. The court agreed, and *Milpurrurru v. Indofurn Pty. Ltd.* became the first case in which a court declared that Aboriginal artists must be compensated for the unauthorized use of their art. This case was seen as a big victory for Aboriginal peoples and as marking the end to the continued pilfering of their heritage. But has it solved the problem? Although the indigenous artists were able to assert copyright successfully, its requirements may still pose problems for other indigenous works. In addition, other copyright problems that are not present in this case have yet to be overcome.

II. THE USES AND ABUSES OF INDIGENOUS ART

The *Milpurrurru* case is not an isolated example. Instead, it is indicative of a trend. Over the last decade there has been a proliferation of reproductions of indigenous peoples' artworks. Increasingly, indigenous designs are being appropriated and used commercially throughout the world. Technological advances have only fanned this fire. Indigenous motifs are used to sell everything from Japanese automobiles like the Mazda Navajo to Barbie dolls to back-to-school clothes. Indigenous art has been reproduced and sold as art reproductions and as craft items, but more commonly it has been reproduced and sold as cheaper commodities, such as T-shirts, tea towels, and other souvenirs. Indigenous art has also been reproduced and used in advertising and marketing. Thus we are seeing indigenous designs more often and in new contexts.

* * *

Significantly, nearly all of these reproductions are unauthorized. Most are reproduced without so much as a request for permission. The consequence is that the indigenous peoples who created the art are not being compensated for its use. Another consequence is that indigenous communities are not exercising control over how their art is being used. This lack of control means that they cannot refuse to have their work put to particular uses and that they cannot ensure that their work is reproduced in a way that maintains its integrity or the reputation of the creator. To better understand the consequences of this unauthorized use, we need to better understand the traditional place of art in indigenous communities.

A. *The Nature of Indigenous Art*

Art is central to the practice of religion in most indigenous communities. Most spiritual rituals involve visual displays, dance, and/or music and song. In the words of one well-known Aboriginal artist, "In song and dance, in rock engraving and bark painting we re-enact the stories of the Dreamtime, and myth and symbol come together to bind us inseparably from our past, and to reinforce the internal structures of our society."

* * *

Often, due to the spiritual connections to art, a song, dance, or image may be reserved for special ceremonies. Often "certain works of folklore ... cannot be shown, nor can the themes in them be disclosed, except to those few who have been admitted to knowledge of ritual secrets and mysteries by undergoing initiation or other special ceremonies" due to the sacred nature of the work. Only members of the community who have achieved a certain level of initiation may be permitted to observe these rituals. Thus, the "law of art" will also dictate who may see these images and dances and who may hear these songs.

* * *

B.   *The Poaching of Indigenous Culture*

The theft of cultural symbols and art must be placed in historical perspective to grasp its implications fully. Many would agree that the survival of indigenous folklore is threatened. For the indigenous communities, the theft of their folklore represents the final blow to their civilization from "invaders." It is simply an extension of the plunder mentality. It signifies "that culture is open to pillage in the same way that Aboriginal lands and resources have been for over 200 years. Survival for indigenous peoples the world over is not merely a question of physical existence, but depends upon maintaining spiritual links with the land and their communities." Protection of their culture has become recognized as a fundamental human right.

* * *

III.   COPYRIGHT PROTECTION FOR FOLKLORE

Over the last few decades there has been an outcry in the United States, Canada, and Australia for governments to do something to protect indigenous communities from the poaching of their artworks. Naturally, indigenous peoples and advocacy groups are concerned about this problem and have sought legal avenues of redress. In an effort to prevent the appropriation and manipulation of their cultural images and texts, indigenous peoples, fighting for their cultural survival, are increasingly turning to intellectual property laws to protect their cultural heritage from external poaching. Significantly, indigenous groups are willing to participate in the western intellectual property rights scheme from which they feel they have been excluded and therefore disadvantaged. They have invoked intellectual property laws to use as a shield to prevent further intrusions into their already pillaged culture.

* * *

What to the consumer market may look like the same problem actually involves two different sets of concerns. First, some indigenous peoples want to be able to benefit from the economic rights provided by intellectual property laws. They want to be compensated for their contribution to the artwork through licensing, and they want to exclude non-indigenous competitors from the market by preventing unauthentic products from being marketed as made by indigenous people. Assuming that the circulation of indigenous art is inevitable, some indigenous artists want to be sure to participate in this celebration of indigenous culture. By gaining control over the circulation of their imagery, they want to ensure that the public gets an accurate account of indigenous culture and that the investment in that culture goes back to their communities. These concerns are illustrated in the first example described at the beginning of this Article involving the use of the Navajo rug patterns. Perhaps a subset of this group is the individual artists who want to be able to draw on and develop the imagery of their ancestors in a way that may lead to commercial success. Throughout this Article, I will refer to this first group as the "realist group."

But the second set of concerns is more profound. Some indigenous peoples also want to use intellectual property laws to prevent what may be characterized as a cultural or psychological harm caused by the unauthorized use of their art. They see intellectual property laws as offering a means to control the circulation of their art. * * *

It is said that indigenous communities are vulnerable to this kind of theft because their artworks do not enjoy comprehensive protection under existing intellectual property regimes. Unfortunately, this claim has been made without supporting analysis. Most commentators begin with the normative question of whether indigenous art should be protected with intellectual property laws. Few even get to the descriptive question of whether or not indigenous art is protected by simply assuming that it is not. By beginning from the standpoint that indigenous art should be protected by intellectual property laws, and by accepting that it is not currently protected based on generalized notions of the originality of indigenous works as a unified group, commentators have failed to understand how indigenous peoples will best be able to meet their needs. Thus this Article will now proceed to that descriptive level and analyze whether some indigenous art is excluded from protection under existing intellectual property laws, whether the protection intellectual property laws offer is adequate and appropriate, or whether intellectual property laws must be reformulated to accommodate the unique challenges that folklore poses.

Of all the existing legal mechanisms, copyright law initially appears to be the best suited to protect indigenous folklore. Copyright law is a logical choice because copyright law is designed to protect artistic works from unauthorized reproduction. Likewise, indigenous groups are seeking to control the reproduction of their paintings, songs, and dances. Why shouldn't copyright law protect indigenous art? Indigenous artists feel that they should be protected to the same extent as non-indigenous artists. In one article, a well-known Aboriginal artist argued that Aboriginal artists should be accorded "the same recognition [as non-Aboriginal artists], that our works be respected and that we be acknowledged as the rightful owners of our own works of art." Thus the question arises as to whether copyright law is capable of accommodating this art form and satisfactorily meeting the needs of the community.

The copyright doctrine, however, presents a myriad of barriers to the full protection of indigenous art and folklore. These barriers include the duration of the protection, the originality requirement, the fixation requirement, the individual nature of the rights, the fair use exception, and the economic focus of the remedies. Each of these barriers will be analyzed in turn to understand whether they are preclusive or whether they can be overcome.

A.   *The Duration of the Rights*

The first problem of affording copyright protection to folklore is the term of protection. In all Berne Convention member states, the term of the protection is the life of the author plus fifty years. In addition to the problem of identifying a particular author by whose life the term may be measured, the more significant problem is that the term is insufficient. Many indigenous rights advocates argue that perpetual protection should be granted to folklore because "the protection of the expression of folklore is not for the benefit of individual creators but a community whose existence is not limited in time." Even assuming that works would be protected, say, for one hundred years as an unpublished anonymous work, that period is still insignificant in the life of artistic traditions that date back thousands of years. One hundred years from now, indigenous peoples will not want to release their sacred texts to the outside to be exploited. Thus, this term of protection is insufficient for the "traditional group." It is also inadequate for the "realist group." This limited term of protection means that most folkloric works may already be in the public domain and may therefore be used without authorization. Therefore, the "realist group" will not be able to prevent outsiders from copying their works or their basic underlying symbols.

* * *

B.   *The Originality Requirement*

The second barrier to the protection of folklore is that copyright law requires that a work be original to be eligible for protection. As the U.S. Supreme Court pronounced in its most recent decision concerning the subject matter of copyright: "The sine qua non of copyright is originality." And, indeed, American (and Continental) copyright law is premised on the concept of authorship and the concomitant notion of originality. The Copyright Act provides protection only to "original works of authorship."

* * *

Still, this requirement may present problems for folklore. Folkloric work is most often ancient, many of the art forms having been developed generations ago. Australian Aboriginal art, for instance, "draw[s] upon custom and tradition" and "represent[s] a . . . continuation of . . . time-honoured myths and legends." Although folklore can be entirely new, it is most often directly derived from preexisting works. Folklore is the product of a slow process of creative development. It is not stagnant, but evolves slowly.

* * *

Therefore, to protect folklore adequately, copyright would need to be extended "beyond the borders of originality." Furthermore, because the underlying work is unprotected, an outsider could adapt a public domain work and copyright her new translation, thereby obtaining a monopoly over the use of those designs. This would obviously be very problematic for indigenous groups.

* * *

C. *The Fixation Requirement*

Often it may be an outsider who first fixes an indigenous work in a tangible medium—a documentary film maker who videotapes a ritual, or a researcher who notes the steps of a dance, or a musician who writes down the words or notes of a song for the first time. These persons, however, are not the authors, and therefore not the initial copyright owners just as a stenographer is not the "author" for copyright purposes of what he or she transcribes. Under the copyright doctrine, the author is the party who actually "creates" the work. The "fixer" is the author in only the original expression that originates with her. That is, the film maker is the author of the film, not of the underlying dances or music that she captures on film. Furthermore, the U.S. Copyright Act, for example, requires that the work be fixed "by or under the authority of the author." So, unauthorized fixation will not result in copyright, nor will it preclude indigenous artists from thereafter fixing and copyrighting the work.

* * *

D. *Group Rights*

The fourth problem for the application of copyright to folklore is more fundamental. Copyright law is premised on individual rights, and recognizes group rights only in limited situations. At its core, copyright is intended to reward individual authors for their creation of intellectual property. Indigenous art, in contrast, is not thought to be owned by the particular artist who created it. Instead, it is seen as the property of the group or clan. That is, it is something passed down through the generations for the enrichment of all.

* * *

This custom poses a problem for copyright law since copyright law vests the rights in the one who executes the work. It is this owner alone who has the exclusive right to reproduce the work. But this formulation is contrary to indigenous custom where the art is seen as something owned by the community.

* * *

Three mechanisms in copyright law could be utilized to attempt to overcome this problem: (1) joint authorship; (2) the transfer of rights; and (3) the work made-for-hire provision. These mechanisms may, however, in the end, be unsatisfactory. The most logical possibility is the provision for joint authorship. This provision is the only nod to collective ownership in the acts. It allows the multiple authors of a work to be co-owners of the copyright in the work. Unfortunately, this provision is very narrow. In order to be deemed a joint author, two requirements must be satisfied.

First, the joint authors must in fact collaborate in the work's preparation, and second, they must intend, at the time the work is prepared, that their contributions be merged into "inseparable or interdependent parts of a unitary whole." Thus, under the first requirement, joint authorship vests the rights only in the persons who actually make the work (or their designees). That is, only those clan members who are involved in the creation of the work can be joint authors. The rest of the clan or community could not be considered co-owners unless they actually contributed to the creation of the work. Furthermore, to be a joint author each person's contribution must be copyrightable. Thus, a clan elder who dictates the composition to an artist who executes it will not be a joint author with the artist.

* * *

E.   *Fair Use*

Under most copyright regimes, the monopoly on speech that the law permits is balanced by a provision that allows the unauthorized use of a copyrighted work where that use is fair—the so-called "fair use" exception. Whether or not an unauthorized use is deemed fair is determined on a case-by-case basis by considering various factors such as the purpose of the use, the nature of the copyrighted work, the amount of the copyrighted work used, and the effect of the use on the value of the copyrighted work. Thus, where a copyrighted work is used for comment or criticism or for an educational purpose, the author of the work may not be able to preclude its use.

* * *

In all instances, the nature of the copyrighted work also makes a harder case for fair use because creative works are thought to deserve more protection than informational works. Even though most indigenous art is used to communicate information to the community, as in the case of art that depicts creation stories, the work itself will still be judged to be creative. Original songs, dances, and paintings, unlike most databases, have a creative element that is impossible to separate from their underlying facts. That is, it is impossible to take only the information about the creation without also taking the design or expression. Moreover, courts are more prone to protect works that are not yet published. Thus, where unpublished sacred texts are used, it will mitigate against a finding of fair use.

* * *

F.   *Damages*

Lastly, some copyright laws may not provide adequate remedies for the unauthorized use of indigenous art. Surely, injunctive relief and the impounding and destruction of infringing works would be helpful. However, the threat of injunctions and destruction of infringing goods may not be enough to deter individuals and companies from using indigenous art without authorization. Damages may be the only way to ensure that outsiders will respect the copyright in indigenous art. For instance, a small company that manufactures infringing T-shirts at a profit may deliberately do so, knowing that the worst that can happen is that it may be ordered to cease at some point. If it were threatened with surrendering its profits, it might not embark on that plan.

Recovering significant damages, however, may not be possible for infringement of indigenous art. Under some copyright laws, only actual damages are awarded for economic harm caused by infringement. The "realist group" will not be negatively affected by this regime since it will be able to show economic harm. But the "traditional group" will fare worse. Where indigenous art would never be put to a economical use by the copyright owners, it may not be possible to prove that the infringement caused any economic loss. That is, where a work is a sacred text, reproduction of which would never be allowed for commercial gain, an infringing use of their work would not deprive the copyright owners of any financial gain. Thus, the true harm done to the copyright owners—the denigration and release of sacred texts—would go unpunished, although it would be halted. This lack of punishment may not adequately deter future infringements.

* * *

IV. INTERNATIONAL PROPOSALS

* * *

B. *Model Law on Copyright*

The Tunis Model Law on Copyright (1976) was written to provide a model for developing countries to enact comprehensive copyright legislation. This model act explicitly refers to folklore at several places "because in developing countries national folklore constitutes an appreciable part of the cultural heritage and is susceptible of economic exploitation, the fruits of which should not be denied to those countries." In Section 6(2) the act provides that "[w]orks of national folklore are protected by all means in accordance with subsection (1), without limitation in time." Thus it seems that the protection of folklore is perpetual under this act. There is, however, no mention of retroactivity of protection. Therefore, although newer works will be protected forever, much folklore will already be in the public domain.

* * *

C. *Model Provisions*

* * *

The Model Provisions enable the collective ownership and control of folklore, grant perpetual protection, and do not require fixation. The major tenet of the Model Provisions is that utilizations of folklore are subject to authorization by the competent authority "when they are made . . . with gainful intent and outside their traditional or customary context." According to the Working Group on the Intellectual Property Aspects of Folklore Protection, three criteria should be used to determine whether a use is unauthorized: (1) whether the intent is gainful; (2) whether the use was made by members or non-members of the community where the expression is derived from; and (3) whether the use is outside of the traditional context of the usual use.

* * *

D.   *The Mataatua Declaration*

In June 1993, over 150 representatives from indigenous populations of fifteen countries convened in New Zealand for the first International Conference on Cultural and Intellectual Property Rights of Indigenous Peoples. There they passed The Mataatua Declaration on Cultural and Intellectual Property Rights of Indigenous Peoples. The Declaration states that existing intellectual property regimes are inadequate to the needs of indigenous peoples and calls for, among other things, new intellectual property mechanisms that provide for collective ownership, retroactive coverage of historical works, protection against debasement of culturally significant items, and multigenerational coverage span. Moreover, the Declaration urges indigenous peoples to define for themselves their own intellectual property and develop a code of ethics that outsiders must observe when interacting with that property. This document thus identifies the key challenges in reconciling the copyright regime with the needs of the indigenous community. However, because it is more a call to action than a proposal, it offers little guidance as to how to achieve a reconciliation. Unfortunately, no action has been taken in response to this declaration thus far.

V.   STRETCHING THE BOUNDARIES OF COPYRIGHT LAW

Another possibility in the protection of folklore may be to look beyond copyright law. Without reformulating the copyright law, it may be that the law, when coupled with other rights, provides sufficient protection to folklore. The following mechanisms may provide a means to stretch and strengthen copyright law's protection of folklore.

A.   *Moral Rights*

Moral Rights, although distinct from economic rights, are usually grouped in with copyright. Moral Rights basically consist of the rights of divulgation, paternity, and integrity. These rights, which are usually inalienable, allow artists to protect their artwork from being denigrated. Indigenous artists may be protected under this doctrine from having their work first published without their authorization, published without attribution, reproduced in poor quality, reproduced only partially causing the message to be distorted, or put to a use which would be inappropriate to the nature of the original work.

* * * The term of protection may also be a problem for folklore, as protection may be extinguished upon the death of the author, or after a set time. The indigenous community, however, would want to ensure the integrity of the work beyond this limited time since it is the community's interest in the work and not the reputation of the artist with which they are concerned. The community's interest in the work is perpetual. On the other hand, moral rights, if applied too zealously, may frustrate the interests of the "realist group" by protecting sacred imagery from any commercial exploitation.

B. *Public Domain Statutes and Domaine Public Payant*

Public Domain statutes basically provide moral rights in perpetuity. Public Domain legislation is intended to "prevent or sanction use of public domain works in such a way as to prejudice their authenticity or identity." Public domain works can be used as the basis of derivative works so long as the use does not violate the work's essence, cultural value, or reputation. Thus, this scheme appears to provide the appropriate safeguard to the indigenous community's cultural interests, especially those who want to protect sacred imagery. Protection is extended, however, only to works whose copyright protection has expired and to works that would have qualified for copyright protection had the legislation existed at the time they were created. For these reasons, folklore will have the same difficulties that it does with copyright law. Namely, the originality and fixation requirements may prevent it from enjoying protection. Furthermore, authority to control public domain works rests with a designated state agency. Public Domain legislation therefore does not present the problem of individual ownership for indigenous peoples, but it may be problematic to have the state exercise this degree of control over indigenous folklore, especially where the state is not representative of the indigenous community.

* * *

C. *The Law of Unfair Competition*

Combining copyright protection with an additional source of intellectual property protection may be a means of providing adequate protection to folklore. Trademark law may provide additional protection against some kinds of unauthorized copying.

In the United States, Canada, and Australia, indigenous arts and crafts have faced competition in their market from cheaper imitations made by non-indigenous persons, often from overseas. The problem is that as soon as any of their art forms gains popularity with the general public, the market is flooded with imitations. Each of these governments has taken special measures to ensure the authenticity of indigenous products.

In the United States, for example, the Indian Arts and Crafts Act of 1935 was enacted to protect Native American Arts and Crafts. The Act attempts to assure authenticity of Native American works by issuing certification marks * * *. The Act provides civil and criminal penalties for counterfeiting the Board's marks and for misrepresenting the works as "Indian made." The Act, however, appears to be "only a paper tiger" since there has never been a single prosecution in the history of the Act. In fact, after more than sixty years on the books, the Interior Department has not even promulgated any regulations for its enforcement.

* * *

Another possible means of supplementing copyright law's protection is through general unfair competition laws. Unfair competition laws are designed to protect consumers and competitors from the misrepresentation of products on the market. Indigenous groups may use these laws to prevent outsiders from marketing goods as "Indian made" or as being produced on indigenous lands. Trademark law has the advantage of granting rights collectively and of providing perpetual protection. To gain protection under these laws, however, folklore must qualify as a commercial good or service. Some aspects of folklore, however, such as rituals or dance, may not generally qualify as commercial activities. Thus this law would benefit the first group of concerns more than it would the second.

* * *

VI.   ARRIVING AT THE NORMATIVE QUESTION

Finally, with the benefit of an analysis of the extent to which indigenous art and folklore are currently protected by intellectual property regimes, we can now ask the normative question: Should indigenous art and folklore be protected by intellectual property regimes? The answer to this question should not be assumed. Along with it one might ask: What are the implications of the application of existing intellectual property laws to folklore? Stated otherwise, what are the consequences of fitting folklore into the existing scheme?

One consequence is that these artistic traditions will be forced to conform to a set of assumptions that are at odds with their traditions. The underlying rationale of intellectual property law privileges individual ownership, economic exploitation, and the dissemination of new expressions of ideas. Intellectual property rights are driven by the economics of free enterprise and profit. The objective is the creation of a limited monopoly right as an incentive for individuals to disseminate their original expressions. However, indigenous art, especially in its sacred forms, is not something that can be owned by any individual, is not something that should be commercially exploited, is not something that can be freely disseminated, and is not something that can be reinterpreted or adapted. These works, which are often sacred in nature, are unlike the types of works anticipated by the copyright law and may require different types of protections. Thus, in some cases, indigenous groups may seek to use intellectual property laws, which imply dissemination, to withhold the circulation of their art. Although they may use the intellectual property regime to get partial protection, they are using it for a purpose that is alien to it.

* * *

CONCLUSION

* * *

The first revelation that the analysis unveils is that those indigenous peoples who want to gain control of their imagery in order to participate in its circulation are, in fact, adequately protected by the existing legal regime. Certainly their protection could be strengthened, but anything more may inhibit free expression and upset the delicate balance that the copyright law has achieved. To the extent we want to grant special protection to these works, this goal may be better achieved through unfair competition law.

———

NOTES AND QUESTIONS

1. Copyright law as a Western concept. Copyrights are widely used in Western countries to protect artists' creations and works but this does not easily translate to indigenous cultures. *See* Dieter Dambiec, *Protecting indigenous peoples' folklore through copyright law, available at* http://www.proutworld.org/features/copyrightindigen.itra(1999). According to Dambiec, copyright law does not easily apply in indigenous cultures because of the differences in the concept of ownership. Western cultures tend to think of ownership in individual terms while many indigenous cultures think in terms of community ownership. An intriguing argument on this point can be found in MICHAEL I. BROWN, WHO OWNS NATIVE CULTURE, Harvard University Press (2003).

2. Questions of identity and ownership. Another important issue in indigenous folklore is identification of the artists and ownership. Unlike Western cultures, it is not as easy to identify work that may have been created hundreds of years ago in indigenous communities. Some works contain the contribution of successive groups of artists, whose work accumulates over time in a serial dynamic process of revision and change. Dambiec says that New Zealand's Maori society has assumed ownership of tribal creations through various levels, meaning different people in the tribe control specific aspects of the creations. This is a possible avenue in giving ownership to indigenous tribes in a manner that allows community ownership and participation.

3. Moral rights or copyrights? As Dambiec argues, copyrights are often insufficient when dealing with indigenous culture and folklore. Because of this, a viable solution could be to merge the moral and legal to best meet the needs of indigenous cultures. According to Dambiec, moral rights comprise three types of rights: the power to control the publication or dissemination of a work; the right to have the artist's or tribe's name associated with the work; and the right to prevent misuse, mutilation, or distortion of a work. *See* Dambiec, *supra* at 847, n.1. Because of the various issues involved in ownership and folklore culture, the most viable means of compensating indigenous peoples is to merge Western and indigenous concepts to best protect their interests. Obviously, the Western concept of ownership and copyright is often insufficient to address indigenous people's concerns, just as their ideas of ownership and identity are often dismissed in the Western legal system.

D. BUSINESS-LIKE IMAGE

Rogers v. American Airlines, Inc.

Southern District of New York, 527 F.Supp. 229 (S.D.N.Y. 1981).

■ JUDGE SOFAER delivered the opinion of the court:

Plaintiff is a black woman who seeks $10,000 damages, injunctive, and declaratory relief against enforcement of a grooming policy of the defendant

American Airlines that prohibits employees in certain employment categories from wearing an all-braided hairstyle. Plaintiff has been an American Airlines employee for approximately eleven years, and has been an airport operations agent for over one year. Her duties involve extensive passenger contact, including greeting passengers, issuing boarding passes, and checking luggage. She alleges that the policy violates her rights under the Thirteenth Amendment of the United States Constitution, under Title VII of the Civil Rights Act, 42 U.S.C. § 2000e et seq. (1976), and under 42 U.S.C. § 1981 (1976), in that it discriminates against her as a woman, and more specifically as a black woman. She claims that denial of the right to wear her hair in the "corn row" style intrudes upon her rights and discriminates against her.* * *

[The court dismissed the plaintiff's Thirteenth Amendment claim]. The [motion to dismiss] is also meritorious with respect to the statutory claims insofar as they challenge the policy on its face. * * * The policy is addressed to both men and women, black and white. Plaintiff's assertion that the policy has practical effect only with respect to women is not supported by any factual allegations. Many men have hair longer than many women. Some men have hair long enough to wear in braids if they choose to do so. Even if the grooming policy imposed different standards for men and women, however, it would not violate Title VII. * * * The complaint does not state a claim for sex discrimination.

The considerations with respect to plaintiff's race discrimination claim would clearly be the same, see *Smith v. Delta Air Lines*, 486 F.2d 512 (5th Cir. 1973), except for plaintiff's assertion that the "corn row" style has a special significance for black women. She contends that it "has been, historically, a fashion and style adopted by Black American women, reflective of cultural, historical essence of the Black women in American society." * * * "The style was 'popularized' so to speak, within the larger society, when Cicely Tyson adopted the same for an appearance on nationally viewed Academy Awards presentation several years ago. * * * It was and is analogous to the public statement by the late Malcolm X regarding the Afro hair style. * * * At the bottom line, the completely braided hair style, sometimes referred to as corn rows, has been and continues to be part of the cultural and historical essence of Black American women." * * * "There can be little doubt that, if American adopted a policy which foreclosed Black women/all women from wearing hair styled as an 'Afro/ bush,' that policy would have very pointedly racial dynamics and consequences reflecting a vestige of slavery unwilling to die (that is, a master mandate that one wear hair divorced from ones historical and cultural perspective and otherwise consistent with the 'white master' dominated society and preference thereof)." * * *

Plaintiff is entitled to a presumption that her arguments, largely repeated in her affidavit, are true. But the grooming policy applies equally to members of all races, and plaintiff does not allege that an all-braided hair style is worn exclusively or even predominantly by black people. Moreover, it is proper to note that defendants have alleged without contravention that plaintiff first appeared at work in the all-braided hairstyle on or about September 25, 1980, soon after the style had been popularized by a white actress in the film "10." Plaintiff may be correct that an employer's policy prohibiting the "Afro/bush" style might offend Title VII and section 1981. But if so, this chiefly would be because banning a natural hairstyle would implicate the policies underlying the prohibition of discrimination on the basis of immutable characteristics. * * * An all-braided hair style is an "easily changed characteristic," and, even if socioculturally associated with a particular race or nationality, is not an impermissible basis for distinctions in the application of employment practices by an employer. * * * The Fifth Circuit recently upheld, without requiring any showing of business purpose, an employer's policy prohibiting the speaking of any language but English in the workplace, despite the importance of Spanish to the ethnic identity of Mexican–Americans. * * *

Although the Act may shield "employees' psychological as well as economic fringes" from employer abuse * * * plaintiff's allegations do not amount to charging American with "a practice of creating a working environment heavily charged with ethnic or racial discrimination," or one "so heavily polluted with discrimination as to destroy completely the emotional and psychological stability of minority group workers." * * * If an even-handed English-only policy that has the effect of prohibiting a Mexican–American from speaking Spanish during working hours is valid without a showing of business purpose, the policy at issue here, even if ill-advised, does not offend the law.

Moreover, the airline did not require plaintiff to restyle her hair. It suggested that she could wear her hair as she liked while off duty, and permitted her to pull her hair into a bun and wrap a hairpiece around the bun during working hours. * * *

Plaintiff has failed to allege sufficient facts to require defendants to demonstrate that the policy has a bona fide business purpose. * * * In this regard, however, plaintiff does not dispute defendant's assertion that the policy was adopted in order to help American project a conservative and business-like image, a consideration recognized as a bona fide business purpose. E.g., *Fagan v. National Cash Register Co.*, 481 F.2d 1115, 1124–25 (D.C. Cir. 1973). * * *

Plaintiff also asserts in her complaint that the regulation has been applied in an uneven and discriminatory manner. She claims that white women in particular have been permitted to wear ponytails and shag cuts. She goes on to claim, in fact, that some black women are permitted to wear the same hairstyle that she has been prohibited from wearing. These claims seriously undercut her assertion that the policy discriminates against women, and her claim that it discriminates against black women in particular. Conceivably, however, the complaint could be construed as alleging that the policy has been applied in a discriminatory manner against plaintiff because she is black by some representative of the defendant. On its face, this allegation is sufficient, although it might be subject to dismissal on a summary judgment motion if it is not supplemented with some factual claims.

This remaining claim—of racially discriminatory application—by its nature is not appropriate for class action treatment. In light of plaintiff's assertions that both white and black women in the purported class have been permitted to wear the all-braided style, she seems to be saying, ultimately, that there are no similarly situated people, and she does not identify any. Therefore, the motion for class certification is denied. * * * Indeed, even as broadly alleged, plaintiff's claims would not warrant certification of a class. Plaintiff seeks specific retroactive monetary relief only for herself and not for any class members. With respect to the class, plaintiff seeks a change in company policy, and a victory in plaintiff's case, with an injunctive and declaratory order, would afford relief to all similarly situated people. * * *

A Hair Piece: Perspective on the Intersection of Race and Gender

1991 DUKE L.J. 365.

■ PAULETTE M. CALDWELL

I. OF SMALL BEGINNINGS

A. *Rediscovering My Hair*

> *When will I cherish my hair again, the way my grandmother cherished it, when fascinated by its beauty, with hands carrying centuries-old secrets of adornment and craftswomanship, she plaited it, twisted it, cornrowed it, finger-curled it, olive-oiled it, on the growing moon cut and shaped it, and wove it like fine strands of gold inlaid with semiprecious stones, coral and ivory, telling with my hair a lost-found story of the people she carried inside her?*

> * * *

B. *On Being the Subject of a Law School Hypothetical*

The case of *Rogers v. American Airlines* upheld the right of employers to prohibit categorically the wearing of braided hairstyles in the workplace. The plaintiff, a black woman, argued that American Airline's policy discriminated against her specifically as a black woman. In effect, she based her claim on the interactive effects of racial and gender discrimination. The court chose, however, to base its decision principally on distinctions between biological and cultural conceptions of race. More importantly, it treated the plaintiff's claims of race and gender discrimination in the alternative and independent of each other, thus denying any interactive relationship between the two.

> * * *

I discovered *Rogers* while reading a newspaper article describing the actual or threatened firing of several black women in metropolitan Washington, D.C. solely for wearing braided hairstyles. The article referred to *Rogers* but actually focused on the case of Cheryl Tatum, who was fired from her job as a restaurant cashier in a Hyatt Hotel under a company policy that prohibited "extreme and unusual hairstyles."

The newspaper description of the Hyatt's grooming policy conjured up an image of a ludicrous and outlandishly-coiffed Cheryl Tatum, one clearly bent on exceeding the bounds of workplace taste and discipline. But the picture that accompanied the article revealed a young, attractive black woman whose hair fell neatly to her shoulders in an all-American, common, everyday pageboy style, distinguished only by the presence of tiny braids in lieu of single strands of hair.

* * *

C.   *Why Would Anyone Want to Wear Their Hair That Way?*
* * *

Hair seems to be such a little thing. Yet it is the little things, the small everyday realities of life, that reveal the deepest meanings and values of a culture, give legal theory its grounding, and test its legitimacy.

II.   To Choose Myself: Interlocking Figurations in the Construction of Race and Gender

A.   *A Black Woman's Hair, A Black Woman's Place*

SUNDAY. School is out, my exams are graded, and I have un-braided my hair a few days before my appointment at the beauty parlor to have it braided again. After a year in braids, my hair is healthy again: long and thick and cottony soft. I decide not to french roll it or twist it or pull it into a ponytail or bun or cover it with a scarf. Instead, I comb it out and leave it natural, in a full and big "Angela Davis" afro style. I feel full and big and regal. I walk the three blocks from my apartment to the subway. I see a white male colleague walking in the opposite direction and I wave to him from across the street. He stops, squints his eyes against the glare of the sun and stares, trying to figure out who has greeted him. He recognizes me and starts to cross over to my side of the street. I keep walking, fearing the possibility of his curiosity and needing to be relieved of the strain of explanation.

MONDAY. My hair is still unbraided, but I blow it out with a hair dryer and pull it back into a ponytail tied at the nape of my neck before I go to the law school. I enter the building and run into four white female colleagues on their way out to a white female lunch. Before I can say hello, one of them blurts out, "It IS weird!" Another drowns out the first: "You look so young, like a teenager!" The third invites me to join them for lunch while the fourth stands silently, observing my hair. I mumble some excuse about lunch and, interject, almost apologetically, that I plan to get my hair braided again the next day. When I arrive at my office suite and run into the white male I had greeted on Sunday, I realize immediately that he has told the bunch on the way to lunch about our encounter the day before. He mutters something about how different I look today, then asks me whether the day before I had been on my way to a ceremony. He and the others are generally nice colleagues, so I half-smile, but say nothing in response. I feel a lot less full and big and regal.

TUESDAY. I walk to the garage under my apartment building, again wearing a big, full "Angela Davis" afro. Another white male colleague passes me by, not recognizing me. I greet him and he smiles broadly saying that he has never seen me look more beautiful. I smile back, continue the chit chat for a moment more and try not to think about whether he is being disingenuous. I slowly get into my car, buckle up, relax, and turn on the radio. It will take me about forty-five minutes to drive uptown to the beauty parlor, park my car, and get something to eat before beginning the long hours of sitting and braiding. I feel good, knowing that the braider will be ecstatic when she sees the results of her healing handiwork. I keep my movements small, easy, and slow, relishing in a rare, short morning of being free.

B. *When Race and Gender Intersect*

My initial outrage notwithstanding, *Rogers* is an unremarkable decision. Courts generally protect employer-mandated hair and dress codes, and they often accord the greatest deference to codes that classify individuals on the basis of socially-conditioned rather than biological differences. And although *Rogers* rests on one line of authority without acknowledging the existence of another, grooming codes are governed by decisional law that clearly lacks conceptual coherence. All in all, such cases are generally considered only marginally significant in the battle to secure equal employment rights.

But *Rogers* is regrettably unremarkable in an important respect. It rests on suppositions that are deeply imbedded in American culture—assumptions so entrenched and so necessary to the maintenance of interlocking, interdependent structures of domination that their mythological bases and political functions have become invisible, especially to those to whom their existence is most detrimental. *Rogers* proceeds from the premise that, although racism and sexism share much in common, they are nonetheless fundamentally unrelated phenomena—a proposition proved false by history and contemporary reality. Racism and sexism are interlocking, mutually-reinforcing components of a system of dominance rooted in patriarchy. No significant and lasting progress in combating either can be made until this interdependent aspect of their relation is acknowledged, and until the perspectives gained from considering their interaction are reflected in legal theory and public policy.

* * *

C. *The Limitations of the Assumptions of Race–Sex Correspondence and Independence*

* * *

Correlative to the assumption of race-sex correspondence, there exists an equally powerful assumption of race-sex independence or distinctiveness. Also rooted in American history, particularly in the politics of emancipation and suffrage, this assumption has contemporary manifestations in the existence of distinct political movements against racism and sexism, the development of social policy along exclusively gender or race lines, and the legal conceptualization of distinct approaches to issues of race and gender.

* * *

Problems arise in the development of legal theory and social policy when the possibility of other relationships between race and gender, such as intersection, are not considered. Black women's issues "slip through the cracks" of legal protection, and the gender components of racism and the race components of sexism remain hidden.

* * *

In one category, courts have considered whether black women may represent themselves or other race or gender discriminatees. Some cases deny black women the right to claim discrimination as a subgroup distinct from black men and white women. Others deny black women the right to represent a class that includes white women in a suit based on sex discrimination, on the ground that race distinguishes them. Still other cases prohibit black women from representing a class in a race discrimination suit that includes black men, on the ground of gender differences. These cases demonstrate the failure of courts to account for race-sex intersection, and are premised on the assumption that discrimination is based on either race or gender, but never both.

A second category of cases concerns the interaction of race and gender in determining the limits of an employer's ability to condition work on reproductive and marital choices associated with black women. Several courts have upheld the firing of black women for becoming pregnant while unmarried if their work involves association with children—especially black teenage girls. These decisions rest on entrenched fears of and distorted images about black female sexuality, stigmatize single black mothers (and by extension their children) and reinforce "culture of poverty" notions that blame poverty on poor people themselves. They also reinforce the notion that the problems of black families are attributable to the deviant and dominant roles of black women and the idea that racial progress depends on black female subordination.

A third category concerns black women's physical images. These cases involve a variety of mechanisms to exclude black women from jobs that involve contact with the public—a tendency particularly evident in traditionally female jobs in which employers place a premium on female attractiveness—including a subtle, and often not so subtle, emphasis on female sexuality. The latter two categories sometimes involve, in addition to the intersection of race and gender, questions that concern the interaction of race, gender, and culture.

* * *

D.   *The Rogers Opinion*

The *Rogers* decision is a classic example of a case concerning the physical image of black women. Renee Rogers, whose work for American Airlines involved extensive passenger contact, claimed that American's prohibition of braided hairstyles in certain job classifications discriminated against her as a woman in general, and as a black woman in particular. The court did not attempt to limit the plaintiff's case by forcing her to proceed on either race or gender grounds, nor did it create a false hierarchy between the two bases by treating one as grounded in statutory law and the other as a "plus" factor that would explain the application of law to a subgroup not technically recognized as a protected group by law. The court also appeared to recognize that the plaintiff's claim was not based on the cumulative effects of race and gender.

* * *

The court gave three principal reasons for dismissing the plaintiff's claim. First, in considering the sex discrimination aspects of the claim, the court disagreed with the plaintiff's argument that, in effect, the application of the company's grooming policy to exclude the category of braided hairstyles from the workplace reached only women. Rather, the court stressed that American's policy was even-handed and applied to men and women alike. Second, the court emphasized that American's grooming policy did not regulate or classify employees on the basis of an immutable gender characteristic. Finally, American's policy did not bear on the exercise of a fundamental right. The plaintiff's racial discrimination claim was analyzed separately but dismissed on the same grounds: neutral application of American's anti-braid policy to all races and absence of any impact of the policy on an immutable racial characteristic or of any effect on the exercise of a fundamental right.

* * *

In support of its view that the plaintiff had failed to establish a factual basis for her claim that American's policy had a disparate impact on black women, thus destroying any basis for the purported neutral application of the policy, the court pointed to American's assertion that the plaintiff had adopted the prohibited hairstyle only shortly after it had been "popularized" by Bo Derek, a white actress, in the film "10." Notwithstanding the factual inaccuracy of American's claim, and notwithstanding the implication that there is no relationship between braided hair and the culture of black women, the court assumed that black and white women are equally motivated (i.e., by the movies) to adopt braided hairstyles.

* * *

The court's reference to Bo Derek presents us with two conflicting images, both of which subordinate black women and black culture. On the one hand, braids are separated from black culture, and, by implication are said to arise from whites. Not only do blacks contribute nothing to the nation's or the world's culture, they copy the fads of whites. On the other hand, whites make fads of black culture, which, by virtue of their popularization, become—like all "pop"—disposable, vulgar, and without lasting value. Braided hairstyles are thus trivialized and protests over them made ludicrous.

* * *

III. TRUTHS AND SOJOURNS: STEREOTYPING AT THE INTERSECTION OF RACE AND GENDER

A. *Of Changes and More*

1985. In a few days I will teach in a four-day workshop for fifty black women. The participants have been chosen primarily because of their status in the corporate world of business and finance. My feelings of performance anxiety seem greatly overshadowed by feelings of happy excitement and expectancy at the prospect of navigating my peers through the murky waters of possibilities and pitfalls for black women in leadership positions. I arrive at the beauty parlor for the grooming of my hair, which, after a year in braids, has grown to my shoulders. Time is short and the hairdresser is late. When she arrives, on impulse, I decide to forgo braids and ask her to apply a chemical straightener to my virgin hair. I return to work a day later and the "significant other" of a male colleague addresses me in that chastising, condescending tone of voice reserved for slaves and women in domestic service: "Every time I see you, you've done something else to your hair!"

Days later I arrive at the workshop site and greet the participants, my hair arranged in a style reminiscent of my former for-profit corporate self. Over the next four days, I am frequently complimented for my competence, unusual insights, and mastery of subject matter, but mostly—especially from those who over the years have watched me alternate between closely-cropped Afros and short, straight bobs—for the beauty of my long, straight hair.

B. *Hair and the Timeless Search for Legitimacy*

* * *

Unlike skin color and other physical manifestations of race, hair has both mutable and immutable characteristics. Change in the mutable and in the appearance of the immutable characteristics of hair can be accomplished with relative ease, albeit, for many blacks, not without long-term consequences. Hair can be cut off, straightened out, curled up, or covered over either in the exercise of individual preference or to comply with the tastes or preferences of others. The uniqueness of hair among physical characteristics correlating with race lies not only in the ability of its true nature to be disguised, but also in its susceptibility to external control.

* * *

Today, Afro hairstyles—or at least some of them—are widely accepted in all forms of employment, although the extent of their legal protection is far from certain. They are considered by many to reflect personal style—aesthetic choice—and are not generally associated with the politics of the period of their origin. However, the rationalizations that accompanied opposition to Afro hairstyles in the 1960s—extreme, too unusual, not businesslike, inconsistent with a conservative image, unprofessional, inappropriate with business attire, too "black" (i.e., too militant), unclean—are used today to justify the categorical exclusion of braided hairstyles in many parts of the workforce, particularly in jobs that are either traditionally conservative or highly structured, involve close immediate supervision, or require significant contact with the public.

C. *In Whose Image? The Application of Antidiscrimination Principles to Employer Grooming and Image Preferences*

By focusing on neutrality, immutability, and the exercise of fundamental rights, the *Rogers* court obscured an underlying principle in the application of antidiscrimination law to a variety of employer image preferences, including—but not limited to—those expressed through grooming codes. A careful analysis of cases in this area reveals that courts pay close attention to the eradication of stereotypes, attention in no way evidenced in *Rogers*. These cases also make clear that stereotyping is impermissible whether or not the standards set forth in *Rogers* are satisfied.

* * *

* * * *Image Discrimination in the Airline Industry*. The fact that the *Rogers* case was brought against a major airline is itself of considerable significance. The airline industry's history of discrimination against women is nothing short of malevolent. Perhaps no industry has fought as hard to control its image and to seek competitive advantage by exploiting stereotypical cultural attitudes concerning the physical appearance, proper place in society, and supposed personal characteristics of blacks and women.

* * *

D. *Public Degradation of Black Women*

Many employers express shock that black women who refuse to unbraid their hair take such a strong stance, one that could cost them their jobs, in defense of a hairstyle. More shocking is the recurrence among unrelated employers of virtually identical solutions to the issue of braids, solutions that embody overt racist caricatures of the past expressed in the subtle, symbolic code of contemporary racism. Invariably, black women are told either to unbraid their hair or to disguise their braids by pulling them into a bun or cover them up with a wig or hairpiece. This latter solution—the forcible covering up of a black woman's hair—connotes a demeaning servitude that persists even in the face of changes in one of America's most cherished and enduring symbols. For the first time in the more than one hundred years of the Aunt Jemima trademark's existence, its current owner has deemed it profitable to reveal Aunt Jemima's hair. But for the color of her skin, the new Aunt Jemima could pass for Betty Crocker. There is nothing wrong or offensive about the similarity of these trademarks, but the marketing judgment of Aunt Jemina's owner does reflect the assumption that the public equates progress for black women with the imitation of white women. Because being black is an occasion for oppression, avoiding blackness and its attached cultural associations becomes the essential mechanism of liberation.

* * *

Judgments about aesthetics do not exist apart from judgments about the social, political, and economic order of a society. They are an essential part of that order. Aesthetic values determine who and what is valued, beautiful, and entitled to control. Thus established, the structure of society at other levels also is justified. What appears to be merely an aesthetic judgment in *Rogers* is part of the subordination of black women and is inextricably connected to the more obvious economic judgments reflected in other cases that affect black women.

IV.   THE NATURE OF KINSHIP

The issues in *Rogers* defy resolution by resort to arguments about mere aesthetic judgments, doctrinal confusion, or minimal effect on employment rights. The application of *Willingham* in *Rogers* reflects patriarchal assumptions about women generally and competing stereotypical images about womanhood determined by race. These competing images limit black women's choices in ways far more fundamental than is readily apparent in controversies about hair. And although *Willingham* and *Rogers* appear to reserve to white women the privilege of their personal and cultural choices, these cases are based on stereotypes that constitute a ready mechanism for denying employment opportunity to white women who refuse to express themselves in ways that satisfy their employers' notions of "white femaleness." These decisions effectively lock men—black and white—and black women out of choices associated with "true" womanhood; read in reverse, they lock white women into such choices.

* * *

V.   HEALING THE SHAME

Eliminating the behavioral consequences of certain stereotypes is a core function of antidiscrimination law. This function can never be adequately performed as long as courts and legal theorists create narrow, inflexible definitions of harm and categories of protection that fail to reflect the actual experience of discrimination. Considering the interactive relationship between racism and sexism from the experiential standpoint and knowledge base of black women can lead to the development of legal theories grounded in reality, and to the consideration by all women of the extent to which racism limits their choices *as women* and by black and other men of color of the extent to which sexism defines their experiences as men of subordinated races.

* * *

NOTES AND QUESTIONS

1. Impact of *Rogers*. The ruling in the case upheld employers' right to prohibit their employees from wearing braided hairstyles. The case relied on *Carswell v. Peachford Hospital*, which upheld the right of a psychiatric hospital to dismiss an employee for wearing beads in their braided hairstyle. The court held that the decision was based on a rule that banned the wearing of jewelry by employees. According to the hospital, the rule was mandated for the patients' safety rather than as a form of racial discrimination. Both cases rely on the premise that braided hairstyles are not the exclusive province of black women. For example, American Airlines claimed the plaintiff only began wearing the braided hairstyle after it was "popularized" by Bo Derek in the movie 10. This argument succeeded because it operated on the premise that braided hairstyles are not immutable physical traits such as an Afro. *See* Caldwell, *supra*.

2. Employee discrimination or customer preference? Caldwell learned of the *Rogers* decision while reading an article concerning Cheryl Tatum, a black woman dismissed from Hyatt Hotel in Washington, D.C. for wearing an inappropriate hairstyle. According to Caldwell, the accompanying picture showed a black woman with a pageboy hairstyle that had small braids also. Tatum claims a Hyatt manager said, "I can't understand why you would want to wear your hair like that anyway. What would our guests think if we allowed you all to wear your hair like that?" *See* Caldwell, *supra* at 850, n.7. The managers' statements exhibit the frequency with which employers invoke customer preference as the reason for banning certain hairstyles. But as Caldwell states, customer preference is usually nothing more than the employer stating its appearance preferences.

3. Black women's place in appearance-focused industries. In the article, Caldwell argues that black women often experience a precarious position in appearance-focused, feminine industries such as airline stewardesses. For example, do the appearance regulations speak to gender or race? Caldwell's article seems to suggest that gender and race are significant factors in the regulations and that black women particularly face both issues. As mentioned in the article, scores of black women have been dismissed from jobs for having inappropriate hairstyles such as braids. In addition, these appearance rules are seen as particularly restricting upon women and decided by men. In this sense black women's appearance has to be pleasing to the white and male eye.

4. Distinction between immutable and mutable traits. American Airlines and the court felt the plaintiff's hairstyle was a voluntary choice. It was not like an Afro, which is an immutable biological trait of blacks. In this sense, the court distinguished between physical and cultural traits and choices. Furthermore, the argument concerning Bo Derek was used by the court and American Airlines to suggest that the prohibition against braided hairstyles was not racial in nature because it was also a style popular with white women. Because of this, it was difficult for the plaintiff to successfully argue that black women were exclusively targeted by the prohibition.

5. Narrow definition of discrimination. Caldwell's article suggests that Rogers was unsuccessful because the court used such a narrow scope of the harm caused by discrimination. She suggests that a more flexible interpretation would take into account the reality of racism and the manner in which it constricts the choices and options of black women and other minorities. Upon suing under the Thirteenth Amendment prohibition on slavery, Rogers' arguments were not supported because the court ruled she was not forced to stay on the job.

E.   THE MARKET VALUE OF POPULAR IMAGES

Madonna: Plantation Mistress or Soul Sister?

BLACK LOOKS: RACE AND REPRESENTATION 157–64 (1992).

■ BELL HOOKS

White women "stars" like Madonna, Sandra Bernhard, and many others publicly name their interest in, and appropriation of, black culture as yet another sign of their radical chic. Intimacy with that "nasty" blackness good white girls stay away from is what they seek. To white and other non-black consumers, this gives them a special flavor, an added spice. After all it is a very recent historical phenomenon for any white girl to be able to get some mileage out of flaunting her fascination and envy of blackness. The thing about envy is that it is always ready to destroy, erase, take-over, and consume the desired object. That's exactly what Madonna attempts to do when she appropriates and commodifies aspects of black culture. Needless to say this kind of fascination is a threat. It endangers. Perhaps that is why so many of the grown black women I spoke with about Madonna had no interest in her as a cultural icon and said things like, "The bitch can't even sing." It was only among young black females that I could find die-hard Madonna fans. Though I often admire and, yes at times, even envy Madonna because she has created a cultural space where she can invent and reinvent herself and receive public affirmation and material reward, I do not consider myself a Madonna fan.

* * *

Fascinated yet envious of black style, Madonna appropriates black culture in ways that mock and undermine, making her presentation one that upstages. This is most evident in the video "Like a Prayer." Though I read numerous articles that discussed public outrage at this video, none focused on the issue of race. No article called attention to the fact that Madonna flaunts her sexual agency by suggesting that she is breaking the ties that bind her as a white girl to white patriarchy, and establishing ties with black men. She, however, and not black men, does the choosing. The message is directed at white men. It suggests that they only labeled black men rapists for fear that white girls would choose black partners over them. Cultural critics commenting on the video did not seem at all interested in exploring the reasons Madonna chooses a black cultural backdrop for this video, i.e., black church and religious experience. Clearly, it was this backdrop that added to the video's controversy.

* * *

Eager to see the documentary *Truth or Dare* because it promised to focus on Madonna's transgressive sexual persona, which I find interesting, I was angered by her visual representation of her domination over not white men (certainly not over Warren Beatty or Alek Keshishian), but people of color and white working-class women. I was too angered by this to appreciate other aspects of the film I might have enjoyed. In *Truth or Dare* Madonna clearly revealed that she can only think of exerting power along very traditional, white supremacist, capitalistic, patriarchal lines. That she made people who were dependent on her for their immediate livelihood submit to her will was neither charming nor seductive to me or the other black folks that I spoke with who saw the film. We thought it tragically ironic that Madonna would choose as her dance partner a black male with dyed blonde hair. Perhaps had he appeared less like a white-identified black male consumed by "blonde ambition" he might have upstaged her. Instead he was positioned as a mirror, into which Madonna and her audience could look and see only a reflection of herself and the worship of "whiteness" she embodies—that white supremacist culture wants everyone to embody. Madonna used her power to ensure that he and the other non-white women and men who worked for her, as well as some of the white subordinates would all serve as the backdrop to her white-girl-makes-good drama. Joking about the film with other black folks, we commented that Madonna must have searched long and hard to find a black female that was not a good dancer, one who would not deflect attention away from her. And it is telling that when the film directly reflects something other than a positive image of Madonna, the camera highlights the rage this black female dancer was suppressing. It surfaces when the "subordinates" have time off and are "relaxing".

* * *

I can only say this doesn't sound like liberation to me. Perhaps when Madonna explores those memories of her white working-class childhood in a troubled family in a way that enables her to understand intimately the politics of exploitation, domination, and submission, she will have a deeper connection with oppositional black culture. If and when this radical critical self-interrogation takes place, she will have the power to create new and different cultural productions, work that will be truly transgressive—acts of resistance that transform rather than simply seduce.

NOTES AND QUESTIONS

1. Minority gay males in the image of white women. The Hooks essay suggests that minority gay males often impersonate and aspire to white womanhood. She also suggests that Madonna capitalizes on this by using a black male dancer who sports blond hair. According to Hooks, Madonna is able to look into a mirror and see a similar reflection staring back. *See* Bell Hooks *Madonna: Plantation Mistress or Soul Sister?, in* BLACK LOOKS: RACE AND REPRESENTATION, 157–64 (1992). As a doubly oppressed minority, many impoverished minority gay males impersonate famous white women including Madonna. In particular, if one looks at the "drag ball" phenomenon depicted in the documentary *Paris Is Burning*, it seems that many poor minority gay males aspire to the "power that is clustered around whiteness, wealth and heterosexuality." *See* Darren Lenard Hutchinson, *Out Yet Unseen: A Racial Critique of Gay and Lesbian Legal Theory and Political Discourse*, CONN. L. REV. 561 (1997). Similarly, Hooks contends that Madonna uses her whiteness as power and property that enable her dominance over her minority subordinates. In particular, Hooks criticizes the manner in which Madonna often humiliates and condescends to her minority dancers and backup singer. It somewhat echoes Hutchinson's argument that subjugated minorities will often suffer various harms to gain entry into the white world. *See* Hooks, *supra*.

2. Class as a division between women. In *Feminist Theory: From Margin to Center*, Hooks suggests that class is a divider in addition to race between white and black women. BELL HOOKS, FEMINIST THEORY FROM MARGIN TO CENTER (1984). According to Hooks, to deny that there is a class division is equivalent to denial of a class struggle in the United States. To Hooks, it is insufficient for an affluent woman to take a poor woman to lunch and cite this as an example of female unity. In the same sense, it is insufficient for Madonna to hire the services of minorities and still subjugate them to abuse. In Hooks' opinion, the documentary film *Truth or Dare: In Bed with Madonna* only reinforces the notion of white dominance over minorities. In particular, she argues that the movie and its images connote white patriarchal power. Hooks, *supra* at 159.

3. The different perceptions of black and white female sexuality. Perhaps an excellent example of this is the recent Super Bowl controversy over Janet Jackson and Justin Timberlake's performance. Here is a sample of some of the headlines in leading national and international newspapers: *FCC is Investigating Super Bowl Show*, THE WASH. POST, Feb. 3, 2004, at A1; *Singer's Boob Sparks Outrage in US*, THE GUARDIAN, Feb. 3, 2004; *Halftime incident sparks FCC inquiry*, ATLANTA J–CONST., Feb. 3, 2004; *Janet's Sorry for Super Strip*, N.Y. DAILY NEWS, Feb. 3, 2004. Interestingly enough, Timberlake's participation was notably absent in much of the outrage and debate. A majority of media outlets treated Jackson as if she were the lone participant in the performance. A number of reasons could explain this. Some view her as solely responsible for the planning of the performance and him as an unknowing accomplice. On the other hand, some argue that Jackson has been severely criticized due to her race. In particular, some have wondered if this would have happened if she were white or Timberlake black. Another issue has been whether Timberlake would have been criticized if he were a black man ripping the bodice of a white female performer.

4. Race, sex, and advertising hyperbole: crossing the line.

Although Hooks's essay was written in 1992, sexuality, race, and power continue to be very controversial topics. The Super Bowl controversy illustrates the notion that the public still rejects certain presentations of female sexuality. In the essay, Hooks asserts that Madonna has built a career on bold sexuality while still being able to retreat to her whiteness. For Hooks, this means Madonna has been able to project sexuality without having the same derogatory labels and exploitation affixed to her suffered by generations of black women.

What accounts for the different reactions to black and white sexuality? The reactions to Madonna and Janet Jackson were disparate. The latter was pilloried and drew major criticism in terms of her morals and values. Of course, there are several possible reasons for this. First, it occurred during the "family hour" of the Super Bowl. Many adults contend that the half-time show was inappropriate for children. Second, it occurred during one of the biggest television events of the year, which could account for the large outpouring of reaction and opinion. Third, she is a black woman who was exposed on national television. The last possibility is one that has been mainly voiced by minority groups. The majority of the mainstream press has not discussed the event as a racial issue. Regardless, the aftermath of the Super Bowl suggests that the public has different standards and notions regarding black and white sexuality.

By contrast to the nearly uniform negative outcry over the Janet Jackson nipple baring "wardrobe malfunction," public reaction was mixed in response to an ad that aired during ABC's Monday Night Football. The ad featured white actress Nicollette Sheridan dropping her towel to flash her naked body to black Philadelphia Eagles receiver Terrell Owens. One columnist thought that the initial public criticism was an "overreaction." *Moral Standards; Under Assault, But Holding Their Own*, ORLANDO SENTI-NEL, Dec. 7, 2004, at A15. Other critics called the "towel-dropping teaser everything from racist to pornographic."

F. MARKET VALUE OF SEXUAL DIFFERENCES

The Sexual Continuum: Transsexual Prisoners

Note, 24 NEW ENG. J. ON CRIM. & CIV. CONFINEMENT 599 (1998).

■ ANITA C. BARNES

I. INTRODUCTION

In a society so bent on the absolute, within a legal system so dependent on identifiable categories, the transsexual prisoner presents a serious problem. Transsexualism protests the confines of gender and sex, questioning the very essence of what is man and what is woman, what is masculine and what is feminine. Transgendered individuals challenge the relationship of sex to gender, specifically, sex does not control gender.

The transsexual inmate faces an even greater struggle due to the narrow definition of sex employed by prison authorities. Courts and prisons strain to place pre-and postoperative transsexuals into recognizable categories and fail to appreciate the uniqueness that transsexualism creates. In effect, transgendered prisoners encounter two forms of imprisonment: (1) they are trapped in a body not their own, and (2) they are oppressed within a legal system just beginning to understand their plight.

    * * *

II. LEGAL RECOGNITION OF GENDER AND SEX

A. *The Definition of Sex and Gender*

Sex refers to one's anatomy, biology, and physiology. This includes one's genitalia, chromosomal structure, and internal sexual organs. Gender refers to an individual's self-image, how others perceive the individual, and the underlying stereotypes surrounding sex. Gender represents the social construction of sex, "gender is to sex as feminine is to female and masculine is to male." Sex defines the system, and gender the function: "sex is the act and gender is the classification."

    * * *

Yet gender is largely more determinative of a person's sex than anatomy or biology. In underestimating the importance of gender in defining sex, "the legal community refuses to accept ... that one's gender is as much an indication of sex as is biology." Gender encompasses one's private experience of sexual roles and his or her public expression of them. Gender influences how sex is perceived, and, ultimately, how society determines identity. Gender identity—the sense of maleness or female-ness—"pervades one's entire concept of one's place in life, of one's place in society." This pervasiveness culminates in actual facts of biology becoming secondary. As Dr. Richard Green, Director of the Gender Identity Research and Treatment Clinic at the University of California School of Medicine in Los Angeles noted, "[g]ender is the usually unshakable conviction of being male or female." The social construction of gender challenges the notion that sex is somehow irrevocably assigned at birth, and that sex in its biological sense exclusively dictates the formation of gender. The medical profession acknowledges that gender identity is generally established early in life. Medical practitioners also recognize that genetic makeup does not wholly determine gender or sexual identity; rather, socialization plays a crucial role as well. In order to better understand the dilemma of the transsexual prisoner, the legal community must embrace the notion that anatomy does not conclusively define gender, and gender identity does not necessarily stem from biological sex. As Leslie Pearlman concluded:

> It is the semantic distinction between sex and gender and the subse-quent jurisprudential construction of gender which the legal communi-ty has failed to understand, but that cannot be ignored. The separate concepts of gender and sex must be respected and accorded their true, individual meanings. If they are not, the uniqueness of the transsexual situation cannot be understood.

B. *Legal Recognition of Gender: Gender Discrimination*

Though the United States Supreme Court hesitates to differentiate gender from sex or to acknowledge gender as separate from sex, Supreme

Court cases implicitly focus on gender stereotyping as grounds for sex discrimination. In *Orr v. Orr*, for example, the Court struck down an Alabama statute that required husbands, but not wives, to pay alimony. Recognizing traditional gender roles of men as breadwinners, and women as homemakers as the impetus behind the statute, the Court reasoned that, in order to survive constitutional scrutiny, the statute must rest on some basis other than antiquated gender stereotypes. The Court in *Orr* concentrated on whether sex is a viable criteria for judging financial need. In analyzing this viability, the Court focused on sex not in terms of biology, but rather in terms, of how society dictates gender *on the basis of sex.*

III.   LEGAL DYNAMICS OF TRANSSEXUALISM

A.   *The Definition of Transsexualism*

* * *

Much of the debate surrounding how the law should recognize transsexuality revolves around the search for the root causes of transsexualism, particularly, whether the origin is psychological or physical. Regardless, transsexualism occurs early in life. Though transsexualism is traditionally viewed as a mental disorder, the medical profession recognizes neurological causes for transsexualism. Studies point to brain size and the role of sexual differentiation during fetal development as the sources of transsexuality. Specifically, research concludes that gender identity is the result of "an interaction between the developing brain and sex hormones." Studies suggest that "transsexuals are right. Their sex was judged in the wrong way at the moment of birth because people look only to the sex organs and not to the brain" to determine sex. Given the medical research regarding brain structure and the sexual differentiation of the brain which occurs after birth, assigning a child's sex on the basis of external genitalia amounts to "an act of faith."

* * *

In *Pinneke v. Preisser*, the United States Court of Appeals for the Eighth Circuit concluded that sex reassignment surgery is medically necessary, therefore, Medicaid cannot deny coverage. Likewise, in *G.B. v. Lackner*, the California Court of Appeals rejected the California Department of Health's argument that sex reassignment amounted to cosmetic surgery, which is excluded from Medi–Cal coverage. Instead, the court concluded that transsexual surgery constitutes a reasonable and medically necessary approach to treating transsexuality.

B.   *Transsexualism and Sex Discrimination*

* * *

In analyzing sex discrimination claims brought by transgendered individuals, courts employ circular reasoning. Courts disallow claims of discrimination on the basis of transsexuality, yet would recognize similar actions if based on a transsexual's anatomic or perceived sex. To succeed, transgendered individuals must prove discrimination due to their sex, whether male or female, not their transsexuality. *Dobre* attests to how difficult a burden this places on transsexuals. In *Dobre* the court went so far as to assume that the plaintiff was female and still found that Dobre failed to state an adequate claim that she was discriminated against as a female. The court concluded, "[if] the plaintiff was discriminated against at all, it was because she was perceived as a male who wanted to become a female."

* * *

By clinging to narrow definitions of sex and gender, courts fail to understand the continuum of sexual identity that transgendered individuals create. Instead, courts continue to struggle to assign pre-and postoperative transsexuals an identifiable "sex" according to the traditional definitions of gender and sex. Some courts adopt the rule that completion of surgery determines sex, recognizing postoperative transsexuals with their new sex while classifying preoperative transsexuals according to their anatomy. For the transitioning transsexual, however, this assignment of gender based on biology and genitalia is essentially a form of "institutionalized oppression."

* * *

C. *Transsexualism and Disability Discrimination*

Title VII of the Americans with Disabilities Act (ADA), which bars discrimination against people with disabilities, expressly excludes transsexuals from such protection. Meanwhile, state and federal courts have struggled to define transsexualism and determine whether it is a handicap. In *Leyland v. Orr*, the Ninth Circuit recognized transsexuality as a disability when it upheld the honorable discharge of a postoperative transsexual from the Air Force Reserves. The Air Force concluded that undergoing transsexual surgery significantly impairs an individual's ability to perform his or her duties, and that such surgery rendered Leyland "psychologically unsuitable and physically unfit" for military service.

* * *

In *Doe v. Blue Cross & Blue Shield of Rhode Island*, a Rhode Island district court recognized the "highly sensitive" nature of transsexuality and the stigma associated with the condition when it allowed a transsexual litigant to pursue his claim under a fictitious name. The judge noted the need for anonymity "[p]articularly in this era of seemingly increased societal intolerance toward 'unconventional' sexual behavior." The judge concluded, "I will not strip [the] plaintiff of the cloak of privacy, which, shields him from the stigmatization he might otherwise endure."

* * *

Transsexuality should fall within this protection. Transsexual individuals are socially marginalized due to intolerance, prejudice, and stereotypes surrounding gender and sexual identity. Transgendered individuals are likely to face any or all of the following pervasive social problems: dismissal from employment upon discovery of their transsexuality, termination of parental rights, being labeled as handicapped by the military due to sex reassignment, and being discriminated against by school boards which perpetuate intolerance. Unfortunately, these consequences all occur with the approval of the legal system. This tolerated marginalization challenges Title VII's exclusion of transsexuality as a disability. Transsexualism, therefore, should fall within the definition of a perceived disability.

IV. THE TRANSSEXUAL PRISONER

* * *

The Eighth Amendment directly addresses the treatment of prisoners and the conditions surrounding incarceration. Specifically, it prohibits the infliction of cruel and unusual punishment, thereby imposing on prison authorities a duty to provide humane conditions of confinement and to ensure that inmates receive adequate food, clothing, shelter, and medical care. The Eighth Amendment also requires that prison officials "take reasonable measures to guarantee the safety of the inmates." As noted:

> "[W]hen the State by the affirmative exercise of its power [through incarceration] so restrains an individual's liberty that it renders him unable to care for himself, and at the same time fails to provide for his basic human needs ... it transgresses the substantive limits on state action set by the Eighth Amendment."

The Supreme Court defines cruel and unusual punishment as the wanton and unnecessary infliction of pain, which includes harm that serves no legitimate penological interest and treatment that is grossly disproportionate to the sentence imposed. The standard underlying the Eighth Amendment is not static; rather, its meaning derives from the evolving principles of dignity, decency, and humanity.

* * *

A. *Placement of Transsexual Prisoners*

In *Farmer v. Brennan*, the Court articulated the standard for use with the Eighth Amendment as one of "deliberate indifference." Under this standard, the petitioner must prove that the deprivation was serious and also show that prison officials acted with a culpable state of mind. In defining culpability, the Court rejected an objective test—that prison officials knew or should have known of the risk—and instead set out that to be culpable, an official must be aware of, yet disregard, an excessive risk to a prisoner's health or safety. This subjective standard requires that an officer "be aware of facts from which the inference could be drawn that a substantial risk of serious harm exists, and he [or she] must also draw the inference." A showing of reckless disregard of a substantial risk satisfies this "culpable state of mind" requirement.

* * *

The Court further stated that an official would not escape liability by refusing to verify, or failing to confirm, a strong suspicion that a substantial risk existed. Likewise, the Court recognized that membership within an identifiable group from which members are frequently singled out for attack, establishes a sufficiently serious risk that warrants Eighth Amendment protection.

* * *

Placing preoperative transsexuals with prisoners of the same anatomical sex exacerbates the risk of harm to transsexual prisoners and challenges the constitutionality of this practice. Adherence to the strict construction that genitalia determines sex places transitioning transsexuals in a "Catch–22." The inevitable dangers of being placed in the general population forces prison officials to segregate transsexual prisoners into protective custody. As the court in Crosby concluded, due to the inherent risk involved in placing preoperative transsexuals according to their biological sex and the limitations associated with segregation, the best solution is to house transsexual prisoners according to their gender identity.

B.   *Medical Care of Transsexual Prisoners*

In *Phillips v. Michigan Department of Corrections*, a district court in Michigan granted a transsexual's preliminary injunction for the continued use of female hormones. In so doing, the court recognized that transsexualism represents a serious medical disorder and that failure to provide treatment constitutes cruel and unusual punishment. The court specifically ordered prison officials to continue estrogen therapy and to afford the plaintiff with "the same standard of care she was receiving prior to incarceration." The *Phillips* court further observed that the failure to provide female hormones to the plaintiff reversed the transitional process, thus adversely affecting the plaintiff by worsening her physical and emotional state. As the court noted,

> [i]t is one thing to fail to provide an inmate with care that would improve his or her medical state, such as refusing to provide sex reassignment surgery or to operate on a long-endured cyst. Taking measures which actually reverse the effects of years of healing medical treatment . . . is measurably worse, making the cruel and unusual determination much easier.

Ironically, prisons continue to support treatment approaches that the medical profession and most courts recognize as futile. Outside the prison walls, courts denounce policies that summarily dismiss hormone treatment and sex reassignment as unnecessary and inappropriate treatment for transsexualism. Instead, courts conclude that such treatment is medically necessary and required to "cure" transsexualism. Prison officials' insistence on providing counseling alone, a treatment recognized as unsuccessful, constitutes the unnecessary and wanton infliction of pain, in violation of the Eighth Amendment.

* * *

C.   *Use of Protective Custody*

Administrative segregation, also known as protective custody or administrative detention, is a form of confinement utilized to separate an inmate from the general population. It is designed to segregate inmates for short periods of time. Where protective custody is not voluntary, heightened standards will attach. Prison officials may place an inmate in administrative detention when that inmate poses a serious threat to the security of the institution, the lives of staff, other inmates, or to him or herself. In addition, prisoners may voluntarily choose segregation for their own protection. Wherever possible, the conditions of administrative detention should mirror those of the general population. Administrative segregation, for nonpunitive reasons, "is the sort of confinement that inmates should reasonably anticipate receiving at some point in their incarceration." Accordingly, the Fourteenth Amendment does not independently protect inmates from such segregation. Conditions of confinement, however, fall under the scrutiny of the Eighth Amendment. The " 'evolving standards of decency" and human dignity govern such protective custody.

* * *

States may create liberty interests governing the use of protective custody. In *Hewitt v. Helms*, for example, the United States Supreme Court held that a Pennsylvania statute created a liberty interest for a prisoner to remain in the general prison population. Focusing on the mandatory language contained in the statute, the Court recognized that the Pennsylvania legislature went "beyond simple procedural guidelines" toward creating a liberty interest in not being held in administrative segregation without first complying with due process requirements. The Court also, recognized how administrative detention puts restraints on an inmate's freedom. As dictated by the statute, the Court emphasized that "administrative segregation may not be used as a pretext for indefinite confinement of an inmate." Prison officials, however, must conduct periodic reviews to prevent such abuse. The lower court in *Hewitt* analogized protective custody with solitary confinement absent a showing of misconduct, and concluded that "inmates' interests in avoiding confinement in Administrative Custody are no less real" than those of the prisoner seeking to avoid solitary confinement.

* * *

The United States Supreme Court has recognized that conditions beyond one's control are not punishable. For example, punishing someone for uncontrollable conduct resulting from a disease or illness violates the Eighth Amendment. In *Robinson v. California*, the Court struck down a California statute making drug addiction a criminal offense. The Court determined that addiction represents a status or condition and not a punishable offense. As such, to punish addiction imposes " 'a continuing offense ... [that] is chronic rather than acute; that it continues after it is complete and subjects the offender to arrest at any time.' " Addiction may also occur innocently or involuntarily, further implicating the Eighth Amendment. In concluding that the punishment of addiction violated the Eighth Amendment, the Court analogized that a statute criminalizing mental illness would undoubtedly entail cruel and unusual punishment as well. As the Court explained:

A state law which imprisons a person thus afflicted [with addiction] as a criminal, inflicts a cruel and unusual punishment in violation of the Fourteenth Amendment. To be sure, imprisonment for ninety days is not, in the abstract, a punishment which is either cruel or unusual. But the question cannot be considered in the abstract. Even one day in prison would be a cruel and unusual punishment for the "crime" of having a common cold.

* * *

Transsexualism falls within the definition of a status. Specifically, it is beyond the person's control, it is acquired innocently and involuntarily, possibly at birth, and those afflicted are powerless to overcome the condition. Transsexualism is the constant, inflexible, and immutable conviction of imprisonment in the wrong body. Placing transsexual prisoners in protective custody, given their status, compounds the unconstitutionality of such a practice.

* * *

V.   Conclusion

Present policies regarding the placement, treatment, and conditions of confinement of transsexual prisoners raise serious constitutional issues. Prisons house transsexual prisoners according to their sex as assigned at birth without recognizing the significance of gender in determining identity. This practice ignores the fact that gender plays a far more crucial role than sex in an individual's self-definition, and in how others perceive that individual. Transsexual prisoners constitute an identifiable group due to their gender identity. Intolerance by other inmates sets transsexual inmates apart and encourages attacks' upon them. Prison authorities' insistence on placing preoperative transsexuals according to their biology represents a conscious disregard, or deliberate indifference, toward the obvious risks inherent in such a policy.

———

Refusal to Hire, or Dismissal From Employment, on Account of Plaintiff's Sexual Lifestyle or Sexual Preference As Violation of Federal Constitution or Federal Civil Rights Statutes

Annotation, 42 A.L.R. Fed. 189, 191, 204–05 (1979 & Supp. 2004).

■ Russell J. Davis

[a]   Scope

This annotation collects and analyzes the federal and state cases, and relevant decisions of the Equal Employment Opportunity Commission which decide whether it is a violation of the United States Constitution or of any federal civil rights statute to dismiss an employee or to refuse to hire an applicant for employment because of his "sexual lifestyle" or "sexual preference." The latter terms are given a rather broad definition for purposes of this annotation and include such matters as homosexuality, transsexuality, "adulterous" relationships, and cohabitation without benefit of marriage; however, the annotation does not include decisions involving isolated instances of unorthodox or disapproved sexual behavior.

* * *

5.   Transsexuality

* * *

In *Grossman v. Bernards Township Board of Education*, [538 F.2d 319 (D.C.N.J. 1975)], the court dismissed the civil rights action of an elementary school music teacher who was dismissed from the school system after undergoing a "sex reassignment operation," holding that jurisdiction over the action could not be based on 42 U.S.C.A. § 1981. The court pointed out that the purpose of § 1981 was clearly to afford protection from discrimination based on race, and that no allegation of racial discrimination appeared anywhere in the plaintiff teacher's pleading.

Plaintiff, who was prospective transsexual and employee in beauty salon operated on premises of department store and who was terminated from employment for not dressing and acting as man while at work, failed to state cause of action under 42 U.S.C.A. § 1985(3), where, under statute, plaintiff must allege that defendants' refusal to allow her to continue work while dressing and acting as woman denied her equal protection, or equal privileges and equal immunities, and where there was no allegation that any other employees who were biologically men, were protected, privileged, or immune so as to have right to work while dressed and acting as women (or vice versa); therefore, plaintiff had failed to allege any manner in which she was treated other than as all other (biological) men were. Further, transsexuals are not suspect class for purposes of equal protection analysis and clearly there was rational basis for employer's requiring its employees who dealt with public to dress and act as persons of their biological sex since allowing employees to do otherwise would disturb customers and cause them to take their business elsewhere. *Kirkpatrick v. Seligman & Latz, Inc.*, [475 F.Supp. 145 (M.D. Fla. 1979)].

[b]   Title VII of Civil Rights Act of 1964

Finding a failure to state a cause of action under Title VII of the Civil Rights Act of 1964, 42 U.S.C.A. § 2000e–2(a)(1), the court in *Grossman v. Bernards Township Board of Education*, [538 F.2d 319 (D.C.N.J. 1975)], dismissed an action brought by a transsexual who had been discharged from her position as a music teacher for elementary schools after undergoing a "sex reassignment operation." As affirmed by the state's commissioner of education, the dismissal resulted from school officials' conclusion that the plaintiff teacher was incapable of teaching children because of the potential that her presence in the classroom would cause them psychological harm. Assuming for the purpose of the instant case that the plaintiff teacher was "a member of the female gender," the court found it apparent that she was discharged by the school board not because of her status as a female, but rather because of her change in sex. Noting the scarcity of legislative history relating to the inclusion of sex as a prohibited source of employment discrimination in Title VII, the court expressed its reluctance to ascribe import to this term other than its plain meaning.

Defendant former employer was entitled to dismissal of sex-discrimination complaint by transsexual, since discrimination against sex-change process is not discrimination based on stereotypic notions of males and females and not within congressional intent in prohibiting "sex" discrimination under Title VII. *Dobre v. National R.R. Passenger Corp.*, [850 F.Supp. 284 (E.D. Pa. 1993)].

––––––––

NOTES AND QUESTIONS

1. Transsexual prisoners' rights and housing. One of the most divisive and controversial issues concerning imprisoned transsexuals is their housing. It is a highly delicate issue in terms of the prisoners' concerns for safety and other inmates' concern for privacy. A determinate of where to place the prisoners is whether the prisoner has had genital replacement surgery. Under *Farmer v. Brennan,* 511 U.S. 825, 829 (1994), prisoners who have not had the surgery will be placed according to their birth sex while those who have will be placed in the reassigned gender space. However positive that sounds, there are also negative aspects. In particular, those reassigned are often excluded from educational and occupational opportunities and associational rights. *See* Darren Rosenblum, *"Trapped" in Sing Sing: Transgendered Prisoners Caught in the Gender Binarism,* 6 MICH. J. GENDER & L. 499, 530 (2000).

2. Hormone therapy use in prison. Like housing, the issue of hormone use for transsexual prisoners has not been clear-cut. While courts have ruled that transsexual prisoners have a right to continue hormone therapy, prison officials have not been strictly required to provide the treatments. Because of this, scores of prisoners have not received hormone therapy while imprisoned. *See* Rosenblum, *supra* at 545, n. 62.

3. Placement rights over privacy issues. Whose rights should receive priority in housing situations? Many female prisoners have felt threatened by male to female prisoners sharing the same quarters with them. On the other hand male to female prisoners are threatened in male quarters. For many, the issue of providing separate quarters for transsexuals rings of special treatment that is unfair. None of these issues are simplified by the overcrowding and violence that are prevalent in the United States prison system. If transsexual prisoners are placed in separate facilities, does that mean people should be segregated by race, handicaps, and sexual orientation also?

4. Impact of unconscious attitudes on sexual orientation discrimination. Some argue that it has been difficult to prove sexual orientation discrimination because courts take a narrow view that overlook the impact of unconscious attitudes toward gays. *See* Elvia R. Arriola, *Gendered Inequality Lesbians, Gays, and Feminist Legal Theory*, 9 BERKELEY WOMEN'S L.J. 103 (1994). Arriola contends that courts should examine how attitudes toward sexual identity and stereotypes lead to discrimination.

G.   THE MARKET FOR COUNTERCULTURE

"The price we pay when pursuing any art or calling, is an intimate knowledge of its ugly side."

—James Baldwin

Black But Not Beautiful: Negative Black Stereotypes Abound in Rap Lyrics, on Music Videos, in Movies and on Cable—and Blacks Are Among Those Doing the Stereotyping

NEWSDAY, Oct. 24, 1993, at 6.

■ ESTHER IVEREM

Spike Lee Tells a college audience that Hollywood only wants to make black films about urban violence and drugs.

Bill Cosby calls "Russell Simmons' Def Comedy Jam" a "minstrel show."

The Rev. Calvin Butts thunders from his Harlem pulpit about black musical artists who refer to all women as "bitches" and "whores."

Is this Blaxploitation II?

* * *

"What's happening now I call the black-on-black film crime, the black-on-black television crime, because a lot of people creating this stuff happen to be African–American," Townsend says. "Nobody wants to blow the whistle because they say, 'Hey, that's a brother trying to make some money. He's getting paid.' "

Women in the entertainment industry are concerned about how young female fans will build self-esteem and self confidence in the face of misogynist lyrics characterizing women as sex-for-sale gold diggers—lyrics embraced by many young male artists who find that their newfound money and fame attract groupies who would otherwise shun them. In a recent interview, rapper Dr. Dre described his Los Angeles-area home as a place where he hangs out with friends "and about twenty to thirty women."

Another element that distinguishes the new blaxploitation from that of 20 years ago is the degree to which much of the art by blacks is also consumed by whites. Artists such as Ice–T, Ice Cube and L.L. Cool J.

generate more sales in America's suburban malls than in city shopping districts. "Def Comedy Jam" has an audience that is 60 percent white.

* * *

MUSIC

* * *

To pinpoint the beginning of the current cultural wave is difficult, but by 1989, there was already criticism of artists in the male-dominated world of rap such as Slick Rick, Too Short, and the group N.W.A. for their sexist lyrics.

Slick Rick, for example, included on his 1989 album, "The Great Adventures of Slick Rick," the cut, "Treat Her Like a Prostitute." The group N.W.A. was one of the first groups to refer to all women as "bitches" and "hos" in its seminal "Straight Outta Compton." Even after N.W.A. disbanded, solo acts spawned by the group, including Dr. Dre, continued the tradition. And as the first popular gangster rappers, N.W.A. also launched a barrage of violent images across the country: "When I'm called off / I gotta sawed off / Squeeze the trigger / And bodies are hauled off," the group also rapped in "Straight Outta Compton."

* * *

But most of the violence in black video (and film) depicts black-on-black crime. And rather than being afraid, young white America embraced gangster rap. During the late '80s, as hip-hop's popularity grew, many white pop and dance-music stations played controversial rap groups banned on black radio stations—and lured young black listeners. Though white pop stations traditionally target youth, black radio stations such as New York's WBLS have historically served a wide variety of musical tastes. Even as some black stations have loosened their restrictions to woo back listeners, it's not uncommon for Onyx, Ice–T and 2Pac to receive their first airplay on white pop stations.

* * *

VIDEO AND PERFORMANCE

Nothing has had a greater impact on the overall music industry in the past decade than music videos. Though record companies were slower to provide video budgets for black artists and MTV was slow to give videos by blacks airplay, videos are now an integral part of the marketing strategy for most artists. Today "MTV Jams," which highlights black music, is one of the most popular programs on the cable channel. Like radio, MTV competes successfully against black-owned BET for young black listeners, even though BET plays a wider variety of black artists.

* * *

Butts, pastor of Harlem's Abyssinian Baptist Church, a leader in the black community's response to offensive messages, says that coming across three videos—one by Luther Campbell, Apache's "Gangsta Bitch" and "Ain't Too Proud to Beg" by TLC—in part spurred him to get involved.

"I was appalled at what I saw and heard," says Butts, sitting at his desk at the church's office. "It was so vulgar. I had seen some things in music before that didn't quite jibe with my sensibilities, but I knew that these things were doing important commentary. However, what I saw that particular night had no socially redemptive value at all."

* * *

FILM

Taken as a whole, the new wave of black filmmakers is producing diverse films such as Mario Van Peebles' "Posse," Spike Lee's "Malcolm X" and Charles Lane's "Sidewalk Stories." But there is no doubt that Hollywood sees green in what some directors call "hood" films, centering on criminal elements of the black community—starting with "New Jack City," and "Boyz in the Hood" in 1991 and followed by films such as "Juice," "South–Central," "Trespass," "A Rage in Harlem" and, this year, "Menace II Society." Some have starred rap artists.

"It becomes a self-fulfilling prophecy," says Helena Echegoyen, director of development for New Line Cinema, which released "Menace II Society." "We have to look at the movies being made, at what is making money, and you make movies like those."

* * *

And once their films are in the market, black filmmakers contend with a virtually all-white corps of arts writers and critics, many of whom, directors say, feel more comfortable with ghetto stereotypes and violence than with other depictions of black life.

For example, when Kenneth Turan panned "Boomerang" last year in the Los Angeles Times, he cited his feeling that the movie's star, Eddie Murphy, had been better in his previous hustler roles, and his sense that an all-black cast playing successful professionals was "silly and arbitrary." The review provoked a rare written outcry from Murphy, Hudlin and members of the public.

"If this were a movie about gun-totin' drug dealers, it would be praised for its gritty authenticity while the complaints would be about encouraging violent behavior in the wake of national riots," Hudlin wrote in a letter to the Times.

* * *

COMEDY

At 36 years of age, Russell Simmons is certainly old enough to have been shaped by the race debates of the 1960s and 1970s. But, in his role as head of Rush Communications, which includes the record label and "Def Comedy Jam," he finds himself championing artists and trends of what writer Nelson George calls the post-soul culture of black America. And

Simmons is not concerned that many of his artists as well as "Def Comedy Jam" serve a largely white audience. Reflecting a general comedy explosion in this country, several black comedy shows have cropped up in the past two years, including The Uptown Comedy Club, The Apollo Comedy Hour and Comic View. But none of these draws the audience or controversy of HBO's "Def Comedy Jam." A recent show, for example, peppered with what is the standard profanity, included several comedians graphically illustrating oral sex.

Responding to criticism leveled by Bill Cosby, Simmons says of his program, "I don't feel it's a minstrel show. If he's offended by their language or whatever they do, hey, those are real people. And they are mostly moral and very straightforward people."

Stan Lathan, director and executive producer of "Comedy Jam," says the show fairly represents the kinds of material being presented in black comedy clubs across the country. "The problem is that people zero in on the raunchy material," Lathan says.

* * *

Sandy Wernick, another executive producer of the show and president of Brillstein–Grey Entertainment, which manages several "Saturday Night Live" artists, including Dana Carvey and Adam Sandler, says the show appeals to whites in part because blacks have become secure enough to laugh at themselves.

Wernick, who is white, says he was intrigued by Simmons' idea because of its crossover appeal, and thought Simmons, who sold rap music to white America, was the right man to make the concept successful.

* * *

WHAT'S NEXT

If those concerned about black messages and images in pop culture are searching for relief, they might find it in the fact that the entertainment machine has to get new parts when the current ones wear down. What is coming could be a backlash against current artists who have reduced the panorama of black life to a single grim snapshot.

Artists who followed Public Enemy in the last wave of "conscious rap," such as X–Clan, A Tribe Called Qwest, Chubb Rock, Heavy D, Queen Latifah, De La Soul, and Poor Righteous Teachers, are being joined by newer artists rejecting images of death and nihilism, such as Arrested Development, Nefertitti, Das EFX and Get Set V.O.P.

"People are tired of hearing about people shooting somebody with their nine," said the rapper Heavy D. "Now it's getting monotonous. In the beginning, it was creative because it was somebody telling the rest of the world about a certain place they are from. Now you have a million and one people making those records who aren't even from the ghettos."

* * *

Status Censorship Report

Entertainment Weekly, June 29, 1990.

In an unprecedented legal decision, a federal judge in Florida ruled on June 6 that As Nasty as They Wanna Be, the controversial, sexually explicit rap album by the Miami-based 2 Live Crew, violated community obscenity laws. Within days, three members of the band and a local record-store owner had been arrested for their involvement in the performance and sale of the record, which has been bought by nearly 2 million people nation-wide—and has jumped 29 places on the Billboard chart since the ruling.

With that announcement, the music censorship movement appeared to lose steam—everywhere but in Florida. There, the 2 Live Crew has been at the center of an antiporn campaign by Gov. Bob Martinez (who called Nasty "audio pornography") and Miami attorney Jack Thompson since the release of the album last year. In March, a record-store clerk in Sarasota, Fla., was arrested for selling Nasty to an 11–year–old girl; charges were dropped, but the message to the record business was clear. In response to that incident and other attempts by local police to quell album sales, Luther Campbell (leader of the 2 Live Crew and owner of Luke's Records, which released Nasty) brought a civil suit against Broward County Sheriff Nick Navarro for prohibiting sales of the album by threatening arrest. But on June 6, in a 62–page decision (which began "This is a case between two ancient enemies: Anything Goes and Enough Already"), U.S. District Court Judge Jose Gonzalez ruled that the album's lyrics were legally obscene under the 1973 Miller v. California Supreme Court decision.

In a related development, police attended a Madonna concert in Toronto on May 29 after complaints of "lewdness" during her Blond Ambition tour, including simulations of masturbation and other sexual acts. No legal action followed. For the moment Madonna is safe, as are most rap albums in local record stores. But developments in the censorship battle have proven that the law can be as nasty as it wants to be, too.

A NOTE ON CONFLICTING VALUES WITHIN AFRICAN AMERICAN COMMUNITIES

In the 1990s, a discernable tension developed between some traditional civil rights leaders and the performers in the so-called "gangsta rap" genre of hip-hop. The conflict of values was in part generational. Older civil rights leaders see the sex and violence-laden lyrics of rappers as an affront to more conservative, traditional values of many church-based civil rights activists.

The conflicts between these opposing views within the black community have often included intellectual property litigation and tort claims for interference with contract, trademark infringement, violation of rights of publicity, defamation, with countercharges of conspiracy, extortion, and fraud.

How would critical race theorists analyze the Rosa Parks and C. Delores Tucker legal disputes described below? How would law and economics scholars analyze these disputes? Are these primarily economic disputes with political implications, or primarily political disputes with economic implications?

Parks v. LaFace Records

329 F.3d 437 (6th Cir. 2003).

■ JUDGE HOLSCHUH delivered the opinion of the court:

This is a dispute over the name of a song. Rosa Parks is a civil rights icon who first gained prominence during the Montgomery, Alabama bus boycott in 1955. She brings suit against LaFace Records, a record producer, and OutKast, a "rap" (or "hip-hop") music duo, as well as several other named affiliates, for using her name as the title of their song, *Rosa Parks*. Parks contends that Defendants' use of her name constitutes false advertising under § 43(a) of the Lanham Act, 15 U.S.C. § 1125(a), and intrudes on her common law right of publicity under Michigan state law. Defendants argue that they are entitled to summary judgment because Parks has failed to show any violation of the Lanham Act or her right of publicity. Defendants further argue that, even if she has shown such a violation, their First Amendment freedom of artistic expression should be a defense as a matter of law to each of these claims. Parks also contends that Defendants' conduct renders them liable under Michigan law for defamation and tortious interference with a business relationship; Defendants have also denied liability with respect to these claims.

* * *

For the reasons hereafter set forth, [the court concludes that the district court erred in granting Defendants' motion for summary judgment on the Lanham Act and right of publicity claim, but that that the district court properly granted summary judgment in favor of Defendants on Rosa Parks' state law claims of defamation and tortious interference with a business relationship].

I. BACKGROUND

A. Facts

Rosa Parks is an historical figure who first gained prominence as a symbol of the civil rights movement in the United States during the 1950's and 1960's. In 1955, while riding in the front of a segregated bus in Montgomery, Alabama, she refused to yield her seat to a white passenger and move to the back of the bus as blacks were required to do by the then-existing laws requiring segregation of the races. A 381–day bus boycott in Montgomery flowed from that one event, which eventually became a catalyst for organized boycotts, sit-ins, and demonstrations all across the South. Her single act of defiance has garnered her numerous public accolades and awards, and she has used that celebrity status to promote various civil and human rights causes as well as television programs and books inspired by her life story. She has also approved a collection of gospel recordings by various artists entitled *Verity Records Presents: A Tribute to Mrs. Rosa Parks* (the *"Tribute"* album), released in 1995.

Defendants are OutKast, comprised of recording artists André "Dré" Benjamin and Antwan "Big Boi" Patton; their record producers, LaFace— * * * and LaFace's record distributors, Arista Records and BMG Entertainment—* * *. In September 1998, Defendants released the album *Aquemini*. The album's first single release was a song titled *Rosa Parks*, described as a "hit single" by a sticker on the album. The same sticker that contained the name *Rosa Parks* also contained a Parental Advisory warning of "explicit content." Because, as later discussed, the critical issue in this case is a determination of the artistic relevance of the title, *Rosa Parks*, to the content of the song, the lyrics obviously must be considered in their entirety. They are as follows:

(Hook)

Ah ha, hush that fuss
Everybody move to the back of the bus
Do you wanna bump and slump with us
We the type of people make the club get crunk

Verse 1: (Big Boi)

Many a day has passed, the night has gone by
But still I find the time to put that bump off in your eye
Total chaos, for these playas, thought we was absent
We takin another route to represent the Dungeon Family
Like Great Day, me and my nigga decide to take the back way
We stabbing every city then we headed to that bat cave
A–T–L, Georgia, what we do for ya
Bull doggin hoes like them Georgetown Hoyas
Boy you sounding silly, thank my Brougham aint sittin pretty
Doing doughnuts round you suckas like then circles around titties
Damn we the committee gone burn it down
But us gone bust you in the mouth with the chorus now

(Hook)

Verse 2: (André)

I met a gypsy and she hipped me to some life game
To stimulate then activate the left and right brain
Said baby boy you only funky as your last cut
You focus on the past your ass'll be a has what
Thats one to live by or either that one to die to
I try to just throw it at you determine your own adventure
Andre, got to her station here's my destination
She got off the bus, the conversation lingered in my head for hours
Took a shower kinda sour cause my favorite group ain't comin with it
But I'm witcha you cause you probably goin through it anyway

But anyhow when in doubt went on out and bought it

Cause I thought it would be jammin but examine all the flawsky-wawsky

Awfully, it's sad and it's costly, but that's all she wrote

And I hope I never have to float in that boat Up shit creek it's weak is the last quote

That I want to hear when I'm goin down when all's said and done

And we got a new joe in town

When the record player get to skippin and slowin down

All yawl can say is them niggas earned that crown but until then . . .

* * *

II.   DISCUSSION

* * *

B.   The Lanham Act

Section 43(a) of the Lanham Act creates a civil cause of action against any person who identifies his or her product in such a way as to likely cause confusion among consumers or to cause consumers to make a mistake or to deceive consumers as to association of the producer of the product with another person or regarding the origin of the product or the sponsorship or approval of the product by another person. * * *

[The court discusses the Lanham Act's primary application to "disputes between producers of commercial products and their competitors," but states that it] also permits celebrities to vindicate property rights in their identities against allegedly misleading commercial use by others. * * *

In order to prevail on a false advertising claim under § 43(a), a celebrity must show that use of his or her name is likely to cause confusion among consumers as to the "affiliation, connection, or association" between the celebrity and the defendant's goods or services or as to the celebrity's participation in the "origin, sponsorship, or approval" of the defendant's goods or services. * * *

Parks contends that Defendants have violated the Lanham Act because the *Rosa Parks* title misleads consumers into believing that the song is about her or that she is affiliated with the Defendants, or has sponsored or approved the *Rosa Parks* song and the *Aquemini* album. * * *

Defendants respond that Parks' Lanham Act claim must fail for two reasons. First, they claim that Parks does not possess a trademark right in her name and Defendants have not made a trademark use of her name, as allegedly required for a cause of action under the Lanham Act. Second, they contend that even if use of the title posed some risk of consumer confusion, the risk is outweighed by Defendants' First Amendment right to free expression.

1. *Trademark Right In and Trademark Use of Parks' Name*

* * *

We find Parks' prior commercial activities and international recognition as a symbol of the civil rights movement endow her with a trademark interest in her name the same as if she were a famous actor or musician.

* * * We turn then to Defendants' second argument, that even if Parks could establish some likelihood of confusion, the First Amendment protects Defendants' choice of title.

2. *The First Amendment Defense—Three Approaches*

* * *

[The court discusses the defendants' First Amendment defenses at length, and determines that the *Rogers v. Grimaldi*, 875 F.2d 994 (1989) test should apply.]

* * * The *Rogers* court, finding that overextension of Lanham Act restrictions in the area of titles might intrude on First Amendment values * * * adopted a two-pronged test:

> In the context of allegedly misleading titles using a celebrity's name, that balance [between avoiding consumer confusion and protecting free expression] will normally not support application of the Act unless [1] the title has no artistic relevance to the underlying work whatsoever, or, if it has some artistic relevance, unless [2] the title explicitly misleads as to the source or the content of the work.

* * *

3. Application of the Rogers Test

a. Artistic Relevance Prong

The first prong of Rogers requires a determination of whether there is any artistic relationship between the title and the underlying work. Parks contends that a cursory review of the *Rosa Parks* title and the lyrics demonstrates that there is no artistic connection between them. Parks also submits two articles in which members of OutKast are purported to have admitted that the song was not about her. As further evidence, she offers a "translation" of the lyrics of the song *Rosa Parks,* derived from various electronic "dictionaries" of the "rap" vernacular to demonstrate that the song truly has nothing to do with Parks herself. * * *

Defendants respond that their use of Parks' name is "metaphorical" or "symbolic." They argue that the historical association between Rosa Parks and the phrase "move to the back of the bus" is beyond dispute and that Parks' argument that the song is not "about" her in a biographical sense is simply irrelevant.

* * *

Contrary to the opinion of the district court, we believe that the artistic relationship between the title and the content of the song is certainly not obvious and, indeed, is "open to reasonable debate" for the following reasons.

It is true that the phrase "move to the back of the bus" is repeatedly used in the "hook" or chorus of the song. When the phrase is considered *in the context of the lyrics,* however, the phrase has absolutely nothing to do with Rosa Parks. * * * The composers did *not* intend it to be about Rosa Parks, and the lyrics are *not* about Rosa Parks. The lyrics' sole message is that OutKast's competitors are of lesser quality and, therefore, must "move to the back of the bus," or in other words, "take a back seat." We believe that reasonable persons could conclude that there is no relationship of any kind between Rosa Parks' name and the content of the song—a song that is nothing more and nothing less than a paean announcing the triumph of superior people in the entertainment business over inferior people in that business.... Choosing Rosa Parks' name as the title to the song unquestionably enhanced the song's potential sale to the consuming public.

* * *

While Defendants' lyrics contain profanity and a great deal of "explicit" language (together with a parental warning), they contain absolutely nothing that could conceivably, by any stretch of the imagination, be considered, explicitly or implicitly, a reference to courage, to sacrifice, to the civil rights movement or to any other quality with which Rosa Parks is identified. If the requirement of "relevance" is to have any meaning at all, it would not be unreasonable to conclude that the title *Rosa Parks* is *not* relevant to the content of the song in question. The use of this woman's name unquestionably was a good marketing tool—*Rosa Parks* was likely to sell far more recordings than *Back of the Bus*—but its use could be found by a reasonable finder of fact to be a flagrant deception on the public regarding the actual content of this song and the creation of an impression that Rosa Parks, who had approved the use of her name in connection with the *Tribute* album, had also approved or sponsored the use of her name on Defendants' composition.

It is certainly not dispositive that, in response to an interview following the filing of this lawsuit, one of the OutKast members said that using Rosa Parks' name was "symbolic." Where an artist proclaims that a celebrity's name is used merely as a "symbol" for the lyrics of a song, and such use is highly questionable when the lyrics are examined, a legitimate question is presented as to whether the artist's claim is sincere or merely a guise to escape liability. Our task, it seems to us, is not to accept without question whatever purpose Defendants may now claim they had in using Rosa Parks' name. It is, instead, to make a determination as to whether, applying the law of *Rogers,* there is a genuine issue of material fact regarding the question of whether the title is artistically relevant to the content of the song. * * *

There is a genuine issue of material fact whether the use of Rosa Parks' name as a title to the song and on the cover of the album is artistically related to the content of the song or whether the use of the name Rosa Parks is nothing more than a misleading advertisement for the sale of the song.

b. Misleading Prong

In *Rogers,* the court held that if the title of the work is artistically relevant to its content, there is no violation of the Lanham Act *unless* the "title explicitly misleads as to the source or the content of the work." * * *

We considered all the facts presented to us and concluded that, with reference to the first prong of the *Rogers* analysis, the issue of artistic relevance of the title *Rosa Parks* to the lyrics of the song is highly questionable and cannot be resolved as a matter of law. However, if, on remand, a trier of fact, after a full evidentiary hearing, concludes that the title *is* used in some symbolic or metaphorical sense, application of the *Rogers* analysis, under the particular facts of this case, would appear to be complete. In the present case, the title *Rosa Parks* "make[s] no explicit statement that the work is about that person in any direct sense." In other words, Defendants did not name the song, for example, *The True Life Story of Rosa Parks* or *Rosa Parks' Favorite Rap.*

* * *

C. Right of Publicity

1. Applicable Law

The right of publicity protects the identity of a celebrity from exploitive commercial use. *See Carson v. Here's Johnny Portable Toilets, Inc.,* 698 F.2d 831, 835 (6th Cir.1983). "The theory of the right is that a celebrity's identity can be valuable in the promotion of products, and the celebrity has an interest that may be protected from the unauthorized commercial exploitation of that identity." *Id.* As such, the common law right of publicity forms a species of property right. * * *

Parks' right of publicity argument tracks that of her Lanham Act claim. She alleges that Defendants have profited from her fame by using her name solely for a commercial purpose. * * *

2. Analysis

A right of publicity claim is similar to a false advertising claim in that it grants a celebrity the right to protect an economic interest in his or her name. However, a right of publicity claim does differ from a false advertising claim in one crucial respect; a right of publicity claim does not require any evidence that a consumer is likely to be confused. All that a plaintiff must prove in a right of publicity action is that she has a pecuniary interest in her identity, and that her identity has been commercially exploited by a defendant.

The parties have stipulated that Parks is famous and that she has used her name to promote other goods and services. She has therefore established an economic interest in her name. Furthermore, Defendants admit that they have used Parks' name as the name of their song, and have used that name to sell the song and their album. * * *

For the same reasons we have stated earlier and need not repeat, we believe that Parks' right of publicity claim presents a genuine issue of material fact regarding the question of whether the title to the song is or is not "wholly unrelated" to the content of the song. A reasonable finder of fact, in our opinion, upon consideration of all the evidence, could find the title to be a "disguised commercial advertisement" or adopted "solely to attract attention" to the work.

D.   Other Michigan State Law Claims

* * *

1.   Defamation

Parks argues that the song defames her character or places her in a false light. To succeed on a defamation claim, a public figure must prove actual malice. *See New York Times Co. v. Sullivan*, 376 U.S. 254, 279–80 (1964). In turn, actual malice requires a showing, by clear and convincing evidence, that a defendant made a false statement with knowledge of the falsity or with reckless disregard for the truth. * * * The song is plainly not about Parks in any biographical sense of the term, and certainly does not make any factual statements about her. As there is no factual statement about her, Parks cannot show even the first element of a defamation claim. Therefore, we find this argument meritless.

Parks' defamation-by-implication argument is likewise meritless. As with a traditional defamation claim, a plaintiff in a defamation-by-implication claim must establish a material falsity. Parks has not done so.* * *

[The court found the plaintiff's claim of intentional interference with a business relationship meritless because there was no "wrongful act" that might have hastened a contract breach or another breakdown of a business relationship].

For the reasons stated, as to Rosa Parks' Lanham Act claim and her common law right of publicity claim, the judgment of the District Court is REVERSED and this case is REMANDED for future proceedings not inconsistent with this Opinion. With respect to Rosa Parks' claims of defamation and tortious interference with a business relationship, the judgment of the District Court is AFFIRMED.

Delores Tucker, Gangsta Busta: She's Playing Defense in Her Offensive Against Rap

WASH. POST, Nov. 29, 1995, at C1.

■ JUDITH WEINRAUB

* * *

C. Delores Tucker, 68, entered the fight for civil rights more than 50 years ago and never left. She is a glamorous, well-to-do master of fundraising—for black causes, black mayors, Democrats, anyone whose needs matched her own need to make a difference. She says she's motivated by "a passionate love affair for God and my people," but she's ready to give it up. "I wish other people could do what I'm doing so I could step back and retire," she says.

Instead she finds herself in deeper than ever. Through the National Political Congress of Black Women, an organization she co-founded more than a decade ago, Tucker has waged her latest and perhaps loudest battle—the one against gangsta rap, the one that has made her the target of two lawsuits.

The plaintiffs are Interscope Records and Death Row Records, music companies whose controversial artists she has campaigned against. They charge Tucker with conspiracy and extortion. Though she has high-profile allies in her campaign—notably former secretary of education William Bennett and Connecticut Sen. Joseph Lieberman—only Tucker is being sued.

The suits contend that last summer Tucker tried to persuade rap impresario Suge Knight, head of Death Row Records, to take his business away from Interscope, a distributor. They charge that Tucker offered to distribute Knight's records through a new company that Tucker would control and from which she would profit. They also allege conspiracy, threats, extortion and bribery.

"The allegations are fictional," says Tucker. "The whole charge was simply to restrain me. They were afraid I was going to damage their business."

* * *

She's been crusading for more than two years, picketing stores that sell the music, blocking their entrances and risking arrest. Distributing anti-gangsta-rap petitions and getting statements of support from dozens of African American organizations. Demanding congressional hearings. Buying stock in Nobody Beats the Wiz, Musicland, Sony and Time Warner in order to protest at shareholder meetings.

* * *

Each side in the legal battle, of course, presents a different version. David Kenner, an attorney for Knight and Death Row Records, says he heard Tucker offer $80 million to Knight to leave Interscope and join her in a black-owned distribution company that Time Warner would back.

But Tucker describes a more benign version: She agreed to a meeting with Knight, along with Warwick and Moore. She encouraged Knight to get his gangsta rap clients to use their talents to deliver positive messages. When she asked him what it would take to produce such music, he said he needed distribution. So Tucker asked Warwick and Moore to identify women in the business who might be interested.

"I was trying to assist [the record industry women] in getting what they came to me to get in the first place," she says.

* * *

The Making of a Leader

* * *

Her husband of 44 years calls her "one of the most fearless individuals I have ever known. She will take on anyone, anything, if that is what she thinks is right. . . . I tell her there are times you have to compromise, but she is not one who will readily entertain the idea of compromise about anything."

* * *

Tucker herself has run for office three times—unsuccessfully—most recently for Congress in Philadelphia three years ago. She says she was urged to run by African American women who wanted representation, and she's not interested in doing it again. "Everything that's happened in my life," she says, "I never planned it. I never sought it."

Now she is focused on causes, like the Bethune–DuBois Fund, an organization she founded to provide educational and training programs for black youth, and a newly formed coalition of African American women intent on voter registration.

* * *

Cloudy Days

The rap lawsuits are not the first time Tucker's activities have been questioned. She was fired as secretary of state of Pennsylvania in 1977 by Gov. Milton Shapp, who had hired her. She had been reprimanded two years earlier, after charges that she used state workers and resources to produce speeches for which she received $65,000 in 28 months.

She brushes aside questions about those problems, maintaining that they started when she refused to support Shapp's designated successor as governor. "That's when the henchmen moved in," she says.

In the battle over gangsta rap, opponents describe her as "robotic . . . unable to discuss complicated issues." Industry executives say she has been promoting her own interests by singling out Time Warner for attention over other major rap distributors: Polygram, Sony and BMG. "She wasn't interested in a serious conversation about a complex issue," says one. "She was interested in going on 'Nightline.' "

* * *

"We . . . Have Power"

Despite the lawsuits, Tucker claims victory in her gangsta rap campaign.

* * *

Tucker's masterstroke was to stand up at the Time Warner stockholder meeting in May and read Tupac Shakur and Snoop Doggy Dogg lyrics aloud. Through the summer and fall, she and Bennett—joined by Lieber-man in the Senate—kept up a steady beat of news conferences, television appearances and radio ads. By September, the Warner Music Group had sold its $115 million interest in Interscope.

* * *

Nevertheless, the day after the Interscope sale, Tucker clenched her fist in triumph. "They said it couldn't be done," she crowed. "It shows that we the people have power."

———

A NOTE ON ARTISTIC REPARATIONS

In the following excerpt, we catch a glimpse of black rock 'n' roll icon Little Richard's bitterness about the economic impact of racism that many black artists endured in the 1930s through 1970s. After he suffered bankruptcy, Little Richard describes his economic subordination in the industry as follows: "I was taken for everything except my toenails—and they would've got them as well, but they were too short to cut."

The exploitation of African American talent during this period is a double tragedy because many of the individual artists who are still alive today do not have a secure retirement, or the financial security of many of their less talented white contemporaries. The second misfortune is that the black music of this period is generally agreed around the world to be the most uniquely American contribution to music. It is a paradox that the cultural contributions of African American artists serve as the foundation of American cultural identity worldwide, while these contributions have not provided a foundation of stable wealth for the communities from which they emerged.

The difficulty in law is fashioning a legal theory that will permit the wealth of the music industry to be redirected to rectify past economic injustice. As we see in *Merchant v. Levy*, below, formal legal rules such as laches (delay in pursuing the claim), estoppel (preclusion to pursue the claim because of some earlier action by the claimant), or statutes of limitation (statutory time limitations imposed on the injured party's right to sue for redress) present formidable barriers to redress.

Can you think of other theories of compensation? What about repara-tions theory? Equitable restitution and constructive trusts? For a careful exploration of the moral and ethical premises of restitution, see Hanoch Dagan, *The Distributive Foundation of Corrective Justice*, 98 MICH. L. REV. 138 (1999) (exploring the corrective justice approach to the doctrine of restitution for wrongs and especially for appropriations); HANOCH DAGAN, THE FOURTH PILLAR: THE LAW AND ETHICS OF RESTITUTION (2004).

———

A Session With Little Richard

Jim Jerome, LIFE MAG., Dec. 1992, at p. 48.

With a crash of piano keys, a flash of mascaraed eyelashes and a dash of awop-bop-aloo-bop-awop-bam-boom, Little Richard baptized a new musical style. Born Richard Penniman in Macon, GA., and raised on gospel music, he ran away from home with Dr. Hudson's traveling medicine show. He later toured small nightclubs in the south and cut records for RCA and the Peacock label in Houston commercial success eluded him—until September 14, 1955, when he entered J & M studios in New Orleans for Specialty Records. That recording session produced "Tutti Frutti," a hit in early 1956. More sessions quickly followed, and out of them came such rock standards as "Long Tall Sally," "Rip it Up," "Keep a Knockin" and "Good Golly, Miss Molly." Then, suddenly, during a tour of Australia in late 1957, Little Richard renounced rock and roll, saying he had dreamed of his own damnation. He went on to become a minister in the Seventh–Day Adventist church, and over the years, while mounting several unsuccessful comebacks, he has preached against drugs and sex (particularly homosexuality), but it was his quavering falsetto shriek that gathered most converts. Jim Jerome talked with the 56–or 59–year–old musician (depending on whether you believe him or his mother) in a Hollywood hotel, his home away from his Riverside, Calif., home, as flamboyant and outrageous as ever. Little Richard didn't hesitate to claim his rightful place in the history of rock and roll.

"Tutti Frutti" was really an accident, wasn't it?

Yes. See, they wanted me to sing like Ray Charles and B.B. King. I did it just to record; it wasn't what I wanted. So after one session I got on the piano and did awop-bop-aloo-bop-awop-bam-boom. They said, "That's the hit. Ain't no one ever put out mess like that." I had to clean up the lyrics. I had "Tutti frutti, good booty" instead of "aw-rooty." And there was worse, believe me.

Does any one show stick in your mind?

I remember one of those early Madison Square Garden shows in New York—runnin' out there with my brothers and my entourage, the lights come up and those screams, and it just ran through my whole body like a shock. I stood there with my arms out, then I sat at the piano, screamin' to the top of my lungs and tears comin' out of my eyes. My orgasm was the stage, gettin' out there and touchin' the piano and goin' wild. You can't buy that feeling.

But money did buy you plenty.

I remember before one of his big New York shows Alan Freed walked up to me—it was my birthday or some celebration—and he handed me an envelope with $10,000 in it, all in hundred dollar bills. He kissed me on the jaw. I put it all in the trunk of my custom gold-and-white Cadillac with the leopard interior. I bought my mother a mansion in L.A., right behind Joe Louis, and my bed was packed with money. My sisters would just count it over and over.

What impact did racism have on your early career?

I was blocked from playing a lot of places. We'd have to drive all night in the car, 'cause there wasn't no blacks allowed in the hotel. If we wanted a sandwich, you had to go to the back door of a restaurant and ask the chef if he would fix you one. This is even after all of those big hits. And no hospitals for us if we got sick on the road down south.

Do you see any link between your music and rap?

Yes. When I see Hammer, I see me. Michael Jackson—I look at him, I see Little Richard. And he's the greatest entertainer ever lived. Little Richard suffered, he went through hell, he was denied, he was deprived. I helped build that bridge across despair. Now the road is paved. That's why Michael Jackson gets a billion-dollar guarantee.

So is Elvis the King of Rock and Roll?

I know they call him the King, but if he is, who crowned him? When was the ceremony—and why was I not invited? How can a white boy be King of Rock and Roll? I'm not downin' white singers. But I been imitated by more people. I, too, have been called the King of Rock and Roll. I been called the Queen. I earned the throne 'cause I am the Originator, the Architect, the Emancipator—The Founding Father of Rock and Roll.

Malcolm X and the Hip Hop Culture

RECONSTRUCTION II 100–03 (1993).

■ MARTHA BAYLES

The looming billboards, the full-page ads, the T-shirts, the baseball caps, the potato chips, the automobile air fresheners—they all say "X." To many admirers of Malcolm X, the hype surrounding Spike Lee's latest movie is an insult. How dare Lee reduce Malcolm X's extraordinary, ultimately tragic life to a logo, a trademark with no more depth than, say, the Batman symbol. As Jonathan Yardley wrote in the *Washington Post*: "This implacably serious man has become that most American of creatures, a brand-name superstar. It is impossible to imagine that anything more demeaning could be done, to his name and his memory." Even Malcolm's widow, Betty Shabazz, expressed doubts, hiring a licensing firm to curb a marketing juggernaut that, in her view, "had gotten out of hand."

* * *

This is not to say that there is nothing good about either hip-hop or Lee's film making. On the contrary, that ubiquitous "X" looks a whole lot better after seeing *Malcolm X*. My expectations for the film were modest, because although Lee is gifted in many areas of filmmaking (such as business, production design, hiring jazz composers and working with actors), he is deficient in the most important one, storytelling. To tell a good story, you must be able to think straight, and Lee shows minimal interest in that activity. Like so many other celebrities, black and white, who play at politics from the vantage point of entertainment, Lee seems, (especially in interviews) to have nothing invested in clarity, everything in obfuscation—or, at best, in a clownish incoherence that would be funny if the issues were not so grave.

* * *

Most people would agree that Malcolm X's legacy has something to do with truth-seeking, and with being unafraid to change one's life, along with one's mind, according to the truth one discovers. I hasten to add that by "truth-seeking" I do not mean total historical accuracy. Was Malcolm X's father a proud follower of Marcus Garvey, or did he beat his wife and children? Probably both, but I don't care. Let the historians quibble about whether Earl Little ever laid a hand on young Malcolm; God may be in the details in health-care reform, but not in legend. What matters is that Malcolm X's father was an upright, demanding, forceful man whose loss destroyed the family and left his most brilliant son alone with the painfully open question of what it means to be a black male in America. The film gets that essential starting point right.

* * *

Malcolm X *was* Detroit Red, of course, and one of the most powerful themes in his autobiography is his revulsion at the hypocrisy of whites, including his girlfriend, Sophia, who secretly pursued sexual liaisons with blacks. This theme is soft-pedaled in the film: there's a veil of contempt in Denzel Washington's eyes when (as Malcolm) he orders Sophia to kiss his foot and feed him like a baby. Later, there's more than a hint of revulsion in the image of Sophia's white husband, a lumpish fellow sunk in an armchair who doesn't even look up when she brings his TV dinner. And finally, there's the judgment rendered through Laura, the black girl who defies her strict upbringing to go with Malcolm, only to sink into drug abuse and prostitution when he drops her for Sophia. Together, these scenes evoke something of the indignation Malcolm X felt at the sick racist stereotypes that reduce black men to the status of stud animals and expose black women to every kind of exploitation.

* * *

Recall that Malcolm X, like so many of his followers, was a child of the Great Migration. In addition to being a Garveyite, his father was also an itinerant Baptist preacher, hailing from Georgia but preaching hellfire sermons among his fellow migrants in Philadelphia, Omaha, Milwaukee and East Lansing, Michigan. Malcolm's mother was a native of Grenada, also uprooted from the world of her black mother and the white man who had raped and impregnated her. Even before the Little family was torn apart, it must have experienced both the exhilaration and the terror of being set adrift in alien territory. It's no wonder that Malcolm and his siblings were drawn to the Nation of Islam; its peculiar ideology gave them, and millions like them, a way of coping with both the exhilaration and the terror.

* * *

The Nation of Islam appealed to this liberating impulse, but it was Malcolm X who expressed it most fully—because, although he was deeply serious, he was not, in Yardley's phrase, "implacably serious." The word "implacably" suggests a relentlessness, and especially a humorlessness, that were alien to the man. Hard as Washington works to imitate Malcolm X's oratorical style, his performance skimps on the quality that most intrigued listeners, both white and black. That quality, a function of Malcolm X's extraordinary courage and intelligence, was his comic sense. I don't mean this frivolously, that Malcolm X was a comedian. I mean comic in the classical sense of irony, detachment, distance on both one's circumstances and oneself. When Malcolm X laid down the rhetoric about the white man being a "pale thing" bred from dogs by the devil Yacub on the Isle of Patmos, the effect was, in the highest sense, satirical. The curl of his lip, the glint in his eye, seemed to say: "This is what you sound like, you dumb crackers. Try it on for size." More effective than the blind rage that followed his death, now sadly ritualized into the pumped-up woofing of young hip-hop poseurs, was this devastating mockery. Malcolm X didn't invent it; it has always been part of Afro–American culture. But he brought it out for the white folks to see.

Why was Malcolm X able to do this, when so many other angry people have not? Because he had also found a way to master the terror of his Great Migration upbringing—terror that came, as always, from uprootedness, from the loss of an accepted belief system by which human beings make sense of the cosmos and distinguish between right and wrong. On this level, the story of Malcolm X's youth is a descent into nihilism.

* * *

The Taming of Malcolm X

RECONSTRUCTION II 93–99 (1993).

■ ALAN A. STONE

* * *

There are many conflicting opinions about Malcolm X, the man—what he came from, who he was, where he was going. But whether those opinions are derived from personal encounter, his autobiography, or other documentary sources, one thing seems clear: he was an intimidating human being—an electrifying presence, a burning firebrand, and a brilliant polemicist. Spike Lee, despite his obvious talents, seems to have been unwilling or unable to portray that intimidating presence. The movie lasts more than three hours and Denzel Washington is on the screen most of that time. But he never projects what Ossie Davis recognized as Malcolm's "style and hallmark, that shocking zing of fire and be damned to you." That real Malcolm X briefly appears at the end of the film to speak his famous phrase, "by any means necessary." You need only keep that jarring authentic moment in the center of your awareness as you reflect on the entire movie to get the measure of how much Lee fails to capture the real Malcolm.

* * *

Malcolm X has become increasingly important to African Americans since his death. Part of his importance is psychological. He is their hero, the oppressed Negro who transformed himself into a "Shining Black Prince," an archetype with whom proud young Black men and women, no matter how desperate their lives have become, can make a positive identification. Malcolm X's actual psychological identity as a young man is therefore of great importance. American history has made Washington (I can not tell a lie), Lincoln (Honest Abe who freed the slaves), J.F.K. (the president as martyred savior), into sanctified beings and by that hagiographic standard there is no basis for criticizing Lee's film. He has given African Americans their own saint. However, in the strange alchemy of history, Malcolm X is emerging as the most important African American of the twentieth century and to sanctify his memory is to mystify racism. The attempt here is therefore to analyze Lee's hagiographic version from a psychological perspective using the *Autobiography* and other sources as a standard for comparison to highlight the forces of racism in Malcolm's life which the hagiography suppresses.

* * *

Each of the big scenes during the first hour of the movie emphasize Malcolm, the child-rascal. Malcolm's first conk, sets the stage. As Shorty straightens Malcolm's hair, he quickly turns into a pain-stricken child as the lye reaches his scalp. That scene is reprised just before Malcolm goes to jail. Malcolm has to put his head in the toilet, when, at the crucial moment in his conking, he finds all the water in the apartment has been turned off. The two conk scenes are Lee's "comic" book ends for Malcolm's technicolor life of crime.

* * *

One of the reasons that *The Autobiography of Malcolm X* is a stunning book is because it is a psychologically coherent and believable indictment of life in a racist world whatever race the reader might be. Whether or not Malcolm invented many of the facts he told Haley, Malcolm was telling his version of his own life and it is authentic in that sense. The *Autobiography* also had a sophisticated psychological agenda. This is how the *Autobiography* ends the section of Malcolm's life that Lee has made into a kind of glamorized musical comedy:

> I want to say before I go on that I have never previously told anyone my sordid past in detail. I haven't done it now to sound as though I might be proud of how bad, how evil, I was. But people are always

speculating—why am I as I am? To understand that of any person, his whole life, from birth, must be reviewed. All of our experiences fuse into our personality. Everything that ever happened to us is an ingredient.

Today, when everything that I do has an urgency, I would not spend one hour in the preparation of a book which had the ambition to perhaps titillate some readers. But I am spending many hours because the full story is the best way that I know to have it seen, and understood, that I had sunk to the very bottom of the American white man's society when—soon now, in prison—I found Allah and the religion of Islam and it completely transformed my life.

When Lee's Malcolm goes to jail he is still psychologically a child-man. Malcolm in contrast saw himself as an embittered hustler who had seen the most sordid side of life, and was appropriately nicknamed Satan by his fellow prisoners. Malcolm tells us how almost entirely by his own efforts he shaped that violent and ignorant man into something else in prison. In Lee's movie the child-man finds the good father in prison just as he found the good father in crime.

* * *

Malcolm believed that both of his parents had been destroyed by White racism; his father murdered by bigots and his mother driven mad by grief and a harassing White social worker. His extended family was all the more important to Malcolm and he kept up his ties with his brothers and sisters. His older step-sister, Ella, by the father's first marriage was a strong woman who took him in when he first came to Boston. It is to his older brother's Black Muslim home in Detroit that he goes when he is released from prison. Malcolm's brothers and sisters, however, are entirely absent from Lee's film. Lee's child-man is a virtual orphan and from prison he goes to the invented Baines' home. We are led to believe that the Black Muslim faith has become his family and Malcolm has found in Elijah the father he had lost in childhood.

Lee's Malcolm has a series of particularly touching scenes with the messenger, Elijah Muhammad who is uncannily portrayed by the actor Al Freeman, Jr. Elijah has a gentle exotic spirituality. He is the ultimate kind and wise father and Malcolm, according to Lee's stage direction, is "completely humble in his presence accepting his authority totally and without reservation." Lee's Malcolm has found the answer to his inner longing and his mission is to be the good son.

* * *

Malcolm made it clear in the *Autobiography* that he "adored" Elijah and Lee has found a way to make the scenes between the two men demonstrate that. Those scenes had stymied the previous screenwriters according to Lee. No doubt the earlier writers were unable to reconcile Malcolm's fiery independent personality with his subordination to Elijah. Lee's "tamed" Malcolm presents no such problem for him. He portrays a filial love affair made possible by Elijah's modesty and a Malcolm completely humble in the older man's presence. The scenes make for inspiring cinema, but as with Malcolm's relation to Baines, they also pose questions about his gullibility that are left unanswered when Malcolm leaves the Black Muslim faith. More importantly, just as Lee downplays the forces of White racism in Malcolm's early life, he downplays the Black racism that Malcolm espoused with his acceptance of Elijah Muhammad's religious beliefs.

* * *

The moments in the film which come closest to epic proportions are when Malcolm and his Black Muslim brothers confront police brutality. The mobilization of oppressed people transformed into a disciplined political force to be reckoned with by White America was Malcolm's dream and Lee captures it on film. Whatever criticism one has of the film's psychological veracity, this is surely a stirring moment of artistic and political achievement for Lee as an African American director.

* * *

Innocence and goodness are the constant elements of the Malcolm in Lee's film. That person is a denial not only of Malcolm's own righteous fury but of the contemporary Black rage that finds its sounding board in Malcolm's personality. Malcolm is the man who always knew the score. He was street-smart and self-educated. Malcolm never denied his rage, he used it. His conversion to the Black Muslim faith focused his grievances on the White man as the Blue-eyed devil. His rage was given an outlet in the focused hatred of Black racism which he embraced. His rage was turned from sordid self-destruction to constructive political and religious goals. From guns and hustling he came to polemics and sermons. He understood the traumas of his own family as part of the continuing degradation of slavery and White racism. Everything he said in his sermons and lectures had an impact because Malcolm X spoke as one who recognized the source of his pain. The people all know the awful truth when the angry prophet, the seer finally tells it. Malcolm, the angry prophet, who terrified his listeners with the truth, is what Lee has left out of his film.

* * *

Given the political pressures on Lee, the most difficult issue must have been the filmed account of the assassination. If Oliver Stone's film *J.F.K.* is the standard of comparison, then Lee deserves an Oscar for reasonableness. Some Blacks believe that a White conspiracy involving the F.B.I. or the C.I.A. killed Malcolm. Minister Farrakhan apparently would have preferred the film to have featured that version of the assassination. His idea is that the growing hostility between Malcolm and the Nation of Islam gave the White power structure cover for their own ends. Others have alleged that Elijah Muhammad himself ordered members of "Temple no.25" in New Jersey to kill Malcolm. Of course, there are many conspiracy theories just as is the case with J.F.K., R.F.K., and Martin Luther King, Jr.

Lee's movie shows that White operatives of the F.B.I./C.I.A. had Malcolm under surveillance. But his screenplay leaves no doubt that the actual killers were Black Muslims. He writes: "Five Black men sit around a table. They do not speak. They are Thomas Haver, Ben Thomas, Lon Davis, William X and Wilbur Kinley. All are Muslims; all are the assassins."

* * *

Lee's depiction of the assassination is brilliant and conveys fanatic and desperate brutality. But then, in keeping with the tone he has established throughout his film, he takes us to South Africa where Black school children proudly announce their identification with Malcolm X who has been enshrined by Lee as the icon of Black pride and the catalyst of international Black unity. And finally there on the screen is the long suffering Nelson Mandela, who in his gentle demeanor is the antithesis of Malcolm X. In a voice, devoid of anger, he embraces Malcolm's credo. The prodigal son has found yet another godlike father.

* * *

The Marketing of Malcolm X; Is Spike Lee's Film Just Capitalizing on an Image?

WASH. POST, Nov. 4, 1996, at C1.

■ ELAINE RIVERA

Twenty-seven years after he was assassinated in an auditorium in upper Manhattan, and a few weeks before he is resurrected on the screen in Spike Lee's $34 million epic, Malcolm X is once again at the center of controversy.

* * *

The revolutionary black leader, who spent much of his life attacking white America, is suddenly big business.

* * *

Just what Malcolm's message is, and how he should be portrayed, remains a matter of some dispute. He began life in Omaha as Malcolm Little, transformed himself into a street hustler known as "Detroit Red," went to prison where he was introduced to the teachings of Elijah Muhammad, became a leader of Muhammad's Nation of Islam, which espoused a black separatist philosophy, then broke away to pursue a more international and interracial vision of human rights.

But the Nation of Islam, which Malcolm denounced in the last year of his life and which is now headed by Louis Farrakhan, is still selling Malcolm X tapes at its Harlem mosque. And some who condemned Malcolm for his militant views in the 1960s—or who have little idea of what he stood for—are now embracing him.

* * *

But Betty Shabazz, Malcolm X's widow and an administrator at Medgar Evers College in Brooklyn, says there is nothing wrong with marketing her husband's image.

"People want to be a part of Malcolm, and this is a way for them to do it," said Shabazz, who, as executor of her husband's estate, hired a management company earlier this year to license his name and likeness. "I think anyone who is wearing a hat or T-shirt has a basic understanding that Malcolm was for justice, equality and parity for all human beings."

Thulani Davis, who wrote the libretto for an opera about Malcolm's life, says it's all part of the process of transforming a man into a myth.

"Malcolm is a modern-day myth and a powerful one," said Davis, who has seen the movie and defends Lee's work. "If Spike is doing anything, he's making a movie about a hero."

* * *

The battle over Malcolm's legacy will likely heat up in coming weeks. Baraka says he plans to see the film, then make up his mind about Lee. But he says many people who rejected Malcolm when he was alive "are pimping off of him now."

* * *

NOTES AND QUESTIONS

1.   What accounts for the alliance between black leaders and conservatives in the face of "gangsta rap"?   Clarence Lusane argues that the alliance between C. Delores Tucker and William Bennett, a former Reagan official, against "gangsta rap" created a false sense of cooperation between blacks and conservatives. *See* CLARENCE LUSANE, RACE IN THE GLOBAL ERA: AFRICAN AMERICANS AT THE MILLENNIUM 87 (1997). In particular, he argues that the seeming alliance between both groups ignores the social forces that have negatively impacted the black community.

Is this similar to the criticism that is being leveled at Bill Cosby for his harsh criticism of African Americans of "lower economic" status who have children who curse in public and commit acts of violence? Many blacks have complained that his comments only served to reinforce conservatives' negative stereotypes of blacks. Also, in what context should we assess the criticisms that Tucker and Cosby have leveled against rap music?

One writer likens the Cosby personal responsibility criticisms and counterreaction to them to the historic intellectual debates at the turn of the twentieth century between W.E.B. DuBois and Booker T. Washington. Kevin Merida, *Cos and Effect; Bill Cosby Sparked a Debate. Will His Own Troubles Snuff it Out?* WASH. POST, Feb. 20, 2005, at D01 (arguing that Cosby's "tough-love tour that had been sweeping the country . . . was the kind of thing that used to go on with a lot greater frequency, part of an honored tradition of unflinching dialogue that African Americans have practiced for generations'').

2. Role of race in rap. Much has been made of the fact that the majority of rap fans are white. It has given rise to questions over whether whites are only willing to accept certain images of blacks. In fact, if one looks at MTV and BET, there is a proliferation of rap videos that depict black rappers as pimps and gangsters with numerous scantily clad black women. Is the image prevalent because it is the one whites are most comfortable with? Would blacks still be on MTV and BET if the images were the exact opposite of those presently shown?

In *Pale Imitation of Gangsta Life Gives Everyone a Bad Rap*, Richard Roeper, a *Chicago Sun–Times* columnist, argues that the prevalence of negative black stereotypes in music and movies negatively impacts all blacks. Roeper, Apr. 24, 2003, *available at* www.freerepublic.com. According to Roeper, most of the stereotypes depict blacks as chicken-eating, 40–ounce drinking, dancing people. He finds these clichés embarrassing and troubling.

Recently, the movie *Precious: Based on the Novel Push by Sapphire*, debuted to mixed reviews in the black community. The film, directed by Lee Daniels (an African American), depicts a troubled, overweight black teenager who has been repeatedly raped by her father and whose mother (played by African American comedian Mo'Nique, who won Oscar for Best Supporting Actress in 2010) is an abusive, vicious monster.

The black community has been divided over its perception of *Precious*. Some, like Juelle Stewart writing in *Colorlines*, argue that the film relies on a ''villainization of the Black matriarch,'' and are concerned that it offers white audiences a spectacle confirming stereotypes about oversexed black men and pathological black families. On the other hand, the film has been praised by financial heavyweights in the black community such as Oprah Winfrey and Tyler Perry (who has also been accused of pandering to stereotypes about black people in his movies). For piercing criticism see Ishmael Reed, *Fade to White*, N.Y. TIMES, Feb. 4th 2010 available at http://www.nytimes.com/2010/02/05/opinion/05reed.html and Felicia R. Lee, '' 'Precious' '' Ignites a Debate on the Black Narrative,'' New York Times, Nov. 20, 2009, available at http://www.nytimes.com/2009/11/21/movies/21 precious.html.

3. ''Gangsta rap'' and violence. In *Black Liberation in Conservative America*, Manning Marable suggests that violence rates increased with the increasing popularity of gangsta rap. MANNING MARABLE, BLACK LIBERATION IN CONSERVATIVE AMERICA (1997). Marable cites the violent lyrics coming from his daughter's bedroom and suggests that the music and its message are inescapable.

How much of the blame placed on rap might be misplaced? Don't inner city problems run deeper than rap lyrics? Many commentators have criticized the glamorization of gangsta life by such rappers as Tupac, Notorious

B.I.G., and Snoop Dogg. These critics believe that rap lyrics are responsible for the violence and strife in urban communities.

In the controversy over violence and misogyny in black music, has similar violence and misogyny in white music been overlooked? Kim Deterline and Art Jones of FAIR (Fairness and Accuracy in Reporting) argue in the affirmative:

> The double standard applied to rap—as compared to rock—was pointed out most clearly in a letter to the editor in the *Washington Post* (7/14/92), which commented on the outcry surrounding the song "Cop Killer."

> ("Cop Killer" was actually a speed metal song in the rock genre, but the singer Ice–T, an African American, was best known as a rapper, and the song was often mistakenly called a rap song in media discussions.)

> Letter-writer Jay Marcus cited other songs that received rave reviews: Elton John's 1977 song "Ticking," about a young man who goes into a bar and kills 14 people; Bruce Springsteen's "Nebraska," featuring a couple on a shooting spree, and his "Johnny 99," about a gun-waving laid-off worker; and Stephen Sondheim's score for *Assassins*, which presented songs mostly in the first person about attempted and successful presidential killers.

> "Each of the above songs uses an artistic device of extreme examples to help us understand antisocial behavior," Marcus wrote.

> All are sung either in me first person (that is, the singer takes the role of the killer) and/or with tremendous empathy for the killer. Each song seeks to point out social problems that lead to the killer's actions. Only one, however, incited any sort of public criticism or controversy—Ice–T's. * * *

> The double standard applied to rap music makes it easier to sell the idea that "gangsta rap" is "more" misogynist, racist, violent and just plain dangerous than other music.

> For example, an Orlando Sentinel article (2/26/92) managed to refer to the Geto Boys' second album *We Can't Be Stopped* as having "some horribly violent and misogynist imagery," while in the same article Guns N' Roses' *Use Your Illusion* is called "merely obnoxious on songs like 'Back Off Bitch' in which Axl Rose declares war on women." Why is a "bitch" reference made by a black "gangsta rapper" considered more offensive than one made by a white "bad boy" rocker?

Kim Deterline and Art Jones, "Fear of a Rap Planet," Extra! March/April, 1994, available at http://www.fair.org/index.php?page=2891.

4.   Malcolm X and black rage. Cornel West devotes much discussion to Malcolm X and the black rage he embodied. *See* CORNEL WEST, RACE MATTERS (1993). Malcolm X has long been associated with rage and fiery passion, but the articles suggest that Spike Lee drastically toned that part of his persona to make it more palatable to a mainstream audience. That argument can be made, but on the other hand, anytime a movie is made of one's life some parts are inevitably going to be left out. But, does concern over marketability or the movie's capacity account for Lee's decision to disregard some of the leader's more confrontational rhetoric?

5.   Race and royalties. Black artists and musicians have long struggled to own their songs. Because of this, many have led impoverished lives and died broke. Nor is this a past phenomenon; one only has to look at the travails of modern artists such as TLC and Toni Braxton to see that unfair recording and publishing contracts are still prevalent. Even more telling is that both TLC and Braxton were top-selling artists who still could not fend off bankruptcy.

As the aforementioned articles about Little Richard highlight, struggles with the recording industry are not new. The articles depict both artists as victims of record companies who did not possess the necessary business knowledge for the industry. However, ignorance of the business side of the recording industry does not completely account for the uneven playing field. In *Kraski, Clint Black Launch Equity*, Clint Black, a country artist, discusses how the recording business works: "The system pays artists advances against future royalties, meaning that the revenues from their album sales first must repay numerous recoupable items, including the cost of the record production and marketing." Chris Lewis, *Kraski, Clint Black Launch Equity*, NASHVILLE CITY PAPER, August 1, 2003. As Black's statement illustrates, artists face an uphill battle in securing fair contracts.

The following excerpt provides an inside look at the way independent recording studios and record labels exploited African American artists.

––––––––

CHARLIE ROSE: Much has been said before in the world, and during these four decades, that a lot of these black artists didn't get what they earned.

AHMET ERTEGUN: Oh, that's true. * * * There were a lot of independent record companies in the '40s, that—it mushroomed because there was a shortage of shellac. * * * And a lot of small companies that found a way of getting shellac, a way of pressing records, started to press anything that they could do. So there are all these independent companies. Many of them made jazz records. Many of them made rhythm and blues records. Many of them made country records. They made the music that the majors didn't make because of the shortage. * * *

And as a result, these—a lot of these independent record companies were owned and run by people who were not really that interested in the music. All they cared about was making a fast buck. And they had no intention of paying anybody royalties. So many of these companies were owned by people who were ex-jukebox operators, or nightclub owners, or whatever. They made these records, and unfortunately many of them [] never paid any royalties. And they only paid the big artists something to keep them from leaving the label.

At the same time, the big artists ... all made 5 percent. Records sold for 75 cents. And they made 5 percent of 75 cents. That was top, that was the top royalty. Beginning artists, like country artists were paid 1 percent or 2 percent. Race record artists were paid either nothing or 1 or 2 percent. * * * In those days, a big hit record sold 50,000 or 100,000 copies. And you know, 100,000 times a nickel is not a lot of money. You know, it's $5,000. [M]y first employee at Atlantic Records was a bookkeeper, ... because we in our naive way thought that we had to pay everybody their royalties, so we had to know how much was owed. So we had a bookkeeper to figure that out. And we paid our royalties, but many companies did not.

And so it's generally said that nobody got paid correctly, or got paid at all. [T]he people who made big hits in those days, compared to people who make big hits today, got very little.

A Conversation With Ahmet Ertegun, Music Producer, Founder of Atlantic Records, CHARLIE ROSE TRANSCRIPTS, Feb. 21, 2005. *See also* AHMET ERTEGUN, WHAT'D I SAY: THE ATLANTIC STORY (2001).

6.   The Paradox of Hip–Hop Sampling. *The Washington Post* writer, John Balz, discusses the increasing number of lawsuits between rappers over the use of hooks and beats. Since rap is built on sampling and appropriating old sounds this is a new and unexpected phenomenon. In the article Balz focuses on disputes between unknown artists and established rappers such as I.O.F. (It's Only Family) and Ludacris. Most of these disputes center on unknown artists' allegations that popular rappers steal their hooks and beats and turn them into popular songs.

As more rappers encounter appropriation disputes, one has to wonder whether the increasing number of lawsuits reflects the influence of corporate business on the nature of rap. When rap first began it was mainly a way to entertain at parties or in parks. However, in the thirty years since it was introduced, it is the most popular music in the United States and often the background for advertising in print and media. The introduction of corporate values into what started as a homegrown music enterprise makes it safe to assume that the financial gain of rap has made settling musical disputes through litigation an attractive option for rappers, who until recently, were happy to avoid judicial resolution of their conflicts over creative and intellectual property issues. John Balz, *Hip–Hopping Mad Over Beats and Hooks*, WASH. POST, May 8, 2005, at B01.

The End of White America?

The Atlantic Magazine January/February 2009.

■ Hua Hsu

* * *

Whether you describe it as the dawning of a post-racial age or just the end of white America, we're approaching a profound demographic tipping point. According to an August 2008 report by the U.S. Census Bureau, those groups currently categorized as racial minorities—blacks and Hispanics, East Asians and South Asians—will account for a majority of the U.S. population by the year 2042. Among Americans under the age of 18, this shift is projected to take place in 2023, which means that every child born in the United States from here on out will belong to the first post-white generation. * * *

What will the new mainstream of America look like, and what ideas or values might it rally around? What will it mean to be white after "whiteness" no longer defines the mainstream? Will anyone mourn the end of white America? Will anyone try to preserve it? * * *

[C]onsider Sean Combs, a hip-hop mogul and one of the most famous African Americans on the planet. Combs grew up during hip-hop's late–1970s rise, and he belongs to the first generation that could safely make a living working in the industry—as a plucky young promoter and record-label intern in the late 1980s and early 1990s, and as a fashion designer, artist, and music executive worth hundreds of millions of dollars a brief decade later.

In the late 1990s, Combs made a fascinating gesture toward New York's high society. He announced his arrival into the circles of the rich and powerful not by crashing their parties, but by inviting them into his own spectacularly over-the-top world. Combs began to stage elaborate annual parties in the Hamptons, not far from where Fitzgerald's novel [*The Great Gatsby*] takes place. These "white parties"—attendees are required to wear white—quickly became legendary for their opulence (in 2004, Combs showcased a 1776 copy of the Declaration of Independence) as well as for the cultures-colliding quality of Hamptons elites paying their respects to someone so comfortably nouveau riche. Prospective business partners angled to get close to him and praised him as a guru of the lucrative "urban" market, while grateful partygoers hailed him as a modern-day Gatsby.

"Have I read The Great Gatsby?" Combs said to a London newspaper in 2001. "I am the Great Gatsby."

Yet whereas Gatsby felt pressure to hide his status as an arriviste, Combs celebrated his position as an outsider-insider—someone who appropriates elements of the culture he seeks to join without attempting to assimilate outright. In a sense, Combs was imitating the old WASP establishment; in another sense, he was subtly provoking it, by over-enunciating its formality and never letting his guests forget that there was something slightly off about his presence. There's a silent power to throwing parties where the best-dressed man in the room is also the one whose public profile once consisted primarily of dancing in the background of Biggie Smalls videos. ("No one would ever expect a young black man to be coming to a party with the Declaration of Independence, but I got it, and it's coming with me,'' Combs joked at his 2004 party, as he made the rounds with the document, promising not to spill champagne on it.)

In this regard, Combs is both a product and a hero of the new cultural mainstream, which prizes diversity above all else, and whose ultimate goal is some vague notion of racial transcendence, rather than subversion or assimilation. Although Combs's vision is far from representative—not many hip-hop stars vacation in St. Tropez with a parasol-toting manservant shading their every step—his industry lies at the heart of this new mainstream. Over the past 30 years, few changes in American culture have been as significant as the rise of hip-hop. The genre has radically reshaped the way we listen to and consume music, first by opposing the pop mainstream and then by becoming it. From its constant sampling of past styles and eras—old records, fashions, slang, anything—to its mythologization of the self-made black antihero, hip-hop is more than a musical genre: it's a philosophy, a political statement, a way of approaching and remaking culture. It's a lingua franca not just among kids in America, but also among young people worldwide. And its economic impact extends beyond the music industry, to fashion, advertising, and film. (Consider the producer Russell Simmons—the ur-Combs and a music, fashion, and television mogul—or the rapper 50 Cent, who has parlayed his rags-to-riches story line into extracurricular successes that include a clothing line; book, video-game, and film deals; and a startlingly lucrative partnership with the makers of Vitamin Water.)

But hip-hop's deepest impact is symbolic. During popular music's rise in the 20th century, white artists and producers consistently ''mainstreamed'' African American innovations. Hip-hop's ascension has been different. Eminem notwithstanding, hip-hop never suffered through anything like an Elvis Presley moment, in which a white artist made a musical form safe for white America. This is no dig at Elvis—the constrictive racial logic of the 1950s demanded the erasure of rock and roll's black roots, and if it hadn't been him, it would have been someone else. But hip-hop—the sound of the post-civil-rights, post-soul generation—found a global audience on its own terms.

Today, hip-hop's colonization of the global imagination, from fashion runways in Europe to dance competitions in Asia, is Disney-esque. This transformation has bred an unprecedented cultural confidence in its black originators. Whiteness is no longer a threat, or an ideal: it's kitsch to be appropriated, whether with gestures like Combs's ''white parties'' or the trickle-down epidemic of collared shirts and cuff links currently afflicting rappers. And an expansive multiculturalism is replacing the us-against-the-world bunker mentality that lent a thrilling edge to hip-hop's mid–1990s rise.

Peter Rosenberg, a self-proclaimed ''nerdy Jewish kid'' and radio personality on New York's Hot 97 FM—and a living example of how hip-hop has created new identities for its listeners that don't fall neatly along lines of black and white—shares another example: ''I interviewed [the St. Louis rapper] Nelly this morning, and he said it's now very cool and in to have multicultural friends. Like you're not really considered hip or 'you've made it' if you're rolling with all the same people."

Just as Tiger Woods forever changed the country-club culture of golf, and Will Smith confounded stereotypes about the ideal Hollywood leading man, hip-hop's rise is helping redefine the American mainstream, which no longer aspires toward a single iconic image of style or class. Successful network-television shows like Lost, Heroes, and Grey's Anatomy feature wildly diverse casts, and an entire genre of half-hour comedy, from The Colbert Report to The Office, seems dedicated to having fun with the persona of the clueless white male. The youth market is following the same pattern: consider the Cheetah Girls, a multicultural, multiplatinum, multiplatform trio of teenyboppers who recently starred in their third movie, or Dora the Explorer, the precocious bilingual 7–year–old Latina adventurer who is arguably the most successful animated character on children's television today. In a recent address to the Association of Hispanic Advertising Agencies, Brown Johnson, the Nickelodeon executive who has overseen Dora's rise, explained the importance of creating a character who does not conform to "the white, middle-class mold." When Johnson pointed out that Dora's wares were outselling Barbie's in France, the crowd hooted in delight.

Pop culture today rallies around an ethic of multicultural inclusion that seems to value every identity—except whiteness. "It's become harder for the blond-haired, blue-eyed commercial actor," remarks Rochelle Newman–Carrasco, of the Hispanic marketing firm Enlace. "You read casting notices, and they like to cast people with brown hair because they could be Hispanic. The language of casting notices is pretty shocking because it's so specific: 'Brown hair, brown eyes, could look Hispanic.' Or, as one notice put it: 'Ethnically ambiguous.' "

"I think white people feel like they're under siege right now—like it's not okay to be white right now, especially if you're a white male," laughs Bill Imada, of the IW Group. Imada and Newman–Carrasco are part of a movement within advertising, marketing, and communications firms to reimagine the profile of the typical American consumer. (Tellingly, every person I spoke with from these industries knew the Census Bureau's projections by heart.)

"There's a lot of fear and a lot of resentment," Newman–Carrasco observes, describing the flak she caught after writing an article for a trade publication on the need for more-diverse hiring practices. "I got a response from a friend—he's, like, a 60–something white male, and he's been involved with multicultural recruiting," she recalls. "And he said, 'I really feel like the hunted. It's a hard time to be a white man in America right now, because I feel like I'm being lumped in with all white males in America, and I've tried to do stuff, but it's a tough time.' "

"I always tell the white men in the room, 'We need you,' " Imada says. "We cannot talk about diversity and inclusion and engagement without you at the table. It's okay to be white!

"But people are stressed out about it. 'We used to be in control! We're losing control!' "

If they're right—if white America is indeed "losing control," and if the future will belong to people who can successfully navigate a post-racial, multicultural landscape—then it's no surprise that many white Americans are eager to divest themselves of their whiteness entirely.

For some, this renunciation can take a radical form. In 1994, a young graffiti artist and activist named William "Upski" Wimsatt, the son of a university professor, published Bomb the Suburbs, the spiritual heir to Norman Mailer's celebratory 1957 essay, "The White Negro." Wimsatt was deeply committed to hip-hop's transformative powers, going so far as to embrace the status of the lowly "wigger," a pejorative term popularized in the early 1990s to describe white kids who steep themselves in black culture. Wimsatt viewed the wigger's immersion in two cultures as an engine for change. "If channeled in the right way," he wrote, "the wigger can go a long way toward repairing the sickness of race in America."

Wimsatt's painfully earnest attempts to put his own relationship with whiteness under the microscope coincided with the emergence of an academic discipline known as "whiteness studies." In colleges and universities across the country, scholars began examining the history of "whiteness" and unpacking its contradictions. Why, for example, had the Irish and the Italians fallen beyond the pale at different moments in our history? Were Jewish Americans white? And, as the historian Matthew Frye Jacobson asked, "Why is it that in the United States, a white woman can have black children but a black woman cannot have white children?"

Much like Wimsatt, the whiteness-studies academics—figures such as Jacobson, David Roediger, Eric Lott, and Noel Ignatiev—were attempting to come to terms with their own relationships with whiteness, in its past and present forms. In the early 1990s, Ignatiev, a former labor activist and the author of How the Irish Became White, set out to "abolish" the idea of the white race by starting the New Abolitionist Movement and founding a journal titled Race Traitor. "There is nothing positive about white identity," he wrote in 1998. "As James Baldwin said, 'As long as you think you're white, there's no hope for you.' "

Although most white Americans haven't read Bomb the Suburbs or Race Traitor, this view of whiteness as something to be interrogated, if not shrugged off completely, has migrated to less academic spheres. The perspective of the whiteness-studies academics is commonplace now, even if the language used to express it is different.

"I get it: as a straight white male, I'm the worst thing on Earth," Christian Lander says. Lander is a Canadian-born, Los Angeles–based satirist who in January 2008 started a blog called Stuff White People Like (stuffwhitepeoplelike.com), which pokes fun at the manners and mores of a specific species of young, hip, upwardly mobile whites. (He has written more than 100 entries about whites' passion for things like bottled water, "the idea of soccer," and "being the only white person around.") At its best, Lander's site—which formed the basis for a recently published book of the same name * * *—is a cunningly precise distillation of the identity crisis plaguing well-meaning, well-off white kids in a post-white world.

"Like, I'm aware of all the horrible crimes that my demographic has done in the world," Lander says. "And there's a bunch of white people who are desperate—desperate—to say, 'You know what? My skin's white, but I'm not one of the white people who's destroying the world.'"

For Lander, whiteness has become a vacuum. The "white identity" he limns on his blog is predicated on the quest for authenticity—usually other people's authenticity. "As a white person, you're just desperate to find something else to grab onto. You're jealous! Pretty much every white person I grew up with wished they'd grown up in, you know, an ethnic home that gave them a second language. White culture is Family Ties and Led Zeppelin and Guns N' Roses—like, this is white culture. This is all we have."

Lander's "white people" are products of a very specific historical moment, raised by well-meaning Baby Boomers to reject the old ideal of white American gentility and to embrace diversity and fluidity instead. ("It's strange that we are the kids of Baby Boomers, right? How the hell do you rebel against that? Like, your parents will march against the World Trade Organization next to you. They'll have bigger white dreadlocks than you. What do you do?") But his lighthearted anthropology suggests that the multicultural harmony they were raised to worship has bred a kind of self-denial.

Matt Wray, a sociologist at Temple University who is a fan of Lander's humor, has observed that many of his white students are plagued by a racial-identity crisis: "They don't care about socioeconomics; they care about culture. And to be white is to be culturally broke. The classic thing white students say when you ask them to talk about who they are is, 'I don't have a culture.' They might be privileged, they might be loaded socioeconomically, but they feel bankrupt when it comes to culture ... They feel disadvantaged, and they feel marginalized. They don't have a culture that's cool or oppositional." Wray says that this feeling of being culturally bereft often prevents students from recognizing what it means to be a child of privilege—a strange irony that the first wave of whiteness-studies scholars, in the 1990s, failed to anticipate.

Of course, the obvious material advantages that come with being born white—lower infant-mortality rates and easier-to-acquire bank loans, for example—tend to undercut any sympathy that this sense of marginalization might generate. And in the right context, cultural-identity crises can turn well-meaning whites into instant punch lines. Consider ego trip's The (White) Rapper Show, a brilliant and critically acclaimed reality show that VH1 debuted in 2007. It depicted 10 (mostly hapless) white rappers living together in a dilapidated house—dubbed "Tha White House"—in the South Bronx. Despite the contestants' best intentions, each one seemed like a profoundly confused caricature, whether it was the solemn graduate student committed to fighting racism or the ghetto-obsessed suburbanite who had, seemingly by accident, named himself after the abolitionist John Brown.

Similarly, Smirnoff struck marketing gold in 2006 with a viral music video titled "Tea Partay," featuring a trio of strikingly bad, V-neck-sweater-clad white rappers called the Prep Unit. "Haters like to clown our Ivy League educations / But they're just jealous 'cause our families run the nation," the trio brayed, as a pair of bottle-blond women in spiffy tennis whites shimmied behind them. There was no nonironic way to enjoy the video; its entire appeal was in its self-aware lampooning of WASP culture: verdant country clubs, "old money," croquet, popped collars, and the like.

"The best defense is to be constantly pulling the rug out from underneath yourself," Wray remarks, describing the way self-aware whites contend with their complicated identity. "Beat people to the punch. You're forced as a white person into a sense of ironic detachment. Irony is what fuels a lot of white subcultures. You also see things like Burning Man, when a lot of white people are going into the desert and trying to invent something that is entirely new and not a form of racial mimicry. That's its own kind of flight from whiteness. We're going through a period where whites are really trying to figure out: Who are we?"

The "flight from whiteness" of urban, college-educated, liberal whites isn't the only attempt to answer this question. You can flee into whiteness as well. This can mean pursuing the authenticity of an imagined past: think of the deliberately white-bread world of Mormon America, where the '50s never ended, or the anachronistic WASP entitlement flaunted in books like last year's *A Privileged Life: Celebrating WASP Style*, a handsome coffee-table book compiled by Susanna Salk, depicting a world of seersucker blazers, whale pants, and deck shoes. (What the book celebrates is the "inability to be outdone," and the "self-confidence and security that comes with it," Salk tells me. "That's why I call it 'privilege.' It's this privilege of time, of heritage, of being in a place longer than anybody else.") But these enclaves of preserved-in-amber whiteness are likely to be less important to the American future than the construction of whiteness as a somewhat pissed-off minority culture.

This notion of a self-consciously white expression of minority empowerment will be familiar to anyone who has come across the comedian Larry the Cable Guy—he of "Farting Jingle Bells"—or witnessed the transformation of Detroit-born-and-bred Kid Rock from teenage rapper into "American Bad Ass" southern-style rocker. The 1990s may have been a decade when multiculturalism advanced dramatically—when American culture became "colorized," as the critic Jeff Chang put it—but it was also an era when a very different form of identity politics crystallized. Hip-hop may have provided the decade's soundtrack, but the highest-selling artist of the '90s was Garth Brooks. Michael Jordan and Tiger Woods may have been the faces of athletic superstardom, but it was NASCAR that emerged as professional sports' fastest-growing institution, with ratings second only to the NFL's.

As with the unexpected success of the apocalyptic Left Behind novels, or the Jeff Foxworthy-organized Blue Collar Comedy Tour, the rise of country music and auto racing took place well off the American elite's radar screen. (None of Christian Lander's white people would be caught dead at a NASCAR race.) These phenomena reflected a growing sense of cultural solidarity among lower-middle-class whites—a solidarity defined by a yearning for American "authenticity," a folksy realness that rejects the global, the urban, and the effete in favor of nostalgia for "the way things used to be."

Like other forms of identity politics, white solidarity comes complete with its own folk heroes, conspiracy theories (Barack Obama is a secret Muslim! The U.S. is going to merge with Canada and Mexico!), and laundry lists of injustices. The targets and scapegoats vary—from multiculturalism and affirmative action to a loss of moral values, from immigration to an economy that no longer guarantees the American worker a fair chance—and so do the political programs they inspire. (Ross Perot and Pat Buchanan both tapped into this white identity politics in the 1990s; today, its tribunes run the ideological gamut, from Jim Webb to Ron Paul to Mike Huckabee to Sarah Palin.) But the core grievance, in each case, has to do with cultural and socioeconomic dislocation—the sense that the system that used to guarantee the white working class some stability has gone off-kilter.

Wray is one of the founders of what has been called "white-trash studies," a field conceived as a response to the perceived elite-liberal marginalization of the white working class. He argues that the economic downturn of the 1970s was the precondition for the formation of an "oppositional" and "defiant" white-working-class sensibility—think of the rugged, anti-everything individualism of 1977's Smokey and the Bandit. But those anxieties took their shape from the aftershocks of the identity-based movements of the 1960s. "I think that the political space that the civil-rights movement opens up in the mid–1950s and '60s is the transformative thing," Wray observes. "Following the black-power movement, all of the other minority groups that followed took up various forms of activism, including brown power and yellow power and red power. Of course the problem is, if you try and have a 'white power' movement, it doesn't sound good."

The result is a racial pride that dares not speak its name, and that defines itself through cultural cues instead—a suspicion of intellectual elites and city dwellers, a preference for folksiness and plainness of speech (whether real or feigned), and the association of a working-class white minority with "the real America." (In the Scots–Irish belt that runs from Arkansas up through West Virginia, the most common ethnic label offered to census takers is "American.") Arguably, this white identity politics helped swing the 2000 and 2004 elections, serving as the powerful counterpunch to urban white liberals, and the McCain–Palin campaign relied on it almost to the point of absurdity (as when a McCain surrogate dismissed Northern Virginia as somehow not part of "the real Virginia") as a bulwark against the threatening multiculturalism of Barack Obama. Their strategy failed, of course, but it's possible to imagine white identity politics growing more potent and more forthright in its racial identifications in the future, as "the real America" becomes an ever-smaller portion of, well, the real America, and as the soon-to-be white minority's sense of being besieged and disdained by a multicultural majority grows apace.

This vision of the aggrieved white man lost in a world that no longer values him was given its most vivid expression in the 1993 film *Falling Down*. Michael Douglas plays Bill Foster, a downsized defense worker with a buzz cut and a pocket protector who rampages through a Los Angeles overrun by greedy Korean shop-owners and Hispanic gangsters, railing against the eclipse of the America he used to know. (The film came out just eight years before California became the nation's first majority-minority state.) *Falling Down* ends with a soulful police officer apprehending Foster on the Santa Monica Pier, at which point the middle-class vigilante asks, almost innocently: "I'm the bad guy?"

But this is a nightmare vision. Of course most of America's Bill Fosters aren't the bad guys—just as civilization is not, in the words of Tom Buchanan, "going to pieces" and America is not, in the phrasing of Pat Buchanan, going "Third World." The coming white minority does not mean that the racial hierarchy of American culture will suddenly become inverted, as in 1995's *White Man's Burden*, an awful thought experiment of a film, starring John Travolta, that envisions an upside-down world in which whites are subjugated to their high-class black oppressors. There will be dislocations and resentments along the way, but the demographic shifts of the next 40 years are likely to reduce the power of racial hierarchies over everyone's lives, producing a culture that's more likely than any before to treat its inhabitants as individuals, rather than members of a caste or identity group.

Consider the world of advertising and marketing, industries that set out to mold our desires at a subconscious level. Advertising strategy once assumed a "general market"—"a code word for 'white people,'" jokes one ad executive—and smaller, mutually exclusive, satellite "ethnic markets." In recent years, though, advertisers have begun revising their assumptions and strategies in anticipation of profound demographic shifts. Instead of herding consumers toward a discrete center, the goal today is to create versatile images and campaigns that can be adapted to highly individualized tastes. (Think of the dancing silhouettes in Apple's iPod campaign, which emphasizes individuality and diversity without privileging—or even representing—any specific group.)

At the moment, we can call this the triumph of multiculturalism, or post-racialism. But just as whiteness has no inherent meaning—it is a vessel we fill with our hopes and anxieties—these terms may prove equally empty in the long run. Does being post-racial mean that we are past race completely, or merely that race is no longer essential to how we identify ourselves? Karl Carter, of Atlanta's youth-oriented GTM Inc. (Guerrilla Tactics Media), suggests that marketers and advertisers would be better off focusing on matrices like "lifestyle" or "culture" rather than race or ethnicity. "You'll have crazy in-depth studies of the white consumer or the Latino consumer," he complains. "But how do skaters feel? How do hip-hoppers feel?"

The logic of online social networking points in a similar direction. The New York University sociologist Dalton Conley has written of a "network nation," in which applications like Facebook and MySpace create "crosscutting social groups" and new, flexible identities that only vaguely overlap with racial identities. Perhaps this is where the future of identity after whiteness lies—in a dramatic departure from the racial logic that has defined American culture from the very beginning. What Conley, Carter, and others are describing isn't merely the displacement of whiteness from our cultural center; they're describing a social structure that treats race as just one of a seemingly infinite number of possible self-identifications.
* * *

The problem of the 20th century, W. E. B. DuBois famously predicted, would be the problem of the color line. Will this continue to be the case in the 21st century, when a black president will govern a country whose social networks increasingly cut across every conceivable line of identification? * * * [W]e aspire to be post-racial, but we still live within the structures of privilege, injustice, and racial categorization that we inherited from an older order. We can talk about defining ourselves by lifestyle rather than skin color, but our lifestyle choices are still racially coded. We know, more or less, that race is a fiction that often does more harm than good, and yet it is something we cling to without fully understanding why—as a social and legal fact, a vague sense of belonging and place that we make solid through culture and speech.

But maybe this is merely how it used to be—maybe this is already an outdated way of looking at things. "You have a lot of young adults going into a more diverse world," Carter remarks. For the young Americans born in the 1980s and 1990s, culture is something to be taken apart and remade in their own image. "We came along in a generation that didn't have to follow that path of race," he goes on. "We saw something different." This moment was not the end of white America; it was not the end of anything. It was a bridge, and we crossed it.

CHAPTER 12

CASH AND CARRY

A. THE UNDERGROUND ECONOMY

The "underground" or "informal" economy roughly consists of the total of all economic transactions minus those transactions that are in compliance with applicable government regulations. This economy can include both transactions where just *full* compliance with the law is avoided, such as in Martha Shirk's article in this chapter about domestic help, or transactions directly prohibited by the law, such as in the other articles in this chapter about the drug trade and prostitution.[1] The underground economy in the United States can include everything from the waiter who neglects to report all of his tip income, to the doctor who takes cash on the side for weekend visits, to the unlicensed street vendor who sells knockoff goods on the sidewalks of a major city.[2] In extreme situations, the underground economy—sometimes referred to as the "black market"—may actually satisfy more of the citizens' basic needs for housing, clothing, food, and the like than the formal economy.[3]

Defining exactly what the boundary is between the informal and formal economies, however, can have significant cultural and legal implications by distorting the data on which the government relies to control the economy.[4] The Internal Revenue Service, for instance, excludes the value of household labor, such as childcare done by family members or do-it-yourself activities around the house, from its calculations of income.[5] National economic welfare, furthermore, is measured by looking at annual reported income and its relation to the poverty line. But, because the income from underground economies is consistently not reported or underreported, using only reported income as a measure of poverty mixes the truly poor with those who have a much higher standard of living as a result of the underground economy.[6]

But what leads to the creation of underground economies in the first place? In some cases, informal economies arise to respond to a market

---

1. *See* George L. Priest, *The Ambiguous Moral Foundations of the Underground Economy*, 103 YALE L.J. 2259, 2259 (1994).

2. Richard A. Epstein, *The Moral and Practical Dilemmas of the Underground Economy*, 103 YALE L.J. 2157, 2157, 2164 (1994).

3. *See* Priest, *supra*, at 2268–70.

4. *Id.* at 2259.

5. *See* Morton Paglin, *The Underground Economy: New Estimates from Household Income and Expenditure Surveys*, 103 YALE L.J 2239, 2244–45 (1994).

6. *Id.* at 2250–51.

failure created by a government prohibition on an activity seen as immoral or undesired.[7] In other cases, they arise because of a governmental inability to provide a particular good or service in a way that is responsive to the demands of the citizenry.[8] And in still other cases, the underground economy rises up because the regulations surrounding certain economic transactions seem unjust or unfair, or their enforcement is seen as arbitrary.[9] As a result, individuals turn away from the formal economy to attempt to correct these problems.

Despite the negative implications of calling these systems "underground" economies, such structures can provide real benefits. Informal economic activity can significantly increase the standard of living for some of the poorest in a population, provide otherwise unavailable or inefficiently distributed goods and services which may be necessary for survival, and even provide work opportunities for those excluded from the formal economy by discrimination.[10] But, on the other hand, a large underground economy may undermine the stability and responsibility of the government institutions that control the economy, and such economies may also be seen as fundamentally dishonest.[11] Furthermore, unregulated underground economies also deprive the state of tax revenues that could otherwise be used for public services and can lead to sweatshop conditions and risks to the general welfare.[12] What do the following articles contribute to the underground-economy discourse?

Cashing in on Domestic Help[1]

St. Louis Post-Dispatch, Feb. 15, 1993, at 1C.

■ Martha Shirk

To my mind, the most stunning revelation from the Zoe Baird controversy has been the apparent lack of interest of many Americans in the lives of the maids and baby sitters they employ in their homes.

The Internal Revenue Service says that only one out of four families with domestic workers contributes to the Social Security system for their employees, as required by law. Among the scofflaws, we've learned recently, are Secretary of Commerce Ron Brown, former attorney general nominee Zoe Baird and at least a half-dozen members of Congress.

---

7. *See* Epstein, *supra*, at 2158–59.

8. Priest, *supra*, at 2271.

9. *See* Epstein, *supra*, at 2162–63.

10. *See* Priest, *supra*, at 2272–73.

11. *See* Priest, *supra*, at 2260.

12. *See* Lora Jo Foo, *The Vulnerable and Exploitable Workforce and the Need for Strengthening Worker Protective Legislation*, 103 Yale L.J. 2179, 2179–80 (1994).

1. For further discussion of the racial, national, and class dimensions of the U.S. domestic labor market, see chapter 7.

Ask around, and you'll find that most of your neighbors and colleagues aren't paying into the Social Security system for their domestic help.

Chances are, you aren't either.

For the most part, employers cite one of two reasons for not complying with the law:

They don't know they're supposed to.

Their domestic workers don't want them to.

Few would admit that one of their motivations is the savings to themselves.

For instance, for my $50-a-half-day housecleaner, I pay $7.50 a week, or almost $400 a year, to make sure she's covered by Social Security. (The law requires the employer to pay only half that much, but I cover her legally required contribution, too.)

OK, you say, but it's not because of greed that you don't do it. It's because your maid, or your baby sitter, would quit if you did. She wants to be paid in cash, with no deductions.

It's true that their employees' resistance keeps a lot of employers from paying by the book. Some people do domestic work to supplement their welfare benefits, which, in Missouri anyway, provide only a third of the amount the federal government says a family needs to survive above the poverty level.

If they reported their income from domestic work, they'd lose part or all of their welfare checks, and they might lose Medicaid coverage for their children as well.

But a lot of household workers insist on cash, with no deductions, simply because they lack information about the consequences, which are considerable.

In the first place, if a worker is paid in cash, she's probably not filing a federal income tax return. That means that she can't claim the Earned Income Credit, a tax credit authorized by Congress to shore up the incomes of America's poorest families.

The IRS believes that 2 million eligible families failed to claim the Earned Income Credit last year, simply because they didn't realize they could. (Almost 14 million families did, becoming $11.3 billion richer—about $807 a family—as a result.)

The woman to whom I pay $50 a week will get an Earned Income Credit of $520 this year.

The tragedy for her is that she could be getting an earned income credit of $1,384, in one lump sum, if just two of her four other employers weren't paying her under the table. That's more money than she's managed to save in 20 years, the beginning of a nice little nest.

And what about 25 years from now, when it comes time for a household worker to retire? She's out of luck if her employers haven't contributed to the Social Security system for her. Social Security is not an entitlement. You have to pay into the system for at least 10 years—or have been married to someone who did—to draw benefits.

My housecleaner isn't going to be entitled to much of a retirement check 25 years from now if I'm the only employer who contributes to Social Security for her.

Most likely, my housecleaner, and yours, will end up among the 40 percent of elderly American women who live in or near poverty. She'll probably have to apply for SSI—Supplementary Security Income—which will put only $434 into her pocketbook each month.

I use the feminine pronoun here for a reason: Most household workers are women.

And as with many economic issues, this is one where race and gender converge. A higher proportion of black women than white women make their livings doing domestic work. By not taking care of their household employees' Social Security payments, many Americans are discriminating disproportionately against African–Americans, as well as against women.

Even at retirement, the lifelong disparities in income between men and women and whites and blacks persist. The median income in 1989 for black women over 65 was only $4,494, compared with $7,655 for over–65 white women. (Men over 65 had a median annual income of $13,107.)

It's something to think about the next time you pay your maid cash, under the table.

And if compassion doesn't make you do the right thing, maybe self-interest will.

At your employee's request, the IRS can come after you 25 years from now for back contributions—with interest and penalties.

————

NOTES AND QUESTIONS

1. Is there an underground economy? In OFF THE BOOKS (2006), Sociologist Sudhir Alladi Venkatesh explored the world of the cash transactions of the urban poor. He tells the story of Maquis Park, a poor African American neighborhood on the Southside of Chicago. We learn about the shape and dynamics of a universe of unregulated work that escapes taxation and provides the basis for survival for a community largely cutoff from the flow of formal consumer lending and conventional employment.

This is the story of preachers who help resolve neighborhood disputes for a fee, off the books; beauticians who rent their shops out at night for a fee for gambling, of street vendors who accept only cash. The story of Maquis Park is no longer unique. In the Great Recession of 2009, throughout the nation, double digit unemployment has converted many once-employed workers into inhabitants of the netherworld of unrecorded cash transactions, living life completely "off the books" to survive.

2. Can you imagine yourself as a low wage worker? Think about it for a minute. How would you fare if the bad economy, or bad luck pushed you to the edge of your survival as a worker earning $6–$7 per hour. If you lived in a city in which the rent for a one bedroom apartment was $400 a month, how would you make it?

Journalist Barbara Ehrenreich, who holds a PhD in biology became a voluntary inhabitant of the world of low wage work. She travelled from Florida, to Minnesota, to Maine. She lived in the cheapest place available. She worked as a waitress, hotel maid, housecleaner, nursing home aide, and salesclerk for Wal–Mart. Ehrenreich tells the fascinating story of her anxiety-ridden life as a low wage worker in the best-seller NICKEL AND DIMED, ON (NOT) GETTING BY IN AMERICA (2001).

3. Nannygate and the Zoë Baird problem. In 1993, President Clinton nominated Zoë Baird for Attorney General during the first days of his presidency. Support from the public and from the Senate for Baird's confirmation, however, quickly faded: Baird and her husband, it turned out, had hired an illegal-immigrant Peruvian couple to serve as their chauffer and children's nanny and neglected to pay Social Security taxes on the couple's wages. The public uproar surrounding what eventually became known as "Nannygate" effectively led to the withdrawal of Baird's nomination and cost her the position. The American public, it seemed, was unsympathetic to the troubles of a woman worth $2.3 million. *See* Gwen Ifill, *Settling In: Anatomy of a Doomed Nomination; The Baird Appointment: In Trouble From the Start, Then a Firestorm*, N.Y. TIMES, Jan. 23, 1993, at A8.

President Clinton's next nominee for Attorney General, Kimba Woods, also failed to pass inspection when she was asked if she had "a Zoë Baird problem," even though she had legally employed an alien as a babysitter and properly filed all her taxes. Following Zoë Baird, asking whether or not a particular nominee had hired immigrant nannies became standard during confirmation hearings:

> It was also the question that helped pluck the childless and unmarried Janet Reno from relative obscurity to become the President's nominee for the job. No kids, no nanny, no Zoe Baird problem. Reno, 54, who appears to be well qualified for the post, doesn't even have an immigrant gardener: she mows her own lawn.

Claudia Wallis, *The Lessons of Nannygate*, TIME MAG., Feb. 22, 1993, at 76. Clinton's top officials, including Vice President Al Gore, Labor Secretary Robert Reich, and U.S. Trade Representative Mickey Cantor were all asked if they had hired illegal aliens. J. Jennings Moss & Carleton R. Bryant, *Domestic Help a Taxing Issue*, WASH. TIMES, Feb. 8, 1993, at A1.

To be fair, Zoë Baird's acts were not criminal. Though, technically, undocumented alien workers are not allowed to start working until they receive their green cards, Baird and her husband, a professor at Yale Law School, reported the hiring to the Immigration and Naturalization Service and obtained a letter from the INS saying that it was aware of the situation and, that as long as Baird helped the couple obtain necessary documentation, there would be no problem. In addition, Baird did not pay taxes for the Peruvian couple because she was informed by a lawyer, albeit incorrectly, that the Internal Revenue Service would not accept payment until the workers were properly documented. STEPHEN L. CARTER, THE CONFIRMATION MESS 23–28 (1994). In January 1993, Baird and her husband made a lump-sum payment of the taxes due. Neither the failure to pay taxes nor the hiring of illegal immigrants is a criminal offense. Employers of illegal immigrants, though rarely prosecuted, are liable only for civil penalties, including fines of up to $3,000. David Johnston, *Clinton's Choice for Justice Dept. Hired Illegal Aliens for Household*, N.Y. TIMES, Jan. 14, 1993, at A1. And yet, support for Baird's confirmation became suddenly non-existent. Should the hiring of illegal immigrants be criminally punishable (*see* chapter 12)? Is what happened to Zoë Baird an example of the arbitrary enforcement of regulations that can lead to underground economies in the first place?

4.   Nanny tax. At the time of Zoe Baird's confirmation hearings, federal statutes enacted over four decades earlier governing household employees mandated certain reporting and withholding requirements for household employers who paid their household employees more than $50 every three months. The law was sharply criticized as being outdated, however, especially since, given the right circumstances, it frequently applied to the casual, teenaged, neighborhood baby-sitter that many families of all economic backgrounds hire to occasionally watch their children. A year-and-a-half after Zoë Baird, Congress passed the Social Security Domestic Employment Reform Act of 1994, changing the threshold to $1,000 annually. Given individual state laws and the statutes enforced by the Department of Labor and the Immigration and Naturalization Service, however, this threshold increase has had little effect on reporting requirements. CHAD R. TURNER, THE NANNY TAX vii (1997).

5.   Need for childcare. Zoë Baird was criticized primarily because she could afford to make other childcare arrangements without breaking the law. However, not only the very wealthy are avoiding immigration and taxation laws for the sake of childcare, though many may not be able to afford *in-home* childcare. Nearly two-thirds of American women with school-age children work and require some sort of childcare arrangement. Moreover, nearly 60 percent of married men with children in America have working wives. At the time of Nannygate, only one in four people who employed household help paid the Social Security taxes required. Wallis, *supra*. In single-parent or two-working-parent homes, how does the Nanny Tax affect the parent's quality of life and ability to work in the marketplace?

6.   Benefits now or later? Martha Shirk's article suggests that "[s]ome people do domestic work to supplement their welfare benefits, which, in Missouri anyway, provide only a third of the amount the federal government says a family needs to survive above the poverty level." She also suggests that reporting the domestic work income might decrease the amount of money the domestic worker was able to receive from welfare, while not reporting means that they won't receive an Earned Income Credit or Social Security Benefits in old age. For a family at or below the poverty line, which is worse? Is avoiding taxes merely short-sighted, or could it be necessary for immediate survival? Then again, Shirk makes the point that the Earned Income Credit would give her domestic "more money than she's managed to save in 20 years." Given Thomas Shapiro's research on intergenerational wealth (see chapter 14), what effect could this wealth accumulation have on the nanny's own children?

7. Outsourcing. In a two-parent home, a mother or father who stays out of the work force to raise the children is not paid for his or her labor, though that parent effectively does the same work as a nanny or house-keeper. As a result, the parent does not receive income, nor does he or she pay the Social Security taxes that ensure future benefits. Is it ultimately more efficient to hire a nanny regardless of the employer's financial status in order to allow the parent to enter the market to obtain greater retire-ment benefits?

8. Domestic workers and the public/private distinction. Because domestic work was traditionally done by housewives for no pay, it has been considered of little or no economic value. Considered part of the private sphere, domestic work is largely unregulated, while the regulations that do exist largely go unenforced. Given Critical Feminist Theory and Frances Olsen's suggestion that the public/private distinction is unsustainable, how does and how should the law regulate the hired domestic worker, who performs private, household work in the public marketplace? How does the reform of the Nanny Tax "protect[] the interests of the propertied class employers who benefit from the public-private distinction?" *See* Taunya Lovell Banks, *Toward a Global Critical Feminist Vision: Domestic Work and the Nanny Tax Debate*, 3 J. GENDER RACE & JUST. 1, 6–9 (1999); *see also* Peggie R. Smith, *Regulating Paid Household Work: Class, Gender, Race and Agendas of Reform*, 48 AM. U. L. REV. 851 (1999).

9. Nanny gendering. Could not Zoë Baird's husband, Yale Law Profes-sor Paul Gewirtz, have stayed at home and raised the couple's children, given Baird's published annual salary of $507,000? How does the natural-ized assumption that women are the caretakers of children interact with the increase of women in the marketplace? Are laws that make it more difficult for families to hire domestic workers discriminatory against wom-en in those families where women want to work? Are those same laws discriminatory against the poor, female domestic worker? *See* Banks, *supra*, at 8–9.

10. Title, race, and national origin. Banks argues that "[t]he term 'domestic worker' invokes the historic image of a native-born Black women, the mammy, an 'ideological construct of the plantation's faithful household servant and the South's most perfect slave.' " She argues further that the "term 'nanny' invokes the image of a 'foreign' woman" and summons " 'vastly sentimentalized notions ... that a typical nanny came to change the diapers and stayed on for the weddings.' " *Id.* at 18–19. How do these terms, as Banks argues, "erase[] the most negative connotations of in-home childcare—low wage work often performed by non-white women in a potentially exploitative environment," and how does the use of such terms influence the debate about the Nanny Tax? *See id.* at 18–24. How do these terms simultaneously mask and highlight the class and racial differences between employer and employee? Given the Critical Legal Theorist's tenet that law and language are indeterminate, is there a better term to use, or are all the terms used for domestic work meant to gloss over the negative aspects of the job?

11. Non-neutrality of immigration law. In 1990, Congress limited the number of foreign "unskilled workers" that could receive permits to work in the United States to 10,000. Included in this category of occupations that require fewer than two years of experience was domestic help such as housekeepers and nannies. Given that most immigrants to the United States are women and that most domestic workers are also women, is this seemingly neutral immigration policy discriminatory against women? Furthermore, does it discriminate against the American woman in the workforce by decreasing the supply of child caretakers in the United States? *See* Joan Fitzpatrick, *The Gender Dimension of U.S. Immigration Policy*, 9 YALE J.L. & FEMINISM 23, 23–37 (1997). For more about immigration law, see chapter 12.

12. For a fictional account of black and white women's domestic relationships in Jackson, Mississippi in the sixties see Kathryn Stockett, THE HELP.

The Diamonds as a Business Enterprise

THE GANG AS AN AMERICAN ENTERPRISE 91–116 (1992).

■ FELIX M. PADILLA

* * *

Several major questions will be considered in the examination. What are the reasons for the gang becoming a business organization? What does the gang look like as an entrepreneurial establishment? That is, what are its defining characteristics as a business enterprise? Which cultural elements are used by youngsters for cementing and reinforcing business relations among themselves? What is the gang's occupational structure? How does the gang generate income for maintaining itself as a business establishment?

* * *

The history of the Diamonds dates back approximately twenty years, a relatively short period compared to other Latino youth gangs in Chicago. At first the Diamonds were a musical group, playing their music on street corners in the neighborhood and in local neighborhood nightclubs. Some members believe that in about 1971 a member of the musical group was mistaken for a gang member and was killed by a gunshot fired by a youngster from an opposition gang. This incident sparked the reorganization of the group into a violent criminal youth gang. And for a period of about six years after that the Diamonds were on a course of vengeance and retaliation, provoking intergang fights with other groups.

Spike, a thirty-year member of the Diamonds, who is still very active in the gang, provides a clear description of the early days: "We were a band, and we would play to pass the time, you know, or in some gigs in the neighborhood. This was not one of your well-known professional bands, but we did OK. We were just a bunch of guys who would get together to have fun, to play music in the hood, you know—out on the streets. You know, we were doing the same thing that other people were doing at the park or in basements, except that we were in our hood. Then the band started to attract followers, people from the neighborhood that liked the music, and they would be there all the time. These people were like body guards, you know, to make sure the band was safe. So the group started growing, and then, all of a sudden, there was talk about forming the group into a gang, so some of them decided to do it. These were the followers and not the band. I don't know what was the problem with some of these guys; maybe one of them had a run-in with the opposition. But, anyway, it was about this time when one of the band players got shot. So, from here on they decided to become a gang and keep the name of the Diamonds, you know, the name of the band. And for a long time they were hard-core, you know— these guys were mean motherf_____. You couldn't go by the neighborhood because they were shooting at everybody. It was really bad. It was worse than what these guys are doing today. There were times we would have these wars with the opposition, and we go out to the park, the two gangs, with bats, clubs, guns, and shit, and just have it out right there. It was crazy. I can tell you of about ten guys from our side who died from gang fights. Some of the fights were right here because the opposition would drive by shooting at us. Some of our guys got killed right here."

During most of this early period the membership of the Diamonds was quite small; the organization had not expanded and divided itself into sections. Gang members' involvement in drugs—in particular, marijuana— was essentially for their own recreational use. The Diamonds had yet to become a profit-making business enterprise. In some instances, a member would purchase a relatively sizable amount of marijuana and sell to others in the gang. Sometimes money was collected to purchase a quantity of marijuana, which would be equally distributed among contributing members, again, most of the drug was for personal and, at times, social use. As indicated by Spike, while describing the early days of the gang, "We would just get high a lot. It seemed that everybody was doing drugs at that time. It's not like today where people are trying to prevent drug use. No, before there used to be stories about movie stars smoking reefer and doing coke, and they were cool and bad. Doctors were doing drugs; attorneys were doing drugs. I tell you, everybody was doing it. So, we started doing it, too. There were the fights between us and some other gangs—that's another thing we used to do. But, besides that, we would be drinking beer and doing drugs. We were not selling drugs at this time. What we did was to buy the drugs and use them ourselves. We still did not know enough to go into business. We didn't know where to sell them, expect for to our friends, who were already one of us."

Then, in the late 1970s, a major change occurred in the operational structure of the Diamonds. It began to take on a businesslike character. No longer were retaliative, violent behavior against opposition gangs and reefer smoking the mainstays of the organization. Money-making through drug dealing came to represent the gang's emerging chief function. Although a great deal of gangbanging persisted as the Diamonds and enemy gangs maintained ongoing feuds, overall the gang embraced and carried out a program that was built around money-making activities.

Why did the Diamonds undergo this change during this particular period? Which factors and conditions were responsible for the transformation?

CONTROLLED SUBSTANCE ACT

"I remember this older guy from the neighborhood who wanted me to sell for him. He asked several of us to be his dealers. He was offering good money, but I was afraid. I didn't know what he was about. We knew that he was doing something because all these people used to come to his house all the time. Hey, like some of us guys sometimes went to him to cop some smokes for us. He was offering us some good money. He said that we could work for him and that he was going to take care of us. He was even talking about cars; you know, if you do real good and if you're reliable, you know, all of that shit, that he would buy us a beamer [BMW]. And that we would not have to worry again about buying smokes because we would have it all the time. But since he had never dealt with us before and then all of sudden he wanted us to work for him, I was scared. I said no to the buy, I couldn't trust the cat."

What Carmelo is describing is in larger terms an event that had a major influence on the business development of the gang—namely, a piece of legislation: the Illinois Controlled Substance Act, which was passed in 1971 and carried heavy criminal penalties for adult heroin and cocaine dealers. The bill called for mandatory twenty-year prison sentences for drug peddling offenders eighteen years and older.

Well aware that juveniles could always beat the penalties of the newly instituted law, those adults who for the most part had controlled drug distribution and dealing up to this point began enlisting some of the youngsters from the Diamonds as well as from other gangs to work the street blocks and corners of particular neighborhoods. Some youngsters, like Carmelo, refused the job offers, while others agreed to them. It did not take some these youngsters or leaders of the gang very long to realize, however, that they could profit substantially by controlling neighborhood drug dealing. In other words, these young people began to ask the question "If this is our neighborhood and people are using it to make money, why can't we develop our own business?"

And indeed, they did. Gang leaders began reorganizing the structure of the Diamonds into a wholesale enterprise or investment; the organization became a business establishment. It now purchased wholesale merchandise itself and hired its own members, especially the younger ones, to retail the street level. Since the Diamonds viewed themselves as landlords of several *puntos* in the neighborhood (literally translated, the word *punto* stands for "points," but here it refers to street corners), the only missing ingredient for developing a business operation was the necessary capital with which to purchase large amounts of drugs for extracting a profit.

* * *

Not one individual within the Diamonds organization possessed the necessary capital for purchasing large enough quantities of drugs for turning a profit. No single member had the money necessary for establishing himself as the sole owner or shareholder of the corporation. Therefore, some members began pooling their money: Sometimes two or three of the older members (usually the leaders, or chiefs) would "go into business"; at other times the group of investors was larger. On other occasions leaders would command all members to make an investment of a certain minimum amount (along with the lines of passing the hat) and would use this sum for purchasing the necessary amount of drugs with which to start the business. And in still other situations leaders of the gang would simply take and use the dues money for the purchase of large amounts of drugs.

Spike recounts this initial stage in the business development of the Diamonds: "At first it was real tough because we didn't have any cash. So, we would try different ways to raise enough to make a profit. You know, we would all chip in; you know there was no hassle about the money or stuff like that. We wanted the business to get off the ground, you know, make it work because we didn't have nothing for us. This was going to be something that was going to be ours, you know, for us. And once we got going we took control. But at first it was real difficult. And then we had to make sure that people did not spend gang money on themselves. So, it took a little while to get going. But we knew that there was a lot of money to be made in this business. This was a business made for us; it was something like it was sent by God. It was a business that we could do straight from the neighborhoods that we controlled and knew real well. How could you go wrong?"

To the question, "Who controlled the money made from dealing?" Spike answered, "It always was the chief or mainheads. They were the leaders. They had earned their position, and we respected them, and we had a lot of trust in them. So when we paid dues we knew that it was our money, but, in fact, it was the gang's money. And, since the chiefs and mainheads were the leaders, it was the same as the gang. That's how we used to see it then."

* * *

PERCEPTIONS OF CONVENTIONAL WORK

Youngsters' images of "traditional" jobs were perhaps the leading force that helped to transform the gang into a business venture. These young men began turning to the gang in search of employment opportunities, believing that available conventional work would not sufficiently provide the kinds of material goods they wished to secure. Some of the more common assessments I heard about conventional work available for Latino youth are captured in the following two expressions:

> There are some jobs that people can still find, but who wants them? They don't pay. I want a job that can support me. I want a job that I could use my talents—speaking, communicating, selling, and a definite goal that I'd be working toward as far as money is concerned.

> We were just tired of factory jobs. We were supposed to go to school and receive an education. For what? To be employed in factory jobs? We were tired of that. At the same time we were watching these other guys making a lot of money, so we said, "Hey, let's follow these guys. Let's do what they were doing."

These remarks also allow us to gain insight into the pessimistic outlook these young people have developed toward job prospects in the regular economy. Members of the Diamonds have become increasingly convinced that the jobs available to them are essentially meaningless, far from representing the vehicles necessary for overcoming societal barriers to upward mobility. Although these youngsters have been socialized with a view in the conventional cultural course to achieving material success, they refuse to buy into its official means. That is, they do not agree to accept the "American achievement ideology" representative of middle-class norms and shown by Horowitz (1983), Kornblum (1985), and others to be widely supported by ethnic and racial minority parents and teenagers. The ideology stresses that success in school leads to the attainment of managerial and professional jobs, which, in turn, pave the way for social and economic advancement. The youngsters' own school experiences and occasional contacts with the job market—as well as their observations of the frustrating and often futile efforts by some adults around them to achieve social advancement through menial, dead-end jobs—combine to serve as overwhelming evidence that the American achievement ideology does not necessarily apply to them. In brief, these young men do not believe in the power of education to be the "great equalizer," nor do they see existing "legitimate work" as capable of leading them to a successful, meaningful life.

The views of these young people point out the poignant paradox between having culturally defined goals and ineffective but socially legitimate means for achieving them, indicated by sociologist Robert Merton several decades ago and since confirmed by researchers and scholars writing on gangs, youth, and employment (Vigil 1988; Kornblum 1987; Horowitz 1983; Moore 1978; Cloward and Ohlin 1960). The contradiction lies in the absence of avenues and resources necessary for securing the rewards that society most values and which it purports to offer its members.

The decision by members of the Diamonds to accept participation in the gang is informed by their assessments of the lack of available opportunities in the regular economy but also by their high level of aspirations. Rather than arising as a deliberate violation of middle-class aspirations, the gang represents a "counter-organization," a response geared to fulfilling the standards of the larger society. The transformation of the gang into a business enterprise was sparked by the will to change, to alter those forces of domination weighing heavily upon its members' lives. In effect, what these youngsters did was reconstruct the "criminal" gang into a income-generating business operation—an alternate form of employment with which they could hope to "make it" in U.S. society. In the words of Spike, "We grew up at a time when people were making money and making it quick. You know, we saw on television people getting rich overnight. You had the professional athletes—these are the guys who are supposed to have natural talents, you know. That's a lot of bullshit. It's true these guys were taking steroids. You had all these reports about how these athletes were pumping iron and taking steroids so they could sell their bodies and so people could pay to watch them. That's one thing we saw. Then we saw, you know, you had the white-collar criminals—you know, those guys who are just like us but never get caught, except that everybody knows that they are crooks. You had all these guys becoming filthy rich. And what do you think that's going to tell us? It didn't tell me to go and get a job at McDonalds and save my nickels and dimes. Who the f___ was doing it that way? Who the f___ is saving nickels and dimes today? You have kids coming up to you today and asking you for a buck, not for a nickel or a dime or a quarter. Where do they see this shit? You tell me. I wasn't going to save my nickels and dimes. That certainly wasn't going to be me because I would still be waiting, and I would be the only one waiting. Things are not done like that anymore. So, we decided to turn to what we have, and that was us."

"Some of us f___ed up. We didn't make it. I'm thirty years old, and I'm still out here hustling everyday. But that's because certain things didn't work out the way that I wanted. I'm not going to make excuses for my mistakes. But you know what? I'm going to continue because there are many people like me, people who have jobs, people who are making only enough to pay the rent, and then they come out here or go into other kinds of illegal business because they know that what society says and gives them are two different things."

SOCIAL AND CULTURAL COMPONENTS OF THE ETHNIC ENTERPRISE

What are the distinguishing characteristics of the gang which enable it to function as a business organization—a type of establishment necessarily built around a great deal of trust and commitment, which allow it to generate and sustain consistent and dependable social relations and mone-tary gains? That is, which social and cultural elements did the youngsters use for organizing the gang into a reliable money-making enterprise?

In the same way that the family unit teaches its young the norms, skills, values, beliefs, and traditions of the larger society, the gang has developed its own culture, including its own myths, norms, values and ways of communicating and reinforcing them. At the heart of the gang culture is a collective ideology that serves as the basis for realizing the overall welfare of all the members. For the gang collectivism is the major determinant of its efficient development as a business operation. The members' responses to their shared conditions and circumstances are collective in the sense that they lead to partnership, therefore uniting many individuals.

For the members of the Diamonds collectivism translates into an ideology of strength. These young men share the belief that their capacity to make a living or improve their life chances can only be realized through a "collective front." In Coco's view, "We are a group, a community, a family—we have to learn to live together. If we separate, we will never have a chance. We need each other even to make sure that we have a spot for selling our supply. You know, there is people around here, like some opposition, that want to take over your *negocio* [business]. And they think that they can do this very easy. So we stick together, and that makes other people thing twice about trying to take over what is yours. In our case, the opposition has never tried messing with our hood, and that's because they know it's protected real good by us fellas."

Rafael echoes Coco's interpretation of collectivism: "Together we have the numbers. We have protection. My business is his business because we protect our interests together. So we talk about our thing—it's nobody's thing; rather, it's our thing. I think that one of the first things we learn when we start off is to feel like a group or a family. That means that we have to share and we have to protect each other and whatever belongs to us." In effect, though gang members can (and in some cases do) pursue individual financial gains, their business ventures are made possible because of the gang, and their individual work is geared to enhancing the common good and to pursuing collective ends.

The collectivist nature of the gang can he said to be an extension of the traditional Puerto Rican family. In Puerto Rican immigrant society, as well as in other societies from which ethnic and racial groups in the United States originated, the family served as the cornerstone of the culture, defining and determining individual and social behavior. Ties between families were cemented by the establishment of *compadrazco* [godparent-godchild] relationships. Relatives by blood and ceremonial ties as well as friends of the family were linked together in an intricate network of reciprocal obligation. Individuals who suffered misfortunes were aided by relatives and friends, and when these individuals had reestablished themselves they shared their good fortunes with those who had helped them.

        * * *

In addition to its stemming directly from Puerto Rican family tradition, ethnic solidarity served as another fundamental cultural element, used by the youngsters for cementing their business relations. As Puerto Ricans, they expressed feelings of a fundamental tie (blood, or kinship, solidarity), believed to represent a major unifying force. Of course, this organic bond, in turn, provided the basis for trust. One explanation about the correlation between ethnicity and group solidarity was offered by Rafael: "The fact that I knew that what I liked was at another person's house—they would talk to me about things like, 'We're going to listen to Salsa music, we're going to have *arroz con candules* [rice and potpies] and some other stuff—I would get more attracted to that than to other things. That brought us more together. And that's how things are with other people from other nationalities. Polish people—have you been over where they have all the stores not far from here? Well, they have their own neighborhood and groups, you know, like they do their own thing together. So, we do our thing together, too, as one people. We have our hood, our own Latin stores and the business we do in our gang works because we are the same people. We trust each other because we understand what we are all about.''

     * * *

It is clear that the collectivist, communitarian underpinning of the gang was also buttressed by a base of local consumers. Their willingness to become faithful customers, to continuously purchase available goods—drugs and stolen merchandise—is viewed by those in the gang as an indication of a sort of surrogate membership in the gang. Additionally, customers protect gang members working as street-level dealers by agreeing to withhold information when interrogated by police officers and other law enforcement agents. These customers become, in the opinion of one youngster, "one of us." Flaco elaborated on this point: "People from the neighborhood know that they can get smoke, caine, and other things from us. It's risky going to other places. They don't know what those other people be about. So they protect us because they feel secure with us. And we are safe with them. So, we think of them as part of the business."

These various sources of collective behavior are thought to have played a leading role in cementing the Diamond's business structure. The significance of collectivism for gang members can also be gleaned from their views about the idea of individualism. These youngsters do not agree with the view that the exercise of individual effort in pursuit of economic and social mobility applies to them. To them individualism means placing oneself in a precarious position: How can they survive without one another? They are fully aware that they do not possess the traditional resources, such as money and high levels of formal education, used by members of the middle class to negotiate and advance their individual life chances.

To them individual behavior leads to obliteration. Tony makes the claim that "by ourselves we are nobody." He says, "We can be had without no problem. I'm always with my partners because when you're by yourself you are easy prey. You are going to fall the bottom of the barrel because, well, who's going to be there for you? So, if people come to you as a bunch, then we need to create our bunch." Other of Tony's remarks are just as straightforward: "This is not a game that you can win by yourself. If you want to win, you do it as a team. We call ourselves a family, but, you know, when you really think about it we're also a team. And, if you want to lose, play alone. Most of our guys who fall, they fall because they sometimes do things without thinking. Sometimes just do stupid things. Myself, I have gotten busted by the police several times because I was alone. I couldn't see them coming. When you're with your boys you have more eyes to check out what's going on—you can see the cops; you can see the opposition. But when you are by yourself sometimes you feel scared, and you know there is so much you see and so much you can do. In the Diamonds we teach the young guys; we practice how to be together all the time. We think that that's our strength. Other people have money. We have each other."

One other major reason for rejecting the individualist stance is that these young people recognize that success in U.S. society, which is structured around the concept of individualism, has one major interpretative implication: As success honors those who have achieved it, failure (and economic failure in particular) stigmatizes those who suffer it. The system, thus, makes those who have "failed" the objects of criticism and scorn. It can also imply that one's inadequacies in the social system are based upon innate deficiency; failure thus evokes pity and concern. The emphasis on the individual in gauging success and failure in U.S. society is unacceptable as far as these young men are concerned. For this reason they see collectivism as a way of giving gang members a special sense of purpose—the driving force with which to pursue economic and social success.

* * *

NOTES AND QUESTIONS

1. **Illinois Controlled Substance Act.** The Illinois Controlled Substance Act, 720 ILL. COMP. STAT. 570/510 et seq. (2002 & Supp. 2003), was intended to effectively remove certain substances from the marketplace. Does this Act fall under one of Milton Freidman's four duties of government? (*See* chapter 3.) In what ways do the Diamonds's business enterprise respond to the market failure created by the act? Does criminalizing a substance or activity simply invite a market response such as the one seen here? Is this act, by strengthening the criminal penalties for its violation, attempting to restructure the market by increasing the risk premium of dealing in those goods it makes illicit? Can it effectively do so?

2. **Gang as government.** In what way do the Diamonds function as a micro-level government for those in their hood? Again, review Freidman's discussion on the duties of government in chapter 3. Does the system of drug trade among gang members function as a system of taxation? How does the Diamonds's business enterprise redistribute wealth? Is the micro-government a more efficient method of wealth redistribution than taxing the drug trade and redistributing wealth through the centralized governments of the United States?

3. **Criminal law approach to the gang problem.** Liza Vertinsky argues that, because American criminal law is essentially "transaction-based," where the wrongdoer is punished only for the harm attributable to his own, individual conduct, it is ineffective at controlling organized criminal activities. LIZA VERTINSKY, A LAW AND ECONOMICS APPROACH TO CRIMINAL GANGS 2 (1999). Where multiple actors are involved, proof of the act (*actus reus*) and intent (*mens rea*) are more difficult to establish for the specific

individual charged. Furthermore, the organizations will likely have their own systems in place to diffuse responsibility for group activity among many, if not all, of their members, as well as incentive systems that offset the deterrent effect of governmental enforcement policies. *See id.* at 178–80. Vertinsky argues instead for a more "enterprise-based," law and economics approach, focusing on how the group as a whole functions as an economic system. *Id.* at 2–5. What might the policies following this approach look like? Does tort law provide any suggestions? *See id.* at 67–87. What are the potential problems with implementing more "enterprise-based" enforcement policies that might not be as problematic in tort law? How might Becker's rational choice paradigm (*see* chapter 4) be overly simplistic in the face of gang organization?

4. Gangs and the racism-oppression thesis. The racism-oppression thesis suggests that American race relations and ethnic conflict, as well as both majority and minority perceptions of race and oppression, leads to the formation of highly racially homogenized gangs. *See* George W. Knox, An Introduction to Gangs 75 (1994). How does the homogenization of neighborhoods along racial lines contribute to the formation of gangs? How does the organization of gangs along racial lines lead to "bias crimes"? How does the functioning of gangs as vehicles of ethnic conflict promote racial and economic inequality? *See id.* at 74–96. Furthermore, is legislating to minimize the "patterns of ethnic conflict and competition in America, the social structure and institutionalized patterns or race relations, the accommodation of poor and minority group members to an affluent society, and the individual experiences, patterns of enduring racial conflict, and perceptions of racism and oppression" a better solution than the Illinois Controlled Substance Act? *Id.* at 75. Assuming the racism-oppression thesis is correct, how can wealth redistribution affect the formation of gangs? (*See* Thomas Shapiro's work in chapters 6 and 13.)

5. Cheap labor below minimum wage. A study of the monthly financial records of a drug-selling gang showed that although the average hourly wage for the gang members who were involved in the drug trade reached up to $11, the hourly wage for street-level drug dealers was less than minimum wage. Furthermore, the gang's largest non-wage expenditure was tribute to higher levels of the gang. While the gang leader made between $50,000 to $130,000 annually in income, "foot-soldiers" typically made less than $200 per year. However, the average hourly wage for the gang far exceeded the legitimate market wage available to those foot-soldiers, who could rarely expect to make more than minimum wage. For a foot-soldier, then, can participation in the gang be an economically rational decision? Stephen D. Levitt & Sudhir Alladi Venkatesh, *An Economic Analysis of a Drug–Selling Gang's Finances*, National Bureau of Economic Research, Working Paper 6592, 1–19 (1998), available at http://www.nber.org/papers/w 6592.

"Measuring Impact of Crack Cocaine"

"There are three primary reasons why crack may have been so devastating to the Black community. First street gangs, which already controlled outdoor spaces, became the logical sellers of crack. Second, the increased returns associated with drug dealing attracted young Black males to gangs and may have reduced educational investment. Third, a large fraction of crack users were young women." STEVEN D. LEVITT & STEPHEN J. DUBNER, FREAKONOMICS: A ROUGE ECONOMIST EXPLORES THE HIDDEN SIDE OF EVERYTHING (2005) at (8–9).

Note on the Financial Pyramid of a Chicago Gang

Net monthly profit accruing to leader $8,500

Combined wages paid to three officers $2,100

Combined wages paid to foot soldiers $7,400

Total monthly gang wages (excluding leader) $9,500

The total monthly gang wages totals only $1,000 more than the net profits accrued to the leader excluding any side money the leader earns. The combination of danger and low profits suggests that low ranking gang members would reject crack dealing, but the hopes of reaching the top of the pyramid are often too high for them to resist. *Id.*

Carole, *Interview with Barbara, in* SEX WORK: WRITINGS BY WOMEN IN THE SEX INDUSTRY

166–74 (Frédérique Delacoste & Pricilla Alexander eds., 1987).

■ FRÉDÉRIQUE DELACOSTE & PRISCILLA ALEXANDER, EDS.

Barbara is a thirty-nine year old woman. She's worked with prostitutes' rights groups and lives in Richmond, California. I interviewed her in her home, which she shares with her daughter, mother and sister.

Carole: How long have you worked as a prostitute?

Barbara: I've been a prostitute for seventeen or eighteen years.

Carole: Where have you worked?

Barbara: Basically California. I've also worked in Alaska, Washington, Hawaii, and Nevada. I've worked on the streets and in the casinos in Nevada. But I don't work the streets anymore. What I do now is really not prostitution, it's domination. I still charge for it and still like doing it. If I could work on the streets I would, but the police make it too dangerous. They arrest you a lot so that you have to spend all your earnings to get out of jail. And then, they make you work in dark corners; you can't work out in the open for any amount of time. They come along and say, "Move on, move on." Basically, that's why I don't work the streets anymore. I'm older, too, but I think if the police didn't bother me and if it was legal, I'd be working the streets still. It's much easier and you don't have to play the boyfriend-girlfriend routine, you know, and it's quicker! (*She laughs.*) If you get a guy off the streets, it usually lasts about twenty minutes. The whole date, from there to the apartment and back.

Carole: What are your experiences with police arrests? Are tricks ever arrested?

Barbara: They never arrest johns. One time, I can remember in particular when they arrested me and four other women in San Francisco. There were five guys there and instead of arresting them, they made them testify in the trial against us.

Carole: Is that typical?

Barbara: That's typical, yes. If they catch you with the guy, no matter what the guy says, they won't arrest him. One time I can remember I was arrested and I was with a guy when the police pulled up behind us. I told him, "Look, don't say nothing, you know, just tell them, hey, I'm talking to you because as long as you don't say anything, I won't." Well, he freaked out and told the police, "Yeah, she solicited me for X amount of money," and they let him go. They wanted him to testify against me, but he didn't. The guy was into domination. At that time I didn't know what domination was, but he wanted me to whip him and beat him, and he wanted me to put him under a table and just do my commands, do whatever I told him to do. I thought he was crazy, but I also didn't know it was domination. (*She laughs.*) I knew he wasn't going to the court, because if he'd come to trial, I would have told everything. They finally dismissed the case, but I had to go to court at least five times.

And the case was not a case. I mean, the guy had actively solicited me. But I had to pay the cost. I had to bail out of jail and make five court appearances.

Carole: How many times have you been arrested?

Barbara: To be honest, I don't know. At least thirty, probably closer to fifty.

Carole: What kind of violent experiences have taken place in your work?

Barbara: Well, I don't know if this is violent or not. To me, it was. It was the first time I was arrested in San Francisco. I was with a girl. I didn't know her. She had two guys with her. She said they wanted to date her, so we walked around to the place that we were supposed to date at, and we find out that the guys were policemen. So the police said, "You're under arrest," and he said, "Bitch, if you make a move, I'll knock you down in the streets right now. Do you hear me?" I said, "I'm not going to do anything," and he said, "Did you hear me bitch?" You know, he screamed and hollered at me.

Carole: This was in San Francisco?

Barbara: Yes, the San Francisco police.

Carole: Have you been raped while working?

Barbara: Yes. The first year. I was working in Oakland. This guy pulled up to me. He was a young black guy, and he told me that he had a friend who had fifty dollars, but who was too ashamed to come in the area. He said he would take me to the guy. At the time, I didn't know any better and I was loaded on reds, so I went with him. He was supposed to take me to this hotel, but he pulled up in this remote area. And when he pulled off, he grabbed my purse and told me, "Bitch, give me all your money." I told him I wasn't going to give him anything. Okay, since then I've learned that you don't fight back. But I fought back that night. He wound up taking my purse and my coat. I wore wigs then, and he took my wig. He took everything. That was the only time something like that really happened ... and I don't blame the guy. I blame myself for it because I was loaded on reds, because I should have known better in the first place, and, believe me, after that I have. That's about the most violent thing that has happened to me.

Carole: So, he didn't rape you?

Barbara: Well, yes, he did. He raped me. But the rape part was nothing. I mean, the devastating part to me was him taking everything I had. He did rape me ... the rape was nothing. You know, he screwed for about twenty minutes, not even that long, maybe about fifteen. That part doesn't really stick with me because that wasn't the devastating part. Everything after that was.

Carole: When that happened, you didn't want to go to the police?

Barbara: I didn't even think about going to the police at all, you know. At that time I was so young. I was twenty-one. I had just started working. I thought because I was a prostitute, how dare I go to the police. . . .

Carole: Was it because you didn't want them to know you were a prostitute?

Barbara: Well, yes. But at that time I didn't think I had any rights. And, I was loaded, too. I figured I'd be in just as much trouble as this guy would be.

Carole: Were you ever raped again while working?

Barbara: I've had them try. It's just that that's the only time anyone's succeeded. I had this guy one time. I was in Emeryville. He pulled up to me and told me he wanted to date me.

I got in his car and we drove like we were going to my apartment. All of a sudden, he pulled over and said, "I don't have any money and you're going to f___ me right now." I said, "In the front seat?" He had a small knife, it was real small, like a pen knife, and he said, "Get in the back seat." So I got in the back seat. And I said, "Look, whatever you want to do, just do it. I won't fight at all, there won't be any trouble." He started dating me and I kept on being so nice. I'd say, "Oh, and you have to put on a rubber." (*She laughs.*) I was just real sweet. He couldn't stand it. He started dating me, he started screwing me and he pushed me out of the car. I think he really wanted me to fight and jump with him. And I wasn't violent at all—"Okay, you want some, fine I understand, just don't mess up my dress, don't mess up my hair." (*She laughs.*) He didn't want anything to do with me because I wouldn't fight him.

One time I was in Alaska. This guy pulled up and when he pulled up I knew that it wasn't someone I should go with, but it was cold. We were in Anchorage, and in Anchorage you have to work on the streets. They won't let you work in any of the hotels or bars. They harass you some on the streets, but you can still work. It was freezing that night and this guy pulled up and he looked wrong, but I went with him anyway. So I'm on my way to the apartment and two blocks before we get there he grabs me. Well, I had some hair spray, those little aqua-net hair sprays, they make good mace. I took it and sprayed it in his face and it sort of blinded him. Then I just got out of the car.

* * *

Carole: Have police officers tried to get sexual favors from you?

Barbara: Several times. But not as bad as the other girls. Once two other girls and I were sharing an apartment and the landlord decided to call the police and tell them were working out of it. He flagged down this police. Well, I knew the guy flagged down and he was really good. One time, he'd seen me turning a car date, doing a blow job in a car, and he didn't do anything on that occasion. And there were a couple of other times, too. Then after about four times, he told me that I owed him a date. He told me if didn't want to go to jail, I should give him something. I said, "Well, I can't do that, I'm a prostitute, and if I do that you're gonna pay me." He wound up giving me a dollar and seventy cents. I didn't mind because I would much rather have dated him for a dollar and seventy cents then go to jail.

I've heard that happening many times. With vice officers, too. Most of the times I hear about it they're trying to scare the girls into something, you know. It's like, if you date me then I'll keep all the rest of the policemen away from you, or I'll tell you who all the police are.

Carole: Do you think it's better for the prostitutes not to give them anything?

Barbara: For me it was always better if I didn't date them. It's like dating a bartender. If you're in a place and he wants you then he'll keep letting you be there until he gets you. Then after he gets you, he won't want to see you anymore. And so that's what I did with the bartender and cops, too. I'd tease them and play like I was going to—"I can't do it right now, you remind me of a trick; you're too nice a guy." But I've dated a lot of police. Lots of them. I didn't know until afterwards.

Carole: It was during their off-hours?

Barbara: I don't know if it was or not. They said they weren't working, but they showed their badges and stuff afterwards. One cop said he wanted his money back. I said, "Bull." I wasn't afraid of him. I knew that if he told people he'd get in more trouble than I would.

Carole: I've also heard a lot more black prostitutes are arrested than white prostitutes, and that black prostitutes are kept in jail longer. Is that true?

Barbara: That's true. I can barely remember any white girls who were in jail with me in Oakland. The black girl has a much harder time on everything. She'll get kicked out of a hotel much faster than a white girl. A white girl, if she's got any kind of class about her, can work anywhere. Whereas if you're black, if you do anything wrong at all, like getting up to go to a guy in a bar when he calls you over instead of making him come over to you, they can kick you. If you're black, they kick you out faster. In Las Vegas, they arrested a lot of white prostitutes, but at first there *were* only white prostitutes.

Carole: A San Francisco study by Mimi Silbert, PhD, of the Delancey Street Foundation, of two hundred street prostitutes revealed that two-thirds had been raped or forced to do things they didn't want to do. What do you think of those numbers?

Barbara: It sounds too high, and I've known quite a few prostitutes. See, people want to downgrade prostitutes and they think that guys can just take advantage of them. But most of the time the prostitutes set the rules. Johns go where we want them to go. We run everything. They pay you first, they come to your place, they wash, they must use a rubber. People think that the tricks call out the rules but I don't know what girls they talked to. Now junkies work totally differently from prostitutes who are not junkies. And they get hurt more.

Carole: Barbara, why did you first get into prostitution?

Barbara: I did it for the money. That was the only reason I got into it. I couldn't find a job that paid more than minimum wage, whatever it was at the time, two dollars and thirty-five cents. I had two children. I had no way of supporting them besides being on welfare. I was always working two jobs but with the one or two jobs I could still barely pay rent.

Carole: At this point, how difficult would it be for you to leave prostitution if you want to?

Barbara: It would be hard. I'm not into prostitution right now. I'm into domination. But if I wanted to leave both of them alone it would be very difficult because my mother stays here with me, and my sister and my daughter. My sister and my daughter have jobs that don't pay much and my mother is on social security, so I'm the breadwinner, have to pay the rent, help take care of them. And I have to care of myself, too.

Carole: What kinds of things would you change about prostitution if you could?

Barbara: First, I'd make it legal. Lots of prostitutes feel they're guilty when they're arrested and that they don't have any rights. I'd like prostitutes to train prostitutes to change that so they don't think that they have to have pimps. If a woman wants a pimp, that's her business, she should be allowed one. But if she doesn't want one, I don't think that she should have one. I'd make it so that prostitutes had a place where they could work. If they wanted to work the streets I'd make it so that they could. I'd make it so the police would do other things besides bother prostitutes. So many times I was harassed by policemen and they'd say: "It's much easier coming here and talking with you because you're not going to do anything to me."

I was in Amsterdam last year. We had a Forum. A lot of the girls were telling me how bad it was even though they have places to work out of. At first, you know, I went along with them and said, "Yeah, I understand," but then I went down to the red light district, and if I had had a red light district when I was a prostitute, I would have loved it. They have little store fronts, and they sit in the window. Some girls wear hardly anything, some are dressed regular. The guy comes up and if he wants you, he knocks on the door. You've got your bodyguard in there in case anybody wants to go off or anybody's drunk or whatever. Now, I don't think we'd have to be limited that way. The women in Amsterdam complained that this was the only place they could work. I think that women should be able to work where they want to. They also complained that if they got a regular job in addition to the prostitution, they had to tell people that they were prostitutes. I think that's totally wrong. I don't think that I should be stigmatized if I want to sell my body.

Carole: So, that was their main complaint, that they had to stay in one area?

Barbara: Yeah. And that the landlords charged them an arm and a quarter. That if they wanted to get out of it, or just take a part-time job, they had to say they were prostitutes. Still, if we had that much! Some of the women who were with us said, "Yeah, but that's horrible—they're standing there like cows and they're taking them out like cattle." Well, fine, but I'd much rather have guys come to me than go to them. (*She laughs.*) And most prostitutes would.

* * *

Carole: Why do you think that prostitution is kept illegal in the United States?

Barbara: Because they're stupid and lazy. The politicians don't want to figure out a way to get the money, they're afraid that prostitutes will cheat and they won't get enough tax money. And men don't want women to have control over anything. Men want to run everything. Especially white middle class businessmen. They can get away with anything and they know they can.

Carole: What other things would you do, if prostitution was decriminalized?

Barbara: Well, a lot of violence would not happen if it wasn't a crime. Men take advantage of women, true enough, but if the girls were more organized and knew more, then they wouldn't let the guys take advantage of them. Beatings and robbings might not be if women would just stick together. There are so many things I could tell prostitutes so that they'd be protected but if I did that now, I'd be committing a felony because I'd be training a prostitute. It's also conspiracy to tell a girl that someone is a policeman. There are so many laws they can use on you. It's completely sickening to me. Just sitting on this bed could probably be illegal. (*Laughter*)

* * *

Carole: If you could have other work options that paid better than the minimum wage, might you leave prostitution?

Barbara: Prostitution is something I'd like to do on my own terms when I felt like doing it. What I mean is that I wouldn't want to do it all the time. I'd go out maybe twice a week instead of five, six times. I think I'd continue because I like the power I have with men. I like making them do whatever I want them to do. But it gets stressful too. You have to be on your toes. But there's so much money in it. And there's a power thing in making them pay for it and in deciding whether or not I'm going to date them. If I want to be nice to you, that's my choice, and if I want to be a straight up bitch, I can do that too. That's my choice.

Phyllis Luman Metal, *One for Ripley's, in* SEX WORKS: WRITINGS BY WOMEN IN THE SEX INDUSTRY

119–21 (Frédérique Delacoste & Priscilla Alexander eds., 1987).

■ PHYLLIS LUMAN METAL

Well, my dear, I must admit your story seems somewhat unusual ... quite unusual as a matter of fact. I would never imagine a woman would begin being a prostitute at the age of fifty-five. I think that's one for Ripley's, if you don't mind me saying so. I guess I thought of prostitution as something unfortunate young girls got talked into by unscrupulous men. That was my impression. But to get into it at that age and of your own free will, although it does seem there was some financial pressure.... Still, there must have been something else you could have done. Tell me, what did you feel about it? Were you overwhelmed by guilt?

No, I was not. It was a hell of a lot better than marriage. And I tried that five times.

Well, I just don't understand. You seem quite normal. You are an attractive woman, of good family, well brought up. The men you married must have been monsters. But five of them? Something just does not fit.

Well . . . I found it very liberating to be a prostitute, and the men must have found it liberating too, for they were much better lovers than my husbands. They seemed to feel free with me and I with them. Why are you so upset? You don't think sex is wrong do you?

Well, no, I don't think sex is wrong between two consenting adults.

You don't think it's wrong to earn a living, for a woman to earn a living that is?

Why no my dear, of course not. Women have jobs now, all sorts of jobs, married or unmarried.

Well then, why is it wrong to get paid for sex? You must be getting upset about putting the two together.

It would be like selling your organs. Some part of your body.

Well, what about selling blood? That doesn't seem to bother you.

Well, that is to save lives.

True, but you would be amazed at how desperate some of the men are to have sex in the way they need to have sex, and how uptight they are about telling their wives about what they need. And then there are always the guys who are between relationships, or can't seem to get anything going.

Well, my dear, the whole subject is quite confusing. Why don't we just go to a hotel and have some relaxation.

Are you willing to pay me?

Well now, we are good friends. You wouldn't charge me would you?

Do you treat your patients who are your friends for nothing? My body is my source of livelihood. I have upkeep to be available and appealing.

I just wouldn't feel right about paying you. It would spoil it for me. I think you should give it to me.

Sorry. We can be good friends, but forget the sex then. When I first charged for it, I hade much more self respect and self worth than I ever had before. I felt appreciated. When I was a wife I was expected to do a lot of shit work and service my husbands and their desire, not mine. I felt used and abused. No trick ever broke my ribs like my husband did. No trick ever took all my money and left me when it was all gone—another husband did that. No trick ever urged me to neglect my children to accommodate him. No trick ever threw a bunch of in-laws who made my life miserable at me. No trick ever came home drunk every night like one of my husbands did. And I always had money, which I did not when I was married. And I never got a venereal disease. And something else. I got to know people of all nationalities in a way I never could have otherwise. My customers in Paris were from all nations. They were Swiss, British, German, Norwegian, Italian, Spanish, French, Syrian, Berber, Algerian, Senegalese, Saudi, Iranian, Japanese. I felt like a citizen of the world. Prostitution made me feel that all of us on the planet were one family.

Well, my dear it is all very interesting. But I am sure you are an anomaly. I can't believe this is how it usually goes. There is something wrong about it. What would happen to the family if it were legal?

I think it is much more prevalent and accepted in Catholic countries where the family is much stronger than here.

Well, my dear, let's have a drink and talk about something else. There are so many aspects to you. You have such a varied life. This surely isn't that important to you. Why don't you just forget about it? I think you just like to take up controversial issues for causes. You just like the role of being a social reformer. What in the world do you have in common with all those girls who stand on corners? They can't do anything else. Don't tell me you are a feminist.

NOTES AND QUESTIONS

1. Sex work in the economically just society. How does economic inequality contribute to prostitution? Do the overt practices of exchanging dowries and arranging marriages for economic gain in some societies, and the less overt determinations of who pays for dates, weddings, and engagement rings reinforce economic inequality and contribute to prostitution? *See* Priscilla Alexander, *Prostitution: Still a Difficult Issue for Feminists, in* SEX WORK, *supra* at 190–92. How do the dangers of prostitution, including violence and sexually transmitted diseases, reduce the economic viability of women in the workforce and perpetuate economic inequality? Is prostitution a way for those who lack the social skills, attractiveness, or life situation that might prohibit them from competing in the non-monetized sex market of dating, marriage, and one-night stands to gain access to the type of sexual interaction they desire? *See* HELEN REYNOLDS, THE ECONOMICS OF PROSTITUTION 189–90 (1986).

Liz Highleyman, also known as Mistress Veronika Frost, suggests that "[f]rom an anticapitalist perspective, sex work is perhaps the ultimate expression of worker ownership of the means of production, as expressed in the slogan 'my body is my business,' as a person's body is the one asset that cannot be taken away from them." Liz Highleyman, *Professional Dominance: Power, Money, and Identity, in* WHORES AND OTHER FEMINISTS 148 (Jill Nagle ed., 1997). She further suggests that, although it is true that some sex workers are badly exploited and hate their work, "body labor" in the form of sex work should not be taken away from those that lack the educational and infrastructural resources necessary for "mind labor" until alternatives are available. *Id.* at 149. If alternative job choices pay less, is paying a prostitute for sex not the most efficient use of her human resources? *See* REYNOLDS, *supra* at 190. Are prohibitions on the sex industry an exercise in capitalistic dominance? In an economically just society, would the sex industry still exist? *See* Highleyman, *supra* at 148–49.

2. Gender and "exploitation." Female prostitutes are traditionally regarded as victimized, degrading to all women, and in need of rescue from their circumstances. Is there anything *inherently* exploitative about adults engaging in consensual sex for money, or is it only after the actors in a sex-for-money exchange are gendered as female and male that the practice becomes seemingly exploitative? In a gay sex-for-money exchange, "[w]hose erect penis represents the 'weaker sex'?" *See* Julian Marlowe, *It's Different for Boys, in* WHORES AND OTHER FEMINISTS, *supra* at 141–44.

3. Prostitution and civil rights. Are prostitutes being systematically deprived of their civil rights? Does prostitution violate the Thirteenth Amendment's prohibition on slavery? *See* Catherine A. Mackinnon, *Prostitution and Civil Rights, in* APPLICATIONS OF FEMINIST LEGAL THEORY TO WOMEN'S LIVES 226–227 (D. Kelley Weisberg ed., 1996). Frequently, female prostitutes are arrested while the soliciting customers, usually men, are let go with a citation or a warning. *Id.* at 224. Does this violate the Equal Protection Clause of the Fourteenth Amendment? *See* People v. Superior Court of Alameda County, 562 P.2d 1315 (Cal. 1977). What about the fact that police usually send men out to solicit prostitutes, resulting in a higher percentage of women arrested than men? Mackinnon, *supra* at 224.

4. Sex work and stigma. How does the fear of being stigmatized as a "whore" interact with the economics of sex work? Does it discourage participation in the sex trade, or merely "provoke and permit violence against prostitute, and ensure poor working conditions and the inability of many sex workers to move on to other kinds of work without lying about their experience?" Alexander, *supra* at 185.

CHAPTER 13

ECONOMIC BORDERS TO COMMUNITY

Introduction

Beyond the calling of race or nation or creed is this vocation of sonship and brotherhood. Because I believe that the Father is deeply concerned, especially for His suffering and helpless and outcast children, I come tonight to speak for them. This I believe to be the privilege and the burden of all of us who deem ourselves bound by allegiances and loyalties which are broader and deeper than nationalism and which go beyond our nation's self-defined goals and positions. We are called to speak for the weak, for the voiceless, for the victims of our nation, for those it calls "enemy," for no document from human hands can make these humans any less our brothers.

Dr. Martin Luther King, Jr., Beyond Vietnam: A Time to Break Silence, Address delivered to the Clergy and Laymen Concerned about Vietnam, at Riverside Church, 4 April 1967, New York City

At the height of the Vietnam War, Dr. Martin Luther King, Jr. declared his vision of moral citizenship beyond the borders of the nation state. For Dr. King, the defined targets of national hatred became the objects of his compassion and religious commitment. In the years since this stirring oration was delivered into the conflicting passions of the Vietnam era, Dr. King's words have come to stand for something more that compassion toward enemies during wartime. His vision of shared humanity beyond citizenship, like his vision of economic distribution beyond markets, has served as a reminder, even in the academy, of the larger verities at stake in defining who may share in the bounty of this prosperous nation.

In this chapter, we look at several views of the meaning and function of national borders. The Supreme Court defines the constitutional framework for exercising the powers of excluding noncitizens. The Plenary Powers doctrine which grants Congress virtually unlimited power, not explicitly enumerated in the Constitution, is a centerpiece of our legal rules and procedures for deciding who may enter, and once inside the nation, who may stay. This chapter is not designed to teach the law of immigration, a fascinating subject itself. Our purpose in what follows is to identify some of the cultural and identity related variables at work in our national definition of ourselves as citizens, and the sentiments that shape our shifting attitudes toward aliens. This chapter is intended to suggest the economic dimensions of immigration control of noncitizens and the class based exclusions that obtain in erecting borders that separate citizens from each other within the nation.

In a much debated essay, University of Chicago philosopher Martha Nussbaum joins the tradition of Dr. King's Vietnam speech by calling for an ideal of "allegiance to the worldwide community of human beings." Drawing on her work in international development ethics, she argues that even in the aftermath of the tragedy of the September 11 World Trade Center attack:

> We find ourselves feeling sympathy for many people who did not even cross our minds before, New York firefighters, that gay rugby player who helped bring down the fourth plane, . . . [w]e even sometimes notice with a new attention the lives of Arab–Americans among us. . . . Sometimes our compassion even crosses that biggest line of all, the national boundary. . . . The world has come to a stop—in a way that it never has for Americans, when disaster befalls human beings in other places.

Martha Nussbaum, *Introduction: Cosmopolitan Emotions?, in* FOR LOVE OF COUNTRY? ix–x (Joshua Cohen ed., Beacon Press 2002) (1996).

In America, the most politically sensitive immigration issue concerns the conflicting policies and attitudes towards Mexican immigration over the southern border. This decades-long snarl of economic and human rights policy invites our attention to questions of the American role in stimulating immigration, the role that culture and household decision making in Mexico plays in sending male heads of household to work temporarily in America to support families back home in Mexico.

Finally, in keeping with our project of close examination of hidden cultural arrangements that increase economic inequality we look inward to see the way in which two facts of contemporary life create invisible domestic borders to economic inequality. First, we ask whether residential segregation sets up domestic economic borders to communities that are just as vigorously enforced as the national border is enforced against noncitizens. Second, we take a look at the escalating use of prisons to fence out a burgeoning population of men and women of color who experience the civil death of felony convictions.

A. THE BASICS: CITIZENSHIP

Patriotism and Cosmopolitanism

FOR LOVE OF COUNTRY? 3–17 (Joshua Cohen ed., Beacon Press 2002) (1996).

■ MARTHA NUSSBAUM

> When anyone asked him where he came from, he said, "I am a citizen of the world."
>
> Diogenes Laertius, *Life of Diogenes the Cynic*

In Rabindranath Tagore's novel, *The Home and the World*, the young wife Bimala, entranced by the patriotic rhetoric of her husband's friend Sandip, becomes an eager devotee of the *Swadeshi* movement, which has organized a boycott of foreign goods. The slogan of the movement is *Bande Mataram*, "Hail Motherland." Bimala complains that her husband, the cosmopolitan Hindu landlord Nikhil, is cool in his devotion to the cause:

> And yet it was not that my husband refused to support *Swadeshi*, or was in any way against the Cause. Only he had not been able whole-heartedly to accept the spirit of *Bande Mataram*.
>
> "I am willing," he said, to serve my country; but my worship I reserve for Right which is far greater than my country. To worship my country as a god is to bring a curse upon it.'

Americans have frequently supported the principle of *Bande Mataram*, giving the fact of being American a special salience in moral and political deliberation, and pride in a specifically American identity and a specifically American citizenship a special power among the motivations to political action. I believe, with Tagore and his character Nikhil, that this emphasis on patriotic pride is both morally dangerous and, ultimately, subversive of some of the worthy goals patriotism sets out to serve—for example, the goal of national unity in devotion to worthy moral ideals of justice and equality. These goals, I shall argue, would be better served by an ideal that is in any case more adequate to our situation in the contemporary world, namely the very old ideal of the cosmopolitan, the person whose primary allegiance is to the community of human beings in the entire world.

My articulation of these issues is motivated, in part, by my experience working on international quality-of-life issues in an institute for development economics connected with the United Nations. It is motivated, as well, by the renewal of appeals to the nation, and national pride, in some recent discussions of American character and American education. In a by now well-known op-ed piece in *The New York Times* (13 February 1994), philosopher Richard Rorty urges Americans, especially the American left, not to disdain patriotism as a value, and indeed to give central importance to "the emotion of national pride" and "a sense of shared national identity." Rorty argues that we cannot even criticize ourselves well unless we also "rejoice" in our American identity and define ourselves fundamentally in terms of that identity. Rorty seems to hold that the primary alternative to a politics based on patriotism and national identity is what he calls a "politics of difference," one based on internal divisions among America's ethnic, racial, religious, and other sub-groups. He nowhere considers the possibility of a more international basis for political emotion and concern.

This is no isolated case. Rorty's piece responds to and defends Sheldon Hackney's recent call for a "national conversation" to discuss American identity. As a participant in an early phase of that project, I was made vividly aware that the project, as initially conceived, proposed an inward-looking task, bounded by the borders of the nation, rather than considering ties of obligation and commitment that join America to the rest of the world. As with Rorty's piece, the primary contrast drawn in the project was between a politics based on ethnic and racial and religious difference and a politics based on a shared national identity. What we share as both rational and mutually dependent human beings was simply not on the agenda.

One might wonder, however, how far the politics of nationalism really is from the "politics of difference." *The Home and the World* (better known, perhaps, in Satyajit Ray's haunting film of the same title) is a tragic story of the defeat of a reasonable and principled cosmopolitanism by the forces of nationalism and ethnocentrism. I believe that Tagore sees deeply when he sees that at bottom nationalism and ethnocentric particularism are not alien to one another, but akin—that to give support to nationalist sentiments subverts, ultimately, even the values that hold a nation together, because it substitutes a colorful idol for the substantive universal values of justice and right. Once one has said, "I am an Indian first, a citizen of the world second," once one has made that morally questionable move of self-definition by a morally irrelevant characteristic, then what, indeed, will stop one from saying, as Tagore's characters so quickly learn to say, "I am a Hindu first, and an Indian second," "I am an upper-caste landlord first, and a Hindu second." Only the cosmopolitan stance of the landlord Nikhil—so boringly flat in the eyes of his young wife Bimala and his passionate nationalist friend Sandip—has the promise of transcending these divisions, because only this stance asks us to give our first allegiance to what is morally good—and that which, being good, I can commend as such to all human beings. Or so I shall argue.

Proponents of nationalism in politics and in education frequently make a thin concession to cosmopolitanism. They may argue, for example, that although nations should in general base education and political deliberation on shared national values, a commitment to basic human rights should be part of any national educational system, and that this commitment will in a sense serve to hold many nations together. This seems to be a fair comment on practical reality; and the emphasis on human rights is certainly necessary for a world in which nations interact all the time on terms, let us hope, of justice and mutual respect.

But is it sufficient? As students here grow up, is it sufficient for them to learn that they are above all citizens of the United States, but that they ought to respect the basic human rights of citizens of India, Bolivia, Nigeria, and Norway? Or should they, as I think—in addition to giving special attention to the history and current situation of their own nation—learn a good deal more than is frequently the case about the rest of the world in which they live, about India and Bolivia and Nigeria and Norway and their histories, problems, and comparative successes? Should they learn only that citizens of India have equal basic human rights, or should they also learn about the problems of hunger and pollution in India, and the implications of these problems for larger problems of global hunger and global ecology? Most important, should they be taught that they are above all citizens of the United States, or should they instead be taught that they are above all citizens of a world of human beings, and that, while they themselves happen to be situated in the United States, they have to share this world of human beings with the citizens of other countries? I shall shortly suggest four arguments for the second conception of education, which I shall call *cosmopolitan education*. But first I introduce a historical digression, which will trace cosmopolitanism to its origins, in the process recovering some excellent arguments that originally motivated it as an educational project.

II

When Diogenes the Cynic replied, "I am a citizen of the world," he meant apparently that he refused to be defined by his local origins and local group memberships, so central to the self-image of a conventional Greek male; instead, he defined himself in terms of more universal aspirations and concerns. The Stoics who followed his lead developed his image of the *kosmou politês* or world citizen more fully, arguing that each of us dwells, in effect, in two communities—the local community of our birth, and the community of human argument and aspiration that "is truly great and truly common, in which we look neither to this corner nor to that, but measure the boundaries of our nation by the sun" (Seneca, *De Otio*). It is this community that is, most fundamentally, the source of our moral obligations. With respect to the most basic moral values such as justice, "we should regard all human beings as our fellow citizens and neighbors" (Plutarch, *On the Fortunes of Alexander*). We should regard our deliberations as, first and foremost, deliberations about human problems of people in particular concrete situations, not problems growing out of a national identity that is altogether unlike that of others. Diogenes knew that the invitation to think as a world citizen was, in a sense, an invitation to be an exile from the comfort of patriotism and its easy sentiments, to see our own ways of life from the point of view of justice and the good. The accident of where one is born is just that, an accident; any human being might have been born in any nation. Recognizing this, his Stoic successors held, we should not allow differences of nationality or class or ethnic membership or even gender to erect barriers between us and our fellow human beings. We should recognize humanity wherever it occurs, and give its fundamental ingredients, reason and moral capacity, our first allegiance and respect.

This clearly did not mean that the Stoics were proposing the abolition of local and national forms of political organization and the creation of a world state. The point was more radical still: that we should give our first allegiance to no mere form of government, no temporal power, but to the moral community made up by the humanity of all human beings. The idea of the world citizen is in this way the ancestor and source of Kant's idea of the "kingdom of ends," and has a similar function in inspiring and regulating moral and political conduct. One should always behave so as to treat with equal respect the dignity of reason and moral choice in every human being. It is this conception, as well, that inspires Tagore's novel, as the cosmopolitan landlord struggles to stem the tide of nationalism and factionalism by appeals to universal moral norms. Many of the speeches of the character Nikhil were drawn from Tagore's own cosmopolitan political writings.

Stoics who hold that good civic education is education for world citizenship recommend this attitude on three grounds. First, they hold that the study of humanity as it is realized in the whole world is valuable for self-knowledge: we see ourselves more clearly when we see our ways in relation to those of other reasonable people.

Second, they argue, as does Tagore, that we will be better able to solve our problems if we face them in this way. No theme is deeper in Stoicism than the damage done by faction and local allegiances to the political life of a group. Political deliberation, they argue, is sabotaged again and again by partisan loyalties, whether to one's team at the Circus or to one's nation. Only by making our fundamental allegiance that to the world community of justice and reason do we avoid these dangers.

Finally, they insist that the stance of the *kosmou politês* is intrinsically valuable. For it recognizes in persons what is especially fundamental about them, most worthy of respect and acknowledgment: their aspirations to justice and goodness and their capacities for reasoning in this connection. This aspect may be less colorful than local or national traditions and identities—and it is on this basis that the young wife in Tagore's novel spurns it in favor of qualities in the nationalist orator Sandip that she later comes to see as superficial; it is, the Stoics argue, both lasting and deep.

The Stoics stress that to be a citizen of the world one does not need to give up local identifications, which can frequently be a source of great richness in life. They suggest that we think of ourselves not as devoid of local affiliations, but as surrounded by a series of concentric circles. The first one is drawn around the self; the next takes in one's immediate family; then follows the extended family; then, in order, one's neighbors or local group, one's fellow city-dwellers, one's fellow countrymen—and we can easily add to this list groupings based on ethnic, linguistic, historical, professional, gender and sexual identities. Outside all these circles is the largest one, that of humanity as a whole. Our task as citizens of the world will be to "draw the circles somehow toward the center" (Stoic philosopher Hierocles, 1st–2nd CE), making all human beings more like our fellow city dwellers, and so on. In other words, we need not give up our special affections and identifications, whether ethnic or gender-based or religious. We need not think of them as superficial, and we may think of our identity as in part constituted by them. We may and should devote special attention to them in education. But we should work to make all human beings part of our community of dialogue and concern, base our political deliberations on that interlocking commonality, and give the circle that defines our humanity a special attention and respect.

This means, in educational terms, that the student in the United States, for example, may continue to regard herself as in part defined by her particular loves—for her family, her religious and/or ethnic and/or racial community or communities, even for her country. But she must also, and centrally, learn to recognize humanity wherever she encounters it, undeterred by traits that are strange to her, and be eager to understand humanity in its "strange" guises. She must learn enough about the different to recognize common aims, aspirations, and values, and enough about these common ends to see how variously they are instantiated in the many cultures and many histories. Stoic writers insist that the vivid imagining of the different is an essential task of education; and that requires in turn, of course, a mastery of many facts about the different. Marcus Aurelius gives himself the following advice, which might be called the basis for cosmopolitan education: "Accustom yourself not to be inattentive to what another person says, and as far as possible enter into that person's mind" (VI. 53). "Generally," he concludes, "one must first learn many things before one can judge another's action with understanding."

A favored exercise, in this process of world thinking, is to conceive of the entire world of human beings as a single body, its many people as so many limbs. Referring to the fact that it takes only the change of a single letter in Greek to convert the word "limb" (*melos*) into the word "[detached] part" (*meros*), Marcus concludes: "If, changing the word, you call yourself merely a [detached] part rather than a limb, you do not yet love your fellow men from the heart, nor derive complete joy from doing good; you will do it merely as a duty, not as doing good to yourself" (VII. 13). It is important to recall that, as Emperor, he gives himself this advice in connection with daily duties that require coming to grips with the cultures of remote and initially strange civilizations such as those of Parthia and Sarmatia.

I would like to see education adopt this cosmopolitan Stoic stance. The organic model could of course be abused—if, for example, it were to be taken to deny the fundamental importance of the separateness of persons and of fundamental personal liberties. Stoics were not always sufficiently attentive to these values and to their political salience; in that sense their thought is not always a good basis for a scheme of democratic deliberation and education. But as the image is primarily intended—as a reminder of the interdependence of all human beings and communities—it has fundamental significance. There is clearly a huge amount to be said about how such ideas might be realized in curricula at many levels. Instead of beginning that more concrete task, however, I shall now return to the present day and offer four arguments for making world citizenship, rather than democratic/national citizenship, education's central focus. (The first two are modern versions of my first two Stoic arguments; the third develops one part of my Stoic argument about intrinsic moral value; the fourth is more local, directed at the pro-patriotism arguments I am criticizing.)

III

1. *Through cosmopolitan education, we learn more about ourselves.*

One of the greatest barriers to rational deliberation in politics is the unexamined feeling that one's own current preferences and ways are neutral and natural. An education that takes national boundaries as morally salient too often reinforces this kind of irrationality, by lending to what is an accident of history a false air of moral weight and glory. By looking at ourselves in the lens of the other, we come to see what in our practices is local and non-necessary, what more broadly or deeply shared. Our nation is appallingly ignorant of most of the rest of the world. I think that this means that it is also, in many crucial ways, ignorant of itself.

To give just one example of this—since 1994 is the United Nations' International Year of the Family—if we want to understand our own history and our choices where the structure of the family and of child-rearing are involved, we are immeasurably assisted by looking around the world to see in what configurations families exist, and through what strategies children are in fact being cared for. (This would include a study of the history of the family, both in our own and in other traditions.) Such a study can show us, for example, that the two-parent nuclear family, in which the mother is the primary homemaker and the father the primary breadwinner is by no means a pervasive style of child-rearing in today's world. The extended family, clusters of families, the village, women's associations—all these groups and still others are in various places regard-ed as having major child-rearing responsibilities. Seeing this, we can begin to ask questions—for example, how much child abuse there is in a family that involves grandparents and other relatives in child-rearing, as com-pared with the relatively isolated Western-style nuclear family; how many different structures of child care have been found to support women's work, and how well each of these is functioning. If we do not undertake this kind of educational project, we risk assuming that the options familiar to us are the only ones there are, and that they are somehow "normal" and "natural" for the human species as such. Much the same can be said about conceptions of gender and sexuality, about conceptions of work and its division, about schemes of property holding, about the treatment of child-hood and old age.

2. *We make headway solving problems that require international cooperation.* The air does not obey national boundaries. This simple fact can be, for children, the beginning of the recognition that, like it or not, we live in a world in which the destinies of nations are closely intertwined with respect to basic goods and survival itself. The pollution of third-world nations who are attempting to attain our high standard of living will, in some cases, end up in our air. No matter what account of these matters we will finally adopt, any intelligent deliberation about ecology—as, also, about the food supply and population—requires global planning, global knowl-edge, and the recognition of a shared future.

To conduct this sort of global dialogue, we need not only knowledge of the geography and ecology of other nations—something that would already entail much revision in our curricula—but also a great deal about the people with whom we shall be talking, so that in talking with them we may be capable of respecting their traditions and commitments. Cosmopolitan education would supply the background necessary for this type of deliberation.

3. *We recognize moral obligations to the rest of the world that are real, and that otherwise would go unrecognized.* What are Americans to make of the fact that the high living standard we enjoy is one that very likely cannot be universalized, at least given the present costs of pollution controls and the present economic situation of developing nations, without ecological disaster? If we take Kantian morality at all seriously, as we should, we need to educate our children to be troubled by this fact. Otherwise we are educating a nation of moral hypocrites, who talk the language of universalizability but whose universe has a self-serving, narrow scope.

This point may appear to presuppose universalism, rather than being an argument in its favor. But here one may note that the values on which Americans may most justly pride themselves are, in a deep sense, Stoic values: respect for human dignity and the opportunity for each person to pursue happiness. If we really do believe that all human beings are created equal and endowed with certain inalienable rights, we are morally required to think about what that conception requires us to do with and for the rest of the world.

Once again, that does not mean that one may not permissibly give one's own sphere a special degree of concern. Politics, like child care, will be poorly done if each thinks herself equally responsible for all, rather than giving the immediate surroundings special attention and care. To give one's own sphere special care is justifiable in universalist terms, and I think that this is its most compelling justification. To take one example, we do not really think that our own children are morally more important than other people's children, even though almost all of us who have children would give our own children far more love and care than we give other people's children. It is good for children, on the whole, that things should work out this way, and that is why our special care is good rather than selfish. Education may and should reflect those special concerns—spending more time, for example, within a given nation, on that nation's history and politics. But my argument does entail that we should not confine our thinking to our own sphere—that in making choices in both political and economic matters we should most seriously consider the right of other human beings to life, liberty, and the pursuit of happiness, and work to acquire the knowledge that will enable us to deliberate well about those rights. I believe that this sort of thinking will have large-scale economic and political consequences.

4. *We make a consistent and coherent argument based on distinctions we are really prepared to defend.* Let me now return to the defense of shared values in Richard Rorty's article and Sheldon Hackney's project. In these eloquent appeals to the common there is something that makes me very uneasy. On the one hand Rorty and Hackney seem to argue well when they insist on the centrality to democratic deliberation of certain values

that bind all citizens together. But why should these values, which instruct us to join hands across boundaries of ethnicity and class and gender and race, lose steam when they get to the borders of the nation? By conceding that a morally arbitrary boundary such as the boundary of the nation has a deep and formative role in our deliberations, we seem to be depriving ourselves of any principled way of arguing to citizens that they should in fact join hands across these other barriers.

For one thing, the very same groups exist both outside and inside. Why should we think of people from China as our fellows the minute they dwell in a certain place, namely the United States, but not when they dwell in a certain other place, namely China? What is it about the national boundary that magically converts people toward whom our education is both incurious and indifferent into people to whom we have duties of mutual respect? I think, in short, that we undercut the very case for multicultural respect within a nation by failing to make a broader world respect central to education. Richard Rorty's patriotism may be a way of bringing all Americans together; but patriotism is very close to jingoism, and I'm afraid I don't see in Rorty's argument any proposal for coping with this very obvious danger.

Furthermore, the defense of shared national values in both Rorty and Hackney, as I understand it, requires appealing to certain basic features of human personhood that obviously also transcend national boundaries. So if we fail to educate children to cross those boundaries in their minds and imaginations, we are tacitly giving them the message that we don't really mean what we say. We say that respect should be accorded to humanity as such, but we really mean that Americans as such are worthy of special respect. And that, I think, is a story that Americans have told for far too long.

IV

Becoming a citizen of the world is often a lonely business. It is, in effect, as Diogenes said, a kind of exile—from the comfort of local truths, from the warm nestling feeling of patriotism, from the absorbing drama of pride in oneself and one's own. In the writings of Marcus Aurelius (as in those of his American followers Emerson and Thoreau), one sometimes feels a boundless loneliness, as if the removal of the props of habit and local boundaries had left life bereft of a certain sort of warmth and security. If one begins life as a child who loves and trusts its parents, it is tempting to want to reconstruct citizenship along the same lines, finding in an idealized image of a nation a surrogate parent who will do one's thinking for one. Cosmopolitanism offers no such refuge; it offers only reason and the love of humanity, which may seem at times less colorful than other sources of belonging.

In Tagore's novel, the appeal to world citizenship fails—fails because patriotism is full of color and intensity and passion, whereas cosmopolitanism seems to have a hard time gripping the imagination. And yet in its very failure, Tagore shows, it succeeds. For the novel is a story of education for world citizenship, since the entire tragic story is told by the widowed Bimala, who understands, if too late, that Nikhil's morality was vastly superior to Sandip's empty symbol-mongering, that what looked like passion in Sandip was egocentric self-exaltation, and that what looked like lack of passion in Nikhil contained a truly loving perception of her as a person. If one goes today to Santiniketan, a town several hours by train from Calcutta, the town where Tagore founded his cosmopolitan university Vishvabharati—whose name means "all the world"—one feels the tragedy once more. For all-the-world university has not achieved the anticipated influence or distinction within India, and the ideals of the cosmopolitan community of Santiniketan are increasingly under siege from militant forces of ethnocentric particularism and Hindu-fundamentalist nationalism. And yet, in the very decline of Tagore's ideal—which now threatens the very existence of the secular and tolerant Indian state—the observer sees its worth. To worship one's country as a god is indeed to bring a curse upon it. Recent electoral reactions against Hindu nationalism give some grounds for optimism that this recognition of worth is widespread and may prove efficacious, averting a tragic ending of the sort that Tagore describes.

And since I am in fact optimistic that Tagore's ideal can be successfully realized in schools and universities in democracies around the world, and in the formation of public policy, let me conclude with a story of cosmopolitanism that has a happy ending. It is told by Diogenes Laertius about the courtship and marriage of the Cynic cosmopolitan philosophers Crates and Hipparchia (one of the most eminent female philosophers of antiquity), in order, presumably, to show that casting off the symbols of status and nation can sometimes be a way to succeed in love. The background is that Hipparchia is from a good family, attached, as most Greek families were, to social status and pedigree. They resent the cosmopolitan philosopher Crates, with his strange ideas of world citizenship and his strange disdain for rank and boundaries.

> [Hipparchia] fell in love with Crates' arguments and his way of life and paid no attention to any of her suitors nor to wealth or high birth or good looks. Crates, though, was everything to her. Moreover, she told her parents that she would kill herself if she were not married off to him. So Crates was called on by her parents to talk their daughter out of it; he did all he could, but in the end he didn't persuade her. So he stood up and threw off his clothes in front of her and said, "Here is your bridegroom; these are his possessions; make your decision accordingly—for you cannot be my companion unless you undertake the same way of life." The girl chose him. Adopting the same clothing and style of life she went around with her husband and they copulated in public and they went off together to dinner parties. And once she went to a dinner party at the house of Lysimachus and there refuted Theodorus the Atheist, with a sophism like this: "If it wouldn't be judged wrong for Theodorus to do something, then it wouldn't be judged wrong for Hipparchia to do it either; but Theodorus does no wrong if he beats himself; so Hipparchia too does no wrong if she beats Theodorus." And when Theodorus could not reply to her argument, he ripped off her cloak. But Hipparchia was not upset or distraught as a woman would normally be. (DL 6.96–8)

I am not exactly recommending Crates and Hipparchia as the marital ideal for students in my hypothetical cosmopolitan schools (or Theodorus the Atheist as their logic teacher). But the story does reveal this: that the life of the cosmopolitan, who puts right before country, and universal reason before the symbols of national belonging, need not be boring, flat, or lacking in love.

NOTES AND QUESTIONS

1. Unrealistic idealism? Consider this opposing view to Nussbaum's argument for humanitarianism:

> Many people oppose immigration reform and argue against controlling immigration because they believe in a new world order, in the rise of internationalism, and in the demise of nation-states. While their vision may be commendable and their ideals unquestionable, their sense of reality is limited. The world is divided into nations. It will be divided into nations for as long as we can see into the future. And the United States, one of the last few nations to accept any appreciable number of migrants, is one of the most desirable nations in the world in which to live. It will continue to attract as many legal immigrants as we allow to come here, and as many illegal immigrants as we refuse to deter.
>
> Another group, the humanitarian idealists, argues that the United States can help deal with world poverty through high levels of immigration. They, too, are probably sincere but unrealistic. The United States is a small part of the world—only 5 percent of the population of the earth. We can voluntarily share the world's poverty; we cannot make the world rich by sharing our wealth.

RICHARD D. LAMM & GARY IMHOFF, THE IMMIGRATION TIME BOMB: THE FRAGMENT-ING OF AMERICA 1–26 (1986).

2. Beyond the nation state? Can we ever expect that national boundaries will become meaningless? Or is Nussbaum's rumination a call to philosophical ideals, not implementation in the world of practical politics and geopolitical interests?

Lamm and Imhoff object to this perspective:

> The immigration laws of the United States should be written and enforced in order to protect and preserve the interests of Americans and of this country. The test of immigration policy must be the interests of Americans. It cannot be whether it hastens the demise of nations, or whether it makes the worldwide distribution of wealth more equitable by lowering the wealth of Americans while imperceptibly raising the wealth of a small proportion of others.
>
> The first priority of any country, the first test for a nation, is to have defined, agreed-upon borders over which the movements of

citizens and noncitizens alike are controlled. By that test, the United States today would hardly qualify as a nation. We have not clearly and distinctly set and enforced the conditions under which individuals are entitled to enter this country and become participants in our polity. By failing to do so, we have failed to pay attention to the needs, the desires, and the interests of our own citizens.

Lamm & Imhoff, *supra*.

3. The moral vision of a preacher and a philosopher. Can we afford to ignore the moral compass of our visionaries like Dr. Martin Luther King and Martha Nussbaum? On the other hand, can we afford to apply their vision? What role does moral authority play in the process of shaping national immigration policy? What role should it play?

One commentator offers this perspective on the question:

This brings us to the role philosophers can play in resolving these issues. It is often thought that the philosopher aims to be the conscience of policymakers, advising what they ought, morally speaking, to do, and perhaps explaining how this might figure in the tough, pragmatic world of politics. * * * [This] portrays the philosopher as one with some special moral gift to impart to those who lack it.

But the moral is not an aspect separable in the way this view suggests from the world's practical or other aspects. Ethics is not a species unto itself—the department of altruistic affairs; it is practical reasoning. * * *

Of course, the philosopher is not an expert on all or even most of the issues relevant to enlightened decision-making. But then who is? . . . Values cannot be wholly eliminated, but they should be revealed. They need not be arbitrary. Again philosophers can contribute their expertise, which consists not in a unique moral vision but rather in knowing how and to what extent value judgments can be supported.

Judith Litchenberg, *Mexican Migration and U.S. Policy: A Guide for the Perplexed, in* THE BORDER THAT JOINS 14 (Peter G. Brown & Henry Shue eds., 1983.)

B. THE BASICS: CONGRESSIONAL POWER TO EXCLUDE, DETAIN, OR DEPORT, PLENARY POWER?

Fiallo v. Bell

Supreme Court of the United States, 430 U.S. 787 (1977).

[Three sets of unwed natural fathers and their illegitimate offspring brought action to permanently enjoin enforcement of those sections of the

Immigration and Nationality Act which have the effect of excluding the relationship between an illegitimate child and his natural father, as opposed to his natural mother, from the special preference immigration status accorded a "child" or "parent" of a United States citizen or lawful permanent resident. The three-judge District Court for the Eastern District of New York, Moore, Circuit Judge, rendered judgment for the Government, and plaintiffs appealed.]

■ MR. JUSTICE POWELL delivered the opinion of the Court.

This case brings before us a constitutional challenge to §§ 101(b)(1)(D) and 101(b)(2) of the Immigration and Nationality Act of 1952 [(The Act)].

I

The Act grants special preference immigration status to aliens who qualify as the "children" or "parents" of United States citizens or lawful permanent residents. Under § 101(b)(1), a "child" is defined as an unmarried person under 21 years of age who is a legitimate or legitimated child, a stepchild, an adopted child, or an illegitimate child seeking preference by virtue of his relationship with his natural mother. The definition does not extend to an illegitimate child seeking preference by virtue of his relationship with his natural father. Moreover, under § 101(b)(2), a person qualifies as a "parent" for purposes of the Act solely on the basis of the person's relationship with a "child." As a result, the natural father of an illegitimate child who is either a United States citizen or permanent resident alien is not entitled to preferential treatment as a "parent."

The special preference immigration status provided for those who satisfy the statutory "parent-child" relationship depends on whether the immigrant's relative is a United States citizen or permanent resident alien. A United States citizen is allowed the entry of his "parent" or "child" without regard to *either* an applicable numerical quota *or* the labor certification requirement.* * * On the other hand, a United States permanent resident alien is allowed the entry of the "parent" or "child" subject to numerical limitations but without regard to the labor certification requirement. * * *

Appellants are three sets of unwed natural fathers and their illegitimate offspring who sought, either as an alien father or an alien child, a special immigration preference by virtue of a relationship to a citizen or resident alien child or parent. In each instance the applicant was informed that he was ineligible for an immigrant visa unless he qualified for admission under the general numerical limitations and, in the case of the alien parents, received the requisite labor certification.

* * *

II

At the outset, it is important to underscore the limited scope of judicial inquiry into immigration legislation. This Court has repeatedly emphasized that "over no conceivable subject is the legislative power of Congress more complete than it is over" the admission of aliens. * * * Our cases "have long recognized the power to expel or exclude aliens as a fundamental sovereign attribute exercised by the Government's political departments largely immune from judicial control." * * * Our recent decisions have not departed from this long-established rule. Just last Term, for example, the Court had occasion to note that "the power over aliens is of a political character and therefore subject only to narrow judicial review." *Hampton v. Mow Sun Wong*, 426 U.S. 88, 101 n.21 (1976), citing *Fong Yue Ting v. United States*, 149 U.S. 698, 713 (1893). And we observed recently that in the exercise of its broad power over immigration and naturalization, "Congress regularly makes rules that would be unacceptable if applied to citizens." * * *

Appellants apparently do not challenge the need for special judicial deference to congressional policy choices in the immigration context, but instead suggest that a "unique coalescing of factors" makes the instant case sufficiently unlike prior immigration cases to warrant more searching judicial scrutiny. * * * Appellants first observe that since the statutory provisions were designed to reunite families wherever possible, the purpose of the statute was to afford rights not to aliens but to United States citizens and legal permanent residents. Appellants then rely on our border-search decisions in *Almeida–Sanchez v. United States*, 413 U.S. 266 (1973), and *United States v. Brignoni–Ponce*, 422 U.S. 873 (1975), for the proposition that the courts must scrutinize congressional legislation in the immigration area to protect against violations of the rights of citizens. At issue in the border-search cases, however, was the nature of the protections mandated by the Fourth Amendment with respect to Government procedures designed to stem the illegal entry of aliens. Nothing in the opinions in those cases suggests that Congress has anything but exceptionally broad power to determine which classes of aliens may lawfully enter the country. * * *

Appellants suggest a second distinguishing factor. They argue that none of the prior immigration cases of this Court involved "double-barreled" discrimination based on sex and illegitimacy, infringed upon the due process rights of citizens and legal permanent residents, or implicated "the fundamental constitutional interests of United States citizens and permanent residents in a familial relationship." * * * But this Court has resolved similar challenges to immigration legislation based on other constitutional rights of citizens, and has rejected the suggestion that more searching judicial scrutiny is required. In *Kleindienst v. Mandel*, * * *, for example, United States citizens challenged the power of the Attorney General to deny a visa to an alien who, as a proponent of "the economic, international, and governmental doctrines of World communism", was ineligible to receive a visa * * * absent a waiver by the Attorney General. The citizen-appellees in that case conceded that Congress could prohibit entry of all aliens falling into the class defined by § 1182(a)(28)(D). They contended, however, that the Attorney General's statutory discretion to approve a waiver was limited by the Constitution and that their First Amendment rights were abridged by the denial of Mandel's request for a visa. The Court held that "when the Executive exercises this [delegated] power negatively on the basis of a facially legitimate and bona fide reason, the courts will neither look behind the exercise of that discretion, nor test it by balancing its justification against the First Amendment interests of those who seek personal communication with the applicant." * * * We can see no reason to review the broad congressional policy choice at issue here under a more exacting standard than was applied in *Kleindienst v. Mandel*, a First Amendment case.

Finally, appellants characterize our prior immigration cases as involving foreign policy matters and congressional choices to exclude or expel groups of aliens that were "specifically and clearly perceived to pose a grave threat to the national security," citing *Harisiades v. Shaughnessy*, 342 U.S. 580 (1952), "or to the general welfare of this country," citing *Boutilier v. INS*, 387 U.S. 118 (1967). * * * We find no indication in our prior cases that the scope of judicial review is a function of the nature of the policy choice at issue. To the contrary, "[s]ince decisions in these matters may implicate our relations with foreign powers, and since a wide variety of classifications must be defined in the light of changing political and economic circumstances, such decisions are frequently of a character more appropriate to either the Legislature or the Executive than to the Judiciary," and "[t]he reasons that preclude judicial review of political questions also dictate a narrow standard of review of decisions made by the Congress or the President in the area of immigration and naturalization." * * * As Mr. Justice Frankfurter observed in his concurrence in *Harisiades v. Shaughnessy*:

> "The conditions of entry for every alien, the particular classes of aliens that shall be denied entry altogether, the basis for determining such classification, the right to terminate hospitality to aliens, the grounds on which such determination shall be based, have been recognized as matters solely for the responsibility of the Congress and wholly outside the power of this Court to control." 342 U.S., at 596–597.

* * *

IV

We hold that §§ 101(b)(1)(D) and 101(b)(2) of the Immigration and Nationality Act of 1952 are not unconstitutional by virtue of the exclusion of the relationship between an illegitimate child and his natural father from the preferences accorded by the Act to the "child" or "parent" of a United States citizen or lawful permanent resident.

Affirmed.

■ Mr. Justice Marshall, with whom Mr. Justice Brennan joins, dissenting.

Until today I thought it clear that when Congress grants benefits to some citizens, but not to others, it is our duty to insure that the decision comports with Fifth Amendment principles of due process and equal protection. Today, however, the Court appears to hold that discrimination among citizens, however invidious and irrational, must be tolerated if it occurs in the context of the immigration laws. Since I cannot agree that Congress has license to deny fundamental rights to citizens according to the most disfavored criteria simply because the Immigration and Nationality Act is involved, I dissent.

* * *

This case, unlike most immigration cases that come before the Court, directly involves the rights of citizens, not aliens. "[C]oncerned with the problem of keeping families of United States citizens and immigrants united," Congress extended to American citizens the right to choose to be reunited in the United States with their immediate families. The focus was on citizens and their need for relief from the hardships occasioned by the immigration laws. The right to seek such relief was given only to the citizen, not the alien. * * * If the citizen does not petition the Attorney General for the special "immediate relative" status for his parent or child, the alien, despite his relationship, can receive no preference. * * * It is irrelevant that aliens have no constitutional right to immigrate and that Americans have no constitutional right to compel the admission of their families. The essential fact here is that Congress did choose to extend such privileges to American citizens but then denied them to a small class of citizens. When Congress draws such lines among citizens, the Constitution requires that the decision comport with Fifth Amendment principles of equal protection and due process. The simple fact that the discrimination is set in immigration legislation cannot insulate from scrutiny the invidious abridgment of citizens' fundamental interests.

* * *

Zadvydas v. Davis

Supreme Court of the United States, 533 U.S. 678 (2001).

■ JUSTICE BREYER, delivered the opinion of the Court.

* * *

We note at the outset that the primary federal habeas corpus statute, * * * confers jurisdiction upon the federal courts to hear these cases. * * * Before 1952, the federal courts considered challenges to the lawfulness of immigration-related detention, including challenges to the validity of a deportation order, in habeas proceedings. * * * Beginning in 1952, an alternative method for review of *deportation orders,* namely, actions brought in federal district court under the Administrative Procedure Act (APA), became available. * * * And in 1961 Congress replaced district court APA review with initial *deportation order* review in courts of appeals. * * * The 1961 Act specified that federal habeas courts were also available to hear statutory and constitutional challenges to *deportation* (and exclusion) *orders.* * * * These statutory changes left habeas untouched as the basic method for obtaining review of continued *custody after* a deportation order had become final. * * *

More recently, Congress has enacted several statutory provisions that limit the circumstances in which judicial review of deportation decisions is available. But none applies here. One provision * * * simply forbids courts to construe *that section* "to create any . . . procedural right or benefit that is legally enforceable"; it does not deprive an alien of the right to rely on [the provision] to challenge detention that is without statutory authority.

Another provision * * * says that "no court shall have jurisdiction to review" decisions "specified . . . to be in the discretion of the Attorney General." The aliens here, however, do not seek review of the Attorney General's exercise of discretion; rather, they challenge the extent of the Attorney General's authority under the post-removal-period detention statute. And the extent of that authority is not a matter of discretion * * *.

We conclude that * * * habeas corpus proceedings remain available as a forum for statutory and constitutional challenges to post-removal-period detention statute.* * *

* * *

A statute permitting indefinite detention of an alien would raise a serious constitutional problem. The Fifth Amendment's Due Process Clause forbids the Government to "depriv[e]" any "person . . . of . . . liberty . . . without due process of law." Freedom from imprisonment—from government custody, detention, or other forms of physical restraint—lies at the heart of the liberty that Clause protects. * * * And this Court has said that government detention violates that Clause unless the detention is ordered in a *criminal* proceeding with adequate procedural protections * * * or, in certain special and "narrow" nonpunitive "circumstances," * * * where a special justification, such as harm-threatening mental illness, outweighs the "individual's constitutionally protected interest in avoiding physical restraint." * * *

The proceedings at issue here are civil, not criminal, and we assume that they are nonpunitive in purpose and effect. There is no sufficiently strong special justification here for indefinite civil detention—at least as administered under this statute. The statute, says the Government, has two regulatory goals: "ensuring the appearance of aliens at future immigration proceedings" and "[p]reventing danger to the community." * * * But by definition the first justification—preventing flight—is weak or nonexistent where removal seems a remote possibility at best. As this Court said in *Jackson v. Indiana*, 406 U.S. 715 (1972), where detention's goal is no longer practically attainable, detention no longer "bear[s][a] reasonable relation to the purpose for which the individual [was] committed." *Id.,* at 738.

The second justification—protecting the community—does not necessarily diminish in force over time. But we have upheld preventive detention based on dangerousness only when limited to specially dangerous individuals and subject to strong procedural protections. * * * In cases in which preventive detention is of potentially *indefinite* duration, we have also demanded that the dangerousness rationale be accompanied by some other special circumstance, such as mental illness, that helps to create the danger. * * * The civil confinement here at issue is not limited, but potentially permanent. * * * The provision authorizing detention does not apply narrowly to "a small segment of particularly dangerous individuals," * * * say, suspected terrorists, but broadly to aliens ordered removed for many and various reasons, including tourist visa violations. And, once the flight risk justification evaporates, the only special circumstance present is the alien's removable status itself, which bears no relation to a detainee's dangerousness. * * *

    * * *

The Government also looks for support to cases holding that Congress has "plenary power" to create immigration law, and that the Judicial Branch must defer to Executive and Legislative Branch decisionmaking in that area. * * * But that power is subject to important constitutional limitations. See *INS v. Chadha,* 462 U.S. 919, 941–942 (1983) (Congress must choose "a constitutionally permissible means of implementing" that power); *The Chinese Exclusion Case,* 130 U.S. 581, 604 (1889) (congressional authority limited "by the Constitution itself and considerations of public policy and justice which control, more or less, the conduct of all civilized nations"). In these cases, we focus upon those limitations. In doing so, we nowhere deny the right of Congress to remove aliens, to subject them to supervision with conditions when released from detention, or to incarcerate them where appropriate for violations of those conditions. * * * The question before us is not one of " 'confer[ring] on those admitted the right to remain against the national will' " or " 'sufferance of aliens' " who should be removed. [*Post* (SCALIA, J., dissenting) (emphasis deleted).] Rather, the issue we address is whether aliens that the Government finds itself unable to remove are to be condemned to an indefinite term of imprisonment within the United States.

    * * *

B

Despite this constitutional problem, if "Congress has made its intent" in the statute "clear, 'we must give effect to that intent.' " * * * We cannot find here, however, any clear indication of congressional intent to grant the Attorney General the power to hold indefinitely in confinement an alien ordered removed. And that is so whether protecting the community from dangerous aliens is a primary or (as we believe) secondary statutory purpose. [Cf. *post* (KENNEDY, J., dissenting).] After all, the provision is part of a statute that has as its basic purpose effectuating an alien's removal. Why should we assume that Congress saw the alien's dangerousness as unrelated to this purpose?

The Government points to the statute's word "may." But while "may" suggests discretion, it does not necessarily suggest unlimited discretion. In that respect the word "may" is ambiguous. Indeed, if Congress had meant to authorize long-term detention of unremovable aliens, it certainly could have spoken in clearer terms. * * *

    * * *

The Fifth Circuit held Zadvydas' continued detention lawful as long as "good faith efforts to effectuate ... deportation continue" and Zadvydas failed to show that deportation will prove "impossible." * * * But this standard would seem to require an alien seeking release to show the absence of *any* prospect of removal—no matter how unlikely or unforeseeable—which demands more than our reading of the statute can bear. The Ninth Circuit held that the Government was required to release Ma from detention because there was no reasonable likelihood of his removal in the foreseeable future. * * * But its conclusion may have rested solely upon the "absence" of an "extant or pending" repatriation agreement without giving due weight to the likelihood of successful future negotiations. * * * Consequently, we vacate the judgments below and remand both cases for further proceedings consistent with this opinion.

It is so ordered.

■ Justice Scalia, with whom Justice Thomas joins, dissenting.

I join Part I of Justice KENNEDY's dissent, which establishes the Attorney General's clear statutory authority to detain criminal aliens with no specified time limit. I write separately because I do not believe that, as Justice KENNEDY suggests in Part II of his opinion, there may be some situations in which the courts can order release. I believe that in both *Zadvydas v. Davis,* No. 99–7791, and *Ashcroft v. Ma,* No. 00–38, a "careful description" of the substantive right claimed, *Reno v. Flores,* 507 U.S. 292, 302 (1993), suffices categorically to refute its existence. A criminal alien under final order of removal who allegedly will not be accepted by any other country in the reasonably foreseeable future claims a constitutional right of supervised release into the United States. This claim can be repackaged as freedom from "physical restraint" or freedom from "indefinite detention," [*ante*] but it is at bottom a claimed right of release into this country by an individual who *concededly* has no legal right to be here. There is no such constitutional right.

Like a criminal alien under final order of removal, an inadmissible alien at the border has no right to be in the United States. *The Chinese Exclusion Case,* 130 U.S. 581, 603 (1889). In *Shaughnessy v. United States ex rel. Mezei,* 345 U.S. 206 (1953), we upheld potentially indefinite detention of such an inadmissible alien whom the Government was unable to return anywhere else. We said that "we [did] not think that respondent's continued exclusion deprives him of any statutory or constitutional right." * * * While four Members of the Court thought that Mezei deserved greater procedural protections the Attorney General had refused to divulge any information as to why Mezei was being detained * * * no Justice asserted that Mezei had a substantive constitutional right to release into this country. And Justice Jackson's dissent, joined by Justice Frankfurter, affirmatively asserted the opposite, with no contradiction from the Court: "Due process does not invest any alien with a right to enter the United States, *nor confer on those admitted the right to remain against the national will.* Nothing in the Constitution requires admission *or sufferance* of aliens hostile to our scheme of government." * * * Insofar as a claimed legal right to release into this country is concerned, an alien under final order of removal stands on an equal footing with an inadmissible alien at the threshold of entry: He has no such right.

* * *

■ JUSTICE KENNEDY, with whom THE CHIEF JUSTICE joins, and with whom JUSTICE SCALIA and JUSTICE THOMAS join as to Part I, dissenting.

The Court says its duty is to avoid a constitutional question. It deems the duty performed by interpreting a statute in obvious disregard of congressional intent; curing the resulting gap by writing a statutory amendment of its own; committing its own grave constitutional error by arrogating to the Judicial Branch the power to summon high officers of the Executive to assess their progress in conducting some of the Nation's most sensitive negotiations with foreign powers; and then likely releasing into our general population at least hundreds of removable or inadmissible aliens who have been found by fair procedures to be flight risks, dangers to the community, or both. Far from avoiding a constitutional question, the Court's ruling causes systemic dislocation in the balance of powers, thus raising serious constitutional concerns not just for the cases at hand but for the Court's own view of its proper authority. Any supposed respect the Court seeks in not reaching the constitutional question is outweighed by the intrusive and erroneous exercise of its own powers. In the guise of judicial restraint the Court ought not to intrude upon the other branches. The constitutional question the statute presents, it must be acknowledged, may be a significant one in some later case; but it ought not to drive us to an incorrect interpretation of the statute. The Court having reached the wrong result for the wrong reason, this respectful dissent is required.

* * *

The majority's unanchored interpretation ignores another indication that the Attorney General's detention discretion was not limited to this truncated period. Section 1231(a)(6) permits continued detention not only of removable aliens but also of inadmissible aliens, for instance those stopped at the border before entry. Congress provides for detention of both categories within the same statutory grant of authority. Accepting the majority's interpretation, then, there are two possibilities, neither of which is sustainable. On the one hand, it may be that the majority's rule applies to both categories of aliens, in which case we are asked to assume that Congress intended to restrict the discretion it could confer upon the Attorney General so that all inadmissible aliens must be allowed into our community within six months. On the other hand, the majority's logic might be that inadmissible and removable aliens can be treated differently. Yet it is not a plausible construction of § 1231(a)(6) to imply a time limit as to one class but not to another. The text does not admit of this possibility. As a result, it is difficult to see why "[a]liens who have not yet gained initial admission to this country would present a very different question."

* * *

The risk to the community posed by the mandatory release of aliens who are dangerous or a flight risk is far from insubstantial; the motivation to protect the citizenry from aliens determined to be dangerous is central to the immigration power itself. The Government cites statistical studies showing high recidivism rates for released aliens. One Government Accounting Office study cited by Congress in floor debates on the Antiterrorism and Effective Death Penalty Act of 1996, 110 Stat. 1214, put the figure as high as 77 percent. * * * It seems evident a criminal record accumulated by an admitted alien during his or her time in the United States is likely to be a better indicator of risk than factors relied upon during the INS's initial decision to admit or exclude. Aliens ordered deported as the result of having committed a felony have proved to be dangerous.

   * * *

II

The aliens' claims are substantial; their plight is real. They face continued detention, perhaps for life, unless it is shown they no longer present a flight risk or a danger to the community. In a later case the specific circumstances of a detention may present a substantial constitutional question. That is not a reason, however, for framing a rule which ignores the law governing alien status.

As persons within our jurisdiction, the aliens are entitled to the protection of the Due Process Clause. Liberty under the Due Process Clause includes protection against unlawful or arbitrary personal restraint or detention. The liberty rights of the aliens before us here are subject to limitations and conditions not applicable to citizens, however. * * * No party to this proceeding contests the initial premise that the aliens have been determined to be removable after a fair hearing under lawful and proper procedures. Section 1229a sets forth the proceedings required for deciding the inadmissibility or removability of an alien, including a hearing before an immigration judge, at which the INS carries "the burden of establishing by clear and convincing evidence that ... the alien is deportable." * * * Aliens ordered removed pursuant to these procedures are given notice of their right to appeal the decision, * * * may move the immigration judge to reconsider, * * * can seek discretionary cancellation of removal, and can obtain habeas review of the Attorney General's decision not to consider waiver of deportation. * * * As a result, aliens like Zadvydas and Ma do not arrive at their removable status without thorough, substantial procedural safeguards.

   * * *

C. National Borders: Economics and Immigration Policy Debates

Border Crossings in An Age of Border Patrols: *Cruzando Fronteras Metaforicas*

26 N.M. L. Rev. 1 (1996).

■ Margaret E. Montoya

   * * * Issues involving immigration, free trade, illicit drugs, affirmative action for Latinos and the English-only movement have pushed relations

with Mexico, Mexicanos, and Chicanos into a prominence in the political discourse that is unusual for recent national elections. No issue is more prominent and more hotly debated by both the Democrats and the Republicans than the legal and illegal migration of low-skilled persons from Mexico into the Southwestern portions of the United States.

Concerns about transborder movement of people, goods, capital, languages, and accompanying legal claims have become global. People throughout the globe are moving from the southern regions with their relative poverty into the northern countries in search of employment and political stability. Within this current political environment borders are embedded with symbolic meaning about national sovereignty, a desired clarity about who "belongs" and who does not, and employment security. Border crossers become media symbols and political scapegoats.

* * *

THE BORDER

The U.S./Mexico border was defined, as many international borders have been, by war, political intrigue, and river morphology. The 1848 Treaty of Guadalupe Hidalgo ended the United States' war with Mexico and established the Rio Grande as the border from the Gulf of Mexico to El Paso. Moving west, the Gila River that runs from New Mexico through Arizona at a point above Tucson and into the Colorado River was the negotiated boundary. From the Colorado River, a straight line was drawn to the Pacific Ocean at a point just below San Diego.

By 1853, Mexico, and its President Santa Anna, had land and needed money; the United States had money and wanted land for a transcontinental railroad system. So James Gadsden, the minister to Mexico, bargained to have the United States buy large portions of northern Mexico. Originally hoping for Baja California and parts of Sonora and Chihuahua, he eventually settled for a smaller section of land, approximately 30,000 acres for which the United States paid $10 million. With the so-called Gadsden Purchase, the border was now drawn below Nogales and Douglas, Arizona.

The border measures 1,951.36 miles from the Gulf of Mexico to the Pacific, with the Rio Grande accounting for 1,253.69 miles, the Colorado for 23.72 miles, and the land border for 697.67 miles. Even after the border had been officially defined, both the meandering of the alluvial channels of the Rio Grande and the cartographic mistakes in the maps which formed the basis for the Treaty of Guadalupe Hidalgo created ongoing disputes between the two governments.

Nonetheless, what has characterized the border for most of its one hundred and fifty year history has been the lack of open hostility among the people who inhabit the territory along the border. According to historians, the process of cultural lending and borrowing began almost immediately with the flows of people, capital, and ideas largely disregarding the political boundary.

During most of the past century, the United States actively encouraged the movement of workers from Mexico. In the late 1800s, miners were recruited from Sonora and Jalisco, and those immigrant laborers were responsible for the feasibility and profitability of open pit copper mines in Arizona and New Mexico. Later as the Imperial and Mesilla Valleys were irrigated, farm labor from Mexico became critical for the planting, weeding and harvesting of crops. Immigration laws were specifically drafted to protect the Mexican labor supply for agribusiness in California and elsewhere.

Much of the current political debate centers on the "violations" and "transgressions" of the border by undocumented workers who cross to work in the United States or who overstay their visas. This debate is in sharp contrast to the original desire of the two countries to facilitate transborder interactions. A series of "sister-cities" were established along the border—Mexicali and Calexico; Nogales, Arizona and Nogales, Sonora; El Paso, Texas and El Paso del Norte (now called Cuidad Juarez); Laredo, Texas, and Nuevo Laredo, Tumaulipas—with the explicit intent, at the time, to create a population along the border with facility in both cultures, a borderlands in which both languages would be spoken and goods, labor, and capital would move fairly freely. These hopes have largely been realized. Current proposals to fortify the border by building impenetrable concrete walls, electrified fences, or a human fence of border guards fail to take into account the considerable advantages of these historic connections, especially those advantages offered by a hybrid population that navigates easily through both societies.

Rep. Duncan Hunter (R–El Cajon, Ca.) has proposed the building of a triple fence along the 14–mile stretch of border from the Pacific Ocean to Otay Mesa, known colloquially as "Smugglers Alley." According to the Los Angeles Times, the idea for the fence is based on a study prepared by the Sandia National Laboratory in New Mexico, which "concluded that if one fence was good, three fences were better." * * * Nevertheless, the border continues to serve the political fortunes of jingoistic politicians.

BORDER AS METAPHOR

More recently, the border has been imbedded with metaphoric and tropic meanings. Applicable to disciplinary, cultural, and epistemological spaces, the border is seen as site, intersection, bridge, and membrane. Borders have been transformed from bilateral national boundaries to borders representing cultural and epistemic sites of contestation.

In her classic book, *Borderlands, La Frontera: The New Mestiza*, Gloria Anzaldúa transformed the concept of the "border" from geographic and physical spaces to one applicable to psychological, sexual, and spiritual sites, "present wherever two or more cultures edge each other, where people of different races occupy the same territory, where under, lower, middle and upper classes touch, where the space between two individuals shrinks with intimacy." * * * The border as an epistemic space for the exploration of cultural production has proven particularly salient to ethnographers. In 1989, the anthropologist Renato Rosaldo observed:

> [O]ur everyday lives are crisscrossed by border zones, pockets and eruptions of all kinds. Social borders frequently become salient around such lines as sexual orientation, gender, class, race, ethnicity, nationality, age, politics, dress, food or taste. Along with "our" supposedly transparent cultural selves, such borderlands should be regarded not as analytically empty transitional zones but as sites of creative cultural production that require investigation.

Dwight Conquergood extended the notion of contested sites to the self, exploring the reframing of borders for purposes of epistemology and identity formation:

> "borders bleed, as much as they contain. Instead of dividing lines to be patrolled or transgressed, boundaries are now understood as crisscrossing sites inside the post-modern subject. Difference is resituated within, instead of beyond, the self. Inside and outside distinctions, like genres, blur and wobble. . . .

> " . . . The major epistemological consequence of displacing the idea of solid centers and unified wholes with borderlands and zones of contest is a rethinking of identity and culture as constructed and relational, instead of ontologically given and essential. This rethinking privileges metonym, 'reasoning part-to-part' over . . . synecdoche, 'reasoning part-to-whole'; it features syntax over semantics. Meaning is contested and struggled for in the interstices, *in between* structures. Identity is invented and contingent, not autonomous: 'I' is, therefore, not a unified subject, a fixed identity, or that solid mass covered with layers of superficialities one has gradually to peel off before one can see its true face. 'I' is, itself, infinite layers."

My personal favorite is Ruth Behar's *Translated Woman: Crossing the Border with Esperanza's Story*. The centerpiece story about an indigenous Mexican woman is told by Behar in her ethnographic voice, but the multilayered translation of Esperanza's story requires Behar to tell her own story. Here the border is integral to the identities of both the Cuban ethnographer and her Indian informant, but, more importantly, both Behar and Esperanza use their relation to the border to create their identity, to name themselves as illegal, as "literary wetbacks," thereby robbing the popular discourse of its power to define epithets, to construct identities, and to stigmatize experience:

> Esperanza has given me her story to smuggle across the border. Just as Mexican laborers export their bodies for labor on American soil, Esperanza has given me her story for export only. Her story, she realizes, is a kind of commodity that will have a value on the other side that it doesn't have at home-why else would I be "using up" my life to write about her life? She has chosen to be a literary wetback, and I am to act as her literary broker, the border crosser who will take her story

to the other side and make it be heard in translation. The question will be whether I can act as literary broker without becoming the worst kind of coyote, getting her across, but only by exploiting her lack of power to make it to *el otro lado* any other way.

[T]here is a special burden that authorship carries if you have ever occupied a borderland place in the dominant culture, especially if you were told at some point in your life that you didn't have what it takes to be an authority on, an author of, anything. It means writing as a "literary wetback," as the Chicana poet Alicia Gaspar de Alba puts it, without "the 'right' credentials . . . to get across."

It is not just Esperanza, then who is a literary wetback. Even though I have borne her story across to this side of the border, I recognize that I, too, in a quite different way, am a literary wetback in the world of academic letters, a wetback despite the papers that tell me I'm okay, I'm in, I'm a legal alien.

* * *

A CAVEAT

Policing the southern border of the United States has become a central issue in the political agenda of both the Democratic and Republican parties in the presidential campaigns of 1996. As this introduction is being written, the House has considered and passed sweeping new immigration legislation, further restricting legal immigration and adding 5000 new border patrol agents. In California, the Riverside police were recently videotaped in a high-speed chase that ended with them viciously billy-clubbing Enrique Funes Flores and Alicia Sotero, two Mexican nationals who put up no resistance when caught. The Mexican male driver had been transporting some twenty Mexican undocumented workers in the bed of a dilapidated truck.

And while the Mexicans were stereotyped as lazy, shiftless, passive siesta seekers, people who patronized *manhexana*, those who knew them realized that just the opposite was true. The Mexican was one of the hardest working individuals on earth, and [s]he proved it just to get into the United States. [S]he walked for weary weeks, forded muddy and violent rivers, clung to the tenuous underside of trucks and trains, stuffed him[/her]self into the sizzling engine compartment of automobiles, slipped through and over jagged fences, risked being murdered by his own people, flattened by traffic as [s]he darted across the freeway, suffocated in tightly enclosed vans and railroad cars, arrested by the Border Patrol, all so [s]he could earn minimum wages toiling with a short hoe from dawn to dusk. If [s]he wasn't an illegal, [s]he would surely have deserved commendation for bravery, perseverance, and endurance. Such are the people whom we expel from our borders.

As Peter McLaren reminds us, "Some people cross borders willingly, some people are forced to cross them, and others are shot in their attempts at crossing." So as we deploy the border as a metaphor, we need to remember that for many people throughout the world crossing borders is not cognitive or rhetorical; border crossings can be life-risking and life-losing endeavors.

We engage in disciplinary and discursive border crossings to ally ourselves with the millions in their diasporic searches for new homelands with their unfulfilled promise of work, food, security, and opportunity. We engage in disciplinary and discursive border crossings to construct new, more fluid, more complex identities, and in doing so we turn our gaze southward towards our ancestral homes. We engage in disciplinary and discursive border crossings to destabilize the meanings and inscriptions that the superordinate cultures, the Euro/Anglo/North American cultures with their Border Patrols, place on borders.

Undocumented Mexican Migration: In Search of a Just Immigration Law and Policy

28 UCLA L. REV. 615 (1981).

■ GERALD P. LÓPEZ

* * *

The informed consensus applies classical push-pull theory to undocumented Mexican migration. The theory's success has been well-earned in view of its broad utility in explaining world mass migration over the past century. Moreover, data taken in by the informed consensus are mostly accurate. The components seem believable, particularly because their descriptive interaction brings order to what can otherwise appear to be an incomprehensible geo-political jumble. At the same time that the theory seems to provide an objective explanation for mass migration, it implies that the destination country has a quite limited moral responsibility for the problem.

Narrow descriptive accuracy is not, for the most part, what distinguishes the informed consensus from the following alternative explanation that sees as critical certain information the informed consensus has overlooked, disregarded or negligibly weighted. The chief distinctions are ones of interpretation.

* * * The great weakness of the informed consensus lies in its central hypothesis that economic disparity is at the source of mass Mexican migration. This position could be translated into a causal relationship: "but for" economic disparity mass undocumented Mexican migration would not occur. This view derives from the obvious observation that economic disparity between the United States and Mexico has always played an important role in contributing to mass migration. Indeed, mass migration in modern times has rarely occurred except where economic disparity has been present.

There have been numerous instances, however, where economic disparity between nations—even adjoining nations—exists but mass migration is absent. In other words, economic disparity is necessary but not sufficient for migration. Certainly this is true of migration from Mexico to the United States. More than one expert has underscored that the same wage differential (13:1) between migrant earning in the United States and average agricultural wage rates in primary Mexican source regions has prevailed since the first decade of this century. In fact, the disparity was probably greater in earlier years. Nevertheless, mass migration from these regions was unknown until later years. Nor does economic disparity account for the pattern of Mexican migration. Primary Mexican source regions for today's undocumented migration are areas that provided labor earlier in this century. Yet the economic disparity between these source regions and the United States is no greater than that existing between numerous other regions in Mexico and this country. Economic disparity hardly accounts for the fact that the great majority of undocumented Mexicans are the strongest, most able-bodied workers who presumably could compete well in the Mexican labor market.

In contrast to conventional push-pull theory, the following hypothesis offers a more complete explanation for migration: Where there is substantial economic disparity between two adjoining countries and the potential destination country promotes, *de jure* or *de facto*, access to its substantially superior minimal wage, that promotion encourages migrants reasonably to rely on the continuing possibility of migration, employment, and residence, until a competitive economic alternative is made available in the source country. Substantial migration from Mexico did not begin until the United States urged and encouraged Mexican workers to fill lower echelon jobs in this country. The now discernible pattern of emigration from certain source regions coincides almost perfectly with active American promotion in those regions. The curious near-exclusivity of young males among all migrant groups is understandable when one fixes on the fact that promotional effort, particularly until recent years, sought only their services.

* * * [The author reviews over one hundred years of U.S. recruitment and solicitation of Mexican workers to show how the U.S. has induced Mexican villages to send young workers to the United States for temporary employment. After documenting how we have created this reliance by formal and informal means, he turns to the other side of the equation—Eds.]

The Decision–Making Calculus

It is necessary to examine whether the decision to migrate is, as much thinking about undocumented Mexican migration assumes, an individual economic calculation. Identifying the actual decision-making unit as the household rather than the individual allows examination of the effect of migration on the household unit and the influence that unit extends on the migrant's aspirations in the United States.

Even so perceptive a commentator as Professor [Wayne] Cornelius has written that the migratory phenomenon can be understood by taking the rational decision making of the individual as the point of departure: "For most [Mexican migrants] the decision to go to the U.S. is an eminently rational one, in terms of differential economic returns to one's labor, as well as the high probability of finding a job in the U.S." Although most evidence supports Cornelius's assertion that the decision, at least in part, is rational, it disputes his contention that the decision is an individual one. Dedicated field researchers such as Raymond Wiest and Richard Mines argue that the relevant decision-making unit is the household, not the individual. Their conclusion is modern confirmation of the findings of earlier anthropological studies: the household is the appropriate unit for analysis of decisions concerning economic cooperation and production. Despite this early consensus, few studies have subsequently examined the interaction between "wage-labor migration" and the operation of the household unit. Nonetheless, the evidence accumulated by Wiest, Mines, and even Cornelius strongly supports the conclusion that the "rational individual" is not a self-contained decision-making unit, but is part of a household that makes decisions according to the demands of its living situation.

Special reasons argue for focusing on the household unit. First, the household decision-making process may differ markedly from an individual one; the difference bears heavily on the issues of aspirational evolution. For instance, it is far more persuasive to hypothesize that values undergo inevitable change sufficient to predict permanent undocumented relocation if the migrant worker is responsible for his own needs and not those of an economic unit beyond himself than if he is a member of a household unit and responsible to it. To emphasize the importance of the household unit is not to deny that some unmarried young men, and even some married men, migrate for primarily individual reasons. It is also not to deny that some migrant workers begin to operate, after awhile, according to individual needs rather than the needs of the household unit that may have initially dictated their temporary migration. These, however, are not the "normal" cases; even the evidence gathered by Cornelius confirms this fact.

Care in identifying the proper unit of economic decision making is also important if we are to determine, in Mines's terminology, the "retentive capability" of the source village. That is, to understand the possibilities for dissuading undocumented migrant workers from leaving their source villages or, from another angle, to determine what must be done to encourage their remaining at home, we must understand the true decision-making process.

Finally, any culturally sensitive theory must select the appropriate decision-making unit. The simple fact is that Mexico's agricultural society, which still provides the bulk of undocumented workers, has long been characterized by close family ties and a communal struggle to survive. The typical household is perennially in danger of being unable to subsist and of disintegration. All working members of the family cooperate to insure the two essential conditions of household survival: adequate income and adequate composition to permit fulfillment of domestic functions (including child care). All members become committed to the notion of shared obligation within the household unit and to the overriding importance of subordinating individual desires to the extent necessary to perpetuate the household. Initially the older generation provides for the younger; in short time the obligation is shared. Finally, the generations' roles are reversed and with the arrival of the next generation the cycle repeats itself. Centuries of economic loyalty to one's household have transformed what was once essentially an economic decision into an entrenched cultural principle.

Adequate income has always been the most difficult of the two conditions of survival to insure. Households in agricultural Mexico traditionally pursued a variety of income-producing activities; dangerous as generalizations are, it is probably accurate to conclude that a household's most dependable means of producing more income to restore equilibrium was stepped-up agricultural production. Other means of intensifying the household effort were explored but inevitably proved unreliable.

Although intensification of agricultural production was the best means of augmenting income, it was at the same time a dangerous and limited solution because of short-term catastrophes, crude productive techniques, and shortages of cultivable land. These combined obstacles to income production often threatened to disintegrate agricultural household the "normal" cases; even the evidence gathered by Cornelius confirms this fact.

Access to a relatively superior wage structure in the United States created an opportunity to avoid household disintegration by selling male labor. For some households, particularly the landless, this new alternative may have been perceived as the only possibility for survival. From the beginning, the male head was selected by the household to migrate temporarily to the United States to earn badly needed income. In part, the male was chosen because he was the object of American promotion; the household also felt it was the role of the husband-father to make the arduous sacrifice.

In his absence, the household adjusted. Domestic functions—daily logistics and socialization of young family members—became the mother's primary responsibility. The more important adjustment, in terms of cultural acceptance of wage-labor migration, was that the contributing father retained his status as the head of the household. As long as his absences were temporary and associated with remittances, the husband-father's place was secure and unthreatened. In effect, the household adjusted to endure wage-labor migration as a necessity, but insisted that it be only temporary in nature.

The recurring nature of the temporary migrations was likely unforeseeable, and certainly undesirable from the household's point of view. Struggling to maintain equilibrium, households found themselves repeatedly sending their men to the United States far more often than would have been hoped by those who left and those who remained at home. Moreover, the process began to feed on itself, becoming, almost imperceptibly, institutionalized. Not only did experienced households begin to rely regularly and predictably on temporary migration, but new and different households began to perceive temporary wage-labor migration as the dominant emerging alternative during periods of economic crisis.

Vague promotional promises were given weight by the return of "wealthy" migrants, men able to provide monetary support out of line with their previous domestic endeavors and capable of relating tales, often exaggerated by "locker room" boastfulness. Word spread that, if a household needed income, relatively superior wages were available for the price of temporary migration to the United States. From the beginning, the persistence of household disequilibrium in the agricultural areas of Mexico and heightened awareness of the continuing availability of wage-producing labor opportunities in the United States ensured a dependable and ballooning response to the wage-labor migration market.

Since 1940, survival of the household has been further endangered by Mexico's extraordinary population growth. Population growth may be able to be matched by increases in arable land, but to date these lands have gone predominantly to Mexico's large landholders who have tended toward machine-intensive and not labor-intensive development if, in fact, they develop the land at all. As a result there is an excess of population relative to cultivable land and the number of nonagricultural employment opportunities. Thus the landless rural working class and *ejidatarios* have been reduced to an almost perpetually marginal economic status and forced to turn to wage-labor migration as a means of insuring household survival.

Most researchers agree that even if the population growth were controlled, the present wage disparity between Mexico and the United States would result in mass wage-labor migration. Holding other factors constant, it appears that wage disparity determines the absolute number of undocumented migrants. The critical variable is, somewhat surprisingly, not the American but the Mexican wage. When American wages have gone up, the rate of undocumented migration remains unaffected, and when Mexican wages have decreased, migration has increased. Other studies tend to support this conclusion with data tying rates of undocumented migration to Mexican agricultural productivity, commodity prices, and farm wages.

This observation about economic conditions in Mexico, combined with the earlier description of the typical Mexican household, leads to the hypothesis that the decision to migrate for wage labor remains a function of household equilibrium. If, as a result of a decrease in Mexican wages, the household's income falls below subsistence level, the household will be sufficiently "economically motivated" to send one or more of its members to the United States to help earn income from wage labor necessary to maintain the household in Mexico.

This hypothesis is supported by the characteristics of the modern undocumented Mexican. These characteristics remain remarkably similar to those that might have been compiled in the 1880s. Although in recent years there has been an increasing number of older men, the majority of migrants are and have long been young men (between twenty-two and thirty) who are usually uneducated (less than three years). Young women seldom have migrated except with a family (an unusual occurrence) or to join a male who has already established permanent residence in the United States. A majority of undocumented migrants are married but, according to one study, fewer than one percent are ever accompanied by their wives. Most come from rural areas, though small towns and larger cities still contribute their share. Although an increasing number claim an urban residence, most are actually arriving in the United States at the end of a two-or three-leg migration from a rural area. While many have held temporary urban jobs, a majority continue to have substantial ties to households in a rural area. It appears that whenever the household is sufficiently motivated, it is still considered the duty of the man to migrate and the duty of the woman to assume a disproportionate share of the domestic obligation during periods of absence.

The evidence of recent years has made increasingly apparent both the extent and permanence of the reliance on employment in the United States. Professor Cornelius reports that forty-nine percent of those who, since 1969, migrated illegally from one long-established source village also had fathers who had previously worked in the United States, primarily in the Bracero Program. Eighty-seven percent of these same undocumented workers also had brothers or sisters who had previously migrated for wage labor. Forty-three percent of the married undocumented workers since 1969 also had one or more children who had worked in the United States. Finally, fully sixty-two percent of the families in Cornelius's study had members of at least two generations simultaneously going to the United States.

The likelihood that this near-permanent reliance will change anytime soon seems remote. Richard Mines's study of Las Animas, a long-time and prototypical source pueblo in the central plateau state of Zacatecas, is illustrative. An analysis of pueblo sources of disposable income revealed that, on the average, fully 60 percent of each household's income was annually derived from wages earned in the United States.

Even destination patterns for wage-labor migrants reflect the household's increasing reliance on the American wage. Professor Wiest's study of Mexican households indicates that husband-fathers working in the United States contribute a relatively high percentage of household income; these men return predictably to the household, continuing their traditional role in the domestic scheme despite their absences. In contrast, husband-fathers migrating within Mexico usually provide only a supplementary source of income, alone insufficient for household survival; these men tend to return much less predictably and to play a far reduced role in the household.

Economically inefficient and unreliable internal wage-labor migration constitutes a genuine threat to the husband-father's traditional status. Given this fact, growing reliance on wage-labor migration to the United States, as evidenced by recent destination patterns, may be seen as the household's judicious attachment to what it perceives as the best available alternative for its economic and cultural survival. Wage-labor migration, which began as a temporary means for restoring household equilibrium, has apparently become the primary source of income for the landless and *ejidatarios* in rural Mexico.

* * * Thus, while households now rely on wage-labor migration as an economic necessity, they nonetheless view migration as a "temporary crutch." However conscious they are of their dependence, most household members still dream that something, most often the superior American wage, will enable them to permanently terminate participation in the migration cycle. Most migrant workers intend to retire to their village in Mexico when they are done with wage labor in the United States. Interestingly, one study indicates that even if offered permanent status in the United States, most Mexicans would still rather live in Mexico and temporarily migrate for wage-labor.

The persistent cyclical and temporary character of undocumented migration is additional evidence that the more significant evolution is not "aspirational" but reliant in nature. Despite years of continual contact, most Mexican migrants remain uninterested in permanent relocation. Although migration has raised many migrants' economic expectations, most remain part of a household that wants nothing more than to remain together, to survive *in* Mexico.

* * * The present predicament tests, in many ways, our capacity and will to meet the just expectations that we have generated, to admit the truth and to accept our responsibilities. What we did in the past and even now is related to what we will decide is the decent thing to do in the future. We cannot wish away past and present hypocrisy; nor should we want to if we appreciate the very nature of a political community that is even minimally just. It may be true that national boundaries and documented status can define, and indeed may once have defined, the limits of our moral obligations. But our experience with undocumented Mexican workers is fundamentally inconsistent with that comfortable and reflex-like moral posture. If we are not accountable for the present condition of undocumented Mexican workers, we are at least responsible for the commitment implicit in our long-standing relationship. If involvement and neighborhood matter, undocumented Mexican workers are part of the living and working community. They are we.

Facts cannot be ignored even by those who reject (if in fact they even consider) fundamental moral obligations. Mexican households seem to have, and certainly perceive, no short-term means of economic survival without continued access to our labor market. If, as it appears, Mexicans cannot humanely be dissuaded from coming, some form of access must be legislatively accommodated or they will simply continue to come and to work outside the boundaries of the law. The available evidence suggests that while risks and costs to present documented residents of legalized access for undocumented Mexican workers are potentially substantial, they are dwarfed by those that accompany other responses. For those who reject any moral obligation, the most compelling reason for legalizing access may well be the predictable cost of failing to do so. Selfish pragmatists may be forced to admit that legalized access encompasses, even from their perspective, the most sober, mutually advantageous and least costly short- or middle-term response to a profoundly tense and complicated dilemma.

* * *

NOTES AND QUESTIONS

1. Is there an immigration crisis? What are the basic underlying differences between, Montoya, López, and the author of the following comments:

> The immigration crisis has grown steadily and slowly, and therefore taken us by surprise. Today, immigration to the United States is massive, and it is out of control. The United States accepts for permanent resettlement twice as many immigrants as do all the other countries of the world combined. Legal immigration is three times as high as it was in the early 1960s; there are now well over 600,000 legal immigrants in an average year. Illegal immigration is estimated to be ten times greater; there are now well over a million apprehensions a year—without any corresponding increase in enforcement activities. Illegal aliens pour into the United States through Swiss-cheese borders. Legal and illegal immigration combined contribute nearly half of the population growth of the United States. And efforts to cope with the breakdown of immigration law or to moderate the high levels of legal immigration are stymied in Congress by an unlikely coalition of the far right and the far left, fueled by a coalition of big business and Hispanic pressure groups.

Richard Lamm & Gary Imhoff, *How Many Can America Absorb?, in* The Immigration Time Bomb: The Fragmenting of America (1986).

2. Cosmopolitanism and border control. Would Martha Nussbaum, who argued for Cosmopolitanism set any limits on immigration? Lamm and Imhoff note that "Some people deny that immigration can ever be a problem. They refuse to let go of the dream. They argue that treating immigration as a problem treats people, human beings, as a problem. In that, they are right: people, large numbers of people pressing against the resources of the earth, are a problem." Lamm & Imhoff, *supra*.

3. The economic questions: Imhoff and Lamm argue that: "at high enough levels, immigration also creates economic problems." In many areas of the world, migrants are moving from less developed to more developed countries. They generally have fewer skills than workers in their host countries, and in those cases migrants move into unskilled jobs at the bottom of the job ladders of those countries. If their numbers are large enough, they displace native workers and when economies are not vibrant and growing at fast enough rates—they contribute to the unemployment of natives and depress the salary levels for the jobs in which they specialize. In West Germany, for example, certain jobs became stigmatized in the late

1960s and 1970s as "Turkish jobs," performed by temporary migrant guestworkers from Turkey. When certain jobs become stigmatized in such a way, a society loses some of its cohesiveness, a large part of its social mobility, and a degree of respect for manual labor. In the United States, our own garment industry has now been stigmatized as a sector in which illegal immigrants work. Wages have fallen, sweatshops have been revived, a noble union has been corrupted by accepting the existence of "shadow locals" and tolerating the exploitation of illegal workers, and—in a self-fulfilling prophecy—employers have created a class of work that "Americans won't do."

4. The competition for status between native and immigrant workers. Again we turn to Lamm and Imhoff who argue that: "Hispanic Americans—who have been misrepresented by national groups claiming to speak for them—also show overwhelming support in polls both for increased border control against illegal immigration and for lower levels of legal immigration. This should not be surprising, though it is to many people. In many areas, Hispanic Americans are exactly those who are most hurt by massive immigration, whose neighborhoods suffer the greatest impact, and whose jobs are most affected by competition. The most comprehensive poll of Hispanic and black American opinions on immigration was conducted early in 1983 by Democratic pollster Peter D. Hart and Republican pollster V. Lance Tarrance. Hart and Tarrance found that 69 percent of black and 63 percent of Hispanic citizens wanted major increases in spending to enable the Border Patrol to stop illegal aliens from entering the United States; 66 percent of blacks and 66 percent of Hispanic citizens favored penalties and fines for employers who hired illegal aliens; and only 12 percent of Hispanic and 5 percent of black citizens felt that we should admit higher levels of legal immigrants from Mexico."

5. The profit motive. Is Gerald López's argument that immigration from Mexico is fueled by the economic self-interest of employers who want cheap labor? Lamm and Imhoff note that "Certainly, in agricultural areas of Texas and California, politicians are affected by the pleas of powerful growers who employ illegal migrants at wages much lower than they could pay Americans. And restaurants, taxi fleets, and ununionized 'home improvement' firms that employ illegals in our cities certainly profit. The employers' argument is ugly and full of self-interest: they want to be able to hire illegal immigrants in preference to Americans so that they don't have to raise wages or improve working conditions. Surely the employers' argument cannot be powerful. It isn't. Its power comes from the fact that it is allied both to the immigration dream and to the politically powerful and seemingly disinterested forces of internationalism, humanitarianism, and opposition to racism." IMHOFF AND LAMM, *supra*.

6. Racism? The most powerful argument against immigration reform is the fear of acting out of racism. Is immigration reform discriminatory? Is it racist to control illegal immigration or to set ceilings on legal immigration? One fact would tend to support the contention of racism. Twenty years ago, about 80 percent of legal immigrants came from western Europe. Today 80 percent of legal immigrants come from Asia and Latin America, and over half of all immigrants speak Spanish as a native tongue. Opponents of immigration control have contended that this shift in the composition of the immigrant stream, this difference in race, culture, language, and religion, is the real cause of concern over immigration.

Legal scholar, Kevin Johnson argues that:

"[L]ike de jure segregation of the public schools, express racial exclusions in the immigration laws, ... is primarily a problem of the past rather than the present. The real problem of race and immigration today, ... is that facially neutral immigration laws have unmistakable racial impacts, including some that arguably are intentional. A number of examples immediately come to mind, such as the public charge exclusion, which disparately impacts poor and working people from developing nations populated primarily by people of color. Consider that the various removal grounds are facially neutral but that over ninety-two percent of the noncitizens deported in fiscal year 1999 were from Mexico or other Latin American countries. Given such glaring disparate impacts, no wonder that Latino/a scholars have been particularly attentive to immigration and immigrant law and policy."

Kevin Johnson, *Race and Immigration Law and Enforcement: A Response to Is There A Plenary Powers Doctrine?*, 14 GEO. IMMIGR. L.J. 289, 291 (2000).

Johnson also makes the persuasive claim that:

"Many Latino/as in the United States firmly believe that race is *the* determinative factor to immigration officers investigating alleged violations of the immigration laws. This belief has basis in fact. In most cases challenging stops by the Border Patrol, one of the factors that the officers have expressly relied upon was the suspect's 'Hispanic appearance.' " The government's rationale, although infrequently stated, is simple:

the government urges the fact that the driver was Hispanic tends to give the agent reasonable suspicion that the driver was involved in illegal activity. *The government reasons that most illegal immigrants in Texas are Hispanic and jumps to the conclusion that this makes it more likely that this driver was also an illegal immigrant, or was involved in the trafficking of aliens.*

Id. at 294–95 (quoting *United States v. Rubio–Hernandez*, 39 F. Supp. 2d 808, 835 (W.D. Tex. 1999)). *See also* Kevin Johnson, *The Case Against Race Profiling in Immigration Enforcement*, 78 WASH. UNIV. L.Q. 675 (2000).

NOTES AND QUESTIONS

1. A nation of immigrants. Imhoff claims that the history that our country was built by immigrants "was never strictly true." As support for this statement he notes that the white population grew from over three million to almost eight million between 1790 and 1820. However, since the entire white population of the United States is a result of immigration from

Europe, does Imhoff's statement about white population growth have any real significance? Shouldn't Imhoff instead be comparing the contributions of white (and non-white) immigrants with the contributions of Native Americans?

2. Letting go of the dream. One recurring argument in immigration debates is that this country needs to let go of the dream embodied in the inscription on the base of the Statue of Liberty. If this view is correct, and the dream of unlimited promise in America is dead, what are the implications of its passing? Must America now emulate the "ancient lands, with their storied pomp" that the immigrants to America fled from? If America is not doomed to become a stratified society, why is the opportunity in America only something that can be gained by people who are currently American citizens, rather than by anyone who chooses to settle here?

3. Extrapolating to the future. One important question is whether flows of immigration and the politics related to immigration display any discernable patterns. If there is no continuity, then can we reliably use past data to project trends in future population growth?

4. Immigration and population growth. What might be the connection between world population growth and immigration. Population growth means more people in the world. Immigration means shifting people from one part of the world into another. Indeed, if Becker's analysis of the family is correct, then immigration from poor countries like Mexico into rich countries like the United States is a good thing because it will lead to a falling birthrate. Given that it seems that immigration from poor to rich nations would lead to a net decrease in the birthrate, don't arguments about world overpopulation actually support the idea of *encouraging* unlimited immigration?

5. Feasibility of restricting immigration. On May 14, 2003, a trailer was discovered containing 70 illegal immigrants who had been smuggled from Mexico. The migrants were exposed to extremes of temperature and water deprivation such that nineteen of them died. Harvey Rice, *Two Plead Not Guilty in Deaths of 19 Migrants in Truck Trailer*, HOUS. CHRON., July 8, 2003, at 13. This was only one among many multiple fatality incidents involving immigrants trying to cross into the United States from Mexico. In the years 2000–2001 on average more than one person died each day trying to cross into the United States. Evelyn Nieves, *Illegal Immigrant Death Rate Rises Sharply in Barren Areas*, N.Y. TIMES, Aug. 6, 2002, at A1. The increasing death rate is intimately connected with increased border patrol activity. "To avoid the stepped-up border patrols in populated areas, the most desperate migrants cross in the more unguarded and desolate deserts of Arizona and eastern California." *Id.* Given that immigrants have demonstrated that they are willing to risk death to enter the United States, do Imhoff's proposals to control illegal immigration make sense?

6. Economics of immigration restriction. It is often claimed that immigrants contribute to the unemployment of citizens and depress the salary levels for the jobs in which they specialize. However, it is unclear that this is true. Economically, there is no difference between allowing free immigration and importing labor intensive goods from countries whose laborers would otherwise immigrate. Shubha Ghosh, *The Legal, Economic, and Policy Roles of Immigrant Entrepreneurs in the Immigration Debate*, 5 UCLA ASIAN PAC. L.J. 15, 17 (1998). Furthermore, people wishing to come to the United States could be a tremendous source of public income. The prices charged by immigrant smuggling "Coyotes" generally run from $1,000 to $4,000. Eliott C. McLaughlin, *"Coyotes" Offer Hope and Danger*, ATHENS BANNER-HERALD, July 6, 2003, *available at* http://www.onlineathens. com/stories/070703/bus_20030707013.shtml. If Imhoff's figure of one and a half million illegal immigrants per year is accurate, the government could make billions of dollars (literally) by simply selling permission to work in the United States. Additionally, once in the country, the "negative economic effects of immigration are ambiguous and unsubstantiated, but the benefits are established and substantial.... [and] basic economics argues that our laws should allow more immigration than they currently do." Larry J. Obhof, *The Irrationality of Enforcement? An Economic Analysis of U.S. Immigration Law*, 7 KAN. J.L. & PUB. POL'Y 163, 180 (2002). Given that the economics of immigration weigh so heavily on loosening controls, why do Imhoff and others argue for spending more resources on stopping immigration?

7. Feasibility of control of international migration. In light of the current status of illegal immigration discussed *supra* at 980, n.5, would it make any difference if there was maximum efficiency in border control strategies, supported by well-conceived and carefully implemented organizational structures?

8. Rationale for immigration restrictions. Piore is in favor of immigration restrictions because "over a very long period of time immigration does have the capacity to erode the employment opportunities of national workers, and because generally, a tight labor market in which labor is in short supply is more conducive to social progress than a loose one." However, might it be that the social progress he desires is thwarted by nativist impulses which can be legitimated by restrictions on immigration? For example, during the campaign in favor and following passage of California's Proposition 187, which, among other things, excluded the children of undocumented immigrants from public schools, harassment of Mexican Americans increased dramatically. Nancy Cervantes et al., *Hate Unleashed: Los Angeles in the Aftermath of Proposition 187*, 17 CHICANO-LATINO L. REV. 1 (1995). Does this correlation between nativism and immigration restriction undermine Piore's arguments?

9. Developments in Immigration Reform. The Immigration Reform and Control Act, Pub. L. No. 99–603, 100 Stat. 3359 (codified as amended in scattered sections of 8 U.S.C.), was enacted in 1986 and made it illegal to hire illegal immigrants and increased the number of authorized border patrol agents by 50 percent. TIMOTHY J. DUNN, THE MILITARIZATION OF THE U.S.–MEXICO BORDER, 1978–1992, at 49 (1996). Additionally, the character of the border patrol has changed substantially, as the border patrol adds drug interdiction to its objectives.

Since the attacks on September 11, 2001, government action relating to immigration control has become increasingly more vigilant. Secretive preventative detentions, mostly of those detained on immigration violations, increased rapidly after September 11, totaling over 1,000 by early November 2001. Many of those detained were held for weeks or months without charges, and all proceedings were conducted in complete secrecy. Futhermore, the U.S. Patriot Act, Pub. L. No. 107–56, 115 Stat. 272 (2001), enacted swiftly after September 11, authorizes the Attorney General to subject any alien to mandatory detention with only a reasonable belief that the alien engaged in certain vaguely specified terrorist activities. Moreover, the Act allows aliens to be deported if they provide any support that they know or reasonably should know would aid an organization in conducting terrorist activities, and allows denial of entry to aliens for ideological endorsements of terrorist activity. David Cole, *Enemy Aliens*, 54 STAN. L. REV. 953, 959–74 (2002); DAVID COLE, ENEMY ALIENS (2003).

Given this recent broadening of immigration control, are the observations and arguments made by Piore still sound?

10. Causes of fluctuations in Mexican immigration. Piore argues that current immigration by Mexicans can be explained by unwillingness of black youth to work low-status secondary jobs. An alternative hypothesis is that the jump in illegal immigration from Mexico was brought about by the termination of the Bracero program, a program in which the United States brought in hundreds of thousands of guest workers annually from Mexico. The Bracero program ran from the years 1942 to 1964. After the end of the Bracero program, the number of deportations skyrocketed, implying that the rise in illegal immigration is caused more by changes in government policy than by changes in employment patterns among blacks. Larry J. Obhof, *The Irrationality of Enforcement? An Economic Analysis of U.S. Immigration Law*, 12 KAN. J.L. & PUB. POL'Y 163, 178 (2002).

11. Border control. Lichtenberg analyzes immigration from Mexico in terms solely of U.S. and Mexican interests. However, the border between the United States and Mexico joins more than just the United States and Mexico, it joins the United States with the rest of the world. A national of a third country could easily travel to Mexico and then cross the border to the United States from Mexico. In the security conscious climate caused by the attacks of September 11, 2001, is Lichtenberg's rights-based analysis, which does not consider the threats to physical security posed by international terrorism, still applicable? For more on the security implications of international migration, see, for example, MICHELLE MALKIN, INVASION: HOW AMERICA STILL WELCOMES TERRORISTS, CRIMINALS, AND OTHER FOREIGN MENACES TO OUR SHORES (2002).

12. Cooperation with Mexico. Lichtenberg concludes that the governments of the United States and Mexico must work together to address the issues of legal and illegal immigration. However, given her analysis that the elite of Mexico have an interest in maintaining massive migration, which is counter to the interests of both the United States and Mexico, why should the U.S. government consult with the Mexican government? If Lichtenberg is truly able to determine the true interests of the Mexican people, as well as the motivations of the Mexican elite, shouldn't the U.S. government ignore the corrupt Mexican government and simply implement policies which advance the interests of the United States and Mexico, properly understood?

13. Consequences of the "escape valve." If Lichtenberg's position is correct, if Mexican migration, by alleviating unemployment and dissatisfaction in Mexico is a bad thing for Mexico, is there anything to stop that logic from being applied, by analogy, to any problem? Won't any measures taken to relieve suffering alleviate the pressure for social change caused by that suffering? Should the fact that Lichtenberg's position can be invoked to justify oppressing the downtrodden work to undermine Lichtenberg's credibility?

14. Guilty and not guilty. The Supreme Court held in *Plyler v. Doe*, 457 U.S. 202 (1982), that it is unlawful for local governments to deny access to public education to children of illegal immigrants. The theory behind that holding is that, while illegal immigrants themselves are guilty of breaking the law, their children are not, and should not be punished for the crimes of their parents. *Plyler* has generated a great deal of controversy, including a ballot initiative in California which, had it not been enjoined by the courts, would have invalidated *Plyler*. Phillip J. Cooper, Plyler *at the Core: Understanding the Proposition 187 Challenge*, 17 Chicano-Latino L. Rev. 64 (1995). Given the discontent with providing services for the children of illegal immigrants, should *Plyler* be reconsidered? What about if a child's parents immigrated to the United States specifically to take advantage of our social services? Would the rationale of *Plyler*, that children are essentially innocent bystanders, be valid in such a case?

15. Additional reading. For additional information on the *Plyler* decision, as well as the ballot initiative to invalidate it, see generally, John T. Ritondo, Jr., Comment, *California's Duty to Educate the World: Proposition 187 and Mere Rationality*, 26 Cumb. L. Rev. 1045 (1995/1996); Peter H. Schuck, *The Message of Proposition 187*, 26 Pac. L.J. 989 (1995); Nancy Cervantes et al., *Hate Unleashed: Los Angeles in the Aftermath of Proposition 187*, 17 Chicano-Latino L. Rev. 1 (1995); Phillip J. Cooper, Plyler *at the Core: Understanding the Proposition 187 Challenge*, 17 Chicano-Latino L. Rev. 64 (1995); Ruben J. Garcia, Comment, *Critical Race Theory and Proposition 187: The Racial Politics of Immigration Law*, 17 Chicano-Latino L. Rev. 118 (1995). For a religious perspective on immigration law and community, see Terry Coonan, *There Are No Strangers Among Us: Catholic Social Teachings and U.S. Immigration Law*, 40 Cath. Law. 105 (2000). For a scholarly perspective on current immigration issues, see Symposium, *Beyond Belonging: Challenging the Boundaries of Nationality: Proxies for Loyalty in Constitutional Immigration Law: Citizenship and Race After September 11*, 52 DePaul L. Rev. 871 (2003). For proposals to restrict immigration for security reasons aimed at a popular audience, see Yeh Ling–Ling, *Stop Immigration if We Are to Fight Terrorism*, Tucson Citizen, Sept. 4, 2002, *available at* http://www.diversityalliance.org/docs/

article_2002sep04.html; Michelle Malkin, Invasion: How America Still Welcomes Terrorists, Criminals, and Other Foreign Menaces to Our Shores (2002). For additional information on the dangers of immigration, see generally Eliott C. McLaughlin, *"Coyotes" Offer Hope and Danger*, Athens Banner-Herald, July 6, 2003, *available at* http://www.onlineathens.com/stories/070703/bus_20030707013.shtml; Juan A. Lozano, *Alleged Leader in Deadly Texas Immigrant-Smuggling Operation Arrested*, A.P., June 17, 2003, *available at* http://www.islandpacket.com/24hour/nation/story/920171 p-6407304c.html; *INS Announces Vast International Immigrant Smuggling Bust*, CNN, Oct. 17, 2000, *available at* http://www.cnn.com/2000/US/10/17/ins.bust/.

D.   Class Borders

Brown v. Artery Organization

654 F.Supp. 1106 (D.D.C. 1987).

■ Judge Greene delivered the opinion of the court.

The Fair Housing Act (42 U.S.C. §§ 3601 *et seq.*) prohibits discrimination with respect to housing, *inter alia*, on the basis of race or national origin. The most basic substantive issue involved in this case—one of first impression in this Circuit—is whether under the Act the overwhelmingly black and Hispanic tenants of a low-rent apartment complex have the right to secure injunctive relief against the conversion of such housing to high-rent units if they are able to establish that (1) the owners are engaging in the conversion for the purpose of displacing the minority tenants or (2) the displacement of these tenants will be the conversion's predictable and inevitable effect. * * *

I

Facts

Plaintiffs, tenants in the Dominion Gardens and Bruce Street apartment complexes in Alexandria, Virginia, filed this suit challenging the renovation of those complexes and the consequent displacement of its tenants, overwhelmingly black and Hispanic, as a violation of the federal Fair Housing Act. * * * Plaintiffs seek preliminary and permanent relief, that is, injunctions to restrain the defendants from taking any action to oust tenants who have already received 120-day eviction notices and from issuing any further notices to vacate. In addition, although following the institution of this action the private defendants withdrew earlier applications for co-insurance with the United States Department of Housing and Urban Development (HUD), plaintiffs also seek injunctive relief against HUD. That relief would require the Department to delete from its governing "Handbook" a provision which delegates to banks and other lenders

HUD's own statutory responsibility to minimize the involuntary displacement of tenants.

　* * *

IV

Framework for Substantive Decision

Plaintiffs' motion for a preliminary injunction alleges violations of the Fair Housing Act. It requests a number of specific injunctions against defendants Dominion Gardens Arlandria Limited Partnership and Potomac Village Limited Partnership, and it further requests that all the private defendants be enjoined from taking any action which would cause or contribute to the eviction of plaintiffs. Defendants oppose plaintiffs' motion primarily on the ground that plaintiffs have not satisfied their burdens under the Fair Housing Act, in that they have not established discriminatory intent or adverse effect, and their motions to dismiss for failure to state a claim upon which relief may be granted proceed on the basis of substantially similar arguments. Since the issues raised with respect to the two principal substantive motions thus overlap to a significant degree, this part of the Opinion discusses both motions within the framework of analysis for the preliminary injunction motion.

　* * * Under familiar principles, in determining whether to grant a preliminary injunction, the Court is required to consider four factors: (1) whether there is a substantial likelihood that plaintiffs will prevail on the merits; (2) whether plaintiffs will be irreparably injured if the injunction does not issue; (3) the hardship to defendants if the injunction is granted is balanced against the hardship to plaintiffs if the injunction is not granted; and (4) whether the public interest favors granting the preliminary relief requested. *Virginia Petroleum Jobbers Ass'n v. Federal Power Commission,* 259 F.2d 921, 925 (D.C.Cir. 1958). Plaintiffs are not required to prevail on each of these factors; rather the factors should be viewed as a continuum— more of one factor compensating for less of another. Preliminary injunctive relief, therefore, would not be precluded, for example, by a relatively weak showing of likelihood of success on the merits if the plaintiffs demonstrated that the other three factors weighed strongly in their favor. *Washington Metropolitan Area Transit Commission v. Holiday Tours, Inc,* 559 F.2d 841, 843–44 (D.C.Cir. 1977); *Massachusetts Law Reform Institute v. Legal Services Corp.,* 581 F.Supp. 1179, 1184 (D.D.C. 1984), *aff'd,* 737 F.2d 1206 (D.C.Cir. 1984). It is with these standards in mind that the Court examines the motions and the issues they present.

V

Precedents on Housing Discrimination

As indicated above, the Fair Housing Act prohibits public and private discrimination in housing on the basis of race or national origin. A central issue here, as in several other cases which have come before the federal courts in various parts of the country, is whether the Act requires proof of the landlord's intentional discrimination, or whether the statute is violated also where no such intention is established but where the conduct can be shown to have a discriminatory effect.

The answer to that question is unfortunately not entirely clear from a reading of the decided cases. Several of the decisions are inconsistent with each other; others are incomplete in significant respects; and still others do not distinguish between the various relevant concepts. While, to be sure, proof of discriminatory intent by the landlord seems everywhere to be regarded as establishing a violation of the statute, *see Betsey v. Turtle Creek Associates*, 736 F.2d 983, 986 (4th Cir. 1984), there is a variety of opinion, usually not reconciled in any systematic fashion, whether a violation may also be predicated solely upon proof that the landlord's actions had a discriminatory effect, that is, a disproportionate effect on minorities.

Some of the decisions hold, or at least intimate, that evidence of discriminatory effect is alone sufficient to establish a *prima facie* case under the Act. *See, e.g., Betsey*, 736 F.2d at 986; *Metropolitan Housing Corp. v. Village of Arlington Heights*, 558 F.2d 1283, 1290–91 (7th Cir. 1977) (hereinafter referred to as *Arlington II*); *Residents Advisory Board v. Rizzo*, 564 F.2d 126, 147–48 (3d Cir. 1977); *United States v. City of Black Jack, Missouri*, 508 F.2d 1179, 1184–85 (8th Cir. 1974). Other decisions—sometimes the same decisions—suggest that effect by itself is never enough; that there must also be a showing that the private landowner intended to discriminate. *See generally Betsey, supra; Arlington II, supra.*

To complicate matters further, of the cases holding that proof of discriminatory effect is alone sufficient, several distinguish between two types of effect: what has been called adverse impact discrimination and what is termed ultimate effect discrimination. *See, e.g., Arlington II*, 558 F.2d at 1290–91. Adverse impact discrimination is said to be established when the practice or policy in question has a disproportionate effect upon the minorities within the group to which the policy is applied (*e.g.*, the tenants in a particular apartment complex). *Id.; see Betsey*, 736 F.2d at 987–88. Ultimate effect discrimination, on the other hand, focuses upon a different pool: the entire population of a particular community. As the court phrased it in *Arlington II*, 558 F.2d at 1290, a violation of the Act will be found if the decision or policy in question "perpetuates segregation [in the community] and thereby prevents interracial association...."

Moreover, in some of the cases involving allegations of ultimate effect discrimination, liability under the Fair Housing Act appears to depend upon whether the defendant is a governmental body or a private entity, suggesting that proof of discriminatory effect alone (without proof of discriminatory intent) is enough only when the defendant is a governmental body. Indeed, the "ultimate effect" decisions generally involve governmental defendants, *see, e.g., Rizzo*, 564 F.2d at 149; *Black Jack*, 508 F.2d at 1184–85, and some of them explicitly hold that an action against a private landlord cannot be premised upon allegations of ultimate effect discrimination. *See, e.g., Boyd v. Lefrak Organization*, 509 F.2d 1110 (2d Cir. 1975); *Dreher v. Rana Management, Inc*, 493 F. Supp. 930 (E.D.N.Y. 1980).

VI

Rules to be Applied

The Court of Appeals for this Circuit has never had occasion to decide these issues, and this Court is thus not bound by any particular rule. After analyzing the decisions elsewhere, and after considering the theoretical underpinnings of the various holdings, this Court has decided that it will apply the following set of rules.

A.   If the defendant is a governmental body, proof of discriminatory impact of its actions on the community for which it serves suffices to establish a *prima facie* case of violation of the Fair Housing Act. It is unclear from the decided cases whether the governmental body involved can overcome that *prima facie* case by proof of a neutral or positive purpose or whether, in view of the objectives of the Fair Housing Act, the perpetuation of racial segregation or other discrimination by government must be regarded as so pernicious that evidence of a benign intent will not save the activity. Since, in the present posture at least, this case does not present that issue, its resolution may properly be left to another day or another court.

B.   If the defendant is not a governmental body, the plaintiff-tenants will be deemed not to have proved a violation of the Fair Housing Act if they demonstrate no more than that the defendant's actions have had or will have a discriminatory effect or impact: some proof of discriminatory intent (*see infra*) is necessary. The reasons for this conclusion are as simple and straightforward as they are significant.

While it makes perfect sense to charge a governmental entity with violations of the statute if its actions—by way of regulations, ordinances, zoning decisions, or the like—have the effect of fostering or perpetuating racial segregation, there is no indication that the Congress had in mind the far-reaching consequences of the application of such a rule on private landlords or developers. A rule which imposed the burden of responsibility on such individuals or entities for the racial effects of their housing conversions *irrespective of their purpose or intent* would not only render them responsible for consequences over which they have no control (*e.g.*, the racial mix in the community as a whole); but for the reasons cited below, it would also be likely to halt in their tracks most, if not all, private efforts to upgrade deteriorated housing stock in many of the large cities of this nation. The perpetuation and the spread of the resulting blight is not in the public interest, and plaintiffs have cited no evidence that it represents an objective of the Fair Housing Act.

It is an unfortunate fact, for which individual private landowners have no more responsibility than any other member of the community, that the income of a disproportionate number of blacks and members of other minority groups is such that, although they are able to afford low income housing, many cannot afford the rentals being charged for upgraded or luxury housing. As a consequence, if a disproportionate effect or impact on minorities were alone sufficient to call for injunctive relief under the statute, the inhabitants of low-rent private housing largely populated by minorities would be entitled on this basis to judicial orders halting the upgrading or conversion of such housing in all or almost all circumstances. That, as indicated, is not what Congress intended.

C. For these reasons, it is the Court's conclusion that the Act, properly construed, also requires proof of discriminatory intent. The question is—what degree of proof? Defendants suggest that such proof must be direct and convincing, and that, absent evidence of defendant expressions of racial animus or their equivalent, the complaint must be dismissed. That position is as faulty in its way as plaintiffs' claim that intent or purpose are irrelevant.

In the view of this Court, the correct standard is that alluded to by the Seventh Circuit in *Arlington II* and by the Fourth Circuit in *Smith*—that the extent of the proof of discriminatory intent required varies with the proof of discriminatory effect adduced; the more devastating to minorities the effect or impact of the landlord's actions, the less evidence will be required of his actual intentions. That is only common sense: if the impact of particular actions falls overwhelmingly on minorities, it is not unreasonable to regard that circumstance as some evidence, at least *prima facie*, that discrimination was the intended result. To put it another way, discrete evidence of discriminatory purpose is not as critical in that situation as when the impact of a landowner's actions falls alike, or more or less alike, on both minorities and non-minorities.

To be sure, for the reasons discussed above, a plaintiff must still offer some evidence of discriminatory intent in addition to the "effects" proof, but once such evidence, direct or circumstantial, has been produced, the burden falls properly upon the defendant to demonstrate that his decision was not the product in any way of racial purpose or motive.

D. Thus, the requirements of discriminatory effect and intent should be viewed from a single perspective: the more overwhelming the proof of discriminatory effect, the less the showing of discriminatory intent that is required to establish a violation of the Fair Housing Act, and vice versa. However, in every action brought against private parties under the Act, plaintiffs must allege and offer some proof of discriminatory intent in addition to the deduction that may be made from the effects of the defendant's actions.

VII

Application of the Principles to this Case

How do these general principles find applicability here on the basis of the present record? Plaintiffs have offered extensive proof of discriminatory effect. According to them, virtually all the tenants at the Bruce Street apartments and ninety per cent of the tenants at Dominion Gardens are members of minority groups, either black or Hispanic. As a consequence of the planned rehabilitation of the Dominion Gardens and Bruce Street apartment complexes, all of the tenants of those complexes will be evicted, and the vast majority of the 2,000 or so minority tenants will be foreclosed, according to plaintiffs' allegations, from obtaining affordable housing either in the rehabilitated complexes or elsewhere in the City of Alexandria. This will be so, say the plaintiffs, because of the combination of a low vacancy rate in Alexandria (1.7 per cent); high rents for available apartments (including those at Dominion Gardens and Bruce Street when rehabilitation is completed); and the continued existence of race discrimination in Alexandria, as evidenced by a statistical study compiled in September 1986. *See* Regional Fair Housing Consortium, *Race Discrimination in the Rental Housing Market: A Study of the Greater Washington Area* at 6 (September 29, 1986). Plaintiffs also allege, with supporting affidavits, that the displacement of these 2,000 minority tenants will significantly reduce the minority population of the City of Alexandria. In sum, according to plaintiffs, such progress as may have been made in recent times with respect to the inclusion of significant numbers of blacks and other minorities in the Alexandria population will largely be wiped out: that city will, once again, be essentially lily-white.

In contrast to plaintiffs' showing of a disproportionate effect of defendants' actions on blacks and Hispanics, their proof of discriminatory intent is not strong. They have offered no direct evidence at all of such intent. In fact, defendants vigorously assert that their objectives and interests are purely economic. However, plaintiffs have alleged, and to some degree proved, the existence of circumstances from which a trier of fact could eventually find discriminatory purpose if additional evidence of such purpose were adduced. Thus, plaintiffs allege that defendants knew, or should have known, that their actions would result overwhelmingly in the displacement of blacks and Hispanics both from the two apartment complexes directly involved and from the City of Alexandria itself. The Cafritz defendants have been intimately involved in the rehabilitation of at least one other apartment complex in Alexandria occupied primarily by minority tenants, and that rehabilitation resulted in the displacement of all or most of those minority tenants.

Moreover, from the evidence presented by both parties, it appears questionable whether the relocation program established by defendants at that apartment complex, which is comparable to the programs established at Dominion Gardens and Bruce Street, was at all effective in relocating the minority tenants in Alexandria. It is not inappropriate therefore to recall the Seventh Circuit's pronouncement that "conduct that has the necessary and foreseeable consequences of perpetuating segregation can be as deleterious as purposefully discriminatory conduct . . ." *Arlington II,* 558 F.2d at 1289.

Beyond this proof, however, there is the fact that plaintiffs have flatly alleged that defendants acted with discriminatory intent. To be sure, allegation is not proof, and absent some proof, in addition to that recited above, to support their allegation, plaintiffs will not be able to prevail. However, in view of the present posture of this case, plaintiffs have had precious little opportunity to engage in discovery—discovery that is particularly critical where intent is the issue.

In short, while plaintiffs have not adduced adequate evidence of intent to meet their burden of proof at trial, they have sufficiently alleged intent and presented a sufficient indication that they may be able to prove that allegation, that the Court would not be justified in foreclosing them from going forward at this juncture. Through discovery, plaintiffs may be able to bolster their showing in this regard. All that is required of plaintiffs at this preliminary stage, is that there be a substantial likelihood that they could succeed at trial. The Court concludes that plaintiffs have carried that burden.

In addition to supporting plaintiffs' case for a preliminary injunction, the above analysis also compels the conclusion that defendants' motions to dismiss must be denied. If there is any likelihood that plaintiffs will prevail on the merits, it cannot be said that they have failed to state a claim upon which relief may be granted.

VIII

Relative Injuries

Plaintiffs have clearly established that if the injunction is not issued they will be irreparably harmed. It is axiomatic that wrongful eviction constitutes irreparable injury. *Johnson v. United States Department of Agriculture*, 734 F.2d 774, 789 (11th Cir. 1984); *Edwards v. Habib*, 366 F.2d 628 (D.C. Cir. 1965). Indeed, plaintiffs allege that, if they are evicted, they will not be able to relocate in Alexandria due to the city's high rents and extremely low vacancy rate. Consequently, according to plaintiffs, many of them will have to attempt to relocate in new areas, find new jobs, and change schools for their children in mid-year. One significant consequence may be to force these generally low-income individuals and families to spend their limited funds and to waste long periods of time every day on transportation between their out-of-Alexandria housing and their in-Alexandria jobs. Others, it is said, will be forced to move into sub-standard housing in order to avoid homelessness. And some may wind up completely homeless. In addition, the search for new housing will itself cause plaintiffs to lose income—which is low and marginal even now—as they will have to take unpaid leave from their jobs and bear increased transportation costs.

By contrast, defendants can claim only that they *may* be harmed financially if the injunction is issued. Defendants assert that they may lose necessary long-term financing upon the issuance of a court order which had the effect of delaying the conversions, but little concrete support has been offered for that intrinsically not compelling speculation. They also allege, with somewhat greater justification, that the costs of rehabilitation will increase if that rehabilitation is delayed, and that even a short delay will negatively affect income from the project. These hardships, however, are not only largely speculative but they are also reparable and clearly not of the same magnitude as the injuries suffered by plaintiffs should they be wrongfully evicted. This would be so particularly if, as seems likely, plaintiffs would be able to find alternative housing only far away from Alexandria, their employment, schools, friends, and such other ties as they may have established. In short, the balance of hardships weighs heavily in favor of granting the preliminary injunction.

Finally, defendants claim that rehabilitation of the two apartment complexes in question will serve the public interest as it preserves the existing housing and neighborhoods. Issuance of an injunction, they argue, would create a strong disincentive for maintenance and rehabilitation programs for deteriorated housing. Defendants' arguments have obvious merit, and they cannot be dismissed lightly. However, since the early 1960s, the Congress has made eradication of discrimination in all facets of public life, including housing, a priority to which many otherwise private interests must give way. Based upon that strong public policy, the Court concludes that the public interest will most readily be served if prevention of the spread of racial discrimination in housing is given priority weight. This is most appropriately accomplished if allegations of race discrimination in housing which *prima facie* have a likelihood of being meritorious, are allowed fully to be developed at trial.

IX

Conclusion

Plaintiffs have alleged that their threatened evictions from the apartment complexes in which they reside were caused by a purpose or intent to discriminate against them on account of their race or national origin. Some support for that allegation is provided by the fact that the negative impact of the actions of the developers would fall almost entirely on blacks and Hispanics, and the fact that prior renovation programs of some of these same developers had the effect of clearing, or almost clearing, members of such groups both from the apartment complexes there involved and from the City of Alexandria itself.

In view of this preliminary showing, plaintiffs are entitled to prove at trial, if they can, that the developers' actions are the products, in whole or in part, of a discriminatory intent, in which case they will have made out a case of violation of the Fair Housing Act, and they will be entitled to permanent injunctive relief. It should be clear, however, that, while the allegations and the evidence before the Court are sufficient to entitle plaintiffs to a trial and to maintenance of the status quo pending that trial, that evidence will not, without more, support an ultimate judgment in plaintiffs' favor. Under the Fair Housing Act, there will have to be some additional proof, direct or circumstantial, of discriminatory intent.

An appropriate Order consistent with this Opinion is being issued herewith.

* * *

Artery's Agreements

WASH. POST, Apr. 11, 1988, at F33.

Artery sold the northernmost section (364 units) of the 960–unit Lee Gardens complex (now renamed Sheffield Court) to the private, nonprofit

Arlington Housing Corporation, which paid $50,000 per unit, or a total of $18.2 million. The complex deal included a variety of components:

The Arlington Housing Authority was given a $33 million tax-exempt loan from the Virginia Housing and Development Authority for the purchase and renovation of the units.

Artery contributed $1.076 million in cash toward the purchase.

The AHC will permanently maintain 200 of the units for lower-income tenants. Section 8 moderate rehabilitation certificates were obtained from the federal Department of Housing and Urban Development to subsidize rents in these units. The remaining 164 units will be rented at market prices.

Arlington guaranteed the VHDA loan by agreeing to a "moral," but not a legal, obligation to take over the loan payments if Arlington Housing Corporation defaults.

According to Artery, 320 households were moved from Lee Gardens. Of those, 238 remained in Arlington, 39 moved to Falls Church and rest scattered.

In addition, 23 of the 320 families decided to remain at Lee in an Artery-owned unit, taking advantage of a one-year subsidy from the company on the new, higher rent.

In the agreement involving Dominion Gardens, reached among Artery, Alexandria, the VHDA and HUD, a quarter of the total 416 units at Dominion Gardens, now named Kingsport, are set aside for lower-income tenants for five years. Forty-one of these units are reserved for an additional five years, and the parties are seeking additional financing so that all 104 units can be set aside.

Section 8 vouchers from HUD will be used to subsidize rents on the units. In order to supplement these HUD payments, which do not cover the costs of renovation, maintenance and utilities on the set-aside units, a package deal was arranged in which:

Artery agreed to forego some of its costs on these units.

Alexandria contributes $450,000.

Some lower-income tenants pay more rent than the 30 percent of their income required by Section 8 vouchers.

Alexandria applied to the VHDA for a loan of between $1.7 million to $7 million that will help subsidize set-aside units and possibly allow the city to preserve all 104 units for 10 years.

According to Artery, 270 households were moved out of Dominion Gardens. Approximately 75 percent remained in Alexandria; the rest moved elsewhere in Northern Virginia or to Maryland.

Of the 270 families, 52 bought a new home or condominium, partly with the help of the relocation money they received from Artery.

Some Tenants Left Out of Lee Gardens Victory

WASH. POST, Oct. 7, 1987, at B1.

■ EVELYN HSU

Mario Castillo is bewildered.

Castillo and other members of the Lee Gardens tenants association felt as if their efforts had paid off last week when the Artery Organization of Bethesda agreed to sell 364 units in the north section of the complex to a nonprofit Arlington housing group.

The deal would set aside 200 units for low-income tenants. The sale is not, final until Artery reaches an agreement with its lenders.

But Castillo and other tenants from the south side of the complex, who were considered the most active in championing the sale to the Arlington Housing Corp., now find they may not get the coveted subsidized units.

Because of regulations governing federal housing subsidies, tenants from the north side of the 961–unit complex will have first priority for the low-income apartments, all of which are located there.

"I'm very disappointed, disheartened." Castillo, secretary of the tenants association, said through an interpreter. "We had started this fight to get something better for all the community and for ourselves. After all this, we're the ones put aside, left out."

Federal regulations vest the tenants in the north section, which will become a separate housing project, with special rights, including first preference for subsidized units, said Arlington County Manager Anton S. Gardner.

Gardner said the county had asked the U.S. Department of Housing and Urban Development for permission to give residents in the south part of Lee Gardens second priority for the units.

HUD also has been asked to allow priority to be given to south Lee Gardens tenants for housing vouchers that will subsidize their rents at privately owned apartments elsewhere in the county, he said.

"I understand how it feels ... and how personally wrenching it is to some individuals," said Gardner.

This has not mollified tenants living in the south side of the complex, some of whom were turned down when they asked permission to move to the north side of the complex to receive priority for the subsidized units. A person familiar with the negotiations said that such a move would have unfairly favored some tenants of south Lee Gardens over others.

"Now we have to move," said Patricia Rodriguez, vice president of the tenants association and a resident of the south part of Lee Gardens. "We worked very hard to help them. We thought they would help us," she said of all the parties involved in the transaction. "I feel very bad."

The Arlington Housing Corp. has begun surveying families in north Lee Gardens to determine which are eligible for federal subsidies and the sizes of the units they will need.

It appears that 19 families are too large to be accommodated at the complex under state occupancy rules, said Wayne E. Rhodes, development coordinator for the county's housing division. Those families will have to move and will be offered relocation benefits, said Rhodes.

A similar, painful sorting out process is taking place at Alexandria's Dominion Gardens. That complex is also owned by Artery, which last week agreed to set aside for five years 104 of 416 units for low-income tenants who qualify for federal housing subsidies.

The agreement was approved by a federal judge as part of a settlement of a lawsuit alleging housing discrimination.

Some Dominion Gardens tenants complained at a court hearing last week that their settlement results in too few units being set aside for them and that occupancy restrictions will force large families from the complex. Also, some tenants complained that some small families can remain at the complex until they find suitable replacement housing, yet large families have been given a deadline to move.

"I was so disappointed in the settlement," said the Rev. Eldridge Harmon, a tenant at Dominion Gardens since 1985.

Attorneys for the tenants said the majority of residents were interested in settling the case.

U.S. District Judge Harold H. Greene, who approved the settlement, said in his ruling that state occupancy laws limiting the number of tenants in a unit would have been enforced even if the tenants had been victorious in their suit.

To qualify for a subsidized unit, a tenant must receive from the city a federal Section 8 voucher that limits a tenant's rent to 30 percent of his income, said Barry Goldstein, an attorney for the NAACP Legal Defense and Education Fund who represented the tenants in the court case.

Only families of four or fewer will be eligible for the subsidized units because of the occupancy requirements, he said. So far, 129 families have applied for the vouchers, he said. Some may not qualify financially, but if there are more applicants than units a lottery may be held.

There also may be room at the nearby Bruce Street apartments, where 68 out of 275 units are being set aside for low-income tenants as a result of a separate settlement with a different developer, said Goldstein.

"This is a very tough situation," said Goldstein.

"What we got was 104 units and a substantial increase in relocation benefits" for some Dominion Gardens families, he said. "We didn't solve all the housing problems in Northern Virginia."

NOTES AND QUESTIONS

1.   Public/private dichotomy. The district court, in granting a preliminary injunction, stated that, because the defendant was a private organization, it was necessary to show proof of discriminatory intent. However, the plaintiffs in this case were not only seeking to enjoin private defendants. In addition to Artery Organization, the plaintiffs sought to enjoin HUD from delegating its authority with respect to minimizing displacement of tenants. Furthermore, government is undoubtedly intimately involved in the business practices of the defendants in this case. Since the end of World War II, the government has actively subsidized the market for residential housing through means such as mortgage guarantees and tax deductions. William E. Nelson & Norman R. Williams, *Suburbanization and Market Failure: An Analysis of Government Policies Promoting Suburban Growth and Ethnic Assimilation*, 27 FORDHAM URB. L.J. 197, 234 (1999). If government subsidies greatly effect (or arguably create) an industry, shouldn't the responsibility for the practices of that industry, to some extent, fall on the government? Further, if the industry in question engages in policies which have a disparate impact on minorities, wouldn't it be more appropriate to use the government-specific disparate impact standard rather than the private industry specific disparate intent standard? If not, how can the government be prevented from engaging in *de facto* discrimination through proxies in the private market?

2.   Theories of responsibility. According to the court in *Brown*, 654 F.Supp. at 1116, "it is an unfortunate fact, for which individual private landowners have no more responsibility than any other member of the community, that the income of a disproportionate number of blacks and members of other minority groups is such that, although they are able to afford low income housing, many cannot afford the rentals being charged for upgraded or luxury housing." Of course, the defendants in this case are not private individuals, they are large real estate firms and private banks. Coincidentally, until the enactment of the FHA, and, to a depressing extent afterwards, large real-estate organizations and private banks engaged in systematic and continuous discrimination against minorities, particularly African–Americans. With this discriminatory history, how is it appropriate to compare the defendants in this case to the mythical "individual private landowner?"

3.   Class and race. *Brown v. Artery* was decided based on the impact that proposed renovations would have had on low income minority tenants as minorities, not on the impact that proposed renovations would have had on low income minority tenants based on their class status. Is the focus on race on *Brown v. Artery* just? If there were an affluent minority community in Alexandria such that the proposed renovations would not have effectively purged the city of minorities, would the same result have been warranted? What if, instead of minority tenants, Lee Gardens had been occupied by low income Caucasians? Is it possible to distinguish between discrimination based on class and discrimination based on race? Would such a distinction be desirable? For a fascinating case study of combined race and class discrimination in the small town of Shaw, Mississippi in the late 1960s, see CHARLES HAAR & DANIEL W. FESSLER, THE WRONG SIDE OF THE TRACKS (1986).

4. Value of property. In American society, home ownership has come to replace the ownership of productive property (e.g., a farm) as the goal to which all citizens are assumed to aspire. Phyliss Craig–Taylor, *To be Free: Liberty, Citizenship, Property, and Race*, 14 HARV. BLACKLETTER L.J. 45 (1998). With this in mind, class discrimination can be especially damaging because it not only injures directly but also denies its victims the chance to participate in the ideal American community.

5. Fair Housing Act of 1988. The Fair Housing Act of 1988 makes discrimination on the basis of family status illegal, specifically prohibiting five classes of behavior, including: refusing to sell or rent, or refusing to negotiate for the sale or rental of, or otherwise making unavailable or denying a dwelling to any person based on familial status. Shelly D. Cutts, *The Fair Housing Amendments Act of 1988: An Incomplete Solution to the Problem of Housing Discrimination Against Families*, 30 ARIZ. ST. L.J. 205, 207 (1998). Would these amendments have addressed the complaints voiced by individuals in large families with regard to the Artery agreements?

6. *Artery* and the Emerald City. When dissenting from denial of certiorari in *Cleveland Board of Education v. Reed*, Justice Rehnquist wrote that "[e]ven if the Constitution required it, and it were possible for federal courts to do it, no equitable decree can fashion an 'Emerald City' where all races, ethnic groups, and persons of various income levels live side by side in a large metropolitan area." *Cleveland Bd. of Educ. v. Reed*, 445 U.S. 935, 938 (1980) (Rehnquist, J., joined by Burger, C.J. & Powell, J., dissenting from denial of cert.). It would seem then that avoiding a racially integrated city was an overriding priority for Justice Rehnquist, given that it would justify ignoring the requirements of the constitution when it was practicable to abide by them. Does the agreement above, along with all statutes that forbid housing discrimination, contravene Rehnquist's imperative to avoid the "Emerald City?"

7. Problems with the status quo? In the case of *Brown v. Artery Organization*, 654 F.Supp. 1106 (D.D.C. 1987), there was never any allegation that the housing in question was losing money for its owners at any time. The only question seems to be lost opportunity for additional profits. Since there was never any question that the housing in question was being run at a loss, why did there have to be any changes made at all? Prevention of housing discrimination is an overriding priority for the government, and, in this case, maintaining the status quo could have solved the possible problem of evicting minority tenants, as well as allowed Artery to continue to operate its low income housing at a profit. Since that was the case, why did these agreements have to be made at all?

8. Additional reading. For additional information about the development of home ownership in America, see William E. Nelson & Norman R. Williams, *Suburbanization and Market Failure: An Analysis of Government Policies Promoting Suburban Growth and Ethnic Assimilation*, 27 FORDHAM URB. L.J. 197 (1999); Phyliss Craig–Taylor, *To be Free: Liberty, Citizenship,*

Property, and Race, 14 HARV. BLACKLETTER L.J. 45 (1998); SHERYLL CASHIN, THE FAILURES OF INTEGRATION: HOW RACE AND CLASS ARE UNDERMINING THE AMERICAN DREAM (2004). For additional information about the intersection of race and class, see Jennifer M. Russell, *The Race/Class Conundrum and the Pursuit of Individualism in the Making of Social Policy*, 46 HASTINGS L.J. 1353 (1995). For additional information on housing discrimination, see Peter E. Mahoney, *The End(s) of Disparate Impact: Doctrinal Reconstruction, Fair Housing and Lending Law, and the Antidiscrimination Principle*, 47 EMORY L.J. 409 (1998); Shelly D. Cutts, *The Fair Housing Amendments Act of 1988: An Incomplete Solution to the Problem of Housing Discrimination Against Families*, 30 ARIZ. ST. L.J. 205 (1998); Robert F. Drinan, S.J., *Untying the White Noose*, 94 YALE L.J. 435 (1984) (book review). For additional information on discrimination against the poor, see generally Gene R. Nichol, *Toward a People's Constitution*, 91 CALIF. L. REV. 621 (2003) (book review); John Shomberg, *Equity v. Autonomy: The Problems of Private Donations to Public Schools*, 1998 ANN. SURV. AM. L. 143 (1998); Susan H. Bitensky, *We "Had a Dream" in* Brown v. Board of Education, 1996 DET. C.L. REV. 1 (1996); Gay Gellhorn, *Justice Thurgood Marshall's Jurisprudence of Equal Protection of the Laws and the Poor*, 26 ARIZ. ST. L.J. 429 (1994).

From the Punitive City to the Gated Community: Security and Segregation Across the Social and Penal Landscape

56 U. MIAMI L. REV. 89 (2001).

■ MONA LYNCH

INTRODUCTION

Just over twenty years ago, criminologist Stanley Cohen articulated his vision of a newly evolving penal world, "The Punitive City," which was distinguished by several elements: The dispersal and penetration of social control beyond prison walls; the blurring of spatial boundaries which mark the differences between inside and outside, freedom and captivity, imprisoned and released, and guilty and innocent; the emergence of a corrections continuum where intervention and control is finely graded to fit individual "need"; and the widening of the controllable population which resulted from fuzzier definitions of deviancy and normalcy. Cohen conceptualized his "punitive city" as a community built on finely graded social control mechanisms with few clear boundaries between classes and categories of citizens.

These representations of a new form of penal control were most apparent in the emerging revolution of what is euphemistically known as "community corrections" or community-based control. Community control ideology embraces the involvement of family, schools, peers, neighborhoods, the police, and an array of community professionals in keeping the criminal in line within the community, rather than isolated in a distinctly segregated penal institution. While Cohen doubted that these new community-based forms of intervention would replace the prison, he did indicate that prison incarceration rates would likely remain static, if not decline, as the prison became a last resort on the continuum of correction, rather than the first resort for penal intervention.

Cohen's imagined new "punitive city" was not the only expression of doubt about the role and purpose of segregated penal institutions during that period. Beginning in the 1970s, the value and necessity of the prison was being broadly and fundamentally challenged by practitioners and theorists across the U.S. and western Europe. Not only were the physical institutions and day-to-day institutional practices in the critical spotlight, but the very foundations upon which they rested, the philosophies, beliefs, and cultural tenets that told all of us why we punish and with what social aims were scrutinized and challenged. As criminologist Andrew Scull suggested at the time, the movement away from incarceration and toward "community corrections" involved a direct assault on the very intellectual foundations underlying the established systems of control. The rehabilitative mission was critiqued by those on both the left and the right of the political spectrum. It was coming to be seen as a failed experiment which denied the moral autonomy of criminal actors, allowed for oppressive institutional conditions under the guise of benevolence, and simply "didn't work".

* * *

Yet what appears to have happened in the US (in particular, although not exclusively) is that this penological crisis and movement toward alternate criminal justice responses in no way lessened the reliance on prison as a central form of social control. Indeed, the explosion in the sheer numbers of people being imprisoned in this country, and in the rate at which people are imprisoned, actually began its upswing right around the time Cohen's piece on the Punitive City was published and the prison's credibility was being overtly challenged.

In this paper, I explore a potential (if partial) explanation for this somewhat ironic prison explosion by looking beyond the machinery of criminal justice, and analytically resituating the prison as a social institution within the broader socio-cultural landscape. The article begins by describing the transformation of the American prison itself over the past several decades from what was, at least in how it was explicitly idealized, an institution that aimed to reform its charges for the betterment of the inmates themselves as well as the broader society, to the current incarnation of the post-rehabilitative, security-oriented prison. Further, this article will illustrate how the underlying logic of the contemporary prison appears to inform many aspects of contemporary community life, which is a direct contrast to the projected course in which the language and elements of "community" were going to permeate and transform the penal realm. I specifically examine the rise of the "gated community" as a fitting exemplar of the segregative, security oriented society which analysts such as Gary Marx describe. This portion of the paper seeks to illustrate the parallels between "free" gated communities and the prison as an involuntary, no-frills gated community. The article concludes by analyzing what are suspected contributing factors in these social and spatial transformations, and discussing the theoretical implications of these changes and the fundamental impact of these new forms of security zone communities on contemporary social and civic life.

A DERAILED DEMISE OF THE PRISON

As noted above, all of the deep doubts openly expressed about the penal institution's purpose and function did not add up to the "death" of the prison but instead coincided with an unprecedented expansion of its use in the United States. Specifically, between 1930 and 1975, the annual prison incarceration rate in the United States was generally fairly stable, varying between the low nineties to a high of about one-hundred-nineteen (in 1961) per one-hundred thousand population. The incarceration rate began its steady and consistent climb upwards in 1976, and by 1998 the overall national rate had more than tripled in two decades to four-hundred-sixty-one per one-hundred-thousand. At the end of the 20th century, there were in excess of 1.3 million people housed in state and federal prisons in the United States, which was about 1 million more than were incarcerated just two decades earlier. When those imprisoned at the local level, in county jails and juvenile facilities are added into the count, there were more than 2,000,000 incarcerated people in the U.S. by year-end 1999. This imprisonment explosion cannot be explained away by rising crime rates. The rate of incarceration per 1000 index crimes has also nearly quadrupled in two decades, suggesting the growth was due in large part to changing crime control policy.

Besides the growth in the rate and sheer number of people imprisoned over the past several decades, there have been several other notable transformations in the use of prisons in the United States over the same period. First, the racial and ethnic composition of the incarcerated population underwent significant change. The percentage of minorities relative to whites in prison, and relative to their percentage in the general population, especially of African–Americans, grew significantly from 1960 through the 1990s, with the sharpest increase beginning around 1980. Indeed, the incarceration rate for African–American men has increased so dramatically that it has literally reshaped the social structure of entire urban communities over the past twenty years.

Second, the kinds of offenders who occupy American prisons are increasingly non-violent offenders, despite the political rhetoric that would suggest otherwise. Drug offenders in particular have made up a disproportionate percentage of the population growth over the past 2 decades, and a disproportionate number of those who are sent to prison have been African American, not white, drug offenders.

Third, life inside institutional walls has been transformed over the same general period at facilities across the country. The emphasis on incapacitation rather than on rehabilitation in the broader criminal justice sphere has meant that prisons are becoming mere containment sites of varying security levels, with fewer resources devoted to traditional rehabilitative activities. The proliferation of "super-max" prisons in the United States, with their hallmark features of extreme isolation combined with high-tech, high-level security, are just one telling example of contemporary life behind bars. Thus, institutional life itself has undergone a dramatic qualitative shift that coincides with the changes in population demographics and numbers.

If one looks at the state of California, which lays claim to one of the most populous prison systems in the country, the incredible growth of the system is also demonstrated in numbers and rates of incarceration over the last two decades. The incarceration rate in the end of the 1978 was about 95/100,000 with an institutional population of around 21,000 inmates. Twenty years later, the rate was nearly five times higher at 481 per 100,000 and a total institutional population stood at 163,000. The growth is also evident in the physical expansion of California's system. Twenty-one of thirty-three prisons in use in the state, or two-thirds of all operating prisons, have been built since 1982, at a cost of about 5.3 billion dollars. The Department of Corrections now accounts for just over seven percent of the entire state budget, up from about two point nine percent in 1980.

A number of criminal justice scholars have begun to examine why this expansion has occurred, especially directly on the heels of the deep cynicism broadly expressed about the prison's utility and necessity. Perhaps the two most prominent categories of explanations for the huge growth can be characterized as economic/structural and political/cultural. For instance, Ted Chiricos and Miriam Delone address the seemingly Marxist paradox of prison expansion in a time of economic prosperity. The researchers have demonstrated that this contemporary period does indeed have a significant surplus labor population despite appearances to the contrary, and that this population size is positively correlated to use of imprisonment. A number of scholars have also linked the vast economic restructuring brought on by post-industrial market changes and general economic globalization over the past several decades to the growth of the prison "industrial complex" especially as directed at non-Whites.

In terms of the role of politics and issue frames, Katherine Beckett has illustrated how crime as political capital, particularly in the Reagan–Bush years, in concert with media attention to state-shaped crime issues, contributed to the expansion of imprisonment as a primary criminal justice policy, especially at the federal level. Indeed, a number of researchers have pointed to the mass media's role in at least fueling, if not creating, panic over crime which can only be remediated through harsh penal policies (e.g., Scheingold's explication of the "myth of crime and punishment, Irwin and Austin's examination of the interplay between economics, politics and media that has contributed to America's 'imprisonment binge'; Chiricos's analysis of the media-hyped cocaine panic in the 1980s which spawned harsh federal mandatory minimum statutes, and Surette's description of the media influence in California's Three Strikes 1990s lawmaking frenzy, to name a few.")

Several theorists have also grappled with the process by which this penal punitiveness has been put into popular and political language. Dario Melossi describes what he calls the "changing hegemonic vocabulary of punitive motive" which flowed from society's elites to the populace during the period of 1970–1992. During this period, the instrumental value of punishment was in essence translated into a form of moral language adopted and acted upon by politicians and the public. Jonathan Simon has suggested that what he calls, "governing through crime" in which elected officials substitute punitive crime control rhetoric and new penological policy-making in the place of substantive governance, accounts in part for the changing penal practices.

There is also, as described above, an important and growing body of work that places the incarceration boom squarely within the political realm, and illuminates the changing role of crime control/penal policy in state and federal politics and governance. Thus far, though, the prison explosion has generally been most extensively documented in terms of its extent, its practical consequences, and its policy implications. Indeed, there are some underlying social and cultural changes that seem to have contributed to this prison explosion, especially in regard to its changing qualitative features, which have been less fully explored. In particular, one of the links in the process which should be addressed is how the prison itself has transformed in meaning so that it could conceptually "fit the bill" in the new post-rehabilitative era. Given its precarious position just twenty-five years ago, one could easily have imagined a new (or retro) set of punitive penal strategies emerging from the confluence of punitive crime and punishment politics, growing concern with risk management, and skepticism about the function of penal intervention, which would have subsumed the prison's role.

PRISONS AS UNDERCLASS "LIFESTYLE COMMUNITIES"

The first aspect of the changing social meaning of the prison has to do with the understanding of its very function as a populated social space. Where the prison has traditionally been understood as an institution of transformation, in which the goals of training, fixing, and rehabilitating were primary, at least rhetorically, thus analogous in some ways to the school or the factory, it is now better understood as a place to be for those sentenced; thus a form of residence. While the prison was founded and firmly rooted in a rehabilitative tradition, its very nature, as well as its social and cultural place in the larger social sphere, has been fundamentally reconstructed in recent years. Prisons today are explicitly justified primarily (although not exclusively) as being useful for incapacitation, and perhaps a bit of retribution. As a result, the contemporary prison need only function as a holding place where the primary obligation to the residents is the famed "three hots and a cot," and the central obligation to the larger community is simply to keep convicted persons out of sight and behind bars. The label that aptly captures this shift in the role of the prison from a place that reforms to an incapacitative residence is one that is applied with more and more frequency to penal institutions—the warehouse prison.

That the prison is thought of in these terms, by the public, politicians, academics, and practitioners alike, is evident in a number of small but telling ways. First, there is the ascension of a strain of criminological theories explaining criminality as a form of lifestyle or career. As David Garland suggests, the contemporary offender is "no longer [viewed as] the poorly socialized misfit in need of assistance, but instead an implicit, opportunistic consumer." Thus, for instance, the "new criminologies of everyday life" exemplified by Felson and Cohen's routine activities theory presupposes that crime is committed by a rational actor who will only choose such behavior when the rewards are greater than the costs.

Implicit in this understanding of criminality, of course, is that a criminal "career" is a matter of individual choice and personal preference. Thus, the most appropriate intervention is mere preventive containment, since the only reform that would work to get the criminal straight is a change in lifestyle choice. Indeed, one of the few transformative programs within correctional settings that is currently popular is a series of classes offered to correctional populations about changing their lifestyle choices, along with other "cognitive" adjustment programs!

It follows, then, that those who go to prison may be seen as opting for that as their lifestyle community. One hears the assumption that convicts choose to go to prison sounded in a variety of venues. My own fieldwork on parole field supervision demonstrated that parole agents and hearing officers sometimes explicitly justified returns to prison as the choice of the wayward parolee. In the public and political realms, recent demands for tougher institutional conditions such as removing weight equipment, limiting television access, smoking bans, clothing and grooming restrictions are implicitly and explicitly justified on the need to lessen the appeal of the "country club" prison for would-be felons. Some prisons have even begun to charge rent to inmates for their stays, ranging from $10–60 a day. This language also extends to the market end of contemporary prisons, as illustrated in the ad campaigns for correctional products. For instance, DLR prison architectural firm, which frequently advertises in the correctional trade periodical, *Corrections Today*, uses the ad copy "Providing Accommodations for Selected Guests," above a photograph of a jailed man's torso with his hands extending through the bars, and a cigarette dangling between his fingers, in one of its display advertisement campaigns.

Institutions themselves appear to be increasingly operating purely as self-contained communities, with fewer connections with, and obligations to, the larger community. For example, Jonathan Simon has demonstrated how corrections in California increasingly operates in terms of internally defined efficiency and accountability goals. The internal goals are employed rather than the previously dominant externally defined goals which linked correctional success to offenders' post-sentence law abiding behavior in the community. I have found on my visits to institutions in California that prison representatives explicitly describe the prison as a "little city", offering a lengthy narrative about how the prison functions like a self-contained community. The guides on these institutional tours present the main activities that go on behind the gates as ones that simply serve to keep the place functioning smoothly. For instance, they explain where bedding and clothes are laundered, how meals are handled, how to make enough coffee for so many residents, and how to move people through the institution without threatening security. Inmate jobs are generally described in terms of their functionality within the institution, not as skill building or otherwise for the rehabilitation of the inmate, as they might be under a rehabilitative model. Even the cells are referred to as "houses" by inmates and staff alike. Those in the business of corrections products can be found to have adopted the same language in their sales pitches, as is illustrated in a long running display advertisement campaign used by KLN Steel Products Company. In it, several photographs of steel bunks, tables, stools, and lockers are featured below the ad copy: "Furniture for Every Room in the House."

If the prison is better understood as a form of residential community rather than as a reformatory, understanding its proliferation may lie in examining the qualitative shifts in residential communities during the same period. First, examining the notion of community, especially as articulated by Cohen, will illuminate where his (and his contemporaries') vision of the new correctional community failed to be realized. In Cohen's imaginary punitive city that appeared on the horizon, criminal deviants intermingled with middle-class law abiding folks, living together, working together, learning together. This kind of diversified community which could be imagined at that time no longer seems so plausible. The potential for all kinds of mixed communities after the Civil Rights revolution of the 1950s, 60s, and 70s appeared to nearly vanish by the 1980s.

A number of scholars have demonstrated the persistence and intractability of race and class segregation in communities across the nation over the last two decades, although its form has changed in shape, given the explicit prohibitions against residential and other forms of discrimination that were the product of the Civil Rights era litigation and legislation. Gregory Squires documents how policies which favor free market control of housing have contributed to the solidification of residential segregation. This segregation has occurred despite laws prohibiting outright discrimination in providing mortgages and in selling and leasing residential properties. Residential areas in many regions are becoming increasingly homogenized, rather than diversified, on a number of dimensions in the post-Civil Rights era. Generally, market forces have become the proxy by which the entrenched racial and class segregation of the pre-Civil Rights period has been allowed to persist.

Perhaps the most striking development along these lines in recent years, and the one most relevant to the subject of this paper, has been the rise of "gated communities". In many ways, these developments, which are planned residential communities of varying sizes and distinguished by their use of gates and barriers to control who may enter into their space, represent the cardinal point on a continuum of segregated residential security zones that has as its opposite end-point the new "warehouse" prison.

According to urban planning scholars Edward Blakely and Mary Snyder, gated communities began to surge in number beginning in the early 1980s. By the mid–1970s there were about two-thousand five hundred of such residential communities and by the mid–1990s, there were about twenty thousand gated communities containing more than three million housing units. Blakely and Snyder suggest that the rate of building gated communities exceeds that of non-gated planned residential developments in a number of areas. This means there will be a continuation of gated community growth for at least some time.

Gated communities have several defining features. First and foremost, as just noted, they are marked by physical boundaries—walls and gates—which define the space within as private and closed to all but residents and authorized visitors. Second, those within tend to be similar to each other. Residents are homogenized by economics—each community is generally built to aim for a particular piece of the market in terms of pricing. The executive developments do not include the modestly priced two bedroom home; the pricing of units within a development ensures that economically similar buyers will become neighbors. In fact, in some of the larger developments, there are gates within gates that protect the highest-end residents from even their more modest neighbors. Residents of gated communities also tend to be relatively racially homogeneous—generally, white, as observed by Blakely and Snyder in their visits to such communities across the country. As they point out, this is one by-product of the design. "The segregation that gated communities represent is intentionally economic, but race and class are closely correlated attributes in our society." Finally, the proliferation of gated communities is driven in significant part by residents' concern for security, anxieties about crime and other social problems, and a desire to be with similar people.

If we look at the prison as another form of gated community or residential security zone, albeit involuntary and state-run, its growth over the past couple of decades is less puzzling. First, it is within the current cultural language to understand criminals as consumers of prison as a lifestyle community. For instance, criminologist Mark Fleisher, addressing a lay audience in USA Today magazine, frames "lifestyle criminals" use of prison in just these kinds of terms. "To [these criminals], prisons are sanctuaries that deliver social, medical, and recreational services. . . . Prison is stable and offers plenty of food, a clean bed, recreation, and access medical and dental services. Social life in prison is good, too. Some inmates continue criminal activity, such as drug dealing, while others just 'lay up' and enjoy the safety and pleasures of not having to hustle for money and food every day."

In justifying the toughening of prison conditions in California prisons in the late 1990s, former Governor Wilson's spokesman argued, "We got into the position . . . of providing a rather comfortable lifestyle in prison— We should not allow prisoners to ride roughshod over the prisons. They're not there to be entertained and catered to." Louisiana state legislator Troy Hebert justified his bills to limit television and smoking in prisons, quaintly entitled the "Party is Over" package, on similar grounds. "It should be a prison; it is not a hotel you are going to when you go to jail ... Inmates now just lie around and watch baseball games and soap operas." He added that some prisoners have it better in jail than at home "with three meals a day, clean sheets and TV". In the case of prisons, the public is also at least conceived as willing consumers of the product of prisons. As the California Department of Corrections boasts on their official website, beginning in 1981, California voters, "enthusiastically supported separate bond issues totaling more than two billion dollars" to support the "most ambitious prison constructions program in the world."

One can make the analogy between prisons and gated communities fairly easily. First, like the free gated community, the prison is also first and foremost marked by physical boundaries—walls and gates—that define the space inside as inaccessible to all but the residents, staff, and authorized visitors. Second, prisons are relatively homogeneous in population, in terms of the constellation of their demographics. A 1991 national survey of American prisoners indicated that over eighty-five percent had an annual income under $25,000 prior to imprisonment (seventy percent of total had an income below $15,000); most prisoners are men who range in age from twenty to forty, and two-thirds are racial minorities, primarily African–American, who by 1997 constituted nearly half of the state and federal prison population. And, as several researchers have illustrated, the proliferation of prison is explicitly justified by concerns for security, and is offered as a remedy to quell anxieties about crime and other social problems. Further, research on racial attitudes and opinion on punishment indicates that public support for punitive crime control policies is negatively correlated with support for integrationist policies and positively associated with negative racial stereotyping by whites.

Finally, the explosion of the post-rehabilitative "warehouse" prison, and the proliferation of gated communities follow a distinctly similar regional pattern, in addition to being contemporaneous in development. In particular, the Sunbelt and the Southwest regions—states like Florida, Texas, Arizona, Nevada, and California, particularly Southern California—have been the site of the most rapid development of both forms of the "gated community". These states have been at the forefront of prison building, including the construction of post-rehabilitative "super-max" units, and in the escalation of imprisonment rates in the past twenty or so years. They are also the same ones that have the highest concentration of gated developments.

Dana Young has even suggested that gated communities might be best viewed as nearly synonymous with prisons, in that they "represent a trend more concerned with regulating and controlling the residents within its gates and demoralizing relatively powerless groups outside its walls than with reducing the overall amount of avoidable social deprivation." She goes on to conclude, "perhaps common interest developments are ironically closer to functioning like prisons rather than like the idyllic Edens they seek to emulate. The epitome of a gated community is surely a prison." Arguably, there is a profound and fundamental difference between prisons and gated communities. Namely, with prisons, people are fenced in against their will by the state, and in the other, residents pay a premium price in private transactions to fence others out. Nonetheless, as Young might suggest, this crucial distinction depends on the target resident's viewpoint of what can be seen as a similar set of underlying logics of security and segregation.

There is a point on the "residential security zone" continuum where this difference becomes blurred and turns on the fenced in/fenced out variable. Specifically, a growing trend in public housing is "gating" for security and crime control. In these developments, while the residents are nominally living there voluntarily, two aspects suggest that this type of gating is both the mid-point and turning point on the continuum suggested.

First, the gating decision is made by a state entity and imposed upon the residents, often with little or no input by them in the decision. Second, some of those living in these public housing gated communities express a sense of real confusion about whether the gates fence outsiders out or fence residents in. Residents in a recently "gated" DC housing project compared their experiences of having their housing development gated by the government to being jailed. As one resident put it, "We aren't animals. We don't need to be caged."

Finally, in Atlanta (among other cities), which has been at the forefront of gating public housing, residents of some communities are being subject to requirements that strongly resemble a criminal justice intervention. This is the case even though their only "offense" is poverty and a reliance on subsidized housing. Residents at some of these developments are subject to criminal records checks and are required to do community service. In addition, there are nightly curfews and limits imposed upon them by the Housing Authority regarding how long extended family and friends may visit in their homes. Some residents are required to carry ID cards to prove they belong, and can be evicted after two violations of these and other rules. As one resident complained to a reporter about the litany of restrictions he lived under, "This is not a prison. People should be able to come and go as they please."

The defining features, then, of these various forms of communities are the emphasis on security technology and boundary maintenance through the use of barriers to maintain variously defined segregated populations. At the "free" end, it tends to be the wealthiest who are shutting others out to maintain an "exclusive" environment, and at the other end, it is the poor and socially defined deviants who are fenced in.

GATES AND FENCES AS MECHANISMS FOR POST-CIVIL RIGHTS SEGREGATION

The question remains, why the expansion of both of these extreme forms of gated communities at this period in time? It does not appear to be happenstance that both occurred at the end of the Civil Rights revolution.

Subsequent to the 1968 enactment of the Fair Housing Act and related civil rights legislation, both the free market and the state have contributed to the maintenance of social and spatial divisions that fall on racial, ethnic, and class lines through less open and direct means than those in practice up until that time. Although neither openly targets populations based on racial categories, both work in ways that result in racialized segregation. The marketers of gated communities promote the "exclusivity" of the community and promise "like-minded neighbors" as pitches to their potential customers.

The use of race restrictive covenants by private housing developments to ensure racial segregation dates back to the early part of the twentieth century. Once these explicit covenants were definitively deemed unenforceable in 1948, however, homeowner associations began to develop and enforce "race-neutral" restrictive covenants which continued to maintain racial, ethnic, and class segregation. The homeowner association was created as a response to the loss of formal racial segregative mechanisms within private residential communities.

Under this model of privatized resident screening, association members and boards had the authority to determine and enforce "qualification" requirements designed for "preserving the character [and] . . . integrity" of the housing development, including occupancy density and other "lifestyle" restrictions. While the most blatant forms of such screening were more effectively controlled by the Fair Housing Act, the increasing level of spatial, political, and governmental distance that community developers put between their developments and urban centers continued to ensure relative homogeneity within. The subsequent fortification of such residential communities with gates and barriers simply added another layer to the privatized segregation.

* * *

The question remains as to how gates, barriers, and security hardware and software become an appropriate response to concerns about security and safety, fears of crime victimization, and anxieties about racial, cultural, and class differences. The changes described above did not just happen from a top down process, where state actors and/or private developers decided to impose a new regime to maintain race and class divisions. Rather, there has been an interactive transformative process that has occurred at multiple levels of society and culture to facilitate the acceptance and spread of this phenomenon. A major component of that transformative process (but by no means the only one), I suggest, has involved the successful mass commodification of both security and "community", in the form of products, technologies, amenities, and services. In turn, this commodification process agnosticized both state punishment and civil society.

Thus, the safe and secure lifestyle community is no longer something to be created through civic participation, but rather purchased as an amenity to one's residence. Additionally, protection against crime and other social ills is no longer a problem solved by human intervention in the form of rehabilitation or social/structural problem-solving. Rather it too can be purchased through the investment in sophisticated software and hardware that promises to incapacitate the problem population, or at least keep them out of the gated neighborhood. Consequently, these aspects of social life which have not always been thought of in terms of pure marketability have now been seized upon by myriad goods and service marketers in a manner that strips each of its underlying human values. Community responsibility is reduced to paying taxes and approving bond measures to fund the expanding prison industry, on the one hand, and paying homeowners fees and assessments to maintain gates and round-the-clock security patrols, on the other. Not surprisingly, there are hordes who are willing to pay.

The growth of security as a marketable commodity in the place of socially created forms of security has been documented in the form of private police and alarm systems. The emerging literature on gated communities and other forms of exclusive communities also suggests that security, community and lifestyle are becoming products to be purchased, rather than social states that are created. Further, the segregative goal of these social spaces is made evident in the sales pitches.

The private gated communities tend to sell both security and segregation more subtly. For example, Scottsdale, Arizona's Desert Mountain development's promotional package uses the descriptive adjectives "exclusive", "gated" and "serene" as single word selling points to describe the myriad amenities and features. The package boasts that this community that offers "members only exclusivity" and is "the envy of all, reserved for a few." DC Ranch, also in Scottsdale, Arizona, which is made up of mostly gated "neighborhoods", except for the low-end developments (in the $200,000 range) on the south side of the development, tells potential buyers in its promotional materials:

> Of course, comfort in your surroundings is dependent on more than the design of your home and neighborhood. Accordingly, DC Ranch has taken a number of steps to heighten peace of mind and provide confidence in your community and its care. Private community patrols are provided on a twenty-four hours a day, seven days a week schedule by officers who are knowledgeable of, and attentive to, each neighborhood. If you happen to live in a gated area, microchip vehicle tags offer convenient access with no need to stop at the guard station. Residents simply push a button, or insert a card into a gate control mechanism. Also available is the advantage of advanced in-home security wiring, which provides for alarm monitoring and other services.

And there is at least one gated development currently under construction that makes explicit its primary emphasis on security as the theme of the community: Front Sight Master Planned Community outside of Las Vegas, Nevada, developed around firearm training, recreation, and protection. The development is centered around a massive training facility, armory, live fire simulation training ranges, more than a dozen shooting ranges, a SWAT training tower, and an underground tunnel network.

Residents can partake in Uzi sub-machine gun classes, enroll in courses in how to shoot from moving vehicles, and receive low light gun-fight training.

The surrounding two hundred home residential development, protected by armed guards, includes plans for an on-site K–12 school, a shopping center to serve all the needs of the residents (including a firearms "pro shop"), a town arsenal, and an airstrip. The developer, who calls Front Sight "a Disneyland for gun lovers" and "Uzi-land", offers free Uzi submachine guns to buyers who pay for their home sites up front. The developer also markets the place to potential buyers for its safety, "Wouldn't it be nice to live in the safest town in America? We won't have any crime at Front Sight, not with everyone trained in firearms." He has even named the residential streets in the spirit of the theme; Second Amendment Drive is one of the addresses available.

Prison products are also more explicit in selling both segregation and security in their marketing campaigns aimed at corrections' managers. In fact some of the companies that sell to correctional markets also supply security products to high-end gated community developers. A 1995 display advertisement for Robot Company's electronic security system is typical of the imagery and captioning used to sell to the prison market. The ad features a photograph of a convict climbing over low-tech institutional fencing, and the caption, "His dream is your worst nightmare."

Similar themes are used in both the Intelli–FLEX fencing and the First Defence company's ad campaigns. Intelli–FLEX features a close-up of a gruff convict behind the fencing, captioned by: "Intelli–FLEX: The really smart fence. It knows the difference between bad weather and a bad guy." First Defence features a picture of a convict helplessly dangling from the inwardly curved fence top, and the copy, "A design so effective they won't get over it."

The centrality of perimeter control to the segregative function of the warehouse prison is not limited to marketers of such products. Prisons in several jurisdictions have begun to install lethal electric fences around their facilities as the ultimate barrier to the free world. These kinds of very expensive containment products, which the warehouse prison industry invests in heavily, explicitly articulate the underlying ethos of the contemporary gated community.

Investing in prisons, like investing in gated communities, literally buys boundaries to distinguish and secure differentiated lifestyle communities, both spatially and socially. So while there is recognized cynicism about the effects of imprisonment on those incarcerated, the contemporary commitment to prison asks for nothing more than containment of its residents. Thus the social anxieties about crime, difference, and social disorder that play a part in the desire for both can be quelled through the simple investment in walls, fences and gates.

The Meaning of Gates

The observations made here have been articulated by many, so I make no claim to originality in identifying the nature and shape of the racialized post-rehabilitative prison, the rise of the gated community, or the growing commodification process underlying both. The goal of this article was to simply pull these individual threads of social inquiry and analysis into a single narrative that might add to our theoretical understanding of the contemporary prison explosion.

It appears that there are multiple processes at work, including those that are political, cultural, economic, social psychological, and social structural. These processes have come together in this period in such a way that our punishment policies and practices are not only "volatile and contradictory," but also brutally punitive and deeply discriminatory. What this suggests for theoretical understanding of these phenomena, then, is that a) race and ethnicity in all their varied meanings are integral to understanding punishment in the United States; b) examinations of punishment processes like imprisonment often need to be imbedded within larger social and cultural processes; and c) the broader theoretical understandings of the "commodity culture" can also give us insights into a state process like punishment.

Finally, while these late-modern developments are theoretically informative and suggest a profound change in the social, cultural, and political landscape, they also have a real and deep impact on the contemporary state of our civic life. Gregory Alexander has commented on the withdrawal for civic responsibility borne from the proliferation of "free" gated communities and related forms of private residential developments. Alexander suggests that, "the primary functions of the modern residential association are socially insulating rather than . . . connective . . . It does not seem too far-fetched, then, to characterize the incredible growth of these private residential governments as the enclosure movement of the late twentieth century in the United States."

Blakely and Snyder's empirical investigation of gated communities also confirms what we might suspect about such places. The residents tend to view those outside of the walls as outside of their concern, so express apathy about issues facing the surrounding communities. Some gated communities have asked to withdraw from fiscal, political, and social involvement with the larger community, and have done so successfully in several instances.

California has at least 3 fully incorporated gated cities. Places like DC Ranch in Scottsdale plan their own "public" schools on community grounds, as well as fire and police stations so residents will have still fewer reasons to go, in their words, "beyond the fence line." Of course, one outcome of this fiscal withdrawal by predominantly mid-to high income taxpayers means that those with fewer resources who remain in the communities outside the walls end up with fewer basic services and lower levels of assistance as urban tax bases shrink.

Prisons have also had their own impact on civic life. In many urban communities, the population of young men has been decimated by the imprisonment binge, contributing to a radical reshaping of family structures, social relations, and local economics. The communities that deal directly with these criminal justice casualties are the same that have been shut out of the economic prosperity enjoyed by a segment of the nation's population. Thus, these areas in many ways have become their own security zones—whether formally, as in those gated public housing, or through the civic and economic abandonment of whole sections of cities and towns where police aggressively patrol, roust, and arrest those left behind.

This is not to romanticize a time that never really was, in which socially, economically, and racially integrated communities were successfully created as the norm. However, what seems to be gone now is even the dream or vision of such communities, which is no doubt a by-product of the same factors that have driven the growth of gates and fences. Thus, we can now read Cohen's articulation of a coming "Punitive City" not with alarm over the blurring of distinctions between corrections and community as he predicted, but with a sense of loss (or at least nostalgia) over the now absent social elements embodied in both community and "corrections" that undergirded his and others' writings of that time.

NOTES AND QUESTIONS

1. **Prison and the family.** Prison is a "lifestyle community" for more than the people who are incarcerated. When parents are locked up, their families suffer. Children from such families are more likely themselves to later enter the juvenile and criminal justice systems. This dynamic transforms the prison system into, essentially, a substitute for the family. Moreover, the family members left behind suffer the ill-effects of incarceration as well in lost emotional support, income, and family cohesion. In addition, the prisoner upon release can become a vector for spreading prison acquired diseases such as AIDS. *See* Lynette Clemetson, *Links Between Prison and AIDS Affecting Blacks Inside and Out*, N.Y. TIMES, Aug. 6, 2004, at A5. Given the importance of family, discussed in *Moore v. East Cleveland*, 431 U.S. 494 (1977), *supra* at pp. 655–669, do the effects of prisons on families cast doubt on the legitimacy of our system which is premised on prison as a lifestyle choice?

2. **Gated communities as prisons.** While there are similarities between prisons and gated communities, the most striking parallel is between the treatment of those who are in prison by those who are not, and those who are not in a gated community by those who are. In both cases, walls and gates are used to restrict the freedom of movement of those who are poor or of a different race. Additionally, the divisions between gated and non-gated and non-imprisoned and imprisoned function to insulate the favored group from problems plaguing the disfavored group.

3. **Standard of living.** Louisiana Governor Troy Hilbert says that prisoners are often better off in prison because they have three meals a day, clean sheets to sleep between, and access to a television. His response, of course, was to worsen conditions in prisons. However, isn't it something of an embarrassment when citizens are lacking in basic necessities such as three meals a day or a clean place to sleep? This seems to be a direct

example of "governing through crime." Instead of working to ameliorate conditions outside of prison, Governor Hilbert works directly to degrade conditions inside of prison.

4. Additional reading. For additional information on the effects of imprisonment on families, see Dorothy E. Roberts, *Criminal Justice and Black Families: The Collateral Damage of Over–Enforcement*, 34 U.C. DAVIS L. REV. 1005 (2001). For perspectives on the intersection of race and criminal law enforcement, see generally Randolph Stone, *Mass Incarceration: Perspectives on U.S. Imprisonment: Race and Imprisonment*, 7 U. CHI. L. SCH. ROUNDTABLE 127 (2000); William Moffitt, *Race and the Criminal Justice System*, 36 GONZ. L. REV. 305 (2000).

CHAPTER 14

CORRECTIVE STRUGGLES

"Let me give you a word of the philosophy of reform. The whole history of the progress of human liberty shows that all concessions yet made to her august claims, have been born of earnest struggle. . . . If there is no struggle there is no progress. Those who profess to favor freedom and yet depreciate agitation, are men who want crops without plowing up the ground, they want rain without thunder and lightening. They want the ocean without the awful roar of its many waters.

This struggle may be a moral one, or it may be a physical one, and it may be both moral and physical, but it must be a struggle. Power concedes nothing without a demand. It never did and it never will."

Frederick Douglass, Canandaigua, New York,
August 3, 1857.

Introduction

This final chapter presents, perhaps, the greatest challenge within our exploration of the meaning and dimensions of economic justice. We have framed this chapter with a set of premises that we now make explicit. First, this is not a chapter of "solutions." In order for there to be a solution, there must be a stable definition of the problem. Our experience is that race and identity subordination are dynamic, changing even as new efforts to redistribute power, realign economic resources, and eliminate inequality are proposed. In this chapter, we survey the landscape of corrective struggles in order to challenge identity-based economic inequality. We have undertaken this task, with modesty born of the recognition, that as Frederick Douglass said about the end of slavery, "power concedes nothing without a demand." We recognize that the ideas and legal remedies discussed here will be no more than hollow rhetoric without a strong connection to the lives of individual people who must resist the daily indignities of economic inequality and material deprivation. Second, as scholars, we are not committed to a fixed set of remedies. Our commitment is to the process of creative resistance to the economic inequalities that we have surveyed in elaborate detail in the preceding twelve chapters. Finally, we expect that, in keeping with our view of the dynamic nature of subordinating strategies, new theories will enter the debate about corrective justice, even as we go to press. We look forward to bringing the most promising ideas to future editions of this book.

We begin the chapter with two cases that represent significant milestones in the development of the Supreme Court jurisprudence on the constitutionality of minority set-asides in government contracting programs These programs represent explicit economic redistribution. *Croson*, the Richmond case, presents a fascinating opportunity to see the dynamic that ensues when a subordinated group captures a majority in a local legislature. *Metro Broadcasting* has been included, nothwithstanding the fact that it has been overruled by *Adarand Constructors v. Pena*, 515 U.S. 200 (1995). In *Metro Broadcasting*, the court adopted the distinction between benign racial classifications intended to assist members of subordinated groups and invidious discrimination that preserves age-old racial stigmas and subordination. Although this view was later repudiated, it is a valuable artifact of the evolution of Supreme Court jurisprudence addressing race-conscious remedies.

Educational opportunity, as we have seen from the beginning to the end of this book, is one of the most important access points to economic mobility. As we have discussed in earlier chapters, educational attainment is also the single biggest predictor of lifetime earnings. The Constitution, however, does not treat primary or secondary education as a fundamental interest, nor is wealth a suspect classification. These two holdings of the *Rodriguez* school financing case of the 1970s, chapter 7 at p. 489, have served to shatter the first rung on the ladder of equal educational access. The absence of well-financed, high quality public education at the primary and secondary level has meant that colleges and universities must select from a pool of applicants that bear all the marks of wealth-and race-based inequality. As Justices Ginsburg and Breyer observe in *Grutter v. Bollinger*, 539 U.S. 306 (2003) (Ginsberg, J. Concurring): "[a]s to public education, data for the years 2000–2001 show that 71.6% of African–American children and 76.3% of Hispanic children attended a school in which minorities made up a majority of the student body.... [I]t remains the current reality that many minority students encounter markedly inadequate and unequal educational opportunities." Grutter, 539 U.S. at 345–46. It is unsurprising, therefore, that we have the much-discussed test score and grade gap between applicants of color and poor white students on one hand, and the wealthy students who, on the other hand, are able to earn high test scores and strong grades through parental support and resources.

Decreasing economic mobility in recent years has meant that, as conservative editorial writer David Brooks notes, we have a "sticky ladder" in which parental wealth is the greatest predictor of future class status for any child born in America today. Brooks argues, with substantial research support, that we have an "inherited meritocracy." Poor whites and students from racially subordinated communities must overcome formidable financial and educational challenges to secure a college education. Thomas Shapiro documents the consequences of the wealth gap and the attitudes of meritocratic entitlement that underlie the structures of economic privilege for families at the top of the economic ladder.

The Supreme Court opinions in *Grutter* give us a fascinating view of all the major arguments that are made in the debate about race-conscious affirmative action admissions policies in higher education. Justice O'Connor's opinion in *Grutter* sets an ominous time limit of twenty-five years for constitutional approval of race-conscious admissions programs. Lani Guinier offers a deep analysis of the political dimensions of admissions policies and suggests a forward-looking alternative for making admissions decisions.

As we have seen in previous chapters, another important element of the American class system is marriage. In this country, we rely on heterosexual marriage to finance the bulk of family dependency needs, from child care to elder care to care of the sick and dying. As we have seen, the place of marriage in the economic order established in the 1950s asked wives to stay out of wage work in order to provide this dependent care, while husbands would receive a "family wage." Marriage also served as a legal access point for benefits such as private health insurance and social insurance. In recent decades, however, marriage as a system for providing dependent care has steadily broken down. As the industrial economy shifted to a service economy, the family wage disappeared, and the resulting economic pressures have forced more and more wives into wage work in order to keep families afloat. Meanwhile, social changes have led to higher divorce rates, a steadily rising age of first marriage, and increasing numbers of never-married people and single mothers. This chapter examines three groups of people caught in the crossfire of these changes: stay-at-home wives, working mothers, and same-sex couples. The human capital theory offers a useful conceptual intervention in the age-old story of individual ownership of degrees earned with spousal support during the term of a marriage. Treating discrimination against mothers as sex discrimination uses litigation as a tool for restructuring the workplace. Finally, we explore the question of same-sex marriage as an interplay of symbolic issues—religious values versus secular egalitarian values—with material issues, including the continuing viability of marriage as the major conduit for dependency care.

Finally, as we have in earlier chapters, we look at the international dimensions of economic inequality. We consider the role of cultural property, and the international development questions that arise from global poverty and economic inequality.

A. AFFIRMATIVE ACTION

Ricci v. DeStefano

Supreme Court of the United States, 129 S.Ct. 2658 (2009).

■ JUSTICE KENNEDY delivered the opinion of the Court in which ROBERTS, C.J., and SCALIA, THOMAS, and ALITO, JJ., joined. SCALIA, J., filed a concurring opinion. ALITO, J., filed a concurring opinion, in which SCALIA and THOMAS, JJ., joined. GINSBURG, J., filed a dissenting opinion, in which STEVENS, SOUTER, and BREYER, JJ., joined.

In the fire department of New Haven, Connecticut—as in emergency-service agencies throughout the Nation—firefighters prize their promotion to and within the officer ranks. An agency's officers command respect within the department and in the whole community; and, of course, added responsibilities command increased salary and benefits. Aware of the intense competition for promotions, New Haven, like many cities, relies on objective examinations to identify the best qualified candidates.

In 2003, 118 New Haven firefighters took examinations to qualify for promotion to the rank of lieutenant or captain. Promotion examinations in New Haven (or City) were infrequent, so the stakes were high. The results would determine which firefighters would be considered for promotions during the next two years, and the order in which they would be considered. Many firefighters studied for months, at considerable personal and financial cost.

When the examination results showed that white candidates had outperformed minority candidates, the mayor and other local politicians opened a public debate that turned rancorous. Some firefighters argued the tests should be discarded because the results showed the tests to be discriminatory. They threatened a discrimination lawsuit if the City made promotions based on the tests. Other firefighters said the exams were neutral and fair. And they, in turn, threatened a discrimination lawsuit if the City, relying on the statistical racial disparity, ignored the test results and denied promotions to the candidates who had performed well. In the end the City took the side of those who protested the test results. It threw out the examinations.

Certain white and Hispanic firefighters who likely would have been promoted based on their good test performance sued the City and some of its officials. Theirs is the suit now before us. The suit alleges that, by discarding the test results, the City and the named officials discriminated against the plaintiffs based on their race, in violation of both Title VII of the Civil Rights Act of 1964, * * *, and the Equal Protection Clause of the Fourteenth Amendment. The City and the officials defended their actions, arguing that if they had certified the results, they could have faced liability under Title VII for adopting a practice that had a disparate impact on the minority firefighters. The District Court granted summary judgment for the defendants, and the Court of Appeals affirmed.

We conclude that race-based action like the City's in this case is impermissible under Title VII unless the employer can demonstrate a strong basis in evidence that, had it not taken the action, it would have been liable under the disparate-impact statute. The respondents, we further determine, cannot meet that threshold standard. As a result, the City's action in discarding the tests was a violation of Title VII. In light of our ruling under the statutes, we need not reach the question whether respondents' actions may have violated the Equal Protection Clause. * * *

Title VII prohibits intentional acts of employment discrimination based on race, color, religion, sex, and national origin, (disparate treatment), as well as policies or practices that are not intended to discriminate but in fact have a disproportionately adverse effect on minorities, * * * (disparate impact). Once a plaintiff has established a prima facie case of disparate impact, the employer may defend by demonstrating that its policy or practice is "job related for the position in question and consistent with business necessity." *Ibid.* If the employer meets that burden, the plaintiff may still succeed by showing that the employer refuses to adopt an available alternative practice that has less disparate impact and serves the employer's legitimate needs. * * * .

Under Title VII, before an employer can engage in intentional discrimination for the asserted purpose of avoiding or remedying an unintentional, disparate impact, the employer must have a strong basis in evidence to believe it will be subject to disparate-impact liability if it fails to take the race-conscious, discriminatory action. The Court's analysis begins with the premise that the City's actions would violate Title VII's disparate-treatment prohibition absent some valid defense. All the evidence demonstrates that the City rejected the test results because the higher scoring candidates were white. Without some other justification, this express, race-based decisionmaking is prohibited. The question, therefore, is whether the purpose to avoid disparate-impact liability excuses what otherwise would be prohibited disparate-treatment discrimination. The Court has considered cases similar to the present litigation, but in the context of the Fourteenth Amendment's Equal Protection Clause. Such cases can provide helpful guidance in this statutory context. See *Watson v. Fort Worth Bank & Trust*, 487 U.S. 977, 993 (1988). In those cases, the Court held that certain government actions to remedy past racial discrimination—actions that are themselves based on race—are constitutional only where there is a "strong basis in evidence" that the remedial actions were necessary. *Richmond v. J. A. Croson Co.*, 488 U.S. 469, 500; see also *Wygant v. Jackson Bd. of Ed.* In announcing the strong-basis-in-evidence standard, the *Wygant* plurality recognized the tension between eliminating segregation and discrimination on the one hand and doing away with all governmentally imposed discrimination based on race on the other. 476 U.S., at 277. It reasoned that "[e]videntiary support for the conclusion that remedial action is warranted becomes crucial when the remedial program is challenged in court by nonminority employees." The same interests are at work in the interplay between Title VII's disparate-treatment and disparate-impact provisions. Applying the strong-basis-in-evidence standard to Title VII gives effect to both provisions, allowing violations of one in the name of compliance with the other only in certain, narrow circumstances. It also allows the disparate-impact prohibition to work in a manner that is consistent with other Title VII provisions, including the prohibition on adjusting employment-related test scores based on race, and the section that expressly protects bona fide promotional exams. Thus, the Court adopts the strong-basis-in-evidence standard as a matter of statutory construction in order to resolve any conflict between Title VII's disparate-treatment and disparate-impact provisions. The City's race-based rejection of the test results cannot satisfy the strong-basis-in-evidence standard.

The racial adverse impact in this litigation was significant, and petitioners do not dispute that the City was faced with a prima facie case of disparate-impact liability. The problem for respondents is that such a prima facie case—essentially, a threshold showing of a significant statistical disparity, *Connecticut v. Teal*, 457 U.S. 440, and nothing more—is far from a strong basis in evidence that the City would have been liable under Title VII had it certified the test results. That is because the City could be liable for disparate-impact discrimination only if the exams at issue were not job related and consistent with business necessity, or if there existed an equally valid, less discriminatory alternative that served the City's needs but that the City refused to adopt. §§ 2000e–2(k)(1)(A), (C). Based on the record the parties developed through discovery, there is no substantial basis in evidence that the test was deficient in either respect. 530 F.3d 87, is therefore reversed and remanded.

■ Justice Ginsburg dissented, joined by Justices Stevens, Souter and Breyer.

In assessing claims of race discrimination, "[c]ontext matters." *Grutter v. Bollinger*, 539 U.S. 306 (2003). In 1972, Congress extended Title VII of the Civil Rights Act of 1964 to cover public employment. At that time, municipal fire departments across the country, including New Haven's, pervasively discriminated against minorities. The extension of Title VII to cover jobs in firefighting effected no overnight change. It took decades of persistent effort, advanced by Title VII litigation, to open firefighting posts to members of racial minorities.

The white firefighters who scored high on New Haven's promotional exams understandably attract this Court's sympathy. But they had no vested right to promotion. Nor have other persons received promotions in preference to them. New Haven maintains that it refused to certify the test results because it believed, for good cause, that it would be vulnerable to a Title VII disparate-impact suit if it relied on those results. The Court today holds that New Haven has not demonstrated "a strong basis in evidence" for its plea. In so holding, the Court pretends that "[t]he City rejected the test results solely because the higher scoring candidates were white." That pretension, essential to the Court's disposition, ignores substantial evidence of multiple flaws in the tests New Haven used. The Court similarly fails to acknowledge the better tests used in other cities, which have yielded less racially skewed outcomes.

By order of this Court, New Haven, a city in which African–Americans and Hispanics account for nearly 60 percent of the population, must today be served—as it was in the days of undisguised discrimination—by a fire department in which members of racial and ethnic minorities are rarely seen in command positions. In arriving at its order, the Court barely acknowledges the pathmarking decision in *Griggs v. Duke Power Co.*, 401 U.S. 424 (1971), which explained the centrality of the disparate-impact concept to effective enforcement of Title VII. The Court's order and opinion, I anticipate, will not have staying power. * * *

This case presents an unfortunate situation, one New Haven might well have avoided had it utilized a better selection process in the first place. But what this case does not present is race-based discrimination in violation of Title VII. I dissent from the Court's judgment, which rests on the false premise that respondents showed "a significant statistical disparity," but "nothing more."

———

Metro Broadcasting, Inc. v. F.C.C.

Supreme Court of the United States, 497 U.S. 547 (1990).

■ Justice Brennan delivered the opinion of the Court.

The issue in these cases, consolidated for decision today, is whether certain minority preference policies of the Federal Communications Commission violate the equal protection component of the Fifth Amendment. The policies in question are (1) a program awarding an enhancement for minority ownership in comparative proceedings for new licenses, and (2) the minority "distress sale" program, which permits a limited category of existing radio and television broadcast stations to be transferred only to minority-controlled firms. We hold that these policies do not violate equal protection principles.

I

A

The policies before us today can best be understood by reference to the history of federal efforts to promote minority participation in the broadcasting industry.* * *

Building on the results of the conference [on minority ownership policies], the recommendations of the task force [to encourage minority participation in broadcasting], the decision [in *TV 9, Inc. v. FCC,* 161 U.S. App. D. C. 349, 938 (1973) that a reasonable expectation of superior community service was sufficient to justify a preference for African American broadcasters], and a petition proposing several minority ownership policies, the FCC adopted in May 1978 its *Statement of Policy on Minority Ownership of Broadcasting Facilities*. After recounting its past efforts to expand broadcast diversity, the FCC concluded:

> [W]e are compelled to observe that the views of racial minorities continue to be inadequately represented in the broadcast media. This situation is detrimental not only to the minority audience but to all of the viewing and listening public. Adequate representation of minority viewpoints in programming serves not only the needs and interests of the minority community but also enriches and educates the non-minority audience. It enhances the diversified programming which is a key objective not only of the Communications Act of 1934 but also of the First Amendment. * * *

Describing its actions as only "first steps," * * * the FCC outlined two elements of a minority ownership policy.

First, the Commission pledged to consider minority ownership as one factor in comparative proceedings for new licenses. * * *

Second, the FCC outlined a plan to increase minority opportunities to receive reassigned and transferred licenses through the so-called "distress sale" policy. * * * As a general rule, a licensee whose qualifications to hold a broadcast license come into question may not assign or transfer that license until the FCC has resolved its doubts in a noncomparative hearing. The distress sale policy is an exception to that practice, allowing a broadcaster whose license has been designated for a revocation hearing, or whose renewal application has been designated for hearing, to assign the license to an FCC-approved minority enterprise.* * *

II

It is of overriding significance in these cases that the FCC's minority ownership programs have been specifically approved—indeed, mandated—by Congress. In *Fullilove v. Klutznick*, 448 U.S. 448 (1980), Chief Justice Burger [gave deference to agency actions making racial preferences based on congressional instructions].

* * *

Our decision last Term in *Richmond v. J. A. Croson Co.*, 488 U.S. 469 (1989), concerning a minority set-aside program adopted by a municipality, does not prescribe the level of scrutiny to be applied to a benign racial classification employed by Congress. As JUSTICE KENNEDY noted, the question of congressional action was not before the Court, * * * and so *Croson* cannot be read to undermine our decision in *Fullilove*. In fact, much of the language and reasoning in *Croson* reaffirmed the lesson of *Fullilove* that race-conscious classifications adopted by Congress to address racial and ethnic discrimination are subject to a different standard than such classifications prescribed by state and local governments. * * *

We hold that the FCC minority ownership policies pass muster under the test we announce today. First, we find that they serve the important governmental objective of broadcast diversity. Second, we conclude that they are substantially related to the achievement of that objective.

A

Congress found that "the effects of past inequities stemming from racial and ethnic discrimination have resulted in a severe under-representation of minorities in the media of mass communications." [H. R. Conf. Rep. No. 97–765.] Congress and the Commission do not justify the minority ownership policies strictly as remedies for victims of this discrimination, however. Rather, Congress and the FCC have selected the minority ownership policies primarily to promote programming diversity, and they urge that such diversity is an important governmental objective that can serve as a constitutional basis for the preference policies. We agree.

* * *

[T]he interest in enhancing broadcast diversity is, at the very least, an important governmental objective and is therefore a sufficient basis for the Commission's minority ownership policies. Just as a "diverse student body" contributing to a "robust exchange of ideas" is a "constitutionally permissible goal" on which a race-conscious university admissions program may be predicated, [*Bakke* (opinion of Powell, J.),] the diversity of views and information on the airwaves serves important First Amendment values. * * * The benefits of such diversity are not limited to the members of minority groups who gain access to the broadcasting industry by virtue of the ownership policies; rather, the benefits redound to all members of the viewing and listening audience. As Congress found, "the American public will benefit by having access to a wider diversity of information sources." * * *

We also find that the minority ownership policies are substantially related to the achievement of the Government's interest. One component of this inquiry concerns the relationship between expanded minority ownership and greater broadcast diversity; both the FCC and Congress have determined that such a relationship exists. Although we do not " 'defer' to the judgment of the Congress and the Commission on a constitutional question," and would not "hesitate to invoke the Constitution should we determine that the Commission has not fulfilled its task with appropriate sensitivity" to equal protection principles, *Columbia Broadcasting System, Inc. v. Democratic National Committee*, [412 U.S. 94 (1973),] we must pay close attention to the expertise of the Commission and the factfinding of Congress when analyzing the nexus between minority ownership and programming diversity. With respect to this "complex" empirical question, we are required to give "great weight to the decisions of Congress and the experience of the Commission." * * *

* * *

C

The judgment that there is a link between expanded minority ownership and broadcast diversity does not rest on impermissible stereotyping. Congressional policy does not assume that in every case minority ownership and management will lead to more minority-oriented programming or to the expression of a discrete "minority viewpoint" on the airwaves. Neither does it pretend that all programming that appeals to minority audiences can be labeled "minority programming" or that programming that might be described as "minority" does not appeal to nonminorities. Rather, both Congress and the FCC maintain simply that expanded minority ownership of broadcast outlets will, in the aggregate, result in greater broadcast diversity. A broadcasting industry with representative minority participation will produce more variation and diversity than will one whose ownership is drawn from a single racially and ethnically homogeneous group. The predictive judgment about the overall result of minority entry into broadcasting is not a rigid assumption about how minority owners will behave in every case but rather is akin to Justice Powell's conclusion in *Bakke* that greater admission of minorities would contribute, on average, "to the 'robust exchange of ideas.' "

* * *

D

We find that the minority ownership policies are in other relevant respects substantially related to the goal of promoting broadcast diversity. First, the Commission adopted and Congress endorsed minority ownership preferences only after long study and painstaking consideration of all available alternatives. * * * For many years, the FCC attempted to encourage diversity of programming content without consideration of the race of station owners.

* * *

Moreover, the considered nature of the Commission's judgment in selecting the particular minority ownership policies at issue today is illustrated by the fact that the Commission has rejected other types of minority preferences. For example, the Commission has studied but refused to implement the more expansive alternative of setting aside certain frequencies for minority broadcasters. * * * In addition, in a ruling released the day after it adopted the comparative hearing credit and the distress sale preference, the FCC declined to adopt a plan to require 45–day advance public notice before a station could be sold, which had been advocated on the ground that it would ensure minorities a chance to bid on stations that might otherwise be sold to industry insiders without ever coming on the market. * * * Soon afterward, the Commission rejected other minority ownership proposals advanced by the Office of Telecommunications Policy and the Department of Commerce that sought to revise the FCC's time brokerage, multiple ownership, and other policies.

* * *

The minority ownership policies are "appropriately limited in extent and duration, and subject to reassessment and reevaluation by the Congress prior to any extension or reenactment." [*Fullilove* (opinion of Burger, C. J.).] Although it has underscored emphatically its support for the minority ownership policies, Congress has manifested that support through a series of appropriations Acts of finite duration, thereby ensuring future reevaluations of the need for the minority ownership program as the number of minority broadcasters increases. In addition, Congress has continued to hold hearings on the subject of minority ownership. * * * Furthermore, there is provision for administrative and judicial review of all Commission decisions, which guarantees both that the minority ownership policies are applied correctly in individual cases, and that there will be frequent opportunities to revisit the merits of those policies. Congress and the Commission have adopted a policy of minority ownership not as an end in itself, but rather as a means of achieving greater programming diversity.

Such a goal carries its own natural limit, for there will be no need for further minority preferences once sufficient diversity has been achieved. The FCC's plan, like the Harvard admissions program discussed in *Bakke*, contains the seed of its own termination. * * *

Finally, we do not believe that the minority ownership policies at issue impose impermissible burdens on nonminorities. * * *

In the context of broadcasting licenses, the burden on nonminorities is slight. The FCC's responsibility is to grant licenses in the "public interest, convenience, or necessity," * * * and the limited number of frequencies on the electromagnetic spectrum means that "[n]o one has a First Amendment right to a license." [*Red Lion*] Applicants have no settled expectation that their applications will be granted without consideration of public interest factors such as minority ownership. Award of a preference in a comparative hearing or transfer of a station in a distress sale thus contravenes "no legitimate firmly rooted expectation[s]" of competing applicants. [*Johnson.*]

Respondent Shurberg insists that because the minority distress sale policy operates to exclude nonminority firms completely from consideration in the transfer of certain stations, it is a greater burden than the comparative hearing preference for minorities, which is simply a "plus" factor considered together with other characteristics of the applicants. * * * The distress sale policy is not a quota or fixed quantity set-aside. Indeed, the nonminority firm exercises control over whether a distress sale will ever occur at all, because the policy operates only where the qualifications of an existing licensee to continue broadcasting have been designated for hearing and no other applications for the station in question have been filed with the Commission at the time of the designation. * * * Thus, a nonminority can prevent the distress sale procedures from ever being invoked by filing a competing application in a timely manner.

In practice, distress sales have represented a tiny fraction—less than 0.4 percent—of all broadcast sales since 1979. * * *

III

The Commission's minority ownership policies bear the *imprimatur* of longstanding congressional support and direction and are substantially related to the achievement of the important governmental objective of broadcast diversity. The judgment in No. 89–453 is affirmed, the judgment in No. 89–700 is reversed, and the cases are remanded for proceedings consistent with this opinion.

It is so ordered.

[Justice Stevens's concurring opinion has been omitted]

■ Justice O'Connor, with whom the Chief Justice, Justice Scalia, and Justice Kennedy join, dissenting.

At the heart of the Constitution's guarantee of equal protection lies the simple command that the Government must treat citizens "as *individuals*,

not 'as simply components of a racial, religious, sexual or national class.' "
Arizona Governing Comm. for Tax Deferred Annuity and Deferred Compensation Plans v. Norris, 463 U.S. 1073, 1083 (1983). Social scientists may debate how peoples' thoughts and behavior reflect their background, but the Constitution provides that the Government may not allocate benefits and burdens among individuals based on the assumption that race or ethnicity determines how they act or think. To uphold the challenged programs, the Court departs from these fundamental principles and from our traditional requirement that racial classifications are permissible only if necessary and narrowly tailored to achieve a compelling interest. This departure marks a renewed toleration of racial classifications and a repudiation of our recent affirmation that the Constitution's equal protection guarantees extend equally to all citizens. The Court's application of a lessened equal protection standard to congressional actions finds no support in our cases or in the Constitution. I respectfully dissent.

I

As we recognized [in *J. A. Croson*], the Constitution requires that the Court apply a strict standard of scrutiny to evaluate racial classifications such as those contained in the challenged FCC distress sale and comparative licensing policies. * * * The Court abandons this traditional safeguard against discrimination for a lower standard of review, and in practice applies a standard like that applicable to routine legislation. Yet the Government's different treatment of citizens according to race is no routine concern. This Court's precedents in no way justify the Court's marked departure from our traditional treatment of race classifications and its conclusion that different equal protection principles apply to these federal actions.

In both the challenged policies, the Federal Communications Commission (FCC) provides benefits to some members of our society and denies benefits to others based on race or ethnicity. Except in the narrowest of circumstances, the Constitution bars such racial classifications as a denial to particular individuals, of any race or ethnicity, of "the equal protection of the laws." U.S. Const., Amdt. 14, § 1. * * * The dangers of such classifications are clear. They endorse race-based reasoning and the conception of a Nation divided into racial blocs, thus contributing to an escalation of racial hostility and conflict. * * * Such policies may embody stereotypes that treat individuals as the product of their race, evaluating their thoughts and efforts—their very worth as citizens—according to a criterion barred to the Government by history and the Constitution. * * * Racial classifications, whether providing benefits to or burdening particular racial or ethnic groups, may stigmatize those groups singled out for different treatment and may create considerable tension with the Nation's widely shared commitment to evaluating individuals upon their individual merit. * * *

The Constitution's guarantee of equal protection binds the Federal Government as it does the States, and no lower level of scrutiny applies to the Federal Government's use of race classifications. * * * Consistent with this view, the Court has repeatedly indicated that "the reach of the equal protection guarantee of the Fifth Amendment is coextensive with that of the Fourteenth." [*United States v. Paradise*, 480 U.S. 149 (1987) (plurality opinion).]

Nor does the congressional role in prolonging the FCC's policies justify any lower level of scrutiny. As with all instances of judicial review of federal legislation, the Court does not lightly set aside the considered judgment of a coordinate branch. Nonetheless, the respect due a coordinate branch yields neither less vigilance in defense of equal protection principles nor any corresponding diminution of the standard of review.

* * *

The guarantee of equal protection extends to each citizen, regardless of race: The Federal Government, like the States, may not "deny to any person within its jurisdiction the equal protection of the laws." * * *

The Court's reliance on "benign racial classifications," * * * is particularly troubling. " 'Benign' racial classification" is a contradiction in terms. Governmental distinctions among citizens based on race or ethnicity, even in the rare circumstances permitted by our cases, exact costs and carry with them substantial dangers. To the person denied an opportunity or right based on race, the classification is hardly benign. * * * Untethered to narrowly confined remedial notions, "benign" carries with it no independent meaning, but reflects only acceptance of the current generation's conclusion that a politically acceptable burden, imposed on particular citizens on the basis of race, is reasonable. The Court provides no basis for determining when a racial classification fails to be "benevolent." By expressly distinguishing "benign" from remedial race-conscious measures, the Court leaves the distinct possibility that any racial measure found to be substantially related to an important governmental objective is also, by definition, "benign." * * *

This dispute regarding the appropriate standard of review may strike some as a lawyers' quibble over words, but it is not. The standard of review establishes whether and when the Court and Constitution allow the Government to employ racial classifications. A lower standard signals that the Government may resort to racial distinctions more readily. The Court's departure from our cases is disturbing enough, but more disturbing still is the renewed toleration of racial classifications that its new standard of review embodies.

II

Our history reveals that the most blatant forms of discrimination have been visited upon some members of the racial and ethnic groups identified in the challenged programs. Many have lacked the opportunity to share in the Nation's wealth and to participate in its commercial enterprises. It is undisputed that minority participation in the broadcasting industry falls markedly below the demographic representation of those groups, * * * and this shortfall may be traced in part to the discrimination and the patterns of exclusion that have widely affected our society. As a nation we aspire to create a society untouched by that history of exclusion, and to ensure that equality defines all citizens' daily experience and opportunities as well as the protection afforded to them under law.

* * *

III

Under the appropriate standard, strict scrutiny, only a compelling interest may support the Government's use of racial classifications. Modern equal protection doctrine has recognized only one such interest: remedying the effects of racial discrimination. The interest in increasing the diversity of broadcast viewpoints is clearly not a compelling interest. It is simply too amorphous, too insubstantial, and too unrelated to any legitimate basis for employing racial classifications. The Court does not claim otherwise. Rather, it employs its novel standard and claims that this asserted interest need only be, and is, "important." This conclusion twice compounds the Court's initial error of reducing its level of scrutiny of a racial classification. First, it too casually extends the justifications that might support racial classifications, beyond that of remedying past discrimination. * * * Second, it has initiated this departure by endorsing an insubstantial interest, one that is certainly insufficiently weighty to justify tolerance of the Government's distinctions among citizens based on race and ethnicity. This endorsement trivializes the constitutional command to guard against such discrimination and has loosed a potentially far-reaching principle disturbingly at odds with our traditional equal protection doctrine.

An interest capable of justifying race-conscious measures must be sufficiently specific and verifiable, such that it supports only limited and carefully defined uses of racial classifications. In *Croson*, we held that an interest in remedying societal discrimination cannot be considered compelling. * * * We determined that a "generalized assertion" of past discrimination "has no logical stopping point" and would support unconstrained uses of race classifications. * * *

The asserted interest in these cases suffers from the same defects. * * * Like the vague assertion of societal discrimination, a claim of insufficiently diverse broadcasting viewpoints might be used to justify equally unconstrained racial preferences, linked to nothing other than proportional representation of various races. And the interest would support indefinite use of racial classifications, employed first to obtain the appropriate mixture of racial views and then to ensure that the broadcasting spectrum continues to reflect that mixture. We cannot deem to be constitutionally adequate an interest that would support measures that amount to the core constitutional violation of "outright racial balancing." [*Croson*.]

* * *

IV

Our traditional equal protection doctrine requires, in addition to a compelling state interest, that the Government's chosen means be necessary to accomplish, and narrowly tailored to further, the asserted interest. * * * This element of strict scrutiny is designed to "ensur[e] that the means chosen 'fit' [the] compelling goal so closely that there is little or no possibility that the motive for the classification was illegitimate racial prejudice or stereotype." [*Croson* (opinion of O'CONNOR, J.).] The chosen means, resting as they do on stereotyping and so indirectly furthering the asserted end, could not plausibly be deemed narrowly tailored. The Court instead finds the racial classifications to be "substantially related" to achieving the Government's interest, * * * a far less rigorous fit requirement. The FCC's policies fail even this requirement.

A

The FCC claims to advance its asserted interest in diverse viewpoints by singling out race and ethnicity as peculiarly linked to distinct views that require enhancement. The FCC's choice to employ a racial criterion embodies the related notions that a particular and distinct viewpoint inheres in certain racial groups, and that a particular applicant, by virtue of race or ethnicity alone, is more valued than other applicants because he/she is "likely to provide [that] distinct perspective." [Brief for FCC.] The policies directly equate race with belief and behavior, for they establish race as a necessary and sufficient condition of securing the preference. The FCC's chosen means rest on the "premise that differences in race, or in the color of a person's skin, reflect real differences that are relevant to a person's right to share in the blessings of a free society. [T]hat premise is utterly irrational and repugnant to the principles of a free and democratic society." [*Wygant* (STEVENS, J., dissenting).] The policies impermissibly value individuals because they presume that persons think in a manner associated with their race. * * *

The majority addresses this point by arguing that the equation of race with distinct views and behavior is not "impermissible" in these particular cases. * * * Apart from placing undue faith in the Government and courts' ability to distinguish "good" from "bad" stereotypes, this reasoning repudiates essential equal protection principles that prohibit racial generalizations. * * *

B

Moreover, the FCC's selective focus on viewpoints associated with race illustrates a particular tailoring difficulty.* * *

Our equal protection doctrine governing intermediate review indicates that the Government may not use race and ethnicity as "a 'proxy for other, more germane bases of classification.'" [*Mississippi Univ. for Women v. Hogan*, 458 U.S. 718 (1982).] The FCC has used race as a proxy for whatever views it believes to be underrepresented in the broadcasting spectrum. This reflexive or unthinking use of a suspect classification is the hallmark of an unconstitutional policy. * * * The ill fit of means to ends is manifest. The policy is overinclusive: Many members of a particular racial or ethnic group will have no interest in advancing the views the FCC believes to be underrepresented, or will find them utterly foreign. The policy is underinclusive: It awards no preference to disfavored individuals who may be particularly well versed in and committed to presenting those views. The FCC has failed to implement a case-by-case determination, and that failure is particularly unjustified when individualized hearings already occur, as in the comparative licensing process. * * * Even in the remedial context, we have required that the Government adopt means to ensure that the award of a particular preference advances the asserted interest. * * *

　　　* * *

The FCC seeks to avoid the tailoring difficulties by focusing on minority ownership rather than the asserted interest in diversity of broadcast viewpoints. The Constitution clearly prohibits allocating valuable goods such as broadcast licenses simply on the basis of race. * * * Yet the FCC refers to the lack of minority ownership of stations to support the existence of a lack of diversity of viewpoints, and has fitted its programs to increase ownership. * * * This repeated focus on ownership supports the inference that the FCC seeks to allocate licenses based on race, an impermissible end, rather than to increase diversity of viewpoints, the asserted interest. And this justification that links the use of race preferences to minority ownership rather than to diversity of viewpoints ensures that the FCC's programs, like that at issue in *Croson*, "cannot be said to be narrowly tailored to any goal, except perhaps outright racial balancing." * * *

C

Even apart from these tailoring defects in the FCC's policies, one particular flaw underscores the Government's ill fit of means to ends. The FCC's policies assume, and rely upon, the existence of a tightly bound "nexus" between the owners' race and the resulting programming.* * *

Three difficulties suggest that the nexus between owners' race and programming is considerably less than substantial. First, the market shapes programming to a tremendous extent. Members of minority groups who own licenses might be thought, like other owners, to seek to broadcast programs that will attract and retain audiences, rather than programs that reflect the owner's tastes and preferences. * * * Second, station owners have only limited control over the content of programming. The distress sale presents a particularly acute difficulty of this sort. Unlike the comparative licensing program, the distress sale policy provides preferences to minority owners who neither intend nor desire to manage the station in any respect. * * * Whatever distinct programming may attend the race of an owner actively involved in managing the station, an absentee owner would have far less effect on programming.

Third, the FCC had absolutely no factual basis for the nexus when it adopted the policies and has since established none to support its existence. * * *

Even apart from the limited nature of the Court's claims, little can be discerned from the congressional action. First, the Court's survey does not purport to establish that the FCC or Congress has identified any particular deficiency in the viewpoints contained in the broadcast spectrum. Second, no degree of congressional endorsement may transform the equation of race with behavior and thoughts into a permissible basis of governmental action. Even the most express and lavishly documented congressional declaration that members of certain races will as owners produce distinct and superior programming would not allow the Government to employ such reasoning to allocate benefits and burdens among citizens on that basis. Third, we should hesitate before accepting as definitive any declaration regarding even the existence of a nexus.* * *

D

Finally, the Government cannot employ race classifications that unduly burden individuals who are not members of the favored racial and ethnic groups. * * * The challenged policies fail this independent requirement, as well as the other constitutional requirements. The comparative licensing and distress sale programs provide the eventual licensee with an exceptionally valuable property and with a rare and unique opportunity to serve the local community. The distress sale imposes a particularly significant burden. The FCC has at base created a specialized market reserved exclusively for minority controlled applicants. There is no more rigid quota than a 100% set-aside. * * * The Court's argument that the distress sale allocates only a small percentage of all license sales, * * * also misses the mark. This argument readily supports complete preferences and avoids scrutiny of particular programs: It is no response to a person denied admission at one school, or discharged from one job, solely on the basis of race, that other schools or employers do not discriminate.

* * *

■ JUSTICE KENNEDY, with whom JUSTICE SCALIA joins, dissenting.

Almost 100 years ago in *Plessy v. Ferguson, 163 U.S. 537 (1896),* this Court upheld a government-sponsored race-conscious measure, a Louisiana law that required "equal but separate accommodations" for "white" and "colored" railroad passengers. The Court asked whether the measures were "reasonable," and it stated that "[i]n determining the question of reasonableness, [the legislature] is at liberty to act with reference to the established usages, customs and traditions of the people, and with a view to the promotion of their comfort." * * * The *Plessy* Court concluded that the "race-conscious measures" it reviewed were reasonable because they served the governmental interest of increasing the riding pleasure of railroad passengers. The fundamental errors in *Plessy*, its standard of review and its validation of rank racial insult by the State, distorted the law for six decades before the Court announced its apparent demise in *Brown v. Board of Education.* * * * *Plessy*'s standard of review and its explication have disturbing parallels to today's majority opinion that should warn us something is amiss here.

* * * The interest the Court accepts to uphold the race-conscious measures of the Federal Communications Commission (Commission or FCC) is "broadcast diversity." Furthering that interest, we are told, is worth the cost of discriminating among citizens on the basis of race because it will increase the listening pleasure of media audiences. In upholding this preference, the majority exhumes *Plessy*'s deferential approach to racial classifications. The Court abandons even the broad societal remedial justification for racial preferences once advocated by JUSTICE MARSHALL, *e.g.*, [*Bakke* (separate opinion)] and now will allow the use of racial classifications by Congress untied to any goal of addressing the effects of past race discrimination. All that need be shown under the new approach, * * * is that the future effect of discriminating among citizens on the basis of race will advance some "important" governmental interest.

Once the Government takes the step, which itself should be forbidden, of enacting into law the stereotypical assumption that the race of owners is linked to broadcast content, it follows a path that becomes ever more tortuous. It must decide which races to favor. * * * The Court's reasoning provides little justification for welcoming the return of racial classifications to our Nation's laws.

I cannot agree with the Court that the Constitution permits the Government to discriminate among its citizens on the basis of race in order to serve interests so trivial as "broadcast diversity." In abandoning strict scrutiny to endorse this interest the Court turns back the clock on the level of scrutiny applicable to federal race-conscious measures. * * * Strict scrutiny is the surest test the Court has yet devised for holding true to the constitutional command of racial equality. * * *

The Court insists that the programs under review are "benign." JUSTICE STEVENS agrees. * * * A fundamental error of the *Plessy* Court was its similar confidence in its ability to identify "benign" discrimination: "We consider the underlying fallacy of the plaintiff's argument to consist in the assumption that the enforced separation of the two races stamps the colored race with a badge of inferiority. If this be so, it is not by reason of anything found in the act, but solely because the colored race chooses to put that construction upon it." * * * Although the majority is "confident" that it can determine when racial discrimination is benign, * * * it offers no explanation as to how it will do so.

* * *

The history of governmental reliance on race demonstrates that racial policies defended as benign often are not seen that way by the individuals affected by them. * * * Although the majority disclaims it, the FCC policy seems based on the demeaning notion that members of the defined racial groups ascribe to certain "minority views" that must be different from those of other citizens. Special preferences also can foster the view that members of the favored groups are inherently less able to compete on their own. And, rightly or wrongly, special preference programs often are perceived as targets for exploitation by opportunists who seek to take advantage of monetary rewards without advancing the stated policy of minority inclusion.

* * *

Though the racial composition of this Nation is far more diverse than the first Justice Harlan foresaw, his warning in dissent is now all the more apposite: "The destinies of the two races, in this country, are indissolubly linked together, and the interests of both require that the common government of all shall not permit the seeds of race hate to be planted under the sanction of law." [*Plessy* (dissenting opinion).] Perhaps the Court can succeed in its assumed role of case-by-case arbiter of when it is desirable and benign for the Government to disfavor some citizens and favor others based on the color of their skin. Perhaps the tolerance and decency to which our people aspire will let the disfavored rise above hostility and the favored escape condescension. But history suggests much peril in this enterprise, and so the Constitution forbids us to undertake it. I regret that after a century of judicial opinions we interpret the Constitution to do no more than move us from "separate but equal" to "unequal but benign."

Note: The FCC affirmative action distress sale policy reviewed in *Metro Broadcasting* was justified, in part, based upon the agency's concern for increasing the public good of diverse viewpoints and images in the broadcast industry. In the article that follows, legal scholar Jerry Kang takes up directly the relationship of broadcast images to the reinforcement of racial bias. Kang, relying on the cognitive bias research that we considered in Chapter 1 at p. 54 above, offers a provocative "thought experiment" to redirect the broadcast media to the task of "disinfecting" racial bias from the national consciousness.

Trojan Horses of Race

118 HARV. L. REV. 1489 (2005).

■ JERRY KANG

* * *

Mugshot. Political scientists Frank Gilliam and Shanto Iyengar created variations of a local newscast: a control version with no crime story, a crime story with no mugshot, a crime story with a Black-suspect mugshot, and a crime story with a White-suspect mugshot. The Black and White suspects were represented by the same morphed photograph, with the only difference being skin hue—thus controlling for facial expression and features. The suspect appeared for only five seconds in a ten-minute newscast; nonetheless, the suspect's race produced statistically significant differences in a criminal law survey completed after the viewing. Having seen the Black suspect, White participants showed 6% more support for punitive remedies than did the control group, which saw no crime story. When participants were instead exposed to the White suspect, their support for punitive remedies increased by only 1%, which was not statistically significant.

* * *

Shooter Bias. Social cognitionist Joshua Correll created a video game that placed photographs of a White or Black individual holding either a gun or other object (wallet, soda can, or cell phone) into diverse photographic backgrounds. Participants were instructed to decide as quickly as possible whether to shoot the target. Severe time pressure designed into the game forced errors. Consistent with earlier findings, participants were more likely to mistake a Black target as armed when he in fact was unarmed (false alarms); conversely, they were more likely to mistake a White target as unarmed when he in fact was armed (misses). Even more striking is that Black participants showed similar amounts of "shooter bias" as Whites.

What is going on here? Quite simply, a revolution. These studies are the tip of the iceberg of recent social cognition research elaborating what I call "racial mechanics"—the ways in which race alters intrapersonal, interpersonal, and intergroup interactions. The results are stunning, reproducible, and valid by traditional scientific metrics. They seriously challenge current understandings of our "rational" selves and our interrelations.

* * *

I start by asking a fundamental question: "Where does bias come from?" One important source is vicarious experience with the racial other, transmitted through the media. If these experiences are somehow skewed, we should not be surprised by the presence of pervasive implicit bias. What, then, might we do about such media programming given the rigid constraints of the First Amendment? To be sure, private actors of good faith can voluntarily adopt best practices that decrease implicit bias and its manifestations. But can the state, through law, do anything?

If there is any room for intervention, it would be in the communications realm of broadcast, which enjoys doctrinal exceptionalism. In broadcast, notwithstanding the First Amendment, we tolerate the licensing of speakers. In broadcast, we tolerate suppression of speech we dislike, such as indecency and violence. In broadcast, we tolerate encouragement of speech we like, such as educational television and local-oriented programming. All this is in the name of the "public interest," the vague standard that Congress has charged the Federal Communications Commission with pursuing.

That "public interest" standard was recently reshaped in the controversial June 2003 Media Ownership Order. There, the FCC repeatedly justified relaxing ownership rules by explaining how such changes would increase, of all things, local news. Since local news was viewed as advancing "diversity" and "localism," two of the three core elements of the "public interest," any structural deregulation that would increase local news was lauded.

* * *

For a race paper, my using social cognition and applying it to communications law are unorthodox, but purposefully so. * * * One way to break current deadlocks is to turn to new bodies of knowledge uncovered by social science, specifically the remarkable findings of social cognition. Not only do they provide a more precise, particularized, and empirically grounded picture of how race functions in our minds, and thus in our societies, they also rattle us out of a complacency enjoyed after the demise of de jure discrimination. Further calls for equality are often derogated as whining by those who cannot compete in a modern meritocracy. Social cognition discoveries dispute that resentful characterization and make us reexamine our individual and collective responsibilities for persistent racial inequality. * * *

[I] am confident that the language, methodologies, and findings of social cognition provide trenchant additions to the philosophical, anthropological, sociological, literary, and political science modes of argument that have so far dominated critical race studies. For better and worse, law has turned sharply in favor of quantified and empirical analyses. Social cognition allows a phalanx of those who study race to take that same turn, instrumentally to fight fire with fire, and substantively to profit from a body of science that supports, particularizes, and checks what we intuit as the truth of our lived experiences. * * *

Another way to generate new insights is to view old topics through new lenses. That explains my invocation of the metaphor of "Trojan Horses," which is more familiar to cyberlaw than to critical race studies. This strategy further explains why I apply my social cognitive model of racial mechanics to FCC regulations. I start with the theory and evidence of racial mechanics.

* * *

II. Trojan Horses

A. *Tuning In to Broadcast*

* * *

To understand my choice of topic, we must start with a fundamental question: "Where do racial meanings come from?" Racial meanings that accrete in our schemas can, on the one hand, come from "direct experiences" with individuals mapped into those categories. On the other hand, the racial meanings can arise from what I call "vicarious experiences," which are stories of or simulated engagements with racial others provided through various forms of the media or narrated by parents and our peers. Given persistent racial segregation, we should not underestimate the significance of vicarious experiences. Even if direct experience with racial minorities more powerfully shapes our schemas, vicarious experiences may well dominate in terms of sheer quantity and frequency.

The next question becomes, "Why are racial meanings biased against racial minorities?" One hypothesis is that people encounter skewed data sets—or as the computer scientists say, "garbage in, garbage out." If these principally vicarious experiences, transmitted through electronic media, are somehow "skewed," then the racial meanings associated with certain racial categories should also be skewed. This analysis invites further study of culture and mass media policy, topics that social cognitionists have largely avoided.

Suppose that social cognitionists identify which types of vicarious experiences trigger and exacerbate bias and which ameliorate it. Private parties will obviously be free to act on the basis of such discoveries. Voluntary attempts to create a "diversity" of role models on television reflect some such impulse, in addition to financial self-interest since "diversity" is sometimes good for business. But what about collective action, mediated through the state and implemented through law?

* * *

In the 1934 Act, Congress created the FCC and charged it with managing the spectrum to further the "public convenience, interest, or necessity"—the public interest standard. In addition to regulating entry by assigning frequencies, the FCC has power to mold, at least softly, the content of broadcast. * * *

In its history, the FCC has promulgated (and the courts have enforced) regulations that restrict the broadcast of content deemed "bad," such as obscenity, indecency, and excessive commercialization. Specific to antiracism, the FCC, at the instruction of the courts, has revoked the broadcast licenses of stations that favored segregation and aired anti-Black racial epithets. Conversely, the FCC has also promulgated regulations that promote content deemed "good" through informational programming guidelines, community needs and interests ascertainment requirements, the fairness doctrine, and children's educational television guidelines. Specific to questions of race, the FCC has also tried to promote "good" and diverse content by increasing minority ownership of stations through affirmative action. Finally, the FCC has regulated market structure at each stage of production, distribution, and consumption. * * *

[G]iven constitutional law as we know it, if we are curious about what the state can do to combat implicit bias transmitted through vicarious experiences, broadcast is the prime site of inquiry.

B.   *Redefining the Public Interest*

The touchstone for governmental management of broadcast is the "public interest" standard. That standard has recently been explicated in an unusual way. At least in the context of ownership policy, the public interest has been functionally equated with the local news.

In June 2003, a divided FCC lifted numerous media ownership restrictions in the name of the "public interest." Some of the changes permitted greater horizontal consolidation in local markets. Specifically, the FCC liberalized the local television multiple ownership rule and the local radio ownership rule. * * * I focus on how the FCC operationalized, and thus arguably redefined, the idea of the "public interest" by equating it with the production of local news.

* * *

Local news * * * played a starring role in one other component of the public interest: "localism." Localism has never been consistently defined in the Commission's analysis. * * * In its order, the FCC did not clarify the term, but it did establish a methodology for measuring localism. It focused again on "programming responsive to local needs and interests, and local news quantity and quality." For two out of the three fundamental components of the "public interest"—diversity and localism—the FCC highlighted the significance of local news production.

* * *

In sum, "local news" has become *the* critical component of the FCC's "public interest" analysis, at least in the media ownership context. Although local news has long played an important role in the idea of "public service," its predominance in the deregulation order is striking. The supervening norm that the FCC must pursue, the "public interest," has now become practically identical to the number of hours of local news a station broadcasts. But what in fact is on the local news?

C. Local News

1. Crime and Punishment.—Violent crime. Crime occupies a heavy share of broadcast news programming. This is true for national news. It is also true for local news, which is "the most widely used source of information about crime." The PEJ's annual study of local news programming consistently finds that local newscasts spend about a quarter of their time on crime stories.

* * *

Violent crime news stories frequently involve racial minorities, especially African Americans. One reason is that racial minorities are arrested for violent crimes more frequently on a per capita basis than Whites. Given our social cognition review, we can predict what watching local news might do to us. If subliminal flashes of Black male faces can raise our frustration, as shown by the Computer Crash study, would it be surprising that consciously received messages couched in violent visual context have impact, too? In fact, we have already seen in the Mugshot study, described in the Introduction, that even ephemeral exposure to race can alter our opinions about crime and punishment. That study, also conducted by Gilliam and Iyengar, is one of the more sophisticated studies in a line of newscast experiments finding similar results.

* * *

2. Trojan Horse Viruses.—I now make explicit what I have so far left implicit: local news programs, dense with images of racial minorities committing violent crimes in one's own community, can be analogized to Trojan Horse viruses. A type of computer virus, a Trojan Horse installs itself on a user's computer without her awareness. That small program then runs in the background, without the user's knowledge, and silently waits to take action—whether by corrupting files, e-mailing pornographic spam, or launching a "denial of service" attack—which the user, if conscious of it, would disavow.

Typically, a Trojan Horse comes attached secretly to a program or information we actively seek. For instance, we might download a new program for a trial run, and embedded inside may be a Trojan Horse that installs itself without our knowledge. Or, we might browse some website in search of information, and a small javascript bug may be embedded in the page we view. Here is the translation to the news context: we turn on the television in search of local news, and with that information comes a Trojan Horse that alters our racial schemas. The images we see are more powerful than mere words. As local news, they speak of threats nearby, not in some abstract, distant land. The stories are not fiction but a brutal reality. They come from the most popular and trusted source.

* * *

How do we know violent crime stories can, like Trojan Horses, exacerbate implicit bias? The Mugshot study and other work by political scientists using the newscast paradigm are suggestive. Further evidence comes from studies that demonstrate media primings of racial schemas. For example, we now know that exposure to violent rap music can increase implicit bias against African Americans and that playing the video game Doom can increase one's implicit self-concept of aggressiveness—all the while having no statistically significant impact on one's explicit, self-reported views. Still further evidence comes indirectly from research Nilanjana Dasgupta calls the "third wave" of implicit bias research, which examines the malleability of implicit bias. This research demonstrates that implicit bias can be exacerbated or mitigated by the information environments we inhabit.

* * *

[C]onsuming positive images can decrease individuals' implicit bias, although they may register no difference on measures of explicit bias. Conversely, it seems reasonable to suppose that consuming negative images can exacerbate implicit bias. Recall the group in the Blair study instructed to imagine stereotypic women. And if mental imagery can produce such effects, watching direct portrayals in electronic media may well have an even stronger impact.

* * *

To summarize: Local news provides data that we use consciously in a rational analysis to produce informed opinions on, say, criminal punishment. But these newscasts also activate and strengthen linkages among certain racial categories, violent crime, and the fear and loathing such crime invokes. In this sense, the local news functions precisely like a Trojan Horse virus. We invite it into our homes, our dens, in through the gates of our minds, and accept it at face value, as an accurate representation of newsworthy events. But something lurks within those newscasts that programs our racial schemas in ways we cannot notice but can, through scientific measurements, detect. And the viruses they harbor deliver a payload with consequences, affecting how we vote for "three strikes and you're out" laws, how awkwardly we interact with folks, and even how quickly we pull the trigger.

3. *The Accuracy Objection.*—A predictable objection is that the violent content, including crime committed by racial minorities, is a feature, not a bug. In other words, the data presented are not skewed and instead faithfully reflect a reality that the local news did not create. I have three responses to this "accuracy objection": the data are likely not fairly presented; our memories and abilities to see patterns are selective; and we interpret the data in self-serving ways.

First, the information broadcast is probably not fair and balanced. There is a prima facie case that the local media give disproportionate attention to violent crime, in which Black suspects feature prominently. Furthermore, ample evidence shows that the media treats Black-perpetrator stories differently, representing and portraying suspects in a more threatening manner than comparable White perpetrators. Specifically, Robert Entman explains that because of production biases in local newscasts, Black suspects are more likely to remain unnamed and in physical custody, and less likely to speak for themselves. As a result, while there is evidence that the statistical prominence of Blacks portrayed in crime news is "not that much out of line with the actual Black arrest rate," the emphasis on violent crime appears to skew public perceptions.

Second, even if local news accurately reflected reality, we see "illusory correlations." Whenever two salient events are noticed together, that combination leaves a deep impression in our memories and leads us to overestimate its frequency. Because racial minorities are numerical minorities (and therefore often salient) and because bad acts (for example, crimes) are also unusual and salient, when racial minorities commit bad acts, the information gets more deeply imprinted and weighted than is statistically warranted.* * *

Third, even if our recollections are accurate, our interpretations may be biased * * * even if the news conveys descriptively accurate information about the *mean* criminality of racial minority groups, the public still may seriously underestimate the *variance*. This would contribute to the fallacy of thinking that simply because 50% of crimes are committed by a group X, 50% of group X commit crimes. Consider how this tendency to view members of outgroups as monolithic could affect Arab Americans during our indefinite war on terror.

Another concern is the "fundamental attribution error" (FAE). The FAE is a general tendency to attribute the causes of behavior to dispositional, instead of situational, factors. In other words, we tend to underweight contingent, environmental factors that cause a particular action and to highlight putatively stable factors such as personality traits instead.* * *

    * * *

[Kang considers the possibility of placing "caps" on local news stories concerning violent crimes.] After answering the empirical question, we must also make a final normative judgment. In other words, even if implicit bias does what I claim it does, is that important enough to count as "compelling"? First Amendment doctrine does not provide a clear test to answer such a question. So we reason through close analogy to other government interests that have been deemed "compelling." We know, for example, that "safeguarding the physical and psychological well-being" of children is a compelling interest. Drawing on equal protection case law, we know that remedying racial discrimination as well as pursuing educational diversity count as compelling interests. In the end, the government interest in decreasing implicit bias should be deemed "compelling" as well.

    * * *

Grutter v. Bollinger

Supreme Court of the United States, 539 U.S. 306 (2003).

■ O'CONNOR, J., delivered the opinion of the Court, in which STEVENS, SOUTER, GINSBURG, and BREYER, JJ., joined, and in which SCALIA and THOMAS, JJ., joined in part insofar as it is consistent with the views expressed in Part VII of the opinion of THOMAS, J. GINSBURG, J., filed a concurring opinion, in which BREYER, J., joined. SCALIA, J., filed an opinion concurring in part and dissenting in part, in which THOMAS, J., joined. THOMAS, J., filed an opinion concurring in part and dissenting in part, in which SCALIA, J., joined as to Parts I–VII. REHNQUIST, C. J., filed a dissenting opinion, in which SCALIA, KENNEDY, and THOMAS, JJ., joined. KENNEDY, J., filed a dissenting opinion.

■ JUSTICE O'CONNOR delivered the opinion of the Court.

This case requires us to decide whether the use of race as a factor in student admissions by the University of Michigan Law School (Law School) is unlawful.

I

A

The Law School ranks among the Nation's top law schools. It receives more than 3,500 applications each year for a class of around 350 students. Seeking to "admit a group of students who individually and collectively are among the most capable," the Law School looks for individuals with "substantial promise for success in law school" and "a strong likelihood of succeeding in the practice of law and contributing in diverse ways to the well-being of others." * * * More broadly, the Law School seeks "a mix of students with varying backgrounds and experiences who will respect and learn from each other." * * *

The hallmark of [the law school's affirmative action] policy is its focus on academic ability coupled with a flexible assessment of applicants' talents, experiences, and potential "to contribute to the learning of those around them." * * * The policy requires admissions officials to evaluate each applicant based on all the information available in the file, including a personal statement, letters of recommendation, and an essay describing the ways in which the applicant will contribute to the life and diversity of the Law School. * * * In reviewing an applicant's file, admissions officials must consider the applicant's undergraduate grade point average (GPA) and Law School Admissions Test (LSAT) score because they are important (if imperfect) predictors of academic success in law school. * * * The policy stresses that "no applicant should be admitted unless we expect that applicant to do well enough to graduate with no serious academic problems."

* * *

The policy aspires to "achieve that diversity which has the potential to enrich everyone's education and thus make a law school class stronger than the sum of its parts." * * * The policy does not restrict the types of diversity contributions eligible for "substantial weight" in the admissions process, but instead recognizes "many possible bases for diversity admissions." * * * The policy does, however, reaffirm the Law School's long-standing commitment to "one particular type of diversity," that is, "racial and ethnic diversity with special reference to the inclusion of students from groups which have been historically discriminated against, like African-Americans, Hispanics and Native Americans, who without this commitment might not be represented in our student body in meaningful numbers." * * * By enrolling a " 'critical mass' of [underrepresented] minority students," the Law School seeks to "ensure their ability to make unique contributions to the character of the Law School." * * *

The policy does not define diversity "solely in terms of racial and ethnic status." * * * Nor is the policy "insensitive to the competition among all students for admission to the Law School." * * * Rather, the policy seeks to guide admissions officers in "producing classes both diverse and academically outstanding, classes made up of students who promise to continue the tradition of outstanding contribution by Michigan Graduates to the legal profession." * * *

B

Petitioner Barbara Grutter is a white Michigan resident who applied to the Law School in 1996 with a 3.8 grade point average and 161 LSAT score. The Law School initially placed petitioner on a waiting list, but subsequently rejected her application. In December 1997, petitioner filed suit in the United States District Court for the Eastern District of Michigan against the Law School, the Regents of the University of Michigan, Lee Bollinger (Dean of the Law School from 1987 to 1994, and President of the University of Michigan from 1996 to 2002), Jeffrey Lehman (Dean of the Law School), and Dennis Shields (Director of Admissions at the Law School from 1991 until 1998). Petitioner alleged that respondents discriminated against her on the basis of race in violation of the Fourteenth Amendment, Title VI of the Civil Rights Act of 1964, and Rev Stat § 1977.

Petitioner further alleged that her application was rejected because the Law School uses race as a "predominant" factor, giving applicants who belong to certain minority groups "a significantly greater chance of admission than students with similar credentials from disfavored racial groups." Petitioner also alleged that respondents "had no compelling interest to justify their use of race in the admissions process." * * * Petitioner requested compensatory and punitive damages, an order requiring the Law School to offer her admission, and an injunction prohibiting the Law School from continuing to discriminate on the basis of race. * * * Petitioner clearly has standing to bring this lawsuit.

* * *

We granted certiorari * * * to resolve the disagreement among the Courts of Appeals on a question of national importance: Whether diversity is a compelling interest that can justify the narrowly tailored use of race in selecting applicants for admission to public universities. Compare *Hopwood v. Texas*, 78 F.3d 932 (5th Cir. 1996) (Hopwood I) (holding that diversity is not a compelling state interest), with *Smith v. University of Washington Law School*, 233 F.3d 1188 (9th Cir. 2000) (holding that it is).

II

A

We last addressed the use of race in public higher education over 25 years ago. In the landmark *Bakke* case, we reviewed a racial set-aside program that reserved 16 out of 100 seats in a medical school class for members of certain minority groups. * * * The decision produced six separate opinions, none of which commanded a majority of the Court. Four Justices would have upheld the program against all attack on the ground that the government can use race to "remedy disadvantages cast on minorities by past racial prejudice." [*Bakke*] (joint opinion of Brennan, White, Marshall, and Blackmun, JJ., concurring in judgment in part and dissenting in part). Four other Justices avoided the constitutional question altogether and struck down the program on statutory grounds. [*Id.*] (opinion of Stevens, J., joined by Burger, C. J., and Stewart and Rehnquist, JJ., concurring in judgment in part and dissenting in part). Justice Powell provided a fifth vote not only for invalidating the set-aside program, but also for reversing the state court's injunction against any use of race whatsoever. The only holding for the Court in *Bakke* was that a "State has a substantial interest that legitimately may be served by a properly devised admissions program involving the competitive consideration of race and ethnic origin." * * * Thus, we reversed that part of the lower court's judgment that enjoined the university "from any consideration of the race of any applicant." * * *

Since this Court's splintered decision in *Bakke*, Justice Powell's opinion announcing the judgment of the Court has served as the touchstone for constitutional analysis of race-conscious admissions policies. Public and private universities across the Nation have modeled their own admissions programs on Justice Powell's views on permissible race-conscious policies. * * * We therefore discuss Justice Powell's opinion in some detail.

Justice Powell began by stating that "the guarantee of equal protection cannot mean one thing when applied to one individual and something else when applied to a person of another color. If both are not accorded the same protection, then it is not equal." * * *

First, Justice Powell rejected an interest in "reducing the historic deficit of traditionally disfavored minorities in medical schools and in the medical profession" as an unlawful interest in racial balancing. * * * Second, Justice Powell rejected an interest in remedying societal discrimination because such measures would risk placing unnecessary burdens on innocent third parties "who bear no responsibility for whatever harm the beneficiaries of the special admissions program are thought to have suffered." * * * Third, Justice Powell rejected an interest in "increasing the number of physicians who will practice in communities currently underserved," concluding that even if such an interest could be compelling in some circumstances the program under review was not "geared to promote that goal." * * *

Justice Powell approved the university's use of race to further only one interest: "the attainment of a diverse student body." * * * In seeking the "right to select those students who will contribute the most to the 'robust exchange of ideas,' " a university seeks to achieve a goal that is of paramount importance in the fulfillment of its mission." * * *

B

The Equal Protection Clause provides that no State shall "deny to any person within its jurisdiction the equal protection of the laws." U.S. Const., Amdt. 14, § 2. Because the Fourteenth Amendment "protects *persons*, not *groups*," all "governmental action based on race—a *group* classification long recognized as in most circumstances irrelevant and therefore prohibited—should be subjected to detailed judicial inquiry to ensure that the *personal* right to equal protection of the laws has not been infringed." *Adarand Constructors, Inc. v. Pena*, 515 U.S. 200, 227 (1995) (emphasis in original; internal quotation marks and citation omitted). We are a "free people whose institutions are founded upon the doctrine of equality." *Loving v. Virginia*, 388 U.S. 1, 11 (1967) (internal quotation marks and citation omitted). It follows from that principle that "government may treat people differently because of their race only for the most compelling reasons." [*Adarand*.]

We have held that all racial classifications imposed by government "must be analyzed by a reviewing court under strict scrutiny." *Ibid.* This means that such classifications are constitutional only if they are narrowly tailored to further compelling governmental interests. * * *

Strict scrutiny is not "strict in theory, but fatal in fact." [*Adarand*.] Although all governmental uses of race are subject to strict scrutiny, not all are invalidated by it. * * * When race-based action is necessary to further a compelling governmental interest, such action does not violate the constitutional guarantee of equal protection so long as the narrow-tailoring requirement is also satisfied.

* * *

III

A

* * *

We first wish to dispel the notion that the Law School's argument has been foreclosed, either expressly or implicitly, by our affirmative-action cases decided since *Bakke*. It is true that some language in those opinions might be read to suggest that remedying past discrimination is the only permissible justification for race-based governmental action. See, e.g., *Richmond v. J. A. Croson Co.*, [488 U.S. 469 (1989) (plurality opinion).] But we have never held that the only governmental use of race that can survive strict scrutiny is remedying past discrimination. Nor, since *Bakke*, have we directly addressed the use of race in the context of public higher education. Today, we hold that the Law School has a compelling interest in attaining a diverse student body.

The Law School's educational judgment that such diversity is essential to its educational mission is one to which we defer. The Law School's assessment that diversity will, in fact, yield educational benefits is substantiated by respondents and their *amici*. Our scrutiny of the interest asserted by the Law School is no less strict for taking into account complex educational judgments in an area that lies primarily within the expertise of the university. Our holding today is in keeping with our tradition of giving a degree of deference to a university's academic decisions, within constitutionally prescribed limits. * * *

We have long recognized that, given the important purpose of public education and the expansive freedoms of speech and thought associated with the university environment, universities occupy a special niche in our constitutional tradition. * * * In announcing the principle of student body diversity as a compelling state interest, Justice Powell invoked our cases recognizing a constitutional dimension, grounded in the First Amendment, of educational autonomy: "The freedom of a university to make its own judgments as to education includes the selection of its student body." [*Bakke*.] From this premise, Justice Powell reasoned that by claiming "the right to select those students who will contribute the most to the 'robust exchange of ideas,'" a university "seeks to achieve a goal that is of paramount importance in the fulfillment of its mission." * * * Our conclusion that the Law School has a compelling interest in a diverse student body is informed by our view that attaining a diverse student body is at the heart of the Law School's proper institutional mission, and that "good faith" on the part of a university is "presumed" absent "a showing to the contrary." * * *

As part of its goal of "assembling a class that is both exceptionally academically qualified and broadly diverse," the Law School seeks to "enroll a 'critical mass' of minority students." * * * The Law School's interest is not simply "to assure within its student body some specified percentage of a particular group merely because of its race or ethnic origin." [*Bakke*.] That would amount to outright racial balancing, which is patently unconstitutional. * * * Rather, the Law School's concept of critical mass is defined by reference to the educational benefits that diversity is designed to produce.

These benefits are substantial. As the District Court emphasized, the Law School's admissions policy promotes "cross-racial understanding," helps to break down racial stereotypes, and "enables [students] to better understand persons of different races." * * * These benefits are "important and laudable," because "classroom discussion is livelier, more spirited, and simply more enlightening and interesting" when the students have "the greatest possible variety of backgrounds." * * *

The Law School's claim of a compelling interest is further bolstered by its *amici*, who point to the educational benefits that flow from student body diversity. In addition to the expert studies and reports entered into evidence at trial, numerous studies show that student body diversity promotes learning outcomes, and "better prepares students for an increasingly diverse workforce and society, and better prepares them as professionals." [Brief for American Educational Research Association et al.]

These benefits are not theoretical but real, as major American businesses have made clear that the skills needed in today's increasingly global marketplace can only be developed through exposure to widely diverse people, cultures, ideas, and viewpoints. [Brief for 3M et al.; Brief for General Motors Corp.] What is more, high-ranking retired officers and civilian leaders of the United States military assert that, "based on [their] decades of experience," a "highly qualified, racially diverse officer corps . . . is essential to the military's ability to fulfill its principle mission to provide national security." [Brief for Julius W. Becton, Jr. et al.] The primary sources for the Nation's officer corps are the service academies and the Reserve Officers Training Corps (ROTC), the latter comprising students already admitted to participating colleges and universities. * * * At present, "the military cannot achieve an officer corps that is *both* highly qualified *and* racially diverse unless the service academies and the ROTC used limited race-conscious recruiting and admissions policies." [*Id.* (emphasis in original).] To fulfill its mission, the military "must be selective in admissions for training and education for the officer corps, *and* it must train and educate a highly qualified, racially diverse officer corps in a racially diverse setting." [*Id.* (emphasis in original).] We agree that "it requires only a small step from this analysis to conclude that our country's

other most selective institutions must remain both diverse and selective.''
* * *

* * *

Moreover, universities, and in particular, law schools, represent the training ground for a large number of our Nation's leaders. *Sweatt v. Painter*, 339 U.S. 629, 634 (1950) (describing law school as a "proving ground for legal learning and practice"). Individuals with law degrees occupy roughly half the state governorships, more than half the seats in the United States Senate, and more than a third of the seats in the United States House of Representatives. [See Brief for Association of American Law Schools.] The pattern is even more striking when it comes to highly selective law schools. A handful of these schools accounts for 25 of the 100 United States Senators, 74 United States Courts of Appeals judges, and nearly 200 of the more than 600 United States District Court judges. * * *

In order to cultivate a set of leaders with legitimacy in the eyes of the citizenry, it is necessary that the path to leadership be visibly open to talented and qualified individuals of every race and ethnicity. All members of our heterogeneous society must have confidence in the openness and integrity of the educational institutions that provide this training. As we have recognized, law schools "cannot be effective in isolation from the individuals and institutions with which the law interacts." [*Sweatt*.] Access to legal education (and thus the legal profession) must be inclusive of talented and qualified individuals of every race and ethnicity, so that all members of our heterogeneous society may participate in the educational institutions that provide the training and education necessary to succeed in America.

The Law School does not premise its need for critical mass on "any belief that minority students always (or even consistently) express some characteristic minority viewpoint on any issue." * * * To the contrary, diminishing the force of such stereotypes is both a crucial part of the Law School's mission, and one that it cannot accomplish with only token numbers of minority students. Just as growing up in a particular region or having particular professional experiences is likely to affect an individual's views, so too is one's own, unique experience of being a racial minority in a society, like our own, in which race unfortunately still matters. The Law School has determined, based on its experience and expertise, that a "critical mass" of underrepresented minorities is necessary to further its compelling interest in securing the educational benefits of a diverse student body.

B

Even in the limited circumstance when drawing racial distinctions is permissible to further a compelling state interest, government is still "constrained in how it may pursue that end: [T]he means chosen to accomplish the [government's] asserted purpose must be specifically and narrowly framed to accomplish that purpose." *Shaw v. Hunt*, 517 U.S. 899, 908 (1996). The purpose of the narrow tailoring requirement is to ensure that "the means chosen 'fit' th[e] compelling goal so closely that there is little or no possibility that the motive for the classification was illegitimate racial prejudice or stereotype." [*Croson* (plurality opinion).]

* * *

To be narrowly tailored, a race-conscious admissions program cannot use a quota system—it cannot "insulate each category of applicants with certain desired qualifications from competition with all other applicants." [*Bakke* (opinion of Powell, J.).] Instead, a university may consider race or ethnicity only as a " 'plus' in a particular applicant's file," without "insulating the individual from comparison with all other candidates for the available seats." [*Id.*] * * *

We find that the Law School's admissions program bears the hallmarks of a narrowly tailored plan. As Justice Powell made clear in *Bakke*, truly individualized consideration demands that race be used in a flexible, nonmechanical way. * * *

We are satisfied that the Law School's admissions program, like the Harvard plan described by Justice Powell, does not operate as a quota. Properly understood, a "quota" is a program in which a certain fixed number or proportion of opportunities are "reserved exclusively for certain minority groups." [*Croson* (plurality opinion).] Quotas " 'impose a fixed number or percentage which must be attained, or which cannot be exceeded,' " *Sheet Metal Workers v. EEOC*, 478 U.S. 421, 445 (1986) (O'CONNOR, J., concurring in part and dissenting in part), and "insulate the individual from comparison with all other candidates for the available seats." [*Bakke* (opinion of Powell, J.).] In contrast, "a permissible goal . . . requires only a good-faith effort . . . to come within a range demarcated by the goal itself," [*Sheet Metal Workers*,] and permits consideration of race as a "plus" factor in any given case while still ensuring that each candidate "competes with all other qualified applicants," *Johnson v. Transportation Agency, Santa Clara Cty.*, 480 U.S. 616, 638 (1987).

* * *

The Law School's goal of attaining a critical mass of underrepresented minority students does not transform its program into a quota. As the Harvard plan described by Justice Powell recognized, there is of course "some relationship between numbers and achieving the benefits to be derived from a diverse student body, and between numbers and providing a reasonable environment for those students admitted." [*Id.*] "Some attention to numbers," without more, does not transform a flexible admissions system into a rigid quota. [*Id.*] Nor, as Justice Kennedy posits, does the Law School's consultation of the "daily reports," which keep track of the racial and ethnic composition of the class (as well as of residency and gender), "suggest[ ] there was no further attempt at individual review save for race itself" during the final stages of the admissions process. * * * To the contrary, the Law School's admissions officers testified without contradiction that they never gave race any more or less weight based on the information contained in these reports. * * * Moreover, as Justice Kennedy concedes, * * * between 1993 and 2000, the number of African–American, Latino, and Native–American students in each class at the Law School varied from 13.5 to 20.1 percent, a range inconsistent with a quota.

The Chief Justice believes that the Law School's policy conceals an attempt to achieve racial balancing, and cites admissions data to contend that the Law School discriminates among different groups within the critical mass. * * * But, as the Chief Justice concedes, the number of underrepresented minority students who ultimately enroll in the Law School differs substantially from their representation in the applicant pool and varies considerably for each group from year to year. * * *

* * *

Here, the Law School engages in a highly individualized, holistic review of each applicant's file, giving serious consideration to all the ways an applicant might contribute to a diverse educational environment. The Law School affords this individualized consideration to applicants of all races. There is no policy, either *de jure* or *de facto*, of automatic acceptance or rejection based on any single "soft" variable. Unlike the program at issue in *Gratz v. Bollinger*, [123 S.Ct. 2411 (2003),] the Law School awards no mechanical, predetermined diversity "bonuses" based on race or ethnicity. * * * Like the Harvard plan, the Law School's admissions policy "is flexible enough to consider all pertinent elements of diversity in light of the particular qualifications of each applicant, and to place them on the same footing for consideration, although not necessarily according them the same weight." [*Bakke* (opinion of Powell, J.).]

We also find that, like the Harvard plan Justice Powell referenced in *Bakke*, the Law School's race-conscious admissions program adequately ensures that all factors that may contribute to student body diversity are meaningfully considered alongside race in admissions decisions. With respect to the use of race itself, all underrepresented minority students admitted by the Law School have been deemed qualified. By virtue of our Nation's struggle with racial inequality, such students are both likely to have experiences of particular importance to the Law School's mission, and less likely to be admitted in meaningful numbers on criteria that ignore those experiences. * * *

* * *

What is more, the Law School actually gives substantial weight to diversity factors besides race. The Law School frequently accepts nonminority applicants with grades and test scores lower than underrepresented minority applicants (and other nonminority applicants) who are rejected. * * * This shows that the Law School seriously weighs many other diversity factors besides race that can make a real and dispositive difference for nonminority applicants as well. By this flexible approach, the Law School sufficiently takes into account, in practice as well as in theory, a wide variety of characteristics besides race and ethnicity that contribute to a diverse student body. Justice Kennedy speculates that "race is likely outcome determinative for many members of minority groups" who do not fall within the upper range of LSAT scores and grades. * * * But the same could be said of the Harvard plan discussed approvingly by Justice Powell in *Bakke*, and indeed of any plan that uses race as one of many factors. * * *

Petitioner and the United States argue that the Law School's plan is not narrowly tailored because race-neutral means exist to obtain the educational benefits of student body diversity that the Law School seeks. We disagree. Narrow tailoring does not require exhaustion of every conceivable race-neutral alternative. * * *

We agree with the Court of Appeals that the Law School sufficiently considered workable race-neutral alternatives. The District Court took the Law School to task for failing to consider race-neutral alternatives such as "using a lottery system" or "decreasing the emphasis for all applicants on undergraduate GPA and LSAT scores." * * * But these alternatives would require a dramatic sacrifice of diversity, the academic quality of all admitted students, or both.

* * *

We acknowledge that "there are serious problems of justice connected with the idea of preference itself." [*Bakke* (opinion of Powell, J.).] Narrow tailoring, therefore, requires that a race-conscious admissions program not unduly harm members of any racial group. Even remedial race-based governmental action generally "remains subject to continuing oversight to assure that it will work the least harm possible to other innocent persons competing for the benefit." * * * To be narrowly tailored, a race-conscious admissions program must not "unduly burden individuals who are not members of the favored racial and ethnic groups." *Metro Broadcasting, Inc. v. FCC*, 497 U.S. 547, 630 (1990) (O'CONNOR, J., dissenting).

* * * We agree that, in the context of its individualized inquiry into the possible diversity contributions of all applicants, the Law School's race-conscious admissions program does not unduly harm nonminority applicants.

We are mindful, however, that "[a] core purpose of the Fourteenth Amendment was to do away with all governmentally imposed discrimination based on race." *Palmore v. Sidoti*, 466 U.S. 429, 432 (1984). Accordingly, race-conscious admissions policies must be limited in time. This requirement reflects that racial classifications, however compelling their goals, are potentially so dangerous that they may be employed no more broadly than the interest demands. Enshrining a permanent justification for racial preferences would offend this fundamental equal protection principle. We see no reason to exempt race-conscious admissions programs from the requirement that all governmental use of race must have a logical end point. The Law School, too, concedes that all "race-conscious programs must have reasonable durational limits." * * *

In the context of higher education, the durational requirement can be met by sunset provisions in race-conscious admissions policies and periodic reviews to determine whether racial preferences are still necessary to achieve student body diversity. Universities in California, Florida, and Washington State, where racial preferences in admissions are prohibited by state law, are currently engaged in experimenting with a wide variety of alternative approaches. Universities in other States can and should draw on the most promising aspects of these race-neutral alternatives as they develop. * * *

The requirement that all race-conscious admissions programs have a termination point "assure[s] all citizens that the deviation from the norm of equal treatment of all racial and ethnic groups is a temporary matter, a measure taken in the service of the goal of equality itself." [*Croson* (plurality opinion).]

We take the Law School at its word that it would "like nothing better than to find a race-neutral admissions formula" and will terminate its race-conscious admissions program as soon as practicable. * * * It has been 25 years since Justice Powell first approved the use of race to further an interest in student body diversity in the context of public higher education. Since that time, the number of minority applicants with high grades and test scores has indeed increased. * * * We expect that 25 years from now, the use of racial preferences will no longer be necessary to further the interest approved today.

* * *

It is so ordered.

■ JUSTICE GINSBURG, with whom JUSTICE BREYER joins, concurring.

* * *

It is well documented that conscious and unconscious race bias, even rank discrimination based on race, remain alive in our land, impeding realization of our highest values and ideals. * * * As to public education, data for the years 2000–2001 show that 71.6% of African–American children and 76.3% of Hispanic children attended a school in which minorities made up a majority of the student body. * * * And schools in predominantly minority communities lag far behind others measured by the educational resources available to them. [See Brief for National Urban League et al.]

However strong the public's desire for improved education systems may be, * * * it remains the current reality that many minority students encounter markedly inadequate and unequal educational opportunities. Despite these inequalities, some minority students are able to meet the high threshold requirements set for admission to the country's finest undergraduate and graduate educational institutions. As lower school education in minority communities improves, an increase in the number of such students may be anticipated. From today's vantage point, one may hope, but not firmly forecast, that over the next generation's span, progress toward nondiscrimination and genuinely equal opportunity will make it safe to sunset affirmative action.

■ CHIEF JUSTICE REHNQUIST, with whom JUSTICE SCALIA, JUSTICE KENNEDY, and JUSTICE THOMAS join, dissenting.

I agree with the Court that, "in the limited circumstance when drawing racial distinctions is permissible," the government must ensure that its means are narrowly tailored to achieve a compelling state interest. * * * I do not believe, however, that the University of Michigan Law School's (Law School) means are narrowly tailored to the interest it asserts. The Law School claims it must take the steps it does to achieve a " 'critical mass' " of underrepresented minority students. * * * But its actual program bears no relation to this asserted goal. Stripped of its "critical mass" veil, the Law School's program is revealed as a naked effort to achieve racial balancing.

As we have explained many times, "any preference based on racial or ethnic criteria must necessarily receive a most searching examination." [*Adarand* (quoting *Wygant*).] Our cases establish that, in order to withstand this demanding inquiry, respondents must demonstrate that their methods of using race "fit" a compelling state interest "with greater precision than any alternative means." [*Id.*]

Before the Court's decision today, we consistently applied the same strict scrutiny analysis regardless of the government's purported reason for using race and regardless of the setting in which race was being used. We rejected calls to use more lenient review in the face of claims that race was being used in "good faith" because "more than good motives should be required when government seeks to allocate its resources by way of an explicit racial classification system." [*Adarand*.] We likewise rejected calls to apply more lenient review based on the particular setting in which race is being used. Indeed, even in the specific context of higher education, we emphasized that "constitutional limitations protecting individual rights may not be disregarded." [*Bakke*.]

Although the Court recites the language of our strict scrutiny analysis, its application of that review is unprecedented in its deference.

Respondents' asserted justification for the Law School's use of race in the admissions process is "obtaining 'the educational benefits that flow from a diverse student body.' " * * *

In practice, the Law School's program bears little or no relation to its asserted goal of achieving "critical mass." Respondents explain that the Law School seeks to accumulate a "critical mass" of *each* underrepresented minority group. * * * But the record demonstrates that the Law School's admissions practices with respect to these groups differ dramatically and cannot be defended under any consistent use of the term "critical mass."

From 1995 through 2000, the Law School admitted between 1,130 and 1,310 students. Of those, between 13 and 19 were Native American, between 91 and 108 were African–Americans, and between 47 and 56 were Hispanic. If the Law School is admitting between 91 and 108 African–Americans in order to achieve "critical mass," thereby preventing African–American students from feeling "isolated or like spokespersons for their race," one would think that a number of the same order of magnitude would be necessary to accomplish the same purpose for Hispanics and

Native Americans. Similarly, even if all of the Native American applicants admitted in a given year matriculate, which the record demonstrates is not at all the case,* how can this possibly constitute a "critical mass" of Native Americans in a class of over 350 students? In order for this pattern of admission to be consistent with the Law School's explanation of "critical mass," one would have to believe that the objectives of "critical mass" offered by respondents are achieved with only half the number of Hispanics and one-sixth the number of Native Americans as compared to African–Americans. But respondents offer no race-specific reasons for such disparities. Instead, they simply emphasize the importance of achieving "critical mass," without any explanation of why that concept is applied differently among the three underrepresented minority groups.

These different numbers, moreover, come only as a result of substantially different treatment among the three underrepresented minority groups, as is apparent in an example offered by the Law School and highlighted by the Court: The school asserts that it "frequently accepts nonminority applicants with grades and test scores lower than underrepresented minority applicants (and other nonminority applicants) who are rejected." * * * Specifically, the Law School states that "sixty-nine minority applicants were rejected between 1995 and 2000 with at least a 3.5 [Grade Point Average (GPA)] and a [score of] 159 or higher on the [Law School Admissions Test (LSAT)]" while a number of Caucasian and Asian–American applicants with similar or lower scores were admitted. * * *

Review of the record reveals only 67 such individuals. Of these 67 individuals, 56 were Hispanic, while only 6 were African–American, and only 5 were Native American. This discrepancy reflects a consistent practice.

These statistics have a significant bearing on petitioner's case. Respondents have *never* offered any race-specific arguments explaining why significantly more individuals from one underrepresented minority group are needed in order to achieve "critical mass" or further student body diversity. They certainly have not explained why Hispanics, who they have said are among "the groups most isolated by racial barriers in our country," should have their admission capped out in this manner. * * * True, petitioner is neither Hispanic nor Native American. But the Law School's disparate admissions practices with respect to these minority groups demonstrate that its alleged goal of "critical mass" is simply a sham. Petitioner may use these statistics to expose this sham, which is the basis for the Law School's admission of less qualified underrepresented minorities in preference to her. Surely strict scrutiny cannot permit these sort of disparities without at least some explanation.

* * *

---

* Indeed, during this 5–year time period, enrollment of Native American students dropped to as low as *three* such students. Any assertion that such a small group constituted a "critical mass" of Native Americans is simply absurd.

The Court, in an unprecedented display of deference under our strict scrutiny analysis, upholds the Law School's program despite its obvious flaws. We have said that when it comes to the use of race, the connection between the ends and the means used to attain them must be precise. But here the flaw is deeper than that; it is not merely a question of "fit" between ends and means. Here the means actually used are forbidden by the Equal Protection Clause of the Constitution.

[Justice Kennedy's dissenting opinion has been omitted].

■ Justice Scalia, with whom Justice Thomas joins, concurring in part and dissenting in part.

    * * *

[T]he "educational benefit" that the University of Michigan seeks to achieve by racial discrimination consists, according to the Court, of " 'cross-racial understanding,' " * * * and " 'better prepar[ation of] students for an increasingly diverse workforce and society,' " * * * all of which is necessary not only for work, but also for good "citizenship." * * * This is not, of course, an "educational benefit" on which students will be graded on their Law School transcript (Works and Plays Well with Others: B+) or tested by the bar examiners (Q: Describe in 500 words or less your cross-racial understanding). For it is a lesson of life rather than law—essentially the same lesson taught to (or rather learned by, for it cannot be "taught" in the usual sense) people three feet shorter and twenty years younger than the full-grown adults at the University of Michigan Law School, in institutions ranging from Boy Scout troops to public-school kindergartens. If properly considered an "educational benefit" at all, it is surely not one that is either uniquely relevant to law school or uniquely "teachable" in a formal educational setting. *And therefore:* If it is appropriate for the University of Michigan Law School to use racial discrimination for the purpose of putting together a "critical mass" that will convey generic lessons in socialization and good citizenship, surely it is no less appropriate—indeed, *particularly* appropriate—for the civil service system of the State of Michigan to do so. There, also, those exposed to "critical masses" of certain races will presumably become better Americans, better Michiganders, better civil servants. And surely private employers cannot be criticized—indeed, should be praised—if they also "teach" good citizenship to their adult employees through a patriotic, all-American system of racial discrimination in hiring. The nonminority individuals who are deprived of a legal education, a civil service job, or any job at all by reason of their skin color will surely understand.

Unlike a clear constitutional holding that racial preferences in state educational institutions are impermissible, or even a clear anticonstitutional holding that racial preferences in state educational institutions are OK, today's *Grutter–Gratz* split double header seems perversely designed to prolong the controversy and the litigation. * * *

■ Justice Thomas, with whom Justice Scalia joins as to Parts I–VII, concurring in part and dissenting in part.

Frederick Douglass, speaking to a group of abolitionists almost 140 years ago, delivered a message lost on today's majority:

"[I]n regard to the colored people, there is always more that is benevolent, I perceive, than just, manifested towards us. What I ask for the negro is not benevolence, not pity, not sympathy, but simply *justice*. The American people have always been anxious to know what they shall do with us. . . . I have had but one answer from the beginning. Do nothing with us! Your doing with us has already played the mischief with us. Do nothing with us! If the apples will not remain on the tree of their own strength, if they are worm-eaten at the core, if they are early ripe and disposed to fall, let them fall! . . . And if the negro cannot stand on his own legs, let him fall also. All I ask is, give him a chance to stand on his own legs! Let him alone! . . . [Y]our interference is doing him positive injury." What the Black Man Wants: An Address Delivered in Boston, Massachusetts, on 26 January 1865, reprinted in 4 The Frederick Douglass Papers 59, 68 (J. Blassingame & J. McKivigan eds. 1991) (emphasis in original).

Like Douglass, I believe blacks can achieve in every avenue of American life without the meddling of university administrators. Because I wish to see all students succeed whatever their color, I share, in some respect, the sympathies of those who sponsor the type of discrimination advanced by the University of Michigan Law School (Law School). The Constitution does not, however, tolerate institutional devotion to the status quo in admissions policies when such devotion ripens into racial discrimination. Nor does the Constitution countenance the unprecedented deference the Court gives to the Law School, an approach inconsistent with the very concept of "strict scrutiny."

No one would argue that a university could set up a lower general admission standard and then impose heightened requirements only on black applicants. Similarly, a university may not maintain a high admission standard and grant exemptions to favored races. The Law School, of its own choosing, and for its own purposes, maintains an exclusionary admissions system that it knows produces racially disproportionate results. Racial discrimination is not a permissible solution to the self-inflicted wounds of this elitist admissions policy.

The majority upholds the Law School's racial discrimination not by interpreting the people's Constitution, but by responding to a faddish slogan of the cognoscenti. Nevertheless, I concur in part in the Court's opinion. First, I agree with the Court insofar as its decision, which approves of only one racial classification, confirms that further use of race in admissions remains unlawful. Second, I agree with the Court's holding that racial discrimination in higher education admissions will be illegal in 25 years. * * * I respectfully dissent from the remainder of the Court's opinion and the judgment, however, because I believe that the Law School's current use of race violates the Equal Protection Clause and that the Constitution means the same thing today as it will in 300 months.

I

* * * The Constitution abhors classifications based on race, not only because those classifications can harm favored races or are based on illegitimate motives, but also because every time the government places citizens on racial registers and makes race relevant to the provision of burdens or benefits, it demeans us all. "Purchased at the price of immeasurable human suffering, the equal protection principle reflects our Nation's understanding that such classifications ultimately have a destructive impact on the individual and our society." [*Adarand* (Thomas, J., concurring in part and concurring in judgment).]

II

Unlike the majority, I seek to define with precision the interest being asserted by the Law School before determining whether that interest is so compelling as to justify racial discrimination. The Law School maintains that it wishes to obtain "educational benefits that flow from student body diversity." * * * This statement must be evaluated carefully, because it implies that both "diversity" and "educational benefits" are components of the Law School's compelling state interest. Additionally, the Law School's refusal to entertain certain changes in its admissions process and status indicates that the compelling state interest it seeks to validate is actually broader than might appear at first glance.

* * *

A distinction between these two ideas (unique educational benefits based on racial aesthetics and race for its own sake) is purely sophistic—so much so that the majority uses them interchangeably. * * * The Law School's argument, as facile as it is, can only be understood in one way: Classroom aesthetics yields educational benefits, racially discriminatory admissions policies are required to achieve the right racial mix, and therefore the policies are required to achieve the educational benefits. It is the *educational benefits* that are the end, or allegedly compelling state interest, not "diversity." * * *

One must also consider the Law School's refusal to entertain changes to its current admissions system that might produce the same educational benefits. The Law School adamantly disclaims any race-neutral alternative that would reduce "academic selectivity," which would in turn "require the Law School to become a very different institution, and to sacrifice a core part of its educational mission." * * * In other words, the Law School seeks to improve marginally the education it offers without sacrificing too much of its exclusivity and elite status.

The proffered interest that the majority vindicates today, then, is not simply "diversity." Instead the Court upholds the use of racial discrimination as a tool to advance the Law School's interest in offering a marginally superior education while maintaining an elite institution. Unless each constituent part of this state interest is of pressing public necessity, the

Law School's use of race is unconstitutional. I find each of them to fall far short of this standard.

III

A

A close reading of the Court's opinion reveals that all of its legal work is done through one conclusory statement: The Law School has a "compelling interest in securing the educational benefits of a diverse student body." * * * No serious effort is made to explain how these benefits fit with the state interests the Court has recognized (or rejected) as compelling * * * or to place any theoretical constraints on an enterprising court's desire to discover still more justifications for racial discrimination. In the absence of any explanation, one might expect the Court to fall back on the judicial policy of *stare decisis*. But the Court eschews even this weak defense of its holding, shunning an analysis of the extent to which Justice Powell's opinion in [*Bakke*] is binding, * * * in favor of an unfounded wholesale adoption of it.

* * *

B

Under the proper standard, there is no pressing public necessity in maintaining a public law school at all and, it follows, certainly not an elite law school. Likewise, marginal improvements in legal education do not qualify as a compelling state interest.

1

While legal education at a public university may be good policy or otherwise laudable, it is obviously not a pressing public necessity when the correct legal standard is applied. * * *

2

* * * Michigan has no compelling interest in having a law school at all, much less an *elite* one. Still, even assuming that a State may, under appropriate circumstances, demonstrate a cognizable interest in having an elite law school, Michigan has failed to do so here.

* * *

[T]he Law School trains few Michigan residents and overwhelmingly serves students, who, as lawyers, leave the State of Michigan. The Law School's decision to be an elite institution does little to advance the welfare of the people of Michigan or any cognizable interest of the State of Michigan. * * *

3

Finally, even if the Law School's racial tinkering produces tangible educational benefits, a marginal improvement in legal education cannot justify racial discrimination where the Law School has no compelling interest in either its existence or in its current educational and admissions policies.

IV

The interest in remaining elite and exclusive that the majority thinks so obviously critical requires the use of admissions "standards" that, in turn, create the Law School's "need" to discriminate on the basis of race. The Court validates these admissions standards by concluding that alternatives that would require "a dramatic sacrifice of . . . the academic quality of all admitted students," * * * need not be considered before racial discrimination can be employed. In the majority's view, such methods are not required by the "narrow tailoring" prong of strict scrutiny because that inquiry demands, in this context, that any race-neutral alternative work " 'about as well.' " * * * The majority errs, however, because race-neutral alternatives must only be "workable," * * * and do "about as well" *in vindicating the compelling state interest.* The Court never explicitly holds that the Law School's desire to retain the status quo in "academic selectivity" is itself a compelling state interest, and, as I have demonstrated, it is not. * * * Therefore, the Law School should be forced to choose between its classroom aesthetic and its exclusionary admissions system—it cannot have it both ways.

With the adoption of different admissions methods, such as accepting all students who meet minimum qualifications, * * * the Law School could achieve its vision of the racially aesthetic student body without the use of racial discrimination. The Law School concedes this, but the Court holds, implicitly and under the guise of narrow tailoring, that the Law School has a compelling state interest in doing what it wants to do. I cannot agree. * * *

A

The Court bases its unprecedented deference to the Law School—a deference antithetical to strict scrutiny—on an idea of "educational autonomy" grounded in the First Amendment. * * * In my view, there is no basis for a right of public universities to do what would otherwise violate the Equal Protection Clause.

* * *

B

1

The Court's deference to the Law School's conclusion that its racial experimentation leads to educational benefits will, if adhered to, have serious collateral consequences. The Court relies heavily on social science evidence to justify its deference. * * * The Court never acknowledges, however, the growing evidence that racial (and other sorts) of heterogeneity actually impairs learning among black students. * * *

* * *

The majority grants deference to the Law School's "assessment that diversity will, in fact, yield educational benefits." * * * It follows, therefore, that an HBC's [historically black college's] assessment that racial homogeneity will yield educational benefits would similarly be given deference. An HBC's rejection of white applicants in order to maintain racial homogeneity seems permissible, therefore, under the majority's view of the Equal Protection Clause. * * * Contained within today's majority opinion is the seed of a new constitutional justification for a concept I thought long and rightly rejected—racial segregation.

2

* * *

C

* * *

The sky has not fallen at Boalt Hall at the University of California, Berkeley, for example. Proposition 209's adopt[ion] of Cal. Const., Art. 1, § 31(a) [1996], bars the State from "granting preferential treatment ... on the basis of race ... in the operation of ... public education." * * * [W]ithout deploying express racial discrimination in admissions * * * total underrepresented minority student enrollment at Boalt Hall now exceeds 1996 levels. Apparently the Law School cannot be counted on to be as resourceful. The Court is willfully blind to the very real experience in California and elsewhere, which raises the inference that institutions with "reputation[s] for excellence," * * * rivaling the Law School's have satisfied their sense of mission without resorting to prohibited racial discrimination.

V

Putting aside the absence of any legal support for the majority's reflexive deference, there is much to be said for the view that the use of tests and other measures to "predict" academic performance is a poor substitute for a system that gives every applicant a chance to prove he can succeed in the study of law. The rallying cry that in the absence of racial discrimination in admissions there would be a true meritocracy ignores the fact that the entire process is poisoned by numerous exceptions to "merit." For example, in the national debate on racial discrimination in higher education admissions, much has been made of the fact that elite institutions utilize a so-called "legacy" preference to give the children of alumni an advantage in admissions. This, and other, exceptions to a "true" meritocracy give the lie to protestations that merit admissions are in fact the order of the day at the Nation's universities. The Equal Protection Clause does not, however, prohibit the use of unseemly legacy preferences or many other kinds of arbitrary admissions procedures. What the Equal Protection Clause does prohibit are classifications made on the basis of race. So while legacy preferences can stand under the Constitution, racial discrimination cannot. I will not twist the Constitution to invalidate legacy preferences or otherwise impose my vision of higher education admissions on the Nation. The majority should similarly stay its impulse to validate faddish racial discrimination the Constitution clearly forbids.

* * *

[N]o modern law school can claim ignorance of the poor performance of blacks, relatively speaking, on the Law School Admissions Test (LSAT). Nevertheless, law schools continue to use the test and then attempt to "correct" for black underperformance by using racial discrimination in admissions so as to obtain their aesthetic student body. The Law School's continued adherence to measures it knows produce racially skewed results is not entitled to deference by this Court. * * *

Having decided to use the LSAT, the Law School must accept the constitutional burdens that come with this decision. The Law School may freely continue to employ the LSAT and other allegedly merit-based standards in whatever fashion it likes. What the Equal Protection Clause forbids, but the Court today allows, is the use of these standards hand-in-hand with racial discrimination. An infinite variety of admissions methods are available to the Law School. Considering all of the radical thinking that has historically occurred at this country's universities, the Law School's intractable approach toward admissions is striking.

* * *

VI

The absence of any articulated legal principle supporting the majority's principal holding suggests another rationale. I believe what lies beneath the Court's decision today are the benighted notions that one can tell when racial discrimination benefits (rather than hurts) minority groups, * * * and that racial discrimination is necessary to remedy general societal ills. This Court's precedents supposedly settled both issues, but clearly the majority still cannot commit to the principle that racial classifications are *per se* harmful and that almost no amount of benefit in the eye of the beholder can justify such classifications.

* * *

The Law School tantalizes unprepared students with the promise of a University of Michigan degree and all of the opportunities that it offers. These overmatched students take the bait, only to find that they cannot succeed in the cauldron of competition. And this mismatch crisis is not restricted to elite institutions. * * * Indeed, to cover the tracks of the aestheticists, this cruel farce of racial discrimination must continue—in selection for the Michigan Law Review * * * and in hiring at law firms and for judicial clerkships—until the "beneficiaries" are no longer tolerated. While these students may graduate with law degrees, there is no evidence that they have received a qualitatively better legal education (or become better lawyers) than if they had gone to a less "elite" law school for which they were better prepared. And the aestheticists will never address the real problems facing "underrepresented minorities," instead continuing their social experiments on other people's children.

Beyond the harm the Law School's racial discrimination visits upon its test subjects, no social science has disproved the notion that this discrimination "engenders attitudes of superiority or, alternatively, provoke[s] resentment among those who believe that they have been wronged by the government's use of race." [*Adarand* (Thomas, J., concurring in part and concurring in judgment).] "These programs stamp minorities with a badge of inferiority and may cause them to develop dependencies or to adopt an attitude that they are 'entitled' to preferences." [*Id.*]

It is uncontested that each year, the Law School admits a handful of blacks who would be admitted in the absence of racial discrimination. * * * Who can differentiate between those who belong and those who do not? The majority of blacks are admitted to the Law School because of discrimination, and because of this policy all are tarred as undeserving. This problem of stigma does not depend on determinacy as to whether those stigmatized are actually the "beneficiaries" of racial discrimination. When blacks take positions in the highest places of government, industry, or academia, it is an open question today whether their skin color played a part in their advancement. The question itself is the stigma—because either racial discrimination did play a role, in which case the person may be deemed "otherwise unqualified," or it did not, in which case asking the question itself unfairly marks those blacks who would succeed without discrimination. Is this what the Court means by "visibly open"? * * *

     * * *

VII

As the foregoing makes clear, I believe the Court's opinion to be, in most respects, erroneous. I do, however, find two points on which I agree.

     * * *

Under today's decision, it is still the case that racial discrimination that does not help a university to enroll an unspecified number, or "critical mass," of underrepresented minority students is unconstitutional.

     * * *

I * * * understand the imposition of a 25–year time limit only as a holding that the deference the Court pays to the Law School's educational judgments and refusal to change its admissions policies will itself expire. * * * With these observations, I join the last sentence of Part III of the opinion of the Court.

* * *

For the immediate future, however, the majority has placed its *imprimatur* on a practice that can only weaken the principle of equality embodied in the Declaration of Independence and the Equal Protection Clause. "Our Constitution is color-blind, and neither knows nor tolerates classes among citizens." *Plessy v. Ferguson*, 163 U.S. 537, 559 (1896) (Harlan, J., dissenting). It has been nearly 140 years since Frederick Douglass asked the intellectual ancestors of the Law School to "[d]o nothing with us!" and the Nation adopted the Fourteenth Amendment. Now we must wait another 25 years to see this principle of equality vindicated. I therefore respectfully dissent from the remainder of the Court's opinion and the judgment.

* * *

Admissions Rituals as Political Acts: Guardians at the Gates of Our Democratic Ideals

117 HARV. L. REV. 113 (2003).

■ LANI GUINIER

* * *

Every year, selective colleges and universities engage in admissions rituals to reconstitute themselves. Institutions presumably align these high-stakes moments of civic pedagogy with their educational agenda: to produce knowledge, to promote learning, and to help individuals realize their intellectual, athletic, or artistic potential. The moment when admissions decisions are mailed is also fraught with political consequences that reach beyond the classroom to the boardroom, the legislature, and the kitchen table. At selective institutions of higher education, admissions decisions have a special political impact: rationing access to societal influence and power, and training leaders for public office and public life. Those admitted as students then graduate to become citizens who shape business, education, the arts, and the law for the next generation. Admissions decisions affect the individuals who apply, the institutional environments that greet those who enroll, and the stability and legitimacy of our democracy. They are political as well as educational acts.

* * *

Some have construed [the *Grutter* decision's focus on the role of higher education in democracy] as a warning, as Justice O'Connor's majority opinion in *Grutter* includes a puzzling clause stating that she expects the need for considerations of race in admissions decisions to expire after twenty-five years. According to former Harvard University President Derek Bok, for example, this twenty-five-year expectation is more than simply a reminder of the need to reevaluate race-consciousness in order to satisfy the narrow tailoring element of strict scrutiny: rather, it is a "warning to do something about the underlying problem." Universities, in other words, are not living up to their educational and democratic missions: they need to do more about the achievement gap that makes affirmative action necessary; the environmental gap that socially isolates white students who, unlike students of color, spend most of their time with same-race friends in college; and the teaching and learning gaps that disable professors from reaching out to mentor students of color.

At the same time, it is important to acknowledge that the appearance of sharp boundary lines in defining race is problematic for many members of the public and the Court. There is a pervasive reluctance to view race in categorical terms. This resistance to racial categorization affects members of the public, not just the crusaders against affirmative action who, despite their defeat at the Supreme Court, seem to have lost none of their zeal.

* * *

Properly deployed, racial literacy, or the ability to read race in conjunction with institutional and democratic structures, may enable the building of a coalition that starts a larger conversation at the point where educational selection and democratic values meet. Race, in other words, reveals rather than produces the stress on institutional resources that undermines the connection between education and democracy, a connection that the Court in *Grutter* and *Gratz* recognized as essential. Because race is inextricably intertwined with every period in American history, from our founding as a constitutional democracy to current patterns of private wealth formation, it is a formidable diagnostic and sociological tool. Used as a lens to peer beyond the pretense of the debate, race helps detect the deeper issues confronting public institutions of higher education.

* * *

I.   THE DEMOCRATIC AND EDUCATIONAL MISSIONS OF HIGHER EDUCATION: ADMISSIONS JUDGMENTS AS POLITICAL ACTS

* * *

Although education has been linked to opportunity since the early days of the republic, higher education was originally a province reserved for wealthy white men. During the first half of the twentieth century, women, Jews, and blacks were the victims of arbitrary quotas or formal exclusionary policies sanctioned by law. During the 1950s and 1960s, however, legal challenges, social movements, and a participatory conception of individual rights helped pressure these institutions of higher education to open their doors—albeit only a crack—to those who had been shut out. Institutions that had once been bastions of elite privilege began admitting women and people of color for the first time.

At the same time, American society increasingly highlighted the importance of higher education to democratic values by extending the opportunity to attend college to more people. The GI Bill, Pell Grants, the Cold War, and the move to a global and information economy made higher education instrumental to our society's understanding of the relationship between an educated populace, a representative group of leaders, a commitment to public service, and national security. These developments also turned college education into a primary engine for economic and social upward mobility in the last part of the century.

Meanwhile, as more people saw higher education as a necessity for societal as well as individual reasons, government funding for this essential public good shrunk: states shifted resources from education to the criminal justice system, the federal government cut Pell grants, and state revenues plummeted, leading to higher tuition and reduced financial aid. This shift in funding priorities was driven in part by an ideological shift during the Reagan era. Higher education was presented as a private benefit to be financed by the individual, instead of a public good to be funded by the government. As a result, higher education became a scarce, indispensable, and competitive individual resource.

As more people wanted in, colleges and universities became more selective. * * * Many of these institutions valued their "selectivity" as an element of their identity or chose for other reasons not to add sufficient resources to keep up with increased interest. * * *

[I]nstitutions began to seek a fair and efficient set of selection criteria that would preserve their elite status, which had been derived from association with bloodlines and reinforced by the appearance of unattainability. Institutions that once used evidence of "good character"—a proxy for privilege and wealth—switched to ostensibly more democratic indicia of merit. College admissions officers began to replace the pedigreed "natural" aristocracy of Edmund Burke's world that had dominated elite higher education through the middle of the twentieth century. In the 1950s a "meritocracy" began to substitute "aptitude" for "character" (or family) as the ticket into colleges and universities. Admissions would proceed from an open calculus rather than a set of private relationships. Excellence through brains, not blood, would become the basis for awarding scarce admission slots.

Excellence did not simply cloak elitism, however. It was also associated with a fairness principle, derived from scientifically designed, and thus presumably more objective, criteria. One of the primary vehicles for apportioning access to an increasingly popular yet scarce public resource was the introduction of standardized tests and other potentially objective measures of excellence; such tests enabled university administrators to compare individuals from different demographic, geographic, and social cohorts. This ability to compare had been previously either unnecessary for the public institutions that admitted almost every (white male) applicant, or reserved to headmasters at private prep schools.

Because of the perceived ability to manufacture objective evidence of desert, excellence became measurable. Applicants who outscored or outranked their peers on standardized aptitude tests were therefore presumed to be the most qualified, regardless of social class. The premium on allocating access to higher education more democratically and meritocratically led to the development of a testing industry that now functions as one of the primary gatekeepers to upward mobility.

Deciding who "deserves" to benefit from admission to selective colleges and universities now occurs within a "testocracy" that claims to sort, evaluate, and rank measurable mental aptitude. The resulting test scores, together with high school grades, purport to tell us in both real and relative terms about each applicant's potential capacity, which is then deemed the most important evidence of his or her "visible, rankable" merit.

To maintain their elite status in terms of democratic "merit" rather than inherited privilege, these institutions had to raise the stakes. Thus, applicants who receive the thick envelopes in April have higher SAT scores than their parents did a generation ago. Unfortunately, along with democratic "merit" came a sense of entitlement without the sense of obligation. Ambition replaced pedigree, but the public spiritedness * * * failed to materialize.

During the second half of the twentieth century, the pendulum swung dramatically from subjective measures of character to objective measures of excellence; for reasons I describe in the next Part, it soon swung back to more subjective evidence of character to supplement the quantifiable standards for measuring academic merit. But now character would mean motivation, work ethic, and the ability to overcome obstacles, rather than charisma, athletic skill, and the ability to fit in. Diversity rather than homogeneity became a value.

Moving back and forth from subjective to objective to subjective measures, the admissions pendulum never settled on a single, fixed view of merit. Without a stable template for admissions choices, shifts in the values and identities of those making the choices, as well as the process of selection itself, came to define qualification. Yet the choice of who attends institutions of higher education, both public and private, has personal, institutional, and societal implications. Thus, admissions decisions are both educational questions and political acts.

The task of constituting each class is a political act because it implicates the institution's sense of itself as a community, as well as the larger society's sense of itself as a democracy. Such acts allocate resources in a way that affects those who are admitted to the institution, those who are rejected, those who fail to apply, and those who simply use the institution's selection criteria as an interpretive guide. Thus, they affect all members of society, both directly, as described above, and indirectly, by helping determine future political, economic, and social leaders. Directly or indirectly, taxpayers support these institutions, which function as gateways to upward mobility and help legitimize democratic ideals of participation, fairness, and equal opportunity. At nonselective public colleges, the opportunity to attend is less a function of admissions criteria per se, and more a question of application fees and tuition costs, as well as historical patterns of recruitment, information networks, social capital, and location that determine the demographics of the student body and faculty.

* * *

The term "political act" also describes inputs that inflect the process of decisionmaking, not just the outputs that help define it. Beyond the democratic significance, the social consequences, and the individual benefits of gaining admission to these institutions, admissions choices have an internal political dynamic. They are located in the heads of the decisionmakers as well as in the world.

II: CONTEST, SPONSORED, AND STRUCTURAL MOBILITY: ALTERNATIVE
WAYS OF CONCEPTUALIZING THE RELATIONSHIP BETWEEN
EDUCATION AND DEMOCRACY

In this Part, I explore two related aspects of admissions rituals: the process used to make admissions decisions, and the values or goals that seem to animate different views of the selection process. Starting with the goals that inform the process, I identify four important values associated with access to higher education: individualism, merit, democracy, and upward mobility. Of these four, the value that seems to integrate the other three with higher education is upward mobility. Yet although upward mobility is the value most closely associated with higher education in our collective imagination, all four values are closely intertwined.

Upward mobility and individualism are both core values of the American Dream; they legitimate our democratic ideal of equal opportunity for all. In his history of the French Enlightenment, Marshall Berman describes individualism in perhaps its most favorable light: the right to be yourself, particularly the right not to have your role or status ascribed to you, but to find it for yourself. Individualism was forged in a revolt against feudalism, a system based entirely on ascribed roles. Thus conceived, individualism is deeply connected to democratic ideals of opportunity and upward mobility.

Likewise, mobility in America means not just moving out, but also moving up; it refers to sociological as well as geographical relocation in order to take advantage of opportunity. Upward mobility also suggests that we live in a "classless" society—or at least a society in which class is floating, not fixed. At the same time, higher education has built into it the idea of nobility as well as mobility. After all, universities predate the modern state—they were historically limited to an elite. Higher education grants upward social mobility because it is a status marker, not merely a private contract that matches one's skills with an appropriate educational setting to enhance one's learning. In our society education means opportunity, higher education offers heightened opportunity, and elite higher education confers not just heightened opportunity, but also elevated status. Admissions officers may not view themselves as the "sorting hats" of our society, but many Americans construe the fat or thin envelopes mailed in April as serving just this purpose.

Like upward mobility and individualism, meritocracy formally rejects ascribed roles, awarding opportunity based on individual merit rather than inherited status. Those who succeed are presumed to be those who do their best because of effort, not birth. Meritocracy also associates selectivity with excellence. The opportunity to choose among many qualified applicants not only confers status; it automatically connotes merit. Indeed, merit has two ideas of mobility built into it. It suggests criteria for identifying individual capacity for upward mobility. It also suggests the potential to change individual capacity through educational opportunity—the opportunity to learn in an environment that values excellence, and the opportunity to learn after graduation as the educational credential opens economic and political doors.

* * *

The different processes that educational institutions employ to navigate these goals, however, reveal that the goals are often mutually inconsistent. Individualism, for example, is in tension with a democratic commitment to equal opportunity; not all who have been disadvantaged by reason of their group status benefit equally when some group members are treated as individuals. Moreover, when taken to extremes, individualism can be a divisive force, driving people to find comfort in racial stereotyping and animosity, which becomes the only respectable reason for their own failures. If "right living and hard work do lead to success," then those who fail have no one to blame but themselves—an uncomfortable conclusion. Stuck in dead-end jobs, denied access to selective institutions, or frustrated that they cannot pass on their own privileges to their children, poor and working-class whites sometimes find it easier to blame blacks, or some other scapegoat, for "stealing" the American Dream. Blacks become personally responsible for their own, as well as everyone else's, failures. This form of one-way individualism, which accepts responsibility for success but not failure, is not only dangerously polarizing; it also ignores the experience of racial disadvantage. Many Americans have been disadvantaged precisely because of their group identity; yet this reality does not recede by simple commitments to treat everyone as an individual. Because individualism values the individual over the group, and individual mobility over community stability, it can contribute to more general feelings of dislocation and disable groups of people from participating in public life.

Moreover, systems of selection often end up perpetuating inherited privilege, even as they disavow any connection to ascribed identity or natural aristocracies. A principled commitment to merit selection can perpetuate ascribed identities in covert ways that are often aligned with the identities and experiences of those in a position to define merit. Access to higher education can become a "world in which inequalities of power are natural, and individuals compete for well-being as individuals at the same time they occupy distinct social locations replete with social roles and expectations." Nor are commitments to democratic legitimacy or upward mobility necessarily satisfied by selecting just a few group members to succeed. Indeed, in many ways, the democratic role of higher education has atrophied; without significant infusions of public funds and other potential sources of accountability, it is in danger of becoming a rhetorical but unrealized ideal.

I borrow and adopt three sociological terms—contest, sponsored, and structural mobility—to help assess the often-confusing interaction among the values that underlie admissions decisions. These three concepts describe the means through which individual upward mobility can be achieved: pure competition, discretionary choice, or structural intervention.

A. Contest Mobility

The term "contest mobility" is a very rough proxy for upward mobility achieved through competitive success on standardized tests. Elite status is the goal and is achieved by the candidate's own efforts in an open contest. Numerical valuations of students provide a scoreboard for this contest, which is either won or lost, with no middle ground. Victors assume that their success, and their resulting elite status, is a justly won prize, not an opportunity for further growth. Since aptitude or ability is presumed to be fixed before the race, the best prepared, rather than the most diligent, win. The ultimate goal of contest mobility is the distribution of opportunity based on individual competition and quantifiable measures of merit.

* * *

Contest mobility reinforces the culture of meritocratic entitlement among its primary beneficiaries, upper-middle-class whites, who feel they have played by the rules and therefore deserve to win. [C]ommitment to the narrative of contest mobility has proved resistant to data refuting its validity and continues to remain extremely persuasive, particularly among affluent whites, whose children are the primary beneficiaries of the traditional admissions regime and its overreliance on narrow, "objective" indicia of success. Survey data suggest that well-educated, well-off whites are among the most antagonistic to affirmative action in higher education, even though they are more supportive of programs designed to increase the representation of people of color in legislatures, public sector jobs, and government contracting positions.

Explicit diversity criteria for admissions are controversial. They are seen as throwbacks to an earlier, now rebuked, age that relied on social criteria rather than mathematically derived ones. Critics argue that, because explicit diversity criteria categorize people rather than their output, they leave room for the subjective exercise of racial prejudice, thus subverting the fairness principle. These critics presume that, because scores are "earned," and diversity is not, diversity criteria allow less "deserving" students of color to gain admission over more "qualified" whites, even though the number of whites adversely affected by affirmative action is miniscule. For critics of affirmative action, diversity represents a dramatic departure from the background commitment to objective measures of merit. Diversity is therefore denigrated as both a process and a substantive goal. Diversity criteria bend the rules of contest mobility.

B. Sponsored Mobility

In order to admit more individuals from underrepresented demographic categories, colleges and universities have modified contest mobility by supplementing the contest with discretion. This hybrid alternative, which I call "sponsored mobility," refers to the contemporary version of the elitist system that was in place when James Conant was President of Harvard.*

---

* Following World War II ... James Conant, then-President of Harvard University [proposed admissions reforms]. Conant wanted to see elite institutions shift from a WASP

In a system of sponsored mobility, modern elites—including admissions officers, alumni, and others who have already enjoyed the spoils of higher education—hand-pick a few candidates to ascend the ladder of higher education. Whereas contest mobility relies solely on a fixed set of "hard" numbers, sometimes called "skinny merit," sponsored mobility relies on an expandable set of "soft" criteria, which might be called "robust merit," to supplement the hard numbers.

Sponsored mobility is an intermediate position between pure contest mobility and structural mobility. This intermediate position allows decisionmakers some room to maneuver; it also acknowledges the limitations of the contest in determining the most "qualified" candidates. The use of soft variables is defended with hard data showing that a purely test-based system suffers from the fallacy of false precision.

Like the hereditary elite system it replaced, modern sponsored mobility retains a discretionary process. * * * This discretion is informed by interviews, letters of recommendation, extracurricular activities, and personal circumstances, including the applicant's race. Sponsored mobility is managed by professional admissions officers for the most part; however, alumni representatives and the headmasters of private secondary schools still play a role in "sponsoring" candidates to elite institutions. Students from elite private schools, for example, still enjoy disproportionate access to Harvard, Yale, and Princeton.

Sponsored mobility enables status elevation at the individual level, but when it comes to issues of diversity, institutions justify it in the name of the group. This justification may take several forms. An institution may believe that diversity in higher education is important because it allows students of all races to "see that people like themselves can succeed" and to "learn the value of interacting with people who are different." Or it may believe that diversity is essential to preserve a "stable polity." Or it may conclude that interracial interaction helps destabilize stereotypes and improve race relations more generally. Whatever the motivation, decisionmakers select a few deserving group members, whose presence then legitimates the institution's educational and democratic missions. The process values associated with sponsored mobility are elite selection and good-faith discretion.

* * *

Sponsored mobility suffers from four serious flaws: First, it enables the unconscious biases of a relatively homogeneous group to thrive by relying on the judgment of individuals who do not have to explain their choices to a third party. Admissions officers rarely enjoy longstanding relationships with the inner-city principals, high school guidance counselors, individual

establishment of hereditary privilege that emphasized entitlement and obligation, to a more democratic accounting that fostered an even greater sense of social responsibility and a less paternalistic view toward public service. In Conant's view, such educated talent would serve the nation in exchange for support from taxpayers. But while Conant wanted to disturb the view that college was a hereditary privilege, he also desired to maintain the elite and selective status of these institutions.

teachers, or community leaders who might know and recommend a student and who can offer information that may not be apparent from the student's file. Second, sponsored mobility does not adequately embrace the idea that individuals change in relation to their environments; thus, although it moderates notions of the intrinsic worth of individuals, sponsored mobility does not adjust sufficiently for the malleability of intelligence in response to effort or encouragement. Third, sponsored mobility perpetuates reliance on the same admissions processes that enabled the current decisionmakers to succeed. Not only do the decisionmakers sponsor students who look like or remind them of themselves, but they also sponsor students who succeeded under the same criteria they faced. This commitment to self-replication is backward-looking; it tends to encourage complacency rather than self-reflection and experimentation. Finally, because adherents of sponsored mobility do not publicly and continuously rethink the relationship between their selection criteria and their mission, their criteria tend to become ends in themselves.

* * *

In the end, sponsored mobility may be only marginally better than contest mobility at allocating access to higher education in a way that is consistent with democratic principles. Although sponsored mobility uses diversity to supplement the hard numbers, it still relies extensively on "the contest" to determine the winners; in this way, diversity becomes a stabilizing norm to legitimate the status quo. Contest mobility at least assumes that individual competition will create churn to upend a complacent view of the status quo. In addition, sponsored mobility gives power to a few decisionmakers to allocate opportunity to "deserving" individuals. Contest mobility gives that power to the institutions that manufacture or referee the rules of the contest, whether a testing bureaucracy or a news magazine; the contest then allocates opportunity to those who "earn" it on their own, with individual competition serving as a tool of accountability. Sponsored mobility, because of its tendency to operate behind closed doors and in isolation from the people who know the candidate best, often lacks such accountability. Because sponsored mobility is still beholden to the hard numbers, operates without much transparency, and tends to reward a limited range of individual attributes, it can also be perceived as a means to co-opt or pacify potential challengers to the governing regime. * * *

C. *Structural Mobility*

In addition to contest mobility, which uses hard numbers to measure academic merit, and sponsored mobility, which employs expandable criteria to measure diversity, there is a third conception of the relationship between opportunity and admissions: "structural mobility." A system of structural mobility seeks to identify qualified students in relation to the greater role of higher education in the political, economic, and social structure of community. A commitment to structural mobility means that an institution's commitments to upward mobility, merit, democracy, and individualism are framed and tempered by an awareness of how structures, including the institution's own admissions criteria, tend to privilege some groups of people over others. Structural mobility would require universities to change those admissions policies to provide access to large numbers of people across class, race, and geographic lines, thereby changing the very structure of educational opportunity in this country. Advocates of structural mobility understand that opening access to higher education benefits the society as a whole, not just the individual admittees.

Structural mobility differs from both contest and sponsored mobility, which are dedicated to individual advancement through a market-oriented contest or a "vote of confidence." Structural mobility places the issue of merit firmly on the table and attempts to define it in the context of democratic values. It takes a future-oriented view of the role of higher education in a multiracial democracy by linking ideas about merit directly to ideas about public service and opportunity broadly construed.

Although structural mobility is committed to *community* advancement, it is not inconsistent with ideals of individualism. Rather, structural mobility values the individual in relation to the community. Because it privileges those who have already served, or those who want to serve, their communities, structural mobility focuses society's educational resources on those who are most likely to fulfill the aims of democracy.

For proponents of structural mobility, contest mobility's preoccupation with competitive individualism fails to fulfill Conant's dream of assembling a more publicly spirited elite; contest mobility promotes short-term winners of the wrong game. Sponsored mobility does a better job of elevating individuals who remain connected to their communities or to the taxpayers who helped subsidize their success, but only through a small segment of all admittees. Structural mobility extends the emphasis on community affiliation and linked fate to all admittees, not just those who bring racial diversity to college campuses. It links the institution and its students to their communities, thereby advancing the goals of public education at the local, state, and national levels. An institution committed to structural mobility might measure its success, for example, not only by the students it admits but also by the changes it precipitates in educational opportunity at the K–12 level. Finally, structural mobility is sustained by a broadly democratic and participatory process of self-reflective and racially literate experimentalism. In a world of structural mobility, individuals are given access to educational opportunities not because they win a "contest" or because they have been hand-picked by elites, but because the relevant stakeholders come together to make a set of public-minded choices.

* * *

All of the salient features of structural mobility—a commitment to public service, the participation of grassroots voluntary organizations or indigenous actors in the construction of the program, and the escalator effect that generates broad public support—connect to democratic values.

III: Enter the Supreme Court: The Promise
and the Caution of Using Race as a lens

Selective public institutions, such as the University of Michigan and
the University of Michigan Law School, are in the position to choose among
a number of qualified candidates who can do the work and be expected to
graduate. Because their admissions decisions have broad social purposes
and important individual consequences, these institutions must be able to
articulate and defend their admissions criteria and processes to their
respective constituencies. Four elements of the Supreme Court's decisions
in *Grutter* and *Gratz* seem particularly relevant to the challenge facing
institutions of higher education like the University of Michigan that are
committed to maintaining their elite status while producing racially literate
graduates who contribute to both the campus community and the larger
society. These elements are: the value of race-conscious diversity as it is
connected to the university's educational mission; a robust view of diversity
that includes class and geography, not just race; the role of democratic
values; and the relationship between data, demographics, and reflective
practice to inform the way institutions operationalize the concepts of
diversity and democracy.

* * *

Although *Gratz* identifies how numbers cannot capture an individual's
worth (or at least are over-and underinclusive as used by the University of
Michigan's undergraduate program), numbers can provide relevant information in the aggregate about relationships of groups of individuals to
economic, social, and political power. And while numbers do not tell us all
that we need to know about an individual (if we respect the notion that
individuals are unique and cannot be compared along a single metric),
numbers can provide context to help situate individuals within larger
domains. Numbers are informative: they are tools for assisting in making
judgments but should not be confused with proxies for those judgments. If
numbers should not be outcome-determinative about race, then neither
should they be outcome-determinative as proxies for individual "merit"
generally.

There is a direct relationship between efforts to quantify race and
efforts to quantify merit. Both are driven in part by efficiency concerns. In
addition, the quantification of merit hides the discretion of those who
develop the quantification tools—standardized tests—which are normed to
reward upper-class and upper-middle-class whites. Thus, the decision by
institutions like the University of Michigan's undergraduate program to
use "hard edges" to capture race is a recognized compensatory response to
the "hard edges" that define quantifiable notions of merit. Both are over-
and underinclusive categories. But it is the underinclusiveness of the hard
variables that contributes to the hyper-visibility of race.

To the extent "merit" is considered largely quantifiable—as opposed to
a set of qualitative judgments that are essentially educated guesses about
future potential made in the context of an institution's educational and
public missions—individualized assessments that include race as one varia-

ble are doomed to be somewhat mechanistic, albeit less transparently so, in order to compensate for the preferences embedded in the hard variables. This use of race is also vulnerable to continued attack by those who feel excluded by the admissions choices being made (mostly working-class and poor whites, but status-seeking upper-middle-class whites as well), unless those choices reflect not only concerns about democratic legitimacy but also a democratic process.

Yet the likely immediate consequence of *Grutter* is that trusted admissions officials are now freer to make their decisions without a great deal of transparency. They need not give reasons for their choices, as long as they avoid the mechanistic use of race. If, for example, the institution has a backward-looking purpose, then it may rely on contest mobility and continue to use admission as a reward or prize. Many universities, however, do not like to speak of their admissions slots as rewards; law schools in particular have a mission to train public citizens who serve their clients and society as a whole. Such institutions might therefore embrace sponsored mobility, since they may use subjective criteria to supplement the hard variables in making predictions about who among their applicants are likely to serve the public. * * *

There is a caution, in other words, voiced by the very different dissents of Justices Ginsburg and Thomas. The caution is that elite self-replication is the problem, not affirmative action. In this sense, sponsored mobility will be co-opted by elites in the same way contest mobility was. Diversity will not be an aesthetic fad; instead, it will become a fig leaf to hide a commitment to the status quo. If admissions decisions are to be made in a more democratic fashion—that is, with transparency and accountability to the institution's public mission and to the taxpayers who subsidize it—then much more than the physical aesthetics of these choices needs to be obvious.

* * *

Like Conant's version of contest mobility, which used "merit" to replace "character" and ended up reproducing privilege, sponsored mobility may also turn out to benefit only those who are already advantaged. It is not the goal of diversity that is the problem. Nor does adverting to democratic legitimacy justify that goal. The problem is the failure to adopt safeguards that ensure that the goal remains connected to its justificatory principle.

The *Grutter* opinion, in conjunction with Chief Justice Rehnquist's opinion for the Court in *Gratz*, holds two other potential limitations as well as a promise. Although the Court expects institutions to sponsor individuals of color rather than racially categorized groups, and to revisit their use of race periodically in light of the availability of race-neutral alternatives, the Court still, paradoxically, requires institutions to consider race differently from the way they consider merit. Simultaneously, the approval of limited forms of race-consciousness may invite complacency rather than vigilance. However, the Court's quixotic hope that consideration of race will be unnecessary in twenty-five years may instead prompt universities to engage the public in a larger conversation about what type of society we want to live in and what higher education institutions must do to bring us closer to that goal. Ultimately, the promise is that the introduction of a soft deadline will trigger bold new experiments in which universities demonstrate renewed involvement in K–12 education, build relationships with local communities to garner more support, and consider multiple ways to realize their twin goals of educational excellence and democratic opportunity.

IV. PURSUING THE PROMISE AND HEEDING THE WARNING: RACIAL LITERACY AND THE ROLE OF HIGHER EDUCATION IN OUR DEMOCRACY

Although the *Grutter* and *Gratz* decisions vindicate the principle of diversity, they do not explain how institutions of higher education should use that principle to help make admissions decisions. This lack of guidance appears to be intentional: as long as institutions do not weight race so heavily that it overdetermines admissions outcomes, their good faith is essentially presumed. It may be that Justice O'Connor and the *Grutter* majority presume good faith because they want the meaning of diversity to emerge from a process of experimentation, feedback, and reflection. It may be that the Court is not prepared to articulate a national definition of diversity and instead prefers for educational institutions to work out the meaning of diversity locally over time. This explanation is consistent with the way Justice O'Connor interpreted narrow tailoring in the context of sponsored mobility, as well as her preference for voluntary self-correction in other contexts.

To the extent that an institution is committed to diversifying its student body, the Court's lack of specificity gives the institution leeway to experiment with ways to link the broad concept of diversity to the specific educational mission of the institution and the public values it aims to serve. For institutions committed to racial diversity, the three forms of mobility are all presumably constitutional as long as they do not use race categorically, overtly, and decisively to fix outcomes. An institution may consider race implicitly in conjunction with class and geography, as is done in percentage plans; it may consider race explicitly as part of a holistic evaluation; and it may consider other indicia of merit that provide democratic legitimacy, such as evidence of an applicant's service commitments, pluck in the face of disadvantage, or residence in an underrepresented geographic area.

In the short term, individualized, holistic review of all candidates will bring colleges and law schools into compliance with *Grutter*. Individualized review will allow institutions to admit students of color "in meaningful numbers" to ensure that students from underrepresented communities contribute to the character of the school and, in the case of law schools, to the legal profession. But in the long run, using affirmative action simply to perpetuate the status quo will likely backfire for practical, financial, and political reasons. Universities may be dogged by complaints that they are not really following *Grutter*, that their methods are too subjective, that their procedures lack transparency, or that their policies leave the decision-making power firmly in the grasp of admissions bureaucrats. Moreover, institutions committed to affirmative action as an add-on will be hard-pressed to keep up with changing demographics: admissions practices that depend on the language of critical mass may unintentionally result in an upper-limit quota that artificially suppresses the number of black and Latino admittees, despite the burgeoning number of such students in the eighteen-to twenty-four-year-old age cohort.

* * *

To gain a deeper understanding of the problem while garnering public confidence in their admissions practices, universities need to become racially literate. A racially literate institution uses race as a diagnostic device, an analytic tool, and an instrument of process.

As a diagnostic or evidentiary device, race helps identify the underlying problems affecting higher education. Racial literacy begins by redefining racism as a structural problem rather than a purely individual one. Race reveals the ways in which demography is often destiny—not just for people of color, but for working-class and poor whites as well. Race constantly influences access to public resources, while also revealing the influence of class and geographical variables. Racial literacy, therefore, continuously links the underrepresentation of blacks and Latinos to the underrepresentation of poor people generally. At a minimum, it reminds public institutions of higher learning that the "idea of access is deeply embedded in [their] genetic code" and thus, the underrepresentation of certain demographic groups illuminates their failure to fulfill their public responsibilities.

When race is engaged directly, as it was in Texas following *Hopwood*, [78 F.3d 932 (5th Cir. 1996),] it can shed light on the confluence of forces that are truly responsible for current public dissatisfaction and that adversely affect people of all colors. At one time, for example, it was commonly accepted that each generation should publicly subsidize educational opportunity for the next generation. Yet today, higher education is no longer the engine of upward mobility and democratic opportunity that it was once imagined to be. Nor has it remained focused on its original purpose: to train leaders who then go on to serve society. Instead, it has become "a national personnel department" that sorts and ranks people and grants "the high scorers a general, long-duration ticket to high status that can be cashed in anywhere." Selective universities, in particular, use their admissions practices to generate a permanent governing elite, in ways that are inconsistent with democratic values of equal opportunity, accountability, and service. * * *

Racial literacy sees the decline in government investment in higher education, along with the accompanying justificatory rhetoric of individual responsibility and individual "desert," as deeply problematic. Racial literacy suggests that admitting a more diverse class of students not only benefits individual students, but is also necessary to realize the social function and values of higher education, including democratic access, equal opportunity, and public service. The idea that each person is alone responsible for her fate and her tuition has allowed government support for higher education to plummet while costs skyrocket. Meanwhile, the goal of training future leaders—once the noble ambition of public institutions and their signature contribution to society—continues to atrophy.

* * *

Racial literacy helps institutions as they choose between contest, sponsored, and structural mobility. Using racially literate criteria to select among the three kinds of upward mobility is permissible under *Grutter*, is not jeopardized by *Gratz*, and is not only defensible, but may be politically necessary. Racial literacy discloses how all of these admissions processes use sociological proxies for assessing "merit" and future potential. Contest mobility purports to rank individuals, yet it relies on data that is closely aligned with group, not individual, attributes and assets, such as parents' education, grandparents' socioeconomic status, and other indicators of privilege. Sponsored mobility also purports to rank individuals, yet it fails to take account of group bias, which may depress individual performance, tilt the preferences of individual sponsors, and systematically distort the opportunity structure for talented individuals. Each type of mobility puts on the table a different understanding of whether merit is fixed or contextual, stable or responsive, real or imagined, performative or service-oriented. By situating merit within structures of opportunity, racial literacy encourages consideration of qualities that current admissions policies overlook. As a result, racially literate yet selective institutions may be able to relax their efforts to predict short-term outcomes and focus more on encouraging long-term commitments to service and community leadership.

* * *

Racial literacy also has a process dimension that uses race to guide participatory problem solving and accountability. In order to change the way race is understood, race has to be directly addressed rather than ignored. Race is often the subtext of public conversations about institutional goals. In fact, informed discussion about why education is now more desirable but less affordable or accessible often gets drowned out by inflammatory and polarizing rhetoric about race or by equally divisive rhetoric about individual responsibility and merit. By contrast, discussion among a diverse group of citizens about the ways race reveals rather than produces these social costs helps institutional policies become more transparent and thus more legitimate. * * *

Institutions could also make their processes more transparent by taking the views of various constituencies into account, even as they develop in the short term their new, holistic methods of reviewing candidate files. A broadly participatory process that includes the relevant stakeholders also helps satisfy the legitimacy concerns articulated by Justice O'Connor and modified by Justice Thomas's critique of elitism. Such a process would include professional educators and administrators, and would respect their expertise and specialized knowledge. But this process would also seek opportunities to communicate openly and engage with a group that is sufficiently diverse and informed to be critical, to mitigate the tendency of socially isolated decisionmakers to select those like themselves, to pay attention to issues of race and power, and to consider the connection between admissions and pedagogy.

* * *

It is out of a deliberative and interactive process that the institution should create its mission and explore the possibilities of reconstituting itself through admissions rituals. Such a process may generate a hybrid form of contest and sponsored mobility, similar to the choices made by the University of Michigan Law School and by the college post-*Gratz*. It is just as plausible, however, that a process that includes relevant stakeholders in a larger public conversation may prefer social engineering to yield structural mobility, similar to the GI Bill and current military programs, which provide educational opportunity in exchange for national or community service. Whatever the outcome, the process of choosing among contest, sponsored, and structural mobility must be understood as a political act with important societal, not just individual, consequences.

* * *

VI.   CONCLUSION

* * * The *Grutter* and *Gratz* decisions may ultimately usher in a historical moment in which institutions of higher education explore issues of access to education and the scarcity of resources—issues that make limitations on that access deeply problematic in democratic terms. Universities need to explain themselves better to the broader public through a conversation rather than a declaration. It is not simply time for a public relations battle; rather, it is an occasion to align educational opportunity with its cousin, democratic participation. The question becomes who should get opportunity given the long-term goals of the institution or the needs of the larger society, rather than who "deserves" a prize because she won a race or because her presence will improve the institution's rankings in a news magazine. To find the answer, university leaders need to consider the long-term needs of the institution, the concerns of local, regional, and national constituencies, and the stability of the larger society, in a manner that is consistent with the expectation that the university will produce a new generation of citizens capable of assuming a broad range of leadership roles. The post-*Grutter* moment is an opportunity to talk more openly about, and investigate more thoroughly and in contemporary terms, the ways in which race helps reveal the relationship between education and democracy. It is a chance to make ourselves more racially literate and to understand the ways in which the choice among contest, sponsored, and structural mobility is a fundamentally political act.

By viewing their admissions decisions as political acts, in the virtuous sense of the phrase, universities can open the door to greater public support and confidence. Ultimately, this reevaluation of admissions choices may enable universities to join with others to create institutional structures that respond to the future while holding on to the best practices of the past. At the very least, it has the potential to transform the discussion from one fixated on ersatz preferences to one that actively confronts the reality of higher education's role in a multiracial democracy with the promise that education makes to us all.

NOTES AND QUESTIONS

1.   Origins of affirmative action. In March 1961, President John F. Kennedy issued Executive Order 10925, in an effort to end employment discrimination among government contractors. It read in part, "The Contractor will take *affirmative action*, to insure that applicants are employed, and that employees are treated during employment, without regard to their race, creed, color, or national origin." Steven M. Cahn, *Introduction, in* THE AFFIRMATIVE ACTION DEBATE, xi (Steven M. Cahn ed., 2d ed. 2002) (emphasis added). Affirmative action emerged during the civil rights movement as a strategy for helping African Americans overcome the debilitating effects of racial oppression. It has since targeted other minority groups, notably Hispanics, Native Americans, and persons of Asian descent. Affirmative action refers to an array of programs that use race as a factor in the allotment of resources with the intent of benefiting racial minorities. It may take the form of generally increasing outreach to minorities, counting race as a "plus" factor in the allocation of resources, or directing a set amount of resources to minorities in specific "percentage plans." For an overview of federal affirmative action programs, see SAMUEL LEITER & WILLIAM M. LEITER, AFFIRMATIVE ACTION IN ANTIDISCRIMINATION LAW AND POLICY 7–22 (2002).

Affirmative action is among the most controversial issues in American law and politics, evoking strong feelings in both supporters and opponents. This controversy has been accompanied by uncertainty in the Supreme Court, which in thirty years of affirmative action jurisprudence has struggled to find a consistent legal framework with which to treat the issue. Political and public support for affirmative action has also been inconsistent. Democrats and the political left have historically supported affirmative action, while Republicans and conservatives have opposed it. In polls, the public generally expresses support for the goals of racial equality and diversity, but is less supportive of specific affirmative action measures. PETER H. SCHUCK, DIVERSITY IN AMERICA 170–72 (2003).

2.   The constitutionality of affirmative action. Challenges to the constitutionality of affirmative action rest on the Equal Protection Clause of the Fourteenth Amendment. The Fourteenth Amendment reads, in part:

Section 1. . . . No State shall make or enforce any law which shall abridge the privileges or immunities of citizens of the United States; nor shall any State deprive any person of life, liberty, or property, without due process of law; nor deny any person within its jurisdiction the equal protection of the laws.

* * *

Section 5. The Congress shall have power to enforce, by appropriate legislation, the provisions of this article.

U.S. CONST. Amend. XIV, §§ 2, 5.

The Thirteenth, Fourteenth, and Fifteenth Amendments were passed in the wake of the Civil War to try and protect the rights of the South's newly-freed black population. These "Reconstruction Amendments" were deemed necessary because, after the Civil War, the Southern states quickly started passing so-called "Black Codes," which returned former slaves to a position of complete social and political subordination. GEOFFREY STONE, ET AL., CONSTITUTIONAL LAW 432–33 (4th ed. 2001). The language of the amendments appears to afford minorities strong protections against governmental discrimination. However, in the years during and after Reconstruction, the Supreme Court read the amendments narrowly, typified in the *Slaughter–House Cases*, 83 U.S. (16 Wall.) 36 (1873), and especially *Plessy v. Ferguson*, 163 U.S. 537 (1896), in which the court validated the Jim Crow system of "separate but equal." The Court interpreted the amendments as having one overriding purpose, the freeing of the slaves, and showed little inclination to interpret them more ambitiously. BRUCE ACKERMAN, WE THE PEOPLE: FOUNDATIONS 81–105 (1991). As a result, governmentally sponsored racial discrimination persisted well into the twentieth century. The civil rights movement of the 1950s and 1960s was in many ways an attempt to fulfill the initial promise of Reconstruction and its three constitutional amendments, and many consider affirmative action a valuable tool for the realization of this goal. *See* Eric Schnapper, *Affirmative Action and the Legislative History of the Fourteenth Amendment*, 71 VA. L. REV. 753 (1985).

Affirmative action raises Fourteenth Amendment questions because by seeking to promote a remedy for racially subordinated groups, it does not adhere to the formalistic notions of equality. This is not to say it is unconstitutional. The term "equal protection" has bedeviled courts who have tried to elucidate its meaning and apply it to governmental classifications, but some principles have emerged. It does *not* mean that all laws must treat or effect all classes of persons identically. There are many federal, state, and local laws that single out certain groups for inclusion or exclusion in receiving a benefit or suffering a detriment. However, the guarantee of equal protection also means that there are classifications that the government *cannot* lawfully make. It has been the task of the Supreme Court to decide what these unlawful classifications are.

The modern Court's approach to this problem has been to create a system of levels of review when dealing with laws that treat a discreet group or groups differently from others. The two baseline levels of review are "rational basis" review and "strict scrutiny" review, though as *Metro Broadcasting* shows these are not exclusive. The majority of classifications made by the government are subject to low-level, "rational basis" review and are overwhelmingly, but not always, upheld. These are laws which the Court believes are a proper use of governmental power and are rationally related to a legitimate governmental interest. However, the Court has held that some classifications are, by their very nature, "suspect" and should be examined with heightened scrutiny. Race is the classic "suspect" classification, and classifications based on race are normally subject to "strict scrutiny," the most stringent form of judicial review.

Some examples may help to flesh out this discussion. In *New York City Transit Authority v. Beazer*, 440 U.S. 568 (1979), the Court asked whether it was constitutional for the Transit Authority to exclude from employment users of methadone, a drug used by heroin addicts as part of their rehabilitation treatment. The Court concluded that safety concerns provided a sufficient "rational basis" for this special classification, and that it was not constitutionally significant that some qualified potential employees would be injured by the plan. The Court said that because the law "does not circumscribe a class of persons characterized by some unpopular trait or affiliation, it does not create or reflect any likelihood of bias on the part of the ruling majority." *Id.* at 593. *Beazer* is an example of a governmental classification which does not affect people equally, but is nevertheless constitutional. Under rational basis review, the Court treats classifications with a great deal of deference, and explicitly does not examine the wisdom or effectiveness of the law.

On the other end of the spectrum are laws that explicitly disadvantage persons based on their race. In *Strauder v. West Virginia*, 100 U.S. (10 Otto) 303 (1880), a West Virginia law which said that blacks may not serve on juries was invalidated as blatant discrimination, which is constitutionally impermissible. *Strauder* is an older case, but today this kind of classification would be subjected to "strict scrutiny" and would obviously be invalidated.

Traditionally, rational basis review nearly always meant a law would be upheld, and strict scrutiny review almost guaranteed disallowance. There are, however, important exceptions. For an example of a law examined under rational basis but nevertheless invalidated, see *City of Cleburne v. Cleburne Living Center*, 473 U.S. 432 (1985) (holding unconstitutional a law which negatively affected the mentally retarded because it had no rational relation to a legitimate governmental interest, but was instead motivated by "negative attitudes, or fear"). For an example of racial classifications upheld under strict scrutiny, see *Korematsu v. United States*, 323 U.S. 214 (1944) (upholding the internment of Japanese–Americans during World War II because the action was motivated by "pressing public necessity" rather than "racial antagonism"). Note that *Korematsu* has been harshly criticized. *See, e.g.,* Eugene V. Rostow, *The Japanese–American Cases–A Disaster, in* THE MASS INTERNMENT OF JAPANESE AMERICANS AND THE QUEST FOR LEGAL REDRESS 189 (Charles McClain ed., 1994).

Between the extremes of *Beazer* and *Strauder*, there are many laws which do not clearly fit into a certain level of scrutiny. These include laws which do not explicitly make racial classifications but have disparate effects on minorities, or laws that make classifications that are less clearly "suspect," such as with women or homosexuals. See, generally, STONE ET. AL., *supra* at 514–53. Affirmative action programs fall into this problematic category because of their unique position as laws which make racial classifications in the interest of *benefiting* racial minorities. This is using racial classification in quite a different way than the law in *Strauder*, and Courts have struggled to determine what level of scrutiny should apply to affirmative action programs.

3. The *Bakke* case. The Supreme Court first ruled on the substance of affirmative action in *Regents of University of California v. Bakke*, 438 U.S. 265 (1978). *Bakke* established the principle that voluntary use by government employers of race-conscious goals and timetables to remedy prior discrimination is not per se unconstitutional, but that explicit "quotas" are not allowable. The case involved an admissions plan at the University of California Davis Medical School, whereby sixteen seats out of a hundred were reserved for minority applicants. Four justices voted to uphold this aggressive affirmative action plan. Four justices voted to strike it down, but not on constitutional grounds. The deciding vote came from Justice Powell, who first articulated the view that affirmative action programs should be subjected to strict scrutiny. He wrote that all racial classifications, including those that are "benign," are suspect and should be treated under the strict scrutiny test. He did not believe that a general history of prior discrimination created a compelling governmental interest because in the *Bakke* case there were no judicial, administrative, or legislative findings of prior racial discrimination, and there were no findings that discrimination was a pervasive problem at the medical school. Justice Powell's other major contribution was his treatment of diversity as a rationale for affirmative action. He wrote that the interest in a diverse student body was reason enough to allow race to be used in admission decisions, but not a rigid system that isolated sixteen spots from competition with others. Justice Powell wrote only for himself, but his opinion has proven to be very influential in affirmative action decisions. Since *Bakke*, the thorny issues associated with affirmative action have led to an often sharply divided Court and few clear guidelines.

Justice Powell retired in 1987, and Justice Kennedy's appointment was seen as creating a strong conservative voting bloc on the Court. *Croson* was the first time that the Court issued a majority opinion in an affirmative action case. Many believed the case marked a shift away from a Supreme Court that had been relatively receptive to affirmative action programs. Taking a rather literalistic view of the Fourteenth Amendment, the Court found that the fact that "the Richmond Plan denies certain citizens the opportunity to compete for a fixed percentage of public contracts based solely upon their races" meant that the plan must be subjected to strict scrutiny, which it was found not to meet. The decision in *Metro Broadcasting* was therefore something of a surprise. It marked the first time a non-remedial rationale was used to validate an affirmative action plan. The other important deviation made in *Metro Broadcasting* was its use of an intermediate level of scrutiny in assessing the FCC plan.

The regime of intermediate scrutiny in affirmative action cases was short lived. In 1995, only five years after *Metro Broadcasting* was decided, the Court decided *Adarand Constructors v. Pena*, 515 U.S. 200 (1995), the last major case prior to *Grutter*. A majority of the Court overruled *Metro Broadcasting*'s intermediate scrutiny standard and held that strict scrutiny applies to *all* affirmative action programs. The attitude toward affirmative action among the members of the Court had shifted once again with the addition of Justice Thomas, and the decision evidences a loss of confidence in Congress's ability to deal with race. *See* Paul J. Mishkin, *Foreword: The Making of a Turning Point*—Metro *and* Adarand, 84 CAL. L. REV. 875 (1996). Justice Scalia wrote in concurrence that there should be *no* group-based remedies for discrimination, only for individual cases of active discrimination, but a majority of the court has never accepted this view. For a detailed review of the Supreme Court's affirmative action jurisprudence prior to *Grutter*, see GIRARDEAU A. SPANN, THE LAW OF AFFIRMATIVE ACTION (2000).

As these cases show, the Court has struggled to find a consistent view on affirmative action, disagreeing over what legal standard should apply and more generally about the value of affirmative action. In the public arena, affirmative action is perhaps best known for its contentiousness. Depending on how the issue is framed, the arguments on both sides are appealing. What makes affirmative action problematic is that it is not intended to compensate for specific acts of overt discrimination; rather, it works more broadly to attempt to correct the general discrimination that has led to the economic and political inequality that exists for minorities. In this way, it focuses on groups rather than individuals. Supporters of affirmative action believe that given this country's history of racial prejudice, race-conscious programs are necessary to compensate for the disadvantage that has been suffered by minorities. Discrimination is still a problem that cannot be overcome through colorblind policies, and active steps must be taken to eclipse racial injustice. In addition, diversity is a valuable goal in a society where racial misunderstanding has so often led to prejudice. Opponents argue that it is wrong to use race as a basis for the allocation of resources, no matter who the intended beneficiaries are. They believe it is unfair to reserve resources for minorities at the expense of whites who have not engaged in discriminatory conduct, and unjust to have "innocent whites" today pay for the sins of past generations. Many also argue that affirmative action has a stigmatizing effect on blacks, casting doubts on the legitimacy of their accomplishments as possibly the result of special treatment.

For more on the affirmative action debate, see generally Erwin Chemerinsky, *Making Sense of the Affirmative Action Debate*, in CIVIL RIGHTS AND SOCIAL WRONGS 86 (John Higham ed., 1997); BARBARA R. BERGMANN, IN DEFENSE OF AFFIRMATIVE ACTION (1996); Ronald Dworkin, *Affirming Affirmative Action*, N.Y. REV. OF BOOKS, Oct. 28, 1998, at 91; JOHN E. ROEMER, EQUALITY OF OPPORTUNITY (1998). On the possible stigmatization of the beneficiaries of affirmative action, see Linda Hamilton Krieger, *Civil Rights Perestroika: Intergroup Relations After Affirmative Action*, 86 CAL. L. REV. 1251 (1998).

4. Affirmative action and equal protection. The Fourteenth Amendment says nothing about heightened standards of scrutiny for racial classifications. What precisely is it that makes racial classifications so troubling and suited for heightened scrutiny? Are they illegitimate in themselves, or only in the context of this country's history of racism against blacks and other minorities? What is the difference between a class of short men and a class of racial minorities? In a famous footnote in *United States v. Carolene Products*, 304 U.S. 144 (1938), Justice Stone argued that "more searching judicial inquiry" for classifications involving race may be necessary because "prejudice against discrete and insular minorities may be a special condition, which tends seriously to curtail the operation of those political processes ordinarily to be relied upon to protect minorities." Consider Charles R. Lawrence, *The Id, the Ego, and Equal Protection: Reckoning with Unconscious Racism*, 39 STAN. L. REV. 317, 322 (1987):

> Traditional notions of intent do not reflect the fact that decisions about racial matters are influenced in large part by factors that can be characterized as neither intentional—in the sense that certain outcomes are self-consciously sought—nor unintentional—in the sense that the outcomes are random, fortuitous, and uninfluenced by the decisionmaker's beliefs, desires, and wishes.

> Americans share a common historical and cultural heritage in which racism has played and still plays a dominant role. Because of this shared experience, we also inevitably share many ideas, attitudes, and beliefs that attach significance to an individual's race and induce negative feelings and opinions about nonwhites. To the extent that this cultural belief system has influenced all of us, we are all racists. At the same time, most of us are unaware of our racism. We do not recognize the ways in which our cultural experience has influenced our beliefs about race or the occasions on which those beliefs affect our actions. In other words, a large part of the behavior that produces racial discrimination is influenced by unconscious racial motivation.

It is evident from this language that strict scrutiny was intended as a means of *protecting* minorities from the effects of discrimination, be it overt or unconscious. Ironically, the use of strict scrutiny in affirmative action cases has led to the defeat of laws intended to *benefit* racial minorities. Does this prove that strict scrutiny in affirmative action programs is inappropriate? What aspect of affirmative action should most inform the Court's decision about the proper level of scrutiny—its goals, its effects, or its actual operation?

In *Washington v. Davis*, 426 U.S. 229 (1976), the Court held that a law that only disproportionately impacts a minority group, but is not race-specific in its application, will be subject to rational basis review. Is there a meaningful difference between a law that explicitly disadvantages minorities and one that does so only in effect? How can the Court justify treating laws which empirically disadvantage minorities with rational basis review, while treating affirmative action laws with strict scrutiny review simply because they explicitly classify using race? For a discussion of the equal protection clause and affirmative action, see MICHEL ROSENFELD, AFFIRMATIVE ACTION AND JUSTICE (1991).

5. Can racial classifications be benign? Affirmative action programs are considered "benign" forms of discrimination because they burden the majority, and are regarded as protecting rather than harming the political interests of minorities. Many opponents of affirmative action doubt the ability of the government to make benign racial classifications. Some believe that "benign racial classification" is a contradiction in terms, and that given the troubled history of racial classifications in this country the government should *never* allocate resources or give preference on the basis of race. This position is strongly articulated in Justice Kennedy's dissent in *Metro Broadcasting*, when he writes that the Court is not able to identify readily which racial classifications are benign, and equates the logic of affirmative action with the Supreme Court's infamous decision in *Plessy*. Is it true that racial classifications are so dangerous that they should never be used? Why should it be difficult to differentiate between laws that are designed to benefit a minority population and those that are designed to oppress minorities?

6. Strict or intermediate scrutiny? Inside the courtroom, perhaps the most controversial issue regarding affirmative action has been what legal standard should apply. As Justice O'Connor wrote in *Croson*, this is not a mere quibble over lawyers' words. Strict scrutiny is a very difficult standard to meet, and prior to *Grutter* no affirmative action program had survived strict scrutiny. Many predicted that *Adarand* would mark the end of affirmative action programs, believing that strict scrutiny would be "strict in theory, fatal in fact." *Grutter* has proved these predictions wrong, at least in the context of higher education. Why was the intermediate scrutiny used in *Metro Broadcasting* abandoned so quickly?

Strict scrutiny dictates that "benign" racial classifications will only be upheld if they are narrowly tailored to achieve a compelling governmental interest. How does Justice O'Connor apply strict scrutiny in *Grutter*? Do you agree that diversity in a university is a compelling state interest? Is it likely that a set-aside program such as the one in *Croson* can meet the strict scrutiny standard? In limited circumstances, the Court has found the remedying of past discrimination to be compelling governmental interest, see *Shaw v. Hunt*, 517 U.S. 899 (1996), but has stipulated that the remedy must attack "identified discrimination" which must be identified with specificity. Why is the remedying of generalized, pervasive discrimination which certainly existed at one time in this country not a compelling interest? Note Justice Marshall's strong assertion in *Croson* that the "interest in ensuring that the government does not reflect and reinforce prior discrimination is every bit as strong as the interest in eliminating private discrimination...."

The Court in *Croson* believed that attempts to remedy generalized, societal discrimination "[have] no logical stopping point." Is the absence of a clear stopping point sufficient reason to invalidate a law? In *Croson*, why did the majority determine that strict scrutiny was necessary? What were the majority's specific objections to the affirmative action plan in question? Was it appropriate for the court to speculate that the real motivation for the law was not past discrimination but simply political favoritism among African–Americans, who held a majority of City Council seats? What is the relevancy of the dissent's mention of Richmond's history as the capital of the confederacy?

Metro Broadcasting represents a relatively brief period of time when the Supreme Court applied an intermediate level of scrutiny to affirmative action programs, holding that the governmental interest served by a given program need only be "important." How does the Court rationalize this lessened standard? How much was the Court's decision in *Metro Broadcasting* a result of deference to Congressional findings and the extensive review procedures of the FCC? Justice O'Connor contends in her *Metro Broadcasting* dissent that treating groups differently based on race "may stigmatize those groups singled out for different treatment and may create considerable tension with the Nation's widely shared commitment to evaluating individuals upon their individual merit." 497 U.S. at 604. What concern is it of the Court's if the beneficiaries of affirmative action are stigmatized in the eyes of some? Does such a commitment to individual merit exist in this country? What "merits" must one possess to secure a broadcasting license? Is it possible that some racial tension must be tolerated to correct the effects of America's history of racism?

7. Colorblindness versus race-consciousness. Justice Blackmun wrote in *Bakke* "In order to get beyond racism, we must first take account of race. There is no other way. And in order to treat some persons equally, we must treat them differently." 438 U.S. at 407. At the core of the debate over affirmative action is disagreement over whether it is possible to overcome the inequality caused by past racial discrimination without taking race into account in the remedy. Implicit in this debate is further disagreement over whether discrimination itself continues to be a problem. Some believe that while overt racism is seldom expressed in public, unconscious discrimination continues to be a very real problem, despite the improvements in race relations that have taken place over the last fifty years. Not only are colorblind solutions ineffective, they are actually detrimental because they mask the discrimination that still occurs and disengaging whites from the unique problems facing minorities. Consider:

> I believe that [whites] today, raised white in a racist society, are often ridden with white solipsism—not the consciously held belief that one race is inherently superior to all others, but a tunnel-vision which simply does not see nonwhite experience or existence as precious or significant, unless in spasmodic, impotent guilt-reflexes, which have little or no long-term, continuing momentum or political usefulness.... A remedial regime predicated on colorblindness will have little influence at this deep level of social and legal consciousness because it cannot adequately challenge white attitudes or recognize a role for black self-definition.

T. Alexander Aleinikoff, *A Case for Race-consciousness*, 91 COLUM. L. REV. 1060, 1060 (1991). *See also* Williams, *supra*, at 544; LANI GUINIER & GERALD TORRES, THE MINER'S CANARY: ENLISTING RACE, RESISTING POWER, TRANSFORMING DEMOCRACY 32–67 (2002).

Conservative opponents of affirmative action argue that discrimination based on race is largely a thing of the past, and that colorblind policies that simply treat everyone equally can be effective. To overcome racial prejudice and inequality we must move beyond race and treat people as individuals, because the race of a person tells us nothing about her abilities, beliefs, moral worthiness, etc. *See* STEPHAN THERNSTROM & ABIGAIL THERNSTROM, AMERICA IN BLACK AND WHITE, ONE NATION, INDIVISIBLE: RACE IN MODERN AMERICA (1997). Whether or not discrimination continues to be a problem, there is considerable evidence that whites and blacks continue to have strongly divergent opinions on issues of race. *See* DONALD R. KINDER & LYNN SANDERS, DIVIDED BY COLOR: RACIAL POLITICS AND DEMOCRATIC IDEALS (1996). For a rebuttal of the Thernstroms' position that examines a range of issues, including education, crime, poverty, and voting, see Michael K. Brown, Martin Carnoy et al., WHITEWASHING RACE: THE MYTH OF A COLOR-BLIND SOCIETY (2003).

8. Purpose of affirmative action. As *Croson*, *Metro Broadcasting*, and *Grutter* show, affirmative action programs have been employed for a variety of purposes in a variety of contexts. The original rationale for affirmative action was to remedy inequality by directing the allocation of resources to those who have been historically disadvantaged by discrimination. The "set-aside" program in *Croson* was premised on the desire to counteract past discrimination and correct the disparities in access to wealth that exists between whites and minorities. The objection opponents make to set-aside programs is that it is unfair and counterproductive to disadvantage those who have not themselves engaged in the harmful, discriminatory conduct. In *Croson*, why was the large disparity between the percentage of blacks in the general population and their share of contracting dollars not proof enough that discrimination had put black businesses at a disadvantage? Does the Court offer any other explanation for this disparity?

Who was most likely to benefit from the plan in *Metro Broadcasting*? The broadcast licenses at issue in *Metro Broadcasting* are valuable commodities, yet the court uses a diversity rationale to uphold the plan. What are the economic implications of the decision? *Metro Broadcasting* has been harshly criticized as a thinly veiled attempt to further enrich a small amount of already wealthy blacks, and characterized as doing very little to help those who have actually been disadvantaged by discrimination. SCHUCK, *supra* at 142. Others have pointed out that once the remedial rationale is removed from affirmative action cases, it becomes very difficult to decide what groups should be receiving benefits. Paul J. Mishkin writes, "Once remedial justification is set aside, there appears to be no explanation why the goal of greater variety in broadcast content would not be equally (or better) served by including among the preferred groups others not defined by race—e.g., older people or Polish–Americans (who may be able to claim even less presence on the airwaves)." Mishkin, *supra* at 882. Even some supporters of the decision in *Metro Broadcasting* questioned the diversity rationale as being the exclusive inspiration for the court's decision:

> [A]lthough the majority described its measures as "not 'remedial' in the sense of being designed to compensate victims of past governmental or societal discrimination," its reasoning is clearly framed as a corrective for historical conditions that are hardly long buried in the shroud of some long-forgotten past, but whose effects are specifically identifiable and endlessly enumerable.

Patricia J. Williams, Metro Broadcasting, Inc. v. FCC: *Regrouping in Singular Times*, 104 HARV. L. REV. 525, 527 (1990).

The dissent in *Metro Broadcasting* strongly questions the correlation between a person's race and a specific set of views that have been underrepresented. In one sense this must be correct; it is impossible to predict someone's views based simply on the color of their skin. Nevertheless, there is a connection between culture and race, and perhaps while minority broadcasters will not bring any particular views that can immediately be identified as "diverse," increasing the minority broadcasting ownership will better represent "a shared heritage of language patterns, habits, history, and experience" that is "black culture." *See* Williams, *supra* at 529–30.

9.   Controversy about affirmative action. Affirmative action, whatever its merits, is unquestionably a hot-button issue in American politics, and the divide has only deepened in the wake of *Grutter*. This may not be surprising given the strong feelings that issues of race inject into any issue. This is accompanied by the high stakes, such as seats in highly selective colleges, and the feeling by some whites that these seats are their societal entitlement. Some opponents of affirmative action have taken to inflammatory and silly methods to try and undermine its goals. At Roger Williams University in Rhode Island, members of the College Republicans who object to the university's use of race-based affirmative action provoked controversy by awarding a whites-only scholarship, the "Students of Non-color Scholarship." Said the president of the group, "If you're going to have race-based scholarships on campus, you just cannot have it to one group of people and not the other. We say that's unequal treatment." The Republican National Committee denounced the award and severed all ties with the college group. *All Things Considered* (NPR radio broadcast Feb. 19, 2004). In another instance, the editor of the conservative magazine National Review has encouraged white college applicants to engage in "civil disobedience" by misrepresenting their race on college admissions forms. Mark Edmundson, *Civil Disobedience Against Affirmative Action*, N.Y. TIMES, Dec. 14, 2003, (Magazine) at 60.

Supporters of affirmative action have entered this fray as well. For example, some point out that white members of the elite have enjoyed the advantages of affirmative action by being the sons and daughters of alumni of elite institutions and being enrolled in prep schools that every year send many students to the nation's best universities. Supporters note the fact that George W. Bush's sub-par academic performance in high school and subsequent acceptance at Yale. "Bush clearly got [into Yale] because of affirmative action. Affirmative action for the son and grandson of alumni. Affirmative action for a member of a politically influential family. Affirmative action for a boy from a fancy prep school. These forms of affirmative action still go on." Michael Kinsley, *How Affirmative Action Helped George W.*, TIME, Jan. 27, 2003, at 70.

Despite the controversy that surrounds affirmative action, Neal Devins points out the overwhelming support that the *Grutter* decision received from universities, the business community, the military, and politicians. Not a single university filed an amicus brief opposing affirmative action, the military submitted a very influential brief in support, and even the Bush administration, though supporting the plaintiff in the case, expressed support for racial diversity and did not suggest that all race-based preferences be done away with. Devins argues that as a political matter it would have been very difficult for the Supreme Court to have disallowed all considerations of race in college admissions, and that "affirmative action has become so entrenched that the costs of taking a stand against it are greater now than ever before." Neal Devins, *Explaining* Grutter v. Bollinger, 152 U. PA. L. REV. 347, 373 (2003). Should this support affect the Supreme Court's ruling? Is it proper for the Court to recognize when it is dealing with a socially and politically controversial issue and perhaps treat it differently than others?

10. Value of diversity in higher education. There is broad disagreement as to whether diversity in the classroom is a worthwhile goal, and whether it should be achieved through affirmative action, as shown in the *Hopwood* decision. While *Grutter* has settled the legal question for now, the debate will continue. Supporters of affirmative action view diversity as promoting the inclusion of marginalized segments of the population, helping to abate the broader segregation that exists in society, breaking down stereotypes, and introducing different and previously underrepresented viewpoints into the classroom. Devon W. Carbado & Mitu Gulati, *What Exactly is Racial Diversity?*, 91 CAL. L. REV. 1149 (2003) (book review).

Conservative commentators are highly skeptical of the benefits of diversity, and agree with Justice Thomas's contention that the support for affirmative action shown by universities is merely evidence of elite institutions' desire to be "aesthetically" diverse. Who benefits from classroom diversity? Is it legitimate to expect members of a certain race to bring a set of views that will be different from the white majority? Consider this attack from an opponent:

> Students of minority groups may be forceful and eloquent spokesmen for their own racial views. But so what? There are many academic courses in which the questions of race and sex are marginal at best. In the arts and sciences, none of the math and science curriculum has a racial message; the same is true of large portions of social sciences and the humanities as well. Within the

law school, tax, business, and procedural courses have little if any content related to race, and it would be odd to say that they could not be taught successfully without any reference to race, or indeed without any minority or female students. After all, many of the lawyers and professors who teach today received excellent education in these subjects before the advent of any affirmative action program.

Richard A. Epstein, *A Rational Basis for Affirmative Action: A Shaky but Classical Liberal Defense*, 100 MICH. L. REV. 2036, 2040–41 (2002).

Another critique of the diversity rationale is that it presumes that certain qualities "inhere in a racial group." SCHUCK, *supra* at 165. *See also* Charles R. Lawrence III, *Two Views of the River: A Critique of the Liberal Defense of Affirmative Action*, 101 COLUM. L. REV. 928 (2001) (criticizing the diversity rationale while supporting affirmative action). Notice Justice Kennedy's claim in *Grutter* that diversity may be a convenient rationale that is not the true basis for support of affirmative action. If diversity does not benefit a university, why is affirmative action overwhelmingly supported by the country's most selective colleges and graduate schools? Admission to top universities increases one's access to elite professions and social circles. Is increasing diversity not only in the classroom but in the upper echelons of society a realistic goal for affirmative action?

Another facet of the debate over university admissions is the value of the traditional tools that universities use for admission decisions, namely grades and standardized tests. Opponents of affirmative action contend that college admission should be based solely on these and other merit-based standards. However, many believe that grades, and especially standardized tests such as the SAT and LSAT, are not predictive of success in college or law school, but do correlate quite closely to race and parental income. How would the elimination of standardized testing affect admissions to elite universities? GUINIER & TORRES, *supra* at 71. Lani Guinier proposes a "structural mobility" framework in which identification of qualified applicants would move beyond traditional indicators such as standardized tests. Take for example two applicants to an Ivy League school. One is a wealthy, white, "A" student from a top prep school who scores extremely well on standardized tests and has a full compliment of extracurricular activities. The other is a black, "B+" student, from a crumbling inner-city high school whose test scores and extracurriculars are good but less impressive. How should an admissions officer assess these two candidates? Is it possible to say who "deserves" admission? What is the goal of an admissions officer in making this decision? Is it who she thinks will better succeed in college? Succeed in life? Add more to the college's student body? Add more to society as a whole? Should the fact that the second student has very likely encountered many more obstacles in her achievements be relevant to an admissions decision?

11. *Gratz v. Bollinger.* *Gratz v. Bollinger*, 539 U.S. 244 (2003), decided on the same day as *Grutter*, dealt with the admissions policy at the undergraduate division of the University of Michigan. The University ranked applicants on a 150 point scale. Students were primarily awarded points for academic achievement, but up to 40 points were available based on qualifications unrelated to academics. An applicant received 20 points for membership in an underrepresented minority group, attendance at a predominately minority or disadvantaged high school, or recruitment for athletics. Other non-academic factors included 10 points for residence in Michigan, 4 points for children of alumni, and up to 3 points for an outstanding essay. This admissions policy was rejected by the Court, primarily because it did not include the individualized review present in *Grutter*, and therefore too closely resembled the kind of quota system disallowed in *Bakke*. Justice Powell wrote in *Bakke* that the fact of an applicant being a minority should be "considered without being decisive," but according to Justice Rehnquist's majority opinion, under Michigan's undergraduate plan "the factor of race [is] decisive for virtually every minimally qualified underrepresented minority applicant." Justice Souter's dissent saw a meaningful difference between the quota system in *Bakke* and the system at issue in *Gratz*, because the *Bakke* plan focused only on race, whereas this plan "lets all applicants compete for all places and values an applicant's offerings for any place not solely on the grounds of [race]." He contended that the "college simply does by a numbered scale what that law school accomplishes by 'holistic review'; the distinction does not imply that applicants to the undergraduate college are denied individualized consideration...."

12. Alternate approaches. Kevin Brown presents a bleak picture of the prospects for black enrollment in selective colleges and graduate schools if affirmative action were stopped. Kevin Brown, Hopwood: *Was This the African–American Nightmare or the African American Dream*? 2 TEX. F. ON C.L. & C.R. 97 (1996):

After the *Hopwood* decision, Texas instituted a plan in which the top 10 percent of students from every public school in the state are automatically accepted by state universities. Florida and California have adopted similar programs. The plan has been described as a compromise between race and merit-based solutions. An obvious goal of the plan is to have minority students from underperforming schools and bad neighborhoods be able to attend state universities, but by not explicitly involving race it ameliorates some of the supposed unfairness of affirmative action. The Texas plan also received support from poor, rural whites who have limited access to opportunities in higher education. Justice Souter criticized these plans in his *Gratz* dissent, writing that they suffer "the disadvantage of obfuscation ... the 'percentage plans' are just as race conscious as the point scheme (and fairly so), but they get their racially diverse results without saying directly what they are doing or why they are doing it." *Id.* at 298. These plans may also have the effect of disadvantaging minority students who attend better schools and do well, but fall outside of the top 10 percent. Does the Texas plan strike you as an effective way to meet the goals of affirmative action without employing race-based preferences?

In California, Proposition 209 prohibited preferential treatment based on race in public education. Justice Thomas contends in *Grutter* that minority admissions at Boalt Hall, the elite law school at the University of California Berkeley, have not significantly suffered since Proposition 209's passage. For a contrary view, see ANDREA GUERRERO, SILENCE AT BOALT HALL: THE DISMANTLING OF AFFIRMATIVE ACTION (2002). One scholar at the University of California–Los Angeles has claimed, based on a statistical analysis of data collected at that university's law school, that eliminating race-conscious admissions programs in law schools would actually increase the number of minority lawyers, because African American law students who are presently unable to perform adequately at top-flight schools would go to lesser schools where they could succeed spectacularly and pass the bar in greater numbers. Richard H. Sander, *A Systematic Analysis of Affirmative Action in American Law Schools*, 57 STAN. L. REV. 367 (2004). Sander's analysis has been attacked by defenders of affirmative action. *See, e.g.,* David L. Chambers et al., *The Real Impact of Eliminating Affirmative Action in American Law Schools: An Empirical Critique of Richard Sander's Study*, 57 STAN. L. REV. 1855 (2005); Cheryl I. Harris & William C. Kidder, *The Black Student Mismatch Myth in Legal Education: The Systemic Flaws in Richard Sander's Affirmative Action Study*, J. BLACKS HIGHER EDUC. 102 (2005). How can we reconcile this controversy with Brown's article?

What kinds of measures might an elite university take to sustain minority enrollment without using explicit, race-based preferences? Is it possible that admissions officers may secretly or even subconsciously continue to give preferential treatment to minorities even after a formal affirmative action program is no longer in place? Justice Ginsburg predicts in her dissent in *Gratz* that this will take place. Is there a value to having race-based preferences out in the open?

Many have argued that affirmative action in college admissions should be based on class rather than race, pointing out that academic achievement is tied to economic status, and that the beneficiaries of race-based admissions preferences are mostly middle and upper-middle class blacks who are not as in need of assistance. *See* RICHARD D. KAHLENBERG, THE REMEDY: CLASS, RACE, AND AFFIRMATIVE ACTION (1996). Despite the victory of the University of Michigan's Law School in *Grutter*, the president of the university has expressed the desire "to create a more 'diverse diversity,' based on students from wider socioeconomic backgrounds ... not[ing] that poor kids are nearly as scarce on campus as minorities. Just one in five of Michigan's 25,000 undergrads comes from a family making less than $50,000 a year." Keith Naughton, *A New Campus Crusader*, NEWSWEEK, Dec. 29, 2003/Jan. 5, 2004, at 78. Who has the most to lose and the most to gain when affirmative action programs are in place? What should be made of poor white students who face great challenges in achieving high levels of educations—should they be the beneficiaries of affirmative action programs? Other proposals, such as those promoted by Shapiro, promote a focus on the root causes of why affirmative action is deemed necessary, namely the poor education available to minority students that renders them unable to compete on an equal footing. Is racial inequality too widespread and deeply-rooted a problem to be solved by affirmative action?

13. Is affirmative action effective? Despite the inequality that still exists, minorities have enjoyed uneven, but noteworthy, improvement in economic and social status in the past fifty years. Some argue that affirmative action has been instrumental in this progress. William Bowen and Derek Bok contend that selective colleges have succeeded in educating "sizable numbers of minority students who have already achieved significant success and seem likely in time to occupy positions of leadership throughout society." William Bowen & Derek Bok, The Shape of the River: Long-Term Consequences of Considering Race in College and University Admissions (1998). Others attribute this progress to a variety of advances and changed circumstances for black Americans unrelated to affirmative action. Schuck, *supra* at 140. To what extent should effectiveness affect future decisions about affirmative action? Justice O'Connor's *Grutter* opinion contains the prediction that in twenty-five years affirmative action will no longer be necessary. Does this seem likely? Why would she feel compelled to include this speculation?

B. The Wealth of Communities

The financial services infrastructure available to make loans and accept deposits is a critical component for creating and sustaining wealth. Two banking statutes, the Equal Credit Opportunity Act and the Community Reinvestment Act, were designed to correct the long-established patterns of discriminatory lending to women, and to poor and minority communities. In what follows, legal scholar Anthony Taibi questions whether either of these statutes contributes significantly to the reversal of financial subordination, and economic isolation that have been sustaining features of wealth and income inequality for Blacks, and other targets of racial discrimination. Taibi proposes, instead, a "community empowerment" paradigm in which local racial cultural identities and civil institutions are accorded central importance beyond the formalistic model of markets and rational choice.

Banking, Finance, and Community Economic Empowerment: Structural Economic Theory, Procedural Civil Rights, and Substantive Racial Justice

107 Harv. L. Rev. 1463 (1994).

■ Anthony D. Taibi

> Practical men, who believe themselves to be quite exempt from any intellectual influences, are usually the slaves of some defunct economist.

> John Maynard Keynes

I.   INTRODUCTION: PARADIGMS OF THE RELATIONSHIP BETWEEN
CIVIL RIGHTS AND BANKING REGULATION

The structure of America's financial system necessarily has a profound effect on the social and economic conditions of our neighborhoods and communities. The current small business credit crunch increasingly stifles those businesses that provide the bulk of new jobs and give regular people a chance for entrepreneurial independence. The continuing discrimination and redlining in both mortgage and consumer credit hinder the ability of Black people to buy and improve their homes and therefore block asset accumulation, stakeholding, and revitalization in Black communities. The ongoing consolidation of the banking industry has had and will continue to have a profound negative impact in low- and moderate-income communities and in non-White communities. Community investment is at the intersection of civil rights and economics, yet the prevailing civil rights paradigms fail to consider the structure of the banking system as a civil rights issue.

Two paradigms dominate civil rights discourse, neither of which aids in understanding how the structure of the financial system disempowers African–American and other non-elite communities. The equality paradigm, embodied in the Equal Credit Opportunity Act (ECOA), seeks to regulate financial institutions to ensure that banks treat like customers alike and make services available according to race neutral criteria. The affirmative action paradigm considers traditional equal treatment policy insufficient to erase the legacy of past discrimination. This latter model, embodied in the Community Reinvestment Act (CRA), seeks to ensure not only that banks apply race neutral criteria in evaluating individual loan applications, but also that banks actually lend in low- and moderate-income communities.

These two prevailing civil rights paradigms cannot address the structural nature of disinvestment, because they implicitly accept a neoclassical economic ideology that is incompatible with genuine reform. According to the neoclassical economic paradigm, every competitively profitable investment will find an investor; therefore, an unfunded investment could not possibly be competitively profitable. Although this postulate has a pleasingly simple logic, it simply is not true. All investments are made with at least some degree of uncertainty. Investment decisions are made before realization, and actual return at realization can be very different from initial assumptions: some investments do not live up to initial expectations and others outperform expectations. Neoclassical ideology refuses to acknowledge that cultural and psychological forces can be as powerful as market forces. To the extent that investors continue to undervalue community investments relative to other investments—due to racial, ethnic, or class biases, or because small investments for working people seem mundane— there is systematic market failure. Neoclassical thinkers would counter that, even if market failure does occur, in the long run, someone will discover the failure and enter the underserved market. Leaving aside for the moment the fact that disinvestment can sometimes become a self-fulfilling prophecy, that "long run" may last until long after our grandchildren are dead.

The equality paradigm implicitly embraces neoclassical assumptions in that it presupposes that the competition for funds in particular real-world marketplaces can operate as competition would in the neutral, rational, theoretically "perfect" market. Thus, the equality paradigm assumes that, to the extent that African–Americans and other people from disempowered communities have an "equal opportunity" to compete for a capital investment with other credit seekers, the outcome of that competition is fair or at least efficient.

The affirmative action paradigm reinforces neoclassical assumptions in more subtle ways. It too incorporates the neoclassical assumption that capital allocations determined in particular marketplaces are in fact "market efficient," but also posits equity as a distinct and competing value from procedural fairness and efficiency and seeks to subsidize favored groups to achieve a desired distributional outcome. It never questions the structure of marketplaces that routinely produce unacceptable results. To the extent that it accepts as given the institutional structures of American life (but for racial disparity), affirmative action reinforces the legitimacy of the very institutions that effectively disempower African–American and other non-elite communities. Thus, affirmative action turns the aspirations of disempowered groups into mere special interest pleadings, and demands for justice into supplications for charity. It divides the disempowered along the lines of who does and does not benefit from "special treatment" instead of uniting them in a common struggle.

Unwittingly accepting these neoclassical assumptions, progressive observers continue to describe community investment problems in terms of industry recalcitrance and insufficient political commitment toward reform. This is a tragic error. The disinvestment faced by lower-middle-class communities is structural—a product of the globalization of markets, capital, and production. Working-class, ethnic, and minority communities must control their own destinies by wresting control of local finance away from non-local institutions; they must not simply ask those institutions to invest a little more in local neighborhoods. The structural economic problems facing America's communities can be addressed in part by creating and reinforcing financial institutions that are community specific in their control, whether in the form of a broad-based community organization or simply a local business elite focused on profits but informed by a sense of its cultural roots.

Liberal perspectives do not treat building community institutions as an end in itself; their assumptions obscure how such institutions might be both fair and efficient given a different structural grounding. Of course, even in a reformed marketplace, not all socially desired investments will be competitive. Ensuring efficiency and structuring markets does not exhaust the role of politics. From health care to roads, from the environment to housing, American citizens must make decisions about whether and how to subsidize and to regulate. But as long as we are mired in the habits of mind engendered by liberal civil rights ideology and neoclassical economics, we will make these decisions myopically.

The creation of empowered communities requires more than new policies tied to community-based political organizations: it requires creating a new economic discourse. Although the "American Dream" of strong communities and financial independence remains an essential part of our culture and politics, the idea that the purpose of economic policy should be to promote this dream has not enjoyed intellectual respectability since the downfall of the Populist movement in the late nineteenth century. The assumptions of neoclassical economic ideology implicitly underlie and undermine the debate across the political spectrum. This Article represents merely a salvo in the battle of scholarly debates, op-ed pieces, think-tank projects, and efforts to shape our understanding of "common sense." Creating a discourse of populist community-empowerment economics and public policy is an ongoing project.

Although the racial dimension is among the most pressing and morally repugnant aspects of community disinvestment, the eroding job base, the small business credit crunch, and the globalization of capital are problems that affect all Americans. These issues are racial, but they require more than racial solutions. The small business credit crunch affects all communities, and U.S. home ownership rates have dropped precipitously in the last decade for all Americans. The "redundancy" of the American workforce to global corporations is now affecting white-collar professionals and middle managers, as well as Black and White working class people. If we are to create a new populist discourse about structural economic changes in our society, our movement must be transracial and have broad appeal across the economic spectrum. Opposing the economic and cultural colonization of our particular racial, ethnic, cultural, and religious communities requires a common struggle. Ironically, we can only promote our own group's interest if we work in concert with other groups.

The creation of a new civil rights consciousness requires that we examine the successes and the failures of existing policies that were informed by the two predominant civil rights paradigms. To that end, Part II examines the expression of the equality paradigm in the Equal Credit Opportunity Act (ECOA) and the effects and shortcomings of that Act. Part II then looks critically at liberal explanations of those shortcomings and offers an understanding of the ECOA's weaknesses from the perspective of community empowerment. Part III examines the manifestation of the affirmative action paradigm in the Community Reinvestment Act (CRA). A review and critique of the CRA's successes and failures demonstrate why a community-empowerment perspective can more effectively improve people's lives and create a multi-racial political consensus than can current paradigms. Part IV describes the emergence of the various types of institutions that comprise the community development financial institutions (CDFI) industry. A critique of the Clinton administration's proposed Community Development Banking and Financial Institutions Act of 1994, informed by a community-empowerment perspective, then reveals the failure of the bill to confront the imperatives of the already-established financial structure. The Article concludes by proposing a number of steps that the government should take if it truly wishes to embrace the community-empowerment paradigm as a model for its vision of the financial sector.

II. The Equal Credit Opportunity Act

A. Background and Aims

The Equal Credit Opportunity Act (ECOA) expresses traditional liberal civil rights policy in the credit arena. The ECOA serves two purposes. First, like other consumer credit legislation, such as the Truth in Lending Act and the Fair Credit Reporting Act, the ECOA is a consumer protection statute designed to provide accurate information to or about consumers involved in credit transactions. Second, the ECOA is an antidiscrimination statute, like the Equal Employment Opportunity Act (EEOA) and the Fair Housing Act (FHA), that seeks to promote wider credit availability by prohibiting the use of stereotypes in credit decisions. For example, the Act prohibits financial institutions from discriminating between otherwise credit-worthy customers on the basis of race, color, national origin, sex, marital status, age, receipt of public assistance income, or the exercise in good faith of the rights guaranteed under the Consumer Credit Protection Act.

ECOA compliance is enforced both by government agencies and through private litigation. The Act authorizes the Federal Reserve Board to prescribe regulations that clarify and amplify specific statutory provisions in light of the Act's legislative purpose. Overall administrative enforcement of the Act rests with the Federal Trade Commission, with limited authority delegated to several other federal agencies. The ECOA and its implementing Regulation B cover all phases of a credit transaction. Regulation B identifies and addresses in detail various phases of the credit-granting procedure, with particular focus on the application process, the evaluation process, and the reporting of reasons for adverse action.

* * *

As amended, the ECOA appeared to be an imposing piece of antidiscrimination legislation. Industry spokesmen feared a substantial increase in administrative activity and litigation, as toughened public and private enforcement mechanisms combined to promote compliance with the Act. As the next section demonstrates, however, the intervening years have produced few public enforcement actions and a only a trickle of private litigation.

B. The ECOA's Performance: Evidence of Inadequacy

Discrimination in lending decisions remains a serious problem. Both systematic study and anecdotal evidence demonstrate that widespread credit discrimination continues to block home ownership, as well as small business creation and expansion, and thereby community economic development in non-White communities. For example, a recent Federal Reserve Bank of Boston study concluded that, all other factors being equal, Black and Latino mortgage applicants are roughly sixty percent more likely to be denied a loan than White applicants. This study may even have underestimated the extent of mortgage loan discrimination by omitting those discouraged from applying for loans by pre-application screening processes, negative institutional reputation, or loan officers' attitudes. Indeed, another recent study revealed that the lack of applications from minority neighborhoods, rather than disproportionately low approval rates, is the principal reason that lenders fail to attain similar lending rates in minority neighborhoods and White neighborhoods in the lenders' service area. Home Mortgage Disclosure Act data from 1992 further revealed that the disparity between Blacks and Whites in gross denial rates for conventional home purchase loans has widened slightly: in 1992, Blacks were 2.26 times more likely to be denied loans than were Whites, compared with 2.16 times in 1991.

Business loans to Black-owned firms present an even more distressing picture. Available data are not as complete as the data on home mortgages because business lenders need not disclose the race of their borrowers, as mortgagees must under the Home Mortgage Disclosure Act; evaluation is also more difficult because business loans are less uniform than home mortgage loans. Nevertheless, the available evidence indicates that Black and White business owners with identical predictive traits—age, educational background, a close family member who is a business owner or self-employed professional, purchase of an ongoing concern, and possession of equity capital—do not receive equal treatment. Black-owned firms are denied loans more frequently than White-owned firms, and the business financing that is approved is usually for smaller amounts and on more onerous terms. Studies indicate that lender caution derived from inaccurate perceptions that similarly situated Black-owned firms are riskier than their White-owned counterparts undermines many otherwise viable Black businesses. It is thus unsurprising that, according to one 1993 study, eighty-three percent of Black entrepreneurs believe that lending bias is a very serious problem for Black-owned businesses, with another nine percent considering the issue a moderately serious problem.

C. Standard Liberal Proposals

The evidence of ongoing and pervasive lending discrimination is extremely persuasive, prompting both explanations and proposals for possible improvement. For example, the speculative nature of actual damages in discrimination cases makes statutory damages particularly important, causing some critics to propose amending the Act to include a minimum statutory recovery. Under such a scheme, even technical violations of the Act would carry a minimum $100 award, regardless of the actual damages. Although such an Amendment might have some marginal benefit for large consumer-credit class actions, as well as for suits in which many individuals claim mortgage discrimination, statutory damages would be of little help to individual small business claims, to which the technical aspects of the Act do not apply.

Other critics attribute the paucity of litigation under the ECOA to the fact that (1) although lenders must supply written notification of adverse action to individual consumers, the lenders need only provide a written statement of reasons if the consumer makes a written request; (2) business creditors need not be notified at all; and (3) a change in credit terms to which the applicant has agreed does not constitute an adverse action. * * *

Finally, some progressive critics target the historical lack of effort on the part of public enforcement bodies. The Justice Department did not file its first "pattern or practice" lawsuit until 1992; the amount of time that went by before the first suit was filed and the paucity of suits since then have left serious doubts about the government's commitment to reform. In creating the ECOA, however, Congress clearly envisioned that private litigation that alleged substantive discrimination crimination would be the main enforcement method. The Act uses the concept of the private attorney general to provide for generous class action recoveries and attorney's fee awards. Despite Congress's expectations, most of the few suits brought under the Act have been based on minor violations of the Act's technical and notification provisions. Only a tiny amount of private litigation has been reported since the enactment of the ECOA in 1974, and most of this litigation has focused on sex rather than on race. Indeed, only a handful of substantive discrimination claims, few of which rested on racial grounds, and only three class actions have been successfully prosecuted.

    * * *

D. A Community–Empowerment Critique of the ECOA

This section presents a community-empowerment critique of the ECOA that attacks both the Act's unrealistic conceptual assumptions and its defective normative vision. This critique explains more compellingly than standard liberal analyses why the ECOA has met with such limited success in extending credit to Black people and shows why the Act's vision may ultimately be undesirable.

The equality paradigm embodied by the ECOA posits an acultural, meritocratic "thing" called "creditworthiness." The paradigm assumes that banks can measure "creditworthiness" objectively and neutrally, and that, having done so, banks have an equal incentive to lend equally to all similarly creditworthy customers. The notion of "equally qualified" borrowers, however, overlooks the cultural specificity of the proxies by which creditworthiness is judged. Rather than reflecting actual ability and willingness to repay debts, particular qualifications are in fact only indicia associated with, but not determinative of, what succeeded in a creditor's past—a past that was typically "White only." The available research suggests that certain credit-scoring-model criteria have different meanings for different populations. For example, credit-scoring systems have typically deemed frequent changes in residence a significant negative, indicative of instability. It may be, however, that for Black people facing housing discrimination and concomitant schooling problems for their children, frequent family moves indicate hard work and responsibility. Such frequent movers might in fact be excellent credit risks. Similarly, frequent job changes may have different meanings for different populations. Indeed, the Federal Financial Institutions Examination Council has concluded that traditional employment stability requirements are discriminatory.

* * *

In addition to the equality paradigm's unrealistic conceptual assumptions, its normative vision is inherently limited. Relatively little non-consumer credit is granted solely on the basis of objective information. For small business loans in general and start-up loans in particular, little lending can be done by the numbers alone. The decision to lend is ultimately based on an inherently subjective determination that the credit-seeker's project has merit and that the credit-seeker is of good character and will go the extra mile to repay debts. Lenders do look to objective criteria like collateral and credit history and may consider how similar projects have fared in the past, but a decision to lend is in the end a decision to trust the judgment of the debtor. Even in mortgage lending, the decision to grant credit often hinges on the lending officer's subjective sense of the applicant's creditworthiness and the officer's extra efforts to work with the borrower to make the numbers come out right. It is at these points that racism may enter the loan-granting process.

In conventional use, "racism" means allowing race, an irrelevant characteristic, to play a part in what ought to be a purely "rational" decision. Banker discretion thus creates an opportunity for conventionally understood racism (either intentional or unconscious) to enter the loan-granting process. However, although racism is conventionally understood to mean not just hate for the other, but affinity for one's own, such subjective moments are both utterly inevitable and potentially desirable. Furthermore, fully "rationalized" settings, with no discretion and thus no conventional racism, may permit worse forms of institutional racism.

* * *

A community-empowerment critique points out that subjective moments in the lending process are not always problematic. People are more comfortable with things that are familiar to them. As a matter of common sense, loan officers feel more comfortable lending money to people with whom they share a common rapport, who belong to institutions with which they are familiar, who have backgrounds similar to their own, who seek loans for homes or business projects in familiar neighborhoods, and whose business plans are for familiar projects. At worst, we can attribute this phenomenon to culturally embedded racist stereotypes that prevent loan officers from seeing good business opportunities. At best, we can see this as good business sense: it is prudent to invest only in neighborhoods that one knows, in projects that one understands, and with people whom one trusts. It not only appears unlikely that we can eliminate subjectivity—which is necessarily culturally bound—from the credit-granting process, but it also seems that we would not want to if we could; what separates good from bad investments in lower-middle-class neighborhoods and small businesses will often be unquantifiable, intangible qualities like the passion, character, and vision of the borrower, or the aesthetic quality of the houses on a particular block. We want lenders to take a chance, based on the intuition that a project will succeed, on projects whose numbers may be less than perfect. This point of subjectivity in the lending process is paradoxically the time when both the worst and the best lending practices might transpire.

* * *

[B]lacks and Whites of the same economic status typically attend different clubs and recreational facilities, send their children to different schools, and therefore serve on different PTA boards, attend different churches, and live in different neighborhoods. Without personal knowledge of a credit seeker's character and reputation in the community, a banker has no basis for a reputational judgment. Even the most well-meaning White loan officer will be unable to make character loans with an acceptable racial balance. To the extent that, in modern America, White people do not know Black people, reputational lending by White institutions cannot help being "discriminatory."

Hiring more employees from Black communities could never be more than a partial solution. To make a large, White-owned bank in a Black neighborhood more responsive to the needs of its customers by staffing that branch with African–Americans might well harm the careers of those African–American loan officers. The management fast track at most large corporations necessitates moving around from position to position rather than remaining in a single location. The best opportunities for career advancement and bonuses are unlikely to be found in lower-middle-class neighborhoods; requiring Black professionals to work in low-income areas might ghettoize these professionals and thereby run afoul of employment discrimination laws. In addition, such a solution would do nothing for the credit problems of lower-middle-class White people.

In summary, as long as the main business of the bank is outside of a particular local community, it is difficult to imagine how members of that community could be treated "equally" by the institution. Within the context of an economy and financial structure driven by highly mobile transnational capital and large corporate interests, community-based economic development will always be a charitable afterthought, not an economic imperative.

III.   THE COMMUNITY REINVESTMENT ACT

Lending discrimination contributes to neighborhood disinvestment, but such discrimination is only a part of the story. Even if all lending discrimination were eliminated, it would have little impact on low-income neighborhoods. Many Americans cannot even conceive of having sufficient economic resources to own their own home; African–Americans are significantly overrepresented in this group. Because lending in lower-income and non-White communities cannot be improved within the framework of conventional business practices, stronger steps must be taken. Such a remedial purpose is envisioned by the Community Reinvestment Act.

The equality paradigm suggests that it is beyond the scope of public policy to remedy inequality that persists after fair and equal procedures have been established. Thus, procedural fairness has no necessary connection to fair outcomes: lending outcomes are considered beyond question as long as lending criteria are arguably rational and clearly non-racial. In contrast, the affirmative action model maintains that the lingering effects of past discrimination cannot be cured by equal treatment alone, but only by affirmative steps to make equal opportunity a reality. As President Johnson stated, "[y]ou do not take a person who, for years, has been hobbled by chains and liberate him, bring him to the starting line of a race and then say, 'you are free to compete with all the others,' and still justly believe that you have been completely fair." Under the more activist affirmative action paradigm, government policy at the intersection of civil rights and banking regulation must do more than simply demand procedural equality; regulations must ensure that an appropriate level of lending actually takes place in all communities.

In this spirit, in 1977, Congress passed the Community Reinvestment Act (CRA). The Act has recently attracted much attention. Unlike the Bush administration, whose attempts to disarm the CRA were thwarted by Congress, President Clinton made community reinvestment a centerpiece of his campaign's economic platform. Clinton promised to "[e]ase the credit crunch in our inner cities by passing a more progressive Community Reinvestment Act to prevent 'redlining'; and requiring financial institutions to invest in their communities." The battle over the CRA has been joined.

A. Background and Aims

The Community Reinvestment Act (CRA) places upon each insured depository institution a "continuing and affirmative obligation to help meet the credit needs of the local communities in which [it is] chartered" and requires that each such institution be assessed on its "record of meeting the credit needs of its entire community, including low-and moderate-income neighborhoods, consistent with the safe and sound operation of such institution." Congress determined that banks were redlining or neglecting important credit needs within their communities and that regulators' efforts to deter such behavior were inadequate.

Although redlining and discrimination are somewhat different, in the credit context, the two practices are clearly interrelated. Discrimination refers to the denial of credit to an individual applicant based on race. Redlining originally referred to the practice of literally drawing a red line around certain neighborhoods on a city map and refusing to make loans for property or businesses located within the demarcated zones. Today the term refers to any set of practices that "systematically den[ies] credit to applicants from low-and moderate-income, and minority neighborhoods." Redlining decisions are sometimes based on a perception that the housing stock in certain neighborhoods is in disrepair. The practice also derives from outright racial discrimination or from the related prejudice that property values in racially changing neighborhoods must decline. Furthermore, herd behavior may result if others follow one major lender's decision not to invest. Consequently, to the extent that Black people live in distinct communities, racially disparate rejection rates indicate that Black communities suffer from systematic under-investment—redlining.

* * *

Despite its weaknesses, the CRA did affect bank behavior by allowing community-based organizations and residents to intervene in expansion and merger application proceedings and to challenge the approval of expansion requests on the basis of alleged inadequacies in the CRA records of the applicants or institutions to be acquired. Public responses to bank expansion requests are authorized by statute or regulation. Regulators must review evidence presented through the public comment process. Community groups have thus brought an estimated three hundred challenges against expansion requests. Although only approximately fifteen applications have been denied outright on CRA grounds since the Act's inception, and although federal regulators have granted conditional approval imposing CRA requirements in only fifty to sixty cases, community groups have successfully used the CRA process to negotiate directly with the applicant institution. A majority of CRA challenges have been withdrawn after applicant institutions and local groups negotiated settlements. Such settlements often specify what measures the applicant institution must take to improve its record in low-and moderate-income and non-White communities. Although this informal dispute resolution mechanism is neither sanctioned nor enforced by regulators, it is preferred by many community groups. These agreements have generated between $7.5 and $20 billion in targeted loan commitments to low-and moderate-income areas, which far exceeds the conditions that would have been imposed by regulators. Thus, the success of the CRA-challenge process depends on how effectively community leaders can obtain specific commitments to community reinvestment from banks in independent negotiations. Furthermore, research suggests that CRA agreements have resulted in significant changes in the institutional behavior of lenders. In addition to the imposed and negotiated commitments, lenders have made additional unilateral commitments of some $23 billion to community-development lending while their expansion requests were pending. It is doubtful that these lenders would have made these commitments without the desire to head off CRA challenges. Further, in the current climate of accelerated merger activity in the banking industry, the primary CRA enforcement mechanism of denying permission for mergers may be increasingly powerful.

In addition, in 1989 Congress greatly enhanced the CRA's impact as part of the comprehensive Financial Institutions Reform, Recovery, and Enforcement Act (FIRREA). Among other changes, the 1989 Amendments mandated public disclosure of regulators' CRA evaluation results and greatly expanded the collection of Home Mortgage Disclosure Act data. These Amendments sent a message to the regulatory agencies to strengthen their CRA enforcement, which has been amplified by the Clinton administration's proposed overhaul of the regulations under the CRA.

B.   The CRA's Performance: Evidence of Inadequacy

Although the CRA has fostered many negotiated partnerships for community lending, low- and moderate-income communities remain underserved by the banking industry. The extent to which these commitments have translated into actual changes in lending practices is unclear. Although eighty-nine percent of the nation's banks and thrifts received outstanding or satisfactory CRA grades from federal banking regulators, widespread evidence indicates that the industry continues to fall short of the law's mandates.

The inadequacy of the CRA is demonstrated both by continuing and pervasive lending discrimination and by evidence demonstrating that banks continue to neglect the credit needs of low-and moderate-income communities. Redlining of many kinds is pervasive and growing. Many of America's lower-and middle-class communities—whether White or Black, urban, rural, or small town—suffer from continuing disinvestment. Even if the CRA's goals were met, it is unclear that their fulfillment would reverse these long-term, structural declines.

C.   The CRA's Inherent Contradictions

The CRA has been sharply criticized from all sides. Liberals attack the Act's enforcement provisions as ineffective and argue that much of what passes for compliance is merely charitable donation instead of serious investment. Conservatives bemoan allegedly excessive compliance costs, anti-competitive effects, and inefficient impacts on market structure. To the extent that speakers on both sides of this debate are correct, these critiques highlight the limitations of the CRA strategy that creates the illusion of a fixed choice between healthy communities and profitable industry. This false dichotomy results from our intellectual and political failure to target directly the structure of the financial industry.

1.   Liberal Critiques of the CRA.—Liberal critics of the CRA see much of what passes for CRA compliance as mere public relations and charitable contribution to community-group causes. According to this view, CRA enforcement merely imposes the requirement of extensive paper trails for marginal activities that have little to do with substantive investment in low- and moderate-income communities. These critics argue that banks refuse to change the way they do business and look to please regulators rather than to comply with the spirit of the law.

Liberal critics argue persuasively that regulators must, among other things, be directed to see CRA evaluation as an integral part of a regulator's job rather than as an additional burden; that better guidelines should emphasize the CRA as an aspect of normal bank operations rather than as a charitable afterthought; that only substantive lending in low- and moderate-income communities rather than negotiated gifts to community groups or other causes should constitute compliance; and that regulators need help in forming substantive policies rather than formalistic rules and in reducing paperwork. Backed by substantial bipartisan political support, various liberal reform proposals have recently emerged on both the legislative and the new administration's regulatory agendas. * * *

The CRA Reform Act also imposes CRA-type duties on non-depository mortgage banks and mortgage insurance companies: "[e]ach mortgage bank shall have an ongoing responsibility to meet the credit needs of all the communities in which such bank makes a significant number of extensions of credit or extends a significant amount of credit, including extensions of credit in low- and moderate-income neighborhoods of such communities." This provision is significant because mortgage banks account for an large share of mortgage-origination activity. The Act would establish an Office of Mortgage Bank and Insurance Supervision within the Department of Housing and Urban Development and require mortgage banks and mortgage insurers to submit reports detailing their efforts at meeting community credit needs. If the Secretary of HUD found that a mortgage bank was maintaining an "inadequate level of community support," the Secretary could issue an order requiring the institution to file a plan within ninety days detailing "concrete goals and timetables for correcting identified deficiencies." The Secretary could further prohibit the bank from using any HUD-administered program or product until all identified deficiencies were met. Violations of such orders would be subject to administrative and judicial review, cease and desist orders, and civil monetary penalties. This portion of the Act could have a dramatic impact on the behavior of mortgage lenders.

The CRA Reform Act is a well-intentioned but inherently limited step in the right direction. Liberal critiques both accept the financial market as it is currently structured and generally fail to respond adequately to the very real difficulties that the CRA creates for financial institutions. Such difficulties are the domain of the conservative critiques to which we now turn.

2. Neoclassical and Conservative Critiques of the CRA.—Despite continuing disinvestment in lower-middle-class communities and clear lack of regulatory enforcement, industry spokespeople and conservative commentators argue that, at least in part as a consequence of the 1989 amendments:

> CRA-based challenges to bank mergers and other transactions subject to CRA scrutiny are now routine, even when the institution in question has received high marks for CRA compliance in recent examinations. Some deals are actually derailed by the statute, and the costs of consummating a transaction in the face of a CRA challenge can be substantial.

Conservative commentators and industry analysts level three main criticisms at the Act: (a) compliance costs are too high, (b) banks are put at a competitive disadvantage vis-a-vis their non-bank competitors, and (c) the Act impedes market trends toward consolidation.

(a) Compliance Costs.—There is considerable disagreement about the direct compliance costs of the CRA. The CRA has been targeted as the most costly banking regulation currently in force; more troubling still, some

studies reveal that smaller banks face the highest relative compliance costs. Conservative critics also charge that CRA regulations are vague and standardless and that bankers thus have little guidance about compliance with the Act. The data are not conclusive, however. Charles A. Bowsher, the Comptroller General of the United States, argues that these industry studies of compliance costs suffer from "serious methodological problems"; the regulatory agencies concluded, based on data received from financial institutions, that the paperwork requirements of the CRA are less time-consuming than the paperwork requirements of other banking consumer regulations. Nevertheless, whatever the precise burden may be, and no matter how the proposed regulatory changes may alter that burden, the CRA does generate substantial paperwork and other bureaucratic compliance costs.

(b) Anti-competitive Effects.—It is also fairly clear that the CRA places depository institutions at a competitive disadvantage compared to their less regulated non-bank competitors. Depository institutions face competition in the lending market from a wide array of other institutions, including pension funds, life insurance companies, finance companies, mortgage banks, venture capital companies, mutual funds, and commercial paper markets. As Professors Macey and Miller argue, "[t]he CRA thus effectively imposes a special, discriminatory tax on banks and savings associations, which are thereby weakened relative to other financial institutions." Given the centrality of banks to a variety of community-development goals, banks' declining importance in the U.S. finance system is troubling. To the extent that the CRA contributes to this trend, such decline runs counter to the Act's own goals.

* * *

A second issue arises if we seek to cure the problem of differential impact by extending the CRA to cover other lenders. Although some non-bank intermediaries—mortgage banks and finance companies—often operate within a geographic community, others—mutual funds, investment banks, and pension funds—operate across extended geographic areas. To bring these lenders within the ambit of CRA regulation, the idea of meeting the credit needs of a lender's "entire community" would have to be reconsidered. Yet the inclusion of this latter group is feasible. If these institutions were given a "safe harbor" from regulatory oversight in return for investing a set percentage of their assets in certain approved investments, a highly sophisticated and liquid market for CRA-approved investments would develop rather quickly. As the last decade proved, Wall Street financiers can securitize almost any investment. In addition, there are several bills before Congress that would create secondary markets—government-sponsored enterprises (GSEs) or private market mechanisms—to facilitate the securitization of small business and community-development lending. The CRA, therefore, could conceivably be extended to more sophisticated lenders with minimal logistical barriers.

* * *

(c) *Impact on Market Consolidation.*—Professors Macey and Miller argue that the CRA impedes the "desirable process of bank mergers and acquisitions." They contend that the consolidation of the industry is inevitable, efficient, and by implication, socially unproblematic. Although bank merger activity continues to increase and CRA protests *can* delay, derail, or raise the costs of an attempted merger, determining the normative value of this effect is a difficult task that requires both consideration of the relevant economic evidence and sensitivity to the contested nature of the implicated political values.

* * *

However, even if we accept the deeply problematic assumption that banking industry mergers take place because they promote efficiency and economies of scale, we should not necessarily permit consolidation. Efficiency is only one of many social goals, and it is legitimate for society to consider other public policy goals and to accept some sacrifice of efficiency.

In a narrow society-as-aggregate-of-individuals welfare calculus, small businesses, community institutions, and traditional forms of authority have no independent significance. But the promotion of small businesses and community institutions may be a legitimate independent political end. Small businesses and family farmers are an important bulwark in the maintenance of community and not just another interest group. Small businesses have been the engine of economic innovation and the sector of much new job creation. Additionally, small Black-owned businesses provide the best employment opportunities for Black workers. Civil rights values will therefore be best served by a structure of finance that supports such businesses.

Greater banking consolidation is inimical to small business and community institutions. Many studies show that local independent banks give small businesses better credit terms and service than do larger, more distant lenders. Local banks can evaluate and monitor the creditworthiness of small local firms more easily than large banks, know more about their small businesses customers, provide more reliable sources of credit, keep loan personnel in place longer, provide better access to these personnel, and make lending decisions faster. Local independent banks tend, therefore, to depend more on the character of the borrower in granting credit than on requiring high collateral. Branches and subsidiaries of large banks, on the other hand, are more likely to rotate personnel and to maintain final approval authority in remote head offices. For this reason, the branches or subsidiaries of out-of-town banks tend to rely on higher collateral requirements and other standardized lending criteria and "to provide less than the amount of credit requested by small" businesses. Larger banks generally do not emphasize small business lending; they view such lending as less profitable than middle market and larger business loans. Larger banks that do compete for small business customers primarily focus on established small businesses.

* * *

3. Further Considerations for CRA Reformers.—Despite the limitations of the CRA as a tool of structural reform, the CRA framework will exist for some time. It is thus useful to consider how the Act could be made more effective. This section argues that, in addition to extending the CRA's reach to all financial intermediaries, the current open-ended examination of institutions' lending policies should be replaced with a determinate requirement that institutions invest a set portion of their funds in approved investments. Such an approach would both reduce the bureaucratic role in the lending process and ensure that financial institutions actually invest in community development. Although such reform stops well short of real structural change to the economic landscape, it offers the possibility that the CRA might more systematically improve the lives of low- and moderate-income Americans.

The simplest way to extend the CRA to all lenders would be to abandon the ideology of community reinvestment and replace it with a conventional affirmative action approach that requires lenders to meet lending volume goals for certain delineated minority groups. A reform of this type would be a terrible mistake. Although the racial dimension of community disinvestment is the most visible and morally repugnant aspect of this problem, the majority of the American people suffer from the effects of disinvestment. These issues are racial, but they are not only racial. If we are to create a new populist discourse about structural economic changes in our society, our movement must be transracial and have broad appeal across the economic spectrum. Communities can only promote their own interests if they work in concert with other communities.

I want to underscore the argument that the CRA's reach should be extended to all financial intermediaries. First, to the extent that there are costs associated with CRA compliance, the CRA puts banks at a competitive disadvantage to non-bank competitors. Given that banks are, for a variety of reasons, already in significant decline compared to their competitors, their use as a tool of reform is of declining importance to the financial structure. The victories won in the realm of banking will be increasingly irrelevant. Moreover, the increasing complexity of America's financial marketplace requires a more comprehensive and unified regulatory structure. More generally, over the past two decades, the United States financial system has been reshaped by the spread of multifunctional financial conglomerates and the emergence of an unregulated parallel banking system. Along with other powerful trends like securitization, these events have broken down the carefully compartmentalized credit and capital marketplace that was established by New Deal legislation sixty years ago. Check-cashing and pawn shops, along with home-repair second mortgage companies, offer expensive services to low-income people bypassed by mainstream financial firms. Mortgage banks constitute a less regulated parallel housing finance system and finance companies constitute a parallel business and consumer lending regime. The commercial paper market cuts banks out of the financing of corporate businesses. Mutual funds and similar services provide the public with depository-like services that banks once provided exclusively.

* * *

In poor neighborhoods, one can find many profitable but marginal, under-regulated, and exploitative institutions that fill this niche—check-cashing outlets, pawn shops, finance companies, rent-to-own stores, and home-repair second mortgage companies—but there are few conventional banks. The data indicate that community lending is no riskier than comparable lending at similar rates of return. The lack of interest that banks show toward these markets helps create the demand for fringe banking services; conventional financial institutions then cash in on the fringe banking boom by issuing lines of credit to finance companies, providing transactional services to check-cashing outlets, purchasing high-interest notes from second mortgage companies, and pursuing other such business services. Thus, conventional financial institutions do help service these markets—but in an indirect way that permits unscrupulous operators to extract a middleman's profit while the banks keep their hands clean. To the extent that these alternative financial service businesses' high prices reflect not the actual extra risks of such lending, but rather the transaction-cost effects of cultural biases, this trend represents a cultural tax on low-and moderate-income communities.

Given current political realities, the view of most CRA supporters that the existing regulatory structure should not be abolished may well be correct. Unless the investment requirements are set high enough, a safe harbor approach will not provide sufficient incentive even to institutions that could easily extend their efforts in low- and moderate-income communities. Nevertheless, if we are to create a politics that promotes market-based community empowerment, we must move beyond marginal improvement in the opportunities for home and small business ownership and ultimately seek to alter the economic power relationships that dominate life in America.

D.   A Structural Critique of the CRA

* * *

The CRA is based on a very limited vision of the nature of the credit problems facing low-and moderate-income communities. Offering no plan for the structure of the financial industry, CRA-based reinvestment strategies assume that industry and firm structure are independent of the investment decisions that firms make. By raising the cost of mergers, the Act has arbitrary and uneven effects that depend upon the zeal of local community groups and the direction of the political winds. Moreover, the incentive structure of the CRA is perverse; in recognition for having engaged in a minimally acceptable level of community investment, a firm is rewarded by being allowed to contribute to undermining the long-term basis of community investment by further concentrating the market. The CRA assumes that, with a little push, all financial institutions, regardless of size and structure, can be made to engage in significant community investment and that structural questions are separate issues. Lacking a vision of what the structure of the industry ought to be, the CRA cannot be a coherent tool of structural change.

For example, CRA ratings for banks are inexact and subjective. The Act's requirement that each depository institution "help meet the credit needs" "of its entire community, including low-and moderate-income neighborhoods, consistent with the safe and sound operation of such institution[s]" is simple and straightforward in the abstract but, as a practical matter, difficult to assess in a uniform, principled manner. The implementing regulations that are currently in place are very vague. Even under the Clinton administration's proposed new regulations, which are somewhat more determinate and emphasize performance over procedural requirements, the CRA will remain without an overall structural image for the banking industry. In an industry of banks of many types and sizes, without credit quotas and with institutional decisionmaking left to bank managers, the best the CRA can do is to prescribe inexact guidelines and then to ask that bureaucrats apply these guidelines to various real-world situations on a case-by-case basis. Unfortunately, as the literature on bureaucratic management suggests, in this sort of environment, more attention will be paid to the imperatives of the bureaucracy than to the underlying goal.

The structural inadequacy of the CRA is symptomatic of the affirmative action paradigm's insufficiency. Although the equality paradigm and the ECOA are inadequate, because they refuse to entertain the possibility that seemingly fair procedures often yield unfair outcomes, the affirmative action paradigm is inadequate because it refuses to inspect and reform the institutional structures that determine the unfair outcomes affirmative action seeks to redress. Like most affirmative action programs, the CRA does not address the way that the structural imperatives of the institutions it seeks to reform inevitably recreate the very difficulties that the Act attempts to eradicate. Unlike most affirmative action programs, the CRA does not take an individualistic and race-specific approach to regulation. The income and neighborhood-based approach mandated by the CRA is a strength of the Act, but the lack of a vision for the structure of the financial industry undermines the Act's ability to achieve its purpose; the CRA approach does not recognize the fundamental incompatibility of the regulatory requirements it seeks to impose with the system it leaves unquestioned. To borrow President Johnson's metaphor, affirmative action does not question the type of race being run or the awards that attend differences in performance.

IV. TOWARD A COMMUNITY-EMPOWERMENT PARADIGM

The above analysis implies that the existing paradigms of civil rights reform are deeply flawed and, in spite of some important gains won under them, hopelessly contradictory and unworkable. The equality paradigm begins with several flawed premises: that neutral standards of merit exist or could exist, that those standards can be measured objectively, and that assimilation to the culture of the standards is a positive social goal upon which we all ought to agree. The affirmative action paradigm, although more realistic than the equality paradigm, is even more problematic in its premises: it seeks to ameliorate directly inequalities produced through the usual course of business in institutional life, but never questions why such institutions continually produce unacceptable results. Racial inequality is not merely an aberration of institutions that are otherwise fair and neutral and that serve the needs of all Americans equally and unproblematically. Rather, racial inequality is simply the most visible manifestation of how institutions like banks, universities, and law firms fail to serve the lower-middle-class and non-elite cultural communities. To the extent that affirmative action accepts as a given the structure of American life (but for racial disparity), it reinforces the legitimacy of the very institutions that colonize and suppress the Black community and its culture, and other non-elite communities and their distinct cultures. The equality and affirmative action paradigms reflect the views of the big business and big government elites who promote them: that cultural identity and religious belief are pathologies that must be cured so that everyone can become national-market consumers and clients of state services.

A community-empowerment paradigm seeks to escape from our current racial impasse and to allow us both to keep our particular cultural and religious identities and to live in economically healthy communities. Traditional civil rights reformers, neoclassical conservatives, and most Marxists fail to see any positive role for racial, ethnic, and cultural identification beyond the shaping of subjective preferences for individual consumption items. Any greater cultural identification is seen as an atavistic impulse, exemplified by the Klan or the tragic situation in the former Yugoslavia, that should be replaced with universal standards that apply equally to everyone. Although few would contest that the concepts of market and jural equality have created much good for the human race, man does not live by bread and procedural rights alone. A realm of authority and meaning exists at a level between the individual and the state—a realm that cannot be comprehended by neoclassical commentators and traditional civil rights reformers. Non-rational processes and forms of authority pervade the institutions—family, church, friendship—that are most central to people's lives. The local institutions of civil society are not understandable in market or bureaucratic terms.

In advocating a move toward a community-empowerment paradigm, one need not be an extreme racial or cultural particularist. Rather, one need merely believe that there is nothing pathological or wicked about the desire most people have to bond with others with whom they feel a common link of family, language, history, religion, and tradition. The universalisms of the market and government bureaucracies weaken the bonds of community. It does not derogate the individual to realize that life is given meaning in the context of family, community, religion, and culture.

* * *

The current view—that procedural fairness and outcome fairness are necessarily in conflict—traps us between two undesirables: big business and big government. Community empowerment shows us that our real interests lie in establishing economic and political structures that strengthen community-based institutions and allow the issues that most directly touch people's lives to be decided at the local level. Community empowerment advances the interests of every non-elite American, regardless of race or ethnicity, and addresses problems of middle-class anomie as well as of lower-class hopelessness. Part of the struggle must be to create a financial structure that ensures that all Americans can buy and improve their own homes, start and maintain their own businesses, and serve their own people. A community-empowerment paradigm sees lower-and middle-class Blacks and Whites as united by their desires to resist the cultural and economic colonization of their respective communities and to engage in self-determination. Moreover, a community-empowerment approach may provide a more legitimate and enduring basis for transracial politics, because unlike existing civil rights paradigms, community empowerment is based on a genuine respect for our differences. Because the structural economic forces that are eroding our communities can only be understood in their larger context, the discussion of community-empowerment public policy begins with a sobering analysis of the local effects of globalization.

* * *

B. A Community–Empowerment Approach in Practice: Community Development Financial Institutions

Despite increasing globalization, some significant positive signs have appeared on the horizon. Quietly, over the past fifteen years, with little governmental support, a billion dollar community development financial institution (CDFI) industry has emerged. Development banks, credit unions, and loan funds have collectively extended more than $2 billion in loans and are currently capitalized with more than $700 million—much of it raised from within the communities served. Although assisted by banks receiving CRA credit for investing in CDFIs, the emergence of the CDFI industry is largely a testament to what can be achieved by committed and visionary grassroots activism coupled with the support of small business.

CDFIs exist in a variety of forms: some are bank holding companies or other insured depository institutions; others are unregulated non-profit corporations. All CDFIs are responsible financial intermediaries primarily devoted to developing the community in which they operate. They are structured so as to encourage community input in making policy. Thus, CDFIs express the community-empowerment mindset: they transcend the liberal-conservative dichotomy, they are not entirely market driven but are not charities, and they are not bureaucratic government programs. Rather, they are responsible local businesses dedicated to helping their local community, institutions, and people to help themselves.

* * *

There are a variety of traditional reasons to support the assistance of the CDFI industry. Developing credit in low-and moderate-income communities is vital to our nation's economic prospects. As corporate downsizing is expected to continue, small businesses will continue to provide the bulk of new job growth; as the conventional financial industry becomes more concentrated and increasingly neglects small business, and as the possibility of direct governmental aid becomes increasingly remote, the role of CDFIs becomes ever more crucial. In addition, CDFI lending programs encourage entrepreneurship, self-sufficiency, and creative problem solving—essential qualities for national and community economic prosperity, and for breaking the cycles of poverty and welfare dependency. Notably, CDFIs measure their success not only by institutional and client economic gains, but also by their contributions to building the civic infrastructure of businesses, professions, voluntary organizations, church groups, families, and other community institutions.

To serve our communities' growing need for locally controlled credit, a national commitment to CDFIs must be cultivated. Yet there is a notable tension between the need that community-empowerment institutions have for independence, local control, and freedom from bureaucratic red tape on the one hand, and their need for active restructuring of the financial marketplace by the federal government and more initial capital input on the other. Public policy aimed at fostering the CDFI movement must do the latter without treating CDFIs as charities. Existing public purpose lenders, particularly community-development banks, community-development credit unions, community-development loan funds, and microloan funds, constitute a solid basis for a national network of CDFIs and provide potential models for structuring new institutions. The discussion that follows offers a look at some of the major models for CDFIs and concludes with a consideration of the policies on the current legislative agenda aimed at fostering CDFIs.

1. Community–Development Banks.—A community-development bank—the most comprehensive of the CDFI models—provides for development credit for its community through the vehicle of a commercial bank, credit union, or savings and loan. It utilizes proactive subsidiaries or affiliates to carry out its mission to develop the community. A community-development bank incorporates a broad range of services rather than specializing in a product or credit service as do other CDFIs. The depository institution subsidiaries of community-development banks are, of course, legally identical to and bound by the same regulations as their conventional insured depository counterparts.

A community-development bank, like any financial institution, must be concerned with operating in a safe and sound manner. In addition, if the institution hopes to grow—both by building on its retained earnings and by attracting additional outside capital—then it must be reasonably profitable. Nevertheless, its primary goal is the impact that both its depository institution and other affiliates have on its community or target population. Thus, a development bank has a dual standard of performance; it must successfully operate a financial institution and support community empowerment and development. The successes of the industry to date demonstrate that these are not necessarily incompatible goals.

* * *

2. *Community–Development Credit Unions.*—Community-development credit unions (CDCUs) are regulated and federally insured depository institutions that are cooperatively owned and operated by their members on a one-person, one-vote system regardless of the amount on deposit. As non-profit cooperative institutions, credit unions are tax exempt. Although their services vary depending on the credit union's size, age, level of organization, and the desires of its members, most CDCUs offer only a basic set of retail banking services.

* * *

CDCUs serve as the only bank for many poor Americans. Members are provided with basic financial services—bank accounts; check cashing; financial planning; and personal, car, tuition, and home-repair loans. By bringing people into the financial mainstream, credit unions help members to develop mainstream creditworthiness. Membership in the credit union offers not only reduced costs for needed services like check cashing and bill paying, but also encouragement to save through regular deposits and payroll deductions. Most importantly, credit union membership encourages better attitudes toward sound personal financial management.

Lending is, of course, central to the mission of most CDCUs. All credit unions make loans to their members, but CDCUs strive to make loans that will contribute to community development as well as benefit individual members. CDCUs typically encourage loans that enable members to get and keep jobs, start and expand businesses, and improve members' property. Many CDCUs also work with other community-development organizations to make loans for such development projects as the rehabilitation of multi-family apartment buildings.

* * *

3. *Community–Development Loan Funds.*—Community-development loan funds (CDLFs) are unregulated and uninsured financial intermediaries that aggregate capital raised from individual and institutional social investors at below market interest rates. They lend this money primarily to non-profit and cooperative housing and business developers in low-income rural and inner-city communities. CDLFs emphasize financing projects that provide new economic opportunities and resources in their communities. By providing low-income people with an economic stake, CDLFs encourage participation in community-business, social, and political affairs. "CDLFs have been leaders in financing community land trusts, cooperative housing (including mobile home parks), and worker/community-owned businesses."

CDLFs provide credit that is neither affordable nor available from mainstream lenders. Frequently, CDLFs' borrowers cannot seek financing from mainstream institutions because they lack credit histories or require too much technical assistance. Because most community-development projects require multiple sources of funding, the loans necessary to make the projects work most often do not comport well with mainstream financial loan packages and must be individually tailored to the project. This lack of standardization means that few projects fit secondary market criteria; these projects are thus unattractive to conventional lenders. In other instances, the loans appear too risky to mainstream lenders, and sometimes the CDLFs engage in outright interest rate subsidy.

CDLFs also operate as a bridge to conventional permanent financing by providing a reliable, low-risk source of information and funding. Conventional lenders often commit to a project once a CDLF loan provides comfort about the adequacy of the project's collateral. CDLFs can provide such assurance because, by involving community members directly in loan fund decisionmaking, CDLFs are able to base lending decisions not only on by-the-numbers financial analysis, but also on direct knowledge of their borrowers, thereby reducing risk. In addition, CDLFs' small, cooperative structure allows low-cost provision of capital because of the superior access to information and a high degree of repayment loyalty. Despite the absence of traditional risk management policies, of the more than $100 million loaned by CDLFs, loan default losses have amounted to less than one percent of all loans made.

* * *

4. Microloan Funds.—Microloan fund programs "make very small, short term loans from a revolving loan fund to people who want to start up or expand very small ... businesses that are often part-time, home-based, and minority-owned." Microloan funds most often appear as one component among many in micro-enterprise development programs that promote and teach entrepreneurship by integrating both economic and human development among low-income people. These micro-enterprise ventures include such businesses as home day care, tailoring, catering and food service, hair and nail styling, engine repair, trucking, and retail sales. Pioneered in the developing world by Accion International and Bangladesh's Grameen Bank, microloan funds are relatively new to the United States; the first such fund was established here in 1983. Approximately 150 funds now exist in the United States, and their successes have engaged the interest of President Clinton and members of the Small Business Administration.

Many microloan programs rely on a peer-group lending model, in which a small group of would-be entrepreneurs come together for the purpose of obtaining credit; after training and analyzing each other's business plans, the group selects a plan to receive the first loan. If payments on the first loan remain current for a certain length of time, other members of the group are eligible to borrow. In most programs, if one member defaults, no one else is eligible to borrow. Members meet regularly to evaluate business plans, track repayments, exchange information, and lend mutual support. Group borrowing creates tremendous peer pressure to repay loans, and by assuming administrative tasks, participants lower operating costs.

* * *

E.   Toward Community Economic Empowerment

There are moments in history in which intense shifts in what constitutes common-sense occur. The Great Depression was such a time. In the wake of the Great Depression, the American people lost their faith in the financial system and the business leadership of the society. The persistence of the Depression and the revelation of scandals involving the most prominent financiers caused a massive shift—one that transcended class—in notions about the proper role of government and the appropriate structure of the financial economy. President Roosevelt's answer was the New Deal's restructuring of financial markets, which was part of the foundation for a generation of expanding economic opportunity. That system collapsed as a result of "deregulation and destabilizing macroeconomic policies." In a similar fashion, shortly after Richard Nixon announced, "I am now a Keynesian," the neoclassical ideal of laissez faire again became the dominant economic paradigm in the United States. We are once more about to undergo such a change in world view.

I have attempted to demonstrate how a community-empowerment paradigm highlights the inadequacy of dominant civil rights paradigms that are based on neoclassical economic thinking; far from solving the problems they address, civil rights paradigms have instead obscured how the structure of the financial system harms all non-rich Americans and their communities, with particularly deleterious effects on the communities of African–Americans. This Article attempts both to disrupt the dominant paradigms and to begin to replace them. The latter ambition requires ongoing commitment, debate, and discussion. The ideas that follow are thus presented as tenuous indicators of potentially fruitful avenues of exploration, designed as much to provoke discussion and suggest areas for further research as to advocate a particular political trajectory.

Changing the nature of financial policy requires a broad-based coalition. Financial debate in Washington currently expresses little more than the scramble for advantage of different segments of the financial industry: big banks versus small banks, securities firms versus banks, and insurance companies versus securities firms. Consumer groups and community activists typically engage in the politics of finance with little more than interest-group aspirations. To achieve far-reaching reform, these groups must go beyond thinking about a hot scandal or a few bits of legislation and integrate financial reform into a larger politics. The logical source of financial reform is all nonrich Americans, whose interests are not addressed by the current financial economy. The interests of those who seek community reinvestment and those who seek decent, union-wage work are linked with those whose savings are inadequate, unguaranteed, or poorly invested, or whose pensions are jeopardized by weak regulatory and guaranty mechanisms. "These seemingly irreconcilable positions can only dovetail to drive reform if both organizing tracks explicitly promote greater financial sector stability and more dynamism in the underlying economy." Savers and borrowers must work together to effect changes in regulatory policy and in the tax code to support a more long-term perspective for investors and managers and to strengthen the foundational assets of the paper economy. "No matter where they fall on the risk-reward spectrum, most non-rich capital suppliers and capital users win when their political demands define the public obligations of financial markets in terms of strengthening domestic employment and living standards."

    * * *

V. CONCLUSION

According to the influential philosopher Thomas Kuhn, when old modes of thought no longer provide a satisfactory explanation of reality or a guide to future activity, a shift in paradigms takes place so that activity and analysis can progress. This Article argues that the old liberal and conservative paradigms have exhausted their power to explain, inspire, or guide public policy. A new community-empowerment paradigm, however, is emerging. I have avoided making any highly specific claims as to the content of this emerging paradigm because, like the modes of thought I believe it will supplant, it is more a sensibility and an approach than it is a body of doctrine.

    * * *

As the major parties stumble in the old grooves and grope toward a new politics, a variety of thriving grassroots organizations are meeting in living rooms and union halls across America to organize working class communities around such issues as hazardous waste dumping, community investment, and affordable housing. Unlike those who lead major activist and lobbying groups, grassroots activists come not from the professional classes, but from among the more typically alienated lower middle classes. "For them, democracy means building their own political organizations, drawing people together in a relationship that leads to real political power. In a sense, they are reinventing democracy from the ground up, starting in their own neighborhoods."

Despite the many local successes that grassroots community groups have won, the community-organizing movement has developed neither a national political presence nor a coherent body of doctrine or theory. Liberals and conservatives, bereft of any workable plans to deal with the nation's ills, look increasingly to community-based organizations for ideas. Unfortunately, mainstream politicians too often attempt to use ideas from the community-organizing movement for their own purposes and develop government programs that adopt the form but reject the substance of community empowerment. Technocratic attempts to "empower" people without challenging the entrenched power of the dominant elite are hollow. This hollowness is evident in the administration's CDFI initiative; although President Clinton genuinely seeks to give low-income communities the tools with which they can help themselves, his plan refuses to confront how the financial industry's structure undermines the economic base of our communities. Politicians now quote the old saying "give a man a fish and you feed him for a day. Teach a man to fish and you feed him for life." A community-empowerment approach argues that what really matters is who owns the fish pond, because skills and tools are not enough to ensure long-term community prosperity, and because man does not live by bread alone.

* * *

Moral values and social policies must be understood in the material economic context out of which they emerge. Moral values in the abstract have little content, and social policies meant to effectuate these values will be of no avail without concrete structural analysis of the nature of the problems being addressed. Racial justice is a moral value, and although the problems caused by the absence of racial justice are manifest everywhere, our old paradigms and attendant mindset obscure the structure within which these problems exist. Manifestations of our absence of racial justice include disinvestment in African–American communities and the difficulties that African–American people face when seeking access to capital. Continuing to understand these social problems solely in terms of the old paradigms, however, will cause us to continue to make largely ineffective public policy. The Equal Credit Opportunity Act and the Community Reinvestment Act, for all their good intentions, have failed to stem the tide of structural economic forces that are disempowering African–American and other low- and moderate-income communities.

The lack of access to capital that disempowers Black people and their communities is only the most visible and extreme manifestation of how the economic structure disempowers all non-elite people and their communities. The old formulations of anti-discrimination, equal treatment, and affirmative action policies are not up to the task of challenging the structural imperatives of the emerging global financial system; indeed, these policies tend to legitimate the very structures that are doing the damage. Within a community-empowerment paradigm, the devastation of particular communities is understood within the structural economic context, and the intellectual, rhetorical, and cultural foundation is laid for the creation of a broad-based transracial politics that can challenge the power of the emerging global business and professional elite.

The Hidden Cost of Being African American

OXFORD UNIV. PRESS (2004) at 183–200 (2004).

■ THOMAS SHAPIRO

CONCLUSION: ASSETS FOR EQUALITY

The enormous racial wealth gap perpetuates racial inequality in the United States. Racial inequality appears intransigent because the way families use wealth transmits advantages from generation to generation. Furthermore, the twenty-first century marks the beginning of a new racial dilemma for the United States: Family wealth and inheritances cancel gains in classrooms, workplaces, and paychecks, worsening racial inequality. I see no means of seriously moving toward racial equality without positive asset policies to address the racial wealth gap.

The racial wealth gap is more then obdurate historical legacy that lives in the present, because it also springs from contemporary public policy and institutional discrimination, not to mention individuals' behavior.

Children's Savings Accounts

Children growing up in families with assets go to school secure in the knowledge that their families will support their dreams and future wellbeing. However, many children in America grow up without such confidence. The majority of children come from families who cannot provide a positive asset legacy. About 4 in 10 of all children grow up in asset poor families. More distressing, over half of African American children grow up asset poor. What difference would it make if every child in America grew up knowing that (s)he had a nest egg to use to go to college, buy a home, or start a business? As a result of acquiring start up money, they would be more confident and competent; they would feel more invested in themselves, their communities, and the future. They would have dreams and a way of making them come true. Benefits would accrue to individuals, families, and society as a whole.

There are many models for Children's Savings Accounts, such as initial government or private contributions at birth, matches of family contributions for low income families throughout the child's formative years, and limited use of account balances at age 18 and older. Imagine, for example, that every child born in the United States had an initial deposit of $1,000 in such an account. Additional yearly deposits would be encouraged and possibly tied to achievements such as school graduations, summer employment, and community service. Acquiring financial literacy throughout the school years would be a strong program component, providing a relevant and stimulating educational content. Government would match contributions from low income parents.

Individual Development Accounts

The vast majority of Americans have not accumulated many assets and are not about to inherit a large nest egg. This lack of assets impedes them from moving ahead, and they watch people jumping ahead who they know have not worked harder, have not tried harder, and do not deserve financial success any more than they do. Start up assets for opportunities like education, businesses and retirement could improve dramatically the lives of average Americans.

Latoya Miton, who would do anything for her daughter's education, dreams of moving to a community with better schools, even calculating sacrifices like going without telephone service and auto insurance. If Latoya's job of managing a dry-cleaning establishment paid a living wage and offered health and pension benefits, moving to Kirkwood, Missouri might not be just a dream. She is an ideal candidate for a program that motivates savings for future mobility. Smart and hardworking, she might use it for higher education or even start a dry-cleaning business of her own.

Individual Development Accounts (IDA) are the first and largest policy initiative in asset-development policy, spearheaded by Michael Sherraden's book *Assets and the Poor,* promoted by policy makers and advocacy groups, and backed by several national foundations. Individual Development Accounts reward savings by asset poor families who aim to buy their first home, acquire postsecondary education, or start a small business. For every dollar a family saves, matching funds that typically come from a variety of private and public sources provide strong incentive. The IDA Tax Credit would work by providing financial institutions with a dollar for dollar tax credit for every dollar they contribute as matching funds for IDAs, up to $500 per IDA per year.

Down Payment Accounts

Homeownership is a signature of the American Dream and, as I have emphasized throughout this book, frames class status, family identity, and schooling opportunities. We also know that homeownership provides the nexus for transformative assets of family wealth. For this reason, and others, I think a hallmark policy idea is Down Payment Accounts for first time homebuyers.

The chief purpose of Down Payment Accounts is to allow families to acquire assets for down payment and closing costs. How would these accounts work? Similar to the home mortgage interest deduction, renters could deduct a portion of their rent on their tax form and have it put aside in a dedicated account to match their own savings for homeownership on a one to one basis. This money would be used for first time homebuyers.

A revealing contrast is that in U.S. history government policies have been very effective in giving other kinds of families start ups to acquire property and assets. I am thinking specifically of the Homestead Act, begun in 1862, which provided up to 160 acres of land, self-reliance, and ultimately wealth to millions of American families. This remarkable government policy set in motion opportunities for upward mobility and a more secure future for oneself and one's children by giving nearly 1.5 million families title to 246 million acres of land, nearly the size of California and Texas combined. One study puts the number of homestead descendents living today at 46 million adults. This means that up to a quarter of the adult population potentially traces its legacy of property ownership, upward mobility, economic stability, class status, and wealth directly to one national policy—a policy that in practice essentially excluded African Americans.

Matching Social Assistance to Asset Policy

Traditional welfare policies have failed to launch families out of poverty, just as they have failed to promote independence and self reliance. Asset policies will not work by themselves, either. In tandem, asset and income policies promise supporting pillars for mobility. To make sure that asset building policies do not become a shell game simply transferring costs from federal to state or from public to private–or creaming monies from social assistance–policy need to be crafted so that asset and traditional social assistance policies synergize one another rather than cancel each other out. For example, Children's Savings Accounts should not replace a public commitment to higher education. Tuition at public institutions of higher education should not rise just because 18 year olds have accumulated a small nest egg to make college affordable. A worst case scenario involves a family raiding their fledgling IDA account, losing matching payments in the process, to buy food at the end of the month because their food stamp allocation was too small. Families should not miss medical appointments, delay renewing prescriptions, stretch out the time between dental visits, or skip meals to scrape together money for monthly IDA contributions. These sacrifices to contribute to asset accounts are damaging bargains families should not be forced to consider because of public policy failures. One lesson from the national IDA demonstration project indicates that these temptations are real and should be avoided.

The single most important housing policy is the home mortgage interest deduction. Because it lowers taxes in proportion to a family's tax rate, the majority of this $55 billion subsidy goes to the highest income families; one third of it goes to families in the top 10 percent.

The nation's housing priorities must change. First, the dynamic housing markets—that is, laws of supply and demand incentives for new housing construction, and the location of new housing—must change. I like an idea that, instead of rewarding taxpayers who pay higher marginal tax rates, converts the interest one can deduct into a flat percentage rate. All families, say, could take 25% of home mortgage interest off their taxes, regardless of earnings or whether they choose the standard deduction or the itemized tax schedule.

Given the increasing prevalence of automated underwriting systems in scoring mortgage applications, fair lending enforcement agencies should develop tools to test for discrimination so that factors weighted against minorities do not become codified into uniform industry standards. Especially as loan pricing according to risk becomes common practice, lenders should be discouraged from generating greater profits by designing systems that make minorities appear to be riskier mortgages.

Mortgage lenders and insurance redliners should be held accountable for the racially specific damages they have imposed on communities of color. Why can't we sue predatory lenders and their suppliers of capital, mortgage and insurance redliners for what they have done to cities and communities?

Without these changes, the extra capital made available to families through various asset policies and other government policies would likely fail because the two tiered housing market would still generate more wealth for the affluent.

Where a family lives largely determines school quality and family wealth largely determines where people live. Local property taxes fund the leading portion of school finances, 45–50 percent; therefore, it is easy to understand how the wealth of a community, its resource base, governs educational resources and the opportunities that go with them. (The federal share is actually only about 5–10 percent, with the state contributing the remaining 45–50 percent.) The disadvantage of low resource communities and the advantage of higher resource communities can be addressed by shifting local school financing up to state and federal levels.

Part of the big picture I have been describing is how communities, families, and individuals try to trap resources and hoard them for their own benefit. Because individuals believe they can personally benefit from it, and because they do not trust government to act in the civic interest, they attempt to buy their way out of social problems on a one at a time basis. This encourages a privatized notion of citizenship at the expense of solutions that work for all.

We can no loner ignore tremendous wealth inequities as we struggle with the thorny issue of racial inequality. Without attending to how equal results–especially concerning wealth–we will continue to repeat the deep and disturbing patterns of racial inequality and conflict that plague our republic. A just society would not wish racial legacies and inheritance to block opportunities and make a mockery of merit, and just individual will rejoice to give merit and democracy a fairer chance to triumph.

NOTE: The following case represents an innovative use of the Uniform Commercial Code and common law doctrine of unconscioniability to challenge the propensity of banks to increase fee income by introducing new fees, for automatic teller transactions for example, or by raising existing fees, such as bounced check (NSF) fees. The trend to unlimited increases in bounced check fees became a point of consumer activism in the 1990's in the immediate aftermath of Federal rules ending the interest rate ceilings on deposit account. Banks lost the government protection from having to pay market rates of interest of deposit accounts, and were forced to compete for deposits by paying higher and higher interest rates. The deposit rate wars created pressures on the profitability of the once secure bank balance sheet. This pressure was relieved in the early 1980's by introducing fees that were unrelated to cost, and that were not disclosed to depositors when the initial deposit agreement was signed.

Although, the *Perdue* case represents a victory. It did not result in a permanent reconfiguration of the fee structure for bounced checks. It did, however, introduce the use of unconscionability doctrine in class actions by plaintiffs seeking to limit the fee structure imposed on retail deposit customers in the federally regulated banking industry. The unconscionability doctrine that you encountered in your contracts course served the more limited purpose of defending a single consumer against a default enforcement action by retail sellers who sought judicial enforcement of a variety of unfair terms contained in boilerplate agreements. When you finish reading Perdue, can you think of any other retail price structures that might be suitable for unconscionability challenges?

NOTES AND QUESTIONS

1. Community economic development. The intransigence of urban poverty and discrimination against African Americans and other minorities has led politicians, legal scholars, and public policy advocates to look beyond affirmative action and to seek out different legal and economic strategies with which to attack inequality. Many of these proposals have been market-based, grounded in the theory that the most effective ways to alleviate the burden of discrimination and poverty are new approaches to economic development and investment in disadvantaged communities. During the economic boom of the 1990s "community economic development . . . emerged as the dominant approach to poverty alleviation, touted by politicians as a market-based alternative to outdated welfare policies and championed by civil rights leaders as a critical link to economic equality." Scott L. Cummings, *Community Economic Development as Progressive Politics: Toward a Grassroots Movement for Economic Justice*, 54 STAN L. REV. 399, 400 (2001). Similarly, some argue that the primary obstacle to minority advancement is the lack of assets such as inheritance and homeownership. Asset-based policy, such as the measures Shapiro proposes in the second excerpted portion of his book, focuses on giving the poor monetary benefits they can use to lift themselves out of poverty. Financial assets are seen as providing the poor with the opportunity to attain the keys to success in American society, such as homeownership, business ownership, and quality education. *See* MICHAEL SHERRADEN, ASSETS AND THE POOR: A NEW AMERICAN WELFARE POLICY (1991).

2. Economic versus social equality. The debate over whether blacks should focus on achieving economic or social equality goes back to the origins of the modern civil rights movement. Booker T. Washington emphasized economic self-sufficiency and downplayed the struggle for civil rights. W.E.B. DuBois rejected this "politically acquiescent strategy," and came to be identified with his concept of building a 'Talented Tenth' of college-trained black leaders to direct the fight for racial equality. Cummings, *supra* at 410–11. Should the goals of economic and social equality be sought in the same manner? Does one naturally follow from the other?

3. Community economic empowerment. The kind of community development encouraged by Anthony Taibi is a model of economic investment wherein the betterment of the individual and community reinforce each other. Taibi expresses skepticism about the value of affirmative action, writing "the affirmative action paradigm is inadequate because it refuses to inspect and reform the institutional structures that determine the unfair outcomes affirmative action seeks to redress." How might a proponent of affirmative action respond to this critique? His proposals are very consciously economic, and this approach has been criticized as ignoring the "political dimensions of poverty." The poor are not only economically disadvantaged. Their interests are also woefully underrepresented in mainstream political discourse, and some believe that it is only through political advocacy as well as sound economic policy that the problems of inequality can truly be eradicated. The localism emphasized by Taibi has also been criticized. Scott L. Cummings argues it inhibits multiracial solutions and "works within the existing spatial distribution of poverty and does not address the nexus between poverty concentration and residential segregation—leaving unchallenged the racial cleavages that dissect urban geographies." Cummings, *supra* at 457.

What is your assessment of Taibi's proposals? Is it true that by focusing so exclusively on economics and localism his proposals will fall short of the broad-based changes many deem necessary? Why does Taibi reject the "equality paradigm" and "affirmative action paradigm" as outmoded approaches to improving the lives of minorities and the poor?

4.   Asset-based policy. Thomas Shapiro, in his book, *The Hidden Cost of Being African American: How Wealth Perpetuates Inequality* (2004), proposes several methods for providing actual monetary assets to those in need to try and foster "wealth" in disadvantaged communities. Affirmative action may also be seen as an attempt to put some minorities on the road to "wealth." What is the importance of "wealth"? Should the government take an active role in providing financial assets to those who lack them? If educational and employment opportunities are severely limited for many minorities, and the government does not take steps to improve the economic condition of minorities, what are the prospects for narrowing economic inequality?

5.   Unconscionabilty doctrine. Judicially developed legal doctrine has also been used as a method for combating the problems of racial and social inequality. The doctrine of unconscionability represents an attempt to protect the interests of those who are disadvantaged in knowledge and/or resources in contractual dealings. The doctrine was introduced in the D.C. Circuit Court case *Williams v. Walker–Thomas Furniture Co.*, 350 F.2d 445 (D.C. Cir. 1965), in response to what the court regarded as oppressive and unfair credit arrangements in low-income communities. Judge Skelly Wright wrote that in "many cases, the meaningfulness of choice is negated by gross inequality of bargaining power." *Id.* at 450. Unconscionability can be seen as undermining the general legal principle of freedom of contract, an extension of market-based rational choice theory, in which individuals are viewed as autonomous actors with perfect information, who may enter into any contractual arrangement they choose, as long as it is not illegal. The argument that the unconscionability doctrine does not violate freedom of contract is that the target of the doctrine, contracts of adhesion, are *not* entered into freely and therefore do not enjoy the same deference as truly bargained-for transactions. Many perceive a fundamental unfairness in form contracts between one economically sophisticated corporation, which writes a lengthy contract in dense, legalistic language, and a party who has no knowledge of contract law and limited resources for finding a different contractual partner. Despite its good intentions, the usefulness of unconscionability has been widely questioned, and there is well-developed criticism of the paternalistic nature of the doctrine. Is it the individual consumer's responsibility to understand every contract he or she enters into?

6. NSF fees and open price terms. One critic of the affirmative use of unconscionability doctrine to limit bank fees argues that "[j]udicial attempts at limiting bank discretion in setting NSF and other fees have been wholly unsuccessful in compensating injured depositors. Rising prices and industry practices . . . are used to maximize the number of NSF checks and have created increasing consumer hostility." Stephanie J. Weber, Note, *Excessive Bank Fees: Theories of Liability and the Need for Legislative Action*, 25 U. Mem. L. Rev. 1439, 1474 (1995). Is it inherently unfair for a contract to have an open price term which the seller may fill with little or no oversight, only a vague duty to engage in "good faith and fair dealing"? Are open price terms in contracts especially subject to abuse when sellers are dealing with individuals it knows have little business knowledge and will be less likely to mount a legal challenge? For an exhaustive discussion of unconscionability doctrine in California see, Harry G. Prince, *Unconscionability in California: A Need for Restraint and Consistency*, 46 Hastings L.J. 459 (1995).

7. Economic effects of discrimination. Shapiro contends that "studies using matching white and black couples with identical job, income, and credit information consistently reveal discrimination by real estate agents and banks." He argues that despite the reduction in overt racism, blacks and other minorities continue to be the victims of unconscious discrimination and stereotyping in employment, housing, loan application, and any number of other areas. Many contend in even stronger terms that white subordination of minorities is alive and well. Eduardo Bonilla–Silva detects a "new racism," in which racial inequality is reproduced in subtler and less facially offensive ways. In the example of housing segregation, "covert behaviors and strategies have largely replaced Jim Crow practices and have maintained the same outcome." Eduardo Bonilla–Silva, *"New Racism," Color–Blind Racism, and the Future of Whiteness in America, in* White Out: The Continuing Significance of Racism 271, 273 (Ashley "Woody" Doane & Eduardo Bonilla–Silva eds., 2003). *See also* Glenn C. Loury, The Anatomy of Racial Inequality (2003).

The economic inequality that exists in the United States, and its relation to race, must have an explanation, and since very few people would contend that blacks are less intelligent or less naturally able to succeed, many draw the conclusion that the best possible explanation is the preservation of subtle forms of white prejudice. What is your experience with racial discrimination, either observing or experiencing it?

David Dante Troutt makes the argument that the promotion of the ideal white-American middle-class neighborhood, the "metamarket," has contributed to the development of ghettoes populated largely by minorities, the "antimarket":

A metamarket * * * describes the dynamic interaction of wealth- and welfare-enhancing public and private forces that stabilize life in middle-income neighborhoods. Meta links not only economic and noneconomic factors, but also the cultural, political, public, and private forces. A metamarket's specific elements reflect degrees of realized psychic and cultural ideals regarding "the good life". * * *

In contrast, the antimarket involves more than just ghetto. It is the antinorm of the metamarket, the urban place never designed to hold stability. The antimarket encompasses the economic, political, and psychic marginalization of inner-city consumers through the subversion of middle-class rules. Its elements typically include a low-credit, high-risk milieu of struggling stores, inadequate public and private services, a preponderance of undermaintained and disproportionately public rental housing, weak schools, unregulated and unlawful commerce, a lack of public safety, a dearth of political capital, and virtually no personal wealth. * * *

African American ghetto poverty remains the quintessential form of inner-city or "underclass" poverty because exclusion of, and discrimination against, African Americans have been the most essential means to sustaining middle-class metamarkets. In many respects, such as the siting of undesirable land uses or the deprivation of basic public infrastructure and maintenance services, ghettoes have made middle-class residential markets possible.

David Dante Troutt, *Ghettoes Made Easy: The Metamarket/Antimarket Dichotomy and the Legal Challenges of Inner–City Economic Development*, 35 Harv. C.R.-C.L. L. Rev. 427, 429–33 (2000); *see also* William Julius Wilson, When Work Disappears: The World of the New Urban Poor (1997).

Troutt also argues that the worst thing that can happen to a poor community is success, because of the inevitable gentrification and displacement of minorities that will follow. Troutt, *supra* at 502. Shapiro shows the importance that one's neighborhood can have for his or her economic prospects, especially with regards to property values and quality public education. There are some who argue that the increased economic viability of currently disadvantaged communities will benefit society. On the other hand, if society has limited resources, and whites are the overwhelming beneficiaries of them, is it likely they will support policies that transfer these resources to others? Is it possible for everyone to live in a good neighborhood and attend a good school? How do Shapiro's points about educational opportunity among African–Americans relate to the goals of affirmative action?

C.   Rethinking the Family as an Economic Institution

In Re Marriage of Sullivan

691 P.2d 1020 (Cal. 1984).

■ Bird, C. J.

Is a spouse, who has made economic sacrifices to enable the other spouse to obtain a professional education, entitled to any compensation for his or her contribution upon dissolution of the marriage?

I

Janet and Mark Sullivan were married in September of 1967. The following year, Mark (respondent) entered medical school at Irvine and Janet (appellant) began her final year of undergraduate college at UCLA.

Appellant gives the following abbreviated account of the ensuing years. From 1968 through 1971, respondent attended medical school. Until 1969, appellant worked part time while completing her undergraduate education. After graduation, she obtained a full-time position which she held through 1971.

In 1972, respondent began his internship at Portland, Oregon. Appellant gave up her full-time job to accompany him there. Shortly after the move, she obtained part-time employment.

The couple's daughter, Treisa, was born in May of 1974. Appellant ceased work until 1975 when she resumed part-time employment. From 1976 through 1977, she worked full-time. During this period, respondent completed his residency.

Both parties then moved back to California. Shortly afterward, they separated. In August 1978, respondent petitioned for dissolution of the marriage.

During the marriage, the couple had accumulated some used furniture and two automobiles, both with payments outstanding. This property was disposed of by agreement. Appellant received $500, some used furniture and her automobile, including the obligation to complete the payments.

At the dissolution proceeding, appellant sought to introduce evidence of the value of respondent's medical education. She argued that the education was obtained by the joint efforts and sacrifices of the couple, that it constituted the greatest asset of the marriage, and that—accordingly—both parties should share in its benefits.

The superior court rejected these arguments and granted respondent's motion *in limine* to exclude all evidence pertaining to the value of the education. At the same time, the court granted partial summary judgment to the effect that respondent's education did not constitute community property. The court indicated that it was barred from awarding appellant any compensation for her contribution to respondent's education by the rule of *In re Marriage of Aufmuth*, [89 Cal. App. 3d 446 (1979)] (professional education does not constitute community property).

In May of 1980, the court issued its interlocutory judgment of dissolution. Appellant was awarded no spousal support, but the court reserved jurisdiction for five years to modify that determination. The parties were awarded joint custody of their daughter. Respondent was ordered to pay appellant $250 per month for child support and to reimburse her for half the cost of the child's medical insurance. Finally, the court directed respondent to pay appellant $1,250 in attorney fees and $1,000 in costs.

Both parties appealed.

II

This court originally granted a hearing in this case primarily to determine whether a spouse, who has made economic sacrifices to enable the other spouse to obtain an education, is entitled to compensation upon dissolution of the marriage. While the case was pending before this court, the Legislature amended the Family Law Act to provide compensation in all cases not yet final on January 1, 1985. * * *

The Amendments provide for the community to be reimbursed, absent an express written agreement to the contrary, for "community contributions to education or training of a party that substantially enhances the earning capacity of the party." [Civ. Code, § 4800.3.] The compensable community contributions are defined as "payments made with community property for education or training or for the repayment of a loan incurred for education or training." * * * The reimbursement award may be reduced or modified where an injustice would otherwise result.[4] * * *

---

4. The reimbursement provision states in full: "Section 4800.3 is added to the Civil Code, to read:

4800.3. (a) As used in this section, 'community contributions to education or training' means payments made with community property for education or training or for the repayment of a loan incurred for education or training.

(b) Subject to the limitations provided in this section, upon dissolution of marriage or legal separation:

(1) The community shall be reimbursed for community contributions to education or training of a party that substantially enhances the earning capacity of the party. The amount reimbursed shall be with interest at the legal rate, accruing from the end of the calendar year in which the contributions were made.

(2) A loan incurred during marriage for the education or training of a party shall not be included among the liabilities of the community for the purpose of division pursuant to Section 4800 but shall be assigned for payment by the party.

(c) The reimbursement and assignment required by this section shall be reduced or modified to the extent circumstances render such a disposition unjust, including but not limited to any of the following:

(1) The community has substantially benefited from the education, training, or loan incurred for the education or training of the party. There is a rebuttable presumption, affecting the burden of proof, that the community has not substantially benefited from community contributions to the education or training made less than 10 years before the commencement of the proceeding, and that the community has substantially benefited from community contributions to the education or training made more than 10 years before the commencement of the proceeding.

(2) The education or training received by the party is offset by the education or training received by the other party for which community contributions have been made.

(3) The education or training enables the party receiving the education or training to engage in gainful employment that substantially reduces the need of the party for support that would otherwise be required.

In addition to providing for reimbursement, the amendments require the court to consider, in awarding spousal support, "the extent to which the supported spouse contributed to the attainment of an education, training, or a license by the other spouse." Civ. Code, § 4801.

Since the property settlement in the present proceeding will not be final on January 1, 1985, appellant is entitled to the benefit of the new amendments. * * *

III

Respondent has cross-appealed from that portion of the trial court's judgment ordering him to pay $1,250 for appellant's attorney fees and $1,000 for her costs. He contends that the decision was an abuse of the trial court's discretion.

Civil Code section 4370 provides that "[in] respect to services rendered or costs incurred after the entry of judgment, the court may award such costs and attorneys' fees as may be reasonably necessary to maintain or defend any subsequent proceeding. . . ." The purpose of the award is to provide one of the parties, if necessary, with an amount adequate to properly litigate the controversy.

In making its determination as to whether or not attorney fees and costs should be awarded, the trial court considers the respective needs and incomes of the parties. * * * Further, the trial court is not restricted in its assessment of ability to pay to a consideration of salary alone, but may consider all the evidence concerning the parties' income, assets and abilities. * * *

Finally, a motion for attorney fees and costs in a dissolution proceeding is left to the sound discretion of the trial court. * * * In the absence of a clear showing of abuse, its determination will not be disturbed on appeal. * * *

Review of the total financial situation of each of the parties reveals that there is substantial evidence to support the trial court's order. The record reflects that the trial court considered the financial statements of both the appellant and respondent before making its award. Appellant's financial statement disclosed a net monthly income that was several hundred dollars less than her monthly expenses. Further, appellant's total separate property assets amounted to even less than her net monthly income. According to her statement, then, appellant's assets would have been depleted within a matter of months and her expenses would continue to exceed her net income.

(d) Reimbursement for community contributions and assignment of loans pursuant to this section is the exclusive remedy of the community or a party for the education or training and any resulting enhancement of the earning capacity of a party. However, nothing in this subdivision shall limit consideration of the effect of the education, training, or enhancement, or the amount reimbursed pursuant to this section, on the circumstances of the parties for the purpose an order for support pursuant to Section 4801."

(e) This section is subject to an express written agreement of the parties to the contrary."

Respondent's financial statement, prepared in the spring of 1980, also reflected monthly expenses which exceeded his net monthly income by over $800. Similarly, respondent's assets, although greater than appellant's, would also have been depleted within a few months if his income and expenses remained the same.

However, the court also had before it a comparative statement of respondent's business revenue and expenditures for the years 1978 and 1979, respondent's first two years of medical practice. Significantly, this comparative statement demonstrated that the fees which respondent collected during his second year of practice were more than double the fees he collected during the first. His annual net income increased by over $40,000 in one year. On the other hand, there was no corresponding statement or testimony to indicate any likelihood of an increase in appellant's income.

Given this evidence, this court can only conclude that the trial court made the reasonable inference that respondent's burgeoning medical practice would continue to flourish and that his income would increase dramatically. The facts of this case fall woefully short of establishing any abuse of discretion by the trial court. "[The] cases have frequently and uniformly held that the court may base its decision on the [paying spouse's] ability to earn, rather than his [or her] current earnings . . ." for the simple reason that in cases such as this, current earnings give a grossly distorted view of the paying spouse's financial ability. [*Meagher v. Meagher*, 190 Cal. App. 2d 62 (1961).]

IV

That portion of the judgment ordering respondent to pay appellant's costs and attorney fees is affirmed. The judgment denying compensation for contributions to spousal education is reversed and the cause remanded for further proceedings consistent with the views expressed in this opinion. Appellant to recover costs on both appeals.

■ Mosk, J., dissenting in part.

While I agree this matter should be returned to the trial court for consideration in the light of recent legislation, I fear that inappropriate language in the majority opinion may mislead the bench and bar. Several times in the majority opinion—indeed, in framing a question at the outset—there is reference to "compensation" for contributions to education. I must assume the repetition of that term was calculated and not inadvertent.

At no place in the relevant legislation does the word "compensation" appear. With clarity and precision, the Legislature referred instead to "reimbursement." The terms are not synonymous; there is a significant distinction that extends beyond mere semantics. Reimbursement implies *re*-payment of a debt or obligation; that is what the Legislature obviously contemplated. Compensation, on the other hand, may be payment in any sum for any lawful purpose; the Legislature also obviously did not intend to give such a blank check to trial courts.

Furthermore, the majority, in their creative reference to "compensation," fail to emphasize to whom it is to be paid. It is not to an individual spouse, in response to the initial query of the majority. The Legislature was crystal clear: reimbursement is to be made to the *community*. The community consists of both the husband and the wife, not one or the other. Thus when reimbursement is made to the community, that reclaimed community asset should be divided between the husband and wife in the same manner as all other community property.

* * *

To review the legislation: Civil Code section 4800.3, subdivision (b)(1), provides "The *community* shall be *reimbursed* for community contributions to education or training of a party that substantially enhances the earning capacity of the party. The amount *reimbursed* shall be with interest...." Subdivision (c) provides "The *reimbursement* and assignment required by this section shall be reduced or modified...." Subdivision (d) is even more precise: "*Reimbursement for community contributions and assignment of loans pursuant to this section is the exclusive remedy of the community or a party* for the education or training and any resulting enhancement of the earning capacity of a party." (Italics added.)

One searches in vain in the statute for a single use of the word "compensation." Thus I find it curious that the majority choose to employ that term rather than to consistently adhere to "reimbursement," the only monetary claim authorized by the Legislature. I trust that trial courts will not be misled into making awards of any sums for any purpose other than that permitted in what the Legislature described with remarkable emphasis as "the exclusive remedy."

———

NOTES AND QUESTIONS

1. Value of human capital. What is the relationship between *Sullivan* and the other materials in this chapter? States have taken different approaches to the issue of educational costs upon divorce. California stands alone as the only community property jurisdiction that permits the community estate to be reimbursed for the educational contributions of the working spouse to the degree awarded upon the dissolution of a marriage. New York courts have held that professional degrees, education leading to professional degrees, and professional licenses are marital property when earned during marriage. Raj Rajan, *Medical Degree in Divorce: New York Versus California*, 11 CONTEMP. LEGAL ISSUES 240 (1997). Texas courts have concluded that the costs of financial support incurred by the supporting spouse are not reimbursable even though made with community funds. Katherine M. Willis, *The True Value of an Education: The Texas Approach to Characterizing and Valuing a Professional Educational Degree Upon Dissolution of Marriage*, 31 TEX. TECH L. REV. 1117 (2000).

Recall the discussion of non-marital contractual relationships in *Marvin* and *Whorton*, *supra* chapter 8. Consensual sexual relationships are by nature intimate and in many ways opaque to those outside them. Can courts do an adequate job of deciding what is "fair" when these relationships dissolve? Does the existence of separate family-law courts in many jurisdictions prove that normal courts do not have the necessary expertise in marital and sexual relationships to adjudicate regarding them?

The court in *Marvin* wrote:

The mores of the society have indeed changed so radically in regard to cohabitation that we cannot impose a standard based on alleged moral considerations that have apparently been so widely abandoned by so many. Lest we be misunderstood, however, we take this occasion to point out that the structure of society itself largely depends upon the institution of marriage, and nothing we have said in this opinion should be taken to derogate from that institution. The joining of the man and woman in marriage is at once the most socially productive and individually fulfilling relationship that one can enjoy in the course of a lifetime.

Marvin, 557 P.2d 122.

Is this stamp of approval for marriage appropriate for a court? Have societal attitudes towards marriage changed significantly since *Marvin* was decided in 1976?

2.   Dependency, marriage, and the state. As the Williams excerpt points out, caretaking, which involves the dependency needs of both children and adults, has traditionally been considered a "private" matter and thus ceded to the heterosexual nuclear family, while at the same time supported by extensive state subsidies and extensive social privileges. This service to the larger society can be seen as a public good of economic and social value. In a time in which (1) divorce rates are very high; (2) women can no longer carry the entire burden of caretaking given the economic pressures forcing them into the workplace (not to mention many women's desire to work for wages); and (3) sexual minorities are both struggling for social recognition and denied access to marriage, what should state policy toward marriage and dependency look like? What are the "legitimate state interests" that the government should be able to directly support, or to indirectly incentivize? What should feminists and sexual minorities be fighting for?

3.   Discrimination against homosexuals? Most agree that homosexuals have historically been a marginalized population, and that a moral and religious stigma attached to same-sex relationships has existed throughout this country's history. However, some do not believe that homosexuals deserve to be treated as a "minority" in the same sense that blacks and Hispanics are. This belief may stem from the view that gays are now generally accepted in society and have every opportunity to attain material success equivalent to straight people. Indeed, gays and lesbians are sometimes painted as an economically privileged group, on the theory that they are less likely to have children. Colorado for Family Values, the group supporting Colorado's Amendment 2, made the disputed claim that "gay and lesbian Americans enjoyed substantially better salaries and higher education levels, and that they tended to be managers and professionals who travel around the world on ample supplies of disposable income . . . [thus] seeking to destroy the image of gays and lesbians as somehow disadvantaged before the law." Sharon E. Debbage Alexander, Romer v. Evans *and the Amendment 2 Controversy: The Rhetoric and Reality of Sexual Orientation Discrimination in America*, 6 TEX. F. ON C.R. & C.L. 261, 278 (2002). Others, especially those on the "Christian right" continue to believe that moral condemnation of homosexuality is acceptable.

Romer has been hailed by many as a landmark decision for the protection of the rights of homosexuals. In this view, Amendment 2 was struck down "for seeking to impose second-class status on gays and lesbians," and by striking down the law "the Supreme Court illuminated the core of equal protection: government must respect the principle that all persons have equal intrinsic worth." Supporters of the decision tend to have little doubt that Amendment 2 was inspired by hostility towards gays and lesbians, but even barring animosity they believe the law invalid because "the principle [of equal protection] bars laws that seek to entrench a social hierarchy—to keep a group 'in its place.'" Joseph S. Jackson, *Persons of Equal Worth:* Romer v. Evans *and the Politics of Equal Protection*, 45 UCLA L. REV. 453, 454 (1997). Why do you think Amendment 2 was passed? Should the legality of the Amendment be affected if it was principally inspired by hostility towards homosexuals? Scalia's dissent strongly criticizes the court's decision as having "no foundation in American constitutional law." If so, why did the court decide as it did? Was Amendment 2 the same as laws prohibiting polygamy, as Scalia suggests? Is the protection of "traditional sexual mores," endorsed by Scalia, an appropriate governmental goal?

The federal courts have not regarded homosexuals as a protected class. On the other hand, many states and municipalities have passed anti-discrimination laws that cover sexual orientation. For example, by 1999, eleven states and the District of Columbia had legislation prohibiting employment discrimination based on sexual orientation, and eighteen states and the District of Columbia prohibited discrimination based on sexual orientation in public employment specifically. By 1999, over half of the Fortune 500 companies included sexual orientation in their anti-discrimination policies, and anti-discrimination policies in universities had become commonplace. Alexander, *supra* at 271. Is the passage of anti-discrimination laws regarding homosexuals proof that they are discriminated against? If the claim made by CFV about homosexuals' material success is accurate, is that proof that they are not being discriminated against?

4.   Homosexuality and the Supreme Court. The success of gays and lesbians before the Supreme Court has been mixed post-*Romer*. In *Lawrence v. Texas, supra* chapter 8, the court struck down laws which outlawed homosexual sex. But in *Boy Scouts of America v. Dale*, 530 U.S. 640 (2000), the Supreme Court allowed private discrimination against homosexuals by ruling that a New Jersey anti-discrimination law violated the Boy Scouts' First Amendment expressive association right to exclude homosexuals from membership.

Same-sex marriage abruptly moved to the foreground of gay and lesbian legal rights in 2003. As Phyllis Bossin recounts:

> The most dramatic legal development in the United States in 2003 was the Massachusetts Supreme Court's decision in *Goodridge v. Department of Public Health* [798 N.E.2d 941, *supra* at chapter 8.] It was without question the shot heard around the world, or at least around the United States. The decision became a call to arms for conservatives to press for a federal constitutional amendment. Although the decision was based upon the Massachusetts, not the United States, Constitution, concern about the spread of legalized same-sex marriage was profound. Numerous amicus briefs were filed by groups presenting legal, religious, and mental health perspectives. The court had amassed before it a wealth of information related to all possible aspects of this highly controversial issue. It is clear from a reading of the opinion that the court weighed all of the information before it, and also considered much of the dicta of *Lawrence*, in rendering its opinion. The court distinguished the Massachusetts Constitution from the federal Constitution, noting that: "The Massachusetts Constitution is, if anything, more protective of individual liberty and equality than the Federal Constitution; it may demand broader protection for fundamental rights; and it is less tolerant of government intrusion into the protected sphere of private life."
>
> The court divided the question before it—whether the marriage restriction violated the Massachusetts Constitution—into two queries: whether the restriction was a denial of equal protection and whether the restriction violated due process of law. It pointed out, however, that in matters of marriage and children, the two concepts overlap. The court recognized the substantial benefits enjoyed by those in marriages and pointed out that: "Because it fulfils yearnings for security, safe haven, and connection that express our common humanity, civil marriage is an esteemed institution, and the decision whether and whom to marry is among life's momentous acts of self-definition." The court then discussed some of the benefits attached to marriage that are not available to unmarried persons, concluding that: "It is undoubtedly for these concrete reasons, as well as for its intimately personal significance, that civil marriage has long been termed a 'civil right.'"
>
> Significantly, the court analogized the prohibition on same-sex marriage to the earlier prohibition on interracial marriage, stating:
>
>> As both *Perez* and *Loving* make clear, the right to marry means little if it does not include the right to marry the person of one's choice, subject to appropriate government restrictions in the interests of public health, safety and wel-

fare. In this case, as in *Perez* and *Loving*, a statute deprives individuals of access to an institution of fundamental legal, personal, and social significance—the institution of marriage—because of a single trait: skin color in *Perez* and *Loving*, sexual orientation here. As it did in *Perez* and *Loving*, history must yield to a more fully developed understanding of the invidious quality of the discrimination.

After analyzing the safeguards of the Massachusetts Constitution to protect liberty and equality, the court found that: "The liberty interest in choosing whether and whom to marry would be hollow if the Commonwealth could, without sufficient justification, foreclose an individual from freely choosing the person with whom to share an exclusive commitment in the unique institution of civil marriage." The court went on to find that the marriage ban could not meet the rational basis test under either due process or equal protection analysis. * * *

The court stayed its order for 180 days to permit the legislature to enact legislation consistent with its decision. Subsequently, the legislature requested an advisory opinion from the court as to whether the enactment of a civil union law would comply with the court's order. The court unequivocally found that it would not. The court found that the proposed legislation suffered from an inherent defect, specifically, that it continued to define "marriage" as between one man and one woman and attempted to create an institution that is parallel but not the same as marriage. The court stated emphatically that "the history of our nation has demonstrated that separate is seldom, if ever, equal." Therefore, the court ordered that only full marriage rights for same-sex couples would pass constitutional muster.

Although the *Goodridge* decision made abundantly clear that the Massachusetts Constitution affords greater protections than does the United States Constitution and further acknowledged that its decision can and should go no further than the state's own borders, the national reaction to the decision was nothing short of mass hysteria. Afraid that homosexual marriage would be imposed throughout the land, Congress and many states urged the passage of constitutional amendments forever banning same-sex marriage.

Phyllis G. Bossin, *Same–Sex Unions: the New Civil Rights Struggle or an Assault on Traditional Marriage?*, 40 TUL. L. REV. 381 (2005).

5. Proposal to create private enforcement of antidiscrimination employment policies against gays through intellectual property law. Legal scholars Ian Ayres and Jennifer Gerarda Brown have proposed an interesting new corrective opinion to expand the range of possible remedies in the struggle against employment discrimination against homosexuals. Ayres and Brown have created a certification mark, a registered trademark. The trademark is **FE** in a circle. The symbol is called the "Fair Employment" mark. Registration with the Patent Office gives the trademark holder the right to enforce the terms of the mark. The non-discrimination policy is provided by Ayres and Brown on an online licensing site that states a detailed non-discrimination policy. Any employer who adopts this mark becomes liable to individual lawsuits from employees who believe they have suffered discrimination because of their sexual orientation. Although the conventional method for enforcing such licenses is for the holder of the intellectual property interest to police and initiate a lawsuit, this mark was created to extend "express third party beneficiary" status to any employee of a covered employer.

Why would any employer ever adopt this mark? If you were the lawyer for an employer with a good record of non-discrimination against homosexuals what advice would you give your client about whether or not to opt into the FE. What would be the relationship of this private remedy to any future federal employment discrimination law? What might the risk calculus for an employer look like? Are employers who are now free to discriminate, including religious institutional employers, likely to adopt this mark? Would this work for race discrimination? As a matter of legal policy is privatizing antidiscrimination law a sound idea? Ian Ayres & Jennifer Gerarda Brown, "Privatizing Gay Rights with Nondiscrimination Promises Instead of Policies," *The Economists' Voice*: Vol. 2: No. 2, Article 11 (2006) *available at* http://www.bepress.com/ev/vol2/iss2/art11.

D.   REPARATIONS

The idea that the federal government owed former slaves material compensation for the economic, social, and psychological injuries of the "peculiar institution of slavery," gained currency with the end of the Civil War. On January 16, 1865, General Sherman's Special Field Order No. 15 granted to former slaves, who were the heads of households, 40 acres of land formerly belonging to land-owning whites in the low lands of South Carolina, and a mule to plow the land. ERIC FONER, RECONSTRUCTION: AMERICAN'S UNFINISHED REVOLUTIONS, 1863–1877 (1988). From this order, soon vetoed by President Johnson, grew the phrase, Forty Acres and a Mule, now emblematic of all forms of reparations for slavery. Through the years, virtually every black liberation movement, from Marcus Garvey to Martin Luther King, called upon the obligation of the federal government to provide redress to the descendents of former slaves.

The twenty-first century has witnessed a revival of earlier calls for reparations in the form of litigation seeking legal compensation for slavery. The defendants have ranged from insurance companies, to elite universities with proven ties to the profit from slavery. The contemporary reparations movement raises complex questions of legal standing, statutes of limitations, the problems of calculating damages, and identifying suitable plaintiffs.

Legal scholar, Roy Brooks takes up many of these questions in his book, *Atonement and Forgiveness: A New Model for Black Reparations*. In the passages that follow, Brooks advances his core conception of the atonement rationale for reparations.

Atonement and Forgiveness: A New Model for Black Reparations

University of California Press, (2004) pages 155–63.

■ Roy L. Brooks

THE ANATOMY OF REPARATIONS

Essence of Reparations

Once the perpetrator of an atrocity has apologized, it now has the burden of making its precious words believable. It must solidify its apology. In other words, the perpetrator of an atrocity cannot expiate the sin it has committed against an innocent people until it has undertaken a great and heroic task of redemption. That task of redemption is a reparation. The second element of the atonement model, a reparation can thus be defined as *the revelation and realization of apology.* It is the act that transforms the rhetoric of apology into a meaningful, material reality. Simply saying "I'm sorry" is never enough when righting an atrocity.

A reparation is by nature asymmetrical. Only victims of the atrocity are eligible to receive a reparation. A scholarship program for African Americans as a form of redress for slavery is a reparation. But a scholarship program for "minority and women students" even when presented as a form of redress for slavery is no more a reparation than are Holocaust payments to American gentiles, including blacks. It is important to understand, however, that asymmetrical civil rights policies-reparations-are not intended to displace ongoing civil rights enforcement or other social reforms. On this point, I wholeheartedly agree with Elazar Barkan. I would add that symmetrical human rights measures, such as traditional U.S. civil rights legislation, are designed to be equally accessible to all victims of discrimination. Employment discrimination laws, for example, are open to blacks, other persons of color, women, and whites. Although there may be some duplication, symmetrical and asymmetrical human rights measures are not mutually exclusive. Japanese Americans who have received reparations from the federal government were not excluded from traditional civil rights laws or even precluded from participating in social welfare programs. That is how it should be. Symmetrical and asymmetrical human rights measures serve different purposes.

Forms of Reparations

Reparations can come in many forms. They need not be directed toward the victims personally nor involve cash payments. Indeed, when one looks

> at the ways in which governments have responded to atrocities committed under their authority, a pattern begins to emerge. A basic

distinction is made between what can be called *compensatory* and *rehabilitative* reparations. Compensatory reparations are directed toward the individual victim or the victim's family. They are intended to be compensatory, but only in a symbolic sense; for nothing can undo the past or truly return the victim to the status quo ante. In contrast, rehabilitative reparations are directed toward the victim's group, or community. They are designed to benefit the victim's group, to nurture the group's self-empowerment and, thus, aid in the nation's social and cultural transformation.

Whether compensatory or rehabilitative, reparations can come in monetary or nonmonetary forms. Unrestricted cash payments or restricted cash payments (such as scholarship funds) given directly to the victims or their immediate families are monetary compensatory reparations. In contrast, unrestricted cash payments or restricted cash payments to the victim's group (such as, scholarship funds or an atonement trust fund that provides an estate for educational purposes or venture capital to eligible members of the victim's group) are examples of monetary rehabilitative reparation. Although nonmonetary reparations can be compensatory, such as a statute commemorating a family member, they are more likely to be rehabilitative. Affirmative action for the victim's group and a museum memorializing the slaves and educating the public about slavery's contribution to our nation are all examples of nonmonetary rehabilitative reparations.

The perpetrator of an atrocity ultimately has the responsibility of coming forward with an appropriate form of reparations. In so doing, the perpetrator must give due respect to the victims' needs or desires. This, of course, is a moral responsibility, part of the perpetrator's atonement. What follows are suggestions concerning the types of reparations that may be appropriate for slave redress. My intention is to be illustrative rather than comprehensive, yet to provide enough details so that we have a pretty good idea as to the direction in which the government ought to be moving.

Solidifying the Apology for Slavery and Jim Crow

There are no dearth of ways in which our government could make its apology for slavery and Jim Crow believable. Compensatory reparations in the form of government checks to slave descendants, usually broached in the context of the tort model, have received the most attention in the national debate. In my view, compensatory reparations are inappropriate for slave redress. Rehabilitative reparations are far more appropriate, for two reasons. First, they are structurally designed to reach a greater number of victims. As such, they are likely to be both more effective than compensatory reparations in solidifying the apology for slavery and Jim Crow and more helpful in fostering racial reconciliation. Second, rehabilitation reparations are narrowly tailored to the harms visited upon slaves and slave descendants. Slavery and Jim Crow operated at the group level— blacks were persecuted, not because of who they were individually, but because of who they were collectively. Rehabilitative reparations proceed at this level of generality; they speak more to the group than to the individual.

The two rehabilitative reparations I favor most are a museum of slavery and an atonement trust fund. The former would be a memorial to the slaves, and the latter would be a governmental response to some of the capital deficiencies today's blacks have inherited from their ancestors. As will become clear in a moment, the museum of slavery envisioned here is very different in structure and purpose from the "National Museum of African American History and Culture" President Bush signed into law in 2003. . . .

Slavery museums modeled on the Holocaust Museum in Washington, D.C., and the Simon Wiesenthal Center Museum of Tolerance in Los Angeles should be built in Washington, D.C.; and every state capital to commemorate the contributions slaves made to our country and educate Americans about them, as well as about the lingering effects slavery has on blacks today. These objectives can be realized through high-tech, interactive experiences. Visitors will be led back in time to witness the horrors of racial slavery, from capture in Africa, to the middle passage, and, finally, to the peculiar institution. Men, women, and children will be able to walk through a recreated slave ship in which hundreds of blacks were packed together for weeks like sardines in incredibly tight spaces as the ship made its way from West Africa to the American colonies (and later to the United States). Visitors will also be able to listen to recordings of slave narratives spoken by the slaves themselves. This experience should give the visitor a close-up view of life on the plantation, including the mind-numbing drudgery of working in the fields under the hot sun from sunup to sundown and the dehumanizing conditions of the slave quarters.

Reenactments of the debates on slavery at the Constitutional Convention in 1787 and in Congress on the eve of southern succession can be presented in a "Point of View Diner" that serves a menu of slave-related topics on video jukeboxes. Was the North's creation of a union with the South a necessary evil or merely a convenience? Was that union ultimately good for the slaves? Did Union soldiers fight to end slavery or to save the Union? Did Confederate soldiers fight to keep slavery or for states' rights? What contributions have slaves made to our nation? How are blacks disadvantaged by slavery? What is racism? Visitors will listen to the debates on these and similar topics, and then input their opinions as to which side of the debate won. After instant tabulation of the results, the visitors might be surprised to learn how little our opinions may have changed over time.

Some might argue that a museum of slavery would be a racially divisive reparation, because it would dwell on the darkest hour in our nation's past. But I believe it would have just the opposite effect. Like the fabulous 1970s TV series *Roots*—at the time, the most watched event in TV history—the museum of slavery will pull a racially divided nation together through a mixture of awareness, understanding, and, in some cases, empathy. The museum of slavery will, in fact, teach many valuable lessons. Among these are:

- Slavery was more than just another everyday tragedy. Millions of innocent lives were sacrificed and families were broken up for personal profit and the socioeconomic development of our country. Human beings were denied liberty at its worst so that other human beings could enjoy liberty at its fullest. We must take into our hearts and minds those who perished at the hands of our country. They were great Americans.

- We need to learn and remember, because none of us was there to see slavery, and because many Americans continue to suffer from the lingering effects of slavery-the psychology and socioeconomics of slavery.

- There is a line drawn in time between those who view human life, liberty, and well-being as expendable in pursuit of personal gain, and those who believe in the dignity of all human beings. We must always look down from time to time to see on which side of the line we stand.

- We must rededicate ourselves to the cause of freedom, tolerance, and human dignity, even when the tide of public opinion flows against us. These are the values that make our nation exceptional. These are the values worth fighting for.

- The emancipation of black slaves redefined our ideas of democracy and freedom. It made America a better nation, truer to her ideals. In this sense, emancipation and slavery transcended skin color.

- By remembering the nation's resolve to end slavery, we gain a positive racial perspective that enables us to move forward with probity and intelligence on racial matters. This racial outlook reminds us that we are on a mission of racial justice, that we must come together to complete this mission, that this is our history's call, which we must answer.

The museum of slavery, in short, will be a national symbol that gives voice to the millions of nameless slaves who made possible the aspirations of others. For the vast majority of Americans, the museum will challenge their thinking about slavery and, it may be hoped, transform them. Certainly, the construction of the museum will cost taxpayers money. But if it was worth constructing memorials to mourn the death of the some 3,000 innocent people who perished in the World Trade Center, the Pentagon, and on a field near Shanksville, Pennsylvania, at the hands of terrorists, then it is surely worth constructing a tribute to the millions of slaves who died in forced service to this country.

My second proposal is the atonement trust fund. As envisioned here, the federal government would finance, and reputable trust administrators selected by prominent black Americans would administer, a trust fund for every newborn black American child born within a certain period of time-five, ten, or more years. The Supreme Court seems to view racial progress in increments of twenty-five years, a generation, but the eligibility period can certainly be negotiated. The purpose of the trust fund is to provide a core group of blacks with one of the most important resources slavery and Jim Crow have denied them—financial capital, family resources, or an estate, handed down from generation to generation. Subject to the restrictions mentioned in a moment, each black child within this group would receive the proceeds from the trust fund annually or upon reaching a certain age. He or she would then have the financial wherewithal to take a meaningful step toward a successful future, including enrolling in and graduating from college. The atonement estate would also be ear-marked for elementary and secondary education, allowing parents to take their children out of inferior public schools.

Before sketching the contours of the atonement trust fund, I should like to take a moment to explain why this particular reparation applies only to slave descendants and not to other racial minorities, who, nonetheless, would continue to receive symmetrical social benefits. Slavery created and Jim Crow sustained a racial hierarchy based on color. Under this system of racial favoritism, presumptions of beauty and intelligence and other manifestations of group privilege are determined in large part by the group's proximity to the European (or white) phenotype. Asians, Latinos, or other racial groups whose phenotype is closer to the European model than that of blacks experience less disadvantage than blacks, although more than whites, *owing to slavery and Jim Crow.* This is true even among blacks. For example, in American society, black women who are admired for their beauty—such as Halle Berry, Tyra Banks, and Vanessa Williams—have predominantly European rather than Negroid features. One could argue, however, that because nonblack minorities experience at least some disadvantage from the lingering effects of slavery and Jim Crow—which is to say, the "black-white paradigm," or "black-white binary," which sees the color line only in black and white, is invalid—the atonement trust fund, which after all is designed to redress the lingering effects of slavery, should be made available to all racial minorities. But to do this, we would have to determine the relative degree of disadvantage each racial group actually sustains because of slavery and Jim Crow. We would have to determine, for example, what percentage of the social problems Latinos experience are fueled by the continuous flow of poor and unskilled immigrants into Latino communities, or how much harm slavery and Jim Crow visits on Asians who continue to experience housing discrimination yet have higher incomes and educational levels than even whites. This exercise would simply run the idea of reparations into the ground—it would make a mockery of an otherwise laudable principle. For that reason, a line has to be drawn somewhere.

I draw the line at blacks for several reasons. First, blacks were the *main target* of slavery and Jim Crow. No other American group inhabited the peculiar institution. No other American group sustained more casualties or lengthier suffering from slavery and Jim Crow. No other American group harbors as much ill will against the federal government for slavery and Jim Crow. Second, this gives blacks a connection to slavery and Jim

Crow—both familial and psychological—that no other racial minority has. There is a collective memory here that only blacks have, and a collective emotional need that only the government can satisfy. Third, unlike Asians and Latinos, blacks did not volunteer for this tour of duty. Blacks were kidnapped from their homeland and brought to this country by brutal force, the likes of which we have not seen before or since in American history. In short, although blacks, Asians, Latinos, Native Americans, Indians, and other people of color are victims of what Joe Feagin calls "systemic racism" (or the "white-created" paradigm of racial subordination), they do not experience and hence do not react to racial subordination in exactly the same way. Each experiences a different pattern, or syndrome, of white oppression, which sometimes overlaps, and each reacts differently, from despair to disregard, from levels of resistance to total acceptance. White-on-black oppression is just different from other white-oppression syndromes, whether racial or gender. "As Patricia Rodriguez has observed, 'White means mostly privilege and black means overcoming obstacles, a history of civil rights. As a Latina, I can't try to claim one of these.'" Black Americans carry the weight of the atrocities—slavery and Jim Crow—for which atonement is being sought. But, again, all racial minorities, including blacks, should continue to receive the protection of symmetrical social measures, including the civil rights laws.

Although the atonement trust fund would apply primarily to blacks, several restrictions would be imposed on the management, transfer, and use of trust funds. Each trust fund would have a life of twenty-five years (the amount of time it would take each child to get through college or many graduate or professional schools) and be maintained by the federal government. A board of commissioners, consisting of reputable citizens selected by blacks, would oversee fund operations in their respective regions of the country. Commissioners and their staff would, for example, help fund recipients make the right choices in schools and business opportunities. All payments from the trust fund would be by electronic transfer. Recipients would never really see or handle the funds.

Money accumulated in the atonement trust fund would only be spent for education or to start or invest in a business. Good primary and secondary education, graduation from a prestigious college or university, and small businesses are important ingredients in building family resources and sustaining their accumulation from one generation to the next. The trust fund would provide resources to help black children escape poor-performing public schools, alleviate the financial burden that causes many black students to leave college before graduating, and finance business opportunities for blacks who do not go to college. Venture capital funds would not, however, be made available until the recipient's twenty-fifth birthday (or later). An eighteen-year-old simply lacks the maturity to know his or her aspirations or to make sound investment decisions. For that reason, vocational education and mandatory consultations with a managerial advisory board, consisting of retired business persons selected by the board of commissioners, would be additional requirements for the receipt of venture capital. Finally, wealthy black families would be excluded from the program. Because wealth is relative—$100,000 in Tupelo, Mississippi, is not the same as $100,000 in New York City—the income level would be set regionally by the board of commissioners.

The amount of money each black recipient should receive for education or business investment could be determined in numerous ways. One way is to base it on projected educational costs. A broader approach is offered by Boris I. Bittker, whose calculation operates upon the relevant assumption that the purpose of monetary relief is to close the considerable net family wealth gap between blacks and whites, discussed in chapter 3. Bittker takes the difference between the average earnings between whites and blacks (let us call this value EG, for earnings gap) and multiplies EG by the number of black Americans (BA) to arrive at the amount of money blacks as a group should receive. This sum (the reparations amount, or RA) is determined annually, and is the amount Congress funds each year until the net family wealth gap is closed. Bittker does not say how long it would take to close the net family wealth gap. I would suggest that the funding period be consistent with the life of the atonement trust fund-twenty-five years for each beneficiary. Bittker's formula, then, is roughly, $EG \times BA = RA$.

Another approach, offered by a former student of mine, the attorney Darrell L. Pugh, takes the racial income gap figure (EG) and capitalizes it to determine the present value of the investment required to realize the income necessary to close the gap. "For example, assume an average income gap of $5,000 a year and an average market rate of return of zero per-cent. Under the capitalization approach, it would take $50,000 of investment capital per eligible worker to close the gap– $5,000/.10 = $50,000$. This figure could then be multiplied by the number of African Americans available in the adult workforce." Pugh's approach would permit funding to be phased in over time, "not only to encourage capacity building but to make the political feasibility of funding more likely."

Bittker and Pugh demonstrate that it is quite possible to calculate a monetary amount to be paid to slave descendants either per capita or through some program of eligibility like the atonement trust fund. Indeed, calculating the value of human life is rather routine in our society. Government agencies, juries, and insurance companies do it everyday. It is also important to note, as one thinks about the reparations calculations, that these calculations are always subject to second guessing. For example, when the Environmental Protection Agency did a cost-benefit analysis of a clean-air proposal that valued the life of a person over seventy years old at $1.4 million less than the life of a younger person-the so-called "senior death discount"—it was criticized by economists on several grounds, including that the calculation was faulty.

I offer the museum of slavery and atonement trust fund as forms of redress for slavery and Jim Crow, not as substitutes for ongoing civil rights reforms. The U.S. government still has an obligation to do what governments are supposed to do—protect its citizens from invidious discrimination. The museum of slavery and atonement trust fund should be viewed as special addenda to the struggle for racial justice in the United States. When viewed in juxtaposition to the milestones of this struggle—the abolition of slavery and Jim Crow—the museum of slavery and the atonement trust fund present easy burdens for our government. The hard question is whether white self-interest or perception of the public good will, once again, impede racial justice.

E.   REDRESS IN THE GLOBAL POLITICAL ECONOMY

What Role for Humanitarian Intellectual Property? The Globalization of Intellectual Property Rights

6 MINN.J.L.SCI. & TECH. 191 (2004).

■ SUSAN K. SELL

* * *

The 1995 Agreement on Trade–Related Aspects of Intellectual Property Rights (TRIPS), administered by the World Trade Organization (WTO), is the most important international law governing intellectual property rights. TRIPS extends patent rights to a wide variety of agricultural biotechnology innovations, including pharmaceutical products, pesticides, and plant varieties. It establishes a twenty-year patent term for these innovations. TRIPS requires states to provide adequate and effective enforcement mechanisms both internally and at their borders. The price of information and technology is increased under TRIPS because monopoly privileges are extended to patent-holders and TRIPS makes WTO dispute settlement procedures available to patent holders claiming violation of intellectually property rights. If a complaining government is successful in its claim, the WTO can authorize trade sanctions against the violating state. These settlement procedures and powers to punish make TRIPS a real force in the world.

Intellectual property rights reflect an inherent tension between the strong desire to promote and reward creative energy and the desire to make the fruits of that creativity available to the public. The granting of exclusive rights must be balanced against the economic effects of higher product and transaction costs and the potential "exclusion from the market of competitors who may be able to imitate or adapt the invention in such a way that social value is increased." Thus, the question is whether intellectual property rights should be treated as "a public goods problem for which the remedy is commodification, or a monopoly of information problem for which the remedy is unfettered competition[?]"

Strong intellectual property protection is justified by a market approach, because such protection provides incentives to "increase the number of commercially available products and thereby serve the public interest." However, it is important to question which public interests these rights serve. In the context of agricultural biotechnology, stakeholders include private sector seed companies, public corporations, research institutions, and resource-poor farmers. Intellectual property rights holders benefit from exclusive control of their innovations, as do those who have the resources to gain access to these innovations via the commercial market. Yet market-based solutions have failed to serve marginalized populations, such as the millions of people afflicted with HIV/AIDS and smallholder subsistence farmers in developing countries. The fact that smallholder farmers account for seventy-five percent of the world's undernourished population is evidence of this failure. In contemporary life science industries, market mechanisms fail to deliver innovation into the public domain. Indeed, "[i]nternational markets for technologies are inherently subject to failure due to distortions attributable to concerns about appropriability, problems of valuing information by buyers and sellers, and market power, all strong justifications for public intervention at both the domestic and global levels." There is a great need to strike a balance between a patentholder's exclusive rights and the provision of agricultural technology to marginalized populations throughout the world. Solutions that will maximize the benefit of protecting innovation and yet minimize the risk of harm created by the potential overextension of this protection must be explored. It is therefore essential that policymakers consider "humanitarian" policies that promote social goals, such as protecting public health and alleviating malnutrition.

* * *

The contemporary global intellectual property regime is embedded in a broad structural context characterized by asymmetrical power relationships. Over the past thirty years, the globalization of financial markets and the shift towards an unfettered faith in laissez faire markets ideology pursued by the Reagan and Thatcher administrations has resulted in an increase in corporate transnational power vis-à-vis the state. States, seeking to be globally competitive, have liberalized markets, engaged in deregulation and privatization, and implemented new regulatory structures designed to promote efficiency and enforce market-friendly behavior. According to Philip Cerny, "[t]he institutions and practices of the state itself are increasingly marketized or 'commodified,' and the state becomes the spearhead of structural transformation to international market norms both at home and abroad." States have increasingly privatized once-public services, such as prisons, hospitals, military support services and even "mission-critical" functions, such as providing protection for the head of the 2003 Coalition Provisional Authority in Iraq, L. Paul Bremer III. The expansion of intellectual property rights and the privatization of federally funded research under the Bayh–Dole Act must be seen as an instance of this larger trend.

These broad economic changes have profoundly affected developing countries. Earlier models of economic development such as import-substituting industrialization, popular in Latin America and India, were discredited by economic stagnation and the debt crises of the 1970s–1980s. Meanwhile, the success of the East Asian "Tigers" vindicated export-led development and integration into global markets. Many developing countries subsequently reversed decades-old policies of economic nationalism in favor of market liberalization and privatization and consequently slashed public budgets. Governments in developing countries began to compete to attract foreign investment and eased former restrictions of foreign investors' activities. The new push toward export-led growth meant that developing countries needed access to industrialized country markets. The dependence of developing nations on trade gave the United States considerable economic leverage. Those developing countries sought access to the expansive United States market. Using the U.S. Trade Act of 1974, the Office of the United States Trade Representative, at the behest of high-technology firms, threatened trade sanctions against developing countries unless they adopted and enforced highly protective intellectual property policies. Such economic coercion was an important factor behind developing countries' ultimate acceptance of TRIPS.

This liberalizing agenda favors "finance capital and other mobile factors of production." Transnational firms in knowledge-intensive sectors such as pharmaceuticals, chemicals, software, and entertainment "have the resources, motivations and capabilities to roam the world searching for the kind of opportunities that promise lucrative rewards." These privileged sectors participate in "globalized" markets insofar as "there are a small number of participants who know one another and operate across countries with a common conception of control." TRIPS reflects the wishes of these privileged sectors and globalizes their preferred conception of control by establishing a high level of protection.

Beyond extending property rights, competitiveness concerns moved the United States to relax its antitrust policies. The Reagan administration codified this approach in the Antitrust Division's Merger Control Guidelines of 1982. Reflecting the influence of the Chicago School of Economics, the new guidelines abandoned the populist focus on market structure in favor of the Chicago school's focus on price theory. "In this view, only business practices that reduce output and increase prices are anti-competitive; business practices that expand output are pro-competitive." In contrast to earlier approaches, according to the Chicago school, "[h]igh levels of market concentration and the exercise of market power may be indicative of efficiencies." The 1982 guidelines presented an expanded definition of relevant markets. The guidelines allowed the introduction of non-structural factors, such as foreign competition or the possession of new technology that was important to long-term competitiveness. The Justice Department argued that "anti-trust laws should not be applied in a way that hinders the renewed emphasis on . . . competitiveness."

This new thinking removed most intellectual property licensing from antitrust scrutiny. As Thomas Hayslett points out, under Reagan's administration, "executive agencies viewed the economic incentives provided by intellectual property rights as legitimate means of extracting the full economic benefit from innovation." In effect then, "[i]ntellectual property rights acted as a 'magic trump card' allowing many previously suspect arrangements to proceed without challenge from the [Federal Trade Commission] or [Department of Justice]." Keith Maskus and Jerome Reichman suggest that today:

> There are virtually no products sold on the general products market that do not come freighted with a bewildering and overlapping array of exclusive property rights that discourage follow-on applications of routine technical know-how. Weak enforcement of antitrust laws then further reinforces the barriers to entry erected upon this thicket of rights, while the need to stimulate and coordinate investment in complex innovation projects justifies patent pools, concentrations of research efforts, and predatory practices formerly thought to constitute misuses of the patent monopoly.

So-called patent "thickets" have proliferated, in which overlapping patent rights require those seeking to commercialize new technology to obtain licenses from multiple patent holders. "A growing thicket of rights surrounds gene fragments, research tools, and other upstream inputs of scientific research, and the resulting transaction costs impede and delay research and development undertaken in both the public and private sectors."

III. ISSUES IN AGRICULTURE

What are the implications of the foregoing for agriculture? "Increasingly ... [intellectual property] rights have invaded the research commons itself and made it both costly and difficult to obtain cutting-edge technologies needed for public health, agricultural production, environmental protection, and the provision of other public goods." Critics of the increasing commodification of what was once treated as the public domain have raised at least six issues of concern: (1) threats to traditional agriculture and food security; (2) abuses of monopoly power; (3) increased dependence on costly commercial agriculture; (4) threats to biodiversity; (5) "biopiracy;" and (6) questions of benefit sharing. The discussion in this article focuses on the first three issues of concern.

Technological, judicial, and legislative changes together have produced a radical shift from public to private provision of seeds. As Professor Keith Aoki points out, "[t]he private seed market for grains was almost nonexistent at the beginning of the twentieth century, due to free government seed distribution and the widespread practice of farmer seed saving." According to Professor Aoki, "the intersection of biotechnical knowledge and methods and expanded legal protections for plant breeders transforms seed germplasm into a paradigm commodity." Legislative changes, including the United States Plant Variety Protection Act of 1970, "increased expectations of seed industry profits and thereby helped to stimulate an upsurge in mergers and acquisitions...." Life sciences corporations "emerged out of a wave of mergers, acquisitions, joint ventures and strategic partnerships involving companies in a wide range of fields such as chemicals, seeds, processed foods, dietary supplements and pharmaceuticals.'' Advances in biotechnology spurred the consolidation process throughout the 1970s and particularly in the 1980s. The 1973 development of the recombinant DNA technique, ''which enabled foreign genes to be inserted into microorganisms,'' helped launch the era of commercial biotechnology. Notably, although ''the Cohen–Boyer method for combining DNA from different organisms'' was patented, ''the patents were licensed nonexclusively and cheaply to encourage firms to take licenses rather than to challenge the patents.'' This technology had been federally funded, and ''[m]any observers attribute the rapid progress of the biotechnology industry to the fact that this technology was made widely available rather than licensed exclusively to a single firm.'' In 1980, the U.S. Supreme Court ruled in Diamond v. Chakrabarty that a man-made, oil-eating bacterium could be patented. This case led to the expansion of rights to own living organisms and injected greater certainty into the development of commercial biotechnology. The ability to acquire patents on altered life forms helped biotechnology startup companies to raise venture capital.

The combination of expanded intellectual property rights and relaxed antitrust enforcement has led to marked economic concentration in the life sciences industries. The ''vertical integration'' of plant breeding, agrochemical, and food processing corporations has led to a situation in which the top ten seed companies control thirty percent of the world's $23 billion commercial seed market. Corporate plant breeders are obtaining broad patents that will have ''far reaching'' consequences. ''Breeders are patenting entire species (cotton), economic characteristics (oil quality), plant reproductive behaviour (apomixes), and basic techniques in biotechnology (gene transfer tools).'' Six major industrial groups now control most of the technology '' 'which gives freedom to undertake commercial research and development in the area of [genetically modified] crops.' These are (i) Agrevo and Plant Genetic Systems (PGS); (ii) Du Pont and Pioneer; (iii) ELM, DNAP, Asgrow and Seminis; (iv) Monsanto, Calgene, DeKalb, Agracetus, PBI, Hybritech and Delta and Pine Land Co.; (v) Novartis; and (vi) Zeneca, Mogen and Avanta.'' Furthermore, six agricultural biotechnology companies alone hold seventy-five percent of all U.S. patents granted to the top thirty patent-holding firms: Monsanto, Du Pont, Syngenta, Dow, Aventis, and Grupo Pulsar. This combination of economic concentration with extensive and broad patenting means that a handful of global corporations are making huge inroads toward control of the world's food supply and are entangling farmers and indigenous peoples in an increasingly complex web of licensing and royalty obligations. As Keith Maskus and Jerome Reichman suggest:

> [T]he natural competitive disadvantages of follower countries may become reinforced by a proliferation of legal monopolies and related entry barriers that result from global minimum [intellectual property] standards. Such external restraints on competition could consign the poorest countries to a quasi-permanent status at the bottom of the technology and growth ladder.

The current system skews research towards rich and middle-income countries' markets and sectors. Most notably, there is a tendency in the public health sector to neglect tropical diseases in favor of focusing on cancer and so-called lifestyle afflictions, requiring drugs to combat obesity, balding, and erectile dysfunction. Consequently, only thirteen of 1,233 new drugs marketed between 1975 and 1997 were approved for tropical diseases in particular. As Professor Hammer suggests, "the rhetoric of strong intellectual property rights leading to innovation that meets social needs rings particularly hollow" for poorer countries most afflicted by tropical diseases. Similarly, there is a focus on the interests of higher-income markets in the agriculture sector, resulting in the development of crops unsuitable for subsistence and smallholder farming and a dearth of research beneficial for less lucrative micro-climates. The disproportionate emphasis on wealthier countries' market needs can be corrected through changes in private-public collaboration and through the allocation of more funding towards "the goal of helping subsistence farmers." Historically, seed companies preferred to develop hybrids because farmers must purchase new hybrid seed every planting season. Since the offspring of hybrid plants do not breed true-to-type, hybrid seeds offer a "form of biological protection." However, for plant varieties that lack this built-in biological protection, plant breeders can appeal to plant breeders' rights. Plant breeders' rights "generally do not encourage breeding related to minor crops with small markets." As a result, the private sector under invests in crops and technologies suitable for smallholder farmers, and these public goods are underprovided.

With the advent of genetic engineering, plant breeders sought to safeguard their investments through strong patent protections. Depending on national law, patents may be available for "the use of the new gene to transform a plant, on the transformation process, and most significantly on the transformed plant itself." The protection of transgenic plants enables genetic engineering firms to have "more confidence in their ability to reap the fruits of their research." That is because transfer or insertion of the patented gene into other plants constitutes patent infringement. Before the adoption of the 1991 Union for the Protection of New Varieties of Plants (UPOV91), plant breeders were forced to choose to protect their plant varieties with either a plant breeders' right or a patent. However, UPOV91 "removed the 1978 [UPOV's] ban on dual protection and now permits member states to protect the same plant variety with both a breeders' right and a patent." Professor Robert Lettington argues that this expansion of intellectual property rights into the agricultural sector has threatened the public sector's traditional focus on the needs of smallholder farmers. First of all, "private sector intellectual property rights may limit public sector access to innovations and germplasm that may be adaptable to smallholder needs and conditions while also limiting public sector research options due to concerns over the unhindered distribution of the products of its research." Second, the "failure of intellectual property systems to preserve the integrity of the public domain, and the consequent development of intellectual property rights strategies in public institutions, risks distorting research priorities to the detriment of smallholder farmers."

In developing countries, a large number of farmers are smallholders who do not participate in the transgenic seed market in any substantial way. Instead, these farmers engage in seed-saving, replanting, and "across-the-fence" exchange. This is particularly the case in many African countries where the public and private sectors play a minimal role in seed production and distribution. The smallholder farming sector plays an important role in contributing to national food needs. For example, such farmers produce "fifty-one percent of Latin America's maize, seventy-seven percent of its beans and sixty-one percent of its potatoes." In Africa, smallholder farmers produce the "majority of grains and legumes and almost all root, tuber and plantain crops." Furthermore, fifty to sixty percent of Peruvians and seventy to eighty percent of Kenyans depend on smallholder agriculture for their livelihood.

According to Professor Lettington, subsistence farmers traditionally save seeds for reuse, trade, and experimentation with new hybrids. Such experimentation contributes to the planet's biodiversity, as evidenced by the farmers in Professor Lettington's study who produced "as many as [thirty or forty] distinct varieties of potato, and [five or ten varieties] of maize, on farms of little more than a hectare." In the past, American laws covering plant varieties incorporated the notion of farmers' rights in which farmers retained their freedom to engage in these important and traditional activities. However, in August 1994 the U.S. Congress amended the Plant Variety Protection Act and removed the farmer's exemption. As a result, "it is now expressly illegal for farmers to sell or save seeds from proprietary crop varieties without receiving permission from breeders and paying royalties." Ironically, according to Professor Aoki, while the U.S. Patent Office in the "early 19th century began to collect and catalogue and make" seed freely available, by the early twenty-first century, the commodification of germplasm had transformed the U.S. patent office, into a "primary means" of attacking the longstanding "practice of farmer seed-saving." Grassroots activists are convinced that American industries are seeking these same results through TRIPS by pushing a particular interpretation of sui generis protection under Article 27.3(b).

Ultimately, TRIPS restricted the patenting of life forms, but Article 27.3(b) requires that members provide intellectual property protection for plant varieties or an "effective sui generis" system. However, there really is no consensus on what a sui generis system needs to include. Additionally, the negotiations leading to the adoption of Article 27 provide little guidance because they provide no record on the meaning of sui generis. American plant breeders have been pushing the UPOV as the model sui generis system. American support of UPOV may be due in part to how generous UPOV is to the corporate plant breeder. Fifty-one countries, many of which are industrialized, have joined the UPOV, which was last amended in 1991. The 1978 version of UPOV provided two limitations on the monopoly rights of plant breeders. First, other breeders could freely use UPOV-protected varieties for research purposes. Second, farmers could reuse the seed for the following year's harvest under certain conditions. The 1991 revision narrowed down the exemption for competing breeders, deleted the so-called farmers' privilege, and extended the breeders' monopoly right to the products of the farmer's harvest. "Although the UPOV system allows on-farm replanting, its rules restrict farmers' freedom to buy seed from sources other than the original breeders." UPOV91 "does not authorize farmers to sell or exchange seeds with other farmers for propagating purposes." To join UPOV today, nations must sign the 1991 treaty. Countries eschewing the UPOV system can adopt sui generis systems of protection that allow "farmers to acquire ... protected seed from any source and/or requiring protected varieties to display qualities that are genuinely superior to existing varieties."

In a comparative study of smallholder farming in Peru and Kenya, Robert J. L. Lettington did not find evidence that plant variety protection (PVP) legislation harmed smallholder agriculture. However, he argued that "the current system of PVP [legislation] is failing to create solutions to existing problems." In particular, PVP legislation has created incentives that direct resources away from subsistence farmers' needs in favor of those of large commercial agricultural enterprises. It also promotes the use of commercial seed as opposed to landraces or "wild" cultivars. "The end result has been a hastening of the deterioration of food security in these areas...." Professor Lettington suggests that governments that seek to limit the cost of seed in economically and climatically marginal areas may "need to place limits on the nature of intellectual property rights."

IV. THE REGULATORY ENVIRONMENT

In examining the regulatory environment in this context, the central question is what degree of discretion states have in limiting intellectual property rights to support smallholder agriculture. There are at least two dimensions to the answer: one addresses the letter of the law, the other addresses the broader context of asymmetrical power. Focusing on the formal features of intellectual property law, texts, and institutions, one sees plenty of room for state discretion and flexibility in adapting the global minimum standards to local concerns. However, this formal universe is embedded in a system of asymmetrical power relationships and global capitalism that constrain weaker states' abilities to exploit the flexibilities crafted into the law.

TRIPS provides substantial flexibility for developing countries. Article 27.3(b) specifies that countries may adopt an "effective sui generis system" to protect plant varieties. Under TRIPS, countries may adopt patent protection for plant varieties, UPOV91, an alternative sui generis system, or some combination of these forms of protection. While corporate plant breeders would prefer that developing countries adopt UPOV91 as their domestic legislative standard, these countries are by no means required to do so. The UPOV treaties are one type of sui generis protection designed to serve the interests of plant breeders. In a searching and thorough analysis of developing countries' options, Professor Laurence Helfer has arrayed the options on a spectrum ranging from maximum discretion to minimal discretion for developing countries to tailor their systems to meet their particular needs. States that adopt TRIPS and ratify or accede to UPOV91 have the least discretion. According to Professor Helfer, states wishing to retain maximum flexibility and discretion to serve the needs of smallholder agriculture would be well-advised to adopt TRIPS only.

The advantages of TRIPS are that its provisions on plant varieties "do not refer to or incorporate any preexisting intellectual property agreements, including the 1978 and 1991 UPOV Acts." TRIPS members are neither required "to become members of UPOV nor to enact national laws consistent with either UPOV Act in order to comply with their obligations under TRIP[S]." Article 27.3(b) preserves "significant leeway for national governments to work out the precise manner in which they will balance protection of IPRs against other international obligations and national objectives." "The chances are, that for a poor nation, neither a UPOV nor a regular patent approach will actually encourage private-sector research. Hence, such a nation is probably best-off adopting minimum compliance with TRIPS. . . ." TRIPS, unlike UPOV91, preserves the right of subsistence farmers to exchange seed. For a nation in which the exchange is an issue, it would be wise to incorporate both subsistence farmer exemptions and research exemptions in national plant breeders' rights legislation. Countries wishing to adopt the stronger UPOV91 system should consider incorporating waivers or exemptions for subsistence and smallholder farmers. In countries lacking significant private sector competition, as is often the case in poor countries, public sector seed provision will be important to promote competition to stimulate both variety and lower prices.

Public-private partnerships in agriculture might stimulate the transfer of technology so that public sector seed providers could adapt technology to subsistence farmers' needs. In order for such arrangements to work, private firms would need to retain opportunities to capture economic benefits in the market sector, while keeping the technology affordable for the subsistence sector. This two-tiered arrangement has some parallels in the control of access to medicines and would require safeguards against diverting subsistence-priced technology into the market sector.

Focusing on TRIPS and the letter of the law, one can conclude, as does Professor Helfer, that:

> States that implement the four core TRIP[S] requirements in good faith—that is, states that grant breeders intellectual property rights and enforcement measures applicable to varieties in all species and botanical genera and that provide those same rights and measures to breeders from other TRIP[S] member states—are unlikely to have their laws challenged successfully.

However, public international law such as TRIPS is embedded in a broader context of asymmetrical power relationships between developed and developing countries, and between producers and consumers of the fruits of biotechnology. This context reduces the amount of leeway that poor states have in devising regulatory approaches most suitable for their individual needs and stages of development. In particular, developing countries increasingly have been subject to bilateral and regional pressure to surrender the flexibilities afforded by TRIPS. Bilateral investment treaties, bilateral intellectual property agreements, and regional free trade agreements concluded between the United States and developing countries and between the European Union and developing countries invariably have been considered to be "TRIPS–Plus."

For example, in the intellectual property provisions covering agriculture in the Central American Free Trade Agreement framework, developing countries are most often required to ratify or accede to UPOV91 as their sui generis system of protection and "to undertake 'all reasonable efforts' to make patent protection available for plants."

Furthermore, developing countries have failed to take full advantage of TRIPS flexibilities not only in the agricultural marketplace, but the pharmaceutical market as well. This is largely because such nations are eager to attract foreign investment and are concerned about alienating potential investors. They also are eager to have access to technologies that may aid in their development, provide reliable nutrition, and which have the potential to address a myriad of pressing social and economic problems. Most of these countries lack significant bargaining leverage and the capacity to resist the high-pressure tactics of the United States Trade Representative and the industries that it represents.

In these circumstances it is imperative that public institutions take the lead in assisting developing countries in the implementation of suitable legislation that conforms to their international legal obligations. Public institutions, such as land grant universities, must also continue to make the fruits of their research available to those who need it most on terms that the recipients accept. The 1980 Bayh–Dole Act allowed "grantees to seek patent rights in government-sponsored research results." The idea behind this was that many inventions with commercial potential lay fallow in university laboratories, and that patenting opportunities would give universities incentives to search research labs for significant and marketable inventions. The Bayh–Dole Act has resulted in at least a ten-fold increase of university patenting activity since 1979. This flurry of patenting activity has had the beneficial effect of generating revenue for cash-strapped public universities. For instance, the patent infringement award that the University of Minnesota won for the development of the drug Ziagen has provided much-needed funding for research and graduate student support. University patent portfolios also help to attract private sector funding, especially in biotechnology.

However, the Bayh–Dole Act also has created new divisions within universities. As Professors Arti Rai and Rebecca Eisenberg point out, the legislation makes no distinction between upstream and downstream research, and as a result, an increasing number of research tools have become patent-protected. An unintended consequence of the Bayh–Dole Act has been the dramatic reduction of open access to research tools. Technology transfer offices are charged with patenting and licensing technology to generate revenue for the institution. Research scientists are more interested in having access to "open science." The Bayh–Dole Act also has increased university collaboration with private sector biotechnology firms, raising many questions about academic freedom, research priorities, and incentives. Some critics have gone so far as to assert that universities have lost their sense of "public mission."

Yet the choices may not be so stark, and there may be ways to navigate the contours of the current system to better balance competing imperatives. For example, in the pharmaceutical sector, there could be clauses in agreements to allow a university to sublicense to generic manufacturers if its patent conflicts with efforts to distribute affordable drugs for HIV/AIDS victims in sub-Saharan Africa. Professors Rai and Eisenberg offer a similarly modest and sensible suggestion for publicly-funded research. They suggest that "decisions about the dividing line between the public domain and private property should be made by institutions that are in a position to appreciate the tensions between widespread access and preservation of commercial incentives without being unduly swayed by institutional interests that diverge from the overall public interest." In other words, they argue that public funding agencies should decide what fruits of their investments to patent. They also advocate addressing the upstream/downstream research tool issue by devising "a system that distinguishes cases in which proprietary claims make sense from cases in which they do not." Research tool exemptions would be useful to help to preserve the domain of "open science."

V. CONCLUSION

This brief overview of some major issues involved in intellectual property protection and agricultural biotechnology underscores the fact that "the institution of property is extremely complex, and more importantly, political." Yet we are no closer to resolving these controversies. "More often than not, rather than being an answer, the issue of property rights is only the beginning of a long series of vexing questions." Developing countries should do what they can to preserve their autonomy in adopting intellectual property policies that suit their levels of development. They should resist TRIPS-plus initiatives in bilateral and regional trade and investment agreements and insist upon TRIPS as their maximum standard. Developing nations should seek technical assistance that encourages them to use existing TRIPS flexibilities. They also need to participate in global standard-setting exercises concerning competition policy and address the ways in which they would prefer to regulate foreign firms' acquisition of local firms.

Promoting genuine competition is an important policy objective. "Nations in which there is limited private sector competition in the seed industry should ensure that public sector varieties are available in competition with private sector ones." Professor Lettington recommends:

The activities of smallholder farmers, in particular the saving, use, exchange, and sale of farm-saved seed, should be explicitly stated as not subject to the rights of intellectual property rights holders. In accordance with the purposes and objectives of TRIPS, effort should be made to develop effective incentives for research targeted at smallholder farmers . . . . Limited exceptions to intellectual property rights should be permitted to promote the adaptation of protected products to the needs of smallholder farmers. These should apply to both research and development and to manufacturing and distribution.

Universities may feel caught between the conflicting imperatives of attracting private sector funding and generating revenue through patenting activity on the one hand, and promoting public goods through "humanitarian intellectual property" policies on the other. It is clear that universities have an important role to play in preserving the balance between exclusion and access as well as paving the way to more informed, effective, and socially responsible agricultural intellectual property policies.

———

Civil Resistance and the "Diversity of Tactics" in the Anti–Globalization Movement: Problems of Violence, Silence, and Solidarity in Activist Politics

41 Osgoode Hall L.J. 505 (2003).

■ Janet Conway

I. INTRODUCTION

With the November 1999 mobilization that shut down the World Trade Organization (WTO) meetings in Seattle, the "anti-globalization" movement erupted onto the world stage. Between the Seattle protest and the events of September 11, 2001 (9/11), massive and growing anti-globalization demonstrations confronted neo-liberal elites wherever they convened. These demonstrations, especially their North American and European variants, have been the forum for the emergence of a debate over "diversity of tactics." The debate has revolved around the acceptability of more disruptive or confrontational forms of direct action, the putative role of property damage, and the use of veiled threats of the escalation of violence in the struggle against neo-liberal globalization.

* * *

In the name of creativity, resistance, and democracy, many anti-globalization activists advocate "respect for diversity of tactics" as a non-negotiable basis of unity. Solidarity with the full range of resistance has meant that no tactics are ruled out in advance and that activists refrain from publicly criticizing tactics with which they disagree. However, embracing diversity of tactics is not without ambiguity and risk: both strategically in terms of provoking repression and losing public support, but also in terms of democratic practice and culture within the movement itself where it may damage any prospect for broad coalition politics.

* * *

II. CIVIL DISOBEDIENCE AND DIRECT ACTION

The terms "civil disobedience" and "direct action" have been used interchangeably in both activist and academic circles; their meanings are often conflated. Further, the meaning of these terms often suffers as assumptions of illegality and violence are imported into their use.

Civil disobedience is a specific form of extra-parliamentary political action involving the deliberate, principled, and public breaking of a law that is perceived to be unjust. Acts of civil disobedience are premised on the existence of liberal democratic institutions and the rule of law. The public and principled breaking of a law by otherwise law-abiding persons is meant to call attention to the unjustness of that law, both through heroic witness (being willing to risk arrest or jail), and through using or gumming-up legal channels themselves (for example, through a trial). Classic examples of the use of civil disobedience from recent movement history include the lunch counter sit-ins of the civil-rights movement, the burning of draft cards in the anti-Vietnam War movement, and the blockades and occupations of the anti-nuclear movement.

Direct action is a larger and more generic category than is civil disobedience. The term refers to forms of political action that bypass parliamentary or bureaucratic channels to directly ameliorate or eliminate an injustice, or to slow down or obstruct regular operations of an unjust system or order. Strikes, street demonstrations, and occupations are classic forms of direct action.

Virtually all contemporary forms of direct action are in some sense symbolic as the action dramatizes conflict of system-wide problems. For example, the act of squatting (moving into and living in) in a vacant building may provide housing for a dozen homeless people thus directly ameliorating their situation. However, as forms of political action, most squats point to a much larger phenomenon of homelessness and create pressure for public agencies to act against the squat or to provide afforda-ble housing. In this sense, a single squat constitutes direct action and is symbolic at the same time.

Direct action can be legal, illegal, or extra-legal (extra-legal is used here to refer to practices that are not currently contemplated by the law). It may or may not be an occasion of police action and arrests. While all civil disobedience is a form of direct action, not all direct action involves the intentional and principled breaking of an unjust law with the purpose of calling attention to it. Direct action can be situated anywhere on what young activists call "the violence/non-violence continuum." Likewise, direct action can be situated anywhere on the illegal/extra-legal/legal continuum. There is no necessary correlation between non-violence and legality or, as activist victims of police brutality are quick to point out, between violence and illegality.

Both civil disobedience and direct action can involve property destruction and can still be considered non-violent by many activists. Here, non-violence is generally understood to mean the eschewing of the use of physical force against another human being. Generally, the mass street actions of the anti-globalization movement have been forms of direct action, some of them legal but many of them not, and have been almost completely non-violent on the part of the protesters. Within the demonstrations, there have been numerous direct actions of a great variety of types. The intensifying debate over diversity of tactics in the movement must be understood within a context of expanding commitment to, and enactment of, a wide variety of expressions of direct action.

III. DIVERSITY OF TACTICS

The debate over diversity of tactics in the anti-globalization movement initially emerged in the context of the Seattle demonstrations in November 1999. By the April 2001 anti-Free Trade Area of the Americas (FTAA) demonstrations in Quebec City, there was a full and specific articulation of the meaning of the term. Respect for diversity of tactics implies support for a bundle of organizing approaches, attitudes, and tactics. Since the Seattle demonstrations, proponents of diversity of tactics in the Canadian anti-globalization movement have argued both for an escalation and for a diversification of tactics beyond the routines of lobbying and legal, stage-managed demonstrations. They have argued for the valuing of a wider range of political activity especially in the institutionalized power centres of the movement such as labour unions and non-governmental organizations (NGOs). Proponents of diversity of tactics have called for and have engaged in popular education, cultural work, and grassroots-community organizing. Driven by a sense of urgency resulting from mounting social and ecological crises, these activists have argued for a return to more militant and confrontational tactics, including direct action and civil disobedience. In the name of both escalation and diversity they have also called for and defended property destruction, from stickering, spray painting, and guerrilla murals, to window smashing and the defacing of signs.

Respect for diversity of tactics as an ethical framework presupposes the existence of "affinity groups" as the unit of organization and democratic decision making. Affinity group organizing has its roots in feminist, anarchist, and anti-nuclear movements in which small, autonomous groups decide on the nature of their participation in a direct action, organizing independently of any centralized movement authority. Commitment to affinity group organizing often implies a repudiation of representative forms of democracy, institutions of the liberal democratic state, as well as labour unions and more bureaucratized movement organizations. Respect for diversity of tactics is part of a commitment to and practice of direct and participatory democracy in which all practitioners participate directly in decision making about tactics within their affinity groups. Large-scale anti-globalization demonstrations have been organized in significant part by networks of affinity groups who gather in spokescouncils. Theoretically, these groups strive for consensus, but practically work towards coordination and mutual tolerance.

The decisive feature of respect for diversity of tactics is an ethic of respect for, and acceptance of, the tactical choices of other activists. This tolerance of pluralism involves an explicit agreement not to publicly denounce the tactics of other activists—most controversially, rock-throwing, window-breaking, garbage can burning, and vandalism. So respect for diversity of tactics precludes, for example, the kind of non-violence agreement proposed by the Direct Action Network (DAN) that undergirded the Seattle organizing. The debate about diversity of tactics first emerged under that name when DAN organizers and other key movement leaders condemned the people throwing rocks and breaking windows in Seattle.

By the time of the demonstrations in Quebec City, those who were advocating diversity of tactics were also repudiating the dogmatism of non-violence, which they understood to be an authoritarian move to render certain forms of political resistance illegitimate. They criticized the overly rigid violence/non-violence binary that characterizes much of the discourse around non-violence. They also critiqued the highly ritualized forms of civil disobedience that had evolved during the peace movement, where protesters passively handed themselves over to the police.

* * *

V. PERSPECTIVES ON PROPERTY DESTRUCTION IN THE ANTI–GLOBALIZATION MOVEMENT

The most contentious debates about violence and non-violence in the North American anti-globalization movement revolve around the nature and status of property destruction as a tactic. Proponents of diversity of tactics specify that property damage includes such political staples as stickering, billboard "corrections," or graffiti. Few activists would dispute the value and creativity of these tactics, either within the context of large demonstrations and in their own right.

They rightly argue that the label violent is used somewhat indiscriminately, both within and beyond the movement, to refer to anyone acting outside the bounds of legitimate, that is routinized, legalized, and bureaucratized, forms of dissent. Those within the movement (including those engaged in non-violent direct action) tend to single out property damage, particularly window breaking, as violent. Notably, the debate here is not about physical violence against persons, but about whether destruction of property is encompassed within the meaning of violent.

The smashing of corporate windows, police cruisers, and media vehicles remain very controversial and have occasionally given rise to fisticuffs on the spot between activists who try to prevent those who attempt to pursue these tactics. Proponents of property destruction in Seattle pointed out the irony of self-proclaimed non-violent protesters physically tackling those targeting corporate property. They reject the notion that property destruction is violent unless it involves causing pain to, or death of, people. Rather than an expression of rage or reaction, proponents claim that property damage is "strategically and specifically targeted direct action against corporate interests." Proponents distinguish between private (capitalist) property and personal (use-value) property, targeting the former. They maintain that, as a tactic, property destruction unsettles middle-class culture and the reification of private property that is so entrenched in North America. "Property destruction allows for a change in landscape, a visual punctuation."

Therefore, proponents argue both ideologically and strategically for certain *kinds* of property destruction. But within the discourse of respect for diversity of tactics there seems to be little room for discussion between affinity groups of what kinds of property can be destroyed and what kinds of damage are appropriate. Further, there is little discussion between groups about the relation of these acts to the larger political context or to any broader movement strategy.

It is a fact that both the mainstream and alternative media are captivated by property destruction and the climate of uncertainty and disorder that it fosters through its threat of escalating conflict. Some forms of property destruction—notably window breaking—have trumped all other movement tactics in terms of the mass production of images. This fact is not recognized as problematic among the proponents of property destruction, despite their rhetoric of respect for (and presumably, a valuing of) diversity of tactics.

VI.   THE BLACK BLOC

Finally, while I support a clear distinction between the destruction of property and violence to people, discussions about property damage in the context of the anti-globalization movement are unavoidably haunted by the spectre of the Black Bloc and the host of political and strategic issues it raises. Because it is the most prominent apologist for, and practitioner of, property destruction, the Black Bloc's discourses and practices as a whole overdetermine the debate about property destruction in the context of the anti-globalization movement.

The Black Bloc originated in the European Autonomen movement in which masked and black-clad anarchists engaged in a range of militant and confrontational tactics and defend each other from the police. In Seattle, the Black Bloc concentrated their efforts on property damage and avoided engaging the police. In post-Seattle actions in Toronto, Ottawa, and Quebec City, the Black Bloc appeared to me to be a masked and costumed group of youths beating tattoos on poles and stop signs and marching in formation within large demonstrations. Yet in other situations, notably in Europe, all manners of mayhem have been attributed to the Black Bloc—hurling rocks, sticks, and Molotov cocktails at the police and looking for a fight. They played particularly explosive roles in Prague and Genoa.

  * * *

Numerous activists do engage in various forms of property destruction without masks and without any identification with the Black Bloc. Moreover, many are explicitly non-violent in their interactions with police. There are also traditions of property destruction in the anti-nuclear movement that are part of traditions of non-violent civil disobedience. But in the current context of the anti-globalization movement, property destruction has also become a tactic favoured by the Black Bloc. And it is this relationship, created by the discourses and practices of the Black Bloc, between property destruction in the context of the large anti-globalization demonstrations and a readiness, even an eagerness, to confront the police physically, that has so problematized property destruction as an acceptable tactic in the current context. Furthermore, when property destruction is enacted by masked activists, it is also vulnerable to appropriation, manipulation, and escalation by masked others: the police or their paid agitators, fascists, or criminal elements, some of whom appear to have participated in Genoa.

According to George Lakey, at its best, non-violent protest is a form of prefiguration. Its power lies in its contrast to the violent power of the state in the theatre of protest—solidarity and pacifism in the face of naked aggression. However, these assumptions were challenged in Seattle, particularly by those who engaged in and defended property destruction, not as a form of violence, but as embodying a distinct (and more militant and therefore better) political and strategic logic. As such, property destruction continues to raise troubling and challenging questions for the movement. In the post-Seattle period, Barbara Ehrenreich states:

> Clearly the left, broadly speaking, has come to a creative impasse. We need to invent some new forms of demonstrating that minimize the danger while maximizing the possibilities for individual self-expression.... We need ways of protesting that are accessible to the uninitiated, untrained, nonvegan population as well as to the seasoned veteran. We need to figure out how to capture public attention while, as often as possible, directly accomplishing some not-entirely-symbolic purpose, such as gumming up a WTO meeting or, for that matter, slowing down latte sales at a Starbucks.

> Rock-throwing doesn't exactly fit these criteria, nor did the old come-as-you-are demos of the sixties. But neither do the elaborately choreographed rituals known as "nonviolent" civil disobedience.

* * *

IX. ELITE RETREAT TO KANANASKIS AND HARD LESSONS FOR THE MOVEMENT

In response to the events of Genoa, the June 2002 meeting of the G8 was set for the remote Rocky Mountain town of Kananaskis. With five thousand troops, fifteen hundred Royal Canadian Mounted Police (RCMP), and an enforced no-fly zone, it was the "largest security operation in Canadian history," with a price tag of three to 500,000,000 dollars. Activists spent months planning a week-long Solidarity Village only to be outspent and outmaneuvered by governments and security forces at every turn. Negotiations with the Stoney Point First Nation over use of land came to an abrupt halt amid accusations of federal interference. The City of Calgary refused permission to use parks. According to David Robbins, an organizer with the Council of Canadians, "there's a desire to disorganize and frustrate coherent organizing around this particular summit in order to create confrontation and discredit opposition to the G–8 and corporate globalization."

Nevertheless, several thousand people turned up to the summit, the snake march, and the picnic without a permit, to muddy corporate facades, and to demonstrate with and without their clothes on. Again, the actions were organized under the rubric of diversity of tactics. Significantly, unions, NGOs, and direct-action protesters in Canada were working together again after a post–9/11 hiatus. In Calgary, unionists were visible in all the activities, including the snake marches that disrupted traffic during Monday morning rush hour, and had participated in the convergence table leading up to and during the events. The demonstrations were completely non-violent, although not without some heated moments. Protesters actively intervened to defuse potentially explosive situations between police and the more confrontational activist factions. Police in Calgary were on bicycles and in soft hat rather than riot gear.

Several thousand people also turned up in Ottawa in response to a call to "take the capital." As in Calgary, the framework for organizing was respect for diversity of tactics. Coordinated separation of spaces allowed for different kinds of events, from an explicitly non-violent World March of Women-led "revolutionary knitting action" to a diversity of tactics, CLAC [La Convergence des Luttes Anti–Capitalistes]-led snake march. A large non-violent convergence march was organized on the second day around the theme that "no one is illegal" in response to repressive anti-terrorist laws.

In the lead-up to Calgary and Ottawa, new language had begun to appear among proponents of diversity of tactics advocating forms of resistance "that maximize respect for life." This did not mean that organizing, especially in Ottawa, was not extremely fractious. A refusal by CLAC, in the name of respect for diversity of tactics, to exclude violent tactics created a serious split in the Ottawa activist community. Most church-, labour-, and NGO-based activists (including Global Democracy Ottawa) simply stayed away from all Take the Capital activities. As a result, the CLAC-organized snake march in particular represented a much narrower cross-section of the movement; it was comprised almost exclusively of young people with a high proportion of self-identified anarchists, including a number who were masked and carrying batons. The batons were used to produce the trademark rhythmic drumming on any available metal surface—stop signs, guardrails, and street grates.

Throughout both the snake march and the "no one is illegal" march, CLAC organizer Jaggi Singh kept reiterating over the bullhorn that "anything could happen," and that people should and will directly confront actions they perceive to be unjust in ways that they deem legitimate. As a participant in both events, I experienced this rhetoric as inflammatory and manipulative. Singh was holding open the possibility of violence as an acceptable aspect of protest in general and in the context of the event in which we were participating. As someone willing to support a militant action organized under the rubric of diversity of tactics, I felt that my presence was being manipulated to support a threat of violent escalation over which I had no say.

On the other hand, the Raging Granny marching beside me had this to say: "Some of our members are uncomfortable taking part in these kinds of events because they're worried about what might happen. But, I think, when you consider the violence all around us, these (gesturing to the sea of young people) are just the lambs."

In Ottawa, there was some spray-painting and paint-bombing of banks. The windows of a police car were smashed during the snake march, but this action was immediately booed by protesters and did not escalate. Police were in regular uniform and kept their distance. Like the events in Calgary, Ottawa was acclaimed by police, press, and protesters alike as completely non-violent, despite the tensions created by those insisting on "solidarity with the full scope of resistance."

In the aftermath of these actions, Starhawk published what amounted to a thorough rethinking of diversity of tactics. Coming from an activist with demonstrated commitment to both non-violent direct action and respectful dialogue with the Black Bloc, her comments are especially persuasive. She argued that the time (post–9/11) and place (oil-rich and right-wing Calgary) demanded a powerful, militant, disruptive, and explicitly non-violent direct action. However, such action could not happen because diversity of tactics had become the movement's default mode.

Although offering a critique of the morality of much non-violence politics and the staleness of its tactics, Starhawk argues that a commitment to strategic non-violence opens up political space that diversity of tactics has, in effect, shut down:

> Strategic nonviolence lets us mobilize broadly around actions that are more than symbolic, that actually interfere with the operations of an institution of power. Unions and NGOs, and at-risk groups can support and participate in such actions, which contain many necessary roles at varied levels of risk.
>
> Committing to nonviolence as a strategic move for a particular action allows us to organize openly, without security culture and with broad participation in decision-making. . . . Transparency allows us to actually educate, mobilize, and inspire people to join us. While security culture may be necessary at times, it works against empowerment and direct democracy. People can only have a voice in the decisions that affect them if they know what is being decided. . . .
>
> If we are to regain momentum in the post–9–11 climate for issues of global justice, we need actions that can mobilize large numbers of

people to do more than simply march. We need to embrace discussion and debate, and trust that our movement is strong, resilient, and mature enough to tolerate our differences of opinion. We might agree that a diversity of tactics are [sic] needed in the long run to undermine global corporate capitalism, and still be willing to commit to strategic nonviolence for an action when it seems the strongest option. Otherwise, we end up without either diversity or tactics.

X.   CONCLUSIONS

The first G8 summit in Europe since Genoa, 9/11, and the war in Iraq is currently taking place in Evian, France and with it has come the return of massive anti-globalization protests. Organizers claim that 120,000 people demonstrated in the mass march on Sunday, June 1, 2003. Through the winter of 2003, the anti-globalization movement was transformed by the explosion of a massive, global anti-war movement in opposition to an American-led attack on Iraq. On February 15, 2003, over four million people took to the streets in over six hundred towns and cities across the world in an extraordinary, globally-coordinated effort to prevent war. In January 2003, over 100,000 people gathered in Porto Alegre, Brazil for the third annual World Social Forum to march against the American Empire, to showcase the existence of political and economic alternatives to neo-liberalism, and to assert that another world is possible. Global opposition to neo-liberalism has been fueled by the war on Iraq. United States-led military aggression is increasingly recognized as an imperial civilizational project of global proportion.

In this new climate, the debate about diversity of tactics appeared increasingly marginalized. Organizers of mass anti-war demonstrations in Canada and elsewhere negotiated routes with police and marshaled the protests. Protesters carefully avoided property destruction or confrontation with police.

Anti-globalization activists were very prominent in the organizing and protesting against the war. But the movement against the war also broadened dramatically, incorporating many more people of color, notably from Muslim and Arab communities, and people who have never before protested anything. New movement coalitions included the more traditional peace groups with their strong traditions of pacificism and non-violent civil disobedience.

There will almost certainly be renewed debates within the movement about tactics. Property destruction has re-appeared in Lausanne, Switzerland, as part of the most recent round of anti-G8 protests. So have non-violent direct actions blockading roads and bridges. But these activities are in the wake of massive anti-war coalitions and demonstrations that may change the conditions for debate within the movement. Most powerfully, in the face of such naked use of deadly force by the United States, Starhawk's argument for strategic non-violence may have greater purchase in the movement.

In Canada, from the late 1990s into the early years of this century, the notion of "respect for diversity of tactics" held great appeal, especially among young activists. Against the historical backdrop of several decades of highly institutionalized forms of movement politics, it both named and validated important new activist practices in the face of growing global crises. More than ever, the movement and the world needs the creativity and courage of this new generation of activists in advancing non-violent strategies for social transformation. But in the face of unprecedented forces of power and domination, we also need to nurture the movement as a space of freedom and democracy, genuine diversity and pluralism, respect for life, and a love of peace in prefiguring the world we want.

NOTES AND QUESTIONS

1. **Global security and poverty:** In February of 2005, UN Secretary General Kofi Annan said "We will not defeat terrorism unless we also tackle the causes of conflict and misgovernment in developing countries. And we will not defeat poverty so long as trade and investment in any major part of the world are inhibited by fear of violence or instability."

In an extended interview with *Mother Jones* magazine, Jeffrey Sachs, an international development economist, author of *The End of Poverty*, laid out his own strategies for eradicating global poverty by 2025. Sachs headed a United Nations panel of development experts that were given the task of drafting global development goals to be met by the year 2015.

Why is it that decades of development economics haven't achieved the elimination of poverty? What makes Sachs' proposals so special? Is eradicating poverty a feasible goal to achieve in our lifetime? Sachs recently discussed his views with *Mother Jones Magazine*. Onnesha Roychoudhuri, *The End of Poverty: An Interview with Jeffrey Sachs*, MOTHER JONES MAG., May 6, 2005, *available at* http://www.motherjones.com/news/qa/2005/05/jeffrey_sachs.html.

2. **Practical investment strategy.** Sachs proposes that the "rich countries need to help poor countries make practical investments that are often really very basic.... For instance, one issue that has been tragically neglected ... is malaria. That's a disease that kills up to 3 million people every year." Sachs decries the failure to address this practical problem "that could be controlled quite dramatically and easily." Sachs argues that development issues got sidetracked during the post–9/11 crisis period. However, he notes that the tsunami in the Indian Ocean in which we could all see the scope of the devastation on our television screens, shifted discussion towards the plight of the world's poor.

3. **The point seven percent solution.** Sachs has proposed that the rich countries, such as the United States, devote 0.7 percent of our Gross National Product to development aid. This proposal has been criticized by former World Bank economist, William Easterly. Easterly calls instead for

"piecemeal reform," in which more limited projects are tried, monitored, and measured to see what really works before a major commitment is given. Sachs' reply to the piecemeal approach is that "I don't think that we should be choosing between whether a young girl has immunizations or water, or between whether her mother and father are alive, because they have access of treatment for AIDS, or whether she has a meal at school, or whether her father and mother, who are farmers are able to grow enough food to feed their family.... Those strike me as quite doable and practical things that can be done at once.... I am proposing that we help people help themselves."

4.   Corruption. Rich countries frequently cite the problem of corruption as a reason to withhold significant contributions of foreign aid. Sachs says, "my experience is that there's corruption everywhere: in the U.S., in Europe, in Asia, and in Africa. It's a bit like infectious disease—you can control it, but it's very hard to eradicate it ... I don't have any magic solution for those situations.... Nothing is done on trust. Everything should be done on a basis of measurement and monitoring.... Don't just send money: send bed nets, send in auditors, make targets quantitative."

5.   Teaching development economics in the universities. Sachs proposes a major change in the way advanced students are taught development economics. "Students in economics write dissertations about countries that they never stepped foot in because their advisor gives them a database from Nigeria or Kenya or some place else, and they do their thesis that way. That is like becoming a doctor without ever seeing a patient. We don't do case studies" Sachs proposes that development economists be trained with "clinical economics." In this mode students would meet in the field of study, then conference with professors to analyze the results of their efforts. This would approximate the hospital "rounds" for residents in training.

6.   Shocking disengagement of World Bank from the AIDS crisis. "I was absolutely shocked and aghast when I learned that in the late 1990s the World Bank and other donors weren't paying a penny to help treat people dying of AIDS.... Rarely do rich countries say, 'Look we're just not prepared to spend money to save poor people's lives'. Instead you get a lot of skepticism. 'You can't do this, this is impossible. We're doing everything we can after all. We've tried everything. Let's go slowly. Let's do one thing at a time' I don't buy those arguments."

7.   Modern direct action. Attempts to affect social change through courts or legislatures can often be a cumbersome process, characterized by delays, compromises, and setbacks. Social activists have often sought more immediate strategies, such as protests and boycotts. Socially and economically disruptive activity has the advantage of gaining immediate and widespread attention from the public, and they may be more forceful both in their methods and results. These tactics include risks as well. Their failure may also be more visible, and they may engender backlash from the public.

The most famous example of a boycott from the American civil rights movement is the Montgomery Bus Boycott. In 1955, Montgomery, Alabama had a municipal law which required black citizens to ride in the back of the city's buses. On December 1, Rosa Parks sparked the boycott when she was arrested for refusing to relinquish her seat at the front of the bus to white passengers. Over the weekend of December 3 and 4, the leaders of Montgomery's black community, including Dr. Martin Luther King, planned a large scale boycott of Montgomery's bus system, in protest of the South's segregation laws. Black ministers urged their congregations to join the boycott, and pamphlets were distributed throughout the city. The boycott was remarkably successful. According to the bus company receipts, about 90 percent of blacks who usually rode the buses joined the boycott and found other means of transportation. The boycott continued into 1956, during which time the leaders and participants of the boycott were subjected to harassment and violence. Bombs were set off at the houses of both Dr. King and E. D. Nixon. In November of 1956, the Supreme Court declared that segregation on public buses was unconstitutional, and the boycott ended. *See* Thomas J. Gilliam, *The Montgomery Bus Boycott of 1955–56, in* THE WALKING CITY: THE MONTGOMERY BUS BOYCOTT (David J. Garrow ed., 1989).

The protest was an invaluable tool for the civil rights movement. Clayborne Carson describes the movement, or in his preferred term the "Black Freedom Struggle," as involving "local protest movements" engaged in by "thousands of protesters, including large numbers of working class blacks, and local organizers who were more concerned with local issues, including employment opportunities and political power, than with achieving national legislation." Clayborne Carson, *Civil Rights Reform and the Black Freedom Struggle, in* THE CIVIL RIGHTS MOVEMENT IN AMERICA 19, 23–4 (Charles W. Eagles ed., 1986). Martin Luther King highly valued the peaceful protest, and admired its participants. In his famous "Letter from a Birmingham Jail," Dr. King responded to criticism made by eight Alabama clergymen of the demonstrations going on in Birmingham in 1963. He wrote:

> I wish you had commended the Negro sit-inners and demonstrators of Birmingham for their sublime courage, their willingness to suffer and their amazing discipline in the midst of great provocation. One day the South will recognize its real heroes. They will be the James Merediths, with the noble sense of purpose that enables them to face jeering, and hostile mobs, and with the agonizing loneliness that characterizes the life of the pioneer. They will be old, oppressed, battered Negro women, symbolized in a seventy-two-year-old woman in Montgomery, Alabama, who rose up with a sense of dignity and with her people decided not to ride segregated buses, and who responded with ungrammatical profundity to one who inquired about her weariness: "My feets is tired, but my soul is at rest." They will be the young high school and college students, the young ministers of the gospel and a host of their elders, courageously and nonviolently sitting in at lunch counters

and willingly going to jail for conscience' sake. One day the South will know that when these disinherited children of God sat down at lunch counters, they were in reality standing up for what is best in the American dream and for the most sacred values in our Judeo–Christian heritage, thereby bringing our nation back to those great wells of democracy which were dug deep by the founding fathers in their formulation of the Constitution and the Declaration of Independence.

8.   Protests and boycotts today. By the end of 2009 and the beginning 2010, the economies of many of the nations belonging to the European Union had begun to falter, drowning in debt. The first to reach the brink of economic collapse was Greece. In the spring of 2010, the Greek Parliament passed a series of austerity measures including cuts to public sector salaries, higher taxes on alcohol and cigarettes, and tighter retirement rules. The austerity package was seen as politically necessary to ensure bailout commitments from the EU and/or the International Monetary Fund, but tens of thousands of Greeks took to the streets in response, unleashing a general strike and a series of demonstrations, some of which turned violent. In early May, for instance, young protesters identified by the police as "anarchists" led efforts to storm the Parliament building, chanting "thieves, thieves," and hurling rocks and gasoline bombs. The police responded with tear gas canisters that spread a choking pall over the crowd. Dan Bilefsky, "Greek Parliament Passes Austerity Measures," New York Times, May 5, 2010, http://www.nytimes.com/2010/05/07/world/europe/07greece.html?pagewanted=1&fta=y. Later that day a firebomb was thrown into a bank, trapping at least 30 people. Three people died of smoke inhalation. The euro sank in value in response to fears that the unrest would lead Greece to abandon its austerity plan, or that the unrest would spread to other nations on shaky financial footing. *Id.*

Are street demonstrations, protests, boycotts, and other examples of "people power" effective against structural economic policy? Are such protests just—or will the people protesting ultimately be more hurt by lasting economic collapse? How should the Greek Parliament balance its commitments to the European Union, the global financial markets, and its own citizens?

9.   Anti-globalization struggles and guerrilla theater. In addition to the direct action tactics of violent and non-violent mass action described by Conway, activists in the anti-globalization movement have engaged in other kinds of tactics. In *No Logo: Taking Aim at the Brand Bullies* (1999), Naomi Klein describes "culture jamming," "the practice of parodying advertisements and hijacking billboards in order to drastically alter their messages." Klein, *supra* at 280. Klein explains:

[J]ammers * * * insist that they aren't inverting ad messages but are rather improving, editing, augmenting or unmasking them. * * * A good jam, in other words, is an X-ray of the subconscious of a campaign, uncovering not an opposite meaning but the deeper truth hiding beneath the layers of advertising euphemisms. So, according to these principles, with a slight turn of the imagery knob, the now-retired Joe Camel turns into Joe Chemo, hooked up to an IV machine. That's what's in his future, isn't it? * * * Apple computers' "Think Different" campaign of famous figures both living and dead has been the subject of numerous simple hacks: a photograph of Stalin appears with the altered slogan "Think Really Different"; the caption for the ad featuring the Dalai Lama is changed to "Think Disillusioned" and the rainbow Apple logo is morphed into a skull * * *. My favorite truth-in-advertising campaign is a simple jam on Exxon that appeared just after the 1989 Valdez spill: "Shit Happens. New Exxon," two towering billboards announced to millions of San Francisco commuters.

KLEIN, *supra* at 281–82.

10. Grassroots global anti-poverty campaigns: the Jubilee movement. "Jubilee 2000" was an international grassroots campaign that mobilized twenty four million people over a five year period, beginning in 1996, to cancel the "unpayable debts of the poorest countries by the year 2000." The term comes from the Old Testament book of Leviticus, which describes a Year of Jubilee that comes once every fifty years, during which slaves are freed and debt is canceled. The Jubilee 2000 campaign—which launched the slogan "Drop the Debt"—was supported by celebrities, including musicians Bono of U2, Bob Geldof, Youssou Ndour, Thom Yorke and others, as well as by mainline Protestant and evangelical church organizations. In 1999, at the Cologne G8 Summit, world leaders agreed to $34 billion in debt relief for 22 countries, 18 of them in Africa. *See ihttp://www.jubilee2000uk.org/* (visited June 9, 2005); Jeff M. Sellers, *How To Spell Debt Relief*, CHRISTIANITY TODAY, May 21, 2001, *available at http://www.christianitytoday.com/ct/2001/007/6.64.html*.

Grassroots organizing under the Jubilee name continues in various countries. According to the Jubilee USA Network website, the United States network began in 1997 "when a diverse gathering of people and organizations came together in response to the international call for Jubilee debt cancellation. Now over sixty organizations including labor, churches, religious communities and institutions, AIDS activists, trade campaigners and over 9,000 individuals are active members of the Jubilee USA Network. Together we are a strong, diverse and growing network dedicated to working for a world free of debt for billions of people." Jubilee USA Network, *About the network*, *http://www.jubileeusa.org* (visited June 9, 2005).

11. Porto Allegre grassroots movement. In January 2001, as a counter to the World Economic Forum—an exclusive annual gathering of economic elites in Davos, Switzerland—a committee of Brazilian non-governmental organizations hosted the first "World Social Forum" in Porto Alegre, Brazil. The World Social Forum became an annual international grassroots event. According to its Charter of Principles, the World Social Forum:

is an open meeting place for reflective thinking, democratic debate of ideas, formulation of proposals, free exchange of experiences and interlinking for effective action, by groups and movements of civil society that are opposed to neoliberalism and to domination of the world by capital and any form of imperialism, and are committed to building a planetary society directed towards fruitful relationships among Humankind and between it and the Earth.

World Social Forum Charter of Principles, *available at http://www.forum socialmundial.org.br/main.php?id_menu=4&cd_language=2* (visited June 9, 2005).

Porto Alegre itself is a place open to alternatives to traditional economic practices. An article reports on "participatory budgeting" in the city:

Porto Alegre is a regional capital of 1.3 million people which since 1989 has been governed by the Partido dos Trabalhadores (PT or Workers' Party), Brazil's largest Left-wing party. Its flagship policy—the Participatory Budget—involves thousands of city residents in decisions about municipal expenditures. In a country where public funds are typically spent through a mixture of corruption, patronage and obscure technocratism, this is a revolution in political practice.

It sprang from a political party's desire to live up to its policy platform, an aim seldom achieved in the world of politics. Since it was formed in the 1980s, the Workers' Party proclaimed its commitment to both citizen participation and redirecting government priorities toward the poor. But when it was elected to municipal office in January 1989, the party found an administration deeply indebted, lacking basic supplies and with buildings and machinery in shambles. At the first neighbourhood assemblies to discuss the budget, community leaders called for hundreds of investments. Not a penny was available.

The local government spent its first year controlling costs and passing tax increases in city council but opinion polls showed high levels of dissatisfaction. So a group within the administration proposed both participatory decision-making and that priority be given to basic infrastructure in the poorest neighbourhoods. This translated as a total commitment, backed by funds, to the decisions made by the neighbourhood budget assemblies.

Since then, residents have met in their neighbourhoods annually to discuss needs for community infrastructure, electing delegates to each of 16 'district budget forums'. Through intense and often conflictual negotiations among neighbourhood representatives, these delegates list priorities for each type of capital expenditure such as basic sanitation, street paving and parks. Every year, open assemblies in each district also elect two members to a city-wide Municipal Budget Council which devises criteria for distributing funds among districts and approves an investment plan that respects the priorities of each one.

This policy gained such popularity in its first years that the administration expanded the programme beyond neighbourhood issues when it was re-elected in 1992. A year later, a series of Thematic Forums were created to discuss city-wide expenditures in areas such as urban planning, transportation and economic development. These forums also elect members to the Municipal Budget Council.

As it has grown, the Council has gained force. Not only does it now approve the entire capital budget but it also deliberates on all city expenditures. Over time a series of other participatory councils have also been created to discuss more qualitative aspects of city programmes on issues such as housing, health, culture and the environment.

The timing was ideal for building support for the idea. The first half of the 1990s was a period of great popular outrage in Brazil against government corruption, leading to the impeachment of President Collor de Mello. By contrast, at a local level, the Participatory Budget demonstrated that the administration was committed to change by challenging 'back room decision-making', mobilizing large numbers of people and visibly improving the quality of life in the poorest neighbourhoods. While opposition politicians privately questioned participatory decision-making, which effectively eliminated them as patronage brokers, they were forced to approve the investment plans since their own supporters were increasingly participating. After just one electoral term, all candidates promised to maintain the Participatory Budget.

As the policy began to gain international recognition, the government also gained local popularity for being innovative and responsible. Those people participating in the Municipal Budget Council gained a certain 'moral authority'. This helped garner the support of groups that still questioned the policy, such as technical personnel within the bureaucracy who doubted the ability of ordinary people to make budget decisions. The result was a bureaucracy that worked better, responding with agility to the demands of budget participants.

One of the outstanding achievements of the Participatory Budget has been its effectiveness in bringing the poor into public decision-making. The poorest neighbourhoods participate in much greater numbers than middle-class ones where streets have already been paved, sewers built and children are sent to private schools. Surveys show assembly participants have lower incomes and education levels than averages for the city as a whole.

However, the most enduring value of the Participatory Budget is that citizen participation has now become a way of life, accepted by people as well as politicians as the modus operandi in all realms of public decision-making. What is more, citizen groups have grown and strengthened in response to increased opportunities for effectively influencing government actions. Contrary to the common assumption that civil society must strengthen before government will improve, in

Porto Alegre a state-initiated policy that has encouraged civic organizing has helped consolidate the new practices at all levels.

While promoting citizen participation may often seem politically risky, in Porto Alegre it has helped build political success for the Workers' Party. Since 1989 the party has been re-elected three times and has gained a reputation for effective administration elsewhere. Today it governs five cities of more than a million people, including São Paulo, as well as three states. Its local successes have directly challenged the idea that the Workers' Party—a party once identified with radical social movements—does not know how to govern. These successes have served as credentials for the Workers' Party in this year's national election campaign, which delivered the presidency to the party's leader, 'Lula' da Silva.

By 2000, more than 100 Brazilian cities were implementing the policy (about half of which are not Workers' Party controlled). Not always have the results been so impressive as in Porto Alegre. In most cases participatory control has remained limited to a small portion of expenditures. Even so, it is clear that the policy has a tremendous potential to mobilize: in major Brazilian cities such as Belém, Brasília and Belo Horizonte, participatory budget programmes have involved hundreds of thousands of participants. In São Paulo alone, 55,000 people participated in budget forums this year.

Rebecca Abers, *Daring Democracy*, New Internationalist 352 (December 2002), *available at http://www.newint.org/issue352/daring.htm*. In fall, 2004, however, the Workers' Party was voted out of office.

The World Social Forum has now moved to a biannual schedule. In its off years, the forum becomes a decentralized series of events all over the world.

COPYRIGHT PERMISSIONS & FURTHER ACKNOWLEDGEMENTS

Krugman, Paul, *For Richer*, N.Y. Times%, Oct. 20, 2002, at s. 6, p. 62. Copyright © 2002 by Paul Krugman and The New York Times Publishing Company. Reprinted by permission of The New York Times Publishing Company in the format Textbook via the Copyright Clearance Center.

Krugman, Paul, *The Sons Also Rise*, N.Y. Times%, Nov. 22, 2002, at A.27. Copyright © 2002 by Paul Krugman and The New York Times Publishing Company. Reprinted by permission of The New York Times Publishing Company in the format Textbook via the Copyright Clearance Center.

Kuttner, Robert, *Everything For Sale* 16 (1996). From Everything for Sale by Robert Kuttner, copyright © 1996 by the Twentieth Century Fund, Inc. Reprinted by permission of Alfred A. Knopf, a division of Random House, Inc.

Lenhardt, R.A., *Understanding the Mark: Race, Stigma, and Equality in Context*, 79 N.Y.U. L. Rev. 803 (2005). Copyright © 2005 by R.A. Lenhardt and the New York University Law Review. Reprinted by permission of the New York University Law Review.

Lopez, Gerald P., *How Much Responsibility Does the U.S. Bear for Undocumented Mexican Migration?, in Undocumented Mexican Migration: In Search of a Just Immigration Law and Policy*, 28 UCLA L. Rev. 615 (1980). Copyright © 1980 by Gerald P. Lopez and the University of California at Los Angeles Law Review. Reprinted by permission of Gerald P. Lopez.

Lupica, Lois R., *The Consumer Debt Crisis and the Reinforcement of Class Position*, 2009 Loyola University Chicago Law Journal, 40 Loy. U. Chi. L.J. 557. Copyright © 2009 by the University of Chicago Press. Reprinted by permission.

Lynch, Mona, *From Punitive City to Gated Community: Security and Segregation Across the Social and Penal Landscape, Symposium*, 56 U. Miami L. Rev. 89 (2001). Copyright © 2001 by Mona Lynch and the University of Miami Law Review. Reprinted by permission.

Malamud, Deborah C., *Class Based Affirmative Action: Lessons and Caveats*, 74 Tex. L. Rev. 1847 (1996). Copyright © 1996 by Deborah C. Malamud and the University of Texas Law Review. Reprinted by permission of the University of Texas Law Review and Deborah C. Malamud.

Mathematics, Words and Music by Dante Beze and Christopher Martin a 1999 EMI BLACKWOOD MUSIC INC., EMPIRE INTERNATIONAL, MEDINA SOUND MUSIC, EMI APRIL MUSIC INC., and GIFT–ED PEARL MUSIC All Rights for EMPIRE INTERNATIONAL and MEDINA SOUND MUSIC Controlled and Administered by EMI BLACKWOOD MUSIC INC. All Rights for GIFTED PEARL MUSIC Controlled and Administered by EMI APRIL MUSIC INC. All Rights Reserved. International Copyright Secured. Reprinted by Permission.

Matsuda, Mari J., *Voices of America: Accent, Antidiscrimination Law, and a Jurisprudence for the Last Reconstruction*, 100 Yale L.J. 1329 (1991). Copyright © 1991 by Yale Law Journal Company, Inc. Reproduced with

Nussbaum, Martha, *Patriotism and Cosmopolitanism*, in For Love of Country? 3–17 (2002). Copyright © 2002 by Beacon Press. Reproduced with the permission of Beacon Press in the format Textbook via Copyright Clearance Center.

Oliver, Melvin L. & Shapiro, Thomas M., *Wealth and Inequality in America*, in Black Wealth/White Wealth: New Perspectives on Racial Inequality 12–18, 53–90 (1997). Copyright © 1997 by Melvin Oliver, Thomas Shapiro, and Routledge Taylor and Francis Group. Reprinted by permission of Routledge.

Olsen, Frances, *The Family and the Market: A Study of Ideology and Legal Reform*, 96 Harv. L. Rev. 1497 (1983). Copyright © 1983 by Frances Olsen and the Harvard Law Review Association. Copyright © 1995 by Harvard Law Review Association. Reproduced with permission of the Harvard Law Review Association in the format Textbook via Copyright Clearance Center.

Padilla, Felix M., *The Diamonds as a Business Enterprise*, in The Gang as an American Enterprise 90–116 (1992). Copyright © 1992 by Felix Padilla and Rutgers University Press. Reprinted by permission of the Rutgers University Press.

Polinsky, A. Mitchell, *Efficiency and Equity*, in Introduction to Law and Economics 7–11 (2003). Copyright © 2003 by A. Mitchell Polinsky and Aspen Publishers. Reprinted by permission of Aspen Publishers.

Polinsky, A. Mitchell, *Efficiency and Equity Reconsidered*, in Introduction to Law and Economics 147–56 (2003). Copyright © 2003 by A. Mitchell Polinsky and Aspen Publishers. Reprinted by permission of Aspen publishers.

Posner, Richard, *Nuance, Narrative, and Empathy in Critical Race Theory*, in Overcoming Law 368–384 (1995). "Nuance, Narrative, and Empathy in Critical Race Theory" reprinted by permission of the publisher of OVERCOMING LAW by Posner, Richard, pp. 368–384, Cambridge, Mass.: Harvard University Press, Copyright © 1995 by the President and Fellows of Harvard College.

Posner, Richard, *The Economic Approach to Law*, in The Problems of Jurisprudence 353–92 (1990). "The Economic Approach to Law" reprinted by permission of the publisher of The Problems of Jurisprudence by Richard Posner, pp. 353–392, Cambridge, Mass.: Harvard University Press, Copyright © 1990 by the President and Fellows of Harvard College.

Radin, Margaret Jane, *Justice and the Market Domain*, in Markets and Justice 165 (John W. Chapman & J. Roland Pennock eds., 1989). Copyright © 1989 by Margaret Jane Radin and Nomos XXXI. Reprinted by permission.

Rankin, Bill, *Domestic Partner Ordinance Quashed: Atlanta to Appeal in Second Defeat*, Atlanta J. Const., Jan. 1, 1997, at D02. Copyright © 1997

INDEX

References are to Pages.

†